TOTAL STANLEY CUP®

DAN DIAMOND
EDITOR

PAUL BONTJE   **RALPH DINGER**   ERIC ZWEIG

MANAGING EDITORS

JAMES DUPLACEY   JOHN PASTERNAK

ASSISTANT EDITOR   DATA MANAGEMENT

PUBLISHED BY
THE WRITERS' COLLECTIVE
CRANSTON, RHODE ISLAND

Dan Diamond and Associates, Inc.
194 Dovercourt Road
Toronto, Ontario M6J 3C8
Canada
e-mail: dda.nhl@sympatico.ca

Data Management and Typesetting: Caledon Data Management, Hillsburgh, Ontario
Film Output and Scanning: Stafford Graphics, Toronto, Ontario
Cover Design: Chad Lawrence
Cover Photo: Scott Levy/Bruce Bennett Studios
Production Management: Dan Diamond and Associates, Inc., Toronto Ontario

Library of Congress Cataloging-in-Publication Data

Total stanley cup : 2003 playoff media guide / Dan Diamond, editor;
Paul Bontje, Ralph Dinger, Eric Zweig, managing editors.
p.   cm.
ISBN 159411077 (alk. paper)
1. Stanley Cup (Hockey)—History. I. Diamond, Dan.
GV847.7.T68 2003
796.962'648—dc21

Printed in the United States of America

Published by The Writers' Collective, Cranston, Rhode Island

10 9 8 7 6 5 4 3 2 1

TOTAL STANLEY CUP
CONTENTS

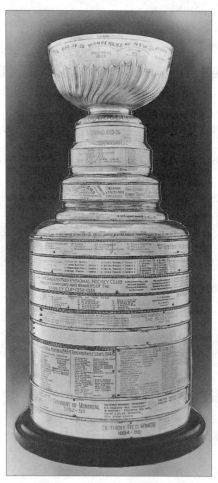

The Changing Trophy

Clockwise from top left: Lord Stanley, Canada's Governor-General, donated the squat English silver bowl that soon bore his name. The custom of engraving the winners' names on the trophy forced it to grow with the addition of silver bands. By 1932, the trophy had become an ungainly cylinder that grew taller by the time Toronto goaltender Turk Broda posed with the Cup in 1947. The silver bands from this cigar-shaped trophy were remounted in 1948, forming a two-piece trophy that split at the top of the wide barrel. The top part would be presented to each year's winning captain; the barrel remained on the presentation table. A new five-band barrel was added in 1958, forming the one-piece Stanley Cup in use today. The inscribed names of each year's winner filled the five bands in 1991. The top band was removed and a new one added at the base. It, too, will be filled after the names of the 2004 Cup winner have been added.

Introduction

*Y*OU CAN TAKE THIS TO THE BANK: *the Stanley Cup probably is the most popular sports trophy in the world... Certainly, it is the most recognizable. And it got that way strictly on merit—no costly promotional campaign of flashing lights and crashing cymbals. It comes closer to being a People's Cup than any other trophy in sport. They line up for hours to get a look at it, peering at the names of hockey idols past and present. The secret of its popularity is its availability. It goes where there are people. It's friendly.*

For more than 100 years the Stanley Cup trophy has been the game's talisman, a focal point shared by players and fans. The shimmering silver bowl, collar and barrels have been displayed everywhere from Miami to Moscow where they have been admired and photographed by hundreds of thousands. It's been the star of the show at small-town rinks and on late-night talk shows, all the while conveying the pride and joy of having reached hockey's pinnacle.

– Milt Dunnell, 1998

*W*ELCOME TO THE FOURTH EDITION of *Total Stanley Cup.* Produced by the editors of the *NHL Official Guide & Record Book* and the *Total Hockey Encyclopedia,* the 2003 edition of *Total Stanley Cup* is an in-depth information package of particular use for journalists and the broadcast media on the hockey playoff beat.

The book is divided into four sections:

- Section I deals with the origins of the trophy and provides background on Lord Stanley, Canada's Governor-General who donated it in 1893 but never saw a Stanley Cup game *(page 6).* The many changes to the trophy itself and the intricacies and idiosyncrasies of the engraving upon it are described as is Cup competition in the early challenge era *(page 13).* A chronology of the NHL's evolving playoff format with special emphasis on the setup of the 2003 playoffs is found here *(page 11).*

- Section II provides comprehensive highlights and playoff records. Each NHL club's all-time playoff record, top playoff scorers and series-by-series results are listed *(page 15)* as are all-time playoff scoring leaders *(page 25),* year-by-year playoff scoring leaders *(page 26)* and Stanley Cup-winning goal scorers *(page 75).* Highlights of each season's playoff competition from 2002 to 1893 along with the score of every playoff game and the roster of each Cup-winning team are found here *(page 27)* as are complete team and individual playoff record books *(page 64).* Also included is a playoff coaching register *(page 73)* and lists of every three-goal-game *(page 76),* over-

time game *(page 78)* and penalty shot *(page 72)* in Stanley Cup play.

- Section III offers similar coverage of the Stanley Cup Finals. A team-by-team Final Series history *(page 91)* and a Final Series record book *(page 94)* is supplemented by year-by-year scoring in the Finals *(page 101),* an alphabetical listing of every player who was a member of a Cup winner from 1893 to 2002 *(page 115)* and Final Series scoring, goaltending and coaching statistics for all NHLers *(page 120).* There is also a statistical summary of every Final Series game played since 1990 complete with team rosters, scoring and penalty statistics, shots on goal and on-ice officials *(page 128).*

- Section IV is comprised of two complete statistical registers, providing year-by-year Stanley Cup playoff statistics for every player and every goaltender to appear in the NHL. More than 5,500 players are listed. The NHL Playoff Player Register is found on page 145. The Goaltender Register begins on page 229.

Several other features in *Total Stanley Cup* are worth noting: This introduction begins with a excerpt from an essay by Milt Dunnell, a recipient of the Hockey Hall of Fame's Elmer Ferguson Memorial Award for writing, who has covered playoff hockey since the 1920s. Eric Zweig's "Lord Stanley and His Cup Revealed" *(page 6)* deals with the donation of the silver trophy, its evolution and engraving the passions ignited by competition for it.

"Odd and Unusual Moments" *(page 62)* details many of the oddest moments in the history of the Stanley Cup trophy. It's been misplaced, drop-kicked, kidnapped and dented more than once in its 110-year existence.

"This Date in Stanley Cup History" *(page 84)* chronicles outstanding and surprising events in the playoffs. April and May have been busy!

"The Post-War Dynasties" *(page 126)* looks at the accomplishments of eight teams of distinction. Three versions of the Montreal Canadiens (1956-60, 1965-69 and 1976-79), two generations of the Toronto Maple Leafs (1947-51 and 1962-64), the Detroit Red Wings (1950-55), the New York Islanders (1980-83) and the Edmonton Oilers (1984-90) make the dynasty list.

Your comments, suggestion and corrections are extremely valuable to the *Total Hockey* editorial team. Please contact us by e-mail at dda.nhl@sympatico.ca.

Dan Diamond
March 2003

CHAPTER 1

Lord Stanley and His Cup Revealed

The Bearded Gent and the Trophy That Bears His Name

Eric Zweig

A Brief Biography

Frederick Arthur, Lord Stanley of Preston, 16th Earl of Derby, was born in London on January 15, 1841. The son of a three-time Prime Minister of England, he himself was a British Member of Parliament from 1865 to 1886. He then sat in the House of Lords, and later served a short stint as the Secretary of State for the British colonies. Publicly shy and politically careful, Lord Stanley was an advocate of closer ties between Britain and its colonies. He was appointed Governor-General of Canada in 1888.

Like most British aristocrats of the day, Lord Stanley was an avid sportsman. He and his family enjoyed the new sports they discovered during his posting to Ottawa. Snowshoeing and toboggan parties became a wintertime feature of life at Rideau Hall, the Governor-General's official residence. Skating and the new sport of ice hockey were also popular. Stanley's daughter Isobel was among the first female hockey players in Canada, while two of his sons, Arthur and Algernon, formed a men's hockey club known as the Rideau Rebels. In 1890, Arthur Stanley helped establish the Ontario Hockey Association. Lord Stanley himself was a patron of the Ottawa Athletic Association, and it was at a dinner for this group on March 18, 1892, that the Governor-General asked Lord Kilcoursie, one of his aides and a member of the Rebels hockey team, to read a letter on his behalf:

> *Gentlemen:*
>
> *I have for some time been thinking that it would be a good thing if there were a challenge cup, which would be held from year to year by the leading hockey club in the Dominion (of Canada). There does not appear to be any outward sign of the championship at present, and considering the general interest which hockey matches now elicit, and the importance of having the game played fairly and under rules generally recognized, I am willing to give a cup which shall be held from year to year by the winning club.*

Lord Stanley's offer was accepted, and a decorative bowl was purchased from a London silversmith for 10 guineas (the equivalent of $48.67). Originally called the Dominion Hockey Challenge Cup, the championship trophy would soon be known by the name of its benefactor. The Stanley Cup was first won by the Montreal Amateur Athletic Association hockey club, champions of the Amateur Hockey Association of Canada (the top hockey league in the country) in 1893. Ironically, Lord Stanley never witnessed a championship game nor attended the presentation of his trophy, having returned home in the midst of the 1893 hockey season. He passed away at Holwood, England, on June 14, 1908.

Terms of the Deal

The Stanley Cup regulations of 1903 outline the rules that Lord Stanley imposed in a document known as the "Deed of Gift" which states that: the then Governor-General, the Earl of Derby, before his departure from Canada in 1893 donated a challenge cup to be held from year to year by the championship Hockey Club of the Dominion. He appointed Sheriff Sweetland and Mr. P.D. Ross, of Ottawa, to act as trustees of the Cup, and requested them to suggest conditions to govern the competition. Meanwhile, his excellency directed that in 1893 the cup should be presented to the M.A.A.A. Hockey team of Montreal, champions of the A.H.A. of Canada, to be held by them until the close of the ensuing year. His excellency laid down the following preliminary conditions:

1. *The winners to give bond for the return of the cup in good order when required by the trustees for the purpose of being handed to any other team who may in turn win.*
2. *Each winning team to have at their own charge engraved on a silver ring fitted on the cup for the purpose the name of the team and the year won. (In the first instance the Montreal Amateur Athletic Association will find the cup already engraved for them.)*
3. *The cup shall remain a challenge cup, and will not become property of any team, even if won more than once.*
4. *In case of any doubt as to the name of any club to claim the position of champions, the cup shall be held or awarded by the trustees as they may think right, their decision being absolute.*
5. *Should either trustee resign or otherwise drop out, the remaining trustee shall nominate a substitute.*

Lord Stanley, in view of the fact of several hockey associations existing in Canada, also asked the trustees to arrange means of making the cup open to all, and thus representative of the hockey championship as completely as possible, rather than of any one association.

The Trustees' Regulations, from 1893:

1. *So far as the Amateur Hockey Association of Canada is concerned, the cup goes with the championship each year, without the necessity of any special or extra contest. Similarly in any other association.*
2. *Challenges from outside the Amateur Hockey Association of Canada are recognized by the trustees only from champion clubs of senior provincial associations, and in the order received.*
3. *When a challenge is accepted, the trustees desire the two competing clubs to arrange by mutual agreement all terms of the contest themselves such as a choice of date, of rink, division of the gate money, selection of officials, etc., etc. The trustees do not wish to interfere in any way, shape or form if it can be avoided.*
4. *Where competing clubs fail to agree, the trustees have observed, and will continue to observe as far as practicable, the following principles.*

a. *Cup to be awarded by the result of one match, or best two out of three, as seems fairest as regards other fixtures. The trustees would be willing, however, if desired, to allow the contest to be decided by a majority of the goals scored in two matches only (instead of best two matches in three).*

b. *Contests to take place on ice in the home city, the date or dates and choice of rink to be made or approved by the trustees.*

c. *The net gate money given by the rink to be equally divided between the competing teams.*

d. *If the clubs fail to agree on a referee, the trustees to appoint one from outside the competing cities, the two clubs to share the expenses equally.*

e. *If the clubs fail to agree on other officials, the trustees to authorize the referee to appoint them, the expense, if any, to be shared equally by the competing clubs.*

f. *No second challenge recognized in one season from the same hockey association.*

How It Got That Way: Physical Changes to the Stanley Cup

THE ORIGINAL STANLEY CUP BOWL purchased in London in 1892 stood 7½ inches (19 cm) tall and measured 11½ inches (29 cm) across the top. It was mounted on a ebony base that made the trophy about one foot tall (29 cm). In accordance with Lord Stanley's terms, the base was fitted with a silver ring that would be used to engrave the names of the winning teams. The first alteration to the physical appearance of the Stanley Cup was made in 1909, when a new bottom section was added. Again, this base was fitted with a ring for engraving. The Cup now stood about 16 inches (40 cm) tall.

No further changes were made to the Stanley Cup until 1924, when the Montreal Canadiens added a silver band between the two engraved rings. When the Victoria Cougars won the Cup the following year, they added an angled band that covered the area between the bottom of the original bowl and the first ring. The Stanley Cup now appeared completely silver from top to bottom. In future years, the silver area beneath the bowl would be known as the collar.

Following the lead of Montreal and Victoria, Stanley Cup-winning teams recorded their victories and the names of their players by adding new silver bands of varying shapes to the trophy, which saw it increase in size by differing amounts almost every year through 1929. From 1930 through 1939, identical-looking thin bands of engraved silver were added every year to commemorate the champions. During the 1940s, the Stanley Cup was standardized as a long "cigar-shaped" trophy which stood almost three feet (90 cm) high. It remained that way until 1948, when it was rebuilt into a two-piece trophy with a wide barrel-shaped base beneath the removable bowl and collar. The barrel-shaped base was sheathed with the rings that had made up the "cigar" of the 1930s and 1940s.

Additional engraving was added to the barrel annually until 1958, when the modern one-piece Stanley Cup was introduced. The silver from the old barrel was then retired to the Hockey Hall of Fame and replaced with five new wide bands, each of which could accommodate the names of 13 winners. The names of Cup winners beginning in 1928 were engraved on the new barrel before the revamped trophy was first presented.

Though the Cup's collar was replaced by a duplicate in 1963, and the original bowl was retired in 1969, the Stanley Cup still appears in the same form as it has since 1958. It is 36 inches (90 cm) tall and 18 inches (45 cm) across the base. It weighs 35 pounds (16 kg). For the opening of the new Hockey Hall of Fame in Toronto in 1993, a replica of the trophy (and all the other NHL trophies) was built so that the Hall would always have version of the Stanley Cup to display when the much-modified "original" trophy was on the road. (The trophy hoisted by the winning captain on the ice after the Cup-clinching game is always the "original.")

While the basic look of the Stanley Cup has not changed for 42 years, one further alteration was made after the 1990–91 season. The Pittsburgh Penguins filled the last available spot on the wide barrel bands that year. (When the trophy was remodeled in 1958 it was designed so that the last space would be filled by the winner during Cup's centennial year of 1991–92. This plan went awry when the names of the 1964–65 Montreal Canadiens were engraved over a space than was larger than normal, advancing the date when the Cup would be filled by one season.)

Rather than make the trophy bigger, and thereby change a shape that had become so familiar to hockey fans throughout the world, the decision was made to remove the top band (which contained the Cup winners from 1928 to 1940) and retire it to the Hockey Hall of Fame. The four remaining bands were then moved up the barrel, and a new fifth band was added at the bottom. With room for 13 teams, the Stanley Cup shouldn't require any alteration until 2005.

What's in a Name: How the Practice of Engraving the Stanley Cup Evolved

THE STANLEY CUP IS THE OLDEST PROFESSIONAL sports trophy in North America. It is also the only trophy in the world that records the name of every single player on every single team that has ever won it.

Well, not exactly.

Though many of the early winners of hockey's most coveted trophy are known to have engaged in some freelance silversmithing with a knife or a nail, the formal engraving of player names on the Stanley Cup first occurred in 1907 and did not become an annual rite until 1924. In between, there are several seasons in which the winning teams are not on the trophy.

Let's start at the very beginning.

In 1892, Lord Stanley, Governor-General of Canada, announced his decision to donate a hockey trophy. One of his initial conditions stipulated that, "each winning team to have at their own charge engraved on a silver ring fitted on the Cup for the purpose, the name of the team and the year won."

In accordance with Lord Stanley's wishes, team names in the earliest years of the Cup's history were engraved on this silver ring, but by 1902, the ring was completely filled. When the Montreal AAA successfully defended their third Stanley Cup title against the Winnipeg Victorias in 1903, they carved their team name right into Lord Stanley's bowl. The Ottawa Silver Seven continued this new practice when they took possession of the Cup later that season, only with a twist. When the Silver Seven successfully turned back a challenge, they engraved not only the year and their name on the bowl but also the name of the team that they had beaten. For this reason, the name Rat Portage appears on the Stanley Cup in 1903. (Rat Portage would win the Stanley Cup under its new name of Kenora in 1907.) By the time the Silver Seven were dethroned in 1906, Ottawa had defeated ten teams and there was no room left on the Cup for hockey's new champions; the Montreal Wanderers.

The Wanderers were certainly not about to let their championship go unrecorded (at least not yet!). The Montreal team chose to engrave its name right into the decorative fluting atop the Stanley Cup bowl. They covered half the bowl's circumference with their first win, then filled the other half when they turned back a challenge from New Glasgow, Nova Scotia. When the Kenora Thistles defeated the Wanderers in January 1907, they had to record their triumph inside the Stanley Cup bowl. This must have inspired the Montreal squad, for when they won the trophy back from Kenora in March, they inscribed the bottom of the bowl's interior with their team name and with the names of all of their players.

The 1908 season was the Wanderers' best yet, as they defeated four different Stanley Cup challengers. And how did these great champions, innovators of engraving that they were, commemorate these triumphs? They didn't! Only months after becoming the first team to engrave the names of its players on the Stanley Cup, the Montreal Wanderers became the first team in hockey history not to record its victory at all.

Why did the Wanderers leave their name off the Cup? No one seems to know. The Hockey Hall of Fame could provide no answer. Current Stanley Cup trustee Brian O'Neill had no explanation. Several Stanley Cup biographers were unable to uncover any stories. The truth may be lost to history forever, but it seems the Wanderers must have lacked the initiative, or felt they lacked the proper authority—or perhaps they were simply not willing to pay—to make additions to the Stanley Cup.

Apparently, Ottawa (now known as the Senators) did not share whatever concern the Wanderers must have had. After the Senators won the trophy in 1909, a new base was built on below the original silver ring and a second silver ring was added, where the team recorded its victory. The Senators entertained two Stanley Cup challenges during the 1910 season, winning them both, but year's end saw the Wanderers win the Cup back from Ottawa. However, not only did the Montreal squad fail to take advantage of the new ring on the Stanley Cup to add their 1908 championship to the trophy, they also did not bother to record their victory for 1910. When Ottawa regained possession of the Cup in 1911, the Senators also left their name off the trophy. Again, no Stanley Cup authority has the answer, so it's only possible to speculate as to what happened.

One thing is certain: hockey, by 1910, had become big business. The formation of the National Hockey Association truly ushered in the era of professional competition for the Stanley Cup. The NHA was formed to confront the hockey powers of the day. The Montreal Wanderers had been frozen out of their old league, the Eastern Canada Hockey Association, when it was realigned as the Canadian Hockey Association. When Ambrose O'Brien, of Renfrew, Ontario, who had been trying to gain admittance for his team in the new league, was turned down by the CHA, he banded with the Wanderers instead.

Like the World Hockey Association versus the NHL in the 1970s, the upstart NHA and the establishment CHA went to war—except in 1910 the upstarts won and the National Hockey Association emerged as the new power in the game. M.J. O'Brien, father of Ambrose, and a multi-millionaire in mining and railroads, donated a new trophy, the O'Brien Cup, and it, the NHA executive decided, would be emblematic of hockey supremacy. It's possible, then, that as champions of the NHA, the 1910 Wanderers and the 1911 Senators would have felt no obligation to engrave their names on the Stanley Cup.

It seems like a good theory to explain why no team names exist on the Stanley Cup for those two seasons, but there are several reasons why it isn't practical. Every league that preceded the NHA had its own championship trophy. The Stanley Cup did not belong to any one league during this era. It was a challenge trophy symbolizing the top team in all of Canada. Also, the reason the O'Briens got involved in hockey in the first place was to try and bring the Stanley Cup to their hometown of Renfrew. As for the Wanderers and Senators, both teams displayed the Stanley Cup prominently in their team photos, even though they had not engraved their names on the Cup, and both teams continued to entertain Stanley Cup challenges from other leagues across Canada. Once again, as in 1908, the truth may be lost to history forever.

The Stanley Cup got back on track in 1912, but was in trouble again by 1915, albeit of a different kind. Between 1915 and 1918, the Ottawa Senators, Portland Rosebuds, and Vancouver Millionaires all put their names on the Cup, even though they had not officially won it. The Cup was no longer a challenge trophy by then. Its playoff had become a World Series-like showdown between the sport's two top pro leagues: the NHA and the Pacific Coast Hockey Association. All three of these teams had defeated the defending Stanley Cup champions to win their own league title, but then lost the Cup to the eventual winner in the NHA-PCHA playoff.

When the Vancouver Millionaires actually won the Stanley Cup in 1915, they placed the team name on the lower ring started by Ottawa in 1909, but also engraved the names of the players within the flutes on the inside of the original bowl. When Vancouver carved its 1918 PCHA title onto the lower ring it completed the space available there. When the Toronto Arenas (of the newly formed NHL), beat Vancouver in the playoffs that year, there was no room left on the Stanley Cup for them. Their name does not appear. In fact, no more names would be added to the Stanley Cup for six seasons. Why? Once again, no one knows. Only 1919 can be logically explained, in that no champion was declared that year. The series between the Montreal Canadiens and Seattle Metropolitans was called off, due to the Spanish Influenza epidemic that killed millions of people around the world, including Joe Hall of the Canadiens. Ottawa's Cup wins in 1920, 1921 and 1923, along with the Toronto St. Pats' victory in 1922, cannot be explained, other than that, perhaps like the Montreal Wanderers, these teams felt they lacked the authority—or the money—to make alterations to the Stanley Cup.

Finally, in 1924, when hockey's most prized trophy involved a three-league battle between the NHL, the PCHA, and the Western Canada Hockey League, a champion's name is once again found on the Stanley Cup. The Montreal Canadiens defeated Ottawa, Vancouver, and Calgary in two-straight games each and celebrated their victory with a gaudy silver band encircling the area between the original rings. Every player, as well as everyone else associated with the team that year, had their name engraved on the Stanley Cup, just as they have every season since.

And what about the teams from 1908, 1910, 1911, and 1918 to 1923? Well, it's true that they did not engrave their names on the trophy in their day, but it's not entirely accurate to say these teams cannot be found anywhere on the trophy. In 1948, when the NHL remodeled the Stanley Cup from a tall, narrow tube into the basic barrel-shape still seen today, the names of all Cup-winning teams were engraved on the newly created "shoulder" of the trophy where the collars met the barrel. So the Stanley Cup won't forget these missing teams, even if the teams didn't leave their mark on the trophy themselves.

CHAPTER 2

Stanley Cup Champions and Finalists

1893 – 2002

YEAR	WINNER	COACH	FINALIST	COACH
2002	Detroit Red Wings	Scotty Bowman	Carolina Hurricanes	Paul Maurice
2001	Colorado Avalanche	Bob Hartley	New Jersey Devils	Larry Robinson
2000	New Jersey Devils	Larry Robinson	Dallas Stars	Ken Hitchcock
1999	Dallas Stars	Ken Hitchcock	Buffalo Sabres	Lindy Ruff
1998	Detroit Red Wings	Scotty Bowman	Washington Capitals	Ron Wilson
1997	Detroit Red Wings	Scotty Bowman	Philadelphia Flyers	Terry Murray
1996	Colorado Avalanche	Marc Crawford	Florida Panthers	Doug MacLean
1995	New Jersey Devils	Jacques Lemaire	Detroit Red Wings	Scotty Bowman
1994	New York Rangers	Mike Keenan	Vancouver Canucks	Pat Quinn
1993	Montreal Canadiens	Jacques Demers	Los Angeles Kings	Barry Melrose
1992	Pittsburgh Penguins	Scotty Bowman	Chicago Blackhawks	Mike Keenan
1991	Pittsburgh Penguins	Bob Johnson	Minnesota North Stars	Bob Gainey
1990	Edmonton Oilers	John Muckler	Boston Bruins	Mike Milbury
1989	Calgary Flames	Terry Crisp	Montreal Canadiens	Pat Burns
1988	Edmonton Oilers	Glen Sather	Boston Bruins	Terry O'Reilly
1987	Edmonton Oilers	Glen Sather	Philadelphia Flyers	Mike Keenan
1986	Montreal Canadiens	Jean Perron	Calgary Flames	Bob Johnson
1985	Edmonton Oilers	Glen Sather	Philadelphia Flyers	Mike Keenan
1984	Edmonton Oilers	Glen Sather	New York Islanders	Al Arbour
1983	New York Islanders	Al Arbour	Edmonton Oilers	Glen Sather
1982	New York Islanders	Al Arbour	Vancouver Canucks	Roger Neilson
1981	New York Islanders	Al Arbour	Minnesota North Stars	Glen Sonmor
1980	New York Islanders	Al Arbour	Philadelphia Flyers	Pat Quinn
1979	Montreal Canadiens	Scotty Bowman	New York Rangers	Fred Shero
1978	Montreal Canadiens	Scotty Bowman	Boston Bruins	Don Cherry
1977	Montreal Canadiens	Scotty Bowman	Boston Bruins	Don Cherry
1976	Montreal Canadiens	Scotty Bowman	Philadelphia Flyers	Fred Shero
1975	Philadelphia Flyers	Fred Shero	Buffalo Sabres	Floyd Smith
1974	Philadelphia Flyers	Fred Shero	Boston Bruins	Armand 'Bep' Guidolin
1973	Montreal Canadiens	Scotty Bowman	Chicago Black Hawks	Billy Reay
1972	Boston Bruins	Tom Johnson	New York Rangers	Emile Francis
1971	Montreal Canadiens	Al MacNeil	Chicago Black Hawks	Billy Reay
1970	Boston Bruins	Harry Sinden	St. Louis Blues	Scotty Bowman
1969	Montreal Canadiens	Claude Ruel	St. Louis Blues	Scotty Bowman
1968	Montreal Canadiens	Hector 'Toe' Blake	St. Louis Blues	Scotty Bowman
1967	Toronto Maple Leafs	George 'Punch' Imlach	Montreal Canadiens	Hector 'Toe' Blake
1966	Montreal Canadiens	Hector 'Toe' Blake	Detroit Red Wings	Sid Abel
1965	Montreal Canadiens	Hector 'Toe' Blake	Chicago Black Hawks	Billy Reay
1964	Toronto Maple Leafs	George 'Punch' Imlach	Detroit Red Wings	Sid Abel
1963	Toronto Maple Leafs	George 'Punch' Imlach	Detroit Red Wings	Sid Abel
1962	Toronto Maple Leafs	George 'Punch' Imlach	Chicago Black Hawks	Rudy Pilous
1961	Chicago Black Hawks	Rudy Pilous	Detroit Red Wings	Sid Abel
1960	Montreal Canadiens	Hector 'Toe' Blake	Toronto Maple Leafs	George 'Punch' Imlach
1959	Montreal Canadiens	Hector 'Toe' Blake	Toronto Maple Leafs	George 'Punch' Imlach
1958	Montreal Canadiens	Hector 'Toe' Blake	Boston Bruins	Milt Schmidt
1957	Montreal Canadiens	Hector 'Toe' Blake	Boston Bruins	Milt Schmidt
1956	Montreal Canadiens	Hector 'Toe' Blake	Detroit Red Wings	Jimmy Skinner
1955	Detroit Red Wings	Jimmy Skinner	Montreal Canadiens	Dick Irvin
1954	Detroit Red Wings	Tommy Ivan	Montreal Canadiens	Dick Irvin
1953	Montreal Canadiens	Dick Irvin	Boston Bruins	Lynn Patrick
1952	Detroit Red Wings	Tommy Ivan	Montreal Canadiens	Dick Irvin
1951	Toronto Maple Leafs	Joe Primeau	Montreal Canadiens	Dick Irvin
1950	Detroit Red Wings	Tommy Ivan	New York Rangers	Lynn Patrick
1949	Toronto Maple Leafs	Clarence 'Hap' Day	Detroit Red Wings	Tommy Ivan
1948	Toronto Maple Leafs	Clarence 'Hap' Day	Detroit Red Wings	Tommy Ivan
1947	Toronto Maple Leafs	Clarence 'Hap' Day	Montreal Canadiens	Dick Irvin
1946	Montreal Canadiens	Dick Irvin	Boston Bruins	Aubrey 'Dit' Clapper
1945	Toronto Maple Leafs	Clarence 'Hap' Day	Detroit Red Wings	Jack Adams
1944	Montreal Canadiens	Dick Irvin	Chicago Black Hawks	Paul Thompson
1943	Detroit Red Wings	Jack Adams	Boston Bruins	Art Ross
1942	Toronto Maple Leafs	Clarence 'Hap' Day	Detroit Red Wings	Jack Adams
1941	Boston Bruins	Ralph 'Cooney' Weiland	Detroit Red Wings	Jack Adams
1940	New York Rangers	Frank Boucher	Toronto Maple Leafs	Dick Irvin
1939	Boston Bruins	Art Ross	Toronto Maple Leafs	Dick Irvin
1938	Chicago Black Hawks	Bill Stewart	Toronto Maple Leafs	Dick Irvin
1937	Detroit Red Wings	Jack Adams	New York Rangers	Lester Patrick

YEAR	WINNER	COACH	FINALIST	COACH
1936	Detroit Red Wings	Jack Adams	Toronto Maple Leafs	Dick Irvin
1935	Montreal Maroons	Tommy Gorman	Toronto Maple Leafs	Dick Irvin
1934	Chicago Black Hawks	Tommy Gorman	Detroit Red Wings	Jack Adams
1933	New York Rangers	Lester Patrick	Toronto Maple Leafs	Dick Irvin
1932	Toronto Maple Leafs	Dick Irvin	New York Rangers	Lester Patrick
1931	Montreal Canadiens	Cecil Hart	Chicago Black Hawks	Dick Irvin
1930	Montreal Canadiens	Cecil Hart	Boston Bruins	Art Ross
1929	Boston Bruins	Cy Denneny	New York Rangers	Lester Patrick
1928	New York Rangers	Lester Patrick	Montreal Maroons	Eddie Gerard
1927	Ottawa Senators	Dave Gill	Boston Bruins	Art Ross
	THE NATIONAL HOCKEY LEAGUE ASSUMED CONTROL OF STANLEY CUP COMPETITION AFTER 1926			
1926	Montreal Maroons	Eddie Gerard	Victoria Cougars	Lester Patrick
1925	Victoria Cougars	Lester Patrick	Montreal Canadiens	Leo Dandurand
1924	Montreal Canadiens	Leo Dandurand	Calgary Tigers	Eddie Oatman
			Vancouver Maroons	Art Duncan/Frank Patrick
1923	Ottawa Senators	Pete Green	Edmonton Eskimos	Ken McKenzie
			Vancouver Maroons	Lloyd Cook/Frank Patrick
1922	Toronto St. Pats	George O'Donoghue	Vancouver Millionaires	Lloyd Cook/Frank Patrick
1921	Ottawa Senators	Pete Green	Vancouver Millionaires	Lloyd Cook/Frank Patrick
1920	Ottawa Senators	Pete Green	Seattle Metropolitans	Pete Muldoon
1919	No decision	Series between Montreal and Seattle cancelled due to influenza epidemic		
1918	Toronto Arenas	Dick Carroll	Vancouver Millionaires	Frank Patrick
1917	Seattle Metropolitans	Pete Muldoon	Montreal Canadiens	Newsy Lalonde
1916	Montreal Canadiens	George Kennedy	Portland Rosebuds	E.H. Savage (manager)
1915	Vancouver Millionaires	Frank Patrick	Ottawa Senators	Frank Shaughnessy (manager)
1914	Toronto Blueshirts	Scotty Davidson (captain)	Victoria Cougars	Lester Patrick
			Montreal Canadiens	Jimmy Gardner
1913	Quebec Bulldogs	Joe Malone (captain)	Sydney Miners	—
1912	Quebec Bulldogs	C. Nolan	Moncton Victories	—
1911	Ottawa Senators	Bruce Stuart (captain)	Port Arthur Bearcats	—
			Galt	—
1910	Montreal Wanderers	Pud Glass (captain)	Berlin Union Jacks	—
	Ottawa Senators	Bruce Stuart (captain)	Edmonton Eskimos	—
			Galt	—
1909	Ottawa Senators	Bruce Stuart (captain)	(no challengers)	
1908	Montreal Wanderers	Cecil Blachford	Edmonton Eskimos	—
			Toronto Trolley Leaguers	—
			Winnipeg Maple Leafs	—
			Ottawa Victorias	—
1907	Montreal Wanderers	Cecil Blachford	Kenora Thistles	—
	Kenora Thistles	Tom Phillips (captain)	Brandon Wheat Kings	—
			Montreal Wanderers	—
1906	Montreal Wanderers	Cecil Blachford (captain)	New Glascow Cubs	—
			Ottawa Silver Seven	—
	Ottawa Silver Seven	Alf Smith	Montreal Wanderers	—
			Smiths Falls	—
			Queen's University	—
1905	Ottawa Silver Seven	Alf Smith	Rat Portage Thistles	—
			Dawson City Nuggets	—
1904	Ottawa Silver Seven	Alf Smith	Brandon Wheat Kings	—
			Montreal Wanderers	—
			Toronto Marlboros	—
			Winnipeg Rowing Club	—
1903	Ottawa Silver Seven	Alf Smith	Rat Portage Thistles	—
			Montreal Victorias	—
	Montreal AAA	Clare McKerrow	Winnipeg Victorias	—
1902	Montreal AAA	Clare McKerrow	Winnipeg Victorias	—
	Winnipeg Victorias	—	Toronto Wellingtons	—
1901	Winnipeg Victorias	Dan Bain (captain)	Montreal Shamrocks	—
1900	Montreal Shamrocks	Harry Trihey (captain)	Halifax Crescents	—
			Winnipeg Victorias	—
1899	Montreal Shamrocks	Harry Trihey (captain)	Queen's University	—
	Montreal Victorias	Mike Grant (captain)	Winnipeg Victorias	—
1898	Montreal Victorias	Frank Richardson	(no challengers)	
1897	Montreal Victorias	Mike Grant (captain)	Ottawa Capitals	—
1896	Montreal Victorias	Mike Grant (captain)	Winnipeg Victorias	—
	Winnipeg Victorias	Jack Armitage	Montreal Victorias	—
1895	Montreal Victorias	Mike Grant (captain)	(no challengers)	
1894	Montreal AAA	—	Ottawa Generals	—
1893	Montreal AAA	—	(no challengers)	

CHAPTER 3

All-Time NHL Playoff Formats

1917-18 – The regular-season was split into two halves. The winners of both halves faced each other in a two-game, total-goals series for the NHL championship and the right to meet the Pacific Coast Hockey Association champion in the best-of-five Stanley Cup Finals.

1918-19 – Same as 1917-18, except that the NHL Finals was extended to a best-of-seven series.

1919-20 – Same as 1917-1918, except that Ottawa won both halves of the split regular-season schedule to earn an automatic berth into the best-of-five Stanley Cup Finals against the PCHA champions.

1921-22 – The top two teams at the conclusion of the regular-season faced each other in a two-game, total-goals series for the NHL championship. The NHL champion then moved on to play the winner of the PCHA-Western Canada Hockey League playoff series in the best-of-five Stanley Cup Finals.

1922-23 – The top two teams at the conclusion of the regular-season faced each other in a two-game, total-goals series for the NHL championship. The NHL champion then moved on to play the PCHA champion in the best-of-three Stanley Cup Semi-Finals, and the winner of the Semi-Finals played the WCHL champion, which had been given a bye, in the best-of-three Stanley Cup Finals.

1923-24 – The top two teams at the conclusion of the regular-season faced each other in a two-game, total-goals series for the NHL championship. The NHL champion then moved on to play the loser of the PCHA-WCHL playoff (the winner of the PCHA-WCHL playoff earned a bye into the Stanley Cup Finals) in the best-of-three Stanley Cup Semi-Finals. The winner of this series met the PCHA-WCHL playoff winner in the best-of-three Stanley Cup Finals.

1924-25 – The first place team (Hamilton) at the conclusion of the regular-season was scheduled to play the winner of a two-game, total goals series between the second (Toronto) and third (Montreal) place clubs. However, Hamilton refused to abide by this new format, demanding greater compensation than offered by the League. Thus, Toronto and Montreal played their two-game, total-goals series, and the winner (Montreal) earned the NHL title and then played the WCHL champion (Victoria) in the best-of-five Stanley Cup Finals.

1925-26 – The format which was intended for 1924-25 went into effect. The winner of the two-game, total-goals series between the second and third place teams squared off against the first place team in the two-game, total-goals NHL championship series. The NHL champion then moved on to play the Western Hockey League champion in the best-of-five Stanley Cup Finals.

After the 1925-26 season, the NHL was the only major professional hockey league still in existence and consequently took over sole control of the Stanley Cup competition.

1926-27 – The 10-team league was divided into two divisions – Canadian and American – of five teams apiece. In each division, the winner of the two-game, total-goals series between the second and third place teams faced the first place team in a two-game, total-goals series for the division title. The two division title winners then met in the best-of-five Stanley Cup Finals.

1928-29 – Both first place teams in the two divisions played each other in a best-of-five series. Both second place teams in the two divisions played each other in a two-game, total-goals series as did the two third place teams. The winners of these latter two series then played each other in a best-of-three series for the right to meet the winner of the series between the two first place clubs. This Stanley Cup Final was a best-of-three.

> Series A: First in Canadian Division versus first in American (best-of-five)
>
> Series B: Second in Canadian Division versus second in American (two-game, total-goals)
>
> Series C: Third in Canadian Division versus third in American (two-game, total-goals)
>
> Series D: Winner of Series B versus winner of Series C (best-of-three)
>
> Series E: Winner of Series A versus winner of Series D (best-of-three) for Stanley Cup

1931-32 – Same as 1928-29, except that Series D was changed to a two-game, total-goals format and Series E was changed to best-of-five.

1936-37 – Same as 1931-32, except that Series B, C, and D were each best-of-three.

1938-39 – With the NHL reduced to seven teams, the two-division system was replaced by one seven-team league. Based on final regular-season standings, the following playoff format was adopted:

> Series A: First versus Second (best-of-seven)
>
> Series B: Third versus Fourth (best-of-three)
>
> Series C: Fifth versus Sixth (best-of-three)
>
> Series D: Winner of Series B versus winner of Series C (best-of-three)
>
> Series E: Winner of Series A versus winner of Series D (best-of-seven)

1942-43 – With the NHL reduced to six teams (the "original six"), only the top four finishers qualified for playoff action. The best-of-seven Semi-Finals pitted Team #1 vs Team #3 and Team #2 vs Team #4. The winners of each Semi-Final series met in the best-of-seven Stanley Cup Finals.

1967-68 – When it doubled in size from 6 to 12 teams, the NHL once again was divided into two divisions – East and West – of six teams apiece. The top four clubs in each division qualified for the playoffs (all series were best-of-seven):

> Series A: Team #1 (East) vs Team #3 (East)
>
> Series B: Team #2 (East) vs Team #4 (East)
>
> Series C: Team #1 (West) vs Team #3 (West)
>
> Series D: Team #2 (West) vs Team #4 (West)
>
> Series E: Winner of Series A vs winner of Series B
>
> Series F: Winner of Series C vs winner of Series D
>
> Series G: Winner of Series E vs Winner of Series F

1970-71 – Same as 1967-68 except that Series E matched the winners of Series A and D, and Series F matched the winners of Series B and C.

1971-72 – Same as 1970-71, except that Series A and C matched Team #1 vs Team #4, and Series B and D matched Team #2 vs Team #3.

1974-75 – With the League now expanded to 18 teams in four divisions, a completely new playoff format was introduced. First, the #2 and #3 teams in each of the four divisions were pooled together in the Preliminary round. These eight (#2 and #3) clubs were ranked #1 to #8 based on regular-season record:

> Series A: Team #1 vs Team #8 (best-of-three)
>
> Series B: Team #2 vs Team #7 (best-of-three)
>
> Series C: Team #3 vs Team #6 (best-of-three)
>
> Series D: Team #4 vs Team #5 (best-of-three)

The winners of this Preliminary round then pooled together with the four division winners, which had received byes into this Quarter-Final round. These eight teams were again ranked #1 to #8 based on regular-season record:

> Series E: Team #1 vs Team #8 (best-of-seven)
>
> Series F: Team #2 vs Team #7 (best-of-seven)
>
> Series G: Team #3 vs Team #6 (best-of-seven)
>
> Series H: Team #4 vs Team #5 (best-of-seven)

The four Quarter-Finals winners, which moved on to the Semi-Finals, were then ranked #1 to #4 based on regular season record:

> Series I: Team #1 vs Team #4 (best-of-seven)
>
> Series J: Team #2 vs Team #3 (best-of-seven)
>
> Series K: Winner of Series I vs winner of Series J (best-of-seven)

1977-78 – Same as 1974-75, except that the Preliminary round consisted of the #2 teams in the four divisions and the next four teams based on regular-season record (not their standings within their divisions).

1979-80 – With the addition of four WHA franchises, the League expanded its playoff structure to include 16 of its 21 teams. The four first place teams in the four divisions automatically earned playoff berths. Among the 17 other clubs, the top 12, according to regular-season record, also earned berths. All 16 teams were then pooled together and ranked #1 to #16 based on regular-season record:

> Series A: Team #1 vs Team #16 (best-of-five)
>
> Series B: Team #2 vs Team #15 (best-of-five)
>
> Series C: Team #3 vs Team #14 (best-of-five)
>
> Series D: Team #4 vs Team #13 (best-of-five)
>
> Series E: Team #5 vs Team #12 (best-of-five)
>
> Series F: Team #6 vs Team #11 (best-of-five)
>
> Series G: Team #7 vs Team #10 (best-of-five)
>
> Series H: Team #8 vs Team #9 (best-of-five)

The eight Preliminary round winners, ranked #1 to #8 based on regular-season record, moved on to the Quarter-Finals:

> Series I: Team #1 vs Team #8 (best-of-seven)
>
> Series J: Team #2 vs Team #7 (best-of-seven)
>
> Series K: Team #3 vs Team #6 (best-of-seven)
>
> Series L: Team #4 vs Team #5 (best-of-seven)

The four Quarter-Finals winners, ranked #1 to #4 based on regular-season record, moved on to the Semi-Finals:

Series M: Team #1 vs Team #4 (best-of-seven)

Series N: Team #2 vs Team #3 (best-of-seven)

Series O: Winner of Series M vs winner of Series N (best-of-seven)

1981-82 – The first four teams in each division earned playoff berths. In each division, the first-place team opposed the fourth-place team and the second-place team opposed the third-place team in a best-of-five Division Semi-Final (DSF) series. In each division, the two winners of the DSF met in a best-of-seven Division Final (DF) series. The two DF winners in each conference met in a best-of-seven Conference Final (CF) series. In the Prince of Wales Conference, the Adams Division winner opposed the Patrick Division winner; in the Clarence Campbell Conference, the Smythe Division winner opposed the Norris Division winner. The two CF winners met in a best-of-seven Stanley Cup Final (F) series.

1986-87 – Division Semi-Final series changed from best-of-five to best-of-seven.

1993-94 – The NHL's playoff draw was conference-based rather than division-based. At the conclusion of the regular season, the top eight teams in each of the Eastern and Western Conferences qualified for the playoffs. The teams that finished in first place in each of the League's divisions are seeded first and second in each conference's playoff draw and were assured of home ice advantage in the first two playoff rounds.

The remaining teams were seeded based on their regular-season point totals. In each conference, the team seeded #1 plays #8; #2 vs. #7; #3 vs. #6; and #4 vs. #5. All series were best-of-seven with home ice rotating on a 2-2-1-1-1 basis, with the exception of matchups between Central and Pacific Division teams. These matchups were played on a 2-3-2 basis to reduce travel. In a 2-3-2 series, the team with the most points could choose to start the series at home or on the road. The Eastern Conference champion faced the Western Conference champion in the Stanley Cup Final.

1994-95 – Same as 1993-94, except that in first, second or third-round playoff series involving Central and Pacific Division teams, the team with the better record had the choice of using either a 2-3-2 or a 2-2-1-1-1 format. When a 2-3-2 format was selected, the higher-ranked team also had the choice of playing games 1, 2, 6 and 7 at home or playing games 3, 4 and 5 at home. The format for the Stanley Cup Final remained 2-2-1-1-1.

1998-99 – The NHL's clubs were re-aligned into two conferences each consisting of three divisions. The number of teams qualifying for the Stanley Cup Playoffs remained unchanged at 16.

First-round playoff berths were awarded to the first-place team in each division as well as to the next five best teams based on regular-season point totals in each conference. The three division winners in each conference were seeded first through third, in order of points, for the playoffs and the next five best teams, in order of points, were seeded fourth through eighth. In each conference, the team seeded #1 played #8; #2 vs. #7; #3 vs. #6; and #4 vs. #5 in the quarter-final round. Home-ice in the Conference Quarter-Finals was granted to those teams seeded first through fourth in each conference.

In the Conference Semi-Finals and Conference Finals, teams were re-seeded according to the same criteria as the Conference Quarter-Finals. Higher seeded teams gained home-ice advantage.

Home-ice advantage for the Stanley Cup Finals to be determined by points.

All series remain best-of-seven.

2003 Playoff Format

The National Hockey League's 30 clubs are aligned into two conferences, each consisting of three divisions (Eastern Conference: Atlantic, Northeast, Southeast; Western Conference: Central, Northwest, Pacific). The number of teams qualifying for the 2003 Stanley Cup Playoffs remains at 16.

First-round playoff berths will be awarded to the first-place team in each division, as well as to the next five best teams (based on regular-season point totals in each conference). The three division winners in each conference will be seeded first through third (in order of points) and the next five best teams (in order of points) will be seeded fourth through eighth. In each conference, the team seeded #1 will play the team seeded #8; #2 vs. #7; #3 vs. #6 and #4 vs. #5 in the Conference Quarter-Final round. Home-ice in the Conference Quarter-Finals is granted to those teams seeded first through fourth in each conference.

In the Conference Semi-Finals and Conference Finals, teams will be re-seeded according to the same criteria as the Conference Quarter-Finals (division leaders will be seeded first and granted home-ice advantage while the remaining teams will be seeded in order of regular-season points).

Home-ice advantage in the Stanley Cup series will be determined by points. All series remain best-of-seven.

Tie-Breaking Procedure

In the event two or more clubs are tied in points at the conclusion of the regular season, the standing of the clubs in each conference will be determined in the following order:

1. The greater number of games won.
2. The greater number of points earned in games between the tied clubs. If two clubs are tied, and have not played an equal number of home games against each other, points earned in the first game played in the city that had the extra game shall not be included. If more than two clubs are tied, the higher percentage of available points earned in games among those clubs (and not including any "odd" games) shall be used to determine the standing.
3. The greater differential between goals for and against for the entire regular season.

Conference Quarter-Finals (Series A – H)

The six regular-season division champions will be ranked in the first three positions in their respective conferences, the clubs with the greatest number of points being ranked first in their respective conferences. The remaining five playoff clubs in each conference will be ranked based on regular-season points. Following are the matchups based on the rankings.

Eastern Conference

Series A　#1 (Division winner) vs. #8
Series B　#2 (Division winner) vs. #7
Series C　#3 (Division winner) vs. #6
Series D　#4 vs. #5

Western Conference

Series E　#1 (Division winner) vs. #8
Series F　#2 (Division winner) vs. #7
Series G　#3 (Division winner) vs. #6
Series H　#4 vs. #5

Conference Semi-Finals (Series I – L)

If one division winner is eliminated in the Conference Quarter-Finals: The remaining division winners would be seeded first and second, followed by the two remaining clubs in order of regular-season points. The #1 seed would face the club with the fewest regular-season points, while the other two clubs would meet.

If two division winners are eliminated in the Conference Quarter-Finals: The remaining division winner would be seeded first, followed by the three remaining clubs in order of regular-season points. The #1 seed would face the club with the fewest regular-season points, while the other two clubs would meet.

If all three division winners are eliminated in the Conference Quarter-Finals: The remaining clubs would be ranked in order of regular-season points. The remaining team with the most regular-season points would be seeded first, followed by the three remaining teams. The #1 seed would face the #4 seed, while the #2 and #3 seeds would meet.

If a division winner meets a non-division winner that compiled more regular-season points: The division winner would receive home-ice advantage.

Conference Finals (Series M and N)

The same criteria used in the selection of order for the Conference Quarter-Finals (Advancing division winners, followed by remaining clubs based on regular-season points) again will be in effect.

If a division winner meets a non-division winner that compiled more regular-season points: The division winner would receive home-ice advantage.

If Conference Semi-Final series end early: Start dates for the Conference Finals may be moved up depending on a number of factors, including building availability and travel schedules.

Stanley Cup Final (Series O)

The Eastern Conference and Western Conference champion will meet in the Stanley Cup Final series. Home ice will be determined by the greater number of regular-season points, subject to the tie-breaking procedures outlined on the previous page. Games will be played on a 2-2-1-1-1 basis.

CHAPTER 4

In the Beginning

From Amateur Challenge Trophy to Pro Hockey Supremacy

Eric Zweig

THE HISTORY OF THE STANLEY CUP prior to the formation of the NHL in 1917 tells the story of how hockey grew from a regionalized amateur pastime into a professional business. Like Darwin's theory of survival of the fittest, the Stanley Cup was able to evolve with the changing times.

When Lord Stanley proposed the idea of a championship trophy in 1892, the "modern" sport of hockey was less than 20 years old. First moved indoors off frozen lakes and rivers in Montreal in 1875, the game was still played most competitively in that city, as well as in nearby Ottawa and Quebec City. The Amateur Hockey Association of Canada, formed in 1886, comprised teams from those cities. Hockey also had a following in Kingston, where outdoor ice games had been played since at least the 1850s. The popularity of hockey in that city helped the game grow through southern Ontario, and in 1890 the Ontario Hockey Association was formed. By that year, the game had also spread to western Canada where it found a particularly fevered following in Winnipeg. Having been home to a variety of outdoor stick and ice games since the early 1800s, Canada's east coast had its own hockey following as well. All of these different areas of interest would eventually be brought together in the quest for Lord Stanley's Cup.

Originally called the Dominion Hockey Challenge Cup, Lord Stanley's trophy was first presented in 1893. It was awarded to the hockey club from the Montreal Amateur Athletic Association, who had won the league title in the Amateur Hockey Association which was recognized as the top league in Canada. But as Lord Stanley wanted his Cup to be truly representative of a national championship, he instructed his trustees, Philip Dansken Ross and Sheriff John Sweetland, to construct a set of terms that would allow teams from across the country to challenge for the trophy. The Stanley Cup, therefore, would not be the sole property of the AHA (or of any hockey league), but could be competed for by the senior champion of any recognized provincial association. However, once a team had won it the Stanley Cup belonged to them until someone defeated them. Defeating them did not necessarily entail issuing a challenge, for the trustees determined that the Stanley Cup could also change hands within a given league. For example, when the Montreal Victorias unseated the AAA for the AHA championship in 1895 they automatically became holders of Stanley Cup. But in order for the Manitoba Hockey League's Winnipeg Victorias to become champions in 1896, they had to issue a challenge to their Montreal counterparts. Once Winnipeg had won the Stanley Cup, it became property of them in the MHL and when the Montreal Vics successfully defended their AHA championship they had to challenge Winnipeg in order to win back the Stanley Cup.

Though the AHA was replaced by the Canadian Amateur Hockey League in 1899, the system of determining Stanley Cup winners that was devised in 1893 went on without a hitch until 1904 when the Ottawa Silver Seven threatened the status quo.

By defeating the defending champion Montreal AAA for the CAHL title in 1903, Ottawa had won the Stanley Cup, but trouble began the following season. On January 30, 1904, the Silver Seven were delayed en route to Montreal for a league game against the Victorias. As a result, the game was not yet over when the two teams agreed to leave the ice at midnight with Ottawa leading 4–1. CAHL officials refused to grant Ottawa the victory, and ordered that the game be replayed. The ensuing debate ended with the Silver Seven withdrawing from the league. CAHL officials hoped the Stanley Cup would then pass to their new league champion (Quebec), but the trustees ruled it would remain with Ottawa. Even though they were no longer a part of any established hockey league, the Silver Seven defeated the OHA champions from Toronto, then had a series with the Montreal Wanderers abandoned due to a scheduling conflict before defeating a team from Brandon, Manitoba that featured a young defenseman named Lester Patrick. Any further problems were resolved when the Silver Seven joined the Federal Amateur Hockey League in 1905. In 1906, the Ottawa club helped form the Eastern Canada Amateur Hockey Association (ECAHA), which replaced the CAHL as the top league in the country.

With a lineup that boasted future Hall of Famers Bouse Hutton, Harvey Pulford, Harry Westwick, Alf Smith, Billy Gilmour, and Frank McGee, the Silver Seven were the first legendary hockey team of the 20th century. Tough and talented, they remained Stanley Cup champions until finally relinquishing the trophy in 1906. During their championship run, the Silver Seven played off for the title ten times—far more than any other team during the Stanley Cup's challenge era.

From 1893 to 1906 the Winnipeg Victorias (1896 and 1901) were the only Stanley Cup winners from outside Montreal and Ottawa. In these early days of Stanley Cup competition, geography and climate played almost as important a role as skill in determining a champion. During this time period, the hockey season in leagues across Canada ran from January to early March—cold weather being a must in arenas that relied on natural ice. This being the case, a Stanley Cup challenge match might be scheduled in late December before the start of hockey season or in mid-March if weather still permitted, but the majority were scheduled in midseason during January and February. The Stanley Cup trustees could only accept as many challenges as time (ie the weather and regular-season schedules) would permit, and an arduous travel agenda didn't make an underdog's role any easier—as the Dawson City Nuggets discovered in 1905.

The most unusual challenge in Stanley Cup history was received by the trustees on September 9, 1904. Spearheaded by businessman and adventurer Joe Boyle, Dawson's Stanley Cup bid was officially sanctioned on December 10. Originally scheduled to be completed by January 10, 1905, the start of the series was pushed back to January 13 in order to accommodate an election that had been called in the Yukon Territory. The hockey players from Dawson City left town on December 18,

1904. Traveling 4,000 miles on foot and on dogsled, by bicycle, boat and by train, they arrived in Ottawa just one day before the start of the series. On the road for almost an entire month, they were in understandably poor condition. After a 9–2 Ottawa victory in the opener, the series concluded with Dawson City being defeated 23–2 on January 16, 1905. Frank McGee scored 14 goals for the Silver Seven that evening.

Ottawa's run as Stanley Cup champions ended when the team lost the ECAHA title to the Montreal Wanderers in March 1906. By November of that year, the Wanderers played a key role in ushering in a new era in Stanley Cup history. At the ECAHA annual meeting prior to the upcoming 1907 season, the Wanderers helped push through a resolution that allowed professional players to play alongside amateurs. The only stipulation was that teams would be required to declare which of their players were pros and which were amateurs, and that the status of these players would be published in the newspapers.

The issue of professionalism was a hot topic in Canada and around the sporting world during the late 19th century and into the 20th. Many people continued to cling to the British aristocratic tradition of sports for sports' sake, but the truth was that many hockey players had been paid to play almost from the beginning—though these payments were usually made in secret. The first openly professional hockey league was the International (Pro) Hockey League, which operated with teams in Pennsylvania, Michigan and northwestern Ontario from 1904 to 1907. Though the issue remained contentious, the Stanley Cup trustees (now P.D. Ross and William Foran) did not impose any moral judgements. If the top league in Canada voted to allow professionals to compete, than the Stanley Cup would be open to competition from professional teams. Once the decision was made, there was no turning back. By 1908, a new trophy (the Allan Cup) was introduced to recognize Canada's amateur champions. The Stanley Cup was now the emblem of professional hockey supremacy. Organizations like the Ontario Professional Hockey League and the Maritime Professional Hockey League would soon arise and send challengers to compete for the Stanley Cup.

In 1910, a new league emerged as the top hockey circuit in Canada. The National Hockey Association (forerunner of the NHL) introduced the Montreal Canadiens to the game during its inaugural season. In 1910–11 (the schedule was now beginning in December) the NHA changed the timing of hockey games from two 30-minute halves to three 20-minute periods. Prior to the 1911-12 season, the NHA eliminated the position of rover and introduced the six-man game. This year would also prove significant in that the Stanley Cup trustees declared that all challenge matches would now take place at the conclusion of the regular season.

Yet another change was introduced to hockey for the 1911–12 season. The Pacific Coast Hockey Association was formed by Frank and Lester Patrick. In addition to running the league, Frank would serve as a player, coach, general manager, and owner of the PCHA's Vancouver Millionaires. Lester held the same duties with the Victoria Aristocrats. (It was hoped the monied monikers would lend the league a touch of class.)

Using proceeds from the sale of their father's British Columbia lumber business, the Patrick brothers built Canada's first artificial ice rinks in Vancouver and Victoria in order to overcome the west coast's non-hockey climate. Using their hockey connections in the east, they raided talent from NHA rosters to stock their teams, as well as the PCHA's third franchise in New Westminster. Notable names like Newsy Lalonde, Tommy Dunderdale, and Moose Watson (Hockey Hall of Famers all) went west that first season, though the man who would give the PCHA the credibility it needed (as he had previously done for the NHA) did not come on board until the league's second season. Fred "Cyclone" Taylor was signed by the Vancouver Millionaires in 1912–13.

The Patricks were innovators, and while it was the NHA that would one day become the NHL it was the PCHA that truly modernized hockey. Though Frank and Lester stubbornly maintained the position of rover, they also painted blue lines on the ice to divide the playing surface into zones, legalized forward passing, and permitted goaltenders to leave their feet. In all, some 20 rules proposed by Frank Patrick would eventually find their way into NHL rule books.

Meanwhile, since its inception in 1910, no team from a rival league had been able to defeat the NHA's champion for the Stanley Cup. As such, the Stanley Cup was passed from the Montreal Wanderers in 1910 to the Ottawa Senators in 1911, to the Quebec Bulldogs in 1912 as the NHA found itself with a new league leader for three straight years. Quebec repeated as champions in 1913, but the Stanley Cup was claimed by the Toronto Blueshirts when they took the NHA title in 1914. That year, Victoria traveled east to take on Toronto for the Stanley Cup. The Aristocrats failed to submit an official request to play for the championship, leading to a statement from trustees Ross and Foran that this series was not regarded as a formal Cup challenge. Prior to the 1914–15 season, the NHA and PCHA simply agreed that their respective league champions would meet to determine the Stanley Cup winner. Because of the distances involved, all games in a given year would be played in one location, the site alternating yearly between the champions of east and west. The two leagues' differing sets of rules would be switched from game to game.

Another significant development in Stanley Cup history took place in the 1914–15 season. The PCHA's New Westminster Royals franchise left British Columbia for Oregon, where it became the Portland Rosebuds. (Portland is known as "The Rose City.") By admitting a United States city into a league that competed for the Stanley Cup, PCHA president Frank Patrick and the Stanley Cup trustees were recognizing that an American-based team might one day be playing for a trophy that had previously been emblematic of Canadian supremacy. In fact, the Rosebuds won the PCHA title in 1916, but they lost the Stanley Cup to the Montreal Canadiens, who won for the first time in franchise history. One year later, the Seattle Metropolitans beat the Canadiens in the NHA–PCHA "World Series" and the Stanley Cup headed south of the border.

Just 25 years after it had been presented, the Stanley Cup was no longer a challenge trophy, nor was it held by the champion team of the Dominion of Canada. These had been the preliminary conditions laid down by Lord Stanley. However, one of the original conditions had also provided that the Cup would be held or awarded by the trustees as they saw fit. By changing with the times, the trustees ensured that the Stanley Cup would always be the top prize in hockey.

CHAPTER 5

Playoff History, Current NHL Clubs

1918–2002

NOTES:
- Calgary totals include Atlanta Flames, 1972-73 to 1979-80.
- Carolina totals include Hartford, 1979–80 to 1996-97.
- Colorado totals include Quebec, 1979-80 to 1994-95.
- Dallas totals include Minnesota North Stars, 1967-68 to 1992-93.
- New Jersey totals include Kansas City, 1974-75 to 1975-76 and Colorado Rockies, 1976-77 to 1981-82.
- Phoenix totals include Winnipeg, 1979-80 to 1995-96.

ANAHEIM

All-Time Playoff Record vs. Other Teams

	Series	W	L	GP	W	L	T	GF	GA	Last Mtg.	Round	Result
Detroit	2	0	2	8	0	8	0	14	30	1999	CQF	L 0-4
Phoenix	1	1	0	7	4	3	0	17	17	1997	CQF	W 4-3
Totals	3	1	2	15	4	11	0	31	47			

Playoff Results 2002-98

Year	Round	Opponent	Result	GF	GA
1999	CQF	Detroit	L 0-4	6	17

Playoff Scoring Leaders

	Player	Years	GP	G	A	PTS
1.	Paul Kariya	97-99	14	8	9	17
2.	Teemu Selanne	97-99	15	9	5	14
3.	Dmitri Mironov	97	11	1	10	11
4.	J.J. Daigneault	97	11	2	7	9
5.	Brian Bellows	97	11	2	4	6
6.	Steve Rucchin	97-99	12	1	5	6
7.	Jari Kurri	97	11	1	2	3
8.	Marty McInnis	99	4	2	0	2
9.	Joe Sacco	97	11	2	0	2
10.	Dave Karpa	97	8	1	1	2
11.	Fredrik Olausson	99	4	0	2	2
12.	Sean Pronger	97	9	0	2	2
13.	Darren Van Impe	97	9	0	2	2
14.	Warren Rychel	97	11	0	2	2

Series Records vs. Other Clubs

Opponent	Year	Series	Winner	W	L	GF	GA
Phx.	1997	CQF	Ana.	4	3	17	17
Det.	1997	CSF	Det.	0	4	8	13
Det.	1999	CQF	Det.	0	4	6	17

BOSTON

All-Time Playoff Record vs. Other Teams

	Series	W	L	GP	W	L	T	GF	GA	Last Mtg.	Round	Result
Buffalo	7	5	2	39	21	18	0	139	130	1999	CSF	L 2-4
Carolina	3	3	0	19	12	7	0	63	48	1999	CQF	W 4-2
Chicago	6	5	1	22	16	5	1	97	63	1978	QF	W 4-0
Colorado	2	1	1	11	6	5	0	37	36	1983	DSF	W 3-1
Dallas	1	0	1	3	0	3	0	13	20	1981	PRE	L 0-3
Detroit	7	4	3	33	19	14	0	96	98	1957	SF	W 4-1
Edmonton	2	0	2	9	1	8	0	20	41	1990	F	L 1-4
Florida	1	0	1	5	1	4	0	16	22	1996	CQF	L 1-4
Los Angeles	2	2	0	13	8	5	0	56	38	1977	QF	W 4-2
Montreal	29	7	22	145	54	91	0	357	450	2002	CQF	L 2-4
New Jersey	3	1	2	18	7	11	0	52	55	1995	CQF	L 1-4
NY Islanders	2	0	2	11	3	8	0	35	49	1983	CF	L 2-4
NY Rangers	9	6	3	42	22	18	2	114	104	1973	QF	L 1-4
Philadelphia	4	2	2	20	11	9	0	60	57	1978	SF	W 4-1
Pittsburgh	4	2	2	19	9	10	0	62	67	1992	CF	L 0-4
St. Louis	2	2	0	8	8	0	0	48	15	1972	SF	W 4-0
Toronto	13	5	8	62	30	31	1	153	150	1974	QF	W 4-0
Washington	2	1	1	10	6	4	0	28	21	1998	CQF	L 2-4
Defunct	3	1	2	11	4	5	2	20	20			
Totals	102	47	55	500	238	256	6	1466	1484			

Playoff Results 2002-98

Year	Round	Opponent	Result	GF	GA
2002	CQF	Montreal	L 2-4	18	20
1999	CSF	Buffalo	L 2-4	14	17
	CQF	Carolina	W 4-2	16	10
1998	CQF	Washington	L 2-4	13	15

Playoff Scoring Leaders

	Player	Years	GP	G	A	PTS
1.	Raymond Bourque	80-99	180	36	125	161
2.	Phil Esposito	68-75	71	46	56	102
3.	Rick Middleton	77-88	111	45	55	100
4.	John Bucyk	58-77	109	40	60	100
5.	Bobby Orr	68-75	74	26	66	92
6.	Wayne Cashman	68-83	145	31	57	88
7.	Cam Neely	87-95	86	55	32	87
8.	Ken Hodge	68-76	86	34	47	81
9.	Brad Park	76-83	91	23	55	78
10.	Peter McNab	77-83	79	38	36	74

Series Records vs. Other Teams

Opponent	Year	Series	Winner	W	L	T	GF	GA
Buf.	1982	DSF	Bos.	3	1		17	11
Buf.	1983	DF	Bos.	4	3		33	23
Buf.	1988	DSF	Bos.	4	2		28	22
Buf.	1989	DSF	Bos.	4	1		16	14
Buf.	1992	DSF	Bos.	4	3		19	24
Buf.	1993	DSF	Buf.	0	4		12	19
Buf.	1999	CSF	Buf.	2	4		14	17
Car.	1999	CQF	Bos.	4	2		16	10
Chi.	1927	QF*	Bos.	1	0	1	10	5
Chi.	1942	QF	Bos.	2	1		5	7
Chi.	1970	SF	Bos.	4	0		20	10
Chi.	1974	SF	Bos.	4	2		28	20
Chi.	1975	PRE	Chi.	1	2		15	12
Chi.	1978	SF	Bos.	4	0		19	9
Det.	1941	F	Bos.	4	0		12	6
Det.	1942	SF	Det.	0	2		5	9
Det.	1943	F	Det.	0	4		5	16
Det.	1945	SF	Det.	3	4		22	22
Det.	1946	SF	Bos.	4	1		16	10
Det.	1953	SF	Bos.	4	2		21	21
Det.	1957	SF	Bos.	4	1		15	14
Edm.	1988	F	Edm.	0	4		12	21
Edm.	1990	F	Edm.	1	4		8	20
Fla.	1996	CQF	Fla.	1	4		16	22
Hfd.	1990	DSF	Bos.	4	3		23	21
Hfd.	1991	DSF	Bos.	4	2		24	17
L.A.	1976	QF	Bos.	4	3		26	14
L.A.	1977	QF	Bos.	4	2		30	24
Min.	1981	PRE	Min.	0	3		13	20
Mtl.	1929	SF	Bos.	3	0		5	2
Mtl.	1930	F	Mtl.	0	2		3	7
Mtl.	1931	SF	Mtl.	2	3		13	13
Mtl.	1943	SF	Bos.	4	1		18	17
Mtl.	1946	F	Mtl.	1	4		13	19
Mtl.	1947	SF	Mtl.	1	4		10	16
Mtl.	1952	SF	Mtl.	3	4		12	18
Mtl.	1953	F	Mtl.	1	4		9	16
Mtl.	1954	SF	Mtl.	0	4		4	16
Mtl.	1955	SF	Mtl.	1	4		9	16
Mtl.	1957	F	Mtl.	1	4		6	15
Mtl.	1958	F	Mtl.	2	4		14	16
Mtl.	1968	QF	Mtl.	0	4		8	15
Mtl.	1969	SF	Mtl.	2	4		16	15
Mtl.	1971	QF	Mtl.	3	4		26	28
Mtl.	1977	F	Mtl.	0	4		6	16
Mtl.	1978	F	Mtl.	2	4		13	18
Mtl.	1979	SF	Mtl.	3	4		20	25
Mtl.	1984	DSF	Mtl.	0	3		2	10
Mtl.	1985	DSF	Mtl.	2	3		17	19
Mtl.	1986	DSF	Mtl.	0	3		6	10
Mtl.	1987	DSF	Mtl.	0	4		11	19
Mtl.	1988	DF	Bos.	4	1		15	10
Mtl.	1989	DF	Mtl.	1	4		13	16
Mtl.	1990	DF	Bos.	4	1		16	12
Mtl.	1991	DF	Bos.	4	3		18	18
Mtl.	1992	DF	Bos.	4	0		14	8
Mtl.	1994	CQF	Bos.	4	3		22	20
Mtl.	2002	CQF	Mtl.	2	4		18	20
N.J.	1988	CF	Bos.	4	3		30	19
N.J.	1994	CSF	N.J.	2	4		17	22
N.J.	1995	CQF	N.J.	1	4		5	14
NYI	1980	QF	NYI	1	4		14	19
NYI	1983	CF	NYI	2	4		21	30
NYR	1927	SF*	Bos.	1	0	1	3	1
NYR	1928	SF*	NYR	0	1	1	2	5
NYR	1929	F	Bos.	2	0		4	1
NYR	1939	SF	Bos.	4	3		14	12
NYR	1940	SF	NYR	2	4		9	15
NYR	1958	SF	Bos.	4	2		28	16
NYR	1970	QF	Bos.	4	2		25	16
NYR	1972	F	Bos.	4	2		18	16
NYR	1973	QF	NYR	1	4		11	22
Phi.	1974	F	Phi.	2	4		13	15
Phi.	1976	SF	Phi.	1	4		12	19
Phi.	1977	SF	Bos.	4	0		14	8
Phi.	1978	SF	Bos.	4	1		21	15
Pit.	1979	QF	Bos.	4	0		16	7
Pit.	1980	PRE	Bos.	3	2		21	14
Pit.	1991	CF	Pit.	2	4		18	27
Pit.	1992	CF	Pit.	0	4		7	19
Que.	1982	DF	Que.	3	4		26	28
Que.	1983	DSF	Bos.	3	1		11	8
St.L.	1970	F	Bos.	4	0		20	7
St.L.	1972	SF	Bos.	4	0		28	8
Tor.	1933	SF	Tor.	2	3		7	9
Tor.	1935	SF	Tor.	1	3		2	7
Tor.	1936	QF*	Tor.	1	1		6	8
Tor.	1938	SF	Tor.	0	3		3	6
Tor.	1939	F	Bos.	4	1		12	6
Tor.	1941	SF	Bos.	4	3		15	17
Tor.	1948	SF	Tor.	1	4		13	20
Tor.	1949	SF	Tor.	1	4		10	16
Tor.	1951	SF	Tor.	1	4	1	5	17
Tor.	1959	SF	Tor.	3	4		21	20
Tor.	1969	QF	Bos.	4	0		24	5
Tor.	1972	QF	Bos.	4	1		18	10
Tor.	1974	QF	Bos.	4	0		17	9
Wsh.	1990	CF	Bos.	4	0		15	6
Wsh.	1998	CQF	Wsh.	2	4		13	15

Defunct Teams

Opponent	Year	Series	Winner	W	L	GF	GA
Mtl.M.	1930	SF	Bos.	3	1	11	5
Mtl.M.	1937	QF	Mtl.M.	1	2	6	8
Ott.	1927	F	Ott.	0	2	3	7

* Total-goals series

BUFFALO

All-Time Playoff Record vs. Other Teams

	Series	W	L	GP	W	L	T	GF	GA	Last Mtg.	Round	Result
Boston	7	2	5	39	18	21	0	130	139	1999	CSF	W 4-2
Chicago	2	2	0	9	8	1	0	36	17	1980	QF	W 4-0
Colorado	2	0	2	8	2	6	0	27	35	1985	DSF	L 2-3
Dallas	3	1	2	13	5	8	0	37	39	1999	F	L 2-4
Montreal	7	3	4	35	17	18	0	111	124	1998	CSF	W 4-0
New Jersey	1	0	1	7	3	4	0	14	14	1994	CQF	L 3-4
NY Islanders	3	0	3	16	4	12	0	45	59	1980	SF	L 2-4
NY Rangers	1	1	0	3	2	1	0	11	6	1978	PRE	W 2-1
Ottawa	2	2	0	11	8	3	0	26	19	1999	CQF	W 4-0
Philadelphia	7	2	5	37	14	23	0	96	110	2001	CQF	W 4-2
Pittsburgh	2	0	2	10	4	6	0	26	26	2001	CSF	L 3-4
St. Louis	1	1	0	3	2	1	0	7	8	1976	PRE	W 2-1
Toronto	1	1	0	5	4	1	0	21	16	1999	CF	W 4-1
Vancouver	2	2	0	7	6	1	0	28	14	1981	PRE	W 3-0
Washington	1	0	1	6	2	4	0	11	13	1998	CF	L 2-4
Totals	**42**	**17**	**25**	**209**	**99**	**110**	**0**	**626**	**639**			

Playoff Results 2002-98

Year	Round	Opponent	Result	GF	GA
2001	CSF	Pittsburgh	L 3-4	17	17
	CQF	Philadelphia	W 4-2	21	13
2000	CQF	Philadelphia	L 1-4	8	14
1999	F	Dallas	L 2-4	9	13
	CF	Toronto	W 4-1	21	16
	CSF	Boston	W 4-2	17	14
	CQF	Ottawa	W 4-0	12	6
1998	CF	Washington	L 2-4	11	13
	CSF	Montreal	W 4-0	17	10
	CQF	Philadelphia	W 4-1	18	9

Playoff Scoring Leaders

	Player	Years	GP	G	A	PTS
1.	Gilbert Perreault	73-85	90	33	70	103
2.	Rick Martin	73-80	62	24	29	53
3.	Craig Ramsay	73-85	89	17	31	48
4.	Danny Gare	75-81	57	23	21	44
5.	Rene Robert	73-79	47	22	17	39
6.	Donald Audette	90-98, 01	61	15	23	38
7.	Don Luce	73-80	62	17	19	36
8.	Miroslav Satan	97-01	51	14	21	35
9.	Dave Andreychuk	83-92, 01	54	13	22	35
10.	Dale Hawerchuk	91-94	28	9	25	34
11.	Jason Woolley	98-01	49	7	27	34

Series Records vs. Other Teams

Opponent	Year	Series	Winner	W	L	GF	GA
Bos.	1982	DSF	Bos.	1	3	11	17
Bos.	1983	DF	Bos.	3	4	23	33
Bos.	1988	DSF	Bos.	2	4	22	28
Bos.	1989	DSF	Bos.	1	4	14	16
Bos.	1992	DSF	Bos.	3	4	24	19
Bos.	1993	DSF	Buf.	4	0	19	12
Bos.	1999	CSF	Buf.	4	2	17	14
Chi.	1975	QF	Buf.	4	1	20	10
Chi.	1980	QF	Buf.	4	0	16	7
Dal.	1999	F	Dal.	2	4	9	13
Min.	1977	PRE	Buf.	2	0	11	3
Min.	1981	QF	Min.	1	4	17	23
Mtl.	1973	QF	Mtl.	2	4	16	21
Mtl.	1975	SF	Buf.	4	2	21	29
Mtl.	1983	DSF	Buf.	3	0	8	2
Mtl.	1990	DSF	Mtl.	2	4	13	17
Mtl.	1991	DSF	Mtl.	2	4	24	29
Mtl.	1993	DF	Mtl.	0	4	12	16
Mtl.	1998	CSF	Buf.	4	0	17	10
N.J.	1994	CQF	N.J.	3	4	14	14
NYI	1976	QF	NYI	2	4	18	21
NYI	1977	QF	NYI	0	4	10	16
NYI	1980	SF	NYI	2	4	17	22
NYR	1978	PRE	Buf.	2	1	11	6
Ott.	1997	CQF	Buf.	4	3	14	13
Ott.	1999	CQF	Buf.	4	0	12	6
Phi.	1975	F	Phi.	2	4	12	19
Phi.	1978	QF	Phi.	1	4	11	16
Phi.	1995	CQF	Phi.	1	4	13	18
Phi.	1997	CSF	Phi.	1	4	13	21
Phi.	1998	CQF	Buf.	4	1	18	9
Phi.	2000	CQF	Phi.	1	4	8	14
Phi.	2001	CQF	Buf.	4	2	21	13
Pit.	1979	PRE	Pit.	1	2	9	9
Pit.	2001	CSF	Pit.	3	4	17	17
Que.	1984	DSF	Que.	0	3	5	13
Que.	1985	DSF	Que.	2	3	22	22
St.L.	1976	PRE	Buf.	2	1	7	8
Tor.	1999	CF	Buf.	4	1	21	16
Van.	1980	PRE	Buf.	3	1	15	7
Van.	1981	PRE	Buf.	3	0	13	7
Wsh.	1998	CF	Wsh.	2	4	11	13

CALGARY

All-Time Playoff Record vs. Other Teams

	Series	W	L	GP	W	L	T	GF	GA	Last Mtg.	Round	Result
Chicago	3	2	1	12	7	5	0	37	33	1996	CQF	L 0-4
Dallas	1	0	1	6	2	4	0	18	25	1981	SF	L 2-4
Detroit	1	0	1	2	0	2	0	5	8	1978	PRE	L 0-2
Edmonton	5	1	4	30	11	19	0	96	132	1991	DSF	L 3-4
Los Angeles	6	2	4	26	13	13	0	102	105	1993	DSF	L 2-4
Montreal	2	1	1	11	5	6	0	32	31	1989	F	W 4-2
NY Rangers	1	0	1	4	1	3	0	8	14	1980	PRE	L 1-3
Philadelphia	2	1	1	11	4	7	0	28	43	1981	QF	W 4-3
Phoenix	3	1	2	13	6	7	0	43	45	1987	DSF	L 2-4
St. Louis	1	1	0	7	4	3	0	28	22	1986	CF	W 4-3
San Jose	1	0	1	7	3	4	0	35	26	1995	CQF	L 3-4
Toronto	1	0	1	2	0	2	0	5	9	1979	PRE	L 0-2
Vancouver	5	3	2	25	13	12	0	82	80	1994	CQF	L 3-4
Totals	**32**	**12**	**20**	**156**	**69**	**87**	**0**	**529**	**590**			

Playoff Results 2002-98

(Last playoff appearance: 1996)

Playoff Scoring Leaders

	Player	Years	GP	G	A	PTS
1.	Al MacInnis	84-94	95	25	77	102
2.	Paul Reinhart	81-88	76	21	51	72
3.	Theoren Fleury	89-96	59	29	33	62
4.	Joel Otto	85-95	87	23	38	61
5.	Joe Nieuwendyk	87-95	66	32	28	60
6.	Joe Mullen	86-90	61	35	20	55
7.	Hakan Loob	84-89	73	26	28	54
8.	Lanny McDonald	82-89	72	24	23	47
9.	Jim Peplinski	81-89	99	15	31	46
10.	Gary Roberts	87-94	58	13	30	43

Series Records vs. Other Clubs

Opponent	Year	Series	Winner	W	L	GF	GA
Chi.	1981	PRE	Cgy.	3	0	15	9
Chi.	1989	CF	Cgy.	4	1	15	8
Chi.	1996	CQF	Chi.	0	4	7	16
Det.	1978	PRE	Det.	0	2	5	8
Edm.	1983	DF	Edm.	1	4	13	35
Edm.	1984	DF	Edm.	3	4	27	33
Edm.	1986	DF	Cgy.	4	3	25	24
Edm.	1988	DF	Edm.	0	4	11	18
Edm.	1991	DSF	Edm.	3	4	20	22
L.A.	1976	PRE	L.A.	0	2	1	3
L.A.	1977	PRE	L.A.	1	2	7	11
L.A.	1988	DSF	Cgy.	4	1	30	18
L.A.	1989	DF	Cgy.	4	0	22	11
L.A.	1990	DSF	L.A.	2	4	24	29
L.A.	1993	DSF	L.A.	2	4	28	33
Min.	1981	SF	Min.	2	4	18	25
Mtl.	1986	F	Mtl.	1	4	13	15
Mtl.	1989	F	Cgy.	4	2	19	16
NYR	1980	PRE	NYR	1	3	8	14
Phi.	1974	QF	Phi.	0	4	6	17
Phi.	1981	QF	Cgy.	4	3	22	26
St.L.	1986	CF	Cgy.	4	3	28	22
S.J.	1995	CQF	S.J.	3	4	35	26
Tor.	1979	PRE	Tor.	0	2	5	9
Van.	1982	DSF	Van.	0	3	5	10
Van.	1983	DSF	Cgy.	3	1	17	14
Van.	1984	DSF	Cgy.	3	1	14	13
Van.	1989	DSF	Cgy.	4	3	26	20
Van.	1994	CQF	Van.	3	4	20	23
Wpg.	1985	DSF	Wpg.	1	3	13	15
Wpg.	1986	DSF	Cgy.	3	0	15	8
Wpg.	1987	DSF	Wpg.	2	4	15	22

CAROLINA

All-Time Playoff Record vs. Other Teams

	Series	W	L	GP	W	L	T	GF	GA	Last Mtg.	Round	Result
Boston	3	0	3	19	7	12	0	48	63	1999	CQF	L 2-4
Colorado	2	1	1	9	5	4	0	35	34	1987	DSF	L 2-4
Detroit	1	0	1	5	1	4	0	7	14	2002	F	L 1-4
Montreal	6	1	5	33	12	21	0	91	108	2002	CSF	W 4-2
New Jersey	2	1	1	12	6	6	0	17	31	2002	CQF	W 4-2
Toronto	1	1	0	6	4	2	0	10	6	2002	CF	W 4-2
Totals	**15**	**4**	**11**	**84**	**35**	**49**	**0**	**208**	**256**			

Playoff Results 2002-98

Year	Round	Opponent	Result	GF	GA
2002	F	Detroit	L 1-4	7	14
	CF	Toronto	W 4-2	10	6
	CSF	Montreal	W 4-2	21	12
	CQF	New Jersey	W 4-2	9	11
2001	CQF	New Jersey	L 2-4	8	20
1999	CQF	Boston	L 2-4	10	16

Playoff Scoring Leaders

	Player	Years	GP	G	A	PTS
1.	Ron Francis	86-90, 99-02	62	14	25	39
2.	Kevin Dineen	86-91, 99	44	17	14	31
3.	Dean Evason	86-91	38	8	15	23
4.	Dave Babych	86-90	31	7	13	20
5.	Bates Battaglia	99-02	35	5	14	19
6.	Ray Ferraro	86-90	33	7	11	18
7.	Jeff O'Neill	99-02	34	9	8	17
8.	John Anderson	86-89	20	6	11	17
9.	Rod Brind'Amour	01-02	29	5	11	16
10.	Sami Kapanen	99-02	34	4	12	16

Series Records vs. Other Teams

Opponent	Year	Series	Winner	W	L	GF	GA
Bos.	1990	DSF	Bos.	3	4	21	23
Bos.	1991	DSF	Bos.	2	4	17	24
Bos.	1999	CQF	Bos.	2	4	14	17
Det.	2002	F	Det.	1	4	7	14
Mtl.	1980	PRE	Mtl.	0	3	8	18
Mtl.	1986	DF	Mtl.	3	4	13	16
Mtl.	1988	DSF	Mtl.	2	4	20	23
Mtl.	1989	DSF	Mtl.	0	4	11	18
Mtl.	1992	DSF	Mtl.	3	4	18	21
Mtl.	2002	CSF	Car.	4	2	21	12
N.J.	2001	CQF	N.J.	2	4	8	20
N.J.	2002	CQF	Car.	4	2	9	11
Que.	1986	DSF	Hfd.	3	0	16	7
Que.	1987	DSF	Que.	2	4	19	27
Tor.	2002	CF	Car.	4	2	10	6

CHICAGO

All-Time Playoff Record vs. Other Teams

	Series	W	L	GP	W	L	T	GF	GA	Last Mtg.	Round	Result
Boston	6	1	5	22	5	16	1	63	97	1978	QF	L 0-4
Buffalo	2	0	2	9	1	8	0	17	36	1980	QF	L 0-4
Calgary	3	1	2	12	5	7	0	33	37	1996	CQF	W 4-0
Colorado	2	0	2	12	4	8	0	28	49	1997	CQF	L 2-4
Dallas	6	4	2	33	19	14	0	120	118	1991	DSF	L 2-4
Detroit	14	8	6	69	38	31	0	210	190	1995	CF	L 1-4
Edmonton	4	1	3	20	8	12	0	77	102	1992	CF	W 4-0
Los Angeles	1	1	0	5	4	1	0	10	7	1974	QF	W 4-1
Montreal	17	5	12	81	29	50	2	185	261	1976	QF	L 0-4
NY Islanders	2	0	2	6	0	6	0	6	21	1979	QF	L 0-4
NY Rangers	5	4	1	24	14	10	0	66	54	1973	SF	W 4-1
Philadelphia	1	1	0	4	4	0	0	20	8	1971	QF	W 4-0
Pittsburgh	2	1	1	8	4	4	0	24	23	1992	F	L 0-4
St. Louis	10	7	3	50	28	22	0	171	142	2002	CQF	L 1-4
Toronto	9	3	6	38	15	22	1	89	111	1995	CQF	W 4-3
Vancouver	2	1	1	9	5	4	0	24	24	1995	CSF	W 4-0
Defunct	4	2	2	9	5	3	1	16	15			
Totals	**90**	**40**	**50**	**411**	**188**	**218**	**5**	**1159**	**1295**			

Playoff Results 2002-98

Year	Round	Opponent	Result	GF	GA
2002	CQF	St. Louis	L 1-4	5	13

Playoff Scoring Leaders

	Player	Years	GP	G	A	PTS
1.	Stan Mikita	60-78	155	59	91	150
2.	Denis Savard	81-90, 95-97	131	61	84	145
3.	Bobby Hull	59-72	116	62	67	129
4.	Steve Larmer	83-93	107	45	66	111
5.	Doug Wilson	78-91	95	19	61	80
6.	Jeremy Roenick	89-96	82	35	42	77

7.	Dennis Hull	65-77	104	33	34	67
8.	Pierre Pilote	59-68	82	8	52	60
9.	Tom Lysiak	79-86	67	23	33	56
10.	Bob Murray	77-90	112	19	37	56

Series Records vs. Other Teams

Opponent	Year	Series	Winner	W	L	T	GF	GA
Bos.	1927	QF*	Bos.	0	1	1	5	10
Bos.	1942	QF	Bos.	1	2		7	5
Bos.	1970	SF	Bos.	0	4		10	20
Bos.	1974	SF	Bos.	2	4		20	28
Bos.	1975	PRE	Chi.	2	1		12	15
Bos.	1978	QF	Bos.	0	4		9	19
Buf.	1975	QF	Buf.	1	4		10	20
Buf.	1980	QF	Buf.	0	4		7	16
Cgy.	1981	PRE	Cgy.	0	3		9	15
Cgy.	1989	CF	Cgy.	1	4		8	15
Cgy.	1996	CQF	Chi.	4	0		16	7
Col.	1996	CSF	Col.	2	4		14	19
Col.	1997	CQF	Col.	2	4		14	28
Det.	1934	F	Chi.	3	1		9	7
Det.	1941	SF	Det.	0	2		2	5
Det.	1944	SF	Chi.	4	1		17	8
Det.	1961	F	Chi.	4	2		19	12
Det.	1963	SF	Det.	2	4		19	25
Det.	1964	SF	Det.	3	4		18	24
Det.	1965	SF	Chi.	4	3		23	19
Det.	1966	SF	Det.	2	4		10	22
Det.	1970	QF	Chi.	4	0		16	8
Det.	1985	DSF	Chi.	3	0		23	8
Det.	1987	DSF	Det.	0	4		6	15
Det.	1989	DSF	Chi.	4	2		25	18
Det.	1992	DF	Chi.	4	0		11	6
Det.	1995	CF	Det.	1	4		12	13
Edm.	1983	CF	Edm.	0	4		11	25
Edm.	1985	CF	Edm.	2	4		25	44
Edm.	1990	CF	Edm.	2	4		20	25
Edm.	1992	CF	Chi.	4	0		21	8
L.A.	1974	QF	Chi.	4	1		10	7
Min.	1982	DSF	Chi.	3	1		14	14
Min.	1983	DF	Chi.	4	1		22	17
Min.	1984	DSF	Min.	2	3		14	18
Min.	1985	DF	Chi.	4	2		32	29
Min.	1990	DSF	Chi.	4	3		21	18
Min.	1991	DSF	Min.	2	4		16	23
Mtl.	1930	QF*	Mtl.	0	1	1	2	3
Mtl.	1931	F	Mtl.	2	3		8	11
Mtl.	1934	QF*	Chi.	1	1		4	3
Mtl.	1938	QF	Chi.	2	1		11	8
Mtl.	1941	QF	Chi.	2	1		8	7
Mtl.	1944	F	Mtl.	0	4		8	16
Mtl.	1946	SF	Mtl.	0	4		7	26
Mtl.	1953	SF	Mtl.	3	4		14	18
Mtl.	1959	SF	Mtl.	2	4		16	21
Mtl.	1960	SF	Mtl.	0	4		6	14
Mtl.	1961	SF	Chi.	4	2		16	15
Mtl.	1962	SF	Chi.	4	2		19	13
Mtl.	1965	F	Mtl.	3	4		12	18
Mtl.	1968	SF	Mtl.	1	4		10	22
Mtl.	1971	F	Mtl.	3	4		18	20
Mtl.	1973	F	Mtl.	2	4		23	33
Mtl.	1976	QF	Mtl.	0	4		3	13
NYI	1977	PRE	NYI	0	2		3	7
NYI	1979	QF	NYI	0	4		3	14
NYR	1931	SF*	Chi.	2	0		3	0
NYR	1968	QF	Chi.	4	2		18	12
NYR	1971	SF	Chi.	4	3		21	14
NYR	1972	SF	NYR	0	4		9	17
NYR	1973	SF	Chi.	4	1		15	11
Phi.	1978	QF	Chi.	4	0		20	8
Pit.	1972	QF	Chi.	4	0		14	8
Pit.	1992	F	Pit.	0	4		10	15
St.L.	1973	QF	Chi.	4	1		22	9
St.L.	1980	PRE	Chi.	3	0		12	4
St.L.	1982	DF	Chi.	4	2		23	19
St.L.	1983	DSF	Chi.	3	1		16	10
St.L.	1988	DSF	St.L.	1	4		17	21
St.L.	1989	DF	Chi.	4	1		19	12
St.L.	1990	DF	Chi.	4	3		28	22
St.L.	1992	DSF	Chi.	4	2		23	19
St.L.	1993	DSF	St.L.	0	4		6	13
St.L.	2002	CQF	St.L.	1	4		5	13
Tor.	1931	QF*	Chi.	1	0	1	4	3
Tor.	1932	QF*	Tor.	1	1		2	6
Tor.	1938	F	Chi.	3	1		10	8
Tor.	1940	QF	Tor.	0	2		3	5
Tor.	1962	F	Tor.	2	4		15	18
Tor.	1967	SF	Tor.	2	4		14	18
Tor.	1986	DSF	Tor.	0	3		9	18
Tor.	1994	CQF	Tor.	2	4		10	15
Tor.	1995	CQF	Chi.	4	3		22	20
Van.	1982	CF	Van.	1	4		13	18
Van.	1995	CSF	Chi.	4	0		11	6

Defunct Teams

Mtl.M.	1934	SF*	Chi.	2	0		6	2
Mtl.M.	1935	QF*	Mtl.M.	0	1	1	0	1
NYA	1936	QF*	NYA	1	1		5	7
NYA	1938	SF	Chi.	2	1		5	5

* Total-goals series

COLORADO

All-Time Playoff Record vs. Other Teams

	Series	W	L	GP	W	L	T	GF	GA	Last Mtg.	Round	Result
Boston	2	1	1	11	5	6	0	36	37	1983	DSF	L 1-3
Buffalo	2	2	0	8	6	2	0	35	27	1985	DSF	W 3-2
Carolina	2	1	1	9	4	5	0	34	35	1987	DSF	W 4-2
Chicago	2	2	0	12	8	4	0	49	28	1997	CQF	W 4-2
Dallas	2	0	2	14	6	8	0	29	37	2000	CF	L 3-4
Detroit	5	3	2	30	17	13	0	79	76	2002	CF	L 3-4
Edmonton	2	1	1	12	7	5	0	35	30	1998	CQF	L 3-4
Florida	1	1	0	4	4	0	0	15	4	1996	F	W 4-0
Los Angeles	2	2	0	14	8	6	0	33	23	2002	CQF	W 4-3
Montreal	5	2	3	31	14	17	0	85	105	1993	DSF	L 2-4
New Jersey	1	1	0	7	4	3	0	19	11	2001	F	W 4-3
NY Islanders	1	0	1	4	0	4	0	9	18	1982	CF	L 0-4
NY Rangers	1	0	1	6	2	4	0	19	25	1995	CQF	L 2-4
Philadelphia	2	0	2	11	4	7	0	29	39	1985	CF	L 2-4
Phoenix	1	1	0	5	4	1	0	17	10	2000	CQF	W 4-1
St. Louis	1	1	0	5	4	1	0	17	11	2001	CF	W 4-1
San Jose	2	2	0	13	8	5	0	44	38	2002	CSF	W 4-3
Vancouver	2	2	0	10	8	2	0	40	26	2001	CQF	W 4-0
Totals	**36**	**22**	**14**	**206**	**113**	**93**	**0**	**624**	**580**			

Playoff Results 2002-98

Year	Round	Opponent	Result	GF	GA
2002	CF	Detroit	L 3-4	13	22
	CSF	San Jose	W 4-3	25	21
	CQF	Los Angeles	W 4-3	16	13
2001	**F**	**New Jersey**	**W 4-3**	**19**	**11**
	CF	St. Louis	W 4-1	17	11
	CSF	Los Angeles	W 4-3	17	10
	CQF	Vancouver	W 4-0	16	9
2000	CF	Dallas	L 3-4	13	14
	CSF	Detroit	W 4-1	13	8
	CQF	Phoenix	W 4-1	17	10
1999	CF	Dallas	L 3-4	16	23
	CSF	Detroit	W 4-2	21	14
	CQF	San Jose	W 4-2	19	17
1998	CQF	Edmonton	L 3-4	16	19

Playoff Scoring Leaders

	Player	Years	GP	G	A	PTS
1.	Joe Sakic	93-02	135	65	83	148
2.	Peter Forsberg	95-02	115	51	84	135
3.	Peter Stastny	81-87	64	24	57	81
4.	Sandis Ozolinsh	96-00	82	18	47	65
5.	Michel Goulet	80-87	66	34	30	64
6.	Valeri Kamensky	93-99	64	25	35	60
7.	Adam Deadmarsh	95-00	88	22	34	56
8.	Claude Lemieux	96-99	62	24	31	55
9.	Anton Stastny	81-87	66	20	32	52
10.	Chris Drury	99-02	80	26	24	50
11.	Milan Hejduk	99-02	72	21	29	50

Series Records vs. Other Teams

Opponent	Year	Series	Winner	W	L	GF	GA
Bos.	1982	DF	Que.	4	3	28	26
Bos.	1983	DSF	Bos.	1	3	8	11
Buf.	1984	DF	Que.	3	0	13	5
Buf.	1985	DSF	Que.	3	2	22	22
Chi.	1996	CSF	Col.	4	2	19	14
Chi.	1997	CQF	Col.	4	2	28	14
Dal.	1999	CF	Dal.	3	4	16	23
Dal.	2000	CF	Dal.	3	4	13	14
Det.	1996	CF	Col.	4	2	20	16
Det.	1997	CF	Det.	2	4	12	16
Det.	1999	CSF	Col.	4	2	21	14
Det.	2000	CSF	Col.	4	1	13	8
Det.	2002	CF	Det.	3	4	13	22
Edm.	1997	CSF	Col.	4	1	19	11
Edm.	1998	CQF	Edm.	3	4	16	19
Fla.	1996	F	Col.	4	0	15	4
Hfd.	1986	DSF	Hfd.	0	3	7	16
Hfd.	1987	DSF	Que.	4	2	27	19
L.A.	2001	CSF	Col.	4	3	17	10
L.A.	2002	CQF	Col.	4	3	16	13
Mtl.	1982	DSF	Que.	3	2	11	16
Mtl.	1984	DF	Mtl.	2	4	13	20
Mtl.	1985	DF	Que.	4	3	24	24
Mtl.	1987	DF	Mtl.	3	4	21	26
Mtl.	1993	DSF	Mtl.	2	4	16	19
N.J.	2001	F	Col.	4	3	19	11
NYI	1982	CF	NYI	0	4	9	18
NYR	1995	CQF	NYR	2	4	19	25
Phi.	1981	PRE	Phi.	2	3	17	22
Phi.	1985	CF	Phi.	2	4	12	17
Phx.	2000	CQF	Col.	4	1	17	10
St.L.	2001	CF	Col.	4	1	17	11
S.J.	1999	CQF	Col.	4	2	19	17
S.J.	2002	CSF	Col.	4	3	25	21
Van.	1996	CQF	Col.	4	2	24	17
Van.	2001	CQF	Col.	4	0	16	9

DALLAS

All-Time Playoff Record vs. Other Teams

	Series	W	L	GP	W	L	T	GF	GA	Last Mtg.	Round	Result
Boston	1	1	0	3	3	0	0	20	13	1981	PRE	W 3-0
Buffalo	3	2	1	13	8	5	0	39	37	1999	F	W 4-2
Calgary	1	1	0	6	4	2	0	25	18	1981	SF	W 4-2
Chicago	6	2	4	33	14	19	0	118	120	1991	DSF	W 4-2
Colorado	2	2	0	14	8	6	0	37	29	2000	CF	W 4-3
Detroit	3	0	3	18	6	12	0	40	55	1998	CF	L 2-4
Edmonton	7	5	2	36	23	13	0	98	93	2001	CQF	W 4-2
Los Angeles	1	1	0	7	4	3	0	26	21	1968	QF	W 4-3
Montreal	2	1	1	13	6	7	0	37	48	1980	QF	W 4-3
New Jersey	1	0	1	6	2	4	0	9	15	2000	F	L 2-4
NY Islanders	1	0	1	5	1	4	0	16	26	1981	F	L 1-4
Philadelphia	2	0	2	11	3	8	0	26	41	1980	SF	L 1-4
Pittsburgh	1	0	1	6	2	4	0	16	28	1991	F	L 2-4
St. Louis	12	6	6	66	34	32	0	197	187	2001	CSF	L 0-4
San Jose	2	2	0	11	8	3	0	31	19	2000	CSF	W 4-1
Toronto	2	2	0	7	6	1	0	35	26	1983	DSF	W 3-1
Vancouver	1	0	1	5	1	4	0	11	18	1994	CSF	L 1-4
Totals	**48**	**25**	**23**	**260**	**133**	**127**	**0**	**782**	**793**			

Playoff Results 2002-98

Year	Round	Opponent	Result	GF	GA
2001	CSF	St. Louis	L 0-4	6	13
	CQF	Edmonton	W 4-2	16	13
2000	F	New Jersey	L 2-4	9	15
	CF	Colorado	W 4-3	14	13
	CSF	San Jose	W 4-1	15	7
	CQF	Edmonton	W 4-1	14	11
1999	**F**	**Buffalo**	**W 4-2**	**13**	**9**
	CF	Colorado	W 4-3	23	16
	CSF	St. Louis	W 4-2	17	12
	CQF	Edmonton	W 4-0	11	7
1998	CF	Detroit	L 2-4	11	15
	CSF	Edmonton	W 4-1	9	5
	CQF	San Jose	W 4-2	16	12

Playoff Scoring Leaders

	Player	Years	GP	G	A	PTS
1.	Mike Modano	89-01	127	45	64	109
2.	Brian Bellows	83-92	81	34	49	83
3.	Neal Broten	81-94, 97	115	28	51	79
4.	Bobby Smith	80-83, 91-92	77	26	50	76
5.	Steve Payne	80-85	71	35	35	70
6.	Dino Ciccarelli	81-86	62	28	23	51
7.	Brad Maxwell	80-84	58	10	39	49
8.	Dave Gagner	90-95	51	22	24	46
9.	Brett Hull	99-01	55	21	25	46
10.	Al MacAdam	80-84	63	20	24	44

Series Records vs. Other Teams

Opponent	Year	Series	Winner	W	L	GF	GA
Bos.	1981	PRE	Min.	3	0	20	13
Buf.	1977	PRE	Buf.	0	2	3	11
Buf.	1981	QF	Min.	4	1	23	17
Buf.	1999	F	Dal.	4	2	13	9

Cgy.	1981	SF	Min.	4	2	25	18
Chi.	1982	DSF	Chi.	1	3	14	14
Chi.	1983	DF	Chi.	1	4	17	22
Chi.	1984	DSF	Min.	3	2	18	14
Chi.	1985	DF	Chi.	2	4	29	32
Chi.	1990	DSF	Chi.	3	4	18	21
Chi.	1991	DSF	Min.	4	2	23	16
Col.	1999	CF	Dal.	4	3	23	16
Col.	2000	CF	Dal.	4	3	14	13
Det.	1992	DSF	Det.	3	4	19	23
Det.	1995	CQF	Det.	1	4	10	17
Det.	1998	CF	Det.	2	4	11	15
Edm.	1984	CF	Edm.	0	4	10	22
Edm.	1991	CF	Min.	4	1	20	14
Edm.	1997	CQF	Edm.	3	4	18	21
Edm.	1998	CSF	Dal.	4	1	9	5
Edm.	1999	CQF	Dal.	4	0	11	7
Edm.	2000	CQF	Dal.	4	1	14	11
Edm.	2001	CQF	Dal.	4	2	16	13
L.A.	1968	QF	Min.	4	3	26	21
Mtl.	1971	SF	Mtl.	2	4	19	27
Mtl.	1980	QF	Min.	4	3	18	21
N.J.	2000	F	N.J.	2	4	9	15
NYI	1981	F	NYI	1	4	16	26
Phi.	1973	QF	Phi.	2	4	12	14
Phi.	1980	SF	Phi.	1	4	14	27
Pit.	1991	F	Pit.	2	4	16	28
St.L.	1968	SF	St.L.	3	4	22	18
St.L.	1970	QF	St.L.	2	4	16	20
St.L.	1971	QF	Min.	4	2	16	15
St.L.	1972	QF	St.L.	3	4	19	19
St.L.	1984	DF	Min.	4	3	19	17
St.L.	1985	DSF	Min.	3	0	9	5
St.L.	1986	DSF	St.L.	2	3	20	18
St.L.	1989	DSF	St.L.	1	4	15	23
St.L.	1991	DF	Min.	4	2	22	17
St.L.	1994	CQF	Dal.	4	0	16	10
St.L.	1999	CSF	Dal.	4	2	17	12
St.L.	2001	CSF	St.L.	0	4	6	13
S.J.	1998	CQF	Dal.	4	2	16	12
S.J.	2000	CSF	Dal.	4	1	15	7
Tor.	1980	PRE	Min.	3	0	17	8
Tor.	1983	DSF	Min.	3	1	18	18
Van.	1994	CSF	Van.	1	4	11	18

DETROIT

All-Time Playoff Record vs. Other Teams

	Series	W	L	GP	W	L	T	GF	GA	Last Mtg.	Round	Result
Anaheim	2	2	0	8	8	0	0	30	14	1999	CQF	W 4-0
Boston	7	3	4	33	14	19	0	98	96	1957	SF	L 1-4
Calgary	1	1	0	2	2	0	0	8	5	1978	PRE	W 2-0
Carolina	1	1	0	5	4	1	0	14	7	2002	F	W 4-1
Chicago	14	6	8	69	31	38	0	190	210	1995	CF	W 4-1
Colorado	5	2	3	30	13	17	0	76	79	2002	CF	W 4-3
Dallas	3	3	0	18	12	6	0	55	40	1998	CF	W 4-2
Edmonton	2	0	2	10	2	8	0	26	39	1988	CF	L 1-4
Los Angeles	2	1	1	10	6	4	0	32	21	2001	CQF	L 2-4
Montreal	12	7	5	62	29	33	0	149	161	1978	QF	L 1-4
New Jersey	1	0	1	4	0	4	0	7	16	1995	F	L 0-4
NY Rangers	5	4	1	23	13	10	0	57	49	1950	F	W 4-3
Philadelphia	1	1	0	4	4	0	0	16	6	1997	F	W 4-0
Phoenix	2	2	0	12	8	4	0	44	28	1998	CQF	W 4-2
St. Louis	7	5	2	40	24	16	0	125	103	2002	CSF	W 4-1
San Jose	2	1	1	11	7	4	0	51	27	1995	CSF	W 4-0
Toronto	23	11	12	117	59	58	0	321	311	1993	DSF	L 3-4
Vancouver	1	1	0	6	4	2	0	22	16	2002	CQF	W 4-2
Washington	1	1	0	4	4	0	0	13	7	1998	F	W 4-0
Defunct	4	3	1	10	7	2	1	21	13			
Totals	**96**	**55**	**41**	**478**	**251**	**226**	**1**	**1355**	**1248**			

Playoff Results 2002-98

Year	Round	Opponent	Result	GF	GA
2002	**F**	**Carolina**	**W 4-1**	**14**	**7**
	CF	Colorado	W 4-3	22	13
	CSF	St. Louis	W 4-1	14	11
	CQF	Vancouver	W 4-2	22	16
2001	CQF	Los Angeles	L 2-4	17	15
2000	CSF	Colorado	L 1-4	8	13
	CQF	Los Angeles	W 4-0	15	6
1999	CSF	Colorado	L 2-4	14	21
	CQF	Anaheim	W 4-0	17	6
1998	**F**	**Washington**	**W 4-0**	**13**	**7**
	CF	Dallas	W 4-2	15	11
	CSF	St. Louis	W 4-2	23	13
	CQF	Phoenix	W 4-2	24	18

Playoff Scoring Leaders

	Player	Years	GP	G	A	PTS
1.	Steve Yzerman	84-02	177	67	108	175
2.	Sergei Fedorov	90-02	158	49	111	160
3.	Gordie Howe	47-70	154	67	91	158
4.	Nicklas Lidstrom	92-02	152	32	75	107
5.	Alex Delvecchio	52-70	121	35	69	104
6.	Ted Lindsay	45-57, 65	123	44	44	88
7.	Vyacheslav Kozlov	93-01	114	42	37	79
8.	Norm Ullman	56-66	80	27	47	74
9.	Brendan Shanahan	97-02	84	30	34	64
10.	Sid Abel	39-52	96	28	30	58
11.	Igor Larionov	96-02	101	20	38	58

Series Records vs. Other Teams

Opponent	Year	Series	Winner	W	L	T	GF	GA
Ana.	1997	CSF	Det.	4	0		13	8
Ana.	1999	CQF	Det.	4	0		17	6
Atl.	1978	PRE	Det.	2	0		8	5
Bos.	1941	F	Bos.	0	4		6	12
Bos.	1942	SF	Det.	2	0		9	5
Bos.	1943	F	Det.	4	0		16	5
Bos.	1945	SF	Det.	4	3		22	22
Bos.	1946	SF	Bos.	1	4		10	16
Bos.	1953	SF	Bos.	2	4		21	21
Bos.	1957	SF	Bos.	1	4		14	15
Car.	2002	F	Det.	4	1		14	7
Chi.	1934	F	Chi.	1	3		7	9
Chi.	1941	SF	Det.	2	0		5	2
Chi.	1944	SF	Chi.	1	4		8	17
Chi.	1961	F	Chi.	2	4		12	19
Chi.	1963	SF	Det.	4	2		25	19
Chi.	1964	SF	Det.	4	3		24	18
Chi.	1965	SF	Chi.	3	4		19	23
Chi.	1966	SF	Det.	4	2		22	10
Chi.	1970	QF	Chi.	0	4		8	16
Chi.	1985	DSF	Chi.	0	3		8	23
Chi.	1987	DSF	Det.	4	0		15	6
Chi.	1989	DSF	Chi.	2	4		18	25
Chi.	1992	DF	Chi.	0	4		6	11
Chi.	1995	CF	Det.	4	1		13	12
Col.	1996	CF	Col.	2	4		16	20
Col.	1997	CF	Det.	4	2		16	12
Col.	1999	CSF	Col.	2	4		14	21
Col.	2000	CSF	Col.	1	4		8	13
Col.	2002	CF	Det.	4	3		22	13
Dal.	1995	CQF	Det.	4	1		17	10
Dal.	1998	CF	Det.	4	2		15	11
Edm.	1987	CF	Edm.	1	4		10	16
Edm.	1988	CF	Edm.	1	4		16	23
L.A.	2000	CQF	Det.	4	0		15	6
L.A.	2001	CQF	L.A.	2	4		17	15
Min.	1992	DSF	Det.	4	3		23	19
Mtl.	1937	SF	Det.	3	2		13	8
Mtl.	1939	QF	Det.	2	1		8	5
Mtl.	1942	QF	Det.	2	1		8	8
Mtl.	1949	SF	Det.	4	3		17	14
Mtl.	1951	SF	Mtl.	2	4		12	13
Mtl.	1952	F	Det.	4	0		11	2
Mtl.	1954	F	Det.	4	3		14	12
Mtl.	1955	F	Det.	4	3		27	20
Mtl.	1956	F	Mtl.	1	4		9	18
Mtl.	1958	SF	Mtl.	0	4		6	19
Mtl.	1966	F	Mtl.	2	4		14	18
Mtl.	1978	QF	Mtl.	1	4		10	24
N.J.	1995	F	N.J.	0	4		7	16
NYR	1933	SF*	NYR	0	2		3	6
NYR	1937	F	Det.	3	2		9	8
NYR	1941	QF	Det.	2	1		6	6
NYR	1948	SF	Det.	4	2		17	12
NYR	1950	F	Det.	4	3		22	17
Phi.	1997	F	Det.	4	0		16	6
Phx.	1998	CQF	Det.	4	2		24	18
St.L.	1984	DSF	St.L.	1	3		12	13
St.L.	1988	DF	Det.	4	1		21	14
St.L.	1991	DSF	St.L.	3	4		20	24
St.L.	1996	CSF	Det.	4	3		22	16
St.L.	1997	CQF	Det.	4	2		13	12
St.L.	1998	CSF	Det.	4	2		23	13
St.L.	2002	CSF	Det.	4	1		14	11
S.J.	1994	CQF	S.J.	3	4		27	21
S.J.	1995	CSF	Det.	4	0		24	6
Tor.	1929	QF*	Tor.	0	2		2	7
Tor.	1934	SF	Det.	3	2		11	12
Tor.	1936	F	Det.	3	1		18	11
Tor.	1939	SF	Tor.	1	2		8	10
Tor.	1940	SF	Tor.	0	2		2	5
Tor.	1942	F	Tor.	3	4		19	25
Tor.	1943	SF	Det.	4	2		20	17
Tor.	1945	F	Tor.	3	4		9	9
Tor.	1947	SF	Tor.	1	4		14	18
Tor.	1948	F	Tor.	0	4		7	18
Tor.	1949	F	Tor.	0	4		5	12
Tor.	1950	SF	Det.	4	3		10	11
Tor.	1952	SF	Det.	4	0		13	3
Tor.	1954	SF	Det.	4	1		15	8
Tor.	1955	SF	Det.	4	0		14	6
Tor.	1956	SF	Det.	4	1		14	10
Tor.	1960	SF	Tor.	2	4		16	20
Tor.	1961	SF	Det.	4	1		15	8
Tor.	1963	F	Tor.	1	4		10	17
Tor.	1964	F	Tor.	3	4		17	22
Tor.	1987	DF	Det.	4	3		20	18
Tor.	1988	DSF	Det.	4	2		32	20
Tor.	1993	DSF	Tor.	3	4		30	24
Van.	2002	CQF	Det.	4	2		22	16
Wsh.	1998	F	Det.	4	0		13	7
Wpg.	1996	CQF	Det.	4	2		20	10
Defunct Teams								
Mtl.M.	1932	QF*	Mtl.M.	0	1	1	1	3
Mtl.M.	1933	QF*	Det.	2	0		5	2
Mtl.M.	1936	SF	Det.	3	0		6	1
NYA	1940	QF	Det.	2	1		9	7

EDMONTON

All-Time Playoff Record vs. Other Teams

	Series	W	L	GP	W	L	T	GF	GA	Last Mtg.	Round	Result
Boston	2	2	0	9	8	1	0	41	20	1990	F	W 4-1
Calgary	5	4	1	30	19	11	0	132	96	1991	DSF	W 4-3
Chicago	4	3	1	20	12	8	0	102	77	1992	CF	L 0-4
Colorado	2	1	1	12	5	7	0	30	35	1998	CQF	W 4-3
Dallas	7	2	5	36	13	23	0	93	98	2001	CQF	L 2-4
Detroit	2	2	0	10	8	2	0	39	26	1988	CF	W 4-1
Los Angeles	7	5	2	36	24	12	0	154	127	1992	DSF	W 4-2
Montreal	1	1	0	3	3	0	0	15	6	1981	PRE	W 3-0
NY Islanders	3	1	2	15	6	9	0	47	58	1984	F	W 4-1
Philadelphia	3	2	1	15	8	7	0	49	44	1987	F	W 4-3
Phoenix	6	6	0	26	22	4	0	120	75	1990	DSF	W 4-3
Vancouver	2	2	0	9	7	2	0	35	20	1992	DF	W 4-2
Totals	**43**	**31**	**12**	**215**	**133**	**82**	**0**	**844**	**666**			

Playoff Results 2002-98

Year	Round	Opponent	Result	GF	GA
2001	CQF	Dallas	L 2-4	13	16
2000	CQF	Dallas	L 1-4	11	14
1999	CQF	Dallas	L 0-4	7	11
1998	CSF	Dallas	L 1-4	5	9
	CQF	Colorado	W 4-3	19	16

Playoff Scoring Leaders

	Player	Years	GP	G	A	PTS
1.	Wayne Gretzky	80-88	120	81	171	252
2.	Mark Messier	80-91	166	80	135	215
3.	Jari Kurri	81-90	146	92	110	202
4.	Glenn Anderson	81-91	164	81	102	183
5.	Paul Coffey	81-87	94	36	67	103
6.	Esa Tikkanen	85-92	114	51	46	97
7.	Charlie Huddy	82-91	138	16	61	77
8.	Craig Simpson	88-92	67	36	32	68
9.	Kevin Lowe	80-92, 97	171	9	43	52
10.	Randy Gregg	82-90	130	13	37	50

Series Records vs. Other Teams

Opponent	Year	Series	Winner	W	L	GF	GA
Bos.	1988	F	Edm.	4	0	21	12
Bos.	1990	F	Edm.	4	1	20	8
Cgy.	1983	DF	Edm.	4	1	35	13
Cgy.	1984	DF	Edm.	4	3	33	27
Cgy.	1986	DF	Cgy.	3	4	24	25
Cgy.	1988	DF	Edm.	4	0	18	11
Cgy.	1991	DSF	Edm.	4	3	22	20
Chi.	1983	CF	Edm.	4	0	25	11

Chi.	1985	CF	Edm.	4	2	44	25
Chi.	1990	CF	Edm.	4	2	25	20
Chi.	1992	CF	Chi.	0	4	8	21
Col.	1997	CSF	Col.	1	4	11	19
Col.	1998	CQF	Edm.	4	3	19	16
Dal.	1997	CQF	Edm.	4	3	21	18
Dal.	1998	CSF	Dal.	1	4	5	9
Dal.	1999	CQF	Dal.	0	4	7	11
Dal.	2000	CQF	Dal.	1	4	11	14
Dal.	2001	CQF	Dal.	2	4	13	16
Det.	1987	CF	Edm.	4	1	16	10
Det.	1988	CF	Edm.	4	1	23	16
L.A.	1982	DSF	L.A.	2	3	23	27
L.A.	1985	DSF	Edm.	3	0	11	7
L.A.	1987	DSF	Edm.	4	1	32	20
L.A.	1989	DSF	L.A.	3	4	20	25
L.A.	1990	DF	Edm.	4	0	24	10
L.A.	1991	DF	Edm.	4	2	21	20
L.A.	1992	DSF	Edm.	4	2	23	18
Min.	1984	CF	Edm.	4	0	22	10
Min.	1991	CF	Min.	1	4	14	20
Mtl.	1981	PRE	Edm.	3	0	15	6
NYI	1981	QF	NYI	2	4	20	29
NYI	1983	F	NYI	0	4	6	17
NYI	1984	F	Edm.	4	1	21	12
Phi.	1980	PRE	Phi.	0	3	6	12
Phi.	1985	F	Edm.	4	1	21	14
Phi.	1987	F	Edm.	4	3	22	18
Van.	1986	DSF	Edm.	3	0	17	5
Van.	1992	DF	Edm.	4	2	18	15
Wpg.	1983	DSF	Edm.	3	0	14	9
Wpg.	1984	DSF	Edm.	3	0	18	7
Wpg.	1985	DF	Edm.	4	0	22	11
Wpg.	1987	DF	Edm.	4	0	17	9
Wpg.	1988	DSF	Edm.	4	1	25	17
Wpg.	1990	DSF	Edm.	4	3	24	22

FLORIDA

All-Time Playoff Record vs. Other Teams

	Series	W	L	GP	W	L	T	GF	GA	Last Mtg.	Round	Result
Boston	1	1	0	5	4	1	0	22	16	1996	CQF	W 4-1
Colorado	1	0	1	4	0	4	0	4	15	1996	F	L 0-4
New Jersey	1	0	1	4	0	4	0	6	12	2000	CQF	L 0-4
NY Rangers	1	0	1	5	1	4	0	10	13	1997	CQF	L 1-4
Philadelphia	1	1	0	6	4	2	0	15	11	1996	CSF	W 4-2
Pittsburgh	1	1	0	7	4	3	0	20	15	1996	CF	W4-3
Totals	**6**	**3**	**3**	**31**	**13**	**18**	**0**	**77**	**82**			

Playoff Results 2002-98

Year	Round	Opponent	Result	GF	GA
2000	CQF	New Jersey	L 0-4	6	12

Playoff Scoring Leaders

	Player	Years	GP	G	A	PTS
1.	Ray Sheppard	96-97	26	10	8	18
2.	Dave Lowry	96-97	27	10	7	17
3.	Stu Barnes	96	22	6	10	16
4.	Rob Niedermayer	96-00	31	8	4	12
5.	Scott Mellanby	96-00	31	3	9	12
6.	Robert Svehla	96-00	31	1	11	12
7.	Bill Lindsay	96-97	25	5	6	11
8.	Tom Fitzgerald	96-97	27	4	5	9
9.	Paul Laus	96-00	30	2	7	9
10.	Ed Jovanovski	96-97	27	1	8	9

Series Records vs. Other Teams

Opponent	Year	Series	Winner	W	L	GF	GA
Bos.	1996	CQF	Fla.	4	1	22	16
Col.	1996	F	Col.	0	4	4	15
N.J.	2000	CQF	N.J.	0	4	6	12
NYR	1997	CQF	NYR	1	4	10	13
Phi.	1996	CSF	Fla.	4	2	15	11
Pit.	1996	CF	Fla.	4	3	20	15

LOS ANGELES

All-Time Playoff Record vs. Other Teams

	Series	W	L	GP	W	L	T	GF	GA	Last Mtg.	Round	Result
Boston	2	0	2	13	5	8	0	38	56	1977	QF	L 2-4
Calgary	6	4	2	26	13	13	0	105	112	1993	DSF	W 4-2
Chicago	1	0	1	5	1	4	0	7	10	1974	QF	L 1-4
Colorado	2	0	2	14	6	8	0	23	33	2002	CQF	L 3-4
Dallas	1	0	1	7	3	4	0	21	26	1968	QF	L 3-4
Detroit	2	1	1	10	4	6	0	21	32	2001	CQF	W 4-2
Edmonton	7	2	5	36	12	24	0	127	154	1992	DSF	L 2-4
Montreal	1	0	1	5	1	4	0	12	15	1993	F	L 1-4
NY Islanders	1	0	1	4	1	3	0	10	21	1980	PRE	L 1-3
NY Rangers	2	0	2	6	1	5	0	14	32	1981	PRE	L 1-3
St. Louis	2	0	2	8	0	8	0	13	32	1998	CQF	L 0-4
Toronto	3	1	2	12	5	7	0	31	41	1993	CF	W 4-3
Vancouver	3	2	1	17	9	8	0	66	60	1993	DF	W 4-2
Defunct	1	1	0	7	4	3	0	23	25	1969	QF	W 4-3
Totals	**34**	**11**	**23**	**170**	**65**	**105**	**0**	**511**	**649**			

Playoff Results 2002-98

Year	Round	Opponent	Result	GF	GA
2002	CQF	Colorado	L 3-4	13	16
2001	CSF	Colorado	L 3-4	10	17
	CQF	Detroit	W 4-2	15	17
2000	CQF	Detroit	L 0-4	6	15
1998	CQF	St. Louis	L 0-4	8	16

Playoff Scoring Leaders

	Player	Years	GP	G	A	PTS
1.	Wayne Gretzky	89-93	60	29	65	94
2.	Luc Robitaille	87-93, 98-01	94	41	48	89
3.	Dave Taylor	78-93	92	26	33	59
4.	Tomas Sandstrom	90-93	50	17	28	45
5.	Marcel Dionne	76-85	43	20	23	43
6.	Steve Duchesne	87-91	43	13	26	39
7.	Bernie Nicholls	82-89	34	16	21	37
8.	Tony Granato	90-93	52	13	24	37
9.	Mike Murphy	74-82	45	11	20	31
10.	Rob Blake	90-00	57	8	16	24

Series Records vs. Other Teams

Opponent	Year	Series	Winner	W	L	GF	GA
Atl.	1976	PRE	L.A.	2	0	3	1
Atl.	1977	PRE	L.A.	2	1	11	7
Bos.	1976	QF	Bos.	3	4	14	26
Bos.	1977	QF	Bos.	2	4	24	30
Cgy.	1988	DSF	Cgy.	1	4	18	30
Cgy.	1989	DF	Cgy.	0	4	11	22
Cgy.	1990	DSF	L.A.	4	2	29	24
Cgy.	1993	DSF	L.A.	4	2	33	28
Chi.	1974	QF	Chi.	1	4	7	10
Col.	2001	CSF	Col.	3	4	10	17
Col.	2002	CQF	Col.	3	4	13	16
Det.	2000	CQF	Det.	0	4	6	15
Det.	2001	CQF	L.A.	4	2	15	17
Edm.	1982	DSF	L.A.	3	2	27	23
Edm.	1985	DSF	Edm.	0	3	7	11
Edm.	1987	DSF	Edm.	1	4	20	32
Edm.	1989	DSF	L.A.	4	3	25	20
Edm.	1990	DF	Edm.	0	4	10	24
Edm.	1991	DF	Edm.	2	4	20	21
Edm.	1992	DSF	Edm.	2	4	18	23
Min.	1968	QF	Min.	3	4	21	26
Mtl.	1993	F	Mtl.	1	4	12	15
NYI	1980	PRE	NYI	1	3	10	21
NYR	1979	PRE	NYR	0	2	2	9
NYR	1981	PRE	NYR	1	3	12	23
St.L.	1969	SF	St.L.	0	4	5	16
St.L.	1998	CQF	St.L.	0	4	8	16
Tor.	1975	PRE	Tor.	1	2	6	7
Tor.	1978	PRE	Tor.	0	2	3	11
Tor.	1993	CF	L.A.	4	3	22	23
Van.	1982	DF	Van.	1	4	14	19
Van.	1991	DSF	L.A.	4	2	26	16
Van.	1993	DF	L.A.	4	2	26	25
Defunct Teams							
Oak.	1969	QF	L.A.	4	3	23	25

MONTREAL

All-Time Playoff Record vs. Other Teams

	Series	W	L	GP	W	L	T	GF	GA	Last Mtg.	Round	Result
Boston	29	22	7	145	91	54	0	450	357	2002	CQF	W 4-2
Buffalo	7	4	3	35	18	17	0	124	111	1998	CSF	L 0-4
Calgary	2	1	1	11	6	5	0	31	32	1989	F	L 2-4
Carolina	6	5	1	33	21	12	0	108	91	2002	CSF	L 2-4
Chicago	17	12	5	81	50	29	2	261	185	1976	QF	W 4-0
Colorado	5	3	2	31	17	14	0	105	85	1993	DSF	W 4-2
Dallas	2	1	1	13	7	6	0	48	37	1980	QF	L 3-4
Detroit	12	5	7	62	33	29	0	161	149	1978	QF	W 4-1
Edmonton	1	0	1	3	0	3	0	6	15	1981	PRE	L 0-3
Los Angeles	1	1	0	5	4	1	0	15	12	1993	F	W 4-1
New Jersey	1	0	1	5	1	4	0	11	22	1997	CQF	L 1-4
NY Islanders	4	3	1	22	14	8	0	64	55	1993	CF	W 4-1
NY Rangers	14	7	7	61	34	25	2	188	158	1996	CQF	L 2-4
Philadelphia	4	3	1	21	14	7	0	72	52	1989	CF	W 4-2
Pittsburgh	1	1	0	6	4	2	0	18	15	1998	CQF	W 4-2
St. Louis	3	3	0	12	12	0	0	42	14	1977	QF	W 4-0
Toronto	15	8	7	71	42	29	0	215	160	1979	QF	W 4-0
Vancouver	1	1	0	5	4	1	0	20	9	1975	QF	W 4-1
Defunct	*10	5	4	28	15	9	4	70	71			
Totals	***135**	**85**	**49**	**650**	**387**	**255**	**8**	**2009**	**1630**			

* 1919 Final suspended due to influenza epidemic.

Playoff Results 2002-98

Year	Round	Opponent	Result	GF	GA
2002	CSF	Carolina	L 2-4	12	21
	CQF	Boston	W 4-2	20	18
1998	CSF	Buffalo	L 0-4	10	17
	CQF	Pittsburgh	W 4-2	18	15

Playoff Scoring Leaders

	Player	Years	GP	G	A	PTS
1.	Jean Beliveau	54-71	162	79	97	176
2.	Jacques Lemaire	68-79	145	61	78	139
3.	Larry Robinson	73-89	203	25	109	134
4.	Guy Lafleur	72-84	124	57	76	133
5.	Henri Richard	56-75	180	49	80	129
6.	Yvan Cournoyer	65-78	147	64	63	127
7.	Maurice Richard	44-60	133	82	44	126
8.	Bernie Geoffrion	51-64	127	56	59	115
9.	Steve Shutt	73-84	96	50	48	98
10.	Dickie Moore	52-63	112	38	56	94

Series Records vs. Other Teams

Opponent	Year	Series	Winner	W	L	T	GF	GA
Bos.	1929	SF	Bos.	0	3		2	5
Bos.	1930	F	Mtl.	2	0		7	3
Bos.	1931	SF	Mtl.	3	2		13	13
Bos.	1943	SF	Bos.	1	4		17	18
Bos.	1946	F	Mtl.	4	1		19	13
Bos.	1947	SF	Mtl.	4	1		16	10
Bos.	1952	SF	Mtl.	4	3		18	12
Bos.	1953	F	Mtl.	4	1		16	9
Bos.	1954	SF	Mtl.	4	0		16	4
Bos.	1955	SF	Mtl.	4	1		16	9
Bos.	1957	F	Mtl.	4	1		15	6
Bos.	1958	F	Mtl.	4	2		16	14
Bos.	1968	QF	Mtl.	4	0		15	8
Bos.	1969	SF	Mtl.	4	2		15	16
Bos.	1971	QF	Mtl.	4	3		28	26
Bos.	1977	F	Mtl.	4	0		16	6
Bos.	1978	F	Mtl.	4	2		18	13
Bos.	1979	SF	Mtl.	4	3		25	20
Bos.	1984	DSF	Mtl.	3	0		10	2
Bos.	1985	DSF	Mtl.	3	2		19	17
Bos.	1986	DSF	Mtl.	3	0		10	6
Bos.	1987	DSF	Mtl.	4	0		19	11
Bos.	1988	DF	Bos.	1	4		10	15
Bos.	1989	DF	Mtl.	4	1		16	13
Bos.	1990	DF	Bos.	1	4		12	16
Bos.	1991	DF	Bos.	3	4		18	18
Bos.	1992	DF	Bos.	0	4		8	14
Bos.	1994	CQF	Bos.	3	4		20	22
Bos.	2002	CQF	Mtl.	4	2		20	18
Buf.	1973	QF	Mtl.	4	2		21	16
Buf.	1975	SF	Buf.	2	4		29	21
Buf.	1983	DSF	Buf.	0	3		2	8
Buf.	1990	DSF	Mtl.	4	2		17	13
Buf.	1991	DSF	Mtl.	4	2		29	24
Buf.	1993	DF	Mtl.	4	0		16	12
Buf.	1998	CSF	Buf.	0	4		10	17
Cgy.	1986	F	Mtl.	4	1		15	13
Cgy.	1989	F	Cgy.	2	4		16	19
Car.	2002	CSF	Car.	2	4		12	21
Chi.	1930	QF*	Mtl.	1	0	1	3	2
Chi.	1931	F	Mtl.	3	2		11	8
Chi.	1934	QF*	Chi.	0	1	1	3	4
Chi.	1938	QF	Chi.	1	2		8	11
Chi.	1941	QF	Chi.	1	2		7	8
Chi.	1944	F	Mtl.	4	0		16	8
Chi.	1946	SF	Mtl.	4	0		26	7
Chi.	1953	SF	Mtl.	4	3		18	14
Chi.	1959	SF	Mtl.	4	2		21	16
Chi.	1960	SF	Mtl.	4	0		14	6
Chi.	1961	SF	Chi.	2	4		15	16
Chi.	1962	SF	Chi.	2	4		13	19
Chi.	1965	F	Mtl.	4	3		18	12
Chi.	1968	SF	Mtl.	4	1		22	10
Chi.	1971	F	Mtl.	4	3		20	18

Chi.	1973	F	Mtl.	4	2		33	23
Chi.	1976	QF	Mtl.	4	0		13	3
Det.	1937	SF	Det.	2	3		8	13
Det.	1939	QF	Det.	1	2		5	8
Det.	1942	QF	Det.	1	2		8	8
Det.	1949	SF	Det.	3	4		14	17
Det.	1951	SF	Mtl.	4	2		13	12
Det.	1952	F	Det.	0	4		2	11
Det.	1954	F	Det.	3	4		12	14
Det.	1955	F	Det.	3	4		20	27
Det.	1956	F	Mtl.	4	1		18	9
Det.	1958	SF	Mtl.	4	0		19	6
Det.	1966	F	Mtl.	4	2		18	14
Det.	1978	QF	Mtl.	4	1		24	10
Edm.	1981	PRE	Edm.	0	3		6	15
Hfd.	1980	PRE	Mtl.	3	0		18	8
Hfd.	1986	DF	Mtl.	4	3		16	13
Hfd.	1988	DSF	Mtl.	4	2		23	20
Hfd.	1989	DSF	Mtl.	4	0		18	11
Hfd.	1992	DSF	Mtl.	4	3		21	18
L.A.	1993	F	Mtl.	4	1		15	12
Min.	1971	SF	Mtl.	4	2		27	19
Min.	1980	QF	Min.	3	4		21	18
N.J.	1997	CQF	N.J.	1	4		11	22
NYI	1976	SF	Mtl.	4	1		17	14
NYI	1977	SF	Mtl.	4	2		19	13
NYI	1984	CF	NYI	2	4		12	17
NYI	1993	CF	Mtl.	4	1		16	11
NYR	1930	SF	Mtl.	2	0		4	1
NYR	1932	SF	NYR	1	3		9	13
NYR	1933	QF*	NYR	0	1	1	5	8
NYR	1935	QF*	NYR	0	1	1	5	6
NYR	1950	SF	NYR	1	4		7	15
NYR	1956	SF	Mtl.	4	1		24	9
NYR	1957	SF	Mtl.	4	1		22	12
NYR	1967	SF	Mtl.	4	0		14	8
NYR	1969	QF	Mtl.	4	0		16	7
NYR	1972	QF	NYR	2	4		14	19
NYR	1974	QF	NYR	2	4		17	21
NYR	1979	F	Mtl.	4	1		19	11
NYR	1986	CF	Mtl.	4	1		15	9
NYR	1996	CQF	NYR	2	4		14	19
Phi.	1973	SF	Mtl.	4	1		19	13
Phi.	1976	F	Mtl.	4	0		14	9
Phi.	1987	CF	Phi.	2	4		22	22
Phi.	1989	CF	Mtl.	4	2		17	8
Pit.	1998	CQF	Mtl.	4	2		18	15
Que.	1982	DSF	Que.	2	3		16	11
Que.	1984	DF	Mtl.	4	2		20	13
Que.	1985	DF	Que.	3	4		24	24
Que.	1987	DF	Mtl.	4	3		26	21
Que.	1993	DSF	Mtl.	4	2		19	16
St.L.	1968	F	Mtl.	4	0		11	7
St.L.	1969	F	Mtl.	4	0		12	3
St.L.	1977	QF	Mtl.	4	0		19	4
Tor.	1918	NHLF*	Tor.	1	1		7	10
Tor.	1925	NHLF*	Mtl.	2	0		5	2
Tor.	1944	SF	Mtl.	4	1		23	6
Tor.	1945	SF	Tor.	2	4		21	15
Tor.	1947	F	Tor.	2	4		13	13
Tor.	1951	F	Tor.	1	4		10	13
Tor.	1959	F	Mtl.	4	1		18	12
Tor.	1960	F	Mtl.	4	0		15	5
Tor.	1963	SF	Tor.	1	4		6	14
Tor.	1964	SF	Tor.	3	4		14	17
Tor.	1965	SF	Mtl.	4	2		17	14
Tor.	1966	SF	Mtl.	4	0		15	6
Tor.	1967	F	Tor.	2	4		16	17
Tor.	1978	SF	Mtl.	4	0		16	6
Tor.	1979	QF	Mtl.	4	0		19	10
Van.	1975	QF	Mtl.	4	1		20	9
Defunct Teams								
Cgy.T.	1924	F	Mtl.	2	0		9	1
Mtl.M.	1927	QF*	Mtl.	1	0	1	2	1
Mtl.M.	1928	SF*	Mtl.M.	0	1	1	2	3
Ott.	1919	NHLF	Mtl.	4	1		26	18
Ott.	1923	NHLF*	Ott.	1	1		2	3
Ott.	1924	NHLF*	Mtl.	2	0		5	2
Ott.	1927	SF*	Ott.	0	1	1	1	5
Sea.	1919	F**	–	2	2	1	10	19
Van.M.	1924	F	Mtl.	2	0		5	3
Vic.	1925	F	Vic.	1	3		8	16

* Total-goals series
** No decision. Series incomplete due to influenza epidemic.

NEW JERSEY

All-Time Playoff Record vs. Other Teams

	Series	W	L	GP	W	L	T	GF	GA	Last Mtg.	Round	Result
Boston	3	2	1	18	11	7	0	55	52	1995	CQF	W 4-1
Buffalo	1	1	0	7	4	3	0	14	14	1994	CQF	W 4-3
Carolina	2	1	1	12	6	6	0	31	17	2002	CQF	L 2-4
Colorado	1	0	1	7	3	4	0	11	19	2001	F	L 3-4
Dallas	1	1	0	6	4	2	0	15	9	2000	F	W 4-2
Detroit	1	1	0	4	4	0	0	16	7	1995	F	W 4-0
Florida	1	1	0	4	4	0	0	12	6	2000	CQF	W 4-0
Montreal	1	1	0	5	4	1	0	22	11	1997	CQF	W 4-1
NY Islanders	1	1	0	6	4	2	0	23	18	1988	DSF	W 4-2
NY Rangers	3	0	3	19	7	12	0	46	56	1997	CSF	L 1-4
Ottawa	1	0	1	6	2	4	0	12	13	1998	CQF	L 2-4
Philadelphia	3	2	1	15	8	7	0	41	35	2000	CF	W 4-3
Pittsburgh	5	2	3	29	15	14	0	86	80	2001	CF	W 4-1
Toronto	2	2	0	13	8	5	0	37	27	2001	CSF	W 4-3
Washington	2	1	1	13	6	7	0	43	44	1990	DSF	L 2-4
Totals	**28**	**16**	**12**	**164**	**90**	**74**	**0**	**464**	**408**			

Playoff Results 2002-98

Year	Round	Opponent	Result	GF	GA
2002	CQF	Carolina	L 2-4	11	9
2001	F	Colorado	L 3-4	11	19
	CF	Pittsburgh	W 4-1	17	7
	CSF	Toronto	W 4-3	21	18
	CQF	Carolina	W 4-2	20	8
2000	**F**	**Dallas**	**W 4-2**	**15**	**9**
	CF	Philadelphia	W 4-3	18	15
	CSF	Toronto	W 4-2	16	9
	CQF	Florida	W 4-0	12	6
1999	CQF	Pittsburgh	L 3-4	18	21
1998	CQF	Ottawa	L 2-4	12	13

Playoff Scoring Leaders

	Player	Years	GP	G	A	PTS
1.	John MacLean	88-97	88	31	44	75
2.	Patrik Elias	97-02	73	20	40	60
3.	Claude Lemieux	91-95, 00	82	34	23	57
4.	Bobby Holik	93-02	121	20	36	56
5.	Scott Stevens	92-02	129	14	39	53
6.	Petr Sykora	97-02	63	22	24	46
7.	Scott Niedermayer	93-02	117	14	31	45
8.	Randy McKay	92-01	116	20	22	42
9.	Bruce Driver	88-95	82	10	32	42
10.	Jason Arnott	98-01	58	18	23	41

Series Records vs. Other Teams

Opponent	Year	Series	Winner	W	L	GF	GA
Bos.	1988	CF	Bos.	3	4	19	30
Bos.	1994	CSF	N.J.	4	2	22	17
Bos.	1995	CQF	N.J.	4	1	14	5
Buf.	1994	CQF	N.J.	4	3	14	14
Car.	2001	CQF	N.J.	4	2	20	8
Car.	2002	CQF	Car.	2	4	11	9
Col.	2001	F	Col.	3	4	11	19
Dal.	2000	F	N.J.	4	2	15	9
Det.	1995	F	N.J.	4	0	16	7
Fla.	2000	F	N.J.	4	0	12	6
Mtl.	1997	CQF	N.J.	4	1	22	11
NYI	1988	DSF	N.J.	4	2	23	18
NYR	1992	DSF	NYR	3	4	25	28
NYR	1994	CF	NYR	3	4	16	18
NYR	1997	CSF	NYR	1	4	5	10
Ott.	1998	CQF	Ott.	2	4	12	13
Phi.	1978	PRE	Phi.	0	2	3	6
Phi.	1995	CF	N.J.	4	2	20	14
Phi.	2000	CF	N.J.	4	3	18	15
Pit.	1991	DSF	Pit.	3	4	21	21
Pit.	1993	DSF	Pit.	1	4	13	23
Pit.	1995	CSF	N.J.	4	1	17	8
Pit.	1999	CQF	Pit.	3	4	18	21
Pit.	2001	CF	N.J.	4	1	17	7
Tor.	2000	CSF	N.J.	4	2	16	9
Tor.	2001	CSF	N.J.	4	3	21	18
Wsh.	1988	DF	N.J.	4	3	25	23
Wsh.	1990	DSF	Wsh.	2	4	18	21

NEW YORK ISLANDERS

All-Time Playoff Record vs. Other Teams

	Series	W	L	GP	W	L	T	GF	GA	Last Mtg.	Round	Result
Boston	2	2	0	11	8	3	0	49	35	1983	CF	W 4-2
Buffalo	3	3	0	16	12	4	0	59	45	1980	SF	W 4-2
Chicago	2	2	0	6	6	0	0	21	6	1979	QF	W 4-0
Colorado	1	1	0	4	4	0	0	18	9	1982	CF	W 4-0
Dallas	1	1	0	5	4	1	0	26	16	1981	F	W 4-1
Edmonton	3	2	1	15	9	6	0	58	47	1984	F	L 1-4
Los Angeles	1	1	0	4	3	1	0	21	10	1980	PRE	W 3-1
Montreal	4	1	3	22	8	14	0	55	64	1993	CF	L 1-4
New Jersey	1	0	1	6	2	4	0	18	23	1988	DSF	L 2-4
NY Rangers	8	5	3	39	20	19	0	129	132	1994	CQF	L 0-4
Philadelphia	4	1	3	25	11	14	0	69	83	1987	DF	L 3-4
Pittsburgh	3	3	0	19	11	8	0	67	58	1993	DF	W 4-3
Toronto	3	1	2	17	9	8	0	54	42	2002	CQF	L 3-4
Vancouver	2	2	0	6	6	0	0	26	14	1982	F	W 4-0
Washington	6	5	1	30	18	12	0	99	88	1993	DSF	W 4-2
Totals	**44**	**30**	**14**	**225**	**131**	**94**	**0**	**769**	**672**			

Playoff Results 2002-98

Year	Round	Opponent	Result	GF	GA
2002	CQF	Toronto	L 3-4	21	22

Playoff Scoring Leaders

	Player	Years	GP	G	A	PTS
1.	Bryan Trottier	76-90	175	64	106	170
2.	Denis Potvin	78-88	185	56	108	164
3.	Mike Bossy	78-87	129	85	75	160
4.	Clark Gillies	75-86	159	47	46	93
5.	Bob Bourne	75-86	129	38	54	92
6.	Bob Nystrom	75-85	157	39	44	83
7.	John Tonelli	79-85	113	28	55	83
8.	Butch Goring	80-84	99	28	40	68
9.	Brent Sutter	82-90	88	24	35	59
10.	Stefan Persson	78-85	102	7	50	57

Series Records vs. Other Teams

Opponent	Year	Series	Winner	W	L	GF	GA
Bos.	1980	QF	NYI	4	1	19	14
Bos.	1983	CF	NYI	4	2	30	21
Buf.	1976	QF	NYI	4	2	21	18
Buf.	1977	QF	NYI	4	0	16	10
Buf.	1980	SF	NYI	4	2	22	17
Chi.	1977	PRE	NYI	2	0	7	3
Chi.	1979	QF	NYI	4	0	14	3
Edm.	1981	QF	NYI	4	2	29	20
Edm.	1983	F	NYI	4	0	17	6
Edm.	1984	F	Edm.	1	4	12	21
L.A.	1980	PRE	NYI	3	1	21	10
Min.	1981	F	NYI	4	1	26	16
Mtl.	1976	SF	Mtl.	1	4	14	17
Mtl.	1977	SF	Mtl.	2	4	13	19
Mtl.	1984	CF	NYI	4	2	17	12
Mtl.	1993	CF	Mtl.	1	4	11	16
N.J.	1988	DSF	N.J.	2	4	18	23
NYR	1975	PRE	NYI	2	1	10	13
NYR	1979	SF	NYR	2	4	13	18
NYR	1981	SF	NYI	4	0	22	8
NYR	1982	DF	NYI	4	2	27	20
NYR	1983	DF	NYI	4	2	28	15
NYR	1984	DSF	NYI	3	2	13	14
NYR	1990	DSF	NYR	1	4	13	22
NYR	1994	CQF	NYR	0	4	3	22
Phi.	1975	SF	Phi.	3	4	16	19
Phi.	1980	F	NYI	4	2	26	25
Phi.	1985	DF	Phi.	1	4	11	16
Phi.	1987	DF	Phi.	3	4	16	23
Pit.	1975	QF	NYI	4	3	21	18
Pit.	1982	DSF	NYI	3	2	22	13
Pit.	1993	DF	NYI	4	3	24	27
Que.	1982	CF	NYI	4	0	18	9
Tor.	1978	QF	Tor.	3	4	13	16
Tor.	1981	PRE	NYI	3	0	20	4
Tor.	2002	CQF	Tor.	3	4	21	22
Van.	1976	PRE	NYI	2	0	8	4
Van.	1982	F	NYI	4	0	18	10
Wsh.	1983	DSF	NYI	3	1	19	11
Wsh.	1984	DF	NYI	4	1	20	13
Wsh.	1985	DSF	NYI	3	2	14	12
Wsh.	1986	DSF	Wsh.	0	3	4	11
Wsh.	1987	DSF	NYI	4	3	19	19
Wsh.	1993	DSF	NYI	4	2	23	22

NEW YORK RANGERS

All-Time Playoff Record vs. Other Teams

	Series	W	L	GP	W	L	T	GF	GA	Last Mtg.	Round	Result
Boston	9	3	6	42	18	22	2	104	114	1973	QF	W 4-1
Buffalo	1	0	1	3	1	2	0	6	11	1978	PRE	L 1-2
Calgary	1	1	0	4	3	1	0	14	8	1980	PRE	W 3-1
Chicago	5	1	4	24	10	14	0	54	66	1973	SF	L 1-4
Colorado	1	1	0	6	4	2	0	25	19	1995	CQF	W 4-2
Detroit	5	1	4	23	10	13	0	49	57	1950	F	L 3-4
Florida	1	1	0	5	4	1	0	13	10	1997	CQF	W 4-1
Los Angeles	2	2	0	6	5	1	0	32	14	1981	PRE	W 3-1
Montreal	14	7	7	61	25	34	2	158	188	1996	CQF	W 4-2
New Jersey	3	3	0	19	12	7	0	56	46	1997	CSF	W 4-1
NY Islanders	8	3	5	39	19	20	0	132	129	1994	CQF	W 4-0
Philadelphia	10	4	6	47	20	27	0	153	158	1997	CF	L 1-4
Pittsburgh	3	0	3	15	3	12	0	45	64	1996	CSF	L 1-4
St. Louis	1	1	0	6	4	2	0	29	22	1981	QF	W 4-2
Toronto	8	5	3	35	19	16	0	86	86	1971	QF	W 4-2
Vancouver	1	1	0	7	4	3	0	21	19	1994	F	W 4-3
Washington	4	2	2	22	11	11	0	71	75	1994	CSF	W 4-1
Defunct	9	6	3	22	11	7	4	43	29			
Totals	**86**	**42**	**44**	**386**	**183**	**195**	**8**	**1091**	**1115**			

Playoff Results 2002-98

(Last playoff appearance: 1997)

Playoff Scoring Leaders

	Player	Years	GP	G	A	PTS
1.	Brian Leetch	88-97	82	28	61	89
2.	Mark Messier	92-97	70	29	51	80
3.	Rod Gilbert	62-75	79	34	33	67
4.	Don Maloney	79-87	85	22	35	57
5.	Walt Tkaczuk	69-80	93	19	32	51
6.	Steve Vickers	73-81	68	24	25	49
7.	Ron Greschner	75-90	84	17	32	49
8.	Ron Duguay	78-87	69	28	19	47
9.	Anders Hedberg	79-85	58	22	24	46
10.	Adam Graves	92-97	68	28	16	44
11.	Brad Park	69-75	64	12	32	44

Series Records vs. Other Teams

Opponent	Year	Series	Winner	W	L	T	GF	GA
Atl.	1980	PRE	NYR	3	1		14	8
Bos.	1927	SF*	Bos.	0	1	1	1	3
Bos.	1928	SF*	NYR	1	0	1	5	2
Bos.	1929	F	Bos.	0	2		1	4
Bos.	1939	SF	Bos.	3	4		12	14
Bos.	1940	SF	NYR	4	2		15	9
Bos.	1958	SF	Bos.	2	4		16	28
Bos.	1970	QF	Bos.	2	4		16	25
Bos.	1972	F	Bos.	2	4		16	18
Bos.	1973	QF	NYR	4	1		22	11
Buf.	1978	PRE	Buf.	1	2		6	11
Chi.	1931	SF*	Chi.	0	2		0	3
Chi.	1968	QF	Chi.	2	4		12	18
Chi.	1971	SF	Chi.	3	4		14	21
Chi.	1972	SF	NYR	4	0		17	9
Chi.	1973	SF	Chi.	1	4		11	15
Det.	1933	SF*	NYR	2	0		6	3
Det.	1937	F	Det.	2	3		8	9
Det.	1941	QF	Det.	1	2		6	6
Det.	1948	SF	Det.	2	4		12	17
Det.	1950	F	Det.	3	4		17	22
Fla.	1997	CQF	NYR	4	1		13	10
L.A.	1979	PRE	NYR	2	0		9	2
L.A.	1981	PRE	NYR	3	1		23	12
Mtl.	1930	SF	Mtl.	0	2		1	4
Mtl.	1932	SF	NYR	3	1		13	9
Mtl.	1933	QF*	NYR	1	0	1	8	5
Mtl.	1935	QF*	NYR	1	0	1	6	5
Mtl.	1950	SF	NYR	4	1		15	7
Mtl.	1956	SF	Mtl.	1	4		9	24
Mtl.	1957	SF	Mtl.	1	4		12	22
Mtl.	1967	SF	Mtl.	0	4		8	14
Mtl.	1969	QF	Mtl.	0	4		7	16
Mtl.	1972	QF	NYR	4	2		19	14
Mtl.	1974	QF	NYR	4	2		21	17
Mtl.	1979	F	Mtl.	1	4		11	19
Mtl.	1986	CF	Mtl.	1	4		9	15
Mtl.	1996	CQF	NYR	4	2		19	14
N.J.	1992	DSF	NYR	4	3		28	25
N.J.	1994	CF	NYR	4	3		18	16
N.J.	1997	CSF	NYR	4	1		10	5
NYI	1975	PRE	NYI	1	2		13	10
NYI	1979	SF	NYR	4	2		18	13
NYI	1981	SF	NYI	0	4		8	22
NYI	1982	DF	NYI	2	4		20	27
NYI	1983	DF	NYI	2	4		15	28
NYI	1984	DSF	NYI	2	3		14	13
NYI	1990	DSF	NYR	4	1		22	13
NYI	1994	CQF	NYR	4	0		22	3
Phi.	1974	SF	Phi.	3	4		17	22
Phi.	1979	QF	NYR	4	1		28	8
Phi.	1980	QF	Phi.	1	4		7	14
Phi.	1982	DSF	NYR	3	1		19	15
Phi.	1983	DSF	NYR	3	0		18	9
Phi.	1985	DSF	Phi.	0	3		10	14
Phi.	1986	DSF	NYR	3	2		18	15
Phi.	1987	DSF	Phi.	2	4		13	22
Phi.	1995	CSF	Phi.	0	4		10	18
Phi.	1997	CF	Phi.	1	4		13	20
Pit.	1989	DSF	Pit.	0	4		11	19
Pit.	1992	DF	Pit.	2	4		19	24
Pit.	1996	CSF	Pit.	1	4		15	21
Que.	1995	CQF	NYR	4	2		25	19
St.L.	1981	QF	NYR	4	2		29	22
Tor.	1929	SF	NYR	2	0		3	1
Tor.	1932	F	Tor.	0	3		10	18
Tor.	1933	F	NYR	3	1		11	5
Tor.	1937	QF	NYR	2	0		5	1
Tor.	1940	F	NYR	4	2		14	11
Tor.	1942	SF	Tor.	2	4		12	13
Tor.	1962	SF	Tor.	2	4		15	22
Tor.	1971	QF	NYR	4	2		16	15
Van.	1994	F	NYR	4	3		21	19
Wsh.	1986	DF	NYR	4	2		20	25
Wsh.	1990	DF	Wsh.	1	4		15	22
Wsh.	1991	DSF	Wsh.	2	4		16	16
Wsh.	1994	CSF	NYR	4	1		20	12

Defunct Teams

Opponent	Year	Series	Winner	W	L	T	GF	GA
Mtl.M.	1928	F	NYR	3	2		5	6
Mtl.M.	1931	QF*	NYR	2	0		8	1
Mtl.M.	1934	QF*	Mtl.M.	0	1	1	1	2
Mtl.M.	1935	SF*	Mtl.M.	0	1	1	4	5
Mtl.M.	1937	SF	NYR	2	0		5	0
NYA	1929	QF*	NYR	1	0	1	1	0
NYA	1938	QF	NYA	1	2		7	8
Ott.	1930	QF*	NYR	1	0	1	6	3
Pit.P.	1928	QF*	NYR	1	1		6	4

* Total-goals series

OTTAWA

All-Time Playoff Record vs. Other Teams

	Series	W	L	GP	W	L	T	GF	GA	Last Mtg.	Round	Result
Buffalo	2	0	2	11	3	8	0	19	26	1999	CQF	L 0-4
New Jersey	1	1	0	6	4	2	0	13	12	1998	CQF	W 4-2
Philadelphia	1	1	0	5	4	1	0	11	2	2002	CQF	W 4-1
Toronto	3	0	3	17	5	12	0	31	43	2002	CSF	L 3-4
Washington	1	0	1	5	1	4	0	7	18	1998	CSF	L 1-4
Totals	**8**	**2**	**6**	**44**	**17**	**27**	**0**	**81**	**101**			

Playoff Results 2002-98

Year	Round	Opponent	Result	GF	GA
2002	CSF	Toronto	L 3-4	18	16
	CQF	Philadelphia	W 4-1	11	2
2001	CQF	Toronto	L 0-4	3	10
2000	CQF	Toronto	L 2-4	10	17
1999	CQF	Buffalo	L 0-4	6	12
1998	CSF	Washington	L 1-4	7	18
	CQF	New Jersey	W 4-2	13	12

Playoff Scoring Leaders

	Player	Years	GP	G	A	PTS
1.	Daniel Alfredsson	97-02	44	22	15	37
2.	Shawn McEachern	97-02	44	4	13	17
3.	Alexei Yashin	97-01	26	6	9	15
4.	Marian Hossa	99-02	26	5	9	14
5.	Wade Redden	97-02	36	5	9	14
6.	Radek Bonk	97-02	36	3	8	11
7.	Andreas Dackell	97-01	32	4	3	7
8.	Igor Kravchuk	98-00	21	3	4	7
9.	Martin Havlat	01-02	16	2	5	7
10.	Jason York	97-01	28	2	4	6

Series Records vs. Other Teams

Opponent	Year	Series	Winner	W	L	GF	GA
Buf.	1997	CQF	Buf.	3	4	13	14
Buf.	1999	CQF	Buf.	0	4	6	12
N.J.	1998	CQF	Ott.	4	2	13	12
Phi.	2002	CQF	Ott.	4	1	11	2
Tor.	2000	CQF	Tor.	2	4	10	17
Tor.	2001	CQF	Tor.	0	4	3	10
Tor.	2002	CSF	Tor.	3	4	18	16
Wsh.	1998	CSF	Wsh.	1	4	7	18

PHILADELPHIA

All-Time Playoff Record vs. Other Teams

	Series	W	L	GP	W	L	T	GF	GA	Last Mtg.	Round	Result
Boston	4	2	2	20	9	11	0	57	60	1978	QF	L 1-4
Buffalo	7	5	2	37	23	14	0	110	96	2001	CQF	L 2-4
Calgary	2	1	1	11	7	4	0	43	28	1981	QF	L 3-4
Chicago	1	0	1	4	0	4	0	8	20	1971	QF	L 0-4
Colorado	2	2	0	11	7	4	0	39	29	1985	CF	W 4-2
Dallas	2	2	0	11	8	3	0	41	26	1980	SF	W 4-1
Detroit	1	0	1	4	0	4	0	6	16	1997	F	L 0-4
Edmonton	3	1	2	15	7	8	0	44	49	1987	F	L 3-4
Florida	1	0	1	6	2	4	0	11	15	1996	CSF	L 2-4
Montreal	4	1	3	21	6	15	0	52	72	1989	CF	L 2-4
New Jersey	3	1	2	15	7	8	0	35	41	2000	CF	L 3-4
NY Islanders	4	3	1	25	14	11	0	83	69	1987	DF	W 4-3
NY Rangers	10	6	4	47	27	20	0	158	153	1997	CF	W 4-1
Ottawa	1	0	1	5	1	4	0	2	11	2002	CQF	L 1-4
Pittsburgh	3	3	0	18	12	6	0	66	51	2000	CSF	W 4-2
St. Louis	2	0	2	11	3	8	0	20	34	1969	QF	L 0-4
Tampa Bay	1	1	0	6	4	2	0	26	13	1996	CQF	W 4-2
Toronto	4	3	1	23	14	9	0	78	56	1999	CQF	L 2-4
Vancouver	1	1	0	3	2	1	0	15	9	1979	PR	W 2-1
Washington	3	1	2	16	7	9	0	55	65	1989	DSF	W 4-2
Totals	**59**	**33**	**26**	**309**	**161**	**148**	**0**	**948**	**913**			

Playoff Results 2002-98

Year	Round	Opponent	Result	GF	GA
2002	CQF	Ottawa	L 1-4	2	11
2001	CQF	Buffalo	L 2-4	13	21
2000	CF	New Jersey	L 3-4	15	18
	CSF	Pittsburgh	W 4-2	15	14
	CQF	Buffalo	W 4-1	14	8
1999	CQF	Toronto	L 2-4	11	9
1998	CQF	Buffalo	L 1-4	9	18

Playoff Scoring Leaders

	Player	Years	GP	G	A	PTS
1.	Bobby Clarke	71-84	136	42	77	119
2.	Brian Propp	80-89	116	52	60	112
3.	Bill Barber	73-83	129	53	55	108
4.	Rick MacLeish	71-81	108	53	52	105
5.	Tim Kerr	81-89	73	39	31	70
6.	Reggie Leach	75-81	91	47	22	69
7.	John LeClair	95-02	85	31	34	65
8.	Rick Tocchet	85-91, 00-01	95	27	33	60
9.	Eric Lindros	95-00	50	24	33	57
10.	Ken Linseman	79-82	41	11	42	53
11.	Mark Howe	83-89	82	8	45	53

Series Records vs. Other Teams

Opponent	Year	Series	Winner	W	L	GF	GA
Atl.	1974	QF	Phi.	4	0	17	6
Bos.	1974	F	Phi.	4	2	15	13
Bos.	1976	SF	Phi.	4	1	19	12
Bos.	1977	SF	Bos.	0	4	8	14
Bos.	1978	SF	Bos.	1	4	15	21
Buf.	1975	F	Phi.	4	2	19	12
Buf.	1978	QF	Phi.	4	1	16	11
Buf.	1995	CQF	Phi.	4	1	18	13
Buf.	1997	CSF	Phi.	4	1	21	13
Buf.	1998	CQF	Buf.	1	4	9	18
Buf.	2000	CQF	Phi.	4	1	14	8
Buf.	2001	CQF	Buf.	2	4	13	21
Cgy.	1981	QF	Cgy.	3	4	26	22
Chi.	1971	QF	Chi.	0	4	8	20
Col.	1978	PRE	Phi.	2	0	6	3
Det.	1997	F	Det.	0	4	6	16
Edm.	1980	PRE	Phi.	3	0	12	6
Edm.	1985	F	Edm.	1	4	14	21
Edm.	1987	F	Edm.	3	4	18	22
Fla.	1996	CSF	Fla.	2	4	11	15
Min.	1973	QF	Phi.	4	2	14	12
Min.	1980	SF	Phi.	4	1	27	14

Mtl.	1973	SF	Mtl.	1	4	13	19
Mtl.	1976	F	Mtl.	0	4	9	14
Mtl.	1987	CF	Phi.	4	2	22	22
Mtl.	1989	CF	Mtl.	2	4	8	17
N.J.	1995	CF	N.J.	2	4	14	20
N.J.	2000	CF	N.J.	3	4	15	18
NYI	1975	SF	Phi.	4	3	19	16
NYI	1980	F	NYI	2	4	25	26
NYI	1985	DF	Phi.	4	1	16	11
NYI	1987	DF	Phi.	4	3	23	16
NYR	1974	SF	Phi.	4	3	22	17
NYR	1979	QF	NYR	1	4	8	28
NYR	1980	QF	Phi.	4	1	14	7
NYR	1982	DSF	NYR	1	3	15	19
NYR	1983	DSF	NYR	0	3	9	18
NYR	1985	DSF	Phi.	3	0	14	10
NYR	1986	DSF	NYR	2	3	15	18
NYR	1987	DSF	Phi.	4	2	22	13
NYR	1995	CSF	Phi.	4	0	18	10
NYR	1997	CF	Phi.	4	1	20	13
Ott.	2002	CQF	Ott.	1	4	2	11
Pit.	1989	DF	Phi.	4	3	31	24
Pit.	1997	CQF	Phi.	4	1	20	13
Pit.	2000	CSF	Phi.	4	2	15	14
Que.	1981	PRE	Phi.	3	2	22	17
Que.	1985	CF	Phi.	4	2	17	12
St.L.	1968	QF	St.L.	3	4	17	17
St.L.	1969	QF	St.L.	0	4	3	17
T.B.	1996	CQF	Phi.	4	2	26	13
Tor.	1975	QF	Phi.	4	0	15	6
Tor.	1976	QF	Phi.	4	3	33	23
Tor.	1977	QF	Phi.	4	2	19	18
Tor.	1999	CQF	Tor.	2	4	11	9
Van.	1979	PRE	Phi.	2	1	15	9
Wsh.	1984	DSF	Wsh.	0	3	5	15
Wsh.	1988	DSF	Wsh.	3	4	25	31
Wsh.	1989	DSF	Phi.	4	2	25	19

PHOENIX

All-Time Playoff Record vs. Other Teams

	Series	W	L	GP	W	L	T	GF	GA	Last Mtg.	Round	Result
Anaheim	1	0	1	7	3	4	0	17	17	1997	CQF	L 3-4
Calgary	3	2	1	13	7	6	0	45	43	1987	DSF	W 4-2
Colorado	1	0	1	5	1	4	0	10	17	2000	CQF	L 1-4
Detroit	2	0	2	12	4	8	0	28	44	1998	CQF	L 2-4
Edmonton	6	0	6	26	4	22	0	75	120	1990	DSF	L 3-4
St. Louis	2	0	2	11	4	7	0	29	39	1999	CQF	L 3-4
San Jose	1	0	1	5	1	4	0	7	13	2002	CQF	L 1-4
Vancouver	2	0	2	13	5	8	0	34	50	1993	DSF	L 2-4
Totals	**18**	**2**	**16**	**92**	**29**	**63**	**0**	**245**	**343**			

Playoff Results 2002-98

Year	Round	Opponent	Result	GF	GA
2002	CQF	San Jose	L 1-4	7	13
2000	CQF	Colorado	L 1-4	10	17
1999	CQF	St. Louis	L 3-4	16	19
1998	CQF	Detroit	L 2-4	18	24

Playoff Scoring Leaders

	Player	Years	GP	G	A	PTS
1.	Dale Hawerchuk	82-90	38	16	33	49
2.	Thomas Steen	82-93	56	12	32	44
3.	Keith Tkachuk	92-00	44	19	9	28
4.	Paul MacLean	82-88	35	16	10	26
5.	Dave Ellett	85-90	33	4	16	20
6.	Jeremy Roenick	97-00	18	9	9	18
7.	Fredrik Olausson	87-93	35	4	13	17
8.	Randy Carlyle	84-92	31	3	14	17
9.	Teppo Numminen	90-02	50	8	8	16
10.	Brian Mullen	83-87	26	7	9	16

Series Records vs. Other Teams

Opponent	Year	Series	Winner	W	L	GF	GA
Ana.	1997	CQF	Ana.	3	4	17	17
Cgy.	1985	DSF	Wpg.	3	1	15	13
Cgy.	1986	DSF	Cgy.	0	3	8	15
Cgy.	1987	DSF	Wpg.	4	2	22	15
Col.	2000	CQF	Col.	1	4	10	17
Det.	1996	CQF	Det.	2	4	10	20
Det.	1998	CQF	Det.	2	4	18	24
Edm.	1983	DSF	Edm.	0	3	9	14
Edm.	1984	DSF	Edm.	0	3	7	18
Edm.	1985	DF	Edm.	0	4	11	22
Edm.	1987	DF	Edm.	0	4	9	17
Edm.	1988	DSF	Edm.	1	4	17	25
Edm.	1990	DSF	Edm.	3	4	22	24
St.L.	1982	DSF	St.L.	1	3	13	20
St.L.	1999	CQF	St.L.	3	4	16	29
S.J.	2002	CQF	S.J.	1	4	7	13
Van.	1992	DSF	Van.	3	4	17	29
Van.	1993	DSF	Van.	2	4	17	21

PITTSBURGH

All-Time Playoff Record vs. Other Teams

	Series	W	L	GP	W	L	T	GF	GA	Last Mtg.	Round	Result
Boston	4	2	2	19	10	9	0	67	62	1992	CF	W 4-0
Buffalo	2	2	0	10	6	4	0	26	26	2001	CSF	W 4-3
Chicago	2	1	1	8	4	4	0	23	24	1992	F	W 4-0
Dallas	1	1	0	6	4	2	0	28	16	1991	F	W 4-2
Florida	1	0	1	7	3	4	0	15	20	1996	CF	L 3-4
Montreal	1	0	1	6	2	4	0	15	18	1998	CQF	L 2-4
New Jersey	5	3	2	29	14	15	0	80	86	2001	CF	L 1-4
NY Islanders	3	0	3	19	8	11	0	58	67	1993	DF	L 3-4
NY Rangers	3	3	0	15	12	3	0	64	45	1996	CSF	W 4-1
Philadelphia	3	0	3	18	6	12	0	51	66	2000	CSF	L 2-4
St. Louis	3	1	2	13	6	7	0	40	45	1981	PRE	L 2-3
Toronto	3	0	3	12	4	8	0	27	39	1999	CSF	L 2-4
Washington	7	6	1	42	26	16	0	137	121	2001	CQF	W 4-2
Defunct	1	1	0	4	4	0	0	13	6	1970	QF	W 4-0
Totals	**36**	**18**	**18**	**190**	**100**	**90**	**0**	**606**	**597**			

Playoff Results 2002-98

Year	Round	Opponent	Result	GF	GA
2001	CF	New Jersey	L 1-4	7	17
	CSF	Buffalo	W 4-3	17	17
	CQF	Washington	W 4-2	14	10
2000	CSF	Philadelphia	L 2-4	14	15
	CQF	Washington	W 4-1	17	8
1999	CSF	Toronto	L 2-4	14	18
	CQF	New Jersey	W 4-3	21	18
1998	CQF	Montreal	L 2-4	15	18

Playoff Scoring Leaders

	Player	Years	GP	G	A	PTS
1.	Mario Lemieux	89-97, 01	107	76	96	172
2.	Jaromir Jagr	91-01	140	65	82	147
3.	Kevin Stevens	89-95, 01	103	46	60	106
4.	Ron Francis	91-98	97	32	68	100
5.	Larry Murphy	91-95	74	15	57	72
6.	Martin Straka	93-94, 98-01	65	19	27	46
7.	Rick Tocchet	92-94	32	15	22	37
8.	Mark Recchi	91	24	10	24	34
9.	Joe Mullen	91-95, 97	62	16	15	31
10.	Alexei Kovalev	99-01	39	11	17	28

Series Records vs. Other Teams

Opponent	Year	Series	Winner	W	L	GF	GA
Bos.	1979	QF	Bos.	0	4	7	16
Bos.	1980	PRE	Bos.	2	3	14	21
Bos.	1991	CF	Pit.	4	2	27	18
Bos.	1992	CF	Pit.	4	0	19	7
Buf.	1979	PRE	Pit.	2	1	9	9
Buf.	2001	CSF	Pit.	4	3	17	17
Chi.	1972	QF	Chi.	0	4	8	14
Chi.	1992	F	Pit.	4	0	15	10
Fla.	1996	CF	Fla.	3	4	15	20
Min.	1991	F	Pit.	4	2	28	16
Mtl.	1998	F	Mon.	2	4	15	18
N.J.	1991	DSF	Pit.	4	3	21	21
N.J.	1993	DSF	Pit.	4	1	23	13
N.J.	1995	CSF	N.J.	1	4	8	17
N.J.	1999	CQF	Pit.	4	3	21	18
N.J.	2001	CQF	N.J.	1	4	7	17
NYI	1975	QF	NYI	3	4	18	21
NYI	1982	DSF	NYI	2	3	13	22
NYI	1993	DF	NYI	3	4	27	24
NYR	1989	DSF	Pit.	4	0	19	11
NYR	1992	DF	Pit.	4	2	24	19
NYR	1996	CSF	Pit.	4	1	21	15
Phi.	1989	DF	Phi.	3	4	24	31
Phi.	1997	CQF	Phi.	1	4	13	20
Phi.	2000	CSF	Phi.	2	4	14	15
St.L.	1970	SF	St.L.	2	4	10	19
St.L.	1975	PRE	Pit.	2	0	9	6
St.L.	1981	PRE	St.L.	2	3	21	20
Tor.	1976	PRE	Tor.	1	2	3	8
Tor.	1977	PRE	Tor.	1	2	10	13
Tor.	1999	CSF	Tor.	2	4	14	18
Wsh.	1991	DF	Pit.	4	1	19	13
Wsh.	1992	DSF	Pit.	4	3	25	27
Wsh.	1994	CQF	Wsh.	2	4	12	20
Wsh.	1995	CQF	Pit.	4	3	29	26
Wsh.	1996	CQF	Pit.	4	2	21	15
Wsh.	2000	CQF	Pit.	4	1	17	8
Wsh.	2001	CQF	Pit.	4	2	14	10
Defunct Teams							
Oak.	1970	QF	Pit.	4	0	13	6

ST. LOUIS

All-Time Playoff Record vs. Other Teams

	Series	W	L	GP	W	L	T	GF	GA	Last Mtg.	Round	Result
Boston	2	0	2	8	0	8	0	15	48	1972	SF	L 0-4
Buffalo	1	0	1	3	1	2	0	8	7	1976	PRE	L 1-2
Calgary	1	0	1	7	3	4	0	22	28	1986	CF	L 3-4
Chicago	10	3	7	50	22	28	0	142	171	2002	CQF	W 4-1
Colorado	1	0	1	5	1	4	0	11	17	2001	CF	L 1-4
Dallas	12	6	6	66	32	34	0	187	197	2001	CSF	W 4-0
Detroit	7	2	5	40	16	24	0	103	125	2002	CSF	L 1-4
Los Angeles	2	2	0	8	8	0	0	32	13	1998	CSF	W 4-0
Montreal	3	0	3	12	0	12	0	14	42	1977	QF	L 0-4
NY Rangers	1	0	1	6	2	4	0	22	29	1981	QF	L 2-4
Philadelphia	2	2	0	11	8	3	0	34	20	1969	QF	W 4-0
Phoenix	2	2	0	11	7	4	0	39	29	1999	CQF	W 4-3
Pittsburgh	3	2	1	13	7	6	0	45	40	1981	PRE	W 3-2
San Jose	2	1	1	13	7	6	0	38	31	2001	CQF	W 4-2
Toronto	5	3	2	31	17	14	0	88	90	1996	CQF	W 4-2
Vancouver	1	0	1	7	3	4	0	27	27	1995	CQF	L 3-4
Totals	**55**	**23**	**32**	**291**	**134**	**157**	**0**	**827**	**914**			

Playoff Results 2002-98

Year	Round	Opponent	Result	GF	GA
2002	CSF	Detroit	L 1-4	11	14
	CQF	Chicago	W 4-1	13	5
2001	CF	Colorado	L 1-4	11	17
	CSF	Dallas	W 4-0	13	6
	CQF	San Jose	W 4-2	16	11
2000	CQF	San Jose	L 3-4	22	20
1999	CSF	Dallas	L 2-4	12	17
	CQF	Phoenix	W 4-3	19	16
1998	CSF	Detroit	L 2-4	13	23
	CQF	Los Angeles	W 4-0	16	8

Playoff Scoring Leaders

	Player	Years	GP	G	A	PTS
1.	Brett Hull	88-98	102	67	50	117
2.	Bernie Federko	77-89	91	35	66	101
3.	Al MacInnis	95-02	79	14	43	57
4.	Doug Gilmour	84-88	49	17	38	55
5.	Chris Pronger	96-02	73	9	37	46
6.	Pierre Turgeon	97-01	50	14	31	45
7.	Frank St. Marseille	68-72	61	19	24	43
8.	Brian Sutter	77-88	65	21	21	42
9.	Jeff Brown	90-93	42	10	28	38
10.	Pavol Demitra	97-02	54	15	21	36

Series Records vs. Other Teams

Opponent	Year	Series	Winner	W	L	GF	GA
Bos.	1970	F	Bos.	0	4	7	20
Bos.	1972	SF	Bos.	0	4	8	28
Buf.	1978	PRE	Buf.	1	2	8	7
Cgy.	1986	CF	Cgy.	3	4	22	28
Chi.	1973	QF	Chi.	1	4	9	22
Chi.	1980	PRE	Chi.	0	3	4	12
Chi.	1982	DF	Chi.	2	4	19	23
Chi.	1983	DSF	Chi.	1	3	10	16
Chi.	1988	DSF	St.L.	4	1	21	17
Chi.	1989	DF	Chi.	1	4	12	19
Chi.	1990	DF	Chi.	3	4	22	28
Chi.	1992	DSF	Chi.	2	4	19	23
Chi.	1993	DSF	St.L.	4	0	13	6
Chi.	2002	CQF	St.L.	4	1	13	5
Col.	2001	CF	Col.	1	4	11	17
Dal.	1994	CQF	Dal.	0	4	10	16
Dal.	1999	CSF	Dal.	2	4	12	17
Dal.	2001	CSF	St.L.	4	0	13	6
Det.	1984	DSF	St.L.	3	1	13	12
Det.	1988	DF	Det.	1	4	14	21
Det.	1991	DSF	St.L.	4	3	24	20
Det.	1996	CSF	Det.	3	4	16	22
Det.	1997	CQF	Det.	2	4	12	13
Det.	1998	CSF	Det.	2	4	13	23
Det.	2002	CSF	Det.	1	4	11	14

L.A.	1969	SF	St.L.	4	0	16	5
L.A.	1998	CQF	St.L.	4	0	16	8
Min.	1968	SF	St.L.	4	3	18	22
Min.	1970	QF	St.L.	4	2	20	16
Min.	1971	QF	Min.	2	4	15	16
Min.	1972	QF	St.L.	4	3	19	19
Min.	1984	DF	Min.	3	4	17	19
Min.	1985	DSF	Min.	0	3	5	9
Min.	1986	DSF	St.L.	3	2	18	20
Min.	1989	DSF	St.L.	4	1	23	15
Min.	1991	DF	Min.	2	4	17	22
Mtl.	1968	F	Mtl.	0	4	7	11
Mtl.	1969	F	Mtl.	0	4	3	12
Mtl.	1977	QF	Mtl.	0	4	4	19
NYR	1981	QF	NYR	2	4	22	29
Phi.	1968	QF	St.L.	4	3	17	17
Phi.	1969	QF	St.L.	4	0	17	3
Phx.	1999	CQF	St.L.	4	3	19	16
Pit.	1970	SF	St.L.	4	2	19	10
Pit.	1975	PRE	Pit.	0	2	6	9
Pit.	1981	PRE	St.L.	3	2	20	21
S.J.	2000	CQF	S.J.	3	4	22	20
S.J.	2001	CQF	St.L.	4	2	16	11
Tor.	1986	DF	St.L.	4	3	24	22
Tor.	1987	DSF	Tor.	2	4	12	15
Tor.	1990	DSF	St.L.	4	1	20	16
Tor.	1993	DF	Tor.	3	4	11	22
Tor.	1996	CQF	St.L.	4	2	21	15
Van.	1995	CQF	Van.	3	4	27	27
Wpg.	1982	DSF	St.L.	3	1	20	13

SAN JOSE

All-Time Playoff Record vs. Other Teams

	Series	W	L	GP	W	L	T	GF	GA	Last Mtg.	Round	Result
Calgary	1	1	0	7	4	3	0	26	35	1995	CQF	W 4-3
Colorado	2	0	2	13	5	8	0	38	44	2002	CSF	L 3-4
Dallas	2	0	2	11	3	8	0	19	31	2000	CSF	L 1-4
Detroit	2	1	1	11	4	7	0	27	51	1995	CSF	L 0-4
Phoenix	1	1	0	5	4	1	0	13	7	2002	CQF	W 4-1
St. Louis	2	1	1	13	6	7	0	31	38	2001	CQF	L 2-4
Toronto	1	0	1	7	3	4	0	21	26	1994	CSF	L 3-4
Totals	**11**	**4**	**7**	**67**	**29**	**38**	**0**	**175**	**232**			

Playoff Results 2002-98

Year	Round	Opponent	Result	GF	GA
2002	CSF	Colorado	L 3-4	21	25
	CQF	Phoenix	W 4-1	13	7
2001	CQF	St. Louis	L 2-4	11	16
2000	CSF	Dallas	L 1-4	7	15
	CQF	St. Louis	W 4-3	20	22
1999	CQF	Colorado	L 2-4	17	19
1998	CQF	Dallas	L 2-4	12	16

Playoff Scoring Leaders

	Player	Years	GP	G	A	PTS
1.	Mike Ricci	98-02	42	12	16	28
2.	Owen Nolan	98-02	40	15	12	27
3.	Igor Larionov	94-95	25	6	21	27
4.	Vincent Damphousse	99-02	36	8	16	24
5.	Patrick Marleau	98-02	34	11	8	19
6.	Ulf Dahlen	94-95	25	11	6	17
7.	Mike Rathje	94-02	54	8	9	17
8.	Sergei Makarov	94-95	25	11	5	16
9.	Marco Sturm	98-02	38	6	9	15
10.	Jeff Friesen	94-00	34	5	10	15
11.	Sandis Ozolinsh	94-95	25	3	12	15
12.	Jeff Norton	95, 99-01	38	1	14	15

Series Records vs. Other Teams

Opponent	Year	Series	Winner	W	L	GF	GA
Cgy.	1995	CQF	S.J.	4	3	26	35
Col.	1999	CQF	Col.	2	4	17	19
Col.	2002	CSF	Col.	3	4	21	25
Dal.	1998	CQF	Dal.	2	4	12	16
Dal.	2000	CSF	Dal.	1	4	7	15
Det.	1994	CQF	S.J.	4	3	21	27
Det.	1995	CSF	Det.	0	4	6	24
Phx.	2002	CQF	S.J.	4	1	13	7
St.L.	2000	CQF	S.J.	4	3	20	22
St.L.	2001	CQF	St.L.	2	4	11	16
Tor.	1994	CSF	Tor.	3	4	21	26

TAMPA BAY

All-Time Playoff Record vs. Other Teams

	Series	W	L	GP	W	L	T	GF	GA	Last Mtg.	Round	Result
Philadelphia	1	0	1	6	2	4	0	13	26	1996	CQF	L 2-4
Totals	**1**	**0**	**1**	**6**	**2**	**4**	**0**	**13**	**26**			

Playoff Results 2002-98

(Last playoff appearance: 1996)

Playoff Scoring Leaders

	Player	Years	GP	G	A	PTS
1.	John Cullen	96	5	3	3	6
2.	Rob Zamuner	96	6	2	3	5
3.	Alex Selivanov	96	6	2	2	4
4.	Brian Bradley	96	5	0	3	3
5.	Petr Klima	96	4	2	0	2
6.	Brian Bellows	96	6	2	0	2
7.	Mikael Andersson	96	6	1	1	2
8.	Shawn Burr	96	6	0	2	2
9.	Chris Gratton	96	6	0	2	2
10.	Jason Wiemer	96	6	1	0	1
11.	Roman Hamrlik	96	5	0	1	1
12.	Bill Houlder	96	6	0	1	1
13.	David Shaw	96	6	0	1	1

Series Records vs. Other Teams

Opponent	Year	Series	Winner	W	L	GF	GA
Phi.	1996	CQF	Phi.	2	4	13	26

TORONTO

All-Time Playoff Record vs. Other Teams

	Series	W	L	GP	W	L	T	GF	GA	Last Mtg.	Round	Result
Boston	13	8	5	62	31	30	1	150	153	1974	QF	L 0-4
Buffalo	1	0	1	5	1	4	0	16	21	1999	CF	L 1-4
Calgary	1	1	0	2	2	0	0	9	5	1979	PR	W 2-0
Carolina	1	0	1	6	2	4	0	6	10	2002	CF	L 2-4
Chicago	9	6	3	38	22	15	1	111	89	1995	CQF	L 3-4
Dallas	2	0	2	7	1	6	0	26	35	1983	DSF	L 1-3
Detroit	23	12	11	117	58	59	0	311	321	1993	DSF	W 4-3
Los Angeles	3	2	1	12	7	5	0	41	31	1993	CF	L 3-4
Montreal	15	7	8	71	29	42	0	160	215	1979	QF	L 0-4
New Jersey	2	0	2	13	5	8	0	27	37	2001	CSF	L 3-4
NY Islanders	3	2	1	17	8	9	0	42	54	2002	CQF	W 4-3
NY Rangers	8	3	5	35	16	19	0	86	86	1971	QF	L 2-4
Ottawa	3	3	0	17	12	5	0	43	31	2002	CSF	W 4-3
Philadelphia	4	1	3	23	9	14	0	56	78	1999	CQF	W 4-2
Pittsburgh	3	3	0	12	8	4	0	39	27	1999	CSF	W 4-2
St. Louis	5	2	3	31	14	17	0	90	88	1996	CQF	L 2-4
San Jose	1	1	0	7	4	3	0	26	21	1994	CSF	W 4-3
Vancouver	1	0	1	5	1	4	0	9	16	1994	CF	L 1-4
Defunct	8	6	2	24	12	10	2	59	57			
Totals	**106**	**57**	**49**	**504**	**242**	**258**	**4**	**1307**	**1375**			

Playoff Results 2002-98

Year	Round	Opponent	Result	GF	GA
2002	CF	Carolina	L 2-4	6	10
	CSF	Ottawa	W 4-3	16	18
	CQF	NY Islanders	W 4-3	22	21
2001	CSF	New Jersey	L 3-4	18	21
	CQF	Ottawa	W 4-0	10	3
2000	CSF	New Jersey	L 2-4	9	16
	CQF	Ottawa	W 4-2	17	10

Playoff Scoring Leaders

	Player	Years	GP	G	A	PTS
1.	Doug Gilmour	93-96	52	17	60	77
2.	Dave Keon	61-75	89	32	35	67
3.	Darryl Sittler	71-81	64	25	40	65
4.	Wendel Clark	86-94, 96, 00	79	34	27	61
5.	Ted Kennedy	44-55	78	29	31	60
6.	George Armstrong	52-71	110	26	34	60
7.	Frank Mahovlich	59-67	84	24	36	60
8.	Mats Sundin	95-02	61	27	30	57
9.	Red Kelly	60-67	70	17	38	55
10.	Syl Apps	37-48	69	25	29	54

Series Records vs. Other Teams

Opponent	Year	Series	Winner	W	L	T	GF	GA
Atl.	1979	PRE	Tor.	2	0		9	5
Bos.	1933	SF	Tor.	3	2		9	7
Bos.	1935	SF	Tor.	3	1		7	2
Bos.	1936	QF*	Tor.	1	1		8	6
Bos.	1938	SF	Tor.	3	0		6	3
Bos.	1939	F	Bos.	1	4		6	12
Bos.	1941	SF	Bos.	3	4		17	15
Bos.	1948	SF	Tor.	4	1		20	13
Bos.	1949	SF	Tor.	4	1		16	10
Bos.	1951	SF	Tor.	4	1	1	17	5
Bos.	1959	SF	Tor.	4	3		20	21
Bos.	1969	QF	Bos.	0	4		5	24
Bos.	1972	QF	Bos.	1	4		10	18
Bos.	1974	QF	Bos.	0	4		9	17
Buf.	1999	CF	Buf.	1	4		16	21
Car.	2002	CF	Car.	2	4		6	10
Chi.	1931	QF*	Chi.	0	1	1	3	4
Chi.	1932	QF*	Tor.	1	1		6	2
Chi.	1938	F	Chi.	1	3		8	10
Chi.	1940	QF	Tor.	2	0		5	3
Chi.	1962	F	Tor.	4	2		18	15
Chi.	1967	SF	Tor.	4	2		18	14
Chi.	1986	DSF	Tor.	3	0		18	9
Chi.	1994	CQF	Tor.	4	2		15	10
Chi.	1995	CQF	Chi.	3	4		20	22
Det.	1929	QF*	Tor.	2	0		7	2
Det.	1934	SF	Det.	2	3		12	11
Det.	1936	F	Det.	1	3		11	18
Det.	1939	SF	Tor.	2	1		10	8
Det.	1940	SF	Tor.	2	0		5	2
Det.	1942	F	Tor.	4	3		25	19
Det.	1943	SF	Det.	2	4		17	10
Det.	1945	F	Tor.	4	3		9	9
Det.	1947	SF	Tor.	4	1		18	14
Det.	1948	F	Tor.	4	0		18	7
Det.	1949	F	Tor.	4	0		12	5
Det.	1950	SF	Det.	3	4		11	10
Det.	1952	SF	Det.	0	4		3	13
Det.	1954	SF	Det.	1	4		8	15
Det.	1955	SF	Det.	0	4		6	14
Det.	1956	SF	Det.	1	4		10	14
Det.	1960	SF	Tor.	4	2		20	16
Det.	1961	SF	Det.	1	4		8	15
Det.	1963	F	Tor.	4	1		17	10
Det.	1964	F	Tor.	4	3		22	17
Det.	1987	DF	Det.	3	4		18	20
Det.	1988	DSF	Det.	2	4		20	32
Det.	1993	DSF	Tor.	4	3		24	30
L.A.	1975	PRE	Tor.	2	1		7	6
L.A.	1978	PRE	Tor.	2	0		11	3
L.A.	1993	CF	L.A.	3	4		23	22
Min.	1980	PRE	Min.	0	3		8	17
Min.	1983	DSF	Min.	1	3		18	18
Mtl.	1918	NHLF*	Tor.	1	1		10	7
Mtl.	1925	NHLF*	Mtl.	0	2		2	5
Mtl.	1944	SF	Mtl.	1	4		6	23
Mtl.	1945	SF	Tor.	4	2		15	21
Mtl.	1947	F	Tor.	4	2		13	13
Mtl.	1951	F	Tor.	4	1		13	10
Mtl.	1959	F	Mtl.	1	4		12	18
Mtl.	1960	F	Mtl.	0	4		5	15
Mtl.	1963	SF	Tor.	4	1		14	6
Mtl.	1964	SF	Tor.	4	3		17	14
Mtl.	1965	SF	Mtl.	2	4		14	17
Mtl.	1966	SF	Mtl.	0	4		6	15
Mtl.	1967	F	Tor.	4	2		17	16
Mtl.	1978	SF	Mtl.	0	4		6	16
Mtl.	1979	QF	Mtl.	0	4		10	19
N.J.	2000	CSF	N.J.	2	4		9	16
N.J.	2001	CSF	N.J.	3	4		18	21
NYI	1978	QF	Tor.	4	3		16	13
NYI	1981	PRE	NYI	0	3		4	20
NYI	2002	CQF	Tor.	4	3		22	21
NYR	1929	SF	NYR	0	2		1	3
NYR	1932	F	Tor.	3	0		18	10
NYR	1933	F	NYR	1	3		5	11
NYR	1937	QF	NYR	0	2		1	5
NYR	1940	F	NYR	2	4		11	14
NYR	1942	SF	Tor.	4	2		13	12
NYR	1962	SF	Tor.	4	2		22	15
NYR	1971	QF	NYR	2	4		15	16
Ott.	2000	CQF	Tor.	4	2		17	10
Ott.	2001	CQF	Tor.	4	0		10	3
Ott.	2002	CSF	Tor.	4	3		16	18
Phi.	1975	QF	Phi.	0	4		6	15
Phi.	1976	QF	Phi.	3	4		23	33
Phi.	1977	QF	Phi.	2	4		18	19
Phi.	1999	CQF	Tor.	4	2		9	11
Pit.	1976	PRE	Tor.	2	1		8	3

Team	Year	Round	Winner	W	L		GF	GA
Pit.	1977	PRE	Tor.	2	1		13	10
Pit.	1999	CSF	Tor.	4	2		18	14
St.L.	1986	DF	St.L.	3	4		22	24
St.L.	1987	DSF	Tor.	4	2		15	12
St.L.	1990	DSF	St.L.	1	4		16	20
St.L.	1993	DF	Tor.	4	3		22	11
St.L.	1996	CQF	St.L.	2	4		15	21
S.J.	1994	CSF	Tor.	4	3		26	21
Van.	1994	CF	Van.	1	4		9	16

Defunct Teams

Team	Year	Round	Winner	W	L	T	GF	GA
Mtl.M.	1932	SF*	Tor.	1	0	1	4	3
Mtl.M.	1935	F	Mtl.M.	0	3		4	10
NYA	1936	SF	Tor.	2	1		6	3
NYA	1939	QF	Tor.	2	0		6	0
Ott.	1921	NHLF*	Ott.	0	2		0	7
Ott.	1922	NHLF*	Tor.	1	0	1	5	4
Van.M.	1918	F	Tor.	3	2		18	21
Van.M.	1922	F	Tor.	3	2		16	9

* Total-goals series

VANCOUVER

All-Time Playoff Record vs. Other Teams

Opponent	Series	W	L	GP	W	L	T	GF	GA	Last Mtg.	Round	Result
Buffalo	2	0	2	7	1	6	0	14	28	1981	PR	L 0-3
Calgary	5	2	3	25	12	13	0	80	82	1994	CQF	W 4-3
Chicago	2	1	1	9	4	5	0	24	24	1995	CSF	L 0-4
Colorado	2	0	2	10	2	8	0	26	40	2001	CQF	L 0-4
Dallas	1	1	0	5	4	1	0	18	11	1994	CSF	W 4-1
Detroit	1	0	1	6	2	4	0	16	22	2002	CQF	L 2-4
Edmonton	2	0	2	9	2	7	0	20	35	1992	DF	L 2-4
Los Angeles	3	1	2	17	8	9	0	60	66	1993	DF	L 2-4
Montreal	1	0	1	5	1	4	0	9	20	1975	QF	L 1-4
NY Islanders	2	0	2	6	0	6	0	14	26	1982	F	L 0-4
NY Rangers	1	0	1	7	3	4	0	19	21	1994	F	L 3-4
Philadelphia	1	0	1	3	1	2	0	9	15	1979	PRE	L 1-2
Phoenix	2	2	0	13	8	5	0	50	34	1993	DSF	W 4-2
St. Louis	1	1	0	7	4	3	0	27	27	1995	CQF	W 4-3
Toronto	1	1	0	5	4	1	0	16	9	1994	CF	W 4-1
Totals	**27**	**9**	**18**	**134**	**56**	**78**	**0**	**402**	**460**			

Playoff Results 2002-98

Year	Round	Opponent	Result	GF	GA
2002	CQF	Detroit	L 2-4	16	22
2001	CQF	Colorado	L 0-4	9	16

Playoff Scoring Leaders

	Player	Years	GP	G	A	PTS
1.	Trevor Linden	89-96, 02	85	31	54	85
2.	Pavel Bure	92-95	60	34	32	66
3.	Geoff Courtnall	91-95	65	26	35	61
4.	Cliff Ronning	91-95	72	24	34	58
5.	Jyrki Lumme	91-96	72	9	31	40
6.	Thomas Gradin	79-86	38	17	21	38
7.	Greg Adams	88-94	53	15	19	34
8.	Stan Smyl	79-89	41	16	17	33
9.	Dave Babych	92-95	60	9	18	27
10.	Murray Craven	93-94	34	8	15	23

Series Records vs. Other Teams

Opponent	Year	Series	Winner	W	L	GF	GA
Buf.	1980	PRE	Buf.	1	3	7	15
Buf.	1981	PRE	Buf.	0	3	7	13
Cgy.	1982	DSF	Van.	3	0	10	5
Cgy.	1983	DSF	Cgy.	1	3	14	17
Cgy.	1984	DSF	Cgy.	1	3	13	14
Cgy.	1989	DSF	Cgy.	3	4	20	26
Cgy.	1994	CQF	Van.	4	3	23	20
Chi.	1982	CF	Van.	4	1	18	13
Chi.	1995	CSF	Chi.	0	4	6	11
Col.	1996	CQF	Col.	2	4	17	24
Col.	2001	CQF	Col.	0	4	9	16
Dal.	1994	CSF	Van.	4	1	18	11
Det.	2002	CQF	Det.	2	4	16	22
Edm.	1986	DSF	Edm.	0	3	5	17
Edm.	1992	DF	Edm.	2	4	15	18
L.A.	1982	DF	Van.	4	1	19	14
L.A.	1991	DSF	L.A.	2	4	16	26
L.A.	1993	DF	L.A.	2	4	25	26
Mtl.	1975	QF	Mtl.	1	4	9	20
NYI	1976	PRE	NYI	0	2	4	8
NYI	1982	F	NYI	0	4	10	18
NYR	1994	F	NYR	3	4	19	21

Opponent	Year	Series	Winner	W	L	GF	GA
Phi.	1979	PRE	Phi.	1	2	9	15
St.L.	1995	CQF	Van.	4	3	27	27
Tor.	1994	CF	Van.	4	1	16	9
Wpg.	1992	DSF	Van.	4	3	29	17
Wpg.	1993	DSF	Van.	4	2	21	17

WASHINGTON

All-Time Playoff Record vs. Other Teams

Opponent	Series	W	L	GP	W	L	T	GF	GA	Last Mtg.	Round	Result
Boston	2	1	1	10	4	6	0	15	13	1998	CQF	W 4-2
Buffalo	1	1	0	6	4	2	0	13	11	1998	CF	W 4-2
Detroit	1	0	1	4	0	4	0	7	13	1998	F	L 0-4
New Jersey	2	1	1	13	7	6	0	44	43	1990	DSF	W 4-2
NY Islanders	6	1	5	30	12	18	0	88	89	1993	DSF	L 2-4
NY Rangers	4	2	2	22	11	11	0	75	71	1994	CSF	L 1-4
Ottawa	1	1	0	5	4	1	0	18	7	1998	CSF	W 4-1
Philadelphia	3	2	1	16	9	7	0	65	55	1989	DSF	L 2-4
Pittsburgh	7	1	6	42	16	26	0	121	137	2001	CQF	L 2-4
Totals	**27**	**10**	**17**	**148**	**67**	**81**	**0**	**452**	**464**			

Playoff Results 2002-98

Year	Round	Opponent	Result	GF	GA
2001	CQF	Pittsburgh	L 2-4	10	14
2000	CQF	Pittsburgh	L 1-4	8	17
1998	F	Detroit	L 0-4	7	13
	CF	Buffalo	W 4-2	13	11
	CSF	Ottawa	W 4-1	18	7
	CQF	Boston	W 4-2	15	13

Playoff Scoring Leaders

	Player	Years	GP	G	A	PTS
1.	Dale Hunter	88-98	100	25	47	72
2.	Mike Ridley	87-94	76	19	41	60
3.	Michal Pivonka	83-98	95	19	36	55
4.	Calle Johansson	89-01	89	12	41	53
5.	Scott Stevens	83-90	67	9	44	53
6.	Peter Bondra	91-01	67	26	24	50
7.	Kevin Hatcher	85-94	83	16	32	48
8.	Kelly Miller	87-98	100	17	30	47
9.	Mike Gartner	83-88	47	16	27	43
10.	Joe Juneau	94-98	44	13	28	41

Series Records vs. Other Teams

Opponent	Year	Series	Winner	W	L	GF	GA
Bos.	1990	CF	Bos.	0	4	6	15
Bos.	1998	CQF	Wsh.	4	2	15	13
Buf.	1998	CF	Wsh.	4	2	13	11
Det.	1998	F	Det.	0	4	7	13
N.J.	1988	DF	N.J.	3	4	23	25
N.J.	1990	DSF	Wsh.	4	2	21	18
NYI	1983	DSF	NYI	1	3	11	19
NYI	1984	DF	NYI	1	4	13	20
NYI	1985	DSF	NYI	2	3	12	14
NYI	1986	DSF	Wsh.	3	0	11	4
NYI	1987	DSF	NYI	3	4	19	19
NYI	1993	DSF	NYI	2	4	22	23
NYR	1986	DF	NYR	2	4	25	20
NYR	1990	DF	Wsh.	4	1	22	15
NYR	1991	DSF	Wsh.	4	2	16	16
NYR	1994	CSF	NYR	1	4	12	20
Ott.	1998	CSF	Wsh.	4	1	18	7
Phi.	1984	DSF	Wsh.	3	0	15	5
Phi.	1988	DSF	Wsh.	4	3	31	25
Phi.	1989	DSF	Phi.	2	4	19	25
Pit.	1991	DF	Pit.	1	4	13	19
Pit.	1992	DSF	Pit.	3	4	27	25
Pit.	1994	CQF	Wsh.	4	2	20	12
Pit.	1995	CQF	Pit.	3	4	26	29
Pit.	1996	CQF	Pit.	2	4	15	21
Pit.	2000	CQF	Pit.	1	4	8	17
Pit.	2001	CQF	Pit.	2	4	10	14

> **NOTE:**
> Atlanta, Columbus, Minnesota and Nashville have not appeared in the Stanley Cup Playoffs.

Stanley Cup Standings, 1918-2002

ranked by Cup wins

Teams	Cup Wins	Yrs.	Series	Wins	Losses	Games	Wins	Losses	Ties	Goals For	Goals Against	Winning %
Montreal	23[1]	73	136[2]	86	49	650	387	255	8	2009	1630	.602
Toronto	13[3]	62	106	57	49	504	242	258	4	1307	1411	.484
Detroit	10	51	96	55	41	478	251	226	1	1355	1248	.526
Boston	5	60	102	47	55	500	238	256	6	1466	1484	.482
Edmonton	5	18	44	31	13	221	135	86	0	857	682	.611
NY Rangers	4	48	86	42	44	386	183	195	8	1091	1114	.484
NY Islanders	4	18	44	30	14	225	131	94	0	769	672	.582
Chicago	3	53	90	40	50	411	188	218	5	1176	1311	.464
Philadelphia	2	28	59	33	26	309	161	148	0	948	913	.521
Pittsburgh	2	21	39	20	19	208	109	99	0	644	641	.524
Colorado[4]	2	16	36	22	14	206	113	93	0	624	580	.549
New Jersey[5]	2	14	28	16	12	164	90	74	0	460	412	.549
Dallas[6]	1	24	48	25	23	260	133	127	0	782	793	.512
Calgary[7]	1	21	32	12	20	156	69	87	0	529	573	.442
St.. Louis	0	32	55	23	32	291	134	157	0	827	914	.460
Buffalo	0	25	42	17	25	209	99	110	0	626	639	.474
Los Angeles	0	23	34	11	23	170	65	105	0	511	649	.382
Vancouver	0	18	27	9	18	134	56	78	0	402	460	.418
Washington	0	17	27	10	17	148	67	81	0	452	464	.453
Phoenix[8]	0	16	18	2	16	92	29	63	0	245	343	.315
Carolina[9]	0	11	15	4	11	84	35	49	0	208	256	.417
San Jose	0	7	11	4	7	67	29	38	0	175	232	.433
Ottawa[10]	0	6	8	2	6	44	17	27	0	81	101	.386
Florida	0	3	6	3	3	31	13	18	0	77	82	.419
Anaheim	0	2	3	1	2	15	4	11	0	31	47	.267
Tampa Bay	0	1	1	0	1	6	2	4	0	13	26	.333

NOTES

[1] Montreal also won the Stanley Cup in 1916.
[2] 1919 final incomplete due to influenza epidemic.
[3] Toronto Blueshirts also won the Stanley Cup in 1914.
[4] Includes totals of Quebec Nordiques 1979-95.
[5] Includes totals of Colorado Rockies 1976-82.
[6] Includes totals of Minnesota North Stars 1967-93.
[7] Includes totals of Atlanta Flames 1972-80.
[8] Includes totals of Winnipeg Jets 1979-96.
[9] Includes totals of Hartford Whalers 1979-97.
[10] Modern Ottawa Senators franchise only, 1992 to date.

CHAPTER 6

All-Time Playoff Scoring Leaders

1918 – 2002

Goals

(40 or more goals)

Player	Teams	Yrs.	GP	G
Wayne Gretzky	Edm., L.A., St.L., NYR	16	208	122
* Mark Messier	Edm., NYR	17	236	109
Jari Kurri	Edm., L.A., NYR, Ana., Col.	15	200	106
* Brett Hull	Cgy., St.L., Dal., Det.	17	186	100
Glenn Anderson	Edm., Tor., NYR, St.L.	15	225	93
Mike Bossy	NYI	10	129	85
Maurice Richard	Mtl.	15	133	82
* Claude Lemieux	Mtl., N.J., Col., Phx.	16	226	80
Jean Beliveau	Mtl.	17	162	79
* Mario Lemieux	Pit.	8	107	76
Dino Ciccarelli	Min., Wsh., Det.	14	141	73
Esa Tikkanen	Edm., NYR, St.L., Van., Wsh.	13	186	72
Bryan Trottier	NYI, Pit.	17	221	71
Gordie Howe	Det., Hfd.	20	157	68
* Steve Yzerman	Det.	17	177	67
Denis Savard	Chi., Mtl.	16	169	66
* Joe Sakic	Que., Col.	9	135	65
* Jaromir Jagr	Pit.	11	140	65
Yvan Cournoyer	Mtl.	12	147	64
Brian Propp	Phi., Bos., Min.	13	160	64
Bobby Smith	Min., Mtl.	13	184	64
Bobby Hull	Chi., Hfd.	14	119	62
Phil Esposito	Chi., Bos., NYR	15	130	61
Jacques Lemaire	Mtl.	11	145	61
Joe Mullen	St.L., Cgy., Pit.	15	143	60
* Doug Gilmour	St.L., Cgy., Tor., N.J., Buf., Mtl.	17	182	60
Stan Mikita	Chi.	18	155	59
Paul Coffey	Edm., Pit., L.A., Det., Phi., Car.	16	194	59
Guy Lafleur	Mtl., NYR	14	128	58
Bernie Geoffrion	Mtl., NYR	16	132	58
Cam Neely	Van., Bos.	9	93	57
Joe Nieuwendyk	Cgy., Dal., N.J.	14	132	57
* Luc Robitaille	L.A., Pit., NYR, Det.	14	155	57
Steve Larmer	Chi., NYR	13	140	56
Denis Potvin	NYI	14	185	56
Rick MacLeish	Phi., Pit., Det.	11	114	54
Bill Barber	Phi.	11	129	53
Stephane Richer	Mtl., N.J., St.L.	12	131	53
* Rick Tocchet	Phi., Pit., Bos., Phx.	13	145	52
* Peter Forsberg	Que., Col.	8	115	51
Frank Mahovlich	Tor., Det., Mtl.	14	137	51
Brian Bellows	Min., Mtl., T.B., Ana., Wsh.	13	143	51
Steve Shutt	Mtl., L.A.	12	99	50
* Brendan Shanahan	N.J., St.L., Det.	13	135	50
* Steve Thomas	Tor., Chi., NYI, N.J.	14	147	50
* Sergei Fedorov	Det.	12	158	49
Henri Richard	Mtl.	18	180	49
Reggie Leach	Bos., Phi.	8	94	47
Ted Lindsay	Det., Chi.	16	133	47
Clark Gillies	NYI, Buf.	13	164	47
Kevin Stevens	Pit.	7	103	46
Dickie Moore	Mtl., Tor., St.L.	14	135	46
* Ron Francis	Hfd., Pit., Car.	16	159	46
Rick Middleton	NYR, Bos.	12	114	45
* Mike Modano	Min., Dal.	10	127	45
* Jeremy Roenick	Chi., Phx., Phi.	13	105	44
Lanny McDonald	Tor., Cgy.	13	117	44
Ken Linseman	Phi., Edm., Bos.	11	113	43
Mike Gartner	Wsh., Min., NYR, Tor., Phx.	15	122	43
* Vyacheslav Kozlov	Det.	9	114	42
Bernie Nicholls	L.A., NYR, Edm., N.J., Chi., S.J.	13	118	42
Bobby Clarke	Phi.	13	136	42
Dale Hunter	Que., Wsh., Col.	18	186	42
John Bucyk	Det., Bos.	14	124	41
Raymond Bourque	Bos., Col.	21	214	41
Tim Kerr	Phi., NYR	10	81	40
Peter McNab	Buf., Bos., Van.	10	107	40
Bob Bourne	NYI, L.A.	13	139	40
John Tonelli	NYI, Cgy., L.A.	13	172	40

Assists

(60 or more assists)

Player	Teams	Yrs.	GP	A
Wayne Gretzky	Edm., L.A., St.L., NYR	16	208	260
* Mark Messier	Edm., NYR	17	236	186
Raymond Bourque	Bos., Col.	21	214	139
Paul Coffey	Edm., Pit., L.A., Det., Phi., Car.	16	194	137
* Doug Gilmour	St.L., Cgy., Tor., N.J., Buf., Mtl.	17	182	128
Jari Kurri	Edm., L.A., NYR, Ana., Col.	15	200	127
Glenn Anderson	Edm., Tor., NYR, St.L.	15	225	121
* Al MacInnis	Cgy., St.L.	18	174	120
Larry Robinson	Mtl., L.A.	20	227	116
Larry Murphy	L.A., Wsh., Min., Pit., Tor., Det.	20	215	115
Bryan Trottier	NYI, Pit.	17	221	113
* Sergei Fedorov	Det.	12	158	111
Denis Savard	Chi., Mtl.	16	169	109
* Steve Yzerman	Det.	17	177	108
Denis Potvin	NYI	14	185	108
* Chris Chelios	Mtl., Chi., Det.	18	210	106
* Adam Oates	Det., St.L., Bos., Wsh., Phi.	14	142	105
Jean Beliveau	Mtl.	17	162	97
* Mario Lemieux	Pit.	8	107	96
Bobby Smith	Min., Mtl.	13	184	96
Ron Francis	Hfd., Pit., Car.	16	159	93
Gordie Howe	Det., Hfd.	20	157	92
Stan Mikita	Chi.	18	155	91
Brad Park	NYR, Bos., Det.	17	161	90
Craig Janney	Bos., St.L., S.J., Wpg., Phx.	11	120	86
* Scott Stevens	Wsh., St.L., N.J.	19	209	86
* Peter Forsberg	Que., Col.	8	115	84
Brian Propp	Phi., Bos., Min.	13	160	84
* Brett Hull	Cgy., St.L., Dal., Det.	17	186	84
* Joe Sakic	Que., Col.	9	135	83
* Jaromir Jagr	Pit.	11	140	82
Henri Richard	Mtl.	18	180	80
Jacques Lemaire	Mtl.	11	145	78
Ken Linseman	Phi., Edm., Bos.	11	113	77
Bobby Clarke	Phi.	13	136	77
* Claude Lemieux	Mtl., N.J., Col., Phx.	16	226	77
Guy Lafleur	Mtl., NYR	14	128	76
Phil Esposito	Chi., Bos., NYR	15	130	76
Dale Hunter	Que., Wsh., Col.	18	186	76
Mike Bossy	NYI	10	129	75
Steve Larmer	Chi., NYR	13	140	75
* Nicklas Lidstrom	Det.	11	152	75
John Tonelli	NYI, Cgy., L.A.	13	172	75
Peter Stastny	Que., N.J., St.L.	12	93	72
Bernie Nicholls	L.A., NYR, Edm., N.J., Chi., S.J.	13	118	72
Brian Bellows	Min., Mtl., T.B., Ana., Wsh.	13	143	71
Gilbert Perreault	Buf.	11	90	70
Geoff Courtnall	Bos., Edm., Wsh., St.L., Van.	15	156	70
Dale Hawerchuk	Wpg., Buf., Phi.	15	97	69
Alex Delvecchio	Det.	14	121	69
* Luc Robitaille	L.A., Pit., NYR, Det.	14	155	69
* Sergei Zubov	NYR, Pit., Dal.	8	125	68
Bobby Hull	Chi., Hfd.	14	119	67
Frank Mahovlich	Tor., Det., Mtl.	14	137	67
Bobby Orr	Bos.	8	74	66
Bernie Federko	St.L.	11	91	66
Jean Ratelle	NYR, Bos.	15	123	66
* Igor Larionov	Van., S.J., Det.	11	145	66
Charlie Huddy	Edm., L.A., Buf., St.L.	14	183	66
* Mike Modano	Min., Dal.	10	127	64
Dickie Moore	Mtl., Tor., St.L.	14	135	64
Doug Harvey	Mtl., NYR, St.L.	15	137	64
Neal Broten	Min., Dal., N.J.	13	135	63
Yvan Cournoyer	Mtl.	12	147	63
John Bucyk	Det., Bos.	14	124	62
* Brian Leetch	NYR	7	82	61
Doug Wilson	Chi.	12	95	61
* Sandis Ozolinsh	S.J., Col., Car.	8	113	61
Steve Duchesne	St.L., A., Que., St.L., Ott., Phi., Det.	14	121	61
Kevin Stevens	Pit.	7	103	60
Bernie Geoffrion	Mtl., NYR	16	132	60
Rick Tocchet	Phi., Pit., Bos., Phx.	13	145	60
Esa Tikkanen	Edm., NYR, St.L., Van., Wsh.	13	186	60

Points

(105 or more points)

Player	Teams	Yrs.	GP	G	A	Pts.
Wayne Gretzky	Edm., L.A., St.L., NYR	16	208	122	260	382
* Mark Messier	Edm., NYR	17	236	109	186	295
Jari Kurri	Edm., L.A., NYR, Ana., Col.	15	200	106	127	233
Glenn Anderson	Edm., Tor., NYR, St.L.	15	225	93	121	214
Paul Coffey	Edm., Pit., L.A., Det., Phi., Car.	16	194	59	137	196
* Doug Gilmour	St.L., Cgy., Tor., N.J., Buf., Mtl.	17	182	60	128	188
* Brett Hull	Cgy., St.L., Dal., Det.	17	186	100	84	184
Bryan Trottier	NYI, Pit.	17	221	71	113	184
Raymond Bourque	Bos., Col.	21	214	41	139	180
Jean Beliveau	Mtl.	17	162	79	97	176
Denis Savard	Chi., Mtl.	16	169	66	109	175
* Steve Yzerman	Det.	17	177	67	108	175
* Mario Lemieux	Pit.	8	107	76	96	172
Denis Potvin	NYI	14	185	56	108	164
Mike Bossy	NYI	10	129	85	75	160
Gordie Howe	Det., Hfd.	20	157	68	92	160
* Sergei Fedorov	Det.	12	158	49	111	160
Bobby Smith	Min., Mtl.	13	184	64	96	160
* Al MacInnis	Cgy., St.L.	18	174	39	120	159
* Claude Lemieux	Mtl., N.J., Col., Phx.	16	226	80	77	157
Larry Murphy	L.A., Wsh., Min., Pit., Tor., Det.	20	215	37	115	152
Stan Mikita	Chi.	18	155	59	91	150
* Joe Sakic	Que., Col.	9	135	65	83	148
Brian Propp	Phi., Bos., Min.	13	160	64	84	148
* Jaromir Jagr	Pit.	11	140	65	82	147
Larry Robinson	Mtl., L.A.	20	227	28	116	144
* Adam Oates	Det., St.L., Bos., Wsh., Phi.	14	142	38	105	143
Jacques Lemaire	Mtl.	11	145	61	78	139
* Ron Francis	Hfd., Pit., Car.	16	159	46	93	139
Phil Esposito	Chi., Bos., NYR	15	130	61	76	137
* Chris Chelios	Mtl., Chi., Det.	18	210	30	106	136
* Peter Forsberg	Que., Col.	8	115	51	84	135
Guy Lafleur	Mtl., NYR	14	128	58	76	134
Esa Tikkanen	Edm., NYR, St.L., Van., Wsh.	13	186	72	60	132
Steve Larmer	Chi., NYR	13	140	56	75	131
Bobby Hull	Chi., Hfd.	14	119	62	67	129
Henri Richard	Mtl.	18	180	49	80	129
Yvan Cournoyer	Mtl.	12	147	64	63	127
Maurice Richard	Mtl.	15	133	82	44	126
* Luc Robitaille	L.A., Pit., NYR, Det.	14	155	57	69	126
Brad Park	NYR, Bos., Det.	17	161	35	90	125
Brian Bellows	Min., Mtl., T.B., Ana., Wsh.	13	143	51	71	122
Ken Linseman	Phi., Edm., Bos.	11	113	43	77	120
Bobby Clarke	Phi.	13	136	42	77	119
Bernie Geoffrion	Mtl., NYR	16	132	58	60	118
Frank Mahovlich	Tor., Det., Mtl.	14	137	51	67	118
Dino Ciccarelli	Min., Wsh., Det.	14	141	73	45	118
Dale Hunter	Que., Wsh., Col.	18	186	42	76	118
John Tonelli	NYI, Cgy., L.A.	13	172	40	75	115
Bernie Nicholls	L.A., NYR, Edm., N.J., Chi., S.J.	13	118	42	72	114
Rick Tocchet	Phi., Pit., Bos., Phx.	13	145	52	60	112
Craig Janney	Bos., St.L., S.J., Wpg., Phx.	11	120	24	86	110
Dickie Moore	Mtl., Tor., St.L.	14	135	46	64	110
* Mike Modano	Min., Dal.	10	127	45	64	109
* Brendan Shanahan	N.J., St.L., Det.	13	135	50	59	109
Geoff Courtnall	Bos., Edm., Wsh., St.L., Van.	15	156	39	70	109
* Scott Stevens	Wsh., St.L., N.J.	19	209	23	86	109
Bill Barber	Phi.	11	129	53	55	108
Rick MacLeish	Phi., Pit., Det.	11	114	54	53	107
* Nicklas Lidstrom	Det.	11	152	32	75	107
Kevin Stevens	Pit.	7	103	46	60	106
Joe Mullen	St.L., Cgy., Pit.	15	143	60	46	106
Peter Stastny	Que., N.J., St.L.	12	93	33	72	105

CHAPTER 7

Leading Playoff Scorers
1918 – 2002

Season	Player and Team	Games Played	Goals	Assists	Points
2001-02	Peter Forsberg, Colorado	20	9	18	27
2000-01	Joe Sakic, Colorado	21	13	13	26
1999-00	Brett Hull, Dallas	23	11	13	24
1998-99	Peter Forsberg, Colorado	19	8	16	24
1997-98	Steve Yzerman, Detroit	22	6	18	24
1996-97	Eric Lindros, Philadelphia	19	12	14	26
1995-96	Joe Sakic, Colorado	22	18	16	34
1994-95	Sergei Fedorov, Detroit	17	7	17	24
1993-94	Brian Leetch, NY Rangers	23	11	23	34
1992-93	Wayne Gretzky, Los Angeles	24	15	25	40
1991-92	Mario Lemieux, Pittsburgh	15	16	18	34
1990-91	Mario Lemieux, Pittsburgh	23	16	28	44
1989-90	Craig Simpson, Edmonton	22	16	15	31
	Mark Messier, Edmonton	22	9	22	31
1988-89	Al MacInnis, Calgary	22	7	24	31
1987-88	Wayne Gretzky, Edmonton	19	12	31	43
1986-87	Wayne Gretzky, Edmonton	21	5	29	34
1985-86	Doug Gilmour, St. Louis	19	9	12	21
	Bernie Federko, St. Louis	19	7	14	21
1984-85	Wayne Gretzky, Edmonton	18	17	30	47
1983-84	Wayne Gretzky, Edmonton	19	13	22	35
1982-83	Wayne Gretzky, Edmonton	16	12	26	38
1981-82	Bryan Trottier, NY Islanders	19	6	23	29
1980-81	Mike Bossy, NY Islanders	18	17	18	35
1979-80	Bryan Trottier, NY Islanders	21	12	17	29
1978-79	Jacques Lemaire, Montreal	16	11	12	23
	Guy Lafleur, Montreal	16	10	13	23
1977-78	Guy Lafleur, Montreal	15	10	11	21
	Larry Robinson, Montreal	15	4	17	21
1976-77	Guy Lafleur, Montreal	14	9	17	26
1975-76	Reggie Leach, Philadelphia	16	19	5	24
1974-75	Rick MacLeish, Philadelphia	17	11	9	20
1973-74	Rick MacLeish, Philadelphia	17	13	9	22
1972-73	Yvan Cournoyer, Montreal	17	15	10	25
1971-72	Phil Esposito, Boston	15	9	15	24
	Bobby Orr, Boston	15	5	19	24
1970-71	Frank Mahovlich, Montreal	20	14	13	27
1969-70	Phil Esposito, Boston	14	13	14	27
1968-69	Phil Esposito, Boston	10	8	10	18
1967-68	Bill Goldsworthy, Minnesota	14	8	7	15
1966-67	Jim Pappin, Toronto	12	7	8	15
1965-66	Norm Ullman, Detroit	12	6	9	15
1964-65	Bobby Hull, Chicago	14	10	7	17
1963-64	Gordie Howe, Detroit	14	9	10	19
1962-63	Gordie Howe, Detroit	11	7	9	16
	Norm Ullman, Detroit	11	4	12	16
1961-62	Stan Mikita, Chicago	12	6	15	21
1960-61	Gordie Howe, Detroit	11	4	11	15
	Pierre Pilote, Chicago	12	3	12	15
1959-60	Henri Richard, Montreal	8	3	9	12
	Bernie Geoffrion, Montreal	8	2	10	12
1958-59	Dickie Moore, Montreal	11	5	12	17
1957-58	Fleming MacKell, Boston	12	5	14	19
1956-57	Bernie Geoffrion, Montreal	11	11	7	18
1955-56	Jean Beliveau, Montreal	10	12	7	19
1954-55	Gordie Howe, Detroit	11	9	11	20
1953-54	Dickie Moore, Montreal	11	5	8	13
1952-53	Ed Sandford, Boston	11	8	3	11
1951-52	Ted Lindsay, Detroit	8	5	2	7
	Floyd Curry, Montreal	11	4	3	7
	Gordie Howe, Detroit	8	2	5	7
	Metro Prystai, Detroit	8	2	5	7
1950-51	Maurice Richard, Montreal	11	9	4	13
	Max Bentley, Toronto	11	2	11	13
1949-50	Pentti Lund, NY Rangers	12	6	5	11
1948-49	Gordie Howe, Detroit	11	8	3	11
1947-48	Ted Kennedy, Toronto	9	8	6	14
1946-47	Maurice Richard, Montreal	10	6	5	11
1945-46	Elmer Lach, Montreal	9	5	12	17
1944-45	Joe Carveth, Detroit	14	5	6	11
1943-44	Toe Blake, Montreal	9	7	11	18
1942-43	Carl Liscombe, Detroit	10	6	8	14
1941-42	Don Grosso, Detroit	12	8	6	14
1940-41	Milt Schmidt, Boston	11	5	6	11
1939-40	Phil Watson, NY Rangers	12	3	6	9
	Neil Colville, NY Rangers	12	2	7	9
1938-39	Bill Cowley, Boston	12	3	11	14
1937-38	Johnny Gottselig, Chicago	10	5	3	8
1936-37	Marty Barry, Detroit	10	4	7	11
1935-36	Buzz Boll, Toronto	9	7	3	10
1934-35	Baldy Northcott, Mtl. Maroons	7	4	1	5
	Busher Jackson, Toronto	7	3	2	5
	Cy Wentworth, Mtl. Maroons	7	3	2	5
1933-34	Larry Aurie, Detroit	9	3	7	10
1932-33	Cecil Dillon, NY Rangers	8	8	2	10
1931-32	Frank Boucher, NY Rangers	7	3	6	9
1930-31	Cooney Weiland, Boston	5	6	3	9
1929-30	Marty Barry, Boston	6	3	3	6
	Cooney Weiland, Boston	6	1	5	6
1928-29	Andy Blair, Toronto	4	3	0	3
	Butch Keeling, NY Rangers	6	3	0	3
	Ace Bailey, Toronto	4	1	2	3
1927-28	Frank Boucher, NY Rangers	9	7	1	8
1926-27	Harry Oliver, Boston	8	4	2	6
	Percy Galbraith, Boston	8	3	3	6
1925-26	Nels Stewart, Mtl. Maroons	8	6	3	9
1924-25	Howie Morenz, Montreal	6	7	1	8
1923-24	Howie Morenz, Montreal	6	7	3	10
1922-23	Punch Broadbent, Ottawa	8	6	1	7
1921-22	Babe Dye, Toronto	7	11	1	12
1920-21	Cy Denneny, Ottawa	7	4	2	6
1919-20	Frank Nighbor, Ottawa	5	6	1	7
	Jack Darragh, Ottawa	5	5	2	7
1918-19	Newsy Lalonde, Montreal	10	17	1	18
1917-18	Alf Skinner, Toronto	7	8	3	11

CHAPTER 8

Year-By-Year Highlights, Scores, and Rosters

2002 – 1893

2002

The Detroit Red Wings became the first team in NHL history to win the Stanley Cup after starting the playoffs with two consecutive losses at home. After losing the first two games in their Conference Quarter-final to the Vancouver Canucks, the Red Wings then won 16 of their next 21 games en route to their third Cup win under coach Scotty Bowman. Bowman established a new coaching record with his ninth Cup victory, surpassing the mark he held with legendary Montreal coach Toe Blake.

After the slow start in their showdown against the Canucks, Detroit proceeded to win the series in six games. They then defeated the St. Louis Blues in five games before eliminating the Colorado Avalanche in a seven-game Conference Final.

Those series wins set up a series against the Eastern Conference champion Carolina Hurricanes. The Hurricanes stunned the Red Wings in game one of the finals on the strength of Ron Francis' overtime goal. That would be Carolina's only win in the series as the Red Wings won four straight including a triple overtime win in game three that proved to be the turning point in the series. The Cup win would be the first for many veterans on the team including goaltender Dominik Hasek, forward Luc Robitaille, as well as defensemen Steve Duchesne and Fredrik Olausson. It also marked the second Cup win for Chris Chelios, 16 years after he first won the Cup as a member of the Montreal Canadiens in 1986.

CONN SMYTHE TROPHY
Nicklas Lidstrom - Defense - Detroit Red Wings

CONFERENCE QUARTER-FINALS

Apr.	18	Montreal	5	at	Boston	2
Apr.	21	Montreal	4	at	Boston	6
Apr.	23	Boston	3	at	Montreal	5
Apr.	25	Boston	5	at	Montreal	2
Apr.	27	Montreal	2	at	Boston	1
Apr.	29	Boston	1	at	Montreal	2

Montreal won best-of-seven series 4-2

Apr.	17	Ottawa	0	at	Philadelphia	1 OT
Apr.	20	Ottawa	3	at	Philadelphia	0
Apr.	22	Philadelphia	0	at	Ottawa	3
Apr.	24	Philadelphia	0	at	Ottawa	3
Apr.	26	Ottawa	2	at	Philadelphia	1 OT

Ottawa won best-of-seven series 4-1

Apr.	17	New Jersey	1	at	Carolina	2
Apr.	19	New Jersey	1	at	Carolina	2 OT
Apr.	21	Carolina	0	at	New Jersey	4
Apr.	23	Carolina	1	at	New Jersey	3
Apr.	24	New Jersey	2	at	Carolina	3 OT
Apr.	27	Carolina	1	at	New Jersey	0

Carolina won best-of-seven series 4-2

Apr.	18	NY Islanders	1	at	Toronto	3
Apr.	20	NY Islanders	0	at	Toronto	2
Apr.	23	Toronto	1	at	NY Islanders	6
Apr.	24	Toronto	3	at	NY Islanders	4
Apr.	26	NY Islanders	3	at	Toronto	6
Apr.	28	Toronto	3	at	NY Islanders	5
Apr.	30	NY Islanders	2	at	Toronto	4

Toronto won best-of-seven series 4-3

Apr.	17	Vancouver	4	at	Detroit	3 OT

Apr.	19	Vancouver	5	at	Detroit	2
Apr.	21	Detroit	3	at	Vancouver	1
Apr.	23	Detroit	4	at	Vancouver	2
Apr.	25	Vancouver	0	at	Detroit	4
Apr.	27	Detroit	6	at	Vancouver	4

Detroit won best-of-seven series 4-2

Apr.	18	Los Angeles	3	at	Colorado	4
Apr.	20	Los Angeles	3	at	Colorado	5
Apr.	22	Colorado	1	at	Los Angeles	3
Apr.	23	Colorado	1	at	Los Angeles	0
Apr.	25	Los Angeles	1	at	Colorado	0 OT
Apr.	27	Colorado	1	at	Los Angeles	3
Apr.	29	Los Angeles	0	at	Colorado	4

Colorado won best-of-seven series 4-3

Apr.	17	Phoenix	1	at	San Jose	2
Apr.	20	Phoenix	3	at	San Jose	1
Apr.	22	San Jose	4	at	Phoenix	1
Apr.	24	San Jose	2	at	Phoenix	1
Apr.	26	Phoenix	1	at	San Jose	4

San Jose won best-of-seven series 4-1

Apr.	18	Chicago	2	at	St. Louis	1
Apr.	20	Chicago	0	at	St. Louis	2
Apr.	21	St. Louis	4	at	Chicago	0
Apr.	23	St. Louis	1	at	Chicago	0
Apr.	25	Chicago	3	at	St. Louis	5

St. Louis won best-of-seven series 4-1

CONFERENCE SEMI-FINALS

May	3	Montreal	0	at	Carolina	2
May	5	Montreal	4	at	Carolina	1
May	7	Carolina	1	at	Montreal	2 OT
May	9	Carolina	4	at	Montreal	3 OT
May	12	Montreal	1	at	Carolina	5
May	13	Carolina	8	at	Montreal	2

Carolina won best-of-seven series 4-2

May	2	Ottawa	5	at	Toronto	0
May	4	Ottawa	2	at	Toronto	3 3OT
May	6	Toronto	2	at	Ottawa	3
May	8	Toronto	2	at	Ottawa	1
May	10	Ottawa	4	at	Toronto	2
May	12	Toronto	4	at	Ottawa	3
May	14	Ottawa	0	at	Toronto	3

Toronto won best-of-seven series 4-3

May	1	San Jose	6	at	Colorado	3
May	4	San Jose	2	at	Colorado	8
May	6	Colorado	4	at	San Jose	6
May	8	Colorado	4	at	San Jose	1
May	11	San Jose	5	at	Colorado	3
May	13	Colorado	2	at	San Jose	1 OT
May	15	San Jose	0	at	Colorado	1

Colorado won best-of-seven series 4-3

May	2	St. Louis	0	at	Detroit	2
May	4	St. Louis	2	at	Detroit	3
May	7	Detroit	1	at	St. Louis	6
May	9	Detroit	4	at	St. Louis	3
May	11	St. Louis	0	at	Detroit	4

Detroit won best-of-seven series 4-1

CONFERENCE FINALS

May	16	Toronto	2	at	Carolina	1
May	19	Toronto	1	at	Carolina	2 OT
May	21	Carolina	2	at	Toronto	1 OT
May	23	Carolina	3	at	Toronto	0
May	25	Toronto	1	at	Carolina	0
May	28	Carolina	2	at	Toronto	1 OT

Carolina won best-of-seven series 4-2

May	18	Colorado	3	at	Detroit	5
May	20	Colorado	4	at	Detroit	3 OT
May	22	Detroit	2	at	Colorado	1 OT
May	25	Detroit	2	at	Colorado	3
May	27	Colorado	2	at	Detroit	1 OT
May	29	Detroit	2	at	Colorado	0
May	31	Colorado	0	at	Detroit	7

Detroit won best-of-seven series 4-3

FINALS

June	4	Carolina	3	at	Detroit	2 OT
June	6	Carolina	1	at	Detroit	3
June	8	Detroit	3	at	Carolina	2 3OT
June	10	Detroit	3	at	Carolina	0
June	13	Carolina	1	at	Detroit	3

Detroit won best-of-seven series 4-1

2001-02 – Detroit Red Wings – Steve Yzerman (Captain), Chris Chelios, Mathieu Dandenault, Pavel Datsyuk, Boyd Devereaux, Kris Draper, Steve Duchesne, Sergei Fedorov, Jiri Fischer, Dominik Hasek, Tomas Holmstrom, Brett Hull, Igor Larionov, Manny Legace, Nicklas Lidstrom, Kirk Maltby, Darren McCarty, Fredrik Olausson, Luc Robitaille, Brendan Shanahan, Jiri Slegr, Jason Williams, Michael Illitch (Owner/Governor), Marian Illitch (Owner/Secretary Treasurer), Ronald Illitch, Michael Illitch, Jr., Lisa Illitch Murray, Atanas Illitch, Carole Illitch Trepeck, Jim Devellano (Senior Vice President), Christopher Illitch (Vice President), Denise Illitch (Alternate Governor), Ken Holland (General Manager), Jim Nill (Assistant General Manager), Scotty Bowman (Head Coach), Dave Lewis, Barry Smith (Associate Coaches), Jim Berard (Goaltending Consultant), Joe Kocur (Video Coordinator), John Wharton (Athletic Trainer), Paul Boyer, Mark Miller (Equipment Managers), Piet Van Zant (Assistant Athletic Trainer), Tim Abbott (Assistant Equipment Manager), Sergei Tchekmarev (Masseur), Dan Belisle, Mark Howe, Bob McCammon (Pro Scouts), Hakan Andersson (Director of European Scouting), Mark Leach, Bruce Haralson, Joe McDonnell, Glenn Merkosky (Scouts).

2001

The Colorado Avalanche capped a remarkable season with a seven-game Stanley Cup victory over the defending champion New Jersey Devils. Raymond Bourque had dubbed the Stanley Cup quest "Mission 16W" for the 16 wins it would take to send him into retirement as a champion for the first time in his 22-year career.

Unlike their first Stanley Cup victory in 1996, when the Avalanche never needed more than six games to win a series and swept past the Florida Panthers in four, Colorado was pushed to the brink twice in 2001. The Avalanche needed seven games to dispose of the Los Angeles Kings in the Western Conference Semi-Final and lost Peter Forsberg to a serious injury in the process. After a five-game victory over the St. Louis Blues in the Conference Final, Colorado scored a decisive 5-0 victory to open the Stanley Cup Finals. However, when the Devils took three of the next four games, the Avalanche found themselves facing elimination in the sixth game at New Jersey. The Avalanche were outshot 24 to 18, but emerged with a 4-0 victory thanks to the brilliance of Patrick Roy and a goal and two assists from Adam Foote. Roy made 25 saves back home in Denver

two nights later, and Joe Sakic had a goal and an assist to give the Avalanche a 3-1 victory and their second Stanley Cup win in six seasons.

CONN SMYTHE TROPHY
Patrick Roy - Goaltender - Colorado Avalanche

CONFERENCE QUARTER-FINALS

Apr.	12	Carolina	1	at	New Jersey	5
Apr.	15	Carolina	0	at	New Jersey	2
Apr.	17	New Jersey	4	at	Carolina	0
Apr.	18	New Jersey	2	at	Carolina	3 OT
Apr.	20	Carolina	3	at	New Jersey	2
Apr.	22	New Jersey	5	at	Carolina	1

New Jersey won best-of-seven series 4-2

Apr.	13	Toronto	1	at	Ottawa	0 OT
Apr.	14	Toronto	3	at	Ottawa	0
Apr.	16	Ottawa	2	at	Toronto	3 OT
Apr.	18	Ottawa	1	at	Toronto	3

Toronto won best-of-seven series 4-0

Apr.	12	Pittsburgh	0	at	Washington	1
Apr.	14	Pittsburgh	2	at	Washington	1
Apr.	16	Washington	0	at	Pittsburgh	3
Apr.	18	Washington	4	at	Pittsburgh	3 OT
Apr.	21	Pittsburgh	2	at	Washington	1
Apr.	23	Washington	3	at	Pittsburgh	4 OT

Pittsburgh won best-of-seven series 4-2

Apr.	11	Buffalo	2	at	Philadelphia	1
Apr.	14	Buffalo	4	at	Philadelphia	3 OT
Apr.	16	Philadelphia	3	at	Buffalo	2
Apr.	17	Philadelphia	3	at	Buffalo	4 OT
Apr.	19	Buffalo	1	at	Philadelphia	3
Apr.	21	Philadelphia	0	at	Buffalo	8

Buffalo won best-of-seven series 4-2

Apr.	12	Vancouver	4	at	Colorado	5
Apr.	14	Vancouver	1	at	Colorado	2
Apr.	16	Colorado	4	at	Vancouver	3 OT
Apr.	18	Colorado	5	at	Vancouver	1

Colorado won best-of-seven series 4-0

Apr.	11	Los Angeles	3	at	Detroit	5
Apr.	14	Los Angeles	0	at	Detroit	4
Apr.	15	Detroit	1	at	Los Angeles	2
Apr.	18	Detroit	3	at	Los Angeles	4 OT
Apr.	21	Los Angeles	3	at	Detroit	2
Apr.	23	Detroit	2	at	Los Angeles	3 OT

Los Angeles won best-of-seven series 4-2

Apr.	11	Edmonton	1	at	Dallas	2 OT
Apr.	14	Edmonton	4	at	Dallas	3
Apr.	15	Dallas	3	at	Edmonton	2 OT
Apr.	17	Dallas	1	at	Edmonton	2
Apr.	19	Edmonton	3	at	Dallas	4 OT
Apr.	21	Dallas	3	at	Edmonton	1

Dallas won best-of-seven series 4-2

Apr.	12	San Jose	1	at	St. Louis	3
Apr.	14	San Jose	1	at	St. Louis	0
Apr.	16	St. Louis	6	at	San Jose	3
Apr.	17	St. Louis	2	at	San Jose	3
Apr.	19	San Jose	2	at	St. Louis	3 OT
Apr.	21	St. Louis	2	at	San Jose	1

St. Louis won best-of-seven series 4-2

CONFERENCE SEMI-FINALS

Apr.	26	Toronto	2	at	New Jersey	0
Apr.	28	Toronto	5	at	New Jersey	6 OT
May	1	New Jersey	3	at	Toronto	2 OT
May	3	New Jersey	1	at	Toronto	3
May	5	Toronto	3	at	New Jersey	2
May	7	New Jersey	4	at	Toronto	2
May	9	Toronto	1	at	New Jersey	5

New Jersey won best-of-seven series 4-3

Apr.	26	Pittsburgh	3	at	Buffalo	0
Apr.	28	Pittsburgh	3	at	Buffalo	1
Apr.	30	Buffalo	4	at	Pittsburgh	1
May	2	Buffalo	5	at	Pittsburgh	2
May	5	Pittsburgh	2	at	Buffalo	3 OT

May	8	Buffalo	2	at	Pittsburgh	3 OT
May	10	Pittsburgh	3	at	Buffalo	2 OT

Pittsburgh won best-of-seven series 4-3

Apr.	26	Los Angeles	4	at	Colorado	3 OT
Apr.	28	Los Angeles	0	at	Colorado	2
Apr.	30	Colorado	4	at	Los Angeles	3
May	2	Colorado	3	at	Los Angeles	0
May	4	Los Angeles	1	at	Colorado	4
May	6	Colorado	0	at	Los Angeles	1 2OT
May	9	Los Angeles	1	at	Colorado	5

Colorado won best-of-seven series 4-3

Apr.	27	St. Louis	4	at	Dallas	2
Apr.	29	St. Louis	2	at	Dallas	1
May	1	Dallas	2	at	St. Louis	3 2OT
May	3	Dallas	1	at	St. Louis	4

St. Louis won best-of-seven series 4-0

CONFERENCE FINALS

May	12	Pittsburgh	1	at	New Jersey	3
May	15	Pittsburgh	4	at	New Jersey	2
May	17	New Jersey	3	at	Pittsburgh	0
May	19	New Jersey	5	at	Pittsburgh	0
May	22	Pittsburgh	2	at	New Jersey	4

New Jersey won best-of-seven series 4-1

May	12	St. Louis	1	at	Colorado	4
May	14	St. Louis	2	at	Colorado	4
May	16	Colorado	3	at	St. Louis	4 2OT
May	18	Colorado	4	at	St. Louis	3 OT
May	21	St. Louis	1	at	Colorado	2 OT

Colorado won best-of-seven series 4-1

FINALS

May	26	New Jersey	0	at	Colorado	5
May	29	New Jersey	2	at	Colorado	1
May	31	Colorado	3	at	New Jersey	1
June	2	Colorado	2	at	New Jersey	3
June	4	New Jersey	4	at	Colorado	1
June	7	Colorado	4	at	New Jersey	0
June	9	New Jersey	1	at	Colorado	3

Colorado won best-of-seven series 4-3

2000-01 – Colorado Avalanche – Joe Sakic (Captain), David Aebischer, Rob Blake, Raymond Bourque, Greg de Vries, Chris Dingman, Chris Drury, Adam Foote, Peter Forsberg, Milan Hejduk, Dan Hinote, Jon Klemm, Eric Messier, Bryan Muir, Ville Nieminen, Scott Parker, Shjon Podein, Nolan Pratt, Dave Reid, Steve Reinprecht, Patrick Roy, Martin Skoula, Alex Tanguay, Stephane Yelle, E. Stanley Kroenke (Owner/Governor), Pierre Lacroix (President/General Manager), Bob Hartley (Head Coach), Bryan Trottier, Jacques Cloutier (Assistant Coaches), Paul Fixter (Video Coach), Francois Giguere (Vice President, Hockey Operations), Brian McDonald (Assistant General Manager), Michel Goulet (Vice President, Player Personnel), Jean Martineau (Vice President, Communications/Team Services), Pat Karns (Head Athletic Trainer), Matthew Sokolowski (Assistant Athletic Trainer), Wayne Flemming, Mark Miller (Equipment Managers), Dave Randolph (Assistant Equipment Manager), Paul Goldberg (Strength and Conditioning Coach), Gregorio Pradera (Massage Therapist), Brad Smith (Pro Scout), Jim Hammett (Chief Scout), Garth Joy, Steve Lyons, Joni Lehto, Orval Tessier (Scouts), Charlotte Grahame (Director of Hockey Operations).

2000

On the strength of Jason Arnott's Cup-winning goal in double overtime, the New Jersey Devils won their second Stanley Cup championship by defeating the Dallas Stars four games to two. Nine members of the Devils' squad were also on their Cup-winning team in 1995. The series marked the first time since 1984 (NY Islanders) that the reigning Cup champion made it to the final but failed to defend their title. New Jersey

was led by veteran defenseman Scott Stevens whose spirited play throughout the postseason earned him the Conn Smythe Trophy as playoff MVP.

Apart from the opening game, which New Jersey won 7-3, the series was closely matched. Four of the remaining five games were decided by one goal including the final two games which were decided in overtime. In fact, game five was not decided until the third overtime period while game six went to a second overtime period. The last time that two games in a final went to at least the second overtime period was back in 1934 (Chicago vs. Detroit). Before getting to the finals the Devils had series wins over Florida, Toronto and Philadelphia. In the series against the Flyers the Devils trailed three games to one before overtaking Philadelphia with three straight wins including two on the road.

CONN SMYTHE TROPHY
Scott Stevens - Defense - New Jersey Devils

CONFERENCE QUARTER-FINALS

Apr.	13	Buffalo	2	at	Philadelphia	3
Apr.	14	Buffalo	1	at	Philadelphia	2
Apr.	16	Philadelphia	2	at	Buffalo	0
Apr.	18	Philadelphia	2	at	Buffalo	3 OT
Apr.	20	Buffalo	2	at	Philadelphia	5

Philadelphia won best-of-seven series 4-1

Apr.	13	Pittsburgh	7	at	Washington	0
Apr.	15	Washington	1	at	Pittsburgh	2 OT
Apr.	17	Washington	3	at	Pittsburgh	4
Apr.	19	Pittsburgh	2	at	Washington	3
Apr.	21	Pittsburgh	2	at	Washington	1

Pittsburgh won best-of-seven series 4-1

Apr.	12	Ottawa	0	at	Toronto	2
Apr.	15	Ottawa	1	at	Toronto	5
Apr.	17	Toronto	3	at	Ottawa	4
Apr.	19	Toronto	1	at	Ottawa	2
Apr.	22	Ottawa	1	at	Toronto	2 OT
Apr.	24	Toronto	4	at	Ottawa	2

Toronto won best-of-seven series 4-2

Apr.	13	Florida	3	at	New Jersey	4
Apr.	16	Florida	1	at	New Jersey	2
Apr.	18	New Jersey	2	at	Florida	1
Apr.	20	New Jersey	4	at	Florida	1

New Jersey won best-of-seven series 4-0

Apr.	12	San Jose	3	at	St. Louis	5
Apr.	15	San Jose	4	at	St. Louis	2
Apr.	17	St. Louis	1	at	San Jose	2
Apr.	19	St. Louis	2	at	San Jose	3
Apr.	21	San Jose	3	at	St. Louis	5
Apr.	23	St. Louis	6	at	San Jose	2
Apr.	25	San Jose	3	at	St. Louis	1

San Jose won best-of-seven series 4-3

Apr.	12	Edmonton	1	at	Dallas	2
Apr.	13	Edmonton	0	at	Dallas	3
Apr.	16	Dallas	2	at	Edmonton	5
Apr.	18	Dallas	4	at	Edmonton	3
Apr.	21	Edmonton	2	at	Dallas	3

Dallas won best-of-seven series 4-1

Apr.	13	Phoenix	3	at	Colorado	6
Apr.	15	Phoenix	1	at	Colorado	3
Apr.	17	Colorado	4	at	Phoenix	2
Apr.	19	Colorado	2	at	Phoenix	3
Apr.	21	Phoenix	1	at	Colorado	2

Colorado won best-of-seven series 4-1

Apr.	13	Los Angeles	0	at	Detroit	2
Apr.	15	Los Angeles	5	at	Detroit	8
Apr.	17	Detroit	2	at	Los Angeles	1
Apr.	19	Detroit	3	at	Los Angeles	2

Detroit won best-of-seven series 4-0

CONFERENCE SEMI-FINALS

Apr.	27	Pittsburgh	2	at	Philadelphia	0
Apr.	29	Pittsburgh	4	at	Philadelphia	1
May	2	Philadelphia	4	at	Pittsburgh	3 OT
May	4	Philadelphia	2	at	Pittsburgh	1 5OT
May	7	Pittsburgh	3	at	Philadelphia	6
May	9	Philadelphia	2	at	Pittsburgh	1

Philadelphia won best-of-seven series 4-2

Apr.	27	New Jersey	1	at	Toronto	2
Apr.	29	New Jersey	1	at	Toronto	0
May	1	Toronto	1	at	New Jersey	5
May	3	Toronto	3	at	New Jersey	2
May	6	New Jersey	4	at	Toronto	3
May	8	Toronto	0	at	New Jersey	3

New Jersey won best-of-seven series 4-2

Apr.	28	San Jose	0	at	Dallas	4
Apr.	30	San Jose	0	at	Dallas	1
May	2	Dallas	1	at	San Jose	4
May	5	Dallas	5	at	San Jose	4
May	7	San Jose	1	at	Dallas	4

Dallas won best-of-seven series 4-1

Apr.	27	Detroit	0	at	Colorado	2
Apr.	29	Detroit	1	at	Colorado	3
May	1	Colorado	1	at	Detroit	3
May	3	Colorado	3	at	Detroit	2 OT
May	5	Detroit	2	at	Colorado	4

Colorado won best-of-seven series 4-1

CONFERENCE FINALS

May	14	New Jersey	4	at	Philadelphia	1
May	16	New Jersey	3	at	Philadelphia	4
May	18	Philadelphia	4	at	New Jersey	2
May	20	Philadelphia	3	at	New Jersey	1
May	22	New Jersey	4	at	Philadelphia	1
May	24	Philadelphia	1	at	New Jersey	2
May	26	New Jersey	2	at	Philadelphia	1

New Jersey won best-of-seven series 4-3

May	13	Colorado	2	at	Dallas	0
May	15	Colorado	2	at	Dallas	3
May	19	Dallas	0	at	Colorado	2
May	21	Dallas	4	at	Colorado	1
May	23	Colorado	2	at	Dallas	3 OT
May	25	Dallas	1	at	Colorado	7
May	27	Colorado	2	at	Dallas	3

Dallas won best-of-seven series 4-3

FINALS

May	30	Dallas	3	at	New Jersey	7
June	1	Dallas	2	at	New Jersey	1
June	3	New Jersey	2	at	Dallas	1
June	5	New Jersey	3	at	Dallas	1
June	8	Dallas	1	at	New Jersey	0 3OT
June	10	New Jersey	2	at	Dallas	1 2OT

New Jersey won best-of-seven series 4-2

1999-2000 – New Jersey Devils – Scott Stevens (Captain), Jason Arnott, Brad Bombardir, Martin Brodeur, Steve Brule, Sergei Brylin, Ken Daneyko, Patrik Elias, Scott Gomez, Bobby Holik, Steve Kelly, Claude Lemieux, John Madden, Vladimir Malakhov, Randy McKay, Alexander Mogilny, Sergei Nemchinov, Scott Niedermayer, Krzysztof Oliwa, Jay Pandolfo, Brian Rafalski, Ken Sutton, Petr Sykora, Chris Terreri, Colin White, Dr. John J. McMullen (Owner/Chairman), Peter S. McMullen (Owner), Lou Lamoriello (President/General Manager), Larry Robinson (Head Coach), Viacheslav Fetisov (Assistant Coach), Bob Carpenter (Assistant Coach), Jacques Caron (Goaltending Coach), John Cuniff (AHL Coach), David Conte (Director of Scouting), Claude Carrier (Assistant Director of Scouting), Milt Fisher, Dan Labraaten, Marcel Pronovost (Scouts), Bob Hoffmeyer (Pro Scout), Dr. Barry Fisher (Orthopedist), Dennis Gendron (AHL Assistant Coach), Robbie Ftorek (Coach), Vladimir Bure (Consultant), Taran Singleton, Marie Carnevale, Callie Smith (Hockey Operations), Bill Murray (Medical Trainer), Michael

Vasalani (Strength/Conditioning Coordinator), Dana McGuane (Equipment Manager), Juergen Merz (Massage Therapist), Harry Bricker, Lou Centanni (Assistant Equipment Managers).

1999

It had been five years since the NHL's best regular-season team had also been its playoff champion, but this year the Dallas Stars won the Stanley Cup after winning the Presidents' Trophy for the second year in a row. The Stars won the first Cup title in franchise history by beating the Buffalo Sabres in a hard-fought series that marked the first time since 1994 that the Stanley Cup final had not ended in a sweep. Dallas took the series in six games, with Brett Hull scoring the winning goal at 14:51 of the third overtime session. The second-longest game in the history of the Stanley Cup finals ended at 1:30 a.m. local time in Buffalo.

The Stars were led by Joe Nieuwendyk, who paced all playoff performers with 11 goals and won the Conn Smythe Trophy. Mike Modano's 18 assists were the best of the postseason, while Ed Belfour provided stellar goaltending, outperforming Buffalo's Dominik Hasek in the Stanley Cup finals after besting Colorado's Patrick Roy in the Western Conference finals. The Stars had opened the playoffs with a four-game sweep over Edmonton before downing St. Louis in a tight six-game series that saw four games decided in OT.

CONN SMYTHE TROPHY
Joe Nieuwendyk - Center - Dallas Stars

CONFERENCE QUARTER-FINALS

Apr.	22	Pittsburgh	1	at	New Jersey	3
Apr.	24	Pittsburgh	4	at	New Jersey	1
Apr.	25	New Jersey	2	at	Pittsburgh	4
Apr.	27	New Jersey	4	at	Pittsburgh	2
Apr.	30	Pittsburgh	3	at	New Jersey	4
May	2	New Jersey	2	at	Pittsburgh	3 OT
May	4	Pittsburgh	4	at	New Jersey	2

Pittsburgh won best-of-seven series 4-3

Apr.	21	Buffalo	2	at	Ottawa	1
Apr.	23	Buffalo	3	at	Ottawa	2 2OT
Apr.	25	Ottawa	0	at	Buffalo	3
Apr.	27	Ottawa	3	at	Buffalo	4

Buffalo won best-of-seven series 4-0

Apr.	22	Boston	2	at	Carolina	0
Apr.	24	Boston	2	at	Carolina	3 OT
Apr.	26	Carolina	3	at	Boston	2
Apr.	28	Carolina	1	at	Boston	4
Apr.	30	Boston	4	at	Carolina	3 2OT
May	2	Carolina	0	at	Boston	2

Boston won best-of-seven series 4-2

Apr.	22	Philadelphia	3	at	Toronto	0
Apr.	24	Philadelphia	1	at	Toronto	2
Apr.	26	Toronto	2	at	Philadelphia	1
Apr.	28	Toronto	2	at	Philadelphia	5
Apr.	30	Philadelphia	1	at	Toronto	2 OT
May	2	Toronto	1	at	Philadelphia	0

Toronto won best-of-seven series 4-2

Apr.	21	Edmonton	1	at	Dallas	2
Apr.	23	Edmonton	2	at	Dallas	3
Apr.	25	Dallas	3	at	Edmonton	2
Apr.	27	Dallas	3	at	Edmonton	2 3OT

Dallas won best-of-seven series 4-0

Apr.	24	Colorado	3	at	San Jose	1
Apr.	26	Colorado	2	at	San Jose	1 OT
Apr.	28	San Jose	4	at	Colorado	2
Apr.	30	San Jose	7	at	Colorado	3
May	1	San Jose	2	at	Colorado	6
May	3	Colorado	3	at	San Jose	2 OT

Colorado won best-of-seven series 4-2

Apr.	21	Anaheim	3	at	Detroit	5
Apr.	23	Anaheim	1	at	Detroit	5
Apr.	25	Detroit	4	at	Anaheim	2
Apr.	27	Detroit	3	at	Anaheim	0

Detroit won best-of-seven series 4-0

Apr.	22	St. Louis	3	at	Phoenix	1
Apr.	24	St. Louis	3	at	Phoenix	4 OT
Apr.	25	Phoenix	5	at	St. Louis	4
Apr.	27	Phoenix	2	at	St. Louis	1
Apr.	30	St. Louis	2	at	Phoenix	1 OT
May	2	Phoenix	3	at	St. Louis	5
May	4	St. Louis	1	at	Phoenix	0 OT

St. Louis won best-of-seven series 4-3

CONFERENCE SEMI-FINALS

May	7	Pittsburgh	2	at	Toronto	0
May	9	Pittsburgh	2	at	Toronto	4
May	11	Toronto	3	at	Pittsburgh	4
May	13	Toronto	3	at	Pittsburgh	2 OT
May	15	Pittsburgh	1	at	Toronto	4
May	17	Toronto	4	at	Pittsburgh	3 OT

Toronto won best-of-seven series 4-2

May	6	Buffalo	2	at	Boston	4
May	9	Buffalo	3	at	Boston	1
May	12	Boston	2	at	Buffalo	3
May	14	Boston	0	at	Buffalo	3
May	16	Buffalo	3	at	Boston	5
May	18	Boston	2	at	Buffalo	3

Buffalo won best-of-seven series 4-2

May	6	St. Louis	0	at	Dallas	3
May	8	St. Louis	4	at	Dallas	5 OT
May	10	Dallas	2	at	St. Louis	3 OT
May	12	Dallas	2	at	St. Louis	3 OT
May	15	St. Louis	1	at	Dallas	3
May	17	Dallas	2	at	St. Louis	1 OT

Dallas won best-of-seven series 4-2

May	7	Detroit	3	at	Colorado	2 OT
May	9	Detroit	4	at	Colorado	0
May	11	Colorado	5	at	Detroit	3
May	13	Colorado	6	at	Detroit	2
May	16	Detroit	0	at	Colorado	3
May	18	Colorado	5	at	Detroit	2

Colorado won best-of-seven series 4-2

CONFERENCE FINALS

May	23	Buffalo	5	at	Toronto	4
May	25	Buffalo	3	at	Toronto	6
May	27	Toronto	2	at	Buffalo	4
May	29	Toronto	2	at	Buffalo	5
May	31	Buffalo	4	at	Toronto	2

Buffalo won best-of-seven series 4-1

May	22	Colorado	2	at	Dallas	1
May	24	Colorado	2	at	Dallas	4
May	26	Dallas	3	at	Colorado	0
May	28	Dallas	2	at	Colorado	3 OT
May	30	Colorado	7	at	Dallas	5
June	1	Dallas	4	at	Colorado	1
June	4	Colorado	1	at	Dallas	4

Dallas won best-of-seven series 4-3

FINALS

June	8	Buffalo	3	at	Dallas	2 OT
June	10	Buffalo	2	at	Dallas	4
June	12	Dallas	2	at	Buffalo	1
June	15	Dallas	1	at	Buffalo	2
June	17	Buffalo	0	at	Dallas	2
June	19	Dallas	2	at	Buffalo	1 3OT

Dallas won best-of-seven series 4-2

1998-99 – Dallas Stars – Derian Hatcher (Captain), Ed Belfour, Guy Carbonneau, Shawn Chambers, Benoit Hogue, Tony Hrkac, Brett Hull, Mike Keane, Jamie Langenbrunner, Jere Lehtinen, Craig Ludwig, Grant Marshall, Richard Matvichuk, Mike Modano, Joe Nieuwendyk, Derek Plante, Dave Reid, Jon Sim, Brian Skrudland, Blake Sloan, Darryl Sydor, Roman Turek, Pat Verbeek, Sergei Zubov, Thomas Hicks (Chairman of the Board/Owner), Jim Lites (President), Bob Gainey (Vice President, Hockey

Operations/General Manager), Doug Armstrong (Assistant General Manager), Craig Button (Director of Player Personnel), Ken Hitchcock (Head Coach), Doug Jarvis, Rick Wilson (Assistant Coaches), Rick McLaughlin (Vice President/Chief Financial Officer), Jeff Cogen (Vice President, Marketing and Promotion), Bill Strong (Vice President, Marketing and Broadcasting), Tim Bernhardt (Director of Amateur Scouting), Doug Overton (Director of Pro Scouting), Bob Gernander (Chief Scout), Stu MacGregor (Western Scout), Dave Suprenant (Medical Trainer), Dave Smith, Rich Matthews (Equipment Managers), J.J. McQueen (Strength and Conditioning Coach), Rick St. Croix (Goaltending Consultant), Dan Stuchal (Director of Team Services), Larry Kelly (Director of Public Relations).

1998

With a four-game sweep of the Washington Capitals, the Detroit Red Wings became the first team since the Pittsburgh Penguins (1991 and 1992) to repeat as Stanley Cup champions. The Wings were led by Steve Yzerman, who became just the fifth player as captain of his team to receive the Conn Smythe Trophy as the most valuable player in the playoffs. Scotty Bowman equalled Toe Blake's NHL record of eight Stanley Cup coaching victories.

Despite the four-game sweep in the finals, Detroit did not have a smooth road to the Cup, as they were forced to play six games in each of the three series leading up to the Stanley Cup finals. Overall, the team had equal success at home and on the road, posting identical 8–3 records. A total of ten Red Wing players contributed the 16 game-winning goals scored en route to the Stanley Cup.

The on-ice celebration produced one of the most emotional moments in NHL history, as injured teammate Vladimir Konstantinov participated in the post-game festivities from his wheelchair. Konstantinov had been a key part of Detroit's Stanley Cup championship in 1997, but nearly lost his life in a car accident one week after the victory.

CONN SMYTHE TROPHY
Steve Yzerman - Center - Detroit Red Wings

CONFERENCE QUARTER-FINALS

Apr.	22	Ottawa	2	at	New Jersey	1 OT
Apr.	24	Ottawa	1	at	New Jersey	3
Apr.	26	New Jersey	1	at	Ottawa	2 OT
Apr.	28	New Jersey	3	at	Ottawa	4
Apr.	30	Ottawa	1	at	New Jersey	3
May	2	New Jersey	1	at	Ottawa	4

Ottawa won best-of-seven series 4-2

Apr.	23	Montreal	3	at	Pittsburgh	2 OT
Apr.	25	Montreal	1	at	Pittsburgh	4
Apr.	27	Pittsburgh	1	at	Montreal	3
Apr.	29	Pittsburgh	6	at	Montreal	3
May	1	Montreal	5	at	Pittsburgh	2
May	3	Pittsburgh	0	at	Montreal	3

Montreal won best-of-seven series 4-2

Apr.	22	Buffalo	3	at	Philadelphia	2
Apr.	24	Buffalo	2	at	Philadelphia	3
Apr.	27	Philadelphia	1	at	Buffalo	6
Apr.	29	Philadelphia	1	at	Buffalo	4
May	1	Buffalo	3	at	Philadelphia	2 OT

Buffalo won best-of-seven series 4-1

Apr.	22	Boston	1	at	Washington	3
Apr.	24	Boston	4	at	Washington	3 2OT
Apr.	26	Washington	3	at	Boston	2 2OT
Apr.	28	Washington	3	at	Boston	0
May	1	Boston	4	at	Washington	0
May	3	Washington	3	at	Boston	2 OT

Washington won best-of-seven series 4-2

Apr.	22	San Jose	1	at	Dallas	4
Apr.	24	San Jose	2	at	Dallas	5
Apr.	26	Dallas	1	at	San Jose	4
Apr.	28	Dallas	0	at	San Jose	1 OT
Apr.	30	San Jose	2	at	Dallas	3
May	2	Dallas	3	at	San Jose	2 OT

Dallas won best-of-seven series 4-2

Apr.	22	Edmonton	3	at	Colorado	2
Apr.	24	Edmonton	2	at	Colorado	5
Apr.	26	Colorado	5	at	Edmonton	4 OT
Apr.	28	Colorado	3	at	Edmonton	1
Apr.	30	Edmonton	3	at	Colorado	1
May	2	Colorado	0	at	Edmonton	2
May	4	Edmonton	4	at	Colorado	0

Edmonton won best-of-seven series 4-3

Apr.	22	Phoenix	3	at	Detroit	6
Apr.	24	Phoenix	7	at	Detroit	4
Apr.	26	Detroit	2	at	Phoenix	3
Apr.	28	Detroit	4	at	Phoenix	2
Apr.	30	Phoenix	1	at	Detroit	3
May	3	Detroit	5	at	Phoenix	2

Detroit won best-of-seven series 4-2

Apr.	23	Los Angeles	3	at	St. Louis	8
Apr.	25	Los Angeles	1	at	St. Louis	2
Apr.	27	St. Louis	4	at	Los Angeles	3
Apr.	30	St. Louis	2	at	Los Angeles	1

St. Louis won best-of-seven series 4-0

CONFERENCE SEMI-FINALS

May	7	Ottawa	2	at	Washington	4
May	9	Ottawa	1	at	Washington	6
May	11	Washington	3	at	Ottawa	4
May	13	Washington	2	at	Ottawa	0
May	15	Ottawa	0	at	Washington	3

Washington won best-of-seven series 4-1

May	8	Montreal	2	at	Buffalo	3 OT
May	10	Montreal	3	at	Buffalo	6
May	12	Buffalo	5	at	Montreal	4 2OT
May	14	Buffalo	3	at	Montreal	1

Buffalo won best-of-seven series 4-0

May	7	Edmonton	1	at	Dallas	3
May	9	Edmonton	2	at	Dallas	0
May	11	Dallas	1	at	Edmonton	0 OT
May	13	Dallas	3	at	Edmonton	1
May	16	Edmonton	1	at	Dallas	2

Dallas won best-of-seven series 4-1

May	8	St. Louis	4	at	Detroit	2
May	10	St. Louis	1	at	Detroit	6
May	12	Detroit	3	at	St. Louis	2 2OT
May	14	Detroit	5	at	St. Louis	2
May	17	St. Louis	3	at	Detroit	1
May	19	Detroit	6	at	St. Louis	1

Detroit won best-of-seven series 4-2

CONFERENCE FINALS

May	23	Buffalo	2	at	Washington	0
May	25	Buffalo	2	at	Washington	3 OT
May	28	Washington	4	at	Buffalo	3 OT
May	30	Washington	2	at	Buffalo	0
June	2	Buffalo	2	at	Washington	1
June	4	Washington	3	at	Buffalo	2 OT

Washington won best-of-seven series 4-2

May	24	Detroit	2	at	Dallas	0
May	26	Detroit	1	at	Dallas	3
May	29	Dallas	3	at	Detroit	5
May	31	Dallas	2	at	Detroit	3
June	3	Detroit	2	at	Dallas	3 OT
June	5	Dallas	0	at	Detroit	2

Detroit won best-of-seven series 4-2

FINALS

June	9	Washington	1	at	Detroit	2
June	11	Washington	4	at	Detroit	5 OT
June	13	Detroit	2	at	Washington	1
June	16	Detroit	4	at	Washington	1

Detroit won best-of-seven series 4-0

1997-98 – Detroit Red Wings – Steve Yzerman (Captain), Doug Brown, Mathieu Dandenault, Kris Draper, Anders Eriksson, Sergei Fedorov, Viacheslav Fetisov, Brent Gilchrist, Kevin Hodson, Tomas Holmstrom, Mike Knuble, Joe Kocur, Vyacheslav Kozlov, Martin Lapointe, Igor Larionov, Nicklas Lidstrom, Jamie Macoun, Kirk Maltby, Darren McCarty, Dmitri Mironov, Larry Murphy, Chris Osgood, Bob Rouse, Brendan Shanahan, Aaron Ward, Mike Ilitch, (Owner/Chairman), Marian Ilitch (Owner), Atanas Ilitch, Christopher Ilitch (Vice Presidents), Denise Ilitch, Ronald Ilitch, Michael Ilitch, Jr., Lisa Ilitch Murray, Carole Ilitch Trepeck, Jim Devellano (Senior Vice President), Scotty Bowman (Head Coach), Ken Holland (General Manager), Don Waddell (Assistant General Manager), Barry Smith, Dave Lewis (Associate Coaches), Jim Bedard (Goaltending Consultant), Jim Nill (Director of Player Development), Dan Belisle, Mark Howe (Pro Scouts), Hakan Andersson (Director of European Scouting), Mark Leach (USA Scout), Moe McDonnell (Eastern Scout), Bruce Haralson (Western Scout), John Wharton (Athletic Trainer), Paul Boyer (Equipment Manager), Tim Abbott (Assistant Equipment Manager), Bob Huddleston (Masseur), Wally Crossman (Dressing Room Assistant).

1997

The Detroit Red Wings won their first Stanley Cup title since 1955 with a four-game final series sweep of the Philadelphia Flyers. The series opened at the CoreStates Center in Philadelphia in front of 20,291 fans, the largest crowd ever to witness a hockey game in the state of Pennsylvania. Goaltender Mike Vernon made 26 saves in a 4–2 Detroit win as unheralded Red Wings Kirk Maltby and Joe Kocur gave Detroit a 2-1 lead after the first period. Sergei Fedorov tallied the game-winner just after the midway point of the second. Maltby scored again in game two, breaking a 2–2 tie in the second period with what would prove to be the game-winning goal. Rod Brind'Amour scored both of the Flyers' goals in the game, connecting for two power-play markers 1:09 apart late in the first period.

The Red Wings returned home to a vocal and supportive home crowd for game three at Joe Louis Arena and responded with a 6–1 win to take a commanding 3–0 lead in the series. The Flyers opened the scoring on a first-period goal by John LeClair, but Detroit replied with three unanswered goals before the period ended. The win snapped Detroit's eight-game and 33-year home-ice losing streak in the Stanley Cup finals. Sergei Fedorov and Martin Lapointe each tallied twice to pace the Red Wings.

The Red Wings completed the series sweep by defeating the Flyers 2-1 in game four. Red Wings defenseman Nicklas Lidstrom's goal late in the first period gave Detroit a lead it would not relinquish and Darren McCarty scored the Stanley Cup-winning goal on a spectacular individual effort at 13:02 of the second period. Goaltender Mike Vernon was named the Conn Smythe Trophy winner as the MVP of the playoffs, finishing the postseason with a 16–4 record and 1.76 goals-against average. He allowed two goals or fewer in 17 of his 20 playoff games.

CONN SMYTHE TROPHY
Mike Vernon - Goaltender - Detroit Red Wings

CONFERENCE QUARTER-FINALS

Apr.	17	Montreal	2	at	New Jersey	5
Apr.	19	Montreal	1	at	New Jersey	4
Apr.	22	New Jersey	6	at	Montreal	4
Apr.	24	New Jersey	3	at	Montreal	4 3OT

| Apr. | 26 | Montreal | 0 | at | New Jersey | 4 |

New Jersey won best-of-seven series 4-1

Apr.	17	Ottawa	1	at	Buffalo	3
Apr.	19	Ottawa	3	at	Buffalo	1
Apr.	21	Buffalo	3	at	Ottawa	2
Apr.	23	Buffalo	0	at	Ottawa	1 OT
Apr.	25	Ottawa	4	at	Buffalo	1
Apr.	27	Buffalo	3	at	Ottawa	0
Apr.	29	Ottawa	2	at	Buffalo	3 OT

Buffalo won best-of-seven series 4-3

Apr.	17	Pittsburgh	1	at	Philadelphia	5
Apr.	19	Pittsburgh	2	at	Philadelphia	3
Apr.	21	Philadelphia	5	at	Pittsburgh	3
Apr.	23	Philadelphia	1	at	Pittsburgh	4
Apr.	26	Pittsburgh	3	at	Philadelphia	6

Philadelphia won best-of-seven series 4-1

Apr.	17	NY Rangers	0	at	Florida	3
Apr.	20	NY Rangers	3	at	Florida	0
Apr.	22	Florida	3	at	NY Rangers	4 OT
Apr.	23	Florida	2	at	NY Rangers	3
Apr.	25	NY Rangers	3	at	Florida	2 OT

NY Rangers won best-of-seven series 4-1

Apr.	16	Chicago	0	at	Colorado	6
Apr.	18	Chicago	1	at	Colorado	3
Apr.	20	Colorado	3	at	Chicago	4 2OT
Apr.	22	Colorado	3	at	Chicago	6
Apr.	24	Chicago	0	at	Colorado	7
Apr.	26	Colorado	6	at	Chicago	3

Colorado won best-of-seven series 4-2

Apr.	16	Edmonton	3	at	Dallas	5
Apr.	18	Edmonton	4	at	Dallas	0
Apr.	20	Dallas	3	at	Edmonton	4 OT
Apr.	22	Dallas	4	at	Edmonton	3
Apr.	25	Edmonton	1	at	Dallas	0 2OT
Apr.	27	Dallas	3	at	Edmonton	2
Apr.	29	Edmonton	4	at	Dallas	3 OT

Edmonton won best-of-seven series 4-3

Apr.	16	St. Louis	2	at	Detroit	0
Apr.	18	St. Louis	1	at	Detroit	2
Apr.	20	Detroit	3	at	St. Louis	2
Apr.	22	Detroit	0	at	St. Louis	4
Apr.	25	St. Louis	2	at	Detroit	5
Apr.	27	Detroit	3	at	St. Louis	1

Detroit won best-of-seven series 4-2

Apr.	16	Phoenix	2	at	Anaheim	4
Apr.	18	Phoenix	2	at	Anaheim	4
Apr.	20	Anaheim	1	at	Phoenix	4
Apr.	22	Anaheim	0	at	Phoenix	2
Apr.	24	Phoenix	5	at	Anaheim	2
Apr.	27	Anaheim	3	at	Phoenix	2 OT
Apr.	29	Phoenix	0	at	Anaheim	3

Anaheim won best-of-seven series 4-3

CONFERENCE SEMI-FINALS

May	2	NY Rangers	0	at	New Jersey	2
May	4	NY Rangers	2	at	New Jersey	0
May	6	New Jersey	2	at	NY Rangers	3
May	8	New Jersey	0	at	NY Rangers	3
May	11	NY Rangers	2	at	New Jersey	1 OT

NY Rangers won best-of-seven series 4-1

May	3	Philadelphia	5	at	Buffalo	3
May	5	Philadelphia	2	at	Buffalo	1
May	7	Buffalo	1	at	Philadelphia	4
May	9	Buffalo	5	at	Philadelphia	4 OT
May	11	Philadelphia	6	at	Buffalo	3

Philadelphia won best-of-seven series 4-1

May	2	Edmonton	1	at	Colorado	5
May	4	Edmonton	1	at	Colorado	4
May	7	Colorado	3	at	Edmonton	4
May	9	Colorado	3	at	Edmonton	2 OT
May	11	Edmonton	3	at	Colorado	4

Colorado won best-of-seven series 4-1

| May | 2 | Anaheim | 1 | at | Detroit | 2 OT |
| May | 4 | Anaheim | 2 | at | Detroit | 3 3OT |

| May | 6 | Detroit | 5 | at | Anaheim | 3 |
| May | 8 | Detroit | 3 | at | Anaheim | 2 2OT |

Detroit won best-of-seven series 4-0

CONFERENCE FINALS

May	16	NY Rangers	1	at	Philadelphia	3
May	18	NY Rangers	5	at	Philadelphia	4
May	20	Philadelphia	6	at	NY Rangers	3
May	23	Philadelphia	3	at	NY Rangers	2
May	25	NY Rangers	2	at	Philadelphia	4

Philadelphia won best-of-seven series 4-1

May	15	Detroit	1	at	Colorado	2
May	17	Detroit	4	at	Colorado	2
May	19	Colorado	1	at	Detroit	2
May	22	Colorado	0	at	Detroit	6
May	24	Detroit	0	at	Colorado	6
May	26	Colorado	1	at	Detroit	3

Detroit won best-of-seven series 4-2

FINALS

May	31	Detroit	4	at	Philadelphia	2
June	3	Detroit	4	at	Philadelphia	2
June	5	Philadelphia	1	at	Detroit	6
June	7	Philadelphia	1	at	Detroit	2

Detroit won best-of-seven series 4-0

1996-97 – Detroit Red Wings – Steve Yzerman (Captain), Doug Brown, Mathieu Dandenault, Kris Draper, Sergei Fedorov, Viacheslav Fetisov, Kevin Hodson, Tomas Holmstrom, Joe Kocur, Vladimir Konstantinov, Vyacheslav Kozlov, Martin Lapointe, Igor Larionov, Nicklas Lidstrom, Kirk Maltby, Darren McCarty, Larry Murphy, Chris Osgood, Jamie Pushor, Bob Rouse, Tomas Sandstrom, Brendan Shanahan, Tim Taylor, Mike Vernon, Aaron Ward, Mike Ilitch (Owner/Chairman), Marian Ilitch (Owner), Atanas Ilitch, Christopher Ilitch (Vice Presidents), Denise Ilitch Lites, Ronald Ilitch, Michael Ilitch, Jr., Lisa Ilitch Murray, Carole Ilitch Trepeck, Jim Devellano (Senior Vice President), Scotty Bowman (Head Coach/Director of Player Personnel), Ken Holland (Assistant General Manager), Barry Smith, Dave Lewis (Associate Coaches), Mike Krushelnyski (Assistant Coach), Jim Nill (Director of Player Development), Dan Belisle, Mark Howe (Pro Scouts), Hakan Andersson (Director of European Scouting), John Wharton (Athletic Trainer), Paul Boyer (Equipment Manager), Tim Abbott (Assistant Equipment Manager), Sergei Mnatsakanov (Masseur).

1996

The Colorado Avalanche became Stanley Cup champions in their first season in the Mile High City after moving west from Quebec, sweeping the surprising Florida Panthers in the final series. Colorado was led by the scoring flash of Joe Sakic, Valeri Kamensky and Peter Forsberg, backed up by a solid defense and the stellar goaltending of Patrick Roy, but it was Uwe Krupp who scored the Cup-winning goal at 4:31 of the third overtime period in the longest 1-0 game in the history of the Stanley Cup finals.

Goaltending had been the story for Florida, as the Panthers, who had made the playoffs in just their third season, relied on the spectacular work of John Vanbiesbrouck to knock off the Boston Bruins, Philadelphia Flyers and Pittsburgh Penguins. Colorado advanced with victories over Vancouver and Chicago before defeating Detroit in the finals of the Western Conference.

Despite the final series sweep, the games were close (with the exception of Colorado's 8-1 win in game two), but the Avalanche clearly had the better of the play. Vanbiesbrouck's heroics gave the Panthers a chance, but ultimately Roy and Sakic, who established himself as a major NHL star, proved to be too much. Sakic led all playoff scorers with 18 goals and 34 points and also won the

Conn Smythe Trophy as playoff MVP.

CONN SMYTHE TROPHY
Joe Sakic - Center - Colorado Avalanche

CONFERENCE QUARTER-FINALS

Apr.	16	Tampa Bay	3	at	Philadelphia	7
Apr.	18	Tampa Bay	2	at	Philadelphia	1 OT
Apr.	21	Philadelphia	4	at	Tampa Bay	5 OT
Apr.	23	Philadelphia	4	at	Tampa Bay	1
Apr.	25	Tampa Bay	1	at	Philadelphia	4
Apr.	27	Philadelphia	6	at	Tampa Bay	1

Philadelphia won best-of-seven series 4-2

Apr.	17	Washington	6	at	Pittsburgh	4
Apr.	19	Washington	5	at	Pittsburgh	3
Apr.	22	Pittsburgh	4	at	Washington	3
Apr.	24	Pittsburgh	3	at	Washington	2 4OT
Apr.	26	Washington	1	at	Pittsburgh	4
Apr.	28	Pittsburgh	3	at	Washington	2

Pittsburgh won best-of-seven series 4-2

Apr.	16	Montreal	3	at	NY Rangers	2 OT
Apr.	18	Montreal	5	at	NY Rangers	3
Apr.	21	NY Rangers	2	at	Montreal	1
Apr.	23	NY Rangers	4	at	Montreal	3
Apr.	26	Montreal	2	at	NY Rangers	3
Apr.	28	NY Rangers	5	at	Montreal	3

NY Rangers won best-of-seven series 4-2

Apr.	17	Boston	3	at	Florida	6
Apr.	22	Boston	2	at	Florida	6
Apr.	24	Florida	4	at	Boston	2
Apr.	25	Florida	2	at	Boston	6
Apr.	27	Boston	3	at	Florida	4

Florida won best-of-seven series 4-1

Apr.	17	Winnipeg	1	at	Detroit	4
Apr.	19	Winnipeg	0	at	Detroit	4
Apr.	21	Detroit	1	at	Winnipeg	4
Apr.	23	Detroit	6	at	Winnipeg	1
Apr.	26	Winnipeg	3	at	Detroit	1
Apr.	28	Detroit	4	at	Winnipeg	1

Detroit won best-of-seven series 4-2

Apr.	16	Vancouver	2	at	Colorado	5
Apr.	18	Vancouver	5	at	Colorado	4
Apr.	20	Colorado	4	at	Vancouver	0
Apr.	22	Colorado	3	at	Vancouver	4
Apr.	25	Vancouver	4	at	Colorado	5 OT
Apr.	27	Colorado	3	at	Vancouver	2

Colorado won best-of-seven series 4-2

Apr.	17	Calgary	1	at	Chicago	4
Apr.	19	Calgary	0	at	Chicago	3
Apr.	21	Chicago	7	at	Calgary	5
Apr.	23	Chicago	2	at	Calgary	1 3OT

Chicago won best-of-seven series 4-0

Apr.	16	St. Louis	3	at	Toronto	1
Apr.	18	St. Louis	4	at	Toronto	5 OT
Apr.	21	Toronto	2	at	St. Louis	3 OT
Apr.	23	Toronto	1	at	St. Louis	5
Apr.	25	St. Louis	4	at	Toronto	5 OT
Apr.	27	Toronto	1	at	St. Louis	2

St. Louis won best-of-seven series 4-2

CONFERENCE SEMI-FINALS

May	2	Florida	2	at	Philadelphia	0
May	4	Florida	2	at	Philadelphia	3
May	7	Philadelphia	3	at	Florida	1
May	9	Philadelphia	2	at	Florida	4 OT
May	12	Florida	2	at	Philadelphia	1 2OT
May	14	Philadelphia	1	at	Florida	4

Florida won best-of-seven series 4-2

May	3	NY Rangers	3	at	Pittsburgh	4
May	5	NY Rangers	6	at	Pittsburgh	3
May	7	Pittsburgh	3	at	NY Rangers	2
May	9	Pittsburgh	4	at	NY Rangers	1
May	11	NY Rangers	3	at	Pittsburgh	7

Pittsburgh won best-of-seven series 4-1

Date	Away		at	Home		
May 3	St. Louis	2	at	Detroit	3	
May 5	St. Louis	3	at	Detroit	8	
May 8	Detroit	4	at	St. Louis	5	OT
May 10	Detroit	0	at	St. Louis	1	
May 12	St. Louis	3	at	Detroit	2	
May 14	Detroit	4	at	St. Louis	2	
May 16	St. Louis	0	at	Detroit	1	2OT

Detroit won best-of-seven series 4-3

Date	Away		at	Home		
May 2	Chicago	3	at	Colorado	2	OT
May 4	Chicago	1	at	Colorado	5	
May 6	Colorado	3	at	Chicago	4	OT
May 8	Colorado	3	at	Chicago	2	3OT
May 11	Chicago	1	at	Colorado	4	
May 13	Colorado	4	at	Chicago	3	2OT

Colorado won best-of-seven series 4-2

CONFERENCE FINALS

Date	Away		at	Home		
May 18	Florida	5	at	Pittsburgh	1	
May 20	Florida	2	at	Pittsburgh	3	
May 24	Pittsburgh	2	at	Florida	5	
May 26	Pittsburgh	2	at	Florida	1	
May 28	Florida	0	at	Pittsburgh	3	
May 30	Pittsburgh	3	at	Florida	4	
June 1	Florida	3	at	Pittsburgh	1	

Florida won best-of-seven series 4-3

Date	Away		at	Home		
May 19	Colorado	3	at	Detroit	2	OT
May 21	Colorado	3	at	Detroit	0	
May 23	Detroit	6	at	Colorado	4	
May 25	Detroit	2	at	Colorado	4	
May 27	Colorado	2	at	Detroit	5	
May 29	Detroit	1	at	Colorado	4	

Colorado won best-of-seven series 4-2

FINALS

Date	Away		at	Home		
June 4	Florida	1	at	Colorado	3	
June 6	Florida	1	at	Colorado	8	
June 8	Colorado	3	at	Florida	2	
June 10	Colorado	1	at	Florida	0	3OT

Colorado won best-of-seven series 4-0

1995-96 – Colorado Avalanche – Joe Sakic (Captain), Rene Corbet, Adam Deadmarsh, Stephane Fiset, Adam Foote, Peter Forsberg, Alexei Gusarov, Dave Hannan, Valeri Kamensky, Mike Keane, Jon Klemm, Uwe Krupp, Sylvain Lefebvre, Claude Lemieux, Curtis Leschyshyn, Troy Murray, Sandis Ozolinsh, Mike Ricci, Patrick Roy, Warren Rychel, Chris Simon, Craig Wolanin, Stephane Yelle, Scott Young, Charlie Lyons (Chairman/CEO), Pierre Lacroix (Executive Vice President/General Manager), Marc Crawford (Head Coach), Joel Quenneville, Jacques Cloutier (Assistant Coaches), Francois Giguere (Assistant General Manager), Michel Goulet (Director of Player Personnel), Dave Draper (Chief Scout), Jean Martineau (Director of Public Relations), Pat Karns (Trainer), Matthew Sokolowski (Assistant Trainer), Rob McLean (Equipment Manager), Mike Kramer, Brock Gibbins (Assistant Equipment Managers), Skip Allen (Strength and Conditioning Coach), Paul Fixter (Video Coordinator), Leo Vyssokov (Massage Therapist).

1995

After 21 seasons and two franchise relocations, the New Jersey Devils captured their first Stanley Cup title by downing the Detroit Red Wings in the championship final. Paced by the stellar goaltending of Martin Brodeur and the timely scoring of Claude Lemieux, the Devils upset the favored Red Wings in four straight games, outscoring, outshooting and outplaying Detroit in each encounter.

Both teams took similar routes to the finals. Detroit lost only two games in the opening three rounds, although they did need a trio of overtime victories to subdue Chicago in the Western Conference final. New Jersey dropped four games in the opening three rounds, including a pair to the Philadelphia Flyers in a stirring six-game Eastern Conference final.

New Jersey's Claude Lemieux, who scored only six times in the regular season, erupted for 13 goals in the postseason and was also awarded the Conn Smythe Trophy. Neal Broten, a 14-year veteran acquired by New Jersey late in the season from Dallas, notched four game-winning goals for the champions. Devils coach Jacques Lemaire, who won eight Stanley Cup rings as a player, became the fourth individual to score a Stanley Cup-winning goal and coach a Stanley Cup-winning team.

CONN SMYTHE TROPHY
Claude Lemieux - Right Wing - New Jersey Devils

CONFERENCE QUARTER-FINALS

Date	Away		at	Home		
May 6	NY Rangers	4	at	Quebec	5	
May 8	NY Rangers	8	at	Quebec	3	
May 10	Quebec	3	at	NY Rangers	4	
May 12	Quebec	2	at	NY Rangers	3	OT
May 14	NY Rangers	2	at	Quebec	4	
May 16	Quebec	2	at	NY Rangers	4	

NY Rangers won best-of-seven series 4-2

Date	Away		at	Home		
May 7	Buffalo	3	at	Philadelphia	4	OT
May 8	Buffalo	1	at	Philadelphia	3	
May 10	Philadelphia	1	at	Buffalo	3	
May 12	Philadelphia	4	at	Buffalo	2	
May 14	Buffalo	4	at	Philadelphia	6	

Philadelphia won best-of-seven series 4-1

Date	Away		at	Home		
May 6	Washington	5	at	Pittsburgh	4	
May 8	Washington	3	at	Pittsburgh	5	
May 10	Pittsburgh	2	at	Washington	6	
May 12	Pittsburgh	2	at	Washington	6	
May 14	Washington	5	at	Pittsburgh	6	OT
May 16	Pittsburgh	7	at	Washington	1	
May 18	Washington	0	at	Pittsburgh	3	

Pittsburgh won best-of-seven series 4-3

Date	Away		at	Home		
May 7	New Jersey	5	at	Boston	0	
May 8	New Jersey	3	at	Boston	0	
May 10	Boston	3	at	New Jersey	2	
May 12	Boston	0	at	New Jersey	1	OT
May 14	New Jersey	3	at	Boston	2	

New Jersey won best-of-seven series 4-1

Date	Away		at	Home		
May 7	Dallas	3	at	Detroit	4	
May 9	Dallas	1	at	Detroit	4	
May 11	Detroit	5	at	Dallas	1	
May 14	Detroit	1	at	Dallas	4	
May 15	Dallas	1	at	Detroit	3	

Detroit won best-of-seven series 4-1

Date	Away		at	Home		
May 7	San Jose	5	at	Calgary	4	
May 9	San Jose	5	at	Calgary	4	OT
May 11	Calgary	9	at	San Jose	2	
May 13	Calgary	6	at	San Jose	4	
May 15	San Jose	0	at	Calgary	5	
May 17	Calgary	3	at	San Jose	5	
May 19	San Jose	5	at	Calgary	4	2OT

San Jose won best-of-seven series 4-3

Date	Away		at	Home		
May 7	Vancouver	1	at	St. Louis	2	
May 9	Vancouver	5	at	St. Louis	3	
May 11	St. Louis	1	at	Vancouver	6	
May 13	St. Louis	5	at	Vancouver	2	
May 15	Vancouver	6	at	St. Louis	5	OT
May 17	St. Louis	8	at	Vancouver	2	
May 19	Vancouver	5	at	St. Louis	3	

Vancouver won best-of-seven series 4-3

Date	Away		at	Home		
May 7	Toronto	5	at	Chicago	3	
May 9	Toronto	3	at	Chicago	0	
May 11	Chicago	3	at	Toronto	2	
May 13	Chicago	3	at	Toronto	1	
May 15	Toronto	2	at	Chicago	4	
May 17	Chicago	4	at	Toronto	5	OT
May 19	Toronto	2	at	Chicago	5	

Chicago won best-of-seven series 4-3

CONFERENCE SEMI-FINALS

Date	Away		at	Home		
May 21	NY Rangers	4	at	Philadelphia	5	OT
May 22	NY Rangers	3	at	Philadelphia	4	OT
May 24	Philadelphia	5	at	NY Rangers	2	
May 26	Philadelphia	4	at	NY Rangers	1	

Philadelphia won best-of-seven series 4-0

Date	Away		at	Home		
May 20	New Jersey	2	at	Pittsburgh	3	
May 22	New Jersey	4	at	Pittsburgh	2	
May 24	Pittsburgh	1	at	New Jersey	5	
May 26	Pittsburgh	1	at	New Jersey	2	OT
May 28	New Jersey	4	at	Pittsburgh	1	

New Jersey won best-of-seven series 4-1

Date	Away		at	Home		
May 21	San Jose	0	at	Detroit	6	
May 23	San Jose	2	at	Detroit	6	
May 25	Detroit	6	at	San Jose	2	
May 27	Detroit	6	at	San Jose	2	

Detroit won best-of-seven series 4-0

Date	Away		at	Home		
May 21	Vancouver	1	at	Chicago	2	OT
May 23	Vancouver	0	at	Chicago	2	
May 25	Chicago	3	at	Vancouver	2	OT
May 27	Chicago	4	at	Vancouver	3	OT

Chicago won best-of-seven series 4-0

CONFERENCE FINALS

Date	Away		at	Home		
June 3	New Jersey	4	at	Philadelphia	1	
June 5	New Jersey	5	at	Philadelphia	2	
June 7	Philadelphia	3	at	New Jersey	2	OT
June 10	Philadelphia	4	at	New Jersey	2	
June 11	New Jersey	3	at	Philadelphia	2	
June 13	Philadelphia	2	at	New Jersey	4	

New Jersey won best-of-seven series 4-2

Date	Away		at	Home		
June 1	Chicago	1	at	Detroit	2	OT
June 4	Chicago	2	at	Detroit	3	
June 6	Detroit	4	at	Chicago	3	2OT
June 8	Detroit	2	at	Chicago	5	
June 11	Chicago	1	at	Detroit	2	2OT

Detroit won best-of-seven series 4-1

FINALS

Date	Away		at	Home		
June 17	New Jersey	2	at	Detroit	1	
June 20	New Jersey	4	at	Detroit	2	
June 22	Detroit	2	at	New Jersey	5	
June 24	Detroit	2	at	New Jersey	5	

New Jersey won best-of-seven series 4-0

1994-95 – New Jersey Devils – Scott Stevens (Captain), Tommy Albelin, Martin Brodeur, Neal Broten, Sergei Brylin, Bob Carpenter, Shawn Chambers, Tom Chorske, Danton Cole, Ken Daneyko, Kevin Dean, Jim Dowd, Bruce Driver (Alternate Captain), Bill Guerin, Bobby Holik, Claude Lemieux, John MacLean (Alternate Captain), Chris McAlpine, Randy McKay, Scott Niedermayer, Mike Peluso, Stephane Richer, Brian Rolston, Chris Terreri, Valeri Zelepukin, Dr. John J. McMullen (Owner/Chairman), Peter S. McMullen (Owner), Lou Lamoriello (President/General Manager), Jacques Lemaire (Head Coach), Jacques Caron (Goaltender Coach), Dennis Gendron, Larry Robinson (Assistant Coaches), Robbie Ftorek (AHL Coach), Alex Abasto (Assistant Equipment Manager), Bob Huddleston (Massage Therapist), David Nichols (Equipment Manager), Ted Schuch (Medical Trainer), Mike Vasalani (Strength Coach), David Conte (Director of Scouting), Claude Carrier, Milt Fisher, Dan Labraaten, Marcel Pronovost (Scouts).

1994

The New York Rangers ended their 54-year Stanley Cup drought with a stirring, seven-game series win over the Vancouver Canucks. The Rangers jumped out to a 3–1 series lead, only to see the Canucks storm back to tie the series, forcing a deciding game seven at Madison Square Garden. Viewed by a record television audience worldwide, the Rangers earned a 3–2 win and the Stanley Cup.

Both the Rangers and Canucks followed a difficult route to the championship series. In the Eastern Conference final, the Rangers were stretched to the limit by the New Jersey Devils before prevailing four games to three with three games in the series decided in double overtime. The Canucks, meanwhile, had faced a 3–1 series deficit in their first-round series versus the Calgary Flames, but rallied to win the last three games in overtime.

Rangers defenseman Brian Leetch became the first U.S.-born player to capture the Conn Smythe Trophy as playoff MVP. Leetch led all players in scoring during the postseason with 34 points (11 goals, 23 assists) in 23 games. Head coach Mike Keenan, in his first season behind the Rangers bench, captured his first Stanley Cup victory. He had previously made championship series appearances with the Philadelphia Flyers (twice) and Chicago Blackhawks.

CONN SMYTHE TROPHY
Brian Leetch - Defense - NY Rangers

CONFERENCE QUARTER-FINALS

Apr.	17	NY Islanders	0	at	NY Rangers	6
Apr.	18	NY Islanders	0	at	NY Rangers	6
Apr.	21	NY Rangers	5	at	NY Islanders	1
Apr.	24	NY Rangers	5	at	NY Islanders	2

NY Rangers won best-of-seven series 4-0

Apr.	17	Washington	5	at	Pittsburgh	3
Apr.	19	Washington	1	at	Pittsburgh	2
Apr.	21	Pittsburgh	0	at	Washington	2
Apr.	23	Pittsburgh	1	at	Washington	4
Apr.	25	Washington	2	at	Pittsburgh	3
Apr.	27	Pittsburgh	3	at	Washington	6

Washington won best-of-seven series 4-2

Apr.	17	Buffalo	2	at	New Jersey	0
Apr.	19	Buffalo	1	at	New Jersey	2
Apr.	21	New Jersey	2	at	Buffalo	1
Apr.	23	New Jersey	3	at	Buffalo	5
Apr.	25	Buffalo	3	at	New Jersey	5
Apr.	27	New Jersey	0	at	Buffalo	1 4OT
Apr.	29	Buffalo	1	at	New Jersey	2

New Jersey won best-of-seven series 4-3

Apr.	16	Montreal	2	at	Boston	3
Apr.	18	Montreal	3	at	Boston	2
Apr.	21	Boston	6	at	Montreal	3
Apr.	23	Boston	2	at	Montreal	5
Apr.	25	Montreal	2	at	Boston	1 OT
Apr.	27	Boston	3	at	Montreal	2
Apr.	29	Montreal	3	at	Boston	5

Boston won best-of-seven series 4-3

Apr.	18	San Jose	5	at	Detroit	4
Apr.	20	San Jose	0	at	Detroit	4
Apr.	22	Detroit	3	at	San Jose	2
Apr.	23	Detroit	3	at	San Jose	4
Apr.	26	Detroit	4	at	San Jose	6
Apr.	28	San Jose	1	at	Detroit	7
Apr.	30	San Jose	3	at	Detroit	2

San Jose won best-of-seven series 4-3

Apr.	18	Vancouver	5	at	Calgary	0
Apr.	20	Vancouver	5	at	Calgary	7
Apr.	22	Calgary	4	at	Vancouver	2
Apr.	24	Calgary	3	at	Vancouver	2
Apr.	26	Vancouver	2	at	Calgary	1 OT
Apr.	28	Calgary	2	at	Vancouver	3 OT
Apr.	30	Vancouver	4	at	Calgary	3 2OT

Vancouver won best-of-seven series 4-3

Apr.	18	Chicago	1	at	Toronto	5
Apr.	20	Chicago	0	at	Toronto	1 OT
Apr.	23	Toronto	4	at	Chicago	5
Apr.	24	Toronto	3	at	Chicago	4 OT
Apr.	26	Chicago	0	at	Toronto	1
Apr.	28	Toronto	1	at	Chicago	0

Toronto won best-of-seven series 4-2

Apr.	17	St. Louis	3	at	Dallas	5
Apr.	20	St. Louis	2	at	Dallas	4
Apr.	22	Dallas	5	at	St. Louis	4 OT
Apr.	24	Dallas	2	at	St. Louis	1

Dallas won best-of-seven series 4-0

CONFERENCE SEMI-FINALS

May	1	Washington	3	at	NY Rangers	6
May	3	Washington	2	at	NY Rangers	5
May	5	NY Rangers	3	at	Washington	0
May	7	NY Rangers	2	at	Washington	4
May	9	Washington	3	at	NY Rangers	4

NY Rangers won best-of-seven series 4-1

May	1	Boston	2	at	New Jersey	1
May	3	Boston	6	at	New Jersey	5 OT
May	5	New Jersey	4	at	Boston	2
May	7	New Jersey	5	at	Boston	4 OT
May	9	Boston	0	at	New Jersey	2
May	11	New Jersey	5	at	Boston	3

New Jersey won best-of-seven series 4-2

May	2	San Jose	3	at	Toronto	2
May	4	San Jose	1	at	Toronto	5
May	6	Toronto	2	at	San Jose	5
May	8	Toronto	8	at	San Jose	3
May	10	Toronto	2	at	San Jose	5
May	12	San Jose	2	at	Toronto	3 OT
May	14	San Jose	2	at	Toronto	4

Toronto won best-of-seven series 4-3

May	2	Vancouver	6	at	Dallas	4
May	4	Vancouver	3	at	Dallas	0
May	6	Dallas	4	at	Vancouver	3
May	8	Dallas	1	at	Vancouver	2 OT
May	10	Dallas	2	at	Vancouver	4

Vancouver won best-of-seven series 4-1

CONFERENCE FINALS

May	15	New Jersey	4	at	NY Rangers	3 2OT
May	17	New Jersey	0	at	NY Rangers	4
May	19	NY Rangers	3	at	New Jersey	2 2OT
May	21	NY Rangers	1	at	New Jersey	3
May	23	New Jersey	4	at	NY Rangers	1
May	25	NY Rangers	4	at	New Jersey	2
May	27	New Jersey	1	at	NY Rangers	2 2OT

NY Rangers won best-of-seven series 4-3

May	16	Vancouver	2	at	Toronto	3 OT
May	18	Vancouver	4	at	Toronto	3
May	20	Toronto	0	at	Vancouver	4
May	22	Toronto	0	at	Vancouver	2
May	24	Toronto	3	at	Vancouver	4 2OT

Vancouver won best-of-seven series 4-1

FINALS

May	31	Vancouver	3	at	NY Rangers	2 OT
June	2	Vancouver	1	at	NY Rangers	3
June	4	NY Rangers	5	at	Vancouver	1
June	7	NY Rangers	4	at	Vancouver	2
June	9	Vancouver	6	at	NY Rangers	3
June	11	NY Rangers	1	at	Vancouver	4
June	14	Vancouver	2	at	NY Rangers	3

NY Rangers won best-of-seven series 4-3

1993-94 – New York Rangers – Mark Messier (Captain), Brian Leetch, Kevin Lowe, Adam Graves, Steve Larmer, Glenn Anderson, Jeff Beukeboom, Greg Gilbert, Mike Hartman, Glenn Healy, Mike Hudson, Alexander Karpovtsev, Joe Kocur, Alexei Kovalev, Nick Kypreos, Doug Lidster, Stephane Matteau, Craig MacTavish, Sergei Nemchinov, Brian Noonan, Ed Olczyk, Mike Richter, Esa Tikkanen, Jay Wells, Sergei Zubov, Robert Gutkowski, Stanley Jaffe, Kenneth Munoz (Governors), Neil Smith (President/General Manager/Governor), Larry Pleau (Assistant General Manager), Mike Keenan (Head Coach), Colin Campbell (Associate Coach), Dick Todd (Assistant Coach), Matthew Loughren (Manager, Team Operations), Barry Watkins (Dir., Communications), Christer Rockstrom, Tony Feltrin, Martin Madden, Herb Hammond, Darwin Bennett (Scouts), Dave Smith, Joe Murphy, Mike Folga, Bruce Lifrieri (Trainers).

1993

The Montreal Canadiens claimed their 24th Stanley Cup title, defeating the Los Angeles Kings in an exciting five-game series. The Kings, led by playoff scoring leader Wayne Gretzky, were making their first appearance in the finals. After dropping the opening game of the series at home, Montreal responded with four straight wins, including three in overtime.

The overtime wins capped a record-setting performance for Montreal in extra time. After losing their first overtime game of the playoffs at Quebec in game one of the opening round, the club posted 10 straight wins in extra time, setting playoff records for most OT wins in one season and most consecutive OT wins. Of the 85 games played in the postseason this year, 28 were decided in overtime, smashing the previous playoff record of 16, set in 1982 and 1991.

Canadiens' goaltender Patrick Roy was awarded the Conn Smythe Trophy as playoff MVP, posting a 16–4 record and 2.13 goals-against average in 20 games. Roy became the fifth multiple winner of the award, having previously won as a rookie in 1986.

CONN SMYTHE TROPHY
Patrick Roy - Goaltender - Montreal Canadiens

DIVISION SEMI-FINALS

Apr.	18	Buffalo	5	at	Boston	4 OT
Apr.	20	Buffalo	4	at	Boston	0
Apr.	22	Boston	3	at	Buffalo	4 OT
Apr.	24	Boston	5	at	Buffalo	6 OT

Buffalo won best-of-seven series 4–0

Apr.	18	Montreal	2	at	Quebec	3 OT
Apr.	20	Montreal	1	at	Quebec	4
Apr.	22	Quebec	1	at	Montreal	2 OT
Apr.	24	Quebec	2	at	Montreal	3
Apr.	26	Montreal	5	at	Quebec	4 OT
Apr.	28	Quebec	2	at	Montreal	6

Montreal won best-of-seven series 4–2

Apr.	18	New Jersey	3	at	Pittsburgh	6
Apr.	20	New Jersey	0	at	Pittsburgh	7
Apr.	22	Pittsburgh	4	at	New Jersey	3
Apr.	25	Pittsburgh	1	at	New Jersey	4
Apr.	26	New Jersey	3	at	Pittsburgh	5

Pittsburgh won best-of-seven series 4–1

Apr.	18	NY Islanders	1	at	Washington	3
Apr.	20	NY Islanders	5	at	Washington	4 2OT
Apr.	22	Washington	3	at	NY Islanders	4 OT
Apr.	24	Washington	3	at	NY Islanders	4 2OT
Apr.	26	NY Islanders	4	at	Washington	6
Apr.	28	Washington	3	at	NY Islanders	5

NY Islanders won best-of-seven series 4–2

Apr.	18	St. Louis	4	at	Chicago	3
Apr.	21	St. Louis	2	at	Chicago	0
Apr.	23	Chicago	0	at	St. Louis	3
Apr.	25	Chicago	3	at	St. Louis	4 OT

St. Louis won best-of-seven series 4–0

Apr.	19	Toronto	3	at	Detroit	6
Apr.	21	Toronto	2	at	Detroit	6
Apr.	23	Detroit	2	at	Toronto	4
Apr.	25	Detroit	2	at	Toronto	3
Apr.	27	Toronto	5	at	Detroit	4 OT
Apr.	29	Detroit	7	at	Toronto	3
May	1	Toronto	4	at	Detroit	3 OT

Toronto won best-of-seven series 4–3

Apr.	19	Winnipeg	2	at	Vancouver	4
Apr.	21	Winnipeg	2	at	Vancouver	3
Apr.	23	Vancouver	4	at	Winnipeg	5
Apr.	25	Vancouver	3	at	Winnipeg	1
Apr.	27	Winnipeg	4	at	Vancouver	3 OT

Apr.	29	Vancouver	4	at Winnipeg	3 OT

Vancouver won best-of-seven series 4–2

Apr.	18	Los Angeles	6	at Calgary	3
Apr.	21	Los Angeles	4	at Calgary	9
Apr.	23	Calgary	5	at Los Angeles	2
Apr.	25	Calgary	1	at Los Angeles	3
Apr.	27	Calgary	9	at Los Angeles	4
Apr.	29	Calgary	6	at Los Angeles	9

Los Angeles won best-of-seven series 4–2

DIVISION FINALS

May	2	Buffalo	3	at Montreal	4
May	4	Buffalo	3	at Montreal	4 OT
May	6	Montreal	4	at Buffalo	3 OT
May	8	Montreal	4	at Buffalo	3 OT

Montreal won best-of-seven series 4–0

May	2	NY Islanders	3	at Pittsburgh	2
May	4	NY Islanders	0	at Pittsburgh	3
May	6	Pittsburgh	3	at NY Islanders	1
May	8	Pittsburgh	5	at NY Islanders	6
May	10	NY Islanders	3	at Pittsburgh	6
May	12	Pittsburgh	5	at NY Islanders	7
May	14	NY Islanders	4	at Pittsburgh	3 OT

NY Islanders won best-of-seven series 4–3

May	3	St. Louis	1	at Toronto	2 2OT
May	5	St. Louis	2	at Toronto	1 2OT
May	7	Toronto	3	at St. Louis	4
May	9	Toronto	4	at St. Louis	1
May	11	St. Louis	1	at Toronto	5
May	13	Toronto	1	at St. Louis	2
May	15	St. Louis	0	at Toronto	6

Toronto won best-of-seven series 4–3

May	2	Los Angeles	2	at Vancouver	5
May	5	Los Angeles	6	at Vancouver	3
May	7	Vancouver	4	at Los Angeles	7
May	9	Vancouver	7	at Los Angeles	2
May	11	Los Angeles	4	at Vancouver	3 2OT
May	13	Vancouver	3	at Los Angeles	5

Los Angeles won best-of-seven series 4–2

CONFERENCE FINALS

May	16	NY Islanders	1	at Montreal	4
May	18	NY Islanders	3	at Montreal	4 2OT
May	20	Montreal	2	at NY Islanders	1 OT
May	22	Montreal	1	at NY Islanders	4
May	24	NY Islanders	2	at Montreal	5

Montreal won best-of-seven series 4–1

May	17	Los Angeles	1	at Toronto	4
May	19	Los Angeles	3	at Toronto	2
May	21	Toronto	2	at Los Angeles	4
May	23	Toronto	4	at Los Angeles	2
May	25	Los Angeles	2	at Toronto	3 OT
May	27	Toronto	4	at Los Angeles	5 OT
May	29	Los Angeles	5	at Toronto	4

Los Angeles won best-of-seven series 4–3

FINALS

June	1	Los Angeles	4	at Montreal	1
June	3	Los Angeles	2	at Montreal	3 OT
June	5	Montreal	4	at Los Angeles	3 OT
June	7	Montreal	3	at Los Angeles	2 OT
June	9	Los Angeles	1	at Montreal	4

Montreal won best-of-seven series 4–1

1992-93 – Montreal Canadiens – Guy Carbonneau (Captain), Patrick Roy, Mike Keane, Eric Desjardins, Stephan Lebeau, Mathieu Schneider, J.J. Daigneault, Denis Savard, Lyle Odelein, Todd Ewen, Kirk Muller, John LeClair, Gilbert Dionne, Benoit Brunet, Patrice Brisebois, Paul Di Pietro, Andre Racicot, Donald Dufresne, Mario Roberge, Sean Hill, Ed Ronan, Kevin Haller, Vincent Damphousse, Brian Bellows, Gary Leeman, Rob Ramage, Ronald Corey (President), Serge Savard (Managing Director/Vice President, Hockey), Jacques Demers (Head Coach), Jacques Laperriere, Charles Thiffault (Assistant Coaches), Francois Allaire (Goaltending Instructor), Jean Béliveau (Senior Vice President, Corporate

Affairs), Fred Steer (Vice President, Finance & Adminstration), Aldo Giampaolo (Vice President, Operations), Bernard Brisset (Vice President, Marketing & Communications), André Boudrias (Assistant to the Managing Director/Director of Scouting), Jacques Lemaire (Assistant to the Managing Director), Gaeten Lefebvre (Athletic Trainer), John Shipman (Assistant to the Athletic Trainer), Eddy Palchak (Equipment Manager), Pierre Gervais, Robert Boulanger, Pierre Ouellete (Assistants to the Equipment Manager).

1992

The Penguins captured their second consecutive Stanley Cup title, winning the championship in four consecutive games from the Chicago Blackhawks, who were making their first appearance in the finals since 1973.

Both finalists established a new record for consecutive playoff wins with 11. The Blackhawks' victories spanned the first three rounds of the playoffs. The Penguins' 11 wins included their four-game final series sweep.

Mario Lemieux captured the Conn Smythe Trophy as playoff MVP for the second straight year, becoming just the second player in NHL history (Bernie Parent, 1974 and 1975) to accomplish the feat.

CONN SMYTHE TROPHY
Mario Lemieux - Center - Pittsburgh Penguins

DIVISION SEMI-FINALS

Apr.	19	Hartford	0	at Montreal	2
Apr.	21	Hartford	2	at Montreal	5
Apr.	23	Montreal	2	at Hartford	5
Apr.	25	Montreal	1	at Hartford	3
Apr.	27	Hartford	4	at Montreal	7
Apr.	29	Montreal	1	at Hartford	2 OT
May	1	Hartford	2	at Montreal	3 2OT

Montreal won best-of-seven series 4–3

Apr.	19	Buffalo	3	at Boston	2
Apr.	21	Buffalo	2	at Boston	3 OT
Apr.	23	Boston	3	at Buffalo	2
Apr.	25	Boston	5	at Buffalo	4 OT
Apr.	27	Buffalo	2	at Boston	0
Apr.	29	Boston	3	at Buffalo	9
May	1	Buffalo	2	at Boston	3

Boston won best-of-seven series 4–3

Apr.	19	New Jersey	1	at NY Rangers	2
Apr.	21	New Jersey	7	at NY Rangers	3
Apr.	23	NY Rangers	1	at New Jersey	3
Apr.	25	NY Rangers	3	at New Jersey	0
Apr.	27	New Jersey	5	at NY Rangers	6
Apr.	29	NY Rangers	3	at New Jersey	5
May	1	New Jersey	4	at NY Rangers	8

NY Rangers won best-of-seven series 4–3

Apr.	19	Pittsburgh	1	at Washington	3
Apr.	21	Pittsburgh	2	at Washington	6
Apr.	23	Washington	4	at Pittsburgh	6
Apr.	25	Washington	7	at Pittsburgh	2
Apr.	27	Pittsburgh	5	at Washington	2
Apr.	29	Washington	4	at Pittsburgh	6
May	1	Pittsburgh	3	at Washington	1

Pittsburgh won best-of-seven series 4–3

Apr.	18	Minnesota	4	at Detroit	3
Apr.	20	Minnesota	4	at Detroit	2
Apr.	22	Detroit	5	at Minnesota	4 OT
Apr.	24	Detroit	4	at Minnesota	5
Apr.	26	Minnesota	0	at Detroit	3
Apr.	28	Detroit	1	at Minnesota	0 OT
Apr.	30	Minnesota	2	at Detroit	5

Detroit won best-of-seven series 4–3

Apr.	18	St. Louis	1	at Chicago	3
Apr.	20	St. Louis	5	at Chicago	3
Apr.	22	Chicago	4	at St. Louis	5 2OT

Apr.	24	Chicago	5	at St. Louis	3
Apr.	26	St. Louis	4	at Chicago	6
Apr.	28	Chicago	2	at St. Louis	1

Chicago won best-of-seven series 4–2

Apr.	18	Winnipeg	3	at Vancouver	2
Apr.	20	Winnipeg	2	at Vancouver	3
Apr.	22	Vancouver	2	at Winnipeg	4
Apr.	24	Vancouver	1	at Winnipeg	3
Apr.	26	Winnipeg	2	at Vancouver	8
Apr.	28	Vancouver	8	at Winnipeg	3
Apr.	30	Winnipeg	0	at Vancouver	5

Vancouver won best-of-seven series 4–3

Apr.	18	Edmonton	3	at Los Angeles	1
Apr.	20	Edmonton	5	at Los Angeles	8
Apr.	22	Los Angeles	2	at Edmonton	4
Apr.	24	Los Angeles	4	at Edmonton	3
Apr.	26	Edmonton	5	at Los Angeles	2
Apr.	28	Los Angeles	0	at Edmonton	3

Edmonton won best-of-seven series 4–2

DIVISION FINALS

May	3	Boston	6	at Montreal	4
May	5	Boston	3	at Montreal	2 OT
May	7	Montreal	2	at Boston	3
May	9	Montreal	0	at Boston	2

Boston won best-of-seven series 4–0

May	3	Pittsburgh	4	at NY Rangers	2
May	5	Pittsburgh	2	at NY Rangers	4
May	7	NY Rangers	6	at Pittsburgh	5 OT
May	9	NY Rangers	4	at Pittsburgh	5 OT
May	11	Pittsburgh	3	at NY Rangers	5
May	13	NY Rangers	1	at Pittsburgh	5

Pittsburgh won best-of-seven series 4–2

May	2	Chicago	2	at Detroit	1
May	4	Chicago	3	at Detroit	1
May	6	Detroit	4	at Chicago	5
May	8	Detroit	0	at Chicago	1

Chicago won best-of-seven series 4–0

May	3	Edmonton	4	at Vancouver	3 OT
May	4	Edmonton	0	at Vancouver	4
May	6	Vancouver	2	at Edmonton	5
May	8	Vancouver	2	at Edmonton	3
May	10	Edmonton	3	at Vancouver	4
May	12	Vancouver	0	at Edmonton	3

Edmonton won best-of-seven series 4–2

CONFERENCE FINALS

May	17	Boston	3	at Pittsburgh	4 OT
May	19	Boston	3	at Pittsburgh	5
May	21	Pittsburgh	5	at Boston	1
May	23	Pittsburgh	5	at Boston	1

Pittsburgh won best-of-seven series 4–0

May	16	Edmonton	2	at Chicago	8
May	18	Edmonton	2	at Chicago	4
May	20	Chicago	4	at Edmonton	3 OT
May	22	Chicago	5	at Edmonton	1

Chicago won best-of-seven series 4–0

FINALS

May	26	Chicago	4	at Pittsburgh	5
May	28	Chicago	1	at Pittsburgh	3
May	30	Pittsburgh	1	at Chicago	0
June	1	Pittsburgh	6	at Chicago	5

Pittsburgh won best-of-seven series 4–0

1991-92 – Pittsburgh Penguins – Mario Lemieux (Captain), Ron Francis, Bryan Trottier, Kevin Stevens, Bob Errey, Phil Bourque, Troy Loney, Rick Tocchet, Joe Mullen, Jaromir Jagr, Jiri Hrdina, Shawn McEachern, Ulf Samuelsson, Kjell Samuelsson, Larry Murphy, Gordie Roberts, Jim Paek, Paul Stanton, Tom Barrasso, Ken Wregget, Jay Caufield, Jamie Leach, Wendell Young, Grant Jennings, Peter Taglianetti, Jock Callander, Dave Michayluk, Mike Needham, Jeff Chychrun, Ken Priestlay, Jeff Daniels, Howard Baldwin (Owner/President), Morris Belzberg, Thomas Ruta (Owners), Donn Patton (Executive Vice

President/Chief Financial Officer), Paul Martha (Executive Vice President/General Counsel), Craig Patrick (Executive Vice President/General Manager), Bob Johnson (Coach), Scotty Bowman (Director of Player Development/Coach), Barry Smith, Rick Kehoe, Pierre McGuire, Gilles Meloche, Rick Paterson (Assistant Coaches), Steve Latin (Equipment Manager), Skip Thayer (Trainer), John Welday (Strength and Conditioning Coach), Greg Malone, Les Binkley, Charlie Hodge, John Gill, Ralph Cox (Scouts).

1991

The Penguins captured their first Stanley Cup championship, defeating the Minnesota North Stars in six games. The North Stars were making their second appearance in the finals.

Pittsburgh center Mario Lemieux, despite missing one game in the series due to a back injury, recorded 12 points (five goals, seven assists) in five games to lead all scorers. His overall playoff performance earned him Conn Smythe Trophy honors.

Penguins defenseman Larry Murphy tallied 10 points (one goal, nine assists) in six games, the second highest total for a defenseman in Stanley Cup finals history.

Four Pittsburgh players — Bryan Trottier, Paul Coffey, Joe Mullen and Jiri Hrdina — won a Stanley Cup championship with their second team. Trottier won four previous titles with the New York Islanders, Coffey captured three with Edmonton, while Mullen and Hrdina were members of the 1989 Stanley Cup-champion Calgary Flames.

CONN SMYTHE TROPHY
Mario Lemieux - Center - Pittsburgh Penguins

DIVISION SEMI-FINALS

Apr.	3	Hartford	5	at	Boston	2
Apr.	5	Hartford	3	at	Boston	4
Apr.	7	Boston	6	at	Hartford	3
Apr.	9	Boston	3	at	Hartford	4
Apr.	11	Hartford	1	at	Boston	6
Apr.	13	Boston	3	at	Hartford	1

Boston won best-of-seven series 4–2

Apr.	3	Buffalo	5	at	Montreal	7
Apr.	5	Buffalo	4	at	Montreal	5
Apr.	7	Montreal	4	at	Buffalo	5
Apr.	9	Montreal	4	at	Buffalo	6
Apr.	11	Buffalo	3	at	Montreal	4 OT
Apr.	13	Montreal	5	at	Buffalo	1

Montreal won best-of-seven series 4–2

Apr.	3	New Jersey	3	at	Pittsburgh	1
Apr.	5	New Jersey	4	at	Pittsburgh	5 OT
Apr.	7	Pittsburgh	4	at	New Jersey	3
Apr.	9	Pittsburgh	1	at	New Jersey	4
Apr.	11	New Jersey	4	at	Pittsburgh	2
Apr.	13	Pittsburgh	4	at	New Jersey	3
Apr.	15	New Jersey	0	at	Pittsburgh	4

Pittsburgh won best-of-seven series 4–3

Apr.	3	Washington	1	at	NY Rangers	2
Apr.	5	Washington	3	at	NY Rangers	0
Apr.	7	NY Rangers	6	at	Washington	0
Apr.	9	NY Rangers	2	at	Washington	3
Apr.	11	Washington	5	at	NY Rangers	4 OT
Apr.	13	NY Rangers	2	at	Washington	4

Washington won best-of-seven series 4–2

Apr.	4	Minnesota	4	at	Chicago	3 OT
Apr.	6	Minnesota	2	at	Chicago	5
Apr.	8	Chicago	6	at	Minnesota	5
Apr.	10	Chicago	1	at	Minnesota	3
Apr.	12	Minnesota	6	at	Chicago	0
Apr.	14	Chicago	1	at	Minnesota	3

Minnesota won best-of-seven series 4–2

Apr.	4	Detroit	6	at	St. Louis	3
Apr.	6	Detroit	2	at	St. Louis	4
Apr.	8	St. Louis	2	at	Detroit	5
Apr.	10	St. Louis	3	at	Detroit	4
Apr.	12	Detroit	1	at	St. Louis	6
Apr.	14	St. Louis	3	at	Detroit	0
Apr.	16	Detroit	2	at	St. Louis	3

St. Louis won best-of-seven series 4–3

Apr.	4	Vancouver	6	at	Los Angeles	5
Apr.	6	Vancouver	2	at	Los Angeles	3 OT
Apr.	8	Los Angeles	1	at	Vancouver	2 OT
Apr.	10	Los Angeles	6	at	Vancouver	1
Apr.	12	Vancouver	4	at	Los Angeles	7
Apr.	14	Los Angeles	4	at	Vancouver	1

Los Angeles won best-of-seven series 4–2

Apr.	4	Edmonton	3	at	Calgary	1
Apr.	6	Edmonton	1	at	Calgary	3
Apr.	8	Calgary	3	at	Edmonton	4
Apr.	10	Calgary	2	at	Edmonton	5
Apr.	12	Edmonton	3	at	Calgary	5
Apr.	14	Calgary	2	at	Edmonton	1 OT
Apr.	16	Edmonton	5	at	Calgary	4 OT

Edmonton won best-of-seven series 4–3

DIVISION FINALS

Apr.	17	Montreal	1	at	Boston	2
Apr.	19	Montreal	4	at	Boston	3 OT
Apr.	21	Boston	3	at	Montreal	2
Apr.	23	Boston	2	at	Montreal	6
Apr.	25	Montreal	1	at	Boston	4
Apr.	27	Boston	2	at	Montreal	3 OT
Apr.	29	Montreal	1	at	Boston	2

Boston won best-of-seven series 4–3

Apr.	17	Washington	4	at	Pittsburgh	2
Apr.	19	Washington	6	at	Pittsburgh	7 OT
Apr.	21	Pittsburgh	3	at	Washington	1
Apr.	23	Pittsburgh	3	at	Washington	1
Apr.	25	Washington	1	at	Pittsburgh	4

Pittsburgh won best-of-seven series 4–1

Apr.	18	Minnesota	2	at	St. Louis	1
Apr.	20	Minnesota	2	at	St. Louis	5
Apr.	22	St. Louis	1	at	Minnesota	5
Apr.	24	St. Louis	4	at	Minnesota	8
Apr.	26	Minnesota	2	at	St. Louis	4
Apr.	28	St. Louis	2	at	Minnesota	3

Minnesota won best-of-seven series 4–2

Apr.	18	Edmonton	3	at	Los Angeles	4 OT
Apr.	20	Edmonton	4	at	Los Angeles	3 2OT
Apr.	22	Los Angeles	3	at	Edmonton	4 2OT
Apr.	24	Los Angeles	3	at	Edmonton	4
Apr.	26	Edmonton	2	at	Los Angeles	5
Apr.	28	Los Angeles	3	at	Edmonton	4 OT

Edmonton won best-of-seven series 4–2

CONFERENCE FINALS

May	1	Pittsburgh	3	at	Boston	6
May	3	Pittsburgh	4	at	Boston	5 OT
May	5	Boston	1	at	Pittsburgh	4
May	7	Boston	1	at	Pittsburgh	4
May	9	Pittsburgh	7	at	Boston	2
May	11	Boston	3	at	Pittsburgh	5

Pittsburgh won best-of-seven series 4–2

May	2	MInnesota	3	at	Edmonton	1
May	4	Minnesota	2	at	Edmonton	7
May	6	Edmonton	3	at	Minnesota	7
May	8	Edmonton	1	at	Minnesota	5
May	10	Minnesota	3	at	Edmonton	2

Minnesota won best-of-seven series 4–1

FINALS

May	15	Minnesota	5	at	Pittsburgh	4
May	17	Minnesota	1	at	Pittsburgh	4
May	19	Pittsburgh	1	at	Minnesota	3
May	21	Pittsburgh	5	at	Minnesota	3
May	23	Minnesota	4	at	Pittsburgh	6
May	25	Pittsburgh	8	at	Minnesota	0

Pittsburgh won best-of-seven series 4–2

1990-91 – Pittsburgh Penguins – Mario Lemieux (Captain), Paul Coffey, Randy Hillier, Bob Errey, Tom Barrasso, Phil Bourque, Jay Caufield, Ron Francis, Randy Gilhen, Jiri Hrdina, Jaromir Jagr, Grant Jennings, Troy Loney, Joe Mullen, Larry Murphy, Jim Paek, Barry Pederson, Frank Pietrangelo, Mark Recchi, Gordie Roberts, Ulf Samuelsson, Paul Stanton, Kevin Stevens, Peter Taglianetti, Bryan Trottier, Scott Young, Wendell Young, Edward J. DeBartolo, Sr. (Owner), Marie D. DeBartolo York (President), Paul Martha (Vice President/General Counsel), Craig Patrick (General Manager), Scotty Bowman (Director of Player Development & Recruitment), Bob Johnson (Coach), Rick Kehoe (Assistant Coach), Gilles Meloche (Goaltending Coach/Scout), Rick Paterson, Barry Smith (Assistant Coaches), Steve Latin (Equipment Manager), Skip Thayer (Trainer), John Welday (Strength & Conditioning Coach), Greg Malone (Scout).

1990

The Oilers captured their fifth Stanley Cup title in seven years (and their first since trading Wayne Gretzky to Los Angeles in 1988), defeating Boston for their second Stanley Cup triumph over the Bruins in three seasons.

The two teams battled for 55:13 of overtime in game one at Boston Garden before Edmonton's Petr Klima ended the marathon encounter with the game-winner. It represented the longest game in Stanley Cup finals history, edging the previous mark of 53:50 set in game three of the 1931 series between Chicago and Montreal.

Edmonton goaltender Bill Ranford, who posted all 16 Oilers victories in the postseason, won the Conn Smythe Trophy as playoff MVP.

Seven players — Glenn Anderson, Grant Fuhr, Randy Gregg, Charlie Huddy, Jari Kurri, Kevin Lowe and Mark Messier — won their fifth Stanley Cup rings as members of the Oilers.

CONN SMYTHE TROPHY
Bill Ranford - Goaltender - Edmonton Oilers

DIVISION SEMI-FINALS

Apr.	5	Hartford	4	at	Boston	3
Apr.	7	Hartford	1	at	Boston	3
Apr.	9	Boston	3	at	Hartford	5
Apr.	11	Boston	6	at	Hartford	5
Apr.	13	Hartford	2	at	Boston	3
Apr.	15	Boston	2	at	Hartford	3 OT
Apr.	17	Hartford	1	at	Boston	3

Boston won best-of-seven series 4–3

Apr.	5	Montreal	1	at	Buffalo	4
Apr.	7	Montreal	3	at	Buffalo	0
Apr.	9	Buffalo	1	at	Montreal	2 OT
Apr.	11	Buffalo	4	at	Montreal	2
Apr.	13	Montreal	4	at	Buffalo	2
Apr.	15	Buffalo	2	at	Montreal	5

Montreal won best-of-seven series 4–2

Apr.	5	NY Islanders	1	at	NY Rangers	2
Apr.	7	NY Islanders	2	at	NY Rangers	5
Apr.	9	NY Rangers	3	at	NY Islanders	4 2OT
Apr.	11	NY Rangers	6	at	NY Islanders	1
Apr.	13	NY Islanders	5	at	NY Rangers	6

NY Rangers won best-of-seven series 4–1

Apr.	5	Washington	5	at	New Jersey	4 OT
Apr.	7	Washington	5	at	New Jersey	6
Apr.	9	New Jersey	2	at	Washington	1
Apr.	11	New Jersey	1	at	Washington	3
Apr.	13	New Jersey	4	at	New Jersey	3
Apr.	15	New Jersey	2	at	Washington	3

Washington won best-of-seven series 4–2

Apr.	4	Minnesota	2	at	Chicago	1
Apr.	6	Minnesota	3	at	Chicago	5

Apr.	8	Chicago	2	at	Minnesota	1
Apr.	10	Chicago	0	at	Minnesota	4
Apr.	12	Minnesota	1	at	Chicago	5
Apr.	14	Chicago	3	at	Minnesota	5
Apr.	16	Minnesota	2	at	Chicago	5

Chicago won best-of-seven series 4–3

Apr.	4	Toronto	2	at	St. Louis	4
Apr.	6	Toronto	2	at	St. Louis	4
Apr.	8	St. Louis	6	at	Toronto	5 OT
Apr.	10	St. Louis	2	at	Toronto	4
Apr.	12	Toronto	3	at	St. Louis	4

St. Louis won best-of-seven series 4–1

Apr.	4	Los Angeles	5	at	Calgary	3
Apr.	6	Los Angeles	5	at	Calgary	8
Apr.	8	Calgary	1	at	Los Angeles	2 OT
Apr.	10	Calgary	4	at	Los Angeles	12
Apr.	12	Los Angeles	1	at	Calgary	5
Apr.	14	Calgary	3	at	Los Angeles	4 2OT

Los Angeles won best-of-seven series 4–2

Apr.	4	Winnipeg	7	at	Edmonton	5
Apr.	6	Winnipeg	2	at	Edmonton	3 OT
Apr.	8	Edmonton	1	at	Winnipeg	2
Apr.	10	Edmonton	3	at	Winnipeg	4 2OT
Apr.	12	Winnipeg	3	at	Edmonton	4
Apr.	14	Edmonton	4	at	Winnipeg	3
Apr.	16	Winnipeg	1	at	Edmonton	4

Edmonton won best-of-seven series 4–3

DIVISION FINALS

Apr.	19	Montreal	0	at	Boston	1
Apr.	21	Montreal	4	at	Boston	5 OT
Apr.	23	Boston	6	at	Montreal	3
Apr.	25	Boston	1	at	Montreal	4
Apr.	27	Montreal	1	at	Boston	3

Boston won best-of-seven series 4–1

Apr.	19	Washington	3	at	NY Rangers	7
Apr.	21	Washington	6	at	NY Rangers	3
Apr.	23	NY Rangers	1	at	Washington	7
Apr.	25	NY Rangers	3	at	Washington	4 OT
Apr.	27	Washington	2	at	NY Rangers	1 OT

Washington won best-of-seven series 4–1

Apr.	18	St. Louis	4	at	Chicago	3
Apr.	20	St. Louis	3	at	Chicago	5
Apr.	22	Chicago	4	at	St. Louis	5
Apr.	24	Chicago	3	at	St. Louis	2
Apr.	26	St. Louis	2	at	Chicago	3
Apr.	28	Chicago	2	at	St. Louis	4
Apr.	30	St. Louis	2	at	Chicago	8

Chicago won best-of-seven series 4–3

Apr.	18	Los Angeles	0	at	Edmonton	7
Apr.	20	Los Angeles	1	at	Edmonton	6
Apr.	22	Edmonton	5	at	Los Angeles	4
Apr.	24	Edmonton	6	at	Los Angeles	5 OT

Edmonton won best-of-seven series 4–0

CONFERENCE FINALS

May	3	Washington	3	at	Boston	5
May	5	Washington	0	at	Boston	3
May	7	Boston	4	at	Washington	1
May	9	Boston	3	at	Washington	2

Boston won best-of-seven series 4–0

May	2	Chicago	2	at	Edmonton	5
May	4	Chicago	4	at	Edmonton	3
May	6	Edmonton	1	at	Chicago	5
May	8	Edmonton	4	at	Chicago	2
May	10	Chicago	3	at	Edmonton	4
May	12	Edmonton	8	at	Chicago	4

Edmonton won best-of-seven series 4–2

FINALS

May	15	Edmonton	3	at	Boston	2 3OT
May	18	Edmonton	7	at	Boston	2
May	20	Boston	2	at	Edmonton	1
May	22	Boston	1	at	Edmonton	5
May	24	Edmonton	4	at	Boston	1

Edmonton won best-of-seven series 4–1

1989-90 – Edmonton Oilers – Kevin Lowe, Steve Smith, Jeff Beukeboom, Mark Lamb, Joe Murphy, Glenn Anderson, Mark Messier (Captain), Adam Graves, Craig MacTavish, Kelly Buchberger, Jari Kurri, Craig Simpson, Martin Gelinas, Randy Gregg, Charlie Huddy, Geoff Smith, Reijo Ruotsalainen, Craig Muni, Bill Ranford, Dave Brown, Pokey Reddick, Petr Klima, Esa Tikkanen, Grant Fuhr, Peter Pocklington (Owner), Glen Sather (President/General Manager), John Muckler (Coach), Ted Green (Co-Coach), Ron Low (Assistant Coach), Bruce MacGregor (Assistant General Manager), Barry Fraser (Director of Player Personnel), John Blackwell (Director of Operations, AHL), Ace Bailey, Ed Chadwick, Lorne Davis, Harry Howell, Matti Vaisanen, Albert Reeves (Scouts), Bill Tuele (Director of Public Relations), Werner Baum (Controller), Dr. Gordon Cameron (Medical Chief of Staff), Dr. David Reid (Team Physician), Barrie Stafford (Athletic Trainer), Ken Lowe (Athletic Therapist), Stuart Poirier (Massage Therapist), Lyle Kulchisky (Assistant Trainer).

1989

The Calgary Flames won their first Stanley Cup title with a 4–2 series victory over the Montreal Canadiens, who had defeated Calgary for the Stanley Cup in 1986. The Flames wrapped up the series with a 4–2 triumph over the Canadiens in game six, becoming the first visiting team to beat the Canadiens for the Stanley Cup on Montreal Forum ice.

Goaltender Mike Vernon tied an NHL playoff record by registering 16 wins during the postseason, tying the mark Edmonton's Grant Fuhr had set the previous year.

Al MacInnis became the fourth defenseman to win the Conn Smythe Trophy since the award was instituted in 1965. MacInnis joined Serge Savard (1969), Bobby Orr (1970 and 1972) and Larry Robinson (1978). MacInnis led the league in playoff scoring with 31 points (seven goals, 24 assists) and amassed a 17-game consecutive point-scoring streak, equaling the second longest in NHL playoff history and the longest ever by a defenseman.

CONN SMYTHE TROPHY
Al MacInnis - Defense - Calgary Flames

DIVISION SEMI-FINALS

Apr.	5	Hartford	2	at	Montreal	6
Apr.	6	Hartford	2	at	Montreal	3
Apr.	8	Montreal	5	at	Hartford	4 OT
Apr.	9	Montreal	4	at	Hartford	3 OT

Montreal won best-of-seven series 4–0

Apr.	5	Buffalo	6	at	Boston	0
Apr.	6	Buffalo	3	at	Boston	5
Apr.	8	Boston	4	at	Buffalo	2
Apr.	9	Boston	3	at	Buffalo	2
Apr.	11	Buffalo	1	at	Boston	4

Boston won best-of-seven series 4–1

Apr.	5	Philadelphia	2	at	Washington	3
Apr.	6	Philadelphia	3	at	Washington	2
Apr.	8	Washington	4	at	Philadelphia	3 OT
Apr.	9	Washington	2	at	Philadelphia	5
Apr.	11	Philadelphia	8	at	Washington	5
Apr.	13	Washington	3	at	Philadelphia	4

Philadelphia won best-of-seven series 4–2

Apr.	5	NY Rangers	1	at	Pittsburgh	3
Apr.	6	NY Rangers	4	at	Pittsburgh	7
Apr.	8	Pittsburgh	5	at	NY Rangers	3
Apr.	9	Pittsburgh	4	at	NY Rangers	3

Pittsburgh won best-of-seven series 4–0

Apr.	5	Chicago	2	at	Detroit	3
Apr.	6	Chicago	5	at	Detroit	4 OT
Apr.	8	Detroit	2	at	Chicago	4
Apr.	9	Detroit	2	at	Chicago	3
Apr.	11	Chicago	4	at	Detroit	6
Apr.	13	Detroit	1	at	Chicago	7

Chicago won best-of-seven series 4–2

Apr.	5	Minnesota	3	at	St. Louis	4 OT
Apr.	6	Minnesota	3	at	St. Louis	4 OT
Apr.	8	St. Louis	5	at	Minnesota	4
Apr.	9	St. Louis	4	at	Minnesota	5
Apr.	11	Minnesota	1	at	St. Louis	6

St. Louis won best-of-seven series 4–1

Apr.	5	Vancouver	4	at	Calgary	3 OT
Apr.	6	Vancouver	2	at	Calgary	5
Apr.	8	Calgary	4	at	Vancouver	0
Apr.	9	Calgary	3	at	Vancouver	5
Apr.	11	Vancouver	0	at	Calgary	4
Apr.	13	Calgary	3	at	Vancouver	6
Apr.	15	Vancouver	3	at	Calgary	4 OT

Calgary won best-of-seven series 4–3

Apr.	5	Edmonton	4	at	Los Angeles	3
Apr.	6	Edmonton	2	at	Los Angeles	5
Apr.	8	Los Angeles	0	at	Edmonton	4
Apr.	9	Los Angeles	3	at	Edmonton	4
Apr.	11	Edmonton	2	at	Los Angeles	4
Apr.	13	Los Angeles	4	at	Edmonton	1
Apr.	15	Edmonton	3	at	Los Angeles	6

Los Angeles won best-of-seven series 4–3

DIVISION FINALS

Apr.	17	Boston	2	at	Montreal	3
Apr.	19	Boston	2	at	Montreal	3 OT
Apr.	21	Montreal	5	at	Boston	4
Apr.	23	Montreal	2	at	Boston	3
Apr.	25	Boston	2	at	Montreal	3

Montreal won best-of-seven series 4–1

Apr.	17	Philadelphia	3	at	Pittsburgh	4
Apr.	19	Philadelphia	4	at	Pittsburgh	2
Apr.	21	Pittsburgh	4	at	Philadelphia	3 OT
Apr.	23	Pittsburgh	1	at	Philadelphia	4
Apr.	25	Pittsburgh	7	at	Philadelphia	10
Apr.	27	Pittsburgh	2	at	Philadelphia	6
Apr.	29	Philadelphia	4	at	Pittsburgh	1

Philadelphia won best-of-seven series 4–3

Apr.	18	Chicago	3	at	St. Louis	1
Apr.	20	Chicago	4	at	St. Louis	5 2OT
Apr.	22	St. Louis	2	at	Chicago	5
Apr.	24	St. Louis	2	at	Chicago	3
Apr.	26	Chicago	4	at	St. Louis	2

Chicago won best-of-seven series 4–1

Apr.	18	Los Angeles	3	at	Calgary	4 OT
Apr.	20	Los Angeles	3	at	Calgary	8
Apr.	22	Calgary	5	at	Los Angeles	3
Apr.	24	Calgary	5	at	Los Angeles	3

Calgary won best-of-seven series 4–0

CONFERENCE FINALS

May	1	Philadelphia	3	at	Montreal	1
May	3	Philadelphia	0	at	Montreal	3
May	5	Montreal	5	at	Philadelphia	1
May	7	Montreal	3	at	Philadelphia	0
May	9	Philadelphia	2	at	Montreal	1 OT
May	11	Montreal	4	at	Philadelphia	2

Montreal won best-of-seven series 4–2

May	2	Chicago	0	at	Calgary	3
May	4	Chicago	4	at	Calgary	2
May	6	Calgary	5	at	Chicago	2
May	8	Calgary	2	at	Chicago	1 OT
May	10	Chicago	1	at	Calgary	3

Calgary won best-of-seven series 4–1

FINALS

May	14	Montreal	2	at	Calgary	3
May	17	Montreal	4	at	Calgary	2
May	19	Calgary	3	at	Montreal	4 2OT
May	21	Calgary	4	at	Montreal	2
May	23	Montreal	2	at	Calgary	3
May	25	Calgary	4	at	Montreal	2

Calgary won best-of-seven series 4–2

1988-89 – Calgary Flames – Mike Vernon, Rick Wamsley, Al MacInnis, Brad McCrimmon, Dana Murzyn, Ric Nattress, Joe Mullen, Lanny McDonald (Co-Captain), Gary Roberts, Colin Patterson, Hakan Loob, Theoren Fleury, Jiri Hrdina, Tim Hunter (Assistant Captain), Gary Suter, Mark Hunter, Jim Peplinski (Co-Captain), Joe Nieuwendyk, Brian MacLellan, Joel Otto, Jamie Macoun, Doug Gilmour, Rob Ramage, Norman Green, Harley Hotchkiss, Norman Kwong, Sonia Scurfield, B.J. Seaman, D.K. Seaman (Owners), Cliff Fletcher (President/General Manager), Al MacNeil (Assistant General Manager), Al Coates (Assistant to the President), Terry Crisp (Head Coach), Doug Risebrough, Tom Watt (Assistant Coaches), Glenn Hall (Goaltending Consultant), Jim Murray (Trainer), Bob Stewart (Equipment Manager), Al Murray (Assistant Trainer).

1988

The Edmonton Oilers won their fourth Stanley Cup title in five years with a 4–0 series victory over the Boston Bruins, who were making their first appearance in the Stanley Cup finals in 10 years.

For the first time since 1927, a Stanley Cup finals game failed to determine a winner. During the fourth game of the series, a power failure at Boston Garden halted play at 16:37 of the second period with the teams tied 3–3. Under NHL bylaws, the match was suspended, to be made up in its entirety only in the event that a seventh and deciding game was necessary.

Thus the series shifted back to Edmonton where the Oilers, still holding a 3–0 series lead, recorded a 6–3 victory to win the Cup. Wayne Gretzky was selected as the Conn Smythe Trophy winner for the second time in his career, establishing a Stanley Cup final series record of 13 points on three goals and ten assists.

CONN SMYTHE TROPHY
Wayne Gretzky - Center - Edmonton Oilers

DIVISION SEMI-FINALS

Apr.	6	Hartford	3	at Montreal	4
Apr.	7	Hartford	3	at Montreal	7
Apr.	9	Montreal	4	at Hartford	3
Apr.	10	Montreal	5	at Hartford	7
Apr.	12	Hartford	3	at Montreal	1
Apr.	14	Montreal	2	at Hartford	1

Montreal won best-of-seven series 4–2

Apr.	6	Buffalo	3	at Boston	7
Apr.	7	Buffalo	1	at Boston	4
Apr.	9	Boston	2	at Buffalo	6
Apr.	10	Boston	5	at Buffalo	6 OT
Apr.	12	Buffalo	4	at Boston	5
Apr.	14	Boston	5	at Buffalo	2

Boston won best-of-seven series 4–2

Apr.	6	New Jersey	3	at NY Islanders	4 OT
Apr.	7	New Jersey	3	at NY Islanders	2
Apr.	9	NY Islanders	0	at New Jersey	3
Apr.	10	NY Islanders	5	at New Jersey	4 OT
Apr.	12	New Jersey	4	at NY Islanders	2
Apr.	14	NY Islanders	5	at New Jersey	6

New Jersey won best-of-seven series 4–2

Apr.	6	Philadelphia	4	at Washington	2
Apr.	7	Philadelphia	4	at Washington	5
Apr.	9	Washington	3	at Philadelphia	4
Apr.	10	Washington	4	at Philadelphia	5 OT
Apr.	12	Philadelphia	2	at Washington	5
Apr.	14	Washington	7	at Philadelphia	2
Apr.	16	Philadelphia	4	at Washington	5 OT

Washington won best-of-seven series 4–3

Apr.	6	Toronto	6	at Detroit	2
Apr.	7	Toronto	2	at Detroit	6
Apr.	9	Detroit	6	at Toronto	3

Apr.	10	Detroit	8	at Toronto	0
Apr.	12	Toronto	6	at Detroit	5 OT
Apr.	14	Detroit	5	at Toronto	3

Detroit won best-of-seven series 4–2

Apr.	6	Chicago	1	at St. Louis	5
Apr.	7	Chicago	2	at St. Louis	3
Apr.	9	St. Louis	3	at Chicago	6
Apr.	10	St. Louis	6	at Chicago	5
Apr.	12	Chicago	3	at St. Louis	5

St. Louis won best-of-seven series 4–1

Apr.	6	Los Angeles	2	at Calgary	9
Apr.	7	Los Angeles	4	at Calgary	6
Apr.	9	Calgary	2	at Los Angeles	5
Apr.	10	Calgary	7	at Los Angeles	3
Apr.	12	Los Angeles	4	at Calgary	6

Calgary won best-of-seven series 4–1

Apr.	6	Winnipeg	4	at Edmonton	7
Apr.	7	Winnipeg	2	at Edmonton	3
Apr.	9	Edmonton	4	at Winnipeg	6
Apr.	10	Edmonton	5	at Winnipeg	3
Apr.	12	Winnipeg	2	at Edmonton	6

Edmonton won best-of-seven series 4–1

DIVISION FINALS

Apr.	18	Boston	2	at Montreal	5
Apr.	20	Boston	4	at Montreal	3
Apr.	22	Montreal	1	at Boston	3
Apr.	24	Montreal	0	at Boston	2
Apr.	26	Boston	4	at Montreal	1

Boston won best-of-seven series 4–1

Apr.	18	New Jersey	1	at Washington	3
Apr.	20	New Jersey	5	at Washington	3
Apr.	22	Washington	4	at New Jersey	10
Apr.	24	Washington	4	at New Jersey	1
Apr.	26	New Jersey	3	at Washington	1
Apr.	28	Washington	7	at New Jersey	2
Apr.	30	New Jersey	3	at Washington	2

New Jersey won best-of-seven series 4–3

Apr.	19	St. Louis	4	at Detroit	5
Apr.	21	St. Louis	0	at Detroit	6
Apr.	23	Detroit	3	at St. Louis	6
Apr.	25	Detroit	3	at St. Louis	1
Apr.	27	St. Louis	3	at Detroit	4

Detroit won best-of-seven series 4–1

Apr.	19	Edmonton	3	at Calgary	1
Apr.	21	Edmonton	5	at Calgary	4 OT
Apr.	23	Calgary	2	at Edmonton	4
Apr.	25	Calgary	4	at Edmonton	6

Edmonton won best-of-seven series 4–0

CONFERENCE FINALS

May	2	New Jersey	3	at Boston	5
May	4	New Jersey	3	at Boston	2 OT
May	6	Boston	6	at New Jersey	1
May	8	Boston	1	at New Jersey	3
May	10	New Jersey	1	at Boston	7
May	12	Boston	3	at New Jersey	6
May	14	New Jersey	2	at Boston	6

Boston won best-of-seven series 4–3

May	3	Detroit	1	at Edmonton	4
May	5	Detroit	3	at Edmonton	5
May	7	Edmonton	2	at Detroit	5
May	9	Edmonton	4	at Detroit	3 OT
May	11	Detroit	4	at Edmonton	8

Edmonton won best-of-seven series 4–1

FINALS

May	18	Boston	1	at Edmonton	2
May	20	Boston	2	at Edmonton	4
May	22	Edmonton	6	at Boston	3
May	24	Edmonton	3	at Boston	3 *
May	26	Boston	3	at Edmonton	6

* Game suspended at 16:37 of second period due to power failure.

Edmonton won best-of-seven series 4–0

1987-88 – Edmonton Oilers – Keith Acton, Glenn Anderson, Jeff Beukeboom, Geoff Courtnall, Grant Fuhr, Randy Gregg, Wayne Gretzky (Captain), Dave Hannan, Charlie Huddy, Mike Krushelnyski, Jari Kurri, Normand Lacombe, Kevin Lowe, Craig MacTavish, Kevin McClelland, Marty McSorley, Mark Messier, Craig Muni, Bill Ranford, Craig Simpson, Steve Smith, Esa Tikkanen, Peter Pocklington (Owner), Glen Sather (General Manager/Coach), John Muckler (Co-Coach), Ted Green (Assistant Coach), Bruce MacGregor (Assistant General Manager), Barry Fraser (Director of Player Personnel), Bill Tuele (Director of Public Relations), Dr. Gordon Cameron (Team Physician), Peter Millar (Athletic Therapist), Barrie Stafford (Trainer), Juergen Mers (Massage Therapist), Lyle Kulchisky (Assistant Trainer).

1987

After a year's absence, the Edmonton Oilers returned to the finals and captured their third Stanley Cup title in four seasons.

Edmonton and Philadelphia carried the championship series to a full seven games for the first time since the Montreal Canadiens — Chicago Black Hawks series in 1971. Philadelphia goaltender Ron Hextall received the Conn Smythe Trophy, joining Roger Crozier (1966 Detroit Red Wings), Glenn Hall (1968 St. Louis Blues) and Reggie Leach (1976 Philadelphia Flyers) as the only players on a losing club to be so honored.

CONN SMYTHE TROPHY
Ron Hextall - Goaltender - Philadelphia Flyers

DIVISION SEMI-FINALS

Apr.	8	Quebec	2	at Hartford	3 OT
Apr.	9	Quebec	4	at Hartford	5
Apr.	11	Hartford	1	at Quebec	5
Apr.	12	Hartford	1	at Quebec	4
Apr.	14	Quebec	7	at Hartford	5
Apr.	16	Hartford	4	at Quebec	5 OT

Quebec won best-of-seven series 4–2

Apr.	8	Boston	2	at Montreal	6
Apr.	9	Boston	3	at Montreal	4 OT
Apr.	11	Montreal	5	at Boston	4
Apr.	12	Montreal	4	at Boston	2

Montreal won best-of-seven series 4–0

Apr.	8	NY Rangers	3	at Philadelphia	0
Apr.	9	NY Rangers	3	at Philadelphia	8
Apr.	11	Philadelphia	3	at NY Rangers	0
Apr.	12	Philadelphia	3	at NY Rangers	6
Apr.	14	NY Rangers	1	at Philadelphia	3
Apr.	16	Philadelphia	5	at NY Rangers	0

Philadelphia won best-of-seven series 4–2

Apr.	8	NY Islanders	3	at Washington	4
Apr.	9	NY Islanders	3	at Washington	1
Apr.	11	Washington	2	at NY Islanders	1
Apr.	12	Washington	4	at NY Islanders	1
Apr.	14	NY Islanders	4	at Washington	2
Apr.	16	Washington	4	at NY Islanders	5
Apr.	18	NY Islanders	3	at Washington	2 4OT

NY Islanders won best-of-seven series 4–3

Apr.	8	Toronto	1	at St. Louis	3
Apr.	9	Toronto	3	at St. Louis	2 OT
Apr.	11	St. Louis	5	at Toronto	3
Apr.	12	St. Louis	1	at Toronto	2
Apr.	14	Toronto	2	at St. Louis	1
Apr.	16	St. Louis	0	at Toronto	4

Toronto won best-of-seven series 4–2

Apr.	8	Chicago	1	at Detroit	3
Apr.	9	Chicago	1	at Detroit	5
Apr.	11	Detroit	4	at Chicago	3 OT
Apr.	12	Detroit	3	at Chicago	1

Detroit won best-of-seven series 4–0

Apr.	8	Los Angeles	5	at Edmonton	2
Apr.	9	Los Angeles	3	at Edmonton	13
Apr.	11	Edmonton	6	at Los Angeles	5
Apr.	12	Edmonton	6	at Los Angeles	3
Apr.	14	Los Angeles	4	at Edmonton	5

Edmonton won best-of-seven series 4–1

Apr.	8	Winnipeg	4	at Calgary	2
Apr.	9	Winnipeg	3	at Calgary	2
Apr.	11	Calgary	3	at Winnipeg	2 OT
Apr.	12	Calgary	3	at Winnipeg	4
Apr.	14	Winnipeg	3	at Calgary	4
Apr.	16	Calgary	1	at Winnipeg	6

Winnipeg won best-of-seven series 4–2

DIVISION FINALS

Apr.	20	Quebec	7	at Montreal	5
Apr.	22	Quebec	2	at Montreal	1
Apr.	24	Montreal	7	at Quebec	2
Apr.	26	Montreal	3	at Quebec	2 OT
Apr.	28	Quebec	2	at Montreal	3
Apr.	30	Montreal	2	at Quebec	3
May	2	Quebec	3	at Montreal	5

Montreal won best-of-seven series 4–3

Apr.	20	NY Islanders	2	at Philadelphia	4
Apr.	22	NY Islanders	2	at Philadelphia	1
Apr.	24	Philadelphia	4	at NY Islanders	1
Apr.	26	Philadelphia	6	at NY Islanders	1
Apr.	28	NY Islanders	2	at Philadelphia	1
Apr.	30	Philadelphia	2	at NY Islanders	4
May	2	NY Islanders	1	at Philadelphia	5

Philadelphia won best-of-seven series 4–3

Apr.	21	Toronto	4	at Detroit	2
Apr.	23	Toronto	7	at Detroit	2
Apr.	25	Detroit	4	at Toronto	2
Apr.	27	Detroit	2	at Toronto	3 OT
Apr.	29	Toronto	0	at Detroit	3
May	1	Detroit	4	at Toronto	2
May	3	Toronto	0	at Detroit	3

Detroit won best-of-seven series 4–3

Apr.	21	Winnipeg	2	at Edmonton	3 OT
Apr.	23	Winnipeg	3	at Edmonton	5
Apr.	25	Edmonton	5	at Winnipeg	2
Apr.	27	Edmonton	4	at Winnipeg	2

Edmonton won best-of-seven series 4–0

CONFERENCE FINALS

May	4	Montreal	3	at Philadelphia	4 OT
May	6	Montreal	5	at Philadelphia	2
May	8	Philadelphia	4	at Montreal	3
May	10	Philadelphia	6	at Montreal	3
May	12	Montreal	5	at Philadelphia	2
May	14	Philadelphia	4	at Montreal	3

Philadelphia won best-of-seven series 4–2

May	5	Detroit	3	at Edmonton	1
May	7	Detroit	1	at Edmonton	4
May	9	Edmonton	2	at Detroit	1
May	11	Edmonton	3	at Detroit	2
May	13	Detroit	3	at Edmonton	6

Edmonton won best-of-seven series 4–1

FINALS

May	17	Philadelphia	2	at Edmonton	4
May	20	Philadelphia	2	at Edmonton	3 OT
May	22	Edmonton	3	at Philadelphia	5
May	24	Edmonton	4	at Philadelphia	1
May	26	Philadelphia	4	at Edmonton	3
May	28	Edmonton	2	at Philadelphia	3
May	31	Philadelphia	1	at Edmonton	3

Edmonton won best-of-seven series 4–3

1986-87 – Edmonton Oilers – Glenn Anderson, Jeff Beukeboom, Kelly Buchberger, Paul Coffey, Grant Fuhr, Randy Gregg, Wayne Gretzky (Captain), Charlie Huddy, Dave Hunter, Mike Krushelnyski, Jari Kurri, Moe Lemay, Kevin Lowe, Craig MacTavish, Kevin McClelland, Marty McSorley, Mark Messier, Andy Moog, Craig Muni, Kent Nilsson, Jaroslav Pouzar,

Reijo Ruotsalainen, Steve Smith, Esa Tikkanen, Peter Pocklington (Owner), Glen Sather (General Manager/Coach), John Muckler (Co-Coach), Ted Green, Ron Low (Assistant Coaches), Bruce MacGregor (Assistant General Manager), Barry Fraser (Director of Player Personnel), Peter Millar (Athletic Therapist), Barrie Stafford (Trainer), Lyle Kulchisky (Assistant Trainer).

1986

The Montreal Canadiens set a new professional record for championships, winning their 23rd Stanley Cup title. Montreal had been tied with the New York Yankees, who had amassed 22 World Series titles through this point in their history. The series between the Canadiens and the Calgary Flames marked the first all-Canadian final since Montreal and Toronto faced each other in 1967.

Brian Skrudland scored nine seconds into overtime in game two to set a new record for the fastest overtime goal in playoff history, eclipsing the old mark of 11 seconds set by J.P. Parise of the NY Islanders on April 11, 1975.

Twenty-year-old goaltender Patrick Roy became the youngest player to earn the Conn Smythe Trophy in the 22-year history of the award. Roy posted a record-tying 15 playoff wins (15–5) and a 1.92 average in 20 postseason games.

CONN SMYTHE TROPHY
Patrick Roy - Goaltender - Montreal Canadiens

DIVISION SEMI-FINALS

Apr.	9	Hartford	3	at Quebec	2 OT
Apr.	10	Hartford	4	at Quebec	1
Apr.	12	Quebec	4	at Hartford	9

Hartford won best-of-five series 3–0

Apr.	9	Boston	1	at Montreal	3
Apr.	10	Boston	2	at Montreal	3
Apr.	12	Montreal	4	at Boston	3

Montreal won best-of-five series 3–0

Apr.	9	NY Rangers	6	at Philadelphia	2
Apr.	10	NY Rangers	1	at Philadelphia	2
Apr.	12	Philadelphia	2	at NY Rangers	5
Apr.	13	Philadelphia	7	at NY Rangers	1
Apr.	15	NY Rangers	5	at Philadelphia	2

NY Rangers won best-of-five series 3–2

Apr.	9	NY Islanders	1	at Washington	3
Apr.	10	NY Islanders	2	at Washington	5
Apr.	12	Washington	3	at NY Islanders	1

Washington won best-of-five series 3–0

Apr.	9	Toronto	5	at Chicago	3
Apr.	10	Toronto	6	at Chicago	4
Apr.	12	Chicago	2	at Toronto	7

Toronto won best-of-five series 3–0

Apr.	9	St. Louis	2	at Minnesota	1
Apr.	10	St. Louis	2	at Minnesota	6
Apr.	12	Minnesota	3	at St. Louis	4
Apr.	13	Minnesota	7	at St. Louis	4
Apr.	15	St. Louis	6	at Minnesota	3

St. Louis won best-of-five series 3–2

Apr.	9	Vancouver	3	at Edmonton	7
Apr.	10	Vancouver	1	at Edmonton	5
Apr.	12	Edmonton	5	at Vancouver	1

Edmonton won best-of-five series 3–0

Apr.	9	Winnipeg	1	at Calgary	5
Apr.	10	Winnipeg	4	at Calgary	6
Apr.	12	Calgary	4	at Winnipeg	3 OT

Calgary won best-of-five series 3–0

DIVISION FINALS

Apr.	17	Hartford	4	at Montreal	1
Apr.	19	Hartford	1	at Montreal	3
Apr.	21	Montreal	4	at Hartford	1
Apr.	23	Montreal	1	at Hartford	2 OT
Apr.	25	Hartford	3	at Montreal	5
Apr.	27	Montreal	0	at Hartford	1
Apr.	29	Hartford	1	at Montreal	2 OT

Montreal won best-of-seven series 4–3

Apr.	17	NY Rangers	4	at Washington	3 OT
Apr.	19	NY Rangers	1	at Washington	8
Apr.	21	Washington	6	at NY Rangers	3
Apr.	23	Washington	5	at NY Rangers	6 OT
Apr.	25	NY Rangers	4	at Washington	2
Apr.	27	Washington	1	at NY Rangers	2

NY Rangers won best-of-seven series 4–2

Apr.	18	Toronto	1	at St. Louis	6
Apr.	20	Toronto	3	at St. Louis	0
Apr.	22	St. Louis	2	at Toronto	5
Apr.	24	St. Louis	7	at Toronto	4
Apr.	26	Toronto	3	at St. Louis	4 OT
Apr.	28	St. Louis	3	at Toronto	5
Apr.	30	Toronto	1	at St. Louis	2

St. Louis won best-of-seven series 4–3

Apr.	18	Calgary	4	at Edmonton	1
Apr.	20	Calgary	5	at Edmonton	6 OT
Apr.	22	Edmonton	2	at Calgary	3
Apr.	24	Edmonton	7	at Calgary	4
Apr.	26	Calgary	4	at Edmonton	1
Apr.	28	Edmonton	5	at Calgary	2
Apr.	30	Calgary	3	at Edmonton	2

Calgary won best-of-seven series 4–3

CONFERENCE FINALS

May	1	NY Rangers	1	at Montreal	2
May	3	NY Rangers	2	at Montreal	6
May	5	Montreal	4	at NY Rangers	3 OT
May	7	Montreal	0	at NY Rangers	2
May	9	NY Rangers	1	at Montreal	3

Montreal won best-of-seven series 4–1

May	2	St. Louis	3	at Calgary	2
May	4	St. Louis	2	at Calgary	8
May	6	Calgary	5	at St. Louis	3
May	8	Calgary	2	at St. Louis	5
May	10	St. Louis	2	at Calgary	4
May	12	Calgary	5	at St. Louis	6 OT
May	14	St. Louis	1	at Calgary	2

Calgary won best-of-seven series 4–3

FINALS

May	16	Montreal	2	at Calgary	5
May	18	Montreal	3	at Calgary	2 OT
May	20	Calgary	3	at Montreal	5
May	22	Calgary	0	at Montreal	1
May	24	Montreal	4	at Calgary	3

Montreal won best-of-seven series 4–1

1985-86 – Montreal Canadiens – Bob Gainey (Captain), Doug Soetaert, Patrick Roy, Rick Green, David Maley, Ryan Walter, Serge Boisvert, Mario Tremblay, Bobby Smith, Craig Ludwig, Tom Kurvers, Kjell Dahlin, Larry Robinson, Guy Carbonneau, Chris Chelios, Petr Svoboda, Mats Naslund, Lucien DeBlois, Steve Rooney, Gaston Gingras, Mike Lalor, Chris Nilan, John Kordic, Claude Lemieux, Mike McPhee, Brian Skrudland, Stephane Richer, Ronald Corey (President), Serge Savard (General Manager), Jean Perron (Coach), Jacques Laperrière (Assistant Coach), Jean Béliveau, Francois-Xavier Seigneur, Fred Steer (Vice Presidents), Jacques Lemaire, André Boudrias (Assistant General Managers), Claude Ruel (Scout), Yves Belanger (Athletic Therapist), Gaetan Lefebvre (Assistant Athletic Therapist), Eddy Palchak (Trainer), Sylvain Toupin (Assistant Trainer).

1985

In the 1985 playoffs, Wayne Gretzky set new records for assists (30) and points (47) in one playoff year. Gretzky also tied the modern record shared by Montreal's Jean Beliveau (1956) and Mike Bossy (1982) for most goals in the Stanley Cup Finals with seven in five games. Jari Kurri scored 19 goals in 18 games to tie the record (Reggie Leach in 1976) for goals in one playoff year. Kurri also broke teammate Mark Messier's record for most hat tricks in a playoff year with four, including one four-goal game. Paul Coffey, who registered 12 goals and 25 assists in 18 games, shattered the one-year playoff records for goals, assists and points by a defenseman. Coffey broke Boston Bruin Bobby Orr's records for goals (nine in 1970) and assists (19 in 1972), and New York Islander Denis Potvin's record for points (25 in 1981). Edmonton's Grant Fuhr tied New York Islanders' goaltender Billy Smith for most wins, 15, in a playoff year. Fuhr posted a 15–3 record in 18 games. Smith amassed 15 wins in both 1980 and 1982. For the first time in the finals, two penalty shots were awarded in the same series. Both were stopped by Fuhr.

CONN SMYTHE TROPHY
Wayne Gretzky - Center - Edmonton Oilers

DIVISION SEMI-FINALS

Apr.	10	Boston	5	at	Montreal	3
Apr.	11	Boston	3	at	Montreal	5
Apr.	13	Montreal	4	at	Boston	2
Apr.	14	Montreal	6	at	Boston	7
Apr.	16	Boston	0	at	Montreal	1

Montreal won best-of-five series 3–2

Apr.	10	Buffalo	2	at	Quebec	5
Apr.	11	Buffalo	2	at	Quebec	3
Apr.	13	Quebec	4	at	Buffalo	6
Apr.	14	Quebec	4	at	Buffalo	7
Apr.	16	Buffalo	5	at	Quebec	6

Quebec won best-of-five series 3–2

Apr.	10	NY Rangers	4	at	Philadelphia	5 OT
Apr.	11	NY Rangers	1	at	Philadelphia	3
Apr.	13	Philadelphia	6	at	NY Rangers	5

Philadelphia won best-of-five series 3–0

Apr.	10	NY Islanders	3	at	Washington	4 OT
Apr.	11	NY Islanders	1	at	Washington	2 2OT
Apr.	13	Washington	1	at	NY Islanders	2
Apr.	14	Washington	4	at	NY Islanders	6
Apr.	16	NY Islanders	2	at	Washington	1

NY Islanders won best-of-five series 3–2

Apr.	10	Minnesota	3	at	St. Louis	2
Apr.	11	Minnesota	4	at	St. Louis	3
Apr.	13	St. Louis	0	at	Minnesota	2

Minnesota won best-of-five series 3–0

Apr.	10	Detroit	5	at	Chicago	9
Apr.	11	Detroit	1	at	Chicago	6
Apr.	13	Chicago	8	at	Detroit	2

Chicago won best-of-five series 3–0

Apr.	10	Los Angeles	2	at	Edmonton	3 OT
Apr.	11	Los Angeles	2	at	Edmonton	4
Apr.	13	Edmonton	4	at	Los Angeles	3 OT

Edmonton won best-of-five series 3–0

Apr.	10	Calgary	4	at	Winnipeg	5 OT
Apr.	11	Calgary	2	at	Winnipeg	5
Apr.	13	Winnipeg	0	at	Calgary	4
Apr.	14	Winnipeg	5	at	Calgary	3

Winnipeg won best-of-five series 3–1

DIVISION FINALS

Apr.	18	Quebec	2	at	Montreal	1 OT
Apr.	21	Quebec	4	at	Montreal	6
Apr.	23	Montreal	6	at	Quebec	7 OT
Apr.	25	Montreal	3	at	Quebec	1

Apr.	27	Quebec	5	at	Montreal	1
Apr.	30	Montreal	5	at	Quebec	2
May	2	Quebec	3	at	Montreal	2 OT

Quebec won best-of-seven series 4–3

Apr.	18	NY Islanders	0	at	Philadelphia	3
Apr.	21	NY Islanders	2	at	Philadelphia	5
Apr.	23	Philadelphia	5	at	NY Islanders	3
Apr.	25	Philadelphia	2	at	NY Islanders	6
Apr.	28	NY Islanders	0	at	Philadelphia	1

Philadelphia won best-of-seven series 4–1

Apr.	18	Minnesota	8	at	Chicago	5
Apr.	21	Minnesota	2	at	Chicago	6
Apr.	23	Chicago	5	at	Minnesota	3
Apr.	25	Chicago	7	at	Minnesota	6 2OT
Apr.	28	Minnesota	5	at	Chicago	4 OT
Apr.	30	Chicago	6	at	Minnesota	5 OT

Chicago won best-of-seven series 4–2

Apr.	18	Winnipeg	2	at	Edmonton	4
Apr.	20	Winnipeg	2	at	Edmonton	5
Apr.	23	Edmonton	5	at	Winnipeg	4
Apr.	25	Edmonton	8	at	Winnipeg	3

Edmonton won best-of-seven series 4–0

CONFERENCE FINALS

May	5	Philadelphia	1	at	Quebec	2 OT
May	7	Philadelphia	4	at	Quebec	2
May	9	Quebec	2	at	Philadelphia	4
May	12	Quebec	5	at	Philadelphia	3
May	14	Philadelphia	2	at	Quebec	1
May	16	Quebec	0	at	Philadelphia	3

Philadelphia won best-of-seven series 4–2

May	4	Chicago	2	at	Edmonton	11
May	7	Chicago	3	at	Edmonton	7
May	9	Edmonton	2	at	Chicago	5
May	12	Edmonton	6	at	Chicago	8
May	14	Chicago	5	at	Edmonton	10
May	16	Edmonton	8	at	Chicago	2

Edmonton won best-of-seven series 4–2

FINALS

May	21	Edmonton	1	at	Philadelphia	4
May	23	Edmonton	3	at	Philadelphia	1
May	25	Philadelphia	3	at	Edmonton	4
May	28	Philadelphia	3	at	Edmonton	5
May	30	Philadelphia	3	at	Edmonton	8

Edmonton won best-of-seven series 4–1

1984-85 – Edmonton Oilers – Glenn Anderson, Billy Carroll, Paul Coffey, Lee Fogolin, Jr., Grant Fuhr, Randy Gregg, Wayne Gretzky (Captain), Charlie Huddy, Pat Hughes, Dave Hunter, Don Jackson, Mike Krushelnyski, Jari Kurri, Willy Lindstrom, Kevin Lowe, Dave Lumley, Kevin McClelland, Larry Melnyk, Mark Messier, Andy Moog, Mark Napier, Jaroslav Pouzar, Dave Semenko, Esa Tikkanen, Peter Pocklington (Owner), Glen Sather (General Manager/Coach), John Muckler, Ted Green (Assistant Coaches), Bruce MacGregor (Assistant General Manager), Barry Fraser (Director of Player Personnel/Chief Scout), Peter Millar (Athletic Therapist), Barrie Stafford, Lyle Kulchisky (Trainers).

1984

The Edmonton Oilers, who joined the NHL in 1979–80 with the Hartford Whalers, Quebec Nordiques and Winnipeg Jets, became the first of the four former World Hockey Association clubs to win the Stanley Cup.

In his first championship game, Oilers' goalie Grant Fuhr posted a shutout to hand the defending champion New York Islanders their first loss in 10 final series games.

Four different Oilers — Kevin McClelland, Glenn Anderson, Mark Messier and Ken Linseman — scored game-winning goals.

Messier won the Conn Smythe Trophy and also

had eight goals and 18 assists for 26 points in 19 games.

CONN SMYTHE TROPHY
Mark Messier - Center - Edmonton Oilers

DIVISION SEMI-FINALS

Apr.	4	Montreal	2	at	Boston	1
Apr.	5	Montreal	3	at	Boston	1
Apr.	7	Boston	0	at	Montreal	5

Montreal won best-of-five series 3–0

Apr.	4	Quebec	3	at	Buffalo	2
Apr.	5	Quebec	6	at	Buffalo	2
Apr.	7	Buffalo	1	at	Quebec	4

Quebec won best-of-five series 3–0

Apr.	4	NY Rangers	1	at	NY Islanders	4
Apr.	5	NY Rangers	3	at	NY Islanders	0
Apr.	7	NY Islanders	2	at	NY Rangers	7
Apr.	8	NY Islanders	4	at	NY Rangers	1
Apr.	10	NY Rangers	2	at	NY Islanders	3 OT

NY Islanders won best-of-five series 3–2

Apr.	4	Philadelphia	4	at	Washington	4
Apr.	5	Philadelphia	2	at	Washington	6
Apr.	7	Washington	5	at	Philadelphia	1

Washington won best-of-five series 3–0

Apr.	4	Chicago	3	at	Minnesota	1
Apr.	5	Chicago	5	at	Minnesota	6
Apr.	7	Minnesota	4	at	Chicago	1
Apr.	8	Minnesota	3	at	Chicago	4
Apr.	10	Chicago	1	at	Minnesota	4

Minnesota won best-of-five series 3–2

Apr.	4	Detroit	2	at	St. Louis	3
Apr.	5	Detroit	5	at	St. Louis	3
Apr.	7	St. Louis	4	at	Detroit	3 2OT
Apr.	8	St. Louis	3	at	Detroit	2 OT

St. Louis won best-of-five series 3–1

Apr.	4	Winnipeg	2	at	Edmonton	9
Apr.	5	Winnipeg	4	at	Edmonton	5 OT
Apr.	7	Edmonton	4	at	Winnipeg	1

Edmonton won best-of-five series 3–0

Apr.	4	Vancouver	3	at	Calgary	5
Apr.	5	Vancouver	2	at	Calgary	4
Apr.	7	Calgary	0	at	Vancouver	7
Apr.	8	Calgary	5	at	Vancouver	1

Calgary won best-of-five series 3–1

DIVISION FINALS

Apr.	12	Montreal	2	at	Quebec	4
Apr.	13	Montreal	4	at	Quebec	1
Apr.	15	Quebec	1	at	Montreal	2
Apr.	16	Quebec	4	at	Montreal	3 OT
Apr.	18	Montreal	4	at	Quebec	0
Apr.	20	Quebec	3	at	Montreal	5

Montreal won best-of-seven series 4–2

Apr.	12	Washington	3	at	NY Islanders	2
Apr.	13	Washington	4	at	NY Islanders	5 OT
Apr.	15	NY Islanders	3	at	Washington	1
Apr.	16	NY Islanders	5	at	Washington	2
Apr.	18	Washington	3	at	NY Islanders	5

NY Islanders won best-of-seven series 4–1

Apr.	12	St. Louis	1	at	Minnesota	2
Apr.	13	St. Louis	4	at	Minnesota	3 OT
Apr.	15	Minnesota	1	at	St. Louis	3
Apr.	16	Minnesota	3	at	St. Louis	2
Apr.	18	St. Louis	0	at	Minnesota	6
Apr.	20	Minnesota	0	at	St. Louis	4
Apr.	22	St. Louis	3	at	Minnesota	4 OT

Minnesota won best-of-seven series 4–3

Apr.	12	Calgary	2	at	Edmonton	5
Apr.	13	Calgary	6	at	Edmonton	5 OT
Apr.	15	Edmonton	3	at	Calgary	2
Apr.	16	Edmonton	5	at	Calgary	3
Apr.	18	Calgary	5	at	Edmonton	4
Apr.	20	Edmonton	4	at	Calgary	5 OT

Apr.	22	Calgary	4	at	Edmonton	7

Edmonton won best-of-seven series 4–3

CONFERENCE FINALS

Apr.	24	NY Islanders	0	at	Montreal	3
Apr.	26	NY Islanders	2	at	Montreal	4
Apr.	28	Montreal	2	at	NY Islanders	5
May	1	Montreal	1	at	NY Islanders	3
May	3	NY Islanders	3	at	Montreal	1
May	5	Montreal	1	at	NY Islanders	4

NY Islanders won best-of-seven series 4–2

Apr.	24	Minnesota	1	at	Edmonton	7
Apr.	26	Minnesota	3	at	Edmonton	4
Apr.	28	Edmonton	8	at	Minnesota	5
May	1	Edmonton	3	at	Minnesota	1

Edmonton won best-of-seven series 4–0

FINALS

May	10	Edmonton	1	at	NY Islanders	0
May	12	Edmonton	1	at	NY Islanders	6
May	15	NY Islanders	2	at	Edmonton	7
May	17	NY Islanders	2	at	Edmonton	7
May	19	NY Islanders	2	at	Edmonton	5

Edmonton won best-of-seven series 4–1

1983-84 – Edmonton Oilers – Glenn Anderson, Paul Coffey, Pat Conacher, Lee Fogolin, Jr., Grant Fuhr, Randy Gregg, Wayne Gretzky (Captain), Charlie Huddy, Pat Hughes, Dave Hunter, Don Jackson, Jari Kurri, Willy Lindstrom, Ken Linseman, Kevin Lowe, Dave Lumley, Kevin McClelland, Mark Messier, Andy Moog, Jaroslav Pouzar, Dave Semenko, Peter Pocklington (Owner), Glen Sather (General Manager/Coach), John Muckler, Ted Green (Assistant Coaches), Bruce MacGregor (Assistant General Manager), Barry Fraser (Director of Player Personnel/Chief Scout), Peter Millar (Athletic Therapist), Barrie Stafford (Trainer).

1983

The New York Islanders won their fourth straight Stanley Cup title to become only the second NHL franchise in history to amass that many championships in a row. The Montreal Canadiens own the all-time record with five consecutive Cup wins from 1956 to 1960. The Canadiens also won four in a row between 1976 and 1979.

Goaltender Billy Smith won the Conn Smythe Trophy after limiting the Edmonton Oilers to just six goals in four games and shutting out the Campbell Conference champions in seven of 12 periods of play.

In his first appearance in the finals, Wayne Gretzky tallied four assists on the Oilers' six goals.

CONN SMYTHE TROPHY
Billy Smith - Goaltender - New York Islanders

DIVISION SEMI-FINALS

Apr.	5	Quebec	3	at	Boston	4	OT
Apr.	7	Quebec	2	at	Boston	4	
Apr.	9	Boston	1	at	Quebec	2	
Apr.	10	Boston	2	at	Quebec	1	

Boston won best-of-five series 3–1

Apr.	6	Buffalo	1	at	Montreal	0
Apr.	7	Buffalo	3	at	Montreal	0
Apr.	9	Montreal	2	at	Buffalo	4

Buffalo won best-of-five series 3–0

Apr.	5	NY Rangers	5	at	Philadelphia	3
Apr.	7	NY Rangers	4	at	Philadelphia	3
Apr.	9	Philadelphia	3	at	NY Rangers	9

NY Rangers won best-of-five series 3–0

Apr.	6	Washington	2	at	NY Islanders	5
Apr.	7	Washington	4	at	NY Islanders	2
Apr.	9	NY Islanders	6	at	Washington	2
Apr.	10	NY Islanders	6	at	Washington	3

NY Islanders won best-of-five series 3–1

Apr.	6	St. Louis	4	at	Chicago	2
Apr.	7	St. Louis	2	at	Chicago	7
Apr.	9	Chicago	2	at	St. Louis	1
Apr.	10	Chicago	5	at	St. Louis	3

Chicago won best-of-five series 3–1

Apr.	6	Toronto	4	at	Minnesota	5	
Apr.	7	Toronto	4	at	Minnesota	5	OT
Apr.	9	Minnesota	3	at	Toronto	6	
Apr.	10	Minnesota	5	at	Toronto	4	OT

Minnesota won best-of-five series 3–1

Apr.	6	Winnipeg	3	at	Edmonton	6
Apr.	7	Winnipeg	3	at	Edmonton	4
Apr.	9	Edmonton	4	at	Winnipeg	3

Edmonton won best-of-five series 3–0

Apr.	6	Vancouver	3	at	Calgary	4	OT
Apr.	7	Vancouver	3	at	Calgary	5	
Apr.	9	Calgary	4	at	Vancouver	5	
Apr.	10	Calgary	4	at	Vancouver	3	OT

Calgary won best-of-five series 3–1

DIVISION FINALS

Apr.	14	Buffalo	7	at	Boston	4	
Apr.	15	Buffalo	3	at	Boston	5	
Apr.	17	Boston	3	at	Buffalo	4	
Apr.	18	Boston	6	at	Buffalo	2	
Apr.	20	Buffalo	0	at	Boston	9	
Apr.	22	Boston	3	at	Buffalo	5	
Apr.	24	Buffalo	2	at	Boston	3	OT

Boston won best-of-seven series 4–3

Apr.	14	NY Rangers	1	at	NY Islanders	4
Apr.	15	NY Rangers	0	at	NY Islanders	5
Apr.	17	NY Islanders	6	at	NY Rangers	7
Apr.	18	NY Islanders	1	at	NY Rangers	3
Apr.	20	NY Rangers	2	at	NY Islanders	7
Apr.	22	NY Islanders	5	at	NY Rangers	2

NY Islanders won best-of-seven series 4–2

Apr.	14	Minnesota	2	at	Chicago	5	
Apr.	15	Minnesota	4	at	Chicago	7	
Apr.	17	Chicago	1	at	Minnesota	5	
Apr.	18	Chicago	4	at	Minnesota	3	OT
Apr.	20	Minnesota	2	at	Chicago	5	

Chicago won best-of-seven series 4–1

Apr.	14	Calgary	3	at	Edmonton	6
Apr.	15	Calgary	1	at	Edmonton	5
Apr.	17	Edmonton	10	at	Calgary	2
Apr.	18	Edmonton	5	at	Calgary	6
Apr.	20	Calgary	1	at	Edmonton	9

Edmonton won best-of-seven series 4–1

CONFERENCE FINALS

Apr.	26	NY Islanders	5	at	Boston	2
Apr.	28	NY Islanders	1	at	Boston	4
Apr.	30	Boston	3	at	NY Islanders	7
May	3	Boston	3	at	NY Islanders	8
May	5	NY Islanders	1	at	Boston	5
May	7	Boston	4	at	NY Islanders	8

NY Islanders won best-of-seven series 4–2

Apr.	24	Chicago	4	at	Edmonton	8
Apr.	26	Chicago	2	at	Edmonton	8
May	1	Edmonton	3	at	Chicago	2
May	3	Edmonton	6	at	Chicago	3

Edmonton won best-of-seven series 4–0

FINALS

May	10	NY Islanders	2	at	Edmonton	0
May	12	NY Islanders	6	at	Edmonton	3
May	14	Edmonton	1	at	NY Islanders	5
May	17	Edmonton	2	at	NY Islanders	4

NY Islanders won best-of-seven series 4–0

1982-83 – New York Islanders – Mike Bossy, Bob Bourne, Paul Boutilier, Billy Carroll, Greg Gilbert, Clark Gillies, Butch Goring, Mats Hallin, Tomas Jonsson, Anders Kallur, Gord Lane, Dave Langevin, Mike McEwen, Roland Melanson, Wayne Merrick, Ken Morrow, Bob Nystrom, Stefan Persson, Denis Potvin (Captain), Billy Smith, Brent Sutter, Duane Sutter, John

Tonelli, Bryan Trottier, Al Arbour (Coach), Lorne Henning (Assistant Coach), Bill Torrey (General Manager), Ron Waske, Jim Pickard (Trainers).

1982

The New York Islanders distinguished themselves as the first U.S.-based team in history to win three consecutive Stanley Cup championships with a sweep of the Vancouver Canucks.

The Canucks, meanwhile, became the first Vancouver team since the 1924 Maroons of the Western Canada Hockey League to appear in the Stanley Cup finals.

Mike Bossy won the Conn Smythe Trophy after scoring seven goals in the four-game series, tying the modern record for most goals in the finals set by Jean Beliveau in 1956.

Bryan Trottier tallied 23 playoff assists in 19 games to set a new record, while goalie Billy Smith amassed a 15–4–0 mark to equal his own record for playoff wins.

CONN SMYTHE TROPHY
Mike Bossy - Right Wing - New York Islanders

DIVISION SEMI-FINALS

Apr.	7	Quebec	1	at	Montreal	5	
Apr.	8	Quebec	3	at	Montreal	2	
Apr.	10	Montreal	1	at	Quebec	2	
Apr.	11	Montreal	6	at	Quebec	2	
Apr.	13	Quebec	3	at	Montreal	2	OT

Quebec won best-of-five series 3–2

Apr.	7	Buffalo	1	at	Boston	3
Apr.	8	Buffalo	3	at	Boston	7
Apr.	10	Boston	2	at	Buffalo	5
Apr.	11	Boston	5	at	Buffalo	2

Boston won best-of-five series 3–1

Apr.	7	Chicago	3	at	Minnesota	2	OT
Apr.	8	Chicago	5	at	Minnesota	3	
Apr.	10	Minnesota	7	at	Chicago	1	
Apr.	11	Minnesota	2	at	Chicago	5	

Chicago won best-of-five series 3–1

Apr.	7	St. Louis	4	at	Winnipeg	3
Apr.	8	St. Louis	2	at	Winnipeg	5
Apr.	10	Winnipeg	3	at	St. Louis	6
Apr.	11	Winnipeg	2	at	St. Louis	8

St. Louis won best-of-five series 3–1

Apr.	7	Pittsburgh	1	at	NY Islanders	8	
Apr.	8	Pittsburgh	2	at	NY Islanders	7	
Apr.	10	NY Islanders	1	at	Pittsburgh	2	OT
Apr.	11	NY Islanders	2	at	Pittsburgh	5	
Apr.	13	Pittsburgh	3	at	NY Islanders	4	OT

NY Islanders won best-of-five series 3–2

Apr.	7	Philadelphia	4	at	NY Rangers	1
Apr.	8	Philadelphia	3	at	NY Rangers	7
Apr.	10	NY Rangers	4	at	Philadelphia	3
Apr.	11	NY Rangers	7	at	Philadelphia	5

NY Rangers won best-of-five series 3–1

Apr.	7	Los Angeles	10	at	Edmonton	8	
Apr.	8	Los Angeles	2	at	Edmonton	3	OT
Apr.	10	Edmonton	5	at	Los Angeles	6	OT
Apr.	12	Edmonton	3	at	Los Angeles	2	
Apr.	13	Los Angeles	7	at	Edmonton	4	

Los Angeles won best-of-five series 3–2

Apr.	7	Calgary	3	at	Vancouver	5	
Apr.	8	Calgary	1	at	Vancouver	2	OT
Apr.	10	Vancouver	3	at	Calgary	1	

Vancouver won best-of-five series 3–0

DIVISION FINALS

Apr.	15	Quebec	3	at	Boston	4	
Apr.	16	Quebec	4	at	Boston	8	
Apr.	18	Boston	2	at	Quebec	3	OT
Apr.	19	Boston	2	at	Quebec	7	

Apr.	21	Quebec	4	at	Boston	3
Apr.	23	Boston	6	at	Quebec	5 OT
Apr.	25	Quebec	2	at	Boston	1

Quebec won best-of-seven series 4–3

Apr.	15	Chicago	5	at	St. Louis	4
Apr.	16	Chicago	1	at	St. Louis	3
Apr.	18	St. Louis	5	at	Chicago	6
Apr.	19	St. Louis	4	at	Chicago	7
Apr.	21	Chicago	2	at	St. Louis	3 OT
Apr.	23	St. Louis	0	at	Chicago	2

Chicago won best-of-seven series 4–2

Apr.	15	NY Rangers	5	at	NY Islanders	4
Apr.	16	NY Rangers	2	at	NY Islanders	7
Apr.	18	NY Islanders	4	at	NY Rangers	3 OT
Apr.	19	NY Islanders	5	at	NY Rangers	3
Apr.	21	NY Rangers	4	at	NY Islanders	2
Apr.	23	NY Islanders	5	at	NY Rangers	3

NY Islanders won best-of-seven series 4–2

Apr.	15	Los Angeles	2	at	Vancouver	3
Apr.	16	Los Angeles	3	at	Vancouver	2 OT
Apr.	18	Vancouver	4	at	Los Angeles	3 OT
Apr.	19	Vancouver	5	at	Los Angeles	4
Apr.	21	Los Angeles	2	at	Vancouver	5

Vancouver won best-of-seven series 4–1

CONFERENCE FINALS

Apr.	27	Quebec	1	at	NY Islanders	4
Apr.	29	Quebec	2	at	NY Islanders	5
May	1	NY Islanders	5	at	Quebec	4 OT
May	4	NY Islanders	4	at	Quebec	2

NY Islanders won best-of-seven series 4–0

Apr.	27	Vancouver	2	at	Chicago	1 2OT
Apr.	29	Vancouver	1	at	Chicago	4
May	1	Chicago	3	at	Vancouver	4
May	4	Chicago	3	at	Vancouver	5
May	6	Vancouver	6	at	Chicago	2

Vancouver won best-of-seven series 4–1

FINALS

May	8	Vancouver	5	at	NY Islanders	6 OT
May	11	Vancouver	4	at	NY Islanders	6
May	13	NY Islanders	3	at	Vancouver	0
May	16	NY Islanders	3	at	Vancouver	1

NY Islanders won best-of-seven series 4–0

1981-82 – New York Islanders – Mike Bossy, Bob Bourne, Billy Carroll, Butch Goring, Greg Gilbert, Clark Gillies, Tomas Jonsson, Anders Kallur, Gord Lane, Dave Langevin, Hector Marini, Mike McEwen, Roland Melanson, Wayne Merrick, Ken Morrow, Bob Nystrom, Stefan Persson, Denis Potvin (Captain), Billy Smith, Brent Sutter, Duane Sutter, John Tonelli, Bryan Trottier, Al Arbour (Coach), Lorne Henning (Assisant Coach), Bill Torrey (General Manager), Jim Devellano (Assistant General Manager/Director of Scouting), Ron Waske, Jim Pickard (Trainers).

1981

The New York Islanders captured a second consecutive Stanley Cup championship, needing five games to defeat the Minnesota North Stars. For Minnesota, it marked the club's first trip to the finals since joining the NHL in 1967–68.

With 17 goals and 18 assists, New York's Mike Bossy established new playoff records for points (35) and power-play goals (nine) in his 18 post-season outings.

Dino Ciccarelli of Minnesota broke Don Maloney's rookie scoring record with 21 playoff points and Steve Christoff's rookie mark for play-off goals with 14.

CONN SMYTHE TROPHY
Butch Goring - Center - New York Islanders

PRELIMINARY ROUND

Apr.	8	Toronto	2	at	NY Islanders	9
Apr.	9	Toronto	1	at	NY Islanders	5
Apr.	11	NY Islanders	6	at	Toronto	1

NY Islanders won best-of-five series 3–0

Apr.	8	Pittsburgh	2	at	St. Louis	4
Apr.	9	Pittsburgh	6	at	St. Louis	4
Apr.	11	St. Louis	5	at	Pittsburgh	4
Apr.	12	St. Louis	3	at	Pittsburgh	6
Apr.	14	Pittsburgh	3	at	St. Louis	4 2OT

St. Louis won best-of-five series 3–2

Apr.	8	Edmonton	6	at	Montreal	3
Apr.	9	Edmonton	3	at	Montreal	1
Apr.	11	Montreal	2	at	Edmonton	6

Edmonton won best-of-five series 3–0

Apr.	8	NY Rangers	3	at	Los Angeles	1
Apr.	9	NY Rangers	4	at	Los Angeles	5
Apr.	11	Los Angeles	3	at	NY Rangers	10
Apr.	12	Los Angeles	3	at	NY Rangers	6

NY Rangers won best-of-five series 3–1

Apr.	8	Vancouver	2	at	Buffalo	3 OT
Apr.	9	Vancouver	2	at	Buffalo	5
Apr.	11	Buffalo	5	at	Vancouver	3

Buffalo won best-of-five series 3–0

Apr.	8	Quebec	4	at	Philadelphia	6
Apr.	9	Quebec	5	at	Philadelphia	8
Apr.	11	Philadelphia	0	at	Quebec	2
Apr.	12	Philadelphia	3	at	Quebec	4 OT
Apr.	14	Quebec	2	at	Philadelphia	5

Philadelphia won best-of-five series 3–2

Apr.	8	Chicago	3	at	Calgary	4
Apr.	9	Chicago	2	at	Calgary	6
Apr.	11	Calgary	5	at	Chicago	4 2OT

Calgary won best-of-five series 3–0

Apr.	8	Minnesota	5	at	Boston	4 OT
Apr.	9	Minnesota	9	at	Boston	6
Apr.	11	Boston	3	at	Minnesota	6

Minnesota won best-of-five series 3–0

QUARTER-FINALS

Apr.	16	Edmonton	2	at	NY Islanders	8
Apr.	17	Edmonton	3	at	NY Islanders	6
Apr.	19	NY Islanders	2	at	Edmonton	5
Apr.	20	NY Islanders	5	at	Edmonton	4 OT
Apr.	22	Edmonton	4	at	NY Islanders	3
Apr.	24	NY Islanders	5	at	Edmonton	2

NY Islanders won best-of-seven series 4–2

Apr.	16	NY Rangers	3	at	St. Louis	6
Apr.	17	NY Rangers	6	at	St. Louis	4
Apr.	19	St. Louis	3	at	NY Rangers	6
Apr.	20	St. Louis	1	at	NY Rangers	4
Apr.	22	NY Rangers	3	at	St. Louis	4
Apr.	24	St. Louis	4	at	NY Rangers	7

NY Rangers won best-of-seven series 4–2

Apr.	16	Minnesota	4	at	Buffalo	3 OT
Apr.	17	Minnesota	5	at	Buffalo	2
Apr.	19	Buffalo	4	at	Minnesota	6
Apr.	20	Buffalo	5	at	Minnesota	4 OT
Apr.	22	Minnesota	4	at	Buffalo	3

Minnesota won best-of-seven series 4–1

Apr.	16	Calgary	0	at	Philadelphia	4
Apr.	17	Calgary	5	at	Philadelphia	4
Apr.	19	Philadelphia	1	at	Calgary	2
Apr.	20	Philadelphia	4	at	Calgary	5
Apr.	22	Calgary	4	at	Philadelphia	9
Apr.	24	Philadelphia	3	at	Calgary	2
Apr.	26	Calgary	4	at	Philadelphia	1

Calgary won best-of-seven series 4–3

SEMI-FINALS

Apr.	28	NY Rangers	2	at	NY Islanders	5
Apr.	30	NY Rangers	3	at	NY Islanders	7
May	2	NY Islanders	5	at	NY Rangers	1
May	5	NY Islanders	5	at	NY Rangers	2

NY Islanders won best-of-seven series 4–0

Apr.	28	Minnesota	4	at	Calgary	1
Apr.	30	Minnesota	2	at	Calgary	3
May	3	Calgary	4	at	Minnesota	6
May	5	Calgary	4	at	Minnesota	7
May	7	Minnesota	1	at	Calgary	3
May	9	Calgary	3	at	Minnesota	5

Minnesota won best-of-seven series 4–2

FINALS

May	12	Minnesota	3	at	NY Islanders	6
May	14	Minnesota	3	at	NY Islanders	6
May	17	NY Islanders	7	at	Minnesota	5
May	19	NY Islanders	2	at	Minnesota	4
May	21	Minnesota	1	at	NY Islanders	5

NY Islanders won best-of-seven series 4–1

1980-81 – New York Islanders – Denis Potvin (Captain), Mike McEwen, Ken Morrow, Gord Lane, Bob Lorimer, Stefan Persson, Dave Langevin, Mike Bossy, Bryan Trottier, Butch Goring, Wayne Merrick, Clark Gillies, John Tonelli, Bob Nystrom, Billy Carroll, Bob Bourne, Hector Marini, Anders Kallur, Duane Sutter, Garry Howatt, Lorne Henning, Billy Smith, Roland Melanson, Al Arbour (Coach), Bill Torrey (General Manager), Jim Devellano (Chief Scout), Ron Waske, Jim Pickard (Trainers).

1980

In their eighth NHL season, the New York Islanders became the second expansion team to win the Stanley Cup. Two players, Billy Smith and Bob Nystrom, had been with the team since its inception in 1972.

In game one, Denis Potvin recorded the first power-play goal ever scored in overtime in Stanley Cup history. The Flyers' Jimmy Watson went off at the 2:08 mark, and Potvin scored 1:59 later to end the game and give the Islanders their first win in the finals. Nystrom also scored an overtime goal, the Cup-winner in game six, to raise his career total to four playoff overtime goals. Maurice "Rocket" Richard, who scored six overtime goals in the playoffs, owns the all-time record.

CONN SMYTHE TROPHY
Bryan Trottier - Center - New York Islanders

PRELIMINARY ROUND

Apr.	8	Edmonton	3	at	Philadelphia	4 OT
Apr.	9	Edmonton	1	at	Philadelphia	5
Apr.	11	Philadelphia	3	at	Edmonton	2 2OT

Philadelphia won best-of-five series 3–0

Apr.	8	Vancouver	1	at	Buffalo	2
Apr.	9	Vancouver	0	at	Buffalo	6
Apr.	11	Buffalo	4	at	Vancouver	5
Apr.	12	Buffalo	3	at	Vancouver	1

Buffalo won best-of-five series 3–1

Apr.	8	Hartford	1	at	Montreal	6
Apr.	9	Hartford	4	at	Montreal	8
Apr.	11	Montreal	4	at	Hartford	3 OT

Montreal won best-of-five series 3–0

Apr.	8	Pittsburgh	4	at	Boston	2
Apr.	10	Pittsburgh	1	at	Boston	4
Apr.	12	Boston	1	at	Pittsburgh	4
Apr.	13	Boston	8	at	Pittsburgh	3
Apr.	14	Pittsburgh	2	at	Boston	6

Boston won best-of-five series 3–2

Apr.	8	Los Angeles	1	at	NY Islanders	8
Apr.	9	Los Angeles	6	at	NY Islanders	3
Apr.	11	NY Islanders	4	at	Los Angeles	3 OT
Apr.	12	NY Islanders	6	at	Los Angeles	0

NY Islanders won best-of-five series 3–1

Apr.	8	Toronto	3	at	Minnesota	6
Apr.	9	Toronto	2	at	Minnesota	7
Apr.	11	Minnesota	4	at	Toronto	3 OT

Minnesota won best-of-five series 3–0

Apr. 8 St. Louis 2 at Chicago 3 OT
Apr. 9 St. Louis 1 at Chicago 5
Apr. 11 Chicago 4 at St. Louis 1
Chicago won best-of-five series 3–0

Apr. 8 Atlanta 1 at NY Rangers 2 OT
Apr. 9 Atlanta 1 at NY Rangers 5
Apr. 11 NY Rangers 2 at Atlanta 4
Apr. 12 NY Rangers 5 at Atlanta 2
NY Rangers won best-of-five series 3–1

QUARTER-FINALS
Apr. 16 NY Rangers 1 at Philadelphia 2
Apr. 17 NY Rangers 1 at Philadelphia 4
Apr. 19 Philadelphia 3 at NY Rangers 0
Apr. 20 Philadelphia 3 at NY Rangers 4
Apr. 22 NY Rangers 1 at Philadelphia 3
Philadelphia won best-of-seven series 4–1

Apr. 16 Chicago 0 at Buffalo 5
Apr. 17 Chicago 4 at Buffalo 6
Apr. 19 Buffalo 2 at Chicago 1
Apr. 20 Buffalo 3 at Chicago 2
Buffalo won best-of-seven series 4–0

Apr. 16 Minnesota 3 at Montreal 0
Apr. 17 Minnesota 4 at Montreal 1
Apr. 19 Montreal 5 at Minnesota 0
Apr. 20 Montreal 5 at Minnesota 1
Apr. 22 Minnesota 2 at Montreal 6
Apr. 24 Montreal 2 at Minnesota 5
Apr. 27 Minnesota 3 at Montreal 2
Minnesota won best-of-seven series 4–3

Apr. 16 NY Islanders 2 at Boston 1 OT
Apr. 17 NY Islanders 5 at Boston 4 OT
Apr. 19 Boston 3 at NY Islanders 5
Apr. 21 Boston 4 at NY Islanders 3 OT
Apr. 22 NY Islanders 4 at Boston 2
NY Islanders won best-of-seven series 4–1

SEMI-FINALS
Apr. 29 Minnesota 6 at Philadelphia 5
May 1 Minnesota 0 at Philadelphia 7
May 4 Philadelphia 5 at Minnesota 3
May 6 Philadelphia 3 at Minnesota 2
May 8 Minnesota 3 at Philadelphia 7
Philadelphia won best-of-seven series 4–1

Apr. 29 NY Islanders 4 at Buffalo 1
May 1 NY Islanders 2 at Buffalo 1 2OT
May 3 Buffalo 4 at NY Islanders 7
May 6 Buffalo 7 at NY Islanders 4
May 8 NY Islanders 0 at Buffalo 2
May 10 Buffalo 2 at NY Islanders 5
NY Islanders won best-of-seven series 4–2

FINALS
May 13 NY Islanders 4 at Philadelphia 3 OT
May 15 NY Islanders 3 at Philadelphia 8
May 17 Philadelphia 2 at NY Islanders 6
May 19 Philadelphia 2 at NY Islanders 5
May 22 NY Islanders 3 at Philadelphia 6
May 24 Philadelphia 4 at NY Islanders 5 OT
NY Islanders won best-of-seven series 4–2

1979-80 – New York Islanders – Gord Lane, Jean Potvin, Bob Lorimer, Denis Potvin (Captain), Stefan Persson, Ken Morrow, Dave Langevin, Duane Sutter, Garry Howatt, Clark Gillies, Lorne Henning, Wayne Merrick, Bob Bourne, Steve Tambellini, Bryan Trottier, Mike Bossy, Bob Nystrom, John Tonelli, Anders Kallur, Butch Goring, Alex McKendry, Glenn Resch, Billy Smith, Al Arbour (Coach), Bill Torrey (General Manager), Jim Devellano (Chief Scout), Ron Waske, Jim Pickard (Trainers).

1979

The Montreal Canadiens captured their fourth straight Stanley Cup championship to record the second longest streak of championships in NHL history. Only the Canadiens' five-year stronghold on the Cup from 1956 to 1960 lasted longer.

Montreal's game five series-winning effort also marked the first time since 1968 that the Canadiens won the Cup on home ice. At the conclusion of the series, Jacques Lemaire, Yvan Cournoyer and Ken Dryden retired from the NHL. The trio left the game with a combined total of 24 Cup victories among them. Scotty Bowman, who had amassed his fifth Cup title in seven seasons behind the Canadiens bench, also made his farewell appearance with the team as he joined the Buffalo Sabres the following season.

CONN SMYTHE TROPHY
Bob Gainey - Left Wing - Montreal Canadiens

PRELIMINARY ROUND
Apr. 10 Vancouver 3 at Philadelphia 2
Apr. 12 Philadelphia 6 at Vancouver 4
Apr. 14 Vancouver 2 at Philadelphia 7
Philadelphia won best-of-three series 2–1

Apr. 10 Los Angeles 1 at NY Rangers 7
Apr. 12 NY Rangers 2 at Los Angeles 1 OT
NY Rangers won best-of-three series 2–0

Apr. 10 Toronto 2 at Atlanta 1
Apr. 12 Atlanta 4 at Toronto 7
Toronto won best-of-three series 2–0

Apr. 10 Pittsburgh 4 at Buffalo 3
Apr. 12 Buffalo 3 at Pittsburgh 1
Apr. 14 Pittsburgh 4 at Buffalo 3 OT
Pittsburgh won best-of-three series 2–1

QUARTER-FINALS
Apr. 16 Chicago 2 at NY Islanders 6
Apr. 18 Chicago 0 at NY Islanders 1 OT
Apr. 20 NY Islanders 4 at Chicago 0
Apr. 22 NY Islanders 3 at Chicago 1
NY Islanders won best-of-seven series 4–0

Apr. 16 Toronto 2 at Montreal 5
Apr. 18 Toronto 1 at Montreal 5
Apr. 21 Montreal 4 at Toronto 3 2OT
Apr. 22 Montreal 5 at Toronto 4 OT
Montreal won best-of-seven series 4–0

Apr. 16 Pittsburgh 2 at Boston 6
Apr. 18 Pittsburgh 3 at Boston 4
Apr. 21 Boston 2 at Pittsburgh 1
Apr. 22 Boston 4 at Pittsburgh 1
Boston won best-of-seven series 4–0

Apr. 16 NY Rangers 2 at Philadelphia 3 OT
Apr. 18 NY Rangers 7 at Philadelphia 1
Apr. 20 Philadelphia 1 at NY Rangers 5
Apr. 22 Philadelphia 0 at NY Rangers 6
Apr. 24 NY Rangers 8 at Philadelphia 3
NY Rangers won best-of-seven series 4–1

SEMI-FINALS
Apr. 26 NY Rangers 4 at NY Islanders 1
Apr. 28 NY Rangers 3 at NY Islanders 4 OT
May 1 NY Islanders 1 at NY Rangers 3
May 3 NY Islanders 3 at NY Rangers 2 OT
May 5 NY Rangers 4 at NY Islanders 3
May 8 NY Islanders 1 at NY Rangers 2
NY Rangers won best-of-seven series 4–2

Apr. 26 Boston 2 at Montreal 4
Apr. 28 Boston 2 at Montreal 5
May 1 Montreal 1 at Boston 2
May 3 Montreal 3 at Boston 4 OT
May 5 Boston 1 at Montreal 5
May 8 Montreal 2 at Boston 5
May 10 Boston 4 at Montreal 5 OT
Montreal won best-of-seven series 4–3

FINALS
May 13 NY Rangers 4 at Montreal 1
May 15 NY Rangers 2 at Montreal 6
May 17 Montreal 4 at NY Rangers 1
May 19 Montreal 4 at NY Rangers 3 OT
May 21 NY Rangers 1 at Montreal 4
Montreal won best-of-seven series 4–1

1978-79 – Montreal Canadiens – Ken Dryden, Larry Robinson, Serge Savard, Guy Lapointe, Brian Engblom, Gilles Lupien, Rick Chartraw, Guy Lafleur, Steve Shutt, Jacques Lemaire, Yvan Cournoyer (Captain), Réjean Houle, Pierre Mondou, Bob Gainey, Doug Jarvis, Doug Risebrough, Pierre Larouche, Yvon Lambert, Mario Tremblay, Cam Connor, Pat Hughes, Rod Langway, Mark Napier, Michel Larocque, Richard Sévigny, Scotty Bowman (Coach), Irving Grundman (Managing Director), Eddy Palchak, Pierre Meilleur (Trainers).

1978

The Montreal Canadiens lost just ten regular-season games in 1977–78 and were favored in the postseason. The Habs needed nine games to reach the finals, where they again met Boston in a rematch of the 1977 series. The Bruins also needed just nine games to advance, winning three overtime games en route to a berth in the final round of the playoffs.

Conn Smythe Trophy winner Larry Robinson led all playoff performers with 17 assists and tied teammate Guy Lafleur (10–11–21) for the overall playoff scoring lead with 21 points. Robinson was one of three Canadiens, including Doug Jarvis and Steve Shutt, to appear in all 95 games during the course of the season.

CONN SMYTHE TROPHY
Larry Robinson - Defense - Montreal Canadiens

PRELIMINARY ROUND
Apr. 11 Colorado 2 at Philadelphia 3 OT
Apr. 13 Philadelphia 3 at Colorado 1
Philadelphia won best-of-three series 2–0

Apr. 11 NY Rangers 1 at Buffalo 4
Apr. 13 Buffalo 3 at NY Rangers 4 OT
Apr. 15 NY Rangers 1 at Buffalo 4
Buffalo won best-of-three series 2–1

Apr. 11 Los Angeles 3 at Toronto 7
Apr. 13 Toronto 4 at Los Angeles 0
Toronto won best-of-three series 2–0

Apr. 11 Detroit 5 at Atlanta 3
Apr. 13 Atlanta 2 at Detroit 3
Detroit won best-of-three series 2–0

QUARTER-FINALS
Apr. 17 Detroit 2 at Montreal 6
Apr. 19 Detroit 4 at Montreal 2
Apr. 21 Montreal 4 at Detroit 2
Apr. 23 Montreal 8 at Detroit 0
Apr. 25 Detroit 2 at Montreal 4
Montreal won best-of-seven series 4–1

Apr. 17 Chicago 1 at Boston 6
Apr. 19 Chicago 3 at Boston 4 OT
Apr. 21 Boston 4 at Chicago 3 OT
Apr. 23 Boston 5 at Chicago 2
Boston won best-of-seven series 4–0

Apr. 17 Toronto 1 at NY Islanders 4
Apr. 19 Toronto 3 at NY Islanders 2 OT
Apr. 21 NY Islanders 0 at Toronto 2
Apr. 23 NY Islanders 1 at Toronto 3
Apr. 25 Toronto 1 at NY Islanders 2 OT
Apr. 27 NY Islanders 2 at Toronto 5
Apr. 29 Toronto 2 at NY Islanders 1 OT
Toronto won best-of-seven series 4–3

Apr. 17 Buffalo 1 at Philadelphia 4
Apr. 19 Buffalo 2 at Philadelphia 3
Apr. 22 Philadelphia 1 at Buffalo 4
Apr. 23 Philadelphia 4 at Buffalo 2
Apr. 25 Buffalo 2 at Philadelphia 4
Philadelphia won best-of-seven series 4–1

SEMI-FINALS

May	2	Toronto	3	at	Montreal	5	
May	4	Toronto	2	at	Montreal	3	
May	6	Montreal	6	at	Toronto	1	
May	9	Montreal	2	at	Toronto	0	

Montreal won best-of-seven series 4–0

May	2	Philadelphia	2	at	Boston	3	OT
May	4	Philadelphia	5	at	Boston	7	
May	7	Boston	1	at	Philadelphia	3	
May	9	Boston	4	at	Philadelphia	2	
May	11	Philadelphia	3	at	Boston	6	

Boston won best-of-seven series 4–1

FINALS

May	13	Boston	1	at	Montreal	4	
May	16	Boston	2	at	Montreal	3	OT
May	18	Montreal	0	at	Boston	4	
May	21	Montreal	3	at	Boston	4	OT
May	23	Boston	1	at	Montreal	4	
May	25	Montreal	4	at	Boston	1	

Montreal won best-of-seven series 4–2

1977-78 – Montreal Canadiens – Ken Dryden, Larry Robinson, Serge Savard, Guy Lapointe, Bill Nyrop, Pierre Bouchard, Brian Engblom, Gilles Lupien, Rick Chartraw, Guy Lafleur, Steve Shutt, Jacques Lemaire, Yvan Cournoyer (Captain), Réjean Houle, Pierre Mondou, Bob Gainey, Doug Jarvis, Yvon Lambert, Doug Risebrough, Pierre Larouche, Mario Tremblay, Michel Larocque, Murray Wilson, Scotty Bowman (Coach), Sam Pollock (General Manager), Eddy Palchak, Pierre Meilleur (Trainers).

1977

Winning their second consecutive Stanley Cup championship, the Canadiens extended their undefeated streak against Boston in the finals to six straight series.

Jacques Lemaire, who scored three of Montreal's game-winning goals including the Cup-winner in overtime, joined Maurice Richard (3) and Don Raleigh (2) as the only players to record more than one overtime goal in Stanley Cup finals play. Lemaire first scored in overtime against the St. Louis Blues in the 1968 finals, and duplicated the feat in the finale of this latest series. In game two, Ken Dryden posted his fourth shutout of the playoffs to tie the record shared by six goaltenders.

Guy Lafleur won the Conn Smythe Trophy and also had nine goals and 17 assists for 26 points in 14 playoff games.

CONN SMYTHE TROPHY
Guy Lafleur - Right Wing - Montreal Canadiens

PRELIMINARY ROUND

Apr.	5	Chicago	2	at	NY Islanders	5
Apr.	7	Chicago	1	at	NY Islanders	2

NY Islanders won best-of-three series 2–0

Apr.	5	Minnesota	2	at	Buffalo	4
Apr.	7	Buffalo	7	at	Minnesota	1

Buffalo won best-of-three series 2–0

Apr.	5	Atlanta	2	at	Los Angeles	5
Apr.	7	Los Angeles	2	at	Atlanta	3
Apr.	9	Atlanta	2	at	Los Angeles	4

Los Angeles won best-of-three series 2–1

Apr.	5	Toronto	4	at	Pittsburgh	2
Apr.	7	Pittsburgh	6	at	Toronto	4
Apr.	9	Toronto	5	at	Pittsburgh	2

Toronto won best-of-three series 2–1

QUARTER-FINALS

Apr.	11	St. Louis	2	at	Montreal	7
Apr.	13	St. Louis	0	at	Montreal	3
Apr.	16	Montreal	5	at	St. Louis	1
Apr.	17	Montreal	4	at	St. Louis	1

Montreal won best-of-seven series 4–0

Apr.	11	Toronto	3	at	Philadelphia	2	
Apr.	13	Toronto	4	at	Philadelphia	1	
Apr.	15	Philadelphia	4	at	Toronto	3	OT
Apr.	17	Philadelphia	6	at	Toronto	5	OT
Apr.	19	Toronto	0	at	Philadelphia	2	
Apr.	21	Philadelphia	4	at	Toronto	3	

Philadelphia won best-of-seven series 4–2

Apr.	11	Los Angeles	3	at	Boston	8
Apr.	13	Los Angeles	2	at	Boston	6
Apr.	15	Boston	7	at	Los Angeles	6
Apr.	17	Boston	4	at	Los Angeles	7
Apr.	19	Los Angeles	3	at	Boston	1
Apr.	21	Boston	4	at	Los Angeles	3

Boston won best-of-seven series 4–2

Apr.	11	Buffalo	2	at	NY Islanders	4
Apr.	13	Buffalo	2	at	NY Islanders	4
Apr.	15	NY Islanders	4	at	Buffalo	3
Apr.	17	NY Islanders	4	at	Buffalo	3

NY Islanders won best-of-seven series 4–0

SEMI-FINALS

Apr.	23	NY Islanders	3	at	Montreal	4	
Apr.	26	NY Islanders	0	at	Montreal	3	
Apr.	28	Montreal	3	at	NY Islanders	5	
Apr.	30	Montreal	4	at	NY Islanders	0	
May	3	NY Islanders	4	at	Montreal	3	OT
May	5	Montreal	2	at	NY Islanders	1	

Montreal won best-of-seven series 4–2

Apr.	24	Boston	4	at	Philadelphia	3	OT
Apr.	26	Boston	5	at	Philadelphia	4	2OT
Apr.	28	Philadelphia	1	at	Boston	2	
May	1	Philadelphia	0	at	Boston	3	

Boston won best-of-seven series 4–0

FINALS

May	7	Boston	3	at	Montreal	7	
May	10	Boston	0	at	Montreal	3	
May	12	Montreal	4	at	Boston	2	
May	14	Montreal	2	at	Boston	1	OT

Montreal won best-of-seven series 4–0

1976-77 – Montreal Canadiens – Ken Dryden, Guy Lapointe, Larry Robinson, Serge Savard, Jimmy Roberts, Rick Chartraw, Bill Nyrop, Pierre Bouchard, Brian Engblom, Yvan Cournoyer (Captain), Guy Lafleur, Jacques Lemaire, Steve Shutt, Pete Mahovlich, Murray Wilson, Doug Jarvis, Yvon Lambert, Bob Gainey, Doug Risebrough, Mario Tremblay, Rejean Houle, Pierre Mondou, Mike Polich, Michel Larocque, Scotty Bowman (Coach), Sam Pollock (General Manager), Eddy Palchak, Pierre Meilleur (Trainers).

1976

The Montreal Canadiens returned to the Stanley Cup finals after a two-year absence. Guy Lafleur scored his first two goals in the finals and both proved to be game winners as the Canadiens swept Philadelphia to end the Flyers' two-year reign as champions.

Philadelphia's Reggie Leach scored four times in the series to finish the playoffs with the all-time record of 19 postseason goals. Leach became the third player on a Stanley Cup finals loser to win the Conn Smythe Trophy.

CONN SMYTHE TROPHY
Reggie Leach - Right Wing - Philadelphia Flyers

PRELIMINARY ROUND

Apr.	6	Buffalo	2	at	St. Louis	5	
Apr.	8	St. Louis	2	at	Buffalo	3	OT
Apr.	9	St. Louis	1	at	Buffalo	2	OT

Buffalo won best-of-three series 2–1

Apr.	6	Vancouver	3	at	NY Islanders	5
Apr.	8	NY Islanders	3	at	Vancouver	1

NY Islanders won best-of-three series 2–0

Apr.	6	Atlanta	1	at	Los Angeles	2
Apr.	8	Los Angeles	1	at	Atlanta	0

Los Angeles won best-of-three series 2–0

Apr.	6	Pittsburgh	1	at	Toronto	4
Apr.	8	Toronto	0	at	Pittsburgh	2
Apr.	9	Pittsburgh	0	at	Toronto	4

Toronto won best-of-three series 2–1

QUARTER-FINALS

Apr.	11	Chicago	0	at	Montreal	4
Apr.	13	Chicago	1	at	Montreal	3
Apr.	15	Montreal	2	at	Chicago	1
Apr.	18	Montreal	4	at	Chicago	1

Montreal won best-of-seven series 4–0

Apr.	12	Toronto	1	at	Philadelphia	4
Apr.	13	Toronto	1	at	Philadelphia	3
Apr.	15	Philadelphia	4	at	Toronto	5
Apr.	17	Philadelphia	3	at	Toronto	4
Apr.	20	Toronto	1	at	Philadelphia	7
Apr.	22	Philadelphia	5	at	Toronto	8
Apr.	25	Toronto	3	at	Philadelphia	7

Philadelphia won best-of-seven series 4–3

Apr.	11	Los Angeles	0	at	Boston	4	
Apr.	13	Los Angeles	3	at	Boston	2	OT
Apr.	15	Boston	4	at	Los Angeles	6	
Apr.	17	Boston	3	at	Los Angeles	0	
Apr.	20	Los Angeles	1	at	Boston	7	
Apr.	22	Boston	3	at	Los Angeles	4	OT
Apr.	25	Los Angeles	0	at	Boston	3	

Boston won best-of-seven series 4–3

Apr.	11	NY Islanders	3	at	Buffalo	5	
Apr.	13	NY Islanders	2	at	Buffalo	3	OT
Apr.	15	Buffalo	3	at	NY Islanders	5	
Apr.	17	Buffalo	2	at	NY Islanders	4	
Apr.	20	NY Islanders	4	at	Buffalo	3	
Apr.	22	Buffalo	2	at	NY Islanders	3	

NY Islanders won best-of-seven series 4–2

SEMI-FINALS

Apr.	27	NY Islanders	2	at	Montreal	3
Apr.	29	NY Islanders	3	at	Montreal	4
May	1	Montreal	3	at	NY Islanders	2
May	4	Montreal	2	at	NY Islanders	5
May	6	NY Islanders	2	at	Montreal	5

Montreal won best-of-seven series 4–1

Apr.	27	Boston	4	at	Philadelphia	2	
Apr.	29	Boston	1	at	Philadelphia	2	OT
May	2	Philadelphia	5	at	Boston	2	
May	4	Philadelphia	4	at	Boston	2	
May	6	Boston	3	at	Philadelphia	6	

Philadelphia won best-of-seven series 4–1

FINALS

May	9	Philadelphia	3	at	Montreal	4
May	11	Philadelphia	1	at	Montreal	2
May	13	Montreal	3	at	Philadelphia	2
May	16	Montreal	5	at	Philadelphia	3

Montreal won best-of-seven series 4–0

1975-76 – Montreal Canadiens – Ken Dryden, Serge Savard, Guy Lapointe, Larry Robinson, Bill Nyrop, Pierre Bouchard, Jimmy Roberts, Guy Lafleur, Steve Shutt, Pete Mahovlich, Yvan Cournoyer (Captain), Jacques Lemaire, Yvon Lambert, Bob Gainey, Doug Jarvis, Doug Risebrough, Murray Wilson, Mario Tremblay, Rick Chartraw, Michel Larocque, Scotty Bowman (Coach), Sam Pollock (General Manager), Eddy Palchak, Pierre Meilleur (Trainers).

1975

Two modern-era expansion teams met in the Stanley Cup finals for the first time in 1975, as the Philadelphia Flyers defeated the Buffalo Sabres in six games. The Sabres had reached the championship series in just their fifth year in the NHL.

Bernie Parent's netminding highlighted the

series as he allowed only 12 goals in six games and clinched the Cup with a shutout for the second straight year. Parent became the first player to win the Conn Smythe Trophy in consecutive years and joined Boston's Bobby Orr as the only players to have won the award twice.

CONN SMYTHE TROPHY
Bernie Parent - Goaltender - Philadelphia Flyers

PRELIMINARY ROUND

Apr.	8	Toronto	2	at	Los Angeles	3	OT
Apr.	10	Los Angeles	2	at	Toronto	3	OT
Apr.	11	Toronto	2	at	Los Angeles	1	

Toronto won best-of-three series 2–1

Apr.	8	Chicago	2	at	Boston	8	
Apr.	10	Boston	3	at	Chicago	4	OT
Apr.	11	Chicago	6	at	Boston	4	

Chicago won best-of-three series 2–1

| Apr. | 8 | St. Louis | 3 | at | Pittsburgh | 4 | |
| Apr. | 10 | Pittsburgh | 5 | at | St. Louis | 3 | |

Pittsburgh won best-of-three series 2–0

Apr.	8	NY Islanders	3	at	NY Rangers	2	
Apr.	10	NY Rangers	8	at	NY Islanders	3	
Apr.	11	NY Islanders	4	at	NY Rangers	3	OT

NY Islanders won best-of-three series 2–1

QUARTER-FINALS

Apr.	13	Toronto	3	at	Philadelphia	6	
Apr.	15	Toronto	0	at	Philadelphia	3	
Apr.	17	Philadelphia	2	at	Toronto	0	
Apr.	19	Philadelphia	4	at	Toronto	3	OT

Philadelphia won best-of-seven series 4–0

Apr.	13	Chicago	1	at	Buffalo	4	
Apr.	15	Chicago	1	at	Buffalo	3	
Apr.	17	Buffalo	4	at	Chicago	5	OT
Apr.	20	Buffalo	6	at	Chicago	2	
Apr.	22	Chicago	1	at	Buffalo	3	

Buffalo won best-of-seven series 4–1

Apr.	13	Vancouver	2	at	Montreal	6	
Apr.	15	Vancouver	2	at	Montreal	1	
Apr.	17	Montreal	4	at	Vancouver	1	
Apr.	19	Montreal	4	at	Vancouver	0	
Apr.	22	Vancouver	4	at	Montreal	5	OT

Montreal won best-of-seven series 4–1

Apr.	13	NY Islanders	4	at	Pittsburgh	5	
Apr.	15	NY Islanders	1	at	Pittsburgh	3	
Apr.	17	Pittsburgh	6	at	NY Islanders	4	
Apr.	20	Pittsburgh	1	at	NY Islanders	3	
Apr.	22	NY Islanders	4	at	Pittsburgh	2	
Apr.	24	Pittsburgh	1	at	NY Islanders	4	
Apr.	26	NY Islanders	1	at	Pittsburgh	0	

NY Islanders won best-of-seven series 4–3

SEMI-FINALS

Apr.	29	NY Islanders	0	at	Philadelphia	4	
May	1	NY Islanders	4	at	Philadelphia	5	OT
May	4	Philadelphia	1	at	NY Islanders	0	
May	7	Philadelphia	3	at	NY Islanders	4	OT
May	8	NY Islanders	5	at	Philadelphia	1	
May	11	Philadelphia	1	at	NY Islanders	2	
May	13	NY Islanders	1	at	Philadelphia	4	

Philadelphia won best-of-seven series 4–3

Apr.	27	Montreal	5	at	Buffalo	6	OT
Apr.	29	Montreal	2	at	Buffalo	4	
May	1	Buffalo	0	at	Montreal	7	
May	3	Buffalo	2	at	Montreal	8	
May	6	Montreal	4	at	Buffalo	5	OT
May	8	Buffalo	4	at	Montreal	3	

Buffalo won best-of-seven series 4–2

FINALS

May	15	Buffalo	1	at	Philadelphia	4	
May	18	Buffalo	1	at	Philadelphia	2	
May	20	Philadelphia	4	at	Buffalo	5	OT
May	22	Philadelphia	2	at	Buffalo	4	
May	25	Buffalo	1	at	Philadelphia	5	
May	27	Philadelphia	2	at	Buffalo	0	

Philadelphia won best-of-seven series 4–2

1974-75 – Philadelphia Flyers – Bernie Parent, Wayne Stephenson, Ed Van Impe, Tom Bladon, André Dupont, Joe Watson, Jimmy Watson, Ted Harris, Larry Goodenough, Rick MacLeish, Bobby Clarke (Captain), Bill Barber, Reggie Leach, Gary Dornhoefer, Ross Lonsberry, Bob Kelly, Terry Crisp, Don Saleski, Dave Schultz, Orest Kindrachuk, Bill Clement, Fred Shero (Coach), Keith Allen (General Manager), Frank Lewis, Jim McKenzie (Trainers).

1974

Owning a 17–0–2 record in their previous 19 outings at home against Philadelphia, Boston was a heavy favorite with home-ice advantage coming into the Stanley Cup finals.

Flyers' captain Bobby Clarke ended his team's drought at the Garden in game two by scoring two goals, the second in overtime, and adding one assist to overcome an early 2–0 deficit.

Goaltender Bernie Parent limited the Bruins to three goals in his three remaining wins, including a sixth game shutout as the Flyers became the first expansion team to win the Stanley Cup, after only seven years in the NHL.

Parent won the Conn Smythe Trophy and had a 12–5–0 record and 2.02 average in 17 games

CONN SMYTHE TROPHY
Bernie Parent - Goaltender - Philadelphia Flyers

QUARTER-FINALS

Apr.	10	Toronto	0	at	Boston	1	
Apr.	11	Toronto	3	at	Boston	6	
Apr.	13	Boston	6	at	Toronto	3	
Apr.	14	Boston	4	at	Toronto	3	OT

Boston won best-of-seven series 4–0

Apr.	10	NY Rangers	4	at	Montreal	1	
Apr.	11	NY Rangers	1	at	Montreal	4	
Apr.	13	Montreal	4	at	NY Rangers	2	
Apr.	14	Montreal	4	at	NY Rangers	6	
Apr.	16	NY Rangers	3	at	Montreal	2	OT
Apr.	18	Montreal	2	at	NY Rangers	5	

NY Rangers won best-of-seven series 4–2

Apr.	9	Atlanta	1	at	Philadelphia	4	
Apr.	11	Atlanta	1	at	Philadelphia	5	
Apr.	12	Philadelphia	4	at	Atlanta	1	
Apr.	14	Philadelphia	4	at	Atlanta	3	OT

Philadelphia won best-of-seven series 4–0

Apr.	10	Los Angeles	1	at	Chicago	3	
Apr.	11	Los Angeles	1	at	Chicago	4	
Apr.	13	Chicago	1	at	Los Angeles	0	
Apr.	14	Chicago	1	at	Los Angeles	5	
Apr.	16	Los Angeles	0	at	Chicago	1	

Chicago won best-of-seven series 4–1

SEMI-FINALS

Apr.	18	Chicago	4	at	Boston	2	
Apr.	21	Chicago	6	at	Boston	8	
Apr.	23	Boston	3	at	Chicago	4	OT
Apr.	25	Boston	5	at	Chicago	2	
Apr.	28	Chicago	2	at	Boston	6	
Apr.	30	Boston	4	at	Chicago	2	

Boston won best-of-seven series 4–2

Apr.	20	NY Rangers	0	at	Philadelphia	4	
Apr.	23	NY Rangers	2	at	Philadelphia	5	
Apr.	25	Philadelphia	3	at	NY Rangers	5	
Apr.	28	Philadelphia	4	at	NY Rangers	2	OT
Apr.	30	NY Rangers	1	at	Philadelphia	4	
May	2	Philadelphia	1	at	NY Rangers	4	
May	5	NY Rangers	3	at	Philadelphia	4	

Philadelphia won best-of-seven series 4–3

FINALS

May	7	Philadelphia	2	at	Boston	3	
May	9	Philadelphia	3	at	Boston	2	OT
May	12	Boston	1	at	Philadelphia	4	
May	14	Boston	2	at	Philadelphia	4	

| May | 16 | Philadelphia | 1 | at | Boston | 5 | |
| May | 19 | Boston | 0 | at | Philadelphia | 1 | |

Philadelphia won best-of-seven series 4–2

1973-74 – Philadelphia Flyers – Bernie Parent, Ed Van Impe, Tom Bladon, André Dupont, Joe Watson, Jimmy Watson, Barry Ashbee, Bill Barber, Dave Schultz, Don Saleski, Gary Dornhoefer, Terry Crisp, Bobby Clarke (Captain), Simon Nolet, Ross Lonsberry, Rick MacLeish, Bill Flett, Orest Kindrachuk, Bill Clement, Bob Kelly, Bruce Cowick, Al MacAdam, Bobby Taylor, Fred Shero (Coach), Keith Allen (General Manager), Frank Lewis, Jim McKenzie (Trainers).

1973

The Canadiens and Black Hawks met in a rematch of the 1971 finals. Chicago's Tony Esposito and Montreal's Ken Dryden, teammates in the noted 1972 Summit Series against the Soviet Union prior to the start of the season, now faced each other at opposite ends of the ice. Yvan Cournoyer, who recorded the game-winning goals in the second and sixth contests, closed out the playoffs setting a modern record of 15 tallies en route to winning the Conn Smythe Trophy. Cournoyer (6–6–12) and Jacques Lemaire (3–9–12) both tied Gordie Howe's record for points in the finals, while the latter also set a new record for assists in the finals with nine. Henri Richard became the first player to play for 11 Stanley Cup champions and tied the overall record held by Toe Blake, who played on three and coached eight more before retiring in 1968. After coaching the St. Louis Blues to three successive finals from 1968 to 1970, Montreal's Scotty Bowman earned his first Stanley Cup championship.

CONN SMYTHE TROPHY
Yvan Cournoyer - Right Wing - Montreal Canadiens

QUARTER-FINALS

Apr.	4	Buffalo	1	at	Montreal	2	
Apr.	5	Buffalo	3	at	Montreal	7	
Apr.	7	Montreal	5	at	Buffalo	2	
Apr.	8	Montreal	1	at	Buffalo	5	
Apr.	10	Buffalo	3	at	Montreal	2	OT
Apr.	12	Montreal	4	at	Buffalo	2	

Montreal won best-of-seven series 4–2

Apr.	4	NY Rangers	6	at	Boston	2	
Apr.	5	NY Rangers	4	at	Boston	2	
Apr.	7	Boston	4	at	NY Rangers	2	
Apr.	8	Boston	0	at	NY Rangers	4	
Apr.	10	NY Rangers	6	at	Boston	3	

NY Rangers won best-of-seven series 4–1

Apr.	4	St. Louis	1	at	Chicago	7	
Apr.	5	St. Louis	0	at	Chicago	1	
Apr.	7	Chicago	5	at	St. Louis	2	
Apr.	8	Chicago	3	at	St. Louis	5	
Apr.	10	St. Louis	1	at	Chicago	6	

Chicago won best-of-seven series 4–1

Apr.	4	Minnesota	3	at	Philadelphia	0	
Apr.	5	Minnesota	1	at	Philadelphia	4	
Apr.	7	Philadelphia	0	at	Minnesota	5	
Apr.	8	Philadelphia	3	at	Minnesota	0	
Apr.	10	Minnesota	2	at	Philadelphia	3	OT
Apr.	12	Philadelphia	4	at	Minnesota	1	

Philadelphia won best-of-seven series 4–2

SEMI-FINALS

Apr.	14	Philadelphia	5	at	Montreal	4	OT
Apr.	17	Philadelphia	3	at	Montreal	4	OT
Apr.	19	Montreal	2	at	Philadelphia	1	
Apr.	22	Montreal	4	at	Philadelphia	1	
Apr.	24	Philadelphia	3	at	Montreal	5	

Montreal won best-of-seven series 4–1

Apr.	12	NY Rangers	4	at Chicago	1
Apr.	15	NY Rangers	4	at Chicago	5
Apr.	17	Chicago	2	at NY Rangers	1
Apr.	19	Chicago	3	at NY Rangers	1
Apr.	24	NY Rangers	1	at Chicago	4

Chicago won best-of-seven series 4–1

FINALS

Apr.	29	Chicago	3	at Montreal	8
May	1	Chicago	1	at Montreal	4
May	3	Montreal	4	at Chicago	7
May	6	Montreal	4	at Chicago	0
May	8	Chicago	8	at Montreal	7
May	10	Montreal	6	at Chicago	4

Montreal won best-of-seven series 4–2

1972-73 – Montreal Canadiens – Ken Dryden, Guy Lapointe, Serge Savard, Larry Robinson, Jacques Laperrière, Bob Murdoch, Pierre Bouchard, Jimmy Roberts, Yvan Cournoyer, Frank Mahovlich, Jacques Lemaire, Pete Mahovlich, Marc Tardif, Henri Richard (Captain), Réjean Houle, Guy Lafleur, Chuck Lefley, Claude Larose, Murray Wilson, Steve Shutt, Michel Plasse, Scotty Bowman (Coach), Sam Pollock (General Manager), Eddy Palchak, Bob Williams (Trainers).

1972

After 43 years of waiting, the New York Rangers finally got a chance to avenge their 1929 loss to the Boston Bruins in the Stanley Cup finals. However, history would repeat itself as the Bruins defeated the Rangers in this six-game confrontation. Bobby Orr, who scored his second Cup-winning goal in three years, became the first two-time winner of the Conn Smythe Trophy. With four goals and four assists in the finals, Orr raised his playoff totals to five goals and 19 assists, breaking Jean Beliveau's assist mark set in 1971.

CONN SMYTHE TROPHY
Bobby Orr - Defense - Boston Bruins

QUARTER-FINALS

Apr.	5	Toronto	0	at Boston	5
Apr.	6	Toronto	4	at Boston	3 OT
Apr.	8	Boston	2	at Toronto	0
Apr.	9	Boston	5	at Toronto	4
Apr.	11	Toronto	2	at Boston	3

Boston won best-of-seven series 4–1

Apr.	5	Montreal	2	at NY Rangers	3
Apr.	6	Montreal	2	at NY Rangers	5
Apr.	8	NY Rangers	1	at Montreal	2
Apr.	9	NY Rangers	6	at Montreal	4
Apr.	11	Montreal	2	at NY Rangers	1
Apr.	13	NY Rangers	3	at Montreal	2

NY Rangers won best-of-seven series 4–2

Apr.	5	Pittsburgh	1	at Chicago	3
Apr.	6	Pittsburgh	2	at Chicago	3
Apr.	8	Chicago	2	at Pittsburgh	0
Apr.	9	Chicago	6	at Pittsburgh	5 OT

Chicago won best-of-seven series 4–0

Apr.	5	St. Louis	0	at Minnesota	3
Apr.	6	St. Louis	5	at Minnesota	6 OT
Apr.	8	Minnesota	1	at St. Louis	2
Apr.	9	Minnesota	2	at St. Louis	3
Apr.	11	St. Louis	3	at Minnesota	4
Apr.	13	Minnesota	2	at St. Louis	4
Apr.	16	St. Louis	2	at Minnesota	1 OT

St. Louis won best-of-seven series 4–3

SEMI-FINALS

Apr.	18	St. Louis	1	at Boston	6
Apr.	20	St. Louis	2	at Boston	10
Apr.	23	Boston	7	at St. Louis	2
Apr.	25	Boston	5	at St. Louis	3

Boston won best-of-seven series 4–0

Apr.	16	NY Rangers	3	at Chicago	2
Apr.	18	NY Rangers	5	at Chicago	3
Apr.	20	Chicago	2	at NY Rangers	3
Apr.	23	Chicago	2	at NY Rangers	6

NY Rangers won best-of-seven series 4–0

FINALS

Apr.	30	NY Rangers	5	at Boston	6
May	2	NY Rangers	1	at Boston	2
May	4	Boston	2	at NY Rangers	5
May	7	Boston	3	at NY Rangers	2
May	9	NY Rangers	3	at Boston	2
May	11	Boston	3	at NY Rangers	0

Boston won best-of-seven series 4–2

1971-72 – Boston Bruins – Gerry Cheevers, Eddie Johnston, Bobby Orr, Ted Green, Carol Vadnais, Dallas Smith, Don Awrey, Phil Esposito, Ken Hodge, John Bucyk, Mike Walton, Wayne Cashman, Garnet Bailey, Derek Sanderson, Fred Stanfield, Ed Westfall, John McKenzie, Don Marcotte, Garry Peters, Chris Hayes, Tom Johnson (Coach), Milt Schmidt (General Manager), Dan Canney, John Forristall (Trainers).

1971

After missing the playoffs for the first time in 22 years in 1970, the Canadiens rebounded in 1971 to win their 16th Stanley Cup title. Brothers Frank and Pete Mahovlich were reunited in mid-season, and the two responded with a total of nine goals in the seven-game final. Frank also set a modern playoff record with 14 goals and tied Phil Esposito's record 27-point performance of 1970. After Chicago went ahead 2–0 in game seven, Henri Richard scored the tying and winning goals to seal the victory. The hero of the playoffs was rookie goaltender Ken Dryden, who appeared in all 20 postseason games after only six starts during the regular season. Dryden's performance, which included a 12–8 record and 3.00 average, earned him the Conn Smythe Trophy. While the series heralded the beginning of Dryden's career, it also marked the conclusion of Jean Beliveau's playing days. Beliveau, who finished the playoffs with six goals and a record 16 assists, left the sport as the all-time leader in playoff assists (97) and points (176) and temporarily shared first place with Henri Richard in Stanley Cup titles won as a player at 10.

CONN SMYTHE TROPHY
Ken Dryden - Goaltender - Montreal Canadiens

QUARTER-FINALS

Apr.	7	Montreal	1	at Boston	3
Apr.	8	Montreal	7	at Boston	5
Apr.	10	Boston	1	at Montreal	3
Apr.	11	Boston	5	at Montreal	2
Apr.	13	Montreal	3	at Boston	7
Apr.	15	Boston	3	at Montreal	8
Apr.	18	Montreal	4	at Boston	2

Montreal won best-of-seven series 4–3

Apr.	7	Toronto	4	at NY Rangers	5
Apr.	8	Toronto	4	at NY Rangers	1
Apr.	10	NY Rangers	1	at Toronto	3
Apr.	11	NY Rangers	4	at Toronto	2
Apr.	13	Toronto	1	at NY Rangers	3
Apr.	15	NY Rangers	2	at Toronto	1 OT

NY Rangers won best-of-seven series 4–2

Apr.	7	Philadelphia	2	at Chicago	5
Apr.	8	Philadelphia	2	at Chicago	6
Apr.	10	Chicago	3	at Philadelphia	2
Apr.	11	Chicago	6	at Philadelphia	2

Chicago won best-of-seven series 4–0

Apr.	7	Minnesota	3	at St. Louis	2
Apr.	8	Minnesota	2	at St. Louis	4

Apr.	10	St. Louis	3	at Minnesota	0
Apr.	11	St. Louis	1	at Minnesota	2
Apr.	13	Minnesota	4	at St. Louis	3
Apr.	15	St. Louis	2	at Minnesota	5

Minnesota won best-of-seven series 4–2

SEMI-FINALS

Apr.	20	Minnesota	2	at Montreal	7
Apr.	22	Minnesota	6	at Montreal	3
Apr.	24	Montreal	6	at Minnesota	3
Apr.	25	Montreal	2	at Minnesota	5
Apr.	27	Minnesota	1	at Montreal	6
Apr.	29	Montreal	3	at Minnesota	2

Montreal won best-of-seven series 4–2

Apr.	18	NY Rangers	2	at Chicago	1 OT
Apr.	20	NY Rangers	0	at Chicago	3
Apr.	22	Chicago	1	at NY Rangers	4
Apr.	25	Chicago	7	at NY Rangers	1
Apr.	27	NY Rangers	2	at Chicago	3 OT
Apr.	29	Chicago	2	at NY Rangers	3 3OT
May	2	NY Rangers	2	at Chicago	4

Chicago won best-of-seven series 4–3

FINALS

May	4	Montreal	1	at Chicago	2 OT
May	6	Montreal	3	at Chicago	5
May	9	Chicago	2	at Montreal	4
May	11	Chicago	2	at Montreal	5
May	13	Montreal	0	at Chicago	2
May	16	Chicago	3	at Montreal	4
May	18	Montreal	3	at Chicago	2

Montreal won best-of-seven series 4–3

1970-71 – Montreal Canadiens – Ken Dryden, Rogie Vachon, Phil Myre, Jacques Laperrière, J.C. Tremblay, Guy Lapointe, Terry Harper, Pierre Bouchard, Jean Béliveau (Captain), Marc Tardif, Yvan Cournoyer, Réjean Houle, Claude Larose, Henri Richard, Phil Roberto, Pete Mahovlich, Leon Rochefort, John Ferguson, Bobby Sheehan, Jacques Lemaire, Frank Mahovlich, Bob Murdoch, Chuck Lefley, Al MacNeil (Coach), Sam Pollock (General Manager), Eddy Palchak, Yvon Belanger (Trainers).

1970

For the third straight year, the St. Louis Blues qualified for the finals but faced new rivals in the Boston Bruins, who featured the first 100-point defenseman in NHL history in Norris Trophy recipient Bobby Orr.

After winning the first three games by margins of five, four and three goals, respectively, the Bruins were extended into overtime in the fourth game. Conn Smythe Trophy winner Orr quickly ended the affair at the 40 second mark of overtime with his first goal of the series. With Orr literally flying through the air on the play, his winning tally has become one of the most memorable images in hockey history.

The series victory marked the Bruins' first Stanley Cup title in 29 years.

CONN SMYTHE TROPHY
Bobby Orr - Defense - Boston Bruins

QUARTER-FINALS

Apr.	8	Detroit	2	at Chicago	4
Apr.	9	Detroit	2	at Chicago	4
Apr.	11	Chicago	4	at Detroit	2
Apr.	12	Chicago	4	at Detroit	2

Chicago won best-of-seven series 4–0

Apr.	8	NY Rangers	2	at Boston	8
Apr.	9	NY Rangers	3	at Boston	5
Apr.	11	Boston	3	at NY Rangers	4
Apr.	12	Boston	2	at NY Rangers	4
Apr.	14	NY Rangers	2	at Boston	3
Apr.	16	Boston	4	at NY Rangers	1

Boston won best-of-seven series 4–2

Apr.	8	Minnesota	2	at St. Louis	6
Apr.	9	Minnesota	1	at St. Louis	2
Apr.	11	St. Louis	2	at Minnesota	4
Apr.	12	St. Louis	0	at Minnesota	4
Apr.	14	Minnesota	3	at St. Louis	6
Apr.	16	St. Louis	4	at Minnesota	2

St. Louis won best-of-seven series 4–2

Apr.	8	Oakland	1	at Pittsburgh	2
Apr.	9	Oakland	1	at Pittsburgh	3
Apr.	11	Pittsburgh	5	at Oakland	2
Apr.	12	Pittsburgh	3	at Oakland	2 OT

Pittsburgh won best-of-seven series 4–0

SEMI-FINALS

Apr.	19	Boston	6	at Chicago	3
Apr.	21	Boston	4	at Chicago	1
Apr.	23	Chicago	2	at Boston	5
Apr.	26	Chicago	4	at Boston	5

Boston won best-of-seven series 4–0

Apr.	19	Pittsburgh	1	at St. Louis	3
Apr.	21	Pittsburgh	1	at St. Louis	4
Apr.	23	St. Louis	2	at Pittsburgh	3
Apr.	26	St. Louis	1	at Pittsburgh	2
Apr.	28	Pittsburgh	0	at St. Louis	5
Apr.	30	St. Louis	4	at Pittsburgh	3

St. Louis won best-of-seven series 4–2

FINALS

May	3	Boston	6	at St. Louis	1
May	5	Boston	6	at St. Louis	2
May	7	St. Louis	1	at Boston	4
May	10	St. Louis	3	at Boston	4 OT

Boston won best-of-seven series 4–0

1969-70 – Boston Bruins – Gerry Cheevers, Eddie Johnston, Bobby Orr, Rick Smith, Dallas Smith, Bill Speer, Gary Doak, Don Awrey, Phil Esposito, Ken Hodge, John Bucyk, Wayne Carleton, Wayne Cashman, Derek Sanderson, Fred Stanfield, Ed Westfall, John McKenzie, Jim Lorentz, Don Marcotte, Bill Lesuk, Danny Schock, Harry Sinden (Coach), Milt Schmidt (General Manager), Dan Canney, John Forristall (Trainers).

1969

Following in his predecessor's footsteps, Claude Ruel won the Stanley Cup in his first season behind the Canadiens' bench and became the 11th rookie coach in NHL history to go the distance with his team.

Goaltender Rogie Vachon limited St. Louis to three goals in four outings and registered his first career playoff and Stanley Cup finals shutout in the third game.

Serge Savard became the first defenseman to win the Conn Smythe Trophy.

CONN SMYTHE TROPHY
Serge Savard - Defense - Montreal Canadiens

QUARTER-FINALS

Apr.	2	NY Rangers	1	at Montreal	3
Apr.	3	NY Rangers	2	at Montreal	5
Apr.	5	Montreal	4	at NY Rangers	1
Apr.	6	Montreal	4	at NY Rangers	3

Montreal won best-of-seven series 4–0

Apr.	2	Toronto	0	at Boston	10
Apr.	3	Toronto	0	at Boston	7
Apr.	5	Boston	4	at Toronto	3
Apr.	6	Boston	3	at Toronto	2

Boston won best-of-seven series 4–0

Apr.	2	Philadelphia	2	at St. Louis	5
Apr.	3	Philadelphia	0	at St. Louis	5
Apr.	5	St. Louis	3	at Philadelphia	0
Apr.	6	St. Louis	4	at Philadelphia	1

St. Louis won best-of-seven series 4–0

Apr.	2	Los Angeles	5	at Oakland	4 OT
Apr.	3	Los Angeles	2	at Oakland	4
Apr.	5	Oakland	5	at Los Angeles	2
Apr.	6	Oakland	1	at Los Angeles	4
Apr.	9	Los Angeles	1	at Oakland	4
Apr.	10	Oakland	3	at Los Angeles	4
Apr.	13	Los Angeles	5	at Oakland	3

Los Angeles won best-of-seven series 4–3

SEMI-FINALS

Apr.	10	Boston	2	at Montreal	3 OT
Apr.	13	Boston	3	at Montreal	4 OT
Apr.	17	Montreal	0	at Boston	5
Apr.	20	Montreal	2	at Boston	3
Apr.	22	Boston	2	at Montreal	4
Apr.	24	Montreal	2	at Boston	1 2OT

Montreal won best-of-seven series 4–2

Apr.	15	Los Angeles	0	at St. Louis	4
Apr.	17	Los Angeles	2	at St. Louis	3
Apr.	19	St. Louis	5	at Los Angeles	2
Apr.	20	St. Louis	4	at Los Angeles	1

St. Louis won best-of-seven series 4–0

FINALS

Apr.	27	St. Louis	1	at Montreal	3
Apr.	29	St. Louis	1	at Montreal	3
May	1	Montreal	4	at St. Louis	0
May	4	Montreal	2	at St. Louis	1

Montreal won best-of-seven series 4–0

1968-69 – Montreal Canadiens – Gump Worsley, Rogie Vachon, Jacques Laperrière, J.C. Tremblay, Ted Harris, Serge Savard, Terry Harper, Larry Hillman, Jean Béliveau (Captain), Ralph Backstrom, Dick Duff, Yvan Cournoyer, Claude Provost, Bobby Rousseau, Henri Richard, John Ferguson, Christian Bordeleau, Mickey Redmond, Jacques Lemaire, Lucien Grenier, Tony Esposito, Claude Ruel (Coach), Sam Pollock (General Manager), Larry Aubut, Eddy Palchak (Trainers).

1968

The NHL doubled in size with the addition of six expansion teams which comprised one of two new divisions. In the playoffs, Montreal won the East Division, and St. Louis won the West Division to earn a chance at the Stanley Cup. The Blues lineup boasted several aging superstars, including two-time Vezina Trophy winner Glenn Hall, two-time Art Ross Trophy winner Dickie Moore and seven-time Norris Trophy recipient Doug Harvey. The three were no strangers to playoff action with 38 years of postseason experience among them. Rookie defenseman Serge Savard, who would amass seven Stanley Cup rings in his career, scored his first two career playoff goals while shorthanded in games two and three to tie a final series record. Toe Blake retired after capturing his eighth Stanley Cup in 13 years as coach of the Canadiens and set a record as the first person to win a total of 11 Stanley Cup championships in a career. Blake also played on championship teams with the Montreal Maroons in 1935 and the Canadiens in 1944 and 1946.

CONN SMYTHE TROPHY
Glenn Hall - Goaltender - St. Louis Blues

QUARTER-FINALS

Apr.	4	Boston	1	at Montreal	2
Apr.	6	Boston	3	at Montreal	5
Apr.	9	Montreal	5	at Boston	2
Apr.	11	Montreal	3	at Boston	2

Montreal won best-of-seven series 4–0

Apr.	4	Chicago	1	at NY Rangers	3
Apr.	9	Chicago	1	at NY Rangers	2
Apr.	11	NY Rangers	4	at Chicago	7
Apr.	13	NY Rangers	1	at Chicago	3
Apr.	14	Chicago	2	at NY Rangers	1
Apr.	16	NY Rangers	1	at Chicago	4

Chicago won best-of-seven series 4–2

Apr.	4	St. Louis	1	at Philadelphia	0
Apr.	6	St. Louis	3	at Philadelphia	4
Apr.	10	Philadelphia	2	at St. Louis	3 2OT
Apr.	11	Philadelphia	2	at St. Louis	5
Apr.	13	St. Louis	1	at Philadelphia	6
Apr.	16	Philadelphia	2	at St. Louis	1 2OT
Apr.	18	St. Louis	3	at Philadelphia	1

St. Louis won best-of-seven series 4–3

Apr.	4	Minnesota	1	at Los Angeles	2
Apr.	6	Minnesota	0	at Los Angeles	2
Apr.	9	Los Angeles	5	at Minnesota	7
Apr.	11	Los Angeles	2	at Minnesota	3
Apr.	13	Minnesota	3	at Los Angeles	4
Apr.	16	Los Angeles	3	at Minnesota	4 OT
Apr.	18	Minnesota	9	at Los Angeles	4

Minnesota won best-of-seven series 4–3

SEMI-FINALS

Apr.	18	Chicago	2	at Montreal	9
Apr.	20	Chicago	1	at Montreal	4
Apr.	23	Montreal	4	at Chicago	2
Apr.	25	Montreal	1	at Chicago	2
Apr.	28	Chicago	3	at Montreal	4 OT

Montreal won best-of-seven series 4–1

Apr.	21	Minnesota	3	at St. Louis	5
Apr.	22	St. Louis	2	at Minnesota	3 OT
Apr.	25	Minnesota	5	at St. Louis	1
Apr.	27	Minnesota	2	at St. Louis	4 OT
Apr.	29	Minnesota	2	at St. Louis	3 OT
May	1	St. Louis	1	at Minnesota	5
May	3	Minnesota	1	at St. Louis	2 2OT

St. Louis won best-of-seven series 4–3

FINALS

May	5	Montreal	3	at St. Louis	2 OT
May	7	Montreal	1	at St. Louis	0
May	9	St. Louis	3	at Montreal	4 OT
May	11	St. Louis	2	at Montreal	3

Montreal won best-of-seven series 4–0

1967-68 – Montreal Canadiens – Gump Worsley, Rogie Vachon, Jacques Laperrière, J.C. Tremblay, Ted Harris, Serge Savard, Terry Harper, Carol Vadnais, Jean Béliveau (Captain), Gilles Tremblay, Ralph Backstrom, Dick Duff, Claude Larose, Yvan Cournoyer, Claude Provost, Bobby Rousseau, Henri Richard, John Ferguson, Danny Grant, Jacques Lemaire, Mickey Redmond, Toe Blake (Coach), Sam Pollock (General Manager), Larry Aubut, Eddy Palchak (Trainers).

1967

With an average age of 31, the Toronto Maple Leafs sported the oldest lineup ever to win the Stanley Cup. Goaltender Johnny Bower (42) and defenseman Allan Stanley (41) were the senior citizens of the squad, which included seven players over 35 and 12 members over 30.

Dave Keon, a 27-year-old "youngster" who scored a goal and assist in the series, captured the Conn Smythe Trophy on the basis of an outstanding defensive performance.

CONN SMYTHE TROPHY
Dave Keon - Center - Toronto Maple Leafs

SEMI-FINALS

Apr.	6	Toronto	2	at Chicago	5
Apr.	9	Toronto	3	at Chicago	1
Apr.	11	Chicago	1	at Toronto	3
Apr.	13	Chicago	4	at Toronto	3
Apr.	15	Toronto	4	at Chicago	2
Apr.	18	Chicago	1	at Toronto	3

Toronto won best-of-seven series 4–2

Apr.	6	NY Rangers	4	at Montreal	6

Apr.	8	NY Rangers	1	at Montreal	3
Apr.	11	Montreal	3	at NY Rangers	2
Apr.	13	Montreal	2	at NY Rangers	1 OT

Montreal won best-of-seven series 4–0

FINALS

Apr.	20	Toronto	2	at Montreal	6
Apr.	22	Toronto	3	at Montreal	0
Apr.	25	Montreal	2	at Toronto	3 2OT
Apr.	27	Montreal	6	at Toronto	2
Apr.	29	Toronto	4	at Montreal	1
May	2	Montreal	1	at Toronto	3

Toronto won best-of-seven series 4–2

1966-67 – Toronto Maple Leafs – Johnny Bower, Terry Sawchuk, Larry Hillman, Marcel Pronovost, Tim Horton, Bob Baun, Aut Erickson, Allan Stanley, Red Kelly, Ron Ellis, George Armstrong (Captain), Pete Stemkowski, Dave Keon, Mike Walton, Jim Pappin, Bob Pulford, Brian Conacher, Eddie Shack, Frank Mahovlich, Milan Marcetta, Larry Jeffrey, Bruce Gamble, Punch Imlach (General Manager/Coach), Bob Haggart (Trainer).

1966

The Canadiens repeated as champions to give coach Toe Blake his seventh title in 11 years behind the Montreal bench. Henri Richard, a member of each of those seven Stanley Cup teams, scored the game-winner in overtime in game six, marking the ninth time in history that a series-winning goal had been scored in overtime.

Despite his team's loss in the finals, goaltender Roger Crozier received the Conn Smythe Trophy after posting a 2.17 average and one shutout in 12 playoff games.

CONN SMYTHE TROPHY
Roger Crozier - Goaltender - Detroit Red Wings

SEMI-FINALS

Apr.	7	Toronto	3	at Montreal	4
Apr.	9	Toronto	0	at Montreal	2
Apr.	12	Montreal	5	at Toronto	2
Apr.	14	Montreal	4	at Toronto	1

Montreal won best-of-seven series 4–0

Apr.	7	Detroit	1	at Chicago	2
Apr.	10	Detroit	7	at Chicago	0
Apr.	12	Chicago	2	at Detroit	1
Apr.	14	Chicago	1	at Detroit	5
Apr.	17	Detroit	5	at Chicago	3
Apr.	19	Chicago	2	at Detroit	3

Detroit won best-of-seven series 4–2

FINALS

Apr.	24	Detroit	3	at Montreal	2
Apr.	26	Detroit	5	at Montreal	2
Apr.	28	Montreal	4	at Detroit	2
May	1	Montreal	2	at Detroit	1
May	3	Detroit	1	at Montreal	5
May	5	Montreal	3	at Detroit	2 OT

Montreal won best-of-seven series 4–2

1965-66 – Montreal Canadiens – Gump Worsley, Charlie Hodge, J.C. Tremblay, Ted Harris, Jean-Guy Talbot, Terry Harper, Jacques Laperrière, Noel Price, Jean Béliveau (Captain), Ralph Backstrom, Dick Duff, Gilles Tremblay, Claude Larose, Yvan Cournoyer, Claude Provost, Bobby Rousseau, Henri Richard, Dave Balon, John Ferguson, Leon Rochefort, Jimmy Roberts, Toe Blake (Coach), Sam Pollock (General Manager), Larry Aubut, Andy Galley (Trainers).

1965

Repeating the feat accomplished in 1955, the home team won every game in the finals. With the extra game at the Montreal Forum, the Canadiens

treated their fans to four victories.

Gump Worsley, appearing in his first Stanley Cup series after 12 seasons in the NHL, recorded two shutouts in four starts, including one in game seven.

Jean Beliveau captured the inaugural Conn Smythe Trophy as the most valuable player for his team in the playoffs after amassing eight goals and eight assists in 13 games.

CONN SMYTHE TROPHY
Jean Beliveau - Center - Montreal Canadiens

SEMI-FINALS

Apr.	1	Chicago	3	at Detroit	4
Apr.	4	Chicago	3	at Detroit	6
Apr.	6	Detroit	2	at Chicago	5
Apr.	8	Detroit	1	at Chicago	2
Apr.	11	Chicago	2	at Detroit	4
Apr.	13	Detroit	0	at Chicago	4
Apr.	15	Chicago	4	at Detroit	2

Chicago won best-of-seven series 4–3

Apr.	1	Toronto	2	at Montreal	3
Apr.	3	Toronto	1	at Montreal	3
Apr.	6	Montreal	2	at Toronto	3 OT
Apr.	8	Montreal	2	at Toronto	4
Apr.	10	Toronto	1	at Montreal	3
Apr.	13	Montreal	4	at Toronto	3 OT

Montreal won best-of-seven series 4–2

FINALS

Apr.	17	Chicago	2	at Montreal	3
Apr.	20	Chicago	0	at Montreal	2
Apr.	22	Montreal	1	at Chicago	3
Apr.	25	Montreal	1	at Chicago	5
Apr.	27	Chicago	0	at Montreal	6
Apr.	29	Montreal	1	at Chicago	2
May	1	Chicago	0	at Montreal	4

Montreal won best-of-seven series 4–3

1964-65 – Montreal Canadiens – Gump Worsley, Charlie Hodge, J.C. Tremblay, Ted Harris, Jean-Guy Talbot, Terry Harper, Jacques Laperrière, Jean Gauthier, Noel Picard, Jean Béliveau (Captain), Ralph Backstrom, Dick Duff, Claude Larose, Yvan Cournoyer, Claude Provost, Bobby Rousseau, Henri Richard, Dave Balon, John Ferguson, Red Berenson, Jimmy Roberts, Toe Blake (Coach), Sam Pollock (General Manager), Larry Aubut, Andy Galley (Trainers).

1964

Tying their club record set from 1947 to 1949, Toronto captured the Stanley Cup for a third consecutive season.

The Maple Leafs advanced by defeating the Canadiens in seven games. In the Finals, the Leafs lost games 2, 3 and 5 by one-goal margins to trail the Detroit Red Wings three games to two.

With the score tied 3–3 late in game six, Maple Leafs defenseman Bob Baun took a Gordie Howe slapshot on his skate and dropped to the ice in pain. After freezing and taping the injury, he returned for overtime and scored the winning goal at 2:43 of the extra period. On crutches for the next two days, Baun would later suit up for the series finale and never miss a shift as Toronto won the Cup. The following day, x-rays confirmed what Baun had known all along, that the ankle was in fact broken. The Leafs blueliner spent two more months on crutches.

SEMI-FINALS

Mar.	26	Toronto	0	at Montreal	2
Mar.	28	Toronto	2	at Montreal	1
Mar.	31	Montreal	3	at Toronto	2
Apr.	2	Montreal	3	at Toronto	5
Apr.	4	Toronto	2	at Montreal	4

Apr.	7	Montreal	0	at Toronto	3
Apr.	9	Toronto	3	at Montreal	1

Toronto won best-of-seven series 4–3

Mar.	26	Detroit	1	at Chicago	4
Mar.	29	Detroit	5	at Chicago	4
Mar.	31	Chicago	0	at Detroit	3
Apr.	2	Chicago	3	at Detroit	2 OT
Apr.	5	Detroit	2	at Chicago	3
Apr.	7	Chicago	2	at Detroit	7
Apr.	9	Detroit	4	at Chicago	2

Detroit won best-of-seven series 4–3

FINALS

Apr.	11	Detroit	2	at Toronto	3
Apr.	14	Detroit	4	at Toronto	3 OT
Apr.	16	Toronto	3	at Detroit	4
Apr.	18	Toronto	4	at Detroit	2
Apr.	21	Detroit	2	at Toronto	1
Apr.	23	Toronto	4	at Detroit	3 OT
Apr.	25	Detroit	0	at Toronto	4

Toronto won best-of-seven series 4–3

1963-64 – Toronto Maple Leafs – Johnny Bower, Don Simmons, Carl Brewer, Tim Horton, Bob Baun, Allan Stanley, Larry Hillman, Al Arbour, Red Kelly, Gerry Ehman, Andy Bathgate, George Armstrong (Captain), Ron Stewart, Dave Keon, Billy Harris, Don McKenney, Jim Pappin, Bob Pulford, Eddie Shack, Frank Mahovlich, Ed Litzenberger, Punch Imlach (General Manager/Coach), Bob Haggert (Trainer).

1963

Five different Maple Leafs — Bob Nevin, Dick Duff, Ron Stewart, Red Kelly and Dave Keon — recorded multiple-goal performances in Toronto's four victories, and 38-year-old goaltender Johnny Bower limited Detroit to 10 goals in five games.

Keon scored twice in game five with Toronto players in the penalty box, establishing a new playoff record for shorthanded goals in one game.

SEMI-FINALS

Mar.	26	Montreal	1	at Toronto	3
Mar.	28	Montreal	2	at Toronto	3
Mar.	30	Toronto	2	at Montreal	0
Apr.	2	Toronto	1	at Montreal	3
Apr.	4	Montreal	0	at Toronto	5

Toronto won best-of-seven series 4–1

Mar.	26	Detroit	4	at Chicago	5
Mar.	28	Detroit	2	at Chicago	5
Mar.	31	Chicago	2	at Detroit	4
Apr.	2	Chicago	1	at Detroit	4
Apr.	4	Detroit	4	at Chicago	2
Apr.	7	Chicago	4	at Detroit	7

Detroit won best-of-seven series 4–2

FINALS

Apr.	9	Detroit	2	at Toronto	4
Apr.	11	Detroit	2	at Toronto	4
Apr.	14	Toronto	2	at Detroit	3
Apr.	16	Toronto	4	at Detroit	2
Apr.	18	Detroit	1	at Toronto	3

Toronto won best-of-seven series 4–1

1962-63 – Toronto Maple Leafs – Johnny Bower, Don Simmons, Carl Brewer, Tim Horton, Kent Douglas, Allan Stanley, Bob Baun, Larry Hillman, Red Kelly, Dick Duff, George Armstrong (Captain), Bob Nevin, Ron Stewart, Dave Keon, Billy Harris, Bob Pulford, Eddie Shack, Ed Litzenberger, Frank Mahovlich, John MacMillan, Punch Imlach (General Manager/Coach), Bob Haggert (Trainer).

1962

The Maple Leafs regained the Stanley Cup after 11 years, putting an end to the club's longest period without a championship in its 45-year NHL history through 1962.

In his Stanley Cup debut, 22-year-old Dave Keon scored a goal and added an assist.

Stan Mikita tallied two assists in game five to set new playoff records for assists (15) and points (21). The latter broke Gordie Howe's mark of 20 points set in the 1955 playoffs.

SEMI-FINALS

Mar. 27	Chicago	1	at	Montreal	2
Mar. 29	Chicago	3	at	Montreal	4
Apr. 1	Montreal	1	at	Chicago	4
Apr. 3	Montreal	3	at	Chicago	5
Apr. 5	Chicago	4	at	Montreal	3
Apr. 8	Montreal	0	at	Chicago	2

Chicago won best-of-seven series 4–2

Mar. 27	NY Rangers	2	at	Toronto	4
Mar. 29	NY Rangers	1	at	Toronto	2
Apr. 1	Toronto	4	at	NY Rangers	5
Apr. 3	Toronto	2	at	NY Rangers	4
Apr. 5	NY Rangers	2	at	Toronto	3 2OT
Apr. 7	NY Rangers	1	at	Toronto	7

Toronto won best-of-seven series 4–2

FINALS

Apr. 10	Chicago	1	at	Toronto	4
Apr. 12	Chicago	2	at	Toronto	3
Apr. 15	Toronto	0	at	Chicago	3
Apr. 17	Toronto	1	at	Chicago	4
Apr. 19	Chicago	4	at	Toronto	8
Apr. 22	Toronto	2	at	Chicago	1

Toronto won best-of-seven series 4–2

1961-62 – Toronto Maple Leafs – Johnny Bower, Don Simmons, Carl Brewer, Tim Horton, Bob Baun, Allan Stanley, Al Arbour, Larry Hillman, Red Kelly, Dick Duff, George Armstrong (Captain), Frank Mahovlich, Bob Nevin, Ron Stewart, Billy Harris, Bert Olmstead, Bob Pulford, Eddie Shack, Dave Keon, Ed Litzenberger, John MacMillan, Punch Imlach (General Manager/Coach), Bob Haggert (Trainer).

1961

The Chicago Black Hawks captured their first Stanley Cup title since 1938, clinching their third championship overall since joining the NHL in 1926-27.

Two of the greatest athletes in Chicago sports history — Bobby Hull and Stan Mikita — made their premier Stanley Cup appearances, and both figured prominently in the outcome. "The Golden Jet" sparkled in game one with his first two Stanley Cup goals, including the game-winner, while Mikita scored the winner in game five.

SEMI-FINALS

Mar. 21	Chicago	2	at	Montreal	6
Mar. 23	Chicago	4	at	Montreal	3
Mar. 26	Montreal	1	at	Chicago	2 2OT
Mar. 28	Montreal	5	at	Chicago	2
Apr. 1	Chicago	3	at	Montreal	0
Apr. 4	Montreal	0	at	Chicago	3

Chicago won best-of-seven series 4–2

Mar. 22	Detroit	2	at	Toronto	3 2OT
Mar. 25	Detroit	4	at	Toronto	2
Mar. 26	Toronto	0	at	Detroit	2
Mar. 28	Toronto	1	at	Detroit	4
Apr. 1	Detroit	3	at	Toronto	2

Detroit won best-of-seven series 4–1

FINALS

Apr. 6	Detroit	2	at	Chicago	3
Apr. 8	Chicago	1	at	Detroit	3
Apr. 10	Detroit	1	at	Chicago	3
Apr. 12	Chicago	1	at	Detroit	2
Apr. 14	Detroit	3	at	Chicago	6
Apr. 16	Chicago	5	at	Detroit	1

Chicago won best-of-seven series 4–2

1960-61 – Chicago Black Hawks – Glenn Hall, Al Arbour, Pierre Pilote (Captain), Moose Vasko, Jack Evans, Dollard St. Laurent, Reggie Fleming, Tod Sloan, Ron Murphy, Ed Litzenberger, Bill Hay, Bobby Hull, Ab McDonald, Eric Nesterenko, Kenny Wharram, Earl Balfour, Stan Mikita, Murray Balfour, Chico Maki, Wayne Hicks, Wayne Hillman, Denis DeJordy, Tommy Ivan (Manager), Rudy Pilous (Coach), Nick Garen (Trainer).

1960

The Canadiens retained the Stanley Cup for an unprecedented fifth straight season. No team has since matched this record-setting achievement.

Jacques Plante, who had introduced the goalie mask to the hockey world on November 1, 1959, in New York, sparkled with his self-designed face guard. His Stanley Cup performance, which included just five goals allowed in four games, played a large role in the acceptance of the mask by goaltenders worldwide.

Maurice Richard played in the last four games of his career. In game three, "The Rocket" scored his 34th goal in the finals, still an all-time record.

SEMI-FINALS

Mar. 24	Chicago	3	at	Montreal	4
Mar. 26	Chicago	3	at	Montreal	4 OT
Mar. 29	Montreal	4	at	Chicago	0
Mar. 31	Montreal	2	at	Chicago	0

Montreal won best-of-seven series 4–0

Mar. 23	Detroit	2	at	Toronto	1
Mar. 26	Detroit	2	at	Toronto	4
Mar. 27	Toronto	5	at	Detroit	4 3OT
Mar. 29	Toronto	1	at	Detroit	2 OT
Apr. 2	Detroit	4	at	Toronto	5
Apr. 3	Toronto	4	at	Detroit	2

Toronto won best-of-seven series 4–2

FINALS

Apr. 7	Toronto	2	at	Montreal	4
Apr. 9	Toronto	1	at	Montreal	2
Apr. 12	Montreal	5	at	Toronto	2
Apr. 14	Montreal	4	at	Toronto	0

Montreal won best-of-seven series 4–0

1959-60 – Montreal Canadiens – Jacques Plante, Charlie Hodge, Doug Harvey, Tom Johnson, Bob Turner, Jean-Guy Talbot, Albert Langlois, Ralph Backstrom, Jean Béliveau, Marcel Bonin, Bernie Geoffrion, Phil Goyette, Bill Hicke, Don Marshall, Ab McDonald, Dickie Moore, André Pronovost, Claude Provost, Henri Richard, Maurice Richard (Captain), Frank Selke (Manager), Toe Blake (Coach), Hector Dubois, Larry Aubut (Trainers).

1959

The Canadiens skated to a fourth consecutive championship, breaking the record of three they had shared with Toronto (1947 to 1949). Maurice Richard was held off the scoresheet during the playoffs for the first time in his career. Injuries had restricted his participation to just four games.

Led by newly appointed general manager/coach Punch Imlach, Toronto made their first appearance in the Stanley Cup finals since 1951, rebounding from a last-place finish in 1957-58. The Leafs had a perfect record of three wins and no losses in overtime games in this postseason.

SEMI-FINALS

Mar. 24	Chicago	2	at	Montreal	4
Mar. 26	Chicago	1	at	Montreal	5
Mar. 28	Montreal	2	at	Chicago	4
Mar. 31	Montreal	1	at	Chicago	3
Apr. 2	Chicago	2	at	Montreal	4
Apr. 4	Montreal	5	at	Chicago	4

Montreal won best-of-seven series 4–2

Mar. 24	Toronto	1	at	Boston	5
Mar. 26	Toronto	2	at	Boston	4
Mar. 28	Boston	2	at	Toronto	3 OT
Mar. 31	Boston	2	at	Toronto	3 OT
Apr. 2	Toronto	4	at	Boston	5
Apr. 4	Boston	5	at	Toronto	4
Apr. 7	Toronto	3	at	Boston	2

Toronto won best-of-seven series 4–3

FINALS

Apr. 9	Toronto	3	at	Montreal	5
Apr. 11	Toronto	1	at	Montreal	3
Apr. 14	Montreal	2	at	Toronto	3 OT
Apr. 16	Montreal	3	at	Toronto	2
Apr. 18	Montreal	5	at	Toronto	3

Montreal won best-of-seven series 4–1

1958-59 – Montreal Canadiens – Jacques Plante, Charlie Hodge, Doug Harvey, Tom Johnson, Bob Turner, Jean-Guy Talbot, Albert Langlois, Bernie Geoffrion, Ralph Backstrom, Bill Hicke, Maurice Richard (Captain), Dickie Moore, Claude Provost, Ab McDonald, Henri Richard, Marcel Bonin, Phil Goyette, Don Marshall, André Pronovost, Jean Béliveau, Ken Mosdell, Frank Selke (Manager), Toe Blake (Coach), Hector Dubois, Larry Aubut (Trainers).

1958

The Canadiens and Bruins met for a second consecutive year in the Stanley Cup finals. Once again, Boston had been an upset winner in the semi-finals, eliminating the New York Rangers in a high-scoring six-game series.

In the finals, the Habs won the Stanley Cup in six games. The Canadiens' third straight Stanley Cup title equalled the NHL record set by the Toronto Maple Leafs from 1947 to 1949.

Maurice Richard was the top overall playoff goal-scorer with 11. In game five of the finals, he notched the third final series overtime goal of his career and his sixth overtime goal in playoff competiton, setting all-time records in each category.

SEMI-FINALS

Mar. 25	Detroit	1	at	Montreal	8
Mar. 27	Detroit	1	at	Montreal	5
Mar. 30	Montreal	2	at	Detroit	1 OT
Apr. 1	Montreal	4	at	Detroit	3

Montreal won best-of-seven series 4–0

Mar. 25	Boston	3	at	NY Rangers	5
Mar. 27	Boston	4	at	NY Rangers	3 OT
Mar. 29	NY Rangers	0	at	Boston	5
Apr. 1	NY Rangers	5	at	Boston	2
Apr. 3	NY Rangers	1	at	Boston	6
Apr. 5	NY Rangers	2	at	Boston	8

Boston won best-of-seven series 4–2

FINALS

Apr. 8	Boston	1	at	Montreal	2
Apr. 10	Boston	5	at	Montreal	2
Apr. 13	Montreal	3	at	Boston	0
Apr. 15	Montreal	1	at	Boston	3
Apr. 17	Boston	2	at	Montreal	3 OT
Apr. 20	Montreal	5	at	Boston	3

Montreal won best-of-seven series 4–2

1957-58 – Montreal Canadiens – Jacques Plante, Gerry McNeil, Doug Harvey, Tom Johnson, Bob Turner, Dollard St. Laurent, Jean-Guy Talbot, Albert Langlois, Jean Béliveau, Bernie Geoffrion, Maurice Richard (Captain), Dickie Moore, Claude Provost, Floyd Curry, Bert Olmstead, Henri Richard, Marcel Bonin, Phil Goyette, Don Marshall, André Pronovost, Connie Broden, Ab McDonald, Frank Selke (Manager), Toe Blake (Coach), Hector Dubois, Larry Aubut (Trainers).

1957

The Boston Bruins were surprise finalists in 1957, eliminating the regular-season champion Detroit Red Wings in five games. Maurice "Rocket" Richard scored four times in game one, including three goals in the second period, to equal Ted Lindsay's modern Stanley Cup record for goals in a game.

Jacques Plante held the Bruins to six goals in five games as Montreal won its second consecutive Stanley Cup championship. Fleming MacKell had four of Boston's six goals.

SEMI-FINALS

Mar.	26	Boston	3	at	Detroit	1
Mar.	28	Boston	2	at	Detroit	7
Mar.	31	Detroit	3	at	Boston	4
Apr.	2	Detroit	0	at	Boston	2
Apr.	4	Boston	4	at	Detroit	3

Boston won best-of-seven series 4–1

Mar.	26	Montreal	4	at	NY Rangers	1
Mar.	28	Montreal	3	at	NY Rangers	4 OT
Mar.	30	NY Rangers	3	at	Montreal	8
Apr.	2	NY Rangers	1	at	Montreal	3
Apr.	4	NY Rangers	3	at	Montreal	4 OT

Montreal won best-of-seven series 4–1

FINALS

Apr.	6	Boston	1	at	Montreal	5
Apr.	9	Boston	0	at	Montreal	1
Apr.	11	Montreal	4	at	Boston	2
Apr.	14	Montreal	0	at	Boston	2
Apr.	16	Boston	1	at	Montreal	5

Montreal won best-of-seven series 4–1

1956-57 – Montreal Canadiens – Jacques Plante, Gerry McNeil, Doug Harvey, Tom Johnson, Bob Turner, Dollard St. Laurent, Jean-Guy Talbot, Jean Béliveau, Bernie Geoffrion, Floyd Curry, Dickie Moore, Maurice Richard (Captain), Claude Provost, Bert Olmstead, Henri Richard, Phil Goyette, Don Marshall, André Pronovost, Connie Broden, Frank Selke (Manager), Toe Blake (Coach), Hector Dubois, Larry Aubut (Trainers).

1956

Two rookies played integral roles on this first of five consecutive Stanley Cup championship teams for the Montreal Canadiens. Former playing star Toe Blake took over for Dick Irvin behind the Canadiens' bench as coach, while rookie center Henri Richard joined his famous brother Maurice on the ice. Blake, who would become the 10th rookie coach in NHL history to win the Cup, won his first game in the finals as a coach, and young Richard notched his first Stanley Cup goal.

Jean Beliveau scored seven times in the series, including at least one in each game, to set a modern record for goals in the finals and tie Maurice Richard's overall NHL playoff record of 12 goals set in 1944.

SEMI-FINALS

Mar.	20	NY Rangers	1	at	Montreal	7
Mar.	22	NY Rangers	4	at	Montreal	2
Mar.	24	Montreal	3	at	NY Rangers	1
Mar.	25	Montreal	5	at	NY Rangers	3
Mar.	27	NY Rangers	0	at	Montreal	7

Montreal won best-of-seven series 4–1

Mar.	20	Toronto	2	at	Detroit	3
Mar.	22	Toronto	1	at	Detroit	3
Mar.	24	Detroit	5	at	Toronto	4 OT
Mar.	27	Detroit	0	at	Toronto	2
Mar.	29	Toronto	1	at	Detroit	3

Detroit won best-of-seven series 4–1

FINALS

Mar.	31	Detroit	4	at	Montreal	6

Apr.	3	Detroit	1	at	Montreal	5
Apr.	5	Montreal	1	at	Detroit	3
Apr.	8	Montreal	3	at	Detroit	0
Apr.	10	Detroit	1	at	Montreal	3

Montreal won best-of-seven series 4–1

1955-56 – Montreal Canadiens – Jacques Plante, Doug Harvey, Butch Bouchard (Captain), Bob Turner, Tom Johnson, Jean-Guy Talbot, Dollard St. Laurent, Jean Béliveau, Bernie Geoffrion, Bert Olmstead, Floyd Curry, Jack Leclair, Maurice Richard, Dickie Moore, Henri Richard, Ken Mosdell, Don Marshall, Claude Provost, Charlie Hodge, Frank Selke (Manager), Toe Blake (Coach), Hector Dubois (Trainer).

1955

On March 17, Maurice Richard had been suspended for the remainder of the regular-season and playoffs for punching a linesman. The high-scoring right-winger's absence was sorely felt by the Canadiens.

In game two of the finals, Detroit's Ted Lindsay scored four times to set a modern record for goals in a championship game, and the Red Wings won their 15th consecutive contest (including the regular season) to establish another NHL record. Lindsay then tallied one assist, his last of the series, in game four to tie Elmer Lach's record of 12 playoff assists set in 1946.

Gordie Howe set two records in the series. He amassed 12 points in the finals (five goals, seven assists) to establish a new mark, and snapped Toe Blake's overall playoff record with 20 points (nine goals, 11 assists) in 11 games.

For the first time in a best-of-seven final, the home team won all seven games.

SEMI-FINALS

Mar.	22	Toronto	4	at	Detroit	7
Mar.	24	Toronto	1	at	Detroit	2
Mar.	26	Detroit	2	at	Toronto	1
Mar.	29	Detroit	3	at	Toronto	0

Detroit won best-of-seven series 4–0

Mar.	22	Boston	0	at	Montreal	2
Mar.	24	Boston	1	at	Montreal	3
Mar.	27	Montreal	2	at	Boston	4
Mar.	29	Montreal	4	at	Boston	3 OT
Mar.	31	Boston	1	at	Montreal	5

Montreal won best-of-seven series 4–1

FINALS

Apr.	3	Montreal	2	at	Detroit	4
Apr.	5	Montreal	1	at	Detroit	7
Apr.	7	Detroit	2	at	Montreal	4
Apr.	9	Detroit	3	at	Montreal	5
Apr.	10	Montreal	1	at	Detroit	5
Apr.	12	Detroit	3	at	Montreal	6
Apr.	14	Montreal	1	at	Detroit	3

Detroit won best-of-seven series 4–3

1954-55 – Detroit Red Wings – Terry Sawchuk, Red Kelly, Bob Goldham, Marcel Pronovost, Benny Woit, Jim Hay, Larry Hillman, Ted Lindsay (Captain), Tony Leswick, Gordie Howe, Alex Delvecchio, Marty Pavelich, Glen Skov, Dutch Reibel, Johnny Wilson, Bill Dineen, Vic Stasiuk, Marcel Bonin, Jack Adams (Manager), Jimmy Skinner (Coach), Carl Mattson (Trainer).

1954

Tony Leswick's Cup-winning tally was only the second goal ever scored in overtime during the seventh and deciding game of a Stanley Cup final series. Leswick, who notched the winner at 4:29 of the first extra period, matched the feat first accomplished by former Red Wing Pete Babando in 1950.

Marguerite Norris, president of the Detroit club, was presented with the Stanley Cup by NHL President Clarence Campbell at the conclusion of the series. She became the first woman in history to have her name engraved on the Stanley Cup.

SEMI-FINALS

Mar.	23	Toronto	0	at	Detroit	5
Mar.	25	Toronto	3	at	Detroit	1
Mar.	27	Detroit	3	at	Toronto	1
Mar.	30	Detroit	2	at	Toronto	1
Apr.	1	Toronto	3	at	Detroit	4 2OT

Detroit won best-of-seven series 4–1

Mar.	23	Boston	0	at	Montreal	2
Mar.	25	Boston	1	at	Montreal	8
Mar.	28	Montreal	4	at	Boston	3
Mar.	30	Montreal	2	at	Boston	0

Montreal won best-of-seven series 4–0

FINALS

Apr.	4	Montreal	1	at	Detroit	3
Apr.	6	Montreal	3	at	Detroit	1
Apr.	8	Detroit	5	at	Montreal	2
Apr.	10	Detroit	2	at	Montreal	0
Apr.	11	Montreal	1	at	Detroit	0 OT
Apr.	13	Detroit	1	at	Montreal	4
Apr.	16	Montreal	1	at	Detroit	2 OT

Detroit won best-of-seven series 4–3

1953-54 – Detroit Red Wings – Terry Sawchuk, Red Kelly, Bob Goldham, Benny Woit, Marcel Pronovost, Al Arbour, Keith Allen, Ted Lindsay (Captain), Tony Leswick, Gordie Howe, Marty Pavelich, Alex Delvecchio, Metro Prystai, Glen Skov, Johnny Wilson, Bill Dineen, Jimmy Peters, Dutch Reibel, Gilles Dube, Dave Gatherum, Jack Adams (Manager), Tommy Ivan (Coach), Carl Mattson (Trainer).

1953

After goaltender Jacques Plante recorded a split decision in the first two games he ever played in the Stanley Cup finals, Canadiens coach Dick Irvin sent Gerry McNeil into the nets. The move resulted in two shutouts in the final three games as Montreal regained the Cup for the first time in seven years.

Elmer Lach scored the series-winning goal at 1:22 of overtime in the fifth and final game.

SEMI-FINALS

Mar.	24	Boston	0	at	Detroit	7
Mar.	26	Boston	5	at	Detroit	3
Mar.	29	Detroit	1	at	Boston	2 OT
Mar.	31	Detroit	2	at	Boston	6
Apr.	2	Boston	4	at	Detroit	6
Apr.	5	Detroit	2	at	Boston	4

Boston won best-of-seven series 4–2

Mar.	24	Chicago	1	at	Montreal	3
Mar.	26	Chicago	3	at	Montreal	4
Mar.	29	Montreal	1	at	Chicago	2 OT
Mar.	31	Montreal	1	at	Chicago	3
Apr.	2	Chicago	4	at	Montreal	2
Apr.	4	Montreal	3	at	Chicago	0
Apr.	7	Chicago	1	at	Montreal	4

Montreal won best-of-seven series 4–3

FINALS

Apr.	9	Boston	2	at	Montreal	4
Apr.	11	Boston	4	at	Montreal	1
Apr.	12	Montreal	3	at	Boston	0
Apr.	14	Montreal	7	at	Boston	3
Apr.	16	Boston	0	at	Montreal	1 OT

Montreal won best-of-seven series 4–1

1952-53 – Montreal Canadiens – Gerry McNeil, Jacques Plante, Doug Harvey, Butch Bouchard (Captain), Tom Johnson, Dollard St. Laurent, Bud MacPherson, Maurice Richard, Elmer Lach, Bert Olmstead, Bernie Geoffrion, Floyd Curry,

Paul Masnick, Billy Reay, Dickie Moore, Ken Mosdell, Dick Gamble, John McCormack, Lorne Davis, Calum MacKay, Eddie Mazur, Paul Meger, Frank Selke (Manager), Dick Irvin (Coach), Hector Dubois (Trainer).

1952

Terry Sawchuk made his debut in the Cup finals and rose to the occasion, recording two shutouts and limiting Montreal to just two goals during the four-game series. Meanwhile, Gordie Howe contributed his first two career goals in a Stanley Cup championship series.

The Red Wings set an NHL record by winning all eight postseason games, including a four-game sweep over Toronto in the first round.

SEMI-FINALS

Mar.	25	Toronto	0	at	Detroit	3
Mar.	27	Toronto	0	at	Detroit	1
Mar.	29	Detroit	6	at	Toronto	2
Apr.	1	Detroit	3	at	Toronto	1

Detroit won best-of-seven series 4–0

Mar.	25	Boston	1	at	Montreal	5
Mar.	27	Boston	0	at	Montreal	4
Mar.	30	Montreal	1	at	Boston	4
Apr.	1	Montreal	2	at	Boston	3
Apr.	3	Boston	1	at	Montreal	0
Apr.	6	Montreal	3	at	Boston	2 2OT
Apr.	8	Boston	1	at	Montreal	3

Montreal won best-of-seven series 4–3

FINALS

Apr.	10	Detroit	3	at	Montreal	1
Apr.	12	Detroit	2	at	Montreal	1
Apr.	13	Montreal	0	at	Detroit	3
Apr.	15	Montreal	0	at	Detroit	3

Detroit won best-of-seven series 4–0

1951-52 – Detroit Red Wings – Terry Sawchuk, Bob Goldham, Benny Woit, Red Kelly, Leo Reise, Jr., Marcel Pronovost, Tony Leswick, Gordie Howe, Metro Prystai, Marty Pavelich, Sid Abel (Captain), Glen Skov, Alex Delvecchio, Johnny Wilson, Vic Stasiuk, Larry Zeidel, Glenn Hall, Jack Adams (Manager), Tommy Ivan (Coach), Carl Mattson (Trainer).

1951

The 1951 series distinguished itself as the only Stanley Cup final in which every game ended in overtime. Sid Smith, Ted Kennedy, Harry Watson and Bill Barilko notched the overtime winners for Toronto, while Maurice "Rocket" Richard scored goals in all five contests for Montreal.

Richard's overtime tally was his second in a final series and the fourth of his playoff career, breaking the record of three set by Boston's Mel Hill in 1939.

For Barilko, his overtime goal would be his last as the rugged defenseman died tragically in a plane crash during the summer.

SEMI-FINALS

Mar.	27	Montreal	3	at	Detroit	2 4OT
Mar.	29	Montreal	1	at	Detroit	0 3OT
Mar.	31	Detroit	2	at	Montreal	0
Apr.	3	Detroit	4	at	Montreal	1
Apr.	5	Montreal	5	at	Detroit	2
Apr.	7	Detroit	2	at	Montreal	3

Montreal won best-of-seven series 4–2

Mar.	28	Boston	2	at	Toronto	0
Mar.	31	Boston	1	at	Toronto	1 OT*
Apr.	1	Toronto	3	at	Boston	0
Apr.	3	Toronto	3	at	Boston	1
Apr.	7	Boston	1	at	Toronto	4
Apr.	8	Toronto	6	at	Boston	0

* game called after one overtime period due to curfew.

Toronto won best-of-seven series 4–1

FINALS

Apr.	11	Montreal	2	at	Toronto	3 OT
Apr.	14	Montreal	3	at	Toronto	2 OT
Apr.	17	Toronto	2	at	Montreal	1 OT
Apr.	19	Toronto	3	at	Montreal	2 OT
Apr.	21	Montreal	2	at	Toronto	3 OT

Toronto won best-of-seven series 4–1

1950-51 – Toronto Maple Leafs – Turk Broda, Al Rollins, Jimmy Thomson, Gus Mortson, Bill Barilko, Bill Juzda, Fern Flaman, Hugh Bolton, Ted Kennedy (Captain), Sid Smith, Tod Sloan, Cal Gardner, Howie Meeker, Harry Watson, Max Bentley, Joe Klukay, Danny Lewicki, Ray Timgren, Fleming MacKell, John McCormack, Bob Hassard, Conn Smythe (Manager), Joe Primeau (Coach), Tim Daly (Trainer).

1950

Bumped from Madison Square Garden by the circus, the New York Rangers opted to play games two and three in Toronto.

Gordie Howe failed to appear for the winners in this series as a result of a serious head injury sustained in the first game of the playoffs. After sliding head first into the boards, Howe required surgery to repair a fractured nose and cheekbone. Despite the seriousness of the injury, he resumed his career the following season.

Even without Howe, Detroit managed to capture the Cup in seven games, but not without a fight. New York battled Detroit to a 3–3 tie at the end of regulation in game seven, which the Red Wings' Pete Babando ultimately ended at the 28:31 mark of overtime. Babando's goal was the first sudden-death tally ever scored in the seventh game of a final series.

New York's Don Raleigh set a record that would remain unmatched until 1993 when he scored two overtime goals in one Stanley Cup final series.

SEMI-FINALS

Mar.	28	Toronto	5	at	Detroit	0
Mar.	30	Toronto	1	at	Detroit	3
Apr.	1	Detroit	0	at	Toronto	2
Apr.	4	Detroit	2	at	Toronto	1 2OT
Apr.	6	Toronto	2	at	Detroit	0
Apr.	8	Detroit	4	at	Toronto	0
Apr.	9	Toronto	0	at	Detroit	1 OT

Detroit won best-of-seven series 4–3

Mar.	29	Montreal	1	at	NY Rangers	3
Apr.	1	NY Rangers	3	at	Montreal	2
Apr.	2	Montreal	1	at	NY Rangers	4
Apr.	4	NY Rangers	4	at	Montreal	3 OT
Apr.	6	NY Rangers	3	at	Montreal	0

NY Rangers won best-of-seven series 4–1

FINALS

Apr.	11	NY Rangers	1	at	Detroit	4
Apr.	13	Detroit	1	vs.	NY Rangers	3 *
Apr.	15	Detroit	4	vs.	NY Rangers	0 *
Apr.	18	NY Rangers	4	at	Detroit	3 OT
Apr.	20	NY Rangers	1	at	Detroit	2 OT
Apr.	22	NY Rangers	4	at	Detroit	5
Apr.	23	NY Rangers	3	at	Detroit	4 2OT

* played in Toronto

Detroit won best-of-seven series 4–3

1949-50 – Detroit Red Wings – Harry Lumley, Jack Stewart, Leo Reise, Jr., Clare Martin, Al Dewsbury, Lee Fogolin, Marcel Pronovost, Red Kelly, Ted Lindsay, Sid Abel (Captain), Gordie Howe, George Gee, Jimmy Peters, Marty Pavelich, Jim McFadden, Pete Babando, Max McNab, Gerry Couture, Joe Carveth, Steve Black, Johnny Wilson, Larry Wilson, Doug McKay, Jack Adams (Manager), Tommy Ivan (Coach), Carl Mattson (Trainer).

1949

The Toronto Maple Leafs established two NHL records in this 1949 series. Most significantly, they captured their third straight Stanley Cup title, a feat last accomplished 44 years earlier by the Ottawa Silver Seven. They had also won an unprecedented ninth straight game in the finals dating back to April 19, 1947.

SEMI-FINALS

Mar.	22	Montreal	1	at	Detroit	2 3OT
Mar.	24	Montreal	4	at	Detroit	3 OT
Mar.	26	Detroit	2	at	Montreal	3
Mar.	29	Detroit	3	at	Montreal	1
Mar.	31	Montreal	1	at	Detroit	3
Apr.	2	Detroit	1	at	Montreal	3
Apr.	5	Montreal	1	at	Detroit	3

Detroit won best-of-seven series 4–3

Mar.	22	Toronto	3	at	Boston	0
Mar.	24	Toronto	3	at	Boston	2
Mar.	26	Boston	5	at	Toronto	4 OT
Mar.	29	Boston	1	at	Toronto	3
Mar.	30	Toronto	3	at	Boston	2

Toronto won best-of-seven series 4–1

FINALS

Apr.	8	Toronto	3	at	Detroit	2 OT
Apr.	10	Toronto	3	at	Detroit	1
Apr.	13	Detroit	1	at	Toronto	3
Apr.	16	Detroit	1	at	Toronto	3

Toronto won best-of-seven series 4–0

1948-49 – Toronto Maple Leafs – Turk Broda, Jimmy Thomson, Gus Mortson, Bill Barilko, Garth Boesch, Bill Juzda, Ted Kennedy (Captain), Howie Meeker, Vic Lynn, Harry Watson, Bill Ezinicki, Cal Gardner, Max Bentley, Joe Klukay, Sid Smith, Don Metz, Ray Timgren, Fleming MacKell, Harry Taylor, Bob Dawes, Tod Sloan, Conn Smythe (Manager), Hap Day (Coach), Tim Daly (Trainer).

1948

The series marked the beginning and end of two great Stanley Cup careers. For Detroit's Gordie Howe, it was an introduction to the rigors of championship competition. For Toronto's Syl Apps, who scored one goal in game four, it meant the conclusion of a Hall-of-Fame career.

Toronto became the fourth NHL team to repeat as Stanley Cup champions, joining the Ottawa Senators (1920-1921), Montreal Canadiens (1930-1931) and Detroit Red Wings (1936-1937).

SEMI-FINALS

Mar.	24	Boston	4	at	Toronto	5 OT
Mar.	27	Boston	3	at	Toronto	5
Mar.	30	Toronto	5	at	Boston	1
Apr.	1	Toronto	2	at	Boston	3
Apr.	3	Boston	2	at	Toronto	3

Toronto won best-of-seven series 4–1

Mar.	24	NY Rangers	1	at	Detroit	2
Mar.	26	NY Rangers	2	at	Detroit	5
Mar.	28	Detroit	2	at	NY Rangers	3
Mar.	30	Detroit	1	at	NY Rangers	3
Apr.	1	NY Rangers	1	at	Detroit	3
Apr.	4	Detroit	4	at	NY Rangers	2

Detroit won best-of-seven series 4–2

FINALS

Apr.	7	Detroit	3	at	Toronto	5
Apr.	10	Detroit	2	at	Toronto	4
Apr.	11	Toronto	2	at	Detroit	0
Apr.	14	Toronto	7	at	Detroit	2

Toronto won best-of-seven series 4–0

1947-48 – Toronto Maple Leafs – Turk Broda, Jimmy Thomson, Wally Stanowski, Garth Boesch, Bill Barilko, Gus Mortson, Phil Samis, Syl Apps (Captain),

Bill Ezinicki, Harry Watson, Ted Kennedy, Howie Meeker, Vic Lynn, Nick Metz, Max Bentley, Joe Klukay, Les Costello, Don Metz, Sid Smith, Conn Smythe (Manager), Hap Day (Coach), Tim Daly (Trainer).

1947

The Toronto Maple Leafs were a "new look" club in 1946–47. Young players like Calder Trophy-winner Howie Meeker, Bill Barilko and Bill Ezinicki were new performers in the Leafs' overhauled lineup.

In the first all-Canadian final in 12 years, the Maple Leafs defeated the Canadiens in six games. Toronto's Ted Kennedy potted three goals in the series, including the Cup-winner in the closing match-up. The Leafs were the youngest NHL team to win the Stanley Cup.

SEMI-FINALS

Mar. 25	Boston	1	at	Montreal	3
Mar. 27	Boston	1	at	Montreal	2 OT
Mar. 29	Montreal	2	at	Boston	4
Apr. 1	Montreal	5	at	Boston	1
Apr. 3	Boston	3	at	Montreal	4 2OT

Montreal won best-of-seven series 4–1

Mar. 26	Detroit	2	at	Toronto	3 OT
Mar. 29	Detroit	9	at	Toronto	1
Apr. 1	Toronto	4	at	Detroit	1
Apr. 3	Toronto	4	at	Detroit	1
Apr. 5	Detroit	1	at	Toronto	6

Toronto won best-of-seven series 4–1

FINALS

Apr. 8	Toronto	0	at	Montreal	6
Apr. 10	Toronto	4	at	Montreal	0
Apr. 12	Montreal	2	at	Toronto	4
Apr. 15	Montreal	1	at	Toronto	2 OT
Apr. 17	Toronto	1	at	Montreal	3
Apr. 19	Montreal	1	at	Toronto	2

Toronto won best-of-seven series 4–2

1946-47 – Toronto Maple Leafs – Turk Broda, Garth Boesch, Gus Mortson, Jimmy Thomson, Wally Stanowski, Bill Barilko, Harry Watson, Bud Poile, Ted Kennedy, Syl Apps (Captain), Don Metz, Nick Metz, Bill Ezinicki, Vic Lynn, Howie Meeker, Gaye Stewart, Joe Klukay, Gus Bodnar, Bob Goldham, Conn Smythe (Manager), Hap Day (Coach), Tim Daly (Trainer).

1946

Two high-scoring forward units met in the NHL's first post-World War II Stanley Cup final. Boston was led by the Kraut Line of Bobby Bauer, Milt Schmidt and Woody Dumart. The Canadiens featured the Punch Line of Maurice "Rocket" Richard, Elmer Lach and Toe Blake. In game one, Richard scored the first of a record six overtime goals in his playoff career and the first of his record three career overtime tallies in the finals.

The Canadiens won a close, hard-fought series in five games, with three contests requiring overtime.

SEMI-FINALS

Mar. 19	Chicago	2	at	Montreal	6
Mar. 21	Chicago	1	at	Montreal	5
Mar. 24	Montreal	8	at	Chicago	2
Mar. 26	Montreal	7	at	Chicago	2

Montreal won best-of-seven series 4–0

Mar. 19	Detroit	1	at	Boston	3
Mar. 21	Detroit	3	at	Boston	0
Mar. 24	Boston	5	at	Detroit	2
Mar. 26	Boston	4	at	Detroit	1
Mar. 28	Detroit	3	at	Boston	4 OT

Boston won best-of-seven series 4–1

FINALS

Mar. 30	Boston	3	at	Montreal	4 OT
Apr. 2	Boston	2	at	Montreal	3 OT
Apr. 4	Montreal	4	at	Boston	2
Apr. 7	Montreal	2	at	Boston	3 OT
Apr. 9	Boston	3	at	Montreal	6

Montreal won best-of-seven series 4–1

1945-46 – Montreal Canadiens – Elmer Lach, Toe Blake (Captain), Maurice Richard, Bob Fillion, Dutch Hiller, Murph Chamberlain, Ken Mosdell, Buddy O'Connor, Glen Harmon, Jimmy Peters, Butch Bouchard, Billy Reay, Ken Reardon, Leo Lamoureux, Frank Eddolls, Gerry Plamondon, Bill Durnan, Tommy Gorman (Manager), Dick Irvin (Coach), Ernie Cook (Trainer).

1945

Two rookie goaltenders — Toronto's Frank McCool and Detroit's Harry Lumley — manned the opposing nets in the Stanley Cup finals for the first time. McCool, who never played in another final series, posted shutouts in the each of the first three games to set a new Stanley Cup record, while Lumley rebounded with two of his own in games five and six to knot the series at three games apiece.

SEMI-FINALS

Mar. 20	Toronto	1	at	Montreal	0
Mar. 22	Toronto	3	at	Montreal	2
Mar. 24	Montreal	4	at	Toronto	1
Mar. 27	Montreal	3	at	Toronto	4 OT
Mar. 29	Toronto	3	at	Montreal	10
Mar. 31	Montreal	2	at	Toronto	3

Toronto won best-of-seven series 4–2

Mar. 20	Boston	4	at	Detroit	3
Mar. 22	Boston	4	at	Detroit	3
Mar. 25	Detroit	3	at	Boston	2
Mar. 27	Detroit	3	at	Boston	2
Mar. 29	Boston	2	at	Detroit	3 OT
Apr. 1	Detroit	3	at	Boston	5
Apr. 3	Boston	3	at	Detroit	5

Detroit won best-of-seven series 4–3

FINALS

Apr. 6	Toronto	1	at	Detroit	0
Apr. 8	Toronto	2	at	Detroit	0
Apr. 12	Detroit	0	at	Toronto	1
Apr. 14	Detroit	5	at	Toronto	3
Apr. 19	Toronto	0	at	Detroit	2
Apr. 21	Detroit	1	at	Toronto	0 OT
Apr. 22	Detroit	2	at	Toronto	1

Toronto won best-of-seven series 4–3

1944-45 – Toronto Maple Leafs – Don Metz, Frank McCool, Wally Stanowski, Reg Hamilton, Moe Morris, John McCreedy, Tom O'Neill, Ted Kennedy, Babe Pratt, Gus Bodnar, Art Jackson, Jack McLean, Mel Hill, Nick Metz, Bob Davidson (Captain), Sweeney Schriner, Lorne Carr, Pete Backor, Ross Johnstone, Conn Smythe (Manager), Frank Selke (Business Manager), Hap Day (Coach), Tim Daly (Trainer).

1944

Making his Stanley Cup debut, Maurice "Rocket" Richard scored five goals, including the first of his NHL-record three career hat tricks in the finals in game two. In total, the Punch Line of Elmer Lach, Toe Blake and Richard combined for 10 of the Canadiens' 16 goals in the series, including all five Montreal scores in the finale. Blake netted the Cup-winning goal at 9:12 of the first overtime period in game four, marking the fourth time an NHL player had clinched the Cup with a sudden-death tally.

In that final overtime contest, Canadiens goaltender Bill Durnan stonewalled Chicago's Virgil Johnson on the first penalty shot ever awarded in a Stanley Cup final.

The victory gave the Canadiens their first Stanley Cup championship since 1931.

SEMI-FINALS

Mar. 21	Toronto	3	at	Montreal	1
Mar. 23	Toronto	1	at	Montreal	5
Mar. 25	Montreal	2	at	Toronto	1
Mar. 28	Montreal	4	at	Toronto	1
Mar. 30	Toronto	0	at	Montreal	11

Montreal won best-of-seven series 4–1

Mar. 21	Chicago	2	at	Detroit	1
Mar. 23	Chicago	1	at	Detroit	4
Mar. 26	Detroit	0	at	Chicago	2
Mar. 28	Detroit	1	at	Chicago	7
Mar. 30	Chicago	5	at	Detroit	2

Chicago won best-of-seven series 4–1

FINALS

Apr. 4	Chicago	1	at	Montreal	5
Apr. 6	Montreal	3	at	Chicago	1
Apr. 9	Montreal	3	at	Chicago	2
Apr. 13	Chicago	4	at	Montreal	5 OT

Montreal won best-of-seven series 4–0

1943-44 – Montreal Canadiens – Toe Blake (Captain), Maurice Richard, Elmer Lach, Ray Getliffe, Murph Chamberlain, Phil Watson, Butch Bouchard, Glen Harmon, Buddy O'Connor, Gerry Heffernan, Mike McMahon, Leo Lamoureux, Fern Majeau, Bob Fillion, Bill Durnan, Tommy Gorman (Manager), Dick Irvin (Coach), Ernie Cook (Trainer).

1943

A new era in hockey history was ushered in with the 1942–43 season. The departure of the New York Americans franchise left the NHL with just the New York Rangers, Boston Bruins, Chicago Black Hawks, Detroit Red Wings, Toronto Maple Leafs and Montreal Canadiens — the so-called "Original Six."

After losing the Stanley Cup in 1941 and 1942, the Red Wings' third straight trip to the finals proved to be the charm as they swept the Bruins, avenging the similar treatment they had received from Boston two years before. Goaltender Johnny Mowers blanked the Bruins at Boston Garden in the last two games to ice the championship.

SEMI-FINALS

Mar. 21	Toronto	2	at	Detroit	4
Mar. 23	Toronto	3	at	Detroit	2 4OT
Mar. 25	Detroit	4	at	Toronto	2
Mar. 27	Detroit	3	at	Toronto	6
Mar. 28	Toronto	2	at	Detroit	4
Mar. 30	Detroit	3	at	Toronto	2 OT

Detroit won best-of-seven series 4–2

Mar. 21	Montreal	4	at	Boston	5 OT
Mar. 23	Montreal	3	at	Boston	5
Mar. 25	Boston	3	at	Montreal	2 OT
Mar. 27	Boston	0	at	Montreal	4
Mar. 30	Montreal	4	at	Boston	5 OT

Boston won best-of-seven series 4–1

FINALS

Apr. 1	Boston	2	at	Detroit	6
Apr. 4	Boston	3	at	Detroit	4
Apr. 7	Detroit	4	at	Boston	0
Apr. 8	Detroit	2	at	Boston	0

Detroit won best-of-seven series 4–0

1942-43 – Detroit Red Wings – Jack Stewart, Jimmy Orlando, Sid Abel, Alex Motter, Harry Watson, Joe Carveth, Mud Bruneteau, Eddie Wares, Johnny Mowers, Cully Simon, Don Grosso, Carl Liscombe, Adam Brown, Syd Howe, Les Douglas, Harold Jackson, Joe Fisher, Connie Brown, Jack Adams (Manager), Ebbie Goodfellow (Playing Coach), Honey Walker (Trainer).

1942

In the most remarkable comeback in Stanley Cup history, Toronto rebounded from a 3–0 deficit to win the series in seven games. The feat has never been duplicated in the finals.

The Maple Leafs hosted the first crowd of over 16,000 in Canada in game seven.

SERIES A - SEMI-FINALS

Mar.	21	NY Rangers	1	at	Toronto	3
Mar.	22	Toronto	4	at	NY Rangers	2
Mar.	24	Toronto	0	at	NY Rangers	3
Mar.	28	NY Rangers	1	at	Toronto	2
Mar.	29	Toronto	1	at	NY Rangers	3
Mar.	31	NY Rangers	2	at	Toronto	3

Toronto won best-of-seven series 4–2

SERIES B AND C - QUARTER-FINALS

Mar.	22	Boston	2	at	Chicago	1 OT
Mar.	24	Chicago	4	at	Boston	0
Mar.	26	Chicago	2	at	Boston	3

Boston won best-of-three series 2–1

Mar.	22	Montreal	1	at	Detroit	2
Mar.	24	Detroit	0	at	Montreal	5
Mar.	26	Montreal	2	at	Detroit	6

Detroit won best-of-three series 2–1

SERIES D - SEMI-FINALS

Mar.	29	Detroit	6	at	Boston	4
Mar.	31	Boston	1	at	Detroit	3

Detroit won best-of-three series 2–0

SERIES E - FINALS

Apr.	4	Detroit	3	at	Toronto	2
Apr.	7	Detroit	4	at	Toronto	2
Apr.	9	Toronto	2	at	Detroit	5
Apr.	12	Toronto	4	at	Detroit	3
Apr.	14	Detroit	3	at	Toronto	9
Apr.	16	Toronto	3	at	Detroit	0
Apr.	18	Detroit	1	at	Toronto	3

Toronto won best-of-seven series 4–3

1941-42 – Toronto Maple Leafs – Wally Stanowski, Syl Apps (Captain), Bob Goldham, Gordie Drillon, Hank Goldup, Ernie Dickens, Sweeney Schriner, Bucko McDonald, Bob Davidson, Nick Metz, Bingo Kampman, Don Metz, Gaye Stewart, Turk Broda, John McCreedy, Lorne Carr, Pete Langelle, Billy Taylor, Reg Hamilton, Conn Smythe (Manager), Hap Day (Coach), Frank Selke (Business Manager), Tim Daly (Trainer).

1941

In the third best-of-seven series ever played in the Stanley Cup finals, Boston became the first to win in four straight games. Since the National Hockey League was formed in 1917, only four teams — the 1929 Boston Bruins and 1930 Montreal Canadiens in two straight and the 1932 Toronto Maple Leafs and 1935 Montreal Maroons in three straight — had ever won the Cup in the fewest possible games.

SERIES A - SEMI-FINALS

Mar.	20	Toronto	0	at	Boston	3
Mar.	22	Toronto	5	at	Boston	3
Mar.	25	Boston	2	at	Toronto	7
Mar.	27	Boston	2	at	Toronto	1
Mar.	29	Toronto	2	at	Boston	1 OT
Apr.	1	Boston	2	at	Toronto	1
Apr.	3	Toronto	1	at	Boston	2

Boston won best-of-seven series 4–3

SERIES B AND C - QUARTER-FINALS

Mar.	20	NY Rangers	1	at	Detroit	2 OT
Mar.	23	Detroit	1	at	NY Rangers	3
Mar.	25	NY Rangers	2	at	Detroit	3

Detroit won best-of-three series 2–1

Mar.	20	Montreal	1	at	Chicago	2
Mar.	22	Chicago	3	at	Montreal	4 2OT
Mar.	25	Montreal	2	at	Chicago	3

Chicago won best-of-three series 2–1

SERIES D - SEMI-FINALS

Mar.	27	Chicago	1	at	Detroit	3
Mar.	30	Detroit	2	at	Chicago	1 OT

Detroit won best-of-three series 2–0

SERIES E - FINALS

Apr.	6	Detroit	2	at	Boston	3
Apr.	8	Detroit	1	at	Boston	2
Apr.	10	Boston	4	at	Detroit	2
Apr.	12	Boston	3	at	Detroit	1

Boston won best-of-seven series 4–0

1940-41 – Boston Bruins – Bill Cowley, Des Smith, Dit Clapper (Captain), Frank Brimsek, Flash Hollett, Jack Crawford, Bobby Bauer, Pat McReavy, Herb Cain, Mel Hill, Milt Schmidt, Woody Dumart, Roy Conacher, Terry Reardon, Art Jackson, Eddie Wiseman, Jack Shewchuck, Art Ross (Manager), Cooney Weiland (Coach), Win Green (Trainer).

1940

With the circus heading towards New York, the Rangers were forced to play the first two games of the finals on consecutive nights before vacating Madison Square Garden for the rest of the series.

Three of the Rangers' four game-winning goals were scored in overtime, including the Cup-winner by Bryan Hextall in game six. It marked the third time in NHL history that the last goal of the season had been tallied in sudden-death.

Lynn and Murray Patrick skated for the winners to become the third and fourth members of the Patrick family, joining father (and Rangers manager) Lester and uncle Frank, to have their names engraved on the Stanley Cup.

SERIES A - SEMI-FINALS

Mar.	19	Boston	0	at	NY Rangers	4
Mar.	21	NY Rangers	2	at	Boston	4
Mar.	24	NY Rangers	3	at	Boston	4
Mar.	26	Boston	0	at	NY Rangers	1
Mar.	28	NY Rangers	1	at	Boston	0
Mar.	30	Boston	1	at	NY Rangers	4

NY Rangers won best-of-seven series 4–2

SERIES B AND C - QUARTER-FINALS

Mar.	19	Chicago	2	at	Toronto	3 OT
Mar.	21	Toronto	2	at	Chicago	1

Toronto won best-of-three series 2–0

Mar.	19	NY Americans	1	at	Detroit	2 OT
Mar.	22	Detroit	4	at	NY Americans	5
Mar.	24	NY Americans	1	at	Detroit	3

Detroit won best-of-three series 2–1

SERIES D - SEMI-FINALS

Mar.	26	Detroit	1	at	Toronto	2
Mar.	28	Toronto	3	at	Detroit	1

Toronto won best-of-three series 2–0

SERIES E - FINALS

Apr.	2	Toronto	1	at	NY Rangers	2 OT
Apr.	3	Toronto	2	at	NY Rangers	6
Apr.	6	NY Rangers	1	at	Toronto	2
Apr.	9	NY Rangers	0	at	Toronto	3
Apr.	11	NY Rangers	2	at	Toronto	1 2OT
Apr.	13	NY Rangers	3	at	Toronto	2 OT

NY Rangers won best-of-seven series 4–2

1939-40 – New York Rangers – Dave Kerr, Art Coulter (Captain), Ott Heller, Alex Shibicky, Mac Colville, Neil Colville, Phil Watson, Lynn Patrick, Clint Smith, Muzz Patrick, Babe Pratt, Bryan Hextall, Kilby MacDonald, Dutch Hiller, Alf Pike, Stan Smith, Lester Patrick (Manager), Frank Boucher (Coach), Harry Westerby (Trainer).

1939

The NHL expanded the Stanley Cup finals to a best-of-seven format, though it took the Bruins only five games to defeat the Maple Leafs.

Boston goaltender Frank Brimsek held Toronto to just six goals in five games as the Bruins took the Cup for the first time in 10 seasons.

Mel Hill of Boston, who earlier set an NHL record with three overtime goals in the first round of the playoffs, scored twice in the series, and Bill Cowley led all playoff scorers with 11 assists and 14 points, setting modern-era playoff records in both categories.

SERIES A - SEMI-FINALS

Mar.	21	Boston	2	at	NY Rangers	1 3OT
Mar.	23	NY Rangers	2	at	Boston	3 OT
Mar.	26	NY Rangers	1	at	Boston	4
Mar.	28	Boston	1	at	NY Rangers	2
Mar.	30	NY Rangers	2	at	Boston	1 OT
Apr.	1	Boston	1	at	NY Rangers	3
Apr.	2	NY Rangers	1	at	Boston	2 3OT

Boston won best-of-seven series 4–3

SERIES B AND C - QUARTER-FINALS

Mar.	21	NY Americans	0	at	Toronto	4
Mar.	23	Toronto	2	at	NY Americans	0

Toronto won best-of-three series 2–0

Mar.	21	Detroit	0	at	Montreal	2
Mar.	23	Montreal	3	at	Detroit	7
Mar.	26	Montreal	0	at	Detroit	1 OT

Detroit won best-of-three series 2–1

SERIES D - SEMI-FINALS

Mar.	28	Detroit	1	at	Toronto	4
Mar.	30	Toronto	1	at	Detroit	3
Apr.	1	Detroit	4	at	Toronto	5 OT

Toronto won best-of-three series 2–1

SERIES E - FINALS

Apr.	6	Toronto	1	at	Boston	2
Apr.	9	Toronto	3	at	Boston	2 OT
Apr.	11	Boston	3	at	Toronto	1
Apr.	13	Boston	2	at	Toronto	0
Apr.	16	Toronto	1	at	Boston	3

Boston won best-of-seven series 4–1

1938-39 – Boston Bruins – Bobby Bauer, Mel Hill, Flash Hollett, Roy Conacher, Gord Pettinger, Milt Schmidt, Woody Dumart, Jack Crawford, Ray Getliffe, Frank Brimsek, Eddie Shore, Dit Clapper, Bill Cowley, Jack Portland, Red Hamill, Cooney Weiland (Captain), Charlie Sands, Art Ross (Manager/Coach), Win Green (Trainer).

1938

The Black Hawks faced the start of the Stanley Cup finals without top goaltender Mike Karakas, who had played every game during the season but broke his big toe on April 3. Chicago was forced to sign journeyman netminder Alfie Moore, who played game one and posted a win in his only Cup appearance.

Following the victory, NHL President Frank Calder ruled Moore ineligible for further play, and Chicago had to call on minor-league goalie Paul Goodman, who lost his first NHL start in game two.

Karakas finally returned with a steel-capped boot to protect his toe and won both starts, while teammate Doc Romnes wore a football helmet to guard a broken nose and scored the winning goal in game three before a record crowd of 18,497.

Eight American-born players — Karakas, Romnes, Alex Levinsky, Carl Voss, Cully Dahlstrom, Roger Jenkins, Lou Trudel and Virgil Johnson — skated for the Black Hawks to set a record (not broken until 1995) for U.S. talent on a Cup winner.

SERIES A - SEMI-FINALS

Mar.	24	Boston	0	at	Toronto	1	2OT
Mar.	26	Boston	1	at	Toronto	2	
Mar.	29	Toronto	3	at	Boston	2	OT

Toronto won best-of-five series 3–0

SERIES B AND C - QUARTER-FINALS

Mar.	22	NY Americans	2	at	NY Rangers	1	2OT
Mar.	24	NY Rangers	4	at	NY Americans	3	
Mar.	27	NY Americans	3	at	NY Rangers	2	4OT

NY Americans won best-of-three series 2–1

Mar.	22	Chicago	4	at	Montreal	6	
Mar.	24	Montreal	0	at	Chicago	4	
Mar.	26	Chicago	3	at	Montreal	2	OT

Chicago won best-of-three series 2–1

SERIES D - SEMI-FINALS

Mar.	29	Chicago	1	at	NY Americans	3	
Mar.	31	NY Americans	0	at	Chicago	1	2OT
Apr.	3	Chicago	3	at	NY Americans	2	

Chicago won best-of-three series 2–1

SERIES E - FINALS

Apr.	5	Chicago	3	at	Toronto	1	
Apr.	7	Chicago	1	at	Toronto	5	
Apr.	10	Toronto	1	at	Chicago	2	
Apr.	12	Toronto	1	at	Chicago	4	

Chicago won best-of-five series 3–1

1937-38 – Chicago Black Hawks – Art Wiebe, Carl Voss, Harold Jackson, Mike Karakas, Mush March, Jack Shill, Earl Seibert, Cully Dahlstrom, Alex Levinsky, Johnny Gottselig (Captain), Lou Trudel, Pete Palangio, Bill MacKenzie, Doc Romnes, Paul Thompson, Roger Jenkins, Alfie Moore, Bert Connelly, Virgil Johnson, Paul Goodman, Bill Stewart (Manager/Coach), Eddie Froelich (Trainer).

1937

The Rangers, turned away from Madison Square Garden once again by the incoming circus after game one, agreed to play the remainder of the series on Detroit's home ice.

First-year goaltender Earl Robertson, who would never play a regular-season game for the Red Wings during his career, became the first rookie netminder to post two shutouts in the finals, blanking the Rangers in the last two games of the series.

With their second straight Stanley Cup title, Detroit became the first U.S.-based squad to repeat as champions.

SERIES A - SEMI-FINALS

Mar.	23	Montreal	0	at	Detroit	4	
Mar.	25	Montreal	1	at	Detroit	5	
Mar.	27	Detroit	1	at	Montreal	3	
Mar.	30	Detroit	1	at	Montreal	3	
Apr.	1	Detroit	2	at	Montreal	1	3OT

Detroit won best-of-five series 3–2

SERIES B AND C - QUARTER-FINALS

Mar.	23	Boston	1	at	Mtl. Maroons	4	
Mar.	25	Mtl. Maroons	0	at	Boston	4	
Mar.	28	Mtl. Maroons	4	at	Boston	1	

Mtl. Maroons won best-of-three series 2–1

Mar.	23	NY Rangers	3	at	Toronto	0	
Mar.	25	Toronto	1	at	NY Rangers	2	OT

NY Rangers won best-of-three series 2–0

SERIES D - SEMI-FINALS

Apr.	1	Mtl. Maroons	0	at	NY Rangers	1	
Apr.	3	NY Rangers	4	at	Mtl. Maroons	0	

NY Rangers won best-of-three series 2–0

SERIES E - FINALS

Apr.	6	Detroit	1	at	NY Rangers	5	
Apr.	8	NY Rangers	2	at	Detroit	4	
Apr.	11	NY Rangers	1	at	Detroit	0	
Apr.	13	NY Rangers	0	at	Detroit	1	
Apr.	15	NY Rangers	0	at	Detroit	3	

Detroit won best-of-five series 3–2

1936-37 – Detroit Red Wings – Normie Smith, Pete Kelly, Larry Aurie, Herbie Lewis, Hec Kilrea, Mud Bruneteau, Syd Howe, Wally Kilrea, Jimmy Franks, Bucko McDonald, Gord Pettinger, Ebbie Goodfellow, John Gallagher, Ralph Bowman, John Sorrell, Marty Barry, Earl Robertson, John Sherf, Howie Mackie, Rolly Roulston, Doug Young (Captain), Jack Adams (Manager/Coach), Honey Walker (Trainer).

1936

Under the coaching guidance of Jack Adams, the Detroit Red Wings captured their first Stanley Cup championship after 10 NHL seasons.

The series marked Frank "King" Clancy's sixth and final appearance as a player in the finals. However, it would not be his last Stanley Cup series, for Clancy went on to earn prominence as an NHL referee, working 20 Stanley Cup games in that capacity.

SERIES A - SEMI-FINALS

Mar.	24	Detroit	1	at	Mtl. Maroons	0	6OT
Mar.	26	Detroit	3	at	Mtl. Maroons	0	
Mar.	28	Mtl. Maroons	1	at	Detroit	2	

Detroit won best-of-five series 3–0

SERIES B AND C - QUARTER-FINALS

Mar.	24	Toronto	0	at	Boston	3	
Mar.	26	Boston	3	at	Toronto	8	

Toronto won total-goals series 8–6

Mar.	24	Chicago	0	at	NY Americans	3	
Mar.	26	NY Americans	4	at	Chicago	5	

NY Americans won total-goals series 7–5

SERIES D - SEMI-FINALS

Mar.	28	NY Americans	1	at	Toronto	3	
Mar.	31	Toronto	0	at	NY Americans	1	
Apr.	2	NY Americans	1	at	Toronto	3	

Toronto won best-of-three series 2-1

SERIES E - FINALS

Apr.	5	Toronto	1	at	Detroit	3	
Apr.	7	Toronto	4	at	Detroit	9	
Apr.	9	Detroit	3	at	Toronto	4	OT
Apr.	11	Detroit	3	at	Toronto	2	

Detroit won best-of-five series 3–1

1935-36 – Detroit Red Wings – John Sorrell, Syd Howe, Marty Barry, Herbie Lewis, Larry Aurie, Mud Bruneteau, Wally Kilrea, Hec Kilrea, Gord Pettinger, Bucko McDonald, Ralph Bowman, Pete Kelly, Doug Young (Captain), Ebbie Goodfellow, Normie Smith, Jack Adams (Manager/Coach), Honey Walker (Trainer).

1935

In the first all-Canadian final since the Montreal Maroons beat Victoria Cougars in 1926, the Montreal team battled to its second Stanley Cup championship with a three-game sweep of Toronto. Maroons netminder Alex Connell allowed just four goals in three games.

Winning coach Tommy Gorman became the first and only coach to win successive Stanley Cup titles with two different teams. He had directed the Chicago Black Hawks to the championship a year earlier. Gorman currently ranks as one of three NHL coaches (Dick Irvin and Scotty Bowman are the others) to have led more than one team to the Stanley Cup.

SERIES A - SEMI-FINALS

Mar.	23	Toronto	0	at	Boston	1	2OT
Mar.	26	Toronto	2	at	Boston	0	
Mar.	28	Boston	0	at	Toronto	3	
Mar.	30	Boston	1	at	Toronto	2	OT

Toronto won best-of-five series 3–1

SERIES B AND C - QUARTER-FINALS

Mar.	23	Chicago	0	at	Mtl. Maroons	0	
Mar.	26	Mtl. Maroons	1	at	Chicago	0	OT

Mtl. Maroons won total-goals series 1–0

Mar.	24	Montreal	1	at	NY Rangers	2	
Mar.	26	NY Rangers	4	at	Montreal	4	

NY Rangers won total-goals series 6–5

SERIES D - SEMI-FINALS

Mar.	28	Mtl. Maroons	2	at	NY Rangers	1	
Mar.	30	NY Rangers	3	at	Mtl. Maroons	3	

Mtl. Maroons won total-goals series 5–4

SERIES E - FINALS

Apr.	4	Mtl. Maroons	3	at	Toronto	2	OT
Apr.	6	Mtl. Maroons	3	at	Toronto	1	
Apr.	9	Toronto	1	at	Mtl. Maroons	4	

Mtl. Maroons won best-of-five series 3–0

1934-35 – Montreal Maroons – Lionel Conacher, Cy Wentworth, Alex Connell, Toe Blake, Stewart Evans, Earl Robinson, Bill Miller, Dave Trottier, Jimmy Ward, Baldy Northcott, Hooley Smith (Captain), Russ Blinco, Al Shields, Sammy McManus, Gus Marker, Bob Gracie, Herb Cain, Tommy Gorman (Manager/Coach), Bill O'Brien (Trainer).

1934

For the second year in a row, the Stanley Cup-winning goal was scored in overtime. When Chicago's Harold "Mush" March netted the series-winner at 30:05 of overtime, the Black Hawks captured their first Cup victory.

Chicago's Charlie Gardiner limited Detroit to two goals in his club's three victories, while Detroit goaltender Wilf Cude led the Red Wings to their only win of the series in game three despite suffering a broken nose midway through the contest. Cude stopped 52 of 53 Detroit shots in the deciding game, while Gardiner turned aside all 40 Black Hawk blasts. Gardiner had been plagued by severe headaches all year. Two months after the Stanley Cup series he died of a brain hemorrhage.

SERIES A - SEMI-FINALS

Mar.	22	Detroit	2	at	Toronto	1	OT
Mar.	24	Detroit	6	at	Toronto	3	
Mar.	26	Toronto	3	at	Detroit	1	
Mar.	28	Toronto	5	at	Detroit	1	
Mar.	30	Toronto	0	at	Detroit	1	

Detroit won best-of-five series 3–2

SERIES B AND C - QUARTER-FINALS

Mar.	22	Chicago	3	at	Montreal	2	
Mar.	25	Montreal	1	at	Chicago	1	OT

Chicago won total-goals series 4–3

Mar.	20	NY Rangers	0	at	Mtl. Maroons	0	
Mar.	25	Mtl. Maroons	2	at	NY Rangers	1	

Mtl. Maroons won total-goals series 2–1

SERIES D - SEMI-FINALS

Mar.	28	Chicago	3	at	Mtl. Maroons	0	
Apr.	1	Mtl. Maroons	2	at	Chicago	3	

Chicago won total-goals series 6–2

SERIES E - FINALS

Apr.	3	Chicago	2	at	Detroit	1	2OT
Apr.	5	Chicago	4	at	Detroit	1	
Apr.	8	Detroit	5	at	Chicago	2	
Apr.	10	Detroit	0	at	Chicago	1	2OT

Chicago won best-of-five series 3–1

1933-34 – Chicago Black Hawks – Clarence Abel, Rosie Couture, Lou Trudel, Lionel Conacher, Paul Thompson, Leroy Goldsworthy, Art Coulter, Roger Jenkins, Don McFadyen, Tom Cook, Doc Romnes, Johnny Gottselig, Mush March, Johnny Sheppard, Charlie Gardiner (Captain), Bill Kendall, Jack Leswick, Tommy Gorman (Manager/Coach), Eddie Froelich (Trainer).

1933

Again the circus forced the Rangers out of New York, with all but game one contested on Toronto's home ice. However, this year the Rangers would not be denied

In the final match, New York's Bill Cook became the first of 15 NHL players to register a Stanley Cup-winning goal in overtime when he snapped a scoreless tie at 7:33 of the fourth period. Goalie Andy Aitkenhead posted the fourth shutout by an NHL rookie in the finals.

SERIES A - SEMI-FINALS

Mar.	25	Toronto	1	at	Boston	2 OT
Mar.	28	Toronto	1	at	Boston	0 OT
Mar.	30	Boston	2	at	Toronto	1 OT
Apr.	1	Boston	3	at	Toronto	5
Apr.	3	Boston	0	at	Toronto	1 6OT

Toronto won best-of-five series 3–2

SERIES B AND C - QUARTER-FINALS

Mar.	25	Detroit	2	at	Mtl. Maroons	0
Mar.	28	Mtl. Maroons	2	at	Detroit	3

Detroit won total-goals series 5–2

Mar.	26	Montreal	2	at	NY Rangers	5
Mar.	28	NY Rangers	3	at	Montreal	3

NY Rangers won total-goals series 8–5

SERIES D - SEMI-FINALS

Mar.	30	Detroit	0	at	NY Rangers	2
Apr.	2	NY Rangers	4	at	Detroit	3

NY Rangers won total-goals series 6–3

SERIES E - FINALS

Apr.	4	Toronto	1	at	NY Rangers	5
Apr.	8	NY Rangers	3	at	Toronto	1
Apr.	11	NY Rangers	2	at	Toronto	3
Apr.	13	NY Rangers	1	at	Toronto	0 OT

NY Rangers won best-of-five series 3–1

1932-33 – New York Rangers – Ching Johnson, Butch Keeling, Frank Boucher, Art Somers, Babe Siebert, Bun Cook, Andy Aitkenhead, Ott Heller, Oscar Asmundson, Gord Pettinger, Doug Brennan, Cecil Dillon, Bill Cook (Captain), Murray Murdoch, Earl Seibert, Lester Patrick (Manager/Coach), Harry Westerby (Trainer).

1932

After losing to Toronto in game one, the Rangers also lost the home-ice advantage because the circus had once again invaded Madison Square Garden. Game two, originally set for New York, was moved to Boston.

Toronto's famed Kid Line of Harvey "Busher" Jackson, Charlie Conacher and Joe Primeau made its Stanley Cup debut, combining for eight goals in the three-game sweep.

The Leafs' Dick Irvin, who lost in the 1931 finals with the Chicago Black Hawks, earned his first title as a coach.

SERIES A - SEMI-FINALS

Mar.	24	NY Rangers	3	at	Montreal	4
Mar.	26	NY Rangers	4	at	Montreal	3 3OT
Mar.	27	Montreal	0	at	NY Rangers	1
Mar.	29	Montreal	2	at	NY Rangers	5

NY Rangers won best-of-five series 3–1

SERIES B AND C - QUARTER-FINALS

Mar.	27	Toronto	0	at	Chicago	1
Mar.	29	Chicago	1	at	Toronto	6

Toronto won total-goals series 6–2

Mar.	27	Mtl. Maroons	1	at	Detroit	1
Mar.	29	Detroit	0	at	Mtl. Maroons	2

Mtl. Maroons won total-goals series 3–1

SERIES D - SEMI-FINALS

Mar.	31	Toronto	1	at	Mtl. Maroons	1

Apr.	2	Mtl. Maroons	2	at	Toronto	3 OT

Toronto won total-goals series 4–3

SERIES E - FINALS

Apr.	5	Toronto	6	at	NY Rangers	4
Apr.	7	Toronto	6	vs	NY Rangers	2 *
Apr.	9	NY Rangers	4	at	Toronto	6

* played in Boston

Toronto won best-of-five series 3–0

1931-32 – Toronto Maple Leafs – Charlie Conacher, Busher Jackson, King Clancy, Andy Blair, Red Horner, Lorne Chabot, Alex Levinsky, Joe Primeau, Harold Darragh, Baldy Cotton, Frank Finnigan, Hap Day (Captain), Ace Bailey, Bob Gracie, Fred Robertson, Earl Miller, Conn Smythe (Manager), Dick Irvin (Coach), Tim Daly (Trainer).

1931

The Montreal Canadiens became the second NHL team to repeat as Stanley Cup champions, duplicating the feat accomplished by the Ottawa Senators in 1920 and 1921. Chicago's Dick Irvin made his coaching debut in the finals against the team which he would later lead to three Stanley Cup titles.

Over 18,000 fans packed Chicago Stadium for game two to set a new record for the largest attendance in hockey history.

SERIES A - SEMI-FINALS

Mar.	24	Montreal	4	at	Boston	5 OT
Mar.	26	Montreal	1	at	Boston	0
Mar.	28	Boston	3	at	Montreal	4 OT
Mar.	30	Boston	3	at	Montreal	1
Apr.	1	Boston	2	at	Montreal	3 OT

Montreal won best-of-five series 3–2

SERIES B AND C - QUARTER-FINALS

Mar.	24	Chicago	2	at	Toronto	2
Mar.	26	Toronto	1	at	Chicago	2 OT

Chicago won total-goals series 4–3

Mar.	24	Mtl. Maroons	1	at	NY Rangers	5
Mar.	26	NY Rangers	3	at	Mtl. Maroons	0

NY Rangers won total-goals series 8–1

SERIES D - SEMI-FINALS

Mar.	29	NY Rangers	0	at	Chicago	2
Mar.	31	Chicago	1	at	NY Rangers	0

Chicago won total-goals series 3–0

SERIES E - FINALS

Apr.	3	Montreal	2	at	Chicago	1
Apr.	5	Montreal	1	at	Chicago	2 2OT
Apr.	9	Chicago	3	at	Montreal	2 3OT
Apr.	11	Chicago	2	at	Montreal	4
Apr.	14	Chicago	0	at	Montreal	2

Montreal won best-of-five series 3–2

1930-31 – Montreal Canadiens – George Hainsworth, Wildor Larochelle, Marty Burke, Sylvio Mantha (Captain), Howie Morenz, Johnny Gagnon, Aurel Joliat, Armand Mondou, Pit Lepine, Albert Leduc, Georges Mantha, Art Lesieur, Nick Wasnie, Bert McCaffrey, Gus Rivers, Jean Pusie, Léo Dandurand (Manager), Cecil Hart (Coach), Ed Dufour (Trainer).

1930

The defending champion Boston Bruins had skated to the NHL's top regular-season record in 1929–30. The Bruins' 38–5–1 record translates into an .875 winning percentage that is still the best in NHL history. The team did not lose back-to-back games all season until being swept by the Canadiens in the best-of-three Stanley Cup finals. Boston's surprising defeat prompted the NHL to lengthen the finals to a best-of-five in the future.

The Canadiens, who had lost all four of their regular-season meetings with the Bruins, were led by captain Sylvio Mantha who tallied a goal in both final series games.

SERIES A - SEMI-FINALS

Mar.	20	Boston	2	at	Mtl. Maroons	1 3OT
Mar.	22	Boston	4	at	Mtl. Maroons	2
Mar.	25	Mtl. Maroons	1	at	Boston	0 2OT
Mar.	27	Mtl. Maroons	1	at	Boston	5

Boston won best-of-five series 3–1

SERIES B AND C - QUARTER-FINALS

Mar.	23	Montreal	1	at	Chicago	0
Mar.	26	Chicago	2	at	Montreal	2 3OT

Montreal won total-goals series 3–2

Mar.	20	NY Rangers	1	at	Ottawa	1
Mar.	23	Ottawa	2	at	NY Rangers	5

NY Rangers won total-goals series 6–3

SERIES D - SEMI-FINALS

Mar.	28	NY Rangers	1	at	Montreal	2 4OT
Mar.	30	Montreal	2	at	NY Rangers	0

Montreal won best-of-three series 2–0

SERIES E - FINALS

Apr.	1	Montreal	3	at	Boston	0
Apr.	3	Boston	3	at	Montreal	4

Montreal won best-of-three series 2–0

1929-30 – Montreal Canadiens – George Hainsworth, Marty Burke, Sylvio Mantha (Captain), Howie Morenz, Bert McCaffrey, Aurel Joliat, Albert Leduc, Pit Lepine, Wildor Larochelle, Nick Wasnie, Gerry Carson, Armand Mondou, Georges Mantha, Gus Rivers, Léo Dandurand (Manager), Cecil Hart (Coach), Ed Dufour (Trainer).

1929

When the Bruins met the Rangers in this series, it marked the first time in Stanley Cup history that two American teams clashed head-on for the prized trophy.

Goalie Cecil "Tiny" Thompson backstopped the Bruins to consecutive wins, allowing just one goal in the two games and posting the third Stanley Cup shutout ever by an NHL rookie as Boston captured its first Cup.

Dit Clapper and Bill Carson scored the two game-winning goals.

SERIES A - SEMI-FINALS

Mar.	19	Montreal	0	at	Boston	1
Mar.	21	Montreal	0	at	Boston	1
Mar.	23	Boston	3	at	Montreal	2

Boston won best-of-five series 3–0

SERIES B AND C - QUARTER-FINALS

Mar.	19	NY Rangers	0	at	NY Americans	0
Mar.	21	NY Americans	0	at	NY Rangers	1 2OT

NY Rangers won total-goals series 1–0

Mar.	19	Toronto	3	at	Detroit	1
Mar.	21	Detroit	1	at	Toronto	4

Toronto won total-goals series 7–2

SERIES D - SEMI-FINALS

Mar.	24	Toronto	0	at	NY Rangers	1
Mar.	26	NY Rangers	2	at	Toronto	1 OT

NY Rangers won best-of-three series 2–0

SERIES E - FINALS

Mar.	28	NY Rangers	0	at	Boston	2
Mar.	29	Boston	2	at	NY Rangers	1

Boston won best-of-three series 2–0

1928-29 – Boston Bruins – Tiny Thompson, Eddie Shore, Lionel Hitchman (Captain), Percy Galbraith, Frank Fredrickson, Mickey Mackay, Red Green, Dutch Gainor, Harry Oliver, Eddie Rodden, Dit Clapper, Cooney Weiland, Lloyd Klein, Cy Denneny, Bill Carson, George Owen, Myles Lane, Art Ross (Manager/Coach), Win Green (Trainer).

1928

Though the Rangers moved into the finals, the circus moved into New York's Madison Square Garden and took priority over the hockey team. As a result, club management decided to play the entire series in Montreal.

After losing goalie Lorne Chabot to an eye injury midway through game two, 44-year-old Rangers coach and early era star player Lester Patrick took over between the pipes, inspiring the New Yorkers to a 2–1 overtime victory. The following day the Rangers signed New York Americans netminder Joe Miller, who responded with two wins including the second shutout by an NHL rookie in Stanley Cup history.

In only their second NHL season, the Rangers captured their first Stanley Cup title and became only the second American team in history, joining the 1917 Seattle Metropolitans of the PCHA, to possess the trophy.

QUARTER-FINALS

Mar.	27	Mtl. Maroons	1	at	Ottawa	0
Mar.	29	Ottawa	1	at	Mtl. Maroons	2

Mtl. Maroons won total-goals series 3–1

Mar.	27	Pittsburgh	0	at	NY Rangers	4
Mar.	29	Pittsburgh	4	at	NY Rangers	2

NY Rangers won total-goals series 6–4

SEMI-FINALS

Mar.	31	Montreal	2	at	Mtl. Maroons	2	
Apr.	3	Mtl. Maroons	1	at	Montreal	0	OT

Mtl. Maroons won total-goals series 3–2

Mar.	31	Boston	1	at	NY Rangers	1
Apr.	3	NY Rangers	4	at	Boston	1

NY Rangers won total-goals series 5–2

FINALS

Apr.	5	NY Rangers	0	at	Mtl. Maroons	2	
Apr.	7	NY Rangers	2	at	Mtl. Maroons	1	OT
Apr.	10	NY Rangers	0	at	Mtl. Maroons	2	
Apr.	12	NY Rangers	1	at	Mtl. Maroons	0	
Apr.	14	NY Rangers	2	at	Mtl. Maroons	1	

NY Rangers won best-of-five series 3–2

1927-28 – New York Rangers – Lorne Chabot, Clarence Abel, Leo Bourgeault, Ching Johnson, Bill Cook (Captain), Bun Cook, Frank Boucher, Bill Boyd, Murray Murdoch, Paul Thompson, Alex Gray, Joe Miller, Patsy Callighen, Lester Patrick (Manager/Coach), Harry Westerby (Trainer).

1927

With the collapse of major professional hockey in the west, the Stanley Cup became sole property of the NHL in 1927. The American Division champion Boston Bruins met the Canadian champion Ottawa Senators in what became the first Stanley Cup of a new era.

Cy Denneny led the Senators with four of the team's seven total goals, including the game-winners in both victories.

QUARTER-FINALS

Mar.	29	Montreal	1	at	Mtl. Maroons	1	
Mar.	31	Mtl. Maroons	0	at	Montreal	1	OT

Montreal won total-goals series 2–1

Mar.	29	Boston	6	vs	Chicago	1	*
Mar.	31	Chicago	4	at	Boston	4	

* played in New York

Boston won total-goals series 10–5

SEMI-FINALS

Apr.	2	Ottawa	4	at	Montreal	0
Apr.	4	Montreal	1	at	Ottawa	1

Ottawa won total-goals series 5–1

Apr.	2	NY Rangers	0	at	Boston	0
Apr.	4	Boston	3	at	NY Rangers	1

Boston won total-goals series 3–1

FINALS

Apr.	7	Ottawa	0	at	Boston	0	OT
Apr.	9	Ottawa	3	at	Boston	1	
Apr.	11	Boston	1	at	Ottawa	1	OT
Apr.	13	Boston	1	at	Ottawa	3	

Ottawa won best-of-five series 2-0-2

1926-27 – Ottawa Senators – Alex Connell, King Clancy, Georges Boucher (Captain), Ed Gorman, Frank Finnigan, Alex Smith, Hec Kilrea, Hooley Smith, Cy Denneny, Frank Nighbor, Jack Adams, Milt Halliday, Dave Gill (Manager/Coach).

1926

The Montreal Maroons became NHL champions in just their second season in the league and hosted the first Stanley Cup series to be played at the Montreal Forum.

Playing in his first career Stanley Cup series, Nels Stewart scored six of Montreal's 10 goals, and goaltender Clint Benedict recorded an unprecedented three shutouts en route to the Maroons' Stanley Cup triumph versus the Victoria Cougars.

With the NHL taking full control of the Stanley Cup following the Western Hockey League's demise soon after this series, the 1926 championship marked the finale of one of the most dynamic eras in Stanley Cup history. Since 1893, Cup play had grown from an amateur challenge in eastern Canada to a professional competition involving teams from across the continent.

FINALS

Mar.	30	Victoria	0	at	Mtl. Maroons	3
Apr.	1	Victoria	0	at	Mtl. Maroons	3
Apr.	3	Victoria	3	at	Mtl. Maroons	2
Apr.	6	Victoria	0	at	Mtl. Maroons	2

Mtl. Maroons won best-of-five series 3-1

1925-26 – Montreal Maroons – Clint Benedict, Reg Noble, Frank Carson, Dunc Munro (Captain), Nels Stewart, Punch Broadbent, Babe Siebert, Chuck Dinsmore, Merlyn Phillips, Hobie Kitchen, Sam Rothschild, Albert Holway, George Horne, Bernie Brophy, Eddie Gerard (Manager/Coach), Bill O'Brien (Trainer).

1925

The Victoria Cougars, who joined the Western Canada Hockey league with the Vancouver Maroons after the Pacific Coast Hockey Association folded, became the last non-NHL team to win the Stanley Cup and only the third west coast club to capture the trophy, joining the 1915 Vancouver Millionaires and the 1917 Seattle Metropolitans as champions.

All eight Montreal goals in the series came from the Canadiens' top line of Howie Morenz, Aurel Joliat and Billy Boucher, but Victoria posted a more balanced attack with eight different skaters combining for 16 goals.

FINALS

Mar.	21	Montreal	2	at	Victoria	5	
Mar.	23	Montreal	1	vs.	Victoria	3	*
Mar.	27	Montreal	4	at	Victoria	2	
Mar.	30	Montreal	1	at	Victoria	6	

* played in Vancouver

Victoria won best-of-five series 3-1

1924-25 – Victoria Cougars – Hap Holmes, Clem Loughlin (Captain), Gord Fraser, Frank Fredrickson, Jack Walker, Gizzy Hart, Harold Halderson, Frank Foyston, Wally Elmer, Harry Meeking, Jocko Anderson, Lester Patrick (Manager-Coach).

1924

As in 1922, the PCHA champions (Vancouver Maroons) and the winners of the WCHL (Calgary Tigers) met in a postseason playoff, only this year it would determine which team got a bye into the Stanley Cup finals against the NHL champion. The best-of-three series was won by the Tigers two games to one.

Billy Boucher scored three of the Canadiens' five goals in the series vs. the Maroons, including both game-winning tallies, to lift Montreal over Vancouver, which lost its chance at the Stanley Cup for the third straight year.

Montreal then faced Calgary in the Stanley Cup finals. A 21-year-old rookie forward named Howie Morenz paced the Canadiens with a hat trick in game one and a goal in game two as Montreal rolled past Calgary to complete a sweep of both series.

Morenz, Aurel Joliat and Sylvio Mantha all made their first appearances on a Stanley Cup winner.

PCHA / WCHL PLAYOFF

Mar.	10	Calgary	1	at	Vancouver	3	
Mar.	12	Vancouver	3	at	Calgary	6	
Mar.	15	Calgary	3	vs.	Vancouver	1	*

* played in Winnipeg

Calgary won best-of-three series 2-1

CUP FINALS (TWO SERIES)

Mar.	18	Vancouver	2	at	Montreal	3	
Mar.	20	Vancouver	1	at	Montreal	2	

Montreal won best-of-three series 2-0

Mar.	22	Calgary	1	at	Montreal	6	
Mar.	25	Calgary	0	vs.	Montreal	3	**

** played in Ottawa

Montreal won best-of-three series 2-0

1923-24 – Montreal Canadiens – Georges Vezina, Sprague Cleghorn (Captain), Billy Coutu, Howie Morenz, Aurel Joliat, Billy Boucher, Odie Cleghorn, Sylvio Mantha, Bobby Boucher, Billy Bell, Billy Cameron, Joe Malone, Charles Fortier, Leo Dandurand (Manager/Coach).

1923

For the first time in Stanley Cup history, brothers opposed each other in the playoffs. In fact, two sets of brothers — Cy and Corb Denneny and Georges and Frank Boucher — stood on opposite sides of the center line for the opening face-off. Cy and Georges skated with Ottawa, while Corb and Frank suited up for Vancouver (who were now known as the Maroons). Each of the Boucher brothers scored twice in the series.

Ottawa's Harry "Punch" Broadbent, who posted the only goal in game one, scored five in the series to lead the Senators, whom Vancouver coach Frank Patrick called the greatest team he had ever seen.

This year the WCHL champions were given the opportunity to compete directly for the Stanley Cup in a best-of-three series. The Eskimos gave the weary Senators a difficult time, but Ottawa came through with a pair of one-goal victories. Cy Denneny and Punch Broadbent scored the game-winning goals.

CUP FINALS (TWO SERIES)

Mar.	16	Ottawa	1	at Vancouver 0
Mar.	19	Ottawa	1	at Vancouver 4
Mar.	23	Ottawa	3	at Vancouver 2
Mar.	26	Ottawa	5	at Vancouver 1

Ottawa won best-of-five series 3-1

Mar.	29	Ottawa	2	vs. Edmonton 1 OT*
Mar.	31	Ottawa	1	vs. Edmonton 0 *

* played in Vancouver

Ottawa won best-of-three series 2-0

1922-23 – Ottawa Senators – Georges Boucher, Lionel Hitchman, Frank Nighbor, King Clancy, Harry Helman, Clint Benedict, Jack Darragh, Eddie Gerard (Captain), Cy Denneny, Punch Broadbent, Tommy Gorman (Manager), Pete Green (Coach), F. Dolan (Trainer).

1922

With the inception of the Western Canada Hockey League (WCHL) in 1921-22, a new playoff structure was designed to match the champions of the two western leagues against each other with the winner to meet the NHL champions for the Stanley Cup. After defeating the WCHL's Regina Capitals in the preliminary series, the PCHA's Vancouver Millionaires set out for Toronto, where the NHL champion St. Pats awaited their arrival.

Cecil "Babe" Dye notched nine of his club's 16 goals, including two game-winners, and goaltender John Ross Roach, who recorded the first Stanley Cup shutout by an NHL rookie, posted a 1.80 goals-against average as Toronto won its second Stanley Cup championship.

Jack Adams, who had been lured away from Toronto by Vancouver in 1920, returned in impressive fashion, scoring six goals in the series.

PCHA / WCHL PLAYOFF

Mar.	8	Regina	2	at Vancouver 1
Mar.	11	Vancouver	4	at Regina 0

Vancouver won total-goals series 5-2

FINAL

Mar.	17	Vancouver	4	at Toronto 3
Mar.	20	Vancouver	1	at Toronto 2 OT
Mar.	23	Vancouver	3	at Toronto 0
Mar.	25	Vancouver	0	at Toronto 6
Mar.	28	Vancouver	1	at Toronto 5

Toronto won best-of-five series 3-2

1921-22 – Toronto St. Pats – Ted Stackhouse, Corb Denneny, Rod Smylie, Lloyd Andrews, John Ross Roach, Harry Cameron, Billy Stuart, Babe Dye, Ken Randall, Reg Noble (Captain), Eddie Gerard (borrowed for one game from Ottawa), Stan Jackson, Ivan Mitchell, Charlie Querrie (Manager), George O'Donoghue (Coach).

1921

A gathering of 11,000 fans, the largest crowd ever to see a hockey game anywhere in the world at the time, jammed the Vancouver arena for the first game of this series, and an estimated record of 51,000 tickets were sold for the entire five-game series.

Jack Darragh was the hero for the second straight year, scoring both Ottawa goals in the finale as the Senators became the first NHL club to capture back-to-back Stanley Cup titles and the first team since the Quebec Bulldogs of 1912 and 1913 to repeat as champions.

FINALS

Mar.	21	Ottawa	1	at Vancouver 3
Mar.	24	Ottawa	4	at Vancouver 3
Mar.	28	Ottawa	3	at Vancouver 2
Mar.	31	Ottawa	2	at Vancouver 3
Apr.	4	Ottawa	2	at Vancouver 1

Ottawa won best-of-five series 3-2

1920-21 – Ottawa Senators – Jack MacKell, Jack Darragh, Morley Bruce, Georges Boucher, Eddie Gerard (Captain), Clint Benedict, Sprague Cleghorn, Frank Nighbor, Punch Broadbent, Cy Denneny, Leth Graham, Tommy Gorman (Manager), Pete Green (Coach), F. Dolan (Trainer).

1920

When the Mets arrived in Ottawa, it became apparent that their red, white and green barber pole uniforms were all too similar to the Senators' red, white and black pattern. Ottawa agreed to play in white jerseys.

Poor ice conditions marred the first three games, and the series was subsequently shifted to the artificial surface of Toronto's Mutual Street Arena. Jack Darragh, who had tallied the winning marker in game one, lifted Ottawa to the championship with a hat trick in the decisive game.

Pete Green became the second rookie coach in the NHL to win the Cup, joining Dick Carroll of the 1918 Toronto Arenas.

FINALS

Mar.	22	Seattle	2	at Ottawa 3
Mar.	24	Seattle	0	at Ottawa 3
Mar.	27	Seattle	3	at Ottawa 1
Mar.	30	Seattle	5	vs Ottawa 2 *
Apr.	1	Seattle	1	vs Ottawa 6 *

* played in Toronto

Ottawa won best-of-five series 3-2

1919-20 – Ottawa Senators – Jack MacKell, Jack Darragh, Morley Bruce, Horrace Merrill, Georges Boucher, Eddie Gerard (Captain), Clint Benedict, Sprague Cleghorn, Frank Nighbor, Punch Broadbent, Cy Denneny, Tommy Gorman (Manager), Pete Green (Coach).

1919

Seattle's Frank Foyston and Montreal's Newsy Lalonde, two of the greatest scorers of the early 20th century, were at their best in this series. Foyston notched nine goals and Lalonde six as the two clubs stood even at two wins and one tie apiece after five games.

Several of the players became seriously ill with the flu, which had reached epidemic proportions throughout North America and the world in 1918 and 1919. So many Montreal players were sick, health officials were forced to cancel the deciding game and the series was abandoned with no winner declared. Canadiens defenseman Joe Hall, hospitalized with a severe case of Spanish Influenza, died on April 5, 1919, in Seattle.

FINALS

Mar.	19	Montreal	0	at Seattle 7
Mar.	22	Montreal	4	at Seattle 2
Mar.	24	Montreal	2	at Seattle 7
Mar.	26	Montreal	0	at Seattle 0 OT
Mar.	30	Montreal	4	at Seattle 3 OT

SERIES CANCELLED DUE TO INFLUENZA EPIDEMIC

1918-19 – No decision – Series halted by Spanish influenza epidemic, illness of several players and death of Joe Hall of Montreal Canadiens from flu. Five games had been played when the series was halted, each team having won two and tied one. Final scores are listed above.

1918

Prior to the start of the 1917-18 campaign, the National Hockey Association dissolved and the NHL took its place. The new league started out with four teams — the Montreal Canadiens and Wanderers, Ottawa and Toronto — but the Wanderers withdrew after the Montreal Arena burned down.

After capturing the first NHL title, Toronto played host to Vancouver in the Stanley Cup finals which meant that eastern rules would be used in games one, three and five. Because neither club seemed comfortable playing an unfamiliar style, Toronto won the series with the advantage of playing the final game under eastern rules.

Alf Skinner led the Arenas with eight goals in five games, while Cyclone Taylor paced Vancouver with nine. Rookie coach Dick Carroll steered his team to the NHL's first Stanley Cup championship.

FINALS

Mar.	20	Vancouver	3	at Toronto 5
Mar.	23	Vancouver	6	at Toronto 4
Mar.	26	Vancouver	3	at Toronto 6
Mar.	28	Vancouver	8	at Toronto 1
Mar.	30	Vancouver	1	at Toronto 2

Toronto won best-of-five series 3-2

1917-18 – Toronto Arenas – Rusty Crawford, Harry Meeking, Ken Randall (Captain), Corb Denneny, Harry Cameron, Jack Adams, Alf Skinner, Harry Mummery, Hap Holmes, Reg Noble, Sammy Hebert, Jack Marks, Jack Coughlin, Charlie Querrie (Manager), Dick Carroll (Coach), Frank Carroll (Trainer).

1917

In only their second season, the Seattle Metropolitans skated to the PCHA title and distinguished themselves as the first U.S. team to host a Stanley Cup series. They also became the first American squad to capture the coveted trophy. Consequently, one of Lord Stanley's original conditions — that the trophy be held by the champion of the Dominion of Canada — had been eradicated.

Seattle's Bernie Morris, who finished second in the PCHA scoring race with 37 goals in 24 games, scored a team-high 14 times against Montreal, including six in the finale, to lead the Mets over the Canadiens.

FINALS

Mar.	17	Montreal	8	at Seattle 4
Mar.	20	Montreal	1	at Seattle 6
Mar.	23	Montreal	1	at Seattle 4
Mar.	25	Montreal	1	at Seattle 9

Seattle won best-of-five series 3-1

1916-17 – Seattle Metropolitans – Hap Holmes, Ed Carpenter, Cully Wilson, Jack Walker, Bernie Morris, Frank Foyston, Roy Rickey, Jim Riley, Bobby Rowe (Captain), Peter Muldoon (Manager).

1916

The PCHA had become the first Canadian league to place a team in the United States in 1915 when the New Westminster Royals moved to Oregon and became the Portland Rosebuds. One year later, Portland became the first American-based team to play for the Stanley Cup

For the first time, the Stanley Cup series came down to a fifth and final game after both participants split the first four games. Portland's Tommy Dunderdale put the Rosebuds ahead early, but the Canadiens bounced back. Skene Ronan tied the game, and Goldie Prodgers netted the Cup-winner.

In his first Stanley Cup appearance, goaltender Georges Vezina backed the Canadiens with a 2.60 average in five games en route to the club's first championship.

FINALS

Mar. 20	Portland	2	at	Montreal	0
Mar. 22	Portland	1	at	Montreal	2
Mar. 25	Portland	3	at	Montreal	6
Mar. 28	Portland	6	at	Montreal	5
Mar. 30	Portland	1	at	Montreal	2

Montreal won best-of-five series 3-2

1915-16 – Montreal Canadiens – Georges Vezina, Bert Corbeau, Jack Laviolette, Newsy Lalonde, Louis Berlinquette, Goldie Prodgers, Howard McNamara, Didier Pitre, Skene Ronan, Amos Arbour, Skinner Poulin, Jack Fournier, George Kennedy (Manager).

1915

An informal agreement was reached between the NHA and PCHA in 1915 that called for the two league's respective champions to meet each year to determine the Stanley Cup winner. The arrangement stated that the series would be played alternately in the east and west, and that the different rules of the two leagues would alternate game by game. (The PCHA still employed the rover, though it had introduced more modern passing rules.)

Deadlocked with 14–6–0 records at the conclusion of the NHA season, the Ottawa Senators and Montreal Wanderers played a two-game total goals series for the league title and the right to face the PCHA champions. The Senators outscored the Canadiens 4–1 and packed up for the first Stanley Cup series to be played west of Winnipeg.

Fred "Cyclone" Taylor notched six goals in three games, and Barney Stanley scored four in the third, to lead the Millionaires to a one-sided sweep of the best-of-five series.

FINALS

Mar. 22	Ottawa	2	at	Vancouver	6
Mar. 24	Ottawa	3	at	Vancouver	8
Mar. 26	Ottawa	3	at	Vancouver	12

Vancouver won best-of-five series 3-0

1914-15 – Vancouver Millionaires – Ken Mallen, Frank Nighbor, Cyclone Taylor, Hugh Lehman, Lloyd Cook, Mickey MacKay, Barney Stanley, Jim Seaborn, Si Griffis (Captain), Johnny Matz, Frank Patrick (Playing Manager).

1914

The Montreal Canadiens, making their first appearance in a Stanley Cup series, faced the Toronto Blueshirts in a two-game showdown for the NHA title and possession of the Cup.

Although each team posted a shutout on its home ice, the Blueshirts, who later became the NHL's Maple Leafs, outscored the Canadiens overall.

Game two in Toronto was the first Stanley Cup matchup ever played on artificial ice.

Three days after the conclusion of the series between the Blueshirts and Canadiens, Victoria of the Pacific Coast Hockey Association came east to play in Toronto. In the first of what would prove to be 13 consecutive east-west confrontations for the Stanley Cup, Victoria overlooked the formality of submitting a challenge, and thus the trustees did not regard the series as legitimate which might have led to quite a dispute if the Aristocrats had won. As it was though, Toronto swept the first best-of-five series in Stanley Cup history. Frank Foyston led the balanced Blueshirts attack with three goals, including the Cup-winner in game three.

FINALS

Mar. 7	Toronto	0	at	Montreal	2
Mar. 11	Montreal	0	at	Toronto	6

Toronto won total-goals series 6-2

Mar. 14	Victoria	2	at	Toronto	5

Mar. 17	Victoria	5	at	Toronto	6 OT
Mar. 19	Victoria	1	at	Toronto	2

Toronto won best-of-five series 3-0

1913-14 – Toronto Blueshirts – Con Corbeau, Roy McGiffen, Jack Walker, George McNamara, Cully Wilson, Frank Foyston, Harry Cameron, Hap Holmes, Scotty Davidson (Captain), Harriston, Jack Marshall (Playing Manager), Frank and Dick Carroll (Trainers).

1913

Quebec repeated as NHA champs and faced the Sydney Miners or "Millionaires", the top Maritime club, in defense of the Stanley Cup. "Phantom" Joe Malone poured in nine goals in the first game. He was not put in the lineup for the second, and the result was closer. Joe Hall scored three times in game two.

After the Sydney series, Victoria challenged Quebec but the Bulldogs refused to put the Stanley Cup in competition so the two teams played an exhibition series with Victoria winning two games to one by scores of 7-5, 3-6, 6-1. It was the first meeting between the Eastern champions and the Western champions from the Pacific Coast Hockey Association. The following year, and until the Western Hockey League disbanded after the 1926 playoffs, the Cup went to the winner of the series between East and West.

CUP CHALLENGE

Mar. 8	Sydney	3	at	Quebec	14
Mar. 10	Sydney	2	at	Quebec	6

Quebec won best-of-three series 2-0

1912-13 – Quebec Bulldogs – Joe Malone (Captain), Joe Hall, Paddy Moran, Harry Mummery, Tommy Smith, Jack Marks, Rusty Crawford, Billy Creighton, Jeff Malone, Rocket Power, M.J. Quinn (Manager), D. Beland (Trainer).

1912

Two major rule changes were introduced at the outset of 1912. The NHA required teams to play for the first time with six men per side instead of seven (abandoning the position of rover), and the Cup trustees declared that all Stanley Cup challenges had to take place after the regular season.

The Quebec Bulldogs, who posted a league-high 10–8–0 record, successfully defended their newly acquired trophy against Moncton of the Maritime Professional Hockey League. Jack MacDonald contributed nine goals while Joe Malone scored five in Quebec's sweep of the best-of-three series.

Although the famed Patrick brothers, Frank and Lester, had started the Pacific Coast Hockey Association, not one of the three original PCHA teams challenged for the Stanley Cup. The Patricks introduced the first artificial ice surfaces in Canada at their new 10,000-seat Arena in Vancouver and in a smaller Victoria facility.

CUP CHALLENGE

Mar. 11	Moncton	3	at	Quebec	9
Mar. 13	Moncton	0	at	Quebec	8

Quebec won best-of-three series 2-0

1911-12 – Quebec Bulldogs – Goldie Prodgers, Joe Hall, Walter Rooney, Paddy Moran, Jack Marks, Jack McDonald, Eddie Oatman, George Leonard, Joe Malone (Captain), C. Nolan (Coach), M.J. Quinn (Manager), D. Beland (Trainer).

1911

Prior to 1912, teams could challenge the Stanley Cup champions for the title at any time, thus there was more than one Championship Series played in most of the seasons between 1894 and 1911. After

defeating Waterloo for the Ontario Professional Hockey League crown, Galt downed Port Hope, champions of the Eastern Professional Hockey League, in what became the second of two playoff series leading up to a challenge for the Stanley Cup.

The NHA champion Senators (13–3–0) had claimed the Cup from the Wanderers before defeating Galt 7-4. Marty Walsh, who had first appeared in Stanley Cup competition with Queen's University in 1906, notched a hat trick for the winning Ottawa side.

Three days after defeating Galt, Ottawa took on the Port Arthur Bearcats, champions of the New (Northern) Ontario Hockey Association who had beaten the Saskatchewan champions from Prince Albert to earn the challenge.

In the one-game confrontation, the Senators' Marty Walsh scored 10 goals to fall four short of the record set by Frank McGee in 1905.

CUP CHALLENGES

Mar. 13	Galt	4	at	Ottawa	7
Mar. 16	Port Arthur	4	at	Ottawa	14

1910-11 – Ottawa Senators – Hamby Shore, Percy LeSueur (Captain), Jack Darragh, Bruce Stuart, Marty Walsh, Bruce Ridpath, Fred Lake, Albert Kerr, Alex Currie, Horace Gaul.

1910 March

When the Senators joined the National Hockey Association they brought the Stanley Cup into what was now unquestionably Canada's top hockey league. By winning the 1910 NHA title, the Montreal Wanderers took possession of the Stanley Cup from Ottawa and accepted a challenge from Berlin, 1910 champions of the OPHL. The Wanderers held on to their trophy in a one-game affair, with Ernie Russell (4) and Harry Hyland (3) scoring all seven goals for the winners.

CUP CHALLENGE

Mar. 12	Berlin	3	at	Mtl. Wanderers	7

1909-10 – (Mar.) – Montreal Wanderers – Cecil Blachford, Moose Johnson, Ernie Russell, Riley Hern, Harry Hyland, Jack Marshall, Pud Glass (Captain), Jimmy Gardner, Dickie Boon (Manager).

1910 January

The Eastern Canada Hockey Association became the Canadian Hockey Association in 1910 in order to freeze out the Montreal Wanderers. The Wanderers then helped to form the NHA, which introduced the Montreal Canadiens, who would eventually become hockey's most prolific champions.

Concerned by the number of "ringers" imported by Cup contestants, the trustees ruled that only players who had skated with their teams during the regular-season could be eligible for the Stanley Cup competition.

The Ottawa Senators were still members of the CHA when the 1910 season began. As holders of the Stanley Cup they defended the trophy against Galt, the 1909 champions of the Ontario Professional Hockey League (OPHL). Marty Walsh scored six goals in the first game en route to a sweep over the challengers.

The Senators had abandoned the CHA for the NHA when they took time out from the regular-season schedule for another Stanley Cup challenge. Edmonton had come east again for what was expected to be a close series, but Ottawa was too strong. The two-game set saw the Senators' Bruce Stuart and Gordie Roberts score seven goals apiece, while Fred Whitcroft notched five for Edmonton.

CUP CHALLENGES

Jan.	5	Galt	3	at Ottawa	12
Jan.	7	Galt	1	at Ottawa	3

Ottawa won total-goals series 15-4

Jan.	18	Edmonton	4	at Ottawa	8
Jan.	20	Edmonton	7	at Ottawa	13

Ottawa won total-goals series 21-11

1909-10 – (Jan.) – Ottawa Senators – Albert Kerr, Fred Lake, Percy LeSueur, Ken Mallen, Bruce Ridpath, Gord Roberts, Hamby Shore, Bruce Stuart (Captain), Marty Walsh.

1909

Prior to the 1909 season Montreal's AAA and Victorias' clubs, who were the last amateur teams in the ECAHA, dropped out of the league. Consequently, the league was renamed the Eastern Canada Hockey Association with "Amateur" dropped from the title.

The Ottawa Senators, formerly the Silver Seven, posted a 10–2–0 record to capture the first all-pro, ECHA championship. Ottawa, as champions of the ECHA, took over the Stanley Cup in 1909 and, although a challenge was accepted by the Cup trustees from the Winnipeg Shamrocks, games could not be arranged because of the lateness of the season. No other challenges were made in 1909.

Fred "Cyclone" Taylor, who tallied eight goals in 11 games, made his debut on a Stanley Cup championship team with the Senators.

1908-09 – Ottawa Senators – Fred Lake, Percy LeSueur, Cyclone Taylor, Billy Gilmour, Albert Kerr, Edgar Dey, Marty Walsh, Bruce Stuart (Captain).

1908 December

As champions of the Alberta Hockey League, the Edmonton Eskimos earned the right to play a challenge series against the defending champions, the Montreal Wanderers.

With six of its seven players brought in especially to face the Wanderers, Edmonton established a new record for ringers on a Cup challenger. Only rover Fred Whitcroft was legitimate. Lester Patrick, Tom Phillips and Didier Pitre headlined the cast of imports.

After dropping the first game, Edmonton replaced two of its ringers with two regulars, Harold Deeton and Jack Miller, who had made the trip to Montreal. They responded, scoring three and two goals, respectively. It marked the Wanderers' first Stanley Cup loss in seven games.

Harry Smith scored six goals, including five in the first game, as the Wanderers successfully defended the Cup on total goals despite splitting the series.

CUP CHALLENGE

Dec.	28	Edmonton	3	at Mtl. Wanderers	7
Dec.	30	Edmonton	7	at Mtl. Wanderers	6

Montreal won total-goals series 13-10

1907-08 – Montreal Wanderers – Riley Hern, Art Ross, Walter Smaill, Pud Glass, Bruce Stuart, Ernie Russell, Moose Johnson, Cecil Blachford (Captain), Tom Hooper, Larry Gilmour, Ernie Liffiton, R.R. Boon (Manager).

1908 March

After retaining the Eastern Canada Amateur Hockey Association crown with an 8–2–0 record, the Wanderers faced the Winnipeg Maple Leafs, champions of the Manitoba Hockey League.

For the first time in Stanley Cup play, every man on the winning team except the goalie scored at least once as the Wanderers took the first game. In the second game, Bruce Stuart and Ernie Johnson each

registered four goals.

The Toronto "Trolley Leaguers", champions of the OPHL, the first entirely pro hockey league ever formed in Canada, played the Wanderers in a one-game, sudden-death affair.

The see-saw battle included four ties until Ernie Johnson scored the Wanderers' game-winning goal and Bruce Stuart tallied an insurance marker.

In his premier Stanley Cup appearance, Newsy Lalonde scored twice for Toronto.

CUP CHALLENGES

Mar.	10	Winnipeg	5	at Mtl. Wanderers	11
Mar.	12	Winnipeg	3	at Mtl. Wanderers	9

Montreal won total-goals series 20-8

Mar.	14	Toronto	4	at Mtl. Wanderers	6

1908 January

The Ottawa Victorias, the latest cast of challengers, had actually finished third in the Federal Amateur Hockey League in 1907, but were awarded the league championship when the first and second place clubs — Montagnards and Cornwall — withdrew from competition. Nevertheless, Ottawa's challenge was accepted by the Cup trustees.

Ernie Russell netted 10 goals in two games, including six in the second, as Montreal easily defended the trophy.

CUP CHALLENGE

Jan.	9	Ottawa	3	at Mtl. Wanderers	9
Jan.	13	Ottawa	1	at Mtl. Wanderers	13

Montreal won total-goals series 22-4

1907 March

Immediately after capturing the ECAHA league title with a perfect record of 10–0–0, the Wanderers submitted a challenge to the Cup trustees, but before the Thistles could play the rematch they had to face the Brandon Wheat Kings in a best-of-three set to determine the champion of the Manitoba league. Kenora swept the series to retain the Cup.

Because the trustees had ruled that Kenora could not use Art Ross against the Wanderers, the Thistles imported Alf Smith and Harry Westwick from Ottawa. Although Smith scored in each game, Montreal's Ernie Russell led a winning attack with four goals in the first game and added a single in the second. Though Kenora won the second game, the Wanderers still took the total-goals series.

All games were played in Winnipeg as a result of unsatisfactory rink conditions in Kenora.

CUP CHALLENGES

Mar.	17	Kenora	8	vs Brandon	6 *
Mar.	18	Kenora	4	vs Brandon	1 *

Montreal won best-of-three series 20-8

Mar.	23	Mtl. Wanderers	7	vs Kenora	2 *
Mar.	25	Mtl. Wanderers	5	vs Kenora	6 *

* played in Winnipeg.

Montreal won total-goals series 12-8.

1906-07 – (Mar.) – Montreal Wanderers – Riley Hern, Billy Strachan, Lester Patrick, Hod Stuart, Pud Glass, Ernie Russell, Cecil Blachford (Captain), Moose Johnson, Rod Kennedy, Jack Marshall, Dickie Boon (Manager).

1906-07 – (Mar.) – Kenora Thistles – Eddie Giroux, Si Griffis, Tom Hooper, Fred Whitcroft, Alf Smith, Harry Westwick, Roxy Beaudro, Tommy Phillips, Russell Phillips

1907 January

Because no ice had been available after the Wanderers took the Stanley Cup title from Ottawa in 1906, this east-west confrontation had to be delayed until the start of the 1907 schedule.

The Kenora Thistles, formerly the Rat Portage Thistles, brought in Art Ross as a ringer in an effort to beef up the lineup which had failed to win its Cup challenges in 1903 and 1905.

Tommy Phillips scored seven times in the two games, including all four Thistles goals in the first contest, as Kenora (with its population of 6,000 people) became the smallest town ever to win a Stanley Cup championship.

CUP CHALLENGE

Jan.	17	Kenora	4	at Mtl. Wanderers	2
Jan.	21	Kenora	8	at Mtl. Wanderers	6

1906-07 – (Jan.) – Kenora Thistles – Eddie Giroux, Art Ross, Si Griffis, Tom Hooper, Billy McGimsie, Roxy Beaudro, Tommy Phillips, Joe Hall, Russell Phillips.

1906 December

A new ruling allowed professionals to play with the amateurs in the ECAHA, and the Wanderers were quick to give contracts to Riley Hern, Pud Glass, Hod Stuart, Moose Johnson and Jack Marshall — who officially became the first five pros in Stanley Cup competition. Players like Cecil Blachford and Ernie Russell chose to remain amateur. A pre-season challenge by a New Glasgow squad stocked with amateur players was accepted.

Amidst the partially pro lineup, it was amateur rover Lester Patrick who led Montreal over New Glasgow with a hat trick in each game.

CUP CHALLENGES

Dec.	27	New Glasgow	3	at Mtl. Wanderers	10
Dec.	29	New Glasgow	2	at Mtl. Wanderers	7

Montreal won total-goals series 17-5

1906-07 – (Dec.) – Montreal Wanderers – Riley Hern, Billy Strachan, Rod Kennedy, Lester Patrick, Pud Glass, Ernie Russell, Moose Johnson, Cecil Blachford (Captain), Dickie Boon (Manager).

1906 March

Late in the ECAHA season, the Cup trustees decided that Ottawa should defend the Cup against Smiths Falls, champions of the reconstituted FAHL. Frank McGee notched nine goals in the two games, which would be the last of Ottawa's nine straight successful Cup defenses.

It is interesting to note that the title "Silver Seven" was given only to the team and not to any particular seven players. Ottawa's line-up included a total of 16 players during its Stanley Cup reign that spanned from 1903 to 1906.

Ottawa and Montreal each concluded the regular-season at 9–1–0, leading to a two-game, total-goals series for the ECAHA championship and possession of the Stanley Cup.

In his Stanley Cup debut, Ernie Russell scored four goals to lift Montreal over Ottawa 9–1 in the first game, which left the defending champs with the task of outscoring the Wanderers by a minimum of nine goals in the second in order to retain the trophy.

Ottawa unveiled Smiths Falls goalie Percy Lesueur in goal for the second game, and after he gave up an early goal, Ottawa stormed to a 9–1 lead on the strength of Harry Smith's five-goal effort to tie the series. However, Montreal rover Lester Patrick scored two late goals for the Wanderers to lock up the club's first Stanley Cup title.

CUP CHALLENGES

Mar.	6	Smiths Falls	5	at	Ottawa	6
Mar.	8	Smiths Falls	2	at	Ottawa	8
Mar	14	Ottawa	1	at	Mtl. Wanderers	9
Mar	17	Mtl. Wanderers	3	at	Ottawa	9

Montreal won total-goals series 12-10

1905-06 – Montreal Wanderers – Henri Menard, Billy Strachan, Rod Kennedy, Lester Patrick, Pud Glass, Ernie Russell, Moose Johnson, Cecil Blachford (Captain), Josh Arnold, Dickie Boon (Manager).

1906 February

Ottawa was among several Federal Amateur and Canadian Amateur Hockey League teams that banded together to form the new Eastern Canada Amateur Hockey Association in 1906. During the ECAHA season, the Silver Seven took time out to host Queen's University, which had challenged for the Stanley Cup for the third time.

Alf and Harry Smith, the best of seven brothers to have tried out for the Ottawa squad, led the Silver Seven to victory. Alf scored five goals in the first game, and Harry duplicated the feat in the second.

CUP CHALLENGE

Feb.	27	Queen's U.	7	at	Ottawa	16
Feb.	28	Queen's U.	7	at	Ottawa	12

1905-06 – (Feb.) – Ottawa Silver Seven – Harvey Pulford (Captain), Arthur Moore, Harry Westwick, Frank McGee, Alf Smith (Playing Coach), Billy Gilmour, Billy Hague, Percy LeSueur, Harry Smith, Tommy Smith, Dion, Ebbs.

1905 March

Having edged out the Montreal Wanderers for the FAHL title, Ottawa retained the Stanley Cup and faced a challenge from the team in Rat Portage (later known as Kenora, Ontario).

Ottawa had lost Frank McGee for the series opener, and the fleet-footed Thistles skated to victory. Tom Phillips put on a show for the fans with the first five-goal performance in a Stanley Cup game by a player other than the high-scoring McGee.

Ottawa's rink crew flooded the ice in the remaining two games, and the move greatly slowed the Thistles' fast-paced attack. McGee returned to score three goals in both games, including the Cup-winner in the finale.

CUP CHALLENGE

Mar.	7	Rat Portage	9	at	Ottawa	3
Mar.	9	Rat Portage	2	at	Ottawa	4
Mar.	11	Rat Portage	4	at	Ottawa	5

Ottawa won best-of-three series 2-1

1904-05 – Ottawa Silver Seven – Dave Finnie, Harvey Pulford (Captain), Arthur Moore, Harry Westwick, Frank McGee, Alf Smith (Playing Coach), Billy Gilmour, Frank White, Horace Gaul, Hamby Shore, Bones Allen.

1905 January

Now a member of the FAHL, Ottawa took on Dawson City in a midseason challenge for the Stanley Cup. The Nuggets, backed by Yukon prospector Colonel Joe Boyle, departed from Dawson City on December 19 to meet the famed Silver Seven nearly a month later. The 4,000-mile excursion included travel by dogsled, boat and train and set the club back by over $3,000.

Wearied from the long trek, the challengers were overwhelmed. In the second game, Ottawa set Stanley Cup scoring records of every variety, including an unparalleled 14-goals from Frank McGee.

CUP CHALLENGE

Jan.	13	Dawson City	2	at	Ottawa	9
Jan.	16	Dawson City	2	at	Ottawa	23

1904 March

The Montreal Wanderers, who had stripped the cross-city rival AAA club of its best players, skated to the inaugural Federal Amateur Hockey League (FAHL) championship with a perfect 6–0–0 record. As such, they were granted a two-game, total-goals challenge for the Stanley Cup.

Following the first game, which ended with a 5–5 tie, a new two-game series was scheduled to be played in Ottawa. However, the Wanderers refused to play unless one of the games would be staged in Montreal. As defenders of the Cup, the Silver Seven did not have to yield to such a demand, and the series was awarded to Ottawa.

Ottawa faced Brandon, the champions of the Manitoba/Northwestern Hockey League, in their fourth Stanley Cup challenge of the season and won in consecutive games. Frank McGee scored eight goals in the two games, including five in the first to tie his own Stanley Cup record set earlier in the year. A 21-year-old Lester Patrick starred for Brandon in his Cup debut.

CUP CHALLENGES

Mar.	2	Ottawa	5	at	Mtl. Wanderers	5
Mar.	9	Brandon	3	at	Ottawa	6
Mar.	11	Brandon	3	at	Ottawa	9

Ottawa won total-goals series 15-6

1903-04 – Ottawa Silver Seven – Suddy Gilmour, Arthur Moore, Frank McGee, Bouse Hutton, Billy Gilmour, Jim McGee, Harry Westwick, Harvey Pulford (Captain), Scott, Alf Smith (Playing Coach).

1904 February

On February 8, Ottawa pulled out of the Canadian Amateur Hockey League over a dispute involving a make-up game with the Montreal Victorias. As a result, the Quebec Bulldogs, who had won the league title, petitioned the trustees to strip the Silver Seven of the Cup and award it to them. The request would be denied, but while the debate continued, Ottawa faced a new challenger, the Toronto Marlboros of the Ontario Hockey Association.

Frank McGee led the Silver Seven with three goals in the first game and the first five-goal performance ever recorded in Stanley Cup competition in the second to insure the sweep.

CUP CHALLENGE

Feb.	23	Tor. Marlboros	3	at	Ottawa	6
Feb.	25	Tor. Marlboros	2	at	Ottawa	11

1904 January

Before beginning the new CAHL season, the Ottawa Silver Seven successfully defended the Cup against the Winnipeg Rowing Club. Ottawa's "One-eyed" Frank McGee registered a hat trick in the first game, but captain Bill Breen rallied the challengers with two goals in the second. In the finale, goalie Bouse Hutton shut down Winnipeg completely, with McGee scoring the game-winner.

Prior to the opening contest, both teams agreed to paint what essentially became the first "goal line" in hockey history. A red line was drawn from goalpost to goalpost in order to aid the referee.

Joe Hall made his Stanley Cup debut with the underdog Rowing Club.

CUP CHALLENGE

Dec.	30	Winnipeg R.C.	1	at	Ottawa	9
Jan.	1	Winnipeg R.C.	6	at	Ottawa	2
Jan.	4	Winnipeg R.C.	0	at	Ottawa	2

Ottawa won best-of-three series 2-1

1903 March

The 1903 CAHL season ended with both Ottawa and the Montreal Victorias finishing ahead of the defending champion Montreal AAA. As both Ottawa and the Vics had identical records of 6–2–0, a two-game total-goals playoff was arranged to determine both the new CAHL and Stanley Cup champion.

After a tie in game one, Ottawa's famed Gilmour brothers — Billy, Dave and Suddy — combined for five goals and Frank McGee added a hat trick en route to a convincing victory. After winning the Stanley Cup, the Ottawa team became known as the Silver Seven.

The Rat Portage Thistles, playing with only one man over the age of 20, journeyed from northwestern Ontario to Ottawa to meet the Silver Seven. The game proved to be a springboard for the Ottawa club, which successfully defended the Cup for the first of nine straight times.

Billy and Dave Gilmour combined with Frank McGee for all 10 Ottawa goals in the series.

SCORES

Mar.	7	Ottawa	1	at	Mtl. Victorias	1
Mar.	10	Mtl. Victorias	0	at	Ottawa	8

Ottawa won total-goals series 9-1

Mar	12	Rat Portage	2	at	Ottawa	6
Mar	14	Rat Portage	2	at	Ottawa	4

Ottawa won total-goals series 10-4

1902-03 – (Mar.) – Ottawa Silver Seven – Suddy Gilmour, Percy Sims, Bouse Hutton, Dave Gilmour, Billy Gilmour, Harry Westwick, Frank McGee, F.H. Wood, A.A. Fraser, Charles Spittal, Harvey Pulford (Captain), Arthur Moore, Alf Smith (Coach).

1903 February

The Montreal AAA took time out from the CAHL schedule to face a challenge from the Winnipeg Victorias in a much-discussed series. The first game was a lopsided contest won by the AAA, but the Vics bounced back in the second. With the score tied 2–2 at midnight after 27 minutes of overtime in this Saturday night affair, the Mayor of Westmount refused to allow the game to continue into the Sabbath. The Cup trustees first decided to resume the overtime the following Monday, but later realized it would be impossible to sell tickets to a game which might end after a few minutes or even a few seconds. Consequently, the game was replayed.

Tommy Phillips, one of the greatest players of the early era, made his Stanley Cup debut with three goals in four games for Montreal. The Winnipeg players all wore tube skates, the first time an entire team had appeared in the east so equipped.

CUP CHALLENGE

Jan.	29	Winnipeg	1	at	Mtl. AAA	8
Jan.	31	Winnipeg	2	at	Mtl. AAA	2 OT
Feb.	2	Winnipeg	4	at	Mtl. AAA	2
Feb.	4	Winnipeg	1	at	Mtl. AAA	4

Montreal won best-of-three series 2-1

1902-03 – (Feb.) – Montreal AAA – Tom Hodge, Dickie Boon, Bill Nicholson, Tommy Phillips, Art Hooper, Billy Bellingham, Charles Liffiton, Jack Marshall, Jimmy Gardner, Cecil Blachford, George Smith.

1902 March

Montreal, having won the championship of the CAHL, challenged Winnipeg, and a best-of-three Stanley Cup series was arranged. Over 4,000 fans packed the Winnipeg Arena for game one, paying as much as $25 for $5 and $10 seats for this battle of the giants. Even larger crowds attended the subsequent games.

After the rival teams split the first two games, Montreal's Art Hooper and Jack Marshall scored early in the third game to give the AAA a 2–0 lead. However, it was a stubborn defense which lifted the Montrealers to victory and earned them the moniker "Little Men of Iron", a nickname which became commonly associated with the Montreal Wanderers who later employed most of the AAA's star players.

CUP CHALLENGE

Mar.	13	Mtl. AAA	0	at Winnipeg	1
Mar.	15	Mtl. AAA	5	at Winnipeg	0
Mar.	17	Mtl. AAA	2	at Winnipeg	1

Montreal won best-of-three series 2-1

1901-02 – (Mar.) – Montreal AAA – Tom Hodge, Dickie Boon, Bill Nicholson, Art Hooper, Billy Bellingham, Charles Liffiton, Jack Marshall, Roland Elliott, Jimmy Gardner.

1902 January

The Cup trustees accepted a challenge from the Toronto Wellingtons of the Ontario Hockey Association, and the Vics easily won the Cup in two games. For unknown reasons, Toronto wore Winnipeg uniforms in the first match and their own in the second.

CUP CHALLENGE

Jan.	21	Tor. Wellingtons	3	at Winnipeg	5
Jan.	23	Tor. Wellingtons	3	at Winnipeg	5

1901-02 – (Jan.) – Winnipeg Victorias – Burke Wood, Tony Gingras, Charles Johnstone, Rod Flett, Magnus Flett, Dan Bain (Captain), Fred Scanlon, F. Cadham, G. Brown.

1901

After a five-year hiatus, the Winnipeg Vics regained the Stanley Cup from the defending champion Shamrocks in consecutive victories. Forward Dan Bain, who scored the Cup-winning goal four minutes into overtime in game two, played both games with a mask as the Vics continued to surprise Montrealers with new innovations from the west.

Winnipeg's victory over the Shamrocks meant the Stanley Cup passed out of the CAHL, so that when Ottawa unseated the Montreal team for the league title their was no Cup to claim. Due to the lateness of the season (March) and the travel to Winnipeg that would be involved, Ottawa declined to issue a Stanley Cup challenge.

CUP CHALLENGE

Jan.	29	Winnipeg	4	at Mtl. Shamrocks	3
Jan.	31	Winnipeg	2	at Mtl. Shamrocks	1 OT

Winnipeg won best-of-three series 2-0

1900-01 – Winnipeg Victorias – Burke Wood, Jack Marshall, Tony Gingras, Charles Johnstone, Rod Flett, Magnus Flett, Dan Bain (Captain), G. Brown.

1900 March

The end of the 1900 season saw the Montreal Shamrocks finish atop the CAHL standings again. Having thus retained their Stanley Cup title, the Shamrocks soundly turned back an attempt by the Halifax Crescents of the Maritime Hockey League to take the Cup. Montreal's Art Farrell established a new Stanley Cup record with four goals in each game to lead the champs.

CUP CHALLENGE

Mar.	5	Halifax	2	at Mtl. Shamrocks	10
Mar.	7	Halifax	0	at Mtl. Shamrocks	11

1899-1900 – Montreal Shamrocks – Joe McKenna, Frank Tansey, Frank Wall, Art Farrell, Fred Scanlon, Harry Trihey (Captain), Jack Brannen.

1900 February

In mid-season, the Shamrocks faced Winnipeg in the first best-of-three challenge to go the limit. The series was evenly played with only one goal separating the teams in each contest. Harry Trihey was the offensive star again with seven goals in three games, including three in the finale.

The Winnipeg club, which had become noted for its innovations, introduced a new hockey stick which had the upper edge of the blade tapered, making it much lighter and considerably more modern.

CUP CHALLENGE

Feb.	12	Winnipeg	4	at Mtl. Shamrocks	3
Feb.	14	Winnipeg	2	at Mtl. Shamrocks	3
Feb.	16	Winnipeg	4	at Mtl. Shamrocks	5

Montreal won best-of-three series 2-1

1899 March

The Montreal Shamrocks, formerly the Crystals, captured the 1899 CAHL title. The key game was a 1–0 victory over the Montreal Victorias in front of 8,000 fans in the brand new Montreal (Westmount) Arena. Harry Trihey scored the lone goal, which gave the Shamrocks a 7–1–0 record on the season to the Victorias' mark of 6–2–0. By defeating the defending champions for their own league title, the Shamrocks won the Stanley Cup, which they successfully defended against Queen's University. Trihey of the Irish netted a hat trick, and Art Farrell posted two more in the 6–2 victory.

CUP CHALLENGE

Mar.	14	Queen's U.	2	at Mtl. Shamrocks	6

1898-99 – (Mar.) – Montreal Shamrocks – Joe McKenna, Frank Tansey, Frank Wall, Harry Trihey (Captain), Art Farrell, Fred Scanlon, Jack Brannen, John Dobby, Charles Hoerner.

Stanley Cup Notebook

First-Game Winners Hold Decisive Edge in Stanley Cup Final

Since the NHL implemented the best-of-seven Stanley Cup Championship format in 1939, the following winning trends have developed:

- Teams winning Game 1 have won the Cup 50 of 64 times (78%).
- Teams winning both Games 1 and 2 have won the Cup 37 of 40 times (93%).
- Teams winning Games 1, 2 and 3 have won the Cup 24 of 25 times (96%).
- Teams winning Game 3 after splitting the first two games have won the Cup 21 of 24 times (88%).
- Teams holding a 2-1 series lead have won the Cup 34 of 39 times (87%).
- Teams winning Game 5 after splitting the first four games have won the Cup 13 of 17 times (76%).
- Teams holding a 3-2 series lead have won the Cup 23 of 28 times (82%).

Sub-.500 Teams in the Stanley Cup Final

Fifteen teams have advanced to the Stanley Cup Final after posting regular-season records below the .500 mark.

The complete list follows with Cup winners shown in bold.

Year	Team	Regular-Season Record	Win. %
1991	Minnesota North Stars	27-39-14	.425
1982	Vancouver Canucks	30-33-17	.481
1968	St. Louis Blues	27-31-16	.473
1961	Detroit Red Wings	25-29-16	.471
1959	Toronto Maple Leafs	27-32-11	.464
1958	Boston Bruins	27-28-15	.493
1953	Boston Bruins	28-29-13	.493
1951	Montreal Canadiens	25-30-15	.464
1950	New York Rangers	28-31-11	.479
1949	**Toronto Maple Leafs**	22-25-13	.475
1944	Chicago Black Hawks	22-23-5	.490
1942	Detroit Red Wings	19-25-4	.438
1939	Toronto Maple Leafs	19-20-9	.490
1938	**Chicago Black Hawks**	14-25-9	.385
1937	New York Rangers	19-20-9	.490

1899 February

The Amateur Hockey Association had dissolved prior to the start of the season with the Canadian Amateur Hockey League (CAHL) taking its place as the top hockey league in the country. The five former AHA franchises now comprised the new league.

The Montreal Vics successfully defended the Cup against their perennial rivals from Winnipeg in a series marred by controversy. After narrowly winning the first game of the set, Montreal's Bob McDougall slashed and injured Winnipeg's Tony Gingras, and the referee imposed a two-minute penalty, which Winnipeg protested was too lenient. The westerners were so incensed, they left the ice.

Insulted by the incident, the referee left the arena. He did reappear over an hour after play had stopped, and gave Winnipeg five minutes to resume play. Upon their failure to return, the game was awarded to Montreal.

CUP CHALLENGE

Feb. 15 Winnipeg 1 at Mtl. Victorias 2
Feb. 18 Winnipeg 2 at Mtl. Victorias 3

1898-99 – (Feb.) – Montreal Victorias – Gordon Lewis, Mike Grant, Graham Drinkwater, Cam Davidson, Bob McDougall, Ernie McLea, Frank Richardson, Jack Ewing, Russell Bowie, Douglas Acer, Fred McRobie.

1898

The Montreal Victorias claimed their fourth consecutive AHA title, romping to the championship with a perfect record of 8–0–0. Vics forward Cam Davidson headlined the cast of scoring leaders with 14 goals in seven regular-season games. As champions of the AHA, the Montreal team retained the Stanley Cup and was not called upon to defend it.

1897-98 – Montreal Victorias – Gordon Lewis, Hartland McDougall, Mike Grant, Graham Drinkwater, Cam Davidson, Bob McDougall, Ernie McLea, Frank Richardson (Captain), Jack Ewing.

1897

The Montreal Victorias were champions of the AHA for a third straight season in 1897 (again with a 7–1–0 record), and accepted a challenge from the Ottawa Capitals, winners of the Central Canada Hockey Association title. The challenge was scheduled for December, which would place it just before the beginning of the next hockey season. Although this Stanley Cup confrontation was originally set as a best-of-three series, the trustees ended the affair after one game because the two teams were unevenly matched.

CUP CHALLENGE

Dec. 27 Ottawa 2 at Mtl. Victorias 14

1896-97 – Montreal Victorias – Gordon Lewis, Harold Henderson, Mike Grant (Captain), Cam Davidson, Graham Drinkwater, Bob McDougall, Ernie McLea, Shirley Davidson, Hartland McDougall, Jack Ewing, Percy Molson, David Gillilan, McLellan.

1896 December

Immediately after winning the AHA championship with a 7–1–0 record, the recently dethroned Cup champion Montreal Vics wasted no time in requesting a challenge against the Winnipeg Vics, but satisfactory ice could not be ensured and the game was put off until the following winter.

The long-awaited rematch was described at the time as the greatest sporting event in Winnipeg history. Throngs of fans jammed the arena, with many paying as much as $12 per seat. Back in Montreal, the *Daily Star* newspaper arranged a public gathering whereby fans received up-to-the-minute game reports via telegraph.

The Montrealers overcame a 4–2 halftime deficit to tie the game 5–5, before Ernie McLea, who posted the first Stanley Cup hat trick, rifled his third goal of the night past goalie George "Whitey" Merritt to win the game in the closing seconds.

CUP CHALLENGE

Dec. 30 Mtl. Victorias 6 at Winnipeg 5

1895-96 – (Dec.) – Montreal Victorias – Harold Henderson, Mike Grant (Captain), Bob McDougall, Graham Drinkwater, Shirley Davidson, Ernie McLea, Robert Jones, Cam Davidson, David Gillilan, Stanley Willett, Gordon Lewis, W. Wallace.

1896 February

The first east-west confrontation in Stanley Cup history pitted the defending Montreal Victorias against the Winnipeg Victorias, champions of the Manitoba Hockey League (MHL).

Whitey Merritt, the Winnipeg netminder, introduced the first set of goalie pads in Stanley Cup history to the Montrealers when he skated onto to the ice with a pair of white cricket pads and proceeded to register a shutout. Dan Bain scored the Cup-winning goal midway through the game, and C.J. Campbell added the other.

CUP CHALLENGE

Feb. 14 Winnipeg 2 at Mtl. Victorias 0

1895-96 – (Feb.) – Winnipeg Victorias – Whitey Merritt, Rod Flett, Fred Higginbotham, Jack Armitage (Captain), Tote Campbell, Dan Bain, Charles Johnstone, H. Howard.

1895

The Montreal Victorias wrapped up the AHA title on March 8, and, having unseated the Montreal AAA, were prepared to defend the Stanley Cup as league champions. However, trustees Sweetland and Ross had already agreed to a challenge match between the 1894 champion AAA club and Queen's University with the game set for March 9.

In what remains one of the most unusual Stanley Cup situations ever, Sweetland and Ross maintained that if the AAA defeated Queen's, the Vics would be declared champions, but if Queen's won, the trophy would pass out of the AHA for the first time and go to the university squad. The first challenge match in Stanley Cup history turned out to be a one-sided affair as the AAA won the game, and the Vics were awarded the trophy.

Clarence McKerrow, playing in place of the injured Billy Barlow, became the first "ringer" in Stanley Cup history and scored once for the AAA in a winning effort.

CUP CHALLENGE

Mar. 9 Queen's U. 1 at Mtl. AAA 5

1894-95 – Montreal Victorias – Robert Jones, Harold Henderson, Mike Grant (Captain), Shirley Davidson, Bob McDougall, Norman Rankin, Graham Drinkwater, Roland Elliot, William Pullan, Hartland McDougall, Art Fenwick, A. McDougall.

1894

The 1894 AHA season ended precariously. Four of the five competing clubs — the Montreal AAA, Montreal Victorias, Ottawa Capitals and Quebec — finished with 5–3–0 records and shares of first place. The determination of a champion, and thus the winner of the Stanley Cup, created many problems for the league's governors who simply could not come to terms on a solution suitable to all involved. With two of the four finalists from Montreal, home-ice advantage became the major issue of contention. After Quebec ultimately withdrew, it was decided that all playoff games would be staged in Montreal and that Ottawa would be given a bye into the finals since it was the sole "road" team.

In what must be termed the first Stanley Cup playoff game ever, the two Montreal clubs battled to a 3–2 decision in favor of the defending champions, who then downed Ottawa in the finale.

Forward Billy Barlow, who finished third overall with eight goals in eight regular-season games, scored twice in each postseason contest as the AAA successfully defended its title.

SCORES

Mar. 17 Mtl. Victorias 2 at Mtl. AAA 3
Mar. 22 Ottawa 1 at Mtl. AAA 3

1893-94 – Montreal AAA – Herb Collins, Allan Cameron, George James, Billy Barlow, Clare Mussen, Archie Hodgson, Haviland Routh, Alex Irving, James Stewart, Toad Wand, A.B. Kingan, E. O'Brien.

1893

In accordance with Lord Stanley's terms, the Montreal AAA Hockey Club captured the inaugural Stanley Cup championship as a result of winning Canada's Amateur Hockey Association (AHA) title. The AAA squad skated to a 7–1–0 record to beat out the 6–2–0 Ottawa Generals, who had handed the Montrealers their lone defeat of the season on opening day. Haviland Routh led the newly crowned champs with a league-high 12 goals in seven games.

Formed in 1886, the AHA was considered the top hockey league in all of Canada. By 1893, its schedule consisted of 20 games played among its' five club members, which included three Montreal teams — the AAA, Victorias and Crystals — as well as Ottawa and Quebec.

Once the AAA had been declared holders of the Cup, any Canadian hockey team deemed acceptable by the trustees could challenge for the trophy, but none would for two years.

1892-93 – Montreal AAA – Tom Paton, James Stewart, Allan Cameron, Haviland Routh, Archie Hodgson, Billy Barlow, A.B. Kingan, G.S. Lowe.

Stanley Cup Notebook
Odd and Unusual Moments in Stanley Cup History

1988: Tie games used to be a part of the NHL playoffs until the practice of two-game total-goals series was abandoned for the 1936–37 postseason. Since then, only two NHL playoff games have ended before a winner was declared, and both involved the Boston Bruins. The first occurred in 1951 (see right). The second took place on May 24, 1988, when a power failure at the Boston Garden stopped a game in the finals between the Bruins and Edmonton Oilers. The game was postponed, and was never replayed as the Oilers went on to defeat the Bruins in four straight games.

After winning, the Oilers took the Cup back to Edmonton to celebrate. One stop on this local victory tour, the Cup was slightly bent in various places, so it was taken to a local autobody shop and repaired. It returned to its home at the Hall of Fame in Toronto looking a little worse for wear, but a quick trip to the silversmith returned the trophy to tip-top condition.

1987: Trailing three games to one in the Finals, Philadelphia coach Mike Keenan uncrated the Cup in the Flyers dressing room as a motivational ploy before Game Five against Edmonton. The Cup's magic worked; the Flyers won 4-3. The Cup was displayed in the dressing room before Game Six and the Flyers won again. Returning to Edmonton for Game Seven, Keenan wanted to stick with his pre-game ritual, but the Cup couldn't be found. Apparently it had been delayed in shipping. Edmonton won the game and the series and celebrated with the trophy. It was later revealed that the Cup had been hidden by Edmonton trainer Sparky Kulchisky.

1984: After the Edmonton Oilers won their Stanley Cup title, owner Peter Pocklington included the name of his father, Basil Pocklington, on the trophy. As Basil had no connection with the team, the name was crossed out with a row of X's that still remain on the Cup. The X's do not appear on the Hockey Hall of Fame's replica Cup.

1977: The current Stanley Cup was almost stolen in 1977, but a keen-eyed employee of the Hall thwarted the attempt. Seven men, with a large gym bag and tools, were seen near the Cup. When spotted, they dashed outside. In their car, police found a series of photos detailing the Hall and the necessary equipment to pull off the heist.

1975: One of the more unusual events in Stanley Cup history took place during the final between the Philadelphia Flyers and Buffalo Sabres. Game Three of the series was played on May 20 on a humid night in Buffalo. Fog inside the old Memorial Auditorium became so thick that the game had to be delayed. Players skated around the ice, waving towels to move the mist away. Suddenly, a bat flew down from the rafters and flew in circles just above the playing surface. The crowd cheered as all the players scattered—except Buffalo's Jim Lorentz, who dispatched the winged creature with a swipe of his hockey stick. The Sabres went on to win the game 3–2 in overtime, but dropped the series in six.

1970: After the Toronto Maple Leafs won the Cup in 1963, the original collar beneath the Stanley Cup bowl was retired to the Hockey Hall of Fame. In January 1970, the collar was stolen. Later, an anonymous phone call told police to check the backroom of a Toronto cleaning store for a very important piece of history. The police weren't sure what they would find, but there, wrapped like a Christmas present was the original collar of the Stanley Cup.

1962: Another attempt to steal the Cup took place in Chicago after the Black Hawks had become playoff champions in 1961, endning the Montreal Canadiens' five-year championship reign. When the Habs lost in the semifinals to the Hawks for the second year in a row in 1962, an unhappy Montreal fan went into the lobby of the Chicago Stadium where the trophy was displayed in a glass case. He broke the glass and made a beeline to freedom with his prize. However, he was quickly caught and the Mug apprehended. He explained that he couldn't stand seeing anybody but the Canadiens win the trophy.

1951: On Saturday, March 31, 1951, the Bruins and Leafs were tied 1–1 after one period of overtime when the game was halted. At that time, the city of Toronto did not allow sports to be played on Sunday, and the clock was just about to strike midnight.

1924: The Montreal Canadiens wanted to celebrate their Cup win in by drinking champagne from the Silver Mug. To this end they headed to owner Leo Dandurand's home to swill the bubbly. As fate would have it, they suffered a flat tire along the way and the boys bolted from the car, leaving Lord Stanley on the curb while they tended to the flat. When they arrived at Dandurand's and prepared to serve the victory wine, they discovered they'd left the Grail behind, on the streets of Montreal. Back into the car (a Tin Lizzie, no less) they rumbled and found the Cup where they had left it, on the sidewalk.

1923: After returning home from the west coast with the Stanley Cup, rookie Frank "King" Clancy asked Ottawa Senator executives if he could bring the Cup home to show his father, a well-known amateur athlete and the original "King."

The following season, NHL president Frank Calder asked the Senators for the Cup, but they couldn't find it. It was then that that Clancy admitted it was at home, sitting on his mantle piece.

1907: The injustices of the Cup continued. The Wanderers quickly forgot the valuable lesson of the previous year and left the Cup at the home of the photographer they hired to document their trophy win. A young fellow happened by and grabbed the Cup, hoping to extract a small ransom for its return. However, no one was interested, so he returned it to the photographer's home, where an astute lady decided it would make a wonderful flower pot. It served that purpose for a few months until the the Wanderers brass remembered it and rescued it from its earthly grave.

1906: The Montreal Wanderers won the Cup this year, dethroning the Silver Seven who had held the trophy since 1903. But when the Montreal players asked to see their prize, the Cup was no where to be found. Someone, somehow remembered that Harry Smith had the Mug and after a quick search, sure enough there it was. It was retrieved and presented to the victorious Wanderers.

1905: The Ottawa Silver Seven felt it necessary to see if one could kick the Cup across Ottawa's Rideau canal. One of them lined it up and gave it a boot, drop-kick style. It didn't make it. The Stanley Cup landed in the canal, which, fortunately, happened to be frozen at the time. The boys went on their merry way, and the Cup stayed on the Canal until the next day when sober heads prevailed and Lord Stanley's mug was rescued.

Stanley Cup Notebook
Comebacks, Upsets, Overtime and Conn Smythe Trophy Winners

Comebacks from Trailing 3–1 in Games

Teams have trailed 3-1 in a best-of-seven series a total of 193 times and have come back to win the series on 16 occasions or 8.3% of the time.

Year	Series Result in Games			
1942	TOR	4	DET	3
1975	NYI	4	PIT	3
1987	NYI	4	WSH	3
1987	DET	4	TOR	3
1988	WSH	4	PHI	3
1989	LA	4	EDM	3
1990	EDM	4	WPG	3
1991	STL	4	DET	3
1992	DET	4	MIN	3
1992	VAN	4	WPG	3
1992	PIT	4	WSH	3
1994	VAN	4	CGY	3
1995	PIT	4	WSH	3
1998	EDM	4	COL	3
1999	STL	4	PHO	3
2000	NJ	4	PHI	3

Comebacks from Trailing 2–0 in Games

Teams have trailed 2-0 in a best-of-seven series a total of 248 times and have come back to win the series on 33 occasions or 13.3% of the time.

Year	Series Result in Games			
1942	TOR	4	DET	3
1945	DET	4	BOS	3
1959	TOR	4	BOS	3
1962	CHI	4	MTL	2
1963	DET	4	CHI	2
1965	CHI	4	DET	3
1966	MTL	4	DET	2
1968	MIN	4	LA	3
1968	CHI	4	NYR	2
1971	MTL	4	CHI	3
1972	STL	4	MIN	3
1975	NYI	4	PIT	3
1976	NYI	4	BUF	2
1977	PHI	4	TOR	2
1978	TOR	4	NYI	3
1982	QUE	4	BOS	3
1984	NYI	4	MTL	2
1987	QUE	4	HFD	2
1987	MTL	4	QUE	3
1987	DET	4	TOR	3
1991	PIT	4	BOS	2
1992	DET	4	MIN	3
1992	PIT	4	WSH	3
1993	MTL	4	QUE	2
1993	TOR	4	DET	3
1994	NJ	4	BOS	2
1995	CHI	4	TOR	3
1996	NYR	4	MTL	2
1996	PIT	4	WSH	2
1999	COL	4	DET	2
2000	PHI	4	PIT	2
2001	LA	4	DET	2
2002	DET	4	VAN	2

Largest Single-Game Playoff Comebacks

Deficit	Date		Final Score			
5	April 10, 1982	LA	6	vs	EDM	5
4	April 8, 1971	MTL	7	at	BOS	5
4	April 28, 1985	MIN	5	at	CHI	4

Largest Regular-Season Point Differential Overcome by Upset Series Winner

Differential	Year	Winner	Pts.	Loser	Pts.
48	1982	LA	63	EDM	111
38	1991	MIN	68	CHI	106
37	1991	MIN	68	STL	105
36	1951	MTL	65	DET	101
33	1981	NYR	74	STL	107
32	1986	NYR	78	PHI	110
32	1993	NYI	87	PIT	119
30	1986	CGY	89	EDM	119

Playoff Overtime, 1990 to 2002

Since the 1990 post season, there have been 235 overtime games. The home team has won 116 games (49.4%) and the road team has won 119 games (50.6%).

Conn Smythe Trophy Update

A total of 32 different players have won the Conn Smythe Trophy, awarded to the most valuable player to his team in the playoffs. The trophy was first awarded in 1965. Patrick Roy is the only three-time winner of the trophy while four players have won the award twice: Bobby Orr, Bernie Parent, Wayne Gretzky and Mario Lemieux.

Four players have won the Conn Smythe Trophy as members of teams that have lost in the Stanley Cup Finals: Roger Crozier (1966, Detroit Red Wings), Glenn Hall (1968, St. Louis Blues), Reggie Leach (1976, Philadelphia Flyers) and Ron Hextall (1987, Philadelphia Flyers).

Twenty-year-old Patrick Roy of the 1986 Montreal Canadiens was the youngest player ever to win the Conn Smythe Trophy.

The Conn Smythe Trophy is voted upon by the Professional Hockey Writers Association (PHWA) at the conclusion of the final game of the Stanley Cup. A complete listing of Conn Smythe winners follows:

Year	Winner	Year	Winner
2002	Nicklas Lidstrom, D, Det.	1983	Billy Smith, G, NYI
2001	Patrick Roy, G, Col.	1982	Mike Bossy, RW, NYI
2000	Scott Stevens, D, N.J.	1981	Butch Goring, C, NYI
1999	Joe Nieuwendyk, C, Dal.	1980	Bryan Trottier, C, NYI
1998	Steve Yzerman, C, Det.	1979	Bob Gainey, LW, Mtl.
1997	Mike Vernon, G, Det.	1978	Larry Robinson, D, Mtl.
1996	Joe Sakic, C, Col.	1977	Guy Lafleur, RW, Mtl.
1995	Claude Lemieux, RW, N.J.	1976	Reggie Leach, RW, Phi.
1994	Brian Leetch, D, NYR	1975	Bernie Parent, G, Phi.
1993	Patrick Roy, G, Mtl.	1974	Bernie Parent, G, Phi.
1992	Mario Lemieux, C, Pit.	1973	Yvan Cournoyer, RW, Mtl.
1991	Mario Lemieux, C. Pit.	1972	Bobby Orr, D, Bos.
1990	Bill Ranford, G, Edm.	1971	Ken Dryden, G, Mtl.
1989	Al MacInnis, D, Cgy.	1970	Bobby Orr, D, Bos.
1988	Wayne Gretzky, C, Edm.	1969	Serge Savard, D, Mtl.
1987	Ron Hextall, G, Phi.	1968	Glenn Hall, G, St.L.
1986	Patrick Roy, G, Mtl.	1967	Dave Keon, C, Tor.
1985	Wayne Gretzky, C, Edm.	1966	Roger Crozier, G, Det.
1984	Mark Messier, C, Edm.	1965	Jean Beliveau, C, Mtl.

CHAPTER 9

Stanley Cup Playoffs Record Book

Team and Individual Records, 1918 – 2002

Team Records

GAMES PLAYED

MOST GAMES PLAYED, ALL TEAMS, ONE PLAYOFF YEAR
92 – **1991.** There were 51 DSF, 24 DF, 11 CF and 6 F games.
90 – 1994. There were 48 CQF, 23 CSF, 12 CF and 7 F games.
 – 2002. There were 47 CQF, 25 CSF, 13 CF and 5 F games.

MOST GAMES PLAYED, ONE TEAM, ONE PLAYOFF YEAR
26 – **Philadelphia Flyers,** 1987. Won DSF 4-2 vs. NY Rangers, DF 4-3 vs. NY Islanders, CF 4-2 vs. Montreal and lost F 4-3 vs. Edmonton.
25 – New Jersey Devils, 2001. Won CQF 4-2 vs. Carolina, CSF 4-3 vs. Toronto, CF 4-1 vs. Pittsburgh and lost F 4-3 vs. Colorado.

PLAYOFF APPEARANCES

MOST STANLEY CUP CHAMPIONSHIPS
23 – **Montreal Canadiens** (1924-30-31-44-46-53-56-57-58-59-60-65-66-68-69-71-73-76-77-78-79-86-93).
13 – Toronto Maple Leafs (1918-22-32-42-45-47-48-49-51-62-63-64-67).
10 – Detroit Red Wings (1936-37-43-50-52-54-55-97-98-02).

MOST CONSECUTIVE STANLEY CUP CHAMPIONSHIPS
5 – **Montreal Canadiens** (1956-57-58-59-60).
4 – Montreal Canadiens (1976-77-78-79).
 – New York Islanders (1980-81-82-83).

MOST FINAL SERIES APPEARANCES
32 – **Montreal Canadiens** in 85-year history.
22 – Detroit Red Wings in 76-year history.
21 – Toronto Maple Leafs in 85-year history.

MOST CONSECUTIVE FINAL SERIES APPEARANCES
10 – **Montreal Canadiens,** (1951-60, inclusive).
5 – Montreal Canadiens, (1965-69, inclusive).
 – New York Islanders, (1980-84, inclusive).

MOST YEARS IN PLAYOFFS
73 – **Montreal Canadiens** in 85-year history.
62 – Toronto Maple Leafs in 85-year history.
60 – Boston Bruins in 78-year history.

MOST CONSECUTIVE PLAYOFF APPEARANCES
29 – **Boston Bruins** (1968-96, inclusive).
28 – Chicago Blackhawks (1970-97, inclusive).
24 – Montreal Canadiens (1971-94, inclusive).
23 – St. Louis Blues (1980-2002, inclusive).
21 – Montreal Canadiens (1949-69, inclusive).

TEAM WINS

MOST HOME WINS, ONE TEAM, ONE PLAYOFF YEAR
11 – **Edmonton Oilers,** 1988. Won three vs. Winnipeg in DSF; two vs. Calgary in DF; three vs. Detroit in CF; three vs. Boston in F.
10 – Edmonton Oilers, 1985. Won two vs. Los Angeles in DSF; two vs. Winnipeg in DF; three vs. Chicago in CF; three vs. Philadelphia in F.
 – Montreal Canadiens, 1986. Won two vs. Boston in DSF; three vs. Hartford in DF; three vs. NY Rangers in CF; two vs. Calgary in F.
 – Montreal Canadiens, 1993. Won three vs. Quebec in DSF; two vs. Buffalo in DF; two vs. NY Islanders in CF; two vs. Los Angeles in F.

MOST ROAD WINS, ONE TEAM, ONE PLAYOFF YEAR
10 – **New Jersey Devils,** 1995. Won three at Boston in CQF; two at Pittsburgh in CSF; three at Philadelphia in CF; two at Detroit in F.
 – **New Jersey Devils,** 2000. Won two at Florida in CQF; two at Toronto in CSF; three at Philadelphia in CF; three at Dallas in F.
8 – New York Islanders, 1980. Won two at Los Angeles in PRE; three at Boston in QF; two at Buffalo in SF; one at Philadelphia in F.
 – Philadelphia Flyers, 1987. Won two at NY Rangers in DSF; two at NY Islanders in DF; three at Montreal in CF; one at Edmonton in F.
 – Edmonton Oilers, 1990. Won one at Winnipeg in DSF; two at Los Angeles in DF; two at Chicago in CF; three at Boston in F.
 – Pittsburgh Penguins, 1992. Won two at Washington in DSF; two at NY Rangers in DF; two at Boston in CF; two at Chicago in F.
 – Vancouver Canucks, 1994. Won three at Calgary in CQF; two at Dallas in CSF; one at Toronto in CF; two at NY Rangers in F.
 – Colorado Avalanche, 1996. Won two at Vancouver in CQF; two at Chicago in CSF; two at Detroit in CF; two at Florida in F.
 – Detroit Red Wings, 1998. Won two at Phoenix in CQF; three at St. Louis in CSF; one at Dallas in CF; two at Washington in F.
 – Colorado Avalanche, 1999. Won three at San Jose in CQF; three at Detroit in CSF; two at Dallas in CF.
 – New Jersey Devils, 2001. Won two at Carolina in CQF; two at Toronto in CSF; two at Pittsburgh in CF; two at Colorado in F.
 – Detroit Red Wings, 2002. Won three at Vancouver in CQF; one at St. Louis in CSF; two at Colorado in CF; two at Carolina in F.

MOST ROAD WINS, ALL TEAMS, ONE PLAYOFF YEAR
46 – **1987.** Of 87 games played, road teams won 46 (22 DSF, 14 DF, 8 CF and 2 in F).

MOST OVERTIME WINS, ONE TEAM, ONE PLAYOFF YEAR
10 – **Montreal Canadiens,** 1993. Won two vs. Quebec in DSF; three vs. Buffalo in DF; two vs. NY Islanders in CF; three vs. Los Angeles in F.
7 – Carolina Hurricanes, 2002. Won two vs. New Jersey in CQF; one vs. Montreal in CSF; three vs. Toronto in CF; one vs. Detroit in F.

MOST OVERTIME WINS AT HOME, ONE TEAM, ONE PLAYOFF YEAR
4 – **St. Louis Blues,** 1968. Won one vs. Philadelphia in QF; three vs. Minnesota North Stars in SF.
 – **Montreal Canadiens,** 1993. Won one vs. Quebec in DSF; one vs. Buffalo in DF; one vs. NY Islanders in CF; one vs. Los Angeles in F.

MOST OVERTIME WINS ON THE ROAD, ONE TEAM, ONE PLAYOFF YEAR
6 – **Montreal Canadiens,** 1993. Won one vs. Quebec in DSF; two vs. Buffalo in DF; one vs. NY Islanders in CF; two vs. Los Angeles in F.

TEAM LOSSES

MOST LOSSES, ONE TEAM, ONE PLAYOFF YEAR
11 – **Philadelphia Flyers,** 1987. Lost two vs. NY Rangers in DSF; three vs. NY Islanders in DF; two vs. Montreal in CF; four vs. Edmonton in F.

MOST HOME LOSSES, ONE TEAM, ONE PLAYOFF YEAR
6 – **Philadelphia Flyers,** 1987. Lost one vs. NY Rangers in DSF; two vs. NY Islanders in DF;

two vs. Montreal in CF; one vs. Edmonton in F.
 – **Washington Capitals,** 1998. Lost two vs. Boston in CQF; two vs. Buffalo in CF; two vs. Detroit in F.
 – **Colorado Avalanche,** 1999. Lost two vs. San Jose in CQF; two vs. Detroit in CSF; two vs. Dallas in CF.
 – **New Jersey Devils,** 2001. Lost one vs. Carolina in CQF; two vs. Toronto in CSF; one vs. Pittsburgh in CF; two vs. Colorado in F.

MOST ROAD LOSSES, ONE TEAM, ONE PLAYOFF YEAR
6 – **St. Louis Blues,** 1968. Lost two at Philadelphia in QF; two at Minnesota North Stars in SF; two at Montreal in F.
 – **St. Louis Blues,** 1970. Lost two at Minnesota North Stars in QF; two at Pittsburgh in SF; two at Boston in F.
 – **New York Islanders,** 1984. Lost one at NY Rangers in DSF; two at Montreal in CF; three at Edmonton in F.
 – **Los Angeles Kings,** 1993. Lost one at Calgary in DSF; one at Vancouver in DF; two at Toronto in CF; two at Montreal in F.

MOST OVERTIME LOSSES, ONE TEAM, ONE PLAYOFF YEAR
4 – **Montreal Canadiens,** 1951. Lost four vs. Toronto in F.
 – **St. Louis Blues,** 1968. Lost one vs. Philadelphia in QF; one vs. Minnesota North Stars in SF; two vs. Montreal in F.
 – **New York Rangers,** 1979. Lost one vs. Philadelphia in QF; two vs. NY Islanders in SF; one vs. Montreal in F.
 – **Los Angeles Kings,** 1991. Lost one vs. Vancouver in DSF; three vs. Edmonton in DF.
 – **Los Angeles Kings,** 1993. Lost one vs. Toronto in CF; three vs. Montreal in F.
 – **New Jersey Devils,** 1994. Lost one vs. Buffalo in CQF; one vs. Boston in CSF; two vs. NY Rangers in CF.
 – **Chicago Blackhawks,** 1995. Lost one vs. Toronto in CQF; three vs. Detroit in CF.
 – **Philadelphia Flyers,** 1996. Lost two vs. Tampa Bay in CQF; two vs. Florida in CSF.
 – **Dallas Stars,** 1999. Lost two vs. St. Louis in CSF; one vs. Colorado in CF; one vs. Buffalo in F.
 – **Detroit Red Wings,** 2002. Lost one vs. Vancouver in CQF; two vs. Colorado in CF; one vs. Carolina in F.

MOST OVERTIME LOSSES AT HOME, ONE TEAM, ONE PLAYOFF YEAR
4 – **Detroit Red Wings,** 2002. Lost one vs. Vancouver in CQF; two vs. Colorado in CF; one vs. Carolina in F.

MOST OVERTIME LOSSES ON THE ROAD, ONE TEAM, ONE PLAYOFF YEAR
3 – **Los Angeles Kings,** 1991. Lost one at Vancouver in DSF; two at Edmonton in DF.
 – **Chicago Blackhawks,** 1995. Lost one at Toronto in CQF; two at Detroit in CF.
 – **St. Louis Blues,** 1996. Lost two at Toronto in CQF; one at Detroit in CSF.
 – **Dallas Stars,** 1999. Lost two at St. Louis in CSF; one at Colorado in CF.

PLAYOFF WINNING STREAKS

LONGEST PLAYOFF WINNING STREAK
14 – **Pittsburgh Penguins.** Streak started on May 9, 1992 as Pittsburgh won the first of three straight games in DF vs. NY Rangers. Continued with four wins vs. Boston in 1992 CF and four wins vs. Chicago in 1992 F. Pittsburgh then won the first three games of

1993 DSF vs. New Jersey. New Jersey ended the streak April 25, 1993, at New Jersey with a 4-1 win vs. Pittsburgh in the fourth game of 1993 DSF.

12 – Edmonton Oilers. Streak started on May 15, 1984 as Edmonton won the first of three straight games in F vs. NY Islanders. Continued with three wins vs. Los Angeles in 1985 DSF and four wins vs. Winnipeg in 1985 DF. Edmonton then won the first two games of 1985 CF vs. Chicago. Chicago ended the streak May 9, 1985, at Chicago with a 5-2 win vs. Edmonton in the third game of 1985 CF.

MOST CONSECUTIVE WINS, ONE TEAM, ONE PLAYOFF YEAR

11 – **Chicago Blackhawks** in 1992. Chicago won last three games of DSF vs. St. Louis to win series 4-2, defeated Detroit 4-0 in DF and Edmonton 4-0 in CF.

– **Pittsburgh Penguins** in 1992. Pittsburgh won last three games of DF vs. NY Rangers to win series 4-2, defeated Boston 4-0 in CF and Chicago 4-0 in F.

– **Montreal Canadiens** in 1993. Montreal won last four games of DSF vs. Quebec to win series 4-2, defeated Buffalo 4-0 in DF and won first three games of CF vs. NY Islanders.

PLAYOFF LOSING STREAKS

LONGEST PLAYOFF LOSING STREAK

16 – **Chicago Black Hawks.** Streak started on April 20, 1975 as Chicago lost the first of two straight games in QF vs. Buffalo. Continued with four losses vs. Montreal in 1976 QF, two losses vs. NY Islanders in 1977 PRE, four losses vs. Boston in 1978 QF and four losses vs. NY Islanders in 1979 QF. Chicago ended the streak April 8, 1980, at Chicago with a 3-2 win vs. St. Louis in the opening game of 1980 PRE.

14 – Los Angeles Kings. Streak started on June 2, 1993 as Los Angeles lost the first of four straight games in F vs. Montreal. Los Angeles failed to qualify for the playoffs the next four years. Continued with four losses vs. St. Louis in 1998 CQF. Los Angeles failed to qualify for the 1999 playoffs. Continued with four losses vs. Detroit in 2000 CQF. Los Angeles then lost the first two games of 2001 CQF vs. Detroit. Los Angeles ended the streak April 15, 2001, at Los Angeles with a 2-1 win vs. Detroit in the third game of 2001 CQF.

MOST GOALS IN A SERIES, ONE TEAM

MOST GOALS, ONE TEAM, ONE PLAYOFF SERIES

44 – **Edmonton Oilers** in 1985 CF. Edmonton won best-of-seven series 4-2, outscoring Chicago 44-25.

35 – Edmonton Oilers in 1983 DF. Edmonton won best-of-seven series 4-1, outscoring Calgary 35-13.

– Calgary Flames in 1995 CQF. Calgary lost best-of-seven series 4-3, outscoring San Jose 35-26.

MOST GOALS, ONE TEAM, TWO-GAME SERIES

11 – **Buffalo Sabres** in 1977 PRE. Buffalo won best-of-three series 2-0, outscoring Minnesota North Stars 11-3.

– **Toronto Maple Leafs** in 1978 PRE. Toronto won best-of-three series 2-0, outscoring Los Angeles 11-3.

10 – Boston Bruins in 1927 QF. Boston won two-game total-goals series, outscoring Chicago 10-5.

MOST GOALS, ONE TEAM, THREE-GAME SERIES

23 – **Chicago Black Hawks** in 1985 DSF. Chicago won best-of-five series 3-0, outscoring Detroit 23-8.

20 – Minnesota North Stars in 1981 PRE. Minnesota won best-of-five series 3-0, outscoring Boston 20-13.

– New York Islanders in 1981 PRE. NY Islanders won best-of-five series 3-0, outscoring Toronto 20-4.

MOST GOALS, ONE TEAM, FOUR-GAME SERIES

28 – **Boston Bruins** in 1972 SF. Boston won best-of-seven series 4-0, outscoring St. Louis 28-8.

MOST GOALS, ONE TEAM, FIVE-GAME SERIES

35 – **Edmonton Oilers** in 1983 DF. Edmonton won best-of-seven series 4-1, outscoring Calgary 35-13.

32 – Edmonton Oilers in 1987 DSF. Edmonton won best-of-seven series 4-1, outscoring Los Angeles 32-20.

MOST GOALS, ONE TEAM, SIX-GAME SERIES

44 – **Edmonton Oilers** in 1985 CF. Edmonton won best-of-seven series 4-2, outscoring Chicago 44-25.

33 – Montreal Canadiens in 1973 F. Montreal won best-of-seven series 4-2, outscoring Chicago 33-23.

– Chicago Black Hawks in 1985 DF. Chicago won best-of-seven series 4-2, outscoring Minnesota North Stars 33-29.

– Los Angeles Kings in 1993 DSF. Los Angeles won best-of-seven series 4-2, outscoring Calgary 33-28.

MOST GOALS, ONE TEAM, SEVEN-GAME SERIES

35 – **Calgary Flames** in 1995 CQF. Calgary lost best-of-seven series 4-3, outscoring San Jose 35-26.

33 – Philadelphia Flyers in 1976 QF. Philadelphia won best-of-seven series 4-3, outscoring Toronto 33-23.

– Boston Bruins in 1983 DF. Boston won best-of-seven series 4-3, outscoring Buffalo 33-23.

– Edmonton Oilers in 1984 DF. Edmonton won best-of-seven series 4-3, outscoring Calgary 33-27.

FEWEST GOALS IN A SERIES, ONE TEAM

FEWEST GOALS, ONE TEAM, TWO-GAME SERIES

0 – **New York Americans** in 1929 SF. NY Americans lost two-game total-goals series 1-0 vs. NY Rangers.

– **Chicago Black Hawks** in 1935 SF. Chicago lost two-game total-goals series 1-0 vs. Mtl. Maroons.

– **Montreal Maroons** in 1937 SF. Mtl. Maroons lost best-of-three series 2-0, outscored by NY Rangers 5-0.

– **New York Americans** in 1939 QF. NY Americans lost best-of-three series 2-0, outscored by Toronto 5-0.

FEWEST GOALS, ONE TEAM, THREE-GAME SERIES

1 – **Montreal Maroons** in 1936 SF. Mtl. Maroons lost best-of-five series 3-0, outscored by Detroit 6-1.

FEWEST GOALS, ONE TEAM, FOUR-GAME SERIES

2 – **Boston Bruins** in 1935 SF. Boston lost best-of-five series 3-1, outscored by Toronto 7-2.

– **Montreal Canadiens** in 1952 F. Montreal lost best-of-seven series 4-0, outscored by Detroit 11-2.

FEWEST GOALS, ONE TEAM, FIVE-GAME SERIES

2 – **Philadelphia Flyers** in 2002 CQF. Ottawa won best-of-seven series 4-1, outscoring Philadelphia 11-2.

FEWEST GOALS, ONE TEAM, SIX-GAME SERIES

5 – **Boston Bruins** in 1951 SF. Toronto won best-of-seven series 4-1 with 1 tie, outscoring Boston 17-5.

FEWEST GOALS, ONE TEAM, SEVEN-GAME SERIES

9 – **Toronto Maple Leafs** in 1945 F. Toronto won best-of-seven series 4-3; teams tied in scoring 9-9.

– **Detroit Red Wings** in 1945 F. Toronto won best-of-seven series 4-3; teams tied in scoring 9-9.

MOST GOALS IN A SERIES, BOTH TEAMS

MOST GOALS, BOTH TEAMS, ONE PLAYOFF SERIES

69 – **Edmonton Oilers (44), Chicago Black Hawks (25)** in 1985 CF. Edmonton won best-of-seven series 4-2.

62 – Chicago Black Hawks (33), Minnesota North Stars (29) in 1985 DF. Chicago won best-of-seven series 4-2.

61 – Los Angeles Kings (33), Calgary Flames (28) in 1993 DSF. Los Angeles won best-of-seven series 4-2.

– Calgary Flames (35), San Jose Sharks (26) in 1995 CQF. San Jose won best-of-seven series 4-3.

MOST GOALS, BOTH TEAMS, TWO-GAME SERIES

17 – **Toronto St. Patricks (10), Montreal Canadiens (7)** in 1918 NHL F. Toronto won two-game total-goals series.

15 – Boston Bruins (10), Chicago Black Hawks (5) in 1927 QF. Boston won two-game total-goals series.

– Pittsburgh Penguins (9), St. Louis Blues (6) in 1975 PRE. Pittsburgh won best-of-three series 2-0.

MOST GOALS, BOTH TEAMS, THREE-GAME SERIES

33 – **Minnesota North Stars (20), Boston Bruins (13)** in 1981 PRE. Minnesota won best-of-five series 3-0.

31 – Chicago Black Hawks (23), Detroit Red Wings (8) in 1985 DSF. Chicago won best-of-five series 3-0.

28 – Toronto Maple Leafs (18), New York Rangers (10) in 1932 F. Toronto won best-of-five series 3-0.

MOST GOALS, BOTH TEAMS, FOUR-GAME SERIES

36 – **Boston Bruins (28), St. Louis Blues (8)** in 1972 SF. Boston won best-of-seven series 4-0.

– **Minnesota North Stars (18), Toronto Maple Leafs (18)** in 1983 DSF. Minnesota won best-of-five series 3-1.

– **Edmonton Oilers (25), Chicago Black Hawks (11)** in 1983 CF. Edmonton won best-of-seven series 4-0.

35 – New York Rangers (23), Los Angeles Kings (12) in 1981 PRE. NY Rangers won best-of-five series 3-1.

MOST GOALS, BOTH TEAMS, FIVE-GAME SERIES

52 – **Edmonton Oilers (32), Los Angeles Kings (20)** in 1987 DSF. Edmonton won best-of-seven series 4-1.

50 – Los Angeles Kings (27), Edmonton Oilers (23) in 1982 DSF. Los Angeles won best-of-five series 3-2.

48 – Edmonton Oilers (35), Calgary Flames (13) in 1983 DF. Edmonton won best-of-seven series 4-1.

– Calgary Flames (30), Los Angeles Kings (18) in 1988 DSF. Calgary won best-of-seven series 4-1.

MOST GOALS, BOTH TEAMS, SIX-GAME SERIES

69 – **Edmonton Oilers (44), Chicago Black Hawks (25)** in 1985 CF. Edmonton won best-of-seven series 4-2.

62 – Chicago Black Hawks (33), Minnesota North Stars (29) in 1985 DF. Chicago won best-of-seven series 4-2.

61 – Los Angeles Kings (33), Calgary Flames (28) in 1993 DSF. Los Angeles won best-of-seven series 4-2.

MOST GOALS, BOTH TEAMS, SEVEN-GAME SERIES

61 – **Calgary Flames (35), San Jose Sharks (26)** in 1995 CQF. San Jose won best-of-seven series 4-3.

60 – Edmonton Oilers (33), Calgary Flames (27) in 1984 DF. Edmonton won best-of-seven series 4-3.

FEWEST GOALS IN A SERIES, BOTH TEAMS

FEWEST GOALS, BOTH TEAMS, TWO-GAME SERIES

1 – **New York Rangers (1), New York Americans (0)** in 1929 SF. NY Rangers won two-game total-goals series.

– **Montreal Maroons (1), Chicago Black Hawks (0)** in 1935 SF. Mtl. Maroons won two-game total-goals series.

FEWEST GOALS, BOTH TEAMS, THREE-GAME SERIES

7 – **Boston Bruins (5), Montreal Canadiens (2)** in 1929 SF. Boston won best-of-five series 3-0.

– **Detroit Red Wings (6), Montreal Maroons (1)** in 1936 SF. Detroit won best-of-five series 3-0.

FEWEST GOALS, BOTH TEAMS, FOUR-GAME SERIES

9 – **Toronto Maple Leafs (7), Boston Bruins (2)** in 1935 SF. Toronto won best-of-five series 3-1.

FEWEST GOALS, BOTH TEAMS, FIVE-GAME SERIES

11 – **Montreal Maroons (6), New York Rangers (5)** in 1928 F. NY Rangers won best-of-five series 3-2.

FEWEST GOALS, BOTH TEAMS, SIX-GAME SERIES

16 – **Carolina Hurricanes (10), Toronto Maple Leafs (6)** in 2002 CF. Carolina won best-of-seven series 4-2.

FEWEST GOALS, BOTH TEAMS, SEVEN-GAME SERIES

18 – **Toronto Maple Leafs (9), Detroit Red Wings (9)** in 1945 F. Toronto won best-of-seven series 4-3.

MOST GOALS IN A GAME OR PERIOD

MOST GOALS, ONE TEAM, ONE GAME

13 – **Edmonton Oilers**, April 9, 1987, vs. Los Angeles at Edmonton . Edmonton won 13-3.

12 – **Los Angeles Kings**, April 10, 1990, vs. Calgary at Los Angeles. Los Angeles won 12-4.

11 – **Montreal Canadiens**, March 30, 1944, vs. Toronto at Montreal. Montreal won 11-0.

– **Edmonton Oilers**, May 4, 1985, vs. Chicago at Edmonton. Edmonton won 11-2.

MOST GOALS, ONE TEAM, ONE PERIOD

7 – **Montreal Canadiens**, March 30, 1944, vs. Toronto at Montreal, third period. Montreal won 11-0.

MOST GOALS, BOTH TEAMS, ONE GAME

18 – **Los Angeles Kings (10), Edmonton Oilers (8)**, April 7, 1982, at Edmonton. Los Angeles won best-of-five DSF 3-2.

17 – Pittsburgh Penguins (10), Philadelphia Flyers (7), April 25, 1989, at Pittsburgh. Philadelphia won best-of-seven DF 4-3.

16 – Edmonton Oilers (13), Los Angeles Kings (3), April 9, 1987, at Edmonton. Edmonton won best-of-seven DSF 4-1.

– Los Angeles Kings (12), Calgary Flames (4), April 10, 1990, at Los Angeles. Los Angeles won best-of-seven DF 4-2.

MOST GOALS, BOTH TEAMS, ONE PERIOD

9 – **New York Rangers (6), Philadelphia Flyers (3)**, April 24, 1979, third period at Philadelphia. NY Rangers won 8-3.

– **Los Angeles Kings (5), Calgary Flames (4)**, April 10, 1990, second period at Los Angeles. Los Angeles won 12-4.

8 – Chicago Black Hawks (8), Montreal Canadiens (7), May 8, 1973, second period at Montreal. Chicago won 8-7.

– Chicago Black Hawks (5), Edmonton Oilers (3), May 12, 1985, first period at Chicago. Chicago won 8-6.

– Edmonton Oilers (6), Winnipeg Jets (2), April 6, 1988, third period at Edmonton. Edmonton won 7-4.

– Hartford Whalers (5), Montreal Canadiens (3), April 10, 1988, third period at Hartford. Hartford won 7-5.

– Vancouver Canucks (5), New York Rangers (3), June 9, 1994, third period at NY Rangers. Vancouver won 6-3.

TEAM POWER-PLAY GOALS

MOST POWER-PLAY GOALS, ALL TEAMS, ONE PLAYOFF YEAR

199 – **1988** in 83 games.

MOST POWER-PLAY GOALS, ONE TEAM, ONE PLAYOFF YEAR

35 – **Minnesota North Stars,** 1991, in 23 games.

32 – Edmonton Oilers, 1988, in 18 games.

31 – New York Islanders, 1981, in 18 games.

MOST POWER-PLAY GOALS, ONE TEAM, ONE SERIES

15 – **New York Islanders** in 1980 F vs. Philadelphia. NY Islanders won series 4-2.

– **Minnesota North Stars** in 1991 DSF vs. Chicago. Minnesota won series 4-2.

13 – New York Islanders in 1981 QF vs. Edmonton. NY Islanders won series 4-2.

– Calgary Flames in 1986 CF vs. St. Louis. Calgary won series 4-3.

MOST POWER-PLAY GOALS, BOTH TEAMS, ONE SERIES

21 – **New York Islanders (15), Philadelphia Flyers (6)** in 1980 F, won by NY Islanders 4-2.

– **New York Islanders (13), Edmonton Oilers (8)** in 1981 QF, won by NY Islanders 4-2.

– **Philadelphia Flyers (11), Pittsburgh Penguins (10)** in 1989 DF, won by Philadelphia 4-3.

– **Minnesota North Stars (15), Chicago Blackhawks (6)** in 1991 DSF, won by Minnesota 4-2.

MOST POWER-PLAY GOALS, ONE TEAM, ONE GAME

6 – **Boston Bruins,** April 2, 1969, vs. Toronto at Boston. Boston won 10-0.

MOST POWER-PLAY GOALS, BOTH TEAMS, ONE GAME

8 – **Minnesota North Stars (4), St. Louis Blues (4),** April 24, 1991, at Minnesota. Minnesota won 8-4.

7 – Minnesota North Stars (4), Edmonton Oilers (3), April 28, 1984, at Minnesota. Edmonton won 8-5.

– Philadelphia Flyers (4), New York Rangers (3), April 13, 1985, at NY Rangers. Philadelphia won 6-5.

– Chicago Black Hawks (5), Edmonton Oilers (2), May 14, 1985, at Edmonton. Edmonton won 10-5.

– Edmonton Oilers (5), Los Angeles Kings (2), April 9, 1987, at Edmonton. Edmonton won 13-3.

– Vancouver Canucks (4), Calgary Flames (3), April 9, 1989, at Vancouver. Vancouver won 5-3.

MOST POWER-PLAY GOALS, ONE TEAM, ONE PERIOD

4 – **Toronto Maple Leafs,** March 26, 1936, second period vs. Boston at Toronto. Toronto won 8-3.

– **Minnesota North Stars,** April 28, 1984, second period vs. Edmonton at Minnesota. Edmonton won 8-5.

– **Boston Bruins,** April 11, 1991, third period vs. Hartford at Boston. Boston won 6-1.

– **Minnesota North Stars,** April 24, 1991, second period vs. St. Louis at Minnesota. Minnesota won 8-4.

– **St. Louis Blues,** April 27, 1998, third period at Los Angeles. St. Louis won 4-3.

MOST POWER-PLAY GOALS, BOTH TEAMS, ONE PERIOD

5 – **Minnesota North Stars (4), Edmonton Oilers (1),** April 28, 1984, second period at Minnesota. Edmonton won 8-5.

– **Vancouver Canucks (3), Calgary Flames (2),** April 9, 1989, third period at Vancouver. Vancouver won 5-3.

– **Minnesota North Stars (4), St. Louis Blues (1),** April 24, 1991, second period at Minnesota. Minnesota won 8-4.

TEAM SHORTHAND GOALS

MOST SHORTHAND GOALS, ALL TEAMS, ONE PLAYOFF YEAR

33 – **1988,** in 83 games.

MOST SHORTHAND GOALS, ONE TEAM, ONE PLAYOFF YEAR

10 – **Edmonton Oilers,** 1983, in 16 games.

9 – New York Islanders, 1981, in 19 games.

8 – Philadelphia Flyers, 1989, in 19 games.

MOST SHORTHAND GOALS, ONE TEAM, ONE SERIES

6 – **Calgary Flames** in 1995 vs. San Jose in CQF won by San Jose 4-3.

– **Vancouver Canucks** in 1995 vs. St. Louis in CQF won by Vancouver 4-3.

5 – New York Rangers in 1979 vs. Philadelphia in QF won by NY Rangers 4-1.

– Edmonton Oilers in 1983 vs. Calgary in DF won by Edmonton 4-1.

MOST SHORTHAND GOALS, BOTH TEAMS, ONE SERIES

7 – **Boston Bruins (4), New York Rangers (3),** in 1958 SF won by Boston 4-2.

– **Edmonton Oilers (5), Calgary Flames (2),** in 1983 DF won by Edmonton 4-1.

– **Vancouver Canucks (6), St. Louis Blues (1),** in 1995 CQF won by Vancouver 4-3.

MOST SHORTHAND GOALS, ONE TEAM, ONE GAME

3 – **Boston Bruins,** April 11, 1981, at Minnesota North Stars. Minnesota won 6-3.

– **New York Islanders,** April 17, 1983, at NY Rangers. NY Rangers won 7-6.

– **Toronto Maple Leafs,** May 8, 1994, at San Jose. Toronto won 8-3.

MOST SHORTHAND GOALS, BOTH TEAMS, ONE GAME

4 – **Boston Bruins (3), Minnesota North Stars (1),** April 11, 1981, at Minnesota. Minnesota won 6-3.

– **New York Islanders (3), New York Rangers (1),** April 17, 1983, at NY Rangers. NY Rangers won 7-6.

– **Toronto Maple Leafs (3), San Jose Sharks (1),** May 8, 1994, at San Jose. Toronto won 8-3.

3 – Toronto Maple Leafs (2), Detroit Red Wings (1), April 5, 1947, at Toronto. Toronto won 6-1.

– New York Rangers (2), Boston Bruins (1), April 1, 1958, at Boston. NY Rangers won 5-2.

– Minnesota North Stars (2), Philadelphia Flyers (1), May 4, 1980, at Minnesota. Philadelphia won 5-3.

– Winnipeg Jets (2), Edmonton Oilers (1), April 9, 1988, at Winnipeg. Winnipeg won 6-4.

– New York Islanders (2), New Jersey Devils (1), April 14, 1988, at New Jersey. New Jersey won 6-5.

– Montreal Canadiens (2), New Jersey Devils (1), April 17, 1997, at New Jersey. New Jersey won 5-2.

– Dallas Stars (2), San Jose Sharks (1), May 5, 2000, at San Jose. Dallas won 5-4.

MOST SHORTHAND GOALS, ONE TEAM, ONE PERIOD

2 – **Toronto Maple Leafs,** April 5, 1947, first period vs. Detroit at Toronto. Toronto won 6-1.

– **Toronto Maple Leafs,** April 13, 1965, first period vs. Montreal at Toronto. Montreal won 4-3.

– **Boston Bruins,** April 20, 1969, first period vs. Montreal at Boston. Boston won 3-2.

– **Boston Bruins,** April 8, 1970, second period vs. NY Rangers at Boston. Boston won 8-2.

– **Boston Bruins,** April 30, 1972, first period vs. NY Rangers at Boston. Boston won 6-5.

– **Chicago Black Hawks,** May 3, 1973, first period vs. Montreal at Chicago. Chicago won 7-4.

– **Montreal Canadiens,** April 23, 1978, first period at Detroit. Montreal won 8-0.

– **New York Islanders,** April 8, 1980, second period vs. Los Angeles at NY Islanders. NY Islanders won 8-1.

– **Los Angeles Kings,** April 9, 1980, first period at NY Islanders. Los Angeles won 6-3.

– **Boston Bruins,** April 13, 1980, second period at Pittsburgh. Boston won 8-3.

- **Minnesota North Stars,** May 4, 1980, second period vs. Philadelphia at Minnesota. Philadelphia won 5-3.
- **Boston Bruins,** April 11, 1981, third period at Minnesota North Stars. Minnesota won 6-3.
- **New York Islanders,** May 12, 1981, first period vs. Minnesota North Stars at NY Islanders. NY Islanders won 6-3.
- **Montreal Canadiens,** April 7, 1982, third period vs. Quebec at Montreal. Montreal won 5-1.
- **Edmonton Oilers,** April 24, 1983, third period vs. Chicago at Edmonton. Edmonton won 8-4.
- **Winnipeg Jets,** April 14, 1985, second period at Calgary. Winnipeg won 5-3.
- **Boston Bruins,** April 6, 1988, first period vs. Buffalo at Boston. Boston won 7-3.
- **New York Islanders,** April 14, 1988, third period at New Jersey. New Jersey won 6-5.
- **Detroit Red Wings,** April 29, 1993, second period at Toronto. Detroit won 7-3.
- **Toronto Maple Leafs,** May 8, 1994, third period at San Jose. Toronto won 8-3.
- **Calgary Flames,** May 11, 1995, first period at San Jose. Calgary won 9-2.
- **Vancouver Canucks,** May 15, 1995, second period at St. Louis. Vancouver won 6-5.
- **Montreal Canadiens,** April 17, 1997, second period at New Jersey. New Jersey won 5-2.
- **Philadelphia Flyers,** April 26, 1997, first period vs. Pittsburgh at Philadelphia. Philadelphia won 6-3.
- **Phoenix Coyotes,** April 24, 1998, second period at Detroit. Phoenix won 7-4.
- **Buffalo Sabres,** April 27, 1998, second period vs. Philadelphia at Buffalo. Buffalo won 6-1.
- **San Jose Sharks,** April 30, 1999, third period at Colorado. San Jose won 7-3.
- **Detroit Red Wings,** April 27, 2002, second period at Vancouver. Detroit won 6-4.

MOST SHORTHAND GOALS, BOTH TEAMS, ONE PERIOD
3 – **Toronto Maple Leafs (2), Detroit Red Wings (1),** April 5, 1947, first period at Toronto. Toronto won 6-1.
- **Toronto Maple Leafs (2), San Jose Sharks (1),** May 8, 1994, third period at San Jose. Toronto won 8-3.

FASTEST GOALS

FASTEST FIVE GOALS, BOTH TEAMS
3:06 – **Minnesota North Stars, Chicago Black Hawks,** April 21, 1985, at Chicago. Keith Brown scored for Chicago at 1:12 of the second period; Ken Yaremchuk, Chicago, 1:27; Dino Ciccarelli, Minnesota, 2:48; Tony McKegney, Minnesota, 4:07; and Curt Fraser, Chicago, 4:18. Chicago won 6-2 and won best-of-seven DF 4-2.
3:20 – Minnesota North Stars, Philadelphia Flyers, April 29, 1980, at Philadelphia. Paul Shmyr scored for Minnesota at 13:20 of the first period; Steve Christoff, Minnesota, 13:59; Ken Linseman, Philadelphia, 14:54; Tom Gorence, Philadelphia, 15:36; and Ken Linseman, Philadelphia, 16:40. Minnesota won 6-5. Philadelphia won best-of-seven SF 4-1.
4:00 – Los Angeles Kings, Detroit Red Wings, April 15, 2000, at Detroit. Brendan Shanahan scored for Detroit at 0:55 of the first period; Martin Lapointe, Detroit, 1:33; Luc Robitaille, Los Angeles, 2:04; Kris Draper, Detroit, 3:32; and Ziggy Palffy, Los Angeles, 4:55. Detroit won 8-5 and best-of-seven CQF 4-0.

FASTEST FIVE GOALS, ONE TEAM
3:36 – **Montreal Canadiens,** March 30, 1944, at Montreal vs. Toronto. Toe Blake scored at 7:58 and 8:37 of the third period; Maurice Richard, 9:17; Ray Getliffe, 10:33; and Buddy O'Connor, 11:34. Canadiens won 11-0 and best-of-seven SF 4-1.

FASTEST FOUR GOALS, BOTH TEAMS
1:33 – **Toronto Maple Leafs, Philadelphia Flyers,** April 20, 1976, at Philadelphia. Don Saleski scored for Philadelphia at 10:04 of the second period; Bob Neely, Toronto, 10:42; Gary Dornhoefer, Philadelphia, 11:24; and Don Saleski, Philadelphia, 11:37. Philadelphia won 7-1 and best-of-seven QF 4-3.

1:34 – Calgary Flames, Montreal Canadiens, May 20, 1986, at Montreal. Joel Otto scored for Calgary at 17:59 of the first period; Bobby Smith, Montreal, 18:25; Mats Naslund, Montreal, 19:17; and Bob Gainey, Montreal, 19:33. Montreal won 5-3 and best-of-seven F 4-1.
1:38 – Boston Bruins, Philadelphia Flyers, April 26, 1977, at Philadelphia. Gregg Sheppard scored for Boston at 14:01 of the second period; Mike Milbury, Boston, 15:01; Gary Dornhoefer, Philadelphia, 15:16; and Jean Ratelle, Boston, 15:39. Boston won 5-4 and best-of-seven SF 4-0.

FASTEST FOUR GOALS, ONE TEAM
2:35 – **Montreal Canadiens,** March 30, 1944, at Montreal, vs. Toronto. Toe Blake scored at 7:58 and 8:37 of third period; Maurice Richard, 9:17; and Ray Getliffe, 10:33. Montreal won 11-0 and best-of-seven SF 4-1.

FASTEST THREE GOALS, BOTH TEAMS
0:21 – **Chicago Black Hawks, Edmonton Oilers,** May 7, 1985, at Edmonton. Behn Wilson scored for Chicago at 19:22 of the third period; Jari Kurri, Edmonton, 19:36; and Glenn Anderson, Edmonton, 19:43. Edmonton won 7-3 and best-of-seven CF 4-2.
0:27 – Phoenix Coyotes, Detroit Red Wings, April 24, 1998, at Detroit. Jeremy Roenick scored for Phoenix at 13:24 of the second period; Mathieu Dandenault, Detroit, 13:32; and Keith Tkachuk, Phoenix, 13:51. Phoenix won 7-4. Detroit won best-of-seven CQF 4-2.
0:30 – Pittsburgh Penguins, Chicago Black Hawks, June 1, 1992, at Chicago. Dirk Graham scored for Chicago at 6:21 of the first period; Kevin Stevens, Pittsburgh, 6:33; and Dirk Graham, Chicago, 6:51. Pittsburgh won 6-5 and best-of-seven F 4-0.

FASTEST THREE GOALS, ONE TEAM
0:23 – **Toronto Maple Leafs,** April 12, 1979, at Toronto vs. Atlanta Flames. Darryl Sittler scored at 4:04 and 4:16 of the first period; and Ron Ellis, 4:27. Toronto won 7-4 and best-of-three PRE 2-0.
0:38 – New York Rangers, April 12, 1986, at NY Rangers vs. Philadelphia. Jim Wiemer scored at 12:29 of the third period; Bob Brooke, 12:43; and Ron Greschner, 13:07. NY Rangers won 5-2 and best-of-five DSF 3-2.
– Colorado Avalanche, April 18, 2001, at Vancouver. Peter Forsberg scored at 9:11 of the third period; Joe Sakic, 9:28; and Eric Messier, 9:49. Colorado won 5-1 and best-of-seven CQF 4-0.

FASTEST TWO GOALS, BOTH TEAMS
0:05 – **Pittsburgh Penguins, Buffalo Sabres,** April 14, 1979, at Buffalo. Gilbert Perreault scored for Buffalo at 12:59 of the first period; and Jim Hamilton, Pittsburgh, 13:04. Pittsburgh won 4-3 and best-of-three PRE 2-1.
0:08 – Minnesota North Stars, St. Louis Blues, April 9, 1989, at Minnesota. Bernie Federko scored for St. Louis at 2:28 of the third period; and Perry Berezan, Minnesota, 2:36. Minnesota won 5-4. St. Louis won best-of-seven DSF 4-1.
– Phoenix Coyotes, Detroit Red Wings, April 24, 1998, at Detroit. Jeremy Roenick scored for Phoenix at 13:24 of the second period; and Mathieu Dandenault, Detroit, 13:32. Phoenix won 7-4. Detroit won best-of-seven CQF 4-2.

FASTEST TWO GOALS, ONE TEAM
0:05 – **Detroit Red Wings,** April 11, 1965, at Detroit vs. Chicago. Norm Ullman scored at 17:35 and 17:40 of the second period. Detroit won 4-2. Chicago won best-of-seven SF 4-3.

OVERTIME

SHORTEST OVERTIME
0:09 – **Montreal Canadiens, Calgary Flames,** May 18, 1986, at Calgary. Montreal won 3-2 on Brian Skrudland's goal at 0:09 of the first overtime period. Montreal won best-of-seven F 4-1.
0:11 – New York Islanders, New York Rangers, April 11, 1975, at NY Rangers. NY Islanders won 4-3 on J.P. Parise's goal at 0:11 of the first overtime period. NY Islanders won best-of-three PRE 2-1.

LONGEST OVERTIME
116:30 – **Detroit Red Wings, Montreal Maroons,** March 24, 1936, at Montreal. Mtl. Maroons won 1-0 on Mud Bruneteau's goal at 16:30 of the sixth overtime period. Detroit won best-of-five SF 3-0.

MOST OVERTIME GAMES, ONE PLAYOFF YEAR
28 – **1993.** 85 games played.
26 – 2001. 86 games played.
21 – 1999. 86 games played.
19 – 1996. 86 games played.
– 1998. 82 games played.

FEWEST OVERTIME GAMES, ONE PLAYOFF YEAR
0 – **1963.** None of the 16 games went into overtime, the only year since 1926 that no overtime was required in any playoff series.

MOST OVERTIME GAMES, ONE SERIES
5 – **Toronto Maple Leafs, Montreal Canadiens** in 1951. Toronto won best-of-seven F 4-1.
4 – Toronto Maple Leafs, Boston Bruins in 1933. Toronto won best-of-five SF 3-2.
– Boston Bruins, New York Rangers in 1939. Boston won best-of-seven SF 4-3.
– St. Louis Blues, Minnesota North Stars in 1968. St. Louis won best-of-seven SF 4-3.
– Dallas Stars, St. Louis Blues in 1999. Dallas won best-of-seven CSF 4-2.
– Dallas Stars, Edmonton Oilers in 2001. Dallas won best-of-seven CQF 4-2.

THREE-OR-MORE GOAL GAMES

MOST THREE-OR-MORE GOAL GAMES, ALL TEAMS, ONE PLAYOFF YEAR
12 – **1983** in 66 games.
– **1988** in 83 games.
11 – 1985 in 70 games.
– 1992 in 86 games.

MOST THREE-OR-MORE GOAL GAMES, ONE TEAM, ONE PLAYOFF YEAR
6 – **Edmonton Oilers** in 16 games, 1983.
– **Edmonton Oilers** in 18 games, 1985.

SHUTOUTS

MOST SHUTOUTS, ALL TEAMS, ONE PLAYOFF YEAR
25 – **2002.** Of 90 games played, Detroit had 6; Ottawa had 4; Carolina, Colorado, St. Louis and Toronto had 3 each; while Los Angeles, New Jersey and Philadelphia had 1 each.
19 – 2001. Of 86 games played, Colorado and New Jersey had 4 each, Toronto had 3, Pittsburgh and Los Angeles had 2 each, while Buffalo, Washington, Detroit and San Jose had 1 each.
18 – 1997. Of 82 games played, Colorado and NY Rangers had 3 each, Edmonton, New Jersey, and St. Louis had 2 each. Anaheim, Buffalo, Detroit, Florida, Ottawa and Phoenix had 1 each.

FEWEST SHUTOUTS, ALL TEAMS, ONE PLAYOFF YEAR
0 – **1959.** 18 games played.

MOST SHUTOUTS, BOTH TEAMS, ONE SERIES
5 – **Toronto Maple Leafs (3), Detroit Red Wings (2)** in 1945 F. Toronto won best-of-seven series 4-3.
– **Toronto Maple Leafs (3), Detroit Red Wings (2)** in 1950 SF. Detroit won best-of-seven series 4-3.

TEAM PENALTIES

FEWEST PENALTIES, BOTH TEAMS, BEST-OF-SEVEN SERIES
19 – **Detroit Red Wings, Toronto Maple Leafs** in 1945 F. Detroit received 10 minors, Toronto received 9 minors. Detroit won best-of-seven series 4-3.

FEWEST PENALTIES, ONE TEAM, BEST-OF-SEVEN SERIES
9 – **Toronto Maple Leafs** in 1945 F vs. Detroit. Toronto received 9 minors. Detroit won best-of-seven series 4-3.

MOST PENALTIES, BOTH TEAMS, ONE SERIES
218 – **New Jersey Devils, Washington Capitals** in 1988 DF. New Jersey received 97 minors, 11 majors, 9 misconducts and 1 match penalty. Washington received 80 minors, 11 majors, 8 misconducts and 1 match penalty. New Jersey won best-of-seven series 4-3.

MOST PENALTY MINUTES, BOTH TEAMS, ONE SERIES
654 – **New Jersey Devils (349), Washington Capitals (305)** in 1988 DF. New Jersey won best-of-seven series 4-3.

MOST PENALTIES, ONE TEAM, ONE SERIES
118 – **New Jersey Devils** in 1988 DF vs. Washington. New Jersey received 97 minors, 11 majors, 9 misconducts and 1 match penalty. New Jersey won best-of-seven series 4-3.

MOST PENALTY MINUTES, ONE TEAM, ONE SERIES
349 – **New Jersey Devils** in 1988 DF vs. Washington. New Jersey won best-of-seven series 4-3.

MOST PENALTIES, BOTH TEAMS, ONE GAME
66 – **Detroit Red Wings, St. Louis Blues,** April 12, 1991, at St. Louis. Detroit received 33 penalties; St. Louis 33. St. Louis won 6-1.
63 – Minnesota North Stars, Chicago Blackhawks, April 6, 1990, at Chicago. Minnesota received 34 penalties; Chicago 29. Chicago won 5-3.
62 – New Jersey Devils, Washington Capitals, April 22, 1988, at New Jersey. New Jersey received 32 penalties; Washington 30. New Jersey won 10-4.

MOST PENALTY MINUTES, BOTH TEAMS, ONE GAME
298 Minutes – **Detroit Red Wings, St. Louis Blues,** April 12, 1991, at St. Louis. Detroit received 33 penalties for 152 minutes; St. Louis 33 penalties for 146 minutes. St. Louis won 6-1.
267 Minutes – New York Rangers, Los Angeles Kings, April 9, 1981, at Los Angeles. NY Rangers received 31 penalties for 142 minutes; Los Angeles 28 penalties for 125 minutes. Los Angeles won 5-4.

MOST PENALTIES, ONE TEAM, ONE GAME
34 – **Minnesota North Stars,** April 6, 1990, at Chicago. Chicago won 5-3.
33 – Detroit Red Wings, April 12,1991, at St. Louis. St. Louis won 6-1.
– St. Louis Blues, April 12, 1991, at St. Louis vs. Detroit. St. Louis won 6-1.

MOST PENALTY MINUTES, ONE TEAM, ONE GAME
152 – **Detroit Red Wings,** April 12, 1991, at St. Louis,. St. Louis won 6-1.
146 – St. Louis Blues, April 12, 1991, at St. Louis vs. Detroit. St. Louis won 6-1.
142 – New York Rangers, April 9, 1981, at Los Angeles. Los Angeles won 5-4.

MOST PENALTIES, BOTH TEAMS, ONE PERIOD
43 – **New York Rangers (24), Los Angeles Kings (19),** April 9, 1981, first period at Los Angeles, Los Angeles won 5-4.

MOST PENALTY MINUTES, BOTH TEAMS, ONE PERIOD
248 – **New York Islanders (124), Boston Bruins (124),** April 17, 1980, first period at Boston. NY Islanders won 5-4.

MOST PENALTIES, ONE TEAM, ONE PERIOD
24 – **New York Rangers,** April 9, 1981, first period at Los Angeles. Los Angeles won 5-4.

MOST PENALTY MINUTES, ONE TEAM, ONE PERIOD
125 – **New York Rangers,** April 9, 1981, first period at Los Angeles. Los Angeles won 5-4.

Individual Records

GAMES PLAYED

MOST YEARS IN PLAYOFFS
21 – **Raymond Bourque,** Boston, Colorado (1980-96 inclusive; 98-2001 inclusive)
20 – Gordie Howe, Detroit, Hartford
– Larry Robinson, Montreal, Los Angeles
– Larry Murphy, Los Angeles, Washington, Minnesota North Stars, Pittsburgh, Toronto, Detroit
19 – Red Kelly, Detroit, Toronto
– Scott Stevens, Washington, St. Louis, New Jersey

MOST CONSECUTIVE YEARS IN PLAYOFFS
20 – **Larry Robinson,** Montreal, Los Angeles (1973-92, inclusive)
18 – Larry Murphy, Washington, Minnesota North Stars, Pittsburgh, Toronto, Detroit (1984-2001, inclusive)
17 – Brad Park, NY Rangers, Boston, Detroit (1969-85, inclusive)
– Raymond Bourque, Boston (1980-96, inclusive)
– Brett Hull, Calgary, St. Louis, Dallas, Detroit (1986-02, inclusive)

MOST PLAYOFF GAMES
240 – **Patrick Roy,** Montreal, Colorado
236 – Mark Messier, Edmonton, NY Rangers
231 – Guy Carbonneau, Montreal, St. Louis, Dallas
227 – Larry Robinson, Montreal, Los Angeles
226 – Claude Lemieux, Montreal, New Jersey, Colorado, Phoenix

GOALS

MOST GOALS IN PLAYOFFS, CAREER
122 – **Wayne Gretzky,** Edmonton, Los Angeles, St. Louis, NY Rangers
109 – Mark Messier, Edmonton, NY Rangers
106 – Jari Kurri, Edmonton, Los Angeles, NY Rangers, Anaheim
100 – Brett Hull, Calgary, St. Louis, Dallas, Detroit
93 – Glenn Anderson, Edmonton, Toronto, NY Rangers, St. Louis

MOST GOALS, ONE PLAYOFF YEAR
19 – **Reggie Leach,** Philadelphia, 1976. 16 games.
– **Jari Kurri,** Edmonton, 1985. 18 games.
18 – Joe Sakic, Colorado, 1996. 22 games.
17 – Newsy Lalonde, Montreal, 1919. 10 games.
– Mike Bossy, NY Islanders, 1981. 18 games.
– Steve Payne, Minnesota North Stars, 1981. 19 games.
– Mike Bossy, NY Islanders, 1982. 19 games.
– Mike Bossy, NY Islanders, 1983. 19 games.
– Wayne Gretzky, Edmonton, 1985. 18 games.
– Kevin Stevens, Pittsburgh, 1991. 24 games.

MOST GOALS IN ONE SERIES (OTHER THAN FINAL)
12 – **Jari Kurri,** Edmonton in 1985 CF, 6 games vs. Chicago.
11 – Newsy Lalonde, Montreal in 1919 NHL F, 5 games vs. Ottawa.
10 – Tim Kerr, Philadelphia in 1989 DF, 7 games vs. Pittsburgh.
9 – Reggie Leach, Philadelphia in 1976 SF, 5 games vs. Boston.
– Bill Barber, Philadelphia in 1980 SF, 5 games vs. Minnesota North Stars.
– Mike Bossy, NY Islanders in 1983 CF, 6 games vs. Boston.
– Mario Lemieux, Pittsburgh in 1989 DF, 7 games vs. Philadelphia.

MOST GOALS IN FINAL SERIES (NHL ONLY)
9 – **Babe Dye,** Toronto in 1922, 5 games vs. Van. Millionaires.
8 – Alf Skinner, Toronto in 1918, 5 games vs. Van. Millionaires.
7 – Jean Beliveau, Montreal in 1956, 5 games vs. Detroit.
– Mike Bossy, NY Islanders in 1982, 4 games vs. Vancouver.
– Wayne Gretzky, Edmonton in 1985, 5 games vs. Philadelphia.

MOST GOALS, ONE GAME
5 – **Newsy Lalonde,** Montreal, March 1, 1919, at Montreal. Final score: Montreal 6, Ottawa 3.

– **Maurice Richard,** Montreal, March 23, 1944, at Montreal. Final score: Montreal 5, Toronto 1.
– **Darryl Sittler,** Toronto, April 22, 1976, at Toronto. Final score: Toronto 8, Philadelphia 5.
– **Reggie Leach,** Philadelphia, May 6, 1976, at Philadelphia. Final score: Philadelphia 6, Boston 3.
– **Mario Lemieux,** Pittsburgh, April 25, 1989, at Pittsburgh. Final score: Pittsburgh 10, Philadelphia 7.

MOST GOALS, ONE PERIOD
4 – **Tim Kerr,** Philadelphia, April 13, 1985, at NY Rangers, second period. Final score: Philadelphia 6, NY Rangers 5.
– **Mario Lemieux,** Pittsburgh, April 25, 1989, at Pittsburgh, first period. Final score: Pittsburgh 10, Philadelphia 7.

ASSISTS

MOST ASSISTS IN PLAYOFFS, CAREER
260 – **Wayne Gretzky,** Edmonton, Los Angeles, St. Louis, NY Rangers
186 – Mark Messier, Edmonton, NY Rangers
139 – Raymond Bourque, Boston, Colorado
137 – Paul Coffey, Edmonton, Pittsburgh, Los Angeles, Detroit, Philadelphia, Carolina
128 – Doug Gilmour, St. Louis, Calgary, Toronto, New Jersey, Buffalo, Montreal

MOST ASSISTS, ONE PLAYOFF YEAR
31 – **Wayne Gretzky,** Edmonton, 1988. 19 games.
30 – Wayne Gretzky, Edmonton, 1985. 18 games.
29 – Wayne Gretzky, Edmonton, 1987. 21 games.
28 – Mario Lemieux, Pittsburgh, 1991. 23 games.
26 – Wayne Gretzky, Edmonton, 1983. 16 games.

MOST ASSISTS IN ONE SERIES (OTHER THAN FINAL)
14 – **Rick Middleton,** Boston in 1983 DF, 7 games vs. Buffalo.
– **Wayne Gretzky,** Edmonton in 1985 CF, 6 games vs. Chicago.
13 – Wayne Gretzky, Edmonton in 1987 DSF, 5 games vs. Los Angeles.
– Doug Gilmour, Toronto in 1994 CSF, 7 games vs. San Jose.
11 – Al MacInnis, Calgary in 1984 DF, 7 games vs. Edmonton.
– Mark Messier, Edmonton in 1989 DSF, 7 games vs. Los Angeles.
– Mike Ridley, Washington in 1992 DSF, 7 games vs. Pittsburgh.
– Ron Francis, Pittsburgh in 1995 CQF, 7 games vs. Washington.

MOST ASSISTS, FINAL SERIES
10 – **Wayne Gretzky,** Edmonton in 1988, 4 games plus suspended game vs. Boston.
9 – Jacques Lemaire, Montreal in 1973, 6 games vs. Chicago.
– Wayne Gretzky, Edmonton in 1987, 7 games vs. Philadelphia.
– Larry Murphy, Pittsburgh in 1991, 6 games vs. Minnesota North Stars.

MOST ASSISTS, ONE GAME
6 – **Mikko Leinonen,** NY Rangers, April 8, 1982, at NY Rangers. Final score: NY Rangers 7, Philadelphia 3.
– **Wayne Gretzky,** Edmonton, April 9, 1987, at Edmonton. Final score: Edmonton 13, Los Angeles 3.
5 – Toe Blake, Montreal, March 23, 1944, at Montreal. Final score: Montreal 5, Toronto 1.
– Maurice Richard, Montreal, March 27, 1956, at Montreal. Final score: Montreal 7, NY Rangers 0.
– Bert Olmstead, Montreal, March 30, 1957, at Montreal. Final score: Montreal 8, NY Rangers 3.
– Don McKenney, Boston, April 5, 1958, at Boston. Final score: Boston 8, NY Rangers 2.
– Stan Mikita, Chicago, April 4, 1973, at Chicago. Final score: Chicago 7, St. Louis 1.
– Wayne Gretzky, Edmonton, April 8, 1981, at Montreal. Final score: Edmonton 6, Montreal 3.
– Paul Coffey, Edmonton, May 14, 1985, at Edmonton. Final score: Edmonton 10, Chicago 5.
– Doug Gilmour, St. Louis, April 15, 1986, at Minnesota North Stars. Final score: St. Louis 6, Minnesota 3.
– Risto Siltanen, Quebec, April 14, 1987, at Hartford. Final score: Quebec 7, Hartford 5.

– Patrik Sundstrom, New Jersey, April 22, 1988, at New Jersey. Final score: New Jersey 10, Washington 4.
– Geoff Courtnall, St. Louis Blues, April 23, 1998, at St. Louis. Final score: St. Louis 8, Los Angeles 3.

MOST ASSISTS, ONE PERIOD

3 – Three assists by one player in one period of a playoff game has been recorded on 74 occasions. Chris Chelios of the Detroit Red Wings is the most recent to equal this mark with 3 assists in the second period at Vancouver, April 27, 2002. Final score: Detroit 6, Vancouver 4.

– **Wayne Gretzky** has had 3 assists in one period 5 times; Raymond Bourque, 3 times; Toe Blake, Jean Beliveau, Doug Harvey and Bobby Orr, twice each. Joe Primeau of Toronto was the first player to be credited with this mark with 3 assists in the third period at NY Rangers, April 7, 1932. Final score: Toronto 6, NY Rangers 2.

POINTS

MOST POINTS IN PLAYOFFS, CAREER

382 – **Wayne Gretzky,** Edmonton, Los Angeles, St. Louis, NY Rangers, 122 goals, 260 assists.
295 – Mark Messier, Edmonton, NY Rangers, 109 goals, 186 assists.
233 – Jari Kurri, Edmonton, Los Angeles, NY Rangers, Anaheim, 106 goals, 127 assists.
214 – Glenn Anderson, Edmonton, Toronto, NY Rangers, St. Louis, 93 goals, 121 assists.
196 – Paul Coffey, Edmonton, Pittsburgh, Los Angeles, Detroit, Philadelphia, Carolina, 59 goals, 137 assists.

MOST POINTS, ONE PLAYOFF YEAR

47 – **Wayne Gretzky,** Edmonton in 1985. 17 goals, 30 assists in 18 games.
44 – Mario Lemieux, Pittsburgh in 1991. 16 goals, 28 assists in 23 games.
43 – Wayne Gretzky, Edmonton in 1988. 12 goals, 31 assists in 19 games.
40 – Wayne Gretzky, Los Angeles in 1993. 15 goals, 25 assists in 24 games.
38 – Wayne Gretzky, Edmonton in 1983. 12 goals, 26 assists in 16 games.

MOST POINTS IN ONE SERIES (OTHER THAN FINAL)

19 – **Rick Middleton,** Boston in 1983 DF, 7 games vs. Buffalo. 5 goals, 14 assists.
18 – Wayne Gretzky, Edmonton in 1985 CF, 6 games vs. Chicago. 4 goals, 14 assists.
17 – Mario Lemieux, Pittsburgh in 1992 DSF, 6 games vs. Washington. 7 goals, 10 assists.
16 – Barry Pederson, Boston in 1983 DF, 7 games vs. Buffalo. 7 goals, 9 assists.
– Doug Gilmour, Toronto in 1994 CSF, 7 games vs. San Jose. 3 goals, 13 assists.

MOST POINTS, FINAL SERIES

13 – **Wayne Gretzky,** Edmonton in 1988, 4 games plus suspended game vs. Boston. 3 goals, 10 assists.
12 – Gordie Howe, Detroit in 1955, 7 games vs. Montreal. 5 goals, 7 assists.
– Yvan Cournoyer, Montreal in 1973, 6 games vs. Chicago. 6 goals, 6 assists.
– Jacques Lemaire, Montreal in 1973, 6 games vs. Chicago. 3 goals, 9 assists.
– Mario Lemieux, Pittsburgh in 1991, 5 games vs. Minnesota North Stars. 5 goals, 7 assists.

MOST POINTS, ONE GAME

8 – **Patrik Sundstrom,** New Jersey, April 22, 1988, at New Jersey, in 10-4 win vs. Washington. 3 goals, 5 assists.
– **Mario Lemieux,** Pittsburgh, April 25, 1989, at Pittsburgh, in 10-7 win vs. Philadelphia. 5 goals, 3 assists.
7 – Wayne Gretzky, Edmonton, April 17, 1983, at Calgary, in 10-2 win. 4 goals, 3 assists.
– Wayne Gretzky, Edmonton, April 25,1985, at Winnipeg, in 8-3 win. 3 goals, 4 assists.
– Wayne Gretzky, Edmonton, April 9, 1987, at Edmonton, in 13-3 win vs. Los Angeles. 1 goal, 6 assists.
6 – Dickie Moore, Montreal, March 25, 1954, at Montreal, in 8-1 win vs. Boston. 2 goals, 4 assists.

– Phil Esposito, Boston, April 2, 1969, at Boston, in 10-0 win vs. Toronto. 4 goals, 2 assists.
– Darryl Sittler, Toronto, April 22, 1976, at Toronto, in 8-5 win vs. Philadelphia. 5 goals, 1 assist.
– Guy Lafleur, Montreal, April 11, 1977, at Montreal, in 7-2 win vs. St. Louis. 3 goals, 3 assists.
– Mikko Leinonen, NY Rangers, April 8, 1982, at NY Rangers, in 7-3 win vs. Philadelphia. 6 assists.
– Paul Coffey, Edmonton, May 14, 1985, at Edmonton, in 10-5 win vs. Chicago. 1 goal, 5 assists.
– John Anderson, Hartford, April 12, 1986, at Hartford, in 9-4 win vs. Quebec. 2 goals, 4 assists.
– Mario Lemieux, Pittsburgh, April 23, 1992, at Pittsburgh, in 6-4 win vs. Washington. 3 goals, 3 assists.
– Geoff Courtnall, St. Louis Blues, April 23, 1998, at St. Louis, in 8-3 win vs. Los Angeles. 1 goal, 5 assists.

MOST POINTS, ONE PERIOD

4 – **Maurice Richard,** Montreal, March 29, 1945, at Montreal, third period, in 10-3 win vs. Toronto. 3 goals, 1 assist.
– **Dickie Moore,** Montreal, March 25, 1954, at Montreal, first period, in 8-1 win vs. Boston. 2 goals, 2 assists.
– **Barry Pederson,** Boston, April 8, 1982, at Boston, second period, in 7-3 win vs. Buffalo. 3 goals, 1 assist.
– **Peter McNab,** Boston, April 11, 1982, at Buffalo, second period, in 5-2 win vs. Buffalo. 1 goal, 3 assists.
– **Tim Kerr,** Philadelphia, April 13, 1985, at NY Rangers, second period, in 6-5 win vs. 4 goals.
– **Ken Linseman,** Boston, April 14, 1985, at Boston, second period, in 7-6 win vs. Montreal. 2 goals, 2 assists.
– **Wayne Gretzky,** Edmonton, April 12, 1987, at Los Angeles, third period, in 6-3 win vs. Los Angeles. 1 goal, 3 assists.
– **Glenn Anderson,** Edmonton, April 6, 1988, at Edmonton, third period, in 7-4 win vs. Winnipeg. 3 goals, 1 assist.
– **Mario Lemieux,** Pittsburgh, April 25, 1989, at Pittsburgh, first period, in 10-7 win vs. Philadelphia. 4 goals.
– **Dave Gagner,** Minnesota North Stars, April 8, 1991, at Minnesota, first period, in 6-5 loss vs. Chicago. 2 goals, 2 assists.
– **Mario Lemieux,** Pittsburgh, April 23, 1992, at Pittsburgh, second period, in 6-4 win vs. Washington. 2 goals, 2 assists.
– **Alexander Mogilny,** New Jersey, April 28, 2001, at New Jersey, second period, in 6-5 win vs. Toronto. 1 goal, 3 assists.

POWER-PLAY GOALS

MOST POWER-PLAY GOALS IN PLAYOFFS, CAREER

37 – **Brett Hull,** St. Louis, Dallas, Detroit
35 – Mike Bossy, NY Islanders
34 – Dino Ciccarelli, Minnesota North Stars, Washington, Detroit
– Wayne Gretzky, Edmonton, Los Angeles, St. Louis, NY Rangers
29 – Mario Lemieux, Pittsburgh

MOST POWER-PLAY GOALS, ONE PLAYOFF YEAR

9 – **Mike Bossy,** NY Islanders, 1981. 18 games vs. Toronto, Edmonton, NY Rangers and Minnesota North Stars.
– **Cam Neely,** Boston, 1991. 19 games vs. Hartford, Montreal and Pittsburgh.
8 – Tim Kerr, Philadelphia, 1989. 19 games.
– John Druce, Washington, 1990. 15 games.
– Brian Propp, Minnesota North Stars, 1991. 23 games.
– Mario Lemieux, Pittsburgh, 1992. 15 games.

MOST POWER-PLAY GOALS, ONE PLAYOFF SERIES

6 – **Chris Kontos,** Los Angeles, 1989 DSF vs. Edmonton, won by Los Angeles 4-3.

5 – Andy Bathgate, Detroit, 1966 SF vs. Chicago, won by Detroit 4-2.
– Denis Potvin, NY Islanders, 1981 QF vs. Edmonton, won by NY Islanders 4-2.
– Ken Houston, Calgary, 1981 QF vs. Philadelphia, won by Calgary 4-3.
– Rick Vaive, Chicago, 1988 DSF vs. St. Louis, won by St. Louis 4-1.
– Tim Kerr, Philadelphia, 1989 DF vs. Pittsburgh, won by Philadelphia 4-3.
– Mario Lemieux, Pittsburgh, 1989 DF vs. Philadelphia, won by Philadelphia 4-3.
– John Druce, Washington, 1990 DF vs. NY Rangers, won by Washington 4-1.
– Pat LaFontaine, Buffalo, 1992 DSF vs. Boston, won by Boston 4-3.
– Adam Graves, NY Rangers, 1996 CQF vs. Montreal, won by NY Rangers 4-2.

MOST POWER-PLAY GOALS, ONE GAME

3 – **Syd Howe,** Detroit, March 23, 1939, at Detroit vs. Montreal. Detroit won 7-3.
– **Sid Smith,** Toronto, April 10, 1949, at Detroit. Toronto won 3-1.
– **Phil Esposito,** Boston, April 2, 1969, at Boston vs. Toronto. Boston won 10-0.
– **John Bucyk,** Boston, April 21, 1974, at Boston vs. Chicago. Boston won 8-6.
– **Denis Potvin,** NY Islanders, April 17, 1981, at NY Islanders vs. Edmonton. NY Islanders won 6-3.
– **Tim Kerr,** Philadelphia, April 13, 1985, at NY Rangers. Philadelphia won 6-5.
– **Jari Kurri,** Edmonton, April 9, 1987, at Edmonton vs. Los Angeles. Edmonton won 13-3.
– **Mark Johnson,** New Jersey, April 22, 1988, at New Jersey vs. Washington. New Jersey won 10-4.
– **Dino Ciccarelli,** Detroit, April 29, 1993, at Toronto. Detroit won 7-3.
– **Dino Ciccarelli,** Detroit, May 11, 1995, at Dallas. Detroit won 5-1.
– **Valeri Kamensky,** Colorado, April 24, 1997, at Colorado vs. Chicago. Colorado won 7-0.

MOST POWER-PLAY GOALS, ONE PERIOD

3 – **Tim Kerr,** Philadelphia, April 13, 1985, at NY Rangers, second period, in 6-5 win.
2 – Two power-play goals have been scored by one player in one period on 53 occasions. Charlie Conacher of Toronto was the first to score two power-play goals in one period, setting the mark with two power-play goals in the second period at Toronto vs. Boston, March 26, 1936. Final score: Toronto 8, Boston 3. Brendan Shanahan of the Detroit Red Wings is the most recent to equal this mark with two power-play goals in the first period at Phoenix, May 3, 1998. Final score: Detroit 5, Phoenix 2.

SHORTHAND GOALS

MOST SHORTHAND GOALS IN PLAYOFFS, CAREER

14 – **Mark Messier,** Edmonton, NY Rangers
11 – Wayne Gretzky, Edmonton, Los Angeles
10 – Jari Kurri, Edmonton, Los Angeles, NY Rangers
8 – Ed Westfall, Boston, NY Islanders
– Hakan Loob, Calgary

MOST SHORTHAND GOALS, ONE PLAYOFF YEAR

3 – **Derek Sanderson,** Boston, 1969. 1 vs. Toronto in QF, won by Boston 4-0; 2 vs. Montreal in SF, won by Montreal, 4-2.
– **Bill Barber,** Philadelphia, 1980. 3 vs. Minnesota North Stars in SF, won by Philadelphia 4-1.
– **Lorne Henning,** NY Islanders, 1980. 1 vs. Boston in QF, won by NY Islanders 4-1, 1 vs. Buffalo in SF, won by NY Islanders 4-2, 1 vs. Philadelphia in F, won by NY Islanders 4-2.
– **Wayne Gretzky,** Edmonton, 1983. 2 against Winnipeg in DSF, won by Edmonton 3-0; 1 against Calgary in DF, won by Edmonton 4-1.
– **Wayne Presley,** Chicago, 1989. 3 against Detroit in DSF, won by Chicago 4-2.
– **Todd Marchant,** Edmonton, 1997. 1 against Dallas in CQF, won by Edmonton 4-3; 2 against Colorado in CSF, won by Colorado 4-1.

MOST SHORTHAND GOALS, ONE PLAYOFF SERIES

- 3 – **Bill Barber,** Philadelphia, 1980 SF vs. Minnesota North Stars, won by Philadelphia 4-1.
  - **Wayne Presley,** Chicago, 1989 DSF vs. Detroit, won by Chicago 4-2.
- 2 – Mac Colville, NY Rangers, 1940 SF vs. Boston, won by NY Rangers 4-2.
  - Jerry Toppazzini, Boston, 1958 SF vs. NY Rangers, won by Boston 4-2.
  - Dave Keon, Toronto, 1963 F vs. Detroit, won by Toronto 4-1.
  - Bob Pulford, Toronto, 1964 F vs. Detroit, won by Toronto 4-3.
  - Serge Savard, Montreal, 1968 F vs. St. Louis, won by Montreal 4-0.
  - Derek Sanderson, Boston, 1969 SF vs. Montreal, won by Montreal 4-2.
  - Bryan Trottier, NY Islanders, 1980 PRE vs. Los Angeles, won by NY Islanders 3-1.
  - Bobby Lalonde, Boston, 1981 PRE vs. Minnesota North Stars, won by Minnesota 3-0.
  - Butch Goring, NY Islanders, 1981 SF vs. NY Rangers, won by NY Islanders 4-0.
  - Wayne Gretzky, Edmonton, 1983 DSF vs. Winnipeg, won by Edmonton 3-0.
  - Mark Messier, Edmonton, 1983 DF vs. Calgary, won by Edmonton 4-1.
  - Jari Kurri, Edmonton, 1983 CF vs. Chicago, won by Edmonton 4-0.
  - Wayne Gretzky, Edmonton, 1985 DF vs. Winnipeg, won by Edmonton 4-0.
  - Kevin Lowe, Edmonton, 1987 F vs. Philadelphia, won by Edmonton 4-3.
  - Bob Gould, Washington, 1988 DSF vs. Philadelphia, won by Washington 4-3.
  - Dave Poulin, Philadelphia, 1989 DF vs. Pittsburgh, won by Philadelphia 4-3.
  - Russ Courtnall, Montreal, 1991 DF vs. Boston, won by Boston 4-3.
  - Sergei Fedorov, Detroit, 1992 DSF vs. Minnesota North Stars, won by Detroit 4-3.
  - Mark Messier, NY Rangers, 1992 DSF vs. New Jersey, won by NY Rangers 4-3.
  - Tom Fitzgerald, NY Islanders, 1993 DF vs. Pittsburgh, won by NY Islanders 4-3.
  - Mark Osborne, Toronto, 1994 CSF vs. San Jose, won by Toronto 4-3.
  - Tony Amonte, Chicago, 1997 CQF vs. Colorado, won by Colorado 4-2.
  - Brian Rolston, New Jersey, 1997 CQF vs. Montreal, won by New Jersey 4-1.
  - Rod Brind'Amour, Philadelphia, 1997 CQF vs. Pittsburgh, won by Philadelphia 4-1.
  - Todd Marchant, Edmonton, 1997 CSF vs. Colorado, won by Colorado 4-1.
  - Jeremy Roenick, Phoenix, 1998 CQF vs. Detroit, won by Detroit 4-2.
  - Vincent Damphousse, San Jose, 1999 CQF vs. Colorado, won by Colorado 4-2.
  - Dixon Ward, Buffalo, 1999 CF vs. Toronto, won by Buffalo 4-1.
  - Curtis Brown, Buffalo, 2001 CSF vs. Pittsburgh, won by Pittsburgh 4-3.

MOST SHORTHAND GOALS, ONE GAME

- 2 – **Dave Keon,** Toronto, April 18, 1963, at Toronto, in 3-1 win vs. Detroit.
  - **Bryan Trottier,** NY Islanders, April 8, 1980, at NY Islanders, in 8-1 win vs. Los Angeles.
  - **Bobby Lalonde,** Boston, April 11, 1981, at Minnesota North Stars, in 6-3 loss vs. Minnesota.
  - **Wayne Gretzky,** Edmonton, April 6, 1983, at Edmonton, in 6-3 win vs. Winnipeg.
  - **Jari Kurri,** Edmonton, April 24, 1983, at Edmonton, in 8-3 win vs. Chicago.
  - **Mark Messier,** NY Rangers, April 21, 1992, at NY Rangers, in 7-3 loss vs. New Jersey.
  - **Tom Fitzgerald,** NY Islanders, May 8, 1993, at NY Islanders, in 6-5 win vs. Pittsburgh.
  - **Rod Brind'Amour,** Philadelphia, April 26, 1997, at Philadelphia, in 6-3 win vs. Pittsburgh.
  - **Jeremy Roenick,** Phoenix, April 24, 1998, at Detroit, in 7-4 win vs. Detroit.
  - **Vincent Damphousse,** San Jose, April 30, 1999, at Colorado, in 7-3 win vs. Colorado.

MOST SHORTHAND GOALS, ONE PERIOD

- 2 – **Bryan Trottier,** NY Islanders, April 8, 1980, second period, at NY Islanders, in 8-1 win vs. Los Angeles.
  - **Bobby Lalonde,** Boston, April 11, 1981, third period, at Minnesota North Stars, in 6-3 loss vs. Minnesota.
  - **Jari Kurri,** Edmonton, April 24, 1983, third period, at Edmonton, in 8-4 win vs. Chicago.
  - **Rod Brind'Amour,** Philadelphia, April 26, 1997, first period, at Philadelphia, in 6-3 win vs. Pittsburgh.
  - **Jeremy Roenick,** Phoenix, April 24, 1998, second period, at Detroit, in 7-4 win vs. Detroit.
  - **Vincent Damphousse,** San Jose, April 30, 1999, third period, at Colorado, in 7-3 win vs. Colorado.

GAME-WINNING GOALS

MOST GAME-WINNING GOALS IN PLAYOFFS, CAREER

- 24 – **Wayne Gretzky,** Edmonton, Los Angeles, St. Louis, NY Rangers
- 23 – Brett Hull, St. Louis, Dallas, Detroit
- 19 – Claude Lemieux, Montreal, New Jersey, Colorado
- 18 – Maurice Richard, Montreal
- 17 – Mike Bossy, NY Islanders
  - Glenn Anderson, Edmonton, Toronto, NY Rangers, St. Louis

MOST GAME-WINNING GOALS, ONE PLAYOFF YEAR

- 6 – **Joe Sakic,** Colorado, 1996. 22 games.
  - **Joe Nieuwendyk,** Dallas, 1999. 23 games.
- 5 – Mike Bossy, NY Islanders, 1983. 19 games.
  - Jari Kurri, Edmonton, 1987. 21 games.
  - Bobby Smith, Minnesota North Stars, 1991. 23 games.
  - Mario Lemieux, Pittsburgh, 1992. 15 games.

MOST GAME-WINNING GOALS, ONE PLAYOFF SERIES

- 4 – **Mike Bossy,** NY Islanders, 1983 CF vs. Boston, won by NY Islanders 4-2.

OVERTIME GOALS

MOST OVERTIME GOALS IN PLAYOFFS, CAREER

- 6 – **Maurice Richard,** Montreal (1 in 1946; 3 in 1951; 1 in 1957; 1 in 1958.)
- 5 – Glenn Anderson, Edmonton, Toronto, St. Louis
- 4 – Bob Nystrom, NY Islanders
  - Dale Hunter, Quebec, Washington
  - Wayne Gretzky, Edmonton, Los Angeles
  - Stephane Richer, Montreal, New Jersey
  - Joe Murphy, Edmonton, Chicago
  - Esa Tikkanen, Edmonton, NY Rangers
  - Jaromir Jagr, Pittsburgh
  - Kirk Muller, Montreal, Dallas
  - Joe Sakic, Colorado

MOST OVERTIME GOALS, ONE PLAYOFF YEAR

- 3 – **Mel Hill,** Boston, 1939. All vs. NY Rangers in best-of-seven SF, won by Boston 4-3.
  - **Maurice Richard,** Montreal, 1951. 2 vs. Detroit in best-of-seven SF, won by Montreal 4-2; 1 vs. Toronto in best-of-seven F, won by Toronto 4-1.

MOST OVERTIME GOALS, ONE PLAYOFF SERIES

- 3 – Mel Hill, Boston, 1939 SF vs. NY Rangers, won by Boston 4-3. Hill scored at 59:25 of overtime March 21 for a 2-1 win; at 8:24 of overtime, March 23 for a 3-2 win; and at 48:00 of overtime, April 2 for a 2-1 win.

SCORING BY A DEFENSEMAN

MOST GOALS BY A DEFENSEMAN, ONE PLAYOFF YEAR

- 12 – **Paul Coffey,** Edmonton, 1985. 18 games.
- 11 – Brian Leetch, NY Rangers, 1994. 23 games.
- 9 – Bobby Orr, Boston, 1970. 14 games.
  - Brad Park, Boston, 1978. 15 games.
- 8 – Denis Potvin, NY Islanders, 1981. 18 games.
  - Raymond Bourque, Boston, 1983. 17 games.
  - Denis Potvin, NY Islanders, 1983. 20 games.
  - Paul Coffey, Edmonton, 1984. 19 games.

MOST GOALS BY A DEFENSEMAN, ONE GAME

- 3 – **Bobby Orr,** Boston, April 11, 1971, at Montreal. Final score: Boston 5, Montreal 2.
  - **Dick Redmond,** Chicago, April 4, 1973, at Chicago. Final score: Chicago 7, St. Louis 1.
  - **Denis Potvin,** NY Islanders, April 17, 1981, at NY Islanders. Final score: NY Islanders 6, Edmonton 3.
  - **Paul Reinhart,** Calgary, April 14, 1983, at Edmonton. Final score: Edmonton 6, Calgary 3.
  - **Doug Halward,** Vancouver, April 7, 1984, at Vancouver. Final score: Vancouver 7, Calgary 0.
  - **Paul Reinhart,** Calgary, April 8, 1984, at Vancouver. Final score: Calgary 5, Vancouver 1.
  - **Al Iafrate,** Washington, April 26, 1993, at Washington. Final score: Washington 6, NY Islanders 4.
  - **Eric Desjardins,** Montreal, June 3, 1993, at Montreal. Final score: Montreal 3, Los Angeles 2.
  - **Gary Suter,** Chicago, April 24, 1994, at Chicago. Final score: Chicago 4, Toronto 3.
  - **Brian Leetch,** NY Rangers, May 22, 1995, at Philadelphia. Final score: Philadelphia 4, NY Rangers 3.
  - **Andy Delmore,** Philadelphia, May 7, 2000, at Philadelphia. Final score: Philadelphia 6, Pittsburgh 3.

MOST ASSISTS BY A DEFENSEMAN, ONE PLAYOFF YEAR

- 25 – **Paul Coffey,** Edmonton, 1985. 18 games.
- 24 – Al MacInnis, Calgary, 1989. 22 games.
- 23 – Brian Leetch, NY Rangers, 1994. 23 games.
- 19 – Bobby Orr, Boston, 1972. 15 games.
- 18 – Raymond Bourque, Boston, 1988. 23 games.
  - Raymond Bourque, Boston, 1991. 19 games.
  - Larry Murphy, Pittsburgh, 1991. 23 games.

MOST ASSISTS BY A DEFENSEMAN, ONE GAME

- 5 – **Paul Coffey,** Edmonton, May 14, 1985, at Edmonton vs. Chicago. Edmonton won 10-5.
  - **Risto Siltanen,** Quebec, April 14, 1987, at Hartford. Quebec won 7-5.

MOST POINTS BY A DEFENSEMAN, ONE PLAYOFF YEAR

- 37 – **Paul Coffey,** Edmonton, in 1985. 12 goals, 25 assists in 18 games.
- 34 – Brian Leetch, NY Rangers, in 1994. 11 goals, 23 assists in 23 games.
- 31 – Al MacInnis, Calgary, in 1989. 7 goals, 24 assists in 22 games.
- 25 – Denis Potvin, NY Islanders, in 1981. 8 goals, 17 assists in 18 games.
  - Raymond Bourque, Boston, in 1991. 7 goals, 18 assists in 19 games.

MOST POINTS BY A DEFENSEMAN, ONE GAME

- 6 – **Paul Coffey,** Edmonton, May 14, 1985, at Edmonton vs. Chicago. 1 goal, 5 assists. Edmonton won 10-5.
- 5 – Eddie Bush, Detroit, April 9, 1942, at Detroit vs. Toronto. 1 goal, 4 assists. Detroit won 5-2.
  - Bob Dailey, Philadelphia, May 1, 1980, at Philadelphia vs. Minnesota North Stars. 1 goal, 4 assists. Philadelphia won 7-0.
  - Denis Potvin, NY Islanders, April 17, 1981, at NY Islanders vs. Edmonton. 3 goals, 2 assists. NY Islanders won 6-3.
  - Risto Siltanen, Quebec, April 14, 1987, at Hartford. 5 assists. Quebec won 7-5.

SCORING BY A ROOKIE

MOST GOALS BY A ROOKIE, ONE PLAYOFF YEAR

- 14 – **Dino Ciccarelli,** Minnesota North Stars, 1981. 19 games.
- 11 – Jeremy Roenick, Chicago, 1990. 20 games.
- 10 – Claude Lemieux, Montreal, 1986. 20 games.
- 9 – Pat Flatley, NY Islanders, 1984. 21 games.
- 8 – Steve Christoff, Minnesota North Stars, 1980. 14 games.
  - Brad Palmer, Minnesota North Stars, 1981. 19 games.
  - Mike Krushelnyski, Boston, 1983. 17 games.
  - Bob Joyce, Boston, 1988. 23 games.

MOST POINTS BY A ROOKIE, ONE PLAYOFF YEAR
21 – **Dino Ciccarelli,** Minnesota North Stars, 1981. 14 goals, 7 assists in 19 games.
20 – Don Maloney, NY Rangers, 1979. 7 goals, 13 assists in 18 games.

THREE-OR-MORE-GOAL GAMES

MOST THREE-OR-MORE-GOAL GAMES IN PLAYOFFS, CAREER
10 – **Wayne Gretzky,** Edmonton, Los Angeles, NY Rangers. 8 three-goal games; 2 four-goal games.
7 – Maurice Richard, Montreal. 4 three-goal games; 2 four-goal games and 1 five-goal game.
– Jari Kurri, Edmonton. 6 three-goal games; 1 four-goal game.
6 – Dino Ciccarelli, Minnesota North Stars, Washington, Detroit. 5 three-goal games; 1 four-goal game.
5 – Mike Bossy, NY Islanders. 4 three-goal games; 1 four-goal game.

MOST THREE-OR-MORE-GOAL GAMES, ONE PLAYOFF YEAR
4 – **Jari Kurri,** Edmonton, 1985. 1 four-goal game, 3 three-goal games.
3 – Mark Messier, Edmonton, 1983. 3 three-goal games.
– Mike Bossy, NY Islanders, 1983. 1 four-goal game, 2 three-goal games.
2 – Newsy Lalonde, Montreal, 1919. 1 five-goal game, 1 four-goal game.
– Maurice Richard, Montreal, 1944. 1 five-goal game; 1 three-goal game.
– Doug Bentley, Chicago, 1944. 2 three-goal games.
– Norm Ullman, Detroit, 1964. 2 three-goal games.
– Phil Esposito, Boston, 1970. 2 three-goal games.
– Pit Martin, Chicago, 1973. 2 three-goal games.
– Rick MacLeish, Philadelphia, 1975. 2 three-goal games.
– Lanny McDonald, Toronto, 1977. 1 three-goal game; 1 four-goal game.
– Wayne Gretzky, Edmonton, 1981. 2 three-goal games.
– Wayne Gretzky, Edmonton, 1983. 2 four-goal games.
– Wayne Gretzky, Edmonton, 1985. 2 three-goal games.
– Petr Klima, Detroit, 1988. 2 three-goal games.
– Cam Neely, Boston, 1991. 2 three-goal games.
– Wayne Gretzky, NY Rangers, 1997. 2 three-goal games.
– Daniel Alfredsson, Ottawa, 1998. 2 three-goal games.

MOST THREE-OR-MORE-GOAL GAMES, ONE PLAYOFF SERIES
3 – **Jari Kurri,** Edmonton, 1985 CF vs. Chicago, won by Edmonton 4-2. Kurri scored 3 goals May 7 at Edmonton in 7-3 win, 3 goals May 14 at Edmonton in 10-5 win and 4 goals May 16 at Chicago in 8-2 win.
2 – Doug Bentley, Chicago, 1944 SF vs. Detroit, won by Chicago 4-1. Bentley scored 3 goals Mar. 28 at Chicago in 7-1 win and 3 goals Mar. 30 at Detroit in 5-2 win.
– Norm Ullman, Detroit, 1964 SF vs. Chicago, won by Detroit 4-3. Ullman scored 3 goals Mar. 29 at Chicago in 5-4 win and 3 goals April 7 at Detroit in 7-2 win.
– Mark Messier, Edmonton, 1983 DF vs. Calgary, won by Edmonton 4-1. Messier scored 4 goals April 14 at Edmonton in 6-3 win and 3 goals April 17 at Calgary in 10-2 win.
– Mike Bossy, NY Islanders, 1983 CF vs. Boston, won by NY Islanders 4-2. Bossy scored 3 goals May 3 at NY Islanders in 8-3 win and 4 goals May 7 at NY Islanders in 8-4 win.

SCORING STREAKS

LONGEST CONSECUTIVE GOAL-SCORING STREAK, ONE PLAYOFF YEAR
10 Games – Reggie Leach, Philadelphia, 1976. Streak started April 17 at Toronto and ended May 9 at Montreal. He scored one goal in each of eight games; two in one game; and five in another; a total of 15 goals.

LONGEST CONSECUTIVE POINT-SCORING STREAK, ONE PLAYOFF YEAR
18 games – Bryan Trottier, NY Islanders, 1981. 11 goals, 18 assists, 29 points.
17 games – Wayne Gretzky, Edmonton, 1988. 12 goals, 29 assists, 41 points.
– Al MacInnis, Calgary, 1989. 7 goals, 19 assists, 26 points.

LONGEST CONSECUTIVE POINT-SCORING STREAK, MORE THAN ONE PLAYOFF YEAR
27 games – Bryan Trottier, NY Islanders, 1980, 1981 and 1982. 7 games in 1980 (3 goals, 5 assists, 8 points), 18 games in 1981 (11 goals, 18 assists, 29 points), and 2 games in 1982 (2 goals, 3 assists, 5 points). Total points: 42.
19 games – Wayne Gretzky, Edmonton, Los Angeles, 1988 and 1989. 17 games in 1988 (12 goals, 29 assists, 41 points with Edmonton) and 2 games in 1989 (1 goal, 2 assists, 3 points with Los Angeles). Total points: 44.

FASTEST GOALS

FASTEST GOAL FROM START OF GAME
0:06 – Don Kozak, Los Angeles, April 17, 1977, at Los Angeles vs. Boston and goaltender Gerry Cheevers. Los Angeles won 7-4.
0:07 – Bob Gainey, Montreal, May 5, 1977, at NY Islanders vs. goaltender Glenn Resch. Montreal won 2-1.
– Terry Murray, Philadelphia, April 12, 1981, at Quebec vs. goaltender Dan Bouchard. Quebec won 4-3 in overtime.

FASTEST GOAL FROM START OF PERIOD (OTHER THAN FIRST)
0:06 – Pelle Eklund, Philadelphia, April 25, 1989, at Pittsburgh vs. goaltender Tom Barrasso, second period. Pittsburgh won 10-7.
0:09 – Bill Collins, Minnesota North Stars, April 9, 1968, at Minnesota vs. Los Angeles and goaltender Wayne Rutledge, third period. Minnesota won 7-5.
– Dave Balon, Minnesota North Stars, April 25, 1968, at St. Louis vs. goaltender Glenn Hall, third period. Minnesota won 5-1.
– Murray Oliver, Minnesota North Stars, April 8, 1971, at St. Louis vs. goaltender Ernie Wakely, third period. St. Louis won 4-2.
– Clark Gillies, NY Islanders, April 15, 1977, at Buffalo vs. goaltender Don Edwards, third period. NY Islanders won 4-3.
– Eric Vail, Atlanta Flames, April 11, 1978, at Atlanta vs. Detroit and goaltender Ron Low, third period. Detroit won 5-3.
– Stan Smyl, Vancouver, April 10, 1979, at Philadelphia vs. goaltender Wayne Stephenson, third period. Vancouver won 3-2.
– Wayne Gretzky, Edmonton, April 6, 1983, at Edmonton vs. Winnipeg and goaltender Brian Hayward, second period. Edmonton won 6-3.
– Mark Messier, Edmonton, April 16, 1984, at Calgary vs. goaltender Don Edwards, third period. Edmonton won 5-3.
– Brian Skrudland, Montreal, May 18, 1986, at Calgary vs. goaltender Mike Vernon, first overtime period. Montreal won 3-2.

FASTEST TWO GOALS
0:05 – Norm Ullman, Detroit, April 11, 1965, at Detroit vs. Chicago and goaltender Glenn Hall. Ullman scored at 17:35 and 17:40 of second period. Detroit won 4-2.

FASTEST TWO GOALS FROM START OF A GAME
1:08 – Dick Duff, Toronto, April 9, 1963, at Toronto vs. Detroit and goaltender Terry Sawchuk. Duff scored at 0:49 and 1:08. Final score: Toronto 4, Detroit 2.

FASTEST TWO GOALS FROM START OF A PERIOD
0:35 – Pat LaFontaine, NY Islanders, May 19, 1984, at Edmonton vs. goaltender Andy Moog. LaFontaine scored at 0:13 and 0:35 of third period. Final score: Edmonton 5, NY Islanders 2.

PENALTIES

MOST PENALTY MINUTES IN PLAYOFFS, CAREER
729 – **Dale Hunter,** Quebec, Washington, Colorado
541 – Chris Nilan, Montreal, NY Rangers, Boston
519 – Claude Lemieux, Montreal, New Jersey, Colorado, Phoenix
471 – Rick Tocchet, Philadelphia, Pittsburgh, Boston, Phoenix
466 – Willi Plett, Atlanta Flames, Calgary, Minnesota North Stars, Boston

MOST PENALTIES, ONE GAME
8 – **Forbes Kennedy,** Toronto, April 2, 1969, at Boston. Kennedy was assessed 4 minors, 2 majors, 1 10-minute misconduct and 1 game misconduct. Boston won 10-0.
– **Kim Clackson,** Pittsburgh, April 14, 1980, at Boston. Clackson was assessed 5 minors, 2 majors and 1 10-minute misconduct. Boston won 6-2.

MOST PENALTY MINUTES, ONE GAME
42 – **Dave Schultz,** Philadelphia, April 22, 1976, at Toronto. Schultz was assessed 1 minor, 2 majors, 1 10-minute misconduct and 2 game misconducts. Toronto won 8-5.

MOST PENALTIES, ONE PERIOD AND MOST PENALTY MINUTES, ONE PERIOD
6 Penalties; 39 Minutes – Ed Hospodar, NY Rangers, April 9, 1981, at Los Angeles, first period. Hospodar was assessed 2 minors, 1 major, 1 10-minute misconduct and 2 game misconducts. Los Angeles won 5-4.

GOALTENDING

MOST PLAYOFF GAMES APPEARED IN BY A GOALTENDER, CAREER
240 – **Patrick Roy,** Montreal, Colorado
150 – Grant Fuhr, Edmonton, Buffalo, St. Louis
141 – Ed Belfour, Chicago, Dallas
138 – Mike Vernon, Calgary, Detroit, San Jose, Florida
132 – Billy Smith, NY Islanders
– Andy Moog, Edmonton, Boston, Dallas, Montreal

MOST MINUTES PLAYED BY A GOALTENDER, CAREER
14,786 – **Patrick Roy,** Montreal, Colorado
8,834 – Grant Fuhr, Edmonton, Buffalo, St. Louis
8,639 – Ed Belfour, Chicago, Dallas
8,214 – Mike Vernon, Calgary, Detroit, San Jose, Florida
7,645 – Billy Smith, NY Islanders

MOST MINUTES PLAYED BY A GOALTENDER, ONE PLAYOFF YEAR
1,544 – **Kirk McLean,** Vancouver, 1994. 24 games.
– **Ed Belfour,** Dallas, 1999. 23 games.
1,540 – Ron Hextall, Philadelphia, 1987. 26 games.
1,505 – Martin Brodeur, 2001. 25 games.

MOST SHUTOUTS IN PLAYOFFS, CAREER
22 – **Patrick Roy,** Montreal, Colorado
15 – Clint Benedict, Ottawa, Mtl. Maroons
– Curtis Joseph, St. Louis, Edmonton, Toronto
14 – Jacques Plante, Montreal, St. Louis
13 – Turk Broda, Toronto
– Martin Brodeur, New Jersey

MOST SHUTOUTS, ONE PLAYOFF YEAR
6 – **Dominik Hasek,** Detroit, 2002. 23 games.
4 – Four shutouts by a goaltender in one playoff year has been recorded 14 times: Clint Benedict (1928, 1929), Dave Kerr (1937), Frank McCool (1945), Terry Sawchuk (1952), Bernie Parent (1975), Ken Dryden (1977), Mike Richter (1994), Kirk McLean (1994), Olaf Kolzig (1998), Ed Belfour (2000), Martin Brodeur (2001), Patrick Roy (2001), Patrick Lalime (2002).

MOST SHUTOUTS, ONE PLAYOFF SERIES

3 – **Clint Benedict,** Mtl. Maroons, 1926 F vs. Victoria. 4 games.
– **Dave Kerr,** NY Rangers, 1940 SF vs. Boston. 6 games.
– **Frank McCool,** Toronto, 1945 F vs. Detroit. 7 games.
– **Turk Broda,** Toronto, 1950 SF vs. Detroit. 7 games.
– **Felix Potvin,** Toronto, 1994 CQF vs. Chicago. 6 games.
– **Martin Brodeur,** New Jersey, 1995 CQF vs. Boston. 5 games.
– **Brent Johnson,** St. Louis, 2002 CQF vs. Chicago. 5 games.
– **Patrick Lalime,** Ottawa, 2002 CQF vs. Philadelphia. 5 games.

MOST WINS BY A GOALTENDER, CAREER

148 – **Patrick Roy,** Montreal, Colorado
92 – Grant Fuhr, Edmonton, Buffalo, St. Louis
88 – Billy Smith, NY Islanders
80 – Ken Dryden, Montreal
79 – Ed Belfour, Chicago, Dallas

MOST WINS BY A GOALTENDER, ONE PLAYOFF YEAR

16 – Sixteen wins by a goaltender in one playoff year has been recorded on 14 occasions. Dominik Hasek of the Detroit Red Wings is the most recent to equal this mark, posting a record of 16 wins and 7 losses in 23 games in 2002. It was first accomplished by Grant Fuhr of Edmonton in 1988 with a record of 16 wins, 2 losses and 1 no decision (suspended game).

MOST CONSECUTIVE WINS BY A GOALTENDER, MORE THAN ONE PLAYOFF YEAR

14 – **Tom Barrasso,** Pittsburgh, 1992, 1993; 3 wins vs. NY Rangers in 1992 DF, won by Pittsburgh 4-2; 4 wins vs. Boston in 1992 CF, won by Pittsburgh 4-0; 4 wins vs. Chicago in 1992 F, won by Pittsburgh 4-0; and 3 wins vs. New Jersey in 1993 DSF, won by Pittsburgh 4-1.

MOST CONSECUTIVE WINS BY A GOALTENDER, ONE PLAYOFF YEAR

11 – **Ed Belfour,** Chicago, 1992. 3 wins vs. St. Louis in DSF, won by Chicago 4-2; 4 wins vs. Detroit in DF, won by Chicago 4-0; and 4 wins vs. Edmonton in CF, won by Chicago 4-0.
– **Tom Barrasso,** Pittsburgh, 1992. 3 wins vs. NY Rangers in DF, won by Pittsburgh 4-2; 4 wins vs. Boston in CF, won by Pittsburgh 4-0; and 4 wins vs. Chicago in F, won by Pittsburgh 4-0.
– **Patrick Roy,** Montreal, 1993. 4 wins vs. Quebec in DSF, won by Montreal 4-2; 4 wins vs. Buffalo in DF, won by Montreal 4-0; and 3 wins vs. NY Islanders in CF, won by Montreal 4-1.

LONGEST SHUTOUT SEQUENCE

248:32– **Normie Smith,** Detroit, 1936. Smith shut out Mtl. Maroons twice, 1-0 March 24 in 116:30 of overtime; 3-0, March 26; and was scored against at 12:02 of first period, March 29, by Gus Marker. Detroit won best-of-five SF 3-0.

MOST CONSECUTIVE SHUTOUTS

3 – **Clint Benedict,** Mtl. Maroons, 1926. Benedict shut out Ottawa 1-0, March 27; he then shut out Victoria twice, 3-0, March 30; 3-0, April 1. Mtl. Maroons won two-game total-goals NHL F vs. Ottawa 2-1 and won best-of-five F vs. Victoria 3-1.
– **John Ross Roach,** NY Rangers, 1929. Roach shut out NY Americans twice, 0-0, March 19; 1-0, March 21; he then shut out Toronto 1-0, March 24. NY Rangers won two-game total-goals QF vs. NY Americans 1-0 and won best-of-three SF vs. Toronto 2-0.
– **Frank McCool,** Toronto, 1945. McCool shut out Detroit three times, 1-0, April 6; 2-0, April 8; 1-0, April 12. Toronto won best-of-seven F 4-3.
– **Brent Johnson,** St. Louis, 2002. Johnson shut out Chicago three times, 2-0, April 20; 4-0, April 21; 1-0, April 23. St. Louis won best-of-seven CQF 4-1.
– **Patrick Lalime,** Ottawa, 2002. Lalime shut out Philadelphia three times, 3-0, April 20; 3-0, April 22; 3-0, April 24. Ottawa won best-of-seven CQF 4-1.

Playoff Statistics, Active Goaltenders

listed alphabetically

Goaltender	GP	Min	W	L	SO	GA	SOG	Avg.	Sv%
Aebischer, David	2	35	0	0	0	1	14	1.71	.929
Aubin, Jean-Sebastien	1	1	0	0	0	0	0	0.00	---
Belfour, Ed	141	8638	79	57	11	308	3815	2.14	.919
Billington, Craig	8	213	0	2	0	15	102	4.23	.853
Boucher, Brian	21	1308	11	8	1	45	534	2.06	.914
Brathwaite, Fred	1	1	0	0	0	0	0	0.00	.000
Brodeur, Martin	115	7211	67	48	13	226	2769	1.88	.918
Burke, Sean	34	2002	12	22	1	111	993	3.33	.888
Cechmanek, Roman	10	574	3	7	1	25	274	2.61	.909
Cloutier, Dan	8	390	2	5	0	25	180	3.85	.861
Dafoe, Byron	27	1686	10	16	3	65	672	2.31	.903
Fernandez, Manny	2	19	0	0	0	1	8	3.16	.875
Hackett, Jeff	9	432	2	5	0	31	233	4.31	.867
Hedberg, Johan	18	1123	9	9	2	43	482	2.30	.911
Hirsch, Corey	6	338	2	3	0	21	166	3.73	.873
Irbe, Arturs	51	2981	23	27	1	142	1449	2.86	.902
Johnson, Brent	12	652	5	6	3	20	288	1.84	.931
Joseph, Curtis	118	7220	58	58	15	304	3577	2.53	.915
Khabibulin, Nikolai	24	1419	10	13	1	65	778	2.75	.916
Kidd, Trevor	9	517	3	5	1	35	221	4.06	.842
Kiprusoff, Miikka	4	157	1	1	0	5	81	1.91	.938
Kolzig, Olaf	39	2395	18	20	5	86	1184	2.15	.927
Lalime, Patrick	16	1029	7	9	4	28	431	1.63	.942
Legace, Manny	1	11	0	0	0	1	2	5.45	.500
McLennan, Jamie	4	134	0	2	0	7	58	3.13	.879
Nabokov, Evgeni	17	950	8	8	1	41	435	2.59	.906
Osgood, Chris	75	4381	41	29	9	161	1826	2.20	.912
Passmore, Steve	3	138	0	2	0	6	62	2.61	.903
Potvin, Felix	72	4435	35	37	8	195	2169	2.64	.910
Richter, Mike	76	4514	41	33	9	202	2228	2.68	.909
Roloson, Dwayne	4	139	1	1	0	10	67	4.32	.851
Roy, Patrick	240	14786	148	90	22	568	6972	2.30	.919
Salo, Tommy	15	998	3	12	0	40	469	2.40	.915
Schwab, Corey	1	12	0	0	0	0	5	0.00	1.000
Shields, Steve	23	1325	9	14	1	68	693	3.08	.902
Skudra, Peter	3	116	0	1	0	6	57	3.10	.895
Snow, Garth	15	735	8	4	0	36	327	2.94	.891
Storr, Jamie	5	181	0	3	0	11	102	3.65	.892
Theodore, Jose	17	974	7	8	0	43	556	2.65	.977
Thibault, Jocelyn	17	840	4	11	0	50	458	3.57	.891
Tugnutt, Ron	25	1482	9	13	3	56	692	2.27	.919
Turek, Roman	21	1323	12	9	0	50	543	2.27	.908
Weekes, Kevin	8	408	3	2	2	11	180	1.62	.939

Playoff Penalty Shots

Date	Player	Goaltender	Scored	Final Score			Series
3/25/37	Lionel Conacher, Mtl.M.	Tiny Thompson, Bos.	N	Mtl.M	0 at Bos.	4	QF
4/15/37	Alex Shibicky, NYR	Earl Robertson, Det.	N	NYR	0 at Det.	3	F
4/13/44	Virgil Johnson, Chi.	Bill Durnan, Mtl. *	N	Chi.	4 at Mtl.	5	F
4/9/68	Wayne Connelly, Min.	Terry Sawchuk, L.A.	Y	L.A.	5 at Min.	7	QF
4/27/68	Jimmy Roberts, St.L.	Cesare Maniago, Min.	N	St.L.	4 at Min.	3	SF
5/16/71	Frank Mahovlich, Mtl.	Tony Esposito, Chi.	N	Chi.	3 at Mtl.	4	F
5/7/75	Bill Barber, Phi.	Glenn Resch, NYI *	N	Phi.	3 at NYI	4	SF
4/20/79	Mike Walton, Chi.	Glenn Resch, NYI	N	NYI	4 at Chi.	0	QF
4/9/81	Peter McNab, Bos.	Don Beaupre, Min. *	N	Min.	5 at Bos.	4	PR
4/17/81	Anders Hedberg, NYR	Mike Liut, St.L.	N	NYR	6 at St.L.	4	QF
4/9/83	Denis Potvin, NYI	Pat Riggin, Wsh.	N	NYI	6 at Wsh.	2	DSF
4/28/84	Wayne Gretzky, Edm.	Don Beaupre, Min.	Y	Edm.	8 at Min.	5	CF
5/1/84	Mats Naslund, Mtl.	Billy Smith, NYI	N	Mtl.	1 at NYI	3	CF
4/14/85	Bob Carpenter, Wsh.	Billy Smith, NYI	N	Wsh.	4 at NYI	6	DF
5/28/85	Ron Sutter, Phi.	Grant Fuhr, Edm.	N	Phi.	3 at Edm.	5	F
5/30/85	Dave Poulin, Phi.	Grant Fuhr, Edm.	N	Phi.	3 at Edm.	5	F
4/9/88	John Tucker, Buf.	Andy Moog, Bos.	Y	Bos.	2 at Buf.	6	DSF
4/9/88	Petr Klima, Det.	Allan Bester, Tor.	Y	Det.	6 at Tor.	3	DSF
4/8/89	Neal Broten, Min.	Greg Millen, St.L.	Y	St.L.	5 at Min.	3	DSF
4/4/90	Al MacInnis, Cgy.	Kelly Hrudey, L.A.	Y	L.A.	5 at Cgy.	3	DSF
4/5/90	Randy Wood, NYI	Mike Richter, NYR	N	NYI	1 at NYR	2	DSF
5/3/90	Kelly Miller, Wsh.	Andy Moog, Bos.	N	Wsh.	3 at Bos.	5	CF
5/18/90	Petr Klima, Edm.	Reggie Lemelin, Bos.	N	Edm.	7 at Bos.	2	F
4/6/91	Basil McRae, Min.	Ed Belfour, Chi.	Y	Min.	2 at Chi.	5	DSF
4/10/91	Steve Duchesne, L.A.	Kirk McLean, Van.	Y	L.A.	6 at Van.	1	DSF
5/11/92	Jaromir Jagr, Pit.	J. Vanbiesbrouck, NYR	Y	Pit.	3 at NYR	2	DF
5/13/92	Shawn McEachern, Pit.	J. Vanbiesbrouck, NYR	N	NYR	1 at Pit.	2	DF
6/7/94	Pavel Bure, Van.	Mike Richter, NYR	N	NYR	4 at Van.	2	F
5/9/95	Patrick Poulin, Chi.	Felix Potvin, Tor.	N	Tor.	3 at Chi.	0	CQF
5/10/95	Michal Pivonka, Wsh.	Tom Barrasso, Pit.	N	Pit.	2 at Wsh.	6	CQF
4/24/96	Joe Juneau, Wsh.	Ken Wregget, Pit.**	N	Pit.	3 at Wsh.	2	CQF
5/11/97	Eric Lindros, Phi.	Steve Shields, Buf.	Y	Phi.	6 at Buf.	3	CSF
4/23/98	Alexei Morozov, Pit.	Andy Moog, Mtl.***	N	Mtl.	3 at Pit.	2	CQF
4/22/99	Mats Sundin, Tor.	J. Vanbiesbrouck, Phi.	N	Tor.	0 at Tor.	0	CQF
5/29/99	Mats Sundin, Tor.	Dominik Hasek, Buf.	Y	Tor.	2 at Buf.	5	CF
4/16/00	Eric Desjardins, Phi.	Dominik Hasek, Buf.	N	Phi.	2 at Buf.	0	CQF
4/11/01	Mark Recchi, Phi.	Dominik Hasek, Buf.	N	Buf.	2 at Phi.	1	CQF
5/2/01	Martin Straka, Pit.	Dominik Hasek, Buf.	N	Buf.	5 at Pit.	2	CSF
5/12/01	Joe Sakic, Col.	Roman Turek, St.L.	Y	St.L.	1 at Col.	4	CF
4/21/02	Todd Bertuzzi, Van.	Dominik Hasek, Det.	N	Det.	3 at Van.	1	CQF
4/24/02	Shawn Bates, NYI	Curtis Joseph, Tor.	Y	Tor.	3 at NYI	4	CQF
4/26/02	Mike Johnson, Phx.	Evgeni Nabokov, S.J.	N	Phx.	1 at S.J.	4	CQF

* The game was decided in overtime, but penalty shot was taken during regulation time.
** Joe Juneau's penalty shot April 24, 1996 was the first attempted in overtime.
*** Penalty shot taken in overtime.

CHAPTER 10

Coaching Register

Career NHL Playoff Records, 1918-2002

Coach	Team	Games Coached	Wins	Losses	Ties	Playoff Years	Cup Wins	Career
Abel, Sid	Chicago	7	3	4	0	1		
	Detroit	69	29	40	0	8		
	Total	76	32	44	0	9		1952-76
Adams, Jack	Detroit	105	52	52	1	15	3	1927-47
Allen, Keith	Philadelphia	11	3	8	0	2		1967-69
Arbour, Al	St. Louis	11	4	7	0	1		
	NY Islanders	198	119	79	0	15	4	
	Total	209	123	86	0	16	4	1970-94
Barber, Bill	Philadelphia	11	3	8	0	2		2000-02
Berenson, Red	St. Louis	14	5	9	0	2		1979-82
Bergeron, Michel	Quebec	68	31	37	0	7		1980-90
Berry, Bob	Los Angeles	10	2	8	0	3		
	Montreal	8	2	6	0	2		
	St. Louis	15	7	8	0	2		
	Total	33	11	22	0	7		1978-94
Beverley, Nick	Toronto	6	2	4	0	1		1995-96
Blackburn, Don	Hartford	3	0	3	0	1		1979-81
Blair, Wren	Minnesota	14	7	7	0	1		1967-70
Blake, Toe	Montreal	119	82	37	0	13	8	1955-68
Boileau, Marc	Pittsburgh	9	5	4	0	1		1973-76
Boivin, Leo	St. Louis	3	1	2	0	1		1975-78
Boucher, Frank	NY Rangers	27	13	14	0	4	1	1939-54
Boucher, Georges	Mtl. Maroons	2	0	2	0	1		1930-50
Bowman, Scotty	St. Louis	52	26	26	0	4		
	Montreal	98	70	28	0	8	5	
	Buffalo	36	18	18	0	5		
	Pittsburgh	33	23	10	0	2	1	
	Detroit	134	86	48	0	9	3	
	Total	353	223	130	0	28	9	1967-02
Bowness, Rick	Boston	15	8	7	0	1		1988-98
Brooks, Herb	NY Rangers	24	12	12	0	3		
	New Jersey	5	1	4	0	1		
	Pittsburgh	11	6	5	0	1		
	Total	40	19	21	0	5		1981-00
Brophy, John	Toronto	19	9	10	0	2		1986-89
Burns, Charlie	Minnesota	6	2	4	0	1		1969-75
Burns, Pat	Montreal	56	30	26	0	4		
	Toronto	46	23	23	0	3		
	Boston	18	8	10	0	3		
	Total	120	61	59	0	9		1988-01
Campbell, Colin	NY Rangers	36	18	18	0	3		1994-98
Carpenter, Doug	Toronto	5	1	4	0	1		1984-91
Carroll, Dick	Toronto	9	4	5	0	2	1	1917-19
Cheevers, Gerry	Boston	34	15	19	0	4		1980-85
Cherry, Don	Boston	55	31	24	0	5		1974-80
Clancy, King	Toronto	14	2	12	0	3		1937-56
Clapper, Dit	Boston	25	8	17	0	4		1945-49
Cleghorn, Odie	Pittsburgh	4	1	2	1	2		1925-29
Cleghorn, Sprague	Mtl. Maroons	4	1	1	2	1		1931-32
Constantine, Kevin	San Jose	25	11	14	0	2		
	Pittsburgh	19	8	11	0	2		
	New Jersey	6	2	4	0	1		
	Total	50	21	29	0	5		1993-02
Crawford, Marc	Quebec	6	2	4	0	1		
	Colorado	46	29	17	0	3	1	
	Vancouver	10	2	8	0	2		
	Total	62	33	29	0	6	1	1994-02
Creighton, Fred	Atlanta	9	2	7	0	4		1974-80
Crisp, Terry	Calgary	37	22	15	0	3	1	
	Tampa Bay	6	2	4	0	1		
	Total	43	24	19	0	4	1	1987-98
Crozier, Joe	Buffalo	6	2	4	0	1		1971-81
Cunniff, John	New Jersey	6	2	4	0	1		1982-91
Curry, Alex	Ottawa	2	0	1	1	1		1925-26
Dandurand, Leo	Montreal	16	10	6	0	4	1	1921-35
Day, Hap	Toronto	80	49	31	0	9	5	1940-50
Demers, Jacques	St. Louis	33	16	17	0	3		
	Detroit	38	20	18	0	3		
	Montreal	27	19	8	0	2	1	
	Total	98	55	43	0	8	1	1979-99
Denneny, Cy	Boston	5	5	0	0	1	1	1928-33
Dudley, Rick	Buffalo	12	4	8	0	2		1989-92
Dugal, Jules	Montreal	3	1	2	0	1		1938-39
Duncan, Art	Toronto	2	0	1	1	1	1	1926-32
Dutton, Red	NY Americans	16	6	10	0	4		1935-42
Esposito, Phil	NY Rangers	10	2	8	0	2		1986-89
Evans, Jack	Hartford	16	8	8	0	2		1975-88
Ferguson, John	Winnipeg	3	0	3	0	1		1975-86
Francis, Bob	Phoenix	10	2	8	0	2		1999-02
Francis, Emile	NY Rangers	75	34	41	0	9		
	St. Louis	14	5	9	0	2		
	Total	89	39	50	0	11		1965-83
Ftorek, Robbie	Los Angeles	16	5	11	0	2		
	New Jersey	7	3	4	0	1		
	Boston	6	2	4	0	1		
	Total	29	10	19	0	4		1987-02
Gainey, Bob	Minnesota	30	17	13	0	2		
	Dallas	14	6	8	0	2		
	Total	44	23	21	0	4		1990-96
Geoffrion, Bernie	Atlanta	4	0	4	0	1		1968-80
Gerard, Eddie	Mtl. Maroons	25	11	9	5	5	1	1917-35
Gill, David	Ottawa	8	3	2	3	2	1	1926-29
Glover, Fred	Oakland	11	3	8	0	2		1968-74
Gordon, Jackie	Minnesota	25	11	14	0	3		1970-75
Goring, Butch	Boston	3	0	3	0	1		1985-01
Gorman, Tommy	NY Americans	2	0	1	1	1		
	Chicago	8	6	1	1	1	1	
	Mtl. Maroons	15	7	6	2	3	1	
	Total	25	13	8	4	5	2	1925-38
Gottselig, Johnny	Chicago	4	0	4	0	1		1944-48
Green, Pete	Ottawa	26	14	9	3	6	3	1919-25
Green, Ted	Edmonton	16	8	8	0	1		1991-94
Guidolin, Bep	Boston	21	11	10	0	2		1972-76
Harris, Ted	Minnesota	2	0	2	0	1		1975-78
Hart, Cecil	Montreal	37	16	17	4	8	2	1926-39
Hartley, Bob	Colorado	80	49	31	0	4	1	1998-02
Hartsburg, Craig	Chicago	16	8	8	0	2		
	Anaheim	4	0	4	0	1		
	Total	20	8	12	0	3		1995-01
Harvey, Doug	NY Rangers	6	2	4	0	1		1961-62
Hay, Don	Phoenix	7	3	4	0	1		1996-01
Henning, Lorne	Minnesota	5	2	3	0	1		1985-01
Hitchcock, Ken	Dallas	80	47	33	0	5	1	1995-02
Hlinka, Ivan	Pittsburgh	18	9	9	0	1		2000-02
Holmgren, Paul	Philadelphia	19	10	9	0	1		1988-96
Imlach, Punch	Toronto	92	44	48	0	11	4	1958-80
Inglis, Bill	Buffalo	3	1	2	0	1		1978-79
Irvin, Dick	Chicago	9	5	3	1	1		
	Toronto	66	33	32	1	9	1	
	Montreal	115	62	53	0	14	3	
	Total	190	100	88	2	24	4	1928-56
Ivan, Tommy	Detroit	67	36	31	0	7	3	1947-58
Johnson, Bob	Calgary	52	25	27	0	5		
	Pittsburgh	24	16	8	0	1	1	
	Total	76	41	35	0	6	1	1982-91
Johnson, Tom	Boston	22	15	7	0	2	1	1970-73
Johnston, Eddie	Chicago	7	3	4	0	1		
	Pittsburgh	46	22	24	0	5		
	Total	53	25	28	0	6		1979-97
Kasper, Steve	Boston	5	1	4	0	1		1995-97
Keenan, Mike	Philadelphia	57	32	25	0	4		
	Chicago	60	33	27	0	4		
	NY Rangers	23	16	7	0	1	1	
	St. Louis	20	10	10	0	2		
	Total	160	91	69	0	11	1	1984-02
Kelly, Pat	Colorado	2	0	2	0	1		1977-79
Kelly, Red	Los Angeles	18	7	11	0	2		
	Pittsburgh	14	6	8	0	2		
	Toronto	30	11	19	0	4		
	Total	62	24	38	0	8		1967-77

Coach	Team	Games Coached	Wins	Losses	Ties	Playoff Years	Cup Wins	Career
King, Dave	Calgary	20	8	12	0	3		1992-02
Kromm, Bobby	Detroit	7	3	4	0	1		1977-80
Lalonde, Newsy	Montreal	16	7	6	3	4		
	Ottawa	2	0	1	1	1		
	Total	18	7	7	4	5		1917-35
Laviolette, Peter	NY Islanders	7	3	4	0	1		2001-02
Lemaire, Jacques	Montreal	27	15	12	0	2		
	New Jersey	56	34	22	0	4	1	
	Total	83	49	34	0	6	1	1983-02
Ley, Rick	Hartford	13	5	8	0	2		
	Vancouver	11	4	7	0	1		
	Total	24	9	15	0	3		1989-96
Long, Barry	Winnipeg	11	3	8	0	2		1983-86
Loughlin, Clem	Chicago	4	1	2	1	2		1934-37
Low, Ron	Edmonton	28	10	18	0	3		1994-02
Lowe, Kevin	Edmonton	5	1	4	0	1		1999-00
MacLean, Doug	Florida	27	13	14	0	2		1995-98
MacNeil, Al	Montreal	20	12	8	0	1	1	
	Atlanta	4	1	3	0	1		
	Calgary	19	9	10	0	2		
	Total	43	22	21	0	4	1	1970-82
MacTavish, Craig	Edmonton	6	2	4	0	1		2000-02
Magnuson, Keith	Chicago	3	0	3	0	1		1980-82
Mahoney, Bill	Minnesota	16	7	9	0	1		1983-85
Maloney, Dan	Toronto	10	6	4	0	1		
	Winnipeg	15	5	10	0	2		
	Total	25	11	14	0	3		1984-89
Maloney, Phil	Vancouver	7	1	6	0	2		1973-77
Martin, Jacques	St. Louis	16	7	9	0	2		
	Ottawa	44	17	27	0	5		
	Total	60	24	36	0	8		1986-02
Maurice, Paul	Carolina	35	17	18	0	3		1995-02
McCammon, Bob	Philadelphia	10	1	9	0	3		
	Vancouver	7	3	4	0	1		
	Total	17	4	13	0	4		1978-91
McLellan, John	Toronto	11	3	8	0	2		1969-73
McVie, Tom	New Jersey	14	6	8	0	2		1975-92
Melrose, Barry	Los Angeles	24	13	11	0	1		1992-95
Milbury, Mike	Boston	40	23	17	0	2		1989-98
Muckler, John	Edmonton	40	25	15	0	2	1	
	Buffalo	27	11	16	0	4		
	Total	67	36	31	0	6	1	1968-00
Muldoon, Pete	Chicago	2	0	1	1	1		1926-27
Munro, Dunc	Mtl. Maroons	4	1	3	0	1		1929-31
Murdoch, Bob	Chicago	5	1	4	0	1		
	Winnipeg	7	3	4	0	1		
	Total	12	4	8	0	2		1987-91
Murphy, Mike	Los Angeles	5	1	4	0	1		1986-98
Murray, Andy	Los Angeles	24	10	14	0	3		1999-02
Murray, Bryan	Washington	53	24	29	0	7		
	Detroit	25	10	15	0	3		
	Total	78	34	44	0	10		1981-02
Murray, Terry	Washington	39	18	21	0	4		
	Philadelphia	46	28	18	0	3		
	Florida	4	0	4	0	1		
	Total	89	46	43	0	8		1989-01
Neale, Harry	Vancouver	14	3	11	0	4		1978-86
Neilson, Roger	Toronto	19	8	11	0	2		
	Buffalo	8	4	4	0	1		
	Vancouver	21	12	9	0	2		
	NY Rangers	29	13	16	0	3		
	Philadelphia	29	14	15	0	3		
	Total	106	51	55	0	11		1977-02
Nolan, Ted	Buffalo	12	5	7	0	1		1995-97
Nykoluk, Mike	Toronto	7	1	6	0	2		1980-84
O'Donoghue, Geo.	Toronto	7	4	2	1	1		1921-23
O'Reilly, Terry	Boston	37	17	19	1	3		1986-89
Oliver, Murray	Minnesota	13	5	8	0	2		1981-83
Paddock, John	Winnipeg	13	5	8	0	2		1991-95
Page, Pierre	Minnesota	12	4	8	0	2		
	Quebec	6	2	4	0	1		
	Calgary	4	0	4	0	1		
	Total	22	6	16	0	4		1988-98
Patrick, Craig	NY Rangers	17	7	10	0	2		
	Pittsburgh	5	1	4	0	1		
	Total	22	8	14	0	3		1980-97
Patrick, Frank	Boston	6	2	4	0	2		1934-36
Patrick, Lester	NY Rangers	65	32	26	7	12	2	1926-39
Patrick, Lynn	NY Rangers	12	7	5	0	4		
	Boston	28	9	18	1	4		
	Total	40	16	23	1	5		1948-76
Perron, Jean	Montreal	48	30	18	0	3	1	1985-89
Perry, Don	Los Angeles	10	4	6	0	1		1981-84
Pilous, Rudy	Chicago	41	19	22	0	5	1	1957-63
Plager, Barclay	St. Louis	4	1	3	0	1		1977-83
Pleau, Larry	Hartford	10	2	8	0	2		1980-89
Polano, Nick	Detroit	7	1	6	0	2		1982-85
Powers, Eddie	Toronto	2	0	2	0	1		1924-26
Primeau, Joe	Toronto	15	8	6	1	2	1	1950-53
Pronovost, Marcel	Buffalo	8	3	5	0	1		1977-79
Pulford, Bob	Los Angeles	26	10	16	0	4		
	Chicago	45	17	28	0	6		
	Total	71	27	44	0	10		1972-00
Quenneville, Joel	St. Louis	61	31	30	0	6		1996-02
Quinn, Pat	Philadelphia	39	22	17	0	3		
	Los Angeles	3	0	3	0	1		
	Vancouver	61	31	30	0	5		
	Toronto	60	32	28	0	4		
	Total	163	85	78	0	13		1978-02
Reay, Billy	Chicago	116	56	60	0	12		1957-77
Risebrough, Doug	Calgary	7	3	4	0	1		1990-92
Roberts, Jim	Hartford	7	3	4	0	1		1981-97
Robinson, Larry	Los Angeles	4	0	4	0	1		
	New Jersey	48	31	17	0	2	1	
	Total	52	31	21	0	3	1	1995-02
Ross, Art	Boston	65	27	33	5	11	1	1917-45
Ruel, Claude	Montreal	27	18	9	0	3	2	1968-81
Ruff, Lindy	Buffalo	54	32	22	0	4		1997-02
Sather, Glen	Edmonton	127	89	37	1	10	4	1979-94
Sator, Ted	NY Rangers	16	8	8	0	1		
	Buffalo	11	3	8	0	2		
	Total	27	11	16	0	3		1985-89
Schinkel, Ken	Pittsburgh	6	2	4	0	2		1972-77
Schmidt, Milt	Boston	34	15	19	0	4		1954-76
Schoenfeld, Jim	New Jersey	20	11	9	0	1		
	Washington	24	10	14	0	3		
	Phoenix	13	5	8	0	2		
	Total	57	26	31	0	6		1985-99
Shero, Fred	Philadelphia	83	48	35	0	6	2	
	NY Rangers	27	15	12	0	2		
	Total	110	63	47	0	8	2	1971-81
Simpson, Terry	NY Islanders	20	9	11	0	2		
	Winnipeg	6	2	4	0	1		
	Total	26	11	15	0	3		1986-96
Sinden, Harry	Boston	43	24	19	0	5	1	1966-85
Skinner, Jimmy	Detroit	26	14	12	0	3	1	1954-58
Smith, Alf	Ottawa	5	1	4	0	1		1918-19
Smith, Floyd	Buffalo	32	16	16	0	3		1971-80
Smythe, Conn	Toronto	4	2	2	0	1		1927-31
Sonmor, Glen	Minnesota	43	25	18	0	3		1978-87
Stasiuk, Vic	Philadelphia	4	0	4	0	1		1969-73
Stewart, Bill	Chicago	10	7	3	0	1	1	1937-39
Stewart, Ron	Los Angeles	2	0	2	0	1		1975-78
Sutter, Brian	St. Louis	41	20	21	0	4		
	Boston	22	7	15	0	3		
	Chicago	5	1	4	0	1		
	Total	68	28	40	0	8		1988-02
Sutter, Darryl	Chicago	26	11	15	0	3		
	San Jose	42	18	24	0	5		
	Total	68	29	39	0	8		1992-02
Talbot, Jean-Guy	St. Louis	5	1	4	0	1		
	NY Rangers	3	1	2	0	1		
	Total	8	2	6	0	2		1972-78
Tessier, Orval	Chicago	18	9	9	0	2		1982-85
Therrien, Michel	Montreal	12	6	6	0	1		2000-02
Thompson, Paul	Chicago	19	7	12	0	4		1938-45
Tobin, Bill	Chicago	4	1	2	1	2		1929-32
Tremblay, Mario	Montreal	11	3	8	0	2		1995-97
Ubriaco, Gene	Pittsburgh	11	7	4	0	1		1988-90
Vigneault, Alain	Montreal	10	4	6	0	1		1997-01
Watson, Phil	NY Rangers	16	4	12	0	3		1955-63
Watt, Tom	Winnipeg	7	1	6	0	2		
	Vancouver	3	0	3	0	1		
	Total	10	1	9	0	3		1981-92
Webster, Tom	Los Angeles	28	12	16	0	3		1986-92
Weiland, Cooney	Boston	17	10	7	0	2	1	1939-41
White, Bill	Chicago	2	0	2	0	1		1976-77
Wilson, Johnny	Pittsburgh	12	4	8	0	2		1969-80
Wilson, Ron	Anaheim	11	4	7	0	1		
	Washington	32	15	17	0	3		
	Total	43	19	24	0	4		1993-02
Young, Garry	St. Louis	2	0	2	0	1		1972-76

CHAPTER 11
Stanley Cup-Winning Goal Scorers
1918 – 2002

Year	Player, Team	Time of Goal	Period	Score	Series	Year	Player, Team	Time of Goal	Period	Score	Series
2002	Brendan Shanahan, Detroit	14:04	2nd	3-1	4-1	1958	Bernie Geoffrion, Montreal	19:26	2nd	5-3	4-2
2001	Alex Tanguay, Colorado	4:57	2nd	3-1	4-3	1957	Dickie Moore, Montreal	0:14	2nd	5-1	4-1
2000	Jason Arnott, New Jersey	28:20	OT	2-1	4-2	1956	Maurice Richard, Montreal	15:08	2nd	3-1	4-1
1999	Brett Hull, Dallas	54:51	OT	3-2	4-2	1955	Gordie Howe, Detroit	19:49	2nd	3-1	4-3
1998	Martin Lapointe, Detroit	2:26	2nd	4-1	4-0	1954	Tony Leswick, Detroit	4:20	OT	2-1	4-3
1997	Darren McCarty, Detroit	13:02	2nd	2-1	4-0	1953	Elmer Lach, Montreal	1:22	OT	1-0	4-1
1996	Uwe Krupp, Colorado	44:31	OT	1-0	4-0	1952	Metro Prystai, Detroit	6:50	1st	3-0	4-0
1995	Neal Broten, New Jersey	7:56	2nd	5-2	4-0	1951	Bill Barilko, Toronto	2:53	OT	3-2	4-1
1994	Mark Messier, NY Rangers	13:29	2nd	3-2	4-3	1950	Pete Babando, Detroit	28:31	OT	4-3	4-3
1993	Kirk Muller, Montreal	3:51	2nd	4-1	4-1	1949	Cal Gardner, Toronto	19:45	2nd	3-1	4-0
1992	Ron Francis, Pittsburgh	7:59	3rd	6-5	4-0	1948	Harry Watson, Toronto	11:13	1st	7-2	4-0
1991	Ulf Samuelsson, Pittsburgh	2:00	1st	8-0	4-2	1947	Ted Kennedy, Toronto	14:39	3rd	2-1	4-2
1990	Craig Simpson, Edmonton	9:31	2nd	4-1	4-1	1946	Toe Blake, Montreal	11:06	3rd	6-3	4-1
1989	Doug Gilmour, Calgary	11:02	3rd	4-2	4-2	1945	Babe Pratt, Toronto	12:14	3rd	2-1	4-3
1988	Wayne Gretzky, Edmonton	9:44	2nd	6-3	4-0	1944	Toe Blake, Montreal	9:12	OT	5-4	4-0
1987	Jari Kurri, Edmonton	14:59	2nd	3-1	4-3	1943	Joe Carveth, Detroit	12:09	1st	2-0	4-0
1986	Bobby Smith, Montreal	10:30	3rd	4-3	4-1	1942	Pete Langelle, Toronto	9:48	3rd	3-1	4-3
1985	Paul Coffey, Edmonton	17:57	1st	8-3	4-1	1941	Bobby Bauer, Boston	8:43	2nd	3-1	4-0
1984	Ken Linseman, Edmonton	0:38	2nd	5-2	4-1	1940	Bryan Hextall, NY Rangers	2:07	OT	3-2	4-2
1983	Mike Bossy, NY Islanders	12:39	1st	4-2	4-0	1939	Roy Conacher, Boston	17:54	2nd	3-1	4-1
1982	Mike Bossy, NY Islanders	5:00	2nd	3-1	4-0	1938	Carl Voss, Chicago	16:45	2nd	4-3	3-1
1981	Wayne Merrick, NY Islanders	5:37	1st	5-1	4-1	1937	Marty Barry, Detroit	19:22	1st	3-0	3-2
1980	Bob Nystrom, NY Islanders	7:11	OT	5-4	4-2	1936	Pete Kelly, Detroit	9:45	3rd	3-2	3-1
1979	Yvon Lambert, Montreal	1:02	2nd	4-1	4-1	1935	Baldy Northcott, Mtl. Maroons	16:18	2nd	4-1	3-0
1978	Mario Tremblay, Montreal	9:20	1st	4-1	4-2	1934	Mush March, Chicago	30:05	OT	1-0	3-1
1977	Jacques Lemaire, Montreal	4:32	OT	2-1	4-1	1933	Bill Cook, NY Rangers	7:34	OT	1-0	3-1
1976	Guy Lafleur, Montreal	14:18	3rd	5-3	4-0	1932	Ace Bailey, Toronto	15:07	3rd	6-4	3-0
1975	Bob Kelly, Philadelphia	0:11	3rd	2-0	4-2	1931	Johnny Gagnon, Montreal	9:59	2nd	2-0	3-2
1974	Rick MacLeish, Philadelphia	14:48	1st	1-0	4-2	1930	Howie Morenz, Montreal	1:00	2nd	4-3	2-0
1973	Yvan Cournoyer, Montreal	8:13	3rd	6-4	4-2	1929	Bill Carson, Boston	18:02	3rd	2-1	2-0
1972	Bobby Orr, Boston	11:18	1st	3-0	4-2	1928	Frank Boucher, NY Rangers	3:35	3rd	2-1	3-2
1971	Henri Richard, Montreal	2:34	3rd	3-2	4-3	1927	Cy Denneny, Ottawa	7:30	2nd	3-1	2-0
1970	Bobby Orr, Boston	0:40	OT	4-3	4-0	1926	Nels Stewart, Mtl. Maroons	2:50	2nd	2-0	3-1
1969	John Ferguson, Montreal	3:02	3rd	2-1	4-1	1925	Gizzy Hart, Victoria	2:35	2nd	6-1	3-1
1968	J.C. Tremblay, Montreal	11:40	3rd	3-2	4-0	1924	Billy Boucher, Montreal	14:00	3rd	2-1	2-0
1967	Jim Pappin, Toronto	19:24	2nd	3-1	4-2		Howie Morenz, Montreal	4:55	1st	3-0	2-0
1966	Henri Richard, Montreal	2:20	OT	3-2	4-2	1923	Eddie Gerard, Ottawa	17:25	1st	5-1	3-1
1965	Jean Beliveau, Montreal	0:14	1st	4-0	4-3		Punch Broadbent, Ottawa	11:23	1st	1-0	2-0
1964	Andy Bathgate, Toronto	3:04	1st	4-0	4-3	1922	Babe Dye, Toronto	4:20	1st	5-1	3-2
1963	Eddie Shack, Toronto	13:28	3rd	3-1	4-1	1921	Jack Darragh, Ottawa	9:40	2nd	2-1	3-2
1962	Dick Duff, Toronto	14:14	3rd	2-1	4-2	1920	Jack Darragh, Ottawa	5:00	3rd	6-1	3-2
1961	Ab McDonald, Chicago	18:49	2nd	5-1	4-2	1919	— no decision —				
1960	Jean Beliveau, Montreal	8:16	1st	4-0	4-0	1918	Corb Denneny, Toronto	10:30	3rd	2-1	3-2
1959	Marcel Bonin, Montreal	9:55	2nd	5-3	4-1						

CHAPTER 12

Three-Or-More-Goal Games, Playoffs

1918 – 2002

Player	Team	Date	City	Total Goals	Opposing Goaltender	Score	
Wayne Gretzky (10)	Edm.	Apr. 11/81	Edm.	3	Richard Sevigny	Edm. 6	Mtl. 2
		Apr. 19/81	Edm.	3	Billy Smith	Edm. 5	NYI 2
		Apr. 6/83	Edm.	4	Brian Hayward	Edm. 6	Wpg. 3
		Apr. 17/83	Cgy.	4	Reggie Lemelin	Edm.10	Cgy. 2
		Apr. 25/85	Wpg.	3	Brian Hayward (2) Marc Behrend (1)	Edm. 8	Wpg. 3
		May 25/85	Edm.	3	Pelle Lindbergh	Edm. 4	Phi. 3
		Apr. 24/86	Cgy.	3	Mike Vernon	Edm. 7	Cgy. 4
	L.A.	May 29/93	Tor.	3	Felix Potvin	L.A. 5	Tor. 4
	NYR	Apr. 23/97	NYR	3	John Vanbiesbrouck	NYR 3	Fla. 2
		May 18/97	Phi.	3	Garth Snow	NYR 5	Phi. 4
Maurice Richard (7)	Mtl.	Mar. 23/44	Mtl.	5	Paul Bibeault	Mtl. 5	Tor. 1
		Apr. 7/44	Chi.	3	Mike Karakas	Mtl. 3	Chi. 1
		Mar. 29/45	Mtl.	4	Frank McCool	Mtl. 10	Tor. 3
		Apr. 14/53	Bos.	3	Gord Henry	Mtl. 7	Bos. 3
		Mar. 20/56	Mtl.	3	Gump Worsley	Mtl. 7	NYR 1
		Apr. 6/57	Mtl.	4	Don Simmons	Mtl. 5	Bos. 1
		Apr. 1/58	Det.	3	Terry Sawchuk	Mtl. 4	Det. 3
Jari Kurri (7)	Edm.	Apr. 4/84	Edm.	3	Doug Soetaert (1) Mike Veisor (2)	Edm. 9	Wpg. 2
		Apr. 25/85	Wpg.	3	Brian Hayward (2) Marc Behrend (1)	Edm. 8	Wpg. 3
		May 7/85	Edm.	3	Murray Bannerman	Edm. 7	Chi. 3
		May 14/85	Edm.	3	Murray Bannerman	Edm.10	Chi. 5
		May 16/85	Chi.	4	Murray Bannerman	Edm. 8	Chi. 2
		Apr. 9/87	Edm.	4	Roland Melanson (2) Darren Eliot (2)	Edm.13	L.A. 3
		May 18/90	Bos.	3	Andy Moog (2) Reggie Lemelin (1)	Edm. 7	Bos. 2
Dino Ciccarelli (6)	Min.	May 5/81	Min.	3	Pat Riggin	Min. 7	Cgy. 4
		Apr. 10/82	Min.	3	Murray Bannerman	Min. 7	Chi. 1
	Wsh.	Apr. 5/90	N.J.	3	Sean Burke	Wsh. 5	N.J. 4
		Apr. 25/92	Pit.	4	Tom Barrasso (1) Ken Wregget (3)	Wsh. 7	Pit. 2
	Det.	Apr. 29/93	Tor.	3	Felix Potvin (2) Daren Puppa (1)	Det. 7	Tor. 3
		May 11/95	Dal.	3	Andy Moog (2) Darcy Wakaluk (1)	Det. 5	Dal. 1
Mike Bossy (5)	NYI	Apr. 16/79	NYI	3	Tony Esposito	NYI 6	Chi. 2
		May 8/82	NYI	3	Richard Brodeur	NYI 6	Van. 5
		Apr. 10/83	Wsh.	3	Al Jensen	NYI 6	Wsh. 3
		May 3/83	NYI	3	Pete Peeters	NYI 8	Bos. 3
		May 7/83	NYI	4	Pete Peeters	NYI 8	Bos. 4
Phil Esposito (4)	Bos.	Apr. 2/69	Bos.	4	Bruce Gamble	Bos.10	Tor. 0
		Apr. 8/70	Bos.	3	Ed Giacomin	Bos. 8	NYR 2
		Apr. 19/70	Chi.	3	Tony Esposito	Bos. 6	Chi. 3
		Apr. 8/75	Bos.	3	Tony Esposito (2) Michel Dumas (1)	Bos. 8	Chi. 2
Mark Messier (4)	Edm.	Apr. 14/83	Edm.	4	Reggie Lemelin	Edm. 6	Cgy. 3
		Apr. 17/83	Cgy.	3	Reggie Lemelin (1) Don Edwards (2)	Edm.10	Cgy. 2
		Apr. 26/83	Edm.	3	Murray Bannerman	Edm. 8	Chi. 2
	NYR	May 25/94	N.J.	3	Martin Brodeur (2) ENG (1)	NYR 4	N.J. 2
Steve Yzerman (4)	Det.	Apr. 6/89	Det.	3	Alain Chevrier	Chi. 5	Det. 4
		Apr. 4/91	St.L.	3	Vincent Riendeau (2) Pat Jablonski (1)	Det. 6	St.L. 3
		May 8/96	St.L.	3	Jon Casey	St.L. 5	Det. 4
		Apr. 21/99	Det.	3	Guy Hebert (2) Pat Jablonski (1)	Det. 5	Ana. 3
Bernie Geoffrion (3)	Mtl.	Mar. 27/52	Mtl.	3	Jim Henry	Mtl. 4	Bos. 0
		Apr. 7/55	Mtl.	3	Terry Sawchuk	Mtl. 4	Det. 2
		Mar. 30/57	Mtl.	3	Gump Worsley	Mtl. 8	NYR 3
Norm Ullman (3)	Det.	Mar. 29/64	Chi.	3	Glenn Hall	Det. 5	Chi. 4
		Apr. 7/64	Det.	3	Glenn Hall (2) Denis DeJordy (1)	Det. 7	Chi. 2
		Apr. 11/65	Det.	3	Glenn Hall	Det. 4	Chi. 2
John Bucyk (3)	Bos.	May 3/70	St.L.	3	Jacques Plante (1) Ernie Wakely (2)	Bos. 6	St.L. 1
		Apr. 20/72	Bos.	3	Jacques Caron (1) Ernie Wakely (2)	Bos.10	St.L. 2
		Apr. 21/74	Bos.	3	Tony Esposito	Bos. 8	Chi. 6
Rick MacLeish (3)	Phi.	Apr. 11/74	Phi.	3	Phil Myre	Phi. 5	Atl. 1
		Apr. 13/75	Phi.	3	Gord McRae	Phi. 6	Tor. 3
		May 13/75	Phi.	3	Glenn Resch	Phi. 4	NYI 1
Denis Savard (3)	Chi.	Apr. 19/82	Chi.	3	Mike Liut	Chi. 7	St.L. 4
		Apr. 10/86	Chi.	4	Ken Wregget	Tor. 6	Chi. 4
		Apr. 9/88	St.L.	3	Greg Millen	Chi. 6	St.L. 3
Tim Kerr (3)	Phi.	Apr. 13/85	NYR	4	Glen Hanlon	Phi. 6	NYR 5
		Apr. 20/87	Phi.	3	Kelly Hrudey	Phi. 4	NYI 2
		Apr. 19/89	Pit.	3	Tom Barrasso	Phi. 4	Pit. 2
Cam Neely (3)	Bos.	Apr. 9/87	Mtl.	3	Patrick Roy	Mtl. 4	Bos. 3
		Apr. 5/91	Bos.	3	Peter Sidorkiewicz	Bos. 4	Hfd. 3
		Apr. 25/91	Bos.	3	Patrick Roy	Bos. 4	Mtl. 1
Petr Klima (3)	Det.	Apr. 7/88	Tor.	3	Alan Bester (2) Ken Wregett (1)	Det. 6	Tor. 2
		Apr. 21/88	St.L.	3	Greg Millen	Det. 6	St.L. 0
	Edm.	May 4/91	Edm.	3	Jon Casey	Edm. 7	Min. 2
Esa Tikkanen (3)	Edm.	May 22/88	Edm.	3	Reggie Lemelin	Edm. 6	Bos. 3
		Apr. 16/91	Cgy.	3	Mike Vernon	Edm. 5	Cgy. 4
		Apr. 26/92	L.A.	3	Kelly Hrudey (2) Tom Askey (1)	Edm. 5	L.A. 2
Mike Gartner (3)	NYR	Apr. 13/90	NYR	3	Mark Fitzpatrick (2) Glenn Healy (1)	NYR 6	NYI 5
		Apr. 27/92	NYR	3	Chris Terreri	NYR 8	N.J. 5
	Tor.	Apr. 25/96	Tor.	3	Jon Casey	Tor. 5	St.L. 4
Mario Lemieux (3)	Pit.	Apr. 25/89	Pit.	5	Ron Hextall	Pit. 10	Phi. 7
		Apr. 23/92	Pit.	3	Don Beaupre	Pit. 6	Wsh. 4
		May 11/96	Pit.	3	Mike Richter	Pit. 7	NYR 3
Newsy Lalonde (2)	Mtl.	Mar. 1/19	Mtl.	5	Clint Benedict	Mtl. 6	Ott. 3
		Mar. 22/19	Sea.	4	Hap Holmes	Mtl. 4	Sea. 2
Howie Morenz (2)	Mtl.	Mar. 22/24	Mtl.	3	Charlie Reid	Mtl. 6	Cgy.T.1
		Mar. 27/25	Mtl.	3	Hap Holmes	Mtl. 4	Vic. 2
Doug Bentley (2)	Chi.	Mar. 28/44	Chi.	3	Connie Dion	Chi. 7	Det. 1
		Mar. 30/44	Det.	3	Connie Dion	Chi. 5	Det. 2
Toe Blake (2)	Mtl.	Mar. 22/38	Mtl.	3	Mike Karakas	Mtl. 6	Chi. 4
		Mar. 26/46	Chi.	3	Mike Karakas	Mtl. 7	Chi. 2
Ted Kennedy (2)	Tor.	Apr. 14/45	Tor.	3	Harry Lumley	Det. 5	Tor. 3
		Mar. 27/48	Tor.	4	Frank Brimsek	Tor. 5	Bos. 3
F. St. Marseille (2)	St.L.	Apr. 28/70	St.L.	3	Al Smith	St.L. 5	Pit. 0
		Apr. 6/72	Min.	3	Cesare Maniago	Min. 6	St.L. 5
Bobby Hull (2)	Chi.	Apr. 7/63	Det.	3	Terry Sawchuk	Det. 7	Chi. 4
		Apr. 9/72	Pit.	3	Jim Rutherford	Chi. 6	Pit. 5
Pit Martin (2)	Chi.	Apr. 4/73	Chi.	3	Wayne Stephenson	Chi. 7	St.L. 1
		May 10/73	Chi.	3	Ken Dryden	Mtl. 6	Chi. 4
Yvan Cournoyer (2)	Mtl.	Apr. 5/73	Mtl.	3	Dave Dryden	Mtl. 7	Buf. 3
		Apr. 11/74	Mtl.	3	Ed Giacomin	Mtl. 4	NYR 1
Guy Lafleur (2)	Mtl.	May 1/75	Mtl.	3	Roger Crozier (1) Gerry Desjardins (2)	Mtl. 7	Buf. 0
		Apr. 11/77	Mtl.	3	Ed Staniowski	Mtl. 7	St.L. 2
Lanny McDonald (2)	Tor.	Apr. 9/77	Pit.	3	Denis Herron	Tor. 5	Pit. 2
		Apr. 17/77	Tor.	4	Wayne Stephenson	Phi. 6	Tor. 5
Bryan Trottier (2)	NYI	Apr. 8/80	NYI	3	Doug Keans	NYI 8	L.A. 1
		Apr. 9/81	NYI	3	Michel Larocque	NYI 5	Tor. 1
Bill Barber (2)	Phi.	May 4/80	Min.	4	Gilles Meloche	Phi. 5	Min. 3
		Apr. 9/81	Phi.	3	Dan Bouchard	Phi. 8	Que. 5
Butch Goring (2)	L.A.	Apr. 9/77	L.A.	3	Phil Myre	L.A. 4	Atl. 2
	NYI	May 17/81	Min.	3	Gilles Meloche	NYI 7	Min. 5
Paul Reinhart (2)	Cgy	Apr. 14/83	Edm.	3	Andy Moog	Edm. 6	Cgy. 3
		Apr. 8/84	Van.	3	Richard Brodeur	Cgy. 5	Van. 1
Brian Propp (2)	Phi.	Apr. 22/81	Phi.	3	Pat Riggin	Phi. 9	Cgy. 4
		Apr. 21/85	Phi.	3	Billy Smith	Phi. 5	NYI 2
Peter Stastny (2)	Que.	Apr. 5/83	Bos.	3	Pete Peeters	Bos. 4	Que. 3
		Apr. 11/87	Que.	3	Mike Liut (2) Steve Weeks (1)	Que. 5	Hfd. 1
Michel Goulet (2)	Que.	Apr. 23/85	Que.	3	Steve Penney	Que. 7	Mtl. 6
		Apr. 12/87	Que.	3	Mike Liut	Que. 4	Hfd. 1
Glenn Anderson (2)	Edm.	Apr. 26/83	Edm.	4	Murray Bannerman	Edm. 8	Chi. 2
		Apr. 6/88	Wpg.	3	Daniel Berthiaume	Edm. 7	Wpg.4
Peter Zezel (2)	Phi.	Apr. 13/86	NYR	3	John Vanbiesbrouck	Phi. 7	NYR 1
	St.L.	Apr. 11/89	St.L.	3	Jon Casey (2) Kari Takko (1)	St.L. 6	Min. 1
Geoff Courtnall (2)	Van.	Apr. 4/91	L.A.	3	Kelly Hrudey	Van. 6	L.A. 5
		Apr. 30/92	Van.	3	Rick Tabaracci	Van. 5	Win. 0
Joe Sakic (2)	Que.	May 6/95	Que.	3	Mike Richter	Que. 5	NYR 4
	Col.	Apr. 25/96	Col.	3	Corey Hirsch	Col. 5	Van. 4
Daniel Alfredsson (2)	Ott.	Apr. 28/98	Ott.	3	Martin Brodeur	Ott. 4	N.J. 3
		May 11/98	Ott.	3	Olaf Kolzig	Ott. 4	Wsh. 3

Player	Team	Date	City	Total Goals	Opposing Goaltender	Score
Harry Meeking	Tor.	Mar. 11/18	Tor.	3	Georges Vezina	Tor. 7 Mtl. 3
Alf Skinner	Tor.	Mar.23/18	Tor.	3	Hugh Lehman	Van.M.6 Tor. 4
Joe Malone	Mtl.	Feb. 23/19	Mtl.	3	Clint Benedict	Mtl. 8 Ott. 4
Odie Cleghorn	Mtl.	Feb. 27/19	Ott.	3	Clint Benedict	Mtl. 5 Ott. 3
Jack Darragh	Ott.	Apr. 1/20	Tor.	3	Hap Holmes	Ott. 6 Sea. 1
Georges Boucher	Ott.	Mar. 10/21	Ott.	3	Jake Forbes	Ott. 5 Tor. 0
Babe Dye	Tor.	Mar.28/22	Tor.	4	Hugh Lehman	Tor. 5 Van.M.1
Percy Galbraith	Bos.	Mar.31/27	Bos.	3	Hugh Lehman	Bos. 4 Chi. 4
Busher Jackson	Tor.	Apr. 5/32	NYR	3	John Ross Roach	Tor. 6 NYR 4
Frank Boucher	NYR	Apr. 9/32	Tor.	3	Lorne Chabot	Tor. 6 NYR 4
Charlie Conacher	Tor.	Mar.26/36	Tor.	3	Tiny Thompson	Tor. 8 Bos. 3
Syd Howe	Det.	Mar.23/39	Det.	3	Claude Bourque	Det. 7 Mtl. 3
Bryan Hextall	NYR	Apr. 3/40	NYR	3	Turk Broda	NYR 6 Tor. 2
Joe Benoit	Mtl.	Mar.22/41	Mtl.	3	Sam LoPresti	Mtl. 4 Chi. 3
Syl Apps	Tor.	Mar.25/41	Tor.	3	Frank Brimsek	Tor. 7 Bos. 2
Jack McGill	Bos.	Mar.29/42	Bos.	3	Johnny Mowers	Det. 6 Bos. 4
Don Metz	Tor.	Apr. 14/42	Tor.	3	Johnny Mowers	Tor. 9 Det. 3
Mud Bruneteau	Det.	Apr. 1/43	Det.	3	Frank Brimsek	Det. 6 Bos. 2
Don Grosso	Det.	Apr. 7/43	Det.	3	Frank Brimsek	Det. 4 Bos. 0
Carl Liscombe	Det.	Apr. 3/45	Det.	4	Paul Bibeault	Det. 5 Bos. 3
Billy Reay	Mtl.	Apr. 1/47	Bos.	4	Frank Brimsek	Mtl. 5 Bos. 1
Gerry Plamondon	Mtl.	Mar. 24/49	Det.	3	Harry Lumley	Mtl. 4 Det. 3
Sid Smith	Tor.	Apr. 10/49	Det.	3	Harry Lumley	Tor. 3 Det. 1
Pentti Lund	NYR	Apr. 2/50	NYR	3	Bill Durnan	NYR 4 Mtl. 1
Ted Lindsay	Det.	Apr. 5/55	Det.	4	Charlie Hodge (1) Jacques Plante (3)	Det. 7 Mtl. 1
Gordie Howe	Det.	Apr. 10/55	Det.	3	Jacques Plante	Det. 5 Mtl. 1
Phil Goyette	Mtl.	Mar.25/58	Mtl.	3	Terry Sawchuk	Mtl. 8 Det. 1
Jerry Toppazzini	Bos.	Apr. 5/58	Bos.	3	Gump Worsley	Bos. 8 NYR 2
Bob Pulford	Tor.	Apr. 19/62	Tor.	3	Glenn Hall	Tor. 8 Chi. 4
Dave Keon	Tor.	Apr. 9/64	Mtl.	3	Charlie Hodge (2) ENG (1)	Tor. 3 Mtl. 1
Henri Richard	Mtl.	Apr. 20/67	Mtl.	3	Terry Sawchuk (2) Johnny Bower (1)	Mtl. 6 Tor. 2
Rosaire Paiement	Phi.	Apr. 13/68	Phi.	3	Glenn Hall (1) Seth Martin (2)	Phi. 6 St.L. 1
Jean Beliveau	Mtl.	Apr. 20/68	Mtl.	3	Denis DeJordy	Mtl. 4 Chi. 1
Red Berenson	St.L.	Apr. 15/69	St.L.	3	Gerry Desjardins	St.L. 4 L.A. 0
Ken Schinkel	Pit.	Apr. 10/70	Oak.	3	Gary Smith	Pit. 5 Oak. 2
Jim Pappin	Chi.	Apr. 10/71	Phi.	3	Bruce Gamble	Chi. 6 Phi. 2
Bobby Orr	Bos.	Apr. 10/71	Mtl.	3	Ken Dryden	Bos. 5 Mtl. 2
Jacques Lemaire	Mtl.	Apr. 20/71	Mtl.	3	Gump Worsley	Mtl. 7 Min. 2
Vic Hadfield	NYR	Apr. 22/71	NYR	3	Tony Esposito	NYR 4 Chi. 1
Fred Stanfield	Bos.	Apr. 18/72	Bos.	3	Jacques Caron	Bos. 6 St.L. 1
Ken Hodge	Bos.	Apr. 30/72	Bos.	3	Ed Giacomin	Bos. 6 NYR 5
Dick Redmond	Chi.	Apr. 4/73	Chi.	3	Wayne Stephenson	Chi. 7 St.L. 1
Steve Vickers	NYR	Apr. 10/73	Bos.	3	Ross Brooks (2) Eddie Johnston (1)	NYR 6 Bos. 3
Tom Williams	L.A.	Apr. 14/74	L.A.	3	Mike Veisor	L.A. 5 Chi. 1
Marcel Dionne	L.A.	Apr. 15/76	L.A.	3	Gilles Gilbert	L.A. 6 Bos. 4
Don Saleski	Phi.	Apr. 20/76	Phi.	3	Wayne Thomas	Phi. 7 Tor. 1
Darryl Sittler	Tor.	Apr. 22/76	Tor.	5	Bernie Parent	Tor. 8 Phi. 5
Reggie Leach	Phi.	May 6/76	Phi.	5	Gilles Gilbert	Phi. 6 Bos. 3
Jim Lorentz	Buf.	Apr. 7/77	Min.	3	Pete LoPresti (2) Gary Smith (1)	Buf. 7 Min. 1
Bobby Schmautz	Bos.	Apr. 11/77	Bos.	3	Rogie Vachon	Bos. 8 L.A. 3
Billy Harris	NYI	Apr. 23/77	Mtl.	3	Ken Dryden	Mtl. 4 NYI 3
George Ferguson	Tor.	Apr. 11/78	Tor.	3	Rogie Vachon	Tor. 7 L.A. 3
Jean Ratelle	Bos.	May 3/79	Bos.	3	Ken Dryden	Bos. 4 Mtl. 3
Stan Jonathan	Bos.	May 8/79	Bos.	3	Ken Dryden	Bos. 5 Mtl. 2
Ron Duguay	NYR	Apr. 20/80	NYR	3	Pete Peeters	NYR 4 Phi. 2
Steve Shutt	Mtl.	Apr. 22/80	Mtl.	3	Gilles Meloche	Mtl. 6 Min. 2
Gilbert Perreault	Buf.	May 6/80	NYI	3	Billy Smith (2) ENG (1)	Buf. 7 NYI 4
Paul Holmgren	Phi.	May15/80	Phi.	3	Billy Smith	Phi. 8 NYI 3
Steve Payne	Min.	Apr. 8/81	Bos.	3	Rogie Vachon	Min. 5 Bos. 4
Denis Potvin	NYI	Apr. 17/81	NYI	3	Andy Moog	NYI 6 Edm. 3
Barry Pederson	Bos.	Apr. 9/82	Bos.	3	Don Edwards	Bos. 7 Buf. 3
Duane Sutter	NYI	Apr. 15/83	NYI	3	Glen Hanlon	NYI 5 NYR 0
Doug Halward	Van.	Apr. 7/84	Van.	3	Reggie Lemelin (2) Don Edwards (1)	Van. 7 Cgy. 0
Jorgen Pettersson	St.L.	Apr. 8/84	Det.	3	Eddie Mio	St.L. 3 Det. 2
Clark Gillies	NYI	May 12/84	NYI	3	Grant Fuhr	NYI 6 Edm. 1
Ken Linseman	Bos.	Apr. 14/85	Bos.	3	Steve Penney	Bos. 7 Mtl. 6
Dave Andreychuk	Buf.	Apr. 14/85	Buf.	3	Dan Bouchard	Buf. 7 Que. 4
Greg Paslawski	St.L.	Apr. 15/86	Min.	3	Don Beaupre	St.L. 6 Min. 3
Doug Risebrough	Cgy.	May 4/86	Cgy.	3	Rick Wamsley	Cgy. 8 St.L. 2
Mike McPhee	Mtl.	Apr. 11/87	Bos.	3	Doug Keans	Mtl. 5 Bos. 4
John Ogrodnick	Que.	Apr. 14/87	Hfd.	3	Mike Liut	Que. 7 Hfd. 5
Pelle Eklund	Phi.	May 10/87	Mtl.	3	Patrick Roy (1) Brian Hayward (2)	Phi. 6 Mtl. 3
John Tucker	Buf.	Apr. 9/88	Bos.	4	Andy Moog	Buf. 6 Bos. 2
Tony Hrkac	St.L.	Apr. 10/88	St.L.	4	Darren Pang	St.L. 6 Chi. 5
Hakan Loob	Cgy.	Apr. 10/88	Cgy.	3	Glenn Healy	Cgy. 7 L.A. 3
Ed Olczyk	Tor.	Apr. 12/88	Tor.	3	Greg Stefan (2) Glen Hanlon (1)	Tor. 6 Det. 5
Aaron Broten	N.J.	Apr. 20/88	N.J.	3	Pete Peeters	N.J. 5 Wsh. 2
Mark Johnson	N.J.	Apr. 22/88	Wsh.	4	Pete Peeters	N.J. 10 Wsh. 4
Patrik Sundstrom	N.J.	Apr. 22/88	Wsh.	3	Pete Peeters (2) Clint Malarchuk (1)	N.J. 10 Wsh. 4
Bob Brooke	Min.	Apr. 5/89	St.L.	3	Greg Millen	St.L. 4 Min. 3
Chris Kontos	L.A.	Apr. 6/89	L.A.	3	Grant Fuhr	L.A. 5 Edm. 2
Wayne Presley	Chi.	Apr. 13/89	Chi.	3	Greg Stefan (1) Glen Hanlon (2)	Chi. 7 Det. 1
Tony Granato	L.A.	Apr. 10/90	L.A.	3	Mike Vernon (1) Rick Wamsley (2)	L.A. 12 Cgy. 4
Tomas Sandstrom	L.A.	Apr. 10/90	L.A.	3	Mike Vernon (1) Rick Wamsley (2)	L.A. 12 Cgy. 4
Dave Taylor	L.A.	Apr. 10/90	L.A.	3	Mike Vernon (1) Rick Wamsley (2)	L.A. 12 Cgy. 4
Bernie Nicholls	NYR	Apr. 19/90	NYR	3	Mike Liut	NYR 7 Wsh. 3
John Druce	Wsh.	Apr. 21/90	NYR	3	John Vanbiesbrouck	Wsh. 6 NYR 3
Adam Oates	St.L.	Apr. 12/91	St.L.	3	Tim Chevaldae	St.L. 6 Det. 1
Luc Robitaille	L.A.	Apr. 26/91	L.A.	3	Grant Fuhr	L.A. 5 Edm. 2
Ray Sheppard	Det.	Apr. 24/92	Min.	3	Jon Casey	Min. 5 Det. 2
Pavel Bure	Van.	Apr. 28/92	Wpg.	3	Rick Tabaracci	Van. 8 Wpg. 3
Joe Murphy	Edm.	May 6/92	Edm.	3	Kirk McLean	Edm. 5 Van. 2
Ron Francis	Pit.	May 9/92	Pit.	3	Mike Richter (2) John V'brouck (1)	Pit. 5 NYR 4
Kevin Stevens	Pit.	May21/92	Bos.	4	Andy Moog	Pit. 5 Bos. 2
Dirk Graham	Chi.	June 1/92	Chi.	3	Tom Barrasso	Pit. 5 Chi. 4
Brian Noonan	Chi.	Apr. 18/93	Chi.	3	Curtis Joseph	St.L. 4 Chi. 3
Dale Hunter	Wsh.	Apr. 20/93	Wsh.	3	Glenn Healy	NYI 5 Wsh. 3
Teemu Selanne	Wpg.	Apr. 23/93	Wpg.	3	Kirk McLean	Wpg. 5 Van. 4
Ray Ferraro	NYI	Apr. 26/93	Wsh.	3	Don Beaupre	Wsh. 6 NYI 4
Al Iafrate	Wsh.	Apr. 26/93	Wsh.	3	Glenn Healy (2) Mark Fitzpatrick (1)	Wsh. 6 NYI 4
Paul Di Pietro	Mtl.	Apr. 28/93	Mtl.	3	Ron Hextall	Mtl. 6 Que. 2
Wendel Clark	Tor.	May27/93	L.A.	3	Kelly Hrudey	L.A. 5 Tor. 4
Eric Desjardins	Mtl.	Jun. 3/93	Mtl.	3	Kelly Hrudey	Mtl. 3 L.A. 2
Tony Amonte	Chi.	Apr. 23/94	Chi.	4	Felix Potvin	Chi. 5 Tor. 4
Gary Suter	Chi.	Apr. 24/94	Chi.	3	Felix Potvin	Chi. 4 Tor. 3
Ulf Dahlen	S.J.	May 6/94	S.J.	3	Felix Potvin	S.J. 5 Tor. 2
Mike Sullivan	Cgy.	May 11/95	S.J.	3	Arturs Irbe (2) Wade Flaherty (1)	Cgy. 9 S.J. 2
Theoren Fleury	Cgy.	May13/95	S.J.	4	Arturs Irbe (3) ENG (1)	Cgy. 6 S.J. 4
Brendan Shanahan	St.L.	May13/95	Van.	3	Kirk McLean	St.L. 5 Van. 2
John LeClair	Phi.	May21/95	Phi.	3	Mike Richter	Phi. 5 NYR 4
Brian Leetch	NYR	May22/95	Phi.	3	Ron Hextall	Phi. 4 NYR 3
Trevor Linden	Van.	Apr. 25/96	Col.	3	Patrick Roy	Col. 5 Van. 4
Jaromir Jagr	Pit.	May 11/96	Pit.	3	Mike Richter	Pit. 7 NYR 3
Peter Forsberg	Col.	Jun. 6/96	Col.	3	John Vanbiesbrouck	Col. 8 Fla. 1
Valeri Zelepukin	N.J.	Apr. 22/97	Mtl.	3	Jocelyn Thibault	N.J. 6 Mtl. 4
Valeri Kamensky	Col.	Apr. 24/97	Col.	3	Jeff Hackett (2) Chris Terreri (1)	Col. 7 Chi. 0
Eric Lindros	Phi.	May 20/97	NYR	3	Mike Richter	Phi. 6 NYR 3
Matthew Barnaby	Buf.	May 10/98	Buf.	3	Andy Moog (2) ENG (1)	Buf. 6 Mtl. 3
Martin Straka	Pit.	Apr. 25/99	Pit.	3	Martin Brodeur	Pit. 4 N.J. 2
Martin Lapointe	Det.	Apr. 15/00	Det.	3	Stephane Fiset (2) Jamie Storr (1)	Det. 8 L.A. 5
Doug Weight	Edm.	Apr. 16/00	Edm.	3	Ed Belfour	Edm. 5 Dal. 2
Bill Guerin	Edm.	Apr. 18/00	Edm.	3	Ed Belfour	Dal. 4 Edm. 3
Scott Young	St.L.	Apr. 23/00	S.J.	3	Steve Shields	St.L. 5 S.J. 2
Andy Delmore	Phi.	May 7/00	Phi.	3	Ron Tugnutt (2) Peter Skudra (1)	Phi. 6 Pit. 3
Brett Hull	Det.	Apr. 27/02	Det.	3	Peter Skudra	Det. 6 Van. 4
Keith Tkachuk	St.L.	May7/02	St.L.	3	Dominik Hasek	St.L. 6 Det. 1
Darren McCarty	Det.	May18/02	Det.	3	Patrick Roy	Det. 5 Col. 3

CHAPTER 13

Overtime

1918 – 2002

Overtime Record of Current Teams

(Listed by number of OT games played)

	Overall				Home					Road				
Team	GP	W	L	T	GP	W	L	T	Last OT Game	GP	W	L	T	Last OT Game
Montreal	122	70	50	2	57	37	19	1	May 9/02	65	33	31	1	May 8/98
Toronto	101	52	48	1	64	34	29	1	May 28/02	37	18	19	0	May 19/02
Boston	98	38	57	3	45	20	24	1	May 3/98	53	18	33	2	Apr. 30/99
Detroit	72	33	39	0	43	16	27	0	Jun. 4/02	29	17	12	0	Jun. 8/02
NY Rangers	63	30	33	0	27	12	15	0	Apr. 22/97	36	18	18	0	May 11/97
Chicago	62	30	30	2	30	16	13	1	Apr. 20/97	32	14	17	1	May 2/96
Philadelphia	52	25	27	0	24	12	12	0	Apr. 26/02	28	13	15	0	May 4/00
Dallas [1]	50	23	27	0	23	10	13	0	Apr. 19/01	27	13	14	0	May 1/01
St. Louis	49	27	22	0	26	20	6	0	May 18/01	23	7	16	0	May 21/01
Buffalo	46	25	21	0	26	16	10	0	May 10/01	20	9	11	0	May 8/01
Colorado [2]	45	27	18	0	18	9	9	0	May 22/02	27	18	9	0	May 27/02
NY Islanders	38	29	9	0	17	14	3	0	May 20/93	21	15	6	0	May 18/93
Edmonton	38	21	17	0	21	11	10	0	Apr. 17/01	17	10	7	0	Apr. 19/01
Los Angeles	35	17	18	0	19	11	8	0	May 6/01	16	6	10	0	Apr. 25/02
Vancouver	31	14	17	0	13	5	8	0	Apr. 16/01	18	9	9	0	Apr. 17/02
Calgary [3]	30	11	19	0	14	4	10	0	Apr. 23/96	16	7	9	0	Apr. 28/94
Washington	29	14	15	0	10	5	5	0	May 25/98	19	9	10	0	Apr. 23/01
Pittsburgh	28	15	13	0	18	10	8	0	May 8/01	10	5	5	0	May 10/01
New Jersey [4]	27	8	19	0	11	3	8	0	Apr. 28/01	16	5	11	0	Apr. 24/02
Carolina [5]	23	14	9	0	14	9	5	0	Jun. 8/02	9	5	4	0	Jun. 4/02
Phoenix [6]	12	5	7	0	8	3	5	0	May 4/99	4	2	2	0	Apr. 27/93
San Jose	9	3	6	0	5	1	4	0	May 13/02	4	2	2	0	Apr. 16/01
Ottawa	8	3	5	0	4	2	2	0	Apr. 13/01	4	1	3	0	Apr. 16/01
Florida	5	2	3	0	3	1	2	0	Apr. 25/97	2	1	1	0	Apr. 22/97
Anaheim	4	1	3	0	1	0	1	0	May 8/97	3	1	2	0	May 4/97
Tampa Bay	2	2	0	0	1	1	0	0	Apr. 21/96	1	1	0	0	Apr. 18/96

[1] Totals include those of Minnesota North Stars 1968-93.
[2] Totals include those of Quebec Nordiques 1980-95.
[3] Totals include those of Atlanta Flames 1973-80.
[4] Totals include those of Kansas City Scouts and Colorado Rockies 1975-82.
[5] Totals include those of Hartford Whalers 1980-97.
[6] Totals include those of Winnipeg Jets 1980-96.

Ten Longest Overtime Games

Date	City	Series	Score			Scorer	Time	Series Winner
Mar. 24/36	Mtl.	SF	Det. 1	Mtl. M. 0		Mud Bruneteau	116:30	Det.
Apr. 3/33	Tor.	SF	Tor. 1	Bos. 0		Ken Doraty	104:46	Tor.
May 4/00	Pit.	CSF	Phi. 2	Pit. 1		Keith Primeau	92:01	Phi.
Apr. 24/96	Wsh.	CQF	Pit. 3	Wsh. 2		Petr Nedved	79:15	Pit.
Mar. 23/43	Det.	SF	Tor. 3	Det. 2		Jack McLean	70:18	Det.
Mar. 28/30	Mtl.	SF	Mtl. 2	NYR 1		Gus Rivers	68:52	Mtl.
Apr. 18/87	Wsh.	DSF	NYI 3	Wsh. 2		Pat LaFontaine	68:47	NYI
Apr. 27/94	Buf.	CQF	Buf. 1	N.J. 0		Dave Hannan	65:43	N.J.
Mar. 27/51	Det.	SF	Mtl. 3	Det. 2		Maurice Richard	61:09	Mtl.
Mar. 27/38	NYR	QF	NYA 3	NYR 2		Lorne Carr	60:40	NYA

Overtime Games since 1918

Abbreviations: Teams/Cities: Ana. - Anaheim; Atl. - Atlanta Flames; Bos. - Boston; Buf. - Buffalo; Cgy. - Calgary; Chi. - Chicago; Col. - Colorado; Dal. - Dallas; Det. - Detroit; Edm. - Edmonton; Edm. E. - Edmonton Eskimos (Western Canada Hockey League); Fla. - Florida; Hfd. - Hartford; L.A. - Los Angeles; Min. - Minnesota North Stars; Mtl. - Montreal; Mtl. M. - Montreal Maroons; N.J. - New Jersey; NYA - New York Americans; NYI - New York Islanders; NYR - New York Rangers; Oak. - Oakland; Ott. - Ottawa; Phi. - Philadelphia; Phx. - Phoenix; Pit. - Pittsburgh; Que. - Quebec; St.L. - St.Louis; Sea. - Seattle Metropolitans (Pacific Coast Hockey Association); S.J. - San Jose; T.B. - Tampa Bay; Tor. - Toronto; Van. - Vancouver; Van. M. - Vancouver Millionaires (PCHA); Wpg. - Winnipeg; Wsh. - Washington.

SERIES CF - conference final; CQF - conference quarter-final; CSF - conference semi-final; DF - division final; DSF - division semi-final; F - final; PRE - preliminary round; QF - quarter final; SF - semi-final.

NOTE: * - scored series clinching goal (in overtime) in second game of two-game total goals series.

Date	City	Series	Score			Scorer	Time	Series Winner
Mar. 26/19	Sea.	F	Mtl. 0	Sea. 0		no scorer	20:00	no winner
Mar. 30/19	Sea.	F	Mtl. 4	Sea. 0		Odie Cleghorn	15:57	no winner
Mar. 20/22	Tor.	F	Tor 2	Van. M. 1		Babe Dye	4:50	Tor.
Mar. 29/23	Van.	F	Ott. 2	Edm. E. 1		Cy Denneny	2:08	Ott.
Mar. 31/27	Mtl.	QF	Mtl. 1	Mtl. M. 0		Howie Morenz	12:05	Mtl.
Apr. 7/27	Bos.	F	Ott. 0	Bos. 0		no scorer	20:00	Ott.
Apr. 11/27	Ott.	F	Bos. 1	Ott. 1		no scorer	20:00	Ott.
Apr. 3/28	Mtl.	QF	Mtl. M. 1	Mtl. 0		Russell Oatman	8:20	Mtl. M.
Apr. 7/28	Mtl.	F	NYR 2	Mtl. M. 1		Frank Boucher	7:05	NYR

Date	City	Series	Score			Scorer	Time	Series Winner
Mar. 21/29	NYR	QF	NYR 1	NYA 0		Butch Keeling	29:50	NYR
Mar. 26/29	Tor.	SF	NYR 2	Tor. 1		Frank Boucher	2:03	NYR
Mar. 20/30	Mtl.	SF	Bos. 2	Mtl. M. 1		Harry Oliver	45:35	Bos.
Mar. 25/30	Bos.	SF	Mtl. M. 1	Bos. 0		Archie Wilcox	26:27	Bos.
Mar. 26/30	Mtl.	QF	Chi. 2	Mtl. 2		Howie Morenz (Mtl.)*	51:43	Mtl.
Mar. 28/30	Mtl.	SF	Mtl. 2	NYR 1		Gus Rivers	68:52	Mtl.
Mar. 24/31	Bos.	SF	Bos. 5	Mtl. 4		Cooney Weiland	18:56	Mtl.
Mar. 26/31	Chi.	QF	Chi. 2	Tor. 1		Stew Adams	19:20	Chi.
Mar. 28/31	Mtl.	SF	Mtl. 4	Bos. 3		Georges Mantha	5:10	Mtl.
Apr. 1/31	Mtl.	SF	Mtl. 3	Bos. 2		Wildor Larochelle	19:00	Mtl.
Apr. 5/31	Chi.	F	Chi. 2	Mtl. 1		Johnny Gottselig	24:50	Mtl.
Apr. 9/31	Mtl.	F	Chi. 3	Mtl. 2		Cy Wentworth	53:50	Mtl.
Mar. 26/32	Mtl.	SF	NYR 4	Mtl. 3		Fred Cook	59:32	NYR
Apr. 2/32	Tor.	SF	Tor. 3	Mtl. M. 2		Bob Gracie	17:59	Tor.
Mar. 25/33	Bos.	SF	Bos. 2	Tor. 1		Marty Barry	14:14	Tor.
Mar. 28/33	Bos.	SF	Tor. 1	Bos. 0		Busher Jackson	15:03	Tor.
Mar. 30/33	Tor.	SF	Bos. 2	Tor. 1		Eddie Shore	4:23	Tor.
Apr. 3/33	Tor.	SF	Tor. 1	Bos. 0		Ken Doraty	104:46	Tor.
Apr. 13/33	Tor.	F	NYR 1	Tor. 0		Bill Cook	7:33	NYR
Mar. 22/34	Tor.	SF	Det. 2	Tor. 1		Herbie Lewis	1:33	Det.
Mar. 25/34	Chi.	QF	Chi. 1	Mtl. 1		Mush March (Chi.)*	11:05	Chi.
Apr. 3/34	Det.	F	Chi. 2	Det. 1		Paul Thompson	21:10	Chi.
Apr. 10/34	Chi.	F	Chi. 1	Det. 0		Mush March	30:05	Chi.
Mar. 23/35	Bos.	SF	Bos. 1	Tor. 0		Dit Clapper	33:26	Tor.
Mar. 26/35	Chi.	QF	Mtl. M. 1	Chi. 0		Baldy Northcott	4:02	Mtl. M.
Mar. 30/35	Tor.	SF	Tor. 2	Bos. 1		Pep Kelly	1:36	Tor.
Apr. 4/35	Tor.	F	Mtl. M 3	Tor. 2		Dave Trottier	5:28	Mtl. M.
Mar. 24/36	Mtl.	SF	Det. 1	Mtl. M. 0		Mud Bruneteau	116:30	Det.
Apr. 9/36	Tor.	F	Tor. 4	Det. 3		Buzz Boll	0:31	Det.
Mar. 25/37	NYR	QF	NYR 2	Tor. 1		Babe Pratt	13:05	NYR
Apr. 1/37	Mtl.	QF	Det. 2	Mtl. 1		Hec Kilrea	51:49	Det.
Mar. 22/38	NYR	QF	NYA 2	NYR 1		John Sorrell	21:25	NYA
Mar. 24/38	Tor.	SF	Tor. 1	Bos. 0		George Parsons	21:31	Tor.
Mar. 26/38	Mtl.	QF	Chi. 3	Mtl. 2		Paul Thompson	11:49	Chi.
Mar. 27/38	NYR	QF	NYA 3	NYR 2		Lorne Carr	60:40	NYA
Mar. 29/38	Bos.	SF	Tor. 3	Bos. 2		Gordie Drillon	10:04	Tor.
Mar. 31/38	Chi.	SF	Chi. 1	NYA 0		Cully Dahlstrom	33:01	Chi.
Mar. 21/39	NYR	SF	Bos. 2	NYR 1		Mel Hill	59:25	Bos.
Mar. 23/39	Bos.	SF	Bos. 3	NYR 2		Mel Hill	8:24	Bos.
Mar. 26/39	Det.	QF	Det. 1	Mtl. 0		Marty Barry	7:47	Det.
Mar. 30/39	Bos.	SF	NYR 2	Bos. 1		Clint Smith	17:19	Bos.
Apr. 1/39	Tor.	SF	Tor. 5	Det. 4		Gordie Drillon	5:42	Tor.
Apr. 2/39	Bos.	SF	Bos. 2	NYR 1		Mel Hill	48:00	Bos.
Apr. 9/39	Bos.	F	Tor. 3	Bos. 2		Doc Romnes	10:38	Bos.
Mar. 19/40	Det.	QF	Det. 2	NYA 1		Syd Howe	0:25	Det.
Mar. 19/40	Tor.	QF	Tor. 3	Chi. 2		Syl Apps	6:35	Tor.
Apr. 2/40	NYR	F	NYR 2	Tor. 1		Alf Pike	15:30	NYR
Apr. 11/40	Tor.	F	NYR 2	Tor. 1		Muzz Patrick	31:43	NYR
Apr. 13/40	Tor.	F	NYR 3	Tor. 2		Bryan Hextall	2:07	NYR
Mar. 20/41	Det.	QF	Det. 2	NYR 1		Gus Giesebrecht	12:01	Det.
Mar. 22/41	Mtl.	QF	Mtl. 4	Chi. 3		Charlie Sands	34:04	Chi.
Mar. 29/41	Bos.	SF	Tor. 2	Bos. 1		Pete Langelle	17:31	Bos.
Mar. 30/41	Chi.	SF	Det. 2	Chi. 1		Gus Giesebrecht	9:15	Det.
Mar. 22/42	Chi.	QF	Bos. 2	Chi. 1		Des Smith	6:51	Bos.
Mar. 21/43	Bos.	SF	Bos. 5	Mtl. 4		Don Gallinger	12:30	Bos.
Mar. 23/43	Det.	SF	Tor. 3	Det. 2		Jack McLean	70:18	Det.
Mar. 25/43	Mtl.	SF	Bos. 3	Mtl. 2		Busher Jackson	3:20	Bos.
Mar. 30/43	Tor.	SF	Det. 3	Tor. 2		Adam Brown	9:21	Det.
Mar. 30/43	Bos.	SF	Bos. 5	Det. 4		Ab DeMarco	3:41	Bos.
Apr. 13/44	Mtl.	F	Mtl. 5	Chi. 4		Toe Blake	9:12	Mtl.
Mar. 27/45	Tor.	SF	Tor. 4	Mtl. 3		Gus Bodnar	12:36	Tor.
Mar. 29/45	Det.	SF	Det. 3	Bos. 2		Mud Bruneteau	17:12	Det.
Apr. 21/45	Tor.	F	Det. 1	Tor. 0		Ed Bruneteau	14:16	Tor.
Mar. 28/46	Bos.	SF	Bos. 4	Det. 3		Don Gallinger	9:51	Bos.
Mar. 30/46	Mtl.	F	Mtl. 4	Bos. 3		Maurice Richard	9:08	Mtl.
Apr. 2/46	Mtl.	F	Mtl. 3	Bos. 2		Jimmy Peters	16:55	Mtl.
Apr. 7/46	Bos.	F	Bos. 3	Mtl. 2		Terry Reardon	15:13	Mtl.
Mar. 26/47	Tor.	SF	Tor. 3	Det. 2		Howie Meeker	3:05	Tor.
Mar. 27/47	Mtl.	SF	Mtl. 2	Bos. 1		Ken Mosdell	5:38	Mtl.
Apr. 3/47	Mtl.	SF	Mtl. 4	Bos. 3		John Quilty	36:40	Mtl.
Apr. 15/47	Tor.	F	Tor. 2	Mtl. 1		Syl Apps	16:36	Tor.
Mar. 24/48	Tor.	SF	Tor. 5	Bos. 4		Nick Metz	17:03	Tor.
Mar. 22/49	Det.	SF	Det. 2	Mtl. 1		Max McNab	44:52	Det.
Mar. 24/49	Det.	SF	Mtl. 4	Det. 3		Gerry Plamondon	2:59	Det.
Mar. 26/49	Tor.	SF	Bos. 5	Tor. 4		Woody Dumart	16:14	Tor.

Date	City	Series	Score		Scorer	Time	Series Winner
Apr. 8/49	Det.	F	Tor. 3	Det. 2	Joe Klukay	17:31	Tor.
Apr. 4/50	Tor.	SF	Det. 2	Tor. 1	Leo Reise Jr.	20:38	Det.
Apr. 4/50	Mtl.	SF	Mtl. 3	NYR 2	Elmer Lach	15:19	NYR
Apr. 9/50	Det.	SF	Det. 1	Tor. 0	Leo Reise Jr.	8:39	Det.
Apr. 18/50	Det.	F	NYR 4	Det. 3	Don Raleigh	8:34	Det.
Apr. 20/50	Det.	F	NYR 2	Det. 1	Don Raleigh	1:38	Det.
Apr. 23/50	Det.	F	Det. 4	NYR 3	Pete Babando	28:31	Det.
Mar. 27/51	Det.	SF	Mtl. 3	Det. 2	Maurice Richard	61:09	Mtl.
Mar. 29/51	Det.	SF	Mtl. 1	Det. 0	Maurice Richard	42:20	Mtl.
Mar. 31/51	Tor.	SF	Bos. 1	Tor. 1	no scorer	20:00	Tor.
Apr. 11/51	Tor.	F	Tor. 3	Mtl. 2	Sid Smith	5:51	Tor.
Apr. 14/51	Tor.	F	Mtl. 3	Tor. 2	Maurice Richard	2:55	Tor.
Apr. 17/51	Mtl.	F	Tor. 2	Mtl. 1	Ted Kennedy	4:47	Tor.
Apr. 19/51	Mtl.	F	Tor. 3	Mtl. 2	Harry Watson	5:15	Tor.
Apr. 21/51	Tor.	F	Tor. 3	Mtl. 2	Bill Barilko	2:53	Tor.
Apr. 6/52	Bos.	SF	Mtl. 3	Bos. 2	Paul Masnick	27:49	Mtl.
Mar. 29/53	Bos.	SF	Bos. 2	Det. 1	Jack McIntyre	12:29	Bos.
Mar. 29/53	Chi.	SF	Chi. 2	Mtl. 1	Al Dewsbury	5:18	Mtl.
Apr. 16/53	Mtl.	F	Mtl. 1	Bos. 0	Elmer Lach	1:22	Mtl.
Apr. 1/54	Det.	SF	Det. 4	Tor. 3	Ted Lindsay	21:01	Det.
Apr. 11/54	Det.	F	Mtl. 1	Det. 0	Ken Mosdell	5:45	Det.
Apr. 16/54	Det.	F	Det. 2	Mtl. 1	Tony Leswick	4:29	Det.
Mar. 29/55	Bos.	SF	Mtl. 4	Bos. 3	Don Marshall	3:05	Mtl.
Mar. 24/56	Tor.	SF	Det. 5	Tor. 4	Ted Lindsay	4:22	Det.
Mar. 28/57	NYR	SF	NYR 4	Mtl. 3	Andy Hebenton	13:38	Mtl.
Apr. 4/57	Mtl.	SF	Mtl. 4	NYR 3	Maurice Richard	1:11	Mtl.
Mar. 27/58	NYR	SF	Bos. 4	NYR 3	Jerry Toppazzini	4:46	Bos.
Mar. 30/58	Det.	SF	Mtl. 2	Det. 1	André Pronovost	11:52	Mtl.
Apr. 17/58	Mtl.	F	Mtl. 3	Bos. 2	Maurice Richard	5:45	Mtl.
Mar. 28/59	Tor.	SF	Tor. 3	Bos. 2	Gerry Ehman	5:02	Tor.
Mar. 31/59	Tor.	SF	Tor. 3	Bos. 2	Frank Mahovlich	11:21	Tor.
Apr. 14/59	Tor.	F	Tor. 3	Mtl. 2	Dick Duff	10:06	Mtl.
Mar. 26/60	Mtl.	SF	Mtl. 4	Chi. 3	Doug Harvey	8:38	Mtl.
Mar. 27/60	Det.	SF	Tor. 5	Det. 4	Frank Mahovlich	43:00	Tor.
Mar. 29/60	Det.	SF	Det. 2	Tor. 1	Gerry Melnyk	1:54	Tor.
Mar. 22/61	Tor.	SF	Tor. 3	Det. 2	George Armstrong	24:51	Det.
Mar. 26/61	Chi.	SF	Chi. 2	Mtl. 1	Murray Balfour	52:12	Chi.
Apr. 5/62	Tor.	SF	Tor. 3	NYR 2	Red Kelly	24:23	Tor.
Apr. 2/64	Det.	SF	Chi. 3	Det. 2	Murray Balfour	8:21	Det.
Apr. 14/64	Tor.	F	Det. 4	Tor. 3	Larry Jeffrey	7:52	Tor.
Apr. 23/64	Det.	F	Tor. 4	Det. 3	Bob Baun	1:43	Tor.
Apr. 6/65	Tor.	SF	Tor. 3	Mtl. 2	Dave Keon	4:17	Mtl.
Apr. 13/65	Tor.	SF	Mtl. 4	Tor. 3	Claude Provost	16:33	Mtl.
May 5/66	Det.	F	Mtl. 3	Det. 2	Henri Richard	2:20	Mtl.
Apr. 13/67	NYR	SF	Mtl. 2	NYR 1	John Ferguson	6:28	Mtl.
Apr. 25/67	Tor.	F	Tor. 3	Mtl. 2	Bob Pulford	28:26	Tor.
Apr. 10/68	St.L.	QF	St.L. 3	Phi. 2	Larry Keenan	24:10	St.L.
Apr. 16/68	St.L.	QF	Phi. 2	St.L. 1	Don Blackburn	31:18	St.L.
Apr. 16/68	Min.	QF	Min. 4	L.A. 3	Milan Marcetta	9:11	Min.
Apr. 22/68	Min.	SF	Min. 3	St.L. 2	Parker MacDonald	3:41	St.L.
Apr. 27/68	St.L.	SF	St.L. 4	Min. 3	Gary Sabourin	1:32	St.L.
Apr. 28/68	Mtl.	SF	Mtl. 4	Chi. 3	Jacques Lemaire	2:14	Mtl.
Apr. 29/68	St.L.	SF	St.L. 3	Min. 2	Bill McCreary	17:27	St.L.
May 3/68	St.L.	SF	St.L. 2	Min. 1	Ron Schock	22:50	St.L.
May 5/68	St.L.	F	Mtl. 3	St.L. 2	Jacques Lemaire	1:41	Mtl.
May 9/68	Mtl.	F	Mtl. 4	St.L. 3	Bobby Rousseau	1:13	Mtl.
Apr. 2/69	Oak.	QF	L.A. 5	Oak. 4	Ted Irvine	0:19	L.A.
Apr. 10/69	Mtl.	SF	Mtl. 3	Bos. 2	Ralph Backstrom	0:42	Mtl.
Apr. 13/69	Mtl.	SF	Mtl. 4	Bos. 3	Mickey Redmond	4:55	Mtl.
Apr. 24/69	Bos.	SF	Mtl. 2	Bos. 1	Jean Béliveau	31:28	Mtl.
Apr. 12/70	Oak.	QF	Pit. 3	Oak. 2	Michel Briere	8:28	Pit.
May 10/70	Bos.	F	Bos. 4	St.L. 3	Bobby Orr	0:40	Bos.
Apr. 15/71	Tor.	QF	NYR 2	Tor. 1	Bob Nevin	9:07	NYR
Apr. 18/71	Chi.	SF	NYR 2	Chi. 1	Pete Stemkowski	1:37	Chi.
Apr. 27/71	Chi.	SF	Chi. 3	NYR 2	Bobby Hull	6:35	Chi.
Apr. 29/71	NYR	SF	NYR 3	Chi. 2	Pete Stemkowski	41:29	Chi.
May 4/71	Chi.	F	Chi. 2	Mtl. 1	Jim Pappin	21:11	Mtl.
Apr. 6/72	Bos.	QF	Tor. 4	Bos. 3	Jim Harrison	2:58	Bos.
Apr. 6/72	Min.	QF	Min. 6	St.L. 5	Bill Goldsworthy	1:36	St.L.
Apr. 9/72	Pit.	QF	Chi. 6	Pit. 5	Pit Martin	0:12	Chi.
Apr. 16/72	Min.	QF	St.L. 2	Min. 1	Kevin O'Shea	10:07	St.L.
Apr. 1/73	Mtl.	QF	Buf. 3	Mtl. 2	René Robert	9:18	Mtl.
Apr. 10/73	Phi.	QF	Phi. 3	Min. 2	Gary Dornhoefer	8:35	Phi.
Apr. 14/73	Mtl.	SF	Phi. 5	Mtl. 4	Rick MacLeish	2:56	Mtl.
Apr. 17/73	Mtl.	SF	Mtl. 4	Phi. 3	Larry Robinson	6:45	Mtl.
Apr. 14/74	Tor.	QF	Bos. 4	Tor. 3	Ken Hodge	1:27	Bos.
Apr. 14/74	Atl.	QF	Phi. 4	Atl. 3	Dave Schultz	5:40	Phi.
Apr. 16/74	Mtl.	QF	NYR 3	Mtl. 2	Ron Harris	4:07	NYR
Apr. 23/74	Chi.	SF	Chi. 4	Bos. 3	Jim Pappin	3:48	Bos.
Apr. 28/74	NYR	SF	NYR 2	Phi. 1	Rod Gilbert	4:20	Phi.
May 9/74	Bos.	F	Phi. 3	Bos. 2	Bobby Clarke	12:01	Phi.
Apr. 8/75	L.A.	PRE	L.A. 3	Tor. 2	Mike Murphy	8:53	Tor.
Apr. 10/75	Tor.	PRE	Tor. 3	L.A. 2	Blaine Stoughton	10:19	Tor.
Apr. 10/75	Chi.	PRE	Chi. 4	Bos. 3	Ivan Boldirev	7:33	Chi.
Apr. 11/75	NYR	PRE	NYI 4	NYR 3	J.P. Parise	0:11	NYI
Apr. 17/75	Chi.	QF	Chi. 5	Buf. 4	Stan Mikita	2:31	Buf.
Apr. 19/75	Tor.	QF	Phi. 4	Tor. 3	André Dupont	1:45	Phi.
Apr. 22/75	Mtl.	QF	Mtl. 5	Van. 4	Guy Lafleur	17:06	Mtl.
Apr. 27/75	Buf.	SF	Buf. 6	Mtl. 5	Danny Gare	4:42	Buf.
May 1/75	Phi.	SF	Phi. 5	NYI 4	Bobby Clarke	2:56	Phi.
May 6/75	Buf.	SF	Buf. 5	Mtl. 4	René Robert	5:56	Buf.
May 7/75	NYI	SF	NYI 4	Phi. 3	Jude Drouin	1:53	Phi.
May 20/75	Buf.	F	Buf. 5	Phi. 4	René Robert	18:29	Phi.
Apr. 8/76	Buf.	PRE	Buf. 3	St.L. 2	Danny Gare	11:43	Buf.
Apr. 9/76	Buf.	PRE	Buf. 2	St.L. 1	Don Luce	14:27	Buf.
Apr. 13/76	Bos.	QF	L.A. 3	Bos. 2	Butch Goring	0:27	Bos.
Apr. 13/76	Buf.	QF	Buf. 3	NYI 2	Danny Gare	14:04	NYI
Apr. 22/76	L.A.	QF	L.A. 4	Bos. 3	Butch Goring	18:28	Bos.
Apr. 29/76	Phi.	SF	Phi. 2	Bos. 1	Reggie Leach	13:38	Phi.
Apr. 15/77	Tor.	QF	Phi. 4	Tor. 3	Rick MacLeish	2:55	Phi.
Apr. 17/77	Tor.	QF	Phi. 6	Tor. 5	Reggie Leach	19:10	Phi.
Apr. 24/77	Phi.	SF	Bos. 4	Phi. 3	Rick Middleton	2:57	Bos.
Apr. 26/77	Phi.	SF	Bos. 5	Phi. 4	Terry O'Reilly	30:07	Bos.
May 3/77	Mtl.	SF	NYI 4	Mtl. 3	Billy Harris	3:58	Mtl.
May 14/77	Bos.	F	Mtl. 2	Bos. 1	Jacques Lemaire	4:32	Mtl.
Apr. 11/78	Phi.	PRE	Phi. 3	Col. 2	Mel Bridgman	0:23	Phi.
Apr. 13/78	NYR	PRE	NYR 4	Buf. 3	Don Murdoch	1:37	Buf.
Apr. 19/78	Bos.	QF	Bos. 4	Chi. 3	Terry O'Reilly	1:50	Bos.
Apr. 19/78	NYI	QF	NYI 3	Tor. 2	Mike Bossy	2:50	Tor.
Apr. 21/78	Chi.	QF	Bos. 4	Chi. 3	Peter McNab	10:17	Bos.
Apr. 25/78	NYI	QF	NYI 2	Tor. 1	Bob Nystrom	8:02	Tor.
Apr. 29/78	NYI	QF	Tor. 2	NYI 1	Lanny McDonald	4:13	Tor.
May 2/78	Bos.	SF	Bos. 3	Phi. 2	Rick Middleton	1:43	Bos.
May 16/78	Mtl.	F	Mtl. 3	Bos. 2	Guy Lafleur	13:09	Mtl.
May 21/78	Bos.	F	Bos. 4	Mtl. 3	Bobby Schmautz	6:22	Mtl.
Apr. 12/79	L.A.	PRE	NYR 2	L.A. 1	Phil Esposito	6:11	NYR
Apr. 14/79	Buf.	PRE	Pit. 4	Buf. 3	George Ferguson	0:47	Pit.
Apr. 16/79	Phi.	QF	Phi. 3	NYR 2	Ken Linseman	0:44	NYR
Apr. 18/79	NYI	QF	NYI 1	Chi. 0	Mike Bossy	2:31	NYI
Apr. 21/79	Tor.	QF	Mtl. 4	Tor. 3	Cam Connor	25:25	Mtl.
Apr. 22/79	Tor.	QF	Mtl. 5	Tor. 4	Larry Robinson	4:14	Mtl.
Apr. 28/79	NYI	SF	NYI 4	NYR 3	Denis Potvin	8:02	NYR
May 3/79	NYR	SF	NYI 3	NYR 2	Bob Nystrom	3:40	NYR
May 3/79	Bos.	SF	Bos. 4	Mtl. 3	Jean Ratelle	3:46	Mtl.
May 10/79	Mtl.	SF	Mtl. 5	Bos. 4	Yvon Lambert	9:33	Mtl.
May 19/79	NYR	F	Mtl. 4	NYR 3	Serge Savard	7:25	Mtl.
Apr. 8/80	NYR	PRE	NYR 2	Atl. 1	Steve Vickers	0:33	NYR
Apr. 8/80	Phi.	PRE	Phi. 4	Edm. 3	Bobby Clarke	8:06	Phi.
Apr. 8/80	Chi.	PRE	Chi. 3	St.L. 2	Doug Lecuyer	12:34	Chi.
Apr. 11/80	Hfd.	PRE	Mtl. 4	Hfd. 3	Yvon Lambert	0:29	Mtl.
Apr. 11/80	Tor.	PRE	Min. 4	Tor. 3	Al MacAdam	0:32	Min.
Apr. 11/80	L.A.	PRE	NYI 4	L.A. 3	Ken Morrow	6:55	NYI
Apr. 11/80	Edm.	PRE	Phi. 3	Edm. 2	Ken Linseman	23:56	Phi.
Apr. 16/80	Bos.	QF	NYI 2	Bos. 1	Clark Gillies	1:02	NYI
Apr. 17/80	Bos.	QF	NYI 5	Bos. 4	Bob Bourne	1:24	NYI
Apr. 21/80	NYI	QF	Bos. 4	NYI 3	Terry O'Reilly	17:13	NYI
May 1/80	Buf.	SF	NYI 2	Buf. 1	Bob Nystrom	21:20	NYI
May 13/80	Phi.	F	NYI 4	Phi. 3	Denis Potvin	4:07	NYI
May 24/80	NYI	F	NYI 5	Phi. 4	Bob Nystrom	7:11	NYI
Apr. 8/81	Buf.	PRE	Buf. 3	Van. 2	Alan Haworth	5:00	Buf.
Apr. 8/81	Bos.	PRE	Min. 5	Bos. 4	Steve Payne	3:34	Min.
Apr. 11/81	Chi.	PRE	Cgy. 5	Chi. 4	Willi Plett	35:17	Cgy.
Apr. 12/81	Que.	PRE	Que. 4	Phi. 3	Dale Hunter	0:37	Phi.
Apr. 14/81	St.L.	PRE	St.L. 4	Pit. 3	Mike Crombeen	25:16	St.L.
Apr. 16/81	Buf.	QF	Min. 4	Buf. 3	Steve Payne	0:22	Min.
Apr. 20/81	Min.	QF	Buf. 5	Min. 4	Craig Ramsay	16:32	Min.
Apr. 20/81	Edm.	QF	NYI 5	Edm. 4	Ken Morrow	5:41	NYI
Apr. 7/82	Min.	DSF	Chi. 3	Min. 2	Greg Fox	3:34	Chi.
Apr. 8/82	Edm.	DSF	Edm. 3	L.A. 2	Wayne Gretzky	6:20	L.A.
Apr. 8/82	Van.	DSF	Van. 2	Cgy. 1	Tiger Williams	14:20	Van.
Apr. 10/82	Pit.	DSF	Pit. 2	NYI 1	Rick Kehoe	4:14	NYI
Apr. 10/82	L.A.	DSF	L.A. 6	Edm. 5	Daryl Evans	2:35	L.A.
Apr. 13/82	Mtl.	DSF	Que. 3	Mtl. 2	Dale Hunter	0:22	Que.
Apr. 13/82	NYI	DSF	NYI 4	Pit. 3	John Tonelli	6:19	NYI
Apr. 16/82	Van.	DF	L.A. 3	Van. 2	Steve Bozek	4:33	Van.
Apr. 18/82	Que.	DF	Que. 3	Bos. 2	Wilf Paiement	11:44	Que.
Apr. 18/82	NYR	DF	NYI 4	NYR 3	Bryan Trottier	3:00	NYI
Apr. 18/82	L.A.	DF	Van. 4	L.A. 3	Colin Campbell	1:23	Van.
Apr. 21/82	St.L.	DF	St.L. 3	Chi. 2	Bernie Federko	3:28	Chi.
Apr. 23/82	Que.	DF	Bos. 6	Que. 5	Peter McNab	10:54	Que.
Apr. 27/82	Chi.	CF	Van. 2	Chi. 1	Jim Nill	28:58	Van.
May 1/82	Que.	CF	NYI 5	Que. 4	Wayne Merrick	16:52	NYI
May 8/82	NYI	F	NYI 6	Van. 5	Mike Bossy	19:58	NYI
Apr. 5/83	Bos.	DSF	Bos. 4	Que. 3	Barry Pederson	1:46	Bos.
Apr. 6/83	Cgy.	DSF	Cgy. 4	Van. 3	Eddy Beers	12:27	Cgy.
Apr. 7/83	Min.	DSF	Min. 5	Tor. 4	Bobby Smith	5:03	Min.
Apr. 10/83	Tor.	DSF	Min. 5	Tor. 4	Dino Ciccarelli	8:05	Min.
Apr. 10/83	Van.	DSF	Cgy. 4	Van. 3	Greg Meredith	1:06	Cgy.
Apr. 18/83	Min.	DF	Chi. 4	Min. 3	Rich Preston	10:34	Chi.
Apr. 24/83	Bos.	DF	Bos. 3	Buf. 2	Brad Park	1:52	Bos.
Apr. 5/84	Edm.	DSF	Edm. 5	Wpg. 4	Randy Gregg	0:21	Edm.
Apr. 7/84	Det.	DSF	St.L. 4	Det. 3	Mark Reeds	37:07	St.L.
Apr. 8/84	Det.	DSF	St.L. 3	Det. 2	Jorgen Pettersson	2:42	St.L.
Apr. 10/84	NYI	DSF	NYI 3	NYR 2	Ken Morrow	8:56	NYI

Date	City	Series	Score		Scorer	Time	Series Winner
Apr. 13/84	Min.	DF	St.L. 4	Min. 3	Doug Gilmour	16:16	Min.
Apr. 13/84	Edm.	DF	Cgy. 6	Edm. 5	Carey Wilson	3:42	Edm.
Apr. 13/84	NYI	DF	NYI 5	Wsh. 4	Anders Kallur	7:35	NYI
Apr. 16/84	Mtl.	DF	Que. 4	Mtl. 3	Bo Berglund	3:00	Mtl.
Apr. 20/84	Cgy.	DF	Cgy. 5	Edm. 4	Lanny McDonald	1:04	Edm.
Apr. 22/84	Min.	DF	Min. 4	St.L. 3	Steve Payne	6:00	Min.
Apr. 10/85	Phi.	DSF	Phi. 5	NYR 4	Mark Howe	8:01	Phi.
Apr. 10/85	Wsh.	DSF	Wsh. 4	NYI 3	Alan Haworth	2:28	NYI
Apr. 10/85	Edm.	DSF	Edm. 3	L.A. 2	Lee Fogolin Jr.	3:01	Edm.
Apr. 10/85	Wpg.	DSF	Wpg. 5	Cgy. 4	Brian Mullen	7:56	Wpg.
Apr. 11/85	Wsh.	DSF	Wsh. 2	NYI 1	Mike Gartner	21:23	NYI
Apr. 13/85	L.A.	DSF	Edm. 4	L.A. 3	Glenn Anderson	0:46	Edm.
Apr. 18/85	Mtl.	DF	Que. 2	Mtl. 1	Mark Kumpel	12:23	Que.
Apr. 23/85	Que.	DF	Que. 7	Mtl. 6	Dale Hunter	18:36	Que.
Apr. 25/85	Min.	DF	Chi. 7	Min. 6	Darryl Sutter	21:57	Chi.
Apr. 28/85	Chi.	DF	Min. 5	Chi. 4	Dennis Maruk	1:14	Chi.
Apr. 30/85	Min.	DF	Chi. 6	Min. 5	Darryl Sutter	15:41	Chi.
May 2/85	Mtl.	DF	Que. 3	Mtl. 2	Peter Stastny	2:22	Que.
May 5/85	Que.	CF	Que. 2	Phi. 1	Peter Stastny	6:20	Phi.
Apr. 9/86	Que.	DSF	Hfd. 3	Que. 2	Sylvain Turgeon	2:36	Hfd.
Apr. 12/86	Wpg.	DSF	Cgy. 4	Wpg. 3	Lanny McDonald	8:25	Cgy.
Apr. 17/86	Wsh.	DF	NYR 4	Wsh. 3	Brian MacLellan	1:16	NYR
Apr. 20/86	Edm.	DF	Edm. 6	Cgy. 5	Glenn Anderson	1:04	Cgy.
Apr. 23/86	Hfd.	DF	Hfd. 2	Mtl. 1	Kevin Dineen	1:07	Mtl.
Apr. 23/86	NYR	DF	NYR 6	Wsh. 5	Bob Brooke	2:40	NYR
Apr. 26/86	St L.	DF	St L. 4	Tor. 3	Mark Reeds	7:11	StL.
Apr. 29/86	Mtl.	DF	Mtl. 2	Hfd. 1	Claude Lemieux	5:55	Mtl.
May 5/86	NYR	CF	Mtl. 4	NYR 3	Claude Lemieux	9:41	Mtl.
May 12/86	St L.	CF	St L. 6	Cgy. 5	Doug Wickenheiser	7:30	Cgy.
May 18/86	Cgy.	F	Mtl. 3	Cgy. 2	Brian Skrudland	0:09	Mtl.
Apr. 8/87	Hfd.	DSF	Hfd. 3	Que. 2	Paul MacDermid	2:20	Que.
Apr. 9/87	Mtl.	DSF	Mtl. 4	Bos. 3	Mats Naslund	2:38	Mtl.
Apr. 9/87	St.L.	DSF	Tor. 3	St.L. 2	Rick Lanz	10:17	Tor.
Apr. 11/87	Wpg.	DSF	Cgy. 3	Wpg. 2	Mike Bullard	3:53	Wpg.
Apr. 11/87	Chi.	DSF	Det. 4	Chi. 3	Shawn Burr	4:51	Det.
Apr. 16/87	Que.	DSF	Que. 5	Hfd. 4	Peter Stastny	6:05	Que.
Apr. 18/87	Wsh.	DSF	NYI 3	Wsh. 2	Pat LaFontaine	68:47	NYI
Apr. 21/87	Edm.	DF	Edm. 3	Wpg. 2	Glenn Anderson	0:36	Edm
Apr. 26/87	Que.	DF	Mtl. 3	Que. 2	Mats Naslund	5:30	Mtl.
Apr. 27/87	Tor.	DF	Tor. 3	Det. 2	Mike Allison	9:31	Det.
May 4/87	Phi.	CF	Phi. 4	Mtl. 3	Ilkka Sinisalo	9:11	Phi.
May 20/87	Edm.	F	Edm. 3	Phi. 2	Jari Kurri	6:50	Edm.
Apr. 6/88	NYI	DSF	NYI 4	N.J. 3	Pat LaFontaine	6:11	N.J.
Apr. 10/88	Phi.	DSF	Phi. 5	Wsh. 4	Murray Craven	1:18	Wsh.
Apr. 10/88	N.J.	DSF	NYI 5	N.J. 4	Brent Sutter	15:07	N.J.
Apr. 10/88	Buf.	DSF	Buf. 6	Bos. 5	John Tucker	5:32	Bos.
Apr. 12/88	Det.	DSF	Tor. 6	Det. 5	Ed Olczyk	0:34	Det.
Apr. 16/88	Wsh.	DSF	Wsh. 5	Phi. 4	Dale Hunter	5:57	Wsh.
Apr. 21/88	Cgy.	DF	Edm. 5	Cgy. 4	Wayne Gretzky	7:54	Edm.
May 4/88	Bos.	CF	N.J. 3	Bos. 2	Doug Brown	17:46	Bos.
May 9/88	Det.	CF	Edm. 4	Det. 3	Jari Kurri	11:02	Edm.
Apr. 5/89	St.L.	DSF	St.L. 4	Min. 3	Brett Hull	11:55	St.L.
Apr. 5/89	Cgy.	DSF	Van. 4	Cgy. 3	Paul Reinhart	2:47	Cgy.
Apr. 6/89	St.L.	DSF	St.L. 4	Min. 3	Rick Meagher	5:30	St.L.
Apr. 6/89	Det.	DSF	Chi. 5	Det. 4	Duane Sutter	14:36	Chi.
Apr. 8/89	Hfd.	DSF	Mtl. 5	Hfd. 4	Stephane Richer	5:01	Mtl.
Apr. 8/89	Phi.	DSF	Wsh. 4	Phi. 3	Kelly Miller	0:51	Phi.
Apr. 9/89	Hfd.	DSF	Mtl. 4	Hfd. 3	Russ Courtnall	15:12	Mtl.
Apr. 15/89	Cgy.	DSF	Cgy. 4	Van. 3	Joel Otto	19:21	Cgy.
Apr. 18/89	Cgy.	DF	Cgy. 4	L.A. 3	Doug Gilmour	7:47	Cgy.
Apr. 19/89	Mtl.	DF	Mtl. 3	Bos. 2	Bobby Smith	12:24	Mtl.
Apr. 20/89	St.L.	DF	St.L. 5	Chi. 4	Tony Hrkac	33:49	Chi.
Apr. 21/89	Phi.	DF	Pit. 4	Phi. 3	Phil Bourque	12:08	Phi.
May 8/89	Chi.	CF	Cgy. 2	Chi. 1	Al MacInnis	15:05	Cgy.
May 9/89	Mtl.	CF	Phi. 2	Mtl. 1	Dave Poulin	5:02	Mtl.
May 19/89	Mtl.	F	Mtl. 4	Cgy. 3	Ryan Walter	38:08	Cgy.
Apr. 5/90	N.J.	DSF	Wsh. 5	N.J. 4	Dino Ciccarelli	5:34	Wsh.
Apr. 6/90	Edm.	DSF	Edm. 3	Wpg. 2	Mark Lamb	4:21	Edm.
Apr. 8/90	Tor.	DSF	St.L. 6	Tor. 5	Sergio Momesso	6:04	St.L.
Apr. 8/90	L.A.	DSF	L.A. 2	Cgy. 1	Tony Granato	8:37	L.A.
Apr. 9/90	Mtl.	DSF	Mtl. 2	Buf. 1	Brian Skrudland	12:35	Mtl.
Apr. 9/90	NYI	DSF	NYI 4	NYR 3	Brent Sutter	20:59	NYR
Apr. 10/90	Wpg.	DSF	Wpg. 4	Edm. 3	Dave Ellett	21:08	Edm.
Apr. 14/90	L.A.	DSF	L.A. 4	Cgy. 3	Mike Krushelnyski	23:14	L.A.
Apr. 15/90	Hfd.	DSF	Hfd. 3	Bos. 2	Kevin Dineen	12:30	Bos.
Apr. 21/90	Bos.	DF	Bos. 5	Mtl. 4	Garry Galley	3:42	Bos.
Apr. 24/90	L.A.	DF	Edm. 6	L.A. 5	Joe Murphy	4:42	Edm.
Apr. 25/90	Wsh.	DF	Wsh. 4	NYR 3	Rod Langway	0:34	Wsh.
Apr. 27/90	NYR	DF	Wsh. 2	NYR 1	John Druce	6:48	Wsh.
May 15/90	Bos.	F	Edm. 3	Bos. 2	Petr Klima	55:13	Edm.
Apr. 4/91	Chi.	DSF	Min. 4	Chi. 3	Brian Propp	4:14	Min.
Apr. 5/91	Pit.	DSF	Pit. 5	N.J. 4	Jaromir Jagr	8:52	Pit.
Apr. 6/91	L.A.	DSF	L.A. 3	Van. 2	Wayne Gretzky	11:08	L.A.
Apr. 8/91	Van.	DSF	Van. 2	L.A. 1	Cliff Ronning	3:12	L.A.
Apr. 11/91	NYR	DSF	Wsh. 5	NYR 4	Dino Ciccarelli	6:44	Wsh.
Apr. 11/91	Mtl.	DSF	Mtl. 4	Buf. 3	Russ Courtnall	5:56	Mtl.
Apr. 14/91	Edm.	DSF	Cgy. 2	Edm. 1	Theoren Fleury	4:40	Edm.
Apr. 16/91	Cgy.	DSF	Edm. 5	Cgy. 4	Esa Tikkanen	6:58	Edm.
Apr. 18/91	L.A.	DF	L.A. 4	Edm. 3	Luc Robitaille	2:13	Edm.
Apr. 19/91	Bos.	DF	Mtl. 4	Bos. 3	Stephane Richer	0:27	Bos.
Apr. 19/91	Pit.	DF	Pit. 7	Wsh. 6	Kevin Stevens	8:10	Pit.
Apr. 20/91	L.A.	DF	Edm. 4	L.A. 3	Petr Klima	24:48	Edm.
Apr. 22/91	Edm.	DF	Edm. 4	L.A. 3	Esa Tikkanen	20:48	Edm.
Apr. 27/91	Mtl.	DF	Mtl. 3	Bos. 2	Shayne Corson	17:47	Bos.
Apr. 28/91	Edm.	DF	Edm. 4	L.A. 3	Craig MacTavish	16:57	Edm.
May 3/91	Bos.	CF	Bos. 5	Pit. 4	Vladimir Ruzicka	8:14	Pit.
Apr. 21/92	Bos.	DSF	Bos. 3	Buf. 2	Adam Oates	11:14	Bos.
Apr. 22/92	Min.	DSF	Det. 5	Min. 4	Yves Racine	1:15	Det.
Apr. 22/92	St.L.	DSF	St.L. 5	Chi. 4	Brett Hull	23:33	Chi.
Apr. 25/92	Buf.	DSF	Bos. 5	Buf. 4	Ted Donato	2:08	Bos.
Apr. 28/92	Min.	DSF	Det. 1	Min. 0	Sergei Fedorov	16:13	Det.
Apr. 29/92	Hfd.	DSF	Hfd. 2	Mtl. 1	Yvon Corriveau	0:24	Mtl.
May 1/92	Mtl.	DSF	Mtl. 3	Hfd. 2	Russ Courtnall	25:26	Mtl.
May 3/92	Van.	DF	Edm. 4	Van. 3	Joe Murphy	8:36	Edm.
May 5/92	Mtl.	DF	Bos. 3	Mtl. 2	Peter Douris	3:12	Bos.
May 7/92	Pit.	DF	NYR 6	Pit. 5	Kris King	1:29	Pit.
May 9/92	Pit.	DF	Pit. 5	NYR 4	Ron Francis	2:47	Pit.
May 17/92	Pit.	CF	Pit. 4	Bos. 3	Jaromir Jagr	9:44	Pit.
May 20/92	Edm.	CF	Chi. 4	Edm. 3	Jeremy Roenick	2:45	Chi.
Apr. 18/93	Bos.	DSF	Buf. 5	Bos. 4	Bob Sweeney	11:03	Buf.
Apr. 18/93	Que.	DSF	Que. 3	Mtl. 2	Scott Young	16:49	Mtl.
Apr. 20/93	Wsh.	DSF	NYI 5	Wsh. 4	Brian Mullen	34:50	NYI
Apr. 22/93	Mtl.	DSF	Mtl. 2	Que. 1	Vincent Damphousse	10:30	Mtl.
Apr. 22/93	Buf.	DSF	Buf. 4	Bos. 3	Yuri Khmylev	1:05	Buf.
Apr. 22/93	NYI	DSF	NYI 4	Wsh. 3	Ray Ferraro	4:46	NYI
Apr. 24/93	Buf.	DSF	Buf. 6	Bos. 5	Brad May	4:48	Buf.
Apr. 24/93	NYI	DSF	NYI 4	Wsh. 3	Ray Ferraro	25:40	NYI
Apr. 25/93	St.L.	DSF	St.L. 4	Chi. 3	Craig Janney	10:43	St.L.
Apr. 26/93	Que.	DSF	Mtl. 5	Que. 4	Kirk Muller	8:17	Mtl.
Apr. 27/93	Det.	DSF	Tor. 5	Det. 4	Mike Foligno	2:05	Tor.
Apr. 27/93	Van.	DSF	Wpg. 4	Van. 3	Teemu Selanne	6:18	Van.
Apr. 29/93	Wpg.	DSF	Van. 4	Wpg. 3	Greg Adams	4:30	Van.
May 1/93	Det.	DSF	Tor. 4	Det. 3	Nikolai Borschevsky	2:35	Tor.
May 3/93	Tor.	DF	Tor. 2	St.L. 1	Doug Gilmour	23:16	Tor.
May 4/93	Mtl.	DF	Mtl. 4	Buf. 3	Guy Carbonneau	2:50	Mtl.
May 5/93	Tor.	DF	St.L. 2	Tor. 1	Jeff Brown	23:03	Tor.
May 6/93	Buf.	DF	Mtl. 4	Buf. 3	Gilbert Dionne	8:28	Mtl.
May 8/93	Buf.	DF	Mtl. 4	Buf. 3	Kirk Muller	11:37	Mtl.
May 11/93	Van.	DF	L.A. 4	Van. 3	Gary Shuchuk	26:31	L.A.
May 14/93	Pit.	DF	NYI 4	Pit. 3	David Volek	5:16	NYI
May 18/93	Mtl.	CF	Mtl. 4	NYI 3	Stephan Lebeau	26:21	Mtl.
May 20/93	NYI	CF	Mtl. 2	NYI 1	Guy Carbonneau	12:34	Mtl.
May 25/93	Tor.	CF	Tor. 3	L.A. 2	Glenn Anderson	19:20	L.A.
May 27/93	L.A.	CF	L.A. 5	Tor. 4	Wayne Gretzky	1:41	L.A.
Jun. 3/93	Mtl.	F	Mtl. 3	L.A. 2	Eric Desjardins	0:51	Mtl.
Jun. 5/93	L.A.	F	Mtl. 4	L.A. 3	John LeClair	0:34	Mtl.
Jun. 7/93	L.A.	F	Mtl. 3	L.A. 2	John LeClair	14:37	Mtl.
Apr. 20/94	Tor.	CQF	Tor. 1	Chi. 0	Todd Gill	2:15	Tor.
Apr. 22/94	St.L.	CQF	Dal. 5	St.L. 4	Paul Cavallini	8:34	Dal.
Apr. 24/94	Chi.	CQF	Chi. 4	Tor. 3	Jeremy Roenick	1:23	Tor.
Apr. 25/94	Bos.	CQF	Mtl. 2	Bos. 1	Kirk Muller	17:18	Bos.
Apr. 26/94	Cgy.	CQF	Van. 2	Cgy. 1	Geoff Courtnall	7:15	Van.
Apr. 27/94	Buf.	CQF	Buf. 1	N.J. 0	Dave Hannan	65:43	N.J.
Apr. 28/94	Van.	CQF	Van. 3	Cgy. 2	Trevor Linden	16:43	Van.
Apr. 30/94	Cgy.	CQF	Van. 4	Cgy. 3	Pavel Bure	22:20	Van.
May 3/94	N.J.	CSF	Bos. 6	N.J. 5	Don Sweeney	9:08	N.J.
May 7/94	Bos.	CSF	N.J. 5	Bos. 4	Stephane Richer	14:19	N.J.
May 8/94	Van.	CSF	Van. 2	Dal. 1	Sergio Momesso	11:01	Van.
May 12/94	Tor.	CSF	Tor. 3	S.J. 2	Mike Gartner	8:53	Tor.
May 15/94	NYR	CF	N.J. 4	NYR 3	Stephane Richer	35:23	NYR
May 16/94	Tor.	CF	Tor. 3	Van. 2	Peter Zezel	16:55	Van.
May 19/94	N.J.	CF	NYR 3	N.J. 2	Stephane Matteau	26:13	NYR
May 24/94	Van.	CF	Van. 4	Tor. 3	Greg Adams	20:14	Van.
May 27/94	NYR	CF	NYR 2	N.J. 1	Stephane Matteau	24:24	NYR
May 31/94	NYR	F	Van. 3	NYR 2	Greg Adams	19:26	NYR
May 7/95	Phi.	CQF	Phi. 4	Buf. 3	Karl Dykhuis	10:06	Phi.
May 9/95	Cgy.	CQF	S.J. 5	Cgy. 4	Ulf Dahlen	12:21	S.J.
May 12/95	NYR	CQF	NYR 3	Que. 2	Steve Larmer	8:09	NYR
May 12/95	N.J.	CQF	N.J. 1	Bos. 0	Randy McKay	8:51	N.J.
May 14/95	Pit.	CQF	Pit. 6	Wsh. 5	Luc Robitaille	4:30	Pit.
May 15/95	St.L.	CQF	Van. 6	St.L. 5	Cliff Ronning	1:48	Van.
May 17/95	Tor.	CQF	Tor. 5	Chi. 4	Randy Wood	10:00	Chi.
May 19/95	Cgy.	CQF	S.J. 5	Cgy. 4	Ray Whitney	21:54	S.J.
May 21/95	Phi.	CSF	Phi. 5	NYR 4	Eric Desjardins	7:03	Phi.
May 21/95	Chi.	CSF	Chi. 2	Van. 1	Joe Murphy	9:04	Chi.
May 22/95	Phi.	CSF	Phi. 4	NYR 3	Kevin Haller	0:25	Phi.
May 25/95	Van.	CSF	Chi. 3	Van. 2	Chris Chelios	6:22	Chi.
May 26/95	N.J.	CSF	N.J. 2	Pit. 1	Neal Broten	18:36	N.J.
May 27/95	Van.	CSF	Chi. 4	Van. 3	Chris Chelios	5:35	Chi.
Jun. 1/95	Det.	CF	Det. 2	Chi. 1	Nicklas Lidstrom	1:01	Det.
Jun. 6/95	Chi.	CF	Det. 4	Chi. 3	Vladimir Konstantinov	29:25	Det.
Jun. 7/95	N.J.	CF	Phi. 3	N.J. 2	Eric Lindros	4:19	N.J.

Date	City	Series	Score		Scorer	Time	Series Winner
Jun. 11/95	Det.	CF	Det. 2	Chi. 1	Vyacheslav Kozlov	22:25	Det.
Apr. 16/96	NYR	CQF	Mtl. 3	NYR 2	Vincent Damphousse	5:04	NYR
Apr. 18/96	Tor.	CQF	Tor. 5	St.L. 4	Mats Sundin	4:02	St.L.
Apr. 18/96	Phi.	CQF	T.B. 2	Phi. 1	Brian Bellows	9:05	Phi.
Apr. 21/96	St.L.	CQF	St.L. 3	Tor. 2	Glenn Anderson	1:24	St.L.
Apr. 21/96	T.B.	CQF	T.B. 5	Phi. 4	Alexander Selivanov	2:04	Phi.
Apr. 23/96	Cgy.	CQF	Chi. 2	Cgy. 1	Joe Murphy	50:02	Chi.
Apr. 24/96	Wsh.	CQF	Pit. 3	Wsh. 2	Petr Nedved	79:15	Pit.
Apr. 25/96	Col.	CQF	Col. 5	Van. 4	Joe Sakic	0:51	Col.
Apr. 25/96	Tor.	CQF	Tor. 5	St.L. 4	Mike Gartner	7:31	St.L.
May 2/96	Col.	CSF	Chi. 3	Col. 2	Jeremy Roenick	6:29	Col.
May 6/96	Chi.	CSF	Chi. 4	Col. 3	Sergei Krivokrasov	0:46	Col.
May 8/96	St.L.	CSF	St.L. 5	Det. 4	Igor Kravchuk	3:23	Det.
May 8/96	Chi.	CSF	Col. 3	Chi. 2	Joe Sakic	44:33	Col.
May 9/96	Fla.	CSF	Fla. 4	Phi. 3	Dave Lowry	4:06	Fla.
May 12/96	Phi.	CSF	Fla. 2	Phi. 1	Mike Hough	28:05	Fla.
May 13/96	Chi.	CSF	Col. 4	Chi. 3	Sandis Ozolinsh	25:18	Col.
May 16/96	Det.	CSF	Det. 1	St.L. 0	Steve Yzerman	21:15	Det.
May 19/96	Det.	CF	Col. 3	Det. 2	Mike Keane	17:31	Col.
Jun. 10/96	Fla.	F	Col. 1	Fla. 0	Uwe Krupp	44:31	Col.
Apr. 20/97	Chi.	CQF	Chi. 4	Col. 3	Sergei Krivokrasov	31:03	Col.
Apr. 20/97	Edm.	CQF	Edm. 4	Dal. 3	Kelly Buchberger	9:15	Edm.
Apr. 22/97	NYR	CQF	NYR 4	Fla. 3	Esa Tikkanen	16:29	NYR
Apr. 23/97	Ott.	CQF	Ott. 1	Buf. 0	Daniel Alfredsson	2:34	Buf.
Apr. 24/97	Mtl.	CQF	Mtl. 4	N.J. 3	Patrice Brisebois	47:37	N.J.
Apr. 25/97	Fla.	CQF	NYR 3	Fla. 2	Esa Tikkanen	12:02	NYR
Apr. 25/97	Dal.	CQF	Edm. 1	Dal. 0	Ryan Smyth	20:22	Edm.
Apr. 27/97	Phx.	CQF	Ana. 3	Phx. 2	Paul Kariya	7:29	Ana.
Apr. 29/97	Buf.	CQF	Buf. 3	Ott. 2	Derek Plante	5:24	Buf.
Apr. 29/97	Edm.	CQF	Edm. 4	Dal. 3	Todd Marchant	12:26	Edm.
May 2/97	Det.	CSF	Det. 2	Ana. 1	Martin Lapointe	0:59	Det.
May 4/97	Det.	CSF	Det. 3	Ana. 2	Vyacheslav Kozlov	41:31	Det.
May 8/97	Ana.	CSF	Det. 3	Ana. 2	Brendan Shanahan	37:03	Det.
May 9/97	Phi.	CSF	Buf. 5	Phi. 4	Ed Ronan	6:24	Phi.
May 9/97	Edm.	CSF	Col. 3	Edm. 2	Claude Lemieux	8:35	Col.
May 11/97	N.J.	CSF	NYR 2	N.J. 1	Adam Graves	14:08	NYR
Apr. 22/98	N.J.	CQF	Ott. 2	N.J. 1	Bruce Gardiner	5:58	Ott.
Apr. 23/98	Pit.	CQF	Mtl. 3	Pit. 2	Benoit Brunet	18:43	Mtl.
Apr. 24/98	Wsh.	CQF	Bos. 4	Wsh. 3	Darren Van Impe	20:54	Wsh.
Apr. 26/98	Ott.	CQF	Ott. 2	N.J. 1	Alexei Yashin	2:47	Ott.
Apr. 26/98	Bos.	CQF	Wsh. 3	Bos. 2	Joe Juneau	26:31	Wsh.
Apr. 26/98	Edm.	CQF	Col. 5	Edm. 4	Joe Sakic	15:25	Edm.
Apr. 28/98	S.J.	CQF	S.J. 1	Dal. 0	Andrei Zyuzin	6:31	Dal.
May 1/98	Phi.	CQF	Buf. 3	Phi. 2	Michal Grosek	5:40	Buf.
May 2/98	S.J.	CQF	Dal. 3	S.J. 2	Mike Keane	3:43	Dal.
May 3/98	Bos.	CQF	Wsh. 3	Bos. 2	Brian Bellows	15:24	Wsh.
May 3/98	Buf.	CQF	Buf. 3	Mtl. 2	Geoff Sanderson	2:37	Buf.
May 11/98	Edm.	CSF	Dal. 1	Edm. 0	Benoit Hogue	13:07	Dal.
May 12/98	Mtl.	CSF	Buf. 5	Mtl. 4	Michael Peca	21:24	Buf.
May 12/98	St.L.	CSF	Det. 3	St.L. 2	Brendan Shanahan	31:12	Det.
May 25/98	Wsh.	CF	Wsh. 3	Buf. 2	Todd Krygier	3:01	Wsh.
May 28/98	Buf.	CF	Wsh. 4	Buf. 3	Peter Bondra	9:37	Wsh.
Jun. 3/98	Dal.	CF	Dal. 3	Det. 2	Jamie Langenbrunner	0:46	Det.
Jun. 4/98	Buf.	CF	Wsh. 3	Buf. 2	Joe Juneau	6:24	Wsh.
Jun. 11/98	Det.	F	Det. 5	Wsh. 4	Kris Draper	15:24	Det.
Apr. 23/99	Ott.	CQF	Buf. 3	Ott. 2	Miroslav Satan	30:35	Buf.
Apr. 24/99	Car.	CQF	Car. 3	Bos. 2	Ray Sheppard	17:05	Bos.
Apr. 24/99	Phx.	CQF	Phx. 4	St.L. 3	Shane Doan	8:58	St.L.
Apr. 26/99	S.J.	CQF	Col. 2	S.J. 1	Milan Hejduk	7:53	Col.
Apr. 27/99	Edm.	CQF	Dal. 3	Edm. 2	Joe Nieuwendyk	57:34	Dal.
Apr. 30/99	Tor.	CQF	Tor. 2	Phi. 1	Yanic Perreault	11:51	Tor.
Apr. 30/99	Car.	CQF	Bos. 4	Car. 3	Anson Carter	34:45	Bos.
Apr. 30/99	Phx.	CQF	St.L. 2	Phx. 1	Scott Young	5:43	St.L.
May 2/99	Pit.	CQF	Pit. 3	N.J. 2	Jaromir Jagr	8:59	Pit.
May 3/99	S.J.	CQF	Col. 3	S.J. 2	Milan Hejduk	13:12	Col.
May 4/99	Phx.	CQF	St.L. 1	Phx. 0	Pierre Turgeon	17:59	St.L.
May 7/99	Col.	CSF	Det. 3	Col. 2	Kirk Maltby	4:18	Col.
May 8/99	Dal.	CSF	Dal. 5	St.L. 4	Joe Nieuwendyk	8:22	Dal.
May 10/99	St.L.	CSF	St.L. 3	Dal. 2	Pavol Demitra	2:43	Dal.
May 12/99	St.L.	CSF	St.L. 3	Dal. 2	Pierre Turgeon	5:52	Dal.
May 13/99	Pit.	CSF	Tor. 3	Pit. 2	Sergei Berezin	2:18	Tor.
May 17/99	Pit.	CSF	Tor. 4	Pit. 3	Garry Valk	1:57	Tor.
May 17/99	St.L.	CSF	Dal. 2	St.L. 1	Mike Modano	2:21	Dal.
May 28/99	Col.	CF	Col. 3	Dal. 2	Chris Drury	19:29	Dal.
Jun. 8/99	Dal.	F	Buf. 3	Dal. 2	Jason Woolley	15:30	Dal.
Jun. 19/99	Buf.	F	Dal. 2	Buf. 1	Brett Hull	54:51	Dal.
Apr. 15/00	Pit.	CQF	Pit. 2	Wsh. 1	Jaromir Jagr	5:49	Pit.
Apr. 18/00	Buf.	CQF	Buf. 3	Phi. 2	Stu Barnes	4:42	Phi.
Apr. 22/00	Tor.	CQF	Tor. 2	Ott. 1	Steve Thomas	14:47	Tor.
May 2/00	Pit.	CSF	Phi. 4	Pit. 3	Andy Delmore	22:01	Phi.
May 4/00	Det.	CSF	Col. 3	Det. 2	Chris Drury	10:21	Col.
May 3/00	Pit.	CSF	Phi. 2	Pit. 1	Keith Primeau	92:01	Phi.
May 23/00	Dal.	CF	Dal. 3	Col. 2	Joe Nieuwendyk	12:10	Dal.
Jun. 8/00	N.J.	F	Dal. 1	N.J. 0	Mike Modano	46:21	N.J.
Jun. 10/00	Dal.	F	N.J. 2	Dal. 1	Jason Arnott	28:20	N.J.
Apr. 11/01	Dal.	CQF	Dal. 2	Edm. 1	Jamie Langenbrunner	2:08	Dal.
Apr. 13/01	Ott.	CQF	Tor. 1	Ott. 0	Mats Sundin	10:49	Tor.
Apr. 14/01	Phi.	CQF	Buf. 4	Phi. 3	Jay McKee	18:02	Buf.
Apr. 15/01	Edm.	CQF	Dal. 3	Edm. 2	Benoit Hogue	19:48	Dal.
Apr. 16/01	Tor.	CQF	Tor. 3	Ott. 2	Cory Cross	2:16	Tor.
Apr. 16/01	Van.	CQF	Col. 4	Van. 3	Peter Forsberg	2:50	Col.
Apr. 17/01	Buf.	CQF	Buf. 4	Phi. 3	Curtis Brown	6:13	Buf.
Apr. 17/01	Edm.	CQF	Edm. 2	Dal. 1	Mike Çomrie	17:19	Dal.
Apr. 18/01	Car.	CQF	Car. 3	N.J. 2	Rod Brind'Amour	0:46	N.J.
Apr. 18/01	Pit.	CQF	Wsh. 4	Pit. 3	Jeff Halpern	4:01	Pit.
Apr. 18/01	L.A.	CQF	L.A. 4	Det. 3	Eric Belanger	2:36	L.A.
Apr. 19/01	Dal.	CQF	Dal. 4	Edm. 3	Kirk Muller	8:01	Dal.
Apr. 19/01	St.L.	CQF	St.L. 3	S.J. 2	Bryce Salvador	9:54	St.L.
Apr. 23/01	Pit.	CQF	Pit. 4	Wsh. 3	Martin Straka	13:04	Pit.
Apr. 23/01	L.A.	CQF	L.A. 3	Det. 2	Adam Deadmarsh	4:48	L.A.
Apr. 26/01	Col.	CSF	L.A. 4	Col. 3	Jaroslav Modry	14:23	Col.
Apr. 28/01	N.J.	CSF	N.J. 6	Tor. 5	Randy McKay	5:31	N.J.
May 1/01	Tor.	CSF	N.J. 3	Tor. 2	Brian Rafalski	7:00	N.J.
May 1/01	St.L.	CSF	St.L. 3	Dal. 2	Cory Stillman	29:26	St.L.
May 5/01	Buf.	CSF	Buf. 3	Pit. 2	Stu Barnes	8:34	Pit.
May 6/01	L.A.	CSF	L.A. 1	Col. 0	Glen Murray	22:41	Col.
May 8/01	Pit.	CSF	Pit. 3	Buf. 2	Martin Straka	11:29	Pit.
May 10/01	Buf.	CSF	Pit. 3	Buf. 2	Darius Kasparaitis	13:01	Pit.
May 16/01	St.L.	CF	St.L. 4	Col. 3	Scott Young	30:27	Col.
May 18/01	St.L.	CF	Col. 4	St.L. 3	Stephane Yelle	4:23	Col.
May 21/01	Col.	CF	Col. 2	St.L. 1	Joe Sakic	0:24	Col.
Apr. 17/02	Phi.	CQF	Phi. 1	Ott. 0	Ruslan Fedotenko	7:47	Ott.
Apr. 17/02	Det.	CQF	Van. 4	Det. 3	Henrik Sedin	13:59	Det.
Apr. 19/02	Car.	CQF	Car. 2	N.J. 1	Bates Battaglia	15:26	Car.
Apr. 24/02	Car.	CQF	Car. 3	N.J. 2	Josef Vasicek	8:16	Car.
Apr. 25/02	Col.	CQF	L.A. 1	Col. 0	Craig Johnson	2:19	Col.
Apr. 26/02	Phi.	CQF	Ott. 2	Phi. 1	Martin Havlat	7:33	Ott.
May 4/02	Tor.	CSF	Tor. 3	Ott. 2	Gary Roberts	44:30	Tor.
May 7/02	Mtl.	CSF	Mtl. 2	Car. 1	Donald Audette	2:26	Car.
May 9/02	Car.	CSF	Car. 4	Mtl. 3	Niclas Wallin	3:14	Car.
May 13/02	S.J.	CSF	Col. 2	S.J. 1	Peter Forsberg	2:47	Col.
May 19/02	Car.	CF	Car. 2	Tor. 1	Niclas Wallin	13:42	Car.
May 20/02	Det.	CF	Col. 4	Det. 3	Chris Drury	2:17	Det.
May 21/02	Tor.	CF	Car. 2	Tor. 1	Jeff O'Neill	6:01	Car.
May 22/02	Col.	CF	Det. 2	Col. 1	Fredrik Olausson	12:44	Det.
May 27/02	Col.	CF	Col. 2	Det. 1	Peter Forsberg	6:24	Det.
May 28/02	Tor.	CF	Car. 2	Tor. 1	Martin Gelinas	8:05	Car.
Jun. 4/02	Det.	F	Car. 3	Det. 2	Ron Francis	0:58	Det.
Jun. 8/02	Car.	F	Det. 3	Car. 2	Igor Larionov	54:47	Det.

Stanley Cup Notebook

Gold Medalist and Stanley Cup Champion

Defenseman Ken Morrow was the first player in hockey history to win both an Olympic Gold Medal and a Stanley Cup title in the same year, having done so as part of the USA's 1980 "Miracle On Ice" and the New York Islanders.

Detroit teammates Steve Yzerman and Brendan Shanahan won gold medals as members of the 2002 Canadian Olympic Team and then went on to win the Stanley Cup in June of 2002 as members of the Detroit Red Wings.

Mario's Magic

Mario Lemieux tied three NHL records on April 25, 1989, in a game against the Philadelphia Flyers. Lemieux's eight-point evening tied a record for most points in a post-season game, his four goals in the opening stanza tied a record for most goals in one period and his five goals matched the mark for most goals in a playoff game.

Active Players Playoff Overtime Record

(Minimum one overtime game played.)

Player	Current Team	GP	G	A	PTS
Craig Adams	CAR	1	0	0	0
Kevyn Adams	CAR	11	0	0	0
Maxim Afinogenov	BUF	5	0	0	0
Tommy Albelin	NJ	13	0	0	0
Daniel Alfredsson	OTT	11	1	0	1
Bryan Allen	VAN	1	0	0	0
Jason Allison	LA	6	0	1	1
Tony Amonte	PHI	16	0	2	2
Dave Andreychuk	TB	27	0	1	1
Nik Antropov	TOR	4	0	1	1
Jason Arnott	DAL	12	1	1	2
Magnus Arvedson	OTT	8	0	0	0
Serge Aubin	COL	2	0	0	0
Adrian Aucoin	NYI	3	0	0	0
Donald Audette	MTL	22	0	2	2
P.J. Axelsson	BOS	5	0	0	0
Matthew Barnaby	NYR	16	0	1	1
Stu Barnes	DAL	15	2	0	2
Murray Baron	VAN	12	0	0	0
Lubos Bartecko	ATL	3	0	0	0
Shawn Bates	NYI	2	0	0	0
Bates Battaglia	COL	12	1	0	1
Jaroslav Bednar	FLA	1	0	0	0
Wade Belak	TOR	3	0	0	0
Eric Belanger	LA	5	1	0	1
Ken Belanger	LA	2	0	0	0
Bryan Berard	BOS	3	0	0	0
Drake Berehowsky	PHX	3	0	0	0
Sergei Berezin	WSH	10	1	3	4
Aki Berg	TOR	8	0	0	0
Marc Bergevin	T.B.	9	0	0	0
Todd Bertuzzi	VAN	2	0	0	0
Craig Berube	CGY	16	0	0	0
Rob Blake	COL	25	0	2	2
Brad Bombardir	MIN	1	0	0	0
Peter Bondra	WSH	14	1	0	1
Radek Bonk	OTT	8	0	1	1
Philippe Boucher	DAL	6	0	0	0
Bob Boughner	CGY	16	0	0	0
Matt Bradley	SJ	1	0	0	0
Donald Brashear	PHI	5	0	0	0
Pavel Brendl	CAR	1	0	0	0
Eric Brewer	EDM	4	0	0	0
Rod Brind'Amour	CAR	23	1	2	3
Patrice Brisebois	MTL	22	1	3	4
Curtis Brown	BUF	13	1	1	2
Andrew Brunette	MIN	1	0	0	0
Sergei Brylin	NJ	9	0	1	1
Kelly Buchberger	PHX	21	1	0	1
Jan Bulis	MTL	2	0	0	0
Pavel Bure	NYR	15	1	2	3
Valeri Bure	STL	2	0	0	0
Keith Carney	ANA	21	0	1	1
Anson Carter	NYR	9	1	1	2
Andrew Cassels	CBJ	5	0	1	1
Zdeno Chara	OTT	3	0	0	0
Brad Chartrand	LA	1	0	0	0
Chris Chelios	DET	45	2	3	5
Artem Chubarov	VAN	1	0	0	0
Dan Cleary	EDM	4	0	0	0
Erik Cole	CAR	9	0	0	0
Mike Comrie	EDM	4	1	0	1
Craig Conroy	CGY	8	0	0	0
Matt Cooke	VAN	2	0	0	0
Shayne Corson	TOR	33	1	5	6
Cory Cross	EDM	10	1	0	1
Jassen Cullimore	TB	4	0	0	0
Mariusz Czerkawski	MTL	8	0	0	0
Andreas Dackell	MTL	10	0	0	0
Ulf Dahlen	DAL	10	1	2	3
Vincent Damphousse	SJ	27	2	2	4
Mathieu Dandenault	DET	9	0	0	0
Ken Daneyko	NJ	26	0	0	0
Jeff Daniels	CAR	11	0	1	1
Pavel Datsyuk	DET	6	0	0	0
Eric Daze	CHI	13	0	1	1
Adam Deadmarsh	LA	21	1	3	4
Andy Delmore	NSH	4	1	0	1
Pavol Demitra	STL	13	1	0	1
Nathan Dempsey	CHI	1	0	0	0
Eric Desjardins	PHI	39	2	2	4
Boyd Devereaux	DET	7	0	0	0
Greg de Vries	COL	21	0	1	1
Rob DiMaio	DAL	12	0	0	0
Chris Dingman	TB	4	0	0	0
Shane Doan	PHX	4	1	0	1
Tie Domi	TOR	16	0	0	0
Ted Donato	NYR	19	1	2	3
Shean Donovan	CGY	2	0	0	0
Jim Dowd	MIN	8	0	0	0
Dallas Drake	STL	11	0	1	1
Kris Draper	DET	21	1	1	2
Harold Druken	CAR	1	0	0	0
Chris Drury	CGY	17	3	0	3
Steve Dubinsky	STL	3	0	0	0
J.P. Dumont	BUF	5	0	1	1
Radek Dvorak	EDM	4	0	0	0
Karl Dykhuis	MTL	12	1	0	1
Mike Eastwood	CHI	25	0	1	1
Mark Eaton	NSH	1	0	0	0
Patrik Elias	NJ	11	0	1	1
Mikko Eloranta	LA	1	0	0	0
Anders Eriksson	TOR	6	0	0	0
Sergei Fedorov	DET	26	1	1	2
Todd Fedoruk	PHI	1	0	0	0
Ruslan Fedotenko	TB	4	1	0	1
Andrew Ference	CGY	5	0	0	0
Scott Ferguson	EDM	4	0	0	0
Jeff Finley	STL	10	0	1	1
Jiri Fischer	DET	8	0	0	0
Mike Fisher	OTT	5	0	0	0
Tom Fitzgerald	TOR	13	0	1	1
Rory Fitzpatrick	BUF	1	0	0	0
Theo Fleury	CHI	19	1	2	3
Adam Foote	COL	31	0	0	0
Peter Forsberg	COL	24	3	2	5
Ron Francis	CAR	29	2	2	4
Jeff Friesen	NJ	6	0	1	1
Simon Gagne	PHI	7	0	0	0
Aaron Gavey	TOR	2	0	0	0
Martin Gelinas	CGY	33	1	3	4
Brent Gilchrist	NSH	19	0	0	0
Hal Gill	BOS	5	0	0	0
Doug Gilmour	TOR	43	3	6	9
Brian Gionta	NJ	2	0	0	0
Scott Gomez	NJ	5	0	0	0
Sergei Gonchar	WSH	12	0	0	0
Jean-Luc Grand-Pierre	CBJ	1	0	0	0
Chris Gratton	PHX	9	0	1	1
Adam Graves	SJ	23	1	1	2
Josh Green	WSH	2	0	0	0
Travis Green	TOR	7	0	0	0
Mike Grier	WSH	11	0	0	0
Michal Grosek	BOS	11	1	1	2
Bill Guerin	DAL	12	0	0	0
Riku Hahl	COL	5	0	0	0
Jeff Halpern	WSH	3	1	0	1
Roman Hamrlik	NYI	4	0	1	1
Michal Handzus	PHI	6	0	0	0
Scott Hannan	SJ	2	0	0	0
Todd Harvey	SJ	5	0	0	0
Derian Hatcher	DAL	25	0	0	0
Martin Havlat	OTT	5	1	0	1
Paul Healey	TOR	2	0	0	0
Jochen Hecht	BUF	9	0	0	0
Bret Hedican	CAR	25	0	1	1
Shawn Heins	PIT	1	0	0	0
Steve Heinze	LA	20	0	1	1
Milan Hejduk	COL	16	2	1	3
Sean Hill	CAR	16	0	0	0
Dan Hinote	COL	11	0	0	0
Jan Hlavac	CAR	1	0	0	0
Shane Hnidy	OTT	3	0	0	0
Jonas Hoglund	TOR	11	0	0	0
Bobby Holik	NYR	23	0	3	3
Tomas Holmstrom	DET	13	0	1	1
Shawn Horcoff	EDM	3	0	0	0
Marian Hossa	OTT	7	0	1	1
Bill Houlder	NSH	13	0	1	1
Phil Housley	TOR	15	0	1	1
Jan Hrdina	PHX	11	0	1	1
Tony Hrkac	ATL	7	1	0	1
Brett Hull	DET	39	3	5	8
Jody Hull	OTT	14	0	2	2
Jarome Iginla	CGY	1	0	0	0
Jaromir Jagr	WSH	22	4	2	6
Calle Johansson	WSH	21	0	0	0
Craig Johnson	LA	1	1	0	1
Greg Johnson	NSH	1	0	0	0
Mike Johnson	PHX	3	0	0	0
Kim Johnsson	PHI	2	0	0	0
Hans Jonsson	PIT	8	0	0	0
Kenny Jonsson	NYI	1	0	0	0
Ed Jovanovski	VAN	7	0	1	1
Joe Juneau	MTL	22	2	2	4
Tomas Kaberle	TOR	12	0	1	1
Dmitri Kalinin	BUF	5	0	0	0
Sami Kapanen	PHI	12	0	2	2
Paul Kariya	ANA	4	1	0	1
David Karpa	NYR	4	0	0	0
Alexander Karpovtsev	CHI	12	0	0	0
Darius Kasparaitis	NYR	20	1	1	2
Mike Keane	COL	57	2	1	3
Alexander Khavanov	STL	5	0	0	0
Chad Kilger	MTL	3	0	0	0
Trent Klatt	VAN	10	0	0	0
Ken Klee	WSH	5	0	0	0
Jon Klemm	CHI	18	0	0	0
Saku Koivu	MTL	6	0	1	1
Steve Konowalchuk	WSH	4	0	1	1
Alexei Kovalev	NYR	18	0	1	1
Slava Kozlov	ATL	16	2	0	2
Milan Kraft	PIT	3	0	0	0
Uwe Krupp	ATL	19	1	0	1
Scott Lachance	CBJ	1	0	0	0
Dan LaCouture	NYR	1	0	0	0
Christian Laflamme	STL	1	0	0	0
Robert Lang	WSH	12	0	2	2
Darren Langdon	VAN	4	0	0	0
Jamie Langenbrunner	NJ	23	2	1	3
Daymond Langkow	PHX	6	0	0	0
Ian Laperriere	LA	6	0	1	1
Claude Lapointe	PHI	4	0	0	0
Martin Lapointe	BOS	14	1	2	3
Georges Laraque	EDM	5	0	0	0
Igor Larionov	DET	23	1	2	3
Brad Larsen	COL	5	0	0	0
Janne Laukkanen	T.B.	14	0	2	2
Paul Laus	FLA	5	0	0	0
John LeClair	PHI	31	2	2	4
Mike Leclerc	ANA	1	0	0	0
Brian Leetch	NYR	14	0	3	3
Sylvain Lefebvre	NYR	30	0	0	0
Jere Lehtinen	DAL	21	0	3	3
Claude Lemieux	DAL	39	3	0	3
Mario Lemieux	PIT	11	0	0	0
Curtis Leschyshyn	OTT	16	0	0	0
Trevor Letowski	VAN	1	0	0	0
Nicklas Lidstrom	DET	26	1	1	2
Andreas Lilja	FLA	1	0	0	0
Trevor Linden	VAN	23	1	1	2
Mats Lindgren	VAN	6	0	1	1
Eric Lindros	NYR	9	1	1	2
Dave Lowry	CGY	16	1	1	2
Brad Lukowich	TB	8	0	0	0
Jyrki Lumme	TOR	24	0	2	2
Craig MacDonald	CAR	1	0	0	0
Al MacInnis	STL	38	1	2	3
John Madden	NJ	7	0	0	0
Adam Mair	BUF	3	0	0	0
Vladimir Malakhov	NYR	12	0	1	1
Marek Malik	VAN	11	0	1	1
Kirk Maltby	DET	17	1	0	1
Kent Manderville	PIT	18	0	0	0
Todd Marchant	EDM	11	1	0	1
Bryan Marchment	COL	7	0	0	0
Andrei Markov	MTL	2	0	0	0
Danny Markov	PHX	8	0	0	0
Patrick Marleau	SJ	6	0	0	0
Grant Marshall	NJ	19	0	0	0
Jason Marshall	MIN	3	0	0	0
Stephane Matteau	FLA	21	2	0	2
Richard Matvichuk	DAL	23	0	1	1
Brad May	VCRg	12	1	0	1
Jamal Mayers	STL	10	0	1	1
Chris McAllister	COL	2	0	0	0
Chris McAlpine	LA	8	0	0	0
Dean McAmmond	CGY	5	0	0	0
Bryan McCabe	TOR	8	0	0	0
Sandy McCarthy	NYR	6	0	0	0
Darren McCarty	DET	22	0	1	1
Alyn McCauley	SJ	8	0	0	0
Shawn McEachern	ATL	17	0	0	0
Dan McGillis	BOS	13	0	1	1
Marty McInnis	BOS	1	0	0	0
Randy McKay	MTL	19	2	0	2
Jay McKee	BUF	7	1	0	1
Jim McKenzie	NJ	6	0	0	0
Kyle McLaren	SJ	5	0	0	0
Scott Mellanby	STL	19	0	2	2
Eric Messier	COL	14	0	0	0
Mark Messier	NYR	37	0	5	5
Aaron Miller	LA	14	0	0	0
Kip Miller	WSH	3	0	0	0
Boris Mironov	NYR	6	0	2	2
Mike Modano	DAL	29	2	3	5
Fredrik Modin	TB	2	0	0	0
Jaroslav Modry	LA	4	1	1	2
Alexander Mogilny	TOR	20	0	0	0
Ian Moran	BOS	14	0	1	1
Ethan Moreau	EDM	4	0	0	0
Aleksey Morozov	PIT	8	0	0	0
Brendan Morrison	VAN	3	0	0	0
Brenden Morrow	DAL	8	0	0	0
Bryan Muir	COL	7	0	0	0
Kirk Muller	DAL	33	4	1	5
Glen Murray	BOS	13	1	0	1
Marty Murray	PHI	2	0	1	1
Rem Murray	NSH	11	0	0	0
Tyson Nash	STL	1	0	0	0
Markus Naslund	VAN	2	0	0	0
Andrei Nazarov	PHX	1	0	0	0
Stan Neckar	TB	4	0	0	0
Petr Nedved	NYR	11	1	1	2
Chris Neil	OTT	3	0	0	0
Rob Niedermayer	ANA	5	0	0	0
Scott Niedermayer	NJ	21	0	0	0
Ville Nieminen	PIT	6	0	1	1
Joe Nieuwendyk	NJ	32	3	0	3
Janne Niinimaa	NYI	8	0	0	0
Andrei Nikolishin	CHI	10	0	2	2
Owen Nolan	TOR	10	0	0	0
Mattias Norstrom	LA	5	0	0	0
Teppo Numminen	PHX	8	0	0	0
Michael Nylander	WSH	4	0	0	0
Adam Oates	ANA	29	1	4	5
Lyle Odelein	DAL	22	0	0	0
Jeff Odgers	ATL	7	0	0	0
Sean O'Donnell	BOS	3	0	0	0
Mattias Ohlund	VAN	2	0	0	0
Fredrik Olausson	ANA	12	1	1	2
Krzysztof Oliwa	BOS	3	0	0	0
Jeff O'Neill	CAR	12	1	2	3
Sandis Ozolinsh	ANA	20	1	3	4
Zigmund Palffy	LA	5	0	2	2
Jay Pandolfo	NJ	10	0	0	0
Richard Park	MIN	5	0	0	0
Scott Parker	COL	1	0	0	0

Player	Current Team	GP	G	A	PTS
James Patrick	BUF	25	0	1	1
Michael Peca	NYI	16	1	0	1
Denis Pederson	NSH	5	0	0	0
Scott Pellerin	PHX	6	0	0	0
Yanic Perreault	MTL	9	1	1	2
Oleg Petrov	NSH	4	0	0	0
Chris Phillips	OTT	7	0	0	0
Domenic Pittis	NSH	3	0	0	0
Steve Poapst	CHI	1	0	0	0
Shjon Podein	STL	22	0	0	0
Tom Poti	NYR	5	0	0	0
Nolan Pratt	TB	1	0	0	0
Keith Primeau	PHI	18	1	1	2
Wayne Primeau	SJ	16	0	0	0
Chris Pronger	STL	18	0	1	1
Sean Pronger	CBJ	3	0	0	0
Vaclav Prospal	TB	4	0	0	0
Deron Quint	PHX	1	0	0	0
Stephane Quintal	MTL	11	0	0	0
Karel Rachunek	OTT	2	0	0	0
Brian Rafalski	NJ	7	1	0	1
Marcus Ragnarsson	PHI	6	0	0	0
Paul Ranheim	PHX	10	0	0	0
Erik Rasmussen	LA	4	0	1	1
Mike Rathje	SJ	8	0	0	0
Rob Ray	OTT	14	0	0	0
Marty Reasoner	EDM	4	0	0	0
Mark Recchi	PHI	16	0	0	0
Wade Redden	OTT	10	0	0	0
Robert Reichel	TOR	14	0	1	1
Steve Reinprecht	COL	10	0	1	1
Mikael Renberg	TOR	10	0	2	2
Pascal Rheaume	ATL	6	0	0	0
Mike Ricci	SJ	19	0	3	3
Luke Richardson	CBJ	16	0	1	1
Craig Rivet	MTL	5	0	0	0
Gary Roberts	TOR	23	1	1	2
Luc Robitaille	DET	32	2	2	4
Jeremy Roenick	PHI	22	3	0	3
Brian Rolston	BOS	6	0	0	0
Cliff Ronning	MIN	23	2	1	3
Andre Roy	TB	2	0	0	0
Michal Rozsival	PIT	1	0	0	0
Steve Rucchin	ANA	4	0	1	1
Martin Rucinsky	STL	7	0	0	0
Jarkko Ruutu	VAN	1	0	0	0
Joe Sacco	PHI	7	0	0	0
Joe Sakic	COL	31	4	5	9
Sami Salo	VAN	3	0	0	0
Bryce Salvador	STL	4	1	0	1
Sergei Samsonov	BOS	5	0	0	0
Geoff Sanderson	CBJ	11	1	1	2
Miroslav Satan	BUF	15	1	1	2
Brian Savage	PHX	6	0	0	0
Mathieu Schneider	DET	21	0	3	3
Daniel Sedin	VAN	2	0	0	0
Henrik Sedin	VAN	2	1	0	1
Teemu Selanne	SJ	8	1	1	2
Brendan Shanahan	DET	24	2	2	4
Jeff Shantz	COL	15	0	0	0
Mike Sillinger	CBJ	5	0	0	0
Chris Simon	CHI	16	0	0	0
Reid Simpson	NSH	2	0	0	0
Martin Skoula	COL	15	0	0	0
Blake Sloan	CGY	7	0	0	0
Richard Smehlik	ATL	26	0	2	2
Jason Smith	EDM	6	0	0	0
Bryan Smolinski	OTT	13	0	0	0
Ryan Smyth	EDM	11	1	1	2
Brent Sopel	VAN	2	0	0	0
Sheldon Souray	MTL	3	0	0	0
Scott Stevens	NJ	32	0	2	2
Turner Stevenson	NJ	8	0	1	1
Cory Stillman	STL	5	1	0	1
Martin Straka	PIT	17	2	1	3
Jason Strudwick	CHI	1	0	0	0
Brad Stuart	SJ	2	0	0	0
Jozef Stumpel	BOS	8	0	2	2
Marco Sturm	SJ	4	0	0	0
Steve Sullivan	CHI	1	0	0	0
Mats Sundin	TOR	18	2	2	4
Niklas Sundstrom	MTL	5	0	0	0
Robert Svehla	TOR	5	0	0	0
Jaroslav Svoboda	CAR	9	0	1	1
Don Sweeney	BOS	19	1	0	1
Darryl Sydor	DAL	29	0	1	1
Petr Sykora	ANA	9	0	0	0
Chris Tamer	ATL	3	0	0	0
David Tanabe	CAR	1	0	0	0
Alex Tanguay	COL	12	0	1	1
Tim Taylor	TB	11	0	0	0
Chris Therien	PHI	18	0	0	0
Steve Thomas	ANA	24	1	1	2
Joe Thornton	BOS	5	0	1	1
Scott Thornton	SJ	8	0	1	1
Keith Tkachuk	STL	11	0	0	0
Patrick Traverse	MTL	1	0	0	0
Darcy Tucker	TOR	10	0	0	0
Pierre Turgeon	DAL	23	2	4	6
Oleg Tverdovsky	NJ	3	0	0	0
Igor Ulanov	FLA	10	0	0	0
Shaun Van Allen	OTT	10	0	1	1
Darren Van Impe	CBJ	9	1	0	1
Vaclav Varada	OTT	15	0	2	2
Josef Vasicek	CAR	10	1	1	2
Lubomir Visnovsky	LA	2	0	0	0
Radim Vrbata	CAR	2	0	0	0
Niclas Wallin	CAR	10	2	0	2
Wes Walz	MIN	3	0	0	0
Aaron Ward	CAR	14	0	0	0
Rhett Warrener	BUF	12	0	0	0
Todd Warriner	NSH	6	0	0	0
Doug Weight	STL	13	0	1	1
Eric Weinrich	PHI	19	0	0	0
Glen Wesley	TOR	31	0	0	0
Colin White	NJ	7	0	0	0
Todd White	OTT	4	0	0	0
Ray Whitney	CBJ	3	1	0	1
Jason Wiemer	NYI	2	0	0	0
Justin Williams	PHI	2	0	0	0
Landon Wilson	PHX	1	0	0	0
Mike Wilson	NYR	8	0	0	0
Brendan Witt	WSH	9	0	0	0
Jason Woolley	DET	15	1	1	2
Tyler Wright	CBJ	7	0	0	0
Alexei Yashin	NYI	7	1	0	1
Stephane Yelle	CGY	25	1	0	1
Jason York	NSH	8	0	0	0
Scott Young	DAL	30	3	1	4
Dmitry Yushkevich	PHI	14	0	0	0
Steve Yzerman	DET	28	1	2	3
Rob Zamuner	BOS	5	0	0	0
Richard Zednik	MTL	6	0	0	0
Alex Zhamnov	CHI	2	0	0	0
Alexei Zhitnik	BUF	25	0	0	0
Sergei Zholtok	MIN	6	0	0	0
Sergei Zubov	DAL	31	0	3	3
Dainius Zubrus	WSH	4	0	0	0
Andrei Zyuzin	MIN	2	1	0	1

Active Goaltenders Playoff Overtime Record

(Minimum one overtime game played.)

Goaltender	Current Team	GP	W	L	MINS	GA	SOG	GAA	SV%
Ed Belfour	TOR	37	20	17	587	17	280	1.74	.939
Brian Boucher	PHX	4	2	2	115	2	48	1.04	.958
Martin Brodeur	NJ	20	6	14	384	14	162	2.19	.914
Sean Burke	PHX	5	1	4	50	4	21	4.77	.810
Roman Cechmanek	PHI	3	1	2	32	2	19	3.75	.895
Dan Cloutier	VAN	1	1	0	14	0	5	0.00	1.000
Byron Dafoe	ATL	5	2	3	115	3	43	1.57	.930
Jeff Hackett	BOS	1	1	0	31	0	21	0.00	1.000
Johan Hedberg	PIT	5	3	2	50	2	16	2.39	.875
Corey Hirsch	DAL	1	0	1	1	1	1	70.59	.000
Arturs Irbe	CAR	12	9	3	176	3	71	1.02	.958
Brent Johnson*	STL	1	0	1	0	1	2	150.00	.500
Curtis Joseph	DET	24	14	10	303	10	161	1.98	.938
Nikolai Khabibulin	TB	4	1	3	40	3	29	4.48	.897
Trevor Kidd	TOR	2	0	1	34	2	16	3.50	.875
Miikka Kiprusoff	SJ	1	0	1	10	1	10	6.06	.900
Olaf Kolzig	WSH	11	6	5	199	5	100	1.50	.950
Patrick Lalime	OTT	5	1	4	73	4	33	3.29	.879
Evgeni Nabokov	SJ	1	0	1	3	1	1	21.56	.000
Chris Osgood	ATL	8	3	5	104	5	42	2.89	.881
Felix Potvin	LA	20	15	5	192	5	89	1.56	.944
Mike Richter	NYR	14	7	7	178	7	85	2.37	.918
Patrick Roy	COL	56	40	16	655	16	343	1.47	.953
Tommy Salo	EDM	5	1	4	105	4	50	2.29	.920
Steve Shields	BOS	3	2	1	14	1	10	4.18	.900
Garth Snow	NYI	1	0	1	6	1	6	9.38	.833
Jose Theodore	MTL	4	2	2	75	2	37	1.61	.946
Jocelyn Thibault	CHI	2	1	1	13	1	4	4.54	.750
Ron Tugnutt	DAL	5	2	3	117	3	62	1.54	.952
Roman Turek	CGY	4	3	1	74	1	32	0.81	.969
Kevin Weekes	CAR	2	1	1	11	1	6	5.61	.833

* Brent Johnson played 24 seconds of overtime vs. Colorado, May 21, 2001. (Winning goal for Colorado by Joe Sakic.)

CHAPTER 14

This Date in Stanley Cup History

December

Dec. 27, 1897 • In the only Stanley Cup challenge of the season, the defending champion Montreal Victorias turned back the Ottawa Capitals 15-2 to retain their champion status.

Dec. 27, 1906 • Riley Hern, "Pud" Glass, "Hod" Stuart, Ernie Johnson and Jack Marshall of the Montreal Wanderers officially became the first professionals to compete for the Stanley Cup. Glass scored four goals as the defending champion Montreal club downed the challenging New Glasgow Cubs 10-3 in the first game of a two-game total-goals series.

Dec. 30, 1896 • Ernie McLea notched the first hat trick in Stanley Cup history as the Montreal Victorias regained possession of the coveted trophy with a 6-5 win versus the defending champion Winnipeg Victorias. Winnipeg had won the Cup earlier in the year, defeating the Montreal Vics 2-0 on February 14, 1896.

Dec. 30, 1904 • In the first game of a best-of-three challenge between the Winnipeg Rowing Club and the defending champion Ottawa Silver Seven, a red line was drawn between each set of goalposts to aid the referee in awarding goals. These lines became the first known "Goal Lines" in hockey history.

January

Jan. 16, 1905 • "One-Eyed" Frank McGee netted an all-time Stanley Cup record 14 goals in the Ottawa Silver Seven's 23-2 win over the Dawson City Nuggets, who had trekked over 4,000 miles by dogsled, boat and train to challenge for the Cup.

Jan. 31, 1901 • The Stanley Cup was won in overtime for the first time when Dan Bain of the Winnipeg Victorias scored four minutes into the extra session for a 2-1 victory over the Montreal Shamrocks. Winnipeg swept the best-of-three series.

February

Feb. 14, 1896 • Winnipeg Victorias goaltender "Whitey" Merritt, credited as the first netminder to wear goalie pads, posted a 2-0 shutout to capture the Stanley Cup from the reigning champion Montreal Victorias. The game marked the first successful challenge in Stanley Cup history.

Feb. 25, 1904 • Ottawa Silver Seven sniper Frank McGee registered the first five-goal performance in Stanley Cup history in an 11-2 win over the challenging Toronto Marlboros.

March

Mar. 5, 1900 • Defending champion Montreal Shamrocks forward Art Farrell led his club to a 10-2 victory against the challenging Halifax Crescents with an unprecedented four-goal Stanley Cup performance.

Mar. 9, 1893 • Upon defeating the Montreal Crystals 2-1, the Montreal Amateur Athletic Association (MAAA) captured the 1893 Amateur Hockey Association (AHA) title and the first Stanley Cup championship. The MAAA lineup consisted of nine players: Billy Barlow (forward), Allan Cameron (defense), Archie Hodgson (forward), Alex Irving (forward), A.B. Kingan (forward), G.S. Lowe (forward), Tom Paton (goaltender), Haviland Routh (forward) and James Stewart (defense).

Mar. 9, 1895 • In the first official challenge for the Stanley Cup, the defending champion Montreal AAA team retained possession of the trophy with a 5-1 triumph over the Queen's University Golden Gaels.

Mar. 11, 1914 • The Toronto Blueshirts (later renamed the Maple Leafs) captured their first Stanley Cup title with a 6-0 home-ice shutout against the Montreal Canadiens in a playoff to determine the NHA champion. The game marked the first Stanley Cup contest ever played on an artificial ice surface.

Mar. 14, 1908 • Making his Stanley Cup debut, "Newsy" Lalonde scored twice, but still the Montreal Wanderers scored a 6-4 win over Lalonde's Toronto Trolley Leaguers for a successful defense of their championship title .

Mar. 16, 1911 • Ottawa Senators forward Marty Walsh scored 10 goals—second in Stanley Cup history only to Frank McGee's 14-goal total (January 16, 1905)—en route to a 13-4 win over the Port Arthur Bearcats.

Mar. 16, 1923 • For the first time in Stanley Cup history, two brothers opposed each other in the Finals. In fact, two sets of brothers—Cy and Corb Denneny, and George and Frank Boucher—lined up on opposite sides of the ice. Cy and George skated for the Ottawa Senators, while Corb and Frank played for Vancouver Maroons. None of the four scored in this opening game, won by Ottawa 1-0.

Mar. 18, 1892 • At a dinner of the Ottawa Amateur Athletic Association, Lord Kilcoursie, a player on the Ottawa Rebels hockey club, read the following message on behalf of Lord Stanley of Preston, the Governor-General of Canada,:"It would be a good thing if there were a challenge cup which should be held from year to year by the champion hockey team in the Dominion (of Canada)...I am willing to give a cup which shall be held...by the winning team." That cup eventually became the Stanley Cup, which has been presented annually since 1893.

Mar. 21, 1921 • More than 11,000 fans jammed the Vancouver Arena for the first game of this best-of-five Stanley Cup series between the hometown Millionaires and the visiting Ottawa Senators. It marked the largest crowd ever to witness a hockey game anywhere in the world up until this date. Vancouver downed Ottawa 2-1.

Mar. 22, 1894 • Forward Billy Barlow netted two goals as the Montreal AAA downed the Ottawa Generals 3-1 in this one-game battle for the 1894 Stanley Cup.

Mar. 22, 1919 • Montreal center "Newsy" Lalonde became the first NHL player ever to score four goals in one Finals game, spurring the Canadiens to a 4-2 win against the PCHA's Seattle Metropolitans. Only "Babe" Dye of the Toronto St. Pats (March 28, 1922), Detroit's Ted Lindsay (April 5, 1955) and Montreal's Maurice "Rocket" Richard (April 6, 1957) have since matched Lalonde's four-goal feat.

Mar. 23, 1918 • Alf Skinner of the Toronto Arenas registered the first hat trick by an NHL player in a Stanley Cup Finals game. The PCHA's Vancouver Millionaires downed Toronto 6-4 in Game Two of the 1918 Finals, the first Stanley Cup series involving an NHL franchise.

Mar. 25, 1917 • The Seattle Metropolitans of the Pacific Coast Hockey Association (PCHA) distinguished themselves as the first United States team to win the Stanley Cup. Seattle's Bernie Morris scored six times en route to a 9-1 triumph over the Montreal Canadiens.

Mar. 25, 1922 • Toronto goaltender John Ross Roach blanked the Vancouver Millionaires 6-0, recording the first Stanley Cup shutout by a goaltender in NHL play.

Mar. 26, 1919 • In the longest game to that point in Finals history, the Montreal Canadiens and Seattle Metropolitans (PCHA) played for 80 minutes (60 minutes of regulation time and 20 minutes of overtime) without scoring a goal. Georges Vezina and Harry Holmes dominated the first scoreless tie in Stanley Cup history with a display of superior goaltending.

Mar. 27, 1925 • Howie Morenz led the Montreal Canadiens to a 4-2 win over the PCHA's Victoria Cougars with the second three-goal output of his Stanley Cup Finals career, setting an NHL record in the process. Maurice "Rocket" Richard later surpassed Morenz's mark with three hat tricks, including one four-goal and two three-goal performances.

Mar. 28, 1922 • "Babe" Dye scores four goals to lead the Toronto St. Pats to a 5-1 win over the Vancouver Millionaires and a three games to one victory in their Stanley Cup series. Dye joined "Newsy" Lalonde (March 22, 1919) as the second player in NHL history to score four goals in a Stanley Cup game.

Mar. 28, 1929 • For the first time in history, two American teams—the Boston Bruins and New York Rangers—clashed in the Finals. The Bruins' "Dit" Clapper and "Dutch" Gainor scored goals, and "Tiny" Thompson posted the third Stanley Cup shutout ever by an NHL rookie to give Boston a 2-0 win in Game One. The Bruins won 2-1 the following night to capture their first championship title.

Mar. 29, 1929 • Harry Oliver scored a goal and an assist, and Bill Carson netted the game-winning tally as the Boston Bruins earned their first Stanley Cup title with a 2-1 win versus the New York Rangers. The victory completed a two-game sweep by Boston in the best-of-three Finals.

Mar. 30, 1916 • In the fifth and final game for the 1916 Stanley Cup title, the Montreal Canadiens downed the PCHA's Portland Rosebuds 2-1 on goals by Skene Ronan and Goldie Prodgers, who netted the winning tally. The victory marked the first of Montreal's 24 championships, a record surpassed only by the New York Yankees in professional sports history.

Mar. 30, 1918 • In the fifth and final game of the 1918 Finals, Alf Skinner and Corb Denneny engineered a successful comeback with unanswered goals in a 2-1 win over the PCHA's Vancouver Millionaires. Denneny notched the game-winner as the Toronto Arenas became the first NHL team to capture Lord Stanley's Cup.

Mar. 30, 1919 • Montreal Canadiens right winger Odie Cleghorn scored the first overtime goal by an NHL player in the Finals, snapping a 3-3 tie at 15:57 of the overtime period. The game knotted the 1919 Finals between Montreal and the Seattle Metropolitans at 2-2-1 after five outings. However, the series never resumed because players from both squads suffered the consequences of a

raging flu epidemic. Montreal's Joe Hall, who had been become ill during this fifth game, died on April 5, 1919, as a result of the sickness.

Mar. 30, 1925 • The Victoria Cougars of the Western Canada Hockey League downed the Montreal Canadiens 6-1 to become the last non-NHL team to capture the Stanley Cup. The win gave Victoria a 3-1 margin over Montreal in the best-of-five championship series.

Mar. 30, 1946 • In Game One, right winger Maurice "Rocket" Richard registered the first of his record three overtime goals in Finals action, snapping a 3-3 tie at 9:08 of the extra period. The goal gave the Montreal Canadiens the first of their four victories versus the Boston Bruins en route to the 1946 Stanley Cup.

April 1 – 10

April 1, 1920 • The Ottawa Senators downed the PCHA's Seattle Metropolitans 6–1 in the fifth and final game in their best-of-five Stanley Cup series. Games Four and Five of the series were played on artificial ice in Toronto because of mild weather in Ottawa. One year later, the Senators would become the first NHL team to win back-to-back Stanley Cup championships.

April 3, 1930 • The Canadiens downed the Bruins 4-3 to complete a two-game sweep of the 1930 Finals. For the defending Stanley Cup champion Boston Bruins, who had posted the NHL's best regular-season record in 1929-30 with a 38-5-1 mark, the games marked their first back-to-back losses of the year.

April 4, 1921 • The Ottawa Senators defeated the Vancouver Millionaires 2-1 in the decisive fifth game of the 1921 Stanley Cup series. Jack Darragh scored both goals for the Senators, who became the first NHL team to capture back-to-back Stanley Cup titles.

April 4, 1944 • Montreal Canadiens rookie right winger Maurice "Rocket" Richard made his Stanley Cup debut, tallying an assist on linemate "Toe" Blake's game-winning goal in this 5-1 victory against the Chicago Black Hawks in Game One of the 1944 Finals. Richard continued to play a key role in Montreal's drive towards the title, scoring four more goals in the remaining three games of the Canadiens' four-game sweep against Chicago.

April 5, 1931 • Over 18,000 fans jammed Chicago Stadium for Game Two of the 1931 championship series, setting a new record for the largest attendance for one game in hockey history. Black Hawks left winger Johnny Gottselig thrilled the hometown fans with the game-winning goal in double overtime as Chicago downed the Montreal Canadiens 2-1. The Canadiens later won the Stanley Cup series three games to two.

April 5, 1955 • Detroit Red Wings left winger Ted Lindsay became the third player in NHL history to score four goals in one Stanley Cup game and tied a Finals record with three goals in one period. Joining "Newsy" Lalonde (March 22, 1919) and "Babe" Dye (March 28, 1922) in achieving the four-goal feat, Lindsay scored the game-winning tally as Detroit downed Montreal 7-1.

April 6, 1926 • Goaltender Clint Benedict backstopped the Montreal Maroons to their first Stanley Cup title, blanking the Victoria Cougars 2-0 to win the best-of-five confrontation 3-1. The shutout was Benedict's third of the series, establishing a new Stanley Cup record for one year.

April 6, 1937 • When regular netminder Normie Smith left Game One of the Finals with an elbow injury, the Detroit Red Wings placed minor leaguer Earl Robertson of the International League's Pittsburgh Hornets into the nets to finish the series. After a 5-1 loss to the New York Rangers in the opener, Robertson, who had never before played an

NHL game, backstopped the Red Wings to three wins in their next four outings to capture the 1937 Stanley Cup.

April 6, 1944 • Rookie right winger Maurice "Rocket" Richard registered the first of his NHL record three Stanley Cup hat tricks as Montreal won Game Two 3-1 over Chicago. The victory was the second of four straight by the Canadiens versus the Black Hawks en route to the 1944 title.

April 6, 1945 • For the first time in Stanley Cup history, two rookie goaltenders—Toronto's Frank McCool and Detroit's Harry Lumley—opposed each other in the Finals. On the strength of Dave "Sweeney" Schriner's first-period goal, McCool and the Leafs blanked the Wings 1-0 to open the best-of-seven series. For McCool, it was the first of a record three straight Stanley Cup shutouts and four victories en route to winning the 1945 title.

April 6, 1954 • Dickie Moore and Maurice "Rocket" Richard of the Montreal Canadiens combined for the fastest three goals by an NHL team in Finals history, scoring three times within 56 seconds. Moore scored at 15:03 of the first period, followed by Richard at 15:28 and 15:59. The Canadiens downed the Red Wings 3-2 in Detroit.

April 6, 1957 • Right winger Maurice "Rocket" Richard tied "Newsy" Lalonde, "Babe" Dye and Ted Lindsay for the NHL record with four goals in one Stanley Cup game, leading Montreal to a 5-1 triumph over the Boston Bruins in Game One of the 1957 Finals. The four-goal effort also distinguished Richard as the only NHL player to record three hat tricks in a Stanley Cup career. Montreal went on to win the best-of-seven series four games to one.

April 6, 1961 • In their Stanley Cup debuts, Bobby Hull (2-0-2) and Stan Mikita (0-2-2) led the Chicago Black Hawks to a 3-2 win against the Detroit Red Wings in Game One of the 1961 Finals. Hull netted the winning tally at 13:15 of the first period. Chicago went on to defeat Detroit four games to two in the best-of-seven series.

April 7, 1927 • The American Division champion Boston Bruins battled the Canadian Division champion Ottawa Senators to a 0-0 overtime tie in the first all-NHL Stanley Cup game. The best-of-five series, eventually won by Ottawa 2-0-2 over Boston, marked the dawn of the modern Stanley Cup era.

April 7, 1928 • After losing starting goaltender Lorne Chabot to an eye injury midway through Game Two, 44-year-old New York Rangers coach and former star player Lester Patrick took over between the pipes and inspired his club to a 2-1 overtime victory in Game Two of the 1928 Finals. After signing New York Americans rookie netminder Joe Miller the following day, the Rangers skated to two wins in their next three outings to win the best-of-five championship series 3-2.

April 7, 1948 • 20-year-old right winger Gordie Howe of Detroit made his Stanley Cup debut in Game One of the 1948 Finals but failed to register a point as the Toronto Maple Leafs downed the Red Wings 5-3. The Leafs later went on to sweep Detroit in four straight games to capture the best-of-seven series and the Stanley Cup. Howe did not score in the series.

April 7, 1960 • In Game One of the 1960 Finals, Montreal right winger Maurice "Rocket" Richard extended his all-time record of Stanley Cup series appearances to 12, while Toronto's Bert Olmstead and Montreal's Doug Harvey, Bernie "Boom Boom" Geoffrion and Tom Johnson extended their records for consecutive Finals appearances to 10. Montreal defeated Toronto 4-2.

April 7, 1982 • The Edmonton Oilers and Los Angeles Kings combined for 18 goals, setting an NHL record for the highest scoring playoff game.

Edmonton won the game 10-8 in Game One of their best-of-five Smythe Division Semifinal. Los Angeles won the series 3-2.

April 8, 1934 • Detroit Red Wings goaltender Wilf Cude suffered a broken nose midway through Game Three but remained in nets until the final buzzer sounded, inspiring his team to a 5-2 upset win against the Black Hawks in Chicago. It was Detroit's only victory during the best-of-five Finals won by Chicago, three games to one.

April 8, 1937 • Referee Clarence Campbell officiated his first Stanley Cup contest in Game Two of the 1937 Finals, a 4-2 win for the Detroit Red Wings over the New York Rangers. Campbell, who later became the third League President in NHL history in 1946, doled out three penalties during the affair.

April 8, 1943 • After blanking Boston 4-0 the previous night, Detroit goalie Johnny Mowers shut out the Bruins 2-0, completing a four-game sweep in the 1943 Finals. Joe Carveth of the Red Wings registered the winning tally at 12:09 of the first period, and teammate Carl Liscombe added an insurance marker to lock up the title.

April 8, 1980 • Gordie Howe established an NHL record for most years in the playoffs (20) by appearing for the Hartford Whalers in Game One of their best-of-three Preliminary round series against Montreal. Howe, making his first NHL playoff appearance since the 1969-70 season, passed former Detroit and Toronto defenseman Red Kelly, who had played in 19 playoff seasons.

April 8, 1982 • Mikko Leinonen of the New York Rangers became the first NHL player to record six assists in a playoff game, helping his club to a 7-3 win over Philadelphia in Game Two of their Patrick Division Final. Leinonen's mark was equalled by Edmonton's Wayne Gretzky during the 1987 playoffs.

April 9, 1932 • The Toronto Maple Leafs defeated the New York Rangers 6-4 to complete a three-game sweep of the 1932 Finals. The series marked the Stanley Cup debut of the Leafs' famed "Kid Line" of Harvey "Busher" Jackson, Charlie Conacher and Joe Primeau, who combined for eight goals in Toronto's three victories.

April 9, 1935 • After winning the first two games of the 1935 Finals in Toronto, the Montreal Maroons completed a three-game sweep of the Maple Leafs with a 4-1 win in the best-of-five Stanley Cup series.

April 9, 1942 • Eddie Bush of the Detroit Red Wings established a new NHL record with five points (1-4-5) by a defenseman in one Stanley Cup Finals game. Bush, who never scored another point in his NHL career, led Detroit to a 5-2 victory over the Toronto Maple Leafs.

April 9, 1946 • In Game Five of the 1946 Finals, Montreal center Elmer Lach scored a goal and two assists in a 6-3 win against the Boston Bruins. The victory gave the Canadiens their second Stanley Cup title in three years.

April 9, 1987 • The Edmonton Oilers established an NHL record for most goals in a playoff game, recording a 13-3 win over Los Angeles in Game Two of their Smythe Division Semifinal. Edmonton went on to win the best-of-seven series 4-1.

April 10, 1934 • The Chicago Black Hawks earned their first Stanley Cup title with a 1-0 overtime victory versus the Detroit Red Wings in Game Four of the best-of-five championship. Harold "Mush" March potted the series-winner at 10:05 of the second overtime period.

April 10, 1949 • Toronto left winger Sid Smith set a new NHL record with three power-play goals in one Finals game. Toronto defeated Detroit 3-1.

April 10, 1956 • Center Jean Beliveau notched a goal and two assists as the Montreal Canadiens took Game Five (3-1) and the 1956 Stanley Cup title

from the Detroit Red Wings. The goal gave Beliveau seven versus Detroit, establishing a modern record for one Final series. New York Islanders right winger Mike Bossy (1982) and Edmonton Oilers center Wayne Gretzky (1985) have since tied Beliveau's Stanley Cup mark.

April 10, 1982 • The Los Angeles Kings scored five third-period goals and added the game-winner in overtime to defeat the Edmonton Oilers 6-5 in Game Three of the 1982 Smythe Division Semifinal in one of the greatest comebacks in NHL playoff history. Trailing 5-0 entering the third period, Los Angeles forward Steve Bozek scored the tying goal with just five seconds remaining and Daryl Evans capped the furious Kings rally by adding the overtime winner at 2:35. Los Angeles went on to win the best-of-five series 3-2.

April 10, 1985 • Detroit Red Wings defenseman Brad Park set an NHL record by appearing in postseason play for the 17th consecutive season. Park, marking his second playoff year in a Red Wings uniform, played in all three games of Detroit's Norris Division Semifinal series against Chicago, which the Black Hawks won 3-0. He had previously made playoff appearances for the New York Rangers (seven seasons) and Boston Bruins (eight seasons).

April 11 – 20

April 11, 1936 • Detroit coach Jack Adams steered the Red Wings to their first Stanley Cup championship with a 3-2 victory over the Toronto Maple Leafs in Game Four of the best-of-five Stanley Cup confrontation. The Wings, who had entered the NHL in 1926-27, became the last of the League's "Original Six" teams to win the Cup.

April 11, 1965 • Detroit Red Wings center Norm Ullman set NHL individual and team playoff records by scoring two goals just five seconds apart in Game Five of their Semifinal series against Chicago. Ullman scored at 17:35 and 17:40 of the second period. Chicago won the best-of-seven series 4-3.

April 11, 1971 • Boston Bruins defenseman Bobby Orr became the first defenseman to score three goals in a playoff game during a 5-2 win over the Montreal Canadiens. Since then, nine other defensemen have equalled Orr's mark.

April 11, 1980 • Montreal's Yvon Lambert scored at 0:29 of overtime to give the Canadiens a 4-3 victory over Hartford and a sweep of the best-of-five series. The game marked the final NHL appearance of two Hall-of-Famers, as Hartford's Gordie Howe and Bobby Hull retired following the Whalers' elimination from the playoffs.

April 11, 1981 • The Boston Bruins set a new playoff record by scoring three shorthanded goals against the Minnesota North Stars in Game Three of their Quarterfinal series. The three shorthanded goals were not enough as Minnesota won the game 6-3 and swept the best-of-five series.

April 11, 1989 • Philadelphia's Ron Hextall was the first goaltender to score a goal in the playoffs with an empty-net goal against the Washington Capitals. The Flyers won the game 8-5.

April 12, 1938 • The Chicago Black Hawks captured the 1938 Stanley Cup title with a 4-1 victory against the Toronto Maple Leafs in Game Four of the best-of-five title series. Eight American-born players— Carl Dahlstrom, Roger Jenkins, Virgil Johnson, Mike Karakas, Alex Levinsky, Elwin "Doc" Romnes, Louis Trudel and Carl Voss—skated for Chicago in the Finals to set a new Stanley Cup record for United States talent on a championship team.

April 12, 1941 • For the first time since the NHL adopted the best-of-seven Finals format in 1939, a team won the Stanley Cup in straight games. The Boston Bruins topped the Detroit Red Wings 3-1 to complete their four-game sweep of the 1941 series.

April 12, 1945 • Maple Leafs rookie netminder Frank McCool set a new record with his third consecutive Stanley Cup shutout, 1-0 against the Red Wings, as Toronto moved to within one game of sweeping Detroit in the Finals. The Leafs later won the championship series in seven games.

April 12, 1960 • Right winger Maurice "Rocket" Richard scored his all-time record 34th and final Stanley Cup goal, helping the Montreal Canadiens to a 5-2 win over the Toronto Maple Leafs in Game Three of the 1960 Finals. The Canadiens' victory was the third in a four-game sweep against the Leafs.

April 12, 1979 • The Toronto Maple Leafs set a playoff record for the fastest three goals by one team during a 7-4 victory over the Atlanta Flames in Game Two of their Preliminary round series. Darryl Sittler scored at 4:04 and 4:16 and Ron Ellis at 4:27 of the first period. Toronto went on to win the best-of-three series 2-0.

April 12, 2001 • Pittsburgh Penguins center Mario Lemieux returned to Stanley Cup Playoff action for the first time since 1997 as the Penguins visited Washington to open their Eastern Conference Quarterfinal. Lemieux had made a triumphant return to the NHL in December, 2000, following three and a half years away from the game. Led by Lemieux's 17 points (six goals, 11 assists), the Penguins advanced to the Eastern Conference Final before bowing to the New Jersey Devils. Lemieux finished the postseason as the only top 10 scorer who did not participate in the Stanley Cup Finals.

April 13, 1985 • Philadelphia Flyers center Tim Kerr set a new playoff record by scoring four goals in one period, eclipsing the mark of three held by many players. Kerr scored the four goals in the second period of a 6-5 win over the New York Rangers. Three of Kerr's goals were scored on the power-play, also setting a new record.

April 13, 1933 • Bill Cook snapped a scoreless tie at 7:33 of overtime to give the New York Rangers a 1-0 victory against the Toronto Maple Leafs. Rangers rookie goaltender Andy Aitkenhead posted the shutout as New York captured the best-of-five series in four games.

April 13, 1940 • Frank Boucher, who played on New York's first two Stanley Cup championship teams in 1928 and 1933, coached the Rangers to a third title with a 3-2 overtime win in Game Six of the best-of-seven series. Among Boucher's players on the team were brothers Lynn and "Muzz" Patrick, the third and fourth members of the legendary Patrick family (including their father Lester and uncle Frank) to have their names engraved on the Cup. Bryan Hextall scored the winning goal.

April 13, 1944 • Montreal's famed Punch Line—left winger "Toe" Blake, center Elmer Lach and right winger Maurice "Rocket" Richard—powered the Canadiens to a 5-4 series-clinching comeback victory versus the Chicago Black Hawks in Game Four of the 1944 Finals. After Chicago had taken a 4-1 lead through two periods, Lach scored at 10:02 of the third, followed by Richard's back-to-back tallies at 16:05 and 17:20 to tie the game at four goals apiece after regulation time. Blake then ended the game and the season with a blast past netminder Mike Karakas at 9:12 of overtime. The win gave the Canadiens their first Stanley Cup title since 1931, ending their longest period without a championship from their first season in the National Hockey Association (NHA), 1909-1910, to the present.

April 13, 1952 • Right winger Gordie Howe registered his first two Stanley Cup goals and goaltender Terry Sawchuk posted a shutout to lead the Detroit Red Wings past the Montreal Canadiens 3-0 in Game Three of the 1952 Finals. The win was Detroit's third straight en route to a four-game sweep of Montreal in the best-of-seven season finale.

April 14, 1928 • In only their second season as an NHL franchise, the New York Rangers captured the 1928 Stanley Cup with a 2-1 triumph over the Montreal Maroons in the final game of the best-of-five title series. The Rangers became only the second American team in history to win the Stanley Cup, joining the 1917 champion Seattle Metropolitans of the Pacific Coast Hockey Association.

April 14, 1931 • Goaltender George Hainsworth blanked the Chicago Black Hawks 2-0 as the Montreal Canadiens became the second NHL team to win Stanley Cup championships in two consecutive seasons. The Ottawa Senators first accomplished the feat in 1920 and 1921.

April 14, 1942 • Brothers Don Metz (3-2-5) and Nick Metz (1-2-3) led the Toronto Maple Leafs to a record-tying 9-3 victory against the Detroit Red Wings in the 1942 Finals. The Leafs' nine-goal outburst matched the Finals scoring mark for an NHL team set by Detroit on April 7, 1936, in a 9-4 win against Toronto.

April 14, 1948 • The Toronto Maple Leafs repeated as Stanley Cup champions with a 7-2 win against the Detroit Red Wings, thus completing a four-game sweep of the 1948 Finals. The game spelled the end of a career for Toronto captain Syl Apps, who punctuated his stint in the NHL with a goal in this series-ending victory.

April 14, 1953 • Maurice "Rocket" Richard became the second NHL player to register two hat tricks in Finals history, joining Howie Morenz in achieving the feat. Richard, who led Montreal to a 7-3 win against Boston, later added a four-goal performance to his record on April 6, 1957.

April 14, 1955 • Right winger Gordie Howe scored the winning goal in Game Seven of the 1955 Stanley Cup Finals to lead the Detroit Red Wings past the Montreal Canadiens 3-1. The goal gave Howe a 5-7-12 scoring mark in the series, setting a new individual mark for Finals competition.

April 14, 1960 • Goaltender Jacques Plante blanked the Toronto Maple Leafs 4-0 as the Montreal Canadiens captured their record-setting fifth straight Stanley Cup championship. The victory marked the end of a career for Maurice "Rocket" Richard, the NHL's all-time leader with 34 goals in Stanley Cup play.

April 15, 1937 • In Game Five of the 1937 Stanley Cup series, referee Mickey Ion awarded Rangers right winger Alex Shibicky the first penalty shot in Finals history. Red Wings rookie goaltender Earl Robertson stopped Shibicky's shot and posted his second straight shutout, 3-0 against New York, as Detroit became the first American team to repeat as Cup champions.

April 15, 1952 • In his fourth shutout in eight postseason games, Detroit Red Wings goalie Terry Sawchuk blanked the Montreal Canadiens 3-0 to complete a four-game sweep of the 1952 Finals. The Wings, who had also swept the Toronto Maple Leafs in the Semifinals, distinguished themselves as the first NHL team to win every postseason game in one year.

April 16, 1939 • Goaltender Frank Brimsek, alias "Mr. Zero", allowed only one goal, his sixth in five Stanley Cup games against Toronto, to lead the Boston Bruins past the Maple Leafs 3-1 to win the 1939 championship.

April 16, 1949 • The Toronto Maple Leafs swept the Detroit Red Wings to become the first NHL team to win three consecutive Stanley Cup titles (1947-49). The 3-1 series-ending victory also marked the Leafs' ninth straight win in Finals action.

April 16, 1953 • Assisted by linemate Maurice "Rocket" Richard, Elmer Lach scored the only goal in Game Five at 1:22 of overtime, and goalie Gerry McNeil blanked the Boston Bruins for the second time in three outings as the Montreal Canadiens earned the 1953 Stanley Cup championship.

April 16, 1954 • Tony Leswick's Stanley Cup-winning tally was the second overtime goal ever scored in the seventh game of a Final series. Leswick, who notched the decisive goal at 4:29 of overtime in Detroit's 2-1 victory over the Montreal Canadiens in Game Seven, matched the feat first accomplished by former Red Wings left winger Pete Babando in 1950.

April 16, 1961 • The Chicago Black Hawks earned their first Stanley Cup championship since 1938 and their third title since joining the NHL in 1926-27. The Black Hawks downed Detroit 5-1 to take the best-of-seven Finals four games to two.

April 16, 1994 • The Boston Bruins opened their Eastern Conference Quarterfinal series against the Montreal Canadiens, extending their NHL record for most consecutive playoff appearances to 27 years.

April 16, 1997 • The Mighty Ducks of Anaheim, making their first playoff appearance, were led by Paul Kariya (2-1-3) and Teemu Selanne (2-1-3) in a 4-2 home win over the Phoenix Coyotes in Game One of their Western Conference Quarterfinal. The win extended the Mighty Ducks home undefeated streak, including regular season, to 15 games (11-0-4).

April 17, 1958 • Right winger Maurice "Rocket" Richard led the Montreal Canadiens to a 3-2 win against the Boston Bruins in Game Five with a goal at 5:45 of overtime. The overtime goal was Richard's third in a Stanley Cup game and sixth in a playoff game, extending his record in each category. The Canadiens went on to win the best-of-seven series in six games.

April 17, 1977 • Don Kozak of the Los Angeles Kings scored the fastest goal from the start of an NHL playoff game, tallying just six seconds into his club's 7-4 win over the Boston Bruins in Game Four of their Quarterfinal series.

April 17, 1997 • The Ottawa Senators made their first playoff appearance since joining the NHL in 1992-93, dropping a 3-1 decision to the Buffalo Sabres at Marine Midland Arena in Game One of their Eastern Conference Quarterfinal.

April 17, 1997 • New Jersey Devils goaltender Martin Brodeur became just the second goaltender in NHL playoff history to score a goal, coming in a 5-2 win over the Montreal Canadiens in Game One of their Eastern Conference Quarterfinal. Philadelphia's Ron Hextall was the first goaltender to score a goal in the playoffs, on April 11, 1989 versus the Washington Capitals.

April 18, 1942 • The Toronto Maple Leafs completed the greatest comeback in Stanley Cup history with their fourth straight victory after losing the first three games of the Finals to the Detroit Red Wings. Leafs goaltender Turk Broda provided the heroics, allowing the Red Wings only seven goals in the last four games, including this 3-1 series-ending victory.

April 18, 1959 • Montreal Canadiens left winger Marcel Bonin scored the Stanley Cup-winning goal at 9:55 of the second period en route to a 5-3 win over the Toronto Maple Leafs in Game Six. This victory ended the series and gave Montreal the fourth of its record five straight Stanley Cup titles.

April 18, 1963 • In Game Five of the 1963 Finals, Toronto Maple Leafs center Dave Keon scored two shorthanded goals against the Detroit Red Wings, setting a single-game playoff record. Keon's heroics led Toronto to a 3-1 Cup-winning triumph over Detroit. It marked the second of three straight Stanley Cups for the Leafs.

April 18, 1987 • Pat LaFontaine scored the dramatic game-winning goal at 8:42 of the fourth overtime period in Game Seven of the Patrick Division Final versus Washington.

April 18, 1994 • The San Jose Sharks defeated the Detroit Red Wings 5-4 at Joe Louis Arena in Detroit in Game One of their Western Conference Quarterfinal series to become the first club since the 1975 New York Islanders to win the first Stanley Cup playoff game in franchise history. Since the Islanders defeated the New York Rangers 3-2 on April 8, 1975, seven clubs had lost their playoff debuts prior to San Jose's win.

April 18, 1994 • The New York Rangers posted their second consecutive 6-0 shutout to open the Stanley Cup playoffs against the New York Islanders. The Rangers became the first club to open the postseason with consecutive shutouts since the Buffalo Sabres defeated Montreal 1-0 and 3-0 in 1983.

April 19, 1947 • After assisting on defenseman Vic Lynn's goal at 5:39 of the second period to tie the game at one goal apiece, Toronto Maple Leafs center Ted "Teeder" Kennedy scored the Cup-winner at 14:39 of the third period to defeat the Montreal Canadiens 2-1 in Game Six. The series-ending victory earned Toronto its third Stanley Cup title in six seasons.

April 20, 1950 • New York center Don Raleigh set a Stanley Cup record with his second overtime goal in as many games as the Rangers downed the Detroit Red Wings 4-3 in Game Five of the 1950 Finals. The win proved to be the Rangers' last of the series as Detroit went on to win the final two games and the Stanley Cup.

April 20, 1967 • In Game One of the 1967 Finals, a 6-2 win for the Montreal Canadiens, defenseman Leonard "Red" Kelly skated in the 12th Stanley Cup series of his career, tying Maurice "Rocket" Richard for the all-time record. Montreal's Henri Richard and Jean Beliveau, both of whom played in the game, would later tie the mark as well.

April 20, 1997 • Chicago Blackhawks forward Sergei Krivokrasov scored at 11:03 of the second overtime period in a 4-3 win over the Colorado Avalanche in Game Three of their Western Conference Quarterfinal at the United Center. The goal stopped Avalanche goaltender Patrick Roy's overtime shutout streak at 162 minutes and 56 seconds, the longest streak in NHL playoff history.

April 20, 1997 • The Edmonton Oilers staged a game-tying, three-goal flurry in the last four minutes of the third period versus the Dallas Stars en route to a 4-3 overtime win in Game Three at Edmonton. It marked the first time since the NHL took exclusive control of the Stanley Cup in 1926-27 that a club had won a playoff game after trailing by three goals with less than five minutes to play. With Dallas leading 3-0 in the third period, Edmonton got goals from Doug Weight (16:00), Andrei Kovalenko (17:44) and Mike Grier (17:56) to tie the game, with Kelly Buchberger adding the game-winner at 9:15 of overtime. Edmonton took a 2-1 lead in the series.

April 20, 1993 • The Pittsburgh Penguins set an NHL playoff record with their 13th consecutive postseason win, a 7-0 decision over the New Jersey Devils in Game Two of their Patrick Division Semifinal. The Penguins passed the previous mark of 12, set by the Edmonton Oilers in the 1984 and 1985 playoff seasons. The Penguins extended their record to 14 games before dropping Game Four to the Devils, ending the streak.

April 21 – 30

April 21, 1951 • Toronto Maple Leafs defenseman Bill Barilko scored the Cup-winning goal at 2:53 of overtime to defeat the Montreal Canadiens 3-2 in Game Five of the 1951 Finals. It was the only Stanley Cup series in which every game had ended in overtime. Toronto's Sid Smith, Ted Kennedy, Harry Watson, Barilko and Montreal's Maurice "Rocket" Richard each netted overtime winners during the five-game matchup. Barilko died in an off-season plane crash in the summer of 1951, though his remains would not be discovered until 1962.

April 22, 1945 • At 12:14 of the third period, Maple Leafs defenseman Walter "Babe" Pratt scored the Cup-winning goal to give Toronto a 2-1 victory over the Detroit Red Wings in Game Seven of the Finals. Leafs rookie goaltender Frank McCool, who allowed only nine goals in seven starts, limited the Wings to one goal or less for the fifth time in the series.

April 22, 1962 • Toronto's Bob Nevin and Dick Duff notched third-period goals to defeat the Chicago Black Hawks 2-1 in Game Six of the 1962 Finals. The win propelled the Maple Leafs to their first of three straight Stanley Cup championships.

April 22, 1976 • Toronto center Darryl Sittler equalled Maurice Richard's 32-year-old record for most goals in one playoff game by scoring five goals in the Maple Leafs' 8-5 Quarterfinal series win over the Philadelphia Flyers. Philadelphia's Reggie Leach joined Richard and Sittler just days later, as Leach scored five of his playoff-record 19 goals on May 6, 1976, in a 6-3 win over the Boston Bruins.

April 22, 1988 • Patrik Sundstrom set an NHL record by recording eight points (3-5-8) in New Jersey's 10-4 win over Washington in Game Three of the Patrick Division Final.

April 23, 1950 • In the first Game Seven overtime in Finals history, left winger Pete Babando, assisted by center George Gee at 8:31 of the second overtime period, gave the Detroit Red Wings a 4-3 win and the 1950 Stanley Cup title. Four years later, another Detroit left winger, Tony Leswick, repeated Babando's overtime feat in Game Seven of the 1954 Finals. Since then, no player has scored the Cup-winning goal in overtime in the seventh and deciding game of the Finals.

April 23, 1996 • The Tampa Bay Lightning established an all-time NHL attendance record as 28,183 fans filled the ThunderDome for Game Four of Tampa Bay's Eastern Conference Quarterfinal series with the Philadelphia Flyers. The Flyers won 4-1, tying the series at two wins apiece. They went on to win the series in six.

April 23, 1997 • Wayne Gretzky scored a natural hat trick in the second period to lead the New York Rangers to a 3-2 victory over the Florida Panthers at Madison Square Garden, opening up a 3-1 series lead. Gretzky scored three goals in a 6:23 span to give the Rangers a 3-1 lead. The hat trick was his ninth in the postseason, extending his playoff record.

April 24, 1994 • Chicago Blackhawks defenseman Gary Suter tallied three goals in a 4-3 overtime win over the Toronto Maple Leafs in Game Four of their Western Conference Quarterfinal series. Suter became the eighth defenseman in Stanley Cup playoffs history to post a hat trick, joining Bobby Orr, Dick Redmond, Denis Potvin, Doug Halward, Paul Reinhart (twice), Al Iafrate and Eric Desjardins.

April 24, 1996 • Petr Nedved of the Penguins scored at the 19:15 mark of the fourth overtime period to give Pittsburgh a 3-2 win over Washington in the third-longest game in NHL history. Washington's Joe Juneau was stopped by Ken Wregget on the first

penalty shot ever taken in overtime of a Stanley Cup playoff game.

April 24, 1997 • The Colorado Avalanche shut out the Chicago Blackhawks 7-0 to gain a 3-2 series lead. It marked the 89th playoff win of Patrick Roy's career, an NHL record.

April 24, 1999 • Colorado Avalanche goaltender Patrick Roy, the NHL's all-time leader for postseason victories, earned his 100th career playoff win as the Avalanche defeated San Jose 3–1 to take a 1-0 lead in their opening-round series.

April 25, 1964 • Toronto goalie Johnny Bower blanked the Detroit Red Wings 4-0 to propel the Maple Leafs to their third straight Stanley Cup title. Four different scorers provided the offensive support for Bower, the Leafs' "China Wall."

April 26, 1975 • Goaltender Glenn Resch and the New York Islanders blanked the Pittsburgh Penguins 1-0 to win Game Seven and capture their 1975 Quarterfinal series. The Islanders became just the second team in NHL history to win a best-of-seven series after losing the first three games, joining the 1942 Toronto Maple Leafs. The Islanders nearly repeated the feat in the Semifinals against Philadelphia. The Islanders again lost the first three games of the series only to bounce back and win the next three. Their bid for an unprecedented second straight 0-3 comeback was stopped as they lost Game Seven, 4-1.

April 26, 1997 • Playing in his final NHL game, Pittsburgh's Mario Lemieux registered a goal and an assist but it wasn't enough as the Philadelphia Flyers defeated the Penguins 6-3, capturing the series 4-1. The sellout crowd at Philadelphia's CoreStates Center acknowledged Lemieux's outstanding career with a rousing standing ovation following the game.

April 27, 1980 • Minnesota's Al MacAdam scored the series-winning goal late in the third period to give the visiting North Stars a 3-2 win over the Montreal Canadiens in Game Seven of the 1980 Quarterfinal series. The Minnesota win stopped the Canadiens' bid for a record- tying fifth consecutive Stanley Cup, a mark that had been set by Montreal from 1956-60.

April 27, 1994 • Buffalo Sabres center Dave Hannan scored at 5:43 of the fourth overtime period in a 1-0 home win over the New Jersey Devils in Game Six of their Eastern Conference Quarterfinal series. This game was the sixth longest in NHL history, beginning at 7:39 p.m. and concluding at 1:51 a.m.—six hours and 12 minutes later. Sabres goaltender Dominik Hasek turned aside all 70 of the shots he faced, while New Jersey netminder Martin Brodeur made 49 saves on 50 shots.

April 27, 1998 • The St. Louis Blues tallied four power-play goals in a span of 3:07 during the third period of a 4-3 win over Los Angeles in Game Three of their Western Conference Quarterfinal. The four fastest power-play goals by one team in NHL history were scored by Pascal Rheaume (9:59), Brett Hull (11:03) Pierre Turgeon (11:59) and Terry Yake (13:06).

April 28, 1996 • A sold-out crowd at the Winnipeg Arena said good-bye to the Winnipeg Jets following a 4-1 loss to the Detroit Red Wings in Game Six of their Western Conference Quarterfinal series. It marked the final game for the Jets before moving to Phoenix and becoming the Coyotes.

April 29, 1973 • Tony Esposito of the Chicago Black Hawks and Ken Dryden of the Montreal Canadiens, who had been Team Canada's goaltending duo in the 1972 Summit Series versus the Soviet Union, faced each other on opposite sides of the ice in Game One of the 1973 Finals. Dryden and the Canadiens won the contest 8-3 and went on to win the title series in six games. Montreal's Henri

Richard tied brother Maurice and Leonard "Red" Kelly for the all-time record for Finals appearances with the 12th of his career.

April 30, 1972 • The New York Rangers made their first appearance in a Stanley Cup finals series game since 1950, losing to the Boston Bruins 6-5 in the opening contest. The 1972 championship clash between New York and Boston marked the first time in 43 years that the two had met in the Finals. Boston won the best-of-seven series in six games.

May 1 – 10

May 1, 1965 • Montreal captain Jean Beliveau notched the winning goal and added one assist to lead the Canadiens past the Chicago Black Hawks in Game Seven of the 1965 Finals. Beliveau, who posted a 5-5-10 scoring total in the seven-game Stanley Cup series, received a new NHL award, the Conn Smythe Trophy, as the most valuable player to his team in the playoffs.

May 2, 1967 • With the oldest lineup in Finals history, the Toronto Maple Leafs defeated the Montreal Canadiens 3-1 in Game Six to win the 1967 Stanley Cup. The Leafs' roster included 42-year-old goalie Johnny Bower and 41-year-old defenseman Allan Stanley as well as seven others at least 30 years old. Toronto defenseman Leonard "Red" Kelly played his 65th game in Finals competition, setting a Stanley Cup record later tied by Montreal's Henri Richard.

May 4, 1969 • With a 2-1 win in Game Four of the 1969 Stanley Cup, the Montreal Canadiens swept the St. Louis Blues in the Finals for the second straight season. The Conn Smythe Trophy was presented to Serge Savard, the first defenseman to receive the award.

May 4, 1972 • New York Rangers defenseman Brad Park registered two power-play goals in the first period of a 5-2 win against the Boston Bruins to tie a Stanley Cup Finals record for one period. Park joined Sid Smith (April 10, 1949) of Toronto and Maurice "Rocket" Richard (April 6, 1954) and Bernie "Boom Boom" Geoffrion (April 7, 1955) in accomplishing this power-play feat.

May 4, 1998 • Curtis Joseph of the Edmonton Oilers blanked the Colorado Avalanche 4-0 to become just the second goaltender in NHL playoff history to post back-to-back shutouts in Games Six and Seven of a playoff series. Joseph and the Oilers recorded a 2-0 win over the Avalanche in Game Six.

May 4, 2000 • The Philadelphia Flyers defeated the Pittsburgh Penguins 2-1 at Mellon Arena in Game Four of their Eastern Conference Semifinal series, ending the third-longest game in NHL history. Philadelphia forward Keith Primeau scored at 12:01 of the fifth overtime period (92:01 into overtime). The game's duration of six hours, 56 minutes set an NHL record.

May 5, 1966 • At 2:30 of overtime in Game Six, Montreal Canadiens center Henri Richard became the ninth player in NHL history to record a Stanley Cup-winning goal in sudden-death. Richard's overtime goal gave Montreal a 3-2 win versus the Detroit Red Wings. Detroit goaltender Roger Crozier, who amassed a 2.17 average and one shutout in 12 playoff games, earned the Conn Smythe Trophy as the most valuable player to his team in postseason competition. Crozier was the first Conn Smythe winner from a losing team.

May 7, 1995 • The Boston Bruins made their 1995 Stanley Cup Playoffs debut, dropping a 5-0 home decision to the New Jersey Devils. The Bruins extended their NHL record by appearing in the playoffs for the 28th consecutive year.

May 8, 1973 • The Chicago Black Hawks and Montreal Canadiens combined to set an NHL record with 15 goals in one Finals game. Led by Stan

Mikita's two-goal, two-assist performance, the Black Hawks edged the Canadiens 8-7 in Game Five at the Montreal Forum. Montreal went on to win the series four games to two.

May 8, 1982 • The Vancouver Canucks became the first team since the 1924 Vancouver Maroons of the Western Canada Hockey League (WCHL) to represent that city in the Stanley Cup Finals. The Canucks lost this opening game 6-5 in overtime to the New York Islanders, who went on to take the series in four straight games.

May 8, 1995 • New York Rangers center Mark Messier scored the 100th goal of his playoff career in an 8-3 win over the Quebec Nordiques in Game Two of their Eastern Conference Quarterfinal. He became just the third player in NHL history to reach the milestone, joining former Oiler teammates Wayne Gretzky (110 career playoff goals) and Jari Kurri (102).

May 9, 1999 • With Detroit's 4-0 win over Colorado in Game Two of their Conference Semifinal series, Red Wings head coach Scotty Bowman recorded his 200th career playoff victory.

May 10, 1970 • Bobby Orr, who had distinguished himself in 1969-70 as the first defenseman in NHL history to record 100 points (33-87-120) in a season, scored just 40 seconds into overtime to give the Boston Bruins a 4-3 win and a four-game sweep versus the St. Louis Blues in the 1970 Finals. For Orr, the Conn Smythe Trophy winner, the goal was his first of the series.

May 10, 1973 • In Montreal's 6-4 series-ending victory in Game Six, Yvan Cournoyer (6-6-12) and Jacques Lemaire (5-7-12) tallied 1-2-3 and 0-2-2 scoring totals, respectively, to tie Gordie Howe's record of 12 points in one Final series. Meanwhile, Montreal's Henri Richard tied Leonard "Red" Kelly's all-time record for Stanley Cup games with the 65th of his career.

May 11 – 20

May 11, 1968 • The Montreal Canadiens swept the St. Louis Blues in straight games with a 3-2 win in Game Four of the 1968 Finals. For Montreal coach "Toe" Blake, it was his 11th Stanley Cup title, setting an all-time record for one individual. Blake, who had won three championships as a player and eight as a coach, retired following the series. Canadiens center Henri Richard later tied Blake's mark with his 11th Stanley Cup in 1973.

May 11, 1972 • For the second time in three seasons, defenseman Bobby Orr scored the Stanley Cup-winning goal as the Boston Bruins blanked the New York Rangers 3-0 in Game Six. The goal gave Orr, who won the Conn Smythe Trophy, a 5-19-24 scoring total in 15 playoff games.

May 11, 1995 • Detroit Red Wings right wing Dino Ciccarelli tallied three power-play goals in a 5-1 win over the Dallas Stars in Game Three of their Western Conference Quarterfinal to tie an NHL playoff record for most power-play goals in one game. Nine players, including Ciccarelli, had previously shared the record. Ciccarelli was the last player to accomplish the feat, on April 29, 1993 versus Toronto, and became the first player in NHL history to post three power-play goals in a playoff game on separate occasions.

May 11, 1996 • Colorado Avalanche goaltender Patrick Roy became the NHL's all-time playoff leader in minutes played by a goaltender, passing former New York Islanders standout Bill Smith. Colorado defeated Chicago 4-1 to take a 3-2 series lead.

May 12, 1995 • New Jersey Devils goaltender Martin Brodeur became just the fifth goaltender since the NHL introduced the best-of-seven format in 1939 to register three shutouts in one playoff series, follow-

ing a 1-0 overtime win over the Boston Bruins in Game Four of their Conference Quarterfinal series. Brodeur joined Dave Kerr of the New York Rangers (1940), and three Toronto Maple Leafs goaltenders—Frank McCool (1945), Turk Broda (1950) and Felix Potvin (1994)—in this select club.

May 14, 1977 • Montreal Canadiens center Jacques Lemaire scored his third game-winning goal of the 1977 Finals and his second career overtime tally in a Stanley Cup game, leading the Montreal Canadiens to a 2-1 series-clinching win against the Boston Bruins. Only Maurice "Rocket" Richard of the Canadiens (3) and Don "Bones" Raleigh of the Rangers (2) have ever posted more than one career overtime goal in Finals history.

May 14, 1993 • The New York Islanders defeated the Pittsburgh Penguins 4-3 in overtime to win their Patrick Division Final in seven games. For Islanders coach Al Arbour, it represented his 30th career playoff series win as a coach, moving him into a tie for the all-time lead with Penguins coach Scott Bowman. The win was also Arbour's 200th postseason game.

May 15, 1990 • Edmonton's Petr Klima scored 15:13 into the third overtime period to lead the Oilers to a 3-2 triumph over the Boston Bruins in Game One of the 1990 Finals at Boston Garden. The 55:13 overtime was the longest in Finals history, 1:23 longer than the 53:50 of overtime played in Game Three of the 1931 Finals between Chicago and Montreal.

May 15, 1995 • The Vancouver Canucks tallied two shorthanded goals in 17 seconds during the second period of their 6-5 win over the St. Louis Blues in Game Five of their Conference Quarterfinal series to set an NHL playoff record for the fastest two shorthanded goals by one team. The Canucks passed the old mark of 24 seconds set by the 1978 Montreal Canadiens versus Detroit on April 23, 1978. Christian Ruuttu scored for Vancouver at 4:31 of the second period, followed by Geoff Courtnall at 4:48.

May 16, 1971 • Center Jean Beliveau tallied two assists, the final two points of his NHL career, as the Montreal Canadiens downed the Chicago Black Hawks 4-3 in Game Six of the 1971 Finals. Beliveau, the all-time leader in Finals history with a 30-31-61 scoring total, helped his club win the Stanley Cup two days later in Game Seven.

May 16, 1976 • In Game Four of the 1976 Finals, Philadelphia Flyers right winger Reggie Leach scored his 19th goal of the playoffs, extending his NHL record in that category. Although the Flyers lost the game 5-3 and the series 4-0 to the Montreal Canadiens, Leach won the Conn Smythe Trophy as the most valuable player to his team in the playoffs.

May 16, 1982 • Right winger Mike Bossy scored twice, including the series-winning goal, to lead the New York Islanders to their third straight Stanley Cup championship. The 3-1 victory gave New York a four-game sweep against the Vancouver Canucks.

May 16, 1996 • The Detroit Red Wings defeated the St. Louis Blues 1-0 in a classic seventh and deciding game of their Western Conference Semifinal series at Joe Louis Arena. Steve Yzerman notched the series-winning goal at 1:15 of the second overtime period as Detroit rallied from three straight losses after opening the series with a pair of wins.

May 17, 1981 • In Game Three of the 1981 Finals, Minnesota North Stars right wing Dino Ciccarelli broke Don Maloney's one-year rookie playoff scoring record (20 points in 1979) with his 21st point, a goal against the New York Islanders. The Islanders won the game 7-5 and later took the series 4-1.

May 17, 1983 • The New York Islanders beat the Edmonton Oilers 4-2 to complete a four-game sweep of the 1983 Finals. It was the Islanders' fourth straight Stanley Cup, one short of the NHL record for consecutive championships set by the

Montreal Canadiens from 1956 to 1960.

May 18, 1971 • The Montreal Canadiens, who had missed the playoffs in 1970, won the 1971 Stanley Cup with a 3-2 triumph over the Chicago Black Hawks in Game Seven. 23-year-old rookie goalie Ken Dryden took the Conn Smythe Trophy with a 12-8 record and a 3.00 average in the playoffs.

May 18, 1986 • Montreal center Brian Skrudland notched the fastest overtime goal in playoff history, scoring just nine seconds into overtime to give the Canadiens a 3-2 victory over the Calgary Flames in Game Two of the 1986 Finals. The win was the first of four straight for Montreal en route to the team's 23rd Stanley Cup title.

May 19, 1974 • The Philadelphia Flyers, who had entered the NHL in 1967-68, became the first expansion team to win the Stanley Cup, downing the Boston Bruins 1-0 in Game Six of the 1974 Finals. Left winger Rick MacLeish scored the game's only goal, while goaltender Bernie Parent, who won the Conn Smythe Trophy as playoff MVP, recorded the shutout.

May 19, 1984 • The Edmonton Oilers, one of four former WHA teams which joined the League in 1979-80, won their first Stanley Cup title. Oilers center Mark Messier, who registered an 8-18-26 scoring mark in 19 playoff games, won the Conn Smythe Trophy.

May 20, 1986 • In the first period of Game Three, Montreal and Calgary combined for the fastest four goals by two teams in a Finals game. Calgary's Joel Otto (17:59) and Montreal's Bobby Smith (18:25), Mats Naslund (19:17) and Bob Gainey (19:33) posted goals within one minute and 34 seconds to set the mark. The Canadiens defeated the Flames 5-3.

May 20, 1993 • The Montreal Canadiens won their seventh overtime game in the postseason, a 2-1 win over the New York Islanders, to set a new playoff record. The Canadiens passed the previous mark of six, set by the Islanders in 1980.

May 21 – 31

May 21, 1979 • Center Jacques Lemaire scored twice, including his second career Stanley Cup-winning goal, to power the Montreal Canadiens past the New York Rangers 4-1 in Game Five. The win gave Montreal its fourth straight Stanley Cup, one short of the record (5) set by the same team, 1956-60.

May 21, 1981 • New York Islanders center Butch Goring notched two goals to help defeat the Minnesota North Stars 5-1 in the fifth and final game of the 1981 Finals. Goring, who assisted on the winning goal in Game Two and scored the winner in Game Three, earned the Conn Smythe Trophy.

May 21, 2001 • Joe Sakic tallied his fourth career playoff overtime goal just 24 seconds into the extra period as the Colorado Avalanche defeated the St. Louis Blues 2-1, clinching the Western Conference Final in five games. Sakic tallied the quickest goal from the start of overtime since Hartford's Yvon Corriveau scored at 24 seconds in a 2-1 victory over Montreal on April 29, 1992.

May 22, 1987 • In Game Three of the 1987 Finals, Edmonton Oilers center Mark Messier set a new playoff record with his eighth career shorthanded goal. Edmonton lost the game 5-3 to the Philadelphia Flyers but went on to win the series in seven games.

May 22, 1999 • The Colorado Avalanche defeated the Dallas Stars 2-1 in the opening game of the Western Conference Final, tying a playoff record for consecutive road victories (seven). The Avalanche equalled a mark previously set by the 1980 and 1982 New York Islanders and the 1995 New Jersey Devils. Dallas went on to defeat Colorado in seven games.

May 24, 1980 • Right winger Bob Nystrom scored at 7:11 of overtime as the New York Islanders defeated the Philadelphia Flyers 5-4 and captured the 1980 Stanley Cup in six games. Nystrom's goal was the fourth and final overtime tally of his playoff career and moved him into second place on the all-time list behind Maurice "Rocket" Richard (6).

May 24, 1986 • The Montreal Canadiens defeated the Calgary Flames 4-3 in Game Five en route to their 23rd Stanley Cup title, a new professional record for the most championship seasons. Montreal had been tied with Major League Baseball's New York Yankees, winners of 22 World Series.

May 24, 1990 • The Edmonton Oilers won their fifth Stanley Cup in seven years with a 4-1 win over the Boston Bruins in Game Five of the 1990 Finals at Boston Garden. Edmonton goaltender Bill Ranford, who registered all 16 wins for the Oilers in the postseason, captured the Conn Smythe Trophy as playoff MVP. Seven Oilers players—Glenn Anderson, Grant Fuhr, Randy Gregg, Charlie Huddy, Jari Kurri, Kevin Lowe and Mark Messier—were members of all five championship clubs.

May 24, 1994 • Greg Adams of the Vancouver Canucks scored at 14 seconds of the second overtime period to give his team a 4-3 win over the Toronto Maple Leafs in Game Five of the Western Conference Final at Pacific Coliseum. The win clinched the series for the Canucks and earned them a berth in the Stanley Cup Championship for the first time since 1982.

May 24, 1995 • New York Rangers center Mark Messier's goal in the second period of a 5-2 loss to the Philadelphia Flyers in Game Three of their Conference Semifinal was the 102nd of his playoff career, tying Jari Kurri for second place on the all-time list.

May 25, 1978 • Conn Smythe Trophy winner Larry Robinson assisted on Mario Tremblay's Stanley Cup-winning goal to lead the Montreal Canadiens past the Boston Bruins 4-1 in Game Six. Robinson was one of three Canadiens, including Doug Jarvis and Steve Shutt, who appeared in all 95 games during the 1977-78 season.

May 25, 1985 • Edmonton Oilers center Wayne Gretzky notched three goals in the first period of a 4-3 win against the Philadelphia Flyers to tie a NHL record for one Finals period. Three players—Toronto's Harvey "Busher" Jackson (April 5, 1932), Detroit's Ted Lindsay (April 5, 1955) and Montreal's Maurice "Rocket" Richard (April 6, 1957)—previously shared the mark.

May 25, 1989 • The Calgary Flames captured their first Stanley Cup title with a 4-2 win over the Montreal Canadiens in Game Six of the 1989 Stanley Cup Championship. Goaltender Mike Vernon recorded his 16th victory of the postseason, tying an NHL playoff record set by Edmonton's Grant Fuhr the previous year, and defenseman Al MacInnis won the Conn Smythe Trophy after leading all playoff scorers with totals of 7-24-31 in 22 games.

May 25, 2002 • Colorado Avalanche goaltender Patrick Roy appeared in his 237th career playoff game, passing Mark Messier to assume first place on the all-time playoff games-played list. The Avalanche defeated the Detroit Red Wings, 3-2, in Game Four of the Western Conference Final. Roy also holds playoff records for career wins, shutouts, and minutes.

May 26, 2000 • The New Jersey Devils defeated the Philadelphia Flyers 2-1 in Game Seven of the Eastern Conference Finals, marking the first time a team overcame a 3-1 series deficit to advance to the Stanley Cup Finals.

May 27, 1975 • Philadelphia goaltender Bernie Parent blanked the Buffalo Sabres 2-0 in Game Six en route to the Flyers' second straight Stanley Cup title. Parent earned the Conn Smythe Trophy to become the first back-to-back winner of the award and the second player, after Bobby Orr, to win it twice. Edmonton's Wayne Gretzky collected his second career Conn Smythe Trophy in 1988, Mario Lemieux of the Penguins won the award in 1991 and 1992 and Patrick Roy of Montreal won in 1986, 1993 and 2001.

May 27, 1994 • Stephane Matteau of the New York Rangers scored at 4:24 of the second overtime period to give his team a 2-1 win over the New Jersey Devils in the seventh and deciding game of the Eastern Conference Final at Madison Square Garden. A record three games in the series were decided in double overtime, with Matteau scoring the winner in two of them. The win earned the Rangers a berth in the Stanley Cup Championship for the first time since 1979.

May 27, 1995 • Detroit Red Wings defenseman Paul Coffey became the all-time leading scorer for defensemen in Stanley Cup playoff history, tallying two points (1-1-2) in Detroit's 6-2 win over the San Jose Sharks in Game Four of their Conference Semifinal. The Red Wings clinched the series in four straight games. Coffey's first-period goal was his 165th point in the postseason (51-114-165 in 146 games), moving him past former New York Islanders rearguard and Hockey Hall of Famer Denis Potvin. Potvin registered 164 points (56-108-164) in 185 career playoff games.

May 30, 1985 • The Edmonton Oilers downed the Philadelphia Flyers 8-3 in Game Five to take the 1985 Stanley Cup and their second straight championship title. Conn Smythe Trophy winner Wayne Gretzky scored a goal and assisted on three others to set playoff records for assists (30) and points (47) in a single postseason, and Jari Kurri tied Reg Leach's record with his 19th goal of the playoffs.

May 30, 1998 • Washington Capitals goaltender Olaf Kolzig became the 10th goaltender in NHL history to record four shutouts in one playoff year, blanking the Buffalo Sabres 2-0 in Game Four of the Eastern Conference Final. Washington went on to win the series in six games and reach the Stanley Cup Finals for the first time.

May 31, 1987 • Right winger Jari Kurri scored the Cup-winning goal at 14:59 of the second period as the Edmonton Oilers beat the Philadelphia Flyers 3-1 in Game Seven of the 1987 Finals. The win marked the third Cup title in four seasons for Edmonton.

May 31, 1997 • The 1997 Stanley Cup Finals opened at the CoreStates Center in Philadelphia in front of 20,291 fans, the largest crowd ever to witness a hockey game in the state of Pennsylvania. The Detroit Red Wings won Game One of the series as goaltender Mike Vernon made 26 saves in a 4-2 win. Unheralded Red Wings Kirk Maltby and Joe Kocur gave Detroit a 2-1 lead after the first period and Sergei Fedorov tallied the game-winner just after the midway point of the second period.

June

June 1, 1992 • In the first NHL game ever played in the month of June, the Pittsburgh Penguins captured their second consecutive Stanley Cup championship with a 6-5 win over the Chicago Blackhawks at Chicago Stadium. The Penguins, who won the best-of-seven series 4-0, tied an NHL playoff record by winning their 11th straight game in the postseason. Mario Lemieux led all playoff scorers and joined Philadelphia goaltender Bernie Parent as just the second player ever to earn back-to-back Conn Smythe Trophy honors.

June 3, 1993 • Montreal Canadiens defenseman Eric Desjardins became the first defenseman in NHL history to record a hat trick in the Stanley Cup Finals. Desjardins tallied a game-tying power-play goal late in the third period and added the overtime winner in a 4-3 win. The tying goal came as a result of a stick measurement requested by Canadiens coach Jacques Demers. The stick used by Los Angeles defenseman Marty McSorley was found to have a curve that exceeded the allowable limit, resulting in a two-minute penalty to McSorley at 18:15 of the third period. Desjardins scored 32 seconds later. His winning goal was scored after just 51 seconds of overtime.

June 4, 1996 • The 1996 Stanley Cup finals opened with the Colorado Avalanche defeating the Florida Panthers 3-1 at McNichols Sports Arena in Denver. For the first time in NHL history, the two competing teams were each making their inaugural appearance in the Stanley Cup finals.

June 5, 1997 • The Detroit Red Wings opened a commanding three-games-to-none lead in the Stanley Cup finals with a 6-1 win over Philadelphia in Game Three at Joe Louis Arena. After the Flyers' John LeClair had opened the scoring at 7:03 of the first period, Detroit replied with three unanswered goals in the opening period. The win broke an eight-game Red Wings home losing streak in the final round of the Stanley Cup dating back to 1964. Detroit forwards Sergei Fedorov and Martin Lapointe each tallied two goals to pace the Red Wings over the Flyers. With the loss, Philadelphia's record dropped to nine wins and two losses when scoring first in the 1997 playoffs.

June 7, 1993 • John LeClair posted his second overtime goal in as many games to lead the Canadiens to a 3-2 win at Los Angeles to take a 3-1 series lead in the Finals. LeClair became the second player in NHL history, after Don Raleigh of the New York Rangers in 1950 versus Detroit, to tally overtime goals in consecutive games in the Finals.

June 8, 1996 • A Stanley Cup game is played in Florida for the first time as the visiting Colorado Avalanche rally to defeat the Florida Panthers 3-2 at the Miami Arena and take a commanding 3-0 lead in the series.

June 8, 2002 • Detroit center Igor Larionov scored at 15:47 of the third overtime period to give the Red Wings a 3-2 victory over the Carolina Hurricanes in Game Three of the Stanley Cup Finals in Raleigh, the first Cup game contested in North Carolina. The 54:47 of overtime made it the third longest Stanley Cup Finals game in history.

June 9, 1993 • The Montreal Canadiens captured their 24th Stanley Cup championship, defeating the Los Angeles Kings 4-1 to win the Stanley Cup Final series in five games. Canadiens goaltender Patrick Roy was awarded the Conn Smythe Trophy as playoff MVP, posting a 16-4 record and an average of 2.13 in 20 games.

June 9, 2001 • Led by 21-year-old Alex Tanguay's two goals and one assist, the Colorado Avalanche defeated the New Jersey Devils 3-1 in Game Seven of the Stanley Cup Finals to capture the club's second championship in six seasons. In a fitting climax to his legendary NHL career, Avalanche defenseman Ray Bourque triumphantly lifted the Stanley Cup for the first time.

June 10, 1996 • Uwe Krupp scored the Stanley Cup-winning goal at 4:31 of the third overtime period, giving the Colorado Avalanche a 1-0 victory over the Florida Panthers in the third-longest game ever played in the Stanley Cup Final. In sweeping the series, the Avalanche, who had relocated to Denver from Quebec, became the first NHL club to win the Stanley Cup after its first season in a new city.

June 10, 2000 • The New Jersey Devils captured their second Stanley Cup in franchise history as forward Jason Arnott scored in double-overtime to defeat the Dallas Stars 2-1 in Game Six of the Finals. Following a Dallas victory in triple-overtime in Game Five, it marked only the second Stanley Cup Finals series to feature consecutive multiple-overtime games. The 1931 Stanley Cup Finals saw Games 2 and 3 between the Chicago Blackhawks and the Montreal Canadiens decided in double and triple overtime, respectively.

June 13, 2002 • The Detroit Red Wings won their third Stanley Cup in six seasons, defeating the Carolina Hurricanes 3-1 in Game Five of the Finals at Joe Louis Arena. Like Colorado Avalanche defenseman Ray Bourque the year before, Red Wings goaltender Dominik Hasek captured his first career Cup in his final game. Hasek, who held the Hurricanes to one goal or fewer in three of the five Finals games, finished the 2002 playoffs with 16-7 record, 1.86 goals-against average and a record six shutouts.

June 14, 1994 • The New York Rangers defeated the Vancouver Canucks 3-2 at Madison Square Garden in Game Seven of the Stanley Cup Finals. This was the first seven-game Final series since 1987 and just the third since 1967. Rangers defenseman Brian Leetch captured the Conn Smythe Trophy as playoff MVP, leading all postseason scorers with 34 points (11-23-34) in 23 games.

June 16, 1998 • The Detroit Red Wings captured their second straight Stanley Cup title, sweeping the Washington Capitals with a 4-1 victory. Scotty Bowman's eighth Stanley Cup win as a coach tied Toe Blake's NHL record.

June 17, 1995 • The 1995 Stanley Cup Championship series opened at Joe Louis Arena and the New Jersey Devils captured Game One with a 2-1 win. Right wing Claude Lemieux scored the game-winning goal early in the third period, his third game-winner of the playoffs and 14th of his career in the postseason. The Devils improved their road record in the playoffs to 9-1, setting a new NHL record for most road wins by one team in the playoffs.

June 19, 1999 • The Dallas Stars captured their first Stanley Cup title in franchise history with a 2-1 win over Buffalo in Game Six of the Finals. Brett Hull scored at 14:51 of the third overtime, ending the second longest game in finals history. The longest was played on May 15, 1990.

June 20, 1995 • The New Jersey Devils defeated the Detroit Red Wings 4-2 at Joe Louis Arena to take a two games to none series lead in the Stanley Cup Championship. New Jersey extended its playoff record by winning its 10th game on the road and tied another playoff record by winning their seventh straight road game.

CHAPTER 15

Final Series History, by Team 1918–2002

All teams played in the National Hockey League unless indicated. Other leagues that played for the Stanley Cup from 1918 to 1926:
PCHA – Pacific Coast Hockey Association; WCHL – Western Canada Hockey League; WHL – Western Hockey League.
These current NHL clubs have not appeared in the Stanley Cup Finals: Mighty Ducks of Anaheim, Atlanta Thrashers, Columbus Blue Jackets,
Minnesota Wild, Nashville Predators, Ottawa Senators, Phoenix Coyotes, San Jose Sharks, Tampa Bay Lightning.

Overall Finals Record
1918-2002

TEAM	SERIES	W	L	GP	W	L	GF	GA
Anaheim	–	–	–	–	–	–	–	–
Atlanta	–	–	–	–	–	–	–	–
Boston [1]	17	5	12	77	28	47	168	219
Buffalo	2	0	2	12	4	8	21	32
Calgary ('20s)	1	0	1	2	0	2	1	9
Calgary	2	1	1	11	5	6	32	31
Carolina	1	0	1	5	1	4	7	14
Chicago	10	3	7	53	22	31	132	158
Colorado	2	2	0	11	8	3	34	15
Dallas [2]	4	1	3	23	9	14	54	78
Detroit	22	10	12	114	54	60	282	290
Edmonton ('20s) [3]	1	0	1	2	0	2	1	3
Edmonton	6	5	1	30	20	10	108	78
Florida	1	0	1	4	0	4	4	11
Los Angeles	1	0	1	5	1	4	12	15
Minnesota	–	–	–	–	–	–	–	–
Montreal [4]	33	23	8	163	105	57	481	381
Mtl. Maroons	3	2	1	12	8	4	26	12
Nashville	–	–	–	–	–	–	–	–
New Jersey	3	2	1	17	11	6	42	35
NY Islanders	5	4	1	24	17	7	99	78
NY Rangers	10	4	6	50	22	28	115	130
Ottawa ('20s) [1,5]	5	4	0	20	13	5	47	33
Ottawa	–	–	–	–	–	–	–	–
Philadelphia	7	2	5	38	14	24	106	124
Phoenix	–	–	–	–	–	–	–	–
Pittsburgh	2	2	0	10	8	2	43	26
St. Louis	3	0	3	12	0	12	24	63
San Jose	–	–	–	–	–	–	–	–
Seattle [4,6]	2	0	1	10	4	5	30	25
Tampa Bay	–	–	–	–	–	–	–	–
Toronto [7]	21	13	8	105	56	49	278	269
Vancouver ('20s) [8]	5	0	5	21	7	14	52	61
Vancouver	2	0	2	11	3	8	29	39
Victoria [9]	2	1	1	8	4	4	19	18
Washington	1	0	1	4	0	4	7	13

[1] Ottawa played two tie games against Boston in 1927. [2] Includes appearances by Minnesota North Stars in 1981 and 1991. [3] An Edmonton team also played for the Stanley Cup in 1908 and 1910. [4] No decision in 1919 Finals, incomplete due to flu epidemic. Seattle and Montreal each had two wins. One game was tied. Note: Montreal also won the Stanley Cup in 1916 for 24 titles overall. [5] Ottawa franchise was also Stanley Cup champion in 1903, 1904, 1905, 1906, 1909, 1910 and 1911. [6] Seattle Metropolitans of the PCHA won the Stanley Cup in 1917. [7] Toronto Blueshirts won the Stanley Cup in 1914 for 14 titles overall. Total also includes Toronto Arenas (1918) and Toronto St. Pats (1922). [8] Vancouver of the PCHA won the Stanley Cup in 1915. [9] Victoria of the PCHA also played for the Stanley Cup in 1914 (Victoria represented the WCHL in 1925 and the WHL in 1926).

BOSTON   1925-2002

All-Time Final Series Record

Opponent	Series	W	L	GP	W	L	GF	GA
Detroit	2	1	1	8	4	4	17	22
Edmonton	2	0	2	9	1	8	17	38
Montreal	7	0	7	33	7	26	64	107
NY Rangers	2	2	0	8	6	2	22	17
Ottawa ('27)*	1	0	1	4	0	2	3	7
Philadelphia	1	0	1	6	2	4	13	15
St. Louis	1	1	0	4	4	0	20	7
Toronto	1	1	0	5	4	1	12	6
TOTALS	**17**	**5**	**12**	**77**	**28**	**47**	**168**	**219**

Final Series Appearances

Opponent	Year	Winner	W	L	GF	GA
Ottawa*	1927	Ottawa	0	2	3	7
NY Rangers	1929	Boston	2	0	4	1
Montreal	1930	Montreal	0	2	3	7
Toronto	1939	Boston	4	1	12	6
Detroit	1941	Boston	4	0	12	6

Detroit	1943	Detroit	0	4	5	16
Montreal	1946	Montreal	1	4	13	19
Montreal	1953	Montreal	1	4	9	16
Montreal	1957	Montreal	1	4	6	15
Montreal	1958	Montreal	2	4	14	16
St. Louis	1970	Boston	4	0	20	7
NY Rangers	1972	Boston	4	2	18	16
Philadelphia	1974	Philadelphia	2	4	13	15
Montreal	1977	Montreal	0	4	6	16
Montreal	1978	Montreal	2	4	13	18
Edmonton	1988	Edmonton	0	4	9	18
Edmonton	1990	Edmonton	1	4	8	20

* includes two ties

Final Series Scoring Leaders

Player	GP	G	A	PTS	PIM
Bobby Orr	16	8	12	20	31
Phil Esposito	16	4	15	19	28
Ken Hodge	16	6	10	16	27
Milt Schmidt	18	6	8	14	4
John Bucyk	16	8	5	13	4

BUFFALO   1971-2002

All-Time Final Series Record

Opponent	Series	W	L	GP	W	L	GF	GA
Dallas	1	0	1	6	2	4	9	13
Philadelphia	1	0	1	6	2	4	12	19
TOTALS	**2**	**0**	**2**	**12**	**4**	**8**	**21**	**32**

Final Series Appearances

Opponent	Year	Winner	W	L	GF	GA
Philadelphia	1975	Philadelphia	2	4	12	19
Dallas	1999	Dallas	2	4	9	13

Final Series Scoring Leaders

Player	GP	G	A	PTS	PIM
Rick Martin	6	2	4	6	6
Don Luce	6	2	3	5	12
Stu Barnes	6	3	0	3	0
Danny Gare	6	2	1	3	4
Jerry Korab	6	2	1	3	6
Jim Lorentz	6	1	2	3	2
Rene Robert	6	1	2	3	6
Alexei Zhitnik	6	1	2	3	18
Richard Smehlik	6	0	3	3	2

CALGARY (WCHL/WHL) 1922-26

All-Time Final Series Record

Opponent	Series	W	L	GP	W	L	GF	GA
Montreal	1	0	1	2	0	2	1	9
TOTALS	**1**	**0**	**1**	**2**	**0**	**2**	**1**	**9**

Final Series Appearances

Opponent	Year	Winner	W	L	GF	GA
Montreal	1924	Montreal	0	2	1	9

Final Series Scoring Leaders

Player	GP	G	A	PTS	PIM
Herb Gardiner	2	1	0	1	0
Bernie Morris	2	0	1	1	0

CALGARY   1973-2002

All-Time Final Series Record

Opponent	Series	W	L	GP	W	L	GF	GA
Montreal	2	1	1	11	5	6	32	31
TOTALS	**2**	**1**	**1**	**11**	**5**	**6**	**32**	**31**

Final Series Appearances

Opponent	Year	Winner	W	L	GF	GA
Montreal	1986	Montreal	1	4	13	15
Montreal	1989	Calgary	4	2	19	16

Final Series Scoring Leaders

Player	GP	G	A	PTS	PIM
Al MacInnis	11	5	8	13	26
Joe Mullen	10	7	4	11	8
Joel Otto	11	3	8	11	14
Doug Gilmour	6	4	3	7	6
Jim Peplinski	9	1	5	6	47

CAROLINA   1980-2002

All-Time Final Series Record

Opponent	Series	W	L	GP	W	L	GF	GA
Detroit	1	0	1	5	1	4	7	14
TOTALS	**1**	**0**	**1**	**5**	**1**	**4**	**7**	**14**

Final Series Appearances

Opponent	Year	Winner	W	L	GF	GA
Detroit	2002	Detroit	1	4	7	14

Final Series Scoring Leaders

Player	GP	G	A	PTS	PIM
Jeff O'Neill	5	3	1	4	2
Ron Francis	5	1	2	3	0
Sean Hill	5	1	1	2	12
Sami Kapanen	5	0	2	2	0
Glen Wesley	5	0	2	2	4

CHICAGO   1927-2002

All-Time Final Series Record

Opponent	Series	W	L	GP	W	L	GF	GA
Detroit	2	2	0	10	7	3	28	19
Montreal	5	0	5	29	10	19	69	98
Pittsburgh	1	0	1	4	0	4	10	15
Toronto	2	1	1	10	5	5	25	26
TOTALS	**10**	**3**	**7**	**53**	**22**	**31**	**132**	**158**

Final Series Appearances

Opponent	Year	Winner	W	L	GF	GA
Montreal	1931	Montreal	2	3	8	11
Detroit	1934	Chicago	3	1	9	7
Toronto	1938	Chicago	3	1	10	8
Montreal	1944	Montreal	0	4	8	16
Detroit	1961	Chicago	4	2	19	12
Toronto	1962	Toronto	2	4	15	18
Montreal	1965	Montreal	3	4	12	18
Montreal	1971	Montreal	3	4	18	20
Montreal	1973	Montreal	2	4	23	33
Pittsburgh	1992	Pittsburgh	0	4	10	15

Final Series Scoring Leaders

Player	GP	G	A	PTS	PIM
Stan Mikita	31	10	21	31	58
Bobby Hull	26	11	17	28	26
Pierre Pilote	17	2	13	15	22
Jim Pappin	13	7	4	11	18
Johnny Gottselig	13	6	5	11	6
Dennis Hull	14	6	5	11	6

COLORADO 1980-2002

All-Time Final Series Record

Opponent	Series	W	L	GP	W	L	GF	GA
Florida	1	1	0	4	4	0	15	4
New Jersey	1	1	0	7	4	3	19	11
TOTALS	**2**	**2**	**0**	**11**	**8**	**3**	**34**	**15**

Final Series Appearances

Opponent	Year	Winner	W	L	GF	GA
Florida	1996	Colorado	4	0	15	4
New Jersey	2001	Colorado	4	3	19	11

Final Series Scoring Leaders

Player	GP	G	A	PTS	PIM
Joe Sakic	11	5	9	14	4
Alex Tanguay	7	4	3	7	4
Peter Forsberg	4	3	2	5	0
Rob Blake	7	2	3	5	4
Adam Foote	11	1	4	5	20

DALLAS   1968-2002

All-Time Final Series Record*

Opponent	Series	W	L	GP	W	L	GF	GA
Buffalo	1	1	0	6	4	2	13	9
New Jersey	1	0	1	6	2	4	9	15
NY Islanders	1	0	1	5	1	4	16	26
Pittsburgh	1	0	1	6	2	4	16	28
TOTALS	**4**	**1**	**3**	**23**	**9**	**14**	**54**	**78**

* Includes final series appearances by Minnesota North Stars in 1981 and 1991.

Final Series Appearances

Opponent	Year	Winner	W	L	GF	GA
NY Islanders	1981	NY Islanders	1	4	16	26
Pittsburgh	1991	Pittsburgh	2	4	16	28
Buffalo	1999	Dallas	4	2	13	9
New Jersey	2000	New Jersey	2	4	9	15

Final Series Scoring Leaders

Player	GP	G	A	PTS	PIM
Mike Modano	18	3	12	15	14
Bobby Smith	11	4	5	9	8
Jere Lehtinen	12	2	6	8	2
Steve Payne	5	5	2	7	2
Brett Hull	11	5	2	7	2

DETROIT 1927-2002

All-Time Final Series Record

Opponent	Series	W	L	GP	W	L	GF	GA
Boston	2	1	1	8	4	4	22	17
Carolina	1	1	0	5	4	1	14	7
Chicago	2	0	2	10	3	7	19	28
Montreal	5	3	2	29	15	14	75	70
New Jersey	1	0	1	4	0	4	7	16
NY Rangers	2	2	0	12	7	5	31	25
Philadelphia	1	1	0	4	4	0	16	6
Toronto	7	1	6	38	13	25	85	114
Washington	1	1	0	4	4	0	13	7
TOTALS	22	10	12	114	54	60	282	290

Final Series Appearances

Opponent	Year	Winner	W	L	GF	GA
Chicago	1934	Chicago	1	3	7	9
Toronto	1936	Detroit	3	1	18	11
NY Rangers	1937	Detroit	3	2	9	8
Boston	1941	Boston	0	4	6	12
Toronto	1942	Toronto	3	4	19	25
Boston	1943	Detroit	4	0	16	5
Toronto	1945	Toronto	3	4	9	9
Toronto	1948	Toronto	0	4	7	18
Toronto	1949	Toronto	0	4	5	12
NY Rangers	1950	Detroit	4	3	22	17
Montreal	1952	Detroit	4	0	11	2
Montreal	1954	Detroit	4	3	14	12
Montreal	1955	Detroit	4	3	27	20
Montreal	1956	Montreal	1	4	9	18
Chicago	1961	Chicago	2	4	12	19
Toronto	1963	Toronto	1	4	10	17
Toronto	1964	Toronto	3	4	17	22
Montreal	1966	Montreal	2	4	14	18
New Jersey	1995	New Jersey	0	4	7	16
Philadelphia	1997	Detroit	4	0	16	6
Washington	1998	Detroit	4	0	13	7
Carolina	2002	Detroit	4	1	14	7

Final Series Scoring Leaders

Player	GP	G	A	PTS	PIM
Gordie Howe	55	18	32	50	94
Alex Delvecchio	47	16	22	38	2
Ted Lindsay	44	19	15	34	48
Sid Abel	34	9	11	20	25
Syd Howe	28	8	12	20	4

EDMONTON (WCHL/WHL) 1922-26

All-Time Final Series Record

Opponent	Series	W	L	GP	W	L	GF	GA
Ottawa ('23)	1	0	1	2	0	2	1	3
TOTALS	1	0	1	2	0	2	1	3

Final Series Appearances

Opponent	Year	Winner	W	L	GF	GA
Ottawa	1923	Ottawa	0	2	1	3

Final Series Scoring Leaders

Player	GP	G	A	PTS	PIM
Crutchy Morrison	2	1	0	1	0
Joe Simpson	2	0	1	1	0

EDMONTON 1980-2002

All-Time Final Series Record

Opponent	Series	W	L	GP	W	L	GF	GA
Boston	2	2	0	9	8	1	38	17
NY Islanders	2	1	1	9	4	5	27	29
Philadelphia	2	2	0	12	8	4	43	32
TOTALS	6	5	1	30	20	10	108	78

Final Series Appearances

Opponent	Year	Winner	W	L	GF	GA
NY Islanders	1983	NY Islanders	0	4	6	17
NY Islanders	1984	Edmonton	4	1	21	12
Philadelphia	1985	Edmonton	4	1	21	14
Philadelphia	1987	Edmonton	4	3	22	18
Boston	1988	Edmonton	4	0	18	9
Boston	1990	Edmonton	4	1	20	8

Final Series Scoring Leaders

Player	GP	G	A	PTS	PIM
Wayne Gretzky	26	16	30	46	6
Jari Kurri	31	14	24	38	14
Glenn Anderson	31	14	12	26	55
Mark Messier	31	9	15	24	35
Paul Coffey	21	7	15	22	24

FLORIDA 1994-2002

All-Time Final Series Record

Opponent	Series	W	L	GP	W	L	GF	GA
Colorado	1	0	1	4	0	4	4	15
TOTALS	1	0	1	4	0	4	4	15

Final Series Appearances

Opponent	Year	Winner	W	L	GF	GA
Colorado	1996	Colorado	0	4	4	15

Final Series Scoring Leaders

Player	GP	G	A	PTS	PIM
Ed Jovanovski	4	0	2	2	11
Tom Fitzgerald	4	1	0	1	0
Ray Sheppard	4	1	0	1	0
Stu Barnes	4	1	0	1	2
Rob Niedermayer	4	1	0	1	4
Martin Straka	4	0	1	1	0
Johan Garpenlov	4	0	1	1	2
Dave Lowry	4	0	1	1	2
Bill Lindsay	4	0	1	1	4
Scott Mellanby	4	0	1	1	4

LOS ANGELES 1968-2002

All-Time Final Series Record

Opponent	Series	W	L	GP	W	L	GF	GA
Montreal	1	0	1	5	1	4	12	15
TOTALS	1	0	1	5	1	4	12	15

Final Series Appearances

Opponent	Year	Winner	W	L	GF	GA
Montreal	1993	Montreal	1	4	12	15

Final Series Scoring Leaders

Player	GP	G	A	PTS	PIM
Wayne Gretzky	5	2	5	7	2
Luc Robitaille	5	3	2	5	4
Tony Granato	5	1	3	4	10
Marty McSorley	5	2	0	2	16
Dave Taylor	3	1	1	2	6
Mike Donnelly	5	1	1	2	0
Tomas Sandstrom	5	0	2	2	4

MONTREAL 1918-2002

All-Time Final Series Record

Opponent	Series	W	L	GP	W	L	GF	GA
Boston	7	7	0	33	26	7	107	64
Calgary	2	1	1	11	6	5	31	32
Chicago	5	5	0	29	19	10	98	69
Detroit	5	2	3	29	14	15	70	75
Los Angeles	1	1	0	5	4	1	15	12
NY Rangers	1	1	0	5	4	1	19	11
Philadelphia	1	1	0	4	4	0	14	9
St. Louis	2	2	0	8	8	0	23	10
Toronto	5	2	3	26	13	13	72	60
Defunct Teams	*4	1	1	13	7	5	32	39
TOTALS	*33	23	8	163	105	57	481	381

Final Series Appearances*

Opponent	Year	Winner	W	L	GF	GA
Seattle*	1919	no decision	2	2	10	19
Vancouver**	1924	Montreal	2	0	5	3
Calgary**	1924	Montreal	2	0	9	1
Victoria	1925	Victoria	1	3	8	16
Boston	1930	Montreal	2	0	7	3
Chicago	1931	Montreal	3	2	11	8
Chicago	1944	Montreal	4	0	16	8
Boston	1946	Montreal	4	1	19	13
Toronto	1947	Toronto	2	4	13	13
Toronto	1951	Toronto	1	4	10	13
Detroit	1952	Detroit	0	4	2	11
Boston	1953	Montreal	4	1	16	9
Detroit	1954	Detroit	3	4	12	14
Detroit	1955	Detroit	3	4	20	27
Boston	1957	Montreal	4	1	15	6
Boston	1958	Montreal	4	2	16	14
Toronto	1959	Montreal	4	1	18	12
Toronto	1960	Montreal	4	0	15	5
Chicago	1965	Montreal	4	3	18	12
Detroit	1966	Montreal	4	2	18	14
Toronto	1967	Toronto	2	4	16	17
St. Louis	1968	Montreal	4	0	11	7
St. Louis	1969	Montreal	4	0	12	3
Chicago	1971	Montreal	4	3	20	18
Chicago	1973	Montreal	4	2	33	23
Philadelphia	1976	Montreal	4	0	14	9
Boston	1977	Montreal	4	0	16	6
Boston	1978	Montreal	4	2	18	13
NY Rangers	1979	Montreal	4	1	19	11
Calgary	1986	Montreal	4	1	15	13
Calgary	1989	Calgary	2	4	16	19
Los Angeles	1993	Montreal	4	1	15	12

* 1919 Finals incomplete due to flu epidemic. Seattle and Montreal each had two wins. One game was tied.

** Montreal defeated PCHA champion (Vancouver) and WCHL champion (Edmonton) in 1924. (counts as one Cup win) (see page 55)

NOTE: Montreal defeated the Portland Rosebuds in the 1916 Stanley Cup Final, prior to the formation of the NHL, giving the franchise 24 championships in all.

Final Series Scoring Leaders

Player	GP	G	A	PTS	PIM
Jean Beliveau	64	30	32	62	78
Henri Richard	65	21	26	47	68
Maurice Richard	59	34	12	46	83
Bernie Geoffrion	53	24	22	46	32
Yvan Cournoyer	50	21	19	40	18

MONTREAL MAROONS 1925-38

All-Time Final Series Record

Opponent	Series	W	L	GP	W	L	GF	GA
NY Rangers	1	0	1	5	2	3	6	5
Toronto	1	1	0	3	3	0	10	4
Victoria	1	1	0	4	3	1	10	3
TOTALS	3	2	1	12	8	4	26	12

Final Series Appearances

Opponent	Year	Winner	W	L	GF	GA
Victoria	1926	Mtl. Maroons	3	1	10	3
NY Rangers	1928	NY Rangers	2	3	6	5
Toronto	1935	Mtl. Maroons	3	0	10	4

Final Series Scoring Leaders

Player	GP	G	A	PTS	PIM
Nels Stewart	9	8	1	9	22
Babe Siebert	8	2	3	5	12
Bill Phillips	9	3	1	4	2
Cy Wentworth	3	2	2	4	0
Baldy Northcott	3	2	1	3	0
Earl Robinson	3	2	1	3	0

NEW JERSEY 1975-2002

All-Time Final Series Record

Opponent	Series	W	L	GP	W	L	GF	GA
Colorado	1	0	1	7	3	4	11	19
Dallas	1	1	0	6	4	2	15	9
Detroit	1	1	0	4	4	0	16	7
TOTALS	3	2	1	17	11	6	42	35

Final Series Appearances

Opponent	Year	Winner	W	L	GF	GA
Detroit	1995	New Jersey	4	0	16	7
Dallas	2000	New Jersey	4	2	15	9
Colorado	2001	Colorado	3	4	11	19

Final Series Scoring Leaders

Player	GP	G	A	PTS	PIM
Patrik Elias	13	2	8	10	2
Jason Arnott	12	5	4	9	6
Petr Sykora	13	5	4	9	8
Sergei Brylin	16	4	3	7	10
Scott Niedermayer	17	2	5	7	10
Brian Rafalski	13	1	6	7	4

NY ISLANDERS 1973-2002

All-Time Final Series Record

Opponent	Series	W	L	GP	W	L	GF	GA
Edmonton	2	1	1	9	5	4	29	27
Minnesota	1	1	0	5	4	1	26	16
Philadelphia	1	1	0	6	4	2	26	25
Vancouver	1	1	0	4	4	0	18	10
TOTALS	5	4	1	24	17	7	99	78

Final Series Appearances

Opponent	Year	Winner	W	L	GF	GA
Philadelphia	1980	NY Islanders	4	2	26	25
Minnesota	1981	NY Islanders	4	1	26	16
Vancouver	1982	NY Islanders	4	0	18	10
Edmonton	1983	NY Islanders	4	0	17	6
Edmonton	1984	Edmonton	1	4	12	21

Final Series Scoring Leaders

Player	GP	G	A	PTS	PIM
Mike Bossy	23	17	17	34	4
Bryan Trottier	24	10	20	30	30
Denis Potvin	24	8	18	26	28
Clark Gillies	24	9	14	23	35
Butch Goring	24	9	7	16	2

NY RANGERS   1927-2002

All-Time Final Series Record

Opponent	Series	W	L	GP	W	L	GF	GA
Boston	2	0	2	8	2	6	17	22
Detroit	2	0	2	12	5	7	25	31
Montreal	1	0	1	5	1	4	11	19
Mtl. Maroons	1	1	0	5	3	2	5	6
Toronto	3	2	1	13	7	6	35	34
Vancouver	1	1	0	7	4	3	21	19
TOTALS	10	4	6	50	22	28	114	131

Final Series Appearances

Opponent	Year	Winner	W	L	GF	GA
Mtl. Maroons	1928	NY Rangers	3	2	5	6
Boston	1929	Boston	0	2	1	4
Toronto	1932	Toronto	0	3	10	18
Toronto	1933	NY Rangers	3	1	11	5
Detroit	1937	Detroit	2	3	8	9
Toronto	1940	NY Rangers	4	2	14	11
Detroit	1950	Detroit	3	4	17	22
Boston	1972	Boston	2	4	16	18
Montreal	1979	Montreal	1	4	11	19
Vancouver	1994	NY Rangers	4	3	21	19

Final Series Scoring Leaders

Player	GP	G	A	PTS	PIM
Frank Boucher	19	8	6	14	6
Brian Leetch	7	5	6	11	4
Bill Cook	14	3	5	8	24

OTTAWA   1918-34

Note: Modern NHL Senators began play in 1992-93.

All-Time Final Series Record

Opponent	Series	W	L	GP	W	L	GF	GA
Boston*	1	1	0	4	2	0	7	3
Defunct Teams	4	4	0	16	11	5	40	30
TOTALS	**5	**4	0	20	13	5	47	33

Final Series Appearances

Opponent	Year	Winner	W	L	GF	GA
Seattle	1920	Ottawa	3	2	15	11
Vancouver	1921	Ottawa	3	2	12	11
Vancouver***	1923	Ottawa	3	1	10	7
Edmonton***	1923	Ottawa	2	0	3	1
Boston*	1927	Ottawa	2	0	7	3

* includes two ties
** Ottawa won seven Stanley Cup titles prior to 1918.
*** Ottawa defeated PCHA champion (Vancouver) and WCHL champion (Edmonton) in 1923. (counts as one Cup win) (see page 56)

Final Series Scoring Leaders

Player	GP	G	A	PTS	PIM
Jack Darragh	10	10	2	12	13
Cy Denneny	20	7	4	11	13
Frank Nighbor	17	7	3	10	0
Punch Broadbent	11	8	0	8	0
Georges Boucher	20	6	0	6	39

PHILADELPHIA   1968-2002

All-Time Final Series Record

Opponent	Series	W	L	GP	W	L	GF	GA
Boston	1	1	0	6	4	2	15	13
Buffalo	1	1	0	6	4	2	19	12
Detroit	1	0	1	4	0	4	6	16
Edmonton	2	0	2	12	4	8	32	43
Montreal	1	0	1	4	0	4	9	14
NY Islanders	1	0	1	6	2	4	25	26
TOTALS	7	2	5	38	14	24	106	124

Final Series Appearances

Opponent	Year	Winner	W	L	GF	GA
Boston	1974	Philadelphia	4	2	15	13
Buffalo	1975	Philadelphia	4	2	19	12
Montreal	1976	Montreal	0	4	9	14
NY Islanders	1980	NY Islanders	2	4	25	26
Edmonton	1985	Edmonton	1	4	14	21
Edmonton	1987	Edmonton	3	4	18	22
Detroit	1997	Detroit	0	4	6	16

Final Series Scoring Leaders

Player	GP	G	A	PTS	PIM
Bobby Clarke	22	9	12	21	22
Brian Propp	18	9	9	18	4
Rick MacLeish	18	6	9	15	8
Bill Barber	22	5	10	15	17
Reggie Leach	16	8	5	13	0

PITTSBURGH   1968-2002

All-Time Final Series Record

Opponent	Series	W	L	GP	W	L	GF	GA
Chicago	1	1	0	4	4	0	15	10
Minnesota	1	1	0	6	4	2	18	16
TOTALS	2	2	0	10	8	2	43	26

Final Series Appearances

Opponent	Year	Winner	W	L	GF	GA
Minnesota	1991	Pittsburgh	4	2	28	16
Chicago	1992	Pittsburgh	4	0	15	10

Final Series Scoring Leaders

Player	GP	G	A	PTS	PIM
Mario Lemieux	9	10	9	19	6
Larry Murphy	10	2	11	13	8
Kevin Stevens	10	6	6	12	27
Ron Francis	10	4	5	9	6
Joe Mullen	6	3	5	8	0
Rick Tocchet	4	2	6	8	2

ST. LOUIS   1968-2002

All-Time Final Series Record

Opponent	Series	W	L	GP	W	L	GF	GA
Boston	1	0	1	4	0	4	7	20
Montreal	2	0	2	8	0	8	17	43
TOTALS	3	0	3	12	0	12	24	63

Final Series Appearances

Opponent	Year	Winner	W	L	GF	GA
Montreal	1968	Montreal	0	4	7	11
Montreal	1969	Montreal	0	4	3	12
Boston	1970	Boston	0	4	7	20

Final Series Scoring Leaders

Player	GP	G	A	PTS	PIM
Frank St. Marseille	12	4	3	7	4
Red Berenson	12	3	1	4	15
Barclay Plager	9	1	2	3	6
Jimmy Roberts	12	1	2	3	10
Noel Picard	12	0	3	3	28

SEATTLE (PCHA/WCHL) 1918-24

All-Time Final Series Record

Opponent	Series	W	L	GP	W	L	GF	GA
Montreal	1	0	0	5	2	2	19	10
Ottawa ('20)	1	0	1	5	2	3	11	15
TOTALS	*2	*0	1	10	4	5	30	25

Final Series Appearances

Opponent	Year	Winner	W	L	GF	GA
Montreal	1919	No Decision*	2	2	19	10
Ottawa	1920	Ottawa	2	3	11	15

* 1919 Finals incomplete due to flu epidemic. Seattle and Montreal each had two wins. One game was tied. NOTE: Seattle Metropolitans defeated the Montreal Canadiens in the 1917 Stanley Cup Final, giving them one championship.

Final Series Scoring Leaders

Player	GP	G	A	PTS	PIM
Frank Foyston	10	15	2	17	7
Jack Walker	10	4	3	7	9
Roy Rickey	10	3	3	6	0
Cully Wilson	5	1	3	4	9
Muzz Murray	10	3	0	3	8
Bobby Rowe	10	3	0	3	19

TORONTO   1918-2002

All-Time Final Series Record

Opponent	Series	W	L	GP	W	L	GF	GA
Boston	1	0	1	5	1	4	6	12
Chicago	2	1	1	10	5	5	26	25
Detroit	7	6	1	38	25	13	114	85
Montreal	5	3	2	26	13	13	60	72
NY Rangers	3	1	2	13	6	7	34	35
Defunct Teams	3	2	1	13	6	7	38	40
TOTALS	21	13	8	105	56	49	278	269

Final Series Appearances

Opponent	Year	Winner	W	L	GF	GA
Vancouver	1918	Toronto	3	2	18	21
Vancouver	1922	Toronto	3	2	16	9
NY Rangers	1932	Toronto	3	0	18	10
NY Rangers	1933	NY Rangers	1	3	5	11
Mtl. Maroons	1935	Mtl. Maroons	0	3	4	10
Detroit	1936	Detroit	1	3	11	18
Chicago	1938	Chicago	1	3	8	10
Boston	1939	Boston	1	4	6	12
NY Rangers	1940	NY Rangers	2	4	11	14
Detroit	1942	Toronto	4	3	25	19
Detroit	1945	Toronto	4	3	9	9
Montreal	1947	Toronto	4	2	13	13
Detroit	1948	Toronto	4	0	18	7
Detroit	1949	Toronto	4	0	12	5
Montreal	1951	Toronto	4	1	13	10
Montreal	1959	Montreal	1	4	12	18
Montreal	1960	Montreal	0	4	5	15
Chicago	1962	Toronto	4	2	18	15
Detroit	1963	Toronto	4	1	17	10
Detroit	1964	Toronto	4	3	22	17
Montreal	1967	Toronto	4	2	17	16

NOTE: Toronto Blueshirts defeated the Victoria Aristocrats in the 1914 Stanley Cup Final, prior to the formation of the NHL, giving the franchise 14 championships in all.

VANCOUVER (PCHA/WCHL/WHL) 1918-26

All-Time Final Series Record

Opponent	Series	W	L	GP	W	L	GF	GA
Montreal	1	0	1	2	0	2	3	5
Ottawa ('20s)	2	0	2	9	3	6	19	22
Toronto	2	0	2	10	4	6	30	34
TOTALS	*5	0	5	21	7	14	52	61

Final Series Appearances*

Opponent	Year	Winner	W	L	GF	GA
Toronto	1918	Toronto	2	3	21	18
Ottawa	1921	Ottawa	2	3	12	12
Toronto	1922	Toronto	2	3	9	16
Ottawa	1923	Ottawa	1	3	7	10
Montreal	1924	Montreal	0	2	3	5

* Vancouver Millionaires defeated the Ottawa Senators in the 1915 Stanley Cup Final, giving them one championship.

Final Series Scoring Leaders

Player	GP	G	A	PTS	PIM
Mickey MacKay	21	7	6	13	16
Cyclone Taylor	10	9	1	10	15
Jack Adams	10	8	2	10	6
Art Duncan	16	4	4	8	10
Alf Skinner	13	5	2	7	16
Lloyd Cook	21	5	2	7	38

VANCOUVER   1971-2002

All-Time Final Series Record

Opponent	Series	W	L	GP	W	L	GF	GA
NY Islanders	1	0	1	4	0	4	10	18
NY Rangers	1	0	1	7	3	4	19	21
TOTALS	2	0	2	11	3	8	29	39

Final Series Appearances

Opponent	Year	Winner	W	L	GF	GA
NY Islanders	1982	NY Islanders	0	4	10	18
NY Rangers	1994	NY Rangers	3	4	19	21

Final Series Scoring Leaders

Player	GP	G	A	PTS	PIM
Pavel Bure	7	3	5	8	15
Cliff Ronning	7	1	6	7	6
Geoff Courtnall	7	4	1	5	11
Thomas Gradin	4	3	2	5	2
Trevor Linden	7	3	2	5	6

VICTORIA (PCHA/WCHL/WHL) 1918-26

All-Time Final Series Record

Opponent	Series	W	L	GP	W	L	GF	GA
Montreal	1	1	0	4	3	1	16	8
Mtl. Maroons	1	0	1	4	1	3	3	10
TOTALS	*2	1	1	8	4	4	19	18

Final Series Appearances*

Opponent	Year	Winner	W	L	GF	GA
Montreal	1925	Victoria	3	1	16	8
Mtl. Maroons	1926	Mtl. Maroons	1	3	3	10

* Victoria Aristocrats won the PCHA title in 1914 but lost to the Toronto Blueshirts in the Stanley Cup Final.

Final Series Scoring Leaders

Player	GP	G	A	PTS	PIM
Frank Fredrickson	8	4	4	8	16
Jack Walker	8	4	2	6	0
Harold Halderson	8	3	1	4	16
Gizzy Hart	8	2	1	3	2
Gord Fraser	8	2	1	3	14

WASHINGTON   1975-2002

All-Time Final Series Record

Opponent	Series	W	L	GP	W	L	GF	GA
Detroit	1	0	1	4	0	4	7	13
TOTALS	1	0	1	4	0	4	7	13

Final Series Appearances

Opponent	Year	Winner	W	L	GF	GA
Detroit	1998	Detroit	0	4	7	13

Final Series Scoring Leaders

Player	GP	G	A	PTS	PIM
Joe Juneau	4	1	3	4	0
Brian Bellows	4	2	1	3	0
Adams Oates	4	1	2	3	0
Peter Bondra	4	1	1	2	0
Jeff Brown	2	0	2	2	0
Andrei Nikolishin	4	0	2	2	2

CHAPTER 16
Final Series Record Book
Team and Individual Records, 1918 – 2002

Team Records

Note: Statistics from the suspended game in 1988 Final have not been included in the compilation of categories in the Team Records section, but are included in the Individual Records section.

MOST STANLEY CUP CHAMPIONSHIPS (1893-2002)
24 – **Montreal Canadiens** (1916-24-30-31-44-46-53-56-57-58-59-60-65-66-68-69-71-73-76-77-78-79-86-93)
14 – **Toronto Maple Leafs** (1914-18-22-32-42-45-47-48-49-51-62-63-64-67)
10 – **Detroit Red Wings** (1936-37-43-50-52-54-55-97-98-02)
NOTE: Montreal Canadiens totals include 1916 victory prior to formation of the NHL. Toronto Maple Leaf totals include those of the pre-NHL Toronto Blueshirts (1914), as well as the Toronto Arenas (1918) and Toronto St. Pats (1922).

MOST CONSECUTIVE STANLEY CUP CHAMPIONSHIPS
5 – **Montreal Canadiens** (1956-57-58-59-60)
4 – New York Islanders (1980-81-82-83)
– Montreal Canadiens (1976-77-78-79)

MOST YEARS IN THE FINALS (1893-2002)
35 – **Montreal Canadiens**
22 – Toronto Maple Leafs
22 – Detroit Red Wings
NOTE: Montreal Canadiens totals include 1916 victory prior to formation of the NHL. Toronto Maple Leaf totals include those of the pre-NHL Toronto Blueshirts (1914), as well as the Toronto Arenas (1918) and Toronto St. Pats (1922).

MOST CONSECUTIVE YEARS IN THE FINALS
10 – **Montreal Canadiens** (1951-60, inclusive)
5 – Montreal Canadiens (1965-69, inclusive)
– New York Islanders (1980-84, inclusive)

MOST GOALS, BOTH TEAMS, ONE SERIES
56 – **Montreal Canadiens, Chicago Black Hawks** in 1973. Montreal won best-of-seven series 4-2, outscoring Chicago 33-23.
51 – New York Islanders, Philadelphia Flyers in 1980. NY Islanders won best-of-seven series 4-2, outscoring Philadelphia 26-25.

MOST GOALS, ONE TEAM, ONE SERIES
33 – **Montreal Canadiens** in 1973. Montreal won best-of-seven series 4-2, outscoring Chicago 33-23.
28 – Pittsburgh Penguins in 1991. Pittsburgh won best-of-seven series 4-2, outscoring Minnesota North Stars 28-16.

MOST GOALS, BOTH TEAMS, FOUR-GAME SERIES
29 – **Detroit Red Wings, Toronto Maple Leafs** in 1936. Detroit won best-of-five series 3-1, outscoring Toronto 18-11.
28 – New York Islanders, Vancouver Canucks in 1982. NY Islanders won best-of-seven series 4-0, outscoring Vancouver 18-10.

MOST GOALS, ONE TEAM, FOUR-GAME SERIES
20 – **Boston Bruins** in 1970. Boston won best-of-seven series 4-0, outscoring St. Louis 20-7.
18 – Detroit Red Wings in 1936. Detroit won best-of-five series 3-1, outscoring Toronto 18-11.
– Toronto Maple Leafs in 1948. Toronto won best-of-seven series 4-0, outscoring Detroit 18-7.
– New York Islanders in 1982. NY Islanders won best-of-seven series 4-0, outscoring Vancouver 18-10.
– Edmonton Oilers in 1988. Edmonton won best-of-seven series 4-0, outscoring Boston 18-9.

MOST GOALS, BOTH TEAMS, FIVE-GAME SERIES
42 – **New York Islanders, Minnesota North Stars** in 1981. NY Islanders won best-of-seven series 4-1, outscoring Minnesota 26-16.
39 – Vancouver Millionaires, Toronto Arenas in 1918. Toronto won best-of-five series 3-2, but were outscored by Vancouver 21-18.
35 – Edmonton Oilers, Philadelphia Flyers in 1985. Edmonton won best-of-seven series 4-1, outscoring Philadelphia 21-14.

MOST GOALS, ONE TEAM, FIVE-GAME SERIES
26 – **New York Islanders** in 1981. NY Islanders won best-of-seven series 4-1, outscoring Minnesota North Stars 26-16.
21 – Vancouver Millionaires in 1918. Vancouver lost best-of-five series 3-2, outscoring Toronto Arenas 21-18
– Edmonton Oilers in 1984. Edmonton won best-of-seven series 4-1, outscoring NY Islanders 21-12.
– Edmonton Oilers in 1985. Edmonton won best-of-seven series 4-1, outscoring Philadelphia 21-14.

MOST GOALS, BOTH TEAMS, SIX-GAME SERIES
56 – **Montreal Canadiens, Chicago Black Hawks** in 1973. Montreal won best-of-seven series 4-2, outscoring Chicago 33-23.
51 – New York Islanders, Philadelphia Flyers in 1980. NY Islanders won best-of-seven series 4-2, outscoring Philadelphia 26-25.

MOST GOALS, ONE TEAM, SIX-GAME SERIES
33 – **Montreal Canadiens** in 1973. Montreal won best-of-seven series 4-2, outscoring Chicago 33-23.
28 – Pittsburgh Penguins in 1991. Pittsburgh won best-of-seven series 4-2, outscoring Minnesota North Stars 28-16.

MOST GOALS, BOTH TEAMS, SEVEN-GAME SERIES
47 – **Detroit Red Wings, Montreal Canadiens** in 1955. Detroit won best-of-seven series 4-3, outscoring Montreal 27-20.
44 – Toronto Maple Leafs, Detroit Red Wings in 1942. Toronto won best-of-seven series 4-3, outscoring Detroit 25-19.

MOST GOALS, ONE TEAM, SEVEN-GAME SERIES
27 – **Detroit Red Wings** in 1955. Detroit won best-of-seven series 4-3, outscoring Montreal 27-20.
25 – Toronto Maple Leafs in 1942. Toronto won best-of-seven series 4-3, outscoring Detroit 25-19.

FEWEST GOALS, BOTH TEAMS, FOUR-GAME SERIES
10 – **Ottawa Senators, Boston Bruins** in 1927. Ottawa won best-of-five series 2-0-2, outscoring Boston 7-3.
13 – Montreal Maroons, Victoria Cougars in 1926. Mtl. Maroons won best-of-five series 3-1, outscoring Victoria 10-3.
– Detroit Red Wings, Montreal Canadiens in 1952. Detroit won best-of-seven series 4-0, outscoring Montreal 11-2.

FEWEST GOALS, ONE TEAM, FOUR-GAME SERIES
2 – **Montreal Canadiens** in 1952. Detroit won best-of-seven series 4-0, outscoring Montreal 11-2.
3 – Victoria Cougars in 1926. Montreal Maroons won best-of-five series 3-1, outscoring Victoria 10-3.
– Boston Bruins in 1927. Ottawa Senators won best-of-five series 2-0-2, outscoring Boston 7-3.
– St. Louis Blues in 1969. Montreal won best-of-seven series 4-0, outscoring St. Louis 12-3.

FEWEST GOALS, BOTH TEAMS, FIVE-GAME SERIES
11 – **New York Rangers, Montreal Maroons** in 1928. NY Rangers won best-of-five series 3-2, but were outscored by Mtl. Maroons 6-5.
17 – Detroit Red Wings, New York Rangers in 1937. Detroit won best-of-five series 3-2, outscoring NY Rangers 9-8.

FEWEST GOALS, ONE TEAM, FIVE-GAME SERIES
5 – **New York Rangers** in 1928. NY Rangers won best-of-five series 3-2, but were outscored by Mtl. Maroons 6-5.
6 – Montreal Maroons in 1928. NY Rangers won best-of-five series 3-2, but were outscored by Mtl. Maroons 6-5.
– Toronto Maple Leafs in 1939. Boston won best-of-seven series 4-1, outscoring Toronto 12-6.
– Boston Bruins in 1957. Montreal won best-of-seven series 4-1, outscoring Boston 15-6.

FEWEST GOALS, BOTH TEAMS, SIX-GAME SERIES
22 – **Dallas Stars, Buffalo Sabres** in 1999. Dallas won best-of-seven series 4-2, outscoring Buffalo 13-9.
24 – New Jersey Devils, Dallas Stars in 2000. New Jersey won best-of-seven series 4-2, outscoring Dallas 15-9.

FEWEST GOALS, ONE TEAM, SIX-GAME SERIES
9 – **Buffalo Sabres** in 1999. Dallas won best-of-seven series 4-2, outscoring Buffalo 13-9.
– Dallas Stars in 2000. New Jersey won best-of-seven series 4-2, outscoring Dallas 15-9.

FEWEST GOALS, BOTH TEAMS, SEVEN-GAME SERIES
18 – **Toronto Maple Leafs, Detroit Red Wings** in 1945. Toronto won best-of-seven series 4-3, teams tied in scoring 9-9.
26 – Detroit Red Wings, Montreal Canadiens in 1954. Detroit won best-of-seven series 4-3, outscoring Montreal 14-12.

FEWEST GOALS, ONE TEAM, SEVEN-GAME SERIES
9 – **Detroit Red Wings** in 1945. Toronto won best-of-seven series 4-3, teams tied in scoring 9-9.
– Toronto Maple Leafs in 1945. Toronto won best-of-seven series 4-3, teams tied in scoring 9-9.
11 – New Jersey Devils in 2001. Colorado won best-of-seven series 4-3, outscoring New Jersey 19-11.

MOST GOALS, BOTH TEAMS, ONE GAME
15 – **Chicago Black Hawks 8 at Montreal Canadiens 7** in Game 5, May 8, 1973. Montreal won best-of-seven series 4-2.
13 – Toronto Maple Leafs 4 at Detroit Red Wings 9 in Game 2, April 7, 1936. Detroit won best-of-five series 3-1.

MOST GOALS, ONE TEAM, ONE GAME
9 – **Detroit Red Wings** in Game 2, April 7, 1936. Toronto 4 at Detroit 9. Detroit won best-of-five series 3-1.
– **Toronto Maple Leafs** in Game 5, April 14, 1942. Detroit 3 at Toronto 9. Toronto won best-of-seven series 4-3.

MOST GOALS, BOTH TEAMS, ONE PERIOD
8 – **Chicago Black Hawks (5), Montreal Canadiens (3)** in 2nd period of Game 5, May 8, 1973. Chicago 8 at Montreal 7. Montreal won best-of-seven series 4-2.
– **Vancouver Canucks (5), New York Rangers (3)** in 3rd period of Game 5, June 9, 1994. Vancouver 6 at NY Rangers 3. NY Rangers won best-of-seven series 4-3.

6 – Toronto Maple Leafs (3), New York Rangers (3) in 3rd period of Game 3, April 9, 1932. NY Rangers 4 at Toronto 6. Toronto won best-of-five series 3-0.

– Montreal Canadiens (4), Calgary Flames (2) in 1st period of Game 3, May 20, 1986. Calgary 3 at Montreal 5. Montreal won best-of-seven series 4-1.

– Pittsburgh Penguins (3), Chicago Blackhawks (3) in 1st period of Game 4, June 1, 1992. Pittsburgh 6 at Chicago 5. Pittsburgh won best-of-seven series 4-0.

MOST GOALS, ONE TEAM, ONE PERIOD

5 – **Toronto Maple Leafs** in 2nd period of Game 5, April 14, 1942. Detroit 3 at Toronto 9. Toronto won best-of-seven series 4-3.

– **Chicago Black Hawks** in 2nd period of Game 5, May 8, 1973. Chicago 8 at Montreal 7. Montreal won best-of-seven series 4-2.

– **Vancouver Canucks** in 3rd period of Game 5, June 9, 1994. Vancouver 6 at NY Rangers 3. NY Rangers won best-of-seven series 4-3.

LONGEST OVERTIME

55:13 – **Edmonton Oilers 3 at Boston Bruins 2** in Game 1, May 15, 1990. Edmonton's Petr Klima, assisted by Jari Kurri and Craig MacTavish, scored at 15:13 of the 3rd overtime period, 115:13 from the start of game. Edmonton won best-of-seven series 4-1.

54:51 – Dallas Stars 2 at Buffalo Sabres 1 in Game 6, 19, 1999. Dallas' Brett Hull, assisted by ▒▒▒en and Mike Modano, scored at ▒▒ 3rd overtime period, 114:51 from the start of game. Dallas won best-of-seven series 4-2.

54:47 – Detroit Red Wings 3 at Carolina Hurricanes 2 in Game 3, June 8, 2002. Detroit's Igor Larionov, assisted by Tomas Holmstrom and Steve Duchesne, scored at 14:47 of the 3rd overtime period, 114:47 from the start of game. Detroit won best-of-seven series 4-1.

SHORTEST OVERTIME

0:09 – **Montreal Canadiens 3 at Calgary Flames 2** in Game 2, May 18, 1986. Montreal's Brian Skrudland, assisted by Mike McPhee and Claude Lemieux, scored nine seconds into overtime. Montreal won best-of-seven series 4-1.

0:31 – Detroit Red Wings 3 at Toronto Maple Leafs 4, in Game 3, April 9, 1936. Toronto's Buzz Boll, assisted by Red Horner and Art Jackson, scored 31 seconds into overtime. Detroit won best-of-five series 3-1.

MOST OVERTIME GAMES, ONE SERIES

5 – **1951.** Of the five games played in the series, all went into overtime. Toronto Maple Leafs won four of the five games to defeat Montreal Canadiens 4-1 in best-of-seven series. Sid Smith, Ted Kennedy, Harry Watson and Bill Barilko scored the overtime winners for Toronto, while Maurice Richard replied for Montreal.

MOST OVERTIME WINS, ONE TEAM, ONE SERIES

4 – **Toronto Maple Leafs** in 1951. Sid Smith, Ted Kennedy, Harry Watson and Bill Barilko scored the overtime winners in games 1,3,4,5, respectively, for Toronto, who defeated Montreal 4-1 in best-of-seven series.

MOST HOME WINS, BOTH TEAMS, ONE SERIES

7 – **Detroit Red Wings (4), Montreal Canadiens (3)** in 1955. Detroit won games 1,2,5,7 at home and Montreal won games 3,4,6 at home. Detroit won best-of-seven series 4-3.

– **Montreal Canadiens (4), Chicago Black Hawks (3)** in 1965. Montreal won games 1,2,5,7 at home and Chicago won games 3,4,6 at home. Montreal won best-of-seven series 4-3.

MOST HOME WINS, ONE TEAM, ONE SERIES

4 – **Detroit Red Wings** in 1955. Detroit won games 1,2,5,7 in Detroit vs. Montreal Canadiens. Detroit won best-of-seven series 4-3.

– **Montreal Canadiens** in 1965. Montreal won games 1,2,5,7 in Montreal vs. Chicago Black Hawks. Montreal won best-of-seven series 4-3.

MOST ROAD WINS, BOTH TEAMS, ONE SERIES

5 – **Toronto Maple Leafs (3), Detroit Red Wings (2)** in 1945. Toronto won games 1,2,7 in Detroit and Detroit won games 4,6 in Toronto. Toronto won best-of-seven series 4-3.

– **Montreal Canadiens (3), Detroit Red Wings (2)** in 1966. Montreal won games 3,4,6 in Detroit and Detroit won games 1,2 in Montreal. Montreal won best-of-seven series 4-2.

– **New Jersey Devils (3), Dallas Stars (2)** in 2000. New Jersey won games 3,4,6 in Dallas and Dallas won games 1,5 in New Jersey. New Jersey won best-of-seven series 4-2.

MOST ROAD WINS, ONE TEAM, ONE SERIES

3 – **Ottawa Senators** in 1921. Ottawa won games 2,3,5 in Vancouver vs. Vancouver Millionaires. All five games were played in Vancouver as per the agreement between the NHL and PCHA. Ottawa won best-of-five series.

– **New York Rangers** in 1928. NY Rangers won games 2,4,5 in Montreal vs. Mtl. Maroons. All five games were played in Montreal as the circus occupied Madison Square Garden. NY Rangers won best-of-five series 3-2.

– **Toronto Maple Leafs** in 1945. Toronto won games 1,2,7 in Detroit vs. Detroit Red Wings. Toronto won best-of-seven series 4-3.

– **Montreal Canadiens** in 1966. Montreal won games 3,4,6 in Detroit vs. Detroit Red Wings. Montreal won best-of-seven series 4-2.

– **Edmonton Oilers** in 1990. Edmonton won games 1,2,5 in Boston vs. Boston Bruins. Edmonton won best-of-seven series 4-1.

– **New Jersey Devils** in 2000. New Jersey won games 3,4,6 in Dallas vs. Dallas Stars. New Jersey won best-of-seven series 4-2.

MOST CONSECUTIVE FINAL SERIES GAME VICTORIES

10 – **Montreal Canadiens.** Streak began May 9, 1976, at Montreal with a 4-3 win vs. Philadelphia in Game 1 and ended May 18, 1978, at Boston with a 4-0 loss in Game 3. Included in the streak were 4 wins vs. Philadelphia in 1976, 4 vs. Boston in 1977 and 2 more vs. Boston in 1978.

9 – Toronto Maple Leafs. Streak began April 19, 1947, at Toronto with a 2-1 win vs. Montreal in Game 6 and ended when the team failed to advance to 1950 Finals. Included in the streak were 1 win vs. Montreal in 1947, 4 vs. Detroit in 1948 and 4 more vs. Detroit in 1949.

– New York Islanders. Streak began May 21, 1981, at NY Islanders with a 5-1 win vs. Minnesota in Game 5 and ended May 10, 1984, at NY Islanders with a 1-0 loss to Edmonton in Game 1. Included in the streak were 1 win vs. Minnesota in 1981, 4 vs. Vancouver in 1982 and 4 vs. Edmonton in 1983.

MOST SHUTOUTS, BOTH TEAMS, ONE SERIES

5 – **Toronto Maple Leafs (3), Detroit Red Wings (2)** in 1945. Toronto won best-of-seven series 4-3.

3 – Montreal Maroons (3), Victoria Cougars (0) in 1926. Mtl. Maroons won best-of-five series 3-1.

– Montreal Maroons (2), New York Rangers (1) in 1928. NY Rangers won best-of-five series 3-2.

– Detroit Red Wings (2), New York Rangers (1) in 1937. Detroit won best-of-five series 3-2.

– Montreal Canadiens (3), Chicago Black Hawks (0) in 1965. Montreal won best-of-seven series 4-3.

MOST SHUTOUTS, ONE TEAM, ONE SERIES

3 – **Montreal Maroons** in 1926. Mtl. Maroons defeated Victoria Cougars 3-1 in best-of-five series

– **Toronto Maple Leafs** in 1945. Toronto defeated Detroit 4-3 in best-of-seven series.

– **Montreal Canadiens** in 1965. Montreal defeated Chicago 4-3 in best-of-seven series.

MOST PENALTIES, BOTH TEAMS, ONE SERIES

142 – **Philadelphia Flyers (75), Boston Bruins (67)** in 1974. Philadelphia won best-of-seven series 4-2.

128 – Philadelphia Flyers (72), New York Islanders (56) in 1980. NY Islanders won best-of-seven series 4-2.

MOST PENALTIES, ONE TEAM, ONE SERIES

75 – **Philadelphia Flyers** in 1974. Philadelphia defeated Boston in best-of-seven series 4-2.

72 – Philadelphia Flyers in 1980. NY Islanders won best-of-seven series 4-2.

MOST PENALTY MINUTES, BOTH TEAMS, ONE SERIES

511 – **Calgary Flames (256), Montreal Canadiens (255)** in 1986. Montreal won best-of-seven series 4-1.

395 – Philadelphia Flyers (219), New York Islanders (176) in 1980. NY Islanders won best-of-seven series 4-2.

MOST PENALTY MINUTES, ONE TEAM, ONE SERIES

256 – **Calgary Flames** in 1986. Montreal won best-of-seven series 4-1.

255 – Montreal Canadiens in 1986. Montreal defeated Calgary in best-of-seven series 4-1.

MOST PENALTIES, BOTH TEAMS, ONE GAME

43 – **Philadelphia Flyers (22) at Boston Bruins (21)** in Game 5, May 16, 1974. Boston 5, Philadelphia 1. Philadelphia won best-of-seven series 4-2.

37 – Boston Bruins (22) at Montreal Canadiens (15) in Game 5, May 23, 1978. Montreal 4, Boston 1. Montreal won best-of-seven series 4-2.

MOST PENALTIES, ONE TEAM, ONE GAME

22 – **Philadelphia Flyers** in Game 5, May 16, 1974. Philadelphia 1 at Boston 5. Philadelphia won best-of-seven series 4-2.

21 – Boston Bruins in Game 5, May 16, 1974. Philadelphia 1 at Boston 5. Philadelphia won best-of-seven series 4-2.

MOST PENALTY MINUTES, BOTH TEAMS, ONE GAME

176 – **Calgary Flames (86) at Montreal Canadiens (90)** in Game 4, May 22, 1986. Montreal 1, Calgary 0. Montreal won best-of-seven series 4-1.

135 – Philadelphia Flyers (67) at Boston Bruins (68) in Game 5, May 16, 1974. Boston 5, Philadelphia 1. Philadelphia won best-of-seven series 4-2.

MOST PENALTY MINUTES, ONE TEAM, ONE GAME

90 – **Montreal Canadiens** in Game 4, May 22, 1986. Calgary 0 at Montreal 1. Montreal won best-of-seven series 4-1.

86 – Calgary Flames in Game 4, May 22, 1986. Calgary 0 at Montreal 1. Montreal won best-of-seven series 4-1.

MOST PENALTIES, BOTH TEAMS, ONE PERIOD

21 – **Boston Bruins (11) at Philadelphia Flyers (10)** in 1st period of Game 4, May 14, 1974. Philadelphia 4, Boston 2. Philadelphia won best-of-seven series 4-2.

20 – Philadelphia Flyers (10) at New York Islanders (10) in 2nd period of Game 3, May 17, 1980. NY Islanders 6, Philadelphia 2. NY Islanders won best-of-seven series 4-2.

– Calgary Flames (10) at Montreal Canadiens (10) in 3rd period of Game 4, May 22, 1986. Montreal 1, Calgary 0. Montreal won best-of-seven series 4-1.

MOST PENALTIES, ONE TEAM, ONE PERIOD

11 – **Boston Bruins** in 1st period of Game 4, May 14, 1974. Boston 2 at Philadelphia 4. Philadelphia won best-of-seven series 4-2.

MOST PENALTY MINUTES, BOTH TEAMS, ONE PERIOD

152 – **Calgary Flames (72) at Montreal Canadiens (80)** in 3rd period of Game 4, May 22, 1986. Montreal 1, Calgary 0. Montreal won best-of-seven series 4-1.

104 – Vancouver Canucks (52) at New York Islanders (52) in 2nd period of Game 1, May 8, 1982. NY Islanders 6, Vancouver 5 (OT). NY Islanders won best-of-seven series 4-0.

MOST PENALTY MINUTES, ONE TEAM, ONE PERIOD

80 – **Montreal Canadiens** in 3rd period of Game 4, May 22, 1986. Montreal 1, Calgary 0. Montreal won best-of-seven series 4-1.

72 – Calgary Flames in 3rd period of Game 4, May 22, 1986. Montreal 1, Calgary 0. Montreal won best-of-seven series 4-1.

FEWEST PENALTIES, BOTH TEAMS, ONE SERIES

19 – **Detroit Red Wings (10), Toronto Maple Leafs (9)** in 1945. Toronto won best-of-seven series 4-3.

FEWEST PENALTIES, ONE TEAM, ONE SERIES

9 – **Toronto Maple Leafs in 1945.** Toronto defeated Detroit in best-of-seven series 4-3.

10 – Detroit Red Wings in 1945. Toronto defeated Detroit in best-of-seven series 4-3.

FEWEST PENALTY MINUTES, BOTH TEAMS, ONE SERIES

41 – **Toronto Maple Leafs (21), Detroit Red Wings (20)** in 1945. Toronto won best-of-seven series 4-3.

FEWEST PENALTY MINUTES, ONE TEAM, ONE SERIES

21 – **Toronto Maple Leafs** in 1945. Toronto defeated Detroit in best-of-seven series 4-3.

20 – Detroit Red Wings in 1945. Toronto defeated Detroit in best-of-seven series 4-3.

FEWEST PENALTIES AND PENALTY MINUTES, BOTH TEAMS, ONE GAME

0 – **Toronto Maple Leafs 1 at Detroit Red Wings 0** in Game 6, April 16, 1942. Toronto won best-of-seven series 4-3.

FEWEST PENALTIES AND PENALTY MINUTES, ONE TEAM, ONE GAME

0 – **Toronto Maple Leafs** in Game 6, April 16, 1942. Toronto 1 at Detroit 0. Toronto won best-of-seven series 4-3.

– **Detroit Red Wings** in Game 6, April 16, 1942. Toronto 1 at Detroit 0. Toronto won best-of-seven series 4-3.

– **Detroit Red Wings** in Game 2, April 8, 1945. Detroit 0 at Toronto 2. Toronto won best-of-seven series 4-3.

– **Toronto Maple Leafs** in Game 3, April 12, 1945. Detroit 0 at Toronto 1. Toronto won best-of-seven series 4-3.

– **New York Rangers** in Game 2, April 13, 1950. NY Rangers 3, Detroit 1 (at Toronto). Detroit won best-of-seven series 4-3.

– **Boston Bruins** in Game 5, April 16, 1953. Boston 0 at Montreal 1 (OT). Montreal won best-of-seven series 4-1.

MOST POWER-PLAY GOALS, BOTH TEAMS, ONE SERIES

21 – **New York Islanders (15), Philadelphia Flyers (6)** in 1980. NY Islanders won best-of-seven series 4-2.

14 – Montreal Canadiens (10), Chicago Black Hawks (4) in 1965. Montreal won best-of-seven series 4-3.

MOST POWER-PLAY GOALS, ONE TEAM, ONE SERIES

15 – **New York Islanders** in 1980. NY Islanders defeated Philadelphia in best-of-seven series 4-2.

10 – Montreal Canadiens in 1965. Montreal defeated Chicago in best-of-seven series 4-3.

MOST POWER-PLAY GOALS, BOTH TEAMS, ONE GAME

5 – seven times.

MOST POWER-PLAY GOALS, ONE TEAM, ONE GAME

5 – **New York Islanders,** May 17, 1980, in Game 3 at NY Islanders. NY Islanders 6, Philadelphia 2. NY Islanders won best-of-seven series 4-2.

4 – Toronto Maple Leafs, April 10, 1947, in Game 2 at Montreal. Toronto 4, Montreal 0. Toronto won best-of-seven series 4-2.

– Montreal Canadiens, April 27, 1965, in Game 5 at Montreal. Montreal 6, Chicago 0. Montreal won best-of-seven series 4-3.

– Edmonton Oilers, May 28, 1985, in Game 4 at Edmonton. Edmonton 5, Philadelphia 3. Edmonton won best-of-seven series 4-1.

– Colorado Avalanche, June 6, 1996, in Game 2 at Colorado. Colorado 8, Florida 1. Colorado won best-of-seven series 4-0.

MOST POWER-PLAY GOALS, BOTH TEAMS, ONE PERIOD

4 – **Florida Panthers (1) at Colorado Avalanche (3),** in 1st period of Game 2, June 6, 1996. Colorado 8, Florida 1. Colorado won best-of-seven series 4-0.

MOST POWER-PLAY GOALS, ONE TEAM, ONE PERIOD

3 – **Montreal Canadiens,** April 6, 1954, in 1st period of Game 2 at Detroit. Montreal 3, Detroit 1. Detroit won best-of-seven series 4-3.

– **New York Rangers,** May 4, 1972, in 1st period of Game 3 at NY Rangers. NY Rangers 5, Boston 2. Boston won best-of-seven series 4-2.

– **Montreal Canadiens,** May 12, 1977, in 1st period of Game 3 at Boston. Montreal 4, Boston 2. Montreal won best-of-seven series 4-0.

– **New York Islanders,** May 17, 1980, in 1st period of Game 3 at NY Islanders. NY Islanders 7, Philadelphia 5. NY Islanders won best-of-seven series 4-2.

– **Colorado Avalanche,** June 6, 1996, in 1st period of Game 2 at Colorado. Colorado 8, Florida 1. Colorado won best-of-seven series 4-0.

MOST SHORTHAND GOALS, BOTH TEAMS, ONE SERIES

6 – **Pittsburgh Penguins (3), Minnesota North Stars (3)** in 1991. Pittsburgh won best-of-seven series 4-2.

4 – New York Rangers (4), Toronto Maple Leafs (0) in 1933. NY Rangers won best-of-five series 3-1.

MOST SHORTHAND GOALS, ONE TEAM, ONE SERIES

4 – **New York Rangers** in 1933. NY Rangers defeated Toronto in best-of-five series 3-1.

3 – Detroit Red Wings in 1955. Detroit defeated Montreal in best-of-seven series 4-3.

– Toronto Maple Leafs in 1963. Toronto defeated Detroit in best-of-seven series 4-1.

– Boston Bruins in 1972. Boston defeated NY Rangers in best-of-seven series 4-2.

– Edmonton Oilers in 1987. Edmonton defeated Philadelphia in best-of-seven series 4-3.

– Pittsburgh Penguins in 1991. Pittsburgh defeated Minnesota North Stars in best-of-seven series 4-2.

– Minnesota North Stars in 1991. Pittsburgh defeated Minnesota North Stars in best-of-seven series 4-2.

MOST SHORTHAND GOALS, BOTH TEAMS, ONE GAME

2 – ten times.

MOST SHORTHAND GOALS, ONE TEAM, ONE GAME

2 – seven times.

MOST SHORTHAND GOALS, BOTH TEAMS, ONE PERIOD

2 – **New York Rangers (0) at Boston Bruins (2),** in 1st period of Game 1, April 30, 1972. Boston 6, NY Rangers 5. Boston won best-of-seven series 4-2.

– **Montreal Canadiens (0) at Chicago Black Hawks (2),** in 1st period of Game 3, May 3, 1973. Chicago 7, Montreal 4. Montreal won best-of-seven series 4-2.

– **Minnesota North Stars (0) at New York Islanders (2),** in 1st period of Game 1, May 12, 1981. NY Islanders 6, Minnesota North Stars 3. NY Islanders won best-of-seven series 4-1.

– **Minnesota North Stars (1), Pittsburgh Penguins (1),** in 2nd period of Game 1, May 15, 1991. Minnesota North Stars 5, Pittsburgh 4. Pittsburgh won best-of-seven series 4-2.

– **Carolina Hurricanes (1) at Detroit Red Wings (1),** in 1st period of Game 2, June 6, 2002. Detroit 3, Carolina 1. Detroit won best-of-seven series 4-1.

MOST SHORTHAND GOALS, ONE TEAM, ONE PERIOD

2 – **Boston Bruins** in 1st period of Game 1, April 30, 1972. Boston 6, NY Rangers 5. Boston won best-of-seven series 4-2.

– **Chicago Black Hawks** in 1st period of Game 3, May 3, 1973. Chicago 7, Montreal 4. Montreal won best-of-seven series 4-2.

– **New York Islanders** in 1st period of Game 1, May 12, 1981. NY Islanders 6, Minnesota North Stars 3. NY Islanders won best-of-seven series 4-1.

FASTEST TWO GOALS, BOTH TEAMS

0:10 – **Toronto Maple Leafs at Detroit Red Wings** in Game 1, April 5, 1936. Detroit's Wally Kilrea and Toronto's Buzz Boll scored at 12:05 and 12:15 of 1st period, respectively. Detroit 3, Toronto 1. Detroit won best-of-five series 3-1.

– **Montreal Canadiens at Toronto Maple Leafs** in Game 3, April 12, 1947. Toronto's Vic Lynn and Montreal's Leo Gravelle scored at 12:23 and 12:33 of 2nd period, respectively. Toronto 4, Montreal 2. Toronto won best-of-seven series 4-2.

0:13 – Detroit Red Wings at Toronto Maple Leafs in Game 1, April 11, 1964. Detroit's Bruce MacGregor and Toronto's George Armstrong scored at 4:31 and 4:44 of 1st period, respectively. Toronto 3, Detroit 2. Toronto won best-of-seven series 4-3.

FASTEST TWO GOALS, ONE T̶̶

0:12 – Montreal Maroons, Ap̶̶ at Mtl. Maroons. Mtl. ̶̶ Baldy Northcott and Cy Wentworth scored at 16:18 and 16:30 of 2nd period, respectively. Mtl. Maroons won best-of-five series 3-0.

– **Montreal Canadiens,** April 7, 1955, in Game 3 at Montreal. Montreal 4, Detroit 2. Bernie Geoffrion scored at 8:30 and 8:42 of first period. Detroit won best-of-seven series 4-3.

– **Dallas Stars,** May 30, 2000, in Game 1 at New Jersey. New Jersey 7, Dallas 3. Jon Sim and Kirk Muller scored at 7:43 and 7:55 of third period, respectively. New Jersey won best-of-seven series 4-2.

FASTEST THREE GOALS, BOTH TEAMS

0:30 – **Pittsburgh Penguins 6 at Chicago Blackhawks 5** in Game 4, June 1, 1992. Chicago's Dirk Graham scored at 6:21 of 1st period, Pittsburgh's Kevin Stevens at 6:33 and Graham at 6:51. Pittsburgh won best-of-seven series 4-0.

0:31 – Philadelphia Flyers 3 at Edmonton Oilers 4 in Game 3, May 25, 1985. Edmonton's Wayne Gretzky scored at 1:10 and 1:25 of first period and Philadelphia's Derrick Smith at 1:41. Edmonton won best-of-seven series 4-1.

1:18 – Calgary Flames 3 at Montreal Canadiens 5 in Game 3, May 20, 1986. Calgary's Joel Otto scored at 17:59 of first period, and Montreal's Bobby Smith at 18:25 and Mats Naslund at 19:17. Montreal won best-of-seven series 4-1.

FASTEST THREE GOALS, ONE TEAM

0:56 – **Montreal Canadiens,** April 6, 1954, in Game 2 at Detroit. Montreal 3, Detroit 1. Dickie Moore scored at 15:03 of first period, and Maurice Richard scored at 15:28 and again at 15:59. Detroit won best-of-seven series 4-3.

1:08 – Montreal Canadiens, May 20, 1986, in Game 3 at Montreal. Montreal 5, Calgary 3. Bobby Smith scored at 18:25 of first period, Mats Naslund at 19:17 and Bob Gainey at 19:33. Montreal won best-of-seven series 4-1.

FASTEST FOUR GOALS, BOTH TEAMS

1:34 – **Calgary Flames 3 at Montreal Canadiens 5** in Game 3, May 20, 1986. Calgary's Joel Otto scored at 17:59 of 1st period, followed by Montreal's Bobby Smith at 18:25, Mats Naslund at 19:17 and Bob Gainey at 19:33. Montreal won best-of-seven series 4-1.

2:54 – New York Rangers 4 at Toronto Maple Leafs 6 in Game 3, April 9, 1932. NY Rangers' Bun Cook scored at 16:32 of 3rd period, followed by Toronto's Bob Gracie at 17:36 and NY Rangers' Frank Boucher at 18:26 and again at 19:26. Toronto won best-of-five series 3-0.

FASTEST FOUR GOALS, ONE TEAM

5:29 – **Montreal Canadiens,** March 31, 1956, in Game 1 at Montreal. Montreal 6, Detroit 4. Jack Leclair, Bernie Geoffrion, Jean Beliveau and Claude Provost scored at 5:20, 6:20, 7:31 and 10:49 of 3rd period, respectively. Montreal won best-of-seven series 4-1.

5:57 – Montreal Canadiens, April 29, 1973, in Game 1 at Montreal. Montreal 8, Chicago 3. Jacques Lemaire, Pete Mahovlich, Frank Mahovlich and Chuck Lefley scored at 8:38, 12:36, 13:34 and 14:35 of 3rd period, respectively. Montreal won best-of-seven series 4-2.

FASTEST FIVE GOALS, BOTH TEAMS

4:20 – **New York Rangers 4 at Toronto Maple Leafs 6** in Game 3, April 9, 1932. Toronto's Ace Bailey scored at 15:07 of 1st period, followed by NY Rangers' Bun Cook at 16:34, Toronto's Bob Gracie at 17:36 and NY Rangers' Frank Boucher at 18:24 and again at 19:27. Toronto won best-of-five series 3-0.

5:34 – Dallas Stars 3 at New Jersey Devils 7 in Game 1, May 30, 2000. New Jersey's Sergei Brylin scored at 2:21 of the 3rd period, followed by New Jersey's Petr Sykora at 3:02 and Jason Arnott at 5:12. Dallas completed the scoring with goals by Jon Sim at 7:43 and Kirk Muller at 7:55. New Jersey won best-of-seven series 4-2.

FASTEST FIVE GOALS, ONE TEAM

10:29 – **Edmonton Oilers,** May 15, 1984, in Game 3 at Edmonton. Edmonton 7, NY Islanders 2. Glenn Anderson scored at 19:12 of 2nd period, followed by Paul Coffey at 19:29, Mark Messier at 5:32 of 3rd period and Dave Semenko at 5:52. Edmonton won best-of-seven series 4-1.

14:20 – New York Islanders, May 12, 1983, in Game 2 at Edmonton. NY Islanders 6, Edmonton 3. Tomas Jonsson scored at 14:21 of 2nd period, followed by Bob Nystrom at 17:55, Mike Bossy at 19:17, Bob Bourne at 8:03 of 3rd period, and Brent Sutter at 8:41. NY Islanders won best-of-seven series 4-0.

Individual Records

Note: Statistics from the suspended game in 1988 Final have not been included in the compilation of categories in the Team Records section, but are included in the Individual Records section.

MOST YEARS IN FINALS

12 – **Maurice Richard,** Montreal (1944-46-47-51-52-53-54-56-57-58-59-60)
– **Red Kelly,** Detroit (1948-49-50-52-54-55-56), Toronto (1960-62-63-64-67)
– **Jean Beliveau,** Montreal (1954-55-56-57-58-60-65-66-67-68-69-71)
– **Henri Richard,** Montreal (1956-57-58-59-60-65-66-67-68-69-71-73)
11 – Bert Olmstead, Montreal (1951-52-53-54-55-56-57-58), Toronto (1959-60-62)
– Doug Harvey, Montreal (1951-52-53-54-55-56-57-58-59-60), St. Louis (1968)
– Jean-Guy Talbot, Montreal (1956-57-58-59-60-65-66-67), St. Louis (1968-69-70)
10 – Gordie Howe, Detroit (1948-49-52-54-55-56-61-63-64-66)
– Claude Provost, Montreal (1956-57-58-59-60-65-66-67-68-69)
– Yvan Cournoyer, Montreal (1965-66-67-68-69-71-73-76-77-78)

MOST CONSECUTIVE YEARS IN FINALS

10 – **Bernie Geoffrion,** Montreal (1951-60 inclusive)
– **Doug Harvey,** Montreal (1951-60 inclusive)
– **Tom Johnson,** Montreal (1951-60 inclusive)
– **Bert Olmstead,** Montreal (1951-58, inclusive), Toronto (1959-60)
9 – Dickie Moore, Montreal (1952-60 inclusive)
8 – Floyd Curry, Montreal (1951-58 inclusive)
7 – Dollard St. Laurent, Montreal (1952-58 inclusive)

MOST GAMES PLAYED IN FINALS

65 – **Red Kelly,** Detroit (37), Toronto (28)
– **Henri Richard,** Montreal
64 – Jean Beliveau, Montreal
59 – Maurice Richard, Montreal
56 – Bert Olmstead, Montreal (43), Toronto (13)
55 – Gordie Howe, Detroit
– Jean-Guy Talbot, Montreal (43), St. Louis (12)

MOST CONSECUTIVE GAMES IN FINALS

53 – **Bernie Geoffrion,** Montreal (Game 1 in 1951 through Game 4 in 1960)
48 – Dickie Moore, Montreal (Game 1 in 1952 through Game 4 in 1960)
41 – Floyd Curry, Montreal (Game 1 in 1951 through Game 3 in 1958)
40 – Bert Olmstead, Montreal (Game 1 in 1951 through Game 2 in 1958)
38 – Tom Johnson, Montreal (Game 1 in 1951 through Game 5 in 1957)

MOST CAREER POINTS IN FINALS

62 – **Jean Beliveau,** Montreal (30G-32A-62PTS in 64 games)
53 – Wayne Gretzky, Edmonton (16G-30A-46PTS in 26 games), Los Angeles (2G-5A-7PTS in 5 games), (18G-35A-53PTS in 31 games overall)
50 – Gordie Howe, Detroit (18G-32A-50PTS in 55 games)
47 – Henri Richard, Montreal (21G-26A-47PTS in 65 games)
46 – Maurice Richard, Montreal (34G-12A-46PTS in 59 games)
– Bernie Geoffrion, Montreal (24G-22A-46PTS in 53 games)

MOST CAREER GOALS IN FINALS

34 – **Maurice Richard,** Montreal (59 games)
30 – Jean Beliveau, Montreal (64 games)
24 – Bernie Geoffrion, Montreal (53 games)
21 – Yvan Cournoyer, Montreal (50 games)
– Henri Richard, Montreal (65 games)
19 – Jacques Lemaire, Montreal (40 games)

MOST CAREER ASSISTS IN FINALS

35 – **Wayne Gretzky,** Edmonton (30A in 26 games), Los Angeles (5A in 5 games), (31 games overall)
32 – Jean Beliveau, Montreal (64 games)
– Gordie Howe, Detroit (55 games)
31 – Doug Harvey, Montreal (30A in 52 games) and St. Louis (1A in 2 games), (54 games overall)
26 – Henri Richard, Montreal (65 games)

MOST CAREER GAME-WINNING GOALS IN FINALS

9 – **Jean Beliveau,** Montreal
8 – Maurice Richard, Montreal
6 – Yvan Cournoyer, Montreal
– Bernie Geoffrion, Montreal

MOST CAREER OVERTIME GOALS IN FINALS

3 – **Maurice Richard,** Montreal (1 in 1946, 1 in 1951, 1 in 1958)
2 – Don Raleigh, NY Rangers (2 in 1950)
– Jacques Lemaire, Montreal (1 in 1968; 1 in 1977)
– John LeClair, Montreal (2 in 1993)

MOST CAREER OVERTIME ASSISTS IN FINALS

2 – **Doc Romnes,** Chicago (2 in 1934)
– **Butch Bouchard,** Montreal (1 in 1944, 1 in 1946)
– **Ed Slowinski,** NY Rangers (2 in 1950)
– **Tod Sloan,** Toronto (2 in 1951)
– **Guy Lafleur,** Montreal (1 in 1977, 1 in 1979)
– **John Tonelli,** NY Islanders (2 in 1980)
– **Harry Watson,** Toronto (1 in 1947, 1 in 1951)

MOST CAREER OVERTIME POINTS IN FINALS

4 – **Maurice Richard,** Montreal (3G-1A-4PTS)
3 – Doc Romnes, Chicago (0G-2A-2PTS) and Toronto (1G-0A-1PTS) (1G-2A-3PTS overall)
– Guy Lafleur, Montreal (1G-2A-3PTS)
– Harry Watson, Toronto (1G-2A-3PTS)

MOST CAREER POWER-PLAY GOALS IN FINALS

11 – **Jean Beliveau,** Montreal
10 – Bernie Geoffrion, Montreal
8 – Mike Bossy, NY Islanders
– Yvan Cournoyer, Montreal
7 – Alex Delvecchio, Detroit

MOST CAREER POWER-PLAY ASSISTS IN FINALS

16 – **Jean Beliveau,** Montreal
14 – Gordie Howe, Detroit
– Wayne Gretzky, Edmonton (11), Los Angeles (3)
12 – Doug Harvey, Montreal (11), St. Louis (1)
– Denis Potvin, NY Islanders

MOST CAREER POWER-PLAY POINTS IN FINALS

27 – **Jean Beliveau,** Montreal (11G-16A-27PTS)
19 – Mike Bossy, NY Islanders (8G-11A-19PTS)
– Wayne Gretzky, Edmonton (5G-11A-16PTS), Los Angeles (0G-3A-3PTS)
18 – Bernie Geoffrion, Montreal (10G-8A-18PTS)
– Yvan Cournoyer, Montreal (8G-10A-18PTS)
– Denis Potvin, NY Islanders (6G-12A-18PTS)
– Gordie Howe, Detroit (4G-14A-18PTS)

MOST CAREER SHORTHAND GOALS IN FINALS

2 – **Cecil Dillon,** NY Rangers (2 in 1933)
– **Dave Keon,** Toronto (2 in 1963)
– **Bob Pulford,** Toronto (2 in 1964)
– **Marcel Pronovost,** Detroit (1 in 1955) and Toronto (1 in 1967)
– **Serge Savard,** Montreal (2 in 1968)
– **Derek Sanderson,** Boston (1 in 1970, 1 in 1972)
– **Pete Mahovlich,** Montreal (1 in 1971, 1 in 1973)
– **Kevin Lowe,** Edmonton (2 in 1987)
– **Mario Lemieux,** Pittsburgh (2 in 1991)
– **Kirk Maltby,** Detroit (1 in 1997, 1 in 2002)

MOST CAREER SHORTHAND ASSISTS IN FINALS

4 – **Bobby Orr,** Boston (2 in 1970, 1 in 1972, 1 in 1974)
2 – George Armstrong, Toronto (2 in 1963)
– Allan Stanley, Toronto (1 in 1963, 1 in 1964)
– Claude Provost, Montreal (1 in 1968, 1 in 1969)
– Bob Bourne, NY Islanders (1 in 1980, 1 in 1982)
– Wayne Gretzky, Edmonton (2 in 1987)
– Kris Draper, Detroit (1 in 1997, 1 in 2002)

MOST CAREER SHORTHAND POINTS IN FINALS

4 – **Bobby Orr,** Boston (0G-4A-4PTS)

MOST CAREER PENALTY MINUTES IN FINALS

94 – **Gordie Howe,** Detroit (in 55 games)
87 – Kevin McClelland, Edmonton (in 22 games)
86 – Duane Sutter, NY Islanders (in 24 games)
83 – Maurice Richard, Montreal (in 59 games)
79 – Wayne Cashman, Boston (in 26 games)

MOST PENALTY MINUTES, ONE GAME

29 – **Kevin McClelland,** Edmonton, in Game 5, May 30, 1985, at Edmonton vs. Philadelphia. McClelland was assessed 2 minors, 1 major, 1 misconduct and 1 game misconduct. Edmonton won 8-3.
27 – Claude Lemieux, Montreal, in Game 4, May 22, 1986, at Montreal vs. Calgary. Lemieux was assessed 1 minor, 1 major, 1 misconduct and 1 game misconduct. Montreal won 1-0.

MOST PENALTY MINUTES, ONE PERIOD

25 – **Kevin McClelland,** Edmonton, May 30, 1985 at Edmonton vs. Philadelphia, third period, Game 5. McClelland was assessed 1 major, 1 misconduct and 1 game misconduct. Edmonton won 8-3.
– Claude Lemieux, Montreal, May 22, 1986 at Montreal vs. Calgary, third period, Game 4. Lemieux was assessed 1 major, 1 misconduct and 1 game misconduct. Montreal won 1-0.

MOST CAREER SHUTOUTS IN FINALS

8 – **Clint Benedict,** Ottawa (1 in 1920, 2 in 1921, 1 in 1923), Mtl. Maroons (3 in 1926, 1 in 1928)
4 – Turk Broda, Toronto (1 in 1940, 1 in 1942, 1 in 1947, 1 in 1948)
– Jacques Plante, Montreal (1 in 1956, 1 in 1957, 1 in 1958, 1 in 1960)
– Patrick Roy, Montreal (1 in 1986), Colorado (1 in 1996, 2 in 2001)
3 – Harry Lumley, Detroit (2 in 1945, 1 in 1950)
– Frank McCool, Toronto (3 in 1945)
– Gerry McNeil, Montreal (2 in 1953, 1 in 1954)
– Terry Sawchuk, Detroit (2 in 1952, 1 in 1954)
– Gump Worsley, Montreal (2 in 1965, 1 in 1968)

MOST CAREER GAMES PLAYED BY A GOALTENDER IN FINALS

41 – **Jacques Plante,** Montreal (38), St.Louis (3)
38 – Turk Broda, Toronto
37 – Terry Sawchuk, Detroit (33), Toronto (4)
32 – Glenn Hall, Detroit (5), Chicago (19), St. Louis (8)
– Ken Dryden, Montreal

MOST CAREER MINUTES PLAYED BY A GOALTENDER IN FINALS
2,423 – Jacques Plante, Montreal (2,279), St. Louis (164)
2,369 – Turk Broda, Toronto
2,185 – Terry Sawchuk, Detroit (1,960), Toronto (225)
1,947 – Ken Dryden, Montreal
1,844 – Glenn Hall, Detroit (300), Chicago (1,060), St. Louis (484)

MOST YEARS BY A GOALTENDER IN FINALS
10 – Jacques Plante, Montreal (8), St. Louis (2)
8 – Turk Broda, Toronto
7 – Terry Sawchuk, Detroit (6), Toronto (1)
– Glenn Hall, Detroit (1), Chicago (3), St. Louis (3)
6 – Johnny Bower, Toronto
– Ken Dryden, Montreal

MOST CONSECUTIVE YEARS BY A GOALTENDER IN FINALS
8 – Jacques Plante, Montreal (1953-60, inclusive)
5 – Billy Smith, NY Islanders (1980-84, inclusive)

MOST CAREER WINS BY A GOALTENDER IN FINALS
25 – Jacques Plante, Montreal
24 – Ken Dryden, Montreal
21 – Turk Broda, Toronto
19 – Terry Sawchuk, Detroit (17), Toronto (2)
18 – Patrick Roy, Montreal (10), Colorado (8)

MOST CONSECUTIVE WINS BY A GOALTENDER IN FINALS
10 – Ken Dryden, Montreal. Streak began May 9, 1976, at Montreal with a 4-3 win vs. Philadelphia in Game 1 and ended May 18, 1978, at Boston with a 4-0 loss in Game 3. Included were four wins vs. Philadelphia in 1976, four vs. Boston in 1977 and two more vs. Boston in 1978.
9 – Turk Broda, Toronto. Streak began April 19, 1947, at Toronto with a 2-1 win vs. Montreal in Game 6 and ended when the team failed to advance to the 1950 Finals. Included were one win vs. Montreal in 1947, four vs. Detroit in 1948 and four vs. Detroit in 1949.
– Billy Smith, NY Islanders. Streak began May 21, 1981, at NY Islanders with a 5-1 win vs. Minnesota North Stars in Game 5 and ended May 10, 1984, at NY Islanders with a 1-0 loss to Edmonton in Game 1. Included were one win vs. Minnesota North Stars in 1981, four vs. Vancouver in 1982 and four vs. Edmonton in 1983.

LOWEST CAREER GOALS-AGAINST AVERAGE (MINIMUM 15 GAMES PLAYED)
1.55 – Clint Benedict, Ottawa, Mtl. Maroons (25 games)
1.82 – Gump Worsley, Montreal (16 games)
1.86 – Gerry McNeil, Montreal (15 games)
1.92 – Patrick Roy, Montreal, Colorado (27 games)
1.98 – Ed Belfour, Chicago, Dallas (16 games)

HIGHEST CAREER WINNING PERCENTAGE, (MINIMUM 15 GAMES PLAYED)
.750 – Ken Dryden, Montreal (24-8)
.739 – Billy Smith, NY Islanders (17-6)
.737 – Grant Fuhr, Edmonton (14-5)
.733 – Gump Worsley, Montreal (11-4)
.667 – Patrick Roy, Montreal, Colorado (18-9)
– Bill Durnan, Montreal (10-5)

MOST POINTS, ONE SERIES
13 – Wayne Gretzky, Edmonton (3G-10A-13PTS in 4 games plus suspended game), in 1988.
12 – Gordie Howe, Detroit, (5G-7A-12PTS in 7 games), in 1955.
– Yvan Cournoyer, Montreal (6G-6A-12PTS in 6 games), in 1973.
– Jacques Lemaire, Montreal (3G-9A-12PTS in 6 games), in 1973.
– Mario Lemieux, Pittsburgh (5G-7A-12PTS in 5 games), in 1991.
11 – Ted Lindsay, Detroit (5G-6A-11PTS in 7 games), in 1955.
– Frank Mahovlich, Montreal (5G-6A-11PTS in 6 games), in 1973.
– Mike Bossy, NY Islanders (4G-7A-11PTS in 6 games), in 1980.
– Wayne Gretzky, Edmonton (7G-4A-11PTS in 5 games), in 1985.
– Paul Coffey, Edmonton (3G-8A-11PTS in 5 games), in 1985.
– Wayne Gretzky, Edmonton (2G-9A-11PTS in 7 games), in 1987.
– Brian Leetch, NY Rangers (5G-6A-11PTS in 7 games), in 1994.

MOST POINTS, FOUR-GAME SERIES
13 – Wayne Gretzky, Edmonton (3G-10A-13PTS in 4 games plus suspended game) in 1988.
9 – Guy Lafleur, Montreal (2G-7A-9PTS in 4 games) in 1977.
– Denis Potvin, NY Islanders (2G-7A-9PTS in 4 games) in 1982.

MOST POINTS, FIVE-GAME SERIES
11 – Wayne Gretzky, Edmonton (7G-4A-11PTS in 5 games) in 1985.
– Paul Coffey, Edmonton (3G-8A-11PTS in 5 games) in 1985.
10 – Alf Skinner, Toronto Arenas (8G-2A-10PTS in 5 games) in 1918.
Mickey MacKay, Vancouver Millionaires (5G-5A-10PTS in 5 games) in 1918.
– Frank Foyston, Seattle Metropolitans (9G-1A-10PTS in 5 games) in 1919.
– Babe Dye, Toronto St. Pats (9G-1A-10PTS in 5 games) in 1922.
– Jean Beliveau, Montreal (7G-3A-10PTS in 5 games) in 1956.

MOST POINTS, SIX-GAME SERIES
12 – Yvan Cournoyer, Montreal (6G-6A-12PTS in 6 games) in 1973.
– Jacques Lemaire, Montreal (3G-9A-12PTS in 6 games) in 1973.
– Mario Lemieux, Pittsburgh (5G-7A-12PTS in 5 games) in 1991.
11 – Frank Mahovlich, Montreal (5G-6A-11PTS in 6 games) in 1973.
– Mike Bossy, NY Islanders (4G-7A-11PTS in 6 games) in 1980.

MOST POINTS, SEVEN-GAME SERIES
12 – Gordie Howe, Detroit (5G-7A-12PTS in 7 games) in 1955.
11 – Ted Lindsay, Detroit (5G-6A-11PTS in 7 games) in 1955.
– Wayne Gretzky, Edmonton (2G-9A-11PTS in 7 games) in 1987.
– Brian Leetch, NY Rangers (5G-6A-11PTS in 7 games) in 1994.

MOST POINTS BY A DEFENSEMAN, ONE SERIES
11 – Paul Coffey, Edmonton (3G-8A-11PTS in 5 games) in 1985.
– Brian Leetch, NY Rangers (5G-6A-11PTS in 7 games) in 1994.
10 – Larry Murphy, Pittsburgh (1G-9A-10PTS in 6 games) in 1991.
9 – Denis Potvin, NY Islanders (5G-4A-9PTS in 6 games) in 1980.
– Denis Potvin, NY Islanders (2G-7A-9PTS in 4 games) in 1982.
– Al MacInnis, Calgary (5G-4A-9PTS in 6 games) in 1989.

MOST POINTS BY A ROOKIE, ONE SERIES
7 – Roy Conacher, Boston, (5G-2A-7PTS in 5 games) in 1939.
– Ralph Backstrom, Montreal, (3G-4A-7PTS in 5 games) in 1959.
6 – Johnny Gagnon, Montreal, (4G-2A-6PTS in 5 games) in 1931.
– Brian Propp, Philadelphia, (3G-3A-6PTS in 6 games) in 1980.

MOST GOALS, ONE SERIES
9 – Cyclone Taylor, Vancouver Millionaires (5 games) in 1918.
– Frank Foyston, Seattle Metropolitans (5 games) in 1919.
– Babe Dye, Toronto St. Pats, (5 games) in 1922.
8 – Alf Skinner, Toronto Arenas, (5 games) in 1918.
7 – Jean Beliveau, Montreal (5 games) in 1956.
– Mike Bossy, NY Islanders (4 games) in 1982.
– Wayne Gretzky, Edmonton (5 games) in 1985.

MOST GOALS, FOUR-GAME SERIES
7 – Mike Bossy, NY Islanders in 1982.
6 – Nels Stewart, Mtl. Maroons in 1926.
– John Bucyk, Boston in 1970.
– Esa Tikkanen, Edmonton in 1988.

MOST GOALS, FIVE-GAME SERIES
9 – Cyclone Taylor, Vancouver Millionaires in 1918.
– Frank Foyston, Seattle Metropolitans in 1919.
– Babe Dye, Toronto St. Pats in 1922.
8 – Alf Skinner, Toronto Arenas in 1918.
7 – Jean Beliveau, Montreal in 1956.
– Wayne Gretzky, Edmonton in 1985.

MOST GOALS, SIX-GAME SERIES
6 – Yvan Cournoyer, Montreal in 1973.
5 – Bernie Geoffrion, Montreal in 1958.
– Ken Hodge, Boston in 1972.
– Pit Martin, Chicago in 1973.
– Frank Mahovlich, Montreal in 1973.
– Denis Potvin, NY Islanders in 1980.
– Al MacInnis, Calgary in 1989.
– Joe Mullen, Calgary in 1989.

MOST GOALS, SEVEN-GAME SERIES
6 – Alex Delvecchio, Detroit in 1955.
– Bernie Geoffrion, Montreal in 1955.

MOST GOALS BY A DEFENSEMAN, ONE SERIES
5 – Denis Potvin, NY Islanders (6 games), in 1980.
– Al MacInnis, Calgary (6 games), in 1989.
– Brian Leetch, NY Rangers (7 games), in 1994.
4 – Bobby Orr, Boston (6 games), in 1972.
– Brad Park, Boston (6 games), in 1978.

MOST GOALS BY A ROOKIE, ONE SERIES
5 – Roy Conacher, Boston (5 games), in 1939.
4 – Johnny Gagnon, Montreal (5 games), in 1931.

MOST ASSISTS, ONE SERIES
10 – Wayne Gretzky, Edmonton (4 games plus suspended game), in 1988.
9 – Jacques Lemaire, Montreal (6 games) in 1973.
– Wayne Gretzky, Edmonton (7 games) in 1987.
– Larry Murphy, Pittsburgh (6 games) in 1991.
8 – Billy Taylor, Toronto (7 games) in 1942.
– Bert Olmstead, Montreal (5 games) in 1956.
– Phil Esposito, Boston (6 games) in 1972.
– Pat Stapleton, Chicago (6 games) in 1973.
– Paul Coffey, Edmonton (5 games) in 1985.

MOST ASSISTS, FOUR-GAME SERIES
10 – Wayne Gretzky, Edmonton in 1988.
7 – Guy Lafleur, Montreal in 1977.
– Denis Potvin, NY Islanders in 1982.
6 – Bernie Geoffrion, Montreal in 1960.
– Phil Esposito, Boston in 1970.
– Rick Tocchet, Pittsburgh in 1992.

MOST ASSISTS, FIVE-GAME SERIES
8 – Bert Olmstead, Montreal in 1956.
– Paul Coffey, Edmonton in 1985.
7 – Bill Cowley, Boston in 1939.

MOST ASSISTS, SIX-GAME SERIES
9 – Jacques Lemaire, Montreal in 1973.
– Larry Murphy, Pittsburgh in 1991.
8 – Phil Esposito, Boston in 1972.
– Pat Stapleton, Chicago in 1973.

MOST ASSISTS, SEVEN-GAME SERIES
9 – **Wayne Gretzky,** Edmonton in 1987.
8 – Billy Taylor, Toronto in 1942.

MOST ASSISTS BY A DEFENSEMAN, ONE SERIES
9 – **Larry Murphy,** Pittsburgh (6 games), in 1991.
8 – Pat Stapleton, Chicago (6 games), in 1973.
– Paul Coffey, Edmonton (5 games), in 1985.
7 – Denis Potvin, NY Islanders (4 games), in 1982.

MOST ASSISTS BY A ROOKIE, ONE SERIES
5 – **Jaromir Jagr,** Pittsburgh (6 games), in 1991.
4 – Ralph Backstrom, Pittsburgh (5 games), in 1959.
– Lars Molin, Vancouver (4 games), in 1982.
– Derrick Smith, Philadelphia (5 games), in 1985.
3 – Brian Propp, Philadelphia (6 games), in 1980.
– Dino Ciccarelli, Minnesota (5 games), in 1981.
– Billy Carroll, NY Islanders (5 games), in 1981.
– Pat Flatley, NY Islanders (5 games), in 1984.
– Janne Niinimaa, Philadelphia (4 games), in 1997.

MOST OVERTIME GOALS, ONE SERIES
2 – **Don Raleigh,** NY Rangers (7 games), in 1950.
– **John LeClair,** Montreal (5 games), in 1993.

MOST POWER-PLAY GOALS, ONE SERIES
4 – **Jean Beliveau,** Montreal (7 games), in 1965.
– **Mike Bossy,** NY Islanders (6 games), in 1980.
3 – Bernie Geoffrion, Montreal (7 games), in 1955.
– Dick Duff, Montreal (4 games), in 1969.
– Steve Shutt, Montreal (4 games), in 1976.
– Denis Potvin, NY Islanders (6 games), in 1980.
– Mike Bossy, NY Islanders (4 games), in 1982.
– Clark Gillies, NY Islanders (5 games), in 1984.
– Joe Mullen, Calgary (6 games), in 1989.

MOST POWER-PLAY ASSISTS, ONE SERIES
6 – **Mike Bossy,** NY Islanders (6 games), in 1980.
– **Wayne Gretzky,** Edmonton (4 games plus suspended game), in 1988.

MOST SHORTHAND GOALS, ONE SERIES
2 – **Cecil Dillon,** NY Rangers (4 games), in 1933.
– **Dave Keon,** Toronto (5 games), in 1963.
– **Bob Pulford,** Toronto (7 games), in 1964.
– **Serge Savard,** Montreal (4 games), in 1968.
– **Kevin Lowe,** Edmonton (7 games), in 1987.

MOST PENALTY MINUTES, ONE SERIES
53 – **Mel Bridgman,** Philadelphia (6 games), in 1980.
49 – Chris Nilan, Montreal (3 games), in 1986.
44 – Eddie Gerard, Ottawa (2 games), in 1921
43 – Brad Marsh, Philadelphia (5 games), in 1985.
– Tim Hunter, Calgary (5 games), in 1986.

MOST SHUTOUTS BY A GOALTENDER, ONE SERIES
3 – **Clint Benedict,** Montreal Maroons (4 games), in 1926
– **Frank McCool,** Toronto (7 games), in 1945.
2 – eight goaltenders tied.

MOST MINUTES PLAYED BY A GOALTENDER, ONE SERIES
459 – **Harry Lumley,** Detroit (7 games), in 1950.
– **Chuck Rayner,** NY Rangers (7 games), in 1950.
441 – Ken Dryden, Montreal (7 games), in 1971.
– Tony Esposito, Chicago (7 games), in 1971.

LONGEST SHUTOUT SEQUENCE BY A GOALTENDER
188:35 – **Frank McCool,** Toronto, in 1945. McCool posted shutouts in each of the first three games against Detroit and did not allow a goal until 8:35 of the first period in Game 4.
166:03 – Dominik Hasek, Detroit, in 2002. Hasek did not allow a Carolina goal from 7:34 of the third period in Game 3 through to 18:50 of the second period in Game 5. NOTE: Game 3 was decided by a Igor Larionov goal at 14:47 of the third overtime period.

FEWEST GOALS ALLOWED BY A GOALTENDER, ONE SERIES (MINIMUM 4 GAMES PLAYED)
2 – **Terry Sawchuk,** Detroit (4 games), in 1952.
3 – Clint Benedict, Montreal Maroons (4 games), in 1926
– Alex Connell, Ottawa (4 games), in 1927
– Rogie Vachon, Montreal (4 games), in 1969.

MOST GOALS ALLOWED BY A GOALTENDER, ONE SERIES
32 – **Tony Esposito,** Chicago (6 games), in 1973.
25 – Johnny Mowers, Detroit (7 games), in 1942.

MOST GOALS, ONE GAME
4 – **Newsy Lalonde,** Montreal, in Game 2, March 22, 1919. Montreal 4 at Seattle 2.
– **Babe Dye,** Toronto, in Game 5, March 28, 1922. Vancouver 1 at Toronto 5.
Ted Lindsay, Detroit, in Game 2, April 5, 1955. Montreal 1 at Detroit 7.
– **Maurice Richard,** Montreal, in Game 1, April 6, 1957. Boston 1 at Montreal 5.
3 – 26 players tied.

MOST ASSISTS, ONE GAME
4 – **Eddie Bush,** Detroit, in Game 3, April 9, 1942. Toronto 2 at Detroit 5.
– **Sid Abel,** Detroit, in Game 1, April 1, 1943. Boston 2 at Detroit 6.
– **Toe Blake,** Montreal, in Game 4, April 13, 1944. Chicago 4 at Montreal 5.
– **Dutch Reibel,** Detroit, in Game 2, April 5, 1955. Montreal 1 at Detroit 7.
– **Brad Maxwell,** Minnesota North Stars, in Game 4, May 19, 1981. NY Islanders 2 at Minnesota 4.
– **Brian Propp,** Philadelphia, in Game 5, May 26, 1987. Philadelphia 4 at Edmonton 3.
– **Wayne Gretzky,** Edmonton, in Game 3, May 22, 1988. Edmonton 6 at Boston 3.
– **Larry Murphy,** Pittsburgh, in Game 5, May 23, 1991. Minnesota North Stars 4 at Pittsburgh 6.
– **Joe Sakic,** Colorado, in Game 2, June 6, 1996. Florida 1 at Colorado 8.

MOST POINTS, ONE GAME
5 – **Eddie Bush** (1G-4A-5PTS), Detroit, in Game 3, April 9, 1942. Toronto 2 at Detroit 5.
– **Syl Apps** (2G-3A-5PTS), Toronto, in Game 5, April 14, 1942. Detroit 3 at Toronto 9.
– **Don Metz** (3G-2A-5PTS), Toronto, in Game 5, April 14, 1942. Detroit 3 at Toronto 9.
– **Sid Abel** (1G-4A-5PTS), Detroit, in Game 1, April 1, 1943. Boston 2 at Detroit 6.
– **Toe Blake** (1G-4A-5PTS), Montreal, in Game 4, April 13, 1944. Chicago 4 at Montreal 5.
– **Jari Kurri** (3G-2A-5PTS), Edmonton, in Game 2, May 17, 1990. Edmonton 7 at Boston 2.

MOST POWER-PLAY GOALS, ONE GAME
3 – **Sid Smith,** Toronto, in Game 2, April 10, 1949. Detroit 1 at Toronto 3.

MOST SHORTHAND GOALS, ONE GAME
2 – **Dave Keon,** Toronto, in Game 5, April 18, 1963. Detroit 1 at Toronto 3.

MOST GOALS, ONE PERIOD
3 – **Busher Jackson,** Toronto, in 2nd period of Game 1, April 5, 1932. Toronto 6 at NY Rangers 4.
– **Ted Lindsay,** Detroit, in 2nd period of Game 2, April 5, 1955. Montreal 4 at Detroit 7.
– **Maurice Richard,** Montreal, in 2nd period of Game 1, April 6, 1957. Boston 1 at Montreal 5.
– **Wayne Gretzky,** Edmonton, in 1st period of Game 3, May 25, 1985. Philadelphia 3 at Edmonton 4.
– **Dirk Graham,** Chicago, in 1st period of Game 4, June 1, 1992. Pittsburgh 6 at Chicago 5.
– **Peter Forsberg,** Colorado, in 1st period of Game 2, June 6, 1996. Florida 1 at Colorado 8.

MOST ASSISTS, ONE PERIOD
3 – **Joe Primeau,** Toronto, in 3rd period of Game 2, April 7, 1932. Toronto 6 at NY Rangers 2.
– **Toe Blake,** Montreal, in 3rd period of Game 4, April 13, 1944. Chicago 4 at Montreal 5 (OT).
– **Doug Harvey,** Montreal, in 2nd period of Game 1, April 6, 1957. Boston 1 at Montreal 5.
– **Henri Richard,** Montreal, in 1st period of Game 1, April 7, 1960. Toronto 2 at Montreal 4.
– **Bobby Rousseau,** Montreal, in 1st period of Game 7, May 1, 1965. Chicago 0 at Montreal 4.
– **Pat Stapleton,** Chicago, in 1st period of Game 1, April 29, 1973. Chicago 3 at Montreal 8.
– **Paul Coffey,** Edmonton, in 1st period of Game 3, May 25, 1985. Philadelphia 3 at Edmonton 4.
– **Larry Murphy,** Pittsburgh, in 1st period of Game 5, May 23, 1991. Minnesota North Stars 4 at Pittsburgh 6.
– **Joe Sakic,** Colorado, in 1st period of Game 2, June 6, 1996. Florida 1 at Colorado 8.

MOST POINTS, ONE PERIOD
3 – 34 players tied.

MOST POWER-PLAY GOALS, ONE PERIOD
2 – **Sid Smith,** Toronto, in 1st period of Game 2, April 10, 1949. Detroit 1 at Toronto 3.
– **Maurice Richard,** Montreal, in 1st period of Game 2, April 6, 1954. Montreal 3 at Detroit 1.
– **Bernie Geoffrion,** Montreal, in 1st period of Game 3, April 7, 1955. Detroit 2 at Montreal 4.
– **Brad Park,** NY Rangers, in 1st period of Game 3, May 4, 1972. Boston 2 at NY Rangers 5.
– **Peter Forsberg,** Colorado, in 1st period of Game 2, June 6, 1996. Florida 1 at Colorado 8.

MOST SHORTHAND GOALS, ONE PERIOD
1 – several players tied.

FASTEST TWO GOALS
0:12 – **Bernie Geoffrion,** Montreal, in Game 3, April 7, 1955. Detroit 2 at Montreal 5. Geoffrion scored at 8:30 and 8:42 of 1st period.
0:15 – Wayne Gretzky, Edmonton, in Game 3, May 25, 1985. Philadelphia 3 at Edmonton 4. Gretzky scored at 1:10 and 1:25 of 1st period.

FASTEST GOAL FROM START OF GAME
0:10 – **Glenn Anderson,** Edmonton, in suspended game, May 24, 1988. Edmonton 3 at Boston 3.
– **John Byce,** Boston, in Game 3, May 20, 1990. Boston 2 at Edmonton 1.

FASTEST GOAL FROM START OF PERIOD
0:09 – **Brian Skrudland,** Montreal, in 1st overtime of Game 2, May 18, 1986. Montreal 3 at Calgary 2 (OT).
0:10 – Glenn Anderson, Edmonton, in 1st period of suspended game, May 24, 1988. Edmonton 3 at Boston 3.
– John Byce, Boston, in 1st period of Game 3, May 20, 1990. Boston 2 at Edmonton 1.

FASTEST OVERTIME GOAL
0:09 – **Brian Skrudland,** Montreal, in Game 2, May 18, 1986. Montreal 3 at Calgary 2 (OT).
0:31 – Buzz Boll, Toronto, in Game 3, April 9, 1936. Detroit 3 at Toronto 4 (OT).

FASTEST TWO GOALS FROM START OF GAME
1:08 – **Dick Duff,** Toronto, in Game 1, April 9, 1963. Detroit 2 at Toronto 4. Duff scored at 0:49 and 1:08 of 1st period.

FASTEST TWO GOALS FROM START OF PERIOD
0:35 – **Pat LaFontaine,** NY Islanders, in Game 5, May 19, 1984. NY Islanders 2 at Edmonton 5. LaFontaine scored at 0:13 and 0:35 of 3rd period.

Coaching

**MOST STANLEY CUP CHAMPIONSHIPS
BY A COACH**
- 9 – **Scotty Bowman,** Montreal (1973-76-77-78-79), Pittsburgh (1992), Detroit (1997-98-2002)
- 8 – Toe Blake, Montreal (1956-57-58-59-60-65-66-68)
- 5 – Hap Day, Toronto (1942-45-47-48-49)
- 4 – Dick Irvin, Toronto (1932), Montreal (1944-46-53)
- – Punch Imlach, Toronto (1962-63-64-67)
- – Al Arbour, NY Islanders (1980-81-82-83)
- – Glen Sather, Edmonton (1984-85-87-88)

MOST YEARS IN THE FINALS BY A COACH
- 16 – Dick Irvin, Chicago (1931), Toronto (1932-33-35-36-38-39-40), Montreal (1944-46-47-51-52-53-54-55)
- 13 – Scotty Bowman, St. Louis (1968-69-70), Montreal (1973-76-77-78-79), Pittsburgh (1992), Detroit (1995-97-98-2002)
- 9 – Toe Blake, Montreal (1956-57-58-59-60-65-66-67-68)
- * 8 – Lester Patrick, Victoria (1914-25-26), NY Rangers (1928-29-32-33-37)
- 6 – Punch Imlach, Toronto (1959-60-62-63-64-67)

MOST GAMES BY A COACH
- 77 – **Dick Irvin,** Chicago (5), Toronto (29), Montreal (43)
- 58 – Scotty Bowman, St. Louis (12), Montreal (25), Pittsburgh (4), Detroit (17)
- 48 – Toe Blake, Montreal
- 33 – Punch Imlach, Toronto
- * 30 – Lester Patrick, Victoria (11), NY Rangers (19)

MOST WINS BY A COACH
- 36 – **Scotty Bowman,** Montreal (20), Pittsburgh (4), Detroit (12)
- 34 – Toe Blake, Montreal
- 32 – Dick Irvin, Chicago (2), Toronto (9), Montreal (21)
- 20 – Hap Day, Toronto
- 17 – Punch Imlach, Toronto
- – Al Arbour, NY Islanders

**BEST WINNING PERCENTAGE BY A COACH
(MINIMUM 15 GAMES)**
- .714 – **Hap Day,** Toronto (20-8 in 28 games)
- .708 – Toe Blake, Montreal (34-14 in 48 games)
- – Al Arbour, NY Islanders (17-7 in 24 games)
- .640 – Glen Sather, Edmonton (16-9 in 25 games)
- .621 – Scotty Bowman, St. Louis (0-12 in 12 games), Montreal (20-5 in 25 games), Pittsburgh (4-0 in 4 games), Detroit (12-5 in 17 games); (36-22 in 58 games overall)

* Lester Patrick's total includes the 1914 Victoria Aristocrats of the Pacific Coast Hockey Association, prior to the formation of the NHL.

Officiating

MOST GAMES OFFICIATED BY A REFEREE
- 42 – **Bill Chadwick** (1941 through 1955)
- 35 – Andy VanHellemond (1977 through 1996)
- 24 – Frank Udvari (1956 through 1966)
- 20 – King Clancy (1940 through 1949)
- 19 – Bill McCreary (1994 through 2001)

MOST GAMES OFFICIATED BY A LINESMAN
- 56 – **Matt Pavelich** (1957 through 1979)
- 54 – George Hayes (1948 through 1964)
- 52 – John D'Amico (1965 through 1987)
- 48 – Neil Armstrong (1960 through 1977)
- – Ray Scapinello (1980 through 2000)

Early Playoff Records
1893-1918

Team Records

MOST GOALS, BOTH TEAMS, ONE GAME:
25 – Ottawa Silver Seven, Dawson City at Ottawa, Jan. 16, 1905. Ottawa 23, Dawson City 2. Ottawa won best-of-three series 2-0.

MOST GOALS, ONE TEAM, ONE GAME:
23 – Ottawa Silver Seven at Ottawa, Jan. 16, 1905. Ottawa defeated Dawson City 23-2.

**MOST GOALS, BOTH TEAMS,
BEST-OF-THREE SERIES:**
42 – Ottawa Silver Seven, Queen's University at Ottawa, 1906. Ottawa defeated Queen's 16-7, Feb. 27, and 12-7, Feb. 28. Ottawa won best-of-three series 2-0.

**MOST GOALS, ONE TEAM,
BEST-OF-THREE SERIES:**
32 – Ottawa Silver Seven in 1905 at Ottawa. Ottawa defeated Dawson City 9-2, Jan. 13, and 23-2, Jan. 16.

**MOST GOALS, BOTH TEAMS,
BEST-OF-FIVE SERIES:**
39 – Toronto Arenas (18), Vancouver Millionaires (21), at Toronto, 1918. Toronto won 5-3, Mar. 20; 6-3, Mar. 26; 2-1, Mar. 30. Vancouver won 6-4, Mar. 23, and 8-1, Mar. 28. Toronto won best-of-five series 3-2.

**MOST GOALS, ONE TEAM,
BEST-OF-FIVE SERIES:**
26 – Vancouver Millionaires in 1915 at Vancouver. Vancouver defeated Ottawa Senators 6-2, Mar. 22; 8-3, Mar. 24; and 12-3 Mar. 26.

Individual Records

MOST GOALS IN PLAYOFFS:
63 – Frank McGee, Ottawa Silver Seven, in 22 playoff games. Seven goals in four games, 1903; 21 goals in eight games, 1904; 18 goals in four games, 1905; 17 goals in six games, 1906.

MOST GOALS, ONE PLAYOFF SERIES:
15 – Frank McGee, Ottawa Silver Seven, in two games in 1905 at Ottawa. Scored one goal, Jan. 13, in 9-2 victory over Dawson City and 14 goals, Jan. 16, in 23-2 victory.

MOST GOALS, ONE PLAYOFF GAME:
14 – Frank McGee, Ottawa Silver Seven, Jan. 16, 1905 at Ottawa in 23-2 victory over Dawson City.

FASTEST THREE GOALS:
0:40 – Marty Walsh, Ottawa Senators, at Ottawa, March 16, 1911, at 3:00, 3:10, and 3:40 of third period. Ottawa defeated Port Arthur 13-4.

CHAPTER 17

Final Series Scoring, Year-By-Year

1918 – 2002

1918

TORONTO

	GP	G	A	PTS	PIM
Alf Skinner	5	8	2	10	18
Harry Mummery	5	0	6	6	21
Harry Cameron	5	3	1	4	12
Corb Denneny	5	3	1	4	0
Reg Noble	5	2	1	3	12
Harry Meeking	5	1	2	3	18
Ken Randall	5	1	0	1	21
GOALTENDER	GP	W	L	MIN GA SO	AVG
Hap Holmes	5	3	2	300 21 0	4.20

VANCOUVER

	GP	G	A	PTS	PIM
Mickey MacKay	5	5	5	10	12
Cyclone Taylor	5	9	0	9	15
Ran MacDonald	5	2	2	4	9
Lloyd Cook	5	2	0	2	12
Barney Stanley	5	2	0	2	6
Si Griffis	5	1	0	1	9
Leo Cook	5	0	0	0	6
Speed Moynes	5	0	0	0	0
GOALTENDER	GP	W	L	MIN GA SO	AVG
Hugh Lehman	5	2	3	300 18 0	3.60

1919

MONTREAL

	GP	G	A	PTS	PIM
Newsy Lalonde	5	6	0	6	3
Didier Pitre	5	0	3	3	0
Odie Cleghorn	5	2	0	2	9
Louis Berlinguette	5	1	1	2	0
Jack MacDonald	5	1	1	2	3
Bert Corbeau	5	0	1	1	3
Billy Coutu	5	0	1	1	0
Joe Hall	5	0	0	0	6
GOALTENDER	GP W	L	T	MIN GA SO	AVG
Georges Vezina	5 2	2	1	336 19 1	3.39

SEATTLE

	GP	G	A	PTS	PIM
Frank Foyston	5	9	1	10	0
Cully Wilson	5	1	3	4	6
Muzz Murray	5	3	0	3	3
Jack Walker	5	3	0	3	9
Roy Rickey	5	1	2	3	0
Ran McDonald	5	1	1	2	3
Bobby Rowe	5	1	0	1	6
GOALTENDER	GP W	L	T	MIN GA SO	AVG
Hap Holmes	5 2	2	1	336 10 2	1.79

1920

OTTAWA

	GP	G	A	PTS	PIM
Frank Nighbor	5	6	1	7	2
Jack Darragh	5	5	2	7	3
Eddie Gerard	2	2	1	3	3
Georges Boucher	5	2	0	2	3
Cy Denneny	5	0	2	2	3
Sprague Cleghorn	5	0	1	1	4
Punch Broadbent	4	0	0	0	0
Jack MacKell	5	0	0	0	0
Morley Bruce	5	0	0	0	0
GOALTENDER	GP	W	L	MIN GA SO	AVG
Clint Benedict	5	3	2	300 11 1	2.20

SEATTLE

	GP	G	A	PTS	PIM
Frank Foyston	5	6	1	7	7
Jack Walker	5	1	3	4	0
Roy Rickey	2	2	1	3	0
Bobby Rowe	5	2	0	2	13
Bernie Morris	2	0	2	2	0
Jim Riley	5	0	1	1	0
Muzz Murray	5	0	0	0	5
Charlie Tobin	5	0	0	0	0
Sibby Nicholls	5	0	0	0	0
GOALTENDER	GP	W	L	MIN GA SO	AVG
Hap Holmes	5	2	3	300 15 0	3.00

1921

OTTAWA

	GP	G	A	PTS	PIM
Jack Darragh	5	5	0	5	7
Cy Denneny	5	2	2	4	10
Georges Boucher	5	2	0	2	9
Punch Broadbent	5	2	0	2	9
Sprague Cleghorn	5	1	1	2	36
Frank Nighbor	2	0	1	1	0
Eddie Gerard	2	0	0	0	44
Jack MacKell	4	0	0	0	0
GOALTENDER	GP	W	L	MIN GA SO	AVG
Clint Benedict	5	3	2	300 12 2	2.40

VANCOUVER

	GP	G	A	PTS	PIM
Alf Skinner	3	4	0	4	12
Jack Adams	5	2	1	3	6
Lloyd Cook	5	2	1	3	20
Art Duncan	5	2	1	3	6
Smokey Harris	5	2	1	3	8
Mickey MacKay	5	0	1	1	0
Cyclone Taylor	5	0	1	1	0
Bill Adams	4	0	0	0	0
Syd Desireau	5	0	0	0	0
GOALTENDER	GP	W	L	MIN GA SO	AVG
Hugh Lehman	5	2	3	300 12 1	2.40

1922

TORONTO

	GP	G	A	PTS	PIM
Babe Dye	5	9	1	10	3
Corb Denneny	5	3	2	5	2
Rod Smylie	5	1	3	4	0
Lloyd Andrews	5	2	0	2	3
Red Stuart	5	0	2	2	6
Harry Cameron	4	0	2	2	11
Ken Randall	4	1	0	1	19
Reg Noble	5	0	1	1	9
Eddie Gerard	1	0	0	0	0
Ted Stackhouse	4	0	0	0	0
GOALTENDER	GP	W	L	MIN GA SO	AVG
John Ross Roach	5	3	2	305 9 1	1.77

VANCOUVER

	GP	G	A	PTS	PIM
Jack Adams	5	6	1	7	-
Ernie Parkes	5	0	3	3	-
Lloyd Cook	5	1	0	1	-
Mickey MacKay	5	1	0	1	-
Eddie Oatman	5	1	0	1	-
Art Duncan	5	0	1	1	-
Alf Skinner	5	0	1	1	-
Charlie Tobin	5	0	0	0	-
Syd Desireau	1	0	0	0	-
GOALTENDER	GP	W	L	MIN GA SO	AVG
Hugh Lehman	5	2	3	305 16 1	3.15

1923

OTTAWA

	GP	G	A	PTS	PIM
Punch Broadbent	6	6	1	7	12
Georges Boucher	6	2	1	3	6
Cy Denneny	6	1	1	2	8
Frank Nighbor	6	1	1	2	10
Lionel Hitchman	5	1	0	1	4
King Clancy	6	1	0	1	4
Eddie Gerard	6	1	0	1	4
Clint Benedict	6	0	0	0	2
Harry Helman	2	0	0	0	0
GOALTENDERS	GP	W	L	MIN GA SO	AVG
Clint Benedict	6	5	1	360 8 1	1.33
King Clancy	1	0	0	2 0 0	0.00

VANCOUVER

	GP	G	A	PTS	PIM
Art Duncan	4	2	2	4	0
Frank Boucher	4	2	0	2	0
Alf Skinner	3	1	1	2	4
Ernie Parkes	4	0	2	2	2
Mickey MacKay	4	1	0	1	4
Smokey Harris	4	1	0	1	8
Lloyd Cook	4	0	1	1	4

Charlie Cotch	2	0	0	0	0
Corb Denneny	3	0	0	0	0
GOALTENDER	GP	W	L	MIN GA SO	AVG
Hugh Lehman	4	1	3	240 10 0	2.50

EDMONTON

	GP	G	A	PTS	PIM
John Morrison	2	1	0	1	0
Joe Simpson	2	0	0	0	0
Johnny Sheppard	1	0	0	0	0
Helge Bostrom	1	0	0	0	0
Art Gagne	2	0	0	0	2
Duke Keats	2	0	0	0	4
Bob Trapp	2	0	0	0	2
Ty Arbour	2	0	0	0	0
Earl Campbell	2	0	0	0	0
GOALTENDER	GP	W	L	MIN GA SO	AVG
Hal Winkler	2	0	2	122 3 0	1.46

1924

MONTREAL

	GP	G	A	PTS	PIM
Billy Boucher	4	5	1	6	6
Howie Morenz	4	4	2	6	4
Aurel Joliat	4	3	1	4	6
Sprague Cleghorn	4	2	2	4	2
Odie Cleghorn	4	0	1	1	0
Bobby Boucher	3	0	0	0	0
Billy Bell	3	0	0	0	0
Billy Coutu	4	0	0	0	0
Billy Cameron	4	0	0	0	0
Sylvio Mantha	4	0	0	0	0
GOALTENDER	GP	W	L	MIN GA SO	AVG
Georges Vezina	4	4	0	240 4 1	1.00

VANCOUVER

	GP	G	A	PTS	PIM
Frank Boucher	2	1	1	2	2
Helge Bostrum	2	1	0	1	0
Joe Matte	2	1	0	1	2
Lloyd Cook	2	0	0	0	2
Art Duncan	2	0	0	0	4
Mickey MacKay	2	0	0	0	0
Charlie Cotch	1	0	0	0	0
Ernie Parkes	2	0	0	0	0
Alf Skinner	2	0	0	0	0
GOALTENDER	GP	W	L	MIN GA SO	AVG
Hugh Lehman	2	0	2	120 5 0	2.50

CALGARY

	GP	G	A	PTS	PIM
Herb Gardiner	2	1	0	1	0
Bernie Morris	2	0	1	1	0
Ernie Anderson	2	0	0	0	2
Bobby Benson	2	0	0	0	0
Rusty Crawford	2	0	0	0	0
Red Dutton	2	0	0	0	4
Eddie Oatman	2	0	0	0	0
Harry Oliver	2	0	0	0	0
Cully Wilson	2	0	0	0	2
GOALTENDER	GP	W	L	MIN GA SO	AVG
Charlie Reid	2	0	2	120 9 0	4.50

1925

VICTORIA

	GP	G	A	PTS	PIM
Jack Walker	4	4	2	6	0
Frank Fredrickson	4	3	3	6	6
Gord Fraser	4	2	1	3	6
Gizzy Hart	4	2	1	3	0
Harold Halderson	4	2	1	3	8
Clem Loughlin	4	1	0	1	4
Frank Foyston	4	1	0	1	0
Jocko Anderson	4	1	0	1	10
Harry Meeking	4	0	1	1	2
Wally Elmer	2	0	0	0	0
GOALTENDER	GP	W	L	MIN GA SO	AVG
Hap Holmes	4	3	1	240 8 0	2.00

MONTREAL

	GP	G	A	PTS	PIM
Howie Morenz	4	4	0	4	4
Aurel Joliat	4	2	0	2	16
Billy Boucher	4	1	1	2	13

Billy Coutu	4	1	0	1	10
Sprague Cleghorn	4	0	0	0	2
Johnny Matz	4	0	0	0	2
Odie Cleghorn	4	0	0	0	0
Fern Headley	4	0	0	0	0
Sylvio Mantha	4	0	0	0	2

GOALTENDER	GP	W	L	MIN	GA	SO	AVG
Georges Vezina	4	1	3	240	16	0	4.00

1926

MTL MAROONS	GP	G	A	PTS	PIM
Nels Stewart	4	6	1	7	14
Babe Siebert	4	1	2	3	2
Bill Phillips	4	1	1	2	0
Punch Broadbent	4	1	0	1	22
Dunc Munro	4	1	0	1	6
Reg Noble	4	0	0	0	4
Chuck Dinsmore	4	0	0	0	2
Frank Carson	4	0	0	0	0
Sam Rothschild	4	0	0	0	0
Albert Holway	2	0	0	0	0

GOALTENDER	GP	W	L	MIN	GA	SO	AVG
Clint Benedict	4	3	1	240	3	3	0.75

VICTORIA	GP	G	A	PTS	PIM
Frank Fredrickson	4	1	1	2	10
Harold Halderson	4	1	0	1	8
Clem Loughlin	4	1	0	1	8
Jack Walker	4	0	0	0	0
Gord Fraser	4	0	0	0	14
Russell Oatman	4	0	0	0	10
Gizzy Hart	4	0	0	0	2
Frank Foyston	4	0	0	0	2
Harry Meeking	4	0	0	0	6
Jocko Anderson	1	0	0	0	0

GOALTENDER	GP	W	L	MIN	GA	SO	AVG
Hap Holmes	4	1	3	240	10	0	2.50

1927

OTTAWA	GP	G	A	PTS	PIM
Cy Denneny	4	4	0	4	0
Frank Finnigan	4	2	0	2	0
King Clancy	4	1	1	2	4
Frank Nighbor	4	0	1	1	0
Hec Kilrea	4	0	1	1	2
Hooley Smith	4	0	1	1	12
Milt Halliday	4	0	0	0	0
Ed Gorman	4	0	0	0	0
Jack Adams	4	0	0	0	2
Alex Smith	4	0	0	0	8
Georges Boucher	4	0	0	0	27

GOALTENDER	GP	W	L	T	MIN	GA	SO	AVG
Alex Connell	4	2	0	2	240	3	1	0.75

BOSTON	GP	G	A	PTS	PIM
Harry Oliver	4	2	1	3	2
Jimmy Herberts	4	1	0	1	18
Harry Meeking	4	0	0	0	0
Percy Galbraith	4	0	0	0	0
Billy Stuart	4	0	0	0	0
Billy Boucher	4	0	0	0	0
Billy Coutu	4	0	0	0	2
Sprague Cleghorn	4	0	0	0	4
Frank Fredrickson	4	0	0	0	16
Lionel Hitchman	4	0	0	0	17
Eddie Shore	4	0	0	0	20

GOALTENDER	GP	W	L	T	MIN	GA	SO	AVG
Hal Winkler	4	0	2	2	240	7	1	1.75

1928

MTL MAROONS	GP	G	A	PTS	PIM
Bill Phillips	5	2	0	2	2
Nels Stewart	5	2	0	2	8
Babe Siebert	4	1	1	2	10
Red Dutton	5	1	1	2	13
Hooley Smith	5	0	2	2	13
Dunc Munro	5	0	1	1	2
Joe Lamb	4	0	0	0	21
Frank Carson	5	0	0	0	0
Fred Brown	5	0	0	0	0
Jimmy Ward	5	0	0	0	2
Russell Oatman	5	0	0	0	12

GOALTENDER	GP	W	L	MIN	GA	SO	AVG
Clint Benedict	5	2	3	307	5	1	0.98

NY RANGERS	GP	G	A	PTS	PIM
Frank Boucher	5	4	0	4	2
Bill Cook	5	1	2	3	16
Ching Johnson	5	0	2	2	26
Bun Cook	5	0	1	1	4
Clarence Abel	5	0	1	1	10
Paul Thompson	3	0	0	0	19
Patsy Callighen	5	0	0	0	0
Alex Gray	5	0	0	0	0
Bill Boyd	5	0	0	0	2
Leo Bourgault	5	0	0	0	6
Murray Murdoch	5	0	0	0	10

GOALTENDERS	GP	W	L	MIN	GA	SO	AVG
Joe Miller	3	2	1	180	3	1	1.00
Lester Patrick	1	1	0	47	1	0	1.28
Lorne Chabot	2	0	1	80	2	0	1.50

1929

NY RANGERS	GP	G	A	PTS	PIM
Butch Keeling	2	1	0	1	0
Russell Oatman	1	0	0	0	0
Gerry Carson	1	0	0	0	0
Bill Boyd	1	0	0	0	0
Leroy Goldsworthy	1	0	0	0	0
Ralph Taylor	1	0	0	0	0
Frank Boucher	2	0	0	0	0
Murray Murdoch	2	0	0	0	0
Sparky Vail	2	0	0	0	0
Leo Bourgault	2	0	0	0	0
Ching Johnson	2	0	0	0	2
Bill Cook	2	0	0	0	4
Bun Cook	2	0	0	0	4
Paul Thompson	2	0	0	0	4
Clarence Abel	2	0	0	0	4

GOALTENDER	GP	W	L	MIN	GA	SO	AVG
John Ross Roach	2	0	2	120	4	0	2.00

BOSTON	GP	G	A	PTS	PIM
Harry Oliver	2	1	1	2	2
Dit Clapper	2	1	0	1	0
Norm Gainor	2	1	0	1	0
Bill Carson	2	1	0	1	2
Red Green	1	0	0	0	0
Eddie Rodden	1	0	0	0	0
Cy Denneny	1	0	0	0	0
Cooney Weiland	2	0	0	0	0
Mickey MacKay	2	0	0	0	0
George Owen	2	0	0	0	0
Myles Lane	2	0	0	0	0
Percy Galbraith	2	0	0	0	2
Eddie Shore	2	0	0	0	8
Lionel Hitchman	2	0	0	0	10

GOALTENDER	GP	W	L	MIN	GA	SO	AVG
Tiny Thompson	2	2	0	120	1	1	0.50

1930

MONTREAL	GP	G	A	PTS	PIM
Albert Leduc	2	1	2	3	0
Sylvio Mantha	2	2	0	2	2
Pit Lepine	2	1	1	2	0
Nick Wasnie	2	1	1	2	6
Bert McCaffrey	2	1	0	1	0
Howie Morenz	2	1	0	1	6
Marty Burke	2	0	1	1	0
Aurel Joliat	2	0	1	1	0
Georges Mantha	2	0	0	0	0
Gerry Carson	2	0	0	0	0
Gus Rivers	2	0	0	0	0
Armand Mondou	2	0	0	0	2
Wildor Larochelle	2	0	0	0	8

GOALTENDER	GP	W	L	MIN	GA	SO	AVG
George Hainsworth	2	2	0	120	3	1	1.50

BOSTON	GP	G	A	PTS	PIM
Dit Clapper	2	1	0	1	0
Percy Galbraith	2	1	0	1	2
Eddie Shore	2	1	0	1	8
Cooney Weiland	2	0	1	1	0
Harry Oliver	2	0	1	1	2
Norm Gainor	1	0	0	0	0
Bill Carson	2	0	0	0	0
Harry Connor	2	0	0	0	0
Myles Lane	2	0	0	0	0
Mickey MacKay	2	0	0	0	2
George Owen	2	0	0	0	2
Lionel Hitchman	2	0	0	0	4
Marty Barry	2	0	0	0	6

GOALTENDER	GP	W	L	MIN	GA	SO	AVG
Tiny Thompson	2	0	2	120	7	0	3.50

1931

MONTREAL	GP	G	A	PTS	PIM
Johnny Gagnon	5	4	2	6	2
Pit Lepine	5	3	1	4	4
Georges Mantha	5	2	1	3	4
Aurel Joliat	5	0	2	2	2
Nick Wasnie	5	1	1	2	2
Howie Morenz	5	1	0	1	6
Albert Leduc	2	1	0	1	0
Marty Burke	5	0	1	1	2
Wildor Larochelle	5	1	0	1	6
Armand Mondou	3	0	0	0	0
Jean Pusie	5	0	0	0	0
Gus Rivers	5	0	0	0	0
Art Lesieur	5	0	0	0	4
Sylvio Mantha	5	0	0	0	16

GOALTENDER	GP	W	L	MIN	GA	SO	AVG
George Hainsworth	5	3	2	379	8	1	1.27

CHICAGO	GP	G	A	PTS	PIM
Johnny Gottselig	5	2	2	4	2
Stew Adams	5	2	1	3	2
Vic Ripley	5	1	1	2	2
Ty Arbour	5	1	0	1	0
Mush March	5	1	0	1	6
Cy Wentworth	5	1	0	1	8
Rosie Couture	5	0	1	1	2
Frank Ingram	5	1	0	1	2
Tom Cook	5	0	1	1	7
Art Somers	5	0	0	0	0
Vic Desjardins	5	0	0	0	0
Doc Romnes	5	0	0	0	2
Clarence Abel	5	0	0	0	6
Helge Bostrum	5	0	0	0	8
Ted Graham	5	0	0	0	10

GOALTENDER	GP	W	L	MIN	GA	SO	AVG
Charlie Gardiner	5	2	3	379	11	0	1.74

1932

TORONTO	GP	G	A	PTS	PIM
Busher Jackson	3	5	2	7	9
Charlie Conacher	3	3	2	5	2
Hap Day	3	1	3	4	4
Joe Primeau	3	0	4	4	0
Andy Blair	3	2	0	2	2
King Clancy	3	2	0	2	8
Bob Gracie	3	1	1	2	0
Red Horner	3	1	1	2	6
Frank Finnigan	3	1	1	2	8
Baldy Cotton	3	1	1	2	10
Ace Bailey	3	0	1	1	0
Earl Miller	2	0	0	0	0
Harold Darragh	3	0	0	0	0
Fred Robertson	3	0	0	0	0
Alex Levinsky	3	0	0	0	2

GOALTENDER	GP	W	L	MIN	GA	SO	AVG
Lorne Chabot	3	3	0	180	10	0	3.33

NY RANGERS	GP	G	A	PTS	PIM
Frank Boucher	3	3	3	6	0
Bun Cook	3	4	1	5	6
Bill Cook	3	0	2	2	0
Cecil Dillon	3	1	0	1	4
Doug Brennan	3	1	0	1	4
Ching Johnson	3	1	0	1	10
Murray Murdoch	3	0	1	1	0
Ott Heller	3	0	1	1	2
Hib Milks	3	0	0	0	0
Vic Desjardins	3	0	0	0	0
Norm Gainor	3	0	0	0	2
Art Somers	3	0	0	0	4
Earl Seibert	3	0	0	0	6
Butch Keeling	3	0	0	0	10

GOALTENDER	GP	W	L	MIN	GA	SO	AVG
John Ross Roach	3	0	3	180	18	0	6.00

1933

NY RANGERS	GP	G	A	PTS	PIM
Cecil Dillon	4	3	1	4	4
Bill Cook	4	2	1	3	4
Art Somers	4	0	3	3	4
Ott Heller	4	2	0	2	4
Murray Murdoch	4	1	1	2	2
Butch Keeling	4	1	1	2	6
Earl Seibert	4	1	0	1	2
Bun Cook	4	1	0	1	4
Oscar Asmundson	4	0	1	1	2
Frank Boucher	4	0	1	1	4
Gord Pettinger	4	0	0	0	2
Doug Brennan	4	0	0	0	2
Ching Johnson	4	0	0	0	8
Babe Siebert	4	0	0	0	10

GOALTENDER	GP	W	L	MIN	GA	SO	AVG
Andy Aitkenhead	4	3	1	248	5	1	1.21

TORONTO

TORONTO	GP	G	A	PTS	PIM
Ken Doraty	4	3	0	3	2
King Clancy	4	0	2	2	6
Alex Levinsky	4	1	0	1	6
Red Horner	4	1	0	1	8
Charlie Sands	4	0	1	1	0
Bob Gracie	4	0	1	1	0
Baldy Cotton	4	0	1	1	2
Joe Primeau	4	0	1	1	4
Buzz Boll	1	0	0	0	0
Andy Blair	4	0	0	0	0
Ace Bailey	4	0	0	0	2
Busher Jackson	4	0	0	0	2
Bill Thoms	4	0	0	0	2
Charlie Conacher	4	0	0	0	6
Hap Day	4	0	0	0	6

GOALTENDER	GP	W	L	MIN	GA	SO	AVG
Lorne Chabot	4	1	3	248	11	0	2.66

1934

CHICAGO	GP	G	A	PTS	PIM
Doc Romnes	4	1	3	4	0
Paul Thompson	4	2	1	3	0
Johnny Gottselig	4	2	1	3	4
Mush March	4	1	1	2	2
Rosie Couture	4	1	1	2	2
Lionel Conacher	4	1	0	1	2
Art Coulter	4	1	0	1	4
Don McFadyen	4	0	1	1	2
Bill Kendall	1	0	0	0	0
Johnny Sheppard	3	0	0	0	0
Roger Jenkins	4	0	0	0	0
Leroy Goldsworthy	4	0	0	0	0
Tom Cook	4	0	0	0	0
Lou Trudel	4	0	0	0	0
Clarence Abel	4	0	0	0	2

GOALTENDER	GP	W	L	MIN	GA	SO	AVG
Charlie Gardiner	4	3	1	291	7	1	1.44

DETROIT	GP	G	A	PTS	PIM
Larry Aurie	4	2	2	4	0
Herbie Lewis	4	2	1	3	2
Cooney Weiland	4	1	1	2	2
Gord Pettinger	3	1	0	1	0
Doug Young	4	1	0	1	2
Frank Carson	2	0	1	1	0
Wilf Starr	3	0	1	1	2
Walt Buswell	4	0	1	1	2
Ted Graham	4	0	1	1	4
Ron Moffatt	2	0	0	0	0
Burr Williams	2	0	0	0	0
Eddie Wiseman	3	0	0	0	0
Gene Carrigan	3	0	0	0	0
Hap Emms	3	0	0	0	2
Gus Marker	3	0	0	0	2
John Sorrell	4	0	0	0	0
Ebbie Goodfellow	4	0	0	0	6

GOALTENDER	GP	W	L	MIN	GA	SO	AVG
Wilf Cude	4	1	3	291	9	0	1.86

1935

MTL MAROONS	GP	G	A	PTS	PIM
Cy Wentworth	3	2	2	4	0
Earl Robinson	3	2	1	3	0
Baldy Northcott	3	2	1	3	0
Jimmy Ward	3	1	1	2	0
Russ Blinco	3	1	1	2	0
Gus Marker	3	1	0	1	0
Dave Trottier	3	1	0	1	4
Al Shields	3	0	1	1	2
Herb Cain	3	0	0	0	0
Bob Gracie	3	0	0	0	0
Bill Miller	3	0	0	0	0
Stewart Evans	3	0	0	0	4
Hooley Smith	3	0	0	0	4
Lionel Conacher	3	0	0	0	8

GOALTENDER	GP	W	L	MIN	GA	SO	AVG
Alex Connell	3	3	0	185	4	0	1.30

TORONTO	GP	G	A	PTS	PIM
Frank Finnigan	3	1	1	2	0
Busher Jackson	3	1	0	1	0
Bill Thoms	3	1	0	1	0
King Clancy	3	1	0	1	4
Nick Metz	3	0	1	1	0
Ken Doraty	1	0	0	0	0
Andy Blair	1	0	0	0	2
Buzz Boll	2	0	0	0	0
Hec Kilrea	2	0	0	0	2
Flash Hollett	3	0	0	0	0
Hap Day	3	0	0	0	0
Baldy Cotton	3	0	0	0	0
Joe Primeau	3	0	0	0	0
Pep Kelly	3	0	0	0	0
Charlie Conacher	3	0	0	0	4
Red Horner	3	0	0	0	4

GOALTENDER	GP	W	L	MIN	GA	SO	AVG
George Hainsworth	3	0	3	185	10	0	3.24

1936

DETROIT	GP	G	A	PTS	PIM
John Sorrell	4	2	3	5	0
Syd Howe	4	2	3	5	2
Gord Pettinger	4	2	2	4	0
Marty Barry	4	2	2	4	2
Bucko McDonald	4	3	0	3	4
Wally Kilrea	4	2	1	3	0
Mud Bruneteau	4	1	2	3	0
Herbie Lewis	4	1	2	3	0
Pete Kelly	4	1	1	2	0
Ralph Bowman	4	1	1	2	2
Doug Young	4	0	2	2	0
Hec Kilrea	4	0	2	2	0
Ebbie Goodfellow	4	1	0	1	2
Larry Aurie	4	0	1	1	2

GOALTENDER	GP	W	L	MIN	GA	SO	AVG
Normie Smith	4	3	1	241	11	0	2.74

TORONTO	GP	G	A	PTS	PIM
Buzz Boll	4	3	1	4	0
Joe Primeau	4	3	1	4	0
Bill Thoms	4	2	2	4	0
Bob Davidson	4	1	2	3	2
Pep Kelly	4	2	0	2	0
Frank Finnigan	4	0	2	2	0
Busher Jackson	4	0	2	2	2
Red Horner	4	0	2	2	8
Art Jackson	4	0	1	1	0
Charlie Conacher	4	0	1	1	2
Jack Shill	4	0	1	1	4
Andy Blair	4	0	0	0	2
King Clancy	4	0	0	0	2
Hap Day	4	0	0	0	4

GOALTENDER	GP	W	L	MIN	GA	SO	AVG
George Hainsworth	4	1	3	241	18	0	4.48

1937

NY RANGERS	GP	G	A	PTS	PIM
Butch Keeling	5	2	1	3	0
Frank Boucher	5	1	2	3	0
Joe Cooper	5	1	2	3	12
Lynn Patrick	5	2	0	2	2
Neil Colville	5	1	1	2	0
Babe Pratt	5	1	1	2	9
Cecil Dillon	5	0	2	2	2
Art Coulter	5	0	2	2	6
Murray Murdoch	5	0	1	1	0
Mac Colville	5	0	1	1	0
Alex Shibicky	5	0	0	0	0
Ching Johnson	5	0	0	0	2
Phil Watson	5	0	0	0	4
Ott Heller	5	0	0	0	5

GOALTENDER	GP	W	L	MIN	GA	SO	AVG
Dave Kerr	5	2	3	300	9	1	1.80

DETROIT	GP	G	A	PTS	PIM
Syd Howe	5	1	4	5	0
Marty Barry	5	3	1	4	0
John Sorrell	5	2	2	4	2
Ebbie Goodfellow	4	0	2	2	12
Mud Bruneteau	5	1	0	1	2
Herbie Lewis	5	1	0	1	4
John Gallagher	5	1	0	1	8
Hec Kilrea	5	0	1	1	0
Gord Pettinger	5	0	1	1	2
John Sherf	5	0	1	1	2
Wally Kilrea	5	0	1	1	4
Pete Kelly	3	0	0	0	0
Howie Mackie	3	0	0	0	0
Bucko McDonald	5	0	0	0	0
Ralph Bowman	5	0	0	0	2

GOALTENDERS	GP	W	L	MIN	GA	SO	AVG
Earl Robertson	5	2	2	280	8	2	1.71
Normie Smith	1	0	0	20	0	0	0.00

1938

CHICAGO	GP	G	A	PTS	PIM
Johnny Gottselig	4	2	2	4	0
Paul Thompson	4	1	2	3	2
Doc Romnes	4	1	2	3	2
Carl Voss	4	2	0	2	0
Mush March	3	1	1	2	6
Cully Dahlstrom	4	1	1	2	0
Jack Shill	4	1	1	2	4
Earl Seibert	4	1	1	2	8
Roger Jenkins	4	0	2	2	6
Lou Trudel	4	0	1	1	0
Virgil Johnson	2	0	0	0	0
Pete Palangio	3	0	0	0	0
Alex Levinsky	4	0	0	0	0
Art Wiebe	4	0	0	0	2
Bill MacKenzie	4	0	0	0	9

GOALTENDERS	GP	W	L	MIN	GA	SO	AVG
Mike Karakas	2	2	0	120	2	0	1.00
Alfie Moore	1	1	0	60	1	0	1.00
Paul Goodman	1	0	1	60	5	0	5.00

TORONTO	GP	G	A	PTS	PIM
Gordie Drillon	4	4	1	5	2
Syl Apps	4	1	2	3	0
George Parsons	3	2	0	2	11
Jimmy Fowler	4	0	2	2	0
Pep Kelly	4	0	2	2	0
Bill Thoms	4	0	2	2	0
Bob Davidson	4	0	2	2	4
Busher Jackson	4	1	0	1	8
Reg Hamilton	4	0	1	1	2
Red Horner	4	0	1	1	8
Murray Armstrong	2	0	0	0	0
Murph Chamberlain	2	0	0	0	2
Nick Metz	4	0	0	0	0
Buzz Boll	4	0	0	0	2
Bingo Kampman	4	0	0	0	6

GOALTENDER	GP	W	L	MIN	GA	SO	AVG
Turk Broda	4	1	3	240	10	0	2.50

1939

BOSTON	GP	G	A	PTS	PIM
Roy Conacher	5	5	2	7	6
Bill Cowley	5	0	7	7	2
Mel Hill	5	2	2	4	4
Bobby Bauer	5	2	1	3	0
Eddie Shore	5	0	3	3	6
Jack Crawford	5	1	1	2	4
Milt Schmidt	5	0	2	2	0
Flash Hollett	5	1	0	1	0
Woody Dumart	5	1	0	1	2
Dit Clapper	5	0	0	0	0
Cooney Weiland	5	0	0	0	0
Gord Pettinger	5	0	0	0	0
Ray Getliffe	5	0	0	0	0
Red Hamill	5	0	0	0	2
Jack Portland	5	0	0	0	2

GOALTENDER	GP	W	L	MIN	GA	SO	AVG
Frank Brimsek	5	4	1	311	6	1	1.16

TORONTO	GP	G	A	PTS	PIM
Doc Romnes	5	1	3	4	0
Gus Marker	5	1	2	3	0
Bingo Kampman	5	1	1	2	12
Gordie Drillon	5	0	2	2	4
Murph Chamberlain	5	0	1	1	0
Syl Apps	5	1	0	1	2
Red Horner	5	1	0	1	6
Busher Jackson	3	0	1	1	2
Nick Metz	5	0	1	1	2
Jack Church	1	0	0	0	0
Don Metz	2	0	0	0	0
Red Heron	2	0	0	0	4
Jimmy Fowler	4	0	0	0	0
Pete Langelle	4	0	0	0	0
Pep Kelly	4	0	0	0	0
Bob Davidson	5	0	0	0	0
Bucko McDonald	5	0	0	0	0
Reg Hamilton	5	0	0	0	4

GOALTENDER	GP	W	L	MIN	GA	SO	AVG
Turk Broda	5	1	4	311	12	0	2.32

1940

NY RANGERS	GP	G	A	PTS	PIM
Bryan Hextall	6	4	1	5	7
Neil Colville	6	2	3	5	12
Phil Watson	6	1	4	5	8
Dutch Hiller	6	1	2	3	0
Alf Pike	6	2	0	2	4
Lynn Patrick	6	1	1	2	6
Babe Pratt	6	1	1	2	6
Alex Shibicky	5	0	2	2	2
Ott Heller	6	0	2	2	8

	GP	G	A	PTS	PIM
Muzz Patrick	6	1	0	1	6
Art Coulter	6	1	0	1	8
Clint Smith	6	0	1	1	2
Mac Colville	6	0	1	1	6
Stan Smith	1	0	0	0	0
Kilby MacDonald	6	0	0	0	4

GOALTENDER	GP	W	L	MIN	GA	SO	AVG
Dave Kerr	6	4	2	394	11	0	1.68

TORONTO	GP	G	A	PTS	PIM
Syl Apps	6	2	2	4	2
Hank Goldup	6	2	1	3	0
Sweeney Schriner	5	0	3	3	3
Gordie Drillon	6	2	0	2	2
Nick Metz	5	1	1	2	9
Gus Marker	6	1	1	2	2
Red Horner	5	0	2	2	14
Pete Langelle	6	0	2	2	0
Billy Taylor	2	1	0	1	0
Red Heron	6	1	0	1	0
Wally Stanowski	6	1	0	1	2
Jack Church	2	0	1	1	2
Bob Davidson	6	0	1	1	11
Reg Hamilton	1	0	0	0	0
Bucko McDonald	1	0	0	0	0
Pep Kelly	2	0	0	0	0
Don Metz	2	0	0	0	0
Murph Chamberlain	3	0	0	0	2
Bingo Kampman	6	0	0	0	19

GOALTENDER	GP	W	L	MIN	GA	SO	AVG
Turk Broda	6	2	4	394	14	1	2.13

1941

BOSTON	GP	G	A	PTS	PIM
Milt Schmidt	4	3	4	7	0
Eddie Wiseman	4	3	0	3	0
Roy Conacher	4	1	2	3	0
Woody Dumart	4	0	3	3	2
Bobby Bauer	4	1	1	2	0
Terry Reardon	4	1	1	2	2
Flash Hollett	4	1	1	2	4
Pat McReavy	4	1	1	2	5
Jack Crawford	4	0	2	2	0
Dit Clapper	4	0	2	2	2
Des Smith	4	0	2	2	2
Art Jackson	4	1	0	1	0
Herb Cain	4	0	1	1	0
Mel Hill	4	0	0	0	0

GOALTENDER	GP	W	L	MIN	GA	SO	AVG
Frank Brimsek	4	4	0	240	6	0	1.50

DETROIT	GP	G	A	PTS	PIM
Carl Liscombe	4	2	1	3	5
Syd Howe	4	1	2	3	0
Bill Jennings	4	1	1	2	0
Sid Abel	4	1	1	2	2
Connie Brown	3	0	2	2	0
Mud Bruneteau	4	1	0	1	0
Gus Giesebrecht	4	0	1	1	0
Don Grosso	4	0	1	1	0
Jack Stewart	4	0	1	1	2
Jimmy Orlando	4	0	1	1	6
Eddie Bruneteau	2	0	0	0	0
Ken Kilrea	2	0	0	0	0
Eddie Wares	3	0	0	0	0
Harold Jackson	4	0	0	0	0
Bob Whitelaw	4	0	0	0	0
Alex Motter	4	0	0	0	2

GOALTENDER	GP	W	L	MIN	GA	SO	AVG
Johnny Mowers	4	0	4	240	12	0	3.00

1942

TORONTO	GP	G	A	PTS	PIM
Billy Taylor	7	1	8	9	2
Sweeney Schriner	7	5	3	8	4
Don Metz	4	4	3	7	0
Syl Apps	7	3	4	7	2
Wally Stanowski	7	2	5	7	0
Lorne Carr	7	3	2	5	6
Nick Metz	7	2	3	5	4
Bob Goldham	7	2	2	4	22
John McCreedy	7	1	2	3	6
Pete Langelle	7	1	1	2	0
Bob Davidson	7	1	1	2	14
Bingo Kampman	7	0	2	2	8
Hank Goldup	3	0	0	0	0
Bucko McDonald	3	0	0	0	0
Gordie Drillon	3	0	0	0	0
Gaye Stewart	3	0	0	0	0
Ernie Dickens	5	0	0	0	4

GOALTENDER	GP	W	L	MIN	GA	SO	AVG
Turk Broda	7	4	3	420	19	1	2.71

DETROIT	GP	G	A	PTS	PIM
Don Grosso	7	4	4	8	14
Syd Howe	7	3	3	6	0
Carl Liscombe	7	2	4	6	2
Eddie Bush	6	1	5	6	16
Mud Bruneteau	7	2	1	3	4
Sid Abel	7	2	1	3	4
Eddie Wares	7	0	3	3	20
Gerry Brown	7	2	0	2	4
Pat McReavy	6	1	1	2	2
Alex Motter	7	1	1	2	6
Jimmy Orlando	7	0	2	2	41
Joe Carveth	7	1	0	1	0
Adam Brown	5	0	1	1	4
Jack Stewart	7	0	1	1	6
Gus Giesebrecht	2	0	0	0	0
Doug McCaig	2	0	0	0	6

GOALTENDER	GP	W	L	MIN	GA	SO	AVG
Johnny Mowers	7	3	4	420	25	0	3.57

1943

DETROIT	GP	G	A	PTS	PIM
Sid Abel	4	1	5	6	2
Carl Liscombe	4	2	3	5	2
Mud Bruneteau	3	3	0	3	0
Joe Carveth	4	3	0	3	0
Don Grosso	4	3	0	3	4
Les Douglas	4	2	1	3	2
Eddie Wares	4	0	3	3	2
Jack Stewart	4	1	1	2	8
Jimmy Orlando	4	2	0	2	6
Syd Howe	3	1	0	1	0
Alex Motter	1	0	1	1	0
Harold Jackson	4	0	1	1	4
Harry Watson	1	0	0	0	0
Joe Fisher	1	0	0	0	0
Cully Simon	3	0	0	0	0
Adam Brown	1	0	0	0	2

GOALTENDER	GP	W	L	MIN	GA	SO	AVG
Johnny Mowers	4	4	0	240	5	2	1.25

BOSTON	GP	G	A	PTS	PIM
Art Jackson	4	3	0	3	7
Herb Cain	2	0	2	2	0
Bill Cowley	4	0	2	2	2
Jack Crawford	3	1	0	1	2
Ab DeMarco	4	1	0	1	0
Flash Hollett	4	0	1	1	0
Don Gallinger	4	0	1	1	4
Murph Chamberlain	4	0	1	1	6
Bep Guidolin	4	0	1	1	8
Ossie Aubuchon	1	0	0	0	0
Jackie Schmidt	2	0	0	0	0
Dit Clapper	4	0	0	0	0
Irvin Boyd	4	0	0	0	2
Busher Jackson	4	0	0	0	2
Jack Shewchuk	4	0	0	0	4

GOALTENDER	GP	W	L	MIN	GA	SO	AVG
Frank Brimsek	4	0	4	240	16	0	4.00

1944

MONTREAL	GP	G	A	PTS	PIM
Toe Blake	4	3	5	8	2
Maurice Richard	4	5	2	7	4
Elmer Lach	4	2	3	5	0
Ray Getliffe	4	2	1	3	4
Phil Watson	4	2	1	3	6
Butch Bouchard	4	0	3	3	0
Murph Chamberlain	4	1	0	1	2
Mike McMahon	4	1	0	1	12
Gerry Heffernan	2	0	1	1	0
Buddy O'Connor	3	0	1	1	2
Leo Lamoureux	4	0	1	1	2
Fern Majeau	1	0	0	0	0
Bob Fillion	2	0	0	0	2
Glen Harmon	4	0	0	0	0

GOALTENDER	GP	W	L	MIN	GA	SO	AVG
Bill Durnan	4	4	0	249	8	0	1.93

CHICAGO	GP	G	A	PTS	PIM
George Allen	4	3	2	5	4
Clint Smith	4	1	3	4	0
John Harms	4	3	0	3	2
Doug Bentley	4	1	2	3	2
Cully Dahlstrom	4	0	2	2	2
Virgil Johnson	4	0	1	1	2
Bill Mosienko	4	0	1	1	2
Art Wiebe	4	0	1	1	4
George Grigor	1	0	0	0	0
Jacques Toupin	1	0	0	0	0
Johnny Gottselig	2	0	0	0	0
Earl Seibert	4	0	0	0	0
Fido Purpur	4	0	0	0	0
Joe Cooper	4	0	0	0	6

GOALTENDER	GP	W	L	MIN	GA	SO	AVG
Mike Karakas	4	0	4	249	16	0	3.86

1945

TORONTO	GP	G	A	PTS	PIM
Ted Kennedy	7	4	1	5	2
Mel Hill	7	1	2	3	4
Babe Pratt	7	1	1	2	4
Gus Bodnar	7	1	0	1	2
Moe Morris	7	1	0	1	2
Sweeney Schriner	7	1	0	1	2
Nick Metz	3	0	1	1	0
Wally Stanowski	7	0	1	1	0
Bob Davidson	7	0	1	1	0
John McCreedy	4	0	0	0	0
Reg Hamilton	7	0	0	0	0
Art Jackson	7	0	0	0	0
Don Metz	7	0	0	0	0
Lorne Carr	7	0	0	0	5

GOALTENDER	GP	W	L	MIN	GA	SO	AVG
Frank McCool	7	4	3	434	9	3	1.24

DETROIT	GP	G	A	PTS	PIM
Flash Hollett	7	2	2	4	0
Joe Carveth	7	2	1	3	0
Eddie Bruneteau	7	2	1	3	0
Murray Armstrong	7	2	0	2	0
Ted Lindsay	7	1	0	1	4
Mud Bruneteau	7	0	1	1	2
Bill Quackenbush	7	0	1	1	2
Tony Bukovich	1	0	0	0	0
Steve Wojciechowski	2	0	0	0	0
Fido Purpur	4	0	0	0	4
Syd Howe	5	0	0	0	0
Carl Liscombe	7	0	0	0	0
Jud McAtee	7	0	0	0	0
Earl Seibert	7	0	0	0	2
Harold Jackson	7	0	0	0	0

GOALTENDER	GP	W	L	MIN	GA	SO	AVG
Harry Lumley	7	3	4	434	9	2	1.24

1946

MONTREAL	GP	G	A	PTS	PIM
Elmer Lach	5	3	4	7	0
Maurice Richard	5	3	2	5	0
Murph Chamberlain	5	2	1	3	0
Dutch Hiller	5	2	1	3	0
Butch Bouchard	5	2	1	3	4
Glen Harmon	5	1	2	3	0
Bob Fillion	5	2	0	2	2
Ken Mosdell	5	2	0	2	2
Frank Eddolls	4	0	1	1	0
Jimmy Peters	5	1	0	1	4
Toe Blake	5	1	0	1	5
Gerry Plamondon	1	0	0	0	0
Buddy O'Connor	5	0	0	0	0
Leo Lamoureux	5	0	0	0	2
Billy Reay	5	0	0	0	0
Ken Reardon	5	0	0	0	4

GOALTENDER	GP	W	L	MIN	GA	SO	AVG
Bill Durnan	5	4	1	341	13	0	2.29

BOSTON	GP	G	A	PTS	PIM
Bep Guidolin	5	2	1	3	9
Don Gallinger	5	1	2	3	0
Bill Cowley	5	1	2	3	2
Milt Schmidt	5	1	2	3	2
Bobby Bauer	5	2	0	2	2
Terry Reardon	5	2	0	2	2
Woody Dumart	5	1	1	2	0
Ken Smith	5	0	2	2	0
Herb Cain	5	0	2	2	2
Murray Henderson	5	1	0	1	0
Jack Crawford	5	1	0	1	0
Pat Egan	5	1	0	1	4
Bill Shill	3	0	1	1	2
Roy Conacher	1	0	0	0	0
Dit Clapper	1	0	0	0	0
Jack McGill	5	0	0	0	0
Jack Church	5	0	0	0	2

GOALTENDER	GP	W	L	MIN	GA	SO	AVG
Frank Brimsek	5	1	4	341	19	0	3.34

1947

TORONTO

	GP	G	A	PTS	PIM
Ted Kennedy	6	3	2	5	2
Vic Lynn	6	3	1	4	12
Harry Watson	6	2	1	3	6
Gaye Stewart	6	1	2	3	6
Howie Meeker	6	0	3	3	6
Bud Poile	5	2	0	2	2
Syl Apps	6	1	1	2	0
Gus Mortson	6	1	1	2	6
Don Metz	6	0	2	2	4
Bill Barilko	6	0	2	2	6
Gus Bodnar	1	0	0	0	0
Nick Metz	1	0	0	0	0
Wally Stanowski	5	0	0	0	0
Joe Klukay	6	0	0	0	0
Garth Boesch	6	0	0	0	6
Jimmy Thomson	6	0	0	0	12
Bill Ezinicki	6	0	0	0	16
GOALTENDER	GP	W	L	MIN	GA	SO	AVG
Turk Broda	6	4	2	377	13	1	2.07

MONTREAL

	GP	G	A	PTS	PIM
Buddy O'Connor	6	3	3	6	0
Toe Blake	6	0	4	4	0
Maurice Richard	5	3	0	3	25
Butch Bouchard	6	0	3	3	14
Leo Gravelle	4	2	0	2	2
Billy Reay	6	2	0	2	2
Glen Harmon	6	1	1	2	0
George Allen	6	1	1	2	6
Roger Leger	6	0	2	2	6
Murph Chamberlain	6	1	0	1	6
John Quilty	2	0	1	1	2
Jimmy Peters	6	0	1	1	4
Leo Lamoureux	2	0	0	0	4
Hub Macey	3	0	0	0	0
Ken Reardon	4	0	0	0	16
Bob Fillion	5	0	0	0	0
Frank Eddolls	5	0	0	0	2
Murdo MacKay	6	0	0	0	0
GOALTENDER	GP	W	L	MIN	GA	SO	AVG
Bill Durnan	6	2	4	377	13	1	2.07

1948

TORONTO

	GP	G	A	PTS	PIM
Harry Watson	4	5	1	6	4
Max Bentley	4	2	4	6	0
Ted Kennedy	4	2	2	4	0
Syl Apps	4	2	2	4	0
Les Costello	4	1	2	3	0
Gus Mortson	1	1	1	2	0
Joe Klukay	4	1	1	2	2
Bill Ezinicki	4	1	1	2	4
Vic Lynn	4	1	1	2	18
Garth Boesch	4	1	0	1	0
Howie Meeker	4	1	0	1	7
Phil Samis	3	0	1	1	2
Wally Stanowski	4	0	1	1	0
Jimmy Thomson	4	0	1	1	5
Nick Metz	4	0	0	0	2
Bill Barilko	4	0	0	0	13
GOALTENDER	GP	W	L	MIN	GA	SO	AVG
Turk Broda	4	4	0	240	7	1	1.75

DETROIT

	GP	G	A	PTS	PIM
Pete Horeck	4	2	2	4	8
Jim McFadden	4	1	1	2	0
Jim Conacher	4	1	0	1	0
Ted Lindsay	4	1	0	1	2
Leo Reise Jr.	4	1	0	1	4
Fern Gauthier	4	1	0	1	5
Pat Lundy	1	0	1	1	0
Lee Fogolin	2	0	1	1	6
Bill Quackenbush	4	0	1	1	0
Marty Pavelich	4	0	1	1	2
Sid Abel	4	0	1	1	9
Enio Sclisizzi	1	0	0	0	0
Al Dewsbury	1	0	0	0	0
Rod Morrison	1	0	0	0	0
Bep Guidolin	1	0	0	0	2
Jack Stewart	3	0	0	0	0
Eddie Bruneteau	3	0	0	0	0
Max McNab	3	0	0	0	2
Red Kelly	4	0	0	0	0
Gordie Howe	4	0	0	0	9
GOALTENDER	GP	W	L	MIN	GA	SO	AVG
Harry Lumley	4	0	4	240	18	0	4.50

1949

TORONTO

	GP	G	A	PTS	PIM
Sid Smith	4	3	1	4	0
Max Bentley	4	2	2	4	0
Ray Timgren	4	1	3	4	0
Jimmy Thomson	4	1	3	4	4
Joe Klukay	4	1	2	3	2
Ted Kennedy	4	1	2	3	2
Fleming MacKell	4	0	3	3	2
Cal Gardner	4	1	1	2	0
Bill Ezinicki	4	1	1	2	10
Gus Mortson	4	1	0	1	2
Harry Watson	4	0	1	1	2
Garth Boesch	4	0	1	1	4
Bill Barilko	4	0	1	1	8
Vic Lynn	4	0	0	0	0
Bob Dawes	4	0	0	0	2
Bill Juzda	4	0	0	0	4
GOALTENDER	GP	W	L	MIN	GA	SO	AVG
Turk Broda	4	4	0	258	5	0	1.16

DETROIT

	GP	G	A	PTS	PIM
Ted Lindsay	4	1	2	3	6
George Gee	4	1	2	3	14
Pete Horeck	4	1	1	2	4
Jack Stewart	4	1	1	2	8
Gordie Howe	4	0	2	2	2
Bill Quackenbush	4	1	0	1	0
Jim McFadden	4	0	1	1	4
Fred Glover	2	0	0	0	2
Gerry Reid	2	0	0	0	0
Marty Pavelich	2	0	0	0	4
Gerry Couture	3	0	0	0	0
Bud Poile	3	0	0	0	0
Lee Fogolin	3	0	0	0	0
Nels Podolsky	3	0	0	0	0
Enio Sclisizzi	3	0	0	0	2
Max McNab	3	0	0	0	2
Red Kelly	4	0	0	0	0
Leo Reise Jr.	4	0	0	0	0
Sid Abel	4	0	0	0	4
GOALTENDER	GP	W	L	MIN	GA	SO	AVG
Harry Lumley	4	0	4	258	12	0	2.79

1950

DETROIT

	GP	G	A	PTS	PIM
Sid Abel	7	5	2	7	2
Ted Lindsay	6	4	2	6	6
Gerry Couture	7	4	2	6	0
George Gee	7	2	3	5	0
Pete Babando	5	2	2	4	2
Joe Carveth	7	1	3	4	4
Jim McFadden	7	2	1	3	2
Marty Pavelich	7	2	1	3	6
Al Dewsbury	5	0	3	3	8
Red Kelly	7	0	3	3	2
Jack Stewart	7	0	3	3	10
Jimmy Peters	5	0	2	2	0
Johnny Wilson	5	0	1	1	0
Marcel Pronovost	6	0	1	1	4
Doug MacKay	1	0	0	0	0
Larry Wilson	2	0	0	0	0
Clare Martin	3	0	0	0	0
Max McNab	4	0	0	0	0
Lee Fogolin	4	0	0	0	2
Steve Black	6	0	0	0	0
Leo Reise Jr.	7	0	0	0	8
GOALTENDER	GP	W	L	MIN	GA	SO	AVG
Harry Lumley	7	4	3	459	17	1	2.22

NY RANGERS

	GP	G	A	PTS	PIM
Edgar Laprade	7	3	3	6	2
Tony Leswick	7	2	4	6	2
Buddy O'Connor	7	3	1	4	2
Dunc Fisher	7	2	2	4	12
Nick Mickoski	7	0	4	4	0
Allan Stanley	7	2	1	3	6
Alex Kaleta	7	0	3	3	0
Ed Slowinski	7	0	3	3	4
Don Raleigh	7	2	0	2	0
Pentti Lund	7	1	1	2	0
Pat Egan	7	1	1	2	4
Gus Kyle	7	1	0	1	14
Jack Gordon	4	0	1	1	2
Jack Lancien	2	0	0	0	0
Fred Shero	4	0	0	0	0
Jack McLeod	5	0	0	0	0
Frank Eddolls	7	0	0	0	2
GOALTENDER	GP	W	L	MIN	GA	SO	AVG
Chuck Rayner	7	3	4	459	22	0	2.88

1951

TORONTO

	GP	G	A	PTS	PIM
Tod Sloan	5	3	4	7	7
Sid Smith	5	5	1	6	0
Ted Kennedy	5	2	4	6	2
Max Bentley	5	0	4	4	2
Harry Watson	5	1	2	3	4
Howie Meeker	5	1	1	2	10
Bill Barilko	5	1	0	1	6
Gus Mortson	5	0	1	1	0
Danny Lewicki	3	0	0	0	0
Fern Flaman	3	0	0	0	6
Ray Timgren	5	0	0	0	0
Joe Klukay	5	0	0	0	0
Cal Gardner	5	0	0	0	0
Bill Juzda	5	0	0	0	2
Fleming MacKell	5	0	0	0	2
Jimmy Thomson	5	0	0	0	4
GOALTENDERS	GP	W	L	MIN	GA	SO	AVG
Al Rollins	3	3	0	193	5	0	1.55
Turk Broda	2	1	1	129	5	0	2.33

MONTREAL

	GP	G	A	PTS	PIM
Maurice Richard	5	5	2	7	4
Billy Reay	5	1	2	3	10
Doug Harvey	5	0	3	3	2
Paul Masnick	5	2	0	2	4
Paul Meger	5	1	1	2	2
Bert Olmstead	5	0	2	2	7
Elmer Lach	5	1	0	1	2
Butch Bouchard	5	0	1	1	0
Bud MacPherson	5	0	1	1	4
Ross Lowe	1	0	0	0	0
Bob Dawes	1	0	0	0	2
Eddie Mazur	2	0	0	0	0
Calum MacKay	5	0	0	0	0
Tom Johnson	5	0	0	0	2
Ken Mosdell	5	0	0	0	2
Floyd Curry	5	0	0	0	2
Bernie Geoffrion	5	0	0	0	4
GOALTENDER	GP	W	L	MIN	GA	SO	AVG
Gerry McNeil	5	1	4	322	13	0	2.42

1952

DETROIT

	GP	G	A	PTS	PIM
Ted Lindsay	4	3	0	3	4
Metro Prystai	4	2	1	3	0
Gordie Howe	4	2	1	3	2
Tony Leswick	4	2	1	3	14
Marty Pavelich	4	1	2	3	2
Glen Skov	4	1	2	3	12
Vic Stasiuk	3	0	1	1	0
Johnny Wilson	4	0	1	1	0
Alex Delvecchio	4	0	1	1	2
Sid Abel	4	0	1	1	2
Leo Reise Jr.	2	0	0	0	0
Red Kelly	3	0	0	0	0
Larry Zeidel	3	0	0	0	0
Benny Woit	4	0	0	0	2
Marcel Pronovost	4	0	0	0	2
Bob Goldham	4	0	0	0	0
GOALTENDER	GP	W	L	MIN	GA	SO	AVG
Terry Sawchuk	4	4	0	240	2	2	0.50

MONTREAL

	GP	G	A	PTS	PIM
Tom Johnson	4	1	0	1	0
Elmer Lach	4	1	0	1	4
Bernie Geoffrion	4	0	1	1	0
Floyd Curry	4	0	1	1	0
Bert Olmstead	4	0	1	1	2
Stan Long	2	0	0	0	0
Dollard St. Laurent	2	0	0	0	0
Dick Gamble	2	0	0	0	0
Billy Reay	3	0	0	0	0
Eddie Mazur	3	0	0	0	4
Paul Meger	4	0	0	0	0
Bud MacPherson	4	0	0	0	4
Maurice Richard	4	0	0	0	4
Butch Bouchard	4	0	0	0	6
Doug Harvey	4	0	0	0	6
Paul Masnick	4	0	0	0	6
Dickie Moore	4	0	0	0	12
GOALTENDER	GP	W	L	MIN	GA	SO	AVG
Gerry McNeil	4	0	4	240	10	0	2.50

1953

MONTREAL

	GP	G	A	PTS	PIM
Maurice Richard	5	4	1	5	0
Ken Mosdell	5	2	2	4	4

	GP	G	A	PTS	PIM
Calum MacKay	5	1	2	3	6
Dickie Moore	5	2	0	2	9
Floyd Curry	5	1	1	2	0
Elmer Lach	5	1	1	2	0
Bert Olmstead	5	1	1	2	2
Dollard St. Laurent	5	0	2	2	2
Doug Harvey	5	0	2	2	4
Paul Masnick	3	1	0	1	0
Bernie Geoffrion	5	1	0	1	0
Lorne Davis	5	1	0	1	2
Tom Johnson	5	1	0	1	4
Butch Bouchard	5	0	1	1	2
Eddie Mazur	5	0	1	1	11
Paul Meger	1	0	0	0	0
John McCormack	2	0	0	0	0
Billy Reay	4	0	0	0	0

GOALTENDERS	GP	W	L	MIN	GA	SO	AVG
Gerry McNeil	3	3	0	181	3	2	0.99
Jacques Plante	2	1	1	120	6	0	3.00

BOSTON	GP	G	A	PTS	PIM
Ed Sandford	5	2	1	3	5
Fleming MacKell	5	0	3	3	2
Milt Schmidt	4	2	0	2	0
Dave Creighton	5	1	1	2	0
Leo Labine	5	1	1	2	4
Woody Dumart	5	0	2	2	0
Jack McIntyre	4	1	0	1	0
Johnny Peirson	5	1	0	1	2
Bob Armstrong	5	1	0	1	6
Bill Quackenbush	5	0	1	1	2
Frank Martin	5	0	1	1	2
Real Chevrefils	5	0	1	1	6
Joe Klukay	5	0	1	1	7
Hal Laycoe	5	0	1	1	10
Warren Godfrey	5	0	0	0	0
Jerry Toppazzini	5	0	0	0	4

GOALTENDERS	GP	W	L	MIN	GA	SO	AVG
Gord Henry	3	1	2	163	10	0	3.68
Jim Henry	3	0	2	138	5	0	2.17

1954

DETROIT	GP	G	A	PTS	PIM
Alex Delvecchio	7	2	4	6	0
Red Kelly	7	3	1	4	0
Metro Prystai	7	2	2	4	0
Ted Lindsay	7	2	2	4	14
Gordie Howe	7	1	2	3	23
Johnny Wilson	7	2	0	2	0
Dutch Reibel	4	1	1	2	0
Tony Leswick	7	1	1	2	8
Bob Goldham	7	0	1	1	0
Benny Woit	7	0	1	1	4
Marty Pavelich	7	0	1	1	4
Marcel Pronovost	7	0	0	0	8
Glen Skov	7	0	1	1	10
Gilles Dube	2	0	0	0	0
Keith Allen	3	0	0	0	0
Jimmy Peters	6	0	0	0	0
Bill Dineen	7	0	0	0	0

GOALTENDER	GP	W	L	MIN	GA	SO	AVG
Terry Sawchuk	7	4	3	430	12	1	1.67

MONTREAL	GP	G	A	PTS	PIM
Floyd Curry	7	3	0	3	2
Maurice Richard	7	3	0	3	20
Bernie Geoffrion	7	2	1	3	16
Dickie Moore	7	1	2	3	8
Paul Masnick	6	0	3	3	4
Elmer Lach	4	0	2	2	2
Jean Beliveau	6	0	2	2	2
Dollard St. Laurent	6	1	0	1	6
Ken Mosdell	7	1	0	1	2
Tom Johnson	7	1	0	1	0
Calum MacKay	3	0	1	1	0
Doug Harvey	6	0	1	1	4
Eddie Mazur	7	0	1	1	0
Bert Olmstead	7	0	1	1	8
Paul Meger	2	0	0	0	2
Bud MacPherson	2	0	0	0	4
Gaye Stewart	3	0	0	0	0
John McCormack	4	0	0	0	0
Butch Bouchard	7	0	0	0	4
Lorne Davis	7	0	0	0	6

GOALTENDERS	GP	W	L	MIN	GA	SO	AVG
Gerry McNeil	3	2	1	190	3	1	0.95
Jacques Plante	4	1	3	240	10	0	2.50

1955

DETROIT	GP	G	A	PTS	PIM
Gordie Howe	7	5	7	12	24
Ted Lindsay	7	5	6	11	6
Alex Delvecchio	7	6	4	10	0
Dutch Reibel	7	2	5	7	2
Vic Stasiuk	7	3	3	6	2
Red Kelly	7	2	3	5	17
Marcel Pronovost	7	1	2	3	2
Marty Pavelich	7	1	2	3	12
Bob Goldham	7	0	2	2	0
Jim Hay	5	1	0	1	0
Glen Skov	7	1	0	1	4
Marcel Bonin	7	0	1	1	4
Tony Leswick	7	0	1	1	10
Johnny Wilson	7	0	0	0	0
Bill Dineen	7	0	0	0	2
Benny Woit	7	0	0	0	4

GOALTENDER	GP	W	L	MIN	GA	SO	AVG
Terry Sawchuk	7	4	3	420	20	0	2.86

MONTREAL	GP	G	A	PTS	PIM
Bernie Geoffrion	7	6	2	8	2
Jean Beliveau	7	3	5	8	12
Floyd Curry	7	5	1	6	2
Calum MacKay	7	2	4	6	2
Ken Mosdell	7	1	4	5	6
Doug Harvey	7	0	5	5	4
Jack Leclair	7	2	0	2	2
Dickie Moore	7	0	2	2	16
Tom Johnson	7	1	0	1	16
Dollard St. Laurent	7	0	1	1	10
Bert Olmstead	7	0	1	1	14
Butch Bouchard	7	0	1	1	31
Jim Bartlett	2	0	0	0	0
Paul Ronty	2	0	0	0	2
Dick Gamble	2	0	0	0	2
George McAvoy	3	0	0	0	0
Don Marshall	7	0	0	0	0

GOALTENDERS	GP	W	L	MIN	GA	SO	AVG
Jacques Plante	7	3	3	403	24	0	3.57
Charlie Hodge	1	0	1	17	3	0	10.59

1956

MONTREAL	GP	G	A	PTS	PIM
Jean Beliveau	5	7	3	10	8
Bert Olmstead	5	0	8	8	4
Bernie Geoffrion	5	3	3	6	2
Maurice Richard	5	2	2	4	12
Floyd Curry	5	1	3	4	4
Henri Richard	5	2	1	3	11
Claude Provost	5	1	2	3	2
Dickie Moore	5	0	3	3	6
Doug Harvey	5	0	3	3	6
Jack Leclair	5	1	1	2	4
Don Marshall	5	1	0	1	0
Ken Mosdell	4	0	1	1	0
Jean-Guy Talbot	4	0	1	1	2
Butch Bouchard	1	0	0	0	0
Dollard St. Laurent	3	0	0	0	2
Bob Turner	5	0	0	0	4
Tom Johnson	5	0	0	0	8

GOALTENDER	GP	W	L	MIN	GA	SO	AVG
Jacques Plante	5	4	1	300	9	1	1.80

DETROIT	GP	G	A	PTS	PIM
Gordie Howe	5	1	5	6	4
Ted Lindsay	5	2	3	5	6
Alex Delvecchio	5	3	1	4	0
Norm Ullman	5	1	1	2	11
Red Kelly	5	1	0	1	2
Bill Dineen	5	1	0	1	4
Al Arbour	4	0	1	1	0
Dutch Reibel	5	0	1	1	2
John Bucyk	5	0	1	1	4
Lorne Ferguson	5	0	1	1	8
Marty Pavelich	5	0	1	1	8
Cummy Burton	1	0	0	0	0
Murray Costello	2	0	0	0	0
Gord Hollingworth	2	0	0	0	2
Gerry Melnyk	4	0	0	0	0
Metro Prystai	4	0	0	0	4
Bob Goldham	5	0	0	0	2
Marcel Pronovost	5	0	0	0	2
Larry Hillman	5	0	0	0	0

GOALTENDER	GP	W	L	MIN	GA	SO	AVG
Glenn Hall	5	1	4	300	18	0	3.60

1957

MONTREAL	GP	G	A	PTS	PIM
Bernie Geoffrion	5	4	2	6	2
Doug Harvey	5	0	5	5	6
Maurice Richard	5	4	0	4	2
Floyd Curry	5	2	2	4	0
Dickie Moore	5	1	3	4	2
Don Marshall	5	1	2	3	2
Phil Goyette	5	1	1	2	2
Jean Beliveau	5	1	1	2	6
Tom Johnson	5	0	2	2	2
Henri Richard	5	0	2	2	8
Bert Olmstead	5	0	2	2	9
Andre Pronovost	3	1	0	1	0
Connie Broden	4	0	1	1	0
Claude Provost	5	0	1	1	2
Dollard St. Laurent	5	0	1	1	9
Bob Turner	2	0	0	0	0
Jean-Guy Talbot	5	0	0	0	6

GOALTENDER	GP	W	L	MIN	GA	SO	AVG
Jacques Plante	5	4	1	300	5	1	1.00

BOSTON	GP	G	A	PTS	PIM
Fleming MacKell	5	4	0	4	2
Don McKenney	5	1	1	2	0
Leo Labine	5	1	1	2	12
Larry Regan	5	0	2	2	4
Doug Mohns	5	0	1	1	0
Bob Armstrong	5	0	1	1	2
Jerry Toppazzini	5	0	1	1	2
Leo Boivin	5	0	1	1	4
Fern Flaman	5	0	1	1	13
Cal Gardner	5	0	0	0	0
Jack Caffery	5	0	0	0	0
Vic Stasiuk	5	0	0	0	2
Real Chevrefils	5	0	0	0	2
Jack Bionda	5	0	0	0	6
Buddy Boone	5	0	0	0	10
Johnny Peirson	5	0	0	0	12

GOALTENDER	GP	W	L	MIN	GA	SO	AVG
Don Simmons	5	1	4	300	15	1	3.00

1958

MONTREAL	GP	G	A	PTS	PIM
Bernie Geoffrion	6	5	3	8	0
Doug Harvey	6	2	5	7	8
Jean Beliveau	6	2	4	6	8
Dickie Moore	6	1	5	6	2
Maurice Richard	6	4	1	5	8
Henri Richard	6	1	2	3	9
Claude Provost	6	1	0	1	2
Bert Olmstead	5	0	1	1	0
Marcel Bonin	5	0	1	1	10
Don Marshall	6	0	1	1	0
Connie Broden	1	0	0	0	0
Ab McDonald	1	0	0	0	0
Tom Johnson	2	0	0	0	0
Albert Langlois	3	0	0	0	0
Floyd Curry	3	0	0	0	0
Dollard St. Laurent	4	0	0	0	8
Bob Turner	6	0	0	0	2
Phil Goyette	6	0	0	0	2
Jean-Guy Talbot	6	0	0	0	0
Andre Pronovost	6	0	0	0	10

GOALTENDER	GP	W	L	MIN	GA	SO	AVG
Jacques Plante	6	4	2	366	14	1	2.30

BOSTON	GP	G	A	PTS	PIM
Larry Regan	6	2	4	6	2
Don McKenney	6	4	1	5	0
Fleming MacKell	6	1	4	5	6
Bronco Horvath	6	3	1	4	4
Allan Stanley	6	1	2	3	4
Vic Stasiuk	6	0	3	3	0
Norm Johnson	6	2	0	2	4
Jerry Toppazzini	6	1	1	2	2
Doug Mohns	6	0	2	2	8
Leo Labine	6	0	2	2	8
Buddy Boone	6	0	1	1	4
Fern Flaman	6	0	1	1	4
Leo Boivin	6	0	1	1	9
Johnny Peirson	2	0	0	0	0
Larry Hillman	5	0	0	0	2
John Bucyk	6	0	0	0	6

GOALTENDER	GP	W	L	MIN	GA	SO	AVG
Don Simmons	6	2	4	366	15	0	2.46

1959

MONTREAL

	GP	G	A	PTS	PIM
Bernie Geoffrion	5	3	4	7	6
Ralph Backstrom	5	3	4	7	8
Henri Richard	5	1	5	6	5
Doug Harvey	5	0	6	6	10
Marcel Bonin	5	3	2	5	2
Dickie Moore	5	2	3	5	8
Claude Provost	5	2	2	4	2
Tom Johnson	5	2	1	3	2
Ab McDonald	5	1	1	2	0
Phil Goyette	5	0	2	2	0
Andre Pronovost	5	1	0	1	0
Don Marshall	5	0	1	1	0
Jean-Guy Talbot	5	0	1	1	6
Bob Turner	5	0	1	1	8
Bill Hicke	1	0	0	0	0
Albert Langlois	4	0	0	0	2
Maurice Richard	4	0	0	0	2

GOALTENDER	GP	W	L	MIN	GA	SO	AVG
Jacques Plante	5	4	1	310	12	0	2.32

TORONTO

	GP	G	A	PTS	PIM
Billy Harris	5	3	1	4	14
Frank Mahovlich	5	2	2	4	6
Gerry Ehman	5	0	4	4	4
Ron Stewart	5	2	1	3	2
Dick Duff	5	2	1	3	4
Bert Olmstead	5	2	1	3	6
Bob Pulford	5	1	2	3	4
George Armstrong	5	0	2	2	6
Carl Brewer	5	0	2	2	18
Dave Creighton	5	0	1	1	0
Tim Horton	5	0	1	1	2
Allan Stanley	5	0	1	1	2
Barry Cullen	1	0	0	0	0
Noel Price	2	0	0	0	2
Larry Regan	3	0	0	0	0
Brian Cullen	3	0	0	0	0
Marc Reaume	4	0	0	0	0
Bob Baun	5	0	0	0	11

GOALTENDER	GP	W	L	MIN	GA	SO	AVG
Johnny Bower	5	1	4	310	18	0	3.48

1960

MONTREAL

	GP	G	A	PTS	PIM
Henri Richard	4	3	5	8	9
Bernie Geoffrion	4	0	6	6	0
Dickie Moore	4	2	3	5	2
Jean Beliveau	4	4	0	4	4
Maurice Richard	4	1	2	3	2
Phil Goyette	4	2	0	2	2
Doug Harvey	4	2	0	2	6
Marcel Bonin	4	0	2	2	6
Albert Langlois	4	0	2	2	12
Don Marshall	4	1	0	1	0
Bill Hicke	4	0	1	1	0
Jean-Guy Talbot	4	0	1	1	4
Claude Provost	4	0	1	1	0
Andre Pronovost	4	0	1	1	0
Bob Turner	4	0	0	0	0
Ralph Backstrom	4	0	0	0	2
Tom Johnson	4	0	0	0	2

GOALTENDER	GP	W	L	MIN	GA	SO	AVG
Jacques Plante	4	4	0	240	5	1	1.25

TORONTO

	GP	G	A	PTS	PIM
Bert Olmstead	4	2	0	2	0
Larry Regan	4	1	1	2	0
Red Kelly	4	0	2	2	2
George Armstrong	4	0	2	2	2
Johnny Wilson	4	1	0	1	2
Bob Baun	4	1	0	1	17
Billy Harris	3	0	1	1	0
Tim Horton	4	0	1	1	0
Dick Duff	4	0	1	1	2
Garry Edmundson	4	0	1	1	2
Carl Brewer	4	0	1	1	6
Gerry Ehman	3	0	0	0	2
Allan Stanley	4	0	0	0	0
Gerry James	4	0	0	0	0
Ron Stewart	4	0	0	0	0
Frank Mahovlich	4	0	0	0	0
Bob Pulford	4	0	0	0	0

GOALTENDER	GP	W	L	MIN	GA	SO	AVG
Johnny Bower	4	0	4	240	15	0	3.75

1961

CHICAGO

	GP	G	A	PTS	PIM
Pierre Pilote	6	2	6	8	2
Stan Mikita	6	3	4	7	2
Bobby Hull	6	2	5	7	2
Murray Balfour	5	3	3	6	4
Bill Hay	6	1	3	4	8
Ron Murphy	6	2	1	3	0
Kenny Wharram	6	2	1	3	10
Ab McDonald	6	1	1	2	2
Eric Nesterenko	6	1	1	2	2
Reggie Fleming	6	1	0	1	2
Jack Evans	6	1	0	1	10
Ed Litzenberger	4	0	1	1	0
Dollard St. Laurent	5	0	1	1	2
Tod Sloan	6	0	1	1	6
Moose Vasko	6	0	1	1	6
Chico Maki	1	0	0	0	0
Wayne Hillman	1	0	0	0	0
Wayne Hicks	1	0	0	0	2
Al Arbour	3	0	0	0	2
Earl Balfour	6	0	0	0	0

GOALTENDER	GP	W	L	MIN	GA	SO	AVG
Glenn Hall	6	4	2	360	12	0	2.00

DETROIT

	GP	G	A	PTS	PIM
Gordie Howe	6	1	7	8	8
Alex Delvecchio	6	3	3	6	0
Al Johnson	6	1	2	3	0
Vic Stasiuk	6	1	2	3	4
Bruce MacGregor	6	1	2	3	6
Howie Young	6	1	1	2	18
Norm Ullman	5	0	2	2	2
Val Fonteyne	6	0	2	2	0
Len Lunde	5	1	0	1	0
Parker MacDonald	6	1	0	1	0
Leo Labine	6	1	0	1	0
Howie Glover	6	1	0	1	0
Marcel Pronovost	4	0	1	1	0
Warren Godfrey	6	0	1	1	10
Gerry Melnyk	6	0	0	0	0
Gerry Odrowski	6	0	0	0	4
Pete Goegan	6	0	0	0	14

GOALTENDERS	GP	W	L	MIN	GA	SO	AVG
Hank Bassen	4	1	2	220	9	0	2.45
Terry Sawchuk	3	1	2	140	10	0	4.29

1962

TORONTO

	GP	G	A	PTS	PIM
Frank Mahovlich	6	4	3	7	21
George Armstrong	6	3	4	7	0
Tim Horton	6	1	6	7	12
Dick Duff	6	1	4	5	16
Ron Stewart	6	0	5	5	2
Bob Pulford	6	3	0	3	14
Billy Harris	6	2	1	3	0
Dave Keon	6	2	1	3	0
Red Kelly	6	1	2	3	0
Bob Baun	6	0	3	3	15
Bob Nevin	6	1	1	2	4
Bert Olmstead	4	0	1	1	0
Allan Stanley	6	0	1	1	2
Carl Brewer	6	0	1	1	18
Al Arbour	2	0	0	0	0
Ed Litzenberger	4	0	0	0	2
Eddie Shack	5	0	0	0	12

GOALTENDERS	GP	W	L	MIN	GA	SO	AVG
Johnny Bower	4	2	1	195	7	0	2.15
Don Simmons	3	2	1	165	8	0	2.91

CHICAGO

	GP	G	A	PTS	PIM
Bobby Hull	6	4	4	8	6
Stan Mikita	6	3	5	8	15
Ab McDonald	6	3	2	5	0
Bill Hay	6	0	4	4	4
Pierre Pilote	6	0	4	4	6
Eric Nesterenko	6	0	4	4	14
Reggie Fleming	6	2	0	2	18
Bronco Horvath	6	1	1	2	2
Murray Balfour	6	1	1	2	11
Bob Turner	6	1	0	1	0
Kenny Wharram	6	0	1	1	4
Dollard St. Laurent	6	0	1	1	8
Merv Kuryluk	2	0	0	0	0
Gerry Melnyk	5	0	0	0	2
Moose Vasko	6	0	0	0	0
Jack Evans	6	0	0	0	12

GOALTENDER	GP	W	L	MIN	GA	SO	AVG
Glenn Hall	6	2	4	360	18	1	3.00

1963

TORONTO

	GP	G	A	PTS	PIM
Dave Keon	5	4	2	6	0
Red Kelly	5	2	2	4	2
Tim Horton	5	1	3	4	4
Allan Stanley	5	0	4	4	4
Bob Nevin	5	3	0	3	0
Dick Duff	5	2	1	3	2
George Armstrong	5	1	2	3	0
Ed Litzenberger	5	1	2	3	4
Bob Pulford	5	0	3	3	8
Ron Stewart	5	2	0	2	2
Eddie Shack	5	1	1	2	4
Frank Mahovlich	4	0	1	1	4
Billy Harris	5	0	1	1	0
Kent Douglas	5	0	1	1	2
Carl Brewer	5	0	1	1	4
Bob Baun	5	0	1	1	6
John MacMillan	1	0	0	0	0

GOALTENDER	GP	W	L	MIN	GA	SO	AVG
Johnny Bower	5	4	1	300	10	0	2.00

DETROIT

	GP	G	A	PTS	PIM
Gordie Howe	5	3	3	6	8
Marcel Pronovost	5	0	4	4	0
Norm Ullman	5	0	4	4	2
Larry Jeffrey	5	2	1	3	4
Alex Delvecchio	5	1	2	3	0
Alex Faulkner	5	2	0	2	2
Floyd Smith	5	0	2	2	4
Vic Stasiuk	4	1	0	1	0
Eddie Joyal	5	1	0	1	0
Bruce MacGregor	5	0	1	1	0
Andre Pronovost	5	0	1	1	0
Parker MacDonald	5	0	1	1	2
Bob Dillabough	1	0	0	0	0
Howie Young	2	0	0	0	0
Gerry Odrowski	2	0	0	0	2
Val Fonteyne	5	0	0	0	0
Pete Goegan	5	0	0	0	2
Doug Barkley	5	0	0	0	6
Bill Gadsby	5	0	0	0	12

GOALTENDER	GP	W	L	MIN	GA	SO	AVG
Terry Sawchuk	5	1	4	300	17	0	3.40

1964

TORONTO

	GP	G	A	PTS	PIM
Frank Mahovlich	7	1	7	8	0
George Armstrong	7	4	3	7	10
Red Kelly	7	2	4	6	2
Don McKenney	5	1	5	6	0
Dave Keon	7	4	1	5	0
Bob Pulford	7	3	2	5	10
Andy Bathgate	7	3	2	5	12
Allan Stanley	7	1	3	4	12
Bob Baun	7	1	2	3	16
Ron Stewart	7	0	3	3	2
Billy Harris	7	1	1	2	4
Tim Horton	7	0	2	2	12
Gerry Ehman	7	1	0	1	2
Carl Brewer	5	0	1	1	10
Al Arbour	1	0	0	0	0
Ed Litzenberger	1	0	0	0	10
Larry Hillman	6	0	0	0	2
Jim Pappin	7	0	0	0	0
Eddie Shack	7	0	0	0	4

GOALTENDER	GP	W	L	MIN	GA	SO	AVG
Johnny Bower	7	4	3	430	17	1	2.37

DETROIT

	GP	G	A	PTS	PIM
Gordie Howe	7	4	4	8	8
Alex Delvecchio	7	1	4	5	0
Norm Ullman	7	1	3	4	2
Floyd Smith	7	3	0	3	0
Bruce MacGregor	7	3	0	3	4
Doug Barkley	7	0	3	3	8
Eddie Joyal	7	2	1	3	6
Larry Jeffrey	7	1	2	3	4
Pit Martin	7	1	2	3	10
Andre Pronovost	7	0	2	2	8
Bill Gadsby	7	0	2	2	14
Paul Henderson	7	1	0	1	4
John MacMillan	4	0	1	1	2
Parker MacDonald	7	0	1	1	0
Alex Faulkner	1	0	0	0	0
Bob Dillabough	1	0	0	0	0
Irv Spencer	7	0	0	0	0
Albert Langlois	7	0	0	0	8
Marcel Pronovost	7	0	0	0	8

GOALTENDER	GP	W	L	MIN	GA	SO	AVG
Terry Sawchuk	7	3	4	430	22	0	3.07

1965

MONTREAL	GP	G	A	PTS	PIM
Jean Beliveau	7	5	5	10	18
Dick Duff	7	3	5	8	5
Bobby Rousseau	7	1	5	6	4
J.C. Tremblay	7	1	5	6	14
Henri Richard	7	3	0	3	20
John Ferguson	7	2	1	3	13
Ted Harris	7	0	3	3	34
Yvan Cournoyer	7	2	0	2	0
Ralph Backstrom	7	1	1	2	4
Claude Provost	7	0	2	2	12
Noel Picard	3	0	1	1	0
Red Berenson	7	0	1	1	2
Jean Gauthier	2	0	0	0	4
Dave Balon	5	0	0	0	0
Claude Larose	7	0	0	0	4
Jimmy Roberts	7	0	0	0	14
Jean-Guy Talbot	7	0	0	0	18
Terry Harper	7	0	0	0	19

GOALTENDERS	GP	W	L	MIN	GA	SO	AVG
Gump Worsley	4	3	1	240	5	2	1.25
Charlie Hodge	3	1	2	180	7	1	2.33

CHICAGO	GP	G	A	PTS	PIM
Bobby Hull	7	2	2	4	10
Chico Maki	7	1	3	4	8
Pierre Pilote	5	0	3	3	14
Stan Mikita	7	0	3	3	35
Fred Stanfield	7	1	1	2	0
Matt Ravlich	7	1	1	2	8
Phil Esposito	7	1	1	2	8
Moose Vasko	7	1	1	2	12
Doug Mohns	7	1	1	2	15
Kenny Wharram	5	1	0	1	2
Bill Hay	7	1	0	1	0
Camille Henry	7	1	0	1	2
Doug Jarrett	7	1	0	1	10
Dennis Hull	1	0	0	0	0
John McKenzie	4	0	0	0	0
Gerry Melnyk	6	0	0	0	0
Eric Nesterenko	7	0	0	0	6
Al MacNeil	7	0	0	0	12

GOALTENDERS	GP	W	L	MIN	GA	SO	AVG
Glenn Hall	7	3	4	400	15	0	2.25
Denis DeJordy	1	0	0	20	3	0	9.00

1966

MONTREAL	GP	G	A	PTS	PIM
J.C. Tremblay	6	1	5	6	0
Jean Beliveau	6	3	2	5	0
Henri Richard	6	1	4	5	2
Gilles Tremblay	6	2	2	4	0
Ralph Backstrom	6	2	2	4	2
Dave Balon	6	2	2	4	16
Dick Duff	6	1	3	4	2
Yvan Cournoyer	6	2	1	3	0
Bobby Rousseau	6	1	2	3	4
Terry Harper	6	1	2	3	4
Leon Rochefort	4	1	1	2	4
Claude Provost	6	1	1	2	2
Noel Price	1	0	1	1	0
Jean-Guy Talbot	6	0	1	1	8
Jimmy Roberts	6	0	1	1	10
Claude Larose	2	0	0	0	0
Ted Harris	6	0	0	0	4
John Ferguson	6	0	0	0	8

GOALTENDER	GP	W	L	MIN	GA	SO	AVG
Gump Worsley	6	4	2	362	14	0	2.32

DETROIT	GP	G	A	PTS	PIM
Norm Ullman	6	4	2	6	6
Floyd Smith	6	3	1	4	0
Paul Henderson	6	1	3	4	4
Andy Bathgate	6	1	3	4	4
Ab McDonald	4	1	2	3	2
Alex Delvecchio	6	0	3	3	0
Dean Prentice	6	1	1	2	2
Bill Gadsby	6	1	1	2	2
Bruce MacGregor	6	1	1	2	2
Gordie Howe	6	1	1	2	6
Bert Marshall	6	0	2	2	4
Gary Bergman	6	0	1	1	4
Warren Godfrey	1	0	0	0	0
Irv Spencer	1	0	0	0	0
Murray Hall	1	0	0	0	0

	GP	W	L	MIN	GA	SO	AVG
Bob Wall	4	0	0	0	2		
Val Fonteyne	6	0	0	0	0		
Parker MacDonald	6	0	0	0	2		
Leo Boivin	6	0	0	0	6		
Bryan Watson	6	0	0	0	12		

GOALTENDERS	GP	W	L	MIN	GA	SO	AVG
Roger Crozier	6	2	3	308	16	0	3.12
Hank Bassen	1	0	1	54	2	0	2.22

1967

TORONTO	GP	G	A	PTS	PIM
Jim Pappin	6	4	4	8	6
Bob Pulford	6	1	6	7	0
Pete Stemkowski	6	2	4	6	4
Tim Horton	6	2	3	5	8
Mike Walton	6	2	1	3	0
Red Kelly	6	0	3	3	2
Larry Hillman	6	1	1	2	0
Dave Keon	6	1	1	2	0
Ron Ellis	6	1	1	2	4
Brian Conacher	6	1	1	2	19
Frank Mahovlich	6	0	2	2	8
Marcel Pronovost	6	1	0	1	4
George Armstrong	6	1	0	1	4
Allan Stanley	6	0	1	1	6
Aut Erickson	1	0	0	0	2
Milan Marcetta	2	0	0	0	0
Eddie Shack	4	0	0	0	8
Bob Baun	5	0	0	0	2

GOALTENDERS	GP	W	L	MIN	GA	SO	AVG
Johnny Bower	3	2	0	163	3	1	1.10
Terry Sawchuk	4	2	2	225	12	0	3.20

MONTREAL	GP	G	A	PTS	PIM
Henri Richard	6	4	3	7	0
Jean Beliveau	6	4	2	6	10
Yvan Cournoyer	6	2	2	4	4
Bobby Rousseau	6	0	4	4	2
Dick Duff	6	1	2	3	4
Ralph Backstrom	6	2	0	2	2
Leon Rochefort	6	1	1	2	2
John Ferguson	6	1	1	2	16
Dave Balon	5	0	2	2	2
J.C. Tremblay	6	0	2	2	0
Jimmy Roberts	3	1	0	1	0
Gilles Tremblay	6	0	1	1	0
Ted Harris	6	0	1	1	12
Claude Larose	6	0	1	1	15
Claude Provost	4	0	0	0	0
Jean-Guy Talbot	6	0	0	0	0
Jacques Laperriere	6	0	0	0	2
Terry Harper	6	0	0	0	6

GOALTENDERS	GP	W	L	MIN	GA	SO	AVG
Rogie Vachon	5	2	3	308	14	0	2.73
Gump Worsley	2	0	1	80	2	0	1.50

1968

MONTREAL	GP	G	A	PTS	PIM
Yvan Cournoyer	4	2	2	4	2
Henri Richard	4	2	1	3	0
John Ferguson	4	0	3	3	4
Serge Savard	4	2	0	2	0
J.C. Tremblay	4	1	1	2	0
Ralph Backstrom	4	1	1	2	0
Dick Duff	4	1	1	2	2
Jacques Lemaire	4	1	1	2	4
Bobby Rousseau	4	1	0	1	6
Claude Larose	4	0	1	1	0
Claude Provost	4	0	1	1	2
Ted Harris	4	0	1	1	6
Jean Beliveau	1	0	0	0	0
Carol Vadnais	1	0	0	0	2
Mickey Redmond	2	0	0	0	0
Danny Grant	4	0	0	0	0
Terry Harper	4	0	0	0	4
Jacques Laperriere	4	0	0	0	6

GOALTENDER	GP	W	L	MIN	GA	SO	AVG
Gump Worsley	4	4	0	243	7	1	1.73

ST. LOUIS	GP	G	A	PTS	PIM
Red Berenson	4	2	1	3	7
Frank St. Marseille	4	1	1	2	0
Barclay Plager	4	1	1	2	6
Craig Cameron	1	1	0	1	0
Gary Sabourin	4	1	0	1	2
Dickie Moore	4	1	0	1	4
Doug Harvey	2	0	1	1	4
Gary Veneruzzo	3	0	1	1	0
Al Arbour	4	0	1	1	0
Tim Ecclestone	4	0	1	1	2

Jean-Guy Talbot	4	0	1	1	4
Noel Picard	4	0	1	1	6
Bill McCreary	3	0	0	0	0
Gerry Melnyk	3	0	0	0	0
Ron Schock	4	0	0	0	0
Larry Keenan	4	0	0	0	0
Terry Crisp	4	0	0	0	0
Jimmy Roberts	4	0	0	0	2
Bob Plager	4	0	0	0	20

GOALTENDER	GP	W	L	MIN	GA	SO	AVG
Glenn Hall	4	0	4	243	11	0	2.72

1969

MONTREAL	GP	G	A	PTS	PIM
Dick Duff	4	4	2	6	2
Jean Beliveau	4	0	5	5	4
Yvan Cournoyer	4	1	3	4	0
John Ferguson	4	2	0	2	20
Ralph Backstrom	4	1	1	2	4
Serge Savard	4	1	1	2	8
J.C. Tremblay	4	0	2	2	6
Bobby Rousseau	4	1	0	1	2
Jacques Lemaire	4	1	0	1	4
Ted Harris	4	1	0	1	6
Claude Provost	3	0	1	1	0
Mickey Redmond	4	0	1	1	0
Henri Richard	4	0	1	1	0
Christian Bordeleau	3	0	0	0	0
Terry Harper	4	0	0	0	4
Jacques Laperriere	4	0	0	0	22

GOALTENDER	GP	W	L	MIN	GA	SO	AVG
Rogie Vachon	4	4	0	240	3	1	0.75

ST. LOUIS	GP	G	A	PTS	PIM
Frank St. Marseille	4	1	1	2	2
Terry Gray	3	1	0	1	8
Larry Keenan	4	1	0	1	8
Barclay Plager	4	0	1	1	0
Terry Crisp	4	0	1	1	2
Jimmy Roberts	4	0	1	1	4
Bill McCreary	4	0	1	1	4
Noel Picard	4	0	1	1	8
Camille Henry	2	0	1	1	0
Craig Cameron	2	0	0	0	0
Bob Plager	2	0	0	0	2
Bill Plager	3	0	0	0	4
Jean-Guy Talbot	4	0	0	0	2
Ron Schock	4	0	0	0	2
Al Arbour	4	0	0	0	4
Red Berenson	4	0	0	0	4
Gary Sabourin	4	0	0	0	4
Ab McDonald	4	0	0	0	4
Tim Ecclestone	4	0	0	0	10

GOALTENDERS	GP	W	L	MIN	GA	SO	AVG
Glenn Hall	2	0	2	120	5	0	2.50
Jacques Plante	2	0	2	120	6	0	3.00

1970

BOSTON	GP	G	A	PTS	PIM
Phil Esposito	4	2	6	8	4
John Bucyk	4	6	0	6	0
Derek Sanderson	4	3	3	6	8
Bobby Orr	4	1	4	5	6
John McKenzie	4	1	4	5	14
Ed Westfall	4	2	1	3	0
Rick Smith	4	1	3	4	2
Fred Stanfield	4	1	3	4	4
Ken Hodge	4	0	3	3	2
Wayne Cashman	4	2	0	2	8
Wayne Carleton	4	1	1	2	0
Dallas Smith	4	0	1	1	6
Don Awrey	4	0	1	1	12
Bill Speer	1	0	0	0	0
Bill Lesuk	2	0	0	0	0
Jim Lorentz	4	0	0	0	0
Don Marcotte	4	0	0	0	2
Gary Doak	4	0	0	0	0

GOALTENDER	GP	W	L	MIN	GA	SO	AVG
Gerry Cheevers	4	4	0	241	7	0	1.74

ST. LOUIS	GP	G	A	PTS	PIM
Frank St. Marseille	4	2	1	3	2
Jimmy Roberts	4	1	1	2	4
Phil Goyette	4	0	2	2	2
Gary Sabourin	4	0	1	1	0
Terry Gray	4	1	0	1	0
Larry Keenan	4	1	0	1	0
Red Berenson	4	1	0	1	4
Bill McCreary	3	0	1	1	0
Ab McDonald	4	0	1	1	0

Tim Ecclestone	4	0	1	1	6
Bob Plager	4	0	1	1	6
Noel Picard	4	0	1	1	14
Barclay Plager	1	0	0	0	0
Ron Anderson	1	0	0	0	2
Norm Dennis	1	0	0	0	2
Bill Plager	2	0	0	0	0
Al Arbour	2	0	0	0	0
Andre Boudrias	3	0	0	0	2
Ray Fortin	3	0	0	0	6
Jean-Guy Talbot	4	0	0	0	0
Terry Crisp	4	0	0	0	0

GOALTENDERS	GP	W	L	MIN	GA	SO	AVG
Jacques Plante	1	0	0	24	1	0	2.50
Glenn Hall	2	0	2	121	8	0	3.97
Ernie Wakely	2	0	2	96	11	0	6.87

1971

MONTREAL	GP	G	A	PTS	PIM
Frank Mahovlich	7	4	4	8	4
Pete Mahovlich	7	5	2	7	16
Yvan Cournoyer	7	4	2	6	6
Jacques Lemaire	7	3	1	4	11
Jean Beliveau	7	1	3	4	6
Henri Richard	7	2	1	3	2
Guy Lapointe	7	1	2	3	19
Jacques Laperriere	7	0	3	3	2
J.C. Tremblay	7	0	3	3	7
Rejean Houle	7	0	3	3	10
Terry Harper	7	0	2	2	10
John Ferguson	6	0	1	1	8
Claude Larose	2	0	0	0	0
Bob Murdoch	2	0	0	0	0
Pierre Bouchard	3	0	0	0	2
Phil Roberto	5	0	0	0	12
Leon Rochefort	6	0	0	0	6
Marc Tardif	7	0	0	0	19

GOALTENDER	GP	W	L	MIN	GA	SO	AVG
Ken Dryden	7	4	3	441	18	0	2.45

CHICAGO	GP	G	A	PTS	PIM
Bobby Hull	7	3	6	9	8
Jim Pappin	7	4	2	6	8
Cliff Koroll	7	2	3	5	4
Stan Mikita	7	1	4	5	6
Dennis Hull	7	3	1	4	2
Lou Angotti	7	2	2	4	9
Chico Maki	7	2	1	3	4
Danny O'Shea	7	1	1	2	12
Pit Martin	6	0	2	2	4
Pat Stapleton	7	0	2	2	0
Bill White	7	0	2	2	10
Rick Foley	4	0	1	1	4
Doug Jarrett	7	0	1	1	2
Dan Maloney	2	0	0	0	4
Jerry Korab	2	0	0	0	14
Paul Shmyr	3	0	0	0	17
Gerry Pinder	5	0	0	0	2
Eric Nesterenko	7	0	0	0	8
Keith Magnuson	7	0	0	0	36

GOALTENDER	GP	W	L	MIN	GA	SO	AVG
Tony Esposito	7	3	4	441	20	1	2.72

1972

BOSTON	GP	G	A	PTS	PIM
Ken Hodge	6	5	3	8	19
Bobby Orr	6	4	4	8	17
Phil Esposito	6	0	8	8	14
Mike Walton	6	1	4	5	6
Wayne Cashman	6	3	1	4	15
Fred Stanfield	6	1	2	3	0
John Bucyk	6	1	2	3	2
Ed Westfall	6	0	2	2	10
John McKenzie	6	0	2	2	25
Don Marcotte	5	1	0	1	6
Garnet Bailey	6	1	0	1	14
Derek Sanderson	6	1	0	1	26
Dallas Smith	6	0	1	1	10
Carol Vadnais	6	0	1	1	13
Ted Green	4	0	0	0	0
Don Awrey	6	0	0	0	21

GOALTENDERS	GP	W	L	MIN	GA	SO	AVG
Eddie Johnston	3	2	1	180	6	0	2.00
Gerry Cheevers	3	2	1	180	10	1	3.33

NY RANGERS	GP	G	A	PTS	PIM
Rod Gilbert	6	4	3	7	11
Brad Park	6	2	4	6	11
Ted Irvine	6	1	4	5	10
Bobby Rousseau	6	2	2	4	5

Pete Stemkowski	6	1	3	4	8
Vic Hadfield	6	1	3	4	16
Bruce MacGregor	6	1	2	3	2
Walt Tkaczuk	6	1	2	3	17
Dale Rolfe	6	2	0	2	10
Rod Seiling	6	1	1	2	6
Bill Fairbairn	6	0	2	2	0
Jim Neilson	3	0	1	1	2
Jean Ratelle	6	0	1	1	0
Ron Stewart	1	0	0	0	0
Jim Dorey	1	0	0	0	0
Ab DeMarco Jr.	1	0	0	0	0
Phil Goyette	3	0	0	0	0
Gary Doak	5	0	0	0	34
Gene Carr	6	0	0	0	9
Glen Sather	6	0	0	0	11

GOALTENDERS	GP	W	L	MIN	GA	SO	AVG
Gilles Villemure	3	1	2	180	7	0	2.33
Ed Giacomin	3	1	2	180	11	0	3.67

1973

MONTREAL	GP	G	A	PTS	PIM
Yvan Cournoyer	6	6	6	12	0
Jacques Lemaire	6	3	9	12	0
Frank Mahovlich	6	5	6	11	0
Pete Mahovlich	6	3	5	8	12
Claude Larose	6	3	4	7	2
Chuck Lefley	6	3	3	6	2
Marc Tardif	6	3	3	6	4
Guy Lapointe	6	1	3	4	8
Henri Richard	6	2	1	3	0
Rejean Houle	6	1	2	3	0
Jacques Laperriere	2	1	1	2	0
Guy Lafleur	6	0	2	2	0
Larry Robinson	6	0	2	2	2
Murray Wilson	6	0	2	2	2
Pierre Bouchard	6	1	0	1	4
Serge Savard	6	1	0	1	6
Bob Murdoch	4	0	0	0	2
Jimmy Roberts	6	0	0	0	6

GOALTENDER	GP	W	L	MIN	GA	SO	AVG
Ken Dryden	6	4	2	360	21	1	3.50

CHICAGO	GP	G	A	PTS	PIM
Stan Mikita	5	3	5	8	0
Pat Stapleton	6	0	8	8	4
Dennis Hull	6	3	4	7	4
Pit Martin	6	5	0	5	4
Jim Pappin	6	3	2	5	10
Ralph Backstrom	6	1	3	4	0
Bill White	6	1	3	4	2
Cliff Koroll	6	1	2	3	2
Dave Kryskow	3	2	0	2	0
Len Frig	4	1	1	2	0
Lou Angotti	6	1	1	2	0
John Marks	6	1	1	2	2
Chico Maki	6	0	2	2	0
J.P. Bordeleau	6	1	0	1	4
Dick Redmond	4	0	1	1	0
Doug Jarrett	6	0	1	1	0
Phil Russell	6	0	1	1	16
Jerry Korab	5	0	0	0	6

GOALTENDERS	GP	W	L	MIN	GA	SO	AVG
Tony Esposito	6	2	4	355	32	0	5.41
Gary Smith	1	0	0	5	0	0	0.00

1974

PHILADELPHIA	GP	G	A	PTS	PIM
Bobby Clarke	6	3	3	6	14
Rick MacLeish	6	2	3	5	4
Andre Dupont	6	2	1	3	33
Dave Schultz	6	1	2	3	38
Bill Flett	6	0	3	3	4
Don Saleski	6	0	3	3	6
Orest Kindrachuk	6	2	0	2	11
Bill Barber	6	1	1	2	2
Ross Lonsberry	6	1	1	2	2
Terry Crisp	6	1	1	2	2
Tom Bladon	6	1	1	2	21
Ed Van Impe	6	0	2	2	13
Joe Watson	6	0	2	2	16
Bill Clement	3	1	0	1	2
Simon Nolet	6	0	1	1	0
Jimmy Watson	6	0	1	1	30
Gary Dornhoefer	3	0	0	0	0
Bruce Cowick	6	0	0	0	7

GOALTENDER	GP	W	L	MIN	GA	SO	AVG
Bernie Parent	6	4	2	372	13	1	2.10

BOSTON	GP	G	A	PTS	PIM
Bobby Orr	6	3	4	7	8
Gregg Sheppard	6	2	3	5	2
Ken Hodge	6	1	4	5	6
Wayne Cashman	6	2	2	4	41
John Bucyk	6	1	3	4	2
Phil Esposito	6	2	1	3	10
Carol Vadnais	6	0	3	3	22
Andre Savard	6	1	1	2	20
Dallas Smith	6	0	2	2	8
Don Marcotte	6	1	0	1	2
Dave Forbes	6	0	1	1	2
Terry O'Reilly	6	0	1	1	25
Rich Leduc	5	0	0	0	9
Darryl Edestrand	6	0	0	0	2
Al Sims	6	0	0	0	4
Bobby Schmautz	6	0	0	0	18

GOALTENDER	GP	W	L	MIN	GA	SO	AVG
Gilles Gilbert	6	2	4	372	15	0	2.42

1975

PHILADELPHIA	GP	G	A	PTS	PIM
Bill Barber	6	2	4	6	0
Bobby Clarke	6	2	3	5	2
Reggie Leach	6	3	1	4	0
Bob Kelly	5	2	2	4	7
Rick MacLeish	6	1	3	4	2
Terry Crisp	4	0	4	4	0
Ross Lonsberry	6	2	1	3	2
Dave Schultz	6	2	0	2	13
Gary Dornhoefer	6	2	0	2	14
Don Saleski	6	1	1	2	8
Larry Goodenough	2	0	2	2	2
Orest Kindrachuk	5	0	2	2	2
Jimmy Watson	6	0	2	2	0
Ted Harris	6	0	2	2	2
Ed Van Impe	6	0	2	2	8
Bill Clement	5	1	0	1	2
Andre Dupont	6	1	0	1	10
Tom Bladon	4	0	1	1	8
Joe Watson	6	0	0	0	2

GOALTENDER	GP	W	L	MIN	GA	SO	AVG
Bernie Parent	6	4	2	378	20	1	3.17

BUFFALO	GP	G	A	PTS	PIM
Rick Martin	6	2	4	6	6
Don Luce	6	2	3	5	12
Danny Gare	6	2	1	3	4
Jerry Korab	6	2	1	3	6
Jim Lorentz	6	1	2	3	2
Rene Robert	6	1	2	3	6
Gilbert Perreault	6	1	1	2	6
Craig Ramsay	6	0	2	2	0
Jim Schoenfeld	6	0	2	2	11
Bill Hajt	6	1	0	1	2
Rick Dudley	4	0	1	1	9
Brian Spencer	6	0	1	1	4
Jocelyn Guevremont	6	0	1	1	8
Lee Fogolin Jr.	4	0	0	0	0
Peter McNab	6	0	0	0	0
Fred Stanfield	6	0	0	0	0
Larry Carriere	6	0	0	0	4

GOALTENDERS	GP	W	L	MIN	GA	SO	AVG
Roger Crozier	2	1	1	118	3	0	1.53
Gerry Desjardins	5	1	3	260	16	0	3.69

1976

MONTREAL	GP	G	A	PTS	PIM
Guy Lafleur	4	2	5	7	2
Steve Shutt	4	3	3	6	0
Pete Mahovlich	4	1	4	5	4
Pierre Bouchard	4	0	2	2	2
Jacques Lemaire	4	2	0	2	2
Yvan Cournoyer	4	1	1	2	0
Larry Robinson	4	1	1	2	4
Doug Risebrough	4	0	2	2	2
Jimmy Roberts	4	1	0	1	0
Guy Lapointe	4	1	0	1	8
Murray Wilson	3	0	1	1	0
Bill Nyrop	4	0	1	1	2
Bob Gainey	4	0	1	1	12
Rick Chartraw	2	0	0	0	0
Mario Tremblay	2	0	0	0	7
Yvon Lambert	3	0	0	0	4
Doug Jarvis	4	0	0	0	0
Serge Savard	4	0	0	0	2

GOALTENDER	GP	W	L	MIN	GA	SO	AVG
Ken Dryden	4	4	0	240	9	0	2.25

PHILADELPHIA

	GP	G	A	PTS	PIM
Reggie Leach	4	4	0	4	0
Tom Bladon	4	0	3	3	2
Bobby Clarke	4	0	3	3	4
Larry Goodenough	4	1	1	2	2
Bill Barber	4	1	1	2	6
Andre Dupont	4	1	1	2	7
Mel Bridgman	4	0	2	2	4
Ross Lonsberry	4	1	0	1	0
Dave Schultz	4	1	0	1	10
Jack McIlhargey	4	0	1	1	4
Gary Dornhoefer	4	0	1	1	6
Terry Crisp	1	0	0	0	0
Terry Murray	2	0	0	0	0
Orest Kindrachuk	4	0	0	0	0
Bob Kelly	4	0	0	0	2
Joe Watson	4	0	0	0	2
Don Saleski	4	0	0	0	4
Jimmy Watson	4	0	0	0	4

GOALTENDER	GP	W	L	MIN	GA	SO	AVG
Wayne Stephenson	4	0	4	240	14	0	3.50

1977

MONTREAL

	GP	G	A	PTS	PIM
Guy Lafleur	4	2	7	9	4
Jacques Lemaire	4	4	2	6	2
Steve Shutt	4	2	3	5	0
Yvon Lambert	4	2	2	4	6
Pete Mahovlich	4	1	3	4	4
Guy Lapointe	4	0	4	4	0
Doug Risebrough	2	2	1	3	2
Larry Robinson	4	0	3	3	6
Mario Tremblay	4	2	0	2	5
Serge Savard	4	0	2	2	0
Rick Chartraw	4	1	0	1	4
Doug Jarvis	4	0	1	1	0
Murray Wilson	4	0	1	1	6
Pierre Bouchard	4	0	1	1	6
Bill Nyrop	1	0	0	0	0
Mike Polich	1	0	0	0	0
Pierre Mondou	2	0	0	0	0
Jimmy Roberts	4	0	0	0	4
Bob Gainey	4	0	0	0	12

GOALTENDER	GP	W	L	MIN	GA	SO	AVG
Ken Dryden	4	4	0	245	6	1	1.47

BOSTON

	GP	G	A	PTS	PIM
Brad Park	4	1	4	5	2
Bobby Schmautz	4	2	0	2	0
Rick Middleton	4	0	2	2	0
Peter McNab	4	1	0	1	2
Gregg Sheppard	4	1	0	1	6
Terry O'Reilly	4	1	0	1	8
Jean Ratelle	4	0	1	1	0
Wayne Cashman	4	0	1	1	13
Matti Hagman	1	0	0	0	0
Earl Anderson	2	0	0	0	0
Darryl Edestrand	2	0	0	0	0
John Bucyk	2	0	0	0	0
Al Sims	2	0	0	0	0
John Wensink	3	0	0	0	4
Mike Milbury	3	0	0	0	20
Dave Forbes	4	0	0	0	0
Gary Doak	4	0	0	0	4
Stan Jonathan	4	0	0	0	4
Don Marcotte	4	0	0	0	4
Rick Smith	4	0	0	0	6

GOALTENDER	GP	W	L	MIN	GA	SO	AVG
Gerry Cheevers	4	0	4	245	16	0	3.92

1978

MONTREAL

	GP	G	A	PTS	PIM
Larry Robinson	6	2	4	6	4
Guy Lafleur	6	3	2	5	8
Steve Shutt	6	3	1	4	2
Pierre Mondou	6	1	3	4	4
Mario Tremblay	3	2	1	3	14
Yvon Lambert	6	1	2	3	2
Yvan Cournoyer	6	1	2	3	6
Jacques Lemaire	6	1	2	3	6
Serge Savard	6	0	3	3	4
Doug Jarvis	6	0	3	3	10
Rejean Houle	6	1	1	2	4
Bob Gainey	6	1	1	2	10
Bill Nyrop	5	0	2	2	6
Guy Lapointe	6	0	2	2	5
Pierre Larouche	2	1	0	1	0
Doug Risebrough	6	1	0	1	7
Brian Engblom	1	0	0	0	0

Gilles Lupien	2	0	0	0	17
Rick Chartraw	3	0	0	0	0
Pierre Bouchard	4	0	0	0	5

GOALTENDER	GP	W	L	MIN	GA	SO	AVG
Ken Dryden	6	4	2	379	13	0	2.06

BOSTON

	GP	G	A	PTS	PIM
Brad Park	6	4	1	5	8
Peter McNab	6	2	3	5	2
Gregg Sheppard	6	1	3	4	2
Don Marcotte	6	1	2	3	4
Bobby Schmautz	6	1	2	3	11
Terry O'Reilly	6	1	2	3	16
Jean Ratelle	6	0	3	3	0
Mike Milbury	6	0	3	3	10
Wayne Cashman	6	0	2	2	2
Rick Middleton	6	1	0	1	0
Gary Doak	6	1	0	1	4
Rick Smith	6	0	1	1	10
Bob Miller	6	0	1	1	9
Al Sims	3	0	0	0	0
Dennis O'Brien	5	0	0	0	6
Stan Jonathan	6	0	0	0	20
John Wensink	6	0	0	0	24

GOALTENDERS	GP	W	L	MIN	GA	SO	AVG
Gerry Cheevers	6	2	4	359	18	1	3.01
Ron Grahame	1	0	0	20	0	0	0.00

1979

MONTREAL

	GP	G	A	PTS	PIM
Jacques Lemaire	5	4	3	7	2
Steve Shutt	5	2	4	6	2
Yvon Lambert	5	2	4	6	4
Bob Gainey	5	3	2	5	6
Rejean Houle	5	1	4	5	2
Guy Lafleur	5	2	1	3	0
Serge Savard	5	1	2	3	2
Doug Risebrough	5	1	2	3	12
Mario Tremblay	5	1	1	2	4
Rick Chartraw	5	1	1	2	12
Doug Jarvis	5	0	2	2	2
Mark Napier	5	1	0	1	2
Larry Robinson	5	0	1	1	0
Pierre Larouche	1	0	0	0	0
Gilles Lupien	4	0	0	0	2
Brian Engblom	5	0	0	0	0
Pierre Mondou	5	0	0	0	2
Rod Langway	5	0	0	0	12

GOALTENDERS	GP	W	L	MIN	GA	SO	AVG
Ken Dryden	5	4	1	287	11	0	2.30
Michel Larocque	1	0	0	20	0	0	0.00

NY RANGERS

	GP	G	A	PTS	PIM
Phil Esposito	5	2	1	3	10
Pat Hickey	5	1	2	3	0
Anders Hedberg	5	1	2	3	2
Dave Maloney	5	1	2	3	10
Ron Duguay	5	2	0	2	4
Steve Vickers	5	1	1	2	0
Don Murdoch	5	1	1	2	2
Mike McEwen	5	0	2	2	4
Carol Vadnais	5	1	0	1	0
Ron Greschner	5	1	0	1	8
Bobby Sheehan	5	0	1	1	0
Walt Tkaczuk	5	0	1	1	4
Don Maloney	5	0	1	1	6
Dave Farrish	1	0	0	0	0
Lucien DeBlois	2	0	0	0	0
Ulf Nilsson	2	0	0	0	2
Pierre Plante	5	0	0	0	0
Eddie Johnstone	5	0	0	0	2
Mario Marois	5	0	0	0	4

GOALTENDER	GP	W	L	MIN	GA	SO	AVG
John Davidson	5	1	4	307	19	0	3.17

1980

NY ISLANDERS

	GP	G	A	PTS	PIM
Mike Bossy	6	4	7	11	4
Denis Potvin	6	5	4	9	6
Bryan Trottier	6	4	4	8	0
Clark Gillies	6	2	6	8	13
Stefan Persson	6	3	4	7	10
Butch Goring	6	3	3	6	0
Bob Nystrom	6	3	1	4	30
Duane Sutter	6	1	3	4	28
Bob Bourne	6	0	4	4	2
John Tonelli	6	0	3	3	4
Lorne Henning	6	1	1	2	0
Garry Howatt	6	0	1	1	21
Wayne Merrick	6	0	0	0	0

Bob Lorimer	6	0	0	0	6
Ken Morrow	6	0	0	0	6
Dave Langevin	6	0	0	0	9
Gord Lane	6	0	0	0	28

GOALTENDERS	GP	W	L	MIN	GA	SO	AVG
Billy Smith	6	4	2	351	23	0	3.93
Glenn Resch	1	0	0	20	2	0	6.00

PHILADELPHIA

	GP	G	A	PTS	PIM
Paul Holmgren	5	4	4	8	15
Ken Linseman	6	1	7	8	16
Bobby Clarke	6	4	3	7	2
Rick MacLeish	6	3	3	6	2
Brian Propp	6	3	3	6	4
Reggie Leach	6	1	4	5	0
Bill Barber	6	1	4	5	9
Bob Dailey	6	1	3	4	4
Mel Bridgman	6	1	3	4	53
Behn Wilson	6	0	4	4	28
Mike Busniuk	6	2	1	3	7
Tom Gorence	5	1	1	2	16
John Paddock	2	2	0	2	0
Bob Kelly	6	1	0	1	9
Jimmy Watson	5	0	1	1	9
Andre Dupont	6	0	1	1	14
Norm Barnes	1	0	0	0	0
Al Hill	6	0	0	0	2
Jack McIlhargey	6	0	0	0	25

GOALTENDERS	GP	W	L	MIN	GA	SO	AVG
Pete Peeters	5	2	3	311	20	0	3.86
Phil Myre	1	0	1	60	6	0	6.00

1981

NY ISLANDERS

	GP	G	A	PTS	PIM
Mike Bossy	5	4	4	8	0
Wayne Merrick	5	3	5	8	0
Butch Goring	5	5	2	7	0
Bryan Trottier	5	2	5	7	14
Denis Potvin	5	2	4	6	8
John Tonelli	5	0	5	5	8
Anders Kallur	5	2	2	4	4
Bob Nystrom	5	2	2	4	10
Billy Carroll	5	1	3	4	0
Mike McEwen	5	2	1	3	2
Bob Bourne	5	1	2	3	12
Clark Gillies	5	0	3	3	8
Dave Langevin	5	0	2	2	10
Ken Morrow	5	1	0	1	2
Gord Lane	5	1	0	1	18
Duane Sutter	5	0	1	1	0
Bob Lorimer	5	0	0	0	9

GOALTENDER	GP	W	L	MIN	GA	SO	AVG
Billy Smith	5	4	1	300	16	0	3.20

MINNESOTA

	GP	G	A	PTS	PIM
Steve Payne	5	5	2	7	2
Dino Ciccarelli	5	3	2	5	19
Bobby Smith	5	2	3	5	2
Craig Hartsburg	5	1	4	5	2
Steve Christoff	5	2	2	4	0
Al MacAdam	5	1	3	4	2
Brad Maxwell	4	0	4	4	9
Tim Young	2	0	3	3	0
Tom McCarthy	3	0	3	3	2
Kent-Erik Andersson	5	1	0	1	0
Brad Palmer	5	1	0	1	4
Neal Broten	5	0	1	1	2
Gordie Roberts	5	0	1	1	2
Greg Smith	5	0	1	1	6
Ken Solheim	1	0	0	0	0
Jack Carlson	2	0	0	0	0
Paul Shmyr	2	0	0	0	2
Kevin Maxwell	2	0	0	0	4
Mike Polich	3	0	0	0	0
Tom Younghans	3	0	0	0	0
Fred Barrett	3	0	0	0	6
Curt Giles	5	0	0	0	2

GOALTENDERS	GP	W	L	MIN	GA	SO	AVG
Don Beaupre	3	1	2	180	13	0	4.33
Gilles Meloche	2	0	2	120	12	0	6.00

1982

NY ISLANDERS

	GP	G	A	PTS	PIM
Denis Potvin	4	2	7	9	4
Mike Bossy	4	7	1	8	0
Bryan Trottier	4	1	6	7	10
Stefan Persson	4	0	5	5	4
Clark Gillies	4	2	1	3	8
Butch Goring	4	1	2	3	2
Bob Nystrom	4	0	2	2	21

	GP	G	A	PTS	PIM
Billy Carroll	4	1	1	2	2
Bob Bourne	4	1	1	2	17
Brent Sutter	4	0	2	2	0
John Tonelli	4	0	2	2	4
Duane Sutter	4	1	0	1	32
Tomas Jonsson	2	0	1	1	2
Wayne Merrick	4	0	1	1	0
Mike McEwen	2	0	0	0	0
Anders Kallur	4	0	0	0	0
Ken Morrow	4	0	0	0	0
Dave Langevin	4	0	0	0	2
Gord Lane	4	0	0	0	22

GOALTENDER	GP	W	L	MIN	GA	SO	AVG
Billy Smith	4	4	0	260	10	1	2.31

VANCOUVER	GP	G	A	PTS	PIM
Thomas Gradin	4	3	2	5	2
Lars Molin	4	0	4	4	2
Gerry Minor	4	1	2	3	0
Tiger Williams	4	0	3	3	14
Curt Fraser	4	0	3	3	28
Ivan Boldirev	4	2	0	2	2
Stan Smyl	4	2	0	2	19
Lars Lindgren	4	1	0	1	2
Jim Nill	3	1	0	1	6
Doug Halward	4	0	1	1	4
Colin Campbell	4	0	1	1	26
Per-Olov Brasar	1	0	0	0	0
Garth Butcher	1	0	0	0	0
Blair MacDonald	1	0	0	0	0
Ivan Hlinka	2	0	0	0	0
Gary Lupul	2	0	0	0	0
Marc Crawford	3	0	0	0	0
Anders Eldebrink	3	0	0	0	2
Ron Delorme	4	0	0	0	4
Neil Belland	4	0	0	0	4
Harold Snepsts	4	0	0	0	16
Darcy Rota	4	0	0	0	19

GOALTENDER	GP	W	L	MIN	GA	SO	AVG
Richard Brodeur	4	0	4	260	17	0	3.92

1983

NY ISLANDERS	GP	G	A	PTS	PIM
Duane Sutter	4	2	5	7	0
Ken Morrow	4	3	2	5	2
Brent Sutter	4	3	2	5	10
Mike Bossy	3	2	2	4	0
Bob Bourne	4	2	2	4	6
Bryan Trottier	4	1	3	4	4
Denis Potvin	4	0	3	3	4
Bob Nystrom	4	1	1	2	2
Anders Kallur	4	1	1	2	4
Tomas Jonsson	4	1	1	2	8
Stefan Persson	4	0	2	2	4
John Tonelli	4	1	0	1	0
Dave Langevin	4	0	1	1	0
Clark Gillies	4	0	1	1	6
Greg Gilbert	1	0	0	0	0
Butch Goring	4	0	0	0	0
Billy Carroll	4	0	0	0	0
Wayne Merrick	4	0	0	0	0
Gord Lane	4	0	0	0	2

GOALTENDER	GP	W	L	MIN	GA	SO	AVG
Billy Smith	4	4	0	240	6	1	1.50

EDMONTON	GP	G	A	PTS	PIM
Wayne Gretzky	4	0	4	4	0
Jari Kurri	4	3	0	3	2
Glenn Anderson	4	1	1	2	11
Lee Fogolin Jr.	4	0	2	2	0
Mark Messier	4	1	0	1	2
Dave Semenko	4	1	0	1	0
Charlie Huddy	4	0	1	1	0
Tom Roulston	4	0	1	1	0
Paul Coffey	4	0	1	1	4
Ray Cote	4	0	0	0	0
Willy Lindstrom	4	0	0	0	0
Randy Gregg	4	0	0	0	0
Pat Hughes	4	0	0	0	2
Kevin Lowe	4	0	0	0	2
Don Jackson	4	0	0	0	4
Ken Linseman	4	0	0	0	4
Dave Hunter	4	0	0	0	8
Dave Lumley	4	0	0	0	9

GOALTENDER	GP	W	L	MIN	GA	SO	AVG
Andy Moog	4	0	4	240	15	0	3.75

1984

EDMONTON	GP	G	A	PTS	PIM
Wayne Gretzky	5	4	3	7	4
Jari Kurri	5	1	5	6	2
Mark Messier	5	3	1	4	7
Paul Coffey	5	2	2	4	0
Kevin McClelland	5	2	2	4	16
Glenn Anderson	5	1	3	4	8
Willy Lindstrom	5	2	1	3	0
Dave Semenko	5	1	2	3	4
Charlie Huddy	5	0	3	3	4
Pat Hughes	5	0	3	3	4
Dave Lumley	5	1	1	2	17
Ken Linseman	5	1	1	2	26
Pat Conacher	2	1	0	1	0
Randy Gregg	5	1	0	1	2
Kevin Lowe	5	1	0	1	4
Dave Hunter	3	0	1	1	6
Lee Fogolin, Jr.	5	0	1	1	6
Jaroslav Pouzar	5	0	0	0	6
Don Jackson	5	0	0	0	13

GOALTENDERS	GP	W	L	MIN	GA	SO	AVG
Andy Moog	3	2	0	128	4	0	1.88
Grant Fuhr	3	2	1	172	8	1	2.79

NY ISLANDERS	GP	G	A	PTS	PIM
Clark Gillies	5	5	3	8	0
Pat Flatley	5	1	3	4	8
Bryan Trottier	5	2	2	4	2
Pat LaFontaine	5	2	1	3	0
Brent Sutter	5	1	2	3	6
Mike Bossy	5	0	3	3	0
Greg Gilbert	5	1	1	2	26
Stefan Persson	4	0	2	2	2
Paul Boutilier	5	0	2	2	0
Anders Kallur	5	0	1	1	0
Ken Morrow	5	0	1	1	4
Denis Potvin	5	0	1	1	6
Billy Carroll	1	0	0	0	0
Mats Hallin	2	0	0	0	0
Bob Nystrom	2	0	0	0	4
Dave Langevin	2	0	0	0	5
Gord Dineen	3	0	0	0	24
Butch Goring	5	0	0	0	0
John Tonelli	5	0	0	0	4
Tomas Jonsson	5	0	0	0	8
Duane Sutter	5	0	0	0	26

GOALTENDERS	GP	W	L	MIN	GA	SO	AVG
Billy Smith	5	1	3	245	17	0	4.16
Roland Melanson	3	0	1	55	3	0	3.27

1985

EDMONTON	GP	G	A	PTS	PIM
Wayne Gretzky	5	7	4	11	0
Paul Coffey	5	3	8	11	6
Jari Kurri	5	1	6	7	0
Mark Messier	5	2	4	6	6
Charlie Huddy	5	1	5	6	6
Mike Krushelnyski	5	2	2	4	4
Willy Lindstrom	5	3	0	3	2
Glenn Anderson	5	1	1	2	12
Dave Hunter	5	1	0	1	25
Randy Gregg	4	0	1	1	2
Kevin McClelland	5	0	1	1	41
Jaroslav Pouzar	1	0	0	0	0
Larry Melnyk	1	0	0	0	0
Dave Lumley	1	0	0	0	2
Billy Carroll	2	0	0	0	0
Esa Tikkanen	3	0	0	0	4
Pat Hughes	4	0	0	0	2
Dave Semenko	4	0	0	0	14
Mark Napier	5	0	0	0	0
Kevin Lowe	5	0	0	0	4
Lee Fogolin, Jr.	5	0	0	0	8
Don Jackson	5	0	0	0	35

GOALTENDER	GP	W	L	MIN	GA	SO	AVG
Grant Fuhr	5	4	1	300	13	0	2.60

PHILADELPHIA	GP	G	A	PTS	PIM
Derrick Smith	5	1	4	5	0
Dave Poulin	5	1	3	4	4
Rich Sutter	3	3	0	3	4
Brian Propp	5	2	1	3	0
Tim Kerr	3	2	1	3	9
Murray Craven	5	1	2	3	4
Ron Sutter	5	1	2	3	6
Todd Bergen	4	1	1	2	0
Mark Howe	5	1	1	2	0
Lindsay Carson	3	0	2	2	2
Doug Crossman	5	0	2	2	12
Rick Tocchet	5	0	2	2	14
Ilkka Sinisalo	5	1	0	1	0
Peter Zezel	5	0	1	1	4
Brad Marsh	5	0	1	1	43
Len Hachborn	1	0	0	0	0
Ray Allison	1	0	0	0	0
Dave Brown	1	0	0	0	19
Thomas Eriksson	4	0	0	0	0
Miroslav Dvorak	5	0	0	0	2
Joe Paterson	5	0	0	0	19
Ed Hospodar	5	0	0	0	34

GOALTENDERS	GP	W	L	MIN	GA	SO	AVG
Pelle Lindbergh	4	1	3	185	11	0	3.57
Bob Froese	3	0	1	115	9	0	4.70

1986

MONTREAL	GP	G	A	PTS	PIM
Mats Naslund	5	3	4	7	0
Bobby Smith	5	2	2	4	8
Chris Chelios	5	1	3	4	19
Gaston Gingras	4	2	1	3	0
David Maley	5	1	2	3	2
Claude Lemieux	5	1	2	3	31
Larry Robinson	5	0	3	3	15
Guy Carbonneau	5	0	3	3	23
Brian Skrudland	5	2	0	2	32
Mike Lalor	5	0	2	2	19
Mike McPhee	5	0	2	2	24
Kjell Dahlin	4	1	0	1	0
Rick Green	5	1	0	1	0
Bob Gainey	5	1	0	1	2
Ryan Walter	5	0	1	1	2
Stephane Richer	1	0	0	0	0
Steve Rooney	1	0	0	0	0
Serge Boisvert	2	0	0	0	0
Chris Nilan	3	0	0	0	49
Craig Ludwig	5	0	0	0	14
John Kordic	5	0	0	0	15

GOALTENDER	GP	W	L	MIN	GA	SO	AVG
Patrick Roy	5	4	1	301	12	1	2.39

CALGARY	GP	G	A	PTS	PIM
Dan Quinn	5	1	4	5	4
Jim Peplinski	5	1	3	4	37
Al MacInnis	5	0	4	4	8
Joe Mullen	4	2	1	3	4
Lanny McDonald	5	2	1	3	6
Joel Otto	5	1	2	3	12
Steve Bozek	4	2	0	2	19
John Tonelli	5	2	0	2	15
Paul Reinhart	5	1	1	2	2
Hakan Loob	5	0	2	2	2
Doug Risebrough	5	1	0	1	12
Nick Fotiu	2	0	1	1	10
Paul Baxter	4	0	1	1	17
Jamie Macoun	5	0	1	1	4
Tim Hunter	5	0	1	1	43
Brian Bradley	1	0	0	0	0
Yves Courteau	1	0	0	0	0
Brett Hull	2	0	0	0	0
Colin Patterson	2	0	0	0	0
Mike Eaves	2	0	0	0	2
Perry Berezan	2	0	0	0	4
Terry Johnson	2	0	0	0	12
Robin Bartel	4	0	0	0	12
Neil Sheehy	5	0	0	0	31

GOALTENDERS	GP	W	L	MIN	GA	SO	AVG
Mike Vernon	5	1	4	260	14	0	3.23
Reggie Lemelin	1	0	0	41	1	0	1.46

1987

EDMONTON	GP	G	A	PTS	PIM
Wayne Gretzky	7	2	9	11	2
Jari Kurri	7	5	4	9	4
Paul Coffey	7	2	4	6	14
Glenn Anderson	7	4	1	5	14
Mark Mesier	7	2	3	5	10
Kevin Lowe	7	2	1	3	4
Randy Gregg	7	1	2	3	0
Mike Krushelnyski	7	1	1	2	6
Craig MacTavish	7	0	2	2	6
Charlie Huddy	7	0	2	2	10
Kevin McClelland	7	1	0	1	4
Marty McSorley	7	1	0	1	10
Jaroslav Pouzar	3	0	1	1	2
Craig Muni	5	0	1	1	0
Kent Nilsson	7	0	1	1	0
Dave Hunter	7	0	1	1	4
Kelly Buchberger	3	0	0	0	5

Steve Smith	3	0	0	0	6
Reijo Ruotsalainen	7	0	0	0	4
Esa Tikkanen	7	0	0	0	6

GOALTENDER	GP	W	L	MIN	GA	SO	AVG
Grant Fuhr	7	4	3	427	17	0	2.39

PHILADELPHIA	GP	G	A	PTS	PIM
Brian Propp	7	4	5	9	0
Pelle Eklund	7	1	7	8	0
Rick Tocchet	7	3	4	7	24
Ron Sutter	7	0	4	4	6
Brad McCrimmon	7	2	1	3	10
Scott Mellanby	7	1	2	3	4
Doug Crossman	7	1	2	3	6
Murray Craven	6	2	0	2	2
Peter Zezel	7	1	1	2	2
Brad Marsh	7	0	2	2	2
J.J. Daigneault	5	1	0	1	0
Lindsay Carson	6	1	0	1	0
Derrick Smith	7	1	0	1	10
Mark Howe	7	0	1	1	0
Kjell Samuelsson	7	0	1	1	10
Dave Brown	7	0	1	1	11
Tim Tookey	1	0	0	0	0
Don Nachbaur	1	0	0	0	0
Daryl Stanley	4	0	0	0	2
Ilkka Sinisalo	5	0	0	0	2
Dave Poulin	7	0	0	0	8

GOALTENDER	GP	W	L	MIN	GA	SO	AVG
Ron Hextall	7	3	4	427	22	0	3.09

1988

Includes suspended game, May 24, 1988

EDMONTON	GP	G	A	PTS	PIM
Wayne Gretzky	5	3	10	13	0
Esa Tikkanen	5	6	3	9	18
Glenn Anderson	5	3	3	6	4
Jari Kurri	5	1	4	5	4
Craig Simpson	5	3	1	4	10
Steve Smith	5	0	4	4	2
Mike Krushelnyski	5	1	2	3	6
Kevin McClelland	5	1	2	3	26
Mark Messier	5	1	2	3	4
Randy Gregg	5	0	3	3	4
Kevin Lowe	5	0	2	2	4
Craig Muni	5	0	2	2	0
Keith Acton	5	1	0	1	0
Normand Lacombe	5	1	0	1	4
Charlie Huddy	1	0	0	0	0
Jeff Beukeboom	4	0	0	0	0
Geoff Courtnall	5	0	0	0	0
Craig MacTavish	5	0	0	0	2
Marty McSorley	5	0	0	0	4

GOALTENDER	GP	W	L	MIN	GA	SO	AVG
Grant Fuhr	5	4	0	277	12	0	2.60

BOSTON	GP	G	A	PTS	PIM
Ken Linseman	5	2	2	4	6
Glen Wesley	5	2	2	4	0
Cam Neely	5	2	1	3	4
Raymond Bourque	5	0	3	3	6
Steve Kasper	5	2	0	2	2
Randy Burridge	5	1	1	2	2
Bob Joyce	5	1	1	2	0
Moe Lemay	5	1	1	2	6
Craig Janney	5	0	2	2	0
Bob Sweeney	5	0	2	2	2
Greg Hawgood	2	1	0	1	0
Greg Johnston	1	0	1	1	0
Keith Crowder	5	0	1	1	10
Gord Kluzak	5	0	1	1	4
Rick Middleton	5	0	1	1	0
Nevin Markwart	1	0	0	0	2
Tom McCarthy	1	0	0	0	0
Willi Plett	2	0	0	0	4
Reed Larson	2	0	0	0	2
Jay Miller	3	0	0	0	24
Allen Pedersen	4	0	0	0	6
Michael Thelven	4	0	0	0	6
Bill O'Dwyer	5	0	0	0	0

GOALTENDERS	GP	W	L	MIN	GA	SO	AVG
Andy Moog	3	0	2	157	11	0	4.20
Reggie Lemelin	2	0	2	120	8	0	4.00

1989

CALGARY	GP	G	A	PTS	PIM
Al MacInnis	6	5	4	9	18
Joe Mullen	6	5	3	8	4
Joel Otto	6	2	6	8	2
Doug Gilmour	6	4	3	7	6
Theoren Fleury	6	1	1	2	2
Joe Nieuwendyk	6	1	1	2	2
Colin Patterson	6	1	1	2	16
Tim Hunter	4	0	2	2	6
Jim Peplinski	4	0	2	2	10
Jamie Macoun	6	0	2	2	8
Rob Ramage	6	0	2	2	10
Lanny McDonald	3	1	0	1	2
Mark Hunter	4	0	1	1	12
Hakan Loob	6	0	1	1	0
Brian MacLellan	6	0	1	1	4
Brad McCrimmon	6	0	1	1	6
Dana Murzyn	6	0	1	1	8
Jiri Hrdina	3	0	0	0	0
Ric Nattress	6	0	0	0	12
Gary Roberts	6	0	0	0	8

GOALTENDER	GP	W	L	MIN	GA	SO	AVG
Mike Vernon	6	4	2	397	16	0	2.42

MONTREAL	GP	G	A	PTS	PIM
Chris Chelios	6	1	6	7	10
Bobby Smith	6	3	2	5	20
Mike McPhee	6	1	3	4	4
Claude Lemieux	4	1	3	4	18
Larry Robinson	6	2	1	3	4
Mike Keane	6	1	2	3	4
Mats Naslund	6	1	2	3	4
Brian Skrudland	6	0	3	3	18
Petr Svoboda	6	0	3	3	8
Russ Courtnall	6	2	0	2	12
Stephane Richer	6	1	1	2	10
Rick Green	6	1	0	1	2
Ryan Walter	6	1	0	1	4
Shayne Corson	6	0	1	1	18
Bob Gainey	6	0	1	1	4
Brent Gilchrist	2	0	0	0	4
Guy Carbonneau	6	0	0	0	6
Eric Desjardins	6	0	0	0	2
Craig Ludwig	6	0	0	0	8

GOALTENDER	GP	W	L	MIN	GA	SO	AVG
Patrick Roy	6	2	4	395	17	0	2.58

1990

EDMONTON	GP	G	A	PTS	PIM
Craig Simpson	5	4	4	8	6
Jari Kurri	5	3	5	8	2
Glenn Anderson	5	4	3	7	6
Esa Tikkanen	5	3	2	5	10
Mark Messier	5	0	5	5	6
Joe Murphy	5	2	2	4	4
Steve Smith	5	1	2	3	13
Mark Lamb	5	0	3	3	2
Adam Graves	5	2	0	2	2
Craig MacTavish	5	0	2	2	2
Reijo Ruotsalainen	5	0	2	2	2
Petr Klima	5	1	0	1	0
Martin Gelinas	5	0	1	1	2
Randy Gregg	5	0	1	1	0
Kelly Buchberger	5	0	0	0	2
Charlie Huddy	5	0	0	0	4
Kevin Lowe	5	0	0	0	0
Craig Muni	5	0	0	0	2

GOALTENDER	GP	W	L	MIN	GA	SO	AVG
Bill Ranford	5	4	1	355	8	0	1.35

BOSTON	GP	G	A	PTS	PIM
Raymond Bourque	5	3	2	5	6
Cam Neely	5	0	4	4	10
Greg Hawgood	5	1	2	3	4
Randy Burridge	5	0	2	2	2
Lyndon Byers	2	1	0	1	0
John Byce	3	1	0	1	0
Greg Johnston	4	1	0	1	4
John Carter	5	1	0	1	19
Bob Sweeney	5	0	1	1	7
Don Sweeney	5	0	1	1	6
Peter Douris	1	0	0	0	0
Andy Brickley	2	0	0	0	0
Dave Poulin	2	0	0	0	0
Jim Wiemer	2	0	0	0	0
Bobby Gould	4	0	0	0	0
Bob Carpenter	5	0	0	0	2
Dave Christian	5	0	0	0	0
Garry Galley	5	0	0	0	4
Craig Janney	5	0	0	0	0
Allen Pedersen	5	0	0	0	2
Brian Propp	5	0	0	0	0
Glen Wesley	5	0	0	0	2

GOALTENDERS	GP	W	L	MIN	GA	SO	AVG
Andy Moog	5	1	4	319	16	0	3.01

	GP	W	L	MIN	GA	SO	AVG
Reggie Lemelin	1	0	0	36	4	0	6.67

1991

PITTSBURGH	GP	G	A	PTS	PIM
Mario Lemieux	5	5	7	12	6
Larry Murphy	6	1	9	10	6
Joe Mullen	6	3	5	8	0
Kevin Stevens	6	4	3	7	27
Ron Francis	6	3	3	6	6
Jaromir Jagr	6	0	5	5	0
Phil Bourque	6	2	2	4	4
Bob Errey	6	2	1	3	8
Mark Recchi	6	2	1	3	8
Ulf Samuelsson	6	2	1	3	12
Bryan Trottier	6	1	2	3	14
Peter Taglianetti	5	0	3	3	8
Scott Young	1	1	1	2	0
Paul Coffey	5	0	2	2	0
Jim Paek	5	1	0	1	2
Troy Loney	6	1	0	1	26
Jiri Hrdina	2	0	0	0	0
Grant Jennings	2	0	0	0	2
Randy Gilhen	5	0	0	0	12
Gordie Roberts	6	0	0	0	23
Paul Stanton	6	0	0	0	8

GOALTENDERS	GP	W	L	MIN	GA	SO	AVG
Tom Barrasso	6	3	2	319	13	1	2.45
Frank Pietrangelo	1	1	0	40	3	0	4.50

MINNESOTA	GP	G	A	PTS	PIM
Dave Gagner	6	4	2	6	14
Neal Broten	6	3	1	4	2
Ulf Dahlen	6	2	2	4	2
Mike Modano	6	2	2	4	6
Bobby Smith	6	1	3	4	4
Brian Propp	6	1	3	4	4
Stew Gavin	6	0	3	3	2
Gaetan Duchesne	6	1	1	2	6
Brian Bellows	6	0	2	2	16
Shawn Chambers	6	0	2	2	6
Marc Bureau	6	1	0	1	8
Chris Dahlquist	6	0	1	1	4
Jim Johnson	6	0	1	1	10
Mark Tinordi	6	0	1	1	15
Perry Berezan	1	0	0	0	0
Doug Smail	1	0	0	0	0
Shane Churla	5	0	0	0	4
Basil McRae	5	0	0	0	26
Brian Glynn	6	0	0	0	6
Neil Wilkinson	6	0	0	0	2

GOALTENDERS	GP	W	L	MIN	GA	SO	AVG
Jon Casey	6	2	3	290	21	0	4.34
Brian Hayward	2	0	1	67	6	0	5.37

1992

PITTSBURGH	GP	G	A	PTS	PIM
Rick Tocchet	4	2	6	8	2
Mario Lemieux	4	5	2	7	0
Kevin Stevens	4	2	3	5	0
Ron Francis	4	1	2	3	0
Larry Murphy	4	1	2	3	2
Jim Paek	4	0	3	3	2
Jaromir Jagr	4	2	0	2	2
Shawn McEachern	4	0	2	2	0
Bob Errey	3	1	0	1	0
Phil Bourque	4	1	0	1	0
Troy Loney	4	0	1	1	0
Kjell Samuelsson	4	0	1	1	2
Paul Stanton	4	0	1	1	20
Dave Michayluk	1	0	0	0	0
Jiri Hrdina	3	0	0	0	0
Jock Callender	4	0	0	0	0
Gordie Roberts	4	0	0	0	8
Ulf Samuelsson	4	0	0	0	0
Bryan Trottier	4	0	0	0	2

GOALTENDER	GP	W	L	MIN	GA	SO	AVG
Tom Barrasso	4	4	0	240	10	1	2.50

CHICAGO	GP	G	A	PTS	PIM
Chris Chelios	4	1	4	5	19
Dirk Graham	4	4	0	4	0
Brian Noonan	4	0	3	3	2
Jeremy Roenick	4	2	0	2	0
Brent Sutter	4	1	1	2	0
Greg Gilbert	3	0	2	2	10
Michel Goulet	4	1	0	1	2
Bryan Marchment	4	1	0	1	2
Stu Grimson	2	0	1	1	0
Rod Buskas	3	0	1	1	0
Steve Larmer	4	0	1	1	2

	GP	G	A	PTS	PIM
Jocelyn Lemieux	4	0	1	1	0
Stephane Matteau	4	0	1	1	0
Cam Russell	1	0	0	0	0
Rob Brown	3	0	0	0	2
Mike Peluso	3	0	0	0	4
Mike Hudson	4	0	0	0	2
Frantisek Kucera	4	0	0	0	0
Steve Smith	4	0	0	0	4
Igor Kravchuk	4	0	0	0	2

GOALTENDERS	GP	W	L	MIN	GA	SO	AVG
Ed Belfour	4	0	3	187	11	0	3.53
Dominik Hasek	1	0	1	53	4	0	4.53

1993

MONTREAL	GP	G	A	PTS	PIM
Eric Desjardins	5	3	1	4	6
John LeClair	5	2	2	4	0
Kirk Muller	5	2	2	4	6
Vincent Damphousse	5	1	3	4	8
Stephan Lebeau	5	1	2	3	4
Mike Keane	4	0	3	3	2
Paul Di Pietro	5	2	0	2	0
Gilbert Dionne	5	1	1	2	4
Brian Bellows	5	1	1	2	4
Ed Ronan	5	1	1	2	6
Mathieu Schneider	5	1	1	2	8
Lyle Odelein	5	0	2	2	6
Kevin Haller	3	0	1	1	0
Benoit Brunet	5	0	1	1	2
Guy Carbonneau	5	0	1	1	0
Gary Leeman	5	0	1	1	2
Donald Dufresne	1	0	0	0	0
Sean Hill	1	0	0	0	0
Denis Savard	1	0	0	0	0
Patrice Brisebois	5	0	0	0	8
J.J. Daigneault	5	0	0	0	6

GOALTENDER	GP	W	L	MIN	GA	SO	AVG
Patrick Roy	5	4	1	315	11	0	2.10

LOS ANGELES	GP	G	A	PTS	PIM
Wayne Gretzky	5	2	5	7	2
Luc Robitaille	5	3	2	5	4
Tony Granato	5	1	3	4	10
Marty McSorley	5	2	0	2	16
Dave Taylor	3	1	1	2	6
Mike Donnelly	5	1	1	2	0
Tomas Sandstrom	5	0	2	2	4
Pat Conacher	5	1	0	1	2
Jari Kurri	5	1	0	1	2
Jimmy Carson	2	0	1	1	0
Mark Hardy	4	0	1	1	4
Rob Blake	5	0	1	1	18
Alexei Zhitnik	5	0	1	1	4
Lonnie Loach	1	0	0	0	0
Charlie Huddy	4	0	0	0	4
Corey Millen	5	0	0	0	2
Warren Rychel	5	0	0	0	2
Gary Shuchuk	5	0	0	0	0
Darryl Sydor	5	0	0	0	4
Tim Watters	5	0	0	0	0

GOALTENDER	GP	W	L	MIN	GA	SO	AVG
Kelly Hrudey	5	1	4	316	15	0	2.85

1994

NY RANGERS	GP	G	A	PTS	PIM
Brian Leetch	7	5	6	11	4
Alexei Kovalev	7	4	3	7	2
Mark Messier	7	2	5	7	17
Sergei Zubov	6	1	5	6	0
Steve Larmer	7	4	0	4	2
Adam Graves	7	1	3	4	4
Glenn Anderson	7	2	1	3	4
Doug Lidster	7	2	0	2	10
Jeff Beukeboom	7	0	2	2	25
Sergei Nemchinov	7	0	2	2	2
Greg Gilbert	7	0	1	1	2
Craig MacTavish	7	0	1	1	6
Stephane Matteau	7	0	1	1	6
Brian Noonan	7	0	1	1	0
Esa Tikkanen	7	0	1	1	12
Nick Kypreos	1	0	0	0	0
Alexander Karpovtsev	2	0	0	0	0
Joe Kocur	6	0	0	0	2
Kevin Lowe	6	0	0	0	6
Jay Wells	7	0	0	0	8

GOALTENDER	GP	W	L	MIN	GA	SO	AVG
Mike Richter	7	4	3	439	19	0	2.60

VANCOUVER	GP	G	A	PTS	PIM
Pavel Bure	7	3	5	8	15
Cliff Ronning	7	1	6	7	6
Geoff Courtnall	7	4	1	5	11
Trevor Linden	7	3	2	5	6
Jeff Brown	7	3	1	4	8
Bret Hedican	7	1	3	4	4
Jyrki Lumme	7	0	4	4	6
Greg Adams	7	1	2	3	2
Nathan LaFayette	7	0	3	3	0
Sergio Momesso	7	1	1	2	17
Murray Craven	7	0	2	2	4
Dave Babych	7	1	0	1	2
Martin Gelinas	7	1	0	1	4
Shawn Antoski	7	0	1	1	8
Gerald Diduck	7	0	1	1	6
Brian Glynn	7	0	1	1	0
Tim Hunter	7	0	0	0	18
John McIntyre	7	0	0	0	6

GOALTENDER	GP	W	L	MIN	GA	SO	AVG
Kirk McLean	7	3	4	437	20	0	2.75

1995

NEW JERSEY	GP	G	A	PTS	PIM
Neal Broten	4	3	3	6	4
John MacLean	4	1	4	5	0
Stephane Richer	4	2	2	4	0
Scott Niedermayer	4	1	3	4	0
Bill Guerin	4	0	4	4	12
Shawn Chambers	4	2	1	3	0
Bruce Driver	4	1	2	3	0
Claude Lemieux	4	2	0	2	4
Jim Dowd	1	1	1	2	2
Sergei Brylin	3	1	1	2	4
Bobby Holik	4	1	1	2	8
Tom Chorske	3	0	2	2	0
Tommy Albelin	4	0	2	2	2
Scott Stevens	4	0	2	2	4
Randy McKay	4	1	0	1	0
Brian Rolston	2	0	1	1	0
Bob Carpenter	4	0	1	1	2
Valeri Zelepukin	3	0	0	0	4
Mike Peluso	4	0	0	0	0
Ken Daneyko	4	0	0	0	6

GOALTENDER	GP	W	L	MIN	GA	SO	AVG
Martin Brodeur	4	4	0	206	7	0	1.75

DETROIT	GP	G	A	PTS	PIM
Sergei Fedorov	4	3	2	5	0
Doug Brown	4	0	3	3	2
Viacheslav Fetisov	4	0	3	3	0
Dino Ciccarelli	4	1	1	2	6
Paul Coffey	4	1	1	2	0
Nicklas Lidstrom	4	0	2	2	0
Steve Yzerman	4	1	0	1	0
Vyacheslav Kozlov	4	1	0	1	0
Martin Lapointe	2	0	1	1	8
Ray Sheppard	3	0	1	1	0
Kris Draper	4	0	0	0	4
Bob Errey	4	0	0	0	4
Bob Rouse	4	0	0	0	0
Vladimir Konstantinov	4	0	0	0	8
Darren McCarty	4	0	0	0	4
Shawn Burr	2	0	0	0	0
Stu Grimson	2	0	0	0	2
Mark Howe	2	0	0	0	0
Mike Krushelnyski	2	0	0	0	0
Mike Ramsey	2	0	0	0	0
Tim Taylor	2	0	0	0	2
Keith Primeau	3	0	0	0	8

GOALTENDERS	GP	W	L	MIN	GA	SO	AVG
Mike Vernon	4	0	4	240	14	0	4.08
Chris Osgood	1	0	0	32	1	0	1.88

1996

COLORADO	GP	G	A	PTS	PIM
Peter Forsberg	4	3	2	5	0
Joe Sakic	4	1	4	5	2
Adam Deadmarsh	4	0	4	4	4
Uwe Krupp	4	2	1	3	2
Rene Corbet	4	2	1	3	0
Valeri Kamensky	4	1	2	3	8
Jon Klemm	4	2	0	2	0
Mike Keane	4	1	1	2	0
Scott Young	4	1	1	2	0
Alexei Gusarov	4	0	2	2	0
Sandis Ozolinsh	4	0	2	2	4
Claude Lemieux	2	1	0	1	4
Mike Ricci	4	1	0	1	6

	GP	G	A	PTS	PIM
Adam Foote	4	0	1	1	4
Sylvain Lefebvre	4	0	1	1	2
Curtis Leschyshyn	4	0	1	1	4
Dave Hannan	3	0	0	0	0
Warren Rychel	3	0	0	0	19

GOALTENDER	GP	W	L	MIN	GA	SO	AVG
Patrick Roy	4	4	0	285	4	1	0.84

FLORIDA	GP	G	A	PTS	PIM
Ed Jovanovski	4	0	2	2	11
Stu Barnes	4	1	0	1	2
Tom Fitzgerald	4	1	0	1	0
Rob Niedermayer	4	1	0	1	2
Ray Sheppard	4	1	0	1	0
Johan Garpenlov	4	0	1	1	2
Bill Lindsay	4	0	1	1	4
Dave Lowery	4	0	1	1	2
Scott Mellanby	4	0	1	1	4
Martin Straka	4	0	1	1	0
Radek Dvorak	1	0	0	0	0
Jody Hull	2	0	0	0	0
Jason Woolley	2	0	0	0	0
Rhett Warrener	3	0	0	0	0
Terry Carkner	4	0	0	0	4
Mike Hough	4	0	0	0	0
Paul Laus	4	0	0	0	2
Gord Murphy	4	0	0	0	0
Brian Skrudland	4	0	0	0	4
Robert Svehla	4	0	0	0	2

GOALTENDERS	GP	W	L	MIN	GA	SO	AVG
John Vanbiesbrouck	4	0	4	245	11	0	2.69
Mark Fitzpatrick	1	0	0	40	4	0	6.00

1997

DETROIT	GP	G	A	PTS	PIM
Sergei Fedorov	4	3	3	6	2
Steve Yzerman	4	3	1	4	0
Brendan Shanahan	4	3	1	4	0
Kirk Maltby	4	2	1	3	2
Martin Lapointe	4	2	1	3	6
Darren McCarty	4	1	2	3	4
Larry Murphy	4	0	3	3	0
Joe Kocur	4	1	1	2	2
Viacheslav Fetisov	4	0	2	2	10
Vyacheslav Kozlov	4	0	2	2	0
Nicklas Lidstrom	4	1	0	1	0
Kris Draper	4	0	1	1	2
Doug Brown	4	0	1	1	2
Tomas Sandstrom	4	0	1	1	4
Mike Vernon	4	0	1	1	0
Igor Larionov	4	0	0	0	4
Vladimir Konstantinov	4	0	0	0	2
Bob Rouse	4	0	0	0	0
Aaron Ward	4	0	0	0	0

GOALTENDER	GP	W	L	MIN	GA	SO	AVG
Mike Vernon	4	4	0	240	6	0	1.50

PHILADELPHIA	GP	G	A	PTS	PIM
Rod Brind'Amour	4	3	1	4	0
John LeClair	4	2	1	3	4
Eric Lindros	4	1	2	3	8
Janne Niinimaa	4	0	3	3	0
Eric Desjardins	4	0	2	2	2
Mikael Renberg	4	0	1	1	0
John Druce	4	0	0	0	0
Joel Otto	4	0	0	0	0
Kjell Samuelsson	4	0	0	0	0
Trent Klatt	4	0	0	0	6
Shjon Podein	4	0	0	0	2
Chris Therien	4	0	0	0	0
Dainius Zubrus	4	0	0	0	0
Dale Hawerchuk	3	0	0	0	2
Karl Dykhuis	3	0	0	0	2
Pat Falloon	3	0	0	0	0
Colin Forbes	3	0	0	0	0
Paul Coffey	2	0	0	0	6
Daniel Lacroix	2	0	0	0	2
Michel Petit	2	0	0	0	2
Petr Svoboda	1	0	0	0	2
Dan Kordic	1	0	0	0	0

GOALTENDERS	GP	W	L	MIN	GA	SO	AVG
Ron Hextall	3	0	3	178	12	0	4.04
Garth Snow	1	0	1	58	4	0	4.11

1998

DETROIT	GP	G	A	PTS	PIM
Doug Brown	4	3	2	5	0
Tomas Holmstrom	4	1	4	5	2
Steve Yzerman	4	2	2	4	2
Martin Lapointe	4	2	1	3	6

	GP	G	A	PTS	PIM
Sergei Fedorov	4	1	2	3	0
Viacheslav Fetisov	4	0	3	3	2
Nicklas Lidstrom	4	1	1	2	2
Larry Murphy	4	1	1	2	0
Igor Larionov	4	0	2	2	4
Darren McCarty	4	0	2	2	2
Kris Draper	4	1	0	1	2
Joe Kocur	4	1	0	1	4
Anders Eriksson	4	0	1	1	4
Vyacheslav Kozlov	4	0	1	1	0
Bob Rouse	4	0	1	1	2
Brendan Shanahan	4	0	1	1	0
Jamie Macoun	4	0	0	0	0
Kirk Maltby	4	0	0	0	6

GOALTENDER	GP	W	L	MIN	GA	SO	AVG
Chris Osgood	4	4	0	254	7	0	1.65

WASHINGTON	GP	G	A	PTS	PIM
Joe Juneau	4	1	3	4	0
Brian Bellows	4	2	1	3	0
Adam Oates	4	1	2	3	0
Peter Bondra	4	1	1	2	4
Jeff Brown	2	0	2	2	0
Andrei Nikolishin	4	0	2	2	2
Chris Simon	4	1	0	1	6
Richard Zednik	4	1	0	1	4
Sergei Gonchar	4	0	1	1	4
Dale Hunter	4	0	1	1	2
Calle Johansson	4	0	1	1	2
Craig Berube	4	0	1	1	0
Phil Housley	4	0	0	0	2
Joe Reekie	4	0	0	0	2
Esa Tikkanen	4	0	0	0	0
Mark Tinordi	4	0	0	0	6
Kelly Miller	3	0	0	0	0
Mike Eagles	2	0	0	0	0
Ken Klee	2	0	0	0	0
Todd Krygier	2	0	0	0	2
Jeff Toms	1	0	0	0	0

GOALTENDER	GP	W	L	MIN	GA	SO	AVG
Olaf Kolzig	4	0	4	251	13	0	3.11

1999

DALLAS	GP	G	A	PTS	PIM
Mike Modano	6	0	7	7	8
Jere Lehtinen	6	2	3	5	0
Brett Hull	5	3	0	3	0
Joe Nieuwendyk	6	2	1	3	9
Jamie Langenbrunner	6	1	2	3	4
Sergei Zubov	6	0	3	3	2
Derian Hatcher	6	1	1	2	10
Craig Ludwig	6	1	1	2	10
Richard Matvichuk	6	0	2	2	6
Dave Reid	6	0	2	2	2
Darryl Sydor	6	1	0	1	8
Pat Verbeek	6	1	0	1	4
Shawn Chambers	6	0	1	1	2
Mike Keane	6	0	1	1	2
Brian Skrudland	6	0	1	1	8
Tony Hrkac	3	0	1	1	2
Guy Carbonneau	6	0	0	0	0
Blake Sloan	6	0	0	0	0
Benoit Hogue	2	0	0	0	2
Jon Sim	2	0	0	0	0

GOALTENDER	GP	W	L	MIN	GA	SO	AVG
Ed Belfour	6	4	2	429	9	1	1.26

BUFFALO	GP	G	A	PTS	PIM
Stu Barnes	6	3	0	3	0
Alexei Zhitnik	6	1	2	3	18
Richard Smehlik	6	0	3	3	2
Wayne Primeau	6	1	1	2	4
Jason Woolley	6	1	1	2	6
Michael Peca	6	1	0	1	2
Geoff Sanderson	6	1	0	1	4
Dixon Ward	6	1	0	1	8
Curtis Brown	6	0	1	1	2
Brian Holzinger	6	0	1	1	9
Joe Juneau	6	0	1	1	0
Miroslav Satan	6	0	1	1	2
Dominik Hasek	6	0	0	0	2
Jay McKee	6	0	0	0	2
James Patrick	6	0	0	0	4
Erik Rasmussen	6	0	0	0	2
Vaclav Varada	6	0	0	0	6
Rhett Warrener	5	0	0	0	6
Michal Grosek	1	0	0	0	0
Paul Kruse	1	0	0	0	0
Rob Ray	1	0	0	0	0

GOALTENDER	GP	W	L	MIN	GA	SO	AVG
Dominik Hasek	6	2	4	428	12	0	1.68

2000

NEW JERSEY	GP	G	A	PTS	PIM
Jason Arnott	6	4	3	7	2
Petr Sykora	6	3	2	5	4
Patrik Elias	6	0	5	5	0
Brian Rafalski	6	1	3	4	4
Sergei Brylin	6	2	1	3	0
Scott Stevens	6	1	2	3	2
Ken Daneyko	6	1	1	2	4
John Madden	6	1	1	2	0
Alexander Mogilny	6	1	1	2	0
Jay Pandolfo	6	0	2	2	0
Scott Niedermayer	6	1	0	1	2
Scott Gomez	6	0	1	1	0
Bobby Holik	6	0	1	1	4
Claude Lemieux	6	0	1	1	4
Vladimir Malakhov	6	0	1	1	4
Randy McKay	6	0	1	1	2
Sergei Nemchinov	6	0	1	1	2
Colin White	6	0	1	1	4

GOALTENDER	GP	W	L	MIN	GA	SO	AVG
Martin Brodeur	6	4	2	434	9	0	1.24

DALLAS	GP	G	A	PTS	PIM
Brett Hull	6	2	2	4	2
Mike Modano	6	1	3	4	0
Jere Lehtinen	6	0	3	3	2
Mike Keane	6	1	1	2	2
Darryl Sydor	6	1	1	2	0
Guy Carbonneau	6	0	2	2	0
Sylvain Cote	6	1	0	1	2
Kirk Muller	6	1	0	1	0
Joe Nieuwendyk	6	1	0	1	0
Jon Sim	6	1	0	1	6
Richard Matvichuk	6	0	1	1	4
Scott Thornton	6	0	1	1	4
Aaron Gavey	1	0	0	0	0
Jamie Langenbrunner	1	0	0	0	0
Grant Marshall	3	0	0	0	0
Blake Sloan	3	0	0	0	2
Roman Lyashenko	4	0	0	0	0
Derian Hatcher	6	0	0	0	6
Dave Manson	6	0	0	0	6
Brenden Morrow	6	0	0	0	4
Sergei Zubov	6	0	0	0	0

GOALTENDERS	GP	W	L	MIN	GA	SO	AVG
Ed Belfour	6	2	4	416	14	1	2.02
Manny Fernandez	1	0	0	17	1	0	3.53

2001

COLORADO	GP	G	A	PTS	PIM
Joe Sakic	7	4	5	9	2
Alex Tanguay	7	4	3	7	4
Rob Blake	7	2	3	5	4
Chris Drury	7	3	1	4	0
Adam Foote	7	1	3	4	16
Dan Hinote	7	1	3	4	11
Ville Nieminen	7	1	2	3	6
Martin Skoula	7	1	2	3	6
Milan Hejduk	7	0	3	3	0
Raymond Bourque	7	1	1	2	2
Steve Reinprecht	7	1	1	2	0
Chris Dingman	7	0	2	2	10
Dave Reid	7	0	2	2	2
Eric Messier	7	0	1	1	6
Shjon Podein	7	0	1	1	6
Greg De Vries	7	0	0	0	6
Jon Klemm	7	0	0	0	2
Stephane Yelle	7	0	0	0	4

GOALTENDER	GP	W	L	MIN	GA	SO	AVG
Patrick Roy	7	4	3	419	11	2	1.58

NEW JERSEY	GP	G	A	PTS	PIM
Patrik Elias	7	2	3	5	2
Petr Sykora	7	2	2	4	4
Alexander Mogilny	7	1	2	3	4
Brian Rafalski	7	0	3	3	0
Jason Arnott	6	1	1	2	4
Bob Corkum	6	1	1	2	0
Sergei Brylin	7	1	1	2	6
Scott Gomez	7	1	1	2	4
Turner Stevenson	7	1	1	2	6
Bobby Holik	7	0	2	2	6
Scott Niedermayer	7	0	2	2	8
John Madden	7	1	0	1	2
Jay Pandolfo	7	0	1	1	0
Randy McKay	1	0	0	0	0

	GP	G	A	PTS	PIM
Jim McKenzie	1	0	0	0	2
Ken Sutton	2	0	0	0	9
Sean O'Donnell	5	0	0	0	25
Ken Daneyko	7	0	0	0	13
Sergei Nemchinov	7	0	0	0	0
Scott Stevens	7	0	0	0	6
Colin White	7	0	0	0	14

GOALTENDER	GP	W	L	MIN	GA	SO	AVG
Martin Brodeur	7	3	4	416	19	0	2.74

2002

DETROIT	GP	G	A	PTS	PIM
Sergei Fedorov	5	1	4	5	6
Igor Larionov	5	3	1	4	4
Steve Yzerman	5	0	4	4	0
Brendan Shanahan	5	3	0	3	6
Brett Hull	5	2	1	3	2
Nicklas Lidstrom	5	1	2	3	2
Chris Chelios	5	0	3	3	4
Kirk Maltby	5	2	0	2	4
Tomas Holmstrom	5	1	1	2	0
Kris Draper	5	1	1	2	4
Fredrik Olausson	5	0	2	2	2
Jiri Fischer	4	0	1	1	4
Darren McCarty	5	0	1	1	2
Boyd Devereaux	5	0	1	1	4
Luc Robitaille	5	0	1	1	4
Steve Duchesne	5	0	1	1	8
Jiri Slegr	1	0	0	0	2
Pavel Datsyuk	5	0	0	0	0
Mathieu Dandenault	5	0	0	0	2

GOALTENDER	GP	W	L	MIN	GA	SO	AVG
Dominik Hasek	5	4	1	355	7	1	1.18

CAROLINA	GP	G	A	PTS	PIM
Jeff O'Neill	5	3	1	4	2
Ron Francis	5	1	2	3	0
Sean Hill	5	1	1	2	12
Sami Kapanen	5	0	2	2	0
Glen Wesley	5	0	2	2	4
Rod Brind'Amour	5	1	0	1	4
Josef Vasicek	5	1	0	1	4
Aaron Ward	5	1	0	1	4
Martin Gelinas	5	0	1	1	4
Jeff Daniels	5	0	0	0	0
Marek Malik	5	0	0	0	0
Tommy Westlund	5	0	0	0	0
Kevyn Adams	5	0	0	0	0
Niclas Wallin	5	0	0	0	2
Bates Battaglia	5	0	0	0	0
Bret Hedican	5	0	0	0	4
Jaroslav Svoboda	5	0	0	0	8
Erik Cole	5	0	0	0	10

GOALTENDER	GP	W	L	MIN	GA	SO	AVG
Arturs Irbe	5	1	4	354	13	0	2.20

CHAPTER 18

Players on Stanley Cup-Winning Teams

1893 – 2002

A TOTAL OF 1,036 PLAYERS HAVE SKATED FOR Stanley Cup championship teams since the trophy was first awarded to the Montreal Amateur Athletic Association (Mtl. AAA) hockey club in 1893. Of the 1036 winners, 551 (53.2%) have won one Cup title, while 485 (46.8%) have won on two or more occasions.

Cup wins	1	2	3	4	5	6	7	8	9	10	11
Players	551	257	83	82	36	18	2	3	1	2	1
Pct.	53.2	24.8	8.0	7.9	3.5	1.7					

Henri Richard holds the record for playing on the most Stanley Cup champions, winning 11 times in his career. During Richard's 20 years with the Montreal Canadiens from 1955-56 to 1974-75, "The Pocket Rocket" never played more than four consecutive seasons without earning a new Stanley Cup ring.

Jean Beliveau and Yvan Cournoyer of the Canadiens share second place behind Richard with 10 Cup wins apiece, and Montreal's Claude Provost ranks third with nine. Red Kelly, Maurice Richard and Jacques Lemaire are tied with eight, while Serge Savard and Jean-Guy Talbot have seven each. Kelly is the only player to rank among these all-time Stanley Cup winners without ever playing for the Canadiens. He won the Cup four times with Detroit in the 1950s and four times with Toronto in the 1960s.

Kelly, Jack Marshall, Bob Goldham, Dick Duff, Frank Mahovlich, Bryan Trottier, Larry Murphy and Patrick Roy (still active) are the only players in history to win multiple Stanley Cup titles with two different teams. Of the 486 players to win more than one Stanley Cup championship, 365 won with the same team every time. Another 112 players won with two teams, while eight won with three and one won with four.

Marshall owns the record for playing with four different teams to win the Stanley Cup. Marshall played on championship teams with the 1901 Winnipeg Victorias, 1902 and 1903 Montreal AAA, 1907 and 1910 Montreal Wanderers and 1914 Toronto Blueshirts.

Eight players have skated for three different Stanley Cup winning franchises in their careers. Frank Foyston, Jack Walker and Mike Keane (still active) had Cup wins with three different clubs, while Claude Lemieux (still active), Hap Holmes, Al Arbour and Gord Pettinger won four Cup titles with three separate teams. Larry Hillman was a six-time winner with Detroit, Toronto and Montreal.

A

Abel, Clarence	NY Rangers 28; Chicago 34
Abel, Sid	Detroit 43,50,52
Acton, Keith	Edmonton 88
Acer, Douglas	Mtl. Victorias 1899
Adams, Jack	Toronto 18; Ottawa 27
Aebischer, David	Colorado 2001
Aitkenhead, Andy	NY Rangers 33
Albelin, Tommy	New Jersey 95
Allen, Bones	Ottawa 05
Allen, Keith	Detroit 54
Anderson, Doug	Montreal 53
Anderson, Glenn	Edmonton 84,85,87,88,90; NY Rangers 94
Anderson, Jocko	Victoria 25
Andrews, Lloyd	Toronto 22
Apps, Syl	Toronto 42,47,48
Arbour, Al	Detroit 54; Chicago 61; Toronto 62,64
Arbour, Amos	Montreal 16
Armitage, Jack	Wpg. Victorias 1896
Armstrong, George	Toronto 62,63,64,67
Arnold, Josh	Mtl. Wanderers 06
Arnott, Jason	New Jersey 2000
Ashbee, Barry	Philadelphia 74
Asmundson, Oscar	NY Rangers 33
Aurie, Larry	Detroit 36,37
Awrey, Don	Boston 70,72

B

Babando, Pete	Detroit 50
Backor, Pete	Toronto 45
Backstrom, Ralph	Montreal 59,60,65,66,68,69

Bailey, Ace	Toronto 32
Bailey, Garnet	Boston 72
Bain, Dan	Wpg. Victorias 1896,01,02
Balfour, Earl	Chicago 61
Balfour, Murray	Chicago 61
Balon, Dave	Montreal 65,66
Barber, Bill	Philadelphia 74,75
Barilko, Bill	Toronto 47,48,49,51
Barlow, Billy	Mtl. AAA 1893,94
Barrasso, Tom	Pittsburgh 91,92
Barry, Marty	Detroit 36,37
Bathgate, Andy	Toronto 64
Bauer, Bobby	Boston 39,41
Baun, Bob	Toronto 62,63,64,67
Beaudro, Roxy	Kenora 07
Belfour, Ed	Dallas 99
Beliveau, Jean	Montreal 56,57,58,59,60,65, 66,68,69,71
Bell, Billy	Montreal 24
Bellingham, Billy	Mtl. AAA 02,03
Bellows, Brian	Montreal 93
Benedict, Clint	Ottawa 20,21,23; Mtl. Maroons 26
Benoit, Joe	Montreal 46
Bentley, Max	Toronto 48,49,51
Berenson, Red	Montreal 65
Berlinquette, Louis	Montreal 16
Beukeboom, Jeff	Edmonton 87,88,90; NY Rangers 94
Blachford, Cecil	Mtl. AAA 03; Mtl. Wanderers 06,07,08,10
Black, Steve	Detroit 50
Bladon, Tom	Philadelphia 74,75
Blair, Andy	Toronto 32

Blake, Rob	Colorado 2001
Blake, Toe	Mtl. Maroons 35; Montreal 44,46
Blinco, Russ	Mtl. Maroons 35
Bodnar, Gus	Toronto 45,47
Boesch, Garth	Toronto 47,48,49
Boisvert, Serge	Montreal 86
Bolton, Hugh	Toronto 51
Bombardir, Brad	New Jersey 2000
Bonin, Marcel	Detroit 55; Montreal 58,59,60
Boon, Dickie	Mtl. AAA 02,03
Bordeleau, Christian	Montreal 69
Bossy, Mike	NY Islanders 80,81,82,83
Bouchard, Butch	Montreal 44,46,53,56
Bouchard, Pierre	Montreal 71,73,76,77,78
Boucher, Billy	Montreal 24
Boucher, Bobby	Montreal 24
Boucher, Frank	NY Rangers 28,33
Boucher, Georges	Ottawa 20,21,23,27
Bourgeault, Leo	NY Rangers 28
Bourne, Bob	NY Islanders 80,81,82,83
Bourque, Phil	Pittsburgh 91,92
Bourque, Raymond	Colorado 2001
Boutilier, Paul	NY Islanders 83
Bower, Johnny	Toronto 62,63,64,67
Bowie, Russell	Mtl. Victorias 1899
Bowman, Ralph	Detroit 36,37
Boyd, Bill	NY Rangers 28
Brannen, Jack	Mtl. Shamrocks 1899,1900
Brennan, Doug	NY Rangers 33
Brewer, Carl	Toronto 62,63,64
Brimsek, Frank	Boston 39,41
Brisebois, Patrice	Montreal 93

Broadbent, Punch — Ottawa 20,21,23; Mtl. Maroons 26
Broda, Turk — Toronto 42,47,48,49,51
Broden, Connie — Montreal 57,58
Brodeur, Martin — New Jersey 95,2000
Brophy, Bernie — Mtl. Maroons 26
Broten, Neal — New Jersey 95
Brown, Adam — Detroit 43
Brown, Connie — Detroit 43
Brown, Dave — Edmonton 90
Brown, Doug — Detroit 97,98
Brown, G. — Wpg. Victorias 01,02
Bruce, Morley — Ottawa 20,21
Brule, Steve — New Jersey 2000
Brunet, Benoit — Montreal 93
Bruneteau, Mud — Detroit 36,37,43
Brylin, Sergei — New Jersey 95,2000
Buchberger, Kelly — Edmonton 87,90
Bucyk, John — Boston 70,72
Burke, Marty — Montreal 30,31

C

Cadham, F. — Wpg. Victorias 02
Cain, Herb — Mtl. Maroons 35; Boston 41
Callander, Jock — Pittsburgh 92
Callighen, Patsy — NY Rangers 28
Cameron, Allan — Mtl. AAA 1893,94
Cameron, Billy — Montreal 24
Cameron, Harry — Toronto 14,18,22
Campbell, Tote — Wpg. Victorias 1896
Carbonneau, Guy — Montreal 86, 93; Dallas 99
Carleton, Wayne — Boston 70
Carpenter, Bob — New Jersey 95
Carpenter, Ed — Seattle 17
Carr, Lorne — Toronto 42,45
Carroll, Billy — NY Islanders 81,82,83; Edmonton 85
Carson, Bill — Boston 29
Carson, Frank — Mtl. Maroons 26
Carson, Gerry — Montreal 30
Carveth, Joe — Detroit 43,50
Cashman, Wayne — Boston 70,72
Caufield, Jay — Pittsburgh 91,92
Chabot, Lorne — NY Rangers 28; Toronto 32
Chamberlain, Murph — Montreal 44,46
Chambers, Shawn — New Jersey 95; Dallas 99
Chartraw, Rick — Montreal 76,77,78,79
Cheevers, Gerry — Boston 70,72
Chelios, Chris — Montreal 86; Detroit 2002
Chorske, Tom — New Jersey 95
Chychrun, Jeff — Pittsburgh 92
Clancy, King — Ottawa 23,27; Toronto 32
Clapper, Dit — Boston 29,39,41
Clarke, Bobby — Philadelphia 74,75
Cleghorn, Odie — Montreal 24
Cleghorn, Sprague — Ottawa 20,21; Montreal 24
Clement, Bill — Philadelphia 74,75
Coffey, Paul — Edmonton 84,85,87; Pittsburgh 91
Cole, Danton — New Jersey 95
Collins, Herb — Mtl. AAA 1894
Colville, Mac — NY Rangers 40
Colville, Neil — NY Rangers 40
Conacher, Brian — Toronto 67
Conacher, Charlie — Toronto 32
Conacher, Lionel — Chicago 34; Mtl. Maroons 35
Conacher, Pat — Edmonton 84
Conacher, Roy — Boston 39,41
Connell, Alex — Ottawa 27; Mtl. Maroons 35
Connelly, Bert — Chicago 38
Connor, Cam — Montreal 79
Cook, Bill — NY Rangers 28,33
Cook, Bun — NY Rangers 28,33
Cook, Lloyd — Vancouver 15
Cook, Tom — Chicago 34
Corbeau, Bert — Montreal 16
Corbeau, Con — Toronto 14
Corbet, Rene — Colorado 96
Costello, Les — Toronto 48
Cotton, Baldy — Toronto 32
Coughlin, Jack — Toronto 18
Coulter, Art — Chicago 34; NY Rangers 40
Cournoyer, Yvan — Montreal 65,66,68,69,71,73, 76,77,78,79
Courtnall, Geoff — Edmonton 88
Coutu, Billy — Montreal 24
Couture, Gerry — Detroit 50

Couture, Rosie — Chicago 34
Cowick, Bruce — Philadelphia 74
Cowley, Bill — Boston 39,41
Crawford, Jack — Boston 39,41
Crawford, Rusty — Quebec 13; Toronto 18
Creighton, Billy — Quebec 13
Crisp, Terry — Philadelphia 74,75
Currie, Alex — Ottawa 11
Curry, Floyd — Montreal 53,56,57,58

D

Dahlin, Kjell — Montreal 86
Dahlstrom, Cully — Chicago 38
Daigneault, J.J. — Montreal 93
Damphousse, Vincent — Montreal 93
Dandenault, Mathieu — Detroit 97,98,2002
Daneyko, Ken — New Jersey 95,2000
Daniels, Jeff — Pittsburgh 92
Darragh, Harold — Toronto 32
Darragh, Jack — Ottawa 11,20,21,23
Datsyuk, Pavel — Detroit 2002
Davidson, Bob — Toronto 42,45
Davidson, Cam — Mtl. Victorias 1896,97,98,99
Davidson, Scotty — Toronto 14
Davidson, Shirley — Mtl. Victorias 1895,96,97
Davis, Lorne — Montreal 53
Dawes, Bob — Toronto 49
Day, Hap — Toronto 32
Deadmarsh, Adam — Colorado 96
Dean, Kevin — New Jersey 95
DeBlois, Lucien — Montreal 86
DeJordy, Denis — Chicago 61
Delvecchio, Alex — Detroit 52,54,55
Denneny, Corb — Toronto 18,22
Denneny, Cy — Ottawa 20,21,23,27; Boston 29
Desjardins, Eric — Montreal 93
de Vries, Greg — Colorado 2001
Devereaux, Boyd — Detroit 2002
Dewsbury, Al — Detroit 50
Dey, Edgar — Ottawa 09
Dickens, Ernie — Toronto 42
Dillon, Cecil — NY Rangers 33
Dineen, Bill — Detroit 54,55
Dingman, Chris — Colorado 2001
Dinsmore, Chuck — Mtl. Maroons 26
Dion — Ottawa 06
Dionne, Gilbert — Montreal 93
Di Pietro, Paul — Montreal 93
Doak, Gary — Boston 70
Dobby, John — Mtl. Shamrocks 1899
Dornhoefer, Gary — Philadelphia 74,75
Douglas, Kent — Toronto 63
Douglas, Les — Detroit 43
Dowd, Jim — New Jersey 95
Draper, Kris — Detroit 97,98,2002
Drillon, Gordie — Toronto 42
Drinkwater, Graham — Mtl. Victorias 1895,96,97,98,99
Driver, Bruce — New Jersey 95
Drury, Chris — Colorado 2001
Dryden, Ken — Montreal 71,73,76,77,78,79
Dube, Gilles — Detroit 54
Duchesne, Steve — Detroit 2002
Duff, Dick — Toronto 62,63; Montreal 65,66,68,69
Dufresne, Donald — Montreal 93
Dumart, Woody — Boston 39,41
Dupont, Andre — Philadelphia 74,75
Durnan, Bill — Montreal 44,46
Dye, Babe — Toronto 22

E

Ebbs — Ottawa 06
Eddolls, Frank — Montreal 46
Ehman, Gerry — Toronto 64
Elias, Patrik — New Jersey 2000
Elliot, Roland — Mtl. Victorias 1895; Mtl. AAA 02
Ellis, Ron — Toronto 67
Elmer, Wally — Victoria 25
Engblom, Brian — Montreal 77,78,79
Erickson, Aut — Toronto 67
Eriksson, Anders — Detroit 98
Errey, Bob — Pittsburgh 91,92
Esposito, Phil — Boston 70,72

Esposito, Tony — Montreal 69
Evans, Jack — Chicago 61
Evans, Stewart — Mtl. Maroons 35
Ewen, Todd — Montreal 93
Ewing, Jack — Mtl. Victorias 1897,98,99
Ezinicki, Bill — Toronto 47,48,49

F

Farrell, Art — Mtl. Shamrocks 1899,1900
Fedorov, Sergei — Detroit 97,98,2002
Fenwick, Art — Mtl. Victorias 1895
Ferguson, John — Montreal 65,66,68,69,71
Fetisov, Viacheslav — Detroit 97,98
Fillion, Bob — Montreal 44,46
Finnie, Dave — Ottawa 05
Finnigan, Frank — Ottawa 27; Toronto 32
Fischer, Jiri — Detroit 2002
Fiset, Stephane — Colorado 96
Fisher, Joe — Detroit 43
Flaman, Fern — Toronto 51
Fleming, Reggie — Chicago 61
Flett, Bill — Philadelphia 74
Flett, Magnus — Wpg. Victorias 01,02
Flett, Rod — Wpg. Victorias 1896,01,02
Fleury, Theoren — Calgary 89
Fogolin, Lee — Detroit 50
Fogolin, Jr., Lee — Edmonton 84,85
Foote, Adam — Colorado 96,2001
Forsberg, Peter — Colorado 96,2001
Fortier, Charles — Montreal 24
Fortier, Charles — Montreal 16
Foyston, Frank — Toronto 14; Seattle 17; Victoria 25
Francis, Ron — Pittsburgh 91,92
Franks, Jimmy — Detroit 37
Fraser, A.A. — Ottawa 03
Fraser, Gord — Victoria 25
Fredrickson, Frank — Victoria 25
Frost, Harry — Boston 39
Fuhr, Grant — Edmonton 84,85,87,88,90

G

Gagnon, Johnny — Montreal 31
Gainey, Bob — Montreal 76,77,78,79,86
Gainor, Dutch — Boston 29
Galbraith, Percy — Boston 29
Gallagher, John — Detroit 37
Gamble, Bruce — Toronto 67
Gamble, Dick — Montreal 53
Gardiner, Charlie — Chicago 34
Gardner, Cal — Toronto 49,51
Gardner, Jimmy — Mtl. AAA 02,03; Mtl. Wanderers 10
Gatherum, Dave — Detroit 54
Gaul, Horace — Ottawa 05,11
Gauthier, Jean — Montreal 65
Gee, George — Detroit 50
Gelinas, Martin — Edmonton 90
Geoffrion, Bernie — Montreal 53,56,57,58,59,60
Gerard, Eddie — Ottawa 20,21,23; Toronto 22
Getliffe, Ray — Boston 39; Montreal 44
Gilbert, Greg — NY Islanders 82,83; NY Rangers 94
Gilchrist, Brent — Detroit 98
Gilhen, Randy — Pittsburgh 91
Gillilan, David — Mtl. Victorias 1896,97
Gillies, Clark — NY Islanders 80,81,82,83
Gilmour, Billy — Ottawa 03,04,05,06,09
Gilmour, Dave — Ottawa 03
Gilmour, Doug — Calgary 89
Gilmour, Larry — Mtl. Wanderers 08
Gilmour, Suddy — Ottawa 03,04
Gingras, Gaston — Montreal 86
Gingras, Tony — Wpg. Victorias 01,02
Giroux, Eddie — Kenora 07
Glass, Pud — Mtl. Wanderers 06,07,08,10
Goldham, Bob — Toronto 42,47; Detroit 52,54,55
Goldsworthy, Leroy — Chicago 34
Goldup, Hank — Toronto 42
Gomez, Scott — New Jersey 2000
Goodenough, Larry — Philadelphia 75
Goodfellow, Ebbie — Detroit 36,37,43
Goodman, Paul — Chicago 38
Goring, Butch — NY Islanders 80,81,82,83
Gorman, Ed — Ottawa 27
Gottselig, Johnny — Chicago 34,38

Goyette, Phil — Montreal 57,58,59,60
Gracie, Bob — Toronto 32; Mtl. Maroons 35
Graham, Leth — Ottawa 21
Grant, Danny — Montreal 68
Grant, Mike — Mtl. Victorias 1895,96,97,98,99
Graves, Adam — Edmonton 90; NY Rangers 94
Gray, Alex — NY Rangers 28
Green, Red — Boston 29
Green, Rick — Montreal 86
Green, Ted — Boston 72
Gregg, Randy — Edmonton 84,85,87,88,90
Grenier, Lucien — Montreal 69
Gretzky, Wayne — Edmonton 84,85,87,88
Griffis, Si — Kenora 07; Vancouver 15
Grosso, Don — Detroit 43
Guerin, Bill — New Jersey 95
Gusarov, Alexei — Colorado 96

H

Hague, Billy — Ottawa 06
Haidy, Gord — Detroit 50
Hainsworth, George — Montreal 30,31
Halderson, Harold — Victoria 25
Hall, Glenn — Detroit 52; Chicago 61
Hall, Joe — Kenora 07; Quebec 12,13
Haller, Kevin — Montreal 93
Halliday, Milt — Ottawa 27
Hallin, Mats — NY Islanders 83
Hamill, Red — Boston 39
Hamilton, Reg — Toronto 42,45
Hannan, Dave — Edmonton 88; Colorado 96
Harmon, Glen — Montreal 44,46
Harper, Terry — Montreal 65,66,68,69,71
Harris, Billy — Toronto 62,63,64
Harris, Ted — Montreal 65,66,68,69; Philadelphia 75
Harriston — Toronto 14
Hart, Gizzy — Victoria 25
Hartman, Mike — NY Rangers 94
Harvey, Doug — Montreal 53,56,57,58,59,60
Hasek, Dominik — Detroit 2002
Hassard, Bob — Toronto 51
Hatcher, Derian — Dallas 99
Hay, Bill — Chicago 61
Hay, Jim — Detroit 55
Hayes, Chris — Boston 72
Healy, Glenn — NY Rangers 94
Hebert, Sammy — Toronto 18
Heffernan, Gerry — Montreal 44
Heller, Ott — NY Rangers 33,40
Hejduk, Milan — Colorado 2001
Helman, Harry — Ottawa 23
Henderson, Harold — Mtl. Victorias 1895,96,97
Henning, Lorne — NY Islanders 80,81
Hern, Riley — Mtl. Wanderers 07,08,10
Hextall, Bryan — NY Rangers 40
Hicke, Bill — Montreal 59,60
Hicks, Wayne — Chicago 61
Higginbotham, Fred — Wpg. Victorias 1896
Hill, Mel — Boston 39,41; Toronto 45
Hill, Sean — Montreal 93
Hiller, Dutch — NY Rangers 40; Montreal 46
Hillier, Randy — Pittsburgh 91
Hillman, Larry — Detroit 55; Toronto 62,63,64,67; Montreal 69
Hillman, Wayne — Chicago 61
Hinote, Dan — Colorado 2001
Hitchman, Lionel — Ottawa 23; Boston 29
Hodge, Charlie — Montreal 56,59,60,65,66
Hodge, Ken — Boston 70,72
Hodge, Tom — Mtl. AAA 02,03
Hodgson, Archie — Mtl. AAA 1893,94
Hodson, Kevin — Detroit 97, 98
Hoerner, Charles — Mtl. Shamrocks 1899
Hogue, Benoit — Dallas 99
Holik, Bobby — New Jersey 95,2000
Hollett, Flash — Boston 39, 41
Holmes, Hap — Toronto 14,18; Seattle 17; Victoria 25
Holmstrom, Tomas — Detroit 97,98,2002
Holway, Albert — Mtl. Maroons 26
Hooper, Art — Mtl. AAA 02,03
Hooper, Tom — Kenora 07; Mtl. Wanderers 08
Horne, George — Mtl. Maroons 26
Horner, Red — Toronto 32

Horton, Tim — Toronto 62,63,64,67
Houle, Rejean — Montreal 71,73,77,78,79
Howard, Attie — Wpg. Victorias 1896
Howatt, Garry — NY Islanders 80,81
Howe, Gordie — Detroit 50,52,54,55
Howe, Syd — Detroit 36,37,43
Hrdina, Jiri — Calgary 89; Pittsburgh 91,92
Hrkac, Tony — Dallas 99
Huddy, Charlie — Edmonton 84,85,87,88,90
Hudson, Mike — NY Rangers 94
Hughes, Pat — Montreal 79; Edmonton 84,85
Hull, Bobby — Chicago 61
Hull, Brett — Dallas 99; Detroit 2002
Hunter, Dave — Edmonton 84,85,87
Hunter, Mark — Calgary 89
Hunter, Tim — Calgary 89
Hutton, Bouse — Ottawa 03,04
Hyland, Harry — Mtl. Wanderers 10

I-J

Irving, Alex — Mtl. AAA 1893, 94
Jackson, Art — Boston 41; Toronto 45
Jackson, Busher — Toronto 32
Jackson, Don — Edmonton 84,85
Jackson, Harold — Chicago 38; Detroit 43
Jackson, Stan — Toronto 22
Jagr, Jaromir — Pittsburgh 91,92
James, George — Mtl. AAA 1894
Jarvis, Doug — Montreal 76,77,78,79
Jeffrey, Larry — Toronto 67
Jenkins, Roger — Chicago 34,38
Jennings, Grant — Pittsburgh 91,92
Johnson, Ching — NY Rangers 28,33
Johnson, Moose — Mtl. Wanderers 06,07,08,10
Johnson, Tom — Montreal 53,56,57,58,59,60
Johnson, Virgil — Chicago 38
Johnston, Eddie — Boston 70,72
Johnstone, Charles — Wpg. Victorias 1896,01,02
Johnstone, Ross — Toronto 45
Joliat, Aurel — Montreal 24,30,31
Jones, Robert — Mtl. Victorias 1895,96
Jonsson, Tomas — NY Islanders 82,83
Juzda, Bill — Toronto 49,51

K

Kallur, Anders — NY Islanders 80,81,82,83
Kamensky, Valeri — Colorado 96
Kampman, Bingo — Toronto 42
Karakas, Mike — Chicago 38
Karpovtsev, Alexander — NY Rangers 94
Keane, Mike — Montreal 93; Colorado 96; Dallas 99
Keeling, Butch — NY Rangers 33
Kelly, Bob — Philadelphia 74,75
Kelly, Pete — Detroit 36,37
Kelly, Red — Detroit 50,52,54,55; Toronto 62,63,64,67
Kelly, Steve — New Jersey 2000
Kendall, Bill — Chicago 34
Kennedy, Rod — Mtl. Wanderers 06,07
Kennedy, Ted — Toronto 45,47,48,49,51
Keon, Dave — Toronto 62,63,64,67
Kerr, Albert — Ottawa 09,10,11
Kerr, Dave — NY Rangers 40
Kilrea, Hec — Ottawa 27; Detroit 36,37
Kilrea, Wally — Detroit 36,37
Kindrachuk, Orest — Philadelphia 74,75
Kingan, A.B. — Mtl. AAA 1893,94
Kitchen, Hobie — Mtl. Maroons 26
Klemm, Jon — Colorado 96,2001
Klima, Petr — Edmonton 90
Klukay, Joe — Toronto 47,48,49,51
Knuble, Mike — Detroit 98
Kocur, Joe — NY Rangers 94; Detroit 97,98
Konstantinov, Vladimir — Detroit 97
Kordic, John — Montreal 86
Kovalev, Alexei — NY Rangers 94
Kozlov, Vyacheslav — Detroit 97,98
Krupp, Uwe — Colorado 96; Detroit 2002
Krushelnyski, Mike — Edmonton 85,87,88
Kurri, Jari — Edmonton 84,85,87,88,90
Kurvers, Tom — Montreal 86
Kypreos, Nick — NY Rangers 94

L

Lach, Elmer — Montreal 44,46,53

Lacombe, Normand — Edmonton 88
Lafleur, Guy — Montreal 73,76,77,78,79
Lake, Fred — Ottawa 09,10,11
Lalonde, Newsy — Montreal 16
Lalor, Mike — Montreal 86
Lamb, Mark — Edmonton 90
Lambert, Yvon — Montreal 76,77,78,79
Lamoureux, Leo — Montreal 44,46
Lane, Gord — NY Islanders 80,81,82,83
Lane, Myles — Boston 29
Langelle, Pete — Toronto 42
Langenbrunner, Jamie — Dallas 99
Langevin, Dave — NY Islanders 80,81,82,83
Langlois, Albert — Montreal 58,59,60
Langway, Rod — Montreal 79
Laperriere, Jacques — Montreal 65,66,68,69,71,73
Lapointe, Guy — Montreal 71,73,76,77,78,79
Lapointe, Martin — Detroit 97,98
Larionov, Igor — Detroit 97,98,2002
Larmer, Steve — NY Rangers 94
Larochelle, Wildor — Montreal 30,31
Larocque, Michel — Montreal 76,77,78,79
Larose, Claude — Montreal 65,66,68,71,73
Larouche, Pierre — Montreal 78,79
Laviolette, Jack — Montreal 16
Leach, Jamie — Pittsburgh 92
Leach, Reggie — Philadelphia 75
Lebeau, Stephan — Montreal 93
Leclair, Jack — Montreal 56
LeClair, John — Montreal 93
Leduc, Albert — Montreal 30,31
Leeman, Gary — Montreal 93
Leetch, Brian — NY Rangers 94
Lefebvre, Sylvain — Colorado 96
Lefley, Chuck — Montreal 71,73
Legace, Manny — Detroit 2002
Lehman, Hugh — Vancouver 15
Lehtinen, Jere — Dallas 99
Lemaire, Jacques — Montreal 68,69,71,73,76, 77,78,79
Lemay, Moe — Edmonton 87
Lemieux, Claude — Montreal 86; New Jersey 95,2000; Colorado 96
Lemieux, Mario — Pittsburgh 91,92
Leonard, George — Quebec 12
Lepine, Pit — Montreal 30,31
Leschyshyn, Curtis — Colorado 96
Lesieur, Art — Montreal 31
LeSueur, Percy — Ottawa 06,09,10,11
Lesuk, Bill — Boston 70
Leswick, Jack — Chicago 34
Leswick, Tony — Detroit 52,54,55
Levinsky, Alex — Toronto 32; Chicago 38
Lewicki, Danny — Toronto 51
Lewis, Gordon — Mtl. Victorias 1896,97,98,99
Lewis, Herbie — Detroit 36,37
Lidster, Doug — NY Rangers 94
Lidstrom, Nicklas — Detroit 97,98,2002
Liffiton, Charles — Mtl. AAA 02,03
Liffiton, Ernie — Mtl. Wanderers 08
Lindsay, Ted — Detroit 50,52,54,55
Lindstrom, Willy — Edmonton 84,85
Linseman, Ken — Edmonton 84
Liscombe, Carl — Detroit 43
Litzenberger, Ed — Chicago 61; Toronto 62,63,64
Loney, Troy — Pittsburgh 91,92
Lonsberry, Ross — Philadelphia 74,75
Loob, Hakan — Calgary 89
Lorentz, Jim — Boston 70
Lorimer, Bob — NY Islanders 80,81
Loughlin, Clem — Victoria 25
Lowe, Jim — Mtl. AAA 1893
Lowe, Kevin — Edmonton 84,85,87,88,90; NY Rangers 94
Ludwig, Craig — Montreal 86; Dallas 99
Lumley, Dave — Edmonton 84,85
Lumley, Harry — Detroit 50
Lupien, Gilles — Montreal 78,79
Lynn, Vic — Toronto 47,48,49

M

MacAdam, Al — Philadelphia 74
MacDonald, Kilby — NY Rangers 40
MacInnis, Al — Calgary 89
MacKay, Calum — Montreal 53

Reddick, Pokey — Edmonton 90
Redmond, Mickey — Montreal 68,69
Reibel, Dutch — Detroit 54,55
Reid, Dave — Dallas 99; Colorado 2001
Reinprecht, Steve — Colorado 2001
Reise, Jr., Leo — Detroit 50,52
Resch, Glenn — NY Islanders 80
Ricci, Mike — Colorado 96
Richard, Henri — Montreal 56,57,58,59,60,65,66,68,69,71,73
Richard, Maurice — Montreal 44,46,53,56,57,58,59,60
Richardson, Frank — Mtl. Victorias 1898,99
Richer, Stephane — Montreal 86; New Jersey 95
Richter, Mike — NY Rangers 94
Rickey, Roy — Seattle 17
Ridpath, Bruce — Ottawa 10,11
Riley, Jim — Seattle 17
Risebrough, Doug — Montreal 76,77,78,79
Rivers, Gus — Montreal 30,31
Roach, John Ross — Toronto 22
Roberge, Mario — Montreal 93
Roberto, Phil — Montreal 71
Roberts, Gary — Calgary 89
Roberts, Gord — Mtl. Wanderers 10
Roberts, Gordie — Pittsburgh 91,92
Roberts, Jimmy — Montreal 65,66,73,76,77
Robertson, Earl — Detroit 37
Robertson, Fred — Toronto 32
Robinson, Earl — Mtl. Maroons 35
Robinson, Larry — Montreal 73,76,77,78,79,86
Robitaille, Luc — Detroit 2002
Rochefort, Leon — Montreal 66,71
Rodden, Eddie — Boston 29
Rollins, Al — Toronto 51
Rolston, Brian — New Jersey 95
Romnes, Doc — Chicago 34,38
Ronan, Ed — Montreal 93
Ronan, Skene — Montreal 16
Rooney, Steve — Montreal 86
Rooney, Walter — Quebec 12
Ross, Art — Kenora 07; Mtl. Wanderers 08
Rothschild, Sam — Mtl. Maroons 26
Roulston, Rolly — Detroit 37
Rouse, Bob — Detroit 97,98
Rousseau, Bobby — Montreal 65,66,68,69
Routh, Haviland — Mtl. AAA 1893,94
Rowe, Bobby — Seattle 17
Roy, Patrick — Montreal 86,93; Colorado 96,2001
Ruotsalainen, Reijo — Edmonton 87,90
Russell, Ernie — Mtl. Wanderers 06,07,08,10
Rychel, Warren — Colorado 96

S

St. Laurent, Dollard — Montreal 53,56,57,58; Chicago 61
Sakic, Joe — Colorado 96,2001
Saleski, Don — Philadelphia 74,75
Samis, Phil — Toronto 48
Samuelsson, Kjell — Pittsburgh 92
Samuelsson, Ulf — Pittsburgh 91,92
Sanderson, Derek — Boston 70,72
Sands, Charlie — Boston 39
Sandstrom, Tomas — Detroit 97
Savard, Denis — Montreal 93
Savard, Serge — Montreal 68,69,73,76,77,78,79
Sawchuk, Terry — Detroit 52,54,55; Toronto 67
Scanlon, Fred — Mtl. Shamrocks 1899,1900; Wpg. Victorias 02
Schmidt, Milt — Boston 39,41
Schneider, Mathieu — Montreal 93
Schock, Danny — Boston 70
Schriner, Sweeney — Toronto 42,45
Schultz, Dave — Philadelphia 74,75
Scott — Ottawa 04
Seaborn, Jim — Vancouver 15
Seibert, Earl — NY Rangers 33; Chicago 38
Semenko, Dave — Edmonton 84,85
Sevigny, Richard — Montreal 79
Shack, Eddie — Toronto 62,63,64,67
Shanahan, Brendan — Detroit 97,98,2002
Sheehan, Bobby — Montreal 71
Sheppard, Johnny — Chicago 34
Sherf, John — Detroit 37
Shewchuck, Jack — Boston 41

Shibicky, Alex — NY Rangers 40
Shields, Al — Mtl. Maroons 35
Shill, Jack — Chicago 38
Shore, Eddie — Boston 29,39
Shore, Hamby — Ottawa 05,10,11
Shutt, Steve — Montreal 73,76,77,78,79
Siebert, Babe — Mtl. Maroons 26; NY Rangers 33
Sim, Jon — Dallas 99
Simmons, Don — Toronto 62,63,64
Simon, Chris — Colorado 96
Simon, Cully — Detroit 43
Simpson, Craig — Edmonton 88,90
Sims, Percy — Ottawa 03
Skinner, Alf — Toronto 18
Skoula, Martin — Colorado 2001
Skov, Glen — Detroit 52,54,55
Skrudland, Brian — Montreal 86; Dallas 99
Slegr, Jiri — Detroit 2002
Sloan, Blake — Dallas 99
Sloan, Tod — Toronto 51; Chicago 61
Smaill, Walter — Mtl. Wanderers 08
Smith, Alex — Ottawa 27
Smith, Alf — Ottawa 04,05,06; Kenora 07
Smith, Billy — NY Islanders 80,81,82,83
Smith, Bobby — Montreal 86
Smith, Clint — NY Rangers 40
Smith, Dallas — Boston 70,72
Smith, Des — Boston 41
Smith, Geoff — Edmonton 90
Smith, George — Mtl. AAA 03
Smith, Harry — Ottawa 06
Smith, Hooley — Ottawa 27; Mtl. Maroons 35
Smith, Normie — Detroit 36,37
Smith, Rick — Boston 70
Smith, Sid — Toronto 48,49,51
Smith, Stan — NY Rangers 40
Smith, Steve — Edmonton 87,88,90
Smith, Tommy — Ottawa 06; Quebec 13
Smylie, Rod — Toronto 22
Soetaert, Doug — Montreal 86
Somers, Art — NY Rangers 33
Sorrell, John — Detroit 36,37
Speer, Bill — Boston 70
Spittal, Charles — Ottawa 03
Stackhouse, Ted — Toronto 22
Stanfield, Fred — Boston 70,72
Stanley, Allan — Toronto 62,63,64,67
Stanley, Barney — Vancouver 15
Stanowski, Wally — Toronto 42,45,47,48
Stanton, Paul — Pittsburgh 91,92
Stasiuk, Vic — Detroit 52,55
Stemkowski, Pete — Toronto 67
Stephenson, Wayne — Philadelphia 75
Stevens, Kevin — Pittsburgh 91,92
Stevens, Scott — New Jersey 95,2000
Stewart, Gaye — Toronto 42,47
Stewart, Jack — Detroit 43,50
Stewart, James — Mtl. AAA 1893,94
Stewart, Nels — Mtl. Maroons 26
Stewart, Ron — Toronto 62,63,64
Strachan, Billy — Mtl. Wanderers 06,07
Stuart, Billy — Toronto 22
Stuart, Bruce — Mtl. Wanderers 08; Ottawa 09,10,11
Stuart, Hod — Mtl. Wanderers 07
Summanen, Raimo — Edmonton 84
Suter, Gary — Calgary 89
Sutter, Brent — NY Islanders 82,83
Sutter, Duane — NY Islanders 80,81,82,83
Sutton, Ken — New Jersey 2000
Svoboda, Petr — Montreal 86
Sydor, Darryl — Dallas 99
Sykora, Petr — New Jersey 2000

T

Taglianetti, Peter — Pittsburgh 91,92
Talbot, Jean-Guy — Montreal 56,57,58,59,60,65,66
Tambellini, Steve — NY Islanders 80
Tanguay, Alex — Colorado 2001
Tansey, Frank — Mtl. Shamrocks 1899,1900
Tardif, Marc — Montreal 71,73
Taylor, Billy — Toronto 42
Taylor, Bobby — Philadelphia 74
Taylor, Cyclone — Ottawa 09; Vancouver 15

Taylor, Harry — Toronto 49
Taylor, Tim — Detroit 97
Terreri, Chris — New Jersey 95,2000
Thompson, Paul — NY Rangers 28; Chicago 34,38
Thompson, Tiny — Boston 29
Thomson, Jimmy — Toronto 47,48,49,51
Tikkanen, Esa — Edmonton 85,87,88,90; NY Rangers 94
Timgren, Ray — Toronto 49,51
Tocchet, Rick — Pittsburgh 92
Tonelli, John — NY Islanders 80,81,82,83
Tremblay, Gilles — Montreal 66,68
Tremblay, J.C. — Montreal 65,66,68,69,71
Tremblay, Mario — Montreal 76,77,78,79,86
Trihey, Harry — Mtl. Shamrocks 1899,1900
Trottier, Bryan — NY Islanders 80,81,82,83; Pittsburgh 91,92
Trottier, Dave — Mtl. Maroons 35
Trudel, Lou — Chicago 34,38
Turek, Roman — Dallas 99
Turner, Bob — Montreal 56,57,58,59,60

V

Vachon, Rogie — Montreal 68,69,71
Vadnais, Carol — Montreal 68; Boston 72
Van Impe, Ed — Philadelphia 74,75
Vasko, Moose — Chicago 61
Verbeek, Pat — Dallas 99
Vernon, Mike — Calgary 89; Detroit 97
Vezina, Georges — Montreal 16,24
Voss, Carl — Chicago 38

W

Walker, Jack — Toronto 14; Seattle 17; Victoria 25
Wall, Frank — Mtl. Shamrocks 1899,1900
Wallace, W. — Mtl. Victorias 1896
Walsh, Marty — Ottawa 09,10,11
Walter, Ryan — Montreal 86
Walton, Mike — Toronto 67; Boston 72
Wamsley, Rick — Calgary 89
Wand, Toad — Mtl. AAA 1894
Ward, Aaron — Detroit 97,98
Ward, Jimmy — Mtl. Maroons 35
Wares, Eddie — Detroit 43
Wasnie, Nick — Montreal 30,31
Watson, Harry — Detroit 43; Toronto 47,48,49,51
Watson, Jimmy — Philadelphia 74,75
Watson, Joe — Philadelphia 74,75
Watson, Phil — NY Rangers 40; Montreal 44
Weiland, Cooney — Boston 29,39
Wells, Jay — NY Rangers 94
Wentworth, Cy — Mtl. Maroons 35
Westfall, Ed — Boston 70,72
Westwick, Harry — Ottawa 03,04,05,06; Kenora 07
Wharram, Kenny — Chicago 61
Whitcroft, Fred — Kenora 07
White, Colin — New Jersey 2000
White, Frank — Ottawa 05
Wiebe, Art — Chicago 38
Willett, Stanley — Mtl. Victorias 1896
Williams, Jason — Detroit 2002
Wilson, Cully — Toronto 14; Seattle 17
Wilson, Johnny — Detroit 50,52,54,55
Wilson, Larry — Detroit 50
Wilson, Murray — Montreal 73,76,77,78
Wiseman, Eddie — Boston 41
Woit, Benny — Detroit 52,54,55
Wolanin, Craig — Colorado 96
Wood, Burke — Wpg. Victorias 01,02
Wood, F.H. — Ottawa 03
Worsley, Gump — Montreal 65,66,68,69
Wregget, Ken — Pittsburgh 92

Y-Z

Yelle, Stephane — Colorado 96,2001
Young, Doug — Detroit 36,37
Young, Scott — Pittsburgh 91; Colorado 96
Young, Wendell — Pittsburgh 91,92
Yzerman, Steve — Detroit 97,98,2002
Zeidel, Larry — Detroit 52
Zelepukin, Valeri — New Jersey 95
Zubov, Sergei — NY Rangers 94; Dallas 99

CHAPTER 19

Final Series Scoring Register

1918 – 2002

A

PLAYER	YRS	GP	G	A	PTS	PIM
Clarence Abel	4	16	0	1	1	22
Sid Abel	7	34	9	11	20	25
Keith Acton	1	5	1	0	1	0
Bill Adams	1	4	0	0	0	0
Greg Adams	1	7	1	2	3	2
Jack Adams	3	14	8	2	10	8
Kevyn Adams	1	5	0	0	0	0
Stewart Adams	1	5	2	1	3	2
Tommy Albelin	1	4	0	2	2	2
George Allen	2	10	4	3	7	10
Keith Allen	1	3	0	0	0	0
Ray Allison	1	1	0	0	0	0
Earl Anderson	1	2	0	0	0	0
Ernie Anderson	1	2	0	0	0	2
Glenn Anderson	7	38	16	13	29	59
Jocko Anderson	2	5	1	0	1	10
Ron Anderson	1	1	0	0	0	2
Kent-Erik Andersson	1	5	1	0	1	0
Lloyd Andrews	1	5	2	0	2	3
Lou Angotti	2	13	3	3	6	9
Shawn Antoski	1	7	0	1	1	8
Syl Apps	6	32	10	11	21	6
Al Arbour	7	20	0	2	2	6
Ty Arbour	2	7	1	0	1	0
Bob Armstrong	2	10	1	1	2	8
George Armstrong	6	33	9	13	22	22
Murray Armstrong	2	9	2	0	2	0
Jason Arnott	2	12	5	4	9	6
Oscar Asmundson	1	4	0	1	1	2
Ossie Aubuchon	1	1	0	0	0	0
Larry Aurie	2	8	2	3	5	2
Don Awrey	2	10	0	1	1	33

B

PLAYER	YRS	GP	G	A	PTS	PIM
Pete Babando	1	5	2	2	4	2
Dave Babych	1	7	1	0	1	2
Ralph Backstrom	8	42	11	12	23	22
Ace Bailey	1	7	1	0	1	2
Garnet Bailey	1	6	1	0	1	14
Earl Balfour	1	6	0	0	0	0
Murray Balfour	2	11	4	4	8	15
Dave Balon	3	16	2	4	6	18
Bill Barber	4	22	5	10	15	17
Bill Barilko	4	19	1	3	4	33
Doug Barkley	2	12	0	3	3	14
Norm Barnes	1	1	0	0	0	4
Stu Barnes	2	10	4	0	4	2
Fred Barrett	1	3	0	0	0	6
Marty Barry	3	11	5	3	8	8
Robin Bartel	1	4	0	0	0	12
Jim Bartlett	1	2	0	0	0	0
Andy Bathgate	2	13	4	5	9	16
Bates Battaglia	1	5	0	0	0	4
Bobby Bauer	3	19	5	2	7	2
Bob Baun	6	32	2	6	8	67
Paul Baxter	1	4	0	1	1	17
Jean Beliveau	12	64	30	32	62	78
Billy Bell	1	3	0	0	0	0
Neil Belland	1	4	0	0	0	4
Brian Bellows	3	15	3	4	7	20
Clint Benedict	1	6	0	0	0	2
Bobby Benson	1	2	0	0	0	0
Doug Bentley	1	4	1	2	3	2
Max Bentley	3	13	4	10	14	2
Red Berenson	4	19	3	2	5	17
Perry Berezan	2	3	0	0	0	4
Todd Bergen	1	4	1	1	2	0
Gary Bergman	1	6	0	1	1	4
Louis Berlinguette	*1	5	1	1	2	0
Craig Berube	1	4	0	0	0	0
Jeff Beukeboom	2	11	0	2	2	25

PLAYER	YRS	GP	G	A	PTS	PIM
Jack Bionda	1	5	0	0	0	6
Steve Black	1	6	0	0	0	0
Tom Bladon	3	14	1	5	6	31
Andy Blair	4	12	2	0	2	6
Rob Blake	2	12	2	4	6	22
Toe Blake	3	15	4	9	13	7
Russ Blinco	1	3	1	1	2	0
Gus Bodnar	2	8	1	0	1	2
Garth Boesch	3	14	1	0	1	10
Serge Boisvert	1	2	0	0	0	0
Leo Boivin	3	17	0	2	2	19
Ivan Boldirev	1	4	2	0	2	2
Buzz Boll	4	11	3	1	4	2
Peter Bondra	1	4	1	1	2	4
Marcel Bonin	4	21	3	6	9	22
Carl Boone	2	11	0	1	1	14
Christian Bordeleau	1	3	0	0	0	0
J.P. Bordeleau	1	6	1	0	1	4
Mike Bossy	5	23	17	17	34	4
Helge Bostrum	3	8	1	0	1	8
Butch Bouchard	9	44	2	10	12	61
Pierre Bouchard	5	21	3	1	4	19
Billy Boucher	1	4	0	0	0	0
Bobby Boucher	3	11	6	2	8	19
Frank Boucher	7	25	11	7	18	8
Georges Boucher	*4	20	6	1	7	45
Andre Boudrias	1	3	0	0	0	2
Leo Bourgeault	2	7	0	0	0	6
Bob Bourne	4	19	4	9	13	37
Phil Bourque	3	17	4	6	10	14
Raymond Bourque	2	10	3	5	8	12
Paul Boutilier	1	5	0	2	2	0
Ralph Bowman	2	9	1	1	2	4
Bill Boyd	2	6	0	0	0	2
Irvin Boyd	1	4	0	0	0	2
Steve Bozek	1	4	2	0	2	19
Connie Braden	2	5	0	1	1	0
Brian Bradley	1	1	0	0	0	0
Per-Olov Brasar	1	1	0	0	0	0
Doug Brennan	2	7	1	0	1	6
Carl Brewer	5	25	0	6	6	56
Andy Brickley	1	2	0	0	0	0
Mel Bridgman	2	10	1	5	6	57
Rod Brind'Amour	2	9	4	1	5	4
Patrice Brisebois	1	5	0	0	0	8
Punch Broadbent	*4	19	9	1	10	34
Neal Broten	3	15	6	5	11	4
Adam Brown	2	9	0	1	1	6
Connie Brown	1	3	0	2	2	0
Curtis Brown	1	6	0	1	1	2
Dave Brown	2	8	0	1	1	30
Doug Brown	3	12	3	6	9	4
Fred Brown	1	5	0	0	0	0
Jeff Brown	2	9	3	3	6	8
Jerry Brown	1	7	2	0	2	4
Rob Brown	1	3	0	0	0	4
Morley Bruce	1	5	0	0	0	0
Benoit Brunet	1	5	0	1	1	2
Eddie Bruneteau	3	12	2	1	3	0
Mud Bruneteau	6	30	8	4	12	8
Sergei Brylin	3	16	4	3	7	10
Kelly Buchberger	2	8	0	0	0	7
John Bucyk	6	29	8	6	14	14
Tony Bukovich	1	1	0	0	0	0
Pavel Bure	1	7	3	5	8	15
Marc Bureau	1	6	1	0	1	8
Marty Burke	2	7	0	2	2	2
Shawn Burr	1	2	0	0	0	0
Randy Burridge	2	10	1	3	4	4
Cummy Burton	1	1	0	0	0	0
Eddie Bush	1	6	1	5	6	16
Rod Buskas	1	3	0	1	1	0
Mike Busniuk	1	6	2	1	3	7
Walter Buswell	4	11	0	1	1	2
Garth Butcher	1	1	0	0	0	0

	YRS	GP	G	A	PTS	PIM
John Byce	1	3	1	0	1	0
Lyndon Byers	1	2	1	0	1	0

C

PLAYER	YRS	GP	G	A	PTS	PIM
Jack Caffery	1	5	0	0	0	0
Herb Cain	4	14	0	5	5	2
Jock Callender	1	4	0	0	0	0
Pat Callighen	1	5	0	0	0	0
Billy Cameron	1	4	0	0	0	0
Craig Cameron	2	3	1	0	1	0
Harry Cameron	*2	9	3	3	6	23
Colin Campbell	1	4	0	1	1	26
Earl Campbell	1	2	0	0	0	0
Guy Carbonneau	5	28	0	6	6	29
Terry Carkner	1	4	0	0	0	4
Wayne Carleton	1	4	1	1	2	0
Jack Carlson	1	2	0	0	0	0
Bob Carpenter	2	9	0	1	1	4
Gene Carr	1	6	0	0	0	9
Lorne Carr	2	14	3	2	5	11
Larry Carriere	1	6	0	0	0	4
Gene Carrigan	1	3	0	0	0	0
Billy Carroll	5	16	2	4	6	2
Bill Carson	2	4	1	0	1	2
Frank Carson	3	11	0	1	1	0
Gerry Carson	2	3	0	0	0	0
Jimmy Carson	1	2	0	1	1	0
Lindsay Carson	2	9	1	2	3	2
John Carter	1	5	1	0	1	19
Joe Carveth	4	25	7	4	11	6
Wayne Cashman	5	26	7	6	13	79
Murph Chamberlain	7	29	5	2	7	18
Shawn Chambers	3	16	2	4	6	8
Rick Chartraw	4	14	2	1	3	16
Chris Chelios	4	20	3	16	19	52
Real Chevrefils	2	10	0	1	1	8
Tom Chorske	1	3	0	2	2	0
Dave Christian	1	5	0	0	0	0
Steve Christoff	1	5	2	2	4	0
Jack Church	3	8	0	1	1	4
Shane Churla	1	5	0	0	0	4
Dino Ciccarelli	2	9	4	3	7	25
King Clancy	6	24	5	3	8	28
Dit Clapper	6	18	2	2	4	2
Bobby Clarke	4	22	9	12	21	22
Odie Cleghorn	3	13	2	1	3	9
Sprague Cleghorn	5	22	3	4	7	48
Bill Clement	2	8	2	0	2	4
Paul Coffey	7	33	8	18	26	30
Erik Cole	1	5	0	0	0	10
Mac Colville	2	11	0	2	2	6
Neil Colville	2	11	3	4	7	12
Brian Conacher	1	6	1	1	2	19
Charlie Conacher	4	13	3	3	6	14
Jim Conacher	4	4	1	0	1	0
Lionel Conacher	2	7	1	0	1	10
Pat Conacher	2	7	2	0	2	2
Roy Conacher	3	10	6	4	10	6
Harry Connor	1	2	0	0	0	0
Bill Cook	4	14	3	5	8	24
Bun Cook	4	14	5	2	7	18
Leo Cook	1	5	0	0	0	6
Lloyd Cook	*5	21	5	2	7	38
Tom Cook	2	9	0	1	1	7
Joe Cooper	2	9	1	2	3	18
Bert Corbeau	*1	5	0	1	1	3
Rene Corbet	1	4	2	1	3	0
Bob Corkum	1	6	1	1	2	0
Shayne Corson	1	6	0	1	1	18
Les Costello	1	4	1	2	3	0
Murray Costello	1	6	0	0	0	0
Charlie Cotch	2	3	0	0	0	0
Ray Cote	1	4	0	0	0	0
Sylvain Cote	1	6	1	0	1	2

PLAYER	YRS	GP	G	A	PTS	PIM
Baldy Cotton	—	3	10	1	2	3	12
Art Coulter	3	15	2	2	4	18
Yvan Cournoyer	9	50	21	19	40	18
Yves Courteau	1	1	0	0	0	0
Geoff Courtnall	2	12	4	1	5	11
Russ Courtnall	1	6	2	0	2	12
Billy Coutu	*4	17	1	1	2	12
Gerry Couture	2	10	4	2	6	0
Rosie Couture	2	9	1	2	3	4
Bruce Cowick	1	6	0	0	0	7
Bill Cowley	3	14	1	11	12	6
Murray Craven	3	18	3	4	7	10
Jack Crawford	4	17	3	3	6	6
Marc Crawford	1	3	0	0	0	0
Rusty Crawford	*1	2	0	0	0	0
Dave Creighton	2	10	1	2	3	0
Terry Crisp	6	23	1	6	7	4
Doug Crossman	2	12	1	4	5	18
Keith Crowder	1	5	0	1	1	10
Barry Cullen	1	1	0	0	0	0
Brian Cullen	1	3	0	0	0	0
Floyd Curry	8	41	12	8	20	10

D

PLAYER	YRS	GP	G	A	PTS	PIM
Ulf Dahlen	1	6	2	2	4	0
Kjell Dahlin	1	4	1	0	1	0
Chris Dahlquist	1	6	0	1	1	4
Cully Dahlstrom	2	8	1	3	4	2
J.J. Daigneault	2	10	1	0	1	6
Bob Dailey	1	6	1	3	4	4
Vincent Damphousse	1	5	1	3	4	8
Mathieu Dandenault	1	5	0	0	0	2
Ken Daneyko	3	17	1	1	2	23
Jeff Daniels	1	5	0	0	0	0
Harry Darragh	1	3	0	0	0	0
Jack Darragh	*2	10	10	2	12	10
Pavel Datsyuk	1	5	0	0	0	0
Bob Davidson	6	33	2	7	9	31
Lorne Davis	2	12	1	0	1	8
Bob Dawes	2	5	0	0	0	4
Hap Day	4	14	1	3	4	14
Adam Deadmarsh	1	4	0	4	4	4
Lucien DeBlois	1	2	0	0	0	0
Ron Delorme	1	4	0	0	0	4
Alex Delvecchio	8	47	16	22	38	2
Ab DeMarco	2	5	1	0	1	0
Corb Denneny	3	13	6	3	9	2
Cy Denneny	5	21	7	5	12	21
Norm Dennis	1	1	0	0	0	2
Syd Desireau	2	6	0	0	0	0
Eric Desjardins	4	15	3	3	6	108
Vic Desjardins	2	8	0	0	0	0
Greg De Vries	1	7	0	0	0	6
Boyd Devereaux	1	5	0	1	1	4
Al Dewsbury	2	6	0	3	3	8
Ernie Dickens	1	5	0	0	0	4
Gerald Diduck	1	7	0	1	1	6
Bob Dillabough	2	2	0	0	0	0
Cecil Dillon	3	12	4	3	7	8
Bill Dineen	3	19	1	0	1	6
Gord Dineen	1	3	0	0	0	24
Chris Dingman	1	7	0	2	2	10
Chuck Dinsmore	1	4	0	0	0	2
Gilbert Dionne	1	5	1	1	2	4
Paul DiPietro	1	5	2	0	2	0
Gary Doak	4	19	1	0	1	44
Mike Donnelly	1	5	1	1	2	0
Ken Doraty	2	5	3	0	3	2
Jim Dorey	1	1	0	0	0	0
Gary Dornhoefer	3	13	2	1	3	20
Kent Douglas	1	5	0	1	1	2
Les Douglas	1	4	2	1	3	2
Peter Douris	1	1	0	0	0	0
Jim Dowd	1	1	1	1	2	2
Kris Draper	4	17	2	2	4	12
Gordie Drillon	4	20	6	3	9	6
Bruce Driver	1	4	1	2	3	0
John Druce	1	4	0	0	0	0
Chris Drury	1	7	3	1	4	0
Gilles Dube	1	2	0	0	0	0
Gaetan Duchesne	1	6	1	1	2	6
Steve Duchesne	1	5	0	1	1	8
Rick Dudley	1	4	0	1	1	9
Dick Duff	9	47	15	20	35	39
Donald Dufresne	1	1	0	0	0	0
Ron Duguay	1	5	2	0	2	4

PLAYER	YRS	GP	G	A	PTS	PIM
Woody Dumart	4	19	2	6	8	4
Art Duncan	4	16	4	4	8	10
Andre Dupont	4	22	4	3	7	64
Red Dutton	2	2	1	1	2	17
Miroslav Dvorak	1	5	0	0	0	2
Radek Dvorak	1	1	0	0	0	0
Babe Dye	1	5	9	1	10	3
Karl Dykhuis	1	3	0	0	0	2

E

PLAYER	YRS	GP	G	A	PTS	PIM
Mike Eagles	1	2	0	0	0	0
Mike Eaves	1	2	0	0	0	2
Tim Ecclestone	3	12	0	2	2	18
Frank Eddolls	3	16	0	1	1	4
Darryl Edestrand	2	8	0	0	0	2
Garry Edmundson	1	4	0	1	1	2
Pat Egan	2	12	2	1	3	8
Gerry Ehman	3	15	1	4	5	8
Pelle Eklund	1	7	1	7	8	0
Anders Eldebrink	1	3	0	0	0	2
Patrik Elias	2	13	2	8	10	2
Ron Ellis	1	6	1	1	2	4
Wally Elmer	1	2	0	0	0	0
Hap Emms	1	3	0	0	0	2
Brian Engblom	2	6	0	0	0	0
Aut Erickson	1	1	0	0	0	0
Anders Eriksson	1	4	0	1	1	4
Thomas Eriksson	1	4	0	0	0	0
Bob Errey	3	13	3	1	4	12
Phil Esposito	5	28	7	17	24	46
Jack Evans	2	12	1	0	1	22
Stewart Evans	1	3	0	0	0	4
Bill Ezinicki	3	14	2	2	4	30

F

PLAYER	YRS	GP	G	A	PTS	PIM
Bill Fairbairn	1	6	0	2	2	0
Pat Falloon	1	3	0	0	0	2
Dave Farrish	1	1	0	0	0	0
Alex Faulkner	2	6	2	0	2	2
Sergei Fedorov	4	17	8	12	20	8
John Ferguson	6	33	5	6	11	69
Lorne Ferguson	1	5	0	1	1	8
Viacheslav Fetisov	3	12	0	8	8	12
Bob Fillion	3	12	2	0	2	4
Frank Finnigan	4	14	4	4	8	8
Jiri Fischer	1	5	0	1	1	4
Dunc Fisher	1	7	2	2	4	12
Joe Fisher	1	1	0	0	0	0
Tom Fitzgerald	1	4	1	0	1	0
Fern Flaman	3	14	0	2	2	23
Pat Flatley	1	5	1	3	4	8
Reg Fleming	2	12	3	0	3	20
Bill Flett	1	6	0	3	3	4
Theoren Fleury	1	6	1	1	2	2
Lee Fogolin	3	9	0	1	1	8
Lee Fogolin, Jr.	4	18	0	3	3	14
Rick Foley	1	4	0	1	1	4
Val Fonteyne	3	17	0	2	2	0
Adam Foote	2	11	1	4	5	20
Colin Forbes	1	3	0	0	0	0
Dave Forbes	2	10	0	1	1	2
Peter Forsberg	1	4	3	2	5	0
Ray Fortin	1	3	0	0	0	6
Nick Fotiu	1	2	0	1	1	10
Jimmy Fowler	2	8	0	2	2	0
Frank Foyston	*4	18	16	2	18	9
Ron Francis	3	15	5	7	12	6
Curt Fraser	1	4	0	3	3	28
Gord Fraser	2	8	2	1	3	20
Frank Fredrickson	3	12	4	4	8	32
Len Frig	1	4	1	1	2	0

G

PLAYER	YRS	GP	G	A	PTS	PIM
Bill Gadsby	3	18	1	3	4	28
Art Gagne	1	2	0	0	0	2
Dave Gagner	1	6	4	2	6	14
Johnny Gagnon	1	5	4	2	6	2
Bob Gainey	6	30	5	5	10	46
Norm Gainor	3	6	1	0	1	2
Percy Galbraith	3	8	1	0	1	4
John Gallagher	1	5	1	0	1	8
Don Gallinger	2	9	1	3	4	4
Garry Galley	1	5	0	0	0	4
Dick Gamble	2	4	0	0	0	2

PLAYER	YRS	GP	G	A	PTS	PIM
Herb Gardiner	1	2	1	0	1	0
Cal Gardner	3	14	1	1	2	0
Danny Gare	1	6	2	1	3	4
Johan Garpenlov	1	4	0	1	1	2
Fern Gauthier	1	4	1	0	1	5
Aaron Gavey	1	1	0	0	0	0
Stew Gavin	1	6	0	3	3	2
George Gee	2	11	3	5	8	14
Martin Gelinas	3	17	1	2	3	10
Bernie Geoffrion	10	53	24	22	46	32
Eddie Gerard	*4	11	3	1	4	51
Ray Getliffe	2	9	2	1	3	6
Gus Giesebrecht	2	6	0	1	1	0
Greg Gilbert	4	16	1	4	5	38
Rod Gilbert	1	6	4	3	7	11
Brent Gilchrist	1	2	0	0	0	4
Curt Giles	1	5	0	0	0	2
Randy Gilhen	1	5	0	0	0	12
Clark Gillies	5	24	9	14	23	35
Doug Gilmour	1	6	4	3	7	6
Gaston Gingras	1	4	2	1	3	0
Fred Glover	1	2	0	0	0	0
Howie Glover	1	6	1	0	1	0
Brian Glynn	2	13	9	1	1	6
Warren Godfrey	3	12	0	1	1	10
Pete Goegan	2	11	0	0	0	16
Bob Goldham	5	30	2	5	7	30
Leroy Goldsworthy	2	5	0	0	0	0
Hank Goldup	2	9	2	1	3	0
Scott Gomez	2	13	1	2	3	4
Sergei Gonchar	1	4	0	1	1	4
Larry Goodenough	2	6	1	3	4	4
Ebbie Goodfellow	3	12	1	2	3	20
Jack Gordon	1	4	0	1	1	2
Tom Gorence	1	5	1	1	2	16
Butch Goring	5	24	9	7	16	2
Ed Gorman	1	4	0	0	0	0
Johnny Gottselig	4	15	6	5	11	6
Bob Gould	1	4	0	0	0	0
Michel Goulet	1	4	1	0	1	2
Phil Goyette	6	27	3	5	8	8
Bob Gracie	3	10	1	2	3	0
Thomas Gradin	1	4	3	2	5	2
Dirk Graham	1	4	4	0	4	0
Ted Graham	2	9	0	1	1	14
Tony Granato	1	5	1	3	4	10
Danny Grant	1	4	0	0	0	0
Leo Gravelle	1	4	2	0	2	2
Adam Graves	2	12	3	3	6	4
Alex Gray	1	5	0	0	0	0
Terry Gray	2	7	2	0	2	8
Red Green	1	1	0	0	0	0
Rick Green	2	11	2	0	2	2
Ted Green	1	4	0	0	0	0
Randy Gregg	6	31	2	7	9	8
Ron Greschner	1	5	1	0	1	8
Wayne Gretzky	6	31	18	35	53	8
Si Griffis	*1	5	1	0	1	9
George Grigor	1	1	0	0	0	0
Stu Grimson	2	4	0	1	1	2
Michal Grosek	1	1	0	0	0	0
Don Grosso	3	15	7	5	12	14
Bill Guerin	1	4	0	4	4	12
Jocelyn Guevremont	1	6	0	1	1	8
Bep Guidolin	3	10	2	2	4	19
Alexei Gusarov	1	4	0	2	2	2

H

PLAYER	YRS	GP	G	A	PTS	PIM
Len Hachborn	1	1	0	0	0	0
Vic Hadfield	1	6	1	3	4	16
Matti Hagman	1	1	0	0	0	0
Bill Hajt	1	6	1	0	1	2
Harold Halderson	2	8	3	1	4	16
Joe Hall	*1	5	0	0	0	6
Murray Hall	1	1	0	0	0	0
Kevin Haller	1	3	0	1	1	0
Milt Halliday	1	4	0	0	0	0
Mats Hallin	1	2	0	0	0	0
Doug Halward	1	4	0	1	1	4
Red Hamill	1	5	0	0	0	0
Reg Hamilton	4	17	0	1	1	6
Dave Hannan	1	3	0	0	0	0
Mark Hardy	1	4	0	1	1	4
Glen Harmon	3	15	2	3	5	0
John Harms	1	4	3	0	3	2
Terry Harper	6	34	1	4	5	47

PLAYER	YRS	GP	G	A	PTS	PIM
Billy Harris	5	26	6	5	11	18
Smokey Harris	*2	9	3	1	4	16
Ted Harris	6	33	1	7	8	64
Gizzy Hart	2	8	5	2	7	18
Craig Hartsburg	1	5	1	4	5	2
Doug Harvey	11	54	4	31	35	60
Dominik Hasek	11	0	0	0	0	2
Derian Hatcher	2	12	1	1	2	16
Dale Hawerchuk	1	3	0	0	0	0
Greg Hawgood	2	7	2	2	4	4
Bill Hay	3	19	2	7	9	12
Jim Hay	1	5	1	0	1	0
Fern Headly	1	4	0	0	0	0
Anders Hedberg	1	5	1	2	3	2
Bret Hedican	2	12	1	3	4	8
Jerry Heffernan	1	2	0	1	1	0
Milan Hejduk	1	7	0	3	3	0
Ott Heller	4	18	2	3	5	19
Harry Helman	1	2	0	0	0	0
Murray Henderson	1	5	1	0	1	0
Paul Henderson	2	13	2	3	5	8
Lorne Henning	1	6	1	1	2	0
Camille Henry	2	9	1	0	1	2
Jimmy Herberts	1	4	1	0	1	18
Red Heron	2	8	1	0	1	4
Bryan Hextall	1	6	4	1	5	7
Bill Hicke	2	5	0	1	1	0
Pat Hickey	1	5	1	2	3	0
Wayne Hicks	1	1	0	0	0	2
Al Hill	1	6	0	0	0	0
Mel Hill	3	16	3	4	7	8
Sean Hill	2	6	1	1	2	12
Dutch Hiller	2	11	3	3	6	0
Larry Hillman	4	22	1	1	2	6
Wayne Hillman	1	1	0	0	0	0
Dan Hinote	1	7	1	3	4	11
Lionel Hitchman	4	13	1	0	1	35
Ivan Hlinka	1	2	0	0	0	0
Ken Hodge	3	16	6	10	16	27
Benoit Hogue	1	2	0	0	0	2
Bobby Holik	3	17	1	4	5	18
Flash Hollett	5	23	4	4	8	4
Gord Hollingworth	1	2	0	0	0	0
Paul Holmgren	1	5	4	4	8	15
Tomas Holmstrom	2	9	2	5	7	2
Albert Holway	1	2	0	0	0	0
Brian Holzinger	1	6	0	1	1	9
Pete Horeck	2	8	3	3	6	12
Red Horner	7	28	3	6	9	54
Tim Horton	6	33	4	16	20	38
Bronco Horvath	2	12	4	2	6	6
Ed Hospodar	1	5	0	0	0	34
Mike Hough	1	4	0	0	0	0
Rejean Houle	4	24	3	10	13	16
Phil Housley	1	4	0	0	0	2
Garry Howatt	1	6	0	1	1	21
Gordie Howe	10	55	18	32	50	94
Mark Howe	3	14	1	2	3	0
Syd Howe	6	28	8	12	20	4
Jiri Hrdina	3	8	0	0	0	0
Tony Hrkac	1	3	0	1	1	2
Charlie Huddy	7	31	1	11	12	28
Mike Hudson	1	4	0	0	0	2
Pat Hughes	3	13	0	3	3	8
Bobby Hull	4	26	11	17	28	26
Brett Hull	4	18	7	3	10	4
Dennis Hull	3	14	6	5	11	6
Jody Hull	1	2	0	0	0	0
Dale Hunter	1	4	0	1	1	2
Dave Hunter	4	19	1	2	3	43
Mark Hunter	1	4	0	1	1	12
Tim Hunter	3	16	0	3	3	67

I-J

PLAYER	YRS	GP	G	A	PTS	PIM
Frank Ingram	1	5	0	1	1	2
Arturs Irbe	1	5	0	0	0	0
Ted Irvine	1	6	1	4	5	10
Art Jackson	4	19	4	1	5	7
Busher Jackson	7	25	7	5	12	25
Don Jackson	3	14	0	0	0	52
Harold Jackson	3	15	0	1	1	8
Jaromir Jagr	2	10	2	5	7	2
Gerry James	1	4	0	0	0	0
Craig Janney	2	10	0	2	2	0
Doug Jarrett	3	20	1	2	3	12
Doug Jarvis	4	19	0	6	6	12

Larry Jeffrey	2	12	3	3	6	8
Roger Jenkins	2	8	0	2	2	6
Bill Jennings	1	4	1	1	2	0
Grant Jennings	1	2	0	0	0	2
Calle Johansson	1	4	0	1	1	2
Allan Johnson	1	6	1	2	3	0
Ching Johnson	5	19	1	2	3	48
Jim Johnson	1	6	0	1	1	10
Norm Johnson	1	6	2	0	2	4
Terry Johnson	1	2	0	0	0	12
Tom Johnson	10	49	6	3	9	44
Virgil Johnson	2	6	0	1	1	2
Greg Johnston	2	5	1	1	2	4
Eddie Johnstone	1	5	0	0	0	2
Aurel Joliat	4	15	5	4	9	24
Stan Jonathan	2	10	0	0	0	24
Tomas Jonsson	3	11	1	2	3	18
Ed Jovanovski	1	4	0	2	2	11
Eddie Joyal	2	12	3	1	4	6
Bob Joyce	1	5	1	1	2	0
Joe Juneau	2	10	1	4	5	0
Bill Juzda	2	9	0	0	0	6

K

PLAYER	YRS	GP	G	A	PTS	PIM
Alex Kaleta	1	7	0	3	3	0
Anders Kallur	4	18	3	4	7	8
Valeri Kamensky	1	4	1	2	3	8
Bingo Kampman	4	22	1	3	4	45
Sami Kapanen	1	5	2	0	2	0
Alexander Karpovtsev	1	2	0	0	0	0
Steve Kasper	1	5	2	0	2	2
Mike Keane	5	26	3	8	11	8
Duke Keats	1	2	0	0	0	4
Butch Keeling	4	14	4	2	6	16
Larry Keenan	3	12	2	0	2	8
Bob Kelly	3	15	3	2	5	18
Pep Kelly	5	17	2	2	4	0
Pete Kelly	2	7	1	1	2	0
Red Kelly	12	65	11	20	31	29
Bill Kendall	1	1	0	0	0	0
Ted Kennedy	5	26	12	11	23	8
Dave Keon	4	24	11	5	16	0
Tim Kerr	1	3	2	1	3	9
Hec Kilrea	4	15	0	4	4	4
Ken Kilrea	1	2	0	0	0	0
Wally Kilrea	2	9	2	2	4	4
Orest Kindrachuk	3	15	2	2	4	13
Trent Klatt	1	4	0	0	0	6
Ken Klee	1	2	0	0	0	0
Lloyd Klein	1	1	0	0	0	0
Jon Klemm	2	11	2	0	2	2
Petr Klima	1	5	1	0	1	0
Joe Klukay	5	24	2	4	6	11
Gord Kluzak	1	5	0	1	1	4
Joe Kocur	3	14	2	1	3	6
Vladimir Konstantinov	2	8	0	0	0	10
Jerry Korab	3	11	2	1	3	26
Dan Kordic	1	1	0	0	0	0
John Kordic	1	5	0	0	0	15
Cliff Koroll	2	13	3	5	8	6
Alexei Kovalev	1	7	4	3	7	2
Vyacheslav Kozlov	3	12	1	3	4	0
Igor Kravchuk	1	4	0	0	0	2
Uwe Krupp	1	4	2	1	3	2
Paul Kruse	1	0	0	0	0	0
Mike Krushelnyski	4	19	4	5	9	16
Todd Krygier	1	2	0	0	0	2
Dave Kryskow	1	3	2	0	2	0
Frantisek Kucera	1	4	0	0	0	0
Jari Kurri	7	36	15	24	39	16
Merv Kuryluk	1	2	0	0	0	0
Gus Kyle	1	7	1	0	1	14
Nick Kypreos	1	1	0	0	0	0

L

PLAYER	YRS	GP	G	A	PTS	PIM
Leo Labine	4	22	3	4	7	24
Elmer Lach	6	27	8	10	18	6
Normand Lacombe	1	5	1	0	1	4
Dan Lacroix	1	2	0	0	0	0
Nathan LaFayette	1	7	0	3	3	0
Guy Lafleur	5	25	9	17	26	14
Pat LaFontaine	1	5	2	1	3	0
Newsy Lalonde	*1	5	6	0	6	3
Mike Lalor	1	5	0	2	2	19
Joe Lamb	1	4	0	0	0	21

Mark Lamb	1	5	0	3	3	2
Yvon Lambert	4	18	5	8	13	16
Leo Lamoureux	3	11	0	1	1	8
Jack Lancien	1	2	0	0	0	0
Gord Lane	4	19	1	0	1	70
Miles Lane	2	4	0	0	0	0
Pete Langelle	3	17	1	3	4	0
Jamie Langenbrunner	2	7	1	2	3	4
Dave Langevin	5	21	0	3	3	26
Albert Langlois	4	18	0	2	2	22
Rod Langway	1	5	0	0	0	12
Jean Lanthier	1	2	0	0	0	4
Jacques Laperriere	5	23	1	4	5	32
Guy Lapointe	5	27	3	11	14	40
Martin Lapointe	3	10	4	3	7	20
Edgar Laprade	1	7	3	3	6	2
Igor Larionov	3	13	3	3	6	12
Steve Larmer	2	11	4	1	5	4
Wildor Larochelle	2	7	0	1	1	14
Claude Larose	6	27	3	6	9	21
Pierre Larouche	2	3	1	0	1	0
Reed Larson	1	2	0	0	0	2
Paul Laus	1	4	0	0	0	2
Hal Laycoe	1	5	0	1	1	10
Reggie Leach	3	16	8	5	13	0
Stephan Lebeau	1	5	1	2	3	4
Jack Leclair	2	12	3	1	4	6
John LeClair	2	9	4	3	7	4
Albert Leduc	2	4	1	3	4	2
Rich LeDuc	1	5	0	0	0	9
Gary Leeman	1	5	0	1	1	2
Brian Leetch	1	7	5	6	11	4
Sylvain Lefebvre	1	4	0	1	1	2
Chuck Lefley	1	6	3	3	6	2
Roger Leger	1	6	0	2	2	6
Jere Lehtinen	2	12	2	6	8	2
Jacques Lemaire	8	40	19	18	37	31
Moe Lemay	1	5	1	1	2	6
Claude Lemieux	5	21	6	4	10	61
Jocelyn Lemieux	1	4	0	1	1	0
Mario Lemieux	2	9	10	9	19	6
Pit Lepine	2	7	4	2	6	4
Curtis Leschyshyn	1	4	0	1	1	4
Art Lesieur	1	5	0	0	0	4
Bill Lesuk	1	2	0	0	0	0
Tony Leswick	4	25	5	7	12	34
Alex Levinsky	3	11	1	0	1	8
Danny Lewicki	1	3	0	0	0	0
Herbie Lewis	3	13	4	3	7	6
Doug Lidster	1	7	2	0	2	10
Nicklas Lidstrom	4	17	3	5	8	4
Trevor Linden	1	7	3	2	5	6
Lars Lindgren	1	4	1	0	1	2
Eric Lindros	1	4	1	2	3	8
Bill Lindsay	1	4	1	1	2	4
Ted Lindsay	8	44	19	15	34	48
Willy Lindstrom	3	14	5	1	6	2
Ken Linseman	4	20	4	10	14	52
Carl Liscombe	4	22	6	8	14	9
Ed Litzenberger	4	14	1	3	4	16
Lonnie Loach	1	1	0	0	0	0
Troy Loney	2	10	1	1	2	26
Stan Long	1	2	0	0	0	0
Ross Lonsberry	3	16	4	2	6	4
Hakan Loob	2	11	0	3	3	2
Jim Lorentz	2	10	1	2	3	2
Bob Lorimer	2	11	0	0	0	15
Clem Loughlin	2	8	2	0	2	12
Kevin Lowe	7	37	3	3	6	24
Ross Lowe	1	1	0	0	0	0
Dave Lowery	1	4	0	1	1	2
Don Luce	1	6	2	3	5	12
Craig Ludwig	3	17	1	1	2	32
Dave Lumley	3	10	1	1	2	28
Jyrki Lumme	1	7	0	4	4	6
Pentti Lund	1	7	1	1	2	0
Len Lunde	1	5	1	0	1	0
Pat Lundy	1	1	1	0	1	0
Gilles Lupien	2	6	0	0	0	19
Gary Lupul	1	2	0	0	0	0
Roman Lyashenko	1	4	0	0	0	0
Vic Lynn	3	14	4	2	6	30

M

PLAYER	YRS	GP	G	A	PTS	PIM
Al MacAdam	1	5	1	3	4	2
Blair MacDonald	1	1	0	0	0	0

PLAYER	YRS	GP	G	A	PTS	PIM
Jack MacDonald	*1	5	1	1	2	3
Kilby MacDonald	1	6	0	0	0	4
Parker MacDonald	4	24	3	1	4	14
Ran MacDonald	2	10	3	3	6	12
Hub Macey	1	3	0	0	0	0
Bruce MacGregor	5	30	6	6	12	14
Al MacInnis	2	11	5	8	13	26
Calum MacKay	4	20	3	7	10	8
Mickey MacKay	*7	25	7	6	13	18
Fleming MacKell	5	25	5	10	15	14
Bill MacKenzie	1	4	0	0	0	9
Howie Mackie	1	3	0	0	0	0
John MacLean	1	4	1	4	5	0
Rick MacLeish	3	18	6	9	15	8
Brian MacLellan	1	6	0	1	1	4
John MacMillan	2	5	0	1	1	2
Al MacNeil	1	7	0	0	0	12
Jamie Macoun	3	15	0	3	3	12
Bud MacPherson	3	11	0	1	1	8
Craig MacTavish	4	24	0	5	5	16
John Madden	2	13	2	1	3	2
Keith Magnuson	1	7	0	0	0	36
Frank Mahovlich	8	45	16	25	41	43
Pete Mahovlich	4	21	10	14	24	36
Fern Majeau	1	1	0	0	0	0
Chico Maki	4	21	3	6	9	12
Vladimir Malakhov	1	6	0	1	1	4
David Maley	1	5	1	2	3	2
Marek Malik	1	5	0	0	0	0
Dan Maloney	1	2	0	0	0	4
Dave Maloney	1	5	1	2	3	10
Don Maloney	1	5	0	1	1	6
Kirk Maltby	3	13	4	1	5	12
Dave Manson	1	6	0	0	0	6
Georges Mantha	2	7	2	1	3	4
Sylvio Mantha	4	15	2	0	2	20
Milan Marcetta	1	2	0	0	0	0
Mush March	3	12	3	2	5	14
Bryan Marchment	1	4	1	0	1	2
Don Marcotte	5	25	3	2	5	16
Gus Marker	4	17	3	3	6	4
John Marks	1	6	1	1	2	2
Nevin Markwart	1	1	0	0	0	2
Mario Marois	1	5	0	0	0	4
Brad Marsh	2	12	0	3	3	45
Bert Marshall	1	6	0	2	2	8
Don Marshall	6	32	3	4	7	4
Grant Marshall	1	3	0	0	0	0
Clare Martin	1	3	0	0	0	0
Frank Martin	1	5	0	1	1	2
Pit Martin	3	19	6	4	10	18
Rick Martin	1	6	2	4	6	6
Paul Masnick	4	18	3	3	6	14
Joe Matte	1	2	1	0	1	2
Stephane Matteau	2	11	0	2	2	6
Richard Matvichuk	2	12	0	3	3	10
John Matz	1	4	0	0	0	2
Brad Maxwell	1	4	0	4	4	9
Kevin Maxwell	1	2	0	0	0	4
Eddie Mazur	4	17	0	2	2	15
Jud McAtee	1	7	0	0	0	0
George McAvoy	1	3	0	0	0	0
Bert McCaffrey	1	2	1	0	1	0
Doug McCaig	1	2	0	0	0	6
Tom McCarthy	2	4	0	3	3	2
Darren McCarty	4	17	1	5	6	12
Kevin McClelland	4	22	4	5	9	87
John McCormack	2	6	0	0	0	0
Bill McCreary	3	10	0	2	2	4
John McCreedy	2	11	1	2	3	6
Brad McCrimmon	2	13	2	2	4	16
Ab McDonald	7	30	6	7	13	8
Bucko McDonald	5	18	3	0	3	4
Lanny McDonald	2	8	3	1	4	8
Shawn McEachern	1	4	0	2	2	0
Mike McEwen	3	12	2	3	5	6
Jim McFadden	3	15	3	3	6	6
Don McFayden	1	4	0	1	1	2
Jack McGill	1	5	0	0	0	0
Jack McIlhargey	2	10	0	1	1	29
Jack McIntyre	1	4	1	0	1	0
Doug McKay	1	1	0	0	0	0
Murdo McKay	1	4	0	0	0	0
Randy McKay	3	11	1	1	2	12
Jay McKee	1	6	0	0	0	2
Jack McKell	2	9	0	0	0	0
Don McKenney	3	16	6	7	13	0
Jim McKenzie	1	1	0	0	0	2
John McKenzie	3	14	1	6	7	39
Jack McLeod	1	5	0	0	0	0
Mike McMahon	1	4	1	0	1	12
Max McNab	3	10	0	0	0	4
Peter McNab	3	16	3	3	6	4
Mike McPhee	2	11	1	5	6	28
Basil McRae	1	5	0	0	0	26
Pat McReavy	2	10	2	2	4	7
Marty McSorley	3	17	3	0	3	30
Howie Meeker	3	15	2	4	6	23
Harry Meeking	4	20	1	3	4	26
Paul Meger	4	12	1	1	2	4
Scott Mellanby	2	11	1	3	4	84
Gerry Melnyk	5	24	0	0	0	2
Larry Melnyk	1	1	0	0	0	0
Wayne Merrick	4	19	3	6	9	0
Eric Messier	1	7	0	1	1	4
Mark Messier	7	38	11	20	31	52
Don Metz	5	21	4	5	9	4
Nick Metz	8	32	3	7	10	17
Dave Michayluk	1	1	0	0	0	0
Nick Mickoski	1	7	0	4	4	0
Rick Middleton	3	15	1	3	4	0
Stan Mikita	5	31	10	21	31	58
Mike Milbury	2	9	0	3	3	30
Hib Milks	1	3	0	0	0	0
Corey Millen	1	5	0	0	0	2
Bill Miller	1	3	0	0	0	0
Bob Miller	1	6	0	1	1	9
Earl Miller	1	2	0	0	0	0
Jay Miller	1	3	0	0	0	24
Kelly Miller	1	3	0	0	0	0
Gerry Minor	1	4	1	2	3	0
Mike Modano	3	18	3	12	15	14
Ron Moffatt	1	2	0	0	0	0
Alexander Mogilny	2	13	2	3	5	4
Doug Mohns	3	18	1	4	5	23
Lars Molin	1	4	0	4	4	0
Sergio Momesso	1	7	1	1	2	17
Armand Mondou	2	5	0	0	0	2
Pierre Mondou	3	13	1	3	4	6
Dickie Moore	10	52	10	21	31	69
Howie Morenz	4	15	10	2	12	20
Bernie Morris	*2	4	0	3	3	0
Moe Morris	1	7	1	0	1	2
John Morrison	1	2	1	0	1	0
Rod Morrison	1	1	0	0	0	0
Brenden Morrow	1	6	0	0	0	4
Ken Morrow	5	24	4	3	7	14
Gus Mortson	4	16	3	3	6	8
Ken Mosdell	6	33	6	7	13	16
Bill Mosienko	1	4	0	1	1	2
Alex Motter	3	12	1	2	3	8
Speed Moynes	1	5	0	0	0	0
Joe Mullen	3	16	10	9	19	8
Kirk Muller	2	11	3	2	5	6
Harry Mummery	*1	5	0	6	6	21
Craig Muni	3	15	0	3	3	2
Dunc Munro	2	9	1	1	2	8
Bob Murdoch	2	6	0	0	0	2
Don Murdoch	1	5	1	1	2	2
Murray Murdoch	5	19	1	3	4	12
Gord Murphy	1	4	0	0	0	0
Joe Murphy	1	5	2	2	4	4
Larry Murphy	4	18	3	15	18	8
Ron Murphy	1	6	2	1	3	0
Muzz Murray	2	10	3	0	3	8
Terry Murray	1	2	0	0	0	0
Dana Murzyn	1	6	0	1	1	8

N

PLAYER	YRS	GP	G	A	PTS	PIM
Don Nachbaur	1	1	0	0	0	0
Mark Napier	2	10	1	0	1	2
Mats Naslund	2	11	4	6	10	4
Ric Nattress	1	6	0	0	0	12
Cam Neely	2	10	2	5	7	14
Jim Neilson	1	3	0	1	1	2
Sergei Nemchinov	3	20	0	3	3	4
Eric Nesterenko	4	26	1	5	6	30
Bob Nevin	2	11	4	1	5	4
Rob Niedermayer	1	4	1	0	1	2
Scott Niedermayer	3	17	2	5	7	10
Ville Nieminen	1	7	1	2	3	6
Joe Nieuwendyk	3	18	4	2	6	11
Sibby Nicholls	1	5	0	0	0	0

PLAYER	YRS	GP	G	A	PTS	PIM
Frank Nighbor	*4	17	7	4	11	12
Janne Niinimaa	1	4	0	3	3	0
Andrei Nikolishin	1	4	0	2	2	2
Chris Nilan	1	3	0	0	0	49
Jim Nill	3	13	1	0	1	6
Kent Nilsson	1	7	0	1	1	0
Ulf Nilsson	1	2	0	0	0	2
Reg Noble	3	14	2	2	4	25
Simon Nolet	1	6	0	1	1	0
Brian Noonan	2	11	0	4	4	2
Baldy Northcott	1	3	2	1	3	0
Bill Nyrop	3	10	0	3	3	8
Bob Nystrom	5	21	8	4	12	67

O

PLAYER	YRS	GP	G	A	PTS	PIM
Adam Oates	1	4	1	2	3	0
Eddie Oatman	*2	7	1	0	1	0
Russell Oatman	3	10	0	0	0	22
Dennis O'Brien	1	5	0	0	0	6
Buddy O'Connor	4	21	6	5	11	4
Lyle Odelein	1	5	0	2	2	6
Sean O'Donnell	1	5	0	0	0	25
Gerry Odrowski	2	8	0	0	0	6
Bill O'Dwyer	1	5	0	0	0	0
Fredrik Olausson	1	5	0	2	2	2
Harry Oliver	4	10	3	3	6	6
Bert Olmstead	11	56	5	19	24	52
Jeff O'Neill	1	5	3	1	4	2
Terry O'Reilly	3	16	2	3	5	49
Jimmy Orlando	3	15	0	5	5	53
Bobby Orr	3	16	8	12	20	31
Danny O'Shea	1	7	1	1	2	12
Joel Otto	3	15	3	8	11	14
George Owen	2	4	0	0	0	2
Sandis Ozolinsh	1	4	0	2	2	4

P-Q

PLAYER	YRS	GP	G	A	PTS	PIM
John Paddock	1	2	2	0	2	0
Jim Paek	2	9	1	3	4	4
Pete Palangio	1	3	0	0	0	0
Brad Palmer	1	5	1	0	1	4
Jay Pandolfo	2	13	0	3	3	0
Jim Pappin	4	26	11	8	19	24
Brad Park	3	16	7	9	16	21
Ernie Parkes	3	11	0	5	5	2
George Parsons	1	3	2	0	2	11
Joe Paterson	1	5	0	0	0	19
James Patrick	1	6	0	0	0	4
Lynn Patrick	2	11	3	1	4	2
Muzz Patrick	1	6	1	0	1	6
Colin Patterson	2	8	1	1	2	16
Marty Pavelich	7	36	4	8	12	38
Steve Payne	1	5	5	2	7	2
Michael Peca	1	6	1	0	1	2
Allen Pedersen	2	9	0	0	0	8
John Peirson	3	12	1	0	1	14
Mike Peluso	2	7	0	0	0	4
Jim Peplinski	2	9	1	5	6	47
Gilbert Perreault	1	6	1	1	2	6
Stefan Persson	4	18	3	13	16	20
Jim Peters	4	22	1	3	4	8
Michel Petit	1	2	0	0	0	2
Gord Pettinger	5	21	3	3	6	2
Merlyn Phillips	2	9	3	1	4	2
Noel Picard	4	15	0	4	4	28
Alf Pike	1	6	2	0	2	4
Pierre Pilote	3	17	2	13	15	22
Gerry Pinder	1	5	0	0	0	0
Didier Pitre	*1	5	0	3	3	0
Barclay Plager	3	9	1	2	3	6
Bill Plager	2	5	0	0	0	4
Bob Plager	3	10	0	1	1	28
Gerry Plamondon	1	1	0	0	0	0
Pierre Plante	1	5	0	0	0	4
Willi Plett	1	2	0	0	0	4
Shjon Podein	2	11	0	1	1	8
Nels Podolsky	1	3	0	0	0	2
Bud Poile	2	8	2	0	2	2
Mike Polich	2	4	0	0	0	0
Jack Portland	1	5	0	0	0	4
Denis Potvin	5	24	9	19	28	28
Dave Poulin	3	14	1	3	4	123
Jaroslav Pouzar	3	9	0	1	1	8
Babe Pratt	3	18	3	3	6	19
Dean Prentice	1	6	1	1	2	2

PLAYER	YRS	GP	G	A	PTS	PIM
Noel Price	2	3	0	1	1	2
Joe Primeau	4	14	3	6	9	4
Keith Primeau	1	3	0	0	0	8
Wayne Primeau	1	6	1	1	2	4
Andre Pronovost	6	30	2	4	6	18
Marcel Pronovost	9	51	2	8	10	30
Brian Propp	5	29	10	12	22	8
Claude Provost	10	49	5	11	16	24
Metro Prystai	3	15	4	3	7	4
Bob Pulford	6	33	8	13	21	44
Fido Purpur	2	8	0	0	0	4
Jean Pusie	1	3	0	0	0	0
Bill Quackenbush	4	20	1	3	4	4
John Quilty	1	2	0	1	1	2
Dan Quinn	1	5	1	4	5	4

R

PLAYER	YRS	GP	G	A	PTS	PIM
Brian Rafalski	2	13	1	6	7	4
Don Raleigh	1	7	2	0	2	0
Rob Ramage	1	6	0	2	2	10
Craig Ramsay	1	6	0	2	2	0
Mike Ramsey	1	2	0	0	0	0
Ken Randall	*2	9	2	0	2	40
Erik Rasmussen	1	6	0	0	0	2
Jean Ratelle	3	16	0	5	5	0
Matt Ravlich	1	7	1	1	2	8
Rob Ray	1	1	0	0	0	0
Ken Reardon	2	9	0	0	0	20
Terry Reardon	2	9	3	1	4	4
Marc Reaume	1	4	0	0	0	0
Billy Reay	5	23	3	2	5	14
Mark Recchi	1	6	2	1	3	8
Dick Redmond	1	4	0	1	1	0
Mickey Redmond	2	6	0	1	1	0
Joe Reekie	1	4	0	0	0	2
Larry Regan	4	18	3	7	10	6
Earl Reibel	3	16	3	7	10	4
Dave Reid	2	13	0	4	4	0
Jerry Reid	1	2	0	0	0	0
Leo Reise, Jr.	4	17	1	0	1	14
Paul Reinhart	1	5	1	1	2	2
Steve Reinprecht	1	7	1	1	2	0
Mikael Renberg	1	4	0	1	1	0
Mike Ricci	1	4	1	0	1	6
Henri Richard	12	65	21	26	47	68
Maurice Richard	12	59	34	12	46	83
Roy Rickey	*2	7	3	3	6	0
Jim Riley	1	5	0	1	1	0
Vic Ripley	1	5	1	1	2	2
Doug Risebrough	5	22	5	5	10	35
Gus Rivers	2	7	0	0	0	0
Rene Robert	1	6	1	2	3	6
Phil Roberto	1	5	0	0	0	12
Gary Roberts	1	6	0	0	0	8
Gordie Roberts	3	15	0	1	1	33
Jimmy Roberts	9	42	3	3	6	44
Fred Robertson	1	3	0	0	0	0
Earl Robinson	1	3	2	1	3	0
Larry Robinson	7	36	5	15	20	35
Luc Robitaille	2	10	3	3	6	8
Leon Rochefort	3	16	2	2	4	12
Ernie Rodden	1	1	0	0	0	0
Jeremy Roenick	1	4	2	0	2	0
Dale Rolfe	1	6	2	0	2	10
Brian Rolston	1	2	0	1	1	0
Doc Romnes	4	18	3	8	11	4
Ed Ronan	1	5	1	1	2	6
Paul Ronty	1	2	0	0	0	2
Steve Rooney	1	1	0	0	0	0
Darcy Rota	1	4	0	0	0	19
Sam Rothschild	1	4	0	0	0	0
Tom Roulston	1	4	0	1	1	0
Bob Rouse	3	12	0	1	1	2
Bobby Rousseau	6	33	6	13	19	23
Bobby Rowe	*2	10	3	0	3	19
Reijo Ruotsalainen	2	12	0	2	2	6
Cam Russell	1	1	0	0	0	0
Phil Russell	1	6	0	1	1	16
Warren Rychel	2	8	0	0	0	21

S

PLAYER	YRS	GP	G	A	PTS	PIM
Gary Sabourin	3	12	2	0	2	6
Joe Sakic	2	11	5	9	14	4
Dollard St. Laurent	9	43	1	6	7	47
Frank St. Marseille	3	12	4	3	7	4
Don Saleski	3	16	1	4	5	18
Kjell Samuelsson	3	15	0	2	2	14
Ulf Samuelsson	2	10	2	1	3	14
Phil Samis	1	3	0	1	1	2
Derek Sanderson	2	10	4	3	7	34
Geoff Sanderson	1	6	1	0	1	4
Ed Sandford	1	5	2	1	3	5
Charlie Sands	1	4	0	1	1	0
Tomas Sandstrom	2	9	0	3	3	8
Miroslav Satan	1	6	0	1	1	2
Glen Sather	1	6	0	0	0	11
Andre Savard	1	6	1	1	2	20
Denis Savard	1	1	0	0	0	0
Serge Savard	7	33	5	8	13	22
Bobby Schmautz	3	16	3	2	5	29
Jackie Schmidt	1	2	0	0	0	0
Milt Schmidt	4	18	6	8	14	44
Mathieu Schneider	1	5	1	1	2	8
Ron Schock	2	8	0	0	0	2
Jim Schoenfeld	1	6	0	2	2	11
Sweeney Schriner	3	19	6	6	12	8
Dave Schultz	3	16	4	2	6	61
Enio Sclisizzi	2	4	0	0	0	2
Earl Seibert	5	22	2	1	3	18
Rod Seiling	1	6	1	1	2	6
Dave Semenko	3	13	2	2	4	18
Eddie Shack	4	21	1	1	2	28
Brendan Shanahan	3	15	6	2	8	6
Bobby Sheehan	1	5	0	1	1	0
Neil Sheehy	1	5	0	0	0	31
Gregg Sheppard	3	16	4	6	10	10
Johnny Sheppard	2	4	0	0	0	0
Ray Sheppard	2	7	1	1	2	0
John Sherf	1	5	0	1	1	2
Fred Shero	1	4	0	0	0	0
Jack Shewchuk	1	4	0	0	0	4
Alex Shibicky	2	10	0	2	2	2
Al Shields	1	3	0	1	1	2
Bill Shill	1	3	0	1	1	2
Jack Shill	2	8	1	2	3	8
Paul Shmyr	2	5	0	0	0	19
Eddie Shore	4	13	1	3	4	42
Gary Shuchuk	1	5	0	0	0	0
Steve Shutt	4	19	10	11	21	4
Babe Siebert	3	12	3	2	5	22
Jon Sim	2	8	1	0	1	6
Chris Simon	1	4	1	0	1	6
John Simon	1	3	0	0	0	0
Craig Simpson	2	10	7	5	12	16
Joe Simpson	1	2	0	1	1	0
Al Sims	3	11	0	0	0	4
Ilkka Sinisalo	2	10	0	1	1	2
Alf Skinner	5	18	13	4	17	34
Martin Skoula	1	7	1	2	3	6
Glen Skov	3	18	2	3	5	26
Brian Skrudland	4	21	2	4	6	62
Jiri Slegr	1	1	0	0	0	2
Blake Sloan	2	9	0	0	0	2
Tod Sloan	2	11	3	5	8	13
Ed Slowinski	1	7	0	3	3	4
Doug Smail	1	1	0	0	0	0
Richard Smehlik	1	6	0	3	3	2
Alex Smith	1	4	0	0	0	8
Bobby Smith	4	22	8	10	18	34
Clint Smith	2	10	1	4	5	2
Dallas Smith	3	16	0	4	4	24
Derrick Smith	2	12	2	4	6	10
Des Smith	1	4	0	2	2	2
Floyd Smith	3	18	6	3	9	4
Greg Smith	1	5	0	1	1	6
Ken Smith	1	5	0	2	2	0
Hooley Smith	3	12	0	3	3	29
Rick Smith	3	14	2	3	5	18
Sid Smith	2	9	8	2	10	0
Stan Smith	1	1	0	0	0	0
Steve Smith	4	17	1	6	7	25
Stan Smyl	1	4	2	0	2	19
Rod Smylie	1	5	1	3	4	0
Harold Snepsts	1	4	0	0	0	16
Ken Solheim	1	1	0	0	0	0
Art Somers	3	12	0	3	3	8
John Sorrell	3	13	4	5	9	2
Bill Speer	1	1	0	0	0	0
Brian Spencer	1	6	0	1	1	4
Irv Spencer	2	8	0	0	0	0
Ted Stackhouse	1	4	0	0	0	0
Fred Stanfield	4	23	3	6	9	4
Allan Stanley	8	46	4	13	17	36
Barney Stanley	*1	5	2	0	2	6
Daryl Stanley	1	4	0	0	0	2
Wally Stanowski	5	29	3	7	10	2
Paul Stanton	2	10	0	1	1	28
Pat Stapleton	2	13	0	10	10	4
Wilf Starr	1	3	0	1	1	2
Vic Stasiuk	6	31	5	9	14	8
Pete Stemkowski	2	12	3	7	10	12
Kevin Stevens	2	10	6	6	12	27
Scott Stevens	3	17	1	4	5	12
Turner Stevenson	1	7	1	1	2	6
Gaye Stewart	3	12	1	2	3	6
Jack Stewart	6	29	2	7	9	34
Nels Stewart	2	9	8	1	9	22
Ron Stewart	6	28	4	9	13	8
Martin Straka	1	4	0	1	1	0
Billy Stuart	2	9	0	2	2	6
Brent Sutter	4	17	5	7	12	16
Duane Sutter	5	24	4	9	13	86
Rich Sutter	1	3	3	0	3	4
Ron Sutter	2	12	1	6	7	12
Ken Sutton	1	2	0	0	0	9
Robert Svehla	1	4	0	0	0	2
Jaroslav Svoboda	1	5	0	0	0	8
Petr Svoboda	2	7	0	3	3	10
Bob Sweeney	2	10	0	3	3	9
Don Sweeney	1	5	0	1	1	6
Darryl Sydor	3	17	2	1	3	12
Petr Sykora	2	13	5	4	9	8

T

PLAYER	YRS	GP	G	A	PTS	PIM
Peter Taglianetti	1	5	0	3	3	8
Jean-Guy Talbot	11	55	0	5	5	56
Alex Tanguay	1	7	4	3	7	4
Marc Tardif	2	13	3	3	6	23
Billy Taylor	2	9	2	8	10	2
Cyclone Taylor	*2	10	9	1	10	15
Dave Taylor	1	3	1	1	2	6
Ralph Taylor	1	1	0	0	0	0
Tim Taylor	1	2	0	0	0	2
Michael Thelven	1	4	0	0	0	6
Chris Therien	1	4	0	0	0	0
Jimmy Thomson	4	19	1	4	5	25
Paul Thompson	4	13	3	3	6	25
Bill Thoms	4	15	3	4	7	2
Scott Thornton	1	6	0	1	1	4
Esa Tikkanen	6	31	9	6	15	54
Ray Timgren	2	9	1	3	4	21
Mark Tinordi	2	10	0	1	1	21
Walt Tkaczuk	2	11	1	3	4	0
Charlie Tobin	*2	10	0	0	0	0
Rick Tocchet	3	16	5	12	17	40
Jeff Toms	1	1	0	0	0	0
John Tonelli	6	29	3	10	13	35
Tim Tookey	1	1	0	0	0	0
Jerry Toppazzini	3	16	1	2	3	8
Jacques Toupin	1	1	0	0	0	0
Bob Trapp	1	2	0	0	0	2
Gilles Tremblay	2	12	2	3	5	0
J.C. Tremblay	6	34	3	18	21	27
Mario Tremblay	4	14	5	2	7	30
Bryan Trottier	7	34	11	22	33	46
Dave Trottier	1	3	1	0	1	4
Lou Trudel	2	8	0	1	1	0
Bob Turner	6	28	1	1	2	14

U-V

PLAYER	YRS	GP	G	A	PTS	PIM
Norm Ullman	5	28	6	12	18	23
Carol Vadnais	4	18	1	4	5	37
Sparky Vail	1	2	0	0	0	0
Ed Van Impe	2	12	0	4	4	21
Vaclav Varada	1	6	0	0	0	6
Josef Vasicek	1	5	1	0	1	4
Moose Vasko	3	19	1	2	3	18
Gary Veneruzzo	1	3	0	1	1	0
Pat Verbeek	1	6	1	0	1	4
Mike Vernon	3	13	0	1	1	0
Steve Vickers	1	5	1	1	2	0
Carl Voss	1	4	2	0	2	0

W

PLAYER	YRS	GP	G	A	PTS	PIM
Jack Walker	*4	18	8	5	13	9
Bob Wall	1	4	0	0	0	2
Niclas Wallin	1	5	0	0	0	2
Ryan Walter	2	11	1	1	2	6
Mike Walton	2	12	3	5	8	6
Aaron Ward	2	9	1	0	0	4
Dixon Ward	1	6	1	0	1	8
Jimmy Ward	2	8	1	1	2	2
Eddie Wares	3	14	0	6	6	22
Rhett Warrener	2	8	0	0	0	6
Nick Wasnie	2	7	2	2	4	8
Bryan Watson	1	6	0	0	0	12
Harry Watson	5	20	8	5	13	10
Jimmy Watson	4	21	0	4	4	43
Joe Watson	3	16	0	2	2	20
Phil Watson	3	15	3	5	8	18
Tim Watters	1	5	0	0	0	4
Cooney Weiland	4	13	1	2	3	2
Jay Wells	1	7	0	0	0	8
John Wensink	2	9	0	0	0	28
Cy Wentworth	2	8	3	2	5	8
Glen Wesley	3	15	2	4	6	6
Ed Westfall	2	10	2	3	5	10
Tommy Westlund	1	5	0	0	0	0
Kenny Wharram	3	17	3	2	5	16
Bill White	2	13	1	5	6	12
Colin White	2	13	0	1	1	18
Bob Whitelaw	1	4	0	0	0	0
Art Wiebe	2	8	0	1	1	6
Jim Wiemer	1	2	0	0	0	0
Neil Wilkinson	1	6	0	0	0	2
Burr Williams	1	2	0	0	0	0
Tiger Williams	1	4	0	3	3	14
Behn Wilson	1	6	0	4	4	28
Cully Wilson	*2	7	1	3	4	8
Johnny Wilson	5	27	3	2	5	2
Larry Wilson	1	2	0	0	0	0
Murray Wilson	3	13	0	4	4	8
Eddie Wiseman	2	7	3	0	3	0
Steve Wojciechowski	1	2	0	0	0	0
Benny Woit	3	18	0	1	1	10
Jason Woolley	2	8	1	1	2	6

Y-Z

PLAYER	YRS	GP	G	A	PTS	PIM
Stephane Yelle	1	7	0	0	0	4
Doug Young	2	8	1	2	3	2
Howie Young	2	8	1	1	2	18
Scott Young	2	5	2	2	4	0
Tim Young	1	2	0	3	3	0
Tom Younghans	1	3	0	0	0	4
Steve Yzerman	4	17	6	7	13	2
Richard Zednik	1	4	1	0	1	4
Larry Zeidel	1	3	0	0	0	0
Valeri Zelepukin	1	3	0	0	0	4
Peter Zezel	2	12	1	2	3	6
Alexei Zhitnik	2	11	1	3	4	22
Sergei Zubov	3	18	1	8	9	2
Dainius Zubrus	1	4	0	0	0	0

* Note: Totals do not include appearances before 1918.

Final Series Goaltending Register

GOALTENDER	YRS	GP	W	L	MIN	GA	SO	AVG
Andy Aitkenhead	1	4	3	1	248	5	1	1.21
Tom Barrasso	2	10	7	2	559	23	2	2.47
Hank Bassen	2	5	1	3	274	11	0	2.41
Don Beaupre	1	3	1	2	180	13	0	4.33
Ed Belfour	3	16	6	9	1032	34	2	1.98
Clint Benedict [1,2]	4	25	16	9	1507	39	8	1.55
Johnny Bower	6	28	13	13	1638	70	2	2.56
Frank Brimsek	4	18	9	9	1132	47	1	2.49
Turk Broda	8	38	21	17	2369	85	4	2.15
Martin Brodeur	3	17	11	6	1056	35	0	1.99
Richard Brodeur	1	4	0	4	260	17	0	3.92
Jon Casey	1	6	2	3	290	21	0	4.34
Lorne Chabot	3	9	4	4	508	23	0	2.72
Gerry Cheevers	4	17	8	9	1020	51	2	3.00
King Clancy [2]	1	1	0	0	2	0	0	0.00
Alex Connell [3]	2	7	5	0	425	7	1	0.99

GOALTENDER	YRS	GP	W	L	MIN	GA	SO	AVG
Roger Crozier	2	8	3	4	426	19	0	2.68
Wilf Cude	1	4	1	3	291	9	0	1.86
John Davidson	1	5	1	4	307	19	0	3.17
Denis DeJordy	1	1	0	0	20	3	0	9.00
Gerry Desjardins	1	5	1	3	260	16	0	3.69
Ken Dryden	6	32	24	8	1947	78	2	2.40
Bill Durnan	3	15	10	5	967	34	1	2.11
Tony Esposito	2	13	5	8	796	52	1	3.92
Manny Fernandez	1	1	0	0	17	1	0	3.53
Mark Fitzpatrick	1	1	0	0	40	4	0	6.00
Bob Froese	1	3	0	1	115	9	0	4.70
Grant Fuhr	4	20	14	5	1176	50	1	2.55
Charlie Gardiner	2	9	5	4	670	18	1	1.61
Ed Giacomin	1	3	1	2	180	11	0	3.67
Gilles Gilbert	1	6	2	4	372	15	0	2.42
Paul Goodman	1	1	0	1	60	5	0	5.00
Ron Grahame	1	1	0	0	20	0	0	0.00
George Hainsworth	4	14	6	8	925	39	2	2.53
Glenn Hall	7	32	10	22	1904	87	1	2.74
Dominik Hasek	3	12	6	6	836	23	1	1.65
Brian Hayward	1	2	0	1	67	6	0	5.37
Gord Henry	1	3	1	2	163	10	0	3.68
Jim Henry	1	3	0	2	138	5	0	2.17
Ron Hextall	2	10	3	7	605	34	0	3.37
Charlie Hodge	2	4	1	3	197	10	1	3.05
Hap Holmes [1,4]	5	23	11	11	1416	64	2	2.71
Kelly Hrudey	1	5	1	4	316	15	0	2.85
Arturs Irbe	1	5	1	4	354	13	0	2.20
Eddie Johnston	1	3	2	1	180	6	0	2.00
Mike Karakas	2	6	2	4	369	18	0	2.93
Dave Kerr	2	11	6	5	694	20	1	1.73
Olaf Kolzig	1	4	0	4	251	13	0	3.11
Michel Larocque	1	1	0	0	20	0	0	0.00
Hugh Lehman [1]	5	21	7	14	1265	61	2	2.89
Reggie Lemelin	3	4	0	2	197	13	0	3.96
Pelle Lindbergh	1	4	1	3	185	11	0	3.57
Harry Lumley	4	22	7	15	1391	56	3	2.42
Frank McCool	1	7	4	3	434	9	3	1.24
Kirk McLean	1	7	3	4	437	20	0	2.75
Gerry McNeil	4	15	6	9	933	29	3	1.86
Roland Melanson	1	3	0	1	55	3	0	3.27
Gilles Meloche	1	2	0	2	120	12	0	6.00
Joe Miller	1	3	2	1	180	3	1	1.00
Andy Moog	4	15	3	10	844	46	0	3.27
Alfie Moore	1	1	1	0	60	1	0	1.00
Johnny Mowers	3	15	7	8	900	42	2	2.80
Phil Myre	1	1	0	1	60	6	0	6.00
Chris Osgood	2	5	4	0	286	8	1	1.68
Bernie Parent	2	12	8	4	750	33	2	2.64
Lester Patrick	1	1	1	0	47	1	0	1.28
Pete Peeters	1	5	2	3	311	20	0	3.86
Frank Pietrangelo	1	1	1	0	40	3	0	4.50
Jacques Plante	10	41	25	14	2423	92	4	2.28
Bill Ranford	1	5	4	1	355	8	0	1.35
Chuck Rayner	1	7	3	4	459	22	0	2.88
Charlie Reid	1	2	0	2	120	9	0	4.50
Glenn Resch	1	1	0	0	20	2	0	6.00
Mike Richter	1	7	4	3	439	19	0	2.60
John Ross Roach	3	10	3	7	605	31	1	3.07
Earl Robertson	1	5	2	2	280	8	2	1.71
Al Rollins	1	3	3	0	193	5	0	1.55
Patrick Roy	5	27	18	9	1715	55	4	1.92
Terry Sawchuk	7	37	19	18	2185	95	3	2.61
Don Simmons	3	14	5	9	831	38	1	2.74
Billy Smith	5	24	17	6	1396	72	3	3.09
Gary Smith	1	1	0	0	5	0	0	0.00
Normie Smith	2	5	4	1	261	11	0	2.53
Garth Snow	1	1	0	1	58	4	0	4.11
Wayne Stephenson	1	4	0	4	240	14	0	3.50
Tiny Thompson	2	4	2	2	240	8	1	2.00
Rogie Vachon	2	9	6	3	548	17	1	1.86
John Vanbiesbrouck	1	4	0	4	245	11	0	2.69
Mike Vernon	4	19	9	10	1137	50	0	2.64
Georges Vezina [1,4]	3	13	7	5	816	39	2	2.87
Gilles Villemure	1	3	1	2	180	7	0	2.33
Ernie Wakely	1	2	0	2	96	11	0	6.87
Hal Winkler [3]	2	6	0	4	362	10	1	1.66
Gump Worsley	4	16	11	5	925	28	3	1.82

[1] Note: Totals do not include appearances before 1918.

[2] Clancy replaced Clint Benedict in goal while Benedict served a two-minute penalty on March 31, 1923.

[3] also recorded two ties in the 1927 Finals.

[4] also recorded a tie in the 1919 Finals.

Final Series Coaching Register

COACH	YRS	CUPS	GC	W	L	PCT
Sid Abel	4	0	24	8	16	.333
Jack Adams	5	3	23	12	11	.522
Al Arbour	5	4	24	17	7	.708
Toe Blake	9	8	48	34	14	.708
Frank Boucher	1	1	6	4	2	.667
Scotty Bowman	13	9	58	36	22	.621
Pat Burns	1	0	6	2	4	.333
Dick Carroll	1	1	5	3	2	.600
Don Cherry	2	0	10	2	8	.200
Dit Clapper	1	0	5	1	4	.200
Lloyd Cook [1]	3	0	14	5	9	.357
Marc Crawford	1	1	4	4	0	1.000
Terry Crisp	1	1	6	4	2	.667
Leo Dandurand	2	1	8	5	3	.625
Hap Day	5	5	28	20	8	.714
Jacques Demers	1	1	5	4	1	.800
Cy Denneny	1	1	2	2	0	1.000
Art Duncan [1]	1	0	2	0	2	.000
Emile Francis	1	0	6	2	4	.333
Bob Gainey	1	0	6	2	4	.333
Eddie Gerard	2	1	9	5	4	.555
Dave Gill [2]	1	1	4	2	0	.750
Ebbie Goodfellow	1	0	4	0	4	.000
Tommy Gorman	2	2	7	6	1	.857
Pete Green	3	3	16	11	5	.688
Bep Guidolin	1	0	6	2	4	.333
Cecil Hart	2	2	7	5	2	.714
Bob Hartley	1	1	7	4	3	.571
Ken Hitchcock	2	1	12	6	6	.500
Punch Imlach	6	4	33	17	16	.515
Dick Irvin	16	4	77	32	45	.416
Tommy Ivan	5	3	26	12	14	.462
Bob Johnson	2	1	11	5	6	.455
Tom Johnson	1	1	6	4	2	.667
Mike Keenan	4	1	23	8	15	.348
Newsy Lalonde [3,4]	2	1	10	5	4	.550
Jacques Lemaire	1	1	4	4	0	1.000
Herbie Lewis	1	0	4	1	3	.250
Doug MacLean	1	0	4	0	4	.000
Al MacNeil	1	1	7	4	3	.571
Paul Maurice	1	0	5	1	4	.200
Ken McKenzie	1	0	2	0	2	.000
Barry Melrose	1	0	5	1	4	.200
Mike Milbury	1	0	5	1	4	.200
John Muckler	1	1	5	4	1	.800
Pete Muldoon [3,4]	3	1	14	7	6	.536
Terry Murray	1	1	4	4	0	.000
Roger Neilson	1	0	4	0	4	.000
Eddie Oatman	1	0	2	0	2	.000
Terry O'Reilly	1	0	4	0	4	.000
Frank Patrick [4]	2	1	8	5	3	.625
Lester Patrick [4]	8	3	30	12	18	.400
Lynn Patrick	2	0	12	4	8	.333
Jean Perron	1	1	5	4	1	.800
Rudy Pilous	2	1	12	6	6	.500
Joe Primeau	1	1	5	4	1	.800
Pat Quinn	2	0	13	5	8	.385
Billy Reay	3	0	20	8	12	.400
Larry Robinson	2	1	13	7	6	.536
Art Ross [2]	4	1	15	4	9	.333
Claude Ruel	1	1	4	4	0	1.000
Lindy Ruff	1	0	6	2	4	.333
Glen Sather	5	4	25	16	9	.640
Milt Schmidt	2	0	11	3	8	.273
Fred Shero	4	2	21	9	12	.429
Harry Sinden	1	1	4	4	0	1.000
Jimmy Skinner	2	1	12	5	7	.417
Floyd Smith	1	0	6	2	4	.333
Glen Sonmor	1	0	5	1	4	.200
Bill Stewart	1	1	4	3	1	.750
Paul Thompson	1	0	4	0	4	.000
Cooney Weiland	1	1	4	4	0	1.000
Ron Wilson	1	0	4	0	4	.000

[1] served as player/coach under manager Frank Patrick.

[2] also recorded two ties in the 1927 Finals.

[3] also recorded a tie in the 1919 Finals.

[4] also includes totals prior to 1918 (Newsy Lalonde 3-2 in 1916, Pete Muldoon 3-1 in 1917, Frank Patrick 3-0 in 1915, Lester Patrick 0-3 in 1914).

CHAPTER 20

The Post-War Dynasties

Eight Benchmark Championship Teams

THE MODERN ECONOMICS OF SPORTS have made it almost impossible to keep a championship team together year after year. For example, eight different teams won the Stanley Cup between 1990 and 1999 for a diversity of titlists not seen since the first decade after the NHL assumed control of the trophy in 1926–27. The Edmonton Oilers' Stanley Cup triumph of 1990 may well have marked the end of an era of hockey dynasties dating back to the days after World War II.

The dynasty teams of the Post-War era also include legendary clubs like the Detroit Red Wings of the early 1950s, two different Toronto Maple Leafs teams, three different Montreal Canadiens teams, and the New York Islanders of the early 1980s.

Although the definition of a sports "dynasty" can be debated, the following criteria have been used here:

a) Three-or-more consecutive Stanley Cup wins
b) Five or six consecutive playoff appearances including four Stanley Cup wins
c) Seven consecutive playoff appearances including five Stanley Cup wins

Eight teams fit this definition of a dynasty:

1)	Toronto	1947-1951
2)	Detroit	1950-1955
3)	Montreal	1956-1960
4)	Toronto	1962-1964
5)	Montreal	1965-1969
6)	Montreal	1976-1979
7)	NY Islanders	1980-1983
8)	Edmonton	1984-1990

Post-War NHL Dynasty Teams

STANDINGS	PLAYERS ON ALL STANLEY CUP TEAMS	ALL-STAR SELECTIONS	INDIVIDUAL HONORS

Toronto 1947-51

	Regular Season					Playoffs			
	GP	W	L	T	PCT	GP	W	L	PCT
*1946-47	60	31	19	10	.600	11	8	3	.727
*1947-48	60	32	15	13	.642	9	8	1	.889
*1948-49	60	22	25	13	.475	9	8	1	.889
1949-50	70	31	27	12	.529	7	3	4	.429
**1950-51	70	41	16	13	.679	11	8	2	.733
	320	157	102	61	.586	47	35	11	.755

* Suspended game vs. Boston counted as a tie

Players on all Stanley Cup teams: Bill Barilko, Turk Broda, Ted Kennedy, Joe Klukay, Howie Meeker, Gus Mortson, Jimmy Thomson, Harry Watson

All-Star Selections:

Turk Broda	G	1st (1948)
Gus Mortson	D	1st (1950)
Ted Kennedy	C	2nd (1950, 1951)
Jimmy Thomson	D	2nd (1951)
Sid Smith	LW	2nd (1951)

Individual Honors:
Howie Meeker, Calder, 1947
Turk Broda, Vezina, 1948
Al Rollins, Vezina, 1951

Detroit 1950-55

	Regular Season					Playoffs			
	GP	W	L	T	PCT	GP	W	L	PCT
*1949-50	70	37	19	14	.629	14	8	6	.571
1950-51	70	44	13	13	.721	6	2	4	.333
*1951-52	70	44	14	12	.714	8	8	0	1.000
1952-53	70	36	16	18	.643	6	2	4	.333
*1953-54	70	37	19	14	.629	12	8	4	.667
*1954-55	70	42	17	11	.679	11	8	3	.727
	420	240	98	82	.659	57	36	21	.632

Players on all Stanley Cup teams: Gordie Howe, Red Kelly, Ted Lindsay, Marty Pavelich, Marcel Pronovost, Johnny Wilson

All-Star Selections:

Sid Abel	C	1st (1950); 2nd (1951)
Ted Lindsay	LW	1st (1950, 1951, 1952, 1953, 1954)
Leo Reise, Jr.	D	2nd (1950, 1951)
Red Kelly	D	1st (1951, 1952, 1953, 1954, 1955); 2nd (1950)
Gordie Howe	RW	1st (1951, 1952, 1953, 1954); 2nd (1950)
Terry Sawchuk	G	1st (1951, 1952, 1953); 2nd (1954, 1955)
Alex Delvecchio	C	2nd (1953)
Bob Goldham	D	2nd (1955)

Individual Honors:
Ted Lindsay, Art Ross, 1950
Gordie Howe, Art Ross, 1951, 1952, 1953, 1964; Hart, 1952, 1953
Red Kelly, Norris, 1954;
    Lady Byng, 1951, 1953, 1954
Terry Sawchuk, Calder, 1951;
    Vezina, 1952, 1953, 1955

Montreal 1956-60

	Regular Season					Playoffs			
	GP	W	L	T	PCT	GP	W	L	PCT
*1955-56	70	45	15	10	.714	10	8	2	.800
*1956-57	70	35	23	12	.586	10	8	2	.800
*1957-58	70	43	17	10	.686	10	8	2	.800
*1958-59	70	39	18	13	.650	11	8	3	.727
*1959-60	70	40	18	12	.657	8	8	0	1.000
	350	202	91	57	.659	49	40	9	.816

Players on all Stanley Cup teams: Jean Beliveau, Bernie Geoffrion, Doug Harvey, Tom Johnson, Don Marshall, Dickie Moore, Jacques Plante, Claude Provost, Henri Richard, Maurice Richard, Jean-Guy Talbot, Bob Turner

All-Star Selections:

Jacques Plante	G	1st (1956, 1959); 2nd (1957, 1958, 1960)
Doug Harvey	D	1st (1956, 1957, 1958, 1960); 2nd (1959)
Jean Beliveau	C	1st (1956, 1957, 1959, 1960); 2nd (1958)
Maurice Richard	RW	1st (1956); 2nd (1957)
Tom Johnson	D	1st (1959); 2nd (1956)
Bert Olmstead	LW	2nd (1956)
Dickie Moore	LW	1st (1958, 1959)
Bernie Geoffrion	RW	2nd (1960)

Individual Honors:
Jean Beliveau, Art Ross, 1956; Hart, 1956
Doug Harvey, Norris, 1956, 1957, 1958, 1960
Jacques Plante, Vezina, 1956, 1957, 1958, 1959, 1960
Dickie Moore, Art Ross, 1958, 1959
Tom Johnson, Norris, 1959
Ralph Backstrom, Calder, 1959

* Stanley Cup winner

Post-War NHL Dynasty Teams

continued

STANDINGS	PLAYERS ON ALL STANLEY CUP TEAMS	ALL-STAR SELECTIONS	INDIVIDUAL HONORS

Toronto 1962-64

	Regular Season					Playoffs		
	GP	W	L	T	PCT	GP	W	L	PCT
*1961-62	70	37	22	11	.607	12	8	4	.667
*1962-63	70	35	23	12	.586	10	8	2	.800
*1963-64	70	33	25	12	.557	14	8	6	.571
	210	**105**	**70**	**35**	**.583**	**36**	**24**	**12**	**.667**

George Armstrong, Bob Baun, Johnny Bower, Carl Brewer, Billy Harris, Tim Horton, Red Kelly, Dave Keon, Frank Mahovlich, Bob Pulford, Eddie Shack, Don Simmons, Allan Stanley, Ron Stewart

Carl Brewer	D	1st (1963); 2nd (1962)
Frank Mahovlich	LW	1st (1963); 2nd (1962, 1964)
Dave Keon	C	2nd (1962)
Tim Horton	D	1st (1964); 2nd (1963)

Dave Keon, Lady Byng, 1962, 1963
Kent Douglas, Calder, 1963

Montreal 1965-69

	Regular Season					Playoffs		
	GP	W	L	T	PCT	GP	W	L	PCT
*1964-65	70	36	23	11	.593	13	8	5	.615
*1965-66	70	41	21	8	.643	10	8	2	.800
1966-67	70	32	25	13	.550	10	6	4	.600
*1967-68	74	42	22	10	.635	13	12	1	.923
*1968-69	76	46	19	11	.678	14	12	2	.857
	360	**197**	**110**	**53**	**.621**	**58**	**48**	**10**	**.767**

Ralph Backstrom, Jean Beliveau, Yvan Cournoyer, Dick Duff, John Ferguson, Terry Harper, Ted Harris, Jacques Laperriere, Claude Provost, Henri Richard, Bobby Rousseau, J.C. Tremblay, Gump Worsley

Jacques Laperriere	D	1st (1965, 1966)
Claude Provost	RW	1st (1965)
Charlie Hodge	G	2nd (1965)
Gump Worsley	G	1st (1968); 2nd (1966)
Jean Beliveau	C	2nd (1966, 1969)
Bobby Rousseau	RW	2nd (1966)
J.C. Tremblay	D	2nd (1968)
Ted Harris	D	2nd (1969)
Yvan Cournoyer	RW	2nd (1969)

Jean Beliveau, Conn Smythe, 1965
Jacques Laperriere, Norris, 1966
Gump Worsley, Vezina, 1966, 1968
Charlie Hodge, Vezina, 1966
Rogie Vachon, Vezina, 1968
Claude Provost, Masterton, 1968
Serge Savard, Conn Smythe, 1969

Montreal 1976-79

	Regular Season					Playoffs		
	GP	W	L	T	PCT	GP	W	L	PCT
*1975-76	80	58	11	11	.794	13	12	1	.923
*1976-77	80	60	8	12	.825	14	12	2	.857
*1977-78	80	59	10	11	.806	15	12	3	.800
*1978-79	80	52	17	11	.719	16	12	4	.750
	320	**229**	**46**	**45**	**.786**	**58**	**48**	**10**	**.828**

Rick Chartraw, Yvan Cournoyer, Ken Dryden, Bob Gainey, Doug Jarvis, Guy Lafleur, Yvon Lambert, Michel Larocque, Jacques Lemaire, Doug Risebrough, Steve Shutt, Mario Tremblay

Ken Dryden	G	1st (1976, 1977, 1978, 1979)
Guy Lafleur	RW	1st (1976, 1977, 1978, 1979)
Guy Lapointe	D	1st (1976, 1977)
Larry Robinson	D	1st (1977, 1979); 2nd (1978)
Steve Shutt	LW	1st (1977); 2nd (1978)
Serge Savard	D	2nd (1979)

Guy Lafleur, Art Ross, 1976, 1977, 1978; Hart, 1977, 1978; Conn Smythe, 1977; Pearson, 1976, 1977, 1978
Ken Dryden, Vezina 1976, 1977, 1978, 1979
Michel Larocque, Vezina, 1977, 1978, 1979
Larry Robinson, Norris, 1977; Conn Smythe, 1978
Bob Gainey, Selke, 1978, 1979; Conn Smythe, 1979
Serge Savard, Masterton, 1979

NY Islanders 1980-83

	Regular Season					Playoffs		
	GP	W	L	T	PCT	GP	W	L	PCT
*1979-80	80	39	28	13	.569	21	15	6	.714
*1980-81	80	48	18	14	.688	18	15	3	.833
*1981-82	80	54	16	10	.738	19	15	4	.789
*1982-83	80	42	26	12	.600	20	15	5	.769
	320	**183**	**88**	**49**	**.648**	**78**	**60**	**18**	**.769**

Mike Bossy, Bob Bourne, Clark Gillies, Butch Goring, Anders Kallur, Gord Lane, Dave Langevin, Wayne Merrick, Ken Morrow, Bob Nystrom, Stefan Persson, Denis Potvin, Billy Smith, Duane Sutter, John Tonelli, Bryan Trottier

Denis Potvin	D	1st (1981)
Mike Bossy	RW	1st (1981, 1982, 1983)
Billy Smith	G	1st (1982)
Bryan Trottier	C	2nd (1982)
John Tonelli	LW	2nd (1982)
Roland Melanson	G	2nd (1983)

Bryan Trottier, Conn Smythe, 1980
Butch Goring, Conn Smythe, 1981
Billy Smith, Vezina, 1982; Jennings, 1983; Conn Smythe, 1983
Mike Bossy, Conn Smythe, 1982; Lady Byng, 1983
Roland Melanson, Jennings, 1983

Edmonton 1984-90

	Regular Season					Playoffs		
	GP	W	L	T	PCT	GP	W	L	PCT
*1984-85	80	49	20	11	.681	18	15	3	.833
1985-86	80	56	17	7	.744	10	6	4	.600
*1986-87	80	50	24	6	.663	21	16	5	.762
*1987-88	80	44	25	11	.619	18	16	2	.889
1988-89	80	38	34	8	.525	7	3	4	.429
*1989-90	80	38	28	14	.563	22	16	6	.727
	560	**332**	**166**	**62**	**.648**	**115**	**87**	**28**	**.757**

Glenn Anderson, Grant Fuhr, Randy Gregg, Charlie Huddy, Jari Kurri, Kevin Lowe, Mark Messier

Wayne Gretzky	C	1st (1984, 1985, 1986, 1987); 2nd (1988)
Paul Coffey	D	1st (1985, 1986); 2nd (1984)
		1st (1985, 1987); 2nd (1984, 1986, 1989)
Mark Messier	C	1st (1990);
	LW	2nd (1984)
Grant Fuhr	G	1st (1988)

Wayne Gretzky, Art Ross, 1984, 1985, 1986, 1987; Hart, 1984, 1985, 1986, 1987; Conn Smythe, 1985, 1988; Pearson, 1984, 1985, 1987
Mark Messier, Conn Smythe, 1984; Hart, 1990; Pearson, 1990
Jari Kurri, Lady Byng, 1985
Paul Coffey, Norris, 1985, 1986
Grant Fuhr, Vezina, 1988
Bill Ranford, Conn Smythe, 1990

* Stanley Cup winner

CHAPTER 21

Final Series Game Summaries

2002–1991

2002

DETROIT RED WINGS - CAROLINA HURRICANES

Game #1 - June 4, 2002 - Joe Louis Arena - Carolina 3, Detroit 2 (OT)

CAROLINA: Kevyn Adams, Bates Battaglia, Rod Brind'Amour, Erik Cole, Jeff Daniels, Ron Francis, Martin Gelinas, Bret Hedican, Sean Hill, Arturs Irbe, Sami Kapanen, Marek Malik, Jeff O'Neill, Jaroslav Svoboda, Josef Vasicek, Niclas Wallin, Aaron Ward, Glen Wesley, Tommy Westlund.
DETROIT: Chris Chelios, Mathieu Dandenault, Pavel Datsyuk, Boyd Devereaux, Kris Draper, Steve Duchesne, Sergei Fedorov, Jiri Fischer, Dominik Hasek, Tomas Holmstrom, Brett Hull, Igor Larionov, Nicklas Lidstrom, Kirk Maltby, Darren McCarty, Fredrik Olausson, Luc Robitaille, Brendan Shanahan, Steve Yzerman.

First Period
1. DETROIT   FEDOROV (YZERMAN)   15:21 (PPG)
Penalties: Hedican (Car) (high sticking) 8:03, Robitaille (Det) (tripping) 10:28, Hill (Car) (tripping) 11:15, Wesley (Car) (interference) 15:03.

Second Period
2. CAROLINA   HILL (KAPANEN, FRANCIS)   3:30 (PPG)
3. DETROIT   MALTBY (McCARTY)   10:39
4. CAROLINA   O'NEILL (WARD)   19:10
Penalties: Carolina bench (too many men) 0:34, Larionov (Det) (high sticking) 2:07, Draper (Det) (hooking) 2:44, Svoboda (Car) (high sticking) 4:28, Wallin (Car) (roughing) 7:41, Dandenault (Det) (tripping) 12:12.

Third Period
No scoring.
Penalties: Devereaux (Det) (holding the stick) 5:49, Larionov (Det) (high sticking) 12:17, Cole (Car) (hooking) 18:19.

First Overtime
5. CAROLINA   FRANCIS (O'NEILL, KAPANEN)   0:58 (GWG)
Penalties: none.

Goalies: Irbe (Car), Hasek (Det)
Shots:	Car	7	-	13	-	5	-	1	26
	Det	8	-	12	-	5	-	0	25

Referees: Bill McCreary, Stephen Walkom
Linesmen: Brad Lazarowich, Brian Murphy

Game #2 - June 6, 2002 - Joe Louis Arena - Detroit 3, Carolina 1

CAROLINA: Kevyn Adams, Bates Battaglia, Rod Brind'Amour, Erik Cole, Jeff Daniels, Ron Francis, Martin Gelinas, Bret Hedican, Sean Hill, Arturs Irbe, Sami Kapanen, Marek Malik, Jeff O'Neill, Jaroslav Svoboda, Josef Vasicek, Niclas Wallin, Aaron Ward, Glen Wesley, Tommy Westlund.
DETROIT: Chris Chelios, Mathieu Dandenault, Pavel Datsyuk, Boyd Devereaux, Kris Draper, Steve Duchesne, Sergei Fedorov, Jiri Fischer, Dominik Hasek, Tomas Holmstrom, Brett Hull, Igor Larionov, Nicklas Lidstrom, Kirk Maltby, Darren McCarty, Fredrik Olausson, Luc Robitaille, Brendan Shanahan, Steve Yzerman.

First Period
1. DETROIT   MALTBY (DRAPER, CHELIOS)   6:33 (SHG)
2. CAROLINA   BRIND'AMOUR (unassisted)   14:47 (SHG)
Penalties: Draper (Det) (boarding) 1:25, Duchesne (Det) (holding) 5:21, Hill (Car) (slashing) 6:33, Svoboda (Car) (roughing) 14:03, Hill (Car) (holding) 16:23.

Second Period
No scoring.
Penalties: Battaglia (Car) (holding) 1:05, Duchesne (Det) (tripping) 3:55, Detroit bench (too many men) 7:23, Gelinas (Car) (interference) 10:10, Ward (Car) (holding) 18:03.

Third Period
3. DETROIT   LIDSTROM (FEDOROV, YZERMAN)   14:52 (PPG,GWG)
4. DETROIT   DRAPER (LIDSTROM, OLAUSSON)   15:05
Penalties: Fischer (Det) (high sticking) 9:38, Gelinas (Car) (slashing) 14:00, Fischer (Det) (slashing) 17:15, Battaglia (Car) (charging) 17:45, Brind'Amour (Car), Cole (Car), McCarty (Det), Maltby (Det), Chelios (Det) (roughing) 19:33, Hull (Det) (tripping) 19:41.

Goalies: Irbe (Car), Hasek (Det)
Shots:	Car	7	-	4	-	6	17
	Det	9	-	8	-	13	30

Referees: Paul Devorski, Don Koharski
Linesmen: Brad Lazarowich, Jean Morin

Game #3 - June 8, 2002 - Entertainment and Sports Arena - Detroit 3, Carolina 2 (3 OT)

DETROIT: Chris Chelios, Mathieu Dandenault, Pavel Datsyuk, Boyd Devereaux, Kris Draper, Steve Duchesne, Sergei Fedorov, Jiri Fischer, Dominik Hasek, Tomas Holmstrom, Brett Hull, Igor Larionov, Nicklas Lidstrom, Kirk Maltby, Darren McCarty, Fredrik Olausson, Luc Robitaille, Brendan Shanahan, Steve Yzerman.
CAROLINA: Kevyn Adams, Bates Battaglia, Rod Brind'Amour, Erik Cole, Jeff Daniels, Ron Francis, Martin Gelinas, Bret Hedican, Sean Hill, Arturs Irbe, Sami Kapanen, Marek Malik, Jeff O'Neill, Jaroslav Svoboda, Josef Vasicek, Niclas Wallin, Aaron Ward, Glen Wesley, Tommy Westlund.

First Period
1. CAROLINA   VASICEK (GELINAS, WESLEY)   14:49
Penalties: Brind'Amour (Car) (holding the stick) 1:45, Hedican (Car) (boarding) 3:32, O'Neill (Car) (boarding) 11:34, Lidstrom (Det) (tripping) 12:30, Devereaux (Det) (slashing) 19:15.

Second Period
2. DETROIT   LARIONOV (HULL)   5:33
Penalties: Maltby (Det), Ward (Car) (unsportsmanlike conduct) 5:13, Chelios (Det) (interference) 8:12, Fedorov (Det), Hill (Car) (holding) 19:44.

Third Period
3. CAROLINA   O'NEILL (FRANCIS)   7:34
4. DETROIT   HULL (LIDSTROM, FEDOROV)   18:46
Penalties: Shanahan (Det), Vasicek (Car) (roughing) 5:25, Duchesne (Det) (holding) 9:58, Shanahan (Det), Hill (Car) (roughing) 19:01.

First Overtime
No scoring.
Penalties: Duchesne (Det), Svoboda (Car) (roughing) 18:23.

Second Overtime
No scoring.
Penalties: Cole (Car) (holding the stick) 8:35, Olausson (Det) (holding) 13:25.

Third Overtime
5. DETROIT   LARIONOV (HOLMSTROM, DUCHESNE)   14:47 (GWG)
Penalties: none.

Goalies: Hasek (Det), Irbe (Car)
Shots:	Det	6	-	7	-	16	-	11	-	6	-	7	53
	Car	8	-	6	-	7	-	5	-	8	-	9	43

Referees: Bill McCreary, Stephen Walkom
Linesmen: Brian Murphy, Dan Schachte

Game #4 - June 10, 2002 - Entertainment and Sports Arena - Detroit 3, Carolina 0

DETROIT: Chris Chelios, Mathieu Dandenault, Pavel Datsyuk, Boyd Devereaux, Kris Draper, Steve Duchesne, Sergei Fedorov, Jiri Fischer, Dominik Hasek, Tomas Holmstrom, Brett Hull, Igor Larionov, Nicklas Lidstrom, Kirk Maltby, Darren McCarty, Fredrik Olausson, Luc Robitaille, Brendan Shanahan, Steve Yzerman.
CAROLINA: Kevyn Adams, Bates Battaglia, Rod Brind'Amour, Erik Cole, Jeff Daniels, Ron Francis, Martin Gelinas, Bret Hedican, Sean Hill, Arturs Irbe, Sami Kapanen, Marek Malik, Jeff O'Neill, Jaroslav Svoboda, Josef Vasicek, Niclas Wallin, Aaron Ward, Glen Wesley, Tommy Westlund.

First Period
No scoring.
Penalties: Wesley (Car) (hooking) 2:05, Fedorov (Det) (high sticking), Cole (Car) (goaltender interference) 16:54.

Second Period
1. DETROIT   HULL (DEVEREAUX, OLAUSSON)   6:32 (GWG)
Penalties: Robitaille (Det) (high sticking) 9:06, Duchesne (Det) (holding the stick) 14:34.

Third Period
2. DETROIT   LARIONOV (FISCHER, ROBITAILLE)   3:43
3. DETROIT   SHANAHAN (FEDOROV, CHELIOS)   14:43
Penalties: Hill (Car) (boarding) 8:34.

Goalies: Hasek (Det), Irbe (Car)
Shots:	Det	10	-	6	-	11	27
	Car	6	-	7	-	4	17

Referees: Paul Devorski, Don Koharski
Linesmen: Jean Morin, Dan Schachte

Game #5 - June 13, 2002 - Joe Louis Arena - Detroit 3, Carolina 1

CAROLINA: Kevyn Adams, Bates Battaglia, Rod Brind'Amour, Erik Cole, Jeff Daniels, Ron Francis, Martin Gelinas, Bret Hedican, Sean Hill, Arturs Irbe, Sami Kapanen, Marek Malik, Jeff O'Neill, Jaroslav Svoboda, Josef Vasicek, Niclas Wallin, Aaron Ward, Glen Wesley, Tommy Westlund.
DETROIT: Chris Chelios, Mathieu Dandenault, Pavel Datsyuk, Boyd Devereaux, Kris Draper, Steve Duchesne, Sergei Fedorov, Dominik Hasek, Tomas Holmstrom, Brett Hull, Igor Larionov, Nicklas Lidstrom, Kirk Maltby, Darren McCarty, Fredrik Olausson, Luc Robitaille, Brendan Shanahan, Jiri Slegr, Steve Yzerman.

First Period
No scoring.
Penalties: Carolina bench (too many men) 12:09.

Second Period
1.	DETROIT	HOLMSTROM (LARIONOV, CHELIOS)	4:07
2.	DETROIT	SHANAHAN (FEDOROV, YZERMAN)	14:04 (PPG,GWG)
3.	CAROLINA	O'NEILL (HILL, WESLEY)	18:50 (PPG)

Penalties: Slegr (Det) (holding) 6:00, Svoboda (Car) (roughing) 13:34, Cole (Car) (roughing) 16:15, Shanahan (Det) (hooking) 16:53.

Third Period
| 4. | DETROIT | SHANAHAN (YZERMAN) | 19:15 (ENG) |

Penalties: Fedorov (Det) (cross-checking) 5:23, Vasicek (Car) (interference) 8:12.

Goalies: Irbe (Car), Hasek (Det)

Shots:	Car	5	-	7	-	5	17
	Det	12	-	8	-	7	27

Referees: Bill McCreary, Stephen Walkom
Linesmen: Brad Lazarowich, Brian Murphy

2001

COLORADO AVALANCHE – NEW JERSEY DEVILS

Game #1 - May 26, 2001 - Pepsi Center - Colorado 5, New Jersey 0

NEW JERSEY: Jason Arnott, Martin Brodeur, Sergei Brylin, Ken Daneyko, Patrik Elias, Scott Gomez, Bobby Holik, John Madden, Randy McKay, Alexander Mogilny, Sergei Nemchinov, Scott Niedermayer, Sean O'Donnell, Jay Pandolfo, Brian Rafalski, Scott Stevens, Turner Stevenson, Petr Sykora, Colin White.
COLORADO: Rob Blake, Raymond Bourque, Greg De Vries, Chris Dingman, Chris Drury, Adam Foote, Milan Hejduk, Dan Hinote, Jon Klemm, Eric Messier, Ville Nieminen, Shjon Podein, Dave Reid, Steve Reinprecht, Patrick Roy, Joe Sakic, Martin Skoula, Alex Tanguay, Stephane Yelle.

First Period
| 1. | COLORADO | SAKIC (HEJDUK, BLAKE) | 11:07 (GWG) |

Penalties: White (NJ) (holding) 4:28, Podein (Col) (elbowing) 13:46.

Second Period
| 2. | COLORADO | DRURY (HINOTE, NIEMINEN) | 9:35 |
| 3. | COLORADO | SAKIC (BLAKE, SKOULA) | 15:06 |

Penalties: De Vries (Col) (boarding) 7:01, Tanguay (Col) (tripping) 10:46, Daneyko (NJ) (boarding), Nieminen (Col) (interference) 14:16.

Third Period
| 4. | COLORADO | BLAKE (TANGUAY, SAKIC) | 5:36 (PPG) |
| 5. | COLORADO | REINPRECHT (DINGMAN, REID) | 17:36 |

Penalties: Hinote (Col) (holding) 3:30, Stevenson (NJ) (interference) 4:45, Sykora (NJ) (charging), White (NJ) (roughing), Foote (Col) (double minor, roughing) 8:04, Daneyko (NJ) (slashing, roughing) 9:43, O'Donnell (NJ) (roughing), Podein (Col) (tripping) 11:34, De Vries (Col) (tripping) 13:20, O'Donnell (NJ) (instigator, fighting, misconduct), Dingman (Col) (fighting) 17:36, Hinote (Col) (roughing) 18:20.

Goalies: Brodeur (NJ), Roy (Col)

Shots:	NJ	7	-	11	-	7	25
	Col	14	-	7	-	9	30

Referees: Paul Devorski, Dan Marouelli
Linesmen: Brad Lazarowich, Dan Schachte

Game #2 - May 29, 2001 - Pepsi Center - New Jersey 2, Colorado 1

NEW JERSEY: Jason Arnott, Martin Brodeur, Sergei Brylin, Bob Corkum, Ken Daneyko, Patrik Elias, Scott Gomez, Bobby Holik, John Madden, Alexander Mogilny, Sergei Nemchinov, Scott Niedermayer, Sean O'Donnell, Jay Pandolfo, Brian Rafalski, Scott Stevens, Turner Stevenson, Petr Sykora, Colin White.
COLORADO: Rob Blake, Raymond Bourque, Greg De Vries, Chris Dingman, Chris Drury, Adam Foote, Milan Hejduk, Dan Hinote, Jon Klemm, Eric Messier, Ville Nieminen, Shjon Podein, Dave Reid, Steve Reinprecht, Patrick Roy, Joe Sakic, Martin Skoula, Alex Tanguay, Stephane Yelle.

First Period
1.	COLORADO	SAKIC (HEJDUK, BLAKE)	5:58 (PPG)
2.	NEW JERSEY	CORKUM (RAFALSKI)	14:29
3.	NEW JERSEY	STEVENSON (NIEDERMAYER, MOGILNY)	17:20 (GWG)

Penalties: Niedermayer (NJ) (cross-checking) 1:43, Brylin (NJ) (interference) 4:53, Elias (NJ) (slashing) 12:28, Messier (Col) (roughing) 14:46, Foote (Col) (holding the stick) 15:17, Holik (NJ) (slashing) 19:39.

Second Period
No scoring.
Penalties: Madden (NJ) (diving), De Vries (Col) (interference) 9:11, Skoula (Col) (holding) 14:47.

Third Period
No scoring.
Penalties: Daneyko (NJ) (cross-checking) 1:28, White (NJ), Nieminen (Col) (roughing) 2:58, Mogilny (NJ) (high sticking) 4:26.

Goalies: Brodeur (NJ), Roy (Col)

Shots:	NJ	12	-	6	-	2	20
	Col	8	-	4	-	8	20

Referees: Bill McCreary, Rob Shick
Linesmen: Brad Lazarowich, Mark Wheler

Game #3 - May 31, 2001 - Continental Airlines Arena - Colorado 3, New Jersey 1

COLORADO: Rob Blake, Raymond Bourque, Greg De Vries, Chris Dingman, Chris Drury, Adam Foote, Milan Hejduk, Dan Hinote, Jon Klemm, Eric Messier, Ville Nieminen, Shjon Podein, Dave Reid, Steve Reinprecht, Patrick Roy, Joe Sakic, Martin Skoula, Alex Tanguay, Stephane Yelle.
NEW JERSEY: Jason Arnott, Martin Brodeur, Sergei Brylin, Bob Corkum, Ken Daneyko, Patrik Elias, Scott Gomez, Bobby Holik, John Madden, Alexander Mogilny, Sergei Nemchinov, Scott Niedermayer, Sean O'Donnell, Jay Pandolfo, Brian Rafalski, Scott Stevens, Turner Stevenson, Petr Sykora, Colin White.

First Period
| 1. | NEW JERSEY | ARNOTT (HOLIK, ELIAS) | 3:16 (PPG) |
| 2. | COLORADO | SKOULA (PODEIN, MESSIER) | 10:38 |

Penalties: Foote (Col) (tripping) 1:29, Yelle (Col) (interference) 6:28, Brylin (NJ) (interference) 14:29, Tanguay (Col) (hooking) 15:03, Nieminen (Col) (boarding) 16:29.

Second Period
No scoring.
Penalties: O'Donnell (NJ) (cross-checking) 2:40, O'Donnell (NJ) (holding) 8:25, Foote (Col) (tripping) 14:52, Arnott (NJ) (boarding) 19:02.

Third Period
| 3. | COLORADO | BOURQUE (SAKIC) | 0:31 (PPG,GWG) |
| 4. | COLORADO | HINOTE (NIEMINEN, DRURY) | 6:28 |

Penalties: Klemm (Col) (holding) 8:22.

Goalies: Roy (Col), Brodeur (NJ)

Shots:	Col	5	-	11	-	5	21
	NJ	8	-	3	-	11	22

Referees: Kerry Fraser, Dan Marouelli
Linesmen: Kevin Collins, Dan Schachte

Game #4 - June 2, 2001 - Continental Airlines Arena - New Jersey 3, Colorado 2

COLORADO: Rob Blake, Raymond Bourque, Greg De Vries, Chris Dingman, Chris Drury, Adam Foote, Milan Hejduk, Dan Hinote, Jon Klemm, Eric Messier, Ville Nieminen, Shjon Podein, Dave Reid, Steve Reinprecht, Patrick Roy, Joe Sakic, Martin Skoula, Alex Tanguay, Stephane Yelle.
NEW JERSEY: Jason Arnott, Martin Brodeur, Sergei Brylin, Bob Corkum, Ken Daneyko, Patrik Elias, Scott Gomez, Bobby Holik, John Madden, Alexander Mogilny, Sergei Nemchinov, Scott Niedermayer, Sean O'Donnell, Jay Pandolfo, Brian Rafalski, Scott Stevens, Turner Stevenson, Petr Sykora, Colin White.

First Period
1.   COLORADO   BLAKE (TANGUAY)   3:58
Penalties: Stevenson (NJ) (interference) 1:36, Gomez (NJ) (goaltender interference) 4:42, Yelle (Col) (diving), Sykora (NJ) (hooking) 7:15, Stevens (NJ) (hooking) 7:42, Sakic (Col) (hooking) 8:26.

Second Period
2.   NEW JERSEY   ELIAS (SYKORA)   3:42 (SHG)
3.   COLORADO   DRURY (DINGMAN, HINOTE)   13:54
Penalties: White (NJ) (roughing) 2:18, Skoula (Col) (interference) 10:16, Stevenson (NJ) (tripping) 16:42.

Third Period
4.   NEW JERSEY   GOMEZ (PANDOLFO, CORKUM)   8:09
5.   NEW JERSEY   SYKORA (ELIAS, HOLIK)   17:23 (GWG)
Penalties: none.

Goalies: Roy (Col), Brodeur (NJ)
          Shots: Col   4 - 4 - 4   12
                   NJ   8 - 11 - 16   35

Referees: Paul Devorski, Bill McCreary
Linesmen: Kevin Collins, Dan Schachte

Game #5 - June 4, 2001 - Pepsi Center - New Jersey 4, Colorado 1

NEW JERSEY: Martin Brodeur, Sergei Brylin, Bob Corkum, Ken Daneyko, Patrik Elias, Scott Gomez, Bobby Holik, John Madden, Jim McKenzie, Alexander Mogilny, Sergei Nemchinov, Scott Niedermayer, Jay Pandolfo, Brian Rafalski, Scott Stevens, Turner Stevenson, Ken Sutton, Petr Sykora, Colin White.
COLORADO: Rob Blake, Raymond Bourque, Greg De Vries, Chris Dingman, Chris Drury, Adam Foote, Milan Hejduk, Dan Hinote, Jon Klemm, Eric Messier, Ville Nieminen, Shjon Podein, Dave Reid, Steve Reinprecht, Patrick Roy, Joe Sakic, Martin Skoula, Alex Tanguay, Stephane Yelle.

First Period
1.   NEW JERSEY   ELIAS (SYKORA, RAFALSKI)   3:09
2.   COLORADO   TANGUAY (SAKIC, BOURQUE)   10:09 (PPG)
3.   NEW JERSEY   MOGILNY (GOMEZ, RAFALSKI)   18:47 (GWG)
Penalties: Holik (NJ) (tripping) 8:56, New Jersey bench (too many men) 19:24.

Second Period
4.   NEW JERSEY   BRYLIN (MOGILNY, NIEDERMAYER)   4:39 (PPG)
Penalties: Blake (Col) (interference) 3:53, Niedermayer (NJ) (interference) 16:33.

Third Period
5.   NEW JERSEY   MADDEN (STEVENSON, BRYLIN)   18:05
Penalties: Stevens (NJ), Foote (Col) (roughing) 10:11, McKenzie (NJ) (holding) 12:54, Sutton (NJ), Hinote (Col) (roughing) 20:00.

Goalies: Brodeur (NJ), Roy (Col)
          Shots: NJ   6 - 10 - 10   26
                   Col   6 - 9 - 8   23

Referees: Kerry Fraser, Rob Shick
Linesmen: Brad Lazarowich, Mark Wheler

Game #6 - June 7, 2001 - Continental Airlines Arena - Colorado 4, New Jersey 0

COLORADO: Rob Blake, Raymond Bourque, Greg De Vries, Chris Dingman, Chris Drury, Adam Foote, Milan Hejduk, Dan Hinote, Jon Klemm, Eric Messier, Ville Nieminen, Shjon Podein, Dave Reid, Steve Reinprecht, Patrick Roy, Joe Sakic, Martin Skoula, Alex Tanguay, Stephane Yelle.
NEW JERSEY: Jason Arnott, Martin Brodeur, Sergei Brylin, Bob Corkum, Ken Daneyko, Patrik Elias, Scott Gomez, Bobby Holik, John Madden, Alexander Mogilny, Sergei Nemchinov, Scott Niedermayer, Jay Pandolfo, Brian Rafalski, Scott Stevens, Turner Stevenson, Ken Sutton, Petr Sykora, Colin White.

First Period
1.   COLORADO   FOOTE (unassisted)   18:02 (GWG)
Penalties: Reid (Col) (obstruction-holding the stick) 5:22, Foote (Col) (high sticking) 7:20, Mogilny (NJ) (hooking) 9:12, Skoula (Col) (hooking) 11:08.

Second Period
2.   COLORADO   NIEMINEN (SKOULA, FOOTE)   2:26 (PPG)
3.   COLORADO   DRURY (REINPRECHT, FOOTE)   18:27
Penalties: Holik (NJ) (roughing) 0:29, Colorado bench (too many men) 8:35, Niedermayer (NJ) (holding) 11:10, Bourque (Col) (obstruction-hooking) 13:01.

Third Period
4.   COLORADO   TANGUAY (REID, SAKIC)   13:46
Penalties: Podein (Col) (interference) 3:24, Niedermayer (NJ) (slashing) 8:26, White (NJ) (slashing) 17:27, Hinote (Col) (fighting), Sutton (NJ) (roughing, fighting) 18:19, White (NJ) (high sticking) 19:43, Dingman (Col), Daneyko (NJ) (fighting) 19:48.

Goalies: Roy (Col), Brodeur (NJ)
          Shots: Col   5 - 7 - 6   18
                   NJ   12 - 7 - 5   24

Referees: Dan Marouelli, Bill McCreary
Linesmen: Kevin Collins, Brad Lazarowich

Game #7 - June 9, 2001 - Pepsi Center - Colorado 3, New Jersey 1

NEW JERSEY: Jason Arnott, Martin Brodeur, Sergei Brylin, Bob Corkum, Ken Daneyko, Patrik Elias, Scott Gomez, Bobby Holik, John Madden, Alexander Mogilny, Sergei Nemchinov, Scott Niedermayer, Sean O'Donnell, Jay Pandolfo, Brian Rafalski, Scott Stevens, Turner Stevenson, Petr Sykora, Colin White.
COLORADO: Rob Blake, Raymond Bourque, Greg De Vries, Chris Dingman, Chris Drury, Adam Foote, Milan Hejduk, Dan Hinote, Jon Klemm, Eric Messier, Ville Nieminen, Shjon Podein, Dave Reid, Steve Reinprecht, Patrick Roy, Joe Sakic, Martin Skoula, Alex Tanguay, Stephane Yelle.

First Period
1.   COLORADO   TANGUAY (HINOTE)   7:58
Penalties: Brylin (NJ) (boarding) 3:20, Gomez (NJ) (holding) 16:06.

Second Period
2.   COLORADO   TANGUAY (SAKIC, FOOTE)   4:57 (GWG)
3.   COLORADO   SAKIC (HEJDUK, TANGUAY)   6:16 (PPG)
4.   NEW JERSEY   SYKORA (ELIAS, ARNOTT)   9:33 (PPG)
Penalties: O'Donnell (NJ) (high sticking) 5:51, Messier (Col) (high sticking) 9:22, Arnott (NJ) (tripping), Messier (Col) (holding) 12:23.

Third Period
No scoring.
Penalties: Blake (Col) (interference) 4:59, White (NJ) (high sticking) 10:32, Foote (Col) (holding the stick) 12:11, Stevens (NJ) (tripping) 14:42.

Goalies: Brodeur (NJ), Roy (Col)
          Shots: NJ   9 - 12 - 5   26
                   Col   10 - 7 - 5   22

Referees: Kerry Fraser, Dan Marouelli
Linesmen: Kevin Collins, Dan Schachte

2000

NEW JERSEY DEVILS - DALLAS STARS

Game #1 - May 30, 2000 - Continental Airlines Arena - New Jersey 7, Dallas 3

DALLAS: Ed Belfour, Guy Carbonneau, Sylvain Cote, Manny Fernandez, Derian Hatcher, Brett Hull, Mike Keane, Jiri Lehtinen, Roman Lyashenko, Dave Manson, Grant Marshall, Richard Matvichuk, Mike Modano, Brenden Morrow, Kirk Muller, Joe Nieuwendyk, Jon Sim, Darryl Sydor, Scott Thornton, Sergei Zubov.

NEW JERSEY: Jason Arnott, Martin Brodeur, Sergei Brylin, Ken Daneyko, Patrik Elias, Scott Gomez, Bobby Holik, Claude Lemieux, John Madden, Vladimir Malakhov, Randy McKay, Alexander Mogilny, Sergei Nemchinov, Scott Niedermayer, Jay Pandolfo, Brian Rafalski, Scott Stevens, Petr Sykora, Colin White.

First Period
1.	NEW JERSEY	ARNOTT (SYKORA, ELIAS)	7:22
2.	DALLAS	SYDOR (LEHTINEN, KEANE)	13:13

Penalties: none.

Second Period
3.	NEW JERSEY	DANEYKO (BRYLIN, MADDEN)	2:52
4.	NEW JERSEY	SYKORA (ELIAS, ARNOTT)	10:28
5.	NEW JERSEY	STEVENS (PANDOLFO, RAFALSKI)	16:04 (GWG)

Penalties: Hatcher (Dal) (slashing) 18:20.

Third Period
6.	NEW JERSEY	BRYLIN (McKAY)	2:21
7.	NEW JERSEY	SYKORA (ARNOTT, ELIAS)	3:02
8.	NEW JERSEY	ARNOTT (HOLIK, SYKORA)	5:12 (PPG)
9.	DALLAS	SIM (CARBONNEAU)	7:43
10.	DALLAS	MULLER (CARBONNEAU)	7:55

Penalties: Thornton (Dal) (roughing) 3:35, Manson (Dal) (slashing) 12:05, Manson (Dal) (elbowing) 19:55.

Goalies: Belfour, Fernandez (Dal), Brodeur (NJ)

Shots:	Dal	5	-	7	-	6	18
	NJ	7	-	9	-	10	26

Referees: Don Koharski, Bill McCreary
Linesmen: Ray Scapinello, Jay Sharrers

Game #2 - June 1, 2000 - Continental Airlines Arena - Dallas 2, New Jersey 1

DALLAS: Ed Belfour, Guy Carbonneau, Sylvain Cote, Derian Hatcher, Brett Hull, Mike Keane, Jiri Lehtinen, Roman Lyashenko, Dave Manson, Richard Matvichuk, Mike Modano, Brenden Morrow, Kirk Muller, Joe Nieuwendyk, Jon Sim, Blake Sloan, Darryl Sydor, Scott Thornton, Sergei Zubov.

NEW JERSEY: Jason Arnott, Martin Brodeur, Sergei Brylin, Ken Daneyko, Patrik Elias, Scott Gomez, Bobby Holik, Claude Lemieux, John Madden, Vladimir Malakhov, Randy McKay, Alexander Mogilny, Sergei Nemchinov, Scott Niedermayer, Jay Pandolfo, Brian Rafalski, Scott Stevens, Petr Sykora, Colin White..

First Period
1.	DALLAS	HULL (MODANO, MATVICHUK)	4:25
2.	NEW JERSEY	MOGILNY (GOMEZ, STEVENS)	12:42

Penalties: Lemieux (NJ) (holding) 8:20, Sloan (Dal), Rafalski (NJ) (roughing) 10:56, Matvichuk (Dal), Holik (NJ) (roughing) 13:52, Matvichuk (Dal) (roughing) 18:27.

Second Period
No scoring.
Penalties: none.

Third Period
3.	DALLAS	HULL (LEHTINEN, MODANO)	15:44 (GWG)

Penalties: Sim (Dal) (holding) 10:48.

Goalies: Belfour (Dal), Brodeur (NJ)

Shots:	Dal	3	-	7	-	7	17
	NJ	9	-	8	-	11	28

Referees: Kerry Fraser, Dan Marouelli
Linesmen: Gord Broseker, Dan Schachte

Game #3 - June 3, 2000 - Reunion Arena - New Jersey 2, Dallas 1

NEW JERSEY: Jason Arnott, Martin Brodeur, Sergei Brylin, Ken Daneyko, Patrik Elias, Scott Gomez, Bobby Holik, Claude Lemieux, John Madden, Vladimir Malakhov, Randy McKay, Alexander Mogilny, Sergei Nemchinov, Scott Niedermayer, Jay Pandolfo, Brian Rafalski, Scott Stevens, Petr Sykora, Colin White.

DALLAS: Ed Belfour, Guy Carbonneau, Sylvain Cote, Derian Hatcher, Brett Hull, Mike Keane, Jiri Lehtinen, Roman Lyashenko, Dave Manson, Richard Matvichuk, Mike Modano, Brenden Morrow, Kirk Muller, Joe Nieuwendyk, Jon Sim, Blake Sloan, Darryl Sydor, Scott Thornton, Sergei Zubov.

First Period
1.	DALLAS	COTE	13:08 (PPG)
2.	NEW JERSEY	ARNOTT (RAFALSKI, WHITE)	18:06

Penalties: Nemchinov (NJ) (slashing) 12:46, Malakhov (NJ) (interference) 13:51, Lemieux (NJ) (cross-checking) 15:02.

Second Period
3.	NEW JERSEY	SYKORA (ARNOTT, RAFALSKI)	12:27 (PPG,GWG)

Penalties: Hull (Dal) (interference) 8:09, Cote (Dal) (elbowing) 11:03.

Third Period
No scoring.
Penalties: Brodeur (NJ) (delay of game) 15:45.

Goalies: Brodeur (NJ), Belfour (Dal)

Shots:	NJ	10	-	16	-	5	31
	Dal	7	-	9	-	7	23

Referees: Terry Gregson, Don Koharski
Linesmen: Ray Scapinello, Jay Sharrers

Game #4 - June 5, 2000 - Reunion Arena - New Jersey 3, Dallas 1

NEW JERSEY: Jason Arnott, Martin Brodeur, Sergei Brylin, Ken Daneyko, Patrik Elias, Scott Gomez, Bobby Holik, Claude Lemieux, John Madden, Vladimir Malakhov, Randy McKay, Alexander Mogilny, Sergei Nemchinov, Scott Niedermayer, Jay Pandolfo, Brian Rafalski, Scott Stevens, Petr Sykora, Colin White.

DALLAS: Ed Belfour, Guy Carbonneau, Sylvain Cote, Aaron Gavey, Derian Hatcher, Brett Hull, Mike Keane, Jamie Langenbrunner, Jiri Lehtinen, Dave Manson, Richard Matvichuk, Mike Modano, Brenden Morrow, Kirk Muller, Joe Nieuwendyk, Jon Sim, Darryl Sydor, Scott Thornton, Sergei Zubov.

First Period
No scoring.
Penalties: Morrow (Dal) (obstruction-tripping) 14:38, Manson (Dal) (slashing) 17:27, Niedermayer (NJ) (obstruction-holding) 19:34.

Second Period
1.	DALLAS	NIEUWENDYK (SYDOR, HULL)	18:02 (PPG)

Penalties: Sykora (NJ) (hooking) 5:45, Keane (Dal) (boarding) 8:45, McKay (NJ) (hooking) 11:59, Malakhov (NJ) (cross-checking) 16:38.

Third Period
3.	NEW JERSEY	BRYLIN (MOGILNY, MALAKHOV)	2:27
4.	NEW JERSEY	MADDEN (NEMCHINOV, DANEYKO)	4:51 (SHG,GWG)
5.	NEW JERSEY	RAFALSKI (ELIAS)	6:08

Penalties: White (NJ) (interference) 3:17, Sim (Dal) (slashing) 11:43.

Goalies: Brodeur (NJ), Belfour (Dal)

Shots:	NJ	8	-	8	-	15	31
	Dal	6	-	7	-	4	17

Referees: Kerry Fraser, Bill McCreary
Linesmen: Gord Broseker, Dan Schachte

Game #5 - June 8, 2000 - Continental Airlines Arena - Dallas 1, New Jersey 0 (3 OT)

DALLAS: Ed Belfour, Guy Carbonneau, Sylvain Cote, Derian Hatcher, Brett Hull, Mike Keane, Jiri Lehtinen, Roman Lyashenko, Dave Manson, Grant Marshall, Richard Matvichuk, Mike Modano, Brenden Morrow, Kirk Muller, Joe Nieuwendyk, Jon Sim, Darryl Sydor, Scott Thornton, Sergei Zubov.
NEW JERSEY: Jason Arnott, Martin Brodeur, Sergei Brylin, Ken Daneyko, Patrik Elias, Scott Gomez, Bobby Holik, Claude Lemieux, John Madden, Vladimir Malakhov, Randy McKay, Alexander Mogilny, Sergei Nemchinov, Scott Niedermayer, Jay Pandolfo, Brian Rafalski, Scott Stevens, Petr Sykora, Colin White.

First Period
No scoring.
Penalties: Hatcher (Dal) (hooking) 11:01, Holik (NJ) (interference) 11:43.

Second Period
No scoring.
Penalties: Sykora (NJ) (high sticking) 14:23, Lehtinen (Dal) (high sticking) 17:01.

Third Period
No scoring.
Penalties: Morrow (Dal) (obstruction-tripping) 13:45.

First Overtime
No scoring.
Penalties: none.

Second Overtime
No scoring.
Penalties: none.

Third Overtime
1. DALLAS   MODANO (HULL, LEHTINEN)   6:21 (GWG)
Penalties: none.

Goalies: Belfour (Dal), Brodeur (NJ)

Shots:	Dal	11	-	6	-	5	-	5	-	12	-	2	41
	NJ	7	-	11	-	9	-	10	-	8	-	3	48

Referees: Don Koharski, Dan Marouelli
Linesmen: Ray Scapinello, Jay Sharrers

Game #6 - June 10, 2000 - Reunion Arena - New Jersey 2, Dallas 1 (2 OT)

NEW JERSEY: Jason Arnott, Martin Brodeur, Sergei Brylin, Ken Daneyko, Patrik Elias, Scott Gomez, Bobby Holik, Claude Lemieux, John Madden, Vladimir Malakhov, Randy McKay, Alexander Mogilny, Sergei Nemchinov, Scott Niedermayer, Jay Pandolfo, Brian Rafalski, Scott Stevens, Petr Sykora, Colin White.
DALLAS: Ed Belfour, Guy Carbonneau, Sylvain Cote, Derian Hatcher, Brett Hull, Mike Keane, Jiri Lehtinen, Dave Manson, Grant Marshall, Richard Matvichuk, Mike Modano, Brenden Morrow, Kirk Muller, Joe Nieuwendyk, Jon Sim, Blake Sloan, Darryl Sydor, Scott Thornton, Sergei Zubov.

First Period
No scoring.
Penalties: Daneyko (NJ) (slashing) 4:46, Sim (Dal) (elbowing) 6:54, Daneyko (NJ) (high sticking) 13:45.

Second Period
1. NEW JERSEY   NIEDERMAYER (LEMIEUX, PANDOLFO)   5:18 (PPG)
2. DALLAS   KEANE (THORNTON, MODANO)   6:27
Penalties: Rafalski (NJ) (holding) 3:30, Stevens (NJ), Hatcher (Dal) (roughing) 13:48, White (NJ), Thornton (Dal) (roughing) 19:21.

Third Period
No scoring.
Penalties: none.

First Overtime
No scoring.
Penalties: Arnott (NJ) (cross-checking) 18:43.

Second Overtime
1. NEW JERSEY   ARNOTT (ELIAS, STEVENS)   8:20 (GWG)
Penalties: none.

Goalies: Brodeur (NJ), Belfour (Dal)

Shots:	NJ	11	-	13	-	7	-	11	-	3	45
	Dal	7	-	9	-	13	-	1	-	1	31

Referees: Terry Gregson, Bill McCreary
Linesmen: Gord Broseker, Dan Schachte

1999

DALLAS STARS - BUFFALO SABRES

Game #1 - June 8, 1999 - Reunion Arena - Buffalo 3, Dallas 2 (OT)

BUFFALO: Stu Barnes, Curtis Brown, Michal Grosek, Dominik Hasek, Brian Holzinger, Joe Juneau, Jay McKee, James Patrick, Michael Peca, Wayne Primeau, Erik Rasmussen, Geoff Sanderson, Miroslav Satan, Richard Smehlik, Vaclav Varada, Dixon Ward, Rhett Warrener, Jason Woolley, Alexei Zhitnik.
DALLAS: Ed Belfour, Guy Carbonneau, Shawn Chambers, Derian Hatcher, Brett Hull, Mike Keane, Jamie Langenbrunner, Jere Lehtinen, Craig Ludwig, Richard Matvichuk, Mike Modano, Joe Nieuwendyk, Dave Reid, Jon Sim, Brian Skrudland, Blake Sloan, Darryl Sydor, Pat Verbeek, Sergei Zubov.

First Period
1. DALLAS   HULL (MODANO, LEHTINEN)   10:17 (PPG)
Penalties: Zubov (Dal) (roughing) 6:36, Satan (Buf) (boarding) 8:18, Patrick (Buf) (double minor, high sticking) 12:46, Ward (Buf) (interference) 19:11.

Second Period
No scoring.
Penalties: Varada (Buf) (goaltender interference) 4:53, Zhitnik (Buf) (interference) 7:07, Ward (Buf) (roughing) 9:34, Ludwig (Dal) (hooking) 12:21, Matvichuk (Dal) (interference) 16:33.

Third Period
2. BUFFALO   BARNES (JUNEAU, SMEHLIK)   8:33
3. BUFFALO   PRIMEAU (ZHITNIK, SMEHLIK)   13:37 (PPG)
4. DALLAS   LEHTINEN (MODANO, ZUBOV)   19:11
Penalties: Sydor (Dal) (obstruction-tripping) 12:10, McKee (Buf) (charging) 14:17.

First Overtime
5. BUFFALO   WOOLLEY (BROWN)   15:30 (GWG)
Penalties: Zhitnik (Buf) (hooking) 6:41, Sanderson (Buf) (boarding) 9:06.

Goalies: Hasek (Buf), Belfour (Dal)

Shots:	Buf	5	-	4	-	10	-	5	24
	Dal	11	-	13	-	6	-	7	37

Referees: Terry Gregson, Bill McCreary
Linesmen: Ray Scapinello, Jay Sharrers

Game #2 - June 10, 1999 - Reunion Arena - Dallas 4, Buffalo 2

BUFFALO: Stu Barnes, Curtis Brown, Dominik Hasek, Brian Holzinger, Joe Juneau, Paul Kruse, Jay McKee, James Patrick, Michael Peca, Wayne Primeau, Erik Rasmussen, Geoff Sanderson, Miroslav Satan, Richard Smehlik, Vaclav Varada, Dixon Ward, Rhett Warrener, Jason Woolley, Alexei Zhitnik.
DALLAS: Ed Belfour, Guy Carbonneau, Shawn Chambers, Derian Hatcher, Tony Hrkac, Brett Hull, Mike Keane, Jamie Langenbrunner, Jere Lehtinen, Craig Ludwig, Richard Matvichuk, Mike Modano, Joe Nieuwendyk, Dave Reid, Brian Skrudland, Blake Sloan, Darryl Sydor, Pat Verbeek, Sergei Zubov.

First Period
No scoring.
Penalties: Skrudland (Dal) (charging) 12:25, Zhitnik (Buf) (boarding) 15:31, Smehlik (Buf) (roughing), Zhitnik (Buf) (cross-checking), Holzinger (Buf) (fighting), Hatcher (Dal) (roughing), Nieuwendyk (Dal) (fighting), Modano (Dal) (tripping) 20:00.

Second Period
1. BUFFALO   PECA (WOOLLEY, SATAN)   7:27 (PPG)
2. DALLAS   LANGENBRUNNER (MATVICHUK, NIEUWENDYK)   18:26
Penalties: Sydor (Dal) (hooking) 5:41, Woolley (Buf) (interference) 9:19, Varada (Buf) (obstruction-tripping) 13:14, Zhitnik (Buf) (tripping) 20:00.

Third Period
3. DALLAS   LUDWIG (SKRUDLAND)   4:25
4. BUFFALO   ZHITNIK (unassisted)   5:36 (PPG)
5. DALLAS   HULL (HRKAC, CHAMBERS)   17:10 (GWG)
6. DALLAS   HATCHER (ZUBOV, KEANE)   19:34 (ENG)
Penalties: Sydor (Dal) (high sticking) 4:50, Varada (Buf) (high sticking) 10:32, Zhitnik (Buf) (hooking) 11:48, Hatcher (Dal) (high sticking) 17:31.

Goalies: Hasek (Buf), Belfour (Dal)

Shots:	Buf	7	-	10	-	4	21
	Dal	5	-	7	-	19	31

Referees: Kerry Fraser, Dan Marouelli
Linesmen: Gord Broseker, Kevin Collins

Game #3 - June 12, 1999 - Marine Midland Arena - Dallas 2, Buffalo 1

DALLAS: Ed Belfour, Guy Carbonneau, Shawn Chambers, Derian Hatcher, Tony Hrkac, Brett Hull, Mike Keane, Jamie Langenbrunner, Jere Lehtinen, Craig Ludwig, Richard Matvichuk, Mike Modano, Joe Nieuwendyk, Dave Reid, Brian Skrudland, Blake Sloan, Darryl Sydor, Pat Verbeek, Sergei Zubov.

BUFFALO: Stu Barnes, Curtis Brown, Dominik Hasek, Brian Holzinger, Joe Juneau, Jay McKee, James Patrick, Michael Peca, Wayne Primeau, Erik Rasmussen, Rob Ray, Geoff Sanderson, Miroslav Satan, Richard Smehlik, Vaclav Varada, Dixon Ward, Rhett Warrener, Jason Woolley, Alexei Zhitnik.

First Period
No scoring.
Penalties: Chambers (Dal) (roughing), Ludwig (Dal) (interference), Rasmussen (Buf) (roughing) 7:45, Matvichuk (Dal) (roughing) 9:43, Skrudland (Dal) (slashing) 18:13, Hatcher (Dal) (roughing) 18:46.

Second Period
1.   BUFFALO   BARNES (SMEHLIK, HOLZINGER)   7:51
2.   DALLAS   NIEUWENDYK (REID, LANGENBRUNNER)   15:33
Penalties: Zhitnik (Buf) (interference) 3:38, Modano (Dal) (tripping) 9:54, Modano (Dal) (slashing) 12:21, Holzinger (Buf) (high sticking) 19:09, Modano (Dal) (interference) 19:23.

Third Period
3.   DALLAS   NIEUWENDYK (LANGENBRUNNER, REID)   9:35 (GWG)
Penalties: Hrkac (Dal) (tripping) 17:38.
Goalies: Belfour (Dal), Hasek (Buf)
          Shots: Dal   8   - 13   -   8   29
                   Buf   3   -   6   -   3   12
Referees: Terry Gregson, Don Koharski
Linesmen: Ray Scapinello, Jay Sharrers

Game #4 - June 15, 1999 - Marine Midland Arena - Buffalo 2, Dallas 1

DALLAS: Ed Belfour, Guy Carbonneau, Shawn Chambers, Derian Hatcher, Tony Hrkac, Mike Keane, Jamie Langenbrunner, Jere Lehtinen, Craig Ludwig, Richard Matvichuk, Mike Modano, Joe Nieuwendyk, Dave Reid, Jon Sim, Brian Skrudland, Blake Sloan, Darryl Sydor, Pat Verbeek, Sergei Zubov.

BUFFALO: Stu Barnes, Curtis Brown, Randy Cunneyworth, Dominik Hasek, Brian Holzinger, Joe Juneau, Jay McKee, James Patrick, Michael Peca, Wayne Primeau, Erik Rasmussen, Geoff Sanderson, Miroslav Satan, Richard Smehlik, Vaclav Varada, Dixon Ward, Rhett Warrener, Jason Woolley, Alexei Zhitnik.

First Period
1.   BUFFALO   SANDERSON (unassisted)   8:09
2.   DALLAS   LEHTINEN (MODANO, HATCHER)   10:14 (PPG)
Penalties: Matvichuk (Dal) (roughing) 3:48, Primeau (Buf) (charging) 9:32, Woolley (Buf) (holding) 19:05.

Second Period
3.   BUFFALO   WARD (unassisted)   7:37 (GWG)
Penalties: Verbeek (Dal) (interference) 0:21, Ludwig (Dal) (interference) 11:07, Skrudland (Dal) (roughing) 14:49, Holzinger (Buf) (boarding) 16:44, Verbeek (Dal), Hatcher (Dal), Hasek (Buf), Zhitnik (Buf) (roughing) 20:00.

Third Period
No scoring.
Penalties: Nieuwendyk (Dal) (hooking) 1:06, Reid (Dal) (roughing), Langenbrunner (Dal) (slashing), Warrener (Buf) (roughing), Ward (Buf) (double minor, roughing) 20:00.
Goalies: Belfour (Dal), Hasek (Buf)
          Shots: Dal   9   -   9   - 13   31
                   Buf   7   -   9   -   2   18
Referees: Dan Marouelli, Bill McCreary
Linesmen: Gord Broseker, Kevin Collins

Game #5 - June 17, 1999 - Reunion Arena - Dallas 2, Buffalo 0

BUFFALO: Stu Barnes, Curtis Brown, Randy Cunneyworth, Dominik Hasek, Brian Holzinger, Joe Juneau, Jay McKee, James Patrick, Michael Peca, Wayne Primeau, Erik Rasmussen, Geoff Sanderson, Miroslav Satan, Richard Smehlik, Vaclav Varada, Dixon Ward, Rhett Warrener, Jason Woolley, Alexei Zhitnik.

DALLAS: Ed Belfour, Guy Carbonneau, Shawn Chambers, Derian Hatcher, Benoit Hogue, Brett Hull, Mike Keane, Jamie Langenbrunner, Jere Lehtinen, Craig Ludwig, Richard Matvichuk, Mike Modano, Joe Nieuwendyk, Dave Reid, Brian Skrudland, Blake Sloan, Darryl Sydor, Pat Verbeek, Sergei Zubov.

First Period
No scoring.
Penalties: Ludwig (Dal) (obstruction-tripping) 2:08.

Second Period
1.   DALLAS   SYDOR (MODANO, ZUBOV)   2:23 (PPG,GWG)
Penalties: Brown (Buf) (interference) 1:42, Woolley (Buf) (obstruction-holding) 3:31, Langenbrunner (Dal) (roughing) 7:44.

Third Period
2.   DALLAS   VERBEEK (MATVICHUK, MODANO)   15:21
Penalties: Primeau (Buf), Sydor (Dal) (roughing) 8:21, Warrener (Buf) (slashing) 16:31, Zhitnik (Buf) (elbowing), Nieuwendyk (Dal) (roughing) 17:27, Skrudland (Dal) (obstruction-tripping) 19:29, Warrener (Buf), Hatcher (Dal), (roughing) 20:00.
Goalies: Hasek (Buf), Belfour (Dal)
          Shots: Buf   9   -   5   -   9   23
                   Dal   8   -   7   -   6   21
Referees: Kerry Fraser, Don Koharski
Linesmen: Ray Scapinello, Jay Sharrers

Game #6 - June 19, 1999 - Marine Midland Arena - Dallas 2, Buffalo 1 (3 OT)

DALLAS: Ed Belfour, Guy Carbonneau, Shawn Chambers, Derian Hatcher, Benoit Hogue, Brett Hull, Mike Keane, Jamie Langenbrunner, Jere Lehtinen, Craig Ludwig, Richard Matvichuk, Mike Modano, Joe Nieuwendyk, Dave Reid, Brian Skrudland, Blake Sloan, Darryl Sydor, Pat Verbeek, Sergei Zubov.

BUFFALO: Stu Barnes, Curtis Brown, Randy Cunneyworth, Dominik Hasek, Brian Holzinger, Joe Juneau, Jay McKee, James Patrick, Michael Peca, Wayne Primeau, Erik Rasmussen, Geoff Sanderson, Miroslav Satan, Darryl Shannon, Richard Smehlik, Vaclav Varada, Dixon Ward, Jason Woolley, Alexei Zhitnik.

First Period
1.   DALLAS   LEHTINEN (MODANO, LUDWIG)   8:09
Penalties: none.

Second Period
2.   BUFFALO   BARNES (PRIMEAU, ZHITNIK)   18:21
Penalties: Sanderson (Buf) (interference) 5:19, Ludwig (Dal) (interference) 10:49, Hogue (Dal) (tripping) 14:28, Peca (Buf) (slashing) 19:27.

Third Period
No scoring.
Penalties: none.

First Overtime
No scoring.
Penalties: none.

Second Overtime
No scoring.
Penalties: none.

Third Overtime
3.   DALLAS   HULL (LEHTINEN, MODANO)   14:51 (GWG)
Penalties: none.
Goalies: Belfour (Dal), Hasek (Buf)
          Shots: Dal   5   - 11   - 10   -   4   - 13   -   7   50
                   Buf 11   - 15   -   6   -   6   - 12   -   4   54
Referees: Terry Gregson, Bill McCreary
Linesmen: Gord Broseker, Kevin Collins

1998

DETROIT RED WINGS - WASHINGTON CAPITALS

Game #1 - June 9, 1998 - Joe Louis Arena - Detroit 2, Washington 1

WASHINGTON: Brian Bellows, Craig Berube, Peter Bondra, Jeff Brown, Mike Eagles, Sergei Gonchar, Phil Housley, Dale Hunter, Calle Johansson, Joe Juneau, Olaf Kolzig, Kelly Miller, Andrei Nikolishin, Adam Oates, Joe Reekie, Chris Simon, Esa Tikkanen, Mark Tinordi, Richard Zednik.

DETROIT: Doug Brown, Kris Draper, Anders Eriksson, Sergei Fedorov, Viacheslav Fetisov, Tomas Holmstrom, Joe Kocur, Vyacheslav Kozlov, Martin Lapointe, Igor Larionov, Nicklas Lidstrom, Jamie Macoun, Kirk Maltby, Darren McCarty, Larry Murphy, Chris Osgood, Bob Rouse, Brendan Shanahan, Steve Yzerman.

First Period
1. DETROIT　　　　KOCUR (BROWN, HOLMSTROM)　　14:04
2. DETROIT　　　　LIDSTROM (YZERMAN, HOLMSTROM) 16:18 (GWG)
Penalties: Lapointe (Det) (tripping) 4:21, Tinordi (Wsh) (interference) 17:22.

Second Period
3. WASHINGTON　　ZEDNIK (NIKOLISHIN, BONDRA)　　15:57
Penalties: Detroit bench (too many men) 5:48, Yzerman (Det) (slashing) 8:51, Simon (Wsh) (roughing) 18:06.

Third Period
No scoring.
Penalties: Nikolishin (Wsh) (interference) 0:38, Kocur (Det) (roughing) 4:19.

Goalies: Kolzig (Wsh), Osgood (Det)
Shots:	Wsh	6	-	4	-	7		17
	Det	10	-	9	-	12		31

Referee: Bill McCreary
Linesmen: Ray Scapinello, Dan Schachte

Game #2 - June 11, 1998 -Joe Louis Arena - Detroit 5, Washington 4 (OT)

WASHINGTON: Brian Bellows, Craig Berube, Peter Bondra, Jeff Brown, Mike Eagles, Sergei Gonchar, Phil Housley, Dale Hunter, Calle Johansson, Joe Juneau, Olaf Kolzig, Todd Krygier, Andrei Nikolishin, Adam Oates, Joe Reekie, Chris Simon, Esa Tikkanen, Mark Tinordi, Richard Zednik.

DETROIT: Doug Brown, Kris Draper, Anders Eriksson, Sergei Fedorov, Viacheslav Fetisov, Tomas Holmstrom, Joe Kocur, Vyacheslav Kozlov, Martin Lapointe,, Igor Larionov, Nicklas Lidstrom, Jamie Macoun, Kirk Maltby, Darren McCarty, Larry Murphy, Chris Osgood, Bob Rouse, Brendan Shanahan, Steve Yzerman.

First Period
1. DETROIT　　　　YZERMAN (HOLMSTROM, LIDSTROM)　7:49
Penalties: Reekie (Wsh) (obstruction-holding) 13:05, Bondra (Wsh) hooking 15:22.

Second Period
2. WASHINGTON　　BONDRA (NIKOLISHIN, BROWN)　　1:51
3. WASHINGTON　　SIMON (BROWN, HUNTER)　　6:11
4. WASHINGTON　　OATES (JUNEAU, JOHANSSON)　　11:03
Penalties: Maltby (Det) (high sticking) 3:09, Zednik (Wsh) (obstruction-hooking) 7:12, Simon (Wsh) (roughing), Osgood (Det) (unsportsmanlike conduct) 14:11, Maltby (Det) (slashing) 16:20.

Third Period
5. DETROIT　　　　YZERMAN (FETISOV, McCARTY)　　6:37 (SHG)
6. WASHINGTON　　JUNEAU (GONCHAR, BELLOWS)　　7:05 (PPG)
7. DETROIT　　　　LAPOINTE (LARIONOV, FETISOV)　　8:08
8. DETROIT　　　　BROWN (unassisted)　　15:46
Penalties: Lidstrom (Det) (interference) 6:23, Zednik (Wsh) (cross-checking) 10:18, Lapointe (Det) (interference) 11:40.

First Overtime
9. DETROIT　　　　DRAPER (LAPOINTE, SHANAHAN)　　15:24 (GWG)
Penalties Tikkanen (Wsh), Kocur (Det) (roughing) 5:24.

Goalies: Kolzig (Wsh), Osgood (Det)
Shots:	Wsh	8	-	15	-	7	-	3		33
	Det	14	-	14	-	20	-	12		60

Referee: Don Koharski
Linesmen: Gord Broseker, Kevin Collins

Game #3 - June 13, 1998 - MCI Center - Detroit 2, Washington 1

DETROIT: Doug Brown, Kris Draper, Anders Eriksson, Sergei Fedorov, Viacheslav Fetisov, Tomas Holmstrom, Joe Kocur, Vyacheslav Kozlov, Martin Lapointe, Igor Larionov, Nicklas Lidstrom, Jamie Macoun, Kirk Maltby, Darren McCarty, Larry Murphy, Chris Osgood, Bob Rouse, Brendan Shanahan, Steve Yzerman.

WASHINGTON: Brian Bellows, Craig Berube, Peter Bondra, Sergei Gonchar, Phil Housley, Dale Hunter, Calle Johansson, Joe Juneau, Ken Klee, Olaf Kolzig, Kelly Miller, Andrei Nikolishin, Adam Oates, Joe Reekie, Chris Simon, Esa Tikkanen, Mark Tinordi, Jeff Toms, Richard Zednik.

First Period
1. DETROIT　　　　HOLMSTROM (YZERMAN, McCARTY)　0:35
Penalties: Simon (Wsh) (slashing) 2:48, Hunter (Wsh) (charging) 8:10, Housley (Wsh) (elbowing) 12:29, Holmstrom (Det) (goaltender interference) 13:11, Lapointe (Det) (interference) 17:01.

Second Period
No scoring.
Penalties: Krygier (Wsh) (roughing) 2:05, Eriksson (Det) (obstruction-holding) 7:29, Larionov (Det) (obstruction-tripping) 10:17, Draper (Det), Gonchar (Wsh) (roughing) 15:23.

Third Period
2. WASHINGTON　　BELLOWS (OATES, JUNEAU)　　10:35 (PPG)
3. DETROIT　　　　FEDOROV (BROWN, FETISOV)　　15:09 (GWG)
Penalties: Gonchar (Wsh) (roughing) 5:50, McCarty (Det) (tripping) 9:22.
Goalies: Osgood (Det), Kolzig (Wsh)
Shots:	Det	13	-	11	-	10		34
	Wsh	1	-	12	-	5		18

Referee: Terry Gregson
Linesmen: Ray Scapinello, Dan Schachte

Game #4 - June 16, 1998 - MCI Center - Detroit 4, Washington 1

DETROIT: Doug Brown, Kris Draper, Anders Eriksson, Sergei Fedorov, Viacheslav Fetisov, Tomas Holmstrom, Joe Kocur, Vyacheslav Kozlov, Martin Lapointe, Igor Larionov, Nicklas Lidstrom, Jamie Macoun, Kirk Maltby, Darren McCarty, Larry Murphy, Chris Osgood, Bob Rouse, Brendan Shanahan, Steve Yzerman.
WASHINGTON: Brian Bellows, Craig Berube, Peter Bondra, Sergei Gonchar, Phil Housley, Dale Hunter, Calle Johansson, Joe Juneau, Ken Klee, Olaf Kolzig, Todd Krygier, Kelly Miller, Andrei Nikolishin, Adam Oates, Joe Reekie, Chris Simon, Esa Tikkanen, Mark Tinordi, Richard Zednik.

First Period
1. DETROIT　　　　BROWN (FEDOROV, MURPHY)　　10:30 (PPG)
Penalties: Eriksson (Det) (interference) 7:17, Bondra (Wsh) (interference) 9:12, Johansson (Wsh) (roughing) 11:01.

Second Period
2. DETROIT　　　　LAPOINTE (LARIONOV, ROUSE)　　2:26 (GWG)
3. WASHINGTON　　BELLOWS (OATES, JUNEAU)　　7:49
4. DETROIT　　　　MURPHY (HOLMSTROM, FEDOROV)　11:46 (PPG)
Penalties: Maltby (Det), Tinordi (Wsh) (roughing) 9:13, Tikkanen (Wsh) (goaltender interference) 11:02, Larionov (Det) (hooking) 12:41, Rouse (Det) (high sticking) 16:07, Tinordi (Wsh) (slashing) 19:53.

Third Period
5. DETROIT　　　　BROWN (KOZLOV, ERIKSSON)　　1:32 (PPG)
Penalties: Fetisov(Det) (interference) 13:08.
Goalies: Osgood (Det), Kolzig (Wsh)
Shots:	Det	14	-	12	-	12		38
	Wsh	6	-	14	-	11		31

Referee: Bill McCreary
Linesmen: Gord Broseker, Kevin Collins

1997

DETROIT RED WINGS - PHILADELPHIA FLYERS

Game #1 - May 31, 1997 - CoreStates Center - Detroit 4, Philadelphia 2

DETROIT: Doug Brown, Kris Draper, Sergei Fedorov, Viacheslav Fetisov, Joe Kocur, Vladimir Konstantinov, Vyacheslav Kozlov, Martin Lapointe, Igor Larionov, Nicklas Lidstrom, Kirk Maltby, Darren McCarty, Larry Murphy, Bob Rouse, Tomas Sandstrom, Brendan Shanahan, Mike Vernon, Aaron Ward, Steve Yzerman.

PHILADELPHIA: Rod Brind'Amour, Paul Coffey, Eric Desjardins, John Druce, Dale Hawerchuk, Ron Hextall, Trent Klatt, Dan Kordic, Daniel Lacroix, John LeClair, Eric Lindros, Janne Niinimaa, Joel Otto, Shjon Podein, Mikael Renberg, Kjell Samuelsson, Petr Svoboda, Chris Therien, Dainius Zubrus.

First Period
1. DETROIT   MALTBY (DRAPER)   6:38 (SHG)
2. PHILADELPHIA   BRIND'AMOUR (LINDROS, NIINIMAA) 7:37 (PPG)
3. DETROIT   KOCUR (unassisted)   15:56
Penalties: Sandstrom (Det) (high sticking) 5:50, Fetisov (Det) (interference) 11:26, Klatt (Phi) (interference) 17:09, Kocur (Det) (interference) 19:42.

Second Period
4. DETROIT   FEDOROV (MURPHY, MCCARTY)   11:41 (GWG)
5. PHILADELPHIA   LeCLAIR (RENBERG, LINDROS)   17:11
Penalties: Lacroix (Phi) (interference) 5:48, Fedorov (Det) (tripping) 7:08, Fetisov (Det) (interference) 15:07, Klatt (Phi) (charging) 17:45.

Third Period
6. DETROIT   YZERMAN (MURPHY)   0:56
Penalties: Svoboda (Phi) (cross-checking) 6:27, Lindros (Phi) (roughing) 17:48.

Goalies: Vernon (Det), Hextall (Phi)

Shots:	Det	8	-	12	-	10	30
	Phi	10	-	9	-	9	28

Referee: Bill McCreary
Linesmen: Ray Scapinello, Dan Schachte

Game #2 - June 3, 1997 - CoreStates Center - Detroit 4, Philadelphia 2

DETROIT: Doug Brown, Kris Draper, Sergei Fedorov, Viacheslav Fetisov, Joe Kocur, Vladimir Konstantinov, Vyacheslav Kozlov, Martin Lapointe, Igor Larionov, Nicklas Lidstrom, Kirk Maltby, Darren McCarty, Larry Murphy, Bob Rouse, Tomas Sandstrom, Brendan Shanahan, Mike Vernon, Aaron Ward, Steve Yzerman.

PHILADELPHIA: Rod Brind'Amour, Paul Coffey, Eric Desjardins, John Druce, Karl Dykhuis, Pat Falloon, Colin Forbes, Dale Hawerchuk, Trent Klatt, John LeClair, Eric Lindros, Janne Niinimaa, Joel Otto, Shjon Podein, Mikael Renberg, Kjell Samuelsson, Garth Snow, Chris Therien, Dainius Zubrus.

First Period
1. DETROIT   SHANAHAN (unassisted)   1:37
2. DETROIT   YZERMAN (MURPHY, FETISOV)   9:22 (PPG)
3. PHILADELPHIA   BRIND'AMOUR (NIINIMAA)   17:42 (PPG)
4. PHILADELPHIA   BRIND'AMOUR (NIINIMAA, LeCLAIR) 18:51 (PPG)
Penalties: Coffey (Phi) (holding) 4:29, Coffey (Phi) (hooking) 7:24, Lapointe (Det) (charging) 10:21, Fetisov (Det) (high sticking) 17:09, Larionov (Det) (hooking) 18:37.

Second Period
5. DETROIT   MALTBY (KOCUR)   2:39 (GWG)
Penalties: Maltby (Det), Coffey (Phi) (roughing) 6:54, Detroit bench (too many men) 9:03, LeClair (Phi) (elbowing) 12:13.

Third Period
6. DETROIT   SHANAHAN (LAPOINTE, FEDOROV)   9:56
Penalties: Lapointe (Det), Dykhuis (Phi) (roughing) 10:27.

Goalies: Vernon (Det), Snow (Phi)

Shots:	Det	14	-	9	-	5	28
	Phi	14	-	9	-	8	31

Referee: Terry Gregson
Linesmen: Wayne Bonney, Gord Broseker

Game #3 - June 5, 1997 - Joe Louis Arena - Detroit 6, Philadelphia 1

PHILADELPHIA: Rod Brind'Amour, Eric Desjardins, John Druce, Karl Dykhuis, Pat Falloon, Colin Forbes, Dale Hawerchuk, Ron Hextall, Trent Klatt, John LeClair, Eric Lindros, Janne Niinimaa, Joel Otto, Michel Petit, Shjon Podein, Mikael Renberg, Kjell Samuelsson, Chris Therien, Dainius Zubrus.

DETROIT: Doug Brown, Kris Draper, Sergei Fedorov, Viacheslav Fetisov, Joe Kocur, Vladimir Konstantinov, Vyacheslav Kozlov, Martin Lapointe, Igor Larionov, Nicklas Lidstrom, Kirk Maltby, Darren McCarty, Larry Murphy, Bob Rouse, Tomas Sandstrom, Brendan Shanahan, Mike Vernon, Aaron Ward, Steve Yzerman.

First Period
1. PHILADELPHIA   LeCLAIR (DESJARDINS, BRIND'AMOUR)7:03 (PPG)
2. DETROIT   YZERMAN (KOZLOV)   9:03 (PPG)
3. DETROIT   FEDOROV   11:05 (GWG)
4. DETROIT   LAPOINTE (BROWN, FEDOROV)   19:00
Penalties: McCarty (Det) (obstruction-interference) 6:10, Desjardins (Phi) (obstruction-holding) 8:44, Fetisov (Det) (obstruction-interference) 12:14, Sandstrom (Det) (obstruction-holding) 12:54, Lapointe (Det) (tripping) 16:43.

Second Period
5. DETROIT   FEDOROV (KOZLOV, SHANAHAN)   3:12 (PPG)
6. DETROIT   SHANAHAN (McCARTY, FETISOV)   19:17
Penalties: Klatt (Phi) (obstruction-hooking) 2:24, Petit (Phi) (holding) 10:14.

Third Period
7. DETROIT   LAPOINTE (FEDOROV, VERNON)   1:08 (PPG)
Penalties: Lindros (Phi) (cross-checking) 0:46, Lindros (Phi) (elbowing) 8:12, McCarty (Det) (obstruction-interference) 8:39, Fetisov (Det) (slashing) 13:02, Brown (Det) (slashing) 19:41.

Goalies: Hextall (Phi), Vernon (Det)

Shots:	Phi	8	-	7	-	7	22
	Det	10	-	12	-	7	29

Referee: Kerry Fraser
Linesmen: Ray Scapinello, Dan Schachte

Game #4 - June 7, 1997 - Joe Louis Arena - Detroit 2, Philadelphia 1

PHILADELPHIA: Rod Brind'Amour, Eric Desjardins, John Druce, Karl Dykhuis, Pat Falloon, Colin Forbes, Ron Hextall, Trent Klatt, Daniel Lacroix, John LeClair, Eric Lindros, Janne Niinimaa, Joel Otto, Michel Petit, Shjon Podein, Mikael Renberg, Kjell Samuelsson, Chris Therien, Dainius Zubrus.

DETROIT: Doug Brown, Kris Draper, Sergei Fedorov, Viacheslav Fetisov, Joe Kocur, Vladimir Konstantinov, Vyacheslav Kozlov, Martin Lapointe, Igor Larionov, Nicklas Lidstrom, Kirk Maltby, Darren McCarty, Larry Murphy, Bob Rouse, Tomas Sandstrom, Brendan Shanahan, Mike Vernon, Aaron Ward, Steve Yzerman.

First Period
1. DETROIT   LIDSTROM (MALTBY)   19:27
Penalties: LeClair (Phi) (obstruction-holding) 3:23, Larionov (Det) (obstruction-interference) 4:31, Lindros (Phi) (obstruction-interference) 9:22, Falloon (Phi) (holding the stick) 13:21.

Second Period
2. DETROIT   McCARTY (SANDSTROM, YZERMAN)   13:02 (GWG)
Penalties: Konstantinov (Det) (obstruction-interference) 9:27.

Third Period
3. PHILADELPHIA   LINDROS (DESJARDINS)   19:45
Penalties: Samuelsson (Phi) (high sticking) 1:32, Podein (Phi) (high sticking) 11:54, Draper (Det) (slashing) 14:39.

Goalies: Hextall (Phi), Vernon (Det)

Shots:	Phi	8	-	12	-	7	27
	Det	9	-	10	-	9	28

Referee: Bill McCreary
Linesmen: Wayne Bonney, Gord Broseker

1996

COLORADO AVALANCHE – FLORIDA PANTHERS

Game #1 - June 4, 1996 - McNichols Sports Arena - Colorado 3, Florida 1

FLORIDA: Stu Barnes, Terry Carkner, Tom Fitzgerald, Johan Garpenlov, Mike Hough, Jody Hull, Ed Jovanovski, Paul Laus, Bill Lindsay, Dave Lowry, Scott Mellanby, Gord Murphy, Rob Niedermayer, Ray Sheppard, Brian Skrudland, Martin Straka, Robert Svehla, John Vanbiesbrouck, Rhett Warrener.

COLORADO: Rene Corbet, Adam Deadmarsh, Adam Foote, Peter Forsberg, Alexei Gusarov, Dave Hannan, Valeri Kamensky, Mike Keane, Jon Klemm, Uwe Krupp, Sylvain Lefebvre, Curtis Leschyshyn, Sandis Ozolinsh, Mike Ricci, Patrick Roy, Warren Rychel, Joe Sakic, Stephane Yelle, Scott Young.

First Period

1.	FLORIDA	FITZGERALD (LINDSAY)	16:51

Penalties: Mellanby (Fla) (roughing) 9:12, Skrudland (Fla) (roughing) 9:21, Krupp (Col) (high sticking) 13:46, Gusarov (Col) (holding) 18:15.

Second Period

2.	COLORADO	YOUNG (DEADMARSH, LEFEBVRE)	10:32
3.	COLORADO	RICCI (OZOLINSH, KEANE)	12:21 (GWG)
4.	COLORADO	KRUPP (KAMENSKY, FORSBERG)	14:21

Penalties: Svehla (Fla) (interference) 0:41, Lindsay (Fla) (roughing) 7:56, Ricci (Col) (roughing) 15:31, Svehla (Fla) (roughing) 17:39, Ricci (Col) (goaltender interference) 18:30.

Third Period

No scoring.
Penalties: Sakic (Col) (holding) 3:35, Carkner (Fla) (slashing) 7:51, Vanbiesbrouck (Fla) (slashing) 9:55, Jovanovski (Fla) (roughing) 19:42.

Goalies: Vanbiesbrouck (Fla), Roy (Col)

Shots:	Fla	12	-	6	-	8	26
	Col	6	-	15	-	9	30

Referee: Bill McCreary
Linesmen: Brian Murphy, Ray Scapinello

Game #2 - June 6, 1996 - McNichols Sports Arena - Colorado 8, Florida 1

FLORIDA: Stu Barnes, Terry Carkner, Tom Fitzgerald, Mark Fitzpatrick, Johan Garpenlov, Mike Hough, Jody Hull, Ed Jovanovski, Paul Laus, Bill Lindsay, Dave Lowry, Scott Mellanby, Gord Murphy, Rob Niedermayer, Ray Sheppard, Brian Skrudland, Martin Straka, Robert Svehla, John Vanbiesbrouck, Rhett Warrener.

COLORADO: Rene Corbet, Adam Deadmarsh, Adam Foote, Peter Forsberg, Alexei Gusarov, Dave Hannan, Valeri Kamensky, Mike Keane, Jon Klemm, Uwe Krupp, Sylvain Lefebvre, Curtis Leschyshyn, Sandis Ozolinsh, Mike Ricci, Patrick Roy, Warren Rychel, Joe Sakic, Stephane Yelle, Scott Young.

First Period

1.	COLORADO	FORSBERG (unassisted)	4:11
2.	FLORIDA	BARNES (LOWRY, JOVANOVSKI)	7:52 (PPG)
3.	COLORADO	CORBET (YOUNG, SAKIC)	10:43 (PPG,GWG)
4.	COLORADO	FORSBERG (SAKIC, OZOLINSH)	13:46 (PPG)
5.	COLORADO	FORSBERG (SAKIC, DEADMARSH)	15:05 (PPG)

Penalties: Deadmarsh (Col) (roughing) 5:53, Lindsay (Fla) (slashing) 8:55, Carkner (Fla) (roughing) 12:51, Vanbiesbrouck (Fla) (interference) 14:50.

Second Period

6.	COLORADO	CORBET (unassisted)	4:37
7.	COLORADO	KAMENSKY (GUSAROV, DEADMARSH)	5:08
8.	COLORADO	KLEMM (CORBET, KRUPP)	10:03

Penalties: Lefebvre (Col) (holding) 6:26, Rychel (Col) (roughing) 17:01.

Third Period

9.	COLORADO	KLEMM (SAKIC)	17:28	(PPG)

Penalties: Kamensky (Col) (double minor, high sticking) 3:11, Jovanovski (Fla), Kamensky (Col) (roughing), Leschyshyn (Col) (charging) 7:28, Jovanovski (Fla) (fighting), Rychel (Col) (instigator, fighting, game misconduct) 9:39, Laus (Fla) (goaltender interference) 11:42, Mellanby (Fla) (roughing) 16:09.

Goalies: Vanbiesbrouck, Fitzpatrick (Fla), Roy (Col)

Shots:	Fla	8	-	15	-	5	28
	Col	11	-	12	-	7	30

Referee: Don Koharski
Linesmen: Kevin Collins, Gerard Gauthier

Game #3 - June 8, 1996 - Miami Arena - Colorado 3, Florida 2

COLORADO: Rene Corbet, Adam Deadmarsh, Adam Foote, Peter Forsberg, Alexei Gusarov, Dave Hannan, Valeri Kamensky, Mike Keane, Jon Klemm, Uwe Krupp, Sylvain Lefebvre, Claude Lemieux, Curtis Leschyshyn, Sandis Ozolinsh, Mike Ricci, Patrick Roy, Joe Sakic, Stephane Yelle, Scott Young.

FLORIDA: Stu Barnes, Terry Carkner, Tom Fitzgerald, Johan Garpenlov, Mike Hough, Ed Jovanovski, Paul Laus, Bill Lindsay, Dave Lowry, Scott Mellanby, Gord Murphy, Rob Niedermayer, Ray Sheppard, Brian Skrudland, Martin Straka, Robert Svehla, John Vanbiesbrouck, Rhett Warrener, Jason Woolley.

First Period

1.	COLORADO	LEMIEUX (KAMENSKY, FORSBERG)	2:44
2.	FLORIDA	SHEPPARD (STRAKA, JOVANOVSKI)	9:14 (PPG)
3.	FLORIDA	NIEDERMAYER (MELLANBY, GARPENLOV)	11:19

Penalties: Deadmarsh (Col) (hooking) 7:40, Foote (Col), Lowry (Fla) (roughing) 12:49.

Second Period

4.	COLORADO	KEANE (FOOTE, GUSAROV)	1:38
5.	COLORADO	SAKIC (DEADMARSH, LESCHYSHYN)	3:00 (GWG)

Penalties: none.

Third Period

No scoring.
Penalties: none.

Goalies: Roy (Col), Vanbiesbrouck (Fla)

Shots:	Col	6	-	10	-	6	22
	Fla	16	-	13	-	5	34

Referee: Andy Van Hellemond
Linesmen: Brian Murphy, Ray Scapinello

Game #4 - June 10, 1996 - Miami Arena - Colorado 1, Florida 0 (3 OT)

COLORADO: Rene Corbet, Adam Deadmarsh, Adam Foote, Peter Forsberg, Alexei Gusarov, Valeri Kamensky, Mike Keane, Jon Klemm, Uwe Krupp, Sylvain Lefebvre, Claude Lemieux, Curtis Leschyshyn, Sandis Ozolinsh, Mike Ricci, Patrick Roy, Warren Rychel, Joe Sakic, Stephane Yelle, Scott Young.

FLORIDA: Stu Barnes, Terry Carkner, Radek Dvorak, Tom Fitzgerald, Johan Garpenlov, Mike Hough, Ed Jovanovski, Paul Laus, Bill Lindsay, Dave Lowry, Scott Mellanby, Gord Murphy, Rob Niedermayer, Ray Sheppard, Brian Skrudland, Martin Straka, Robert Svehla, John Vanbiesbrouck, Jason Woolley.

First Period

No scoring.
Penalties: Svehla (Fla) (roughing) 18:51.

Second Period

No scoring.
Penalties: Kamensky (Col) (hooking), Ozolinsh (Col), Niedermayer (Fla) (roughing) 5:21, Foote (Col) (roughing) 9:28, Jovanovski (Fla) (cross-checking) 12:27, Leschyshyn (Col) (hooking) 15:33, Ricci (Col), Barnes (Fla) (roughing) 18:05.

Third Period

No scoring.
Penalties: Vanbiesbrouck (Fla) (interference) 5:15, Lemieux (Col) (high sticking) 6:29.

First Overtime

No scoring.
Penalties: Ozolinsh (Col), Garpenlov (Fla) (roughing) 13:04.

Second Overtime

No scoring.
Penalties: Lemieux (Col) (roughing), Skrudland (Fla) (slashing) 9:57.

Third Overtime

1.	COLORADO	KRUPP (unassisted)	4:31 (GWG)

Penalties: none.

Goalies: Roy (Col), Vanbiesbrouck (Fla)

Shots:	Col	9	-	10	-	10	-	11	-	12	-	4	56
	Fla	10	-	17	-	8	-	7	-	18	-	3	63

Referee: Bill McCreary
Linesmen: Kevin Collins, Gerard Gauthier

1995

NEW JERSEY DEVILS - DETROIT RED WINGS

Game #1 - June 17, 1995 - Joe Louis Arena - New Jersey 2, Detroit 1

NEW JERSEY: Tommy Albelin, Martin Brodeur, Neal Broten, Sergei Brylin, Bob Carpenter, Shawn Chambers, Tom Chorske, Ken Daneyko, Bruce Driver, Bill Guerin, Bobby Holik, Claude Lemieux, John MacLean, Randy McKay, Scott Niedermayer, Mike Peluso, Stephane Richer, Scott Stevens, Valeri Zelepukin.

DETROIT: Doug Brown, Shawn Burr, Dino Ciccarelli, Paul Coffey, Kris Draper, Bob Errey, Sergei Fedorov, Viacheslav Fetisov, Stu Grimson, Mark Howe, Vladimir Konstantinov, Vyacheslav Kozlov, Nicklas Lidstrom, Darren McCarty, Keith Primeau, Bob Rouse, Ray Sheppard, Mike Vernon, Steve Yzerman.

First Period
No scoring.
Penalties: Guerin (NJ) (holding) 6:47, Konstantinov (Det) (holding the stick) 11:05.

Second Period
1.	NEW JERSEY	RICHER (ALBELIN, BROTEN)	9:41	(PPG)
2.	DETROIT	CICCARELLI (LIDSTROM, COFFEY)	13:08	(PPG)

Penalties: Draper (Det) (roughing) 9:35, Holik (NJ) (high sticking) 11:37, Lemieux (NJ) (hooking) 13:41, Daneyko (NJ), Ciccarelli (Det) (roughing) 15:54.

Third Period
3.	NEW JERSEY	LEMIEUX (MacLEAN, CHORSKE)	3:17	(GWG)

Penalties: Brown (Det) (tripping) 4:48.

Goalies: Brodeur (NJ), Vernon (Det)
Shots:	NJ	9	-	10	-	9	28
	Det	7	-	5	-	5	17

Referee: Bill McCreary
Linesmen: Brian Murphy, Kevin Collins

Game #2 - June 20, 1995 - Joe Louis Arena - New Jersey 4, Detroit 2

NEW JERSEY: Tommy Albelin, Martin Brodeur, Neal Broten, Bob Carpenter, Shawn Chambers, Ken Daneyko, Jim Dowd, Bruce Driver, Bill Guerin, Bobby Holik, Claude Lemieux, John MacLean, Randy McKay, Scott Niedermayer, Mike Peluso, Stephane Richer, Brian Rolston, Scott Stevens, Valeri Zelepukin.

DETROIT: Doug Brown, Shawn Burr, Dino Ciccarelli, Paul Coffey, Kris Draper, Bob Errey, Sergei Fedorov, Viacheslav Fetisov, Mark Howe, Vladimir Konstantinov, Vyacheslav Kozlov, Mike Krushelnyski, Nicklas Lidstrom, Darren McCarty, Bob Rouse, Ray Sheppard, Tim Taylor, Mike Vernon, Steve Yzerman.

First Period
No scoring.
Penalties: Stevens (NJ) (roughing) 0:37, Ciccarelli (Det) (slashing) 5:57, McCarty (Det) (roughing) 8:49, Broten (NJ) (high sticking) 9:27.

Second Period
1.	DETROIT	KOZLOV (CICCARELLI, FEDOROV)	7:17	(PPG)
2.	NEW JERSEY	MacLEAN (NIEDERMAYER, BROTEN)	9:40	

Penalties: Brodeur (NJ) (delay of game) 6:56, Guerin (NJ), McCarty (Det) (slashing) 8:58, Errey (Det) (charging) 16:01, Dowd (NJ) (interference) 18:30.

Third Period
3.	DETROIT	FEDOROV (BROWN, FETISOV)	1:36	
4.	NEW JERSEY	NIEDERMAYER (DOWD)	9:47	
5.	NEW JERSEY	DOWD (CHAMBERS, ALBELIN)	18:36	(GWG)
6.	NEW JERSEY	RICHER (NIEDERMAYER)	19:36	(ENG)

Penalties: Holik (NJ) (boarding) 4:58.

Goalies: Brodeur (NJ), Vernon (Det)
Shots:	NJ	3	-	9	-	11	23
	Det	7	-	6	-	5	18

Referee: Terry Gregson
Linesmen: Wayne Bonney, Ray Scapinello

Game #3 - June 22, 1995 - Meadowlands Arena - New Jersey 5, Detroit 2

DETROIT: Doug Brown, Dino Ciccarelli, Paul Coffey, Kris Draper, Bob Errey, Sergei Fedorov, Viacheslav Fetisov, Vladimir Konstantinov, Vyacheslav Kozlov, Martin Lapointe, Nicklas Lidstrom, Darren McCarty, Chris Osgood, Keith Primeau, Mike Ramsey, Bob Rouse, Ray Sheppard, Tim Taylor, Mike Vernon, Steve Yzerman.

NEW JERSEY: Tommy Albelin, Martin Brodeur, Neal Broten, Sergei Brylin, Bob Carpenter, Shawn Chambers, Tom Chorske, Ken Daneyko, Bruce Driver, Bill Guerin, Bobby Holik, Claude Lemieux, John MacLean, Randy McKay, Scott Niedermayer, Mike Peluso, Stephane Richer, Scott Stevens, Valeri Zelepukin.

First Period
1.	NEW JERSEY	DRIVER (BROTEN, MacLEAN)	10:30	(PPG)
2.	NEW JERSEY	LEMIEUX (CARPENTER, STEVENS)	16:52	

Penalties: Primeau (Det) (slashing), Lemieux (NJ) (roughing) 1:09, Konstantinov (Det) (holding the stick) 8:56, Holik (NJ) (tripping) 10:58, Lapointe (Det), Guerin (NJ) (unsportsmanlike conduct) 16:58.

Second Period
3.	NEW JERSEY	BROTEN (STEVENS, MacLEAN)	6:59	(GWG)
4.	NEW JERSEY	McKAY (HOLIK, DRIVER)	8:20	

Penalties: Broten (NJ) (holding the stick) 11:01, Primeau (Det) (tripping) 16:03, Carpenter (NJ) (cross-checking) 19:47.

Third Period
5.	NEW JERSEY	HOLIK (GUERIN, RICHER)	8:14	(PPG)
6.	DETROIT	FEDOROV (FETISOV, BROWN)	16:57	(PPG)
7.	DETROIT	YZERMAN (SHEPPARD, LIDSTROM)	18:27	(PPG)

Penalties: Albelin (NJ) (high sticking) 2:30, Konstantinov (Det) (high sticking) 4:25, Draper (Det) (high sticking) 5:17, Primeau (Det) (cross-checking) 6:31, Holik (NJ) (interference) 8:44, Richer (NJ) (hooking) 12:28, Ciccarelli (Det), Taylor (Det) (roughing), Lapointe (Det), Zelepukin (NJ) (double minor, roughing), Guerin (NJ) (boarding, roughing), Brylin (NJ) (high sticking, roughing) 15:37.

Goalies: Vernon, Osgood (Det), Brodeur (NJ)
Shots:	Det	7	-	5	-	12	24
	NJ	15	-	8	-	8	31

Referee: Kerry Fraser
Linesmen: Kevin Collins, Brian Murphy

Game #4 - June 24, 1995 - Meadowlands Arena - New Jersey 5, Detroit 2

DETROIT: Doug Brown, Dino Ciccarelli, Paul Coffey, Kris Draper, Bob Errey, Sergei Fedorov, Viacheslav Fetisov, Stu Grimson, Vladimir Konstantinov, Vyacheslav Kozlov, Mike Krushelnyski, Martin Lapointe, Nicklas Lidstrom, Darren McCarty, Keith Primeau, Mike Ramsey, Bob Rouse, Mike Vernon, Steve Yzerman.

NEW JERSEY: Tommy Albelin, Martin Brodeur, Neal Broten, Sergei Brylin, Bob Carpenter, Shawn Chambers, Tom Chorske, Ken Daneyko, Bruce Driver, Bill Guerin, Bobby Holik, Claude Lemieux, John MacLean, Randy McKay, Scott Niedermayer, Mike Peluso, Stephane Richer, Brian Rolston, Scott Stevens.

First Period
1.	NEW JERSEY	BROTEN (RICHER, CHORSKE)	1:08	
2.	DETROIT	FEDOROV (LAPOINTE, FETISOV)	2:03	
3.	DETROIT	COFFEY (BROWN, FEDOROV)	13:01	(SHG)
4.	NEW JERSEY	CHAMBERS (DRIVER, MacLEAN)	17:45	

Penalties: Errey (Det) (hooking) 11:03, Daneyko (NJ) (roughing) 13:36, Primeau (Det) (goaltender interference) 15:35.

Second Period
5.	NEW JERSEY	BROTEN (NIEDERMAYER, GUERIN)	7:56	(GWG)

Penalties: Daneyko (NJ) (slashing) 0:30, Lapointe (Det), Stevens (NJ) (roughing) 10:09, Guerin (NJ) (interference) 12:43, Konstantinov (Det) (hooking) 19:12.

Third Period
6.	NEW JERSEY	BRYLIN (ROLSTON, GUERIN)	7:46	
7.	NEW JERSEY	CHAMBERS (BRYLIN, GUERIN)	12:32	

Penalties: Grimson (Det) (roughing) 10:24.

Goalies: Vernon (Det), Brodeur (NJ)
Shots:	Det	8	-	7	-	1	16
	NJ	8	-	8	-	10	26

Referee: Bill McCreary
Linesmen: Wayne Bonney, Ray Scapinello

1994

NEW YORK RANGERS – VANCOUVER CANUCKS

Game #1 - May 31, 1994 - Madison Square Garden - Vancouver 3, NY Rangers 2 (OT)

VANCOUVER: Greg Adams, Shawn Antoski, Dave Babych, Jeff Brown, Pavel Bure, Geoff Courtnall, Murray Craven, Gerald Diduck, Martin Gelinas, Brian Glynn, Bret Hedican, Tim Hunter, Nathan LaFayette, Trevor Linden, Jyrki Lumme, John McIntyre, Kirk McLean, Sergio Momesso, Cliff Ronning.

NY RANGERS: Glenn Anderson, Jeff Beukeboom, Greg Gilbert, Adam Graves, Joe Kocur, Alexei Kovalev, Steve Larmer, Brian Leetch, Doug Lidster, Kevin Lowe, Craig MacTavish, Stephane Matteau, Mark Messier, Sergei Nemchinov, Brian Noonan, Mike Richter, Esa Tikkanen, Jay Wells, Sergei Zubov.

First Period
1.   NY RANGERS   LARMER (KOVALEV, LEETCH)   3:32
Penalties: Wells (NYR) (cross-checking) 1:47, Linden (Van) (tripping) 2:27, McIntyre (Van) (roughing) 8:50, Craven (Van) (slashing) 10:35, Beukeboom (NYR) (interference) 15:54.

Second Period
No scoring.
Penalties: Messier (NYR) (hooking) 0:20, Lidster (NYR) (tripping) 8:49, Lowe (NYR) (roughing) 8:50, Courtnall (Van) (interference) 13:18, Momesso (Van) (goaltender interference) 16:15, Beukeboom (NYR) (high sticking) 19:34.

Third Period
2.   VANCOUVER   HEDICAN (ADAMS, LUMME)   5:45
3.   NY RANGERS   KOVALEV (LEETCH, ZUBOV)   8:29
4.   VANCOUVER   GELINAS (RONNING, MOMESSO)   19:00
Penalties: none.

First Overtime
5.   VANCOUVER   ADAMS (RONNING, BURE)   19:26 (GWG)
Penalties: Momesso (Van), Gilbert (NYR) (roughing) 9:31.

Goalies: McLean (Van), Richter (NYR)
Shots: Van   10 - 5 - 7 - 9   31
              NYR   15 - 9 - 13 - 17   54

Referee: Terry Gregson
Linesmen: Randy Mitton, Ray Scapinello

Game #2 - June 2, 1994 - Madison Square Garden - NY Rangers 3, Vancouver 1

VANCOUVER: Greg Adams, Shawn Antoski, Dave Babych, Jeff Brown, Pavel Bure, Geoff Courtnall, Murray Craven, Gerald Diduck, Martin Gelinas, Brian Glynn, Bret Hedican, Tim Hunter, Nathan LaFayette, Trevor Linden, Jyrki Lumme, John McIntyre, Kirk McLean, Sergio Momesso, Cliff Ronning.

NY RANGERS: Glenn Anderson, Jeff Beukeboom, Greg Gilbert, Adam Graves, Alexander Karpovtsev, Joe Kocur, Alexei Kovalev, Steve Larmer, Brian Leetch, Doug Lidster, Craig MacTavish, Stephane Matteau, Mark Messier, Sergei Nemchinov, Brian Noonan, Mike Richter, Esa Tikkanen, Jay Wells, Sergei Zubov.

First Period
1.   NY RANGERS   LIDSTER (unassisted)   6:22
2.   VANCOUVER   MOMESSO (RONNING, HEDICAN)   14:04
Penalties: Craven (Van) (tripping) 2:03, Lidster (NYR) (interference) 7:44, Hunter (Van) (roughing) 10:21, Hunter (Van) (misconduct) 15:26, Anderson (NYR) (interference) 16:55.

Second Period
3.   NY RANGERS   ANDERSON (MESSIER)   11:42 (SHG,GWG)
Penalties: Brown (Van) (hooking) 4:27, Matteau (NYR) (holding) 6:12, Graves (NYR) (tripping) 10:35, Antoski (Van) (roughing) 13:58, Tikkanen (NYR) (goaltender interference) 17:08.

Third Period
4.   NY RANGERS   LEETCH (unassisted)   19:55 (ENG)
Penalties: Lidster (NYR) (interference) 1:43, Diduck (Van), Kovalev (NYR) (high sticking) 4:32, Brown (Van), Matteau (NYR) (roughing) 15:29.

Goalies: McLean (Van), Richter (NYR)
Shots: Van   10 - 6 - 13   29
              NYR   14 - 13 - 13   40

Referee: Bill McCreary
Linesmen: Kevin Collins, Gerard Gauthier

Game #3 - June 4, 1994 - Pacific Coliseum - NY Rangers 5, Vancouver 1

NY RANGERS: Glenn Anderson, Jeff Beukeboom, Greg Gilbert, Adam Graves, Alexander Karpovtsev, Joe Kocur, Alexei Kovalev, Steve Larmer, Brian Leetch, Doug Lidster, Kevin Lowe, Craig MacTavish, Stephane Matteau, Mark Messier, Sergei Nemchinov, Brian Noonan, Mike Richter, Esa Tikkanen, Jay Wells.

VANCOUVER: Greg Adams, Shawn Antoski, Dave Babych, Jeff Brown, Pavel Bure, Geoff Courtnall, Murray Craven, Gerald Diduck, Martin Gelinas, Brian Glynn, Bret Hedican, Tim Hunter, Nathan LaFayette, Trevor Linden, Jyrki Lumme, John McIntyre, Kirk McLean, Sergio Momesso, Cliff Ronning.

First Period
1.   VANCOUVER   BURE (LINDEN, ADAMS)   1:03
2.   NY RANGERS   LEETCH (unassisted)   13:39
3.   NY RANGERS   ANDERSON (NEMCHINOV, BEUKEBOOM)   19:19 (GWG)
Penalties: Wells (NYR) (tripping) 2:54, Anderson (NYR) (roughing), Hunter (Van) (charging) 5:42, Lumme (Van) (holding) 9:57, MacTavish (NYR) (holding) 15:04, Leetch (NYR) (tripping) 17:56, Lowe (NYR) (high sticking), Messier (NYR) (roughing), Ronning (Van) (high sticking), Momesso (Van) (roughing), Bure (Van) (high sticking major, game misconduct) 18:12.

Second Period
4.   NY RANGERS   LEETCH (TIKKANEN, BEUKEBOOM)   18:32
Penalties: Lowe (NYR) (roughing) 5:34, Messier (NYR), Antoski (Van) (roughing) 16:28.

Third Period
5.   NY RANGERS   LARMER (unassisted)   0:25
6.   NY RANGERS   KOVALEV (GRAVES, MESSIER)   13:03 (PPG)
Penalties: Tikkanen (NYR) (hooking) 3:13, Hedican (Van) (holding) 5:34, McIntyre (Van) (holding) 7:58, MacTavish (NYR) (holding) 9:46, Momesso (Van) (cross-checking) 11:42, Gelinas (Van) (roughing) 16:35, Antoski (Van) (cross-checking, roughing) 19:19.

Goalies: Richter (NYR), McLean (Van)
Shots: NYR   11 - 5 - 9   25
              Van   9 - 10 - 6   25

Referee: Andy Van Hellemond
Linesmen: Randy Mitton, Ray Scapinello

Game #4 - June 7, 1994 - Pacific Coliseum - NY Rangers 4, Vancouver 2

NY RANGERS: Glenn Anderson, Jeff Beukeboom, Greg Gilbert, Adam Graves, Joe Kocur, Alexei Kovalev, Steve Larmer, Brian Leetch, Doug Lidster, Kevin Lowe, Craig MacTavish, Stephane Matteau, Mark Messier, Sergei Nemchinov, Brian Noonan, Mike Richter, Esa Tikkanen, Jay Wells, Sergei Zubov.

VANCOUVER: Greg Adams, Shawn Antoski, Dave Babych, Jeff Brown, Pavel Bure, Geoff Courtnall, Murray Craven, Gerald Diduck, Martin Gelinas, Brian Glynn, Bret Hedican, Tim Hunter, Nathan LaFayette, Trevor Linden, Jyrki Lumme, John McIntyre, Kirk McLean, Sergio Momesso, Cliff Ronning.

First Period
1.   VANCOUVER   LINDEN (LUMME, BROWN)   13:25 (PPG)
2.   VANCOUVER   RONNING (BURE, CRAVEN)   16:19
Penalties: Courtnall (Van) (elbowing) 3:11, Beukeboom (NYR) (high sticking) 6:35, Graves (NYR) (holding) 13:02, Messier (NYR) (boarding major) 14:17, Linden (Van) (holding the stick) 15:07, Courtnall (Van) (interference) 17:54, Tikkanen (NYR) (roughing) 18:45.

Second Period
3.   NY RANGERS   LEETCH (MacTAVISH, GILBERT)   4:03
4.   NY RANGERS   ZUBOV (MESSIER, LEETCH)   19:44 (PPG)
Penalties: Lidster (NYR) (holding) 1:13, Brown (Van) (tripping) 7:19, Lidster (NYR) (holding) 16:58, Adams (Van) (boarding) 18:55.

Third Period
5.   NY RANGERS   KOVALEV (LEETCH, ZUBOV)   15:05 (PPG,GWG)
6.   NY RANGERS   LARMER (ZUBOV, LEETCH)   17:56
Penalties: NY Rangers bench (too many men) 3:53, Lumme (Van) (holding) 4:48, Tikkanen (NYR), Diduck (Van) (roughing) 10:42, Messier (NYR) (slashing) 11:29, Gelinas (Van) (roughing) 14:31.

Goalies: Richter (NYR), McLean (Van)
Shots: NYR   8 - 8 - 11   27
              Van   8 - 12 - 10   30

Referee: Terry Gregson
Linesmen: Kevin Collins, Gerard Gauthier

(NOTE: Vancouver's Pavel Bure was awarded a penalty shot at 6:31 of the second period. He was unsuccessful against NY Ranger's Mike Richter.)

Game #5 - June 9, 1994 - Madison Square Garden - Vancouver 6, NY Rangers 3

VANCOUVER: Greg Adams, Shawn Antoski, Dave Babych, Jeff Brown, Pavel Bure, Geoff Courtnall, Murray Craven, Gerald Diduck, Martin Gelinas, Brian Glynn, Bret Hedican, Tim Hunter, Nathan LaFayette, Trevor Linden, Jyrki Lumme, John McIntyre, Kirk McLean, Sergio Momesso, Cliff Ronning.

NY RANGERS: Glenn Anderson, Jeff Beukeboom, Greg Gilbert, Adam Graves, Joe Kocur, Alexei Kovalev, Steve Larmer, Brian Leetch, Doug Lidster, Kevin Lowe, Craig MacTavish, Stephane Matteau, Mark Messier, Sergei Nemchinov, Brian Noonan, Mike Richter, Esa Tikkanen, Jay Wells, Sergei Zubov.

First Period
No scoring.
Penalties: Hunter (Van) (elbowing) 0:49, Momesso (Van) (slashing, fighting), Ronning (Van) (roughing), Matteau (NYR) (roughing), Beukeboom (NYR) (instigator, fighting, game misconduct), Wells (NYR) (high sticking) 12:06, Hunter (Van), Wells (NYR) (roughing) 13:20, Ronning (Van), Larmer (NYR) (holding) 17:20, Nemchinov (NYR) (elbowing) 19:32.

Second Period
1.	VANCOUVER	BROWN (RONNING, ANTOSKI)	8:10

Penalties: Courtnall (Van) (elbowing major) 10:13, Messier (NYR) (hooking) 18:19.

Third Period
2.	VANCOUVER	COURTNALL (LaFAYETTE, HEDICAN)	0:26	
3.	VANCOUVER	BURE (CRAVEN)	2:48	
4.	NY RANGERS	LIDSTER (KOVALEV)	3:27	
5.	NY RANGERS	LARMER (MATTEAU, NEMCHINOV)	6:20	
6.	NY RANGERS	MESSIER (ANDERSON, GRAVES)	9:02	
7.	VANCOUVER	BABYCH (BURE)	9:31	(GWG)
8.	VANCOUVER	COURTNALL (LaFAYETTE, LUMME)	12:20	
9.	VANCOUVER	BURE (RONNING, HEDICAN)	13:04	

Penalties: Kocur (NYR) (slashing) 18:41.

Goalies: McLean (Van), Richter (NYR)

Shots:	Van	12	-	8	-	17	37
	NYR	10	-	13	-	15	38

Referee: Andy Van Hellemond
Linesmen: Randy Mitton, Ray Scapinello

Game #6 - June 11, 1994 - Pacific Coliseum - Vancouver 4, NY Rangers 1

NY RANGERS: Glenn Anderson, Jeff Beukeboom, Greg Gilbert, Adam Graves, Joe Kocur, Alexei Kovalev, Steve Larmer, Brian Leetch, Doug Lidster, Kevin Lowe, Craig MacTavish, Stephane Matteau, Mark Messier, Sergei Nemchinov, Brian Noonan, Mike Richter, Esa Tikkanen, Jay Wells, Sergei Zubov.

VANCOUVER: Greg Adams, Shawn Antoski, Dave Babych, Jeff Brown, Pavel Bure, Geoff Courtnall, Murray Craven, Gerald Diduck, Martin Gelinas, Brian Glynn, Bret Hedican, Tim Hunter, Nathan LaFayette, Trevor Linden, Jyrki Lumme, John McIntyre, Kirk McLean, Sergio Momesso, Cliff Ronning.

First Period
1.	VANCOUVER	BROWN (LINDEN)	9:42	(PPG)

Penalties: Beukeboom (NYR) (elbowing) 3:02, Leetch (NYR) (interference) 9:39.

Second Period
2.	VANCOUVER	COURTNALL (LUMME, BURE)	12:29	(GWG)
3.	NY RANGERS	KOVALEV (MESSIER, LEETCH)	14:42	(PPG)

Penalties: Momesso (Van) (interference) 2:26, Diduck (Van) (tripping) 7:27, McIntyre (Van) (interference) 13:23.

Third Period
4.	VANCOUVER	BROWN (unassisted)	8:35
5.	VANCOUVER	COURTNALL (LaFAYETTE, DIDUCK)	18:28

Penalties: none.

Goalies: Richter (NYR), McLean (Van)

Shots:	NYR	7	-	12	-	10	29
	Van	16	-	8	-	7	31

Referee: Bill McCreary
Linesmen: Kevin Collins, Gerard Gauthier

Game #7 - June 14, 1994 - Madison Square Garden - NY Rangers 3, Vancouver 2

VANCOUVER: Greg Adams, Shawn Antoski, Dave Babych, Jeff Brown, Pavel Bure, Geoff Courtnall, Murray Craven, Gerald Diduck, Martin Gelinas, Brian Glynn, Bret Hedican, Tim Hunter, Nathan LaFayette, Trevor Linden, Jyrki Lumme, John McIntyre, Kirk McLean, Sergio Momesso, Cliff Ronning.

NY RANGERS: Glenn Anderson, Jeff Beukeboom, Greg Gilbert, Adam Graves, Joe Kocur, Alexei Kovalev, Steve Larmer, Brian Leetch, Doug Lidster, Kevin Lowe, Craig MacTavish, Stephane Matteau, Mark Messier, Sergei Nemchinov, Brian Noonan, Mike Richter, Esa Tikkanen, Jay Wells, Sergei Zubov.

First Period
1.	NY RANGERS	LEETCH (ZUBOV, MESSIER)	11:02	
2.	NY RANGERS	GRAVES (KOVALEV, ZUBOV)	14:45	(PPG)

Penalties: Lumme (Van) (cross-checking) 14:03, Hedican (Van), Tikkanen (NYR) (roughing) 18:50.

Second Period
3.	VANCOUVER	LINDEN (GLYNN, BURE)	5:21	(SHG)
4.	NY RANGERS	MESSIER (GRAVES, NOONAN)	13:29	(PPG,GWG)

Penalties: Brown (Van) (interference) 4:38, Babych (Van) (tripping) 12:36, Messier (NYR) (hooking) 16:39.

Third Period
5.	VANCOUVER	LINDEN (COURTNALL, RONNING)	4:50	(PPG)

Penalties: Tikkanen (NYR) (hooking) 4:16, Linden (Van), MacTavish (NYR) (roughing) 10:55.

Goalies: McLean (Van), Richter (NYR)

Shots:	Van	9	-	12	-	9	30
	NYR	12	-	14	-	9	35

Referee: Terry Gregson
Linesmen: Kevin Collins, Ray Scapinello

1993
MONTREAL CANADIENS – LOS ANGELES KINGS

Game #1 - June 1, 1993 - Montreal Forum - Los Angeles 4, Montreal 1

LOS ANGELES: Rob Blake, Pat Conacher, Gord Donnelly, Tony Granato, Wayne Gretzky, Mark Hardy, Kelly Hrudey, Charlie Huddy, Jari Kurri, Marty McSorley, Corey Millen, Luc Robitaille, Warren Rychel, Tomas Sandstrom, Gary Shuchuk, Darryl Sydor, Dave Taylor, Tim Watters, Alexei Zhitnik.

MONTREAL: Brian Bellows, Patrice Brisebois, Benoit Brunet, Guy Carbonneau, J.J. Daigneault, Vincent Damphousse, Eric Desjardins, Gilbert Dionne, Paul Di Pietro, Sean Hill, Stephan Lebeau, John LeClair, Gary Leeman, Kirk Muller, Lyle Odelein, Ed Ronan, Patrick Roy, Denis Savard, Mathieu Schneider.

First Period
1.	LOS ANGELES	ROBITAILLE (ZHITNIK, GRETZKY)	3:30	(PPG)
2.	MONTREAL	RONAN (unassisted)	18:09	

Penalties: Odelein (Mtl) (holding) 2:42, Dionne (Mtl) (high sticking) 6:12, McSorley (LA) (delay of game) 11:03, Kurri (LA) (holding) 15:54.

Second Period
3.	LOS ANGELES	ROBITAILLE (BLAKE, GRETZKY)	17:41	(PPG,GWG)

Penalties: Granato (LA) (goaltender interference) 5:08, Taylor (LA), Muller (Mtl) (roughing) 6:23, McSorley (LA), Odelein (Mtl) (unsportsmanlike conduct) 7:16, Damphousse (Mtl) (slashing) 10:23, Millen (LA), Desjardins (Mtl) (high sticking), Brisebois (Mtl) (holding) 17:23, Roy (Mtl) (delay of game) 18:33, Gretzky (LA) (hooking) 19:32.

Third Period
4.	LOS ANGELES	KURRI (GRETZKY, GRANATO)	1:51	
5.	LOS ANGELES	GRETZKY (SANDSTROM)	18:02	(ENG)

Penalties: Huddy (LA) (hooking) 6:41, Daigneault (Mtl) (cross-checking) 18:41.

Goalies: Hrudey (LA), Roy (Mtl)

Shots:	LA	11	-	20	-	7	38
	Mtl	11	-	10	-	11	32

Referee: Andy Van Hellemond
Linesmen: Gerard Gauthier, Ray Scapinello

Game #2 - June 3, 1993 - Montreal Forum - Montreal 3, Los Angeles 2 (OT)

LOS ANGELES: Rob Blake, Pat Conacher, Gord Donnelly, Tony Granato, Wayne Gretzky, Kelly Hrudey, Charlie Huddy, Marty McSorley, Corey Millen, Luc Robitaille, Warren Rychel, Tomas Sandstrom, Gary Shuchuk, Darryl Sydor, Dave Taylor, Tim Watters, Alexei Zhitnik.

MONTREAL: Brian Bellows, Patrice Brisebois, Benoit Brunet, Guy Carbonneau, J.J. Daigneault, Vincent Damphousse, Eric Desjardins, Gilbert Dionne, Paul Di Pietro, Kevin Haller, Mike Keane, Stephan Lebeau, John LeClair, Gary Leeman, Kirk Muller, Lyle Odelein, Ed Ronan, Patrick Roy, Mathieu Schneider.

First Period
1. MONTREAL   DESJARDINS (DAMPHOUSSE, LEBEAU)   18:31

Penalties: Odelein (Mtl) (roughing) 5:57, Robitaille (LA) (hooking) 6:40, Brisebois (Mtl) (interference) 7:05, Blake (LA) (tripping) 10:25, Roy (Mtl) (high sticking) 10:38, Watters (LA) (holding) 10:38, Muller (Mtl) (tripping) 13:01, Sydor (LA) (holding) 14:44, Schneider (Mtl) (high sticking) 17:02, Granato (LA) (holding) 17:53.

Second Period
2. LOS ANGELES   TAYLOR (unassisted)   5:12 (SHG)

Penalties: Muller (Mtl) (cross-checking) 0:35, Huddy (LA) (cross-checking) 4:20, McSorley (LA), Damphousse (Mtl) (roughing) 9:43, Robitaille (LA), Dionne (Mtl) (roughing) 16:02.

Third Period
3. LOS ANGELES   CONACHER (TAYLOR, GRANATO)   8:32
4. MONTREAL   DESJARDINS (DAMPHOUSSE, SCHNEIDER)   18:47 (PPG)

Penalties: Brunet (Mtl) (slashing) 1:31, Damphousse (Mtl) (cross-checking) 2:30, Zhitnik (LA) (tripping) 4:17, Taylor (LA) (goaltender interference) 11:56, Brisebois (Mtl) (cross-checking) 13:16, McSorley (LA) (illegal stick) 18:15).

First Overtime
5. MONTREAL   DESJARDINS (BRUNET, RONAN)   0:51 (GWG)

Penalties: Blake (LA) (misconduct) 0:51.

Goalies: Hrudey (LA), Roy (Mtl)

Shots:						
LA	5	- 9	- 9	- 1	24
Mtl	16	- 12	- 11	- 2	41

Referee: Kerry Fraser
Linesmen: Kevin Collins, Ray Scapinello

Game #3 - June 5, 1993 - Great Western Forum - Montreal 4, Los Angeles 3 (OT)

MONTREAL: Brian Bellows, Patrice Brisebois, Benoit Brunet, Guy Carbonneau, J.J. Daigneault, Vincent Damphousse, Eric Desjardins, Gilbert Dionne, Paul Di Pietro, Kevin Haller, Mike Keane, Stephan Lebeau, John LeClair, Gary Leeman, Kirk Muller, Lyle Odelein, Ed Ronan, Patrick Roy, Mathieu Schneider.

LOS ANGELES: Rob Blake, Pat Conacher, Gord Donnelly, Tony Granato, Wayne Gretzky, Mark Hardy, Kelly Hrudey, Charlie Huddy, Marty McSorley, Corey Millen, Luc Robitaille, Warren Rychel, Tomas Sandstrom, Gary Shuchuk, Darryl Sydor, Dave Taylor, Tim Watters, Alexei Zhitnik.

First Period
1. MONTREAL   BELLOWS (HALLER, MULLER)   10:26 (PPG)

Penalties: Zhitnik (LA) (tripping) 4:23, Bellows (Mtl) (cross-checking) 5:21, Desjardins (Mtl) (interference) 7:40, Watters (LA) (tripping) 10:21, Ronan (Mtl) (goaltender interference) 13:09, Lebeau (Mtl) (slashing) 16:37, Blake (LA) (roughing) 19:59.

Second Period
2. MONTREAL   DIONNE (KEANE, LEBEAU)   2:41
3. MONTREAL   SCHNEIDER (CARBONNEAU)   3:02
4. LOS ANGELES   ROBITAILLE (GRETZKY, SANDSTROM)   7:52
5. LOS ANGELES   GRANATO (unassisted)   11:02
6. LOS ANGELES   GRETZKY (DONNELLY, HARDY)   17:07

Penalties: Ronan (Mtl), Taylor (LA) (slashing) 11:42.

Third Period
No scoring.
Penalties: Lebeau (Mtl) (holding) 6:48, Sandstrom (LA) (goaltender interference) 10:50.

First Overtime
7. MONTREAL   LeCLAIR (MULLER, BELLOWS)   0:34 (GWG)

Penalties: none.

Goalies: Roy (Mtl), Hrudey (LA)

Shots:						
Mtl	12	- 9	- 12	- 3	36
LA	10	- 13	- 10	- 0	33

Referee: Terry Gregson
Linesmen: Wayne Bonney, Ray Scapinello

Game #4 - June 7, 1993 - Great Western Forum - Montreal 3, Los Angeles 2 (OT)

MONTREAL: Brian Bellows, Patrice Brisebois, Benoit Brunet, Guy Carbonneau, J.J. Daigneault, Vincent Damphousse, Eric Desjardins, Gilbert Dionne, Paul Di Pietro, Kevin Haller, Mike Keane, Stephan Lebeau, John LeClair, Gary Leeman, Kirk Muller, Lyle Odelein, Ed Ronan, Patrick Roy, Mathieu Schneider.

LOS ANGELES: Rob Blake, Jimmy Carson, Pat Conacher, Gord Donnelly, Tony Granato, Wayne Gretzky, Mark Hardy, Kelly Hrudey, Jari Kurri, Lonnie Loach, Marty McSorley, Corey Millen, Luc Robitaille, Warren Rychel, Tomas Sandstrom, Gary Shuchuk, Darryl Sydor, Tim Watters, Alexei Zhitnik.

First Period
1. MONTREAL   MULLER (unassisted)   10:57

Penalties: Conacher (LA) (cross-checking) 1:53, Desjardins (Mtl) (high sticking), Granato (LA) (roughing) 4:24, Schneider (Mtl) (elbowing) 16:50.

Second Period
2. MONTREAL   DAMPHOUSSE (KEANE, DESJARDINS)   5:24 (PPG)
3. LOS ANGELES   DONNELLY (GRANATO)   6:33
4. LOS ANGELES   McSORLEY (GRETZKY, ROBITAILLE)   19:55 (PPG)

Penalties: Hardy (LA) (holding) 3:32, McSorley (LA) (misconduct) 5:24, Daigneault (Mtl) (roughing), Rychel (LA) (goaltender interference) 7:37, Brisebois (Mtl), Blake (LA) (roughing) 12:09, Sydor (LA) (interference) 15:58, Bellows (Mtl) (hooking) 19:10.

Third Period
No scoring.
Penalties: Daigneault (Mtl) (cross-checking) 2:42, Schneider (Mtl), Granato (LA) (roughing) 19:30.

First Overtime
5. MONTREAL   LeCLAIR (unassisted)   14:37 (GWG)

Penalties: none.

Goalies: Roy (Mtl), Hrudey (LA)

Shots:						
Mtl	13	- 7	- 12	- 7	39
LA	6	- 11	- 15	- 10	42

Referee: Andy Van Hellemond
Linesmen: Kevin Collins, Gerard Gauthier

Game #5 - June 9, 1993 - Montreal Forum - Montreal 4, Los Angeles 1

LOS ANGELES: Rob Blake, Jimmy Carson, Pat Conacher, Gord Donnelly, Tony Granato, Wayne Gretzky, Mark Hardy, Kelly Hrudey, Charlie Huddy, Jari Kurri, Marty McSorley, Corey Millen, Luc Robitaille, Warren Rychel, Tomas Sandstrom, Gary Shuchuk, Darryl Sydor, Tim Watters, Alexei Zhitnik.

MONTREAL: Brian Bellows, Patrice Brisebois, Benoit Brunet, Guy Carbonneau, J.J. Daigneault, Vincent Damphousse, Eric Desjardins, Gilbert Dionne, Paul Di Pietro, Donald Dufresne, Mike Keane, Stephan Lebeau, John LeClair, Gary Leeman, Kirk Muller, Lyle Odelein, Ed Ronan, Patrick Roy, Mathieu Schneider.

First Period
1. MONTREAL   Di PIETRO (LEEMAN, LeCLAIR)   15:10

Penalties: Schneider (Mtl) (tripping) 4:35, Keane (Mtl) (charging) 10:46, Granato (LA) (tripping) 12:49, Blake (LA), Sandstrom (LA), Ronan (Mtl) (roughing) 19:23.

Second Period
2. LOS ANGELES   McSORLEY (CARSON, ROBITAILLE)   2:40
3. MONTREAL   MULLER (DAMPHOUSSE, ODELEIN)   3:51 (GWG)
4. MONTREAL   LEBEAU (KEANE, LeCLAIR)   11:31 (PPG)

Penalties: Leeman (Mtl) (tripping) 5:52, Damphousse (Mtl) (elbowing) 7:40, Hardy (LA) (holding) 10:29.

Third Period
5. MONTREAL   Di PIETRO (DIONNE, ODELEIN)   12:06

Penalties: none.

Goalies: Hrudey (LA), Roy (Mtl)

Shots:					
LA	7	- 7	- 5	19
Mtl	10	- 12	- 7	29

Referee: Terry Gregson
Linesmen: Wayne Bonney, Ray Scapinello

1992

PITTSBURGH PENGUINS - CHICAGO BLACKHAWKS

Game #1 - May 26, 1992 - Civic Arena - Pittsburgh 5, Chicago 4

CHICAGO: Ed Belfour, Rob Brown, Chris Chelios, Michel Goulet, Dirk Graham, Mike Hudson, Igor Kravchuk, Frantisek Kucera, Steve Larmer, Jocelyn Lemieux, Bryan Marchment, Stephane Matteau, Brian Noonan, Mike Peluso, Jeremy Roenick, Cam Russell, Steve Smith, Brent Sutter.

PITTSBURGH: Tom Barrasso, Phil Bourque, Jock Callander, Bob Errey, Ron Francis, Jiri Hrdina, Jaromir Jagr, Mario Lemieux, Troy Loney, Shawn McEachern, Larry Murphy, Jim Paek, Gordie Roberts, Kjell Samuelsson, Ulf Samuelsson, Paul Stanton, Kevin Stevens, Rick Tocchet, Bryan Trottier.

First Period

1.	CHICAGO	CHELIOS (SUTTER)	6:34	(PPG)
2.	CHICAGO	GOULET (unassisted)	13:17	
3.	CHICAGO	GRAHAM (CHELIOS)	13:43	
4.	PITTSBURGH	BOURQUE (TOCCHET, FRANCIS)	17:26	(PPG)

Penalties: Hudson (Chi) (interference) 2:07, Roberts (Pit) (holding) 6:27, Peluso (Chi) (hooking) 9:34, Kravchuk (Chi) (holding) 15:44, Trottier (Pit) (interference) 18:39.

Second Period

5.	CHICAGO	SUTTER (LARMER, CHELIOS)	11:36
6.	PITTSBURGH	TOCCHET (STANTON, McEACHERN)	15:24
7.	PITTSBURGH	LEMIEUX (STEVENS)	16:23

Penalties: Brown (Chi) (elbowing) 2:17, Chicago bench (too many men) 13:21.

Third Period

8.	PITTSBURGH	JAGR (unassisted)	15:05	
9.	PITTSBURGH	LEMIEUX (MURPHY, FRANCIS)	19:47	(PPG,GWG)

Penalties: Stanton (Pit) (hooking) 1:24, Murphy (Pit) (hooking) 17:39, Smith (Chi) (hooking) 19:42.

Goalies: Belfour (Chi), Barrasso (Pit)

Shots:	Chi	11	-	11	-	12	34
	Pit	15	-	10	-	14	39

Referee: Andy Van Hellemond
Linesmen: Kevin Collins, Gerard Gauthier

Game #2 - May 28, 1992 - Civic Arena - Pittsburgh 3, Chicago 1

CHICAGO: Ed Belfour, Rod Buskas, Chris Chelios, Greg Gilbert, Michel Goulet, Dirk Graham, Stu Grimson, Mike Hudson, Igor Kravchuk, Frantisek Kucera, Steve Larmer, Jocelyn Lemieux, Bryan Marchment, Stephane Matteau, Brian Noonan, Mike Peluso, Jeremy Roenick, Steve Smith, Brent Sutter.

PITTSBURGH: Tom Barrasso, Phil Bourque, Jock Callander, Bob Errey, Ron Francis, Jiri Hrdina, Jaromir Jagr, Mario Lemieux, Troy Loney, Shawn McEachern, Larry Murphy, Jim Paek, Gordie Roberts, Kjell Samuelsson, Ulf Samuelsson, Paul Stanton, Kevin Stevens, Rick Tocchet, Bryan Trottier.

First Period

1.	PITTSBURGH	ERREY (PAEK)	9:52	(SHG)

Penalties: Peluso (Chi) (roughing) 2:07, Stanton (Pit) (delay of game, tripping) 7:38, Smith (Chi) (interference) 11:05, Noonan (Chi) (cross-checking) 18:36.

Second Period

2.	CHICAGO	MARCHMENT (NOONAN, GILBERT)	10:24	
3.	PITTSBURGH	LEMIEUX (TOCCHET)	12:55	(PPG,GWG)
4.	PITTSBURGH	LEMIEUX (TOCCHET, K. SAMUELSSON)	15:23	

Penalties: Marchment (Chi) (elbowing) 12:12, Chicago bench (too many men) 19:43.

Third Period

No scoring.
Penalties: Roberts (Pit) (holding) 5:09.

Goalies: Belfour (Chi), Barrasso (Pit)

Shots:	Chi	11	-	4	-	4	19
	Pit	8	-	11	-	6	25

Referee: Terry Gregson
Linesmen: Swede Knox, Ray Scapinello

Game #3 - May 30, 1992 - Chicago Stadium - Pittsburgh 1, Chicago 0

PITTSBURGH: Tom Barrasso, Phil Bourque, Jock Callander, Ron Francis, Jiri Hrdina, Jaromir Jagr, Mario Lemieux, Troy Loney, Shawn McEachern, Dave Michayluk, Larry Murphy, Jim Paek, Gordie Roberts, Kjell Samuelsson, Ulf Samuelsson, Paul Stanton, Kevin Stevens, Rick Tocchet, Bryan Trottier.

CHICAGO: Ed Belfour, Rob Brown, Rod Buskas, Chris Chelios, Greg Gilbert, Michel Goulet, Dirk Graham, Mike Hudson, Igor Kravchuk, Frantisek Kucera, Steve Larmer, Jocelyn Lemieux, Bryan Marchment, Stephane Matteau, Brian Noonan, Mike Peluso, Jeremy Roenick, Steve Smith, Brent Sutter.

First Period

1.	PITTSBURGH	STEVENS (PAEK, TOCCHET)	15:26	(GWG)

Penalties: K. Samuelsson (Pit) (high sticking) 5:43, Roberts (Pit) (tripping) 11:50, Goulet (Chi) (holding) 16:47, Jagr (Pit) (holding) 19:14.

Second Period

No scoring.
Penalties: Larmer (Chi) (cross-checking) 4:38, Stanton (Pit) (holding) 7:04, Chelios (Chi) (slashing) 10:56.

Third Period

No scoring.
Penalties: Paek (Pit) (interference) 10:05, Chelios (Chi) (fighting, game misconduct) 19:29.

Goalies: Barrasso (Pit), Belfour (Chi)

Shots:	Pit	6	-	8	-	6	20
	Chi	13	-	6	-	8	27

Referee: Don Koharski
Linesmen: Kevin Collins, Gerard Gauthier

Game #4 - June 1, 1992 - Chicago Stadium - Pittsburgh 6, Chicago 5

PITTSBURGH: Tom Barrasso, Phil Bourque, Jock Callander, Bob Errey, Ron Francis, Jiri Hrdina, Jaromir Jagr, Mario Lemieux, Troy Loney, Shawn McEachern, Larry Murphy, Jim Paek, Gordie Roberts, Kjell Samuelsson, Ulf Samuelsson, Paul Stanton, Kevin Stevens, Rick Tocchet, Bryan Trottier.

CHICAGO: Ed Belfour, Rob Brown, Rod Buskas, Chris Chelios, Greg Gilbert, Michel Goulet, Dirk Graham, Stu Grimson, Dominik Hasek, Mike Hudson, Igor Kravchuk, Frantisek Kucera, Steve Larmer, Jocelyn Lemieux, Bryan Marchment, Stephane Matteau, Brian Noonan, Jeremy Roenick, Steve Smith, Brent Sutter.

First Period

1.	PITTSBURGH	JAGR (LONEY)	1:37
2.	CHICAGO	GRAHAM (MATTEAU, CHELIOS)	6:21
3.	PITTSBURGH	STEVENS (LEMIEUX, TOCCHET)	6:33
4.	CHICAGO	GRAHAM (CHELIOS)	6:51
5.	PITTSBURGH	LEMIEUX (MURPHY, STEVENS)	10:13 (PPG)
6.	CHICAGO	GRAHAM (LEMIEUX, NOONAN)	16:18

Penalties: U. Samuelsson (Pit) (interference), Stanton (Pit), Gilbert (Chi) (misconduct) 7:28, Chelios (Chi) (elbowing) 8:17, Roberts (Pit) (roughing) 12:44.

Second Period

7.	PITTSBURGH	TOCCHET (LEMIEUX, STEVENS)	0:58
8.	CHICAGO	ROENICK (NOONAN, GILBERT)	15:40

Penalties: Stanton (Pit) (hooking) 2:21; Tocchet (Pit) (holding) 5:41.

Third Period

9.	PITTSBURGH	MURPHY (TOCCHET)	4:51
10.	PITTSBURGH	FRANCIS (McEACHERN, PAEK)	7:59 (GWG)
11.	CHICAGO	ROENICK (GRIMSON, BUSKAS)	11:18

Penalties: none.

Goalies: Barrasso (Pit), Belfour, Hasek (Chi)

Shots:	Pit	12	-	9	-	8	29
	Chi	8	-	14	-	7	29

Referee: Andy Van Hellemond
Linesmen: Swede Knox, Ray Scapinello

1991
PITTSBURGH PENGUINS - MINNESOTA NORTH STARS

Game #1 - May 15, 1991 - Civic Arena - Minnesota 5, Pittsburgh 4

MINNESOTA: Brian Bellows, Neal Broten, Marc Bureau, Jon Casey, Shawn Chambers, Shane Churla, Ulf Dahlen, Chris Dahlquist, Gaetan Duchesne, Dave Gagner, Stew Gavin, Brian Glynn, Jim Johnson, Basil McRae, Mike Modano, Brian Propp, Bobby Smith, Mark Tinordi, Neil Wilkinson.

PITTSBURGH: Tom Barrasso, Phil Bourque, Bob Errey, Ron Francis, Jiri Hrdina, Jaromir Jagr, Grant Jennings, Mario Lemieux, Troy Loney, Joe Mullen, Larry Murphy, Mark Recchi, Gordie Roberts, Ulf Samuelsson, Paul Stanton, Kevin Stevens, Peter Taglianetti, Bryan Trottier, Scott Young.

First Period
1.	PITTSBURGH	SAMUELSSON (FRANCIS)	3:45
2.	MINNESOTA	BROTEN (unassisted)	6:32
3.	MINNESOTA	DAHLEN (SMITH, CHAMBERS)	9:49

Penalties: Propp (Min) (slashing) 4:17, Loney (Pit) (roughing) 7:45, Chambers (Min) (hooking) 12:32, Tinordi (Min) (high sticking) 13:45, Recchi (Pit) (interference) 15:02, McRae (Min) (unsportsmanlike conduct) 18:13, Bureau (Min) (boarding) 19:39.

Second Period
4.	PITTSBURGH	LEMIEUX (FRANCIS)	3:54 (SHG)
5.	MINNESOTA	BUREAU (GAVIN)	6:53 (SHG)
6.	PITTSBURGH	YOUNG (MURPHY, JAGR)	7:43 (PPG)
7.	MINNESOTA	BROTEN (MODANO)	17:01

Penalties: Roberts (Pit) (interference) 2:01, Johnson (Min) (slashing) 5:58, Bureau (Min) (holding) 10:25, Stanton (Pit) (hooking) 19:11.

Third Period
8.	MINNESOTA	SMITH (DAHLEN)	1:39 (GWG)
9.	PITTSBURGH	MULLEN (JAGR, YOUNG)	10:35

Penalties: Jennings (Pit) (cross-checking) 4:08, Casey (Min) (slashing) 8:25.

Goalies: Casey (Min), Barrasso (Pit)

Shots:	Min	9	-	12	-	8	29
	Pit	17	-	11	-	10	38

Referee: Don Koharski
Linesmen: Wayne Bonney, Ray Scapinello

Game #2 - May 17, 1991 - Civic Arena - Pittsburgh 4, Minnesota 1

MINNESOTA: Brian Bellows, Perry Berezan, Neal Broten, Marc Bureau, Jon Casey, Shawn Chambers, Ulf Dahlen, Chris Dahlquist, Gaetan Duchesne, Dave Gagner, Stew Gavin, Brian Glynn, Jim Johnson, Mike Modano, Brian Propp, Doug Smail, Bobby Smith, Mark Tinordi, Neil Wilkinson.

PITTSBURGH: Tom Barrasso, Phil Bourque, Paul Coffey, Bob Errey, Ron Francis, Randy Gilhen, Jaromir Jagr, Mario Lemieux, Troy Loney, Joe Mullen, Larry Murphy, Jim Paek, Mark Recchi, Gordie Roberts, Ulf Samuelsson, Paul Stanton, Kevin Stevens, Peter Taglianetti, Bryan Trottier.

First Period
1.	PITTSBURGH	ERREY (TAGLIANETTI)	14:26 (SHG)
2.	PITTSBURGH	STEVENS (LEMIEUX, MURPHY)	19:10 (PPG,GWG)

Penalties: Francis (Pit) (hooking) 1:07, Errey (Pit) (boarding) 9:08, Recchi (Pit) (cross-checking) 13:06, Samuelsson (Pit) (holding) 15:12, Bellows (Min) (hooking) 16:36, Chambers (Min) (interference) 18:59, Pittsburgh bench (too many men) 20:00.

Second Period
3.	MINNESOTA	MODANO (CHAMBERS, CASEY)	0:55 (PPG)
4.	PITTSBURGH	LEMIEUX (BOURQUE)	15:04
5.	PITTSBURGH	STEVENS (MULLEN, MURPHY)	16:32

Penalties: Duchesne (Min) (holding) 6:22, Murphy (Pit) (hooking) 6:37, Smith (Min) (interference) 9:30, Glynn (Min) (roughing) 17:27, Wilkinson (Min) (roughing) 19:58, Bureau (Min) (roughing), Tinordi (Min) (fighting), Loney (Pit) (roughing, fighting) 20:00.

Third Period
No scoring.
Penalties: Modano (Min) (high sticking) 5:29, Duchesne (Min) (hooking) 10:39, Samuelsson (Pit) (holding) 12:58, Bureau (Min), Stevens (Pit) (roughing), Trottier (Pit) (misconduct) 16:20, Gagner (Min), Stanton (Pit) (roughing) 17:03, Roberts (Pit) (holding, spearing major, game misconduct) 17:34, Minnesota bench (too many men) 19:41, Francis (Pit) (holding) 20:00.

Goalies: Casey (Min), Barrasso (Pit)

Shots:	Min	12	-	12	-	16	40
	Pit	14	-	12	-	5	31

Referee: Andy Van Hellemond
Linesmen: Gord Broseker, Kevin Collins

Game #3 - May 19, 1991 - Met Center - Minnesota 3, Pittsburgh 1

PITTSBURGH: Tom Barrasso, Phil Bourque, Paul Coffey, Bob Errey, Ron Francis, Randy Gilhen, Jiri Hrdina, Jaromir Jagr, Troy Loney, Joe Mullen, Larry Murphy, Jim Paek, Mark Recchi, Gordie Roberts, Ulf Samuelsson, Paul Stanton, Kevin Stevens, Bryan Trottier.

MINNESOTA: Brian Bellows, Neal Broten, Marc Bureau, Jon Casey, Shawn Chambers, Shane Churla, Ulf Dahlen, Chris Dahlquist, Gaetan Duchesne, Dave Gagner, Stew Gavin, Brian Glynn, Jim Johnson, Basil McRae, Mike Modano, Brian Propp, Bobby Smith, Mark Tinordi, Neil Wilkinson.

First Period
No scoring.
Penalties: Errey (Pit) (charging) 9:08, Francis (Pit) (holding) 13:44, Smith (Min) (interference) 16:21.

Second Period
1.	MINNESOTA	GAGNER (MODANO, JOHNSON)	7:21
2.	MINNESOTA	SMITH (BELLOWS, DAHLQUIST)	7:54 (GWG)

Penalties: McRae (Min) (boarding) 4:08, Recchi (Pit), Chambers (Min) (unsportsmanlike conduct) 5:23, Duchesne (Min) (holding) 8:38, Taglianetti (Pit) (high sticking) 12:36, Loney (Pit), Johnson (Min) (roughing) 17:28.

Third Period
3.	PITTSBURGH	BOURQUE (JAGR, TROTTIER)	1:23
4.	MINNESOTA	DUCHESNE (GAVIN, BROTEN)	2:09

Penalties: Bourque (Pit) (slashing), Johnson (Min) (high sticking), 7:20, Stanton (Pit), Bellows (Min) (roughing) 8:09, Gilhen (Pit) (holding), Gagner (Min) (roughing) 8:13, Samuelsson (Pit) (elbowing) 8:53, Dahlquist (Min) (tripping) 13:34, Stevens (Pit) (spearing major, game misconduct) 18:47, Barrasso (Pit) (slashing) 19:21, Gilhen (Pit), Bellows (Min) (misconduct) 19:53, Errey (Pit) (charging), Smith (Min) (high sticking) 20:00.

Goalies: Barrasso (Pit), Casey (Min)

Shots:	Pit	7	-	8	-	15	30
	Min	12	-	8	-	13	33

Referee: Kerry Fraser
Linesmen: Wayne Bonney, Ray Scapinello

Game #4 - May 21, 1991 - Met Center - Pittsburgh 5, Minnesota 3

PITTSBURGH: Tom Barrasso, Phil Bourque, Paul Coffey, Bob Errey, Ron Francis, Randy Gilhen, Jaromir Jagr, Grant Jennings, Mario Lemieux, Troy Loney, Joe Mullen, Larry Murphy, Jim Paek, Mark Recchi, Gordie Roberts, Ulf Samuelsson, Paul Stanton, Kevin Stevens, Bryan Trottier.

MINNESOTA: Brian Bellows, Neal Broten, Marc Bureau, Jon Casey, Shawn Chambers, Shane Churla, Ulf Dahlen, Chris Dahlquist, Gaetan Duchesne, Dave Gagner, Stew Gavin, Brian Glynn, Jim Johnson, Basil McRae, Mike Modano, Brian Propp, Bobby Smith, Mark Tinordi, Neil Wilkinson.

First Period
1.	PITTSBURGH	STEVENS (unassisted)	0:58
2.	PITTSBURGH	FRANCIS (STEVENS, MULLEN)	2:36
3.	PITTSBURGH	LEMIEUX (RECCHI, MURPHY)	2:58
4.	MINNESOTA	GAGNER (BELLOWS, DAHLEN)	18:22

Penalties: Samuelsson (Pit) (charging) 7:27, Stanton (Pit), Propp (Min) (high sticking) 7:44, Johnson (Min) (holding) 14:45, Samuelsson (Pit) (holding) 18:38.

Second Period
5.	PITTSBURGH	TROTTIER (ERREY, JAGR)	9:55 (GWG)
6.	MINNESOTA	PROPP (GAGNER)	13:10 (PPG)
7.	MINNESOTA	MODANO (PROPP, GAGNER)	18:25 (PPG)

Penalties: Modano (Min) (slashing) 4:28, Murphy (Pit), McRae (Min) (roughing) 11:22, Stevens (Pit) (holding) 11:49, Lemieux (Pit) (interference), Bellows (Min) (roughing) 12:34, Lemieux (Pit) (roughing) 13:10, Murphy (Pit) (roughing) 16:59, Errey (Pit) (high sticking) 18:06, Gagner (Min) (roughing) 18:50.

Third Period
8.	PITTSBURGH	BOURQUE (MULLEN, LEMIEUX)	19:45 (ENG)

Penalties: Loney (Pit) (high sticking major, game misconduct) 13:03, Casey (Min) (interference) 16:52.

Goalies: Barrasso (Pit), Casey (Min)

Shots:	Pit	13	-	5	-	6	24
	Min	14	-	17	-	7	38

Referee: Andy Van Hellemond
Linesmen: Gord Broseker, Kevin Collins

Game #5 - May 23, 1991 - Civic Arena - Pittsburgh 6, Minnesota 4

MINNESOTA: Brian Bellows, Neal Broten, Marc Bureau, Jon Casey, Shawn Chambers, Shane Churla, Ulf Dahlen, Chris Dahlquist, Gaetan Duchesne, Dave Gagner, Stew Gavin, Brian Glynn, Brian Hayward, Jim Johnson, Basil McRae, Mike Modano, Brian Propp, Bobby Smith, Mark Tinordi, Neil Wilkinson.

PITTSBURGH: Tom Barrasso, Phil Bourque, Paul Coffey, Bob Errey, Ron Francis, Randy Gilhen, Jaromir Jagr, Mario Lemieux, Troy Loney, Joe Mullen, Larry Murphy, Jim Paek, Frank Pietrangelo, Mark Recchi, Gordie Roberts, Ulf Samuelsson, Paul Stanton, Kevin Stevens, Peter Taglianetti, Bryan Trottier.

First Period

1.	PITTSBURGH	LEMIEUX (MURPHY, COFFEY)	5:36	(PPG)
2.	PITTSBURGH	STEVENS (COFFEY, MURPHY)	10:08	(PPG)
3.	PITTSBURGH	RECCHI (LEMIEUX, BOURQUE)	11:45	
4.	PITTSBURGH	RECCHI (LEMIEUX, MURPHY)	13:41	
5.	MINNESOTA	BROTEN (TINORDI)	14:52	(SHG)

Penalties: Glynn (Min) (cross-checking) 3:38, Trottier (Pit) (cross-checking) 7:07, Tinordi (Min) (hooking) 9:54, McRae (Min) (charging, roughing, unsportsmanlike conduct), Churla (Min), Paek (Pit), Stevens (Pit) (roughing) 14:26.

Second Period

| 6. | MINNESOTA | GAGNER (PROPP) | 6:54 | (SHG) |
| 7. | PITTSBURGH | FRANCIS (MULLEN) | 16:26 | (GWG) |

Penalties: Dahlquist (Min) (hooking) 5:23, Trottier (Pit) (tripping) 10:46, Gagner (Min) (interference), Taglianetti (Pit) (holding) 14:53, Bourque (Pit) (illegal stick) 17:20.

Third Period

8.	MINNESOTA	DAHLEN (SMITH, DUCHESNE)	1:36	
9.	MINNESOTA	GAGNER (PROPP, GAVIN)	7:41	
10.	PITTSBURGH	LONEY (MURPHY, FRANCIS)	18:21	

Penalties: Taglianetti (Pit) (cross-checking) 8:40, Gagner (Min) (tripping) 9:49, Glynn (Min) (cross-checking) 10:05, Tinordi (Min), Stevens (Pit) (roughing) 12:00, Gagner (Min), Lemieux (Pit) (roughing) 19:02.

Goalies: Casey, Hayward (Min), Barrasso, Pietrangelo (Pit)

| Shots: | Min | 7 | - | 9 | - | 9 | 25 |
| | Pit | 18 | - | 5 | - | 8 | 31 |

Referee: Kerry Fraser
Linesmen: Wayne Bonney, Ray Scapinello

Game #6 - May 25, 1991 - Met Center - Pittsburgh 8, Minnesota 0

PITTSBURGH: Tom Barrasso, Phil Bourque, Paul Coffey, Bob Errey, Ron Francis, Randy Gilhen, Jaromir Jagr, Mario Lemieux, Troy Loney, Joe Mullen, Larry Murphy, Jim Paek, Mark Recchi, Gordie Roberts, Ulf Samuelsson, Paul Stanton, Kevin Stevens, Peter Taglianetti, Bryan Trottier.

MINNESOTA: Brian Bellows, Neal Broten, Marc Bureau, Jon Casey, Shawn Chambers, Shane Churla, Ulf Dahlen, Chris Dahlquist, Gaetan Duchesne, Dave Gagner, Stew Gavin, Brian Glynn, Brian Hayward, Jim Johnson, Basil McRae, Mike Modano, Brian Propp, Bobby Smith, Mark Tinordi, Neil Wilkinson.

First Period

1.	PITTSBURGH	SAMUELSSON (TAGLIANETTI, TROTTIER)	2:00	(PPG,GWG)
2.	PITTSBURGH	LEMIEUX (MURPHY)	12:19	(SHG)
3.	PITTSBURGH	MULLEN (STEVENS, TAGLIANETTI)	13:14	(PPG)

Penalties: Broten (Min) (interference) 0:09, Johnson (Min) (high sticking) 6:20, Stevens (Pit) (holding) 10:25, Roberts (Pit) (roughing) 10:59, Modano (Min) (interference) 11:17, Roberts (Pit) (interference) 13:58, Taglianetti (Pit) (tripping) 17:35.

Second Period

4.	PITTSBURGH	ERREY (JAGR, LEMIEUX)	13:15	
5.	PITTSBURGH	FRANCIS (MULLEN)	14:28	
6.	PITTSBURGH	MULLEN (STEVENS, SAMUELSSON)	18:44	

Penalties: Samuelsson (Pit), Recchi (Pit), Churla (Min) (roughing), Tinordi (Min) (double minor, roughing), McRae (Min) (misconduct) 8:03, Gagner (Min) (roughing), 15:18.

Third Period

| 7. | PITTSBURGH | PAEK (LEMIEUX) | 1:19 | |
| 8. | PITTSBURGH | MURPHY (LEMIEUX) | 13:45 | (PPG) |

Penalties: McRae (Min) (slashing) 12:27, Stevens (Pit), Gavin (Min) (slashing) 13:03.

Goalies: Barrasso (Pit), Casey, Hayward (Min)

| Shots: | Pit | 11 | - | 9 | - | 8 | 28 |
| | Min | 16 | - | 7 | - | 16 | 39 |

Referee: Don Koharski
Linesmen: Gord Broseker, Kevin Collins

1990

EDMONTON OILERS - BOSTON BRUINS

Game #1 - May 15, 1990 - Boston Garden - Edmonton 3, Boston 2 (3 OT)

EDMONTON: Glenn Anderson, Kelly Buchberger, Martin Gelinas, Adam Graves, Randy Gregg, Charlie Huddy, Petr Klima, Jari Kurri, Mark Lamb, Kevin Lowe, Craig MacTavish, Mark Messier, Craig Muni, Joe Murphy, Bill Ranford, Reijo Ruotsalainen, Craig Simpson, Steve Smith, Esa Tikkanen.

BOSTON: Raymond Bourque, Randy Burridge, Lyndon Byers, Bob Carpenter, John Carter, Dave Christian, Garry Galley, Bob Gould, Greg Hawgood, Craig Janney, Andy Moog, Cam Neely, Allen Pedersen, Dave Poulin, Brian Propp, Bob Sweeney, Don Sweeney, Glen Wesley, Jim Wiemer.

First Period

| 1. | EDMONTON | GRAVES (MURPHY, SIMPSON) | 9:46 | |

Penalties: Anderson (Edm) (cross-checking) 3:05, Neely (Bos) (interference) 4:41, Messier (Edm) (tripping) 12:24, Carter (Bos) (roughing) 15:53.

Second Period

| 2. | EDMONTON | ANDERSON (MESSIER, RUOTSALAINEN) | 13:00 | |

Penalties: Tikkanen (Edm) (holding) 9:44, Huddy (Edm) (hooking) 14:38.

Third Period

| 3. | BOSTON | BOURQUE (HAWGOOD, NEELY) | 3:43 | |
| 4. | BOSTON | BOURQUE (NEELY, HAWGOOD) | 18:31 | |

Penalties: none.

First Overtime

No scoring.
Penalties: none.

Second Overtime

No scoring.
Penalties: none.

Third Overtime

| 5. | EDMONTON | KLIMA (KURRI, MacTAVISH) | 15:13 | (GWG) |

Penalties: Smith (Edm), Neely (Bos) (roughing) 2:41, Tikkanen (Edm), Moog (Bos) (slashing) 13:48.

Goalies: Ranford (Edm), Moog (Bos)

| Shots: | Edm | 6 | - | 4 | - | 6 | - | 7 | - | 5 | - | 3 | 31 |
| | Bos | 10 | - | 6 | - | 15 | - | 6 | - | 7 | - | 8 | 52 |

Referee: Don Koharski
Linesmen: Swede Knox, Ray Scapinello

Game #2 - May 18, 1990 - Boston Garden - Edmonton 7, Boston 2

EDMONTON: Glenn Anderson, Kelly Buchberger, Martin Gelinas, Adam Graves, Randy Gregg, Charlie Huddy, Petr Klima, Jari Kurri, Mark Lamb, Kevin Lowe, Craig MacTavish, Mark Messier, Craig Muni, Joe Murphy, Bill Ranford, Reijo Ruotsalainen, Craig Simpson, Steve Smith, Esa Tikkanen.

BOSTON: Raymond Bourque, Randy Burridge, Bob Carpenter, John Carter, Dave Christian, Garry Galley, Bob Gould, Greg Hawgood, Craig Janney, Greg Johnston, Reggie Lemelin, Andy Moog, Cam Neely, Allen Pedersen, Dave Poulin, Brian Propp, Bob Sweeney, Don Sweeney, Glen Wesley, Jim Wiemer.

First Period

1.	EDMONTON	GRAVES (MURPHY, GREGG)	8:38	
2.	EDMONTON	KURRI (TIKKANEN)	10:53	(PPG)
3.	BOSTON	BOURQUE (NEELY)	19:07	

Penalties: Messier (Edm) (roughing) 0:49, Anderson (Edm) (tripping) 4:45, Carter (Bos) (high sticking major, game misconduct) 6:20, Smith (Edm) (hooking) 6:45, Buchberger (Edm) (unsportsmanlike conduct), D. Sweeney (Bos) (elbowing) 12:55, Lamb (Edm) (tripping) 14:56.

Second Period

4.	BOSTON	HAWGOOD (BOURQUE, BURRIDGE)	2:56	(PPG)
5.	EDMONTON	KURRI (TIKKANEN)	4:21	(GWG)
6.	EDMONTON	SIMPSON (KURRI)	15:28	
7.	EDMONTON	TIKKANEN (KURRI)	17:10	
8.	EDMONTON	MURPHY (SMITH)	19:12	

Penalties: Tikkanen (Edm) (holding) 1:14, Smith (Edm), Neely (Bos) (roughing) 2:27, Tikkanen (Edm), Hawgood (Bos) (roughing) 11:00, Ranford (Edm) (delay of game) 11:14.

Third Period

| 9. | EDMONTON | KURRI (RUOTSALAINEN, LAMB) | 7:27 | (PPG) |

Penalties: B. Sweeney (Bos) (holding) 5:30, Murphy (Edm) (roughing, unsportsmanlike conduct), Johnston (Bos) (double minor, roughing) 12:50.

Goalies: Ranford (Edm), Moog, Lemelin (Bos)

| Shots: | Edm | 2 | - | 9 | - | 11 | 22 |
| | Bos | 10 | - | 12 | - | 5 | 27 |

Referee: Kerry Fraser
Linesmen: Wayne Bonney, Ron Finn

(NOTE: Edmonton's Petr Klima was awarded a penalty shot at 19:00 of the second period. He was unsuccessful against Boston's Reggie Lemelin.)

Game #3 - May 20, 1990 - Northlands Coliseum - Boston 2, Edmonton 1

BOSTON: Raymond Bourque, Andy Brickley, Randy Burridge, John Byce, Bob Carpenter, John Carter, Dave Christian, Garry Galley, Bob Gould, Greg Hawgood, Craig Janney, Greg Johnston, Andy Moog, Cam Neely, Allen Pedersen, Brian Propp, Bob Sweeney, Don Sweeney, Glen Wesley.

EDMONTON: Glenn Anderson, Kelly Buchberger, Martin Gelinas, Adam Graves, Randy Gregg, Charlie Huddy, Petr Klima, Jari Kurri, Mark Lamb, Kevin Lowe, Craig MacTavish, Mark Messier, Craig Muni, Joe Murphy, Bill Ranford, Reijo Ruotsalainen, Craig Simpson, Steve Smith, Esa Tikkanen.

First Period
1. BOSTON   BYCE (NEELY)   0:10
2. BOSTON   JOHNSTON (BURRIDGE, B. SWEENEY)   16:18 (GWG)
Penalties: D. Sweeney (Bos) (holding) 3:16, Gelinas (Edm) (hooking) 6:32, MacTavish (Edm) (tripping) 12:18, Kurri (Edm) (interference) 17:17.

Second Period
No scoring.
Penalties: Simpson (Edm) (interference) 12:28, Pedersen (Bos) (holding) 15:37.

Third Period
3. EDMONTON   TIKKANEN (KURRI, SMITH)   5:54 (PPG)
Penalties: D. Sweeney (Bos) (holding) 1:30, Galley (Bos) (holding) 5:32, Bourque (Bos) (holding) 6:01, Smith (Edm) (interference) 6:33.

Goalies: Moog (Bos), Ranford (Edm)

Shots:	Bos	13	-	7	-	2	22
	Edm	11	-	4	-	14	29

Referee: Andy Van Hellemond
Linesmen: Swede Knox, Ray Scapinello

Game #4 - May 22, 1990 - Northlands Coliseum - Edmonton 5, Boston 1

BOSTON: Raymond Bourque, Andy Brickley, Randy Burridge, John Byce, Bob Carpenter, John Carter, Dave Christian, Peter Douris, Garry Galley, Greg Hawgood, Craig Janney, Greg Johnston, Andy Moog, Cam Neely, Allen Pedersen, Brian Propp, Bob Sweeney, Don Sweeney, Glen Wesley.

EDMONTON: Glenn Anderson, Kelly Buchberger, Martin Gelinas, Adam Graves, Randy Gregg, Charlie Huddy, Petr Klima, Jari Kurri, Mark Lamb, Kevin Lowe, Craig MacTavish, Mark Messier, Craig Muni, Joe Murphy, Bill Ranford, Reijo Ruotsalainen, Craig Simpson, Steve Smith, Esa Tikkanen.

First Period
1. EDMONTON   ANDERSON (SIMPSON, LAMB)   2:13 (PPG)
2. EDMONTON   ANDERSON (MESSIER, SIMPSON)   16:27 (GWG)
Penalties: Carpenter (Bos) (interference) 0:24, Neely (Bos), Muni (Edm) (roughing) 3:16, Messier (Edm) (boarding) 13:33, Carter (Bos), Ruotsalainen (Edm) (unsportsmanlike conduct) 16:11, Hawgood (Bos) (slashing) 18:52.

Second Period
3. EDMONTON   SIMPSON (MESSIER, ANDERSON)   1:00
4. EDMONTON   TIKKANEN (KURRI, MacTAVISH)   19:15
Penalties: Wesley (Bos) (hooking) 6:20, Simpson (Edm) (tripping) 12:39, Anderson (Edm) (tripping) 19:50.

Third Period
5. BOSTON   CARTER (unassisted)   15:02
6. EDMONTON   SIMPSON (ANDERSON, MESSIER)   18:36
Penalties: Simpson (Edm) (elbowing) 5:04, Burridge (Bos) (slashing) 12:14, Neely (Bos) (high sticking) 15:14, B. Sweeney (Bos), Smith (Edm) (fighting) 17:06.

Goalies: Moog (Bos), Ranford (Edm)

Shots:	Bos	7	-	11	-	7	25
	Edm	12	-	10	-	11	33

Referee: Don Koharski
Linesmen: Wayne Bonney, Ron Finn

Game #5 - May 24, 1990 - Boston Garden - Edmonton 4, Boston 1

EDMONTON: Glenn Anderson, Kelly Buchberger, Martin Gelinas, Adam Graves, Randy Gregg, Charlie Huddy, Petr Klima, Jari Kurri, Mark Lamb, Kevin Lowe, Craig MacTavish, Mark Messier, Craig Muni, Joe Murphy, Bill Ranford, Reijo Ruotsalainen, Craig Simpson, Steve Smith, Esa Tikkanen.

BOSTON: Raymond Bourque, Randy Burridge, John Byce, Lyndon Byers, Bob Carpenter, John Carter, Dave Christian, Garry Galley, Bob Gould, Greg Hawgood, Craig Janney, Greg Johnston, Andy Moog, Cam Neely, Allen Pedersen, Brian Propp, Bob Sweeney, Don Sweeney, Glen Wesley.

First Period
No scoring.
Penalties: Bourque (Bos) (cross-checking) 2:56, Tikkanen (Edm) (holding) 4:32, Galley (Bos) (holding) 4:45.

Second Period
1. EDMONTON   ANDERSON (unassisted)   1:17
2. EDMONTON   SIMPSON (ANDERSON)   9:31 (GWG)
Penalties: none.

Third Period
3. EDMONTON   SMITH (MESSIER, SIMPSON)   6:09
4. EDMONTON   MURPHY (LAMB, GELINAS)   14:53
5. BOSTON   BYERS (B. SWEENEY, BOURQUE)   16:30
Penalties: Huddy (Edm) (hooking) 7:09, Bourque (Bos) (holding) 11:46.

Goalies: Ranford (Edm), Moog (Bos)

Shots:	Edm	10	-	5	-	7	22
	Bos	10	-	10	-	10	30

Referee: Andy Van Hellemond
Linesmen: Swede Knox, Ray Scapinello

CHAPTER 22

Player Register

Career NHL Playoff Records, 1918-2002

Abbreviations: A – assists; **G** – goals; **GP** – games played; **GW** – game-winning goals; **PIM** – penalties in minutes; **PP** – powerplay goals; **Pts** – points; **SH** – shorthand goals; **•** – active player; * – league-leading total; ♦ – member of Stanley Cup winning team.
Statistics for 1918 to 1926 are NHL only and do not include series vs. PCHA/WCHL/WHL opponents. Goaltender Register begins on page 229.

Season	Team	GP	G	A	Pts	PIM	PP	SH	GW
•AALTO, Antti	Center								
1999	Anaheim	4	0	0	0	2	0	0	0
Playoff Totals		**4**	**0**	**0**	**0**	**2**	**0**	**0**	**0**
ABBOTT, Reg *No Playoffs*	Center								
ABEL, Clarence	Defense								
1927	NY Rangers	2	0	1	1	8	....	....	....
1928♦	NY Rangers	9	1	0	1	14	....	....	....
1929	NY Rangers	6	0	0	0	8	....	....	....
1930	Chicago	2	0	0	0	10	....	....	....
1931	Chicago	9	0	0	0	8	....	....	....
1932	Chicago	2	0	0	0	2	....	....	....
1934♦	Chicago	8	0	0	0	8	....	....	....
Playoff Totals		**38**	**1**	**1**	**2**	**58**	....	....	....
ABEL, Gerry *No Playoffs*	Left wing								
ABEL, Sid	Center/Left wing								
1939	Detroit	6	1	1	2	2	....	....	....
1940	Detroit	5	0	3	3	21	....	....	....
1941	Detroit	9	2	2	4	2	....	....	....
1942	Detroit	12	4	2	6	8	....	....	....
1943♦	Detroit	10	5	8	13	4	....	....	....
1946	Detroit	3	0	0	0	0	....	....	....
1947	Detroit	3	1	1	2	2	....	....	....
1948	Detroit	10	0	3	3	16	....	....	....
1949	Detroit	11	3	3	6	6	....	....	....
1950♦	Detroit	14	*6	2	8	6	....	....	....
1951	Detroit	6	4	3	7	0	....	....	....
1952♦	Detroit	7	2	2	4	12	....	....	....
1953	Chicago	1	0	0	0	0	....	....	....
Playoff Totals		**97**	**28**	**30**	**58**	**79**	....	....	....
ABGRALL, Dennis *No Playoffs*	Right wing								
•ABID, Ramzi *No Playoffs*	Left wing								
ABRAHAMSSON, Thommy *No Playoffs*	Defense								
ACHTYMICHUK, Gene *No Playoffs*	Center								
ACOMB, Doug *No Playoffs*	Center								
ACTON, Keith	Center								
1981	Montreal	2	0	0	0	6	0	0	0
1982	Montreal	5	0	4	4	16	0	0	0
1983	Montreal	3	0	0	0	0	0	0	0
1984	Minnesota	15	4	7	11	12	1	0	1
1985	Minnesota	9	4	4	8	6	1	0	2
1986	Minnesota	5	0	3	3	6	0	0	0
1988♦	Edmonton	7	2	0	2	16	0	0	2
1989	Philadelphia	16	2	3	5	18	0	0	0
1994	NY Islanders	4	0	0	0	8	0	0	0
Playoff Totals		**66**	**12**	**21**	**33**	**88**	**2**	**0**	**5**
ADAM, Douglas *No Playoffs*	Left wing								
ADAM, Russ *No Playoffs*	Center								
•ADAMS, Bryan *No Playoffs*	Left wing								
•ADAMS, Craig	Right wing								
2001	Carolina	3	0	0	0	0	0	0	0
2002	Carolina	1	0	0	0	0	0	0	0
Playoff Totals		**4**	**0**	**0**	**0**	**0**	**0**	**0**	**0**
ADAMS, Greg	Left wing								
1984	Washington	1	0	0	0	0	0	0	0
1985	Washington	5	0	0	0	9	0	0	0
1986	Washington	9	1	3	4	27	0	0	0
1987	Washington	7	1	3	4	38	1	0	0
1988	Washington	14	0	5	5	58	0	0	0
1989	Vancouver	7	0	0	0	21	0	0	0
Playoff Totals		**43**	**2**	**11**	**13**	**153**	**1**	**0**	**0**
ADAMS, Greg	Left wing								
1989	Vancouver	7	2	3	5	2	0	0	0
1991	Vancouver	5	0	0	0	2	0	0	0
1992	Vancouver	6	0	2	2	4	0	0	0
1993	Vancouver	12	7	6	13	6	5	0	1
1994	Vancouver	23	6	8	14	2	2	0	2
1995	Dallas	5	2	0	2	0	0	0	0
1997	Dallas	3	0	1	1	0	0	0	0
1998	Dallas	12	2	2	4	0	0	0	2
1999	Phoenix	3	1	0	1	0	0	0	0
2000	Phoenix	5	0	0	0	0	0	0	0
Playoff Totals		**81**	**20**	**22**	**42**	**16**	**7**	**0**	**5**

Season	Team	GP	G	A	Pts	PIM	PP	SH	GW
ADAMS, Jack	Center								
1918♦	Toronto	2	0	0	0	6	....	....	....
1925	Toronto	2	1	0	1	7	....	....	....
1927♦	Ottawa	6	0	0	0	0	....	....	....
Playoff Totals		**10**	**1**	**0**	**1**	**13**	....	....	....
ADAMS, John	Left wing								
1941	Montreal	3	0	0	0	0	0	0	0
Playoff Totals		**3**	**0**	**0**	**0**	**0**	**0**	**0**	**0**
•ADAMS, Kevyn	Center								
1999	Toronto	7	0	2	2	14	0	0	0
2000	Toronto	12	1	0	1	7	0	1	0
2002	Carolina	23	1	0	1	4	0	0	0
Playoff Totals		**42**	**2**	**2**	**4**	**25**	**0**	**1**	**0**
ADAMS, Stew	Left wing								
1930	Chicago	2	0	0	0	6	....	....	....
1931	Chicago	9	3	3	6	8	....	....	....
Playoff Totals		**11**	**3**	**3**	**6**	**14**	....	....	....
ADDUONO, Rick *No Playoffs*	Center								
•AFANASENKOV, Dmitry *No Playoffs*	Left wing								
AFFLECK, Bruce	Defense								
1975	St. Louis	1	0	0	0	0	0	0	0
1976	St. Louis	3	0	0	0	0	0	0	0
1977	St. Louis	4	0	0	0	0	0	0	0
Playoff Totals		**8**	**0**	**0**	**0**	**0**	**0**	**0**	**0**
•AFINOGENOV, Maxim	Right wing								
2000	Buffalo	5	0	1	1	2	0	0	0
2001	Buffalo	11	2	3	5	4	0	0	0
Playoff Totals		**16**	**2**	**4**	**6**	**6**	**0**	**0**	**0**
AGNEW, Jim	Defense								
1992	Vancouver	4	0	0	0	6	0	0	0
Playoff Totals		**4**	**0**	**0**	**0**	**6**	**0**	**0**	**0**
AHERN, Fred	Right wing								
1978	Colorado	2	0	1	1	2	0	0	0
Playoff Totals		**2**	**0**	**1**	**1**	**2**	**0**	**0**	**0**
AHLIN, Tony *No Playoffs*	Left wing								
AHOLA, Peter	Defense								
1992	Los Angeles	6	0	0	0	2	0	0	0
Playoff Totals		**6**	**0**	**0**	**0**	**2**	**0**	**0**	**0**
AHRENS, Chris	Defense								
1973	Minnesota	1	0	0	0	0	0	0	0
Playoff Totals		**1**	**0**	**0**	**0**	**0**	**0**	**0**	**0**
AILSBY, Lloyd *No Playoffs*	Defense								
AITKEN, Brad *No Playoffs*	Left wing								
•AITKEN, Johnathan *No Playoffs*	Defense								
AIVAZOFF, Micah *No Playoffs*	Center								
•ALATALO, Mika	Left wing								
2000	Phoenix	5	0	0	0	2	0	0	0
Playoff Totals		**5**	**0**	**0**	**0**	**2**	**0**	**0**	**0**
•ALBELIN, Tommy	Defense								
1991	New Jersey	3	0	1	1	2	0	0	0
1992	New Jersey	1	1	1	2	0	0	0	0
1993	New Jersey	5	2	0	2	0	1	0	1
1994	New Jersey	20	2	5	7	14	1	0	1
1995♦	New Jersey	20	1	7	8	2	0	0	0
1996	Calgary	4	0	0	0	0	0	0	0
2002	New Jersey	6	0	0	0	0	0	0	0
Playoff Totals		**59**	**6**	**14**	**20**	**18**	**2**	**0**	**2**
ALBRIGHT, Clint *No Playoffs*	Center								
ALDCORN, Gary	Left wing								
1960	Detroit	6	1	2	3	4	0	0	0
Playoff Totals		**6**	**1**	**2**	**3**	**4**	**0**	**0**	**0**
ALDRIDGE, Keith *No Playoffs*	Defense								
ALEXANDER, Claire	Defense								
1975	Toronto	7	0	0	0	0	0	0	0
1976	Toronto	9	2	4	6	4	1	0	0
Playoff Totals		**16**	**2**	**4**	**6**	**4**	**1**	**0**	**0**
ALEXANDRE, Art	Left wing								
1932	Montreal	4	0	0	0	0	0	0	0
Playoff Totals		**4**	**0**	**0**	**0**	**0**	**0**	**0**	**0**
•ALEXEEV, Nikita *No Playoffs*	Right wing								

Season	Team	GP	G	A	Pts	PIM	PP	SH	GW
•ALFREDSSON, Daniel	Right wing								
1997	Ottawa	7	5	2	7	6	3	0	2
1998	Ottawa	11	7	2	9	20	2	1	1
1999	Ottawa	4	1	2	3	4	1	0	0
2000	Ottawa	6	1	3	4	2	1	0	0
2001	Ottawa	4	1	0	1	2	0	0	0
2002	Ottawa	12	7	6	13	4	3	0	3
Playoff Totals		**44**	**22**	**15**	**37**	**38**	**10**	**1**	**6**
ALLAN, Jeff *No Playoffs*	Defense								
•ALLEN, Bobby *No Playoffs*	Defense								
•ALLEN, Bryan	Defense								
2001	Vancouver	2	0	0	0	2	0	0	0
Playoff Totals		**2**	**0**	**0**	**0**	**2**	**0**	**0**	**0**
ALLEN, Chris *No Playoffs*	Defense								
ALLEN, George	Left wing/Defense								
1939	NY Rangers	7	0	0	0	4	....	....	....
1940	Chicago	2	0	0	0	0	....	....	....
1941	Chicago	5	2	2	4	10	....	....	....
1942	Chicago	3	1	1	2	0	....	....	....
1944	Chicago	9	5	4	9	8	....	....	....
1946	Chicago	4	0	0	0	4	....	....	....
1947	Montreal	11	1	3	4	6	....	....	....
Playoff Totals		**41**	**9**	**10**	**19**	**32**	....	....	....
ALLEN, Keith	Defense								
1954♦	Detroit	5	0	0	0	0	0	0	0
Playoff Totals		**5**	**0**	**0**	**0**	**0**	**0**	**0**	**0**
ALLEN, Peter *No Playoffs*	Defense								
ALLEN, Vivian *No Playoffs*	Right wing								
ALLEY, Steve	Left wing								
1980	Hartford	3	0	1	1	0	0	0	0
Playoff Totals		**3**	**0**	**1**	**1**	**0**	**0**	**0**	**0**
ALLISON, Dave *No Playoffs*	Defense								
•ALLISON, Jamie *No Playoffs*	Defense								
•ALLISON, Jason	Center								
1998	Boston	6	2	6	8	4	1	0	0
1999	Boston	12	2	9	11	6	1	0	0
2002	Los Angeles	7	3	3	6	4	0	0	1
Playoff Totals		**25**	**7**	**18**	**25**	**14**	**2**	**0**	**1**
ALLISON, Mike	Left wing								
1981	NY Rangers	14	3	1	4	20	1	0	2
1982	NY Rangers	10	1	3	4	18	0	0	0
1983	NY Rangers	8	0	5	5	10	0	0	0
1984	NY Rangers	5	0	1	1	6	0	0	0
1986	NY Rangers	16	0	2	2	38	0	0	0
1987	Toronto	13	3	5	8	15	1	0	2
1988	Los Angeles	5	0	0	0	16	0	0	0
1989	Los Angeles	7	1	0	1	10	0	0	0
1990	Los Angeles	4	1	0	1	2	0	1	0
Playoff Totals		**82**	**9**	**17**	**26**	**135**	**2**	**1**	**4**
ALLISON, Ray	Right wing								
1980	Hartford	2	0	1	1	0	0	0	0
1982	Philadelphia	3	2	0	2	2	2	0	0
1983	Philadelphia	3	0	1	1	12	0	0	0
1984	Philadelphia	3	0	1	1	4	0	0	0
1985	Philadelphia	1	0	0	0	2	0	0	0
Playoff Totals		**12**	**2**	**3**	**5**	**20**	**2**	**0**	**0**
ALLUM, Bill *No Playoffs*	Defense								
AMADIO, Dave	Defense								
1968	Los Angeles	7	0	2	2	8	0	0	0
1969	Los Angeles	9	1	0	1	10	0	0	0
Playoff Totals		**16**	**1**	**2**	**3**	**18**	**0**	**0**	**0**
AMBROZIAK, Peter *No Playoffs*	Left wing								
AMODEO, Mike *No Playoffs*	Defense								
•AMONTE, Tony	Right wing								
1991	NY Rangers	2	0	2	2	2	0	0	0
1992	NY Rangers	13	3	6	9	2	2	0	0
1994	Chicago	6	4	2	6	4	1	0	1
1995	Chicago	16	3	3	6	10	0	0	0
1996	Chicago	7	2	4	6	6	1	0	0
1997	Chicago	6	4	2	6	8	0	0	0
2002	Chicago	5	0	1	1	4	0	0	0
Playoff Totals		**55**	**16**	**20**	**36**	**36**	**4**	**0**	**1**

Season	Team	GP	G	A	Pts	PIM	PP	SH	GW
ANDERSON, Bill									Defense
1943	Boston	1	0	0	0	0	0	0	0
Playoff Totals		**1**	**0**	**0**	**0**	**0**	**0**	**0**	**0**
ANDERSON, Dale									Defense
1957	Detroit	2	0	0	0	0	0	0	0
Playoff Totals		**2**	**0**	**0**	**0**	**0**	**0**	**0**	**0**
ANDERSON, Doug									Center
1953♦	Montreal	2	0	0	0	0	0	0	0
Playoff Totals		**2**	**0**	**0**	**0**	**0**	**0**	**0**	**0**
ANDERSON, Earl									Right wing
1975	Boston	3	0	1	1	0	0	0	0
1977	Boston	2	0	0	0	0	0	0	0
Playoff Totals		**5**	**0**	**1**	**1**	**0**	**0**	**0**	**0**
ANDERSON, Glenn									Right wing
1981	Edmonton	9	5	7	12	12	3	0	0
1982	Edmonton	5	2	5	7	8	0	0	1
1983	Edmonton	16	10	10	20	32	1	0	2
1984♦	Edmonton	19	6	11	17	33	1	0	1
1985♦	Edmonton	18	10	16	26	38	2	0	1
1986	Edmonton	10	8	3	11	14	1	0	2
1987♦	Edmonton	21	14	13	27	59	4	0	2
1988♦	Edmonton	19	9	16	25	49	4	0	1
1989	Edmonton	7	1	2	3	8	1	0	0
1990♦	Edmonton	22	10	12	22	20	2	0	2
1991	Edmonton	18	6	7	13	41	3	0	0
1993	Toronto	21	7	11	18	31	0	0	2
1994♦	NY Rangers	23	3	3	6	42	0	1	2
1995	St. Louis	6	1	1	2	*49	0	0	0
1996	St. Louis	11	1	4	5	6	0	0	1
Playoff Totals		**225**	**93**	**121**	**214**	**442**	**22**	**1**	**17**
ANDERSON, Jim *No Playoffs*									Left wing
ANDERSON, John									Right wing
1978	Toronto	2	0	0	0	0	0	0	0
1979	Toronto	6	0	2	2	0	0	0	0
1980	Toronto	3	1	1	2	0	0	0	0
1981	Toronto	2	0	0	0	0	0	0	0
1983	Toronto	4	2	4	6	0	1	0	0
1986	Hartford	10	5	8	13	0	3	0	0
1987	Hartford	6	1	2	3	0	1	0	0
1989	Hartford	4	0	1	1	2	0	0	0
Playoff Totals		**37**	**9**	**18**	**27**	**2**	**5**	**0**	**0**
ANDERSON, Murray *No Playoffs*									Defense
ANDERSON, Perry									Left wing
1982	St. Louis	10	2	0	2	4	1	0	0
1984	St. Louis	9	0	0	0	27	0	0	0
1985	St. Louis	3	0	0	0	7	0	0	0
1988	New Jersey	10	0	0	0	113	0	0	0
1991	New Jersey	4	0	1	1	10	0	0	0
Playoff Totals		**36**	**2**	**1**	**3**	**161**	**1**	**0**	**0**
ANDERSON, Ron *No Playoffs*									Right wing
ANDERSON, Ron									Right wing
1969	Los Angeles	4	0	0	0	2	0	0	0
1970	St. Louis	1	0	0	0	2	0	0	0
Playoff Totals		**5**	**0**	**0**	**0**	**4**	**0**	**0**	**0**
ANDERSON, Russ									Defense
1977	Pittsburgh	3	0	1	1	14	0	0	0
1979	Pittsburgh	2	0	0	0	0	0	0	0
1980	Pittsburgh	5	0	2	2	14	0	0	0
Playoff Totals		**10**	**0**	**3**	**3**	**28**	**0**	**0**	**0**
ANDERSON, Shawn									Defense
1989	Buffalo	5	0	1	1	4	0	0	0
1993	Washington	6	0	0	0	0	0	0	0
1994	Washington	8	1	0	1	12	0	0	0
Playoff Totals		**19**	**1**	**1**	**2**	**16**	**0**	**0**	**0**
ANDERSON, Tom									Left wing/Defense
1936	NY Americans	5	0	0	0	6	....	....	....
1938	NY Americans	6	1	4	5	2	....	....	....
1939	NY Americans	2	0	0	0	0	....	....	....
1940	NY Americans	3	1	3	4	0	....	....	....
Playoff Totals		**16**	**2**	**7**	**9**	**8**	....	....	....
ANDERSSON, Erik *No Playoffs*									Center
•**ANDERSSON, Jonas** *No Playoffs*									Right wing
ANDERSSON, Kent-Erik									Right wing
1980	Minnesota	13	2	4	6	2	0	0	1
1981	Minnesota	19	2	4	6	2	0	0	0
1982	Minnesota	4	0	2	2	0	0	0	0
1983	NY Rangers	9	0	0	0	0	0	0	0
1984	NY Rangers	5	0	1	1	0	0	0	0
Playoff Totals		**50**	**4**	**11**	**15**	**4**	**0**	**0**	**1**
ANDERSSON, Mikael									Left wing
1988	Buffalo	1	1	0	1	0	0	0	0
1990	Hartford	5	0	3	3	2	0	0	0
1992	Hartford	7	0	2	2	6	0	0	0
1996	Tampa Bay	6	1	1	2	0	0	0	0
1999	Philadelphia	6	0	1	1	2	0	0	0
Playoff Totals		**25**	**2**	**7**	**9**	**10**	**0**	**0**	**0**
•**ANDERSSON, Niklas** *No Playoffs*									Left wing
ANDERSSON, Peter *No Playoffs*									Defense

Season	Team	GP	G	A	Pts	PIM	PP	SH	GW
ANDERSSON, Peter									Defense
1984	Washington	3	0	1	1	2	0	0	0
1985	Washington	2	0	0	0	0	0	0	0
1986	Quebec	2	0	1	1	0	0	0	0
Playoff Totals		**7**	**0**	**2**	**2**	**2**	**0**	**0**	**0**
ANDRASCIK, Steve									Right wing
1972	NY Rangers	1	0	0	0	0	0	0	0
Playoff Totals		**1**	**0**	**0**	**0**	**0**	**0**	**0**	**0**
ANDREA, Paul *No Playoffs*									Right wing
ANDREWS, Lloyd									Left wing
1922♦	Toronto	2	0	0	0	0	....	....	....
Playoff Totals		**2**	**0**	**0**	**0**	**0**	....	....	....
•**ANDREYCHUK, Dave**									Left wing
1983	Buffalo	4	1	0	1	4	0	0	0
1984	Buffalo	2	0	1	1	2	0	0	0
1985	Buffalo	5	4	2	6	4	0	0	2
1988	Buffalo	6	2	4	6	0	1	0	0
1989	Buffalo	5	0	3	3	0	0	0	0
1990	Buffalo	6	2	5	7	2	1	0	0
1991	Buffalo	6	2	2	4	8	1	0	0
1992	Buffalo	7	1	3	4	12	0	0	0
1993	Toronto	21	12	7	19	35	4	0	3
1994	Toronto	18	5	5	10	16	3	1	0
1995	Toronto	7	3	2	5	25	2	0	0
1997	New Jersey	1	0	0	0	0	0	0	0
1998	New Jersey	6	1	0	1	4	1	0	0
1999	New Jersey	4	2	0	2	4	0	0	0
2000	Colorado	17	3	2	5	18	2	0	0
2001	Buffalo	13	1	2	3	4	1	0	0
Playoff Totals		**128**	**39**	**38**	**77**	**138**	**16**	**1**	**5**
ANDRIEVSKI, Alexander *No Playoffs*									Right wing
ANDRUFF, Ron									Center
1978	Colorado	2	0	0	0	0	0	0	0
Playoff Totals		**2**	**0**	**0**	**0**	**0**	**0**	**0**	**0**
ANDRUSAK, Greg									Defense
1999	Pittsburgh	12	1	0	1	6	0	0	1
2000	Toronto	3	0	0	0	2	0	0	0
Playoff Totals		**15**	**1**	**0**	**1**	**8**	**0**	**0**	**1**
ANGOTTI, Lou									Center/Right wing
1966	Chicago	6	0	0	0	2	0	0	0
1967	Chicago	6	2	1	3	2	0	0	0
1968	Philadelphia	7	0	0	0	2	0	0	0
1970	Chicago	8	0	0	0	0	0	0	0
1971	Chicago	16	3	3	6	9	0	0	1
1972	Chicago	6	0	0	0	0	0	0	0
1973	Chicago	16	3	4	7	2	0	0	2
Playoff Totals		**65**	**8**	**8**	**16**	**17**	**0**	**0**	**3**
ANHOLT, Darrel *No Playoffs*									Defense
ANSLOW, Hub *No Playoffs*									Center
ANTONOVICH, Mike *No Playoffs*									Center
ANTOSKI, Shawn									Left wing
1994	Vancouver	16	0	1	1	36	0	0	0
1995	Philadelphia	13	0	1	1	10	0	0	0
1996	Philadelphia	7	1	1	2	28	0	0	1
Playoff Totals		**36**	**1**	**3**	**4**	**74**	**0**	**0**	**1**
•**ANTROPOV, Nik**									Center
2000	Toronto	3	0	0	0	4	0	0	0
2001	Toronto	9	2	1	3	12	1	0	1
Playoff Totals		**12**	**2**	**1**	**3**	**16**	**1**	**0**	**1**
APPS, Syl Jr.									Center
1972	Pittsburgh	4	1	0	1	2	0	0	0
1975	Pittsburgh	9	2	3	5	9	1	0	1
1976	Pittsburgh	3	0	1	1	0	0	0	0
1977	Pittsburgh	3	1	0	1	12	1	0	0
1978	Los Angeles	2	0	1	1	0	0	0	0
1979	Los Angeles	2	1	0	1	0	1	0	0
Playoff Totals		**23**	**5**	**5**	**10**	**23**	**3**	**0**	**1**
APPS, Syl									Center
1937	Toronto	2	0	1	1	0	....	....	....
1938	Toronto	7	1	4	5	0	....	....	....
1939	Toronto	10	2	6	8	2	....	....	....
1940	Toronto	10	*5	2	7	2	....	....	....
1941	Toronto	7	3	2	5	2	....	....	....
1942♦	Toronto	13	5	*9	*14	2	....	....	....
1947♦	Toronto	11	5	1	6	0	....	....	....
1948♦	Toronto	9	4	4	8	0	....	....	....
Playoff Totals		**69**	**25**	**29**	**54**	**8**	....	....	....

Season	Team	GP	G	A	Pts	PIM	PP	SH	GW
ARBOUR, Al									Defense
1954♦	Detroit	....	....	....	....	....	....	....	....
1956	Detroit	4	0	1	1	0	0	0	0
1957	Detroit	5	0	0	0	6	0	0	0
1958	Detroit	4	0	1	1	4	0	0	0
1959	Chicago	6	1	2	3	26	0	0	0
1960	Chicago	4	0	0	0	4	0	0	0
1961♦	Chicago	7	0	0	0	2	0	0	0
1962♦	Toronto	8	0	0	0	6	0	0	0
1964♦	Toronto	1	0	0	0	0	0	0	0
1965	Toronto	1	0	0	0	2	0	0	0
1968	St. Louis	14	0	3	3	10	0	0	0
1969	St. Louis	12	0	0	0	10	0	0	0
1970	St. Louis	14	0	1	1	16	0	0	0
1971	St. Louis	6	0	0	0	6	0	0	0
Playoff Totals		**86**	**1**	**8**	**9**	**92**	**0**	**0**	**0**
ARBOUR, Amos *No Playoffs*									Left wing
ARBOUR, Jack *No Playoffs*									Defense
ARBOUR, John									Defense
1971	St. Louis	5	0	0	0	0	0	0	0
Playoff Totals		**5**	**0**	**0**	**0**	**0**	**0**	**0**	**0**
ARBOUR, Ty									Left wing
1930	Chicago	2	1	0	1	0	....	....	....
1931	Chicago	9	1	0	1	6	....	....	....
Playoff Totals		**11**	**2**	**0**	**2**	**6**	....	....	....
ARCHAMBAULT, Michel *No Playoffs*									Left wing
ARCHIBALD, Dave									Center/Left wing
1989	Minnesota	5	0	1	1	0	0	0	0
Playoff Totals		**5**	**0**	**1**	**1**	**0**	**0**	**0**	**0**
ARCHIBALD, Jim *No Playoffs*									Right wing
ARESHENKOFF, Ron *No Playoffs*									Center
•**ARKHIPOV, Denis** *No Playoffs*									Right wing
ARMSTRONG, Bill *No Playoffs*									Center
ARMSTRONG, Bob									Defense
1952	Boston	5	0	0	0	2	....	....	....
1953	Boston	11	1	1	2	10	....	....	....
1954	Boston	4	0	1	1	0	....	....	....
1955	Boston	5	0	0	0	2	....	....	....
1957	Boston	10	0	3	3	10	....	....	....
1959	Boston	7	0	2	2	4	....	....	....
Playoff Totals		**42**	**1**	**7**	**8**	**28**	....	....	....
•**ARMSTRONG, Chris** *No Playoffs*									Defense
•**ARMSTRONG, Derek** *No Playoffs*									Center
ARMSTRONG, George									Right wing
1952	Toronto	4	0	0	0	2	....	....	....
1954	Toronto	5	1	0	1	2	....	....	....
1955	Toronto	4	1	0	1	4	....	....	....
1956	Toronto	5	4	2	6	0	....	....	....
1959	Toronto	12	0	4	4	10	....	....	....
1960	Toronto	10	1	4	5	4	....	....	....
1961	Toronto	5	1	1	2	0	....	....	....
1962♦	Toronto	12	7	5	12	2	....	....	....
1963♦	Toronto	10	3	6	9	4	....	....	....
1964♦	Toronto	14	5	8	13	10	....	....	....
1965	Toronto	6	1	0	1	4	....	....	....
1966	Toronto	4	0	1	1	4	....	....	....
1967♦	Toronto	9	2	1	3	6	....	....	....
1969	Toronto	4	0	0	0	0	0	0	0
1971	Toronto	6	0	2	2	0	0	0	0
Playoff Totals		**110**	**26**	**34**	**60**	**52**	**0**	**0**	**0**
ARMSTRONG, Murray									Center
1938	Toronto	3	0	0	0	0	....	....	....
1940	NY Americans	3	0	0	0	0	....	....	....
1944	Detroit	5	0	2	2	0	....	....	....
1945	Detroit	14	4	2	6	2	....	....	....
1946	Detroit	5	0	2	2	0	....	....	....
Playoff Totals		**30**	**4**	**6**	**10**	**2**	....	....	....
ARMSTRONG, Norm *No Playoffs*									Right Wing/Defense
ARMSTRONG, Tim *No Playoffs*									Center
ARNASON, Chuck									Right wing
1975	Pittsburgh	9	2	4	6	4	1	0	0
Playoff Totals		**9**	**2**	**4**	**6**	**4**	**1**	**0**	**0**
•**ARNASON, Tyler**									Center
2002	Chicago	3	0	0	0	0	0	0	0
Playoff Totals		**3**	**0**	**0**	**0**	**0**	**0**	**0**	**0**
ARNIEL, Scott									Left wing
1982	Winnipeg	3	0	0	0	0	0	0	0
1983	Winnipeg	2	0	0	0	0	0	0	0
1984	Winnipeg	2	0	0	0	5	0	0	0
1985	Winnipeg	8	1	2	3	9	0	0	1
1986	Winnipeg	3	0	0	0	12	0	0	0
1988	Buffalo	6	0	1	1	5	0	0	0
1989	Buffalo	5	1	0	1	4	0	1	0
1990	Buffalo	5	1	0	1	4	0	0	0
Playoff Totals		**34**	**3**	**3**	**6**	**39**	**0**	**1**	**1**

Season	Team	GP	G	A	Pts	PIM	PP	SH	GW
•ARNOTT, Jason									Center
1997	Edmonton	12	3	6	9	18	1	0	0
1998	New Jersey	5	0	2	2	0	0	0	0
1999	New Jersey	7	2	2	4	4	1	0	0
2000◆	New Jersey	23	8	12	20	18	3	0	1
2001	New Jersey	23	8	7	15	16	5	0	0
Playoff Totals		**70**	**21**	**29**	**50**	**56**	**10**	**0**	**1**
ARTHUR, Fred									Defense
1982	Philadelphia	4	0	0	0	2	0	0	0
Playoff Totals		**4**	**0**	**0**	**0**	**2**	**0**	**0**	**0**
ARUNDEL, John *No Playoffs*									Defense
•ARVEDSON, Magnus									Center
1998	Ottawa	11	0	1	1	6	0	0	0
1999	Ottawa	3	0	1	1	2	0	0	0
2000	Ottawa	6	0	0	0	6	0	0	0
2001	Ottawa	2	0	0	0	0	0	0	0
2002	Ottawa	12	2	1	3	4	0	0	0
Playoff Totals		**34**	**2**	**3**	**5**	**18**	**0**	**0**	**0**
•ASHAM, Arron									Right wing
2002	Montreal	3	0	1	1	0	0	0	0
Playoff Totals		**3**	**0**	**1**	**1**	**0**	**0**	**0**	**0**
ASHBEE, Barry									Defense
1973	Philadelphia	11	0	4	4	20	0	0	0
1974◆	Philadelphia	6	0	0	0	2	0	0	0
Playoff Totals		**17**	**0**	**4**	**4**	**22**	**0**	**0**	**0**
ASHBY, Don									Center
1977	Toronto	9	1	0	1	4	0	0	0
1980	Edmonton	3	0	0	0	0	0	0	0
Playoff Totals		**12**	**1**	**0**	**1**	**4**	**0**	**0**	**0**
ASHTON, Brent									Left wing
1980	Vancouver	4	1	0	1	6	0	0	0
1981	Vancouver	3	0	0	0	0	0	0	0
1984	Minnesota	12	1	2	3	22	0	0	0
1985	Quebec	18	6	4	10	13	1	1	1
1986	Quebec	3	2	1	3	9	0	1	0
1987	Detroit	16	4	9	13	6	2	0	0
1988	Detroit	16	7	5	12	10	2	1	0
1990	Winnipeg	7	3	1	4	2	2	0	1
1993	Calgary	6	0	3	3	2	0	0	0
Playoff Totals		**85**	**24**	**25**	**49**	**70**	**7**	**3**	**2**
ASHWORTH, Frank *No Playoffs*									Center
ASMUNDSON, Oscar									Center
1933◆	NY Rangers	8	0	2	2	4	0	0	0
1934	NY Rangers	1	0	0	0	0	0	0	0
Playoff Totals		**9**	**0**	**2**	**2**	**4**	**0**	**0**	**0**
•ASTASHENKO, Kaspars *No Playoffs*									Wing
ASTLEY, Mark									Defense
1995	Buffalo	2	0	0	0	0	0	0	0
Playoff Totals		**2**	**0**	**0**	**0**	**0**	**0**	**0**	**0**
ATANAS, Walt *No Playoffs*									Right wing
ATCHEYNUM, Blair									Right wing
1998	St. Louis	10	0	0	0	2	0	0	0
1999	St. Louis	13	1	3	4	6	0	0	0
Playoff Totals		**23**	**1**	**3**	**4**	**8**	**0**	**0**	**0**
ATKINSON, Steve									Right wing
1973	Buffalo	1	0	0	0	0	0	0	0
Playoff Totals		**1**	**0**	**0**	**0**	**0**	**0**	**0**	**0**
ATTWELL, Bob *No Playoffs*									Right wing
ATTWELL, Ron *No Playoffs*									Right wing
AUBIN, Norm									Center
1983	Toronto	1	0	0	0	0	0	0	0
Playoff Totals		**1**	**0**	**0**	**0**	**0**	**0**	**0**	**0**
•AUBIN, Serge									Center
2000	Colorado	17	0	1	1	6	0	0	0
Playoff Totals		**17**	**0**	**1**	**1**	**6**	**0**	**0**	**0**
AUBRY, Pierre									Left wing
1982	Quebec	15	1	1	2	30	0	0	1
1983	Quebec	2	0	0	0	0	0	0	0
1984	Detroit	3	0	0	0	2	0	0	0
Playoff Totals		**20**	**1**	**1**	**2**	**32**	**0**	**0**	**1**
AUBUCHON, Ossie									Left wing
1943	Boston	6	1	0	1	0	....	....	....
Playoff Totals		**6**	**1**	**0**	**1**	**0**	....	....	....
•AUCOIN, Adrian									Defense
1995	Vancouver	4	1	0	1	0	1	0	0
1996	Vancouver	6	0	0	0	2	0	0	0
2002	NY Islanders	7	2	5	7	4	2	0	0
Playoff Totals		**17**	**3**	**5**	**8**	**6**	**3**	**0**	**0**
AUDET, Philippe *No Playoffs*									Left wing

Season	Team	GP	G	A	Pts	PIM	PP	SH	GW
•AUDETTE, Donald									Right wing
1990	Buffalo	2	0	0	0	0	0	0	0
1993	Buffalo	8	2	2	4	6	0	0	0
1994	Buffalo	7	0	1	1	6	0	0	0
1995	Buffalo	5	1	1	2	4	1	0	0
1997	Buffalo	11	4	5	9	6	3	0	0
1998	Buffalo	15	5	8	13	10	3	0	2
2001	Buffalo	13	3	6	9	4	0	0	0
2002	Montreal	12	6	4	10	10	2	0	2
Playoff Totals		**73**	**21**	**27**	**48**	**46**	**9**	**0**	**4**
AUGE, Les *No Playoffs*									Defense
AUGUSTA, Patrik *No Playoffs*									Right wing
•AULIN, Jared *No Playoffs*									Center
AURIE, Larry									Right wing
1929	Detroit	2	1	0	1	2	....	....	....
1932	Detroit	2	0	0	0	0	....	....	....
1933	Detroit	4	1	0	1	4	....	....	....
1934	Detroit	9	3	*7	*10	2	....	....	....
1936◆	Detroit	7	1	2	3	2	....	....	....
1937◆	Detroit	....	....	....	....	....	....	....	....
Playoff Totals		**24**	**6**	**9**	**15**	**10**	....	....	....
•AVERY, Sean *No Playoffs*									Center
AWREY, Don									Defense
1968	Boston	4	0	1	1	4	0	0	0
1969	Boston	10	0	1	1	28	0	0	0
1970◆	Boston	14	0	5	5	32	0	0	0
1971	Boston	7	0	0	0	17	0	0	0
1972◆	Boston	15	0	4	4	45	0	0	0
1973	Boston	4	0	0	0	6	0	0	0
1975	Montreal	11	0	6	6	12	0	0	0
1976◆	Montreal	....	....	....	....	....	....	....	....
1977	Pittsburgh	3	0	1	1	0	0	0	0
1978	NY Rangers	3	0	0	0	6	0	0	0
Playoff Totals		**71**	**0**	**18**	**18**	**150**	**0**	**0**	**0**
•AXELSSON, P.J.									Left wing
1998	Boston	6	1	0	1	0	0	0	0
1999	Boston	12	1	1	2	4	0	0	0
2002	Boston	6	2	1	3	6	0	1	1
Playoff Totals		**24**	**4**	**2**	**6**	**10**	**0**	**1**	**1**
AYRES, Vern *No Playoffs*									Defense
BABANDO, Pete									Left wing
1948	Boston	5	1	1	2	2	....	....	....
1949	Boston	4	0	0	0	2	....	....	....
1950◆	Detroit	8	2	2	4	2	....	....	....
Playoff Totals		**17**	**3**	**3**	**6**	**6**	....	....	....
BABCOCK, Bobby *No Playoffs*									Defense
BABE, Warren									Left wing
1989	Minnesota	2	0	0	0	0	0	0	0
Playoff Totals		**2**	**0**	**0**	**0**	**0**	**0**	**0**	**0**
•BABENKO, Yuri *No Playoffs*									Center
BABIN, Mitch *No Playoffs*									Center
BABY, John *No Playoffs*									Defense
BABYCH, Dave									Defense
1982	Winnipeg	4	1	2	3	29	1	0	0
1983	Winnipeg	3	0	0	0	0	0	0	0
1984	Winnipeg	3	1	1	2	0	1	0	0
1985	Winnipeg	8	2	7	9	6	2	0	0
1986	Hartford	8	1	3	4	14	0	0	0
1987	Hartford	6	1	1	2	14	1	0	0
1988	Hartford	6	3	2	5	2	0	0	0
1989	Hartford	4	1	5	6	2	0	0	0
1990	Hartford	7	1	2	3	0	0	0	0
1992	Vancouver	13	2	6	8	10	1	0	1
1993	Vancouver	12	2	5	7	6	1	0	0
1994	Vancouver	24	3	5	8	12	0	0	1
1995	Vancouver	11	2	2	4	14	1	1	0
1998	Philadelphia	5	1	0	1	4	1	0	0
Playoff Totals		**114**	**21**	**41**	**62**	**113**	**9**	**1**	**2**
BABYCH, Wayne									Right wing
1980	St. Louis	3	1	2	3	2	0	0	0
1981	St. Louis	11	2	0	2	8	1	0	0
1982	St. Louis	7	3	2	5	8	0	0	1
1984	St. Louis	10	1	4	5	4	0	0	0
1986	Hartford	10	0	1	1	2	0	0	0
Playoff Totals		**41**	**7**	**9**	**16**	**24**	**1**	**0**	**1**
BACA, Jergus *No Playoffs*									Defense
•BACKMAN, Christian *No Playoffs*									Defense
BACKMAN, Mike									Right wing
1982	NY Rangers	1	0	0	0	2	0	0	0
1983	NY Rangers	9	2	2	4	0	0	0	1
Playoff Totals		**10**	**2**	**2**	**4**	**2**	**0**	**0**	**1**
BACKOR, Pete *No Playoffs*									Defense

Season	Team	GP	G	A	Pts	PIM	PP	SH	GW
BACKSTROM, Ralph									Center
1959◆	Montreal	11	3	5	8	12	....	....	....
1960◆	Montreal	7	0	3	3	2	....	....	....
1961	Montreal	5	0	0	0	4	....	....	....
1962	Montreal	5	0	1	1	6	....	....	....
1963	Montreal	5	0	0	0	2	....	....	....
1964	Montreal	7	2	1	3	8	....	....	....
1965◆	Montreal	13	2	3	5	10	....	....	....
1966◆	Montreal	10	3	4	7	4	....	....	....
1967	Montreal	10	5	2	7	6	....	....	....
1968◆	Montreal	13	4	3	7	4	0	0	2
1969◆	Montreal	14	3	4	7	10	0	1	1
1973	Chicago	16	5	6	11	0	0	1	0
Playoff Totals		**116**	**27**	**32**	**59**	**68**	**0**	**2**	**3**
BAILEY, Ace									Right wing
1929	Toronto	4	1	*2	*3	4	....	....	....
1931	Toronto	2	1	1	2	0	....	....	....
1932◆	Toronto	7	1	0	1	4	....	....	....
1933	Toronto	8	0	1	1	4	....	....	....
Playoff Totals		**21**	**3**	**4**	**7**	**12**	....	....	....
BAILEY, Bob									Right wing
1954	Toronto	5	0	2	2	4	0	0	0
1955	Toronto	1	0	0	0	0	0	0	0
1957	Detroit	5	0	2	2	2	0	0	0
1958	Detroit	4	0	0	0	16	0	0	0
Playoff Totals		**15**	**0**	**4**	**4**	**22**	**0**	**0**	**0**
BAILEY, Garnet									Left wing
1969	Boston	1	0	0	0	2	0	0	0
1970◆	Boston	....	....	....	....	....	....	....	....
1971	Boston	1	0	0	0	10	0	0	0
1972◆	Boston	13	2	4	6	16	0	0	1
Playoff Totals		**15**	**2**	**4**	**6**	**28**	**0**	**0**	**1**
BAILEY, Reid									Defense
1981	Philadelphia	12	0	2	2	23	0	0	0
1982	Philadelphia	2	0	0	0	0	0	0	0
1983	Toronto	2	0	0	0	2	0	0	0
Playoff Totals		**16**	**0**	**2**	**2**	**25**	**0**	**0**	**0**
BAILLARGEON, Joel *No Playoffs*									Left wing
BAIRD, Ken *No Playoffs*									Defense
BAKER, Bill									Defense
1982	St. Louis	4	0	0	0	0	0	0	0
1983	NY Rangers	2	0	0	0	0	0	0	0
Playoff Totals		**6**	**0**	**0**	**0**	**0**	**0**	**0**	**0**
BAKER, Jamie									Center
1994	San Jose	14	3	2	5	30	0	0	1
1995	San Jose	11	2	2	4	12	0	0	1
Playoff Totals		**25**	**5**	**4**	**9**	**42**	**0**	**0**	**2**
BAKOVIC, Peter *No Playoffs*									Right wing
•BALA, Chris *No Playoffs*									Left wing
BALDERIS, Helmut *No Playoffs*									Right wing
BALDWIN, Doug *No Playoffs*									Defense
BALFOUR, Earl									Left wing
1952	Toronto	1	0	0	0	0	0	0	0
1956	Toronto	3	0	1	1	2	0	0	0
1959	Chicago	6	0	2	2	0	0	0	0
1960	Chicago	4	0	0	0	0	0	0	0
1961◆	Chicago	12	0	0	0	2	0	0	0
Playoff Totals		**26**	**0**	**3**	**3**	**4**	**0**	**0**	**0**
BALFOUR, Murray									Right wing
1960	Chicago	4	1	0	1	0	....	....	....
1961◆	Chicago	11	5	5	10	14	....	....	....
1962	Chicago	12	1	1	2	15	....	....	....
1963	Chicago	6	0	2	2	12	....	....	....
1964	Chicago	7	2	2	4	4	....	....	....
Playoff Totals		**40**	**9**	**10**	**19**	**45**	....	....	....
BALL, Terry *No Playoffs*									Defense
•BALMOCHNYKH, Maxim *No Playoffs*									Left wing
BALON, Dave									Left wing
1962	NY Rangers	6	2	3	5	2	0	0	2
1964	Montreal	7	1	1	2	25	0	0	0
1965◆	Montreal	10	0	0	0	10	0	0	0
1966◆	Montreal	9	2	3	5	16	0	0	0
1967	Montreal	9	0	2	2	6	0	0	0
1968	Minnesota	14	4	*9	13	14	1	0	1
1969	NY Rangers	4	1	0	1	0	0	0	0
1970	NY Rangers	6	1	1	2	32	0	1	0
1971	NY Rangers	13	3	2	5	4	2	0	1
Playoff Totals		**78**	**14**	**21**	**35**	**109**	**3**	**1**	**4**
BALTIMORE, Bryon *No Playoffs*									Defense
BALUIK, Stan *No Playoffs*									Center
•BANCROFT, Steve *No Playoffs*									Defense
BANDURA, Jeff *No Playoffs*									Defense
BANHAM, Frank *No Playoffs*									Right wing
BANKS, Darren *No Playoffs*									Left wing
•BANNISTER, Drew									Defense
1997	Edmonton	12	0	0	0	30	0	0	0
Playoff Totals		**12**	**0**	**0**	**0**	**30**	**0**	**0**	**0**

Season	Team	GP	G	A	Pts	PIM	PP	SH	GW
BARAHONA, Ralph *No Playoffs* — Center									
BARBE, Andy *No Playoffs* — Right wing									
BARBER, Bill — Left wing									
1973	Philadelphia	11	3	2	5	22	0	0	0
1974♦	Philadelphia	17	3	6	9	18	0	0	1
1975♦	Philadelphia	17	6	9	15	8	0	0	0
1976	Philadelphia	16	6	7	13	18	3	0	0
1977	Philadelphia	10	1	4	5	2	0	0	0
1978	Philadelphia	12	6	3	9	2	1	0	0
1979	Philadelphia	8	3	4	7	10	0	0	0
1980	Philadelphia	19	12	9	21	23	1	3	4
1981	Philadelphia	12	11	5	16	0	3	1	1
1982	Philadelphia	4	1	5	6	4	0	1	0
1983	Philadelphia	3	1	1	2	2	1	0	0
Playoff Totals		**129**	**53**	**55**	**108**	**109**	**9**	**5**	**6**
BARBER, Don — Wing									
1989	Minnesota	4	1	1	2	2	0	0	1
1990	Minnesota	7	3	3	6	8	2	0	1
Playoff Totals		**11**	**4**	**4**	**8**	**10**	**2**	**0**	**2**
BARILKO, Bill — Defense									
1947♦	Toronto	11	0	3	3	18	....	....	....
1948♦	Toronto	9	1	0	1	17	....	....	....
1949♦	Toronto	9	0	1	1	20	....	....	....
1950	Toronto	7	1	1	2	18	....	....	....
1951♦	Toronto	11	3	2	5	31	....	....	....
Playoff Totals		**47**	**5**	**7**	**12**	**104**	....	....	....
BARKLEY, Doug — Defense									
1963	Detroit	11	0	3	3	16	0	0	0
1964	Detroit	14	0	5	5	33	0	0	0
1965	Detroit	5	0	1	1	14	0	0	0
Playoff Totals		**30**	**0**	**9**	**9**	**63**	**0**	**0**	**0**
BARLOW, Bob — Left wing									
1970	Minnesota	6	2	2	4	6	1	0	0
Playoff Totals		**6**	**2**	**2**	**4**	**6**	**1**	**0**	**0**
•BARNABY, Matthew — Right wing									
1993	Buffalo	1	0	1	1	4	0	0	0
1994	Buffalo	3	0	0	0	17	0	0	0
1997	Buffalo	8	0	4	4	36	0	0	0
1998	Buffalo	15	7	6	13	22	3	0	1
1999	Pittsburgh	13	0	0	0	35	0	0	0
2000	Pittsburgh	11	0	2	2	29	0	0	0
Playoff Totals		**51**	**7**	**13**	**20**	**143**	**3**	**0**	**1**
BARNES, Blair *No Playoffs* — Right wing									
BARNES, Norm — Defense									
1979	Philadelphia	2	0	0	0	0	0	0	0
1980	Philadelphia	10	0	0	0	8	0	0	0
Playoff Totals		**12**	**0**	**0**	**0**	**8**	**0**	**0**	**0**
•BARNES, Stu — Center									
1993	Winnipeg	6	1	3	4	2	0	0	0
1996	Florida	22	6	10	16	4	2	0	2
1997	Pittsburgh	5	0	1	1	0	0	0	0
1998	Pittsburgh	6	3	3	6	2	0	0	1
1999	Buffalo	21	7	3	10	6	4	0	1
2000	Buffalo	5	3	0	3	2	2	0	1
2001	Buffalo	13	4	4	8	2	2	0	2
Playoff Totals		**78**	**24**	**24**	**48**	**18**	**10**	**0**	**7**
BARNEY, Scott *No Playoffs* — Center									
•BARON, Murray — Defense									
1992	St. Louis	2	0	0	0	2	0	0	0
1993	St. Louis	11	0	0	0	12	0	0	0
1994	St. Louis	4	0	0	0	10	0	0	0
1995	St. Louis	7	1	1	2	2	0	0	0
1996	St. Louis	13	1	0	1	20	0	1	0
1997	Phoenix	1	0	0	0	0	0	0	0
1998	Phoenix	6	0	2	2	6	0	0	0
2001	Vancouver	4	0	0	0	0	0	0	0
2002	Vancouver	6	0	1	1	10	0	0	0
Playoff Totals		**54**	**2**	**4**	**6**	**62**	**0**	**1**	**0**
BARON, Normand — Left wing									
1984	Montreal	3	0	0	0	22	0	0	0
Playoff Totals		**3**	**0**	**0**	**0**	**22**	**0**	**0**	**0**
BARR, Dave — Right wing									
1982	Boston	5	1	0	1	0	0	0	0
1983	Boston	10	0	0	0	2	0	0	0
1985	St. Louis	2	0	0	0	2	0	0	0
1986	St. Louis	11	1	1	2	14	1	0	0
1987	Detroit	13	1	0	1	14	0	0	0
1988	Detroit	16	5	7	12	22	2	0	0
1989	Detroit	6	3	1	4	6	1	0	1
1993	New Jersey	5	1	0	1	6	0	0	0
1994	Dallas	3	0	1	1	4	0	0	0
Playoff Totals		**71**	**12**	**10**	**22**	**70**	**4**	**0**	**1**
BARRAULT, Doug *No Playoffs* — Right wing									

Season	Team	GP	G	A	Pts	PIM	PP	SH	GW
BARRETT, Fred — Defense									
1973	Minnesota	6	0	0	0	4	0	0	0
1977	Minnesota	2	0	0	0	2	0	0	0
1980	Minnesota	14	0	0	0	22	0	0	0
1981	Minnesota	14	0	1	1	16	0	0	0
1982	Minnesota	4	0	1	1	16	0	0	0
1983	Minnesota	4	0	0	0	0	0	0	0
Playoff Totals		**44**	**0**	**2**	**2**	**60**	**0**	**0**	**0**
BARRETT, John — Defense									
1984	Detroit	4	0	0	0	4	0	0	0
1985	Detroit	3	0	1	1	11	0	0	0
1986	Washington	9	2	1	3	35	0	0	1
Playoff Totals		**16**	**2**	**2**	**4**	**50**	**0**	**0**	**1**
BARRIE, Doug *No Playoffs* — Defense									
BARRIE, Len — Center									
1995	Pittsburgh	4	1	0	1	8	1	0	0
2000	Florida	4	0	0	0	0	0	0	0
Playoff Totals		**8**	**1**	**0**	**1**	**8**	**1**	**0**	**0**
BARRY, Ed *No Playoffs* — Left wing									
BARRY, Marty — Center									
1930	Boston	6	3	3	*6	14	....	....	....
1931	Boston	5	1	1	2	4	....	....	....
1933	Boston	5	2	2	4	6	....	....	....
1935	Boston	4	0	0	0	2	....	....	....
1936♦	Detroit	7	2	4	6	6	....	....	....
1937♦	Detroit	10	*4	*7	*11	2	....	....	....
1939	Detroit	6	3	1	4	0	....	....	....
Playoff Totals		**43**	**15**	**18**	**33**	**34**	....	....	....
BARRY, Ray *No Playoffs* — Center									
•BARTECKO, Lubos — Left wing									
1999	St. Louis	5	0	0	0	2	0	0	0
2000	St. Louis	7	1	1	2	0	0	0	0
Playoff Totals		**12**	**1**	**1**	**2**	**2**	**0**	**0**	**0**
BARTEL, Robin — Defense									
1986	Calgary	6	0	0	0	16	0	0	0
Playoff Totals		**6**	**0**	**0**	**0**	**16**	**0**	**0**	**0**
BARTLETT, Jim — Left wing									
1955	Montreal	2	0	0	0	0	0	0	0
Playoff Totals		**2**	**0**	**0**	**0**	**0**	**0**	**0**	**0**
BARTON, Cliff *No Playoffs* — Right wing									
•BARTOS, Peter *No Playoffs* — Left wing									
•BASHKIROV, Andrei *No Playoffs* — Left wing									
BASSEN, Bob — Center									
1986	NY Islanders	3	0	1	1	0	0	0	0
1987	NY Islanders	14	1	2	3	21	0	0	0
1988	NY Islanders	6	0	1	1	23	0	0	0
1989	Chicago	10	1	1	2	34	0	0	0
1990	Chicago	1	0	0	0	2	0	0	0
1991	St. Louis	13	1	3	4	24	0	0	0
1992	St. Louis	6	0	2	2	4	0	0	0
1993	St. Louis	11	0	0	0	10	0	0	0
1995	Quebec	5	2	4	6	0	0	0	0
1997	Dallas	7	3	1	4	4	0	0	0
1998	Dallas	17	1	0	1	12	0	0	0
Playoff Totals		**93**	**9**	**15**	**24**	**134**	**0**	**0**	**0**
•BAST, Ryan *No Playoffs* — Defense									
•BATES, Shawn — Center									
1999	Boston	12	0	0	0	4	0	0	0
2002	NY Islanders	7	2	4	6	11	1	0	1
Playoff Totals		**19**	**2**	**4**	**6**	**15**	**1**	**0**	**1**
BATHE, Frank — Defense									
1979	Philadelphia	6	1	0	1	12	0	0	0
1980	Philadelphia	1	0	0	0	0	0	0	0
1981	Philadelphia	12	0	3	3	16	0	0	0
1982	Philadelphia	4	0	0	0	2	0	0	0
1983	Philadelphia	3	0	0	0	12	0	0	0
1984	Philadelphia	1	0	0	0	0	0	0	0
Playoff Totals		**27**	**1**	**3**	**4**	**42**	**0**	**0**	**0**
BATHGATE, Andy — Right wing									
1956	NY Rangers	5	1	2	3	2	....	....	....
1957	NY Rangers	5	2	0	2	27	....	....	....
1958	NY Rangers	6	5	3	8	6	....	....	....
1962	NY Rangers	6	1	2	3	4	....	....	....
1964♦	Toronto	14	5	4	9	25	....	....	....
1965	Toronto	6	1	0	1	6	....	....	....
1966	Detroit	12	*6	3	9	6	....	....	....
Playoff Totals		**54**	**21**	**14**	**35**	**76**	....	....	....
BATHGATE, Frank *No Playoffs* — Center									
•BATTAGLIA, Bates — Left wing									
1999	Carolina	6	0	3	3	8	0	0	0
2001	Carolina	6	0	2	2	2	0	0	0
2002	Carolina	23	5	9	14	14	1	0	1
Playoff Totals		**35**	**5**	**14**	**19**	**24**	**1**	**0**	**1**
BATTERS, Jeff *No Playoffs* — Defense									
BATYRSHIN, Ruslan *No Playoffs* — Defense									

Season	Team	GP	G	A	Pts	PIM	PP	SH	GW
BAUER, Bobby — Right wing									
1937	Boston	1	0	0	0	0	....	....	....
1938	Boston	3	0	0	0	2	....	....	....
1939♦	Boston	12	3	2	5	0	....	....	....
1940	Boston	6	1	0	1	2	....	....	....
1941♦	Boston	11	2	2	4	0	....	....	....
1946	Boston	10	4	3	7	2	....	....	....
1947	Boston	5	1	1	2	0	....	....	....
Playoff Totals		**48**	**11**	**8**	**19**	**6**	....	....	....
BAUMGARTNER, Ken — Left wing									
1988	Los Angeles	5	0	1	1	28	0	0	0
1989	Los Angeles	5	0	0	0	8	0	0	0
1990	NY Islanders	4	0	0	0	27	0	0	0
1993	Toronto	7	1	0	1	0	0	0	0
1994	Toronto	10	0	0	0	18	0	0	0
1997	Anaheim	11	0	1	1	11	0	0	0
1998	Boston	6	0	0	0	14	0	0	0
1999	Boston	3	0	0	0	0	0	0	0
Playoff Totals		**51**	**1**	**2**	**3**	**106**	**0**	**0**	**0**
BAUMGARTNER, Mike *No Playoffs* — Defense									
•BAUMGARTNER, Nolan — Defense									
1996	Washington	1	0	0	0	10	0	0	0
Playoff Totals		**1**	**0**	**0**	**0**	**10**	**0**	**0**	**0**
BAUN, Bob — Defense									
1959	Toronto	12	0	0	0	24	0	0	0
1960	Toronto	10	1	0	1	17	0	0	0
1961	Toronto	3	0	0	0	8	0	0	0
1962♦	Toronto	12	0	3	3	19	0	0	0
1963♦	Toronto	10	0	3	3	6	0	0	0
1964♦	Toronto	14	2	3	5	*42	0	0	1
1965	Toronto	6	0	1	1	14	0	0	0
1966	Toronto	4	0	1	1	8	0	0	0
1967♦	Toronto	10	0	0	0	4	0	0	0
1970	Detroit	4	0	0	0	6	0	0	0
1971	Toronto	6	0	1	1	19	0	0	0
1972	Toronto	5	0	0	0	4	0	0	0
Playoff Totals		**96**	**3**	**12**	**15**	**171**	**0**	**0**	**1**
BAUTIN, Sergei — Defense									
1993	Winnipeg	6	0	0	0	2	0	0	0
Playoff Totals		**6**	**0**	**0**	**0**	**2**	**0**	**0**	**0**
BAWA, Robin — Right wing									
1992	Vancouver	1	0	0	0	0	0	0	0
Playoff Totals		**1**	**0**	**0**	**0**	**0**	**0**	**0**	**0**
BAXTER, Paul — Defense									
1981	Pittsburgh	5	0	1	1	28	0	0	0
1982	Pittsburgh	5	0	0	0	14	0	0	0
1984	Calgary	11	0	2	2	37	0	0	0
1985	Calgary	4	0	1	1	18	0	0	0
1986	Calgary	13	0	1	1	55	0	0	0
1987	Calgary	2	0	0	0	10	0	0	0
Playoff Totals		**40**	**0**	**5**	**5**	**162**	**0**	**0**	**0**
•BAYDA, Ryan *No Playoffs* — Left wing									
BEADLE, Sandy *No Playoffs* — Left wing									
BEATON, Frank *No Playoffs* — Left wing									
BEATTIE, Red — Left wing									
1931	Boston	4	0	0	0	0	....	....	....
1933	Boston	5	0	0	0	2	....	....	....
1935	Boston	4	1	0	1	2	....	....	....
1936	Boston	2	0	0	0	2	....	....	....
1937	Boston	3	1	0	1	0	....	....	....
1938	NY Americans	6	2	2	4	2	....	....	....
Playoff Totals		**24**	**4**	**2**	**6**	**8**	....	....	....
BEAUDIN, Norm *No Playoffs* — Right wing									
•BEAUDOIN, Eric *No Playoffs* — Left wing									
BEAUDOIN, Serge *No Playoffs* — Defense									
BEAUDOIN, Yves *No Playoffs* — Defense									
•BEAUFAIT, Mark *No Playoffs* — Center									
BECK, Barry — Defense									
1978	Colorado	2	0	1	1	0	0	0	0
1980	NY Rangers	9	1	4	5	6	1	0	0
1981	NY Rangers	14	5	8	13	32	1	1	0
1982	NY Rangers	10	1	5	6	14	1	0	0
1983	NY Rangers	9	2	4	6	8	0	0	0
1984	NY Rangers	4	1	0	1	6	0	0	0
1985	NY Rangers	3	0	1	1	11	0	0	0
Playoff Totals		**51**	**10**	**23**	**33**	**77**	**3**	**1**	**0**
BECKETT, Bob *No Playoffs* — Center									
BEDARD, James *No Playoffs* — Defense									
BEDDOES, Clayton *No Playoffs* — Center									
•BEDNAR, Jaroslav — Right wing									
2002	Los Angeles	3	0	0	0	0	0	0	0
Playoff Totals		**3**	**0**	**0**	**0**	**0**	**0**	**0**	**0**
BEDNARSKI, John — Defense									
1975	NY Rangers	1	0	0	0	17	0	0	0
Playoff Totals		**1**	**0**	**0**	**0**	**17**	**0**	**0**	**0**
•BEECH, Kris *No Playoffs* — Center									

Season	Team	GP	G	A	Pts	PIM	PP	SH	GW
BEERS, Bob	Defense								
1990	Boston	14	1	1	2	18	0	0	0
1991	Boston	6	0	0	0	4	0	0	0
1992	Boston	1	0	0	0	0	0	0	0
Playoff Totals		**21**	**1**	**1**	**2**	**22**	**0**	**0**	**0**
BEERS, Eddy	Left wing								
1983	Calgary	8	1	1	2	27	0	0	1
1984	Calgary	11	2	5	7	12	0	0	0
1985	Calgary	3	1	0	1	0	1	0	0
1986	St. Louis	19	3	4	7	8	2	0	1
Playoff Totals		**41**	**7**	**10**	**17**	**47**	**3**	**0**	**2**
•BEGIN, Steve *No Playoffs*	Center								
BEHLING, Dick *No Playoffs*	Defense								
BEISLER, Frank *No Playoffs*	Defense								
•BEKAR, Derek *No Playoffs*	Left wing								
•BELAK, Wade	Defense								
2002	Toronto	16	1	0	1	18	0	0	0
Playoff Totals		**16**	**1**	**0**	**1**	**18**	**0**	**0**	**0**
BELANGER, Alain *No Playoffs*	Right wing								
•BELANGER, Eric	Center								
2001	Los Angeles	13	1	4	5	2	0	0	1
2002	Los Angeles	7	0	0	0	4	0	0	0
Playoff Totals		**20**	**1**	**4**	**5**	**6**	**0**	**0**	**1**
•BELANGER, Francis *No Playoffs*	Left wing								
BELANGER, Jesse	Center								
1993♦	Montreal	9	0	1	1	0	0	0	0
1996	Vancouver	3	0	2	2	2	0	0	0
Playoff Totals		**12**	**0**	**3**	**3**	**2**	**0**	**0**	**0**
•BELANGER, Ken	Left wing								
1999	Boston	12	1	0	1	16	0	0	0
Playoff Totals		**12**	**1**	**0**	**1**	**16**	**0**	**0**	**0**
BELANGER, Roger *No Playoffs*	Center								
BELISLE, Danny *No Playoffs*	Right wing								
BELIVEAU, Jean	Center								
1954	Montreal	10	2	*8	10	4	....	....	....
1955	Montreal	12	6	7	13	18	....	....	....
1956♦	Montreal	10	*12	7	*19	22	....	....	....
1957♦	Montreal	10	6	6	12	15	....	....	....
1958♦	Montreal	10	4	8	12	10	....	....	....
1959♦	Montreal	3	1	4	5	4	....	....	....
1960♦	Montreal	8	5	2	7	6	....	....	....
1961	Montreal	6	0	5	5	0	....	....	....
1962	Montreal	6	2	1	3	4	....	....	....
1963	Montreal	5	2	1	3	2	....	....	....
1964	Montreal	5	2	0	2	18	....	....	....
1965♦	Montreal	13	8	8	16	34	....	....	....
1966♦	Montreal	10	5	5	10	6	....	....	....
1967	Montreal	10	6	5	11	*26	....	....	....
1968♦	Montreal	10	7	4	11	6	3	0	1
1969♦	Montreal	14	5	*10	15	8	1	1	0
1971♦	Montreal	20	6	*16	22	28	2	0	0
Playoff Totals		**162**	**79**	**97**	**176**	**211**	**6**	**1**	**1**
BELL, Billy	Center/Right wing								
1922	Ottawa	1	0	0	0	0	0	0	0
1923	Montreal	2	0	0	0	0	0	0	0
1924♦	Montreal	2	0	0	0	0	0	0	0
Playoff Totals		**5**	**0**	**0**	**0**	**0**	**0**	**0**	**0**
BELL, Bruce	Defense								
1985	Quebec	16	2	2	4	21	1	0	0
1986	St. Louis	14	0	2	2	13	0	0	0
1987	St. Louis	4	1	1	2	7	0	0	0
Playoff Totals		**34**	**3**	**5**	**8**	**41**	**1**	**0**	**0**
BELL, Harry *No Playoffs*	Right wing/Defense								
BELL, Joe *No Playoffs*	Left wing								
•BELL, Mark	Center								
2002	Chicago	5	0	0	0	8	0	0	0
Playoff Totals		**5**	**0**	**0**	**0**	**8**	**0**	**0**	**0**
BELLAND, Neil	Defense								
1982	Vancouver	17	1	7	8	16	1	0	0
1984	Vancouver	4	1	2	3	7	0	0	1
Playoff Totals		**21**	**2**	**9**	**11**	**23**	**1**	**0**	**1**
•BELLEFEUILLE, Blake *No Playoffs*	Right wing								
BELLEFEUILLE, Pete *No Playoffs*	Right wing								
BELLEMER, Andy *No Playoffs*	Defense								

Season	Team	GP	G	A	Pts	PIM	PP	SH	GW
BELLOWS, Brian	Left wing								
1983	Minnesota	9	5	4	9	18	2	0	0
1984	Minnesota	16	2	12	14	6	0	1	0
1985	Minnesota	9	2	4	6	9	0	1	0
1986	Minnesota	5	5	0	5	16	3	0	0
1989	Minnesota	5	2	3	5	8	2	0	0
1990	Minnesota	7	4	3	7	10	3	0	1
1991	Minnesota	23	10	19	29	30	6	0	1
1992	Minnesota	7	4	4	8	14	2	0	1
1993♦	Montreal	18	6	9	15	18	2	0	0
1994	Montreal	6	1	2	3	2	0	0	0
1996	Tampa Bay	6	2	0	2	4	0	0	1
1997	Anaheim	11	2	4	6	2	1	0	0
1998	Washington	21	6	7	13	6	2	0	1
Playoff Totals		**143**	**51**	**71**	**122**	**143**	**23**	**2**	**5**
BEND, Lin *No Playoffs*	Center								
BENDA, Jan *No Playoffs*	Center								
BENNETT, Adam *No Playoffs*	Defense								
BENNETT, Bill *No Playoffs*	Left wing								
BENNETT, Curt	Left wing								
1971	St. Louis	2	0	0	0	0	0	0	0
1972	St. Louis	10	0	0	0	12	0	0	0
1974	Atlanta	4	0	1	1	34	0	0	0
1976	Atlanta	2	0	0	0	4	0	0	0
1977	Atlanta	3	1	0	1	7	0	0	0
Playoff Totals		**21**	**1**	**1**	**2**	**57**	**0**	**0**	**0**
BENNETT, Frank *No Playoffs*	Left wing/Defense								
BENNETT, Harvey	Center								
1977	Philadelphia	4	0	0	0	2	0	0	0
Playoff Totals		**4**	**0**	**0**	**0**	**2**	**0**	**0**	**0**
BENNETT, Max *No Playoffs*	Right wing								
BENNETT, Rick *No Playoffs*	Left wing								
BENNING, Brian	Defense								
1986	St. Louis	6	1	2	3	13	1	0	0
1987	St. Louis	6	0	4	4	9	0	0	0
1988	St. Louis	10	1	6	7	25	1	0	0
1989	St. Louis	7	1	1	2	11	1	0	0
1990	Los Angeles	7	0	2	2	10	0	0	0
1991	Los Angeles	12	0	5	5	6	0	0	0
Playoff Totals		**48**	**3**	**20**	**23**	**74**	**3**	**0**	**0**
BENNING, Jim	Defense								
1983	Toronto	4	1	1	2	2	0	0	0
1989	Vancouver	3	0	0	0	0	0	0	0
Playoff Totals		**7**	**1**	**1**	**2**	**2**	**0**	**0**	**0**
BENOIT, Joe	Right wing								
1941	Montreal	3	4	0	4	2	....	....	....
1942	Montreal	3	1	0	1	5	....	....	....
1943	Montreal	5	1	3	4	4	....	....	....
1946♦	Montreal	....	....	....	....	....	....	....	....
Playoff Totals		**11**	**6**	**3**	**9**	**11**	....	....	....
BENSON, Bill *No Playoffs*	Center								
BENSON, Bobby *No Playoffs*	Defense								
BENTLEY, Doug	Left wing								
1940	Chicago	2	0	0	0	0	....	....	....
1941	Chicago	5	1	1	2	4	....	....	....
1942	Chicago	3	0	1	1	4	....	....	....
1944	Chicago	9	8	4	12	4	....	....	....
1946	Chicago	4	0	2	2	0	....	....	....
Playoff Totals		**23**	**9**	**8**	**17**	**12**	....	....	....
BENTLEY, Max	Center								
1941	Chicago	4	1	3	4	2	....	....	....
1942	Chicago	3	2	0	2	0	....	....	....
1946	Chicago	4	1	0	1	4	....	....	....
1948♦	Toronto	9	4	*7	11	0	....	....	....
1949♦	Toronto	9	4	3	7	2	....	....	....
1950	Toronto	7	3	3	6	0	....	....	....
1951♦	Toronto	11	2	*11	*13	4	....	....	....
1952	Toronto	4	1	0	1	2	....	....	....
Playoff Totals		**51**	**18**	**27**	**45**	**14**	....	....	....
BENTLEY, Reg *No Playoffs*	Left wing								
•BENYSEK, Ladislav *No Playoffs*	Defense								
BERALDO, Paul *No Playoffs*	Right wing								
•BERANEK, Josef	Left wing/Center								
1992	Edmonton	12	2	1	3	0	1	0	1
1995	Vancouver	11	1	1	2	12	0	0	0
1996	Vancouver	3	2	1	3	0	0	0	0
1997	Pittsburgh	5	0	0	0	2	0	0	0
1999	Edmonton	2	0	0	0	4	0	0	0
2000	Pittsburgh	11	0	3	3	4	0	0	0
2001	Pittsburgh	13	0	2	2	2	0	0	0
Playoff Totals		**57**	**5**	**8**	**13**	**24**	**1**	**0**	**1**
•BERARD, Bryan	Defense								
1999	Toronto	17	1	8	9	8	1	0	0
Playoff Totals		**17**	**1**	**8**	**9**	**8**	**1**	**0**	**0**

Season	Team	GP	G	A	Pts	PIM	PP	SH	GW
•BEREHOWSKY, Drake	Defense								
1995	Pittsburgh	1	0	0	0	0	0	0	0
1998	Edmonton	12	1	2	3	14	0	0	1
2001	Vancouver	4	0	0	0	12	0	0	0
2002	Phoenix	5	0	1	1	4	0	0	0
Playoff Totals		**22**	**1**	**3**	**4**	**30**	**0**	**0**	**1**
BERENSON, Red	Center								
1962	Montreal	5	2	0	2	0	0	0	0
1963	Montreal	5	0	0	0	0	0	0	0
1964	Montreal	7	0	0	0	4	0	0	0
1965♦	Montreal	9	0	1	1	2	0	0	0
1967	NY Rangers	4	0	1	1	2	0	0	0
1968	St. Louis	18	5	2	7	9	1	1	0
1969	St. Louis	12	7	3	10	20	2	1	0
1970	St. Louis	16	7	5	12	8	3	1	1
1975	St. Louis	2	1	0	1	0	1	0	0
1976	St. Louis	3	1	2	3	0	0	0	0
1977	St. Louis	4	0	0	0	4	0	0	0
Playoff Totals		**85**	**23**	**14**	**37**	**49**	**7**	**3**	**1**
•BERENZWEIG, Bubba *No Playoffs*	Defense								
BEREZAN, Perry	Center								
1985	Calgary	2	1	0	1	4	1	0	0
1986	Calgary	8	1	1	2	6	0	0	1
1987	Calgary	2	0	2	2	7	0	0	0
1988	Calgary	8	0	2	2	13	0	0	0
1989	Minnesota	5	1	2	3	4	0	0	0
1990	Minnesota	5	1	0	1	0	0	0	0
1991	Minnesota	1	0	0	0	0	0	0	0
Playoff Totals		**31**	**4**	**7**	**11**	**34**	**1**	**0**	**1**
•BEREZIN, Sergei	Left wing								
1999	Toronto	17	6	6	12	4	2	0	2
2000	Toronto	12	4	4	8	0	0	0	1
2001	Toronto	11	2	5	7	2	0	0	2
2002	Montreal	6	1	1	2	0	1	0	0
Playoff Totals		**46**	**13**	**16**	**29**	**6**	**3**	**0**	**5**
•BERG, Aki	Defense								
1998	Los Angeles	4	0	3	3	0	0	0	0
2000	Los Angeles	2	0	0	0	2	0	0	0
2001	Toronto	11	0	2	2	4	0	0	0
2002	Toronto	20	0	1	1	37	0	0	0
Playoff Totals		**37**	**0**	**6**	**6**	**43**	**0**	**0**	**0**
BERG, Bill	Left wing								
1993	Toronto	21	1	1	2	18	0	0	0
1994	Toronto	18	1	2	3	10	0	0	0
1995	Toronto	7	0	1	1	4	0	0	0
1996	NY Rangers	10	1	0	1	0	0	0	0
1997	NY Rangers	3	0	0	0	2	0	0	0
1999	Ottawa	2	0	0	0	0	0	0	0
Playoff Totals		**61**	**3**	**4**	**7**	**34**	**0**	**0**	**0**
BERGDINON, Fred *No Playoffs*	Right wing								
BERGEN, Todd	Center								
1985	Philadelphia	17	4	9	13	8	2	0	1
Playoff Totals		**17**	**4**	**9**	**13**	**8**	**2**	**0**	**1**
BERGER, Mike *No Playoffs*	Defense								
BERGERON, Michel *No Playoffs*	Right wing								
BERGERON, Yves *No Playoffs*	Right wing								
•BERGEVIN, Marc	Defense								
1985	Chicago	6	0	3	3	2	0	0	0
1986	Chicago	3	0	0	0	0	0	0	0
1987	Chicago	3	1	0	1	2	0	0	0
1992	Hartford	5	0	0	0	2	0	0	0
1996	Detroit	17	1	0	1	14	1	0	0
1997	St. Louis	6	1	0	1	8	0	0	0
1998	St. Louis	10	0	1	1	8	0	0	0
2000	St. Louis	7	0	1	1	6	0	0	0
2001	Pittsburgh	12	0	1	1	2	0	0	0
2002	St. Louis	7	0	0	0	4	0	0	0
Playoff Totals		**76**	**3**	**6**	**9**	**48**	**1**	**0**	**0**
BERGKVIST, Stefan	Defense								
1996	Pittsburgh	4	0	0	0	2	0	0	0
Playoff Totals		**4**	**0**	**0**	**0**	**2**	**0**	**0**	**0**
BERGLAND, Tim	Right wing								
1990	Washington	15	1	1	2	10	0	0	0
1991	Washington	11	1	1	2	12	0	0	0
Playoff Totals		**26**	**2**	**2**	**4**	**22**	**0**	**0**	**0**
BERGLOFF, Bob *No Playoffs*	Defense								
BERGLUND, Bo	Right wing								
1984	Quebec	7	2	0	2	4	0	0	1
1985	Minnesota	2	0	0	0	2	0	0	0
Playoff Totals		**9**	**2**	**0**	**2**	**6**	**0**	**0**	**1**
•BERGLUND, Christian	Left wing								
2002	New Jersey	3	0	0	0	2	0	0	0
Playoff Totals		**3**	**0**	**0**	**0**	**2**	**0**	**0**	**0**
BERGMAN, Gary	Defense								
1965	Detroit	5	0	1	1	4	0	0	0
1966	Detroit	12	0	3	3	14	0	0	0
1970	Detroit	4	0	1	1	2	0	0	0
Playoff Totals		**21**	**0**	**5**	**5**	**20**	**0**	**0**	**0**

Season	Team	GP	G	A	Pts	PIM	PP	SH	GW
BERGMAN, Thommie — Defense									
1978	Detroit	7	0	2	2	2	0	0	0
Playoff Totals		**7**	**0**	**2**	**2**	**2**	**0**	**0**	**0**
BERGQVIST, Jonas *No Playoffs* — Right wing									
BERLINQUETTE, Louis — Left wing									
1918	Montreal	2	0	0	0	0	....	....	....
1919	Montreal	5	0	2	2	9	....	....	....
1923	Montreal	2	0	2	2	0	....	....	....
1926	Pittsburgh	2	0	0	0	0	....	....	....
Playoff Totals		**11**	**0**	**4**	**4**	**9**	....	....	....
BERNIER, Serge — Right wing									
1971	Philadelphia	4	1	1	2	0	1	0	0
1981	Quebec	1	0	0	0	0	0	0	0
Playoff Totals		**5**	**1**	**1**	**2**	**0**	**1**	**0**	**0**
BERRY, Bob — Left wing									
1974	Los Angeles	5	0	0	0	0	0	0	0
1975	Los Angeles	3	1	2	3	2	0	0	0
1976	Los Angeles	9	1	1	2	0	0	0	1
1977	Los Angeles	9	0	3	3	4	0	0	0
Playoff Totals		**26**	**2**	**6**	**8**	**6**	**0**	**0**	**1**
BERRY, Brad — Defense									
1986	Winnipeg	3	0	0	0	0	0	0	0
1987	Winnipeg	7	0	1	1	14	0	0	0
1990	Winnipeg	1	0	0	0	0	0	0	0
1992	Minnesota	2	0	0	0	2	0	0	0
Playoff Totals		**13**	**0**	**1**	**1**	**16**	**0**	**0**	**0**
BERRY, Doug *No Playoffs* — Center									
BERRY, Fred *No Playoffs* — Center									
BERRY, Ken *No Playoffs* — Left wing									
•BERRY, Rick *No Playoffs* — Defense									
BERTRAND, Eric *No Playoffs* — Left wing									
•BERTUZZI, Todd — Center									
2001	Vancouver	4	2	2	4	8	0	0	0
2002	Vancouver	6	2	2	4	14	1	0	0
Playoff Totals		**10**	**4**	**4**	**8**	**22**	**1**	**0**	**0**
•BERUBE, Craig — Left wing									
1987	Philadelphia	5	0	0	0	17	0	0	0
1989	Philadelphia	16	0	0	0	56	0	0	0
1993	Calgary	6	0	1	1	21	0	0	0
1994	Washington	8	0	0	0	21	0	0	0
1995	Washington	7	0	0	0	29	0	0	0
1996	Washington	2	0	0	0	19	0	0	0
1998	Washington	21	1	0	1	21	0	0	1
1999	Philadelphia	6	1	0	1	4	0	0	0
2000	Philadelphia	18	1	0	1	23	0	0	1
Playoff Totals		**89**	**3**	**1**	**4**	**211**	**0**	**0**	**2**
BESLER, Phil *No Playoffs* — Right wing									
BESSONE, Pete *No Playoffs* — Defense									
BETHEL, John *No Playoffs* — Left wing									
BETIK, Karel *No Playoffs* — Defense									
BETS, Maxim *No Playoffs* — Left wing									
BETTIO, Sam *No Playoffs* — Left wing									
•BETTS, Blair *No Playoffs* — Center									
BEUKEBOOM, Jeff — Defense									
1986	Edmonton	1	0	0	0	4	0	0	0
1987♦	Edmonton	....	....	....	....	....	....	....	....
1988♦	Edmonton	7	0	0	0	16	0	0	0
1989	Edmonton	1	0	0	0	2	0	0	0
1990♦	Edmonton	2	0	0	0	0	0	0	0
1991	Edmonton	18	1	3	4	28	0	0	0
1992	NY Rangers	13	2	3	5	47	0	0	0
1994♦	NY Rangers	22	0	6	6	50	0	0	0
1995	NY Rangers	9	0	0	0	10	0	0	0
1996	NY Rangers	11	0	3	3	6	0	0	0
1997	NY Rangers	15	0	1	1	34	0	0	0
Playoff Totals		**99**	**3**	**16**	**19**	**197**	**0**	**0**	**0**
BEVERLEY, Nick — Defense									
1973	Boston	4	0	0	0	0	0	0	0
1975	NY Rangers	3	0	1	1	0	0	0	0
Playoff Totals		**7**	**0**	**1**	**1**	**0**	**0**	**0**	**0**
BIALOWAS, Dwight *No Playoffs* — Defense									
BIALOWAS, Frank *No Playoffs* — Left wing									
BIANCHIN, Wayne — Left wing									
1977	Pittsburgh	3	0	1	1	6	0	0	0
Playoff Totals		**3**	**0**	**1**	**1**	**6**	**0**	**0**	**0**
•BICANEK, Radim — Defense									
1997	Ottawa	7	0	0	0	8	0	0	0
Playoff Totals		**7**	**0**	**0**	**0**	**8**	**0**	**0**	**0**
•BICEK, Jiri *No Playoffs* — Left wing									
BIDNER, Todd *No Playoffs* — Left wing									
BIGGS, Don *No Playoffs* — Center									
BIGNELL, Larry — Defense									
1975	Pittsburgh	3	0	0	0	2	0	0	0
Playoff Totals		**3**	**0**	**0**	**0**	**2**	**0**	**0**	**0**
BILODEAU, Gilles *No Playoffs* — Left wing									

Season	Team	GP	G	A	Pts	PIM	PP	SH	GW
BIONDA, Jack — Defense									
1957	Boston	10	0	1	1	14	0	0	0
1959	Boston	1	0	0	0	0	0	0	0
Playoff Totals		**11**	**0**	**1**	**1**	**14**	**0**	**0**	**0**
•BIRON, Mathieu *No Playoffs* — Defense									
BISSETT, Tom *No Playoffs* — Center									
BJUGSTAD, Scott — Right wing									
1986	Minnesota	5	0	1	1	0	0	0	0
1990	Los Angeles	2	0	0	0	2	0	0	0
1991	Los Angeles	2	0	0	0	0	0	0	0
Playoff Totals		**9**	**0**	**1**	**1**	**2**	**0**	**0**	**0**
•BLACK, James — Left wing									
1996	Chicago	8	1	0	1	2	0	0	0
1997	Chicago	5	1	1	2	2	0	0	0
Playoff Totals		**13**	**2**	**1**	**3**	**4**	**0**	**0**	**0**
BLACK, Steve — Left wing									
1950♦	Detroit	13	0	0	0	13	0	0	0
Playoff Totals		**13**	**0**	**0**	**0**	**13**	**0**	**0**	**0**
BLACKBURN, Bob — Defense									
1970	Pittsburgh	6	0	0	0	4	0	0	0
Playoff Totals		**6**	**0**	**0**	**0**	**4**	**0**	**0**	**0**
BLACKBURN, Don — Left wing									
1968	Philadelphia	7	3	0	3	8	1	0	1
1969	Philadelphia	4	0	0	0	2	0	0	0
1970	NY Rangers	1	0	0	0	0	0	0	0
Playoff Totals		**12**	**3**	**0**	**3**	**10**	**1**	**0**	**1**
BLADE, Hank *No Playoffs* — Left wing									
BLADON, Tom — Defense									
1973	Philadelphia	11	0	4	4	2	0	0	0
1974♦	Philadelphia	16	4	6	10	25	3	0	1
1975♦	Philadelphia	13	1	3	4	12	1	0	0
1976	Philadelphia	16	2	6	8	14	1	0	0
1977	Philadelphia	10	1	3	4	4	0	0	0
1978	Philadelphia	12	0	2	2	11	0	0	0
1979	Pittsburgh	7	0	4	4	2	0	0	0
1980	Pittsburgh	1	0	1	1	0	0	0	0
Playoff Totals		**86**	**8**	**29**	**37**	**70**	**5**	**0**	**1**
BLAINE, Garry *No Playoffs* — Right wing									
BLAIR, Andy — Center									
1929	Toronto	4	*3	0	*3	2	....	....	....
1931	Toronto	2	1	0	1	0	....	....	....
1932♦	Toronto	7	2	2	4	6	....	....	....
1933	Toronto	9	0	2	2	4	....	....	....
1934	Toronto	5	0	2	2	16	....	....	....
1935	Toronto	2	0	0	0	2	....	....	....
1936	Toronto	9	0	0	0	2	....	....	....
Playoff Totals		**38**	**6**	**6**	**12**	**32**	....	....	....
BLAIR, Chuck *No Playoffs* — Right wing									
BLAIR, Dusty *No Playoffs* — Center									
BLAISDELL, Mike — Right wing									
1988	Toronto	6	1	2	3	10	0	0	0
Playoff Totals		**6**	**1**	**2**	**3**	**10**	**0**	**0**	**0**
BLAKE, Bob *No Playoffs* — Left wing									
•BLAKE, Jason — Center									
2000	Los Angeles	3	0	0	0	0	0	0	0
2002	NY Islanders	7	0	1	1	13	0	0	0
Playoff Totals		**10**	**0**	**1**	**1**	**13**	**0**	**0**	**0**
BLAKE, Mickey *No Playoffs* — Left wing/Defense									
•BLAKE, Rob — Defense									
1990	Los Angeles	8	1	3	4	4	1	0	0
1991	Los Angeles	12	1	4	5	26	1	0	0
1992	Los Angeles	6	2	1	3	12	0	0	0
1993	Los Angeles	23	4	6	10	46	1	1	0
1998	Los Angeles	4	0	0	0	6	0	0	0
2000	Los Angeles	4	0	2	2	4	0	0	0
2001♦	Colorado	23	6	13	19	16	3	0	0
2002	Colorado	20	6	6	12	16	1	0	0
Playoff Totals		**100**	**20**	**35**	**55**	**130**	**7**	**1**	**0**
BLAKE, Toe — Left wing									
1935♦	Mtl. Maroons	1	0	0	0	0	....	....	....
1937	Montreal	5	1	0	1	0	....	....	....
1938	Montreal	3	3	1	4	2	....	....	....
1939	Montreal	3	1	1	2	2	....	....	....
1941	Montreal	3	0	3	3	5	....	....	....
1942	Montreal	3	0	3	3	2	....	....	....
1943	Montreal	5	4	3	7	0	....	....	....
1944♦	Montreal	9	7	*11	*18	2	....	....	....
1945	Montreal	6	0	2	2	5	....	....	....
1946♦	Montreal	9	*7	6	13	5	....	....	....
1947	Montreal	11	2	*7	9	0	....	....	....
Playoff Totals		**58**	**25**	**37**	**62**	**23**	....	....	....
BLIGHT, Rick — Right wing									
1976	Vancouver	2	0	1	1	0	0	0	0
1979	Vancouver	3	0	4	4	2	0	0	0
Playoff Totals		**5**	**0**	**5**	**5**	**2**	**0**	**0**	**0**

Season	Team	GP	G	A	Pts	PIM	PP	SH	GW
BLINCO, Russ — Center									
1934	Mtl. Maroons	4	0	1	1	0	....	....	....
1935♦	Mtl. Maroons	7	2	2	4	2	....	....	....
1936	Mtl. Maroons	3	0	0	0	0	....	....	....
1937	Mtl. Maroons	5	1	0	1	2	....	....	....
Playoff Totals		**19**	**3**	**3**	**6**	**4**	....	....	....
BLOCK, Ken *No Playoffs* — Defense									
BLOEMBERG, Jeff — Defense									
1990	NY Rangers	7	0	3	3	5	0	0	0
Playoff Totals		**7**	**0**	**3**	**3**	**5**	**0**	**0**	**0**
BLOMQVIST, Timo — Defense									
1983	Washington	3	0	0	0	16	0	0	0
1984	Washington	8	0	0	0	8	0	0	0
1985	Washington	2	0	0	0	0	0	0	0
Playoff Totals		**13**	**0**	**0**	**0**	**24**	**0**	**0**	**0**
BLOMSTEN, Arto *No Playoffs* — Defense									
BLOOM, Mike *No Playoffs* — Left wing									
•BLOUIN, Sylvain *No Playoffs* — Left wing									
BLUM, John — Defense									
1984	Boston	3	0	0	0	4	0	0	0
1985	Boston	5	0	0	0	13	0	0	0
1986	Boston	3	0	0	0	6	0	0	0
1987	Washington	6	0	1	1	4	0	0	0
1988	Boston	3	0	1	1	0	0	0	0
Playoff Totals		**20**	**0**	**2**	**2**	**27**	**0**	**0**	**0**
BODAK, Bob *No Playoffs* — Left wing									
BODDY, Gregg — Defense									
1975	Vancouver	3	0	0	0	0	0	0	0
Playoff Totals		**3**	**0**	**0**	**0**	**0**	**0**	**0**	**0**
BODGER, Doug — Defense									
1989	Buffalo	5	1	1	2	11	1	0	0
1990	Buffalo	6	1	5	6	6	0	0	0
1991	Buffalo	4	0	1	1	0	0	0	0
1992	Buffalo	7	2	1	3	2	2	0	1
1993	Buffalo	8	2	3	5	0	2	0	0
1994	Buffalo	7	0	3	3	6	0	0	0
1995	Buffalo	5	0	4	4	0	0	0	0
1998	New Jersey	5	0	0	0	0	0	0	0
Playoff Totals		**47**	**6**	**18**	**24**	**25**	**5**	**0**	**1**
BODNAR, Gus — Center									
1944	Toronto	5	0	0	0	0	....	....	....
1945♦	Toronto	13	3	1	4	4	....	....	....
1947♦	Toronto	1	0	0	0	0	....	....	....
1953	Chicago	7	1	1	2	2	....	....	....
1954	Boston	1	0	0	0	0	....	....	....
1955	Boston	5	0	1	1	4	....	....	....
Playoff Totals		**32**	**4**	**3**	**7**	**10**	....	....	....
BOEHM, Ron *No Playoffs* — Left wing									
BOESCH, Garth — Defense									
1947♦	Toronto	11	0	2	2	6	....	....	....
1948♦	Toronto	8	2	1	3	2	....	....	....
1949♦	Toronto	9	0	2	2	6	....	....	....
1950	Toronto	6	0	0	0	4	....	....	....
Playoff Totals		**34**	**2**	**5**	**7**	**18**	....	....	....
•BOGUNIECKI, Eric — Center									
2002	St. Louis	1	0	1	1	0	0	0	0
Playoff Totals		**1**	**0**	**1**	**1**	**0**	**0**	**0**	**0**
BOH, Rick *No Playoffs* — Center									
•BOHONOS, Lonny — Right wing									
1999	Toronto	9	3	6	9	2	0	0	0
Playoff Totals		**9**	**3**	**6**	**9**	**2**	**0**	**0**	**0**
•BOIKOV, Alexandre *No Playoffs* — Defense									
BOILEAU, Marc *No Playoffs* — Center									
•BOILEAU, Patrick *No Playoffs* — Defense									
BOILEAU, Rene *No Playoffs* — Center									
BOIMISTRUCK, Fred *No Playoffs* — Defense									
BOISVERT, Serge — Right wing									
1985	Montreal	12	3	5	8	2	1	0	0
1986♦	Montreal	8	0	1	1	0	0	0	0
1988	Montreal	3	0	1	1	2	0	0	0
Playoff Totals		**23**	**3**	**7**	**10**	**4**	**1**	**0**	**0**
BOIVIN, Claude *No Playoffs* — Left wing									
BOIVIN, Leo — Defense									
1954	Toronto	5	0	0	0	2	0	0	0
1955	Boston	5	0	1	1	4	0	0	0
1957	Boston	10	2	3	5	12	0	0	0
1958	Boston	12	0	3	3	21	0	0	0
1959	Boston	7	1	2	3	4	0	0	0
1966	Detroit	12	0	1	1	16	0	0	0
1970	Minnesota	3	0	0	0	0	0	0	0
Playoff Totals		**54**	**3**	**10**	**13**	**59**	**0**	**0**	**0**
BOLAND, Mike *No Playoffs* — Right wing									
BOLAND, Mike J. — Defense									
1979	Buffalo	3	1	0	1	2	0	0	0
Playoff Totals		**3**	**1**	**0**	**1**	**2**	**0**	**0**	**0**

Season	Team	GP	G	A	Pts	PIM	PP	SH	GW
BOLDIREV, Ivan	Center								
1975	Chicago	8	4	2	6	2	1	0	1
1976	Chicago	4	0	1	1	0	0	0	0
1977	Chicago	2	0	1	1	0	0	0	0
1978	Chicago	4	0	2	2	2	0	0	0
1979	Atlanta	2	0	2	2	2	0	0	0
1980	Vancouver	4	0	2	2	0	0	0	0
1981	Vancouver	1	1	1	2	0	0	0	0
1982	Vancouver	17	8	3	11	4	3	0	1
1984	Detroit	4	0	5	5	4	0	0	0
1985	Detroit	2	0	1	1	0	0	0	0
Playoff Totals		**48**	**13**	**20**	**33**	**14**	**4**	**0**	**2**
BOLDUC, Danny	Left wing								
1984	Calgary	1	0	0	0	0	0	0	0
Playoff Totals		**1**	**0**	**0**	**0**	**0**	**0**	**0**	**0**
BOLDUC, Michel *No Playoffs*	Defense								
BOLL, Buzz	Left wing								
1933	Toronto	1	0	0	0	0	....	....	....
1934	Toronto	5	0	0	0	9	....	....	....
1935	Toronto	6	0	0	0	0	....	....	....
1936	Toronto	9	*7	3	*10	2	....	....	....
1937	Toronto	2	0	0	0	0	....	....	....
1938	Toronto	7	0	0	0	2	....	....	....
1940	NY Americans	1	0	0	0	0	....	....	....
Playoff Totals		**31**	**7**	**3**	**10**	**13**	....	....	....
BOLONCHUK, Larry *No Playoffs*	Defense								
BOLTON, Hugh	Defense								
1951♦	Toronto	....	....	....	....	....	....	....	....
1952	Toronto	3	0	0	0	4	0	0	0
1954	Toronto	5	0	1	1	4	0	0	0
1955	Toronto	4	0	3	3	6	0	0	0
1956	Toronto	5	0	1	1	0	0	0	0
Playoff Totals		**17**	**0**	**5**	**5**	**14**	**0**	**0**	**0**
•BOMBARDIR, Brad	Defense								
1999	New Jersey	5	0	0	0	0	0	0	0
2000♦	New Jersey	1	0	0	0	0	0	0	0
Playoff Totals		**6**	**0**	**0**	**0**	**0**	**0**	**0**	**0**
BONAR, Dan	Center								
1981	Los Angeles	4	1	1	2	11	0	1	0
1982	Los Angeles	10	2	3	5	11	0	0	0
Playoff Totals		**14**	**3**	**4**	**7**	**22**	**0**	**1**	**0**
•BONDRA, Peter	Right wing								
1991	Washington	4	0	1	1	2	0	0	0
1992	Washington	7	6	2	8	4	1	0	0
1993	Washington	6	0	6	6	0	0	0	0
1994	Washington	9	2	4	6	4	0	0	1
1995	Washington	7	5	3	8	10	2	0	1
1996	Washington	6	3	2	5	8	2	0	1
1998	Washington	17	7	5	12	12	3	0	2
2000	Washington	5	1	1	2	4	1	0	0
2001	Washington	6	2	0	2	2	2	0	1
Playoff Totals		**67**	**26**	**24**	**50**	**46**	**11**	**0**	**6**
•BONIN, Brian	Center								
1999	Pittsburgh	3	0	0	0	0	0	0	0
Playoff Totals		**3**	**0**	**0**	**0**	**0**	**0**	**0**	**0**
BONIN, Marcel	Wing								
1953	Detroit	5	0	1	1	0	0	0	0
1955♦	Detroit	11	0	2	2	4	0	0	0
1958♦	Montreal	9	0	1	1	2	0	0	0
1959♦	Montreal	11	*10	5	15	4	4	0	3
1960♦	Montreal	8	1	4	5	12	0	0	0
1961	Montreal	6	0	1	1	29	0	0	0
Playoff Totals		**50**	**11**	**14**	**25**	**51**	**4**	**0**	**3**
•BONK, Radek	Center								
1997	Ottawa	7	0	1	1	4	0	0	0
1998	Ottawa	5	0	0	0	2	0	0	0
1999	Ottawa	4	0	0	0	6	0	0	0
2000	Ottawa	6	0	0	0	8	0	0	0
2001	Ottawa	2	0	0	0	2	0	0	0
2002	Ottawa	12	3	7	10	6	2	0	1
Playoff Totals		**36**	**3**	**8**	**11**	**28**	**2**	**0**	**1**
•BONNI, Ryan *No Playoffs*	Defense								
BONSIGNORE, Jason *No Playoffs*	Center								
•BONVIE, Dennis	Right wing/Defense								
2002	Boston	1	0	0	0	0	0	0	0
Playoff Totals		**1**	**0**	**0**	**0**	**0**	**0**	**0**	**0**
BOO, Jim *No Playoffs*	Defense								
BOONE, Buddy	Right wing								
1957	Boston	10	1	0	1	12	0	0	0
1958	Boston	12	1	1	2	13	0	0	0
Playoff Totals		**22**	**2**	**1**	**3**	**25**	**0**	**0**	**0**
BOOTHMAN, George	Center/Defense								
1944	Toronto	5	2	1	3	2	....	....	....
Playoff Totals		**5**	**2**	**1**	**3**	**2**	....	....	....

Season	Team	GP	G	A	Pts	PIM	PP	SH	GW
BORDELEAU, Christian	Center								
1969♦	Montreal	6	1	0	1	0	0	0	1
1971	St. Louis	5	0	1	1	17	0	0	0
1972	Chicago	8	3	6	9	0	0	0	1
Playoff Totals		**19**	**4**	**7**	**11**	**17**	**0**	**0**	**2**
BORDELEAU, J.P.	Right wing								
1970	Chicago	1	0	0	0	0	0	0	0
1973	Chicago	14	1	0	1	4	1	0	0
1974	Chicago	11	0	2	2	2	0	0	0
1975	Chicago	7	2	2	4	2	0	0	0
1976	Chicago	4	0	0	0	0	0	0	0
1977	Chicago	2	0	0	0	2	0	0	0
1978	Chicago	4	0	1	1	0	0	0	0
1979	Chicago	4	0	1	1	2	0	0	0
1980	Chicago	1	0	0	0	0	0	0	0
Playoff Totals		**48**	**3**	**6**	**9**	**12**	**1**	**0**	**0**
BORDELEAU, Paulin	Right wing								
1975	Vancouver	5	2	1	3	0	1	0	0
Playoff Totals		**5**	**2**	**1**	**3**	**0**	**1**	**0**	**0**
•BORDELEAU, Sebastien	Center								
1998	Montreal	5	0	0	0	2	0	0	0
Playoff Totals		**5**	**0**	**0**	**0**	**2**	**0**	**0**	**0**
BOROTSIK, Jack *No Playoffs*	Center								
BORSATO, Luciano	Center								
1992	Winnipeg	1	0	0	0	0	0	0	0
1993	Winnipeg	6	1	0	1	4	0	1	0
Playoff Totals		**7**	**1**	**0**	**1**	**4**	**0**	**1**	**0**
BORSCHEVSKY, Nikolai	Right wing								
1993	Toronto	16	2	7	9	0	0	0	1
1994	Toronto	15	2	2	4	4	1	0	0
Playoff Totals		**31**	**4**	**9**	**13**	**4**	**1**	**0**	**1**
BOSCHMAN, Laurie	Center								
1980	Toronto	3	1	1	2	18	1	0	0
1981	Toronto	3	0	0	0	7	0	0	0
1982	Edmonton	3	0	1	1	4	0	0	0
1983	Winnipeg	3	0	1	1	12	0	0	0
1984	Winnipeg	3	0	1	1	5	0	0	0
1985	Winnipeg	8	2	1	3	21	0	1	0
1986	Winnipeg	3	0	1	1	6	0	0	0
1987	Winnipeg	10	2	3	5	32	1	0	0
1988	Winnipeg	5	1	3	4	9	0	0	0
1990	Winnipeg	2	0	0	0	2	0	0	0
1991	New Jersey	7	1	1	2	16	0	0	0
1992	New Jersey	7	1	0	1	8	0	0	1
Playoff Totals		**57**	**8**	**13**	**21**	**140**	**2**	**1**	**1**
BOSSY, Mike	Right wing								
1978	NY Islanders	7	2	2	4	2	0	0	1
1979	NY Islanders	10	6	2	8	2	2	0	1
1980♦	NY Islanders	16	10	13	23	8	6	0	1
1981♦	NY Islanders	18	*17	*18	*35	4	9	0	3
1982♦	NY Islanders	19	*17	10	27	0	6	0	3
1983♦	NY Islanders	19	*17	9	26	10	6	0	5
1984	NY Islanders	21	8	10	18	4	2	0	3
1985	NY Islanders	10	5	6	11	4	2	0	0
1986	NY Islanders	3	1	2	3	4	0	0	0
1987	NY Islanders	6	2	3	5	0	2	0	0
Playoff Totals		**129**	**85**	**75**	**160**	**38**	**35**	**0**	**17**
BOSTROM, Helge	Defense								
1930	Chicago	2	0	0	0	0	0	0	0
1931	Chicago	9	0	0	0	16	0	0	0
1932	Chicago	2	0	0	0	0	0	0	0
Playoff Totals		**13**	**0**	**0**	**0**	**16**	**0**	**0**	**0**
BOTELL, Mark *No Playoffs*	Defense								
BOTHWELL, Tim	Defense								
1980	NY Rangers	9	0	0	0	8	0	0	0
1984	St. Louis	11	0	2	2	14	0	0	0
1985	St. Louis	3	0	0	0	2	0	0	0
1986	Hartford	10	0	0	0	8	0	0	0
1987	St. Louis	6	0	0	0	6	0	0	0
1988	St. Louis	10	0	1	1	18	0	0	0
Playoff Totals		**49**	**0**	**3**	**3**	**56**	**0**	**0**	**0**
•BOTTERILL, Jason *No Playoffs*	Left wing								
BOTTING, Cam *No Playoffs*	Right wing								
BOUCHA, Henry *No Playoffs*	Center								
BOUCHARD, Butch	Defense								
1942	Montreal	3	1	1	2	0	....	....	....
1943	Montreal	5	0	1	1	4	....	....	....
1944♦	Montreal	9	1	3	4	4	....	....	....
1945	Montreal	6	3	4	7	4	....	....	....
1946♦	Montreal	9	2	1	3	17	....	....	....
1947	Montreal	11	0	3	3	21	....	....	....
1949	Montreal	7	0	0	0	6	....	....	....
1950	Montreal	5	0	2	2	2	....	....	....
1951	Montreal	11	1	1	2	2	....	....	....
1952	Montreal	11	0	2	2	14	....	....	....
1953♦	Montreal	12	1	1	2	6	....	....	....
1954	Montreal	11	2	1	3	4	....	....	....
1955	Montreal	12	0	1	1	37	....	....	....
1956♦	Montreal	1	0	0	0	0	....	....	....
Playoff Totals		**113**	**11**	**21**	**32**	**121**	....	....	....

Season	Team	GP	G	A	Pts	PIM	PP	SH	GW
BOUCHARD, Dick *No Playoffs*	Right wing								
BOUCHARD, Edmond *No Playoffs*	Left wing/Defense								
•BOUCHARD, Joel *No Playoffs*	Defense								
BOUCHARD, Pierre	Defense								
1971♦	Montreal	13	0	1	1	10	0	0	0
1972	Montreal	1	0	0	0	0	0	0	0
1973♦	Montreal	17	1	3	4	13	0	0	0
1974	Montreal	6	0	2	2	4	0	0	0
1975	Montreal	10	0	2	2	10	0	0	0
1976♦	Montreal	13	2	0	2	8	1	0	1
1977♦	Montreal	6	0	1	1	6	0	0	0
1978♦	Montreal	10	0	1	1	5	0	0	0
Playoff Totals		**76**	**3**	**10**	**13**	**56**	**1**	**0**	**1**
•BOUCHARD, Pierre-Marc *No Playoffs*	Center								
BOUCHER, Billy	Right wing								
1923	Montreal	2	1	0	1	2	....	....	....
1924♦	Montreal	2	1	0	1	9	....	....	....
1925	Montreal	2	1	0	1	4	....	....	....
1927	Boston	8	0	0	0	2	....	....	....
Playoff Totals		**14**	**3**	**0**	**3**	**17**	....	....	....
BOUCHER, Bobby	Center								
1924♦	Montreal	2	0	0	0	0	0	0	0
Playoff Totals		**2**	**0**	**0**	**0**	**0**	**0**	**0**	**0**
BOUCHER, Clarence *No Playoffs*	Defense								
BOUCHER, Frank	Center								
1922	Ottawa	1	0	0	0	0	....	....	....
1927	NY Rangers	2	0	0	0	4	....	....	....
1928♦	NY Rangers	9	*7	3	*10	2	....	....	....
1929	NY Rangers	6	1	0	1	0	....	....	....
1930	NY Rangers	3	1	1	2	0	....	....	....
1931	NY Rangers	4	0	2	2	0	....	....	....
1932	NY Rangers	7	3	*6	*9	0	....	....	....
1933♦	NY Rangers	8	2	2	4	6	....	....	....
1934	NY Rangers	2	0	0	0	0	....	....	....
1935	NY Rangers	4	0	3	3	0	....	....	....
1937	NY Rangers	9	2	3	5	0	....	....	....
Playoff Totals		**55**	**16**	**20**	**36**	**12**	....	....	....
BOUCHER, Georges	Defense								
1919	Ottawa	5	2	0	2	9	....	....	....
1920♦	Ottawa	....	....	....	....	....	....	....	....
1921♦	Ottawa	2	3	0	3	10	....	....	....
1922	Ottawa	2	0	0	0	4	....	....	....
1923♦	Ottawa	2	0	1	1	2	....	....	....
1924	Ottawa	2	0	1	1	4	....	....	....
1926	Ottawa	2	0	0	0	10	....	....	....
1927♦	Ottawa	6	0	0	0	43	....	....	....
1928	Ottawa	2	0	0	0	4	....	....	....
1930	Mtl. Maroons	3	0	0	0	2	....	....	....
1932	Chicago	2	0	1	1	0	....	....	....
Playoff Totals		**28**	**5**	**3**	**8**	**88**	....	....	....
•BOUCHER, Philippe	Defense								
1994	Buffalo	7	1	1	2	2	1	0	0
2001	Los Angeles	13	0	1	1	2	0	0	0
2002	Los Angeles	5	0	1	1	2	0	0	0
Playoff Totals		**25**	**1**	**3**	**4**	**6**	**1**	**0**	**0**
•BOUCK, Tyler	Right wing								
2001	Dallas	1	0	0	0	0	0	0	0
Playoff Totals		**1**	**0**	**0**	**0**	**0**	**0**	**0**	**0**
BOUDREAU, Bruce	Center								
1977	Toronto	3	0	0	0	0	0	0	0
1981	Toronto	2	1	0	1	0	0	0	0
1983	Toronto	4	1	0	1	0	0	0	0
Playoff Totals		**9**	**2**	**0**	**2**	**0**	**0**	**0**	**0**
BOUDRIAS, Andre	Left wing								
1968	Minnesota	14	3	6	9	8	0	0	1
1970	St. Louis	14	2	4	6	4	1	0	0
1975	Vancouver	5	1	0	1	0	0	0	0
1976	Vancouver	1	0	0	0	0	0	0	0
Playoff Totals		**34**	**6**	**10**	**16**	**12**	**1**	**0**	**1**
BOUGHNER, Barry *No Playoffs*	Left wing								
•BOUGHNER, Bob	Defense								
1997	Buffalo	11	0	1	1	9	0	0	0
1998	Buffalo	14	0	4	4	15	0	0	0
2000	Pittsburgh	11	0	2	2	15	0	0	0
2001	Pittsburgh	18	0	1	1	22	0	0	0
Playoff Totals		**54**	**0**	**8**	**8**	**61**	**0**	**0**	**0**
•BOUILLON, Francis *No Playoffs*	Defense								
•BOULERICE, Jesse *No Playoffs*	Right wing								
•BOULTON, Eric *No Playoffs*	Left wing								
•BOUMEDIENNE, Josef *No Playoffs*	Defense								
BOURBONNAIS, Dan *No Playoffs*	Left wing								
BOURBONNAIS, Rick	Right wing								
1977	St. Louis	4	0	1	1	0	0	0	0
Playoff Totals		**4**	**0**	**1**	**1**	**0**	**0**	**0**	**0**
BOURCIER, Conrad *No Playoffs*	Center								
BOURCIER, Jean *No Playoffs*	Left wing								

Season	Team	GP	G	A	Pts	PIM	PP	SH	GW
BOURGEAULT, Leo	Defense								
1927	NY Rangers	2	0	0	0	4	....	....	....
1928♦	NY Rangers	9	0	0	0	8	....	....	....
1929	NY Rangers	6	0	0	0	0	....	....	....
1930	NY Rangers	3	1	1	2	6	....	....	....
1933	Montreal	2	0	0	0	0	....	....	....
1934	Montreal	2	0	0	0	0	....	....	....
Playoff Totals		**24**	**1**	**1**	**2**	**18**	....	....	....
BOURGEOIS, Charlie	Defense								
1982	Calgary	3	0	0	0	7	0	0	0
1984	Calgary	8	0	1	1	27	0	0	0
1985	Calgary	4	0	0	0	17	0	0	0
1986	St. Louis	19	2	2	4	116	1	0	0
1987	St. Louis	6	0	0	0	27	0	0	0
Playoff Totals		**40**	**2**	**3**	**5**	**194**	**1**	**0**	**0**
BOURNE, Bob	Center								
1975	NY Islanders	9	1	2	3	4	1	0	0
1977	NY Islanders	8	2	0	2	4	0	0	0
1978	NY Islanders	7	2	3	5	2	1	0	0
1979	NY Islanders	10	1	3	4	6	0	0	0
1980♦	NY Islanders	21	10	10	20	10	5	2	1
1981♦	NY Islanders	14	4	6	10	19	1	1	1
1982♦	NY Islanders	19	9	7	16	36	3	1	0
1983♦	NY Islanders	20	8	20	28	14	0	1	2
1984	NY Islanders	8	1	1	2	7	0	0	1
1985	NY Islanders	10	0	2	2	6	0	0	0
1986	NY Islanders	3	0	0	0	0	0	0	0
1987	Los Angeles	5	2	1	3	0	0	0	0
1988	Los Angeles	5	0	1	1	0	0	0	0
Playoff Totals		**139**	**40**	**56**	**96**	**108**	**11**	**5**	**5**
BOURQUE, Phil	Left wing								
1989	Pittsburgh	11	4	1	5	66	0	0	1
1991♦	Pittsburgh	24	6	7	13	16	0	0	0
1992♦	Pittsburgh	21	3	4	7	25	2	0	0
Playoff Totals		**56**	**13**	**12**	**25**	**107**	**2**	**0**	**1**
BOURQUE, Raymond	Defense								
1980	Boston	10	2	9	11	27	0	0	0
1981	Boston	3	0	1	1	2	0	0	0
1982	Boston	9	1	5	6	16	0	0	1
1983	Boston	17	8	15	23	10	2	0	1
1984	Boston	3	0	2	2	0	0	0	0
1985	Boston	5	0	3	3	4	0	0	0
1986	Boston	3	0	0	0	0	0	0	0
1987	Boston	4	1	2	3	0	0	0	0
1988	Boston	23	3	18	21	26	0	0	1
1989	Boston	10	0	4	4	6	0	0	0
1990	Boston	17	5	12	17	16	1	0	0
1991	Boston	19	7	18	25	12	3	0	0
1992	Boston	12	3	6	9	12	2	0	0
1993	Boston	4	1	0	1	2	1	0	0
1994	Boston	13	2	8	10	0	1	0	0
1995	Boston	5	0	3	3	0	0	0	0
1996	Boston	5	1	6	7	2	1	0	0
1998	Boston	6	1	4	5	2	1	0	0
1999	Boston	12	1	9	10	14	0	0	0
2000	Colorado	13	1	8	9	8	0	0	0
2001♦	Colorado	21	4	6	10	12	3	0	1
Playoff Totals		**214**	**41**	**139**	**180**	**171**	**15**	**0**	**4**
BOUTETTE, Pat	Center/Right wing								
1976	Toronto	10	1	4	5	16	0	0	0
1977	Toronto	9	0	4	4	17	0	0	0
1978	Toronto	13	3	3	6	40	0	0	0
1979	Toronto	6	2	2	4	22	0	0	0
1980	Hartford	3	1	0	1	6	0	1	0
1982	Pittsburgh	5	3	1	4	8	2	0	0
Playoff Totals		**46**	**10**	**14**	**24**	**109**	**2**	**1**	**0**
BOUTILIER, Paul	Defense								
1983♦	NY Islanders	2	0	0	0	2	0	0	0
1984	NY Islanders	21	1	7	8	10	0	0	1
1985	NY Islanders	10	0	2	2	16	0	0	0
1986	NY Islanders	3	0	0	0	2	0	0	0
1988	Winnipeg	5	0	0	0	15	0	0	0
Playoff Totals		**41**	**1**	**9**	**10**	**45**	**0**	**0**	**1**
•BOUWMEESTER, Jay *No Playoffs*	Defense								
BOWEN, Jason *No Playoffs*	Defense								
•BOWLER, Bill *No Playoffs*	Center								
BOWMAN, Kirk	Left wing								
1977	Chicago	2	1	0	1	0	1	0	0
1978	Chicago	3	0	0	0	0	0	0	0
1979	Chicago	2	0	0	0	0	0	0	0
Playoff Totals		**7**	**1**	**0**	**1**	**0**	**1**	**0**	**0**
BOWMAN, Ralph	Defense								
1936♦	Detroit	7	2	1	3	2	....	....	....
1937♦	Detroit	10	0	1	1	4	....	....	....
1939	Detroit	5	0	0	0	0	....	....	....
Playoff Totals		**22**	**2**	**2**	**4**	**6**	....	....	....
BOWNASS, Jack *No Playoffs*	Defense								

Season	Team	GP	G	A	Pts	PIM	PP	SH	GW
BOWNESS, Rick	Right wing								
1978	Detroit	4	0	0	0	2	0	0	0
1982	Winnipeg	1	0	0	0	0	0	0	0
Playoff Totals		**5**	**0**	**0**	**0**	**2**	**0**	**0**	**0**
BOYD, Bill	Right wing								
1928♦	NY Rangers	9	0	0	0	4	0	0	0
1929	NY Rangers	1	0	0	0	0	0	0	0
Playoff Totals		**10**	**0**	**0**	**0**	**4**	**0**	**0**	**0**
BOYD, Irvin	Right wing								
1943	Boston	5	0	1	1	4	0	0	0
Playoff Totals		**5**	**0**	**1**	**1**	**4**	**0**	**0**	**0**
BOYD, Randy	Defense								
1982	Pittsburgh	3	0	0	0	11	0	0	0
1985	Chicago	3	0	1	1	7	0	0	0
1986	NY Islanders	3	0	0	0	2	0	0	0
1987	NY Islanders	4	0	1	1	6	0	0	0
Playoff Totals		**13**	**0**	**2**	**2**	**26**	**0**	**0**	**0**
BOYER, Wally	Center								
1966	Toronto	4	0	1	1	0	0	0	0
1967	Chicago	1	0	0	0	0	0	0	0
1970	Pittsburgh	10	1	2	3	0	0	1	0
Playoff Totals		**15**	**1**	**3**	**4**	**0**	**0**	**1**	**0**
BOYER, Zac	Right wing								
1995	Dallas	2	0	0	0	0	0	0	0
Playoff Totals		**2**	**0**	**0**	**0**	**0**	**0**	**0**	**0**
BOYKO, Darren *No Playoffs*	Center								
•BOYLE, Dan *No Playoffs*	Defense								
•BOYNTON, Nick	Defense								
2002	Boston	6	1	2	3	8	0	0	0
Playoff Totals		**6**	**1**	**2**	**3**	**8**	**0**	**0**	**0**
BOZEK, Steve	Left wing								
1982	Los Angeles	10	4	1	5	6	2	0	1
1984	Calgary	10	3	1	4	15	1	0	0
1985	Calgary	3	1	0	1	4	1	0	0
1986	Calgary	14	2	6	8	32	0	0	0
1987	Calgary	4	1	0	1	2	0	0	0
1988	St. Louis	7	1	1	2	6	0	0	0
1989	Vancouver	7	0	2	2	4	0	0	0
1991	Vancouver	3	0	0	0	0	0	0	0
Playoff Totals		**58**	**12**	**11**	**23**	**69**	**4**	**0**	**1**
BOZON, Philippe	Left wing								
1992	St. Louis	6	1	0	1	27	0	0	0
1993	St. Louis	9	1	0	1	0	0	0	0
1994	St. Louis	4	0	0	0	4	0	0	0
Playoff Totals		**19**	**2**	**0**	**2**	**31**	**0**	**0**	**0**
BRACKENBOROUGH, John *No Playoffs*	Left wing/Center								
BRACKENBURY, Curt	Right wing								
1981	Edmonton	2	0	0	0	0	0	0	0
Playoff Totals		**2**	**0**	**0**	**0**	**0**	**0**	**0**	**0**
BRADLEY, Bart *No Playoffs*	Center								
BRADLEY, Brian	Center								
1986	Calgary	1	0	0	0	0	0	0	0
1989	Vancouver	7	3	4	7	10	1	0	0
1996	Tampa Bay	5	0	3	3	6	0	0	0
Playoff Totals		**13**	**3**	**7**	**10**	**16**	**1**	**0**	**0**
BRADLEY, Lyle *No Playoffs*	Center/Right wing								
•BRADLEY, Matt	Right wing								
2002	San Jose	10	0	0	0	0	0	0	0
Playoff Totals		**10**	**0**	**0**	**0**	**0**	**0**	**0**	**0**
BRADY, Neil *No Playoffs*	Center								
BRAGNALO, Rick *No Playoffs*	Center								
BRANIGAN, Andy *No Playoffs*	Defense								
BRASAR, Per-Olov	Left wing								
1980	Vancouver	4	1	2	3	0	0	0	1
1981	Vancouver	3	0	0	0	0	0	0	0
1982	Vancouver	6	0	0	0	0	0	0	0
Playoff Totals		**13**	**1**	**2**	**3**	**0**	**0**	**0**	**1**
•BRASHEAR, Donald	Left wing								
1994	Montreal	2	0	0	0	0	0	0	0
1996	Montreal	6	0	0	0	2	0	0	0
2001	Vancouver	4	0	0	0	0	0	0	0
2002	Philadelphia	5	0	0	0	19	0	0	0
Playoff Totals		**17**	**0**	**0**	**0**	**21**	**0**	**0**	**0**
BRAYSHAW, Russ *No Playoffs*	Left wing								
BREAULT, Francois *No Playoffs*	Right wing								
BREITENBACH, Ken	Defense								
1976	Buffalo	1	0	0	0	0	0	0	0
1977	Buffalo	4	0	0	0	0	0	0	0
1979	Buffalo	3	0	1	1	4	0	0	0
Playoff Totals		**8**	**0**	**1**	**1**	**4**	**0**	**0**	**0**
•BRENDL, Pavel	Right wing								
2002	Philadelphia	2	0	0	0	0	0	0	0
Playoff Totals		**2**	**0**	**0**	**0**	**0**	**0**	**0**	**0**
BRENNAN, Dan *No Playoffs*	Left wing								

Season	Team	GP	G	A	Pts	PIM	PP	SH	GW
BRENNAN, Doug	Defense								
1932	NY Rangers	7	1	0	1	10	....	....	....
1933♦	NY Rangers	8	0	0	0	11	....	....	....
1934	NY Rangers	1	0	0	0	0	....	....	....
Playoff Totals		**16**	**1**	**0**	**1**	**21**	....	....	....
•BRENNAN, Kip *No Playoffs*	Left wing								
•BRENNAN, Rich *No Playoffs*	Defense								
BRENNAN, Tom *No Playoffs*	Right wing								
BRENNEMAN, John *No Playoffs*	Left wing								
BRETTO, Joe *No Playoffs*	Defense								
BREWER, Carl	Defense								
1959	Toronto	12	0	6	6	*40	0	0	0
1960	Toronto	10	2	3	5	16	0	0	0
1961	Toronto	5	0	0	0	4	0	0	0
1962♦	Toronto	8	0	2	2	22	0	0	0
1963♦	Toronto	10	0	1	1	12	0	0	0
1964♦	Toronto	12	0	1	1	30	0	0	0
1965	Toronto	6	1	2	3	12	0	0	0
1970	Detroit	4	0	0	0	2	0	0	0
1971	St. Louis	5	0	2	2	8	0	0	0
Playoff Totals		**72**	**3**	**17**	**20**	**146**	**0**	**0**	**0**
•BREWER, Eric	Defense								
2001	Edmonton	6	1	5	6	2	1	0	0
Playoff Totals		**6**	**1**	**5**	**6**	**2**	**1**	**0**	**0**
BRICKLEY, Andy	Left wing/Center								
1988	New Jersey	4	0	1	1	4	0	0	0
1989	Boston	10	0	2	2	0	0	0	0
1990	Boston	2	0	0	0	0	0	0	0
1993	Winnipeg	1	1	1	2	0	0	0	0
Playoff Totals		**17**	**1**	**4**	**5**	**4**	**0**	**0**	**0**
BRIDEN, Archie *No Playoffs*	Left wing								
BRIDGMAN, Mel	Center								
1976	Philadelphia	16	6	8	14	31	0	0	2
1977	Philadelphia	7	1	0	1	8	0	1	0
1978	Philadelphia	12	1	7	8	36	0	0	1
1979	Philadelphia	8	1	2	3	17	0	0	0
1980	Philadelphia	19	2	9	11	70	0	0	0
1981	Philadelphia	12	2	4	6	39	0	0	0
1982	Calgary	3	2	0	2	14	0	0	0
1983	Calgary	9	3	4	7	33	2	0	0
1987	Detroit	16	5	2	7	28	0	1	1
1988	Detroit	16	4	1	5	12	0	0	0
1989	Vancouver	7	1	2	3	10	1	0	0
Playoff Totals		**125**	**28**	**39**	**67**	**298**	**3**	**2**	**4**
•BRIERE, Daniel	Center								
2000	Phoenix	1	0	0	0	0	0	0	0
2002	Phoenix	5	2	1	3	2	1	0	1
Playoff Totals		**6**	**2**	**1**	**3**	**2**	**1**	**0**	**1**
BRIERE, Michel	Center								
1970	Pittsburgh	10	5	3	8	17	1	3	0
Playoff Totals		**10**	**5**	**3**	**8**	**17**	**1**	**3**	**0**
•BRIGLEY, Travis *No Playoffs*	Left wing								
•BRIMANIS, Aris *No Playoffs*	Defense								
•BRIND'AMOUR, Rod	Center								
1989	St. Louis	5	2	0	2	4	0	0	0
1990	St. Louis	12	5	8	13	6	1	0	0
1991	St. Louis	13	2	5	7	10	1	0	0
1995	Philadelphia	15	6	9	15	8	2	1	1
1996	Philadelphia	12	2	5	7	6	1	0	0
1997	Philadelphia	19	*13	8	21	10	4	2	1
1998	Philadelphia	5	2	2	4	7	0	0	0
1999	Philadelphia	6	1	3	4	0	0	0	0
2001	Carolina	6	1	3	4	6	0	0	1
2002	Carolina	23	4	8	12	16	2	1	1
Playoff Totals		**116**	**38**	**51**	**89**	**73**	**11**	**4**	**4**
BRINDLEY, Doug *No Playoffs*	Left wing/Center								
BRINK, Milt *No Playoffs*	Center								
•BRISEBOIS, Patrice	Defense								
1992	Montreal	11	2	4	6	6	1	0	1
1993♦	Montreal	20	0	4	4	18	0	0	0
1994	Montreal	7	0	4	4	6	0	0	0
1996	Montreal	6	1	2	3	6	0	0	0
1997	Montreal	3	1	1	2	24	0	0	1
1998	Montreal	10	1	0	1	0	0	0	0
2002	Montreal	10	1	1	2	2	0	0	0
Playoff Totals		**67**	**6**	**16**	**22**	**62**	**1**	**0**	**2**
BRISSON, Gerry *No Playoffs*	Right wing								
BRITZ, Greg *No Playoffs*	Right wing								

Season	Team	GP	G	A	Pts	PIM	PP	SH	GW
BROADBENT, Punch									Right wing
1919	Ottawa	5	2	1	3	*18	....	....	....
1920♦	Ottawa	....	....	....	....	....	....	....	....
1921♦	Ottawa	2	0	2	2	4	....	....	....
1922	Ottawa	2	0	1	1	8	....	....	....
1923♦	Ottawa	2	0	0	0	2	....	....	....
1924	Ottawa	2	0	0	0	2	....	....	....
1926♦	Mtl. Maroons	4	2	1	3	14	....	....	....
1927	Mtl. Maroons	2	0	0	0	0	....	....	....
1928	Ottawa	2	0	0	0	0	....	....	....
1929	NY Americans	2	0	0	0	2	....	....	....
Playoff Totals		**23**	**4**	**5**	**9**	**50**	....	....	....
BROCHU, Stephane	*No Playoffs*								Defense
BRODEN, Connie									Center
1957♦	Montreal	6	0	1	1	0	0	0	0
1958♦	Montreal	1	0	0	0	0	0	0	0
Playoff Totals		**7**	**0**	**1**	**1**	**0**	**0**	**0**	**0**
BROOKE, Bob									Center
1984	NY Rangers	5	0	0	0	7	0	0	0
1985	NY Rangers	3	0	0	0	8	0	0	0
1986	NY Rangers	16	6	9	15	28	0	2	2
1989	Minnesota	5	3	0	3	2	0	0	0
1990	New Jersey	5	0	0	0	14	0	0	0
Playoff Totals		**34**	**9**	**9**	**18**	**59**	**0**	**2**	**2**
BROOKS, Gord	*No Playoffs*								Right wing
BROPHY, Bernie									Left wing
1926♦	Mtl. Maroons	....	....	....	....	....	....	....	....
1929	Detroit	2	0	0	0	2	0	0	0
Playoff Totals		**2**	**0**	**0**	**0**	**2**	**0**	**0**	**0**
BROSSART, Willie									Defense
1974	Toronto	1	0	0	0	0	0	0	0
Playoff Totals		**1**	**0**	**0**	**0**	**0**	**0**	**0**	**0**
BROTEN, Aaron									Left wing/Center
1988	New Jersey	20	5	11	16	20	3	0	1
1990	Minnesota	7	0	5	5	8	0	0	0
1992	Winnipeg	7	2	2	4	12	0	0	0
Playoff Totals		**34**	**7**	**18**	**25**	**40**	**3**	**0**	**1**
BROTEN, Neal									Center
1981	Minnesota	19	1	7	8	9	0	0	1
1982	Minnesota	4	0	2	2	0	0	0	0
1983	Minnesota	9	1	6	7	10	1	0	0
1984	Minnesota	16	5	5	10	4	2	0	1
1985	Minnesota	9	2	5	7	10	0	0	0
1986	Minnesota	5	3	2	5	2	1	0	0
1989	Minnesota	5	2	2	4	4	1	1	0
1990	Minnesota	7	2	2	4	18	1	0	0
1991	Minnesota	23	9	13	22	6	2	1	0
1992	Minnesota	7	1	5	6	2	0	0	0
1994	Dallas	9	2	1	3	6	0	0	1
1995♦	New Jersey	20	7	12	19	6	1	0	4
1997	Dallas	2	0	1	1	0	0	0	0
Playoff Totals		**135**	**35**	**63**	**98**	**77**	**9**	**2**	**7**
BROTEN, Paul									Right wing
1990	NY Rangers	6	1	1	2	2	0	1	0
1991	NY Rangers	5	0	0	0	2	0	0	0
1992	NY Rangers	13	1	2	3	10	0	0	0
1994	Dallas	9	1	1	2	2	0	0	0
1995	Dallas	5	1	2	3	2	0	0	0
Playoff Totals		**38**	**4**	**6**	**10**	**18**	**0**	**1**	**0**
•BROUSSEAU, Paul	*No Playoffs*								Right wing
BROWN, Adam									Left wing
1942	Detroit	10	0	2	2	4	....	....	....
1943♦	Detroit	6	1	1	2	2	....	....	....
1944	Detroit	5	0	0	0	8	....	....	....
1946	Detroit	5	1	1	2	0	....	....	....
Playoff Totals		**26**	**2**	**4**	**6**	**14**	....	....	....
BROWN, Arnie									Defense
1967	NY Rangers	4	0	0	0	6	0	0	0
1968	NY Rangers	6	0	1	1	8	0	0	0
1969	NY Rangers	4	0	1	1	0	0	0	0
1970	NY Rangers	4	0	4	4	9	0	0	0
1974	Atlanta	4	0	0	0	0	0	0	0
Playoff Totals		**22**	**0**	**6**	**6**	**23**	**0**	**0**	**0**
•BROWN, Brad	*No Playoffs*								Defense
BROWN, Cam	*No Playoffs*								Left wing
BROWN, Connie									Center
1940	Detroit	5	2	1	3	0	....	....	....
1941	Detroit	9	0	2	2	0	....	....	....
1943♦	Detroit	....	....	....	....	....	....	....	....
Playoff Totals		**14**	**2**	**3**	**5**	**0**	....	....	....
•BROWN, Curtis									Center/Left wing
1998	Buffalo	13	1	2	3	10	1	0	0
1999	Buffalo	21	7	6	13	10	3	0	3
2000	Buffalo	5	1	3	4	6	1	0	0
2001	Buffalo	13	5	0	5	8	0	2	1
Playoff Totals		**52**	**14**	**11**	**25**	**34**	**5**	**2**	**4**

Season	Team	GP	G	A	Pts	PIM	PP	SH	GW
BROWN, Dave									Right wing
1984	Philadelphia	2	0	0	0	12	0	0	0
1985	Philadelphia	11	0	0	0	59	0	0	0
1986	Philadelphia	5	0	0	0	16	0	0	0
1987	Philadelphia	26	1	2	3	59	0	0	0
1988	Philadelphia	7	1	0	1	27	0	0	0
1989	Edmonton	7	0	0	0	6	0	0	0
1990♦	Edmonton	3	0	0	0	0	0	0	0
1991	Edmonton	16	0	1	1	30	0	0	0
1995	Philadelphia	3	0	0	0	0	0	0	0
Playoff Totals		**80**	**2**	**3**	**5**	**209**	**0**	**0**	**0**
BROWN, Doug									Right wing
1988	New Jersey	19	5	1	6	6	0	1	1
1990	New Jersey	6	0	1	1	2	0	0	0
1991	New Jersey	7	2	2	4	2	0	1	0
1994	Pittsburgh	6	0	0	0	2	0	0	0
1995	Detroit	18	4	8	12	2	0	1	1
1996	Detroit	13	3	3	6	4	0	1	0
1997♦	Detroit	14	3	3	6	2	0	0	0
1998♦	Detroit	9	4	2	6	0	3	0	1
1999	Detroit	10	2	2	4	4	1	0	1
2000	Detroit	3	0	1	1	0	0	0	0
2001	Detroit	4	0	0	0	2	0	0	0
Playoff Totals		**109**	**23**	**23**	**46**	**26**	**4**	**4**	**4**
BROWN, Fred									Left wing
1928	Mtl. Maroons	9	0	0	0	0	0	0	0
Playoff Totals		**9**	**0**	**0**	**0**	**0**	**0**	**0**	**0**
BROWN, George									Center
1937	Montreal	4	0	0	0	0	0	0	0
1938	Montreal	3	0	0	0	2	0	0	0
Playoff Totals		**7**	**0**	**0**	**0**	**2**	**0**	**0**	**0**
BROWN, Gerry									Left wing
1942	Detroit	12	2	1	3	4	....	....	....
Playoff Totals		**12**	**2**	**1**	**3**	**4**	....	....	....
BROWN, Greg									Defense
1994	Pittsburgh	6	0	1	1	4	0	0	0
Playoff Totals		**6**	**0**	**1**	**1**	**4**	**0**	**0**	**0**
BROWN, Harold	*No Playoffs*								Right wing
BROWN, Jeff									Defense
1986	Quebec	1	0	0	0	0	0	0	0
1987	Quebec	13	3	3	6	2	2	0	0
1990	St. Louis	12	2	10	12	4	1	0	1
1991	St. Louis	13	3	9	12	6	0	0	0
1992	St. Louis	6	2	1	3	2	0	0	1
1993	St. Louis	11	3	8	11	6	1	0	2
1994	Vancouver	24	6	9	15	37	3	0	0
1995	Vancouver	5	1	3	4	2	0	0	0
1998	Washington	2	0	2	2	0	0	0	0
Playoff Totals		**87**	**20**	**45**	**65**	**59**	**7**	**0**	**4**
BROWN, Jim	*No Playoffs*								Defense
BROWN, Keith									Defense
1980	Chicago	6	0	0	0	4	0	0	0
1981	Chicago	3	0	2	2	2	0	0	0
1982	Chicago	4	0	2	2	5	0	0	0
1983	Chicago	7	0	0	0	11	0	0	0
1984	Chicago	5	0	1	1	10	0	0	0
1985	Chicago	11	2	7	9	31	1	0	0
1986	Chicago	3	0	1	1	9	0	0	0
1987	Chicago	4	0	1	1	6	0	0	0
1988	Chicago	5	0	2	2	10	0	0	0
1989	Chicago	13	1	3	4	25	0	0	0
1990	Chicago	18	0	4	4	43	0	0	0
1991	Chicago	6	1	0	1	8	0	0	0
1992	Chicago	14	0	8	8	18	0	0	0
1993	Chicago	4	0	1	1	2	0	0	0
Playoff Totals		**103**	**4**	**32**	**36**	**184**	**1**	**0**	**0**
•BROWN, Kevin									Right wing
2000	Edmonton	1	0	0	0	0	0	0	0
Playoff Totals		**1**	**0**	**0**	**0**	**0**	**0**	**0**	**0**
BROWN, Larry									Defense
1971	NY Rangers	11	0	1	1	0	0	0	0
1974	Los Angeles	2	0	0	0	0	0	0	0
1975	Los Angeles	3	0	2	2	0	0	0	0
1976	Los Angeles	9	0	0	0	2	0	0	0
1977	Los Angeles	9	0	1	1	6	0	0	0
1978	Los Angeles	1	0	0	0	2	0	0	0
Playoff Totals		**35**	**0**	**4**	**4**	**10**	**0**	**0**	**0**
•BROWN, Mike	*No Playoffs*								Left wing
•BROWN, Rob									Right wing
1989	Pittsburgh	11	5	3	8	22	1	0	3
1991	Hartford	5	1	0	1	7	1	0	1
1992	Chicago	8	2	4	6	4	1	0	0
1998	Pittsburgh	6	1	0	1	4	1	0	0
1999	Pittsburgh	13	2	5	7	8	2	0	0
2000	Pittsburgh	11	1	2	3	0	0	0	0
Playoff Totals		**54**	**12**	**14**	**26**	**45**	**6**	**0**	**4**

Season	Team	GP	G	A	Pts	PIM	PP	SH	GW
•BROWN, Sean									Defense
1999	Edmonton	1	0	0	0	10	0	0	0
2000	Edmonton	3	0	0	0	23	0	0	0
2002	Boston	4	0	0	0	2	0	0	0
Playoff Totals		**8**	**0**	**0**	**0**	**35**	**0**	**0**	**0**
BROWN, Stan									Defense
1927	NY Rangers	2	0	0	0	0	0	0	0
Playoff Totals		**2**	**0**	**0**	**0**	**0**	**0**	**0**	**0**
BROWN, Wayne									Right wing
1954	Boston	4	0	0	0	2	0	0	0
Playoff Totals		**4**	**0**	**0**	**0**	**2**	**0**	**0**	**0**
BROWNE, Cecil	*No Playoffs*								Left wing
BROWNSCHIDLE, Jack									Defense
1980	St. Louis	3	0	0	0	0	0	0	0
1981	St. Louis	11	0	3	3	2	0	0	0
1982	St. Louis	8	0	2	2	14	0	0	0
1983	St. Louis	4	0	0	0	2	0	0	0
Playoff Totals		**26**	**0**	**5**	**5**	**18**	**0**	**0**	**0**
BROWNSCHIDLE, Jeff	*No Playoffs*								Defense
BRUBAKER, Jeff									Left wing
1982	Montreal	2	0	0	0	27	0	0	0
Playoff Totals		**2**	**0**	**0**	**0**	**27**	**0**	**0**	**0**
BRUCE, David									Left wing
1986	Vancouver	1	0	0	0	0	0	0	0
1991	St. Louis	2	0	0	0	2	0	0	0
Playoff Totals		**3**	**0**	**0**	**0**	**2**	**0**	**0**	**0**
BRUCE, Gordie									Left wing
1941	Boston	2	0	0	0	0	....	....	....
1942	Boston	5	2	3	5	4	....	....	....
Playoff Totals		**7**	**2**	**3**	**5**	**4**	....	....	....
BRUCE, Morley									Defense/Center
1920♦	Ottawa	....	....	....	....	....	....	....	....
1921♦	Ottawa	2	0	0	0	2	0	0	0
1922	Ottawa	1	0	0	0	0	0	0	0
Playoff Totals		**3**	**0**	**0**	**0**	**2**	**0**	**0**	**0**
•BRULE, Steve									Right wing
2000♦	New Jersey	1	0	0	0	0	0	0	0
Playoff Totals		**1**	**0**	**0**	**0**	**0**	**0**	**0**	**0**
BRUMWELL, Murray									Defense
1982	Minnesota	2	0	0	0	2	0	0	0
Playoff Totals		**2**	**0**	**0**	**0**	**2**	**0**	**0**	**0**
•BRUNET, Benoit									Left wing
1993♦	Montreal	20	2	8	10	8	1	0	1
1994	Montreal	7	1	4	5	16	0	0	0
1996	Montreal	3	0	2	2	0	0	0	0
1997	Montreal	4	1	3	4	4	0	1	0
1998	Montreal	8	1	0	1	4	0	0	1
2002	Ottawa	12	0	3	3	0	0	0	0
Playoff Totals		**54**	**5**	**20**	**25**	**32**	**1**	**1**	**2**
BRUNETEAU, Eddie									Right wing
1941	Detroit	3	0	0	0	0	....	....	....
1945	Detroit	14	5	2	7	0	....	....	....
1946	Detroit	4	1	0	1	0	....	....	....
1947	Detroit	4	1	4	5	0	....	....	....
1948	Detroit	6	0	0	0	0	....	....	....
Playoff Totals		**31**	**7**	**6**	**13**	**0**	....	....	....
BRUNETEAU, Mud									Right wing
1936♦	Detroit	7	2	2	4	4	....	....	....
1937♦	Detroit	10	2	0	2	6	....	....	....
1939	Detroit	6	0	0	0	0	....	....	....
1940	Detroit	5	3	2	5	0	....	....	....
1941	Detroit	9	2	1	3	2	....	....	....
1942	Detroit	12	5	1	6	6	....	....	....
1943♦	Detroit	9	5	4	9	0	....	....	....
1944	Detroit	5	1	2	3	2	....	....	....
1945	Detroit	14	3	2	5	2	....	....	....
Playoff Totals		**77**	**23**	**14**	**37**	**22**	....	....	....
•BRUNETTE, Andrew									Left wing
1996	Washington	6	1	3	4	0	0	0	0
Playoff Totals		**6**	**1**	**3**	**4**	**0**	**0**	**0**	**0**
BRYDGE, Bill									Defense
1929	Detroit	2	0	0	0	4	0	0	0
Playoff Totals		**2**	**0**	**0**	**0**	**4**	**0**	**0**	**0**
BRYDGES, Paul	*No Playoffs*								Center
BRYDSON, Glenn									Right wing
1931	Mtl. Maroons	2	0	0	0	0	0	0	0
1932	Mtl. Maroons	4	0	0	0	4	0	0	0
1933	Mtl. Maroons	2	0	0	0	0	0	0	0
1934	Mtl. Maroons	1	0	0	0	0	0	0	0
1936	Chicago	2	0	0	0	4	0	0	0
Playoff Totals		**11**	**0**	**0**	**0**	**8**	**0**	**0**	**0**
BRYDSON, Gord	*No Playoffs*								Center/Right wing

Season	Team	GP	G	A	Pts	PIM	PP	SH	GW
•BRYLIN, Sergei — Center									
1995♦	New Jersey	12	1	2	3	4	0	0	0
1999	New Jersey	5	3	1	4	4	1	0	1
2000♦	New Jersey	17	3	5	8	0	0	0	0
2001	New Jersey	20	3	4	7	6	1	0	1
2002	New Jersey	6	0	2	2	2	0	0	0
Playoff Totals		**60**	**10**	**14**	**24**	**16**	**2**	**0**	**2**
BUBLA, Jiri — Defense									
1983	Vancouver	1	0	0	0	5	0	0	0
1984	Vancouver	2	0	0	0	0	0	0	0
1986	Vancouver	3	0	0	0	2	0	0	0
Playoff Totals		**6**	**0**	**0**	**0**	**7**	**0**	**0**	**0**
BUCHANAN, Al *No Playoffs* — Left wing									
BUCHANAN, Bucky *No Playoffs* — Center/Right wing									
BUCHANAN, Jeff *No Playoffs* — Defense									
BUCHANAN, Mike *No Playoffs* — Defense									
BUCHANAN, Ron *No Playoffs* — Center									
•BUCHBERGER, Kelly — Right wing									
1987♦	Edmonton	3	0	1	1	5	0	0	0
1990♦	Edmonton	19	0	5	5	13	0	0	0
1991	Edmonton	12	2	1	3	25	0	0	0
1992	Edmonton	16	1	4	5	32	0	0	0
1997	Edmonton	12	5	2	7	16	0	0	1
1998	Edmonton	12	1	2	3	25	0	0	0
1999	Edmonton	4	0	0	0	0	0	0	0
2000	Los Angeles	4	0	0	0	4	0	0	0
2001	Los Angeles	8	1	0	1	2	0	0	0
2002	Los Angeles	7	0	0	0	7	0	0	0
Playoff Totals		**97**	**10**	**15**	**25**	**129**	**0**	**0**	**1**
BUCYK, John — Left wing									
1956	Detroit	10	1	1	2	8	0	0	0
1957	Detroit	5	0	1	1	0	0	0	0
1958	Boston	12	0	4	4	16	0	0	0
1959	Boston	7	2	4	6	6	0	0	0
1968	Boston	3	0	2	2	0	0	0	0
1969	Boston	10	5	6	11	0	2	1	0
1970♦	Boston	14	11	8	19	2	4	1	0
1971	Boston	7	2	5	7	0	0	0	0
1972♦	Boston	15	9	11	20	6	0	0	0
1973	Boston	5	0	3	3	0	0	0	0
1974	Boston	16	8	10	18	4	3	0	1
1975	Boston	3	1	0	1	0	0	0	0
1976	Boston	12	2	7	9	0	2	0	0
1977	Boston	5	0	0	0	0	0	0	0
Playoff Totals		**124**	**41**	**62**	**103**	**42**	**11**	**2**	**1**
BUCYK, Randy — Center									
1986	Montreal	2	0	0	0	0	0	0	0
Playoff Totals		**2**	**0**	**0**	**0**	**0**	**0**	**0**	**0**
BUHR, Doug *No Playoffs* — Left wing									
BUKOVICH, Tony — Left wing/Center									
1945	Detroit	6	0	1	1	0	0	0	0
Playoff Totals		**6**	**0**	**1**	**1**	**0**	**0**	**0**	**0**
•BULIS, Jan — Center									
2002	Montreal	6	0	0	0	6	0	0	0
Playoff Totals		**6**	**0**	**0**	**0**	**6**	**0**	**0**	**0**
BULLARD, Mike — Center									
1981	Pittsburgh	4	3	3	6	0	1	0	1
1982	Pittsburgh	5	1	1	2	4	0	0	0
1987	Calgary	6	4	3	7	2	3	0	1
1988	Calgary	6	0	2	2	6	0	0	0
1989	Philadelphia	19	3	9	12	32	1	0	0
Playoff Totals		**40**	**11**	**18**	**29**	**44**	**5**	**0**	**2**
BULLER, Hy *No Playoffs* — Defense									
BULLEY, Ted — Left wing									
1978	Chicago	4	1	1	2	2	0	0	0
1979	Chicago	2	0	0	0	0	0	0	0
1980	Chicago	7	2	3	5	10	0	0	0
1982	Chicago	15	2	1	3	12	0	0	1
1983	Washington	1	0	0	0	0	0	0	0
Playoff Totals		**29**	**5**	**5**	**10**	**24**	**0**	**0**	**1**
BURAKOVSKY, Robert *No Playoffs* — Right wing									
BURCH, Billy — Center/Left wing									
1929	NY Americans	2	0	0	0	0	0	0	0
Playoff Totals		**2**	**0**	**0**	**0**	**0**	**0**	**0**	**0**
BURCHELL, Fred *No Playoffs* — Center									
BURDON, Glen *No Playoffs* — Center									
•BURE, Pavel — Right wing									
1992	Vancouver	13	6	4	10	14	0	0	0
1993	Vancouver	12	5	7	12	8	0	0	1
1994	Vancouver	24	*16	15	31	40	3	0	2
1995	Vancouver	11	7	6	13	10	2	2	0
2000	Florida	4	1	3	4	2	1	0	0
Playoff Totals		**64**	**35**	**35**	**70**	**74**	**6**	**2**	**3**
•BURE, Valeri — Right wing									
1996	Montreal	6	0	1	1	6	0	0	0
1997	Montreal	5	0	1	1	2	0	0	0
Playoff Totals		**11**	**0**	**2**	**2**	**8**	**0**	**0**	**0**

Season	Team	GP	G	A	Pts	PIM	PP	SH	GW
BUREAU, Marc — Center									
1991	Minnesota	23	3	2	5	20	0	1	0
1992	Minnesota	5	0	0	0	14	0	0	0
1996	Montreal	6	1	1	2	4	0	0	0
1998	Montreal	10	1	2	3	6	0	0	0
1999	Philadelphia	6	0	2	2	2	0	0	0
Playoff Totals		**50**	**5**	**7**	**12**	**46**	**0**	**1**	**0**
BUREGA, Bill *No Playoffs* — Defense									
BURKE, Eddie *No Playoffs* — Right wing/Center									
BURKE, Marty — Defense									
1928	Pittsburgh	2	1	0	1	2	....	....	....
1929	Montreal	3	0	0	0	8	....	....	....
1930♦	Montreal	6	0	1	1	6	....	....	....
1931♦	Montreal	10	1	2	3	10	....	....	....
1932	Montreal	4	0	0	0	12	....	....	....
1934	Montreal	2	0	1	1	2	....	....	....
1935	Chicago	2	0	0	0	2	....	....	....
1936	Chicago	2	0	0	0	2	....	....	....
Playoff Totals		**31**	**2**	**4**	**6**	**44**	....	....	....
BURMEISTER, Roy *No Playoffs* — Left wing									
BURNETT, Kelly *No Playoffs* — Center									
BURNS, Bobby *No Playoffs* — Left wing									
BURNS, Charlie — Center									
1970	Minnesota	6	1	0	1	2	0	0	0
1971	Minnesota	12	3	3	6	2	0	0	1
1972	Minnesota	7	1	1	2	2	0	0	0
1973	Minnesota	6	0	0	0	0	0	0	0
Playoff Totals		**31**	**5**	**4**	**9**	**6**	**0**	**0**	**1**
BURNS, Gary — Left wing/Center									
1981	NY Rangers	1	0	0	0	2	0	0	0
1982	NY Rangers	4	0	0	0	0	0	0	0
Playoff Totals		**5**	**0**	**0**	**0**	**2**	**0**	**0**	**0**
BURNS, Norm *No Playoffs* — Center									
BURNS, Robin *No Playoffs* — Left wing									
BURR, Shawn — Left wing/Center									
1987	Detroit	16	7	2	9	20	0	0	2
1988	Detroit	9	3	1	4	14	0	0	1
1989	Detroit	6	1	2	3	6	0	0	0
1991	Detroit	7	0	4	4	15	0	0	0
1992	Detroit	11	1	5	6	10	0	0	0
1993	Detroit	7	2	1	3	2	0	1	0
1994	Detroit	7	2	0	2	6	0	0	2
1995	Detroit	16	0	2	2	6	0	0	0
1996	Tampa Bay	6	0	2	2	8	0	0	0
1998	San Jose	6	0	0	0	8	0	0	0
Playoff Totals		**91**	**16**	**19**	**35**	**95**	**0**	**1**	**5**
BURRIDGE, Randy — Left wing									
1986	Boston	3	0	4	4	12	0	0	0
1987	Boston	2	1	0	1	2	0	0	0
1988	Boston	23	2	10	12	16	0	0	0
1989	Boston	10	5	2	7	6	1	1	0
1990	Boston	21	4	11	15	14	0	1	0
1991	Boston	19	0	3	3	39	0	0	0
1992	Washington	2	0	1	1	0	0	0	0
1993	Washington	4	1	0	1	0	0	0	0
1994	Washington	11	0	2	2	12	0	0	0
1997	Buffalo	12	5	1	6	2	3	0	0
Playoff Totals		**107**	**18**	**34**	**52**	**103**	**4**	**2**	**0**
BURROWS, Dave — Defense									
1972	Pittsburgh	4	0	0	0	4	0	0	0
1975	Pittsburgh	9	1	1	2	12	0	0	1
1976	Pittsburgh	3	0	0	0	0	0	0	0
1977	Pittsburgh	3	0	2	2	0	0	0	0
1979	Toronto	6	0	1	1	7	0	0	0
1980	Toronto	3	0	1	1	2	0	0	0
1981	Pittsburgh	1	0	0	0	0	0	0	0
Playoff Totals		**29**	**1**	**5**	**6**	**25**	**0**	**0**	**1**
BURRY, Bert *No Playoffs* — Defense									
BURT, Adam — Defense									
1990	Hartford	2	0	0	0	0	0	0	0
1992	Hartford	2	0	0	0	0	0	0	0
1999	Philadelphia	6	0	0	0	4	0	0	0
2000	Philadelphia	11	0	1	1	4	0	0	0
Playoff Totals		**21**	**0**	**1**	**1**	**8**	**0**	**0**	**0**
BURTON, Cummy — Right wing									
1956	Detroit	3	0	0	0	0	0	0	0
Playoff Totals		**3**	**0**	**0**	**0**	**0**	**0**	**0**	**0**
BURTON, Nelson *No Playoffs* — Left wing									
BUSH, Eddie — Defense									
1942	Detroit	11	1	6	7	23	....	....	....
Playoff Totals		**11**	**1**	**6**	**7**	**23**	....	....	....
BUSKAS, Rod — Defense									
1989	Pittsburgh	10	0	0	0	23	0	0	0
1991	Los Angeles	2	0	2	2	22	0	0	0
1992	Chicago	6	0	1	1	0	0	0	0
Playoff Totals		**18**	**0**	**3**	**3**	**45**	**0**	**0**	**0**

Season	Team	GP	G	A	Pts	PIM	PP	SH	GW
BUSNIUK, Mike — Defense									
1980	Philadelphia	19	2	4	6	23	0	0	0
1981	Philadelphia	6	0	1	1	11	0	0	0
Playoff Totals		**25**	**2**	**5**	**7**	**34**	**0**	**0**	**0**
BUSNIUK, Ron *No Playoffs* — Right wing									
BUSWELL, Walt — Defense									
1933	Detroit	4	0	0	0	4	....	....	....
1934	Detroit	9	0	1	1	2	....	....	....
1937	Montreal	5	0	0	0	2	....	....	....
1938	Montreal	3	0	0	0	0	....	....	....
1939	Montreal	3	2	0	2	2	....	....	....
Playoff Totals		**24**	**2**	**1**	**3**	**10**	....	....	....
BUTCHER, Garth — Defense									
1982	Vancouver	1	0	0	0	0	0	0	0
1983	Vancouver	3	1	0	1	2	0	0	0
1986	Vancouver	3	0	0	0	0	0	0	0
1989	Vancouver	7	1	1	2	22	0	0	1
1991	St. Louis	13	2	1	3	54	0	0	0
1992	St. Louis	5	1	2	3	16	0	0	0
1993	St. Louis	11	1	1	2	20	0	0	1
1995	Toronto	7	0	0	0	8	0	0	0
Playoff Totals		**50**	**6**	**5**	**11**	**122**	**0**	**0**	**2**
•BUTENSCHON, Sven *No Playoffs* — Defense									
BUTLER, Dick *No Playoffs* — Right wing									
BUTLER, Jerry — Right wing									
1974	NY Rangers	12	0	2	2	25	0	0	0
1975	NY Rangers	3	1	0	1	16	0	0	0
1976	St. Louis	3	0	0	0	0	0	0	0
1977	St. Louis	4	0	0	0	14	0	0	0
1978	Toronto	13	1	1	2	18	0	0	0
1979	Toronto	6	0	0	0	4	0	0	0
1980	Vancouver	4	0	0	0	2	0	0	0
1981	Vancouver	3	1	0	1	0	0	0	0
Playoff Totals		**48**	**3**	**3**	**6**	**79**	**0**	**0**	**0**
BUTSAYEV, Viacheslav *No Playoffs* — Center									
•BUTSAYEV, Yuri *No Playoffs* — Center									
BUTTERS, Bill *No Playoffs* — Defense									
BUTTREY, Gord *No Playoffs* — Wing									
BUYNAK, Gord *No Playoffs* — Defense									
•BUZEK, Petr *No Playoffs* — Defense									
BYAKIN, Ilja *No Playoffs* — Defense									
BYCE, John — Center									
1990	Boston	8	2	0	2	2	0	0	0
Playoff Totals		**8**	**2**	**0**	**2**	**2**	**0**	**0**	**0**
BYERS, Gord *No Playoffs* — Defense									
BYERS, Jerry *No Playoffs* — Left wing									
BYERS, Lyndon — Right wing									
1987	Boston	1	0	0	0	0	0	0	0
1988	Boston	11	1	2	3	62	0	0	0
1989	Boston	2	0	0	0	0	0	0	0
1990	Boston	17	1	0	1	12	0	0	0
1991	Boston	1	0	0	0	10	0	0	0
1992	Boston	5	0	0	0	12	0	0	0
Playoff Totals		**37**	**2**	**2**	**4**	**96**	**0**	**0**	**0**
BYERS, Mike — Right wing									
1969	Philadelphia	4	0	1	1	0	0	0	0
Playoff Totals		**4**	**0**	**1**	**1**	**0**	**0**	**0**	**0**
•BYKOV, Dmitri *No Playoffs* — Defense									
•BYLSMA, Dan — Right wing									
1998	Los Angeles	2	0	0	0	0	0	0	0
2000	Los Angeles	3	0	0	0	0	0	0	0
Playoff Totals		**5**	**0**	**0**	**0**	**0**	**0**	**0**	**0**
BYRAM, Shawn *No Playoffs* — Left wing									
CAFFERY, Jack — Center									
1957	Boston	10	1	0	1	4	0	0	0
Playoff Totals		**10**	**1**	**0**	**1**	**4**	**0**	**0**	**0**
CAFFERY, Terry — Center									
1971	Minnesota	1	0	0	0	0	0	0	0
Playoff Totals		**1**	**0**	**0**	**0**	**0**	**0**	**0**	**0**
CAHAN, Larry — Defense									
1955	Toronto	4	0	0	0	0	0	0	0
1957	NY Rangers	3	0	0	0	2	0	0	0
1958	NY Rangers	5	0	0	0	4	0	0	0
1962	NY Rangers	6	0	0	0	10	0	0	0
1969	Los Angeles	11	1	1	2	22	0	1	0
Playoff Totals		**29**	**1**	**1**	**2**	**38**	**0**	**1**	**0**
CAHILL, Charles *No Playoffs* — Right wing									
CAIN, Francis *No Playoffs* — Defense									

Season	Team	GP	G	A	Pts	PIM	PP	SH	GW
CAIN, Herb									Left wing
1934	Mtl. Maroons	4	0	0	0	0	....	....	....
1935♦	Mtl. Maroons	7	1	0	1	2	....	....	....
1936	Mtl. Maroons	3	0	1	1	0	....	....	....
1937	Mtl. Maroons	5	1	1	2	0	....	....	....
1939	Montreal	3	0	0	0	2	....	....	....
1940	Boston	6	1	3	4	2	....	....	....
1941♦	Boston	11	3	2	5	5	....	....	....
1942	Boston	5	1	0	1	0	....	....	....
1943	Boston	7	4	2	6	0	....	....	....
1945	Boston	7	5	2	7	0	....	....	....
1946	Boston	9	0	2	2	2	....	....	....
Playoff Totals		**67**	**16**	**13**	**29**	**13**	....	....	....
CAIRNS, Don *No Playoffs*									Left wing
•CAIRNS, Eric									Defense
1997	NY Rangers	3	0	0	0	0	0	0	0
2002	NY Islanders	7	0	0	0	15	0	0	0
Playoff Totals		**10**	**0**	**0**	**0**	**15**	**0**	**0**	**0**
•CAJANEK, Petr *No Playoffs*									Center
CALDER, Eric *No Playoffs*									Defense
•CALDER, Kyle									Center
2002	Chicago	5	2	0	2	2	1	0	0
Playoff Totals		**5**	**2**	**0**	**2**	**2**	**1**	**0**	**0**
CALLADINE, Norm *No Playoffs*									Center
CALLANDER, Drew *No Playoffs*									Center/Right wing
CALLANDER, Jock									Right wing
1989	Pittsburgh	10	2	5	7	10	0	0	0
1992♦	Pittsburgh	12	1	3	4	2	0	0	0
Playoff Totals		**22**	**3**	**8**	**11**	**12**	**0**	**0**	**0**
CALLIGHEN, Brett									Center
1980	Edmonton	3	0	2	2	0	0	0	0
1981	Edmonton	9	4	4	8	6	1	0	1
1982	Edmonton	2	0	0	0	2	0	0	0
Playoff Totals		**14**	**4**	**6**	**10**	**8**	**1**	**0**	**1**
CALLIGHEN, Patsy									Defense
1928♦	NY Rangers	9	0	0	0	0	0	0	0
Playoff Totals		**9**	**0**	**0**	**0**	**0**	**0**	**0**	**0**
•CALOUN, Jan *No Playoffs*									Right wing
CAMAZZOLA, James *No Playoffs*									Left wing
CAMAZZOLA, Tony *No Playoffs*									Defense
CAMERON, Al									Defense
1978	Detroit	7	0	1	1	2	0	0	0
Playoff Totals		**7**	**0**	**1**	**1**	**2**	**0**	**0**	**0**
CAMERON, Billy									Right wing
1924♦	Montreal	2	0	0	0	0	0	0	0
Playoff Totals		**2**	**0**	**0**	**0**	**0**	**0**	**0**	**0**
CAMERON, Craig									Right wing
1968	St. Louis	14	1	0	1	11	0	0	0
1969	St. Louis	2	0	0	0	0	0	0	0
1971	St. Louis	6	2	0	2	4	0	0	0
1972	Minnesota	5	0	1	1	2	0	0	0
Playoff Totals		**27**	**3**	**1**	**4**	**17**	**0**	**0**	**0**
CAMERON, Dave *No Playoffs*									Center
CAMERON, Harry									Defense
1918♦	Toronto	2	1	2	3	0	....	....	....
1919	Ottawa	5	4	0	4	6	....	....	....
1921	Toronto	2	0	0	0	2	....	....	....
1922♦	Toronto	2	0	2	2	8	....	....	....
Playoff Totals		**11**	**5**	**4**	**9**	**16**	....	....	....
CAMERON, Scotty *No Playoffs*									Center
•CAMMALLERI, Michael *No Playoffs*									Center
•CAMPBELL, Brian *No Playoffs*									Defense
CAMPBELL, Bryan									Center
1969	Los Angeles	6	2	1	3	0	0	0	1
1970	Chicago	8	1	2	3	0	1	0	0
1971	Chicago	4	0	1	1	0	0	0	0
1972	Chicago	4	0	0	0	2	0	0	0
Playoff Totals		**22**	**3**	**4**	**7**	**2**	**1**	**0**	**1**
CAMPBELL, Colin									Defense
1975	Pittsburgh	9	1	3	4	21	0	1	1
1976	Pittsburgh	3	0	0	0	0	0	0	0
1979	Pittsburgh	7	1	4	5	30	0	0	0
1980	Edmonton	3	0	0	0	11	0	0	0
1981	Vancouver	3	0	1	1	9	0	0	0
1982	Vancouver	16	2	2	4	89	0	0	1
1984	Detroit	4	0	0	0	21	0	0	0
Playoff Totals		**45**	**4**	**10**	**14**	**181**	**0**	**1**	**2**
CAMPBELL, Dave *No Playoffs*									Defense
CAMPBELL, Don *No Playoffs*									Left wing
CAMPBELL, Earl									Defense
1924	Ottawa	1	0	0	0	6	0	0	0
Playoff Totals		**1**	**0**	**0**	**0**	**6**	**0**	**0**	**0**

Season	Team	GP	G	A	Pts	PIM	PP	SH	GW
•CAMPBELL, Jim									Right wing
1997	St. Louis	4	1	0	1	6	1	0	0
1998	St. Louis	10	7	3	10	12	4	0	2
Playoff Totals		**14**	**8**	**3**	**11**	**18**	**5**	**0**	**2**
CAMPBELL, Scott *No Playoffs*									Defense
CAMPBELL, Wade									Defense
1984	Winnipeg	3	0	0	0	7	0	0	0
1985	Winnipeg	3	0	0	0	2	0	0	0
1987	Boston	4	0	0	0	11	0	0	0
Playoff Totals		**10**	**0**	**0**	**0**	**20**	**0**	**0**	**0**
CAMPEAU, Tod									Center
1949	Montreal	1	0	0	0	0	0	0	0
Playoff Totals		**1**	**0**	**0**	**0**	**0**	**0**	**0**	**0**
CAMPEDELLI, Dom *No Playoffs*									Defense
CAPUANO, Dave									Left wing
1991	Vancouver	6	1	1	2	5	0	0	0
Playoff Totals		**6**	**1**	**1**	**2**	**5**	**0**	**0**	**0**
CAPUANO, Jack *No Playoffs*									Defense
CARBOL, Leo *No Playoffs*									Defense
CARBONNEAU, Guy									Center
1983	Montreal	3	0	0	0	2	0	0	0
1984	Montreal	15	4	3	7	12	0	0	1
1985	Montreal	12	4	3	7	8	0	1	1
1986♦	Montreal	20	7	5	12	35	0	2	1
1987	Montreal	17	3	8	11	20	0	0	0
1988	Montreal	11	0	4	4	2	0	0	0
1989	Montreal	21	4	5	9	10	0	1	0
1990	Montreal	11	2	3	5	6	0	0	0
1991	Montreal	13	1	5	6	10	0	0	1
1992	Montreal	11	1	1	2	6	0	0	0
1993♦	Montreal	20	3	3	6	10	0	1	2
1994	Montreal	7	1	3	4	4	0	0	0
1995	St. Louis	7	1	2	3	6	0	0	0
1997	Dallas	7	0	1	1	6	0	0	0
1998	Dallas	16	3	1	4	6	0	0	0
1999♦	Dallas	17	2	4	6	6	0	0	1
2000	Dallas	23	2	4	6	12	0	1	1
Playoff Totals		**231**	**38**	**55**	**93**	**161**	**0**	**6**	**8**
CARDIN, Claude *No Playoffs*									Left wing
CARDWELL, Steve									Left wing
1972	Pittsburgh	4	0	0	0	2	0	0	0
Playoff Totals		**4**	**0**	**0**	**0**	**2**	**0**	**0**	**0**
CAREY, George *No Playoffs*									Right wing
CARKNER, Terry									Defense
1987	NY Rangers	1	0	0	0	0	0	0	0
1989	Philadelphia	19	1	5	6	28	0	1	0
1994	Detroit	7	0	0	0	4	0	0	0
1996	Florida	22	0	4	4	10	0	0	0
1997	Florida	5	0	0	0	6	0	0	0
Playoff Totals		**54**	**1**	**9**	**10**	**48**	**0**	**1**	**0**
CARLETON, Wayne									Left wing
1970♦	Boston	14	2	4	6	14	0	0	0
1971	Boston	4	0	0	0	0	0	0	0
Playoff Totals		**18**	**2**	**4**	**6**	**14**	**0**	**0**	**0**
CARLIN, Brian *No Playoffs*									Left wing
CARLSON, Jack									Left wing
1981	Minnesota	15	1	2	3	50	0	0	0
1982	Minnesota	1	0	0	0	15	0	0	0
1983	St. Louis	4	0	0	0	5	0	0	0
1984	St. Louis	5	0	0	0	2	0	0	0
Playoff Totals		**25**	**1**	**2**	**3**	**72**	**0**	**0**	**0**
CARLSON, Kent									Defense
1986	St. Louis	5	0	0	0	11	0	0	0
1988	St. Louis	3	0	0	0	2	0	0	0
Playoff Totals		**8**	**0**	**0**	**0**	**13**	**0**	**0**	**0**
CARLSON, Steve									Center
1980	Los Angeles	4	1	1	2	7	0	0	0
Playoff Totals		**4**	**1**	**1**	**2**	**7**	**0**	**0**	**0**
CARLSSON, Anders									Center
1988	New Jersey	3	1	0	1	2	0	0	1
Playoff Totals		**3**	**1**	**0**	**1**	**2**	**0**	**0**	**1**
CARLYLE, Randy									Defense
1977	Toronto	9	0	1	1	20	0	0	0
1978	Toronto	7	0	1	1	8	0	0	0
1979	Pittsburgh	7	0	0	0	12	0	0	0
1980	Pittsburgh	5	1	0	1	4	0	0	0
1981	Pittsburgh	5	4	5	9	9	0	1	0
1982	Pittsburgh	5	1	3	4	16	0	0	0
1984	Winnipeg	3	0	2	2	4	0	0	0
1985	Winnipeg	8	1	5	6	13	1	0	0
1987	Winnipeg	10	1	5	6	18	0	0	0
1988	Winnipeg	5	0	2	2	10	0	0	0
1992	Winnipeg	5	1	0	1	6	0	0	0
Playoff Totals		**69**	**9**	**24**	**33**	**120**	**1**	**1**	**0**
CARNBACK, Patrik *No Playoffs*									Center

Season	Team	GP	G	A	Pts	PIM	PP	SH	GW
•CARNEY, Keith									Defense
1992	Buffalo	7	0	3	3	0	0	0	0
1993	Buffalo	8	0	3	3	6	0	0	0
1994	Chicago	6	0	1	1	4	0	0	0
1995	Chicago	4	0	1	1	0	0	0	0
1996	Chicago	10	0	3	3	4	0	0	0
1997	Chicago	6	1	1	2	2	0	0	0
1998	Phoenix	6	0	0	0	4	0	0	0
1999	Phoenix	7	1	2	3	10	0	0	0
2000	Phoenix	5	0	0	0	17	0	0	0
Playoff Totals		**59**	**2**	**14**	**16**	**47**	**0**	**0**	**0**
CARON, Alain *No Playoffs*									Right wing
CARPENTER, Bob									Center
1983	Washington	4	1	0	1	2	0	0	0
1984	Washington	8	2	1	3	25	1	0	0
1985	Washington	5	1	4	5	8	0	0	0
1986	Washington	9	5	4	9	12	2	0	1
1987	Los Angeles	5	1	2	3	2	0	0	0
1988	Los Angeles	5	1	1	2	0	0	0	0
1989	Boston	8	1	1	2	4	1	0	1
1990	Boston	21	4	6	10	39	2	0	1
1991	Boston	1	0	1	1	2	0	0	0
1992	Boston	8	0	1	1	6	0	0	0
1993	Washington	6	1	4	5	6	0	0	0
1994	New Jersey	20	1	7	8	20	0	0	0
1995♦	New Jersey	17	1	4	5	6	1	0	0
1997	New Jersey	10	1	2	3	2	0	0	0
1998	New Jersey	6	1	0	1	0	0	0	0
1999	New Jersey	7	0	0	0	2	0	0	0
Playoff Totals		**140**	**21**	**38**	**59**	**136**	**7**	**0**	**3**
CARPENTER, Ed *No Playoffs*									Defense
CARR, Gene									Center
1972	NY Rangers	16	1	3	4	21	0	0	0
1973	NY Rangers	1	0	1	1	0	0	0	0
1974	Los Angeles	5	2	1	3	14	1	0	0
1975	Los Angeles	3	1	2	3	29	0	0	0
1977	Los Angeles	9	1	1	2	2	0	0	0
1979	Atlanta	1	0	0	0	0	0	0	0
Playoff Totals		**35**	**5**	**8**	**13**	**66**	**1**	**0**	**0**
CARR, Lorne									Right wing
1936	NY Americans	5	1	1	2	0	....	....	....
1938	NY Americans	6	3	1	4	2	....	....	....
1939	NY Americans	2	0	0	0	0	....	....	....
1940	NY Americans	3	0	0	0	0	....	....	....
1942♦	Toronto	13	3	2	5	6	....	....	....
1943	Toronto	6	1	2	3	0	....	....	....
1944	Toronto	5	0	1	1	0	....	....	....
1945♦	Toronto	13	2	2	4	5	....	....	....
Playoff Totals		**53**	**10**	**9**	**19**	**13**	....	....	....
CARR, Red *No Playoffs*									Left wing
CARRIERE, Larry									Defense
1973	Buffalo	6	0	1	1	8	0	0	0
1975	Buffalo	17	0	2	2	32	0	0	0
1976	Atlanta	2	0	0	0	2	0	0	0
1980	Toronto	2	0	0	0	0	0	0	0
Playoff Totals		**27**	**0**	**3**	**3**	**42**	**0**	**0**	**0**
CARRIGAN, Gene									Center
1934	Detroit	4	0	0	0	0	0	0	0
Playoff Totals		**4**	**0**	**0**	**0**	**0**	**0**	**0**	**0**
CARROLL, Billy									Center
1981♦	NY Islanders	18	3	9	12	4	0	1	1
1982♦	NY Islanders	19	2	2	4	8	0	2	0
1983♦	NY Islanders	20	1	1	2	2	0	1	0
1984	NY Islanders	5	0	0	0	0	0	0	0
1985♦	Edmonton	9	0	0	0	4	0	0	0
Playoff Totals		**71**	**6**	**12**	**18**	**18**	**0**	**4**	**1**
CARROLL, George *No Playoffs*									Defense
CARROLL, Greg *No Playoffs*									Center
CARRUTHERS, Dwight *No Playoffs*									Defense
CARSE, Bill									Center
1939	NY Rangers	6	1	1	2	0	....	....	....
1940	Chicago	2	1	0	1	0	....	....	....
1941	Chicago	2	0	0	0	0	....	....	....
1942	Chicago	3	1	1	2	0	....	....	....
Playoff Totals		**13**	**3**	**2**	**5**	**0**	....	....	....
CARSE, Bob									Left wing
1940	Chicago	2	0	0	0	0	0	0	0
1941	Chicago	5	0	0	0	2	0	0	0
1942	Chicago	3	0	2	2	0	0	0	0
Playoff Totals		**10**	**0**	**2**	**2**	**2**	**0**	**0**	**0**
CARSON, Bill									Center
1929♦	Boston	5	2	0	2	8	....	....	....
1930	Boston	6	1	0	1	6	....	....	....
Playoff Totals		**11**	**3**	**0**	**3**	**14**	....	....	....

Season	Team	GP	G	A	Pts	PIM	PP	SH	GW
CARSON, Frank	Right wing								
1926♦	Mtl. Maroons	4	0	0	0	0	0	0	0
1927	Mtl. Maroons	2	0	0	0	2	0	0	0
1928	Mtl. Maroons	9	0	0	0	0	0	0	0
1932	Detroit	2	0	0	0	2	0	0	0
1933	Detroit	4	0	1	1	0	0	0	0
1934	Detroit	6	0	1	1	5	0	0	0
Playoff Totals		**27**	**0**	**2**	**2**	**9**	**0**	**0**	**0**
CARSON, Gerry	Defense								
1929	NY Rangers	5	0	0	0	0	0	0	0
1930♦	Montreal	6	0	0	0	0	0	0	0
1933	Montreal	2	0	0	0	2	0	0	0
1934	Montreal	2	0	0	0	2	0	0	0
1935	Montreal	2	0	0	0	4	0	0	0
1937	Mtl. Maroons	5	0	0	0	4	0	0	0
Playoff Totals		**22**	**0**	**0**	**0**	**12**	**0**	**0**	**0**
CARSON, Jimmy	Center								
1987	Los Angeles	5	1	2	3	6	0	0	0
1988	Los Angeles	5	5	3	8	4	1	0	0
1989	Edmonton	7	2	1	3	6	1	0	1
1991	Detroit	7	2	1	3	4	0	0	1
1992	Detroit	11	2	3	5	0	0	0	0
1993	Los Angeles	18	5	4	9	2	2	0	0
1994	Vancouver	2	0	1	1	0	0	0	0
Playoff Totals		**55**	**17**	**15**	**32**	**22**	**4**	**0**	**2**
CARSON, Lindsay	Center								
1983	Philadelphia	1	0	0	0	0	0	0	0
1984	Philadelphia	1	0	0	0	5	0	0	0
1985	Philadelphia	17	0	3	3	24	0	0	0
1986	Philadelphia	1	0	0	0	5	0	0	0
1987	Philadelphia	24	3	5	8	22	0	0	0
1988	Hartford	5	1	2	3	0	0	0	0
Playoff Totals		**49**	**4**	**10**	**14**	**56**	**0**	**0**	**0**
•CARTER, Anson	Right wing								
1998	Boston	6	1	1	2	0	0	0	0
1999	Boston	12	4	3	7	0	1	0	1
2001	Edmonton	6	3	1	4	4	1	0	1
Playoff Totals		**24**	**8**	**5**	**13**	**4**	**2**	**0**	**2**
CARTER, Billy *No Playoffs*	Center								
CARTER, John	Left wing								
1989	Boston	10	1	2	3	6	0	0	0
1990	Boston	21	6	3	9	45	0	1	0
Playoff Totals		**31**	**7**	**5**	**12**	**51**	**0**	**1**	**0**
CARTER, Ron *No Playoffs*	Right wing								
CARVETH, Joe	Right wing								
1942	Detroit	9	4	0	4	0	....	....	....
1943♦	Detroit	10	*6	2	8	4	....	....	....
1944	Detroit	5	2	1	3	8	....	....	....
1945	Detroit	14	5	*6	*11	2	....	....	....
1946	Detroit	5	0	1	1	0	....	....	....
1947	Boston	5	2	1	3	0	....	....	....
1949	Montreal	7	0	1	1	8	....	....	....
1950♦	Detroit	14	2	4	6	6	....	....	....
Playoff Totals		**69**	**21**	**16**	**37**	**28**	....	....	....
CASHMAN, Wayne	Left wing								
1968	Boston	1	0	0	0	0	0	0	0
1969	Boston	6	0	1	1	0	0	0	0
1970♦	Boston	14	5	4	9	50	0	2	0
1971	Boston	7	3	2	5	15	0	0	1
1972♦	Boston	15	4	7	11	42	1	0	0
1973	Boston	5	1	1	2	4	0	0	0
1974	Boston	16	5	9	14	46	1	0	1
1975	Boston	1	0	2	2	0	0	0	0
1976	Boston	11	1	5	6	16	0	0	0
1977	Boston	14	1	8	9	18	0	0	0
1978	Boston	15	4	6	10	13	3	0	2
1979	Boston	10	4	5	9	8	1	0	1
1980	Boston	10	3	3	6	32	1	0	0
1981	Boston	3	0	1	1	0	0	0	0
1982	Boston	9	0	2	2	6	0	0	0
1983	Boston	8	0	1	1	0	0	0	0
Playoff Totals		**145**	**31**	**57**	**88**	**250**	**7**	**2**	**5**
CASSELMAN, Mike *No Playoffs*	Center								
•CASSELS, Andrew	Center								
1991	Montreal	8	0	2	2	2	0	0	0
1992	Hartford	7	2	4	6	6	1	0	0
2002	Vancouver	6	2	1	3	0	1	0	0
Playoff Totals		**21**	**4**	**7**	**11**	**8**	**2**	**0**	**0**
CASSIDY, Bruce	Defense								
1989	Chicago	1	0	0	0	0	0	0	0
Playoff Totals		**1**	**0**	**0**	**0**	**0**	**0**	**0**	**0**
CASSIDY, Tom *No Playoffs*	Center								
CASSOLATO, Tony *No Playoffs*	Right wing								
CAUFIELD, Jay	Right wing								
1987	NY Rangers	3	0	0	0	12	0	0	0
1989	Pittsburgh	9	0	0	0	28	0	0	0
1991♦	Pittsburgh	....	....	....	....	....	....	....	....
1992♦	Pittsburgh	5	0	0	0	2	0	0	0
Playoff Totals		**17**	**0**	**0**	**0**	**42**	**0**	**0**	**0**

Season	Team	GP	G	A	Pts	PIM	PP	SH	GW
CAVALLINI, Gino	Left wing								
1985	Calgary	3	0	0	0	4	0	0	0
1986	St. Louis	17	4	5	9	10	0	0	2
1987	St. Louis	6	3	1	4	2	1	0	1
1988	St. Louis	10	5	5	10	19	2	0	0
1989	St. Louis	9	0	2	2	17	0	0	0
1990	St. Louis	12	1	3	4	12	0	0	1
1991	St. Louis	13	1	3	4	2	0	0	0
1993	Quebec	4	0	0	0	0	0	0	0
Playoff Totals		**74**	**14**	**19**	**33**	**66**	**3**	**0**	**4**
CAVALLINI, Paul	Defense								
1988	St. Louis	10	1	6	7	26	0	1	0
1989	St. Louis	10	2	2	4	14	0	0	0
1990	St. Louis	12	2	3	5	20	0	0	0
1991	St. Louis	13	2	3	5	20	1	0	0
1992	St. Louis	4	0	1	1	6	0	0	0
1993	Washington	6	0	2	2	18	0	0	0
1994	Dallas	9	1	8	9	4	1	0	1
1995	Dallas	5	0	2	2	6	0	0	0
Playoff Totals		**69**	**8**	**27**	**35**	**114**	**2**	**1**	**1**
CERESINO, Ray *No Playoffs*	Right wing								
CERNIK, Frantisek *No Playoffs*	Wing								
CHABOT, John	Center								
1984	Montreal	11	1	4	5	0	0	0	1
1988	Detroit	16	4	15	19	2	1	0	0
1989	Detroit	6	1	1	2	0	0	0	1
Playoff Totals		**33**	**6**	**20**	**26**	**2**	**1**	**0**	**2**
CHAD, John	Right wing								
1940	Chicago	2	0	0	0	0	0	0	0
1941	Chicago	5	0	0	0	2	0	0	0
1946	Chicago	3	0	1	1	0	0	0	0
Playoff Totals		**10**	**0**	**1**	**1**	**2**	**0**	**0**	**0**
CHALMERS, Chick *No Playoffs*	Center								
CHALUPA, Milan *No Playoffs*	Defense								
CHAMBERLAIN, Murph	Left wing								
1938	Toronto	5	0	0	0	2	....	....	....
1939	Toronto	10	2	5	7	4	....	....	....
1940	Toronto	3	0	0	0	0	....	....	....
1941	Montreal	3	0	2	2	11	....	....	....
1943	Boston	6	1	1	2	12	....	....	....
1944♦	Montreal	9	5	3	8	12	....	....	....
1945	Montreal	6	1	1	2	10	....	....	....
1946♦	Montreal	9	4	2	6	18	....	....	....
1947	Montreal	11	1	3	4	19	....	....	....
1949	Montreal	4	0	0	0	8	....	....	....
Playoff Totals		**66**	**14**	**17**	**31**	**96**	....	....	....
CHAMBERS, Shawn	Defense								
1989	Minnesota	3	0	2	2	0	0	0	0
1990	Minnesota	7	2	1	3	10	1	0	0
1991	Minnesota	23	0	7	7	16	0	0	0
1995♦	New Jersey	20	4	5	9	2	2	0	0
1997	New Jersey	10	1	6	7	6	1	0	0
1998	Dallas	14	0	3	3	20	0	0	0
1999♦	Dallas	17	0	2	2	18	0	0	0
Playoff Totals		**94**	**7**	**26**	**33**	**72**	**4**	**0**	**0**
CHAMPAGNE, Andre *No Playoffs*	Left wing								
CHAPDELAINE, Rene *No Playoffs*	Defense								
CHAPMAN, Art	Center								
1931	Boston	5	0	1	1	7	....	....	....
1933	Boston	5	0	0	0	2	....	....	....
1936	NY Americans	5	0	3	3	0	....	....	....
1938	NY Americans	6	0	1	1	0	....	....	....
1939	NY Americans	2	0	0	0	0	....	....	....
1940	NY Americans	3	1	0	1	0	....	....	....
Playoff Totals		**26**	**1**	**5**	**6**	**9**	....	....	....
CHAPMAN, Blair	Right wing								
1977	Pittsburgh	3	1	1	2	7	0	0	0
1979	Pittsburgh	7	1	0	1	2	0	0	0
1980	St. Louis	3	0	0	0	0	0	0	0
1981	St. Louis	9	2	5	7	6	0	0	0
1982	St. Louis	3	0	0	0	0	0	0	0
Playoff Totals		**25**	**4**	**6**	**10**	**15**	**0**	**0**	**0**
CHAPMAN, Brian *No Playoffs*	Defense								
•CHARA, Zdeno	Defense								
2002	Ottawa	10	0	1	1	12	0	0	0
Playoff Totals		**10**	**0**	**1**	**1**	**12**	**0**	**0**	**0**
CHARBONNEAU, Jose	Right wing								
1988	Montreal	8	0	0	0	4	0	0	0
1994	Vancouver	3	1	0	1	4	0	0	0
Playoff Totals		**11**	**1**	**0**	**1**	**8**	**0**	**0**	**0**
CHARBONNEAU, Stephane *No Playoffs*	Right wing								
CHARLEBOIS, Bob *No Playoffs*	Left wing								
CHARLESWORTH, Todd *No Playoffs*	Defense								
CHARRON, Eric	Defense								
1996	Washington	6	0	0	0	8	0	0	0
Playoff Totals		**6**	**0**	**0**	**0**	**8**	**0**	**0**	**0**
CHARRON, Guy *No Playoffs*	Center								

Season	Team	GP	G	A	Pts	PIM	PP	SH	GW
CHARTIER, Dave *No Playoffs*	Center								
•CHARTRAND, Brad	Right wing								
2000	Los Angeles	4	0	0	0	6	0	0	0
2002	Los Angeles	7	1	1	2	2	0	0	1
Playoff Totals		**11**	**1**	**1**	**2**	**8**	**0**	**0**	**1**
CHARTRAW, Rick	Defense/Right wing								
1976♦	Montreal	2	0	0	0	0	0	0	0
1977♦	Montreal	13	2	1	3	17	0	0	0
1978♦	Montreal	10	1	0	1	10	0	0	1
1979♦	Montreal	16	2	1	3	24	0	0	0
1980	Montreal	10	2	2	4	0	0	0	0
1981	Los Angeles	4	0	1	1	4	0	0	0
1982	Los Angeles	10	0	2	2	17	0	0	0
1983	NY Rangers	9	0	2	2	6	0	0	0
1984	Edmonton	1	0	0	0	2	0	0	0
Playoff Totals		**75**	**7**	**9**	**16**	**80**	**0**	**0**	**1**
CHASE, Kelly	Right wing								
1990	St. Louis	9	1	0	1	46	0	0	0
1991	St. Louis	6	0	0	0	18	0	0	0
1992	St. Louis	1	0	0	0	7	0	0	0
1994	St. Louis	4	0	1	1	6	0	0	0
1998	St. Louis	7	0	0	0	23	0	0	0
Playoff Totals		**27**	**1**	**1**	**2**	**100**	**0**	**0**	**0**
CHASSE, Denis	Right wing								
1995	St. Louis	7	1	7	8	23	0	0	0
Playoff Totals		**7**	**1**	**7**	**8**	**23**	**0**	**0**	**0**
•CHEBATURKIN, Vladimir	Defense								
2002	Chicago	3	0	0	0	2	0	0	0
Playoff Totals		**3**	**0**	**0**	**0**	**2**	**0**	**0**	**0**
CHECK, Lude *No Playoffs*	Left wing								
•CHEECHOO, Jonathan *No Playoffs*	Right wing								
•CHELIOS, Chris	Defense								
1984	Montreal	15	1	9	10	17	1	0	0
1985	Montreal	9	2	8	10	17	2	0	0
1986♦	Montreal	20	2	9	11	49	1	0	0
1987	Montreal	17	4	9	13	38	2	1	0
1988	Montreal	11	3	1	4	29	1	0	0
1989	Montreal	21	4	15	19	28	1	0	2
1990	Montreal	5	0	1	1	8	0	0	0
1991	Chicago	6	1	7	8	46	1	0	0
1992	Chicago	18	6	15	21	37	3	0	1
1993	Chicago	4	0	2	2	14	0	0	0
1994	Chicago	6	1	1	2	8	1	0	0
1995	Chicago	16	4	7	11	12	0	1	3
1996	Chicago	9	0	3	3	8	0	0	0
1997	Chicago	6	0	1	1	8	0	0	0
1999	Detroit	10	0	4	4	14	0	0	0
2000	Detroit	9	0	1	1	8	0	0	0
2001	Detroit	5	0	1	1	2	0	0	0
2002♦	Detroit	23	1	13	14	44	1	0	0
Playoff Totals		**210**	**30**	**106**	**136**	**387**	**14**	**2**	**6**
CHERNOFF, Mike *No Playoffs*	Left wing								
CHERNOMAZ, Rich *No Playoffs*	Right wing								
CHERRY, Dick	Defense								
1969	Philadelphia	4	1	0	1	4	0	0	0
Playoff Totals		**4**	**1**	**0**	**1**	**4**	**0**	**0**	**0**
CHERRY, Don	Defense								
1955	Boston	1	0	0	0	0	0	0	0
Playoff Totals		**1**	**0**	**0**	**0**	**0**	**0**	**0**	**0**
CHERVYAKOV, Denis *No Playoffs*	Defense								
CHEVREFILS, Real	Left wing								
1952	Boston	7	1	1	2	6	....	....	....
1953	Boston	7	0	1	1	6	....	....	....
1955	Boston	5	2	1	3	4	....	....	....
1957	Boston	10	2	1	3	4	....	....	....
1958	Boston	1	0	0	0	0	....	....	....
Playoff Totals		**30**	**5**	**4**	**9**	**20**	....	....	....
CHIASSON, Steve	Defense								
1987	Detroit	2	0	0	0	19	0	0	0
1988	Detroit	9	2	2	4	31	1	0	0
1989	Detroit	5	2	1	3	6	1	0	0
1991	Detroit	5	3	1	4	19	1	0	0
1992	Detroit	11	1	5	6	12	1	0	0
1993	Detroit	7	2	2	4	19	1	0	1
1994	Detroit	7	2	3	5	2	2	0	1
1995	Calgary	7	1	2	3	9	1	0	0
1996	Calgary	4	2	1	3	0	0	0	0
1999	Carolina	6	1	2	3	2	1	0	0
Playoff Totals		**63**	**16**	**19**	**35**	**119**	**9**	**0**	**2**
CHIBIREV, Igor *No Playoffs*	Center								
CHICOINE, Dan	Right wing								
1980	Minnesota	1	0	0	0	0	0	0	0
Playoff Totals		**1**	**0**	**0**	**0**	**0**	**0**	**0**	**0**
•CHIMERA, Jason *No Playoffs*	Center								
CHINNICK, Rick *No Playoffs*	Right wing								
CHIPPERFIELD, Ron *No Playoffs*	Center								
CHISHOLM, Art *No Playoffs*	Center/Defense								
CHISHOLM, Colin *No Playoffs*	Defense								

Season	Team	GP	G	A	Pts	PIM	PP	SH	GW
CHISHOLM, Lex	Center/Right wing								
1941	Toronto	3	1	0	1	0	....	....	....
Playoff Totals		**3**	**1**	**0**	**1**	**0**	....	....	....
•CHISTOV, Stanislav *No Playoffs*	Left wing								
CHORNEY, Marc	Defense								
1981	Pittsburgh	2	0	1	1	2	0	0	0
1982	Pittsburgh	5	0	0	0	0	0	0	0
Playoff Totals		**7**	**0**	**1**	**1**	**2**	**0**	**0**	**0**
CHORSKE, Tom	Left wing								
1992	New Jersey	7	0	3	3	4	0	0	0
1993	New Jersey	1	0	0	0	0	0	0	0
1994	New Jersey	20	4	3	7	0	0	0	1
1995♦	New Jersey	17	1	5	6	4	0	0	0
1997	Ottawa	5	0	1	1	2	0	0	0
Playoff Totals		**50**	**5**	**12**	**17**	**10**	**0**	**0**	**1**
•CHOUINARD, Eric *No Playoffs*	Center								
CHOUINARD, Gene *No Playoffs*	Defense								
CHOUINARD, Guy	Center								
1976	Atlanta	2	0	0	0	0	0	0	0
1977	Atlanta	3	2	0	2	0	1	0	0
1978	Atlanta	2	1	0	1	0	0	0	0
1979	Atlanta	2	1	2	3	0	1	0	0
1980	Atlanta	4	1	3	4	4	1	0	0
1981	Calgary	16	3	14	17	4	0	0	0
1982	Calgary	3	0	1	1	0	0	0	0
1983	Calgary	9	1	6	7	4	0	0	0
1984	St. Louis	5	0	2	2	0	0	0	0
Playoff Totals		**46**	**9**	**28**	**37**	**12**	**3**	**0**	**0**
•CHOUINARD, Marc *No Playoffs*	Center								
CHRISTIAN, Dave	Right wing								
1982	Winnipeg	4	0	1	1	2	0	0	0
1983	Winnipeg	3	0	0	0	0	0	0	0
1984	Washington	8	5	4	9	5	1	0	0
1985	Washington	5	1	1	2	0	0	0	0
1986	Washington	9	4	4	8	0	1	0	0
1987	Washington	7	1	3	4	6	0	0	1
1988	Washington	14	5	6	11	6	1	0	0
1989	Washington	6	1	1	2	0	1	0	0
1990	Boston	21	4	1	5	4	1	0	0
1991	Boston	19	8	4	12	4	0	0	2
1992	St. Louis	4	3	0	3	0	0	0	0
1993	Chicago	1	0	0	0	0	0	0	0
1994	Chicago	1	0	0	0	0	0	0	0
Playoff Totals		**102**	**32**	**25**	**57**	**27**	**5**	**0**	**3**
•CHRISTIAN, Jeff *No Playoffs*	Left wing								
CHRISTIE, Mike	Defense								
1978	Colorado	2	0	0	0	0	0	0	0
Playoff Totals		**2**	**0**	**0**	**0**	**0**	**0**	**0**	**0**
•CHRISTIE, Ryan *No Playoffs*	Left wing								
CHRISTOFF, Steve	Center								
1980	Minnesota	14	8	4	12	7	2	0	0
1981	Minnesota	18	8	8	16	16	5	0	1
1982	Minnesota	2	0	0	0	2	0	0	0
1983	Calgary	1	0	0	0	0	0	0	0
Playoff Totals		**35**	**16**	**12**	**28**	**25**	**7**	**0**	**1**
CHRYSTAL, Bob *No Playoffs*	Defense								
•CHUBAROV, Artem	Center								
2002	Vancouver	6	0	1	1	0	0	0	0
Playoff Totals		**6**	**0**	**1**	**1**	**0**	**0**	**0**	**0**
•CHURCH, Brad *No Playoffs*	Left wing								
CHURCH, Jack	Defense								
1939	Toronto	1	0	0	0	0	....	....	....
1940	Toronto	10	1	1	2	6	....	....	....
1941	Toronto	5	0	0	0	8	....	....	....
1946	Boston	9	0	0	0	4	....	....	....
Playoff Totals		**25**	**1**	**1**	**2**	**18**	....	....	....
CHURLA, Shane	Right wing								
1987	Hartford	2	0	0	0	42	0	0	0
1988	Calgary	7	0	1	1	17	0	0	0
1990	Minnesota	7	0	0	0	44	0	0	0
1991	Minnesota	22	2	1	3	90	0	0	1
1994	Dallas	9	1	3	4	35	1	0	0
1995	Dallas	5	0	0	0	20	0	0	0
1996	NY Rangers	11	2	2	4	14	0	0	0
1997	NY Rangers	15	0	0	0	20	0	0	0
Playoff Totals		**78**	**5**	**7**	**12**	**282**	**1**	**0**	**1**
CHYCHRUN, Jeff	Defense								
1989	Philadelphia	19	0	2	2	65	0	0	0
1992♦	Pittsburgh	....	....	....	....	....	....	....	....
Playoff Totals		**19**	**0**	**2**	**2**	**65**	**0**	**0**	**0**
CHYNOWETH, Dean	Defense								
1994	NY Islanders	2	0	0	0	2	0	0	0
1996	Boston	4	0	0	0	24	0	0	0
Playoff Totals		**6**	**0**	**0**	**0**	**26**	**0**	**0**	**0**
CHYZOWSKI, Dave	Left wing								
1994	NY Islanders	2	0	0	0	0	0	0	0
Playoff Totals		**2**	**0**	**0**	**0**	**0**	**0**	**0**	**0**
CIAVAGLIA, Peter *No Playoffs*	Center								

Season	Team	GP	G	A	Pts	PIM	PP	SH	GW
•CIBAK, Martin *No Playoffs*	Center								
CICCARELLI, Dino	Right wing								
1981	Minnesota	19	14	7	21	25	5	0	3
1982	Minnesota	4	3	1	4	2	2	0	1
1983	Minnesota	9	4	6	10	11	1	0	2
1984	Minnesota	16	4	5	9	27	1	0	1
1985	Minnesota	9	3	3	6	8	1	0	0
1986	Minnesota	5	0	1	1	6	0	0	0
1989	Washington	6	3	3	6	12	3	0	0
1990	Washington	8	8	3	11	6	1	0	1
1991	Washington	11	5	4	9	22	3	0	2
1992	Washington	7	5	4	9	14	1	0	0
1993	Detroit	7	4	2	6	16	3	0	0
1994	Detroit	7	5	2	7	14	1	0	0
1995	Detroit	16	9	2	11	22	6	0	2
1996	Detroit	17	6	2	8	26	6	0	1
Playoff Totals		**141**	**73**	**45**	**118**	**211**	**34**	**0**	**13**
CICCONE, Enrico	Defense								
1996	Chicago	9	1	0	1	30	0	0	0
1997	Chicago	4	0	0	0	18	0	0	0
Playoff Totals		**13**	**1**	**0**	**1**	**48**	**0**	**0**	**0**
CICHOCKI, Chris *No Playoffs*	Right wing								
•CIERNIK, Ivan *No Playoffs*	Left wing								
CIERNY, Jozef *No Playoffs*	Left wing								
CIESLA, Hank	Center								
1958	NY Rangers	6	0	2	2	0	0	0	0
Playoff Totals		**6**	**0**	**2**	**2**	**0**	**0**	**0**	**0**
•CIGER, Zdeno	Left wing								
1991	New Jersey	6	0	2	2	4	0	0	0
1992	New Jersey	7	2	4	6	0	0	0	1
Playoff Totals		**13**	**2**	**6**	**8**	**4**	**0**	**0**	**1**
CIMELLARO, Tony *No Playoffs*	Center								
CIMETTA, Rob	Wing								
1989	Boston	1	0	0	0	15	0	0	0
Playoff Totals		**1**	**0**	**0**	**0**	**15**	**0**	**0**	**0**
CIRELLA, Joe	Defense								
1988	New Jersey	19	0	7	7	49	0	0	0
1991	NY Rangers	6	0	2	2	26	0	0	0
1992	NY Rangers	13	0	4	4	23	0	0	0
Playoff Totals		**38**	**0**	**13**	**13**	**98**	**0**	**0**	**0**
CIRONE, Jason *No Playoffs*	Center								
•CISAR, Marian *No Playoffs*	Right wing								
CLACKSON, Kim	Defense								
1980	Pittsburgh	3	0	0	0	37	0	0	0
1981	Quebec	5	0	0	0	33	0	0	0
Playoff Totals		**8**	**0**	**0**	**0**	**70**	**0**	**0**	**0**
CLANCY, King	Defense								
1922	Ottawa	2	0	0	0	2	....	....	....
1923♦	Ottawa	2	0	0	0	0	....	....	....
1924	Ottawa	2	0	0	0	6	....	....	....
1926	Ottawa	2	1	0	1	8	....	....	....
1927♦	Ottawa	6	1	1	2	14	....	....	....
1928	Ottawa	2	0	0	0	6	....	....	....
1930	Ottawa	2	0	1	1	2	....	....	....
1931	Toronto	2	1	0	1	0	....	....	....
1932♦	Toronto	7	2	1	3	14	....	....	....
1933	Toronto	9	0	3	3	14	....	....	....
1934	Toronto	3	0	0	0	8	....	....	....
1935	Toronto	7	1	0	1	8	....	....	....
1936	Toronto	9	2	2	4	10	....	....	....
Playoff Totals		**55**	**8**	**8**	**16**	**92**	....	....	....
CLANCY, Terry *No Playoffs*	Right wing								
CLAPPER, Dit	Right wing/Defense								
1928	Boston	2	0	0	0	2	....	....	....
1929♦	Boston	5	1	0	1	0	....	....	....
1930	Boston	6	4	0	4	4	....	....	....
1931	Boston	5	2	4	6	4	....	....	....
1933	Boston	5	1	1	2	2	....	....	....
1935	Boston	3	1	0	1	0	....	....	....
1936	Boston	2	0	1	1	0	....	....	....
1937	Boston	3	2	0	2	5	....	....	....
1938	Boston	3	0	0	0	12	....	....	....
1939♦	Boston	12	0	1	1	6	....	....	....
1940	Boston	5	0	2	2	2	....	....	....
1941♦	Boston	11	0	5	5	4	....	....	....
1943	Boston	9	2	3	5	9	....	....	....
1945	Boston	7	0	0	0	0	....	....	....
1946	Boston	4	0	0	0	0	....	....	....
Playoff Totals		**82**	**13**	**17**	**30**	**50**	....	....	....
•CLARK, Brett *No Playoffs*	Defense								
•CLARK, Chris *No Playoffs*	Right wing								
CLARK, Dan *No Playoffs*	Defense								
CLARK, Dean *No Playoffs*	Defense								
CLARK, Gordie	Right wing								
1976	Boston	1	0	0	0	0	0	0	0
Playoff Totals		**1**	**0**	**0**	**0**	**0**	**0**	**0**	**0**
CLARK, Nobby *No Playoffs*	Defense								

Season	Team	GP	G	A	Pts	PIM	PP	SH	GW
CLARK, Wendel	Left wing/Defense								
1986	Toronto	10	5	1	6	47	1	0	1
1987	Toronto	13	6	5	11	38	3	0	1
1990	Toronto	5	1	1	2	19	0	0	0
1993	Toronto	21	10	10	20	51	2	0	1
1994	Toronto	18	9	7	16	24	2	0	1
1995	Quebec	6	1	2	3	6	0	0	0
1996	Toronto	6	2	2	4	2	1	0	0
1999	Detroit	10	2	3	5	10	1	0	0
2000	Toronto	6	1	1	2	4	0	0	0
Playoff Totals		**95**	**37**	**32**	**69**	**201**	**10**	**0**	**4**
CLARKE, Bobby	Center								
1971	Philadelphia	4	0	0	0	2	0	0	0
1973	Philadelphia	11	2	6	8	6	2	0	1
1974♦	Philadelphia	17	5	11	16	42	1	0	2
1975♦	Philadelphia	17	4	*12	16	16	2	1	2
1976	Philadelphia	16	2	*14	16	28	1	0	0
1977	Philadelphia	10	5	5	10	8	2	0	0
1978	Philadelphia	12	4	7	11	8	1	0	0
1979	Philadelphia	8	2	4	6	8	1	0	0
1980	Philadelphia	19	8	12	20	16	3	0	2
1981	Philadelphia	12	3	3	6	6	0	1	0
1982	Philadelphia	4	4	2	6	4	1	1	0
1983	Philadelphia	3	1	0	1	2	0	0	0
1984	Philadelphia	3	2	1	3	6	0	0	0
Playoff Totals		**136**	**42**	**77**	**119**	**152**	**14**	**3**	**7**
•CLARKE, Dale *No Playoffs*	Defense								
•CLASSEN, Greg *No Playoffs*	Center								
•CLEARY, Daniel	Left wing								
2000	Edmonton	4	0	1	1	2	0	0	0
2001	Edmonton	6	1	1	2	8	1	0	0
Playoff Totals		**10**	**1**	**2**	**3**	**10**	**1**	**0**	**0**
CLEGHORN, Odie	Right wing/Center								
1919	Montreal	5	7	0	7	0	....	....	....
1923	Montreal	2	0	0	0	2	....	....	....
1924♦	Montreal	2	0	0	0	0	....	....	....
1925	Montreal	2	0	1	1	0	....	....	....
1926	Pittsburgh	1	0	0	0	0	....	....	....
Playoff Totals		**12**	**7**	**1**	**8**	**2**	....	....	....
CLEGHORN, Sprague	Defense								
1919	Ottawa	5	2	0	2	11	....	....	....
1920♦	Ottawa	....	....	....	....	....	....	....	....
1921	Toronto	1	0	0	0	0	....	....	....
1923	Montreal	1	0	0	0	7	....	....	....
1924♦	Montreal	2	0	0	0	0	....	....	....
1925	Montreal	2	1	2	3	2	....	....	....
1927	Boston	8	1	0	1	8	....	....	....
1928	Boston	2	0	0	0	0	....	....	....
Playoff Totals		**21**	**4**	**2**	**6**	**28**	....	....	....
CLEMENT, Bill	Center								
1973	Philadelphia	2	0	0	0	0	0	0	0
1974♦	Philadelphia	4	1	0	1	4	0	0	0
1975♦	Philadelphia	12	1	0	1	8	0	0	0
1976	Atlanta	2	0	1	1	0	0	0	0
1977	Atlanta	3	1	1	2	0	0	1	0
1978	Atlanta	2	0	0	0	2	0	0	0
1979	Atlanta	2	0	0	0	0	0	0	0
1980	Atlanta	4	0	0	0	4	0	0	0
1981	Calgary	16	2	1	3	6	0	0	0
1982	Calgary	3	0	0	0	2	0	0	0
Playoff Totals		**50**	**5**	**3**	**8**	**26**	**0**	**1**	**0**
CLINE, Bruce *No Playoffs*	Right wing								
CLIPPINGDALE, Steve	Left wing								
1977	Los Angeles	1	0	0	0	0	0	0	0
Playoff Totals		**1**	**0**	**0**	**0**	**0**	**0**	**0**	**0**
CLOUTIER, Real	Right wing								
1981	Quebec	3	0	0	0	10	0	0	0
1982	Quebec	16	7	5	12	10	1	0	1
1983	Quebec	4	0	0	0	0	0	0	0
1984	Buffalo	2	0	0	0	0	0	0	0
Playoff Totals		**25**	**7**	**5**	**12**	**20**	**1**	**0**	**1**
CLOUTIER, Rejean *No Playoffs*	Defense								
CLOUTIER, Roland *No Playoffs*	Center								
CLOUTIER, Sylvain *No Playoffs*	Center								
CLUNE, Wally *No Playoffs*	Defense								
•CLYMER, Ben *No Playoffs*	Left wing								
COALTER, Gary *No Playoffs*	Right wing								
COATES, Steve *No Playoffs*	Right wing								
COCHRANE, Glen	Defense								
1981	Philadelphia	6	1	1	2	18	0	0	0
1982	Philadelphia	2	0	0	0	2	0	0	0
1983	Philadelphia	3	0	0	0	4	0	0	0
1986	Vancouver	2	0	0	0	5	0	0	0
1988	Chicago	5	0	0	0	2	0	0	0
Playoff Totals		**18**	**1**	**1**	**2**	**31**	**0**	**0**	**0**

Season	Team	GP	G	A	Pts	PIM	PP	SH	GW
COFFEY, Paul	Defense								
1981	Edmonton	9	4	3	7	22	1	0	0
1982	Edmonton	5	1	1	2	6	1	0	0
1983	Edmonton	16	7	7	14	14	2	2	0
1984♦	Edmonton	19	8	14	22	21	2	0	1
1985♦	Edmonton	18	12	25	37	44	3	1	4
1986	Edmonton	10	1	9	10	30	1	0	0
1987♦	Edmonton	17	3	8	11	30	1	0	1
1989	Pittsburgh	11	2	13	15	31	2	0	1
1991♦	Pittsburgh	12	2	9	11	6	0	0	0
1992	Los Angeles	6	4	3	7	2	3	0	0
1993	Detroit	7	2	9	11	2	0	0	0
1994	Detroit	7	1	6	7	8	0	0	0
1995	Detroit	18	6	12	18	10	2	1	0
1996	Detroit	17	5	9	14	30	3	2	1
1997	Philadelphia	17	1	8	9	6	0	0	0
1999	Carolina	5	0	1	1	2	0	0	0
Playoff Totals		**194**	**59**	**137**	**196**	**264**	**21**	**6**	**8**
COFLIN, Hugh *No Playoffs*	Defense								
•**COLAIACOVO, Carlo** *No Playoffs*	Defense								
COLE, Danton	Center/Right wing								
1995♦	New Jersey	1	0	0	0	0	0	0	0
Playoff Totals		**1**	**0**	**0**	**0**	**0**	**0**	**0**	**0**
•**COLE, Erik**	Left wing								
2002	Carolina	23	6	3	9	30	1	0	1
Playoff Totals		**23**	**6**	**3**	**9**	**30**	**1**	**0**	**1**
COLLEY, Tom *No Playoffs*	Center								
COLLINGS, Norm *No Playoffs*	Forward								
COLLINS, Bill	Right wing								
1968	Minnesota	10	2	4	6	4	0	0	1
1970	Minnesota	6	0	1	1	8	0	0	0
1975	St. Louis	2	1	0	1	0	0	0	0
Playoff Totals		**18**	**3**	**5**	**8**	**12**	**0**	**0**	**1**
COLLINS, Gary	Center								
1959	Toronto	2	0	0	0	0	0	0	0
Playoff Totals		**2**	**0**	**0**	**0**	**0**	**0**	**0**	**0**
COLLYARD, Bob *No Playoffs*	Center								
COLMAN, Michael *No Playoffs*	Defense								
COLVILLE, Mac	Right wing/Defense								
1937	NY Rangers	9	1	2	3	2	....	....	....
1938	NY Rangers	3	0	2	2	0	....	....	....
1939	NY Rangers	7	1	2	3	4	....	....	....
1940♦	NY Rangers	12	3	2	5	6	....	....	....
1941	NY Rangers	3	1	1	2	2	....	....	....
1942	NY Rangers	6	3	1	4	0	....	....	....
Playoff Totals		**40**	**9**	**10**	**19**	**14**	....	....	....
COLVILLE, Neil	Center/Defense								
1937	NY Rangers	9	3	3	6	0	....	....	....
1938	NY Rangers	3	0	1	1	0	....	....	....
1939	NY Rangers	7	0	2	2	2	....	....	....
1940♦	NY Rangers	12	2	*7	*9	18	....	....	....
1941	NY Rangers	3	1	1	2	0	....	....	....
1942	NY Rangers	6	0	5	5	6	....	....	....
1948	NY Rangers	6	1	0	1	6	....	....	....
Playoff Totals		**46**	**7**	**19**	**26**	**32**	....	....	....
COLWILL, Les *No Playoffs*	Right wing								
COMEAU, Rey	Center								
1974	Atlanta	4	2	1	3	6	1	0	0
1977	Atlanta	3	0	0	0	2	0	0	0
1978	Atlanta	2	0	0	0	0	0	0	0
Playoff Totals		**9**	**2**	**1**	**3**	**8**	**1**	**0**	**0**
•**COMMODORE, Mike** *No Playoffs*	Defense								
•**COMRIE, Mike**	Center								
2001	Edmonton	6	1	2	3	0	1	0	1
Playoff Totals		**6**	**1**	**2**	**3**	**0**	**1**	**0**	**1**
COMRIE, Paul *No Playoffs*	Center								
CONACHER, Brian	Left wing								
1967♦	Toronto	12	3	2	5	21	0	0	2
Playoff Totals		**12**	**3**	**2**	**5**	**21**	**0**	**0**	**2**
CONACHER, Charlie	Right wing								
1931	Toronto	2	0	1	1	0	....	....	....
1932♦	Toronto	7	*6	2	8	6	....	....	....
1933	Toronto	9	1	1	2	10	....	....	....
1934	Toronto	5	3	2	5	0	....	....	....
1935	Toronto	7	1	*4	*5	6	....	....	....
1936	Toronto	9	3	2	5	12	....	....	....
1937	Toronto	2	0	0	0	5	....	....	....
1939	Detroit	5	2	5	7	2	....	....	....
1940	NY Americans	3	1	1	2	8	....	....	....
Playoff Totals		**49**	**17**	**18**	**35**	**49**	....	....	....
CONACHER, Jim	Center								
1946	Detroit	5	1	1	2	0	....	....	....
1947	Detroit	5	2	1	3	2	....	....	....
1948	Detroit	9	2	0	2	2	....	....	....
Playoff Totals		**19**	**5**	**2**	**7**	**4**	....	....	....

Season	Team	GP	G	A	Pts	PIM	PP	SH	GW
CONACHER, Lionel	Defense								
1926	Pittsburgh	2	0	0	0	0	....	....	....
1929	NY Americans	2	0	0	0	10	....	....	....
1931	Mtl. Maroons	2	0	0	0	2	....	....	....
1932	Mtl. Maroons	4	0	0	0	2	....	....	....
1933	Mtl. Maroons	2	0	1	1	0	....	....	....
1934♦	Chicago	8	2	0	2	4	....	....	....
1935♦	Mtl. Maroons	7	0	0	0	14	....	....	....
1936	Mtl. Maroons	3	0	0	0	0	....	....	....
1937	Mtl. Maroons	5	0	1	1	2	....	....	....
Playoff Totals		**35**	**2**	**2**	**4**	**34**	....	....	....
CONACHER, Pat	Left wing								
1980	NY Rangers	3	0	1	1	2	0	0	0
1984♦	Edmonton	3	1	0	1	2	0	0	0
1988	New Jersey	17	2	2	4	14	0	1	1
1990	New Jersey	5	1	0	1	10	0	0	0
1991	New Jersey	7	0	2	2	2	0	0	0
1992	New Jersey	7	1	1	2	4	0	1	0
1993	Los Angeles	24	6	4	10	6	0	0	0
Playoff Totals		**66**	**11**	**10**	**21**	**40**	**0**	**2**	**1**
CONACHER, Pete	Left wing								
1953	Chicago	2	0	0	0	0	0	0	0
1956	NY Rangers	5	0	0	0	0	0	0	0
Playoff Totals		**7**	**0**	**0**	**0**	**0**	**0**	**0**	**0**
CONACHER, Roy	Left wing								
1939♦	Boston	12	6	4	10	12	....	....	....
1940	Boston	6	2	1	3	0	....	....	....
1941♦	Boston	11	1	5	6	0	....	....	....
1942	Boston	5	2	1	3	0	....	....	....
1946	Boston	3	0	0	0	0	....	....	....
1947	Detroit	5	4	4	8	2	....	....	....
Playoff Totals		**42**	**15**	**15**	**30**	**14**	....	....	....
CONN, Red *No Playoffs*	Left wing								
CONN, Rob *No Playoffs*	Wing								
CONNELLY, Bert	Left wing								
1935	NY Rangers	4	1	0	1	0	....	....	....
1938♦	Chicago	10	0	0	0	0	....	....	....
Playoff Totals		**14**	**1**	**0**	**1**	**0**	....	....	....
CONNELLY, Wayne	Center								
1968	Minnesota	14	*8	3	11	2	3	0	0
1970	Detroit	4	1	3	4	2	1	0	0
1971	St. Louis	6	2	1	3	0	1	0	1
Playoff Totals		**24**	**11**	**7**	**18**	**4**	**5**	**0**	**1**
•**CONNOLLY, Tim** *No Playoffs*	Center								
CONNOR, Cam	Right wing								
1979♦	Montreal	8	1	0	1	0	0	0	1
1980	NY Rangers	2	0	0	0	2	0	0	0
1982	NY Rangers	10	4	0	4	4	1	0	1
Playoff Totals		**20**	**5**	**0**	**5**	**6**	**1**	**0**	**2**
CONNOR, Harry	Left wing								
1928	Boston	2	0	0	0	0	0	0	0
1929	NY Americans	2	0	0	0	2	0	0	0
1930	Boston	6	0	0	0	0	0	0	0
Playoff Totals		**10**	**0**	**0**	**0**	**2**	**0**	**0**	**0**
CONNORS, Bob	Left wing/Defense								
1929	Detroit	2	0	0	0	10	0	0	0
Playoff Totals		**2**	**0**	**0**	**0**	**10**	**0**	**0**	**0**
CONROY, Al *No Playoffs*	Center								
•**CONROY, Craig**	Center								
1997	St. Louis	6	0	0	0	8	0	0	0
1998	St. Louis	10	1	2	3	8	0	0	1
1999	St. Louis	13	2	1	3	6	0	0	0
2000	St. Louis	7	0	2	2	2	0	0	0
Playoff Totals		**36**	**3**	**5**	**8**	**24**	**0**	**0**	**1**
CONTINI, Joe	Center								
1978	Colorado	2	0	0	0	0	0	0	0
Playoff Totals		**2**	**0**	**0**	**0**	**0**	**0**	**0**	**0**
CONVERY, Brandon	Center								
1996	Toronto	5	0	0	0	2	0	0	0
Playoff Totals		**5**	**0**	**0**	**0**	**2**	**0**	**0**	**0**
CONVEY, Eddie *No Playoffs*	Left wing/Center								
COOK, Bill	Right wing								
1927	NY Rangers	2	1	0	1	6	....	....	....
1928♦	NY Rangers	9	2	3	5	26	....	....	....
1929	NY Rangers	6	0	0	0	6	....	....	....
1930	NY Rangers	4	0	1	1	11	....	....	....
1931	NY Rangers	4	3	0	3	4	....	....	....
1932	NY Rangers	7	3	3	6	2	....	....	....
1933♦	NY Rangers	8	3	2	5	4	....	....	....
1934	NY Rangers	2	0	0	0	2	....	....	....
1935	NY Rangers	4	1	2	3	7	....	....	....
Playoff Totals		**46**	**13**	**11**	**24**	**68**	....	....	....
COOK, Bob *No Playoffs*	Right wing								
COOK, Bud *No Playoffs*	Center								

Season	Team	GP	G	A	Pts	PIM	PP	SH	GW
COOK, Bun	Left wing								
1927	NY Rangers	2	0	0	0	6	....	....	....
1928♦	NY Rangers	9	2	1	3	10	....	....	....
1929	NY Rangers	6	1	0	1	12	....	....	....
1930	NY Rangers	4	2	0	2	2	....	....	....
1931	NY Rangers	4	0	0	0	2	....	....	....
1932	NY Rangers	7	6	2	8	12	....	....	....
1933♦	NY Rangers	8	2	0	2	4	....	....	....
1934	NY Rangers	2	0	0	0	2	....	....	....
1935	NY Rangers	4	2	0	2	0	....	....	....
Playoff Totals		**46**	**15**	**3**	**18**	**50**	....	....	....
COOK, Lloyd *No Playoffs*	Defense								
COOK, Tom	Center								
1930	Chicago	2	0	1	1	4	....	....	....
1931	Chicago	9	1	3	4	11	....	....	....
1932	Chicago	2	0	0	0	2	....	....	....
1934♦	Chicago	8	1	0	1	0	....	....	....
1935	Chicago	2	0	0	0	2	....	....	....
1936	Chicago	1	0	0	0	0	....	....	....
Playoff Totals		**24**	**2**	**4**	**6**	**19**	....	....	....
•**COOKE, Matt**	Left wing								
2001	Vancouver	4	0	0	0	4	0	0	0
2002	Vancouver	6	3	2	5	0	1	0	0
Playoff Totals		**10**	**3**	**2**	**5**	**4**	**1**	**0**	**0**
COOPER, Carson	Right wing								
1927	Montreal	3	0	0	0	0	0	0	0
1929	Detroit	2	0	0	0	2	0	0	0
1932	Detroit	2	0	0	0	0	0	0	0
Playoff Totals		**7**	**0**	**0**	**0**	**2**	**0**	**0**	**0**
•**COOPER, David** *No Playoffs*	Defense								
COOPER, Ed *No Playoffs*	Left wing								
COOPER, Hal *No Playoffs*	Right wing								
COOPER, Joe	Defense								
1937	NY Rangers	9	1	1	2	12	....	....	....
1938	NY Rangers	3	0	0	0	4	....	....	....
1940	Chicago	2	0	0	0	0	....	....	....
1941	Chicago	5	1	0	1	8	....	....	....
1942	Chicago	3	0	2	2	2	....	....	....
1944	Chicago	9	1	1	2	18	....	....	....
1946	Chicago	4	0	1	1	14	....	....	....
Playoff Totals		**35**	**3**	**5**	**8**	**58**	....	....	....
COPP, Bob *No Playoffs*	Defense								
CORBEAU, Bert	Defense								
1918	Montreal	2	1	1	2	11	....	....	....
1919	Montreal	5	1	1	2	17	....	....	....
1925	Toronto	2	0	0	0	10	....	....	....
Playoff Totals		**9**	**2**	**2**	**4**	**38**	....	....	....
CORBET, Rene	Left wing								
1995	Quebec	2	0	1	1	0	0	0	0
1996♦	Colorado	8	3	2	5	2	1	0	1
1997	Colorado	17	2	2	4	27	0	0	0
1998	Colorado	2	0	0	0	2	0	0	0
2000	Pittsburgh	7	1	1	2	9	0	0	0
2001	Pittsburgh	17	1	0	1	12	0	0	1
Playoff Totals		**53**	**7**	**6**	**13**	**52**	**1**	**0**	**2**
CORBETT, Mike	Right wing/Defense								
1968	Los Angeles	2	0	1	1	2	0	0	0
Playoff Totals		**2**	**0**	**1**	**1**	**2**	**0**	**0**	**0**
CORCORAN, Norm	Center/Right wing								
1955	Boston	4	0	0	0	6	0	0	0
Playoff Totals		**4**	**0**	**0**	**0**	**6**	**0**	**0**	**0**
•**CORKUM, Bob**	Center								
1990	Buffalo	5	1	0	1	4	0	0	0
1992	Buffalo	4	1	0	1	0	1	0	0
1993	Buffalo	5	0	0	0	2	0	0	0
1996	Philadelphia	12	1	2	3	6	0	0	0
1997	Phoenix	7	2	2	4	4	0	0	1
1998	Phoenix	6	1	0	1	4	0	0	0
1999	Phoenix	7	0	1	1	4	0	0	0
2000	Los Angeles	4	0	0	0	0	0	0	0
2001	New Jersey	12	1	2	3	0	0	0	0
Playoff Totals		**62**	**7**	**7**	**14**	**24**	**1**	**0**	**1**
CORMIER, Roger *No Playoffs*	Right wing								
CORNFORTH, Mark *No Playoffs*	Defense								
CORRIGAN, Chuck *No Playoffs*	Right wing								
CORRIGAN, Mike	Left wing								
1974	Los Angeles	3	0	1	1	4	0	0	0
1975	Los Angeles	3	0	0	0	4	0	0	0
1976	Los Angeles	9	2	2	4	12	0	0	0
1977	Pittsburgh	2	0	0	0	0	0	0	0
Playoff Totals		**17**	**2**	**3**	**5**	**20**	**0**	**0**	**0**
•**CORRINET, Chris** *No Playoffs*	Right wing								
CORRIVEAU, Andre *No Playoffs*	Right wing								

Season	Team	GP	G	A	Pts	PIM	PP	SH	GW
CORRIVEAU, Yvon	Left wing								
1986	Washington	4	0	3	3	2	0	0	0
1988	Washington	13	1	2	3	30	0	0	0
1989	Washington	1	0	0	0	0	0	0	0
1990	Hartford	4	1	0	1	0	0	0	0
1992	Hartford	7	3	2	5	18	2	0	1
Playoff Totals		**29**	**5**	**7**	**12**	**50**	**2**	**0**	**1**
•CORSO, Daniel	Center								
2001	St. Louis	12	0	1	1	0	0	0	0
2002	St. Louis	2	0	0	0	0	0	0	0
Playoff Totals		**14**	**0**	**1**	**1**	**0**	**0**	**0**	**0**
•CORSON, Shayne	Left wing								
1987	Montreal	17	6	5	11	30	1	1	1
1988	Montreal	3	1	0	1	12	0	0	0
1989	Montreal	21	4	5	9	65	2	0	2
1990	Montreal	11	2	8	10	20	0	0	0
1991	Montreal	13	9	6	15	36	4	1	3
1992	Montreal	10	2	5	7	15	0	0	0
1996	St. Louis	13	8	6	14	22	6	1	1
1997	Montreal	5	1	0	1	4	0	1	0
1998	Montreal	10	3	6	9	26	1	0	1
2001	Toronto	11	1	1	2	14	0	0	0
2002	Toronto	19	1	6	7	33	0	0	0
Playoff Totals		**133**	**38**	**48**	**86**	**277**	**14**	**4**	**8**
•CORVO, Joe	*No Playoffs* — Defense								
CORY, Ross	*No Playoffs* — Defense								
COSSETTE, Jacques	Right wing								
1979	Pittsburgh	3	0	1	1	4	0	0	0
Playoff Totals		**3**	**0**	**1**	**1**	**4**	**0**	**0**	**0**
COSTELLO, Les	Left wing								
1948♦	Toronto	5	2	2	4	2	....	....	....
1950	Toronto	1	0	0	0	0	....	....	....
Playoff Totals		**6**	**2**	**2**	**4**	**2**	....	....	....
COSTELLO, Murray	Center								
1955	Boston	1	0	0	0	2	0	0	0
1956	Detroit	4	0	0	0	0	0	0	0
Playoff Totals		**5**	**0**	**0**	**0**	**2**	**0**	**0**	**0**
COSTELLO, Rich	*No Playoffs* — Center								
COTCH, Charlie	*No Playoffs* — Left wing								
COTE, Alain	Left wing								
1981	Quebec	4	0	0	0	6	0	0	0
1982	Quebec	16	1	2	3	8	0	0	0
1983	Quebec	4	0	3	3	0	0	0	0
1984	Quebec	9	0	2	2	17	0	0	0
1985	Quebec	18	5	5	10	11	0	0	1
1986	Quebec	3	1	0	1	0	0	0	0
1987	Quebec	13	2	3	5	2	0	0	0
Playoff Totals		**67**	**9**	**15**	**24**	**44**	**0**	**0**	**1**
COTE, Alain	Defense								
1991	Montreal	11	0	2	2	26	0	0	0
Playoff Totals		**11**	**0**	**2**	**2**	**26**	**0**	**0**	**0**
COTE, Patrick	*No Playoffs* — Left wing								
COTE, Ray	Center								
1983	Edmonton	14	3	2	5	0	0	0	0
Playoff Totals		**14**	**3**	**2**	**5**	**0**	**0**	**0**	**0**
•COTE, Sylvain	Defense								
1987	Hartford	2	0	2	2	2	0	0	0
1988	Hartford	6	1	1	2	4	1	0	0
1989	Hartford	3	0	1	1	4	0	0	0
1990	Hartford	5	0	0	0	2	0	0	0
1991	Hartford	6	0	2	2	2	0	0	0
1992	Washington	7	1	2	3	4	0	0	0
1993	Washington	6	1	1	2	4	0	0	0
1994	Washington	9	1	8	9	6	0	0	0
1995	Washington	7	1	3	4	2	0	0	0
1996	Washington	6	2	0	2	12	1	0	0
1999	Toronto	17	2	1	3	10	0	0	0
2000	Dallas	23	2	1	3	8	2	0	0
2001	Washington	5	0	0	0	2	0	0	0
Playoff Totals		**102**	**11**	**22**	**33**	**62**	**4**	**0**	**0**
COTTON, Baldy	Left wing								
1926	Pittsburgh	2	1	0	1	0	....	....	....
1928	Pittsburgh	2	1	1	2	2	....	....	....
1929	Toronto	4	0	0	0	2	....	....	....
1931	Toronto	2	0	0	0	2	....	....	....
1932♦	Toronto	7	2	2	4	8	....	....	....
1933	Toronto	9	0	3	3	6	....	....	....
1934	Toronto	5	0	2	2	0	....	....	....
1935	Toronto	7	0	0	0	17	....	....	....
1936	NY Americans	5	0	1	1	9	....	....	....
Playoff Totals		**43**	**4**	**9**	**13**	**46**	....	....	....
COUGHLIN, Jack	*No Playoffs* — Right wing								
COULIS, Tim	Left wing								
1985	Minnesota	3	1	0	1	2	0	0	1
Playoff Totals		**3**	**1**	**0**	**1**	**2**	**0**	**0**	**1**
COULSON, D'arcy	*No Playoffs* — Defense								

Season	Team	GP	G	A	Pts	PIM	PP	SH	GW
COULTER, Art	Defense								
1932	Chicago	2	1	0	1	0	....	....	....
1934♦	Chicago	8	1	0	1	10	....	....	....
1935	Chicago	2	0	0	0	5	....	....	....
1937	NY Rangers	9	0	3	3	15	....	....	....
1939	NY Rangers	7	1	1	2	6	....	....	....
1940♦	NY Rangers	12	1	0	1	21	....	....	....
1941	NY Rangers	3	0	0	0	0	....	....	....
1942	NY Rangers	6	0	1	1	4	....	....	....
Playoff Totals		**49**	**4**	**5**	**9**	**61**	....	....	....
COULTER, Neal	*No Playoffs* — Right wing								
COURNOYER, Yvan	Right wing								
1965♦	Montreal	12	3	1	4	0	3	0	1
1966♦	Montreal	10	2	3	5	2	1	0	1
1967	Montreal	10	2	3	5	6	2	0	1
1968♦	Montreal	13	6	8	14	4	3	0	1
1969♦	Montreal	14	4	7	11	5	0	2	2
1971♦	Montreal	20	10	12	22	6	2	0	1
1972	Montreal	6	2	1	3	2	0	0	0
1973♦	Montreal	17	*15	10	*25	2	3	0	3
1974	Montreal	6	5	2	7	2	0	0	2
1975	Montreal	11	5	6	11	4	2	0	0
1976♦	Montreal	13	3	6	9	4	2	0	1
1977♦	Montreal	....	....	....	....	....	....	....	....
1978♦	Montreal	15	7	4	11	10	0	0	2
1979♦	Montreal	....	....	....	....	....	....	....	....
Playoff Totals		**147**	**64**	**63**	**127**	**47**	**18**	**2**	**15**
COURTEAU, Yves	Right wing								
1986	Calgary	1	0	0	0	0	0	0	0
Playoff Totals		**1**	**0**	**0**	**0**	**0**	**0**	**0**	**0**
COURTENAY, Ed	*No Playoffs* — Right wing								
COURTNALL, Geoff	Left wing								
1985	Boston	5	0	2	2	7	0	0	0
1986	Boston	3	0	0	0	2	0	0	0
1987	Boston	1	0	0	0	0	0	0	0
1988♦	Edmonton	19	0	3	3	23	0	0	0
1989	Washington	6	2	5	7	12	1	0	0
1990	Washington	15	4	9	13	32	1	0	2
1991	Vancouver	6	3	5	8	4	0	0	0
1992	Vancouver	12	6	8	14	20	2	0	1
1993	Vancouver	12	4	10	14	12	1	0	1
1994	Vancouver	24	9	10	19	51	0	1	3
1995	Vancouver	11	4	2	6	34	3	1	1
1996	St. Louis	13	0	3	3	14	0	0	0
1997	St. Louis	6	3	1	4	23	1	0	2
1998	St. Louis	10	2	8	10	18	1	0	0
1999	St. Louis	13	2	4	6	10	2	0	0
Playoff Totals		**156**	**39**	**70**	**109**	**262**	**12**	**2**	**10**
COURTNALL, Russ	Right wing								
1986	Toronto	10	3	6	9	8	1	0	0
1987	Toronto	13	3	4	7	11	1	0	0
1988	Toronto	6	2	1	3	0	0	0	0
1989	Montreal	21	8	5	13	18	1	0	2
1990	Montreal	11	5	1	6	10	0	0	0
1991	Montreal	13	8	3	11	7	2	2	1
1992	Montreal	10	1	1	2	4	0	0	1
1994	Dallas	9	1	8	9	0	0	0	0
1995	Vancouver	11	4	8	12	21	0	2	1
1996	Vancouver	6	1	3	4	2	0	0	0
1997	NY Rangers	15	3	4	7	0	1	0	0
1998	Los Angeles	4	0	0	0	2	0	0	0
Playoff Totals		**129**	**39**	**44**	**83**	**83**	**6**	**4**	**5**
COURVILLE, Larry	*No Playoffs* — Left wing								
COUTU, Billy	Defense								
1918	Montreal	2	0	0	0	3	....	....	....
1919	Montreal	5	0	1	1	6	....	....	....
1923	Montreal	1	0	0	0	*22	....	....	....
1924♦	Montreal	2	0	0	0	0	....	....	....
1925	Montreal	2	0	0	0	0	....	....	....
1927	Boston	7	1	0	1	4	....	....	....
Playoff Totals		**19**	**1**	**1**	**2**	**35**	....	....	....
COUTURE, Gerry	Right wing								
1945	Detroit	2	0	0	0	0	....	....	....
1946	Detroit	5	0	2	2	0	....	....	....
1947	Detroit	1	0	0	0	0	....	....	....
1949	Detroit	10	2	0	2	2	....	....	....
1950♦	Detroit	14	5	4	9	2	....	....	....
1951	Detroit	6	1	1	2	0	....	....	....
1953	Chicago	7	1	0	1	0	....	....	....
Playoff Totals		**45**	**9**	**7**	**16**	**4**	....	....	....
COUTURE, Rosie	Right wing								
1930	Chicago	2	0	0	0	2	....	....	....
1931	Chicago	9	0	3	3	2	....	....	....
1932	Chicago	2	0	0	0	2	....	....	....
1934♦	Chicago	8	1	2	3	4	....	....	....
1935	Chicago	2	0	0	0	5	....	....	....
Playoff Totals		**23**	**1**	**5**	**6**	**15**	....	....	....
COUTURIER, Sylvain	*No Playoffs* — Center								
•COWAN, Jeff	*No Playoffs* — Left wing								

Season	Team	GP	G	A	Pts	PIM	PP	SH	GW
COWICK, Bruce	Left wing								
1974♦	Philadelphia	8	0	0	0	9	0	0	0
Playoff Totals		**8**	**0**	**0**	**0**	**9**	**0**	**0**	**0**
COWIE, Rob	*No Playoffs* — Defense								
COWLEY, Bill	Center								
1936	Boston	2	2	1	3	2	....	....	....
1937	Boston	3	0	3	3	0	....	....	....
1938	Boston	3	2	0	2	0	....	....	....
1939♦	Boston	12	3	11	*14	2	....	....	....
1940	Boston	6	0	1	1	7	....	....	....
1941♦	Boston	2	0	0	0	0	....	....	....
1942	Boston	5	0	3	3	5	....	....	....
1943	Boston	9	1	7	8	4	....	....	....
1945	Boston	7	3	3	6	0	....	....	....
1946	Boston	10	1	3	4	2	....	....	....
1947	Boston	5	0	2	2	0	....	....	....
Playoff Totals		**64**	**12**	**34**	**46**	**22**	....	....	....
COX, Danny	Left wing								
1929	Toronto	4	0	1	1	4	0	0	0
1930	Ottawa	2	0	0	0	0	0	0	0
1932	Detroit	2	0	0	0	2	0	0	0
1934	NY Rangers	2	0	0	0	0	0	0	0
Playoff Totals		**10**	**0**	**1**	**1**	**6**	**0**	**0**	**0**
COXE, Craig	Left wing								
1986	Vancouver	3	0	0	0	2	0	0	0
1988	Calgary	2	1	0	1	16	0	0	0
Playoff Totals		**5**	**1**	**0**	**1**	**18**	**0**	**0**	**0**
•CRAIG, Mike	Right wing								
1991	Minnesota	10	1	1	2	20	1	0	1
1992	Minnesota	4	1	0	1	7	0	0	0
1994	Dallas	4	0	0	0	2	0	0	0
1995	Toronto	2	0	1	1	2	0	0	0
1996	Toronto	6	0	0	0	18	0	0	0
Playoff Totals		**26**	**2**	**2**	**4**	**49**	**1**	**0**	**1**
CRAIGHEAD, John	*No Playoffs* — Right wing								
CRAIGWELL, Dale	*No Playoffs* — Center								
CRASHLEY, Bart	*No Playoffs* — Defense								
CRAVEN, Murray	Left wing								
1985	Philadelphia	19	4	6	10	11	1	1	1
1986	Philadelphia	5	0	3	3	4	0	0	0
1987	Philadelphia	12	3	1	4	9	2	0	0
1988	Philadelphia	7	2	5	7	4	0	0	1
1989	Philadelphia	1	0	0	0	0	0	0	0
1992	Hartford	7	3	3	6	6	0	1	0
1993	Vancouver	12	4	6	10	4	1	0	1
1994	Vancouver	22	4	9	13	18	0	0	1
1995	Chicago	16	5	5	10	4	0	0	1
1996	Chicago	9	1	4	5	2	1	0	0
1997	Chicago	2	0	0	0	2	0	0	0
1998	San Jose	6	1	1	2	0	0	0	0
Playoff Totals		**118**	**27**	**43**	**70**	**64**	**5**	**2**	**5**
CRAWFORD, Bob	Right wing								
1983	St. Louis	4	0	0	0	0	0	0	0
1986	NY Rangers	7	0	1	1	8	0	0	0
Playoff Totals		**11**	**0**	**1**	**1**	**8**	**0**	**0**	**0**
CRAWFORD, Bobby	*No Playoffs* — Right wing								
CRAWFORD, Jack	Defense								
1939♦	Boston	12	1	1	2	9	....	....	....
1940	Boston	6	0	0	0	0	....	....	....
1941♦	Boston	11	0	2	2	7	....	....	....
1942	Boston	5	0	1	1	4	....	....	....
1943	Boston	6	1	1	2	10	....	....	....
1945	Boston	7	0	5	5	0	....	....	....
1946	Boston	10	1	2	3	4	....	....	....
1947	Boston	2	0	0	0	0	....	....	....
1948	Boston	4	0	1	1	2	....	....	....
1949	Boston	3	0	0	0	0	....	....	....
Playoff Totals		**66**	**3**	**13**	**16**	**36**	....	....	....
CRAWFORD, Lou	Left wing								
1990	Boston	1	0	0	0	0	....	....	....
Playoff Totals		**1**	**0**	**0**	**0**	**0**	....	....	....
CRAWFORD, Marc	Left wing								
1982	Vancouver	14	1	0	1	11	0	0	0
1983	Vancouver	3	0	1	1	25	0	0	0
1986	Vancouver	3	0	1	1	8	0	0	0
Playoff Totals		**20**	**1**	**2**	**3**	**44**	**0**	**0**	**0**
CRAWFORD, Rusty	Left wing								
1918♦	Toronto	2	2	1	3	9	....	....	....
Playoff Totals		**2**	**2**	**1**	**3**	**9**	....	....	....
CREIGHTON, Adam	Center								
1989	Chicago	15	5	6	11	44	3	1	0
1990	Chicago	20	3	6	9	59	0	1	0
1991	Chicago	6	0	1	1	10	0	0	0
1995	St. Louis	7	2	0	2	16	1	0	1
1996	St. Louis	13	1	1	2	8	0	0	0
Playoff Totals		**61**	**11**	**14**	**25**	**137**	**4**	**2**	**1**

Season	Team	GP	G	A	Pts	PIM	PP	SH	GW
CREIGHTON, Dave	Center								
1949	Boston	3	0	0	0	0	....	....	....
1951	Boston	5	0	1	1	0	....	....	....
1952	Boston	7	2	1	3	2	....	....	....
1953	Boston	11	4	5	9	10	....	....	....
1954	Boston	4	0	0	0	0	....	....	....
1956	NY Rangers	5	0	0	0	4	....	....	....
1957	NY Rangers	5	2	2	4	2	....	....	....
1958	NY Rangers	6	3	3	6	2	....	....	....
1959	Toronto	5	0	1	1	0	....	....	....
Playoff Totals		**51**	**11**	**13**	**24**	**20**	....	....	....
CREIGHTON, Jimmy *No Playoffs*	Forward								
CRESSMAN, Dave *No Playoffs*	Left wing								
CRESSMAN, Glen *No Playoffs*	Center								
CRISP, Terry	Center								
1968	St. Louis	18	1	5	6	6	0	0	0
1969	St. Louis	12	3	4	7	20	0	2	0
1970	St. Louis	16	2	3	5	2	1	0	0
1971	St. Louis	6	1	0	1	2	0	0	0
1972	St. Louis	11	1	3	4	2	0	0	0
1973	Philadelphia	11	3	2	5	2	1	0	0
1974♦	Philadelphia	17	2	2	4	4	0	1	1
1975♦	Philadelphia	9	2	4	6	0	0	0	0
1976	Philadelphia	10	0	5	5	2	0	0	0
Playoff Totals		**110**	**15**	**28**	**43**	**40**	**2**	**3**	**1**
CRISTOFOLI, Ed *No Playoffs*	Right wing								
CROGHAN, Maurice *No Playoffs*	Defense								
CROMBEEN, Mike	Right wing								
1980	St. Louis	2	0	0	0	0	0	0	0
1981	St. Louis	11	3	0	3	8	0	0	2
1982	St. Louis	10	3	1	4	20	0	0	1
1983	St. Louis	4	0	1	1	4	0	0	0
Playoff Totals		**27**	**6**	**2**	**8**	**32**	**0**	**0**	**3**
CRONIN, Shawn	Defense								
1990	Winnipeg	5	0	0	0	7	0	0	0
1992	Winnipeg	4	0	0	0	6	0	0	0
1994	San Jose	14	1	0	1	20	0	0	0
1995	San Jose	9	0	0	0	5	0	0	0
Playoff Totals		**32**	**1**	**0**	**1**	**38**	**0**	**0**	**0**
•CROSS, Cory	Defense								
1996	Tampa Bay	6	0	0	0	22	0	0	0
2000	Toronto	12	0	2	2	2	0	0	0
2001	Toronto	11	2	1	3	10	0	0	1
2002	Toronto	12	0	0	0	8	0	0	0
Playoff Totals		**41**	**2**	**3**	**5**	**42**	**0**	**0**	**1**
CROSSETT, Stan *No Playoffs*	Defense								
CROSSMAN, Doug	Defense								
1982	Chicago	11	0	3	3	4	0	0	0
1983	Chicago	13	3	7	10	6	1	0	0
1984	Philadelphia	3	0	0	0	0	0	0	0
1985	Philadelphia	19	4	6	10	38	3	0	0
1986	Philadelphia	5	0	1	1	4	0	0	0
1987	Philadelphia	26	4	14	18	31	2	0	0
1988	Philadelphia	7	1	1	2	8	1	0	0
1989	Los Angeles	2	0	1	1	2	0	0	0
1990	NY Islanders	5	0	1	1	6	0	0	0
1991	Detroit	6	0	5	5	6	0	0	0
Playoff Totals		**97**	**12**	**39**	**51**	**105**	**7**	**0**	**0**
CROTEAU, Gary	Left wing								
1969	Los Angeles	11	3	2	5	8	1	0	0
Playoff Totals		**11**	**3**	**2**	**5**	**8**	**1**	**0**	**0**
CROWDER, Bruce	Right wing								
1982	Boston	11	5	3	8	9	1	0	0
1983	Boston	17	3	1	4	32	0	0	1
1984	Boston	3	0	0	0	0	0	0	0
Playoff Totals		**31**	**8**	**4**	**12**	**41**	**1**	**0**	**1**
CROWDER, Keith	Right wing								
1981	Boston	3	2	0	2	9	0	0	0
1982	Boston	11	2	2	4	14	0	0	0
1983	Boston	17	1	6	7	54	1	0	0
1984	Boston	3	0	0	0	7	0	0	0
1985	Boston	4	3	2	5	19	0	0	1
1986	Boston	3	2	0	2	21	0	0	0
1987	Boston	4	0	1	1	4	0	0	0
1988	Boston	23	3	9	12	44	1	0	0
1989	Boston	10	0	2	2	37	0	0	0
1990	Los Angeles	7	1	0	1	9	0	0	0
Playoff Totals		**85**	**14**	**22**	**36**	**218**	**2**	**0**	**1**
CROWDER, Troy	Right wing								
1988	New Jersey	1	0	0	0	12	0	0	0
1990	New Jersey	2	0	0	0	10	0	0	0
1992	Detroit	1	0	0	0	0	0	0	0
Playoff Totals		**4**	**0**	**0**	**0**	**22**	**0**	**0**	**0**
CROWE, Phil	Left wing								
1997	Ottawa	3	0	0	0	16	0	0	0
Playoff Totals		**3**	**0**	**0**	**0**	**16**	**0**	**0**	**0**
•CROWLEY, Mike *No Playoffs*	Defense								
CROWLEY, Ted *No Playoffs*	Defense								
•CROZIER, Greg *No Playoffs*	Left wing								

Season	Team	GP	G	A	Pts	PIM	PP	SH	GW
CROZIER, Joe *No Playoffs*	Defense								
CRUTCHFIELD, Nels	Center								
1935	Montreal	2	0	1	1	22	0	0	0
Playoff Totals		**2**	**0**	**1**	**1**	**22**	**0**	**0**	**0**
CULHANE, Jim *No Playoffs*	Defense								
CULLEN, Barry	Right wing								
1959	Toronto	2	0	0	0	0	0	0	0
1960	Detroit	4	0	0	0	2	0	0	0
Playoff Totals		**6**	**0**	**0**	**0**	**2**	**0**	**0**	**0**
CULLEN, Brian	Center								
1955	Toronto	4	1	0	1	0	1	0	0
1956	Toronto	5	1	0	1	2	1	0	0
1959	Toronto	10	1	0	1	0	0	0	0
Playoff Totals		**19**	**3**	**0**	**3**	**2**	**2**	**0**	**0**
•CULLEN, David *No Playoffs*	Defense								
CULLEN, John	Center								
1989	Pittsburgh	11	3	6	9	28	0	0	0
1991	Hartford	6	2	7	9	10	0	0	0
1992	Hartford	7	2	1	3	12	1	0	1
1993	Toronto	12	2	3	5	0	1	0	0
1994	Toronto	3	0	0	0	0	0	0	0
1995	Pittsburgh	9	0	2	2	8	0	0	0
1996	Tampa Bay	5	3	3	6	0	0	1	0
Playoff Totals		**53**	**12**	**22**	**34**	**58**	**2**	**1**	**1**
•CULLEN, Matt	Center								
1999	Anaheim	4	0	0	0	0	0	0	0
Playoff Totals		**4**	**0**	**0**	**0**	**0**	**0**	**0**	**0**
CULLEN, Ray	Center								
1968	Minnesota	14	2	6	8	2	1	0	0
1970	Minnesota	6	1	4	5	0	0	0	0
Playoff Totals		**20**	**3**	**10**	**13**	**2**	**1**	**0**	**0**
•CULLIMORE, Jassen	Defense								
1995	Vancouver	11	0	0	0	12	0	0	0
1997	Montreal	2	0	0	0	2	0	0	0
Playoff Totals		**13**	**0**	**0**	**0**	**14**	**0**	**0**	**0**
CUMMINS, Barry *No Playoffs*	Defense								
•CUMMINS, Jim	Right wing								
1995	Chicago	14	1	1	2	4	0	0	1
1996	Chicago	10	0	0	0	2	0	0	0
1997	Chicago	6	0	0	0	24	0	0	0
1998	Phoenix	3	0	0	0	4	0	0	0
1999	Phoenix	3	0	1	1	0	0	0	0
2002	NY Islanders	1	0	0	0	9	0	0	0
Playoff Totals		**37**	**1**	**2**	**3**	**43**	**0**	**0**	**1**
CUNNEYWORTH, Randy	Left wing								
1989	Pittsburgh	11	3	5	8	26	1	0	1
1990	Hartford	4	0	0	0	2	0	0	0
1991	Hartford	1	0	0	0	0	0	0	0
1992	Hartford	7	3	0	3	9	1	1	1
1994	Chicago	6	0	0	0	8	0	0	0
1997	Ottawa	7	1	1	2	10	0	0	0
1998	Ottawa	6	0	1	1	6	0	0	0
1999	Buffalo	3	0	0	0	0	0	0	0
Playoff Totals		**45**	**7**	**7**	**14**	**61**	**2**	**1**	**2**
CUNNINGHAM, Bob *No Playoffs*	Center								
CUNNINGHAM, Jim *No Playoffs*	Left wing								
CUNNINGHAM, Les	Center								
1940	Chicago	1	0	0	0	0	0	0	0
Playoff Totals		**1**	**0**	**0**	**0**	**0**	**0**	**0**	**0**
CUPOLO, Bill	Right wing								
1945	Boston	7	1	2	3	0	....	....	....
Playoff Totals		**7**	**1**	**2**	**3**	**0**	....	....	....
CURRAN, Brian	Defense								
1984	Boston	3	0	0	0	7	0	0	0
1986	Boston	2	0	0	0	4	0	0	0
1987	NY Islanders	8	0	0	0	51	0	0	0
1988	Toronto	6	0	0	0	41	0	0	0
1990	Toronto	5	0	1	1	19	0	0	0
Playoff Totals		**24**	**0**	**1**	**1**	**122**	**0**	**0**	**0**
CURRIE, Dan *No Playoffs*	Left wing								
CURRIE, Glen	Center								
1983	Washington	4	0	3	3	4	0	0	0
1984	Washington	8	1	0	1	0	0	0	0
Playoff Totals		**12**	**1**	**3**	**4**	**4**	**0**	**0**	**0**
CURRIE, Hugh *No Playoffs*	Defense								
CURRIE, Tony	Right wing								
1980	St. Louis	2	0	0	0	0	0	0	0
1981	St. Louis	11	4	12	16	4	1	0	0
1982	Vancouver	3	0	0	0	10	0	0	0
Playoff Totals		**16**	**4**	**12**	**16**	**14**	**1**	**0**	**0**

Season	Team	GP	G	A	Pts	PIM	PP	SH	GW
CURRY, Floyd	Right wing								
1949	Montreal	2	0	0	0	2	....	....	....
1950	Montreal	5	1	0	1	2	....	....	....
1951	Montreal	11	0	2	2	2	....	....	....
1952	Montreal	11	4	3	*7	6	....	....	....
1953♦	Montreal	12	2	1	3	2	....	....	....
1954	Montreal	11	4	0	4	4	....	....	....
1955	Montreal	12	8	4	12	4	....	....	....
1956♦	Montreal	10	1	5	6	12	....	....	....
1957♦	Montreal	10	3	2	5	2	....	....	....
1958♦	Montreal	7	0	0	0	2	....	....	....
Playoff Totals		**91**	**23**	**17**	**40**	**38**	....	....	....
CURTALE, Tony *No Playoffs*	Defense								
CURTIS, Paul	Defense								
1973	St. Louis	5	0	0	0	2	0	0	0
Playoff Totals		**5**	**0**	**0**	**0**	**2**	**0**	**0**	**0**
CUSHENAN, Ian *No Playoffs*	Defense								
CUSSON, Jean *No Playoffs*	Left wing								
•CUTTA, Jakub *No Playoffs*	Defense								
CYR, Denis	Right wing								
1983	Chicago	1	0	0	0	0	0	0	0
1985	St. Louis	3	0	0	0	0	0	0	0
Playoff Totals		**4**	**0**	**0**	**0**	**0**	**0**	**0**	**0**
CYR, Paul	Left wing								
1983	Buffalo	10	1	3	4	6	1	0	0
1984	Buffalo	3	0	1	1	0	0	0	0
1985	Buffalo	5	2	2	4	15	0	0	0
1991	Hartford	6	1	0	1	10	0	0	0
Playoff Totals		**24**	**4**	**6**	**10**	**31**	**1**	**0**	**0**
•CZERKAWSKI, Mariusz	Right wing								
1994	Boston	13	3	3	6	4	1	0	0
1995	Boston	5	1	0	1	0	0	0	0
1997	Edmonton	12	2	1	3	10	0	0	0
2002	NY Islanders	7	2	2	4	4	1	0	0
Playoff Totals		**37**	**8**	**6**	**14**	**18**	**2**	**0**	**0**
•DACKELL, Andreas	Right wing								
1997	Ottawa	7	1	0	1	0	0	0	0
1998	Ottawa	11	1	1	2	2	1	0	0
1999	Ottawa	4	0	1	1	0	0	0	0
2000	Ottawa	6	2	1	3	2	0	0	1
2001	Ottawa	4	0	0	0	0	0	0	0
2002	Montreal	12	1	2	3	6	0	0	0
Playoff Totals		**44**	**5**	**5**	**10**	**10**	**1**	**0**	**1**
•DAGENAIS, Pierre *No Playoffs*	Right wing								
•DAHL, Kevin	Defense								
1993	Calgary	6	0	2	2	8	0	0	0
1994	Calgary	6	0	0	0	4	0	0	0
1995	Calgary	3	0	0	0	0	0	0	0
1996	Calgary	1	0	0	0	0	0	0	0
Playoff Totals		**16**	**0**	**2**	**2**	**12**	**0**	**0**	**0**
•DAHLEN, Ulf	Right wing								
1989	NY Rangers	4	0	0	0	0	0	0	0
1990	Minnesota	7	1	4	5	2	0	0	0
1991	Minnesota	15	2	6	8	4	0	0	0
1992	Minnesota	7	0	3	3	2	0	0	0
1994	San Jose	14	6	2	8	0	3	0	1
1995	San Jose	11	5	4	9	0	3	0	1
1997	Chicago	5	0	1	1	0	0	0	0
2000	Washington	5	0	1	1	2	0	0	0
2001	Washington	6	0	1	1	2	0	0	0
Playoff Totals		**74**	**14**	**22**	**36**	**12**	**6**	**0**	**2**
DAHLIN, Kjell	Right wing								
1986♦	Montreal	16	2	3	5	4	0	0	0
1987	Montreal	8	2	4	6	0	0	0	0
1988	Montreal	11	2	4	6	2	0	0	0
Playoff Totals		**35**	**6**	**11**	**17**	**6**	**0**	**0**	**0**
•DAHLMAN, Toni *No Playoffs*	Right wing								
DAHLQUIST, Chris	Defense								
1989	Pittsburgh	2	0	0	0	0	0	0	0
1991	Minnesota	23	1	6	7	20	0	0	0
1992	Minnesota	7	0	0	0	6	0	0	0
1993	Calgary	6	3	1	4	4	0	0	0
1994	Calgary	1	0	0	0	0	0	0	0
Playoff Totals		**39**	**4**	**7**	**11**	**30**	**0**	**0**	**0**
DAHLSTROM, Cully	Center								
1938♦	Chicago	10	3	1	4	2	....	....	....
1940	Chicago	2	0	0	0	0	....	....	....
1941	Chicago	5	3	3	6	2	....	....	....
1942	Chicago	3	0	0	0	0	....	....	....
1944	Chicago	9	0	4	4	0	....	....	....
Playoff Totals		**29**	**6**	**8**	**14**	**4**	....	....	....
DAIGLE, Alain	Right wing								
1975	Chicago	2	0	0	0	0	0	0	0
1976	Chicago	4	0	0	0	0	0	0	0
1977	Chicago	1	0	0	0	0	0	0	0
1978	Chicago	4	0	1	1	0	0	0	0
1979	Chicago	4	0	0	0	0	0	0	0
1980	Chicago	2	0	0	0	0	0	0	0
Playoff Totals		**17**	**0**	**1**	**1**	**0**	**0**	**0**	**0**

Season	Team	GP	G	A	Pts	PIM	PP	SH	GW
•DAIGLE, Alexandre	Center								
1997	Ottawa	7	0	0	0	2	0	0	0
1998	Philadelphia	5	0	2	2	0	0	0	0
Playoff Totals		**12**	**0**	**2**	**2**	**2**	**0**	**0**	**0**
DAIGNEAULT, J.J.	Defense								
1986	Vancouver	3	0	2	2	0	0	0	0
1987	Philadelphia	9	1	0	1	0	0	0	1
1990	Montreal	9	0	0	0	2	0	0	0
1991	Montreal	5	0	1	1	0	0	0	0
1992	Montreal	11	0	3	3	4	0	0	0
1993♦	Montreal	20	1	3	4	22	0	0	0
1994	Montreal	7	0	1	1	12	0	0	0
1996	Pittsburgh	17	1	9	10	36	1	0	1
1997	Anaheim	11	2	7	9	16	1	0	1
1999	Phoenix	6	0	0	0	8	0	0	0
2000	Phoenix	1	0	0	0	0	0	0	0
Playoff Totals		**99**	**5**	**26**	**31**	**100**	**2**	**0**	**3**
DAILEY, Bob	Defense								
1975	Vancouver	5	1	3	4	14	0	0	0
1976	Vancouver	2	1	1	2	0	1	0	0
1977	Philadelphia	10	4	9	13	15	2	0	0
1978	Philadelphia	12	1	5	6	22	0	0	0
1979	Philadelphia	8	1	2	3	14	0	0	0
1980	Philadelphia	19	4	13	17	22	1	1	2
1981	Philadelphia	7	0	1	1	18	0	0	0
Playoff Totals		**63**	**12**	**34**	**46**	**105**	**4**	**1**	**2**
DALEY, Frank	Left wing/Center								
1929	Detroit	2	0	0	0	0	0	0	0
Playoff Totals		**2**	**0**	**0**	**0**	**0**	**0**	**0**	**0**
DALEY, Pat *No Playoffs*	Left wing								
DALGARNO, Brad	Right wing								
1987	NY Islanders	1	0	1	1	0	0	0	0
1988	NY Islanders	4	0	0	0	19	0	0	0
1993	NY Islanders	18	2	2	4	14	0	0	0
1994	NY Islanders	4	0	1	1	4	0	0	0
Playoff Totals		**27**	**2**	**4**	**6**	**37**	**0**	**0**	**0**
DALLMAN, Marty *No Playoffs*	Center								
DALLMAN, Rod	Left wing								
1990	NY Islanders	1	0	1	1	0	0	0	0
Playoff Totals		**1**	**0**	**1**	**1**	**0**	**0**	**0**	**0**
DAME, Bunny *No Playoffs*	Left wing								
DAMORE, Hank *No Playoffs*	Center								
•DAMPHOUSSE, Vincent	Center								
1987	Toronto	12	1	5	6	8	1	0	0
1988	Toronto	6	0	1	1	10	0	0	0
1990	Toronto	5	0	2	2	2	0	0	0
1992	Edmonton	16	6	8	14	8	1	0	0
1993♦	Montreal	20	11	12	23	16	5	0	3
1994	Montreal	7	1	2	3	8	0	0	0
1996	Montreal	6	4	4	8	0	0	1	2
1997	Montreal	5	0	0	0	2	0	0	0
1998	Montreal	10	3	6	9	22	1	0	0
1999	San Jose	6	3	2	5	6	0	2	0
2000	San Jose	12	1	7	8	16	1	0	0
2001	San Jose	6	2	1	3	14	0	1	0
2002	San Jose	12	2	6	8	12	1	0	0
Playoff Totals		**123**	**34**	**56**	**90**	**124**	**10**	**4**	**5**
•DANDENAULT, Mathieu	Right wing/Defense								
1997♦	Detroit	....	....	....	....	....	....	....	....
1998♦	Detroit	3	1	0	1	0	1	0	0
1999	Detroit	10	0	1	1	0	0	0	0
2000	Detroit	6	0	0	0	2	0	0	0
2001	Detroit	6	0	1	1	0	0	0	0
2002♦	Detroit	23	1	2	3	8	0	1	0
Playoff Totals		**48**	**2**	**4**	**6**	**10**	**1**	**1**	**0**
•DANEYKO, Ken	Defense								
1988	New Jersey	20	1	6	7	83	0	0	1
1990	New Jersey	6	2	0	2	21	0	0	0
1991	New Jersey	7	0	1	1	10	0	0	0
1992	New Jersey	7	0	3	3	16	0	0	0
1993	New Jersey	5	0	0	0	8	0	0	0
1994	New Jersey	20	0	1	1	45	0	0	0
1995♦	New Jersey	20	1	0	1	22	0	0	0
1997	New Jersey	10	0	0	0	28	0	0	0
1998	New Jersey	6	0	1	1	10	0	0	0
1999	New Jersey	7	0	0	0	8	0	0	0
2000♦	New Jersey	23	1	2	3	14	0	0	0
2001	New Jersey	25	0	3	3	21	0	0	0
2002	New Jersey	6	0	0	0	8	0	0	0
Playoff Totals		**162**	**5**	**17**	**22**	**294**	**0**	**0**	**1**
•DANIELS, Jeff	Left wing								
1992♦	Pittsburgh	....	....	....	....	....	....	....	....
1993	Pittsburgh	12	3	2	5	0	0	0	1
2001	Carolina	6	0	2	2	2	0	0	0
2002	Carolina	23	0	1	1	0	0	0	0
Playoff Totals		**41**	**3**	**5**	**8**	**2**	**0**	**0**	**1**
DANIELS, Kimbi *No Playoffs*	Center								
DANIELS, Scott	Left wing								
1998	New Jersey	1	0	0	0	0	0	0	0
Playoff Totals		**1**	**0**	**0**	**0**	**0**	**0**	**0**	**0**

Season	Team	GP	G	A	Pts	PIM	PP	SH	GW
•DANTON, Mike *No Playoffs*	Center								
DAOUST, Dan	Center								
1986	Toronto	10	2	2	4	19	0	0	0
1987	Toronto	13	5	2	7	42	0	0	2
1988	Toronto	4	0	0	0	2	0	0	0
1990	Toronto	5	0	1	1	20	0	0	0
Playoff Totals		**32**	**7**	**5**	**12**	**83**	**0**	**0**	**2**
•DARBY, Craig *No Playoffs*	Center								
•DARCHE, Mathieu *No Playoffs*	Left wing								
DARK, Michael *No Playoffs*	Defense								
DARRAGH, Harold	Left wing								
1926	Pittsburgh	2	1	0	1	0	....	....	....
1928	Pittsburgh	2	0	1	1	0	....	....	....
1931	Boston	5	0	1	1	2	....	....	....
1932♦	Toronto	7	0	1	1	2	....	....	....
Playoff Totals		**16**	**1**	**3**	**4**	**4**	....	....	....
DARRAGH, Jack	Right wing								
1919	Ottawa	5	2	0	2	3	....	....	....
1920♦	Ottawa	....	....	....	....	....	....	....	....
1921♦	Ottawa	2	0	0	0	2	....	....	....
1923♦	Ottawa	2	1	0	1	2	....	....	....
1924	Ottawa	2	0	0	0	2	....	....	....
Playoff Totals		**11**	**3**	**0**	**3**	**9**	....	....	....
•DATSYUK, Pavel	Center								
2002♦	Detroit	21	3	3	6	2	1	0	1
Playoff Totals		**21**	**3**	**3**	**6**	**2**	**1**	**0**	**1**
DAVID, Richard	Left wing								
1982	Quebec	1	0	0	0	0	0	0	0
Playoff Totals		**1**	**0**	**0**	**0**	**0**	**0**	**0**	**0**
DAVIDSON, Bob	Left wing								
1936	Toronto	9	1	3	4	2	....	....	....
1937	Toronto	2	0	0	0	5	....	....	....
1938	Toronto	4	0	2	2	7	....	....	....
1939	Toronto	10	1	1	2	6	....	....	....
1940	Toronto	10	0	3	3	16	....	....	....
1941	Toronto	7	0	2	2	7	....	....	....
1942♦	Toronto	13	1	2	3	20	....	....	....
1943	Toronto	6	1	2	3	7	....	....	....
1944	Toronto	5	0	0	0	4	....	....	....
1945♦	Toronto	13	1	2	3	2	....	....	....
Playoff Totals		**79**	**5**	**17**	**22**	**76**	....	....	....
DAVIDSON, Gord *No Playoffs*	Defense								
•DAVIDSON, Matt *No Playoffs*	Right wing								
•DAVIDSSON, Johan	Center								
1999	Anaheim	1	0	0	0	0	0	0	0
Playoff Totals		**1**	**0**	**0**	**0**	**0**	**0**	**0**	**0**
DAVIE, Bob *No Playoffs*	Defense								
DAVIES, Buck	Center								
1948	NY Rangers	1	0	0	0	0	0	0	0
Playoff Totals		**1**	**0**	**0**	**0**	**0**	**0**	**0**	**0**
DAVIS, Bob *No Playoffs*	Right wing								
DAVIS, Kim	Center								
1980	Pittsburgh	4	0	0	0	0	0	0	0
Playoff Totals		**4**	**0**	**0**	**0**	**0**	**0**	**0**	**0**
DAVIS, Lorne	Right wing								
1953♦	Montreal	7	1	1	2	2	....	....	....
1954	Montreal	11	2	0	2	8	....	....	....
Playoff Totals		**18**	**3**	**1**	**4**	**10**	....	....	....
DAVIS, Mal	Left wing								
1983	Buffalo	6	1	0	1	0	0	0	0
1984	Buffalo	1	0	0	0	0	0	0	0
Playoff Totals		**7**	**1**	**0**	**1**	**0**	**0**	**0**	**0**
DAVISON, Murray *No Playoffs*	Defense								
DAVYDOV, Evgeny	Left wing								
1992	Winnipeg	7	2	2	4	2	1	0	0
1993	Winnipeg	4	0	0	0	0	0	0	0
Playoff Totals		**11**	**2**	**2**	**4**	**2**	**1**	**0**	**0**
•DAW, Jeff *No Playoffs*	Center								
•DAWE, Jason	Right wing								
1994	Buffalo	6	0	1	1	6	0	0	0
1995	Buffalo	5	2	1	3	6	0	0	0
1997	Buffalo	11	2	1	3	6	0	0	0
Playoff Totals		**22**	**4**	**3**	**7**	**18**	**0**	**0**	**0**
DAWES, Bob	Defense/Center								
1949♦	Toronto	9	0	0	0	2	0	0	0
1951	Montreal	1	0	0	0	0	0	0	0
Playoff Totals		**10**	**0**	**0**	**0**	**2**	**0**	**0**	**0**

Season	Team	GP	G	A	Pts	PIM	PP	SH	GW
DAY, Hap	Defense								
1925	Toronto	2	0	0	0	0	....	....	....
1929	Toronto	4	1	0	1	4	....	....	....
1931	Toronto	2	0	3	3	7	....	....	....
1932♦	Toronto	7	3	3	6	6	....	....	....
1933	Toronto	9	0	1	1	*21	....	....	....
1934	Toronto	5	0	0	0	6	....	....	....
1935	Toronto	7	0	0	0	4	....	....	....
1936	Toronto	9	0	0	0	8	....	....	....
1937	Toronto	2	0	0	0	0	....	....	....
1938	NY Americans	6	0	0	0	0	....	....	....
Playoff Totals		**53**	**4**	**7**	**11**	**56**	....	....	....
DAY, Joe *No Playoffs*	Center								
•DAZE, Eric	Left wing								
1995	Chicago	16	0	1	1	4	0	0	0
1996	Chicago	10	3	5	8	0	0	0	1
1997	Chicago	6	2	1	3	2	0	0	0
2002	Chicago	5	0	0	0	2	0	0	0
Playoff Totals		**37**	**5**	**7**	**12**	**8**	**0**	**0**	**1**
DEA, Billy	Left wing								
1957	Detroit	5	2	0	2	2	1	0	0
1967	Chicago	2	0	0	0	2	0	0	0
1970	Detroit	4	0	1	1	2	0	0	0
Playoff Totals		**11**	**2**	**1**	**3**	**6**	**1**	**0**	**0**
DEACON, Don	Left wing								
1939	Detroit	2	2	1	3	0	....	....	....
Playoff Totals		**2**	**2**	**1**	**3**	**0**	....	....	....
•DEADMARSH, Adam	Left wing/Center								
1995	Quebec	6	0	1	1	0	0	0	0
1996♦	Colorado	22	5	12	17	25	1	0	0
1997	Colorado	17	3	6	9	24	1	0	1
1998	Colorado	7	2	0	2	4	1	0	0
1999	Colorado	19	8	4	12	20	3	0	0
2000	Colorado	17	4	11	15	21	1	0	1
2001	Los Angeles	13	3	3	6	4	0	0	2
2002	Los Angeles	4	1	3	4	2	0	0	0
Playoff Totals		**105**	**26**	**40**	**66**	**100**	**7**	**0**	**4**
DEADMARSH, Butch	Left wing								
1974	Atlanta	4	0	0	0	17	0	0	0
Playoff Totals		**4**	**0**	**0**	**0**	**17**	**0**	**0**	**0**
DEAN, Barry *No Playoffs*	Left wing								
•DEAN, Kevin	Defense								
1995♦	New Jersey	3	0	2	2	0	0	0	0
1997	New Jersey	1	1	0	1	0	0	0	1
1998	New Jersey	5	1	0	1	2	0	0	0
1999	New Jersey	7	0	0	0	0	0	0	0
Playoff Totals		**16**	**2**	**2**	**4**	**2**	**0**	**0**	**1**
DEBENEDET, Nelson *No Playoffs*	Left wing								
DeBLOIS, Lucien	Center								
1978	NY Rangers	3	0	0	0	2	0	0	0
1979	NY Rangers	9	2	0	2	4	1	0	0
1982	Winnipeg	4	2	1	3	4	0	0	0
1983	Winnipeg	3	0	0	0	5	0	0	0
1984	Winnipeg	3	0	1	1	4	0	0	0
1985	Montreal	8	2	4	6	4	1	0	0
1986♦	Montreal	11	0	0	0	7	0	0	0
1987	NY Rangers	2	0	0	0	2	0	0	0
1989	NY Rangers	4	0	0	0	4	0	0	0
1992	Winnipeg	5	1	0	1	2	0	0	1
Playoff Totals		**52**	**7**	**6**	**13**	**38**	**2**	**0**	**1**
DEBOL, Dave	Center								
1980	Hartford	3	0	0	0	0	0	0	0
Playoff Totals		**3**	**0**	**0**	**0**	**0**	**0**	**0**	**0**
•DeBRUSK, Louie	Left wing								
1997	Edmonton	6	0	0	0	4	0	0	0
1999	Phoenix	6	2	0	2	6	0	0	0
2000	Phoenix	3	0	0	0	0	0	0	0
Playoff Totals		**15**	**2**	**0**	**2**	**10**	**0**	**0**	**0**
DEFAZIO, Dean *No Playoffs*	Left wing								
DEGRAY, Dale	Defense								
1988	Toronto	5	0	1	1	16	0	0	0
1989	Los Angeles	8	1	2	3	12	1	0	0
Playoff Totals		**13**	**1**	**3**	**4**	**28**	**1**	**0**	**0**
•DELISLE, Jonathan *No Playoffs*	Right wing								
•DELISLE, Xavier *No Playoffs*	Center								
DELMONTE, Armand *No Playoffs*	Right wing								
•DELMORE, Andy	Defense								
2000	Philadelphia	18	5	2	7	14	1	0	1
2001	Philadelphia	2	1	0	1	2	0	0	1
Playoff Totals		**20**	**6**	**2**	**8**	**16**	**1**	**0**	**2**
DELORME, Gilbert	Defense								
1983	Montreal	3	0	0	0	2	0	0	0
1984	St. Louis	11	1	3	4	11	0	0	0
1985	St. Louis	3	0	0	0	0	0	0	0
1986	Quebec	2	0	0	0	5	0	0	0
1987	Detroit	16	0	2	2	14	0	0	0
1988	Detroit	15	0	3	3	22	0	0	0
1989	Detroit	6	0	1	1	2	0	0	0
Playoff Totals		**56**	**1**	**9**	**10**	**56**	**0**	**0**	**0**

Season	Team	GP	G	A	Pts	PIM	PP	SH	GW
DELORME, Ron	Center								
1978	Colorado	2	0	0	0	10	0	0	0
1982	Vancouver	15	0	2	2	31	0	0	0
1983	Vancouver	4	0	0	0	10	0	0	0
1984	Vancouver	4	1	0	1	8	0	0	0
Playoff Totals		**25**	**1**	**2**	**3**	**59**	**0**	**0**	**0**
DELORY, Val *No Playoffs*	Left wing								
DELPARTE, Guy *No Playoffs*	Left wing								
DELVECCHIO, Alex	Center/Left wing								
1952♦	Detroit	8	0	3	3	4	....	....	....
1953	Detroit	6	2	4	6	2	....	....	....
1954♦	Detroit	12	2	7	9	7	....	....	....
1955♦	Detroit	11	7	8	15	2	....	....	....
1956	Detroit	10	7	3	10	2	....	....	....
1957	Detroit	5	3	2	5	2	....	....	....
1958	Detroit	4	0	1	1	0	....	....	....
1960	Detroit	6	2	6	8	0	....	....	....
1961	Detroit	11	4	5	9	0	....	....	....
1963	Detroit	11	3	6	9	2	....	....	....
1964	Detroit	14	3	8	11	0	....	....	....
1965	Detroit	7	2	3	5	4	....	....	....
1966	Detroit	12	0	*11	11	4	....	....	....
1970	Detroit	4	0	2	2	0	0	0	0
Playoff Totals		**121**	**35**	**69**	**104**	**29**	**0**	**0**	**0**
DEMARCO, Ab	Center								
1940	Chicago	2	0	0	0	0	....	....	....
1943	Boston	9	3	0	3	2	....	....	....
Playoff Totals		**11**	**3**	**0**	**3**	**2**	....	....	....
DEMARCO, Ab Jr.	Defense								
1970	NY Rangers	5	0	0	0	2	0	0	0
1972	NY Rangers	4	0	1	1	0	0	0	0
1973	St. Louis	4	1	1	2	2	1	0	0
1975	Vancouver	2	0	0	0	0	0	0	0
1976	Los Angeles	9	0	0	0	11	0	0	0
1977	Los Angeles	1	0	0	0	2	0	0	0
Playoff Totals		**25**	**1**	**2**	**3**	**17**	**1**	**0**	**0**
DEMERS, Tony	Right wing								
1941	Montreal	2	0	0	0	0	0	0	0
Playoff Totals		**2**	**0**	**0**	**0**	**0**	**0**	**0**	**0**
•DEMITRA, Pavol	Left wing								
1997	St. Louis	6	1	3	4	6	0	0	0
1998	St. Louis	10	3	3	6	2	0	0	0
1999	St. Louis	13	5	4	9	4	3	0	1
2001	St. Louis	15	2	4	6	2	0	0	1
2002	St. Louis	10	4	7	11	6	2	1	1
Playoff Totals		**54**	**15**	**21**	**36**	**20**	**5**	**1**	**3**
•DEMPSEY, Nathan	Defense								
2002	Toronto	6	0	2	2	0	0	0	0
Playoff Totals		**6**	**0**	**2**	**2**	**0**	**0**	**0**	**0**
DENIS, Jean-Paul *No Playoffs*	Right wing								
DENIS, Lulu *No Playoffs*	Right wing								
DENNENY, Corb	Center								
1918♦	Toronto	2	0	0	0	0	....	....	....
1921	Toronto	2	0	0	0	4	....	....	....
1922♦	Toronto	2	1	0	1	0	....	....	....
Playoff Totals		**6**	**1**	**0**	**1**	**4**	....	....	....
DENNENY, Cy	Left wing								
1919	Ottawa	5	3	2	5	0	....	....	....
1920♦	Ottawa	....	....	....	....	....	....	....	....
1921♦	Ottawa	2	2	0	2	5	....	....	....
1922	Ottawa	2	2	0	2	4	....	....	....
1923♦	Ottawa	2	2	0	2	2	....	....	....
1924	Ottawa	2	2	0	2	2	....	....	....
1926	Ottawa	2	0	0	0	4	....	....	....
1927♦	Ottawa	6	*5	0	5	0	....	....	....
1928	Ottawa	2	0	0	0	0	....	....	....
1929♦	Boston	2	0	0	0	0	....	....	....
Playoff Totals		**25**	**16**	**2**	**18**	**17**	....	....	....
DENNIS, Norm	Center								
1970	St. Louis	2	0	0	0	2	0	0	0
1971	St. Louis	3	0	0	0	0	0	0	0
Playoff Totals		**5**	**0**	**0**	**0**	**2**	**0**	**0**	**0**
DENOIRD, Gerry *No Playoffs*	Center								
DePALMA, Larry	Left wing								
1989	Minnesota	2	0	0	0	6	0	0	0
1994	Pittsburgh	1	0	0	0	0	0	0	0
Playoff Totals		**3**	**0**	**0**	**0**	**6**	**0**	**0**	**0**
DERLAGO, Bill	Center								
1980	Toronto	3	0	0	0	4	0	0	0
1981	Toronto	3	1	0	1	2	1	0	0
1983	Toronto	4	3	0	3	2	2	0	0
1986	Winnipeg	3	1	0	1	0	0	0	0
Playoff Totals		**13**	**5**	**0**	**5**	**8**	**3**	**0**	**0**
DESAULNIERS, Gerard *No Playoffs*	Center								
•DESCOTEAUX, Matthieu *No Playoffs*	Defense								

Season	Team	GP	G	A	Pts	PIM	PP	SH	GW
DESILETS, Joffre	Right wing								
1937	Montreal	5	1	0	1	0	....	....	....
1938	Montreal	2	0	0	0	7	....	....	....
Playoff Totals		**7**	**1**	**0**	**1**	**7**	....	....	....
•DESJARDINS, Eric	Defense								
1989	Montreal	14	1	1	2	6	1	0	0
1990	Montreal	6	0	0	0	10	0	0	0
1991	Montreal	13	1	4	5	8	1	0	0
1992	Montreal	11	3	3	6	4	1	0	0
1993♦	Montreal	20	4	10	14	23	1	0	1
1994	Montreal	7	0	2	2	4	0	0	0
1995	Philadelphia	15	4	4	8	10	1	0	2
1996	Philadelphia	12	0	6	6	2	0	0	0
1997	Philadelphia	19	2	8	10	12	0	0	0
1998	Philadelphia	5	0	1	1	0	0	0	0
1999	Philadelphia	6	2	2	4	4	1	0	1
2000	Philadelphia	18	2	10	12	2	1	0	1
2001	Philadelphia	6	1	1	2	0	0	0	0
2002	Philadelphia	5	0	1	1	2	0	0	0
Playoff Totals		**157**	**20**	**53**	**73**	**87**	**7**	**0**	**5**
DESJARDINS, Martin *No Playoffs*	Center								
DESJARDINS, Vic	Center								
1931	Chicago	9	0	0	0	0	0	0	0
1932	NY Rangers	7	0	0	0	0	0	0	0
Playoff Totals		**16**	**0**	**0**	**0**	**0**	**0**	**0**	**0**
DESLAURIERS, Jacques *No Playoffs*	Defense								
•DEULING, Jarrett *No Playoffs*	Left wing								
•DEVEREAUX, Boyd	Center								
1999	Edmonton	1	0	0	0	0	0	0	0
2001	Detroit	2	0	0	0	0	0	0	0
2002♦	Detroit	21	2	4	6	4	0	0	0
Playoff Totals		**24**	**2**	**4**	**6**	**4**	**0**	**0**	**0**
DEVINE, Kevin *No Playoffs*	Left wing								
•de VRIES, Greg	Defense								
1997	Edmonton	12	0	1	1	8	0	0	0
1998	Edmonton	7	0	0	0	21	0	0	0
1999	Colorado	19	0	2	2	22	0	0	0
2000	Colorado	5	0	0	0	4	0	0	0
2001♦	Colorado	23	0	1	1	20	0	0	0
2002	Colorado	21	4	9	13	2	0	0	1
Playoff Totals		**87**	**4**	**13**	**17**	**77**	**0**	**0**	**1**
DEWAR, Tom *No Playoffs*	Defense								
DEWSBURY, Al	Defense								
1947	Detroit	2	0	0	0	4	....	....	....
1948	Detroit	1	0	0	0	0	....	....	....
1950♦	Detroit	4	0	3	3	8	....	....	....
1953	Chicago	7	1	2	3	4	....	....	....
Playoff Totals		**14**	**1**	**5**	**6**	**16**	....	....	....
DEZIEL, Michel	Left wing								
1975	Buffalo	1	0	0	0	0	0	0	0
Playoff Totals		**1**	**0**	**0**	**0**	**0**	**0**	**0**	**0**
DHEERE, Marcel	Left wing								
1943	Montreal	5	0	0	0	6	0	0	0
Playoff Totals		**5**	**0**	**0**	**0**	**6**	**0**	**0**	**0**
DIACHUK, Edward *No Playoffs*	Left wing								
DICK, Harry *No Playoffs*	Defense								
DICKENS, Ernie	Defense								
1942♦	Toronto	13	0	0	0	4	0	0	0
Playoff Totals		**13**	**0**	**0**	**0**	**4**	**0**	**0**	**0**
DICKENSON, Herb *No Playoffs*	Wing								
DIDUCK, Gerald	Defense								
1987	NY Islanders	14	0	1	1	35	0	0	0
1988	NY Islanders	6	1	0	1	42	1	0	0
1990	NY Islanders	5	0	0	0	12	0	0	0
1991	Vancouver	6	1	0	1	11	1	0	0
1992	Vancouver	5	0	0	0	10	0	0	0
1993	Vancouver	12	4	2	6	12	0	0	0
1994	Vancouver	24	1	7	8	22	0	0	0
1995	Chicago	16	1	3	4	22	0	0	0
1997	Phoenix	7	0	0	0	10	0	0	0
1998	Phoenix	6	0	2	2	20	0	0	0
1999	Phoenix	3	0	0	0	2	0	0	0
2000	Toronto	10	0	1	1	14	0	0	0
Playoff Totals		**114**	**8**	**16**	**24**	**212**	**2**	**0**	**0**
DIETRICH, Don *No Playoffs*	Defense								
DILL, Bob *No Playoffs*	Defense								
DILLABOUGH, Bob	Center								
1963	Detroit	1	0	0	0	0	0	0	0
1964	Detroit	1	0	0	0	0	0	0	0
1965	Detroit	4	0	0	0	0	0	0	0
1969	Oakland	7	3	0	3	0	0	1	0
1970	Oakland	4	0	0	0	0	0	0	0
Playoff Totals		**17**	**3**	**0**	**3**	**0**	**0**	**1**	**0**

Season	Team	GP	G	A	Pts	PIM	PP	SH	GW
DILLON, Cecil	Right wing								
1931	NY Rangers	4	0	1	1	2	....	....	....
1932	NY Rangers	7	2	1	3	4	....	....	....
1933♦	NY Rangers	8	*8	2	*10	6	....	....	....
1934	NY Rangers	2	0	1	1	2	....	....	....
1935	NY Rangers	4	2	1	3	0	....	....	....
1937	NY Rangers	9	0	3	3	0	....	....	....
1938	NY Rangers	3	1	0	1	0	....	....	....
1939	NY Rangers	1	0	0	0	0	....	....	....
1940	Detroit	5	1	0	1	0	....	....	....
Playoff Totals		**43**	**14**	**9**	**23**	**14**	....	....	....
DILLON, Gary *No Playoffs*	Center								
DILLON, Wayne	Center								
1978	NY Rangers	3	0	1	1	0	0	0	0
Playoff Totals		**3**	**0**	**1**	**1**	**0**	**0**	**0**	**0**
•DiMAIO, Rob	Center								
1990	NY Islanders	1	1	0	1	4	0	0	0
1995	Philadelphia	15	2	4	6	4	0	1	1
1996	Philadelphia	3	0	0	0	0	0	0	0
1998	Boston	6	1	0	1	8	0	0	0
1999	Boston	12	2	0	2	8	0	0	1
2001	Carolina	6	0	0	0	4	0	0	0
Playoff Totals		**43**	**6**	**4**	**10**	**28**	**0**	**1**	**2**
•DIMITRAKOS, Nico *No Playoffs*	Right wing								
DINEEN, Bill	Right wing								
1954♦	Detroit	12	0	0	0	2	0	0	0
1955♦	Detroit	11	0	1	1	8	0	0	0
1956	Detroit	10	1	0	1	8	0	0	0
1957	Detroit	4	0	0	0	0	0	0	0
Playoff Totals		**37**	**1**	**1**	**2**	**18**	**0**	**0**	**0**
DINEEN, Gary *No Playoffs*	Center								
DINEEN, Gord	Defense								
1984	NY Islanders	9	1	1	2	28	0	0	0
1985	NY Islanders	10	0	0	0	26	0	0	0
1986	NY Islanders	3	0	0	0	2	0	0	0
1987	NY Islanders	7	0	4	4	4	0	0	0
1989	Pittsburgh	11	0	2	2	8	0	0	0
Playoff Totals		**40**	**1**	**7**	**8**	**68**	**0**	**0**	**0**
•DINEEN, Kevin	Right wing								
1986	Hartford	10	6	7	13	18	1	0	2
1987	Hartford	6	2	1	3	31	1	0	0
1988	Hartford	6	4	4	8	8	1	0	1
1989	Hartford	4	1	0	1	10	0	0	0
1990	Hartford	6	3	2	5	18	0	0	1
1991	Hartford	6	1	0	1	16	0	0	0
1995	Philadelphia	15	6	4	10	18	1	0	1
1999	Carolina	6	0	0	0	8	0	0	0
Playoff Totals		**59**	**23**	**18**	**41**	**127**	**4**	**0**	**5**
DINEEN, Peter *No Playoffs*	Defense								
•DINGMAN, Chris	Left wing								
2001♦	Colorado	16	0	4	4	14	0	0	0
Playoff Totals		**16**	**0**	**4**	**4**	**14**	**0**	**0**	**0**
DINSMORE, Chuck	Center								
1926♦	Mtl. Maroons	4	1	0	1	2	....	....	....
1930	Mtl. Maroons	4	0	0	0	0	....	....	....
Playoff Totals		**8**	**1**	**0**	**1**	**2**	....	....	....
DIONNE, Gilbert	Left wing								
1992	Montreal	11	3	4	7	10	1	0	1
1993♦	Montreal	20	6	6	12	20	1	0	1
1994	Montreal	5	1	2	3	0	0	0	0
1995	Philadelphia	3	0	0	0	4	0	0	0
Playoff Totals		**39**	**10**	**12**	**22**	**34**	**2**	**0**	**2**
DIONNE, Marcel	Center								
1976	Los Angeles	9	6	1	7	0	3	0	0
1977	Los Angeles	9	5	9	14	2	1	0	1
1978	Los Angeles	2	0	0	0	0	0	0	0
1979	Los Angeles	2	0	1	1	0	0	0	0
1980	Los Angeles	4	0	3	3	4	0	0	0
1981	Los Angeles	4	1	3	4	7	1	0	0
1982	Los Angeles	10	7	4	11	0	4	0	0
1985	Los Angeles	3	1	2	3	2	1	0	0
1987	NY Rangers	6	1	1	2	2	1	0	0
Playoff Totals		**49**	**21**	**24**	**45**	**17**	**11**	**0**	**1**
Di PIETRO, Paul	Center								
1993♦	Montreal	17	8	5	13	8	0	0	1
1994	Montreal	7	2	4	6	2	2	0	1
1995	Toronto	7	1	1	2	0	0	0	0
Playoff Totals		**31**	**11**	**10**	**21**	**10**	**2**	**0**	**2**
DIRK, Robert	Defense								
1988	St. Louis	6	0	1	1	2	0	0	0
1990	St. Louis	3	0	0	0	0	0	0	0
1991	Vancouver	6	0	0	0	13	0	0	0
1992	Vancouver	13	0	0	0	20	0	0	0
1993	Vancouver	9	0	0	0	6	0	0	0
1994	Chicago	2	0	0	0	15	0	0	0
Playoff Totals		**39**	**0**	**1**	**1**	**56**	**0**	**0**	**0**
•DIVISEK, Tomas *No Playoffs*	Center								
DJOOS, Per *No Playoffs*	Defense								

Season	Team	GP	G	A	Pts	PIM	PP	SH	GW
DOAK, Gary	Defense								
1968	Boston	4	0	0	0	4	0	0	0
1970♦	Boston	8	0	0	0	9	0	0	0
1972	NY Rangers	12	0	0	0	46	0	0	0
1973	Boston	2	0	0	0	2	0	0	0
1975	Boston	3	0	0	0	4	0	0	0
1976	Boston	12	1	0	1	22	0	0	0
1977	Boston	14	0	2	2	26	0	0	0
1978	Boston	12	1	0	1	4	0	0	1
1979	Boston	7	0	2	2	4	0	0	0
1980	Boston	4	0	0	0	0	0	0	0
Playoff Totals		**78**	**2**	**4**	**6**	**121**	**0**	**0**	**1**
•DOAN, Shane	Right wing								
1996	Winnipeg	6	0	0	0	6	0	0	0
1997	Phoenix	4	0	0	0	2	0	0	0
1998	Phoenix	6	1	0	1	6	0	0	0
1999	Phoenix	7	2	2	4	6	0	0	2
2000	Phoenix	4	1	2	3	8	1	0	0
2002	Phoenix	5	2	2	4	6	0	0	0
Playoff Totals		**32**	**6**	**6**	**12**	**34**	**1**	**0**	**2**
DOBBIN, Brian	Right wing								
1989	Philadelphia	2	0	0	0	17	0	0	0
Playoff Totals		**2**	**0**	**0**	**0**	**17**	**0**	**0**	**0**
DOBSON, Jim *No Playoffs*	Right wing								
DOHERTY, Fred *No Playoffs*	Right wing								
•DOIG, Jason *No Playoffs*	Defense								
DOLLAS, Bobby	Defense								
1986	Winnipeg	3	0	0	0	2	0	0	0
1991	Detroit	7	1	0	1	13	0	0	0
1992	Detroit	2	0	1	1	0	0	0	0
1997	Anaheim	11	0	0	0	4	0	0	0
1998	Edmonton	11	0	0	0	16	0	0	0
1999	Pittsburgh	13	1	0	1	6	0	0	0
Playoff Totals		**47**	**2**	**1**	**3**	**41**	**0**	**0**	**0**
•DOME, Robert *No Playoffs*	Right wing								
•DOMENICHELLI, Hnat *No Playoffs*	Center								
•DOMI, Tie	Right wing								
1992	NY Rangers	6	1	1	2	32	0	0	0
1993	Winnipeg	6	1	0	1	23	0	0	0
1995	Toronto	7	1	0	1	0	0	0	0
1996	Toronto	6	0	2	2	4	0	0	0
1999	Toronto	14	0	2	2	24	0	0	0
2000	Toronto	12	0	1	1	20	0	0	0
2001	Toronto	8	0	1	1	20	0	0	0
2002	Toronto	19	1	3	4	*61	0	0	1
Playoff Totals		**78**	**4**	**10**	**14**	**184**	**0**	**0**	**1**
DONALDSON, Gary *No Playoffs*	Right wing								
DONATELLI, Clark	Left wing								
1992	Boston	2	0	0	0	0	0	0	0
Playoff Totals		**2**	**0**	**0**	**0**	**0**	**0**	**0**	**0**
•DONATO, Ted	Left wing								
1992	Boston	15	3	4	7	4	0	0	1
1993	Boston	4	0	1	1	0	0	0	0
1994	Boston	13	4	2	6	10	2	0	1
1995	Boston	5	0	0	0	4	0	0	0
1996	Boston	5	1	2	3	2	1	0	0
1998	Boston	5	0	0	0	2	0	0	0
1999	Ottawa	1	0	0	0	0	0	0	0
2001	Dallas	8	0	1	1	0	0	0	0
Playoff Totals		**56**	**8**	**10**	**18**	**22**	**3**	**0**	**2**
DONNELLY, Babe	Defense								
1927	Mtl. Maroons	2	0	0	0	0	0	0	0
Playoff Totals		**2**	**0**	**0**	**0**	**0**	**0**	**0**	**0**
DONNELLY, Dave	Center								
1984	Boston	3	0	0	0	0	0	0	0
1985	Boston	1	0	0	0	0	0	0	0
1987	Chicago	1	0	0	0	0	0	0	0
Playoff Totals		**5**	**0**	**0**	**0**	**0**	**0**	**0**	**0**
DONNELLY, Gord	Defense								
1986	Quebec	1	0	0	0	0	0	0	0
1987	Quebec	13	0	0	0	53	0	0	0
1990	Winnipeg	6	0	1	1	8	0	0	0
1992	Buffalo	6	0	1	1	0	0	0	0
Playoff Totals		**26**	**0**	**2**	**2**	**61**	**0**	**0**	**0**
DONNELLY, Mike	Left wing								
1991	Los Angeles	12	5	4	9	6	0	0	0
1992	Los Angeles	6	1	0	1	4	0	0	0
1993	Los Angeles	24	6	7	13	14	0	0	0
1995	Dallas	5	0	1	1	6	0	0	0
Playoff Totals		**47**	**12**	**12**	**24**	**30**	**0**	**0**	**0**
•DONOVAN, Shean	Right wing								
1995	San Jose	7	0	1	1	6	0	0	0
1999	Colorado	5	0	0	0	2	0	0	0
Playoff Totals		**12**	**0**	**1**	**1**	**8**	**0**	**0**	**0**
•DOPITA, Jiri *No Playoffs*	Center								
DORAN, John	Defense								
1936	NY Americans	3	0	0	0	0	0	0	0
Playoff Totals		**3**	**0**	**0**	**0**	**0**	**0**	**0**	**0**
DORAN, Lloyd *No Playoffs*	Center								

Season	Team	GP	G	A	Pts	PIM	PP	SH	GW
DORATY, Ken	Forward								
1933	Toronto	9	5	0	5	2	....	....	....
1934	Toronto	5	2	2	4	0	....	....	....
1935	Toronto	1	0	0	0	0	....	....	....
Playoff Totals		**15**	**7**	**2**	**9**	**2**	....	....	....
DORE, Andre	Defense								
1982	NY Rangers	10	1	1	2	16	0	0	0
1983	St. Louis	4	0	1	1	8	0	0	0
1984	Quebec	9	0	0	0	8	0	0	0
Playoff Totals		**23**	**1**	**2**	**3**	**32**	**0**	**0**	**0**
DORE, Daniel *No Playoffs*	Right wing								
DOREY, Jim	Defense								
1969	Toronto	4	0	1	1	21	0	0	0
1971	Toronto	6	0	1	1	19	0	0	0
1972	NY Rangers	1	0	0	0	0	0	0	0
Playoff Totals		**11**	**0**	**2**	**2**	**40**	**0**	**0**	**0**
DORION, Dan *No Playoffs*	Center								
DORNHOEFER, Gary	Right wing								
1968	Philadelphia	3	0	0	0	15	0	0	0
1969	Philadelphia	4	0	1	1	20	0	0	0
1971	Philadelphia	2	0	0	0	4	0	0	0
1973	Philadelphia	11	3	3	6	16	1	0	1
1974♦	Philadelphia	14	5	6	11	43	2	1	1
1975♦	Philadelphia	17	5	5	10	33	0	0	2
1976	Philadelphia	16	3	4	7	43	1	0	0
1977	Philadelphia	9	1	0	1	22	0	0	0
1978	Philadelphia	4	0	0	0	7	0	0	0
Playoff Totals		**80**	**17**	**19**	**36**	**203**	**4**	**1**	**4**
DOROHOY, Eddie *No Playoffs*	Center/Left wing								
DOUGLAS, Jordy	Left wing								
1983	Minnesota	5	0	0	0	2	0	0	0
1984	Winnipeg	1	0	0	0	2	0	0	0
Playoff Totals		**6**	**0**	**0**	**0**	**4**	**0**	**0**	**0**
DOUGLAS, Kent	Defense								
1963♦	Toronto	10	1	1	2	2	0	0	0
1964♦	Toronto	....	....	....	....	....	....	....	....
1965	Toronto	5	0	1	1	19	0	0	0
1966	Toronto	4	0	1	1	12	0	0	0
1967♦	Toronto	....	....	....	....	....	....	....	....
Playoff Totals		**19**	**1**	**3**	**4**	**33**	**0**	**0**	**0**
DOUGLAS, Les	Center								
1943♦	Detroit	10	3	2	5	2	....	....	....
Playoff Totals		**10**	**3**	**2**	**5**	**2**	....	....	....
DOURIS, Peter	Right wing								
1988	Winnipeg	1	0	0	0	0	0	0	0
1990	Boston	8	0	1	1	8	0	0	0
1991	Boston	7	0	1	1	6	0	0	0
1992	Boston	7	2	3	5	0	0	0	1
1993	Boston	4	1	0	1	0	0	0	0
Playoff Totals		**27**	**3**	**5**	**8**	**14**	**0**	**0**	**1**
•DOWD, Jim	Center								
1994	New Jersey	19	2	6	8	8	0	0	0
1995♦	New Jersey	11	2	1	3	8	0	0	1
1996	Vancouver	1	0	0	0	0	0	0	0
2000	Edmonton	5	2	1	3	4	0	0	0
Playoff Totals		**36**	**6**	**8**	**14**	**20**	**0**	**0**	**1**
•DOWNEY, Aaron	Right wing								
2002	Chicago	4	0	0	0	8	0	0	0
Playoff Totals		**4**	**0**	**0**	**0**	**8**	**0**	**0**	**0**
DOWNIE, Dave *No Playoffs*	Center/Right wing								
DOYON, Mario *No Playoffs*	Defense								
•DRAKE, Dallas	Right wing								
1993	Detroit	7	3	3	6	6	1	0	0
1996	Winnipeg	3	0	0	0	0	0	0	0
1997	Phoenix	7	0	1	1	2	0	0	0
1998	Phoenix	4	0	1	1	2	0	0	0
1999	Phoenix	7	4	3	7	4	2	0	1
2000	Phoenix	5	0	1	1	4	0	0	0
2001	St. Louis	15	4	2	6	16	0	1	1
2002	St. Louis	8	0	0	0	8	0	0	0
Playoff Totals		**56**	**11**	**11**	**22**	**42**	**3**	**1**	**2**
DRAPER, Bruce *No Playoffs*	Center								
•DRAPER, Kris	Center								
1992	Winnipeg	2	0	0	0	0	0	0	0
1994	Detroit	7	2	2	4	4	0	1	0
1995	Detroit	18	4	1	5	12	0	1	1
1996	Detroit	18	4	2	6	18	0	1	0
1997♦	Detroit	20	2	4	6	12	0	1	0
1998♦	Detroit	19	1	3	4	12	0	0	1
1999	Detroit	10	0	1	1	6	0	0	0
2000	Detroit	9	2	0	2	6	0	0	0
2001	Detroit	6	0	1	1	2	0	0	0
2002♦	Detroit	23	2	3	5	20	0	0	0
Playoff Totals		**132**	**17**	**17**	**34**	**92**	**0**	**4**	**2**

Season	Team	GP	G	A	Pts	PIM	PP	SH	GW
DRILLON, Gordie	Right wing								
1937	Toronto	2	0	0	0	0	....	....	....
1938	Toronto	7	*7	1	8	2	....	....	....
1939	Toronto	10	*7	6	13	4	....	....	....
1940	Toronto	10	3	1	4	0	....	....	....
1941	Toronto	7	3	2	5	2	....	....	....
1942♦	Toronto	9	2	3	5	2	....	....	....
1943	Montreal	5	4	2	6	0	....	....	....
Playoff Totals		**50**	**26**	**15**	**41**	**10**	....	....	....
DRISCOLL, Peter	Left wing								
1980	Edmonton	3	0	0	0	0	0	0	0
Playoff Totals		**3**	**0**	**0**	**0**	**0**	**0**	**0**	**0**
DRIVER, Bruce	Defense								
1988	New Jersey	20	3	7	10	14	3	0	0
1990	New Jersey	6	1	5	6	6	0	0	0
1991	New Jersey	7	1	2	3	12	1	0	0
1992	New Jersey	7	0	4	4	2	0	0	0
1993	New Jersey	5	1	3	4	4	0	1	0
1994	New Jersey	20	3	5	8	12	2	0	0
1995♦	New Jersey	17	1	6	7	8	1	0	0
1996	NY Rangers	11	0	7	7	4	0	0	0
1997	NY Rangers	15	0	1	1	2	0	0	0
Playoff Totals		**108**	**10**	**40**	**50**	**64**	**7**	**1**	**0**
DROLET, Rene *No Playoffs*	Right wing								
DROPPA, Ivan *No Playoffs*	Defense								
DROUILLARD, Clarence *No Playoffs*	Center								
DROUIN, Jude	Center								
1971	Minnesota	12	5	7	12	10	1	0	0
1972	Minnesota	7	4	4	8	6	1	0	1
1973	Minnesota	6	1	3	4	0	0	0	0
1975	NY Islanders	17	6	*12	18	6	1	0	1
1976	NY Islanders	13	6	9	15	0	1	0	1
1977	NY Islanders	12	5	6	11	6	1	0	0
1978	NY Islanders	5	0	0	0	5	0	0	0
Playoff Totals		**72**	**27**	**41**	**68**	**33**	**5**	**0**	**3**
DROUIN, P.C. *No Playoffs*	Left wing								
DROUIN, Polly	Left wing								
1938	Montreal	1	0	0	0	0	0	0	0
1939	Montreal	3	0	1	1	5	0	0	0
1940	Montreal	1	0	0	0	0	0	0	0
Playoff Totals		**5**	**0**	**1**	**1**	**5**	**0**	**0**	**0**
DRUCE, John	Right wing								
1989	Washington	1	0	0	0	0	0	0	0
1990	Washington	15	14	3	17	23	8	1	4
1991	Washington	11	1	1	2	7	1	0	0
1992	Washington	7	1	0	1	2	0	0	1
1993	Winnipeg	2	0	0	0	0	0	0	0
1996	Philadelphia	2	0	2	2	2	0	0	0
1997	Philadelphia	13	1	0	1	2	0	1	0
1998	Philadelphia	2	0	0	0	2	0	0	0
Playoff Totals		**53**	**17**	**6**	**23**	**38**	**9**	**2**	**5**
•DRUKEN, Harold	Center								
2001	Vancouver	4	0	1	1	0	0	0	0
Playoff Totals		**4**	**0**	**1**	**1**	**0**	**0**	**0**	**0**
DRULIA, Stan *No Playoffs*	Right wing								
DRUMMOND, Jim *No Playoffs*	Defense								
•DRURY, Chris	Center								
1999	Colorado	19	6	2	8	4	0	0	4
2000	Colorado	17	4	10	14	4	1	0	2
2001♦	Colorado	23	11	5	16	4	2	0	2
2002	Colorado	21	5	7	12	10	1	0	3
Playoff Totals		**80**	**26**	**24**	**50**	**22**	**4**	**0**	**11**
DRURY, Herb	Defense/Right wing								
1926	Pittsburgh	2	1	0	1	0	....	....	....
1928	Pittsburgh	2	0	1	1	0	....	....	....
Playoff Totals		**4**	**1**	**1**	**2**	**0**	....	....	....
•DRURY, Ted	Center								
1997	Anaheim	10	1	0	1	4	0	0	0
1999	Anaheim	4	0	0	0	0	0	0	0
Playoff Totals		**14**	**1**	**0**	**1**	**4**	**0**	**0**	**0**
DUBE, Christian	Center								
1997	NY Rangers	3	0	0	0	0	0	0	0
Playoff Totals		**3**	**0**	**0**	**0**	**0**	**0**	**0**	**0**
DUBE, Gilles	Left wing								
1954♦	Detroit	2	0	0	0	0	0	0	0
Playoff Totals		**2**	**0**	**0**	**0**	**0**	**0**	**0**	**0**
DUBE, Norm *No Playoffs*	Left wing								
DUBERMAN, Justin *No Playoffs*	Right wing								
•DUBINSKY, Steve	Center								
1994	Chicago	6	0	0	0	10	0	0	0
1997	Chicago	4	1	0	1	4	0	0	0
Playoff Totals		**10**	**1**	**0**	**1**	**14**	**0**	**0**	**0**

Season	Team	GP	G	A	Pts	PIM	PP	SH	GW
DUCHESNE, Gaetan	Left wing								
1983	Washington	4	1	1	2	4	0	0	0
1984	Washington	8	2	1	3	2	0	0	1
1985	Washington	5	0	1	1	7	0	0	0
1986	Washington	9	4	3	7	12	0	1	0
1987	Washington	7	3	0	3	14	0	0	0
1990	Minnesota	7	0	0	0	6	0	0	0
1991	Minnesota	23	2	3	5	34	0	0	0
1992	Minnesota	7	1	0	1	6	0	0	0
1994	San Jose	14	1	4	5	12	0	0	0
Playoff Totals		**84**	**14**	**13**	**27**	**97**	**0**	**1**	**1**
DUCHESNE, Steve	Defense								
1987	Los Angeles	5	2	2	4	4	1	0	0
1988	Los Angeles	5	1	3	4	14	1	0	0
1989	Los Angeles	11	4	4	8	12	2	0	0
1990	Los Angeles	10	2	9	11	6	1	0	0
1991	Los Angeles	12	4	8	12	8	1	0	0
1993	Quebec	6	0	5	5	6	0	0	0
1994	St. Louis	4	0	2	2	2	0	0	0
1995	St. Louis	7	0	4	4	2	0	0	0
1997	Ottawa	7	1	4	5	0	1	0	1
1998	St. Louis	10	0	4	4	6	0	0	0
1999	Philadelphia	6	0	2	2	2	0	0	0
2000	Detroit	9	0	4	4	10	0	0	0
2001	Detroit	6	2	4	6	0	2	0	0
2002♦	Detroit	23	0	6	6	24	0	0	0
Playoff Totals		**121**	**16**	**61**	**77**	**96**	**9**	**0**	**1**
DUDLEY, Rick	Left wing								
1975	Buffalo	10	3	1	4	26	1	0	1
1979	Buffalo	3	1	1	2	2	0	0	0
1980	Buffalo	12	3	0	3	41	1	0	1
Playoff Totals		**25**	**7**	**2**	**9**	**69**	**2**	**0**	**2**
DUERDEN, Dave *No Playoffs*	Left wing								
DUFF, Dick	Left wing								
1956	Toronto	5	1	4	5	2	....	....	....
1959	Toronto	12	4	3	7	8	....	....	....
1960	Toronto	10	2	4	6	6	....	....	....
1961	Toronto	5	0	1	1	2	....	....	....
1962♦	Toronto	12	3	10	13	20	....	....	....
1963♦	Toronto	10	4	1	5	2	....	....	....
1965♦	Montreal	13	3	6	9	17	....	....	....
1966♦	Montreal	10	2	5	7	2	....	....	....
1967	Montreal	10	2	3	5	4	....	....	....
1968♦	Montreal	13	3	4	7	4	0	0	1
1969♦	Montreal	14	6	8	14	11	3	1	0
Playoff Totals		**114**	**30**	**49**	**79**	**78**	**3**	**1**	**1**
DUFOUR, Luc	Left wing								
1983	Boston	17	1	0	1	30	0	0	1
1985	St. Louis	1	0	0	0	2	0	0	0
Playoff Totals		**18**	**1**	**0**	**1**	**32**	**0**	**0**	**1**
DUFOUR, Marc *No Playoffs*	Right wing								
DUFRESNE, Donald	Defense								
1989	Montreal	6	1	1	2	4	0	0	0
1990	Montreal	10	0	1	1	18	0	0	0
1991	Montreal	10	0	1	1	21	0	0	0
1993♦	Montreal	2	0	0	0	0	0	0	0
1995	St. Louis	3	0	0	0	4	0	0	0
1997	Edmonton	3	0	0	0	0	0	0	0
Playoff Totals		**34**	**1**	**3**	**4**	**47**	**0**	**0**	**0**
DUGGAN, John	Left wing								
1926	Ottawa	2	0	0	0	0	0	0	0
Playoff Totals		**2**	**0**	**0**	**0**	**0**	**0**	**0**	**0**
DUGGAN, Ken *No Playoffs*	Defense								
DUGUAY, Ron	Center/Right wing								
1978	NY Rangers	3	1	1	2	2	1	0	0
1979	NY Rangers	18	5	4	9	11	0	1	0
1980	NY Rangers	9	5	2	7	11	2	0	0
1981	NY Rangers	14	8	9	17	16	0	1	1
1982	NY Rangers	10	5	1	6	31	1	0	0
1983	NY Rangers	9	2	2	4	28	0	0	0
1984	Detroit	4	2	3	5	2	1	0	0
1985	Detroit	3	1	0	1	7	1	0	0
1987	NY Rangers	6	2	0	2	4	1	0	0
1988	Los Angeles	2	0	0	0	0	0	0	0
1989	Los Angeles	11	0	0	0	6	0	0	0
Playoff Totals		**89**	**31**	**22**	**53**	**118**	**7**	**2**	**1**
DUGUID, Lorne	Left wing								
1933	Mtl. Maroons	2	0	0	0	4	0	0	0
1936	Boston	2	1	0	1	2	....	....	....
Playoff Totals		**4**	**1**	**0**	**1**	**6**	**0**	**0**	**0**
DUKOWSKI, Duke	Defense								
1927	Chicago	2	0	0	0	0	0	0	0
1930	Chicago	2	0	0	0	6	0	0	0
1934	NY Rangers	2	0	0	0	0	0	0	0
Playoff Totals		**6**	**0**	**0**	**0**	**6**	**0**	**0**	**0**

Season	Team	GP	G	A	Pts	PIM	PP	SH	GW
DUMART, Woody	Left wing								
1937	Boston	3	0	0	0	0	....	....	....
1938	Boston	3	0	0	0	0	....	....	....
1939♦	Boston	12	1	3	4	6	....	....	....
1940	Boston	6	1	0	1	0	....	....	....
1941♦	Boston	11	1	3	4	9	....	....	....
1946	Boston	10	4	3	7	0	....	....	....
1947	Boston	5	1	1	2	8	....	....	....
1948	Boston	5	0	0	0	0	....	....	....
1949	Boston	5	3	0	3	0	....	....	....
1951	Boston	6	1	2	3	0	....	....	....
1952	Boston	7	0	1	1	0	....	....	....
1953	Boston	11	0	2	2	0	....	....	....
1954	Boston	4	0	0	0	0	....	....	....
Playoff Totals		**88**	**12**	**15**	**27**	**23**	....	....	....
•DUMONT, J-P	Right wing								
2001	Buffalo	13	4	3	7	8	0	0	0
Playoff Totals		**13**	**4**	**3**	**7**	**8**	**0**	**0**	**0**
DUNBAR, Dale *No Playoffs*	Defense								
DUNCAN, Art	Defense								
1929	Toronto	4	0	0	0	4	0	0	0
1931	Toronto	1	0	0	0	0	0	0	0
Playoff Totals		**5**	**0**	**0**	**0**	**4**	**0**	**0**	**0**
DUNCAN, Iain	Left wing								
1987	Winnipeg	7	0	2	2	6	0	0	0
1988	Winnipeg	4	0	1	1	0	0	0	0
Playoff Totals		**11**	**0**	**3**	**3**	**6**	**0**	**0**	**0**
DUNCANSON, Craig *No Playoffs*	Left wing								
DUNDAS, Rocky *No Playoffs*	Right wing								
DUNLAP, Frank *No Playoffs*	Wing								
DUNLOP, Blake	Center								
1979	Philadelphia	8	1	1	2	4	0	0	0
1980	St. Louis	3	0	2	2	2	0	0	0
1981	St. Louis	11	0	3	3	4	0	0	0
1982	St. Louis	10	2	2	4	4	0	0	0
1983	St. Louis	4	1	1	2	0	1	0	0
1984	Detroit	4	0	1	1	4	0	0	0
Playoff Totals		**40**	**4**	**10**	**14**	**18**	**1**	**0**	**0**
DUNN, Dave	Defense								
1975	Toronto	7	1	1	2	24	0	0	0
1976	Toronto	3	0	0	0	17	0	0	0
Playoff Totals		**10**	**1**	**1**	**2**	**41**	**0**	**0**	**0**
DUNN, Richie	Defense								
1978	Buffalo	1	0	0	0	2	0	0	0
1980	Buffalo	14	2	8	10	8	2	0	0
1981	Buffalo	8	0	5	5	6	0	0	0
1982	Buffalo	4	0	1	1	0	0	0	0
1983	Calgary	9	1	1	2	8	0	0	0
Playoff Totals		**36**	**3**	**15**	**18**	**24**	**2**	**0**	**0**
DUPERE, Denis	Left wing								
1971	Toronto	6	0	0	0	0	0	0	0
1972	Toronto	5	0	0	0	0	0	0	0
1974	Toronto	3	0	0	0	0	0	0	0
1978	Colorado	2	1	0	1	0	1	0	0
Playoff Totals		**16**	**1**	**0**	**1**	**0**	**1**	**0**	**0**
DUPONT, Andre	Defense								
1972	St. Louis	11	1	0	1	20	0	0	0
1973	Philadelphia	11	1	2	3	29	0	0	0
1974♦	Philadelphia	16	4	3	7	67	0	0	0
1975♦	Philadelphia	17	3	2	5	49	1	0	2
1976	Philadelphia	15	2	2	4	46	2	0	0
1977	Philadelphia	10	1	1	2	35	0	0	0
1978	Philadelphia	12	2	1	3	13	0	0	0
1979	Philadelphia	8	0	0	0	17	0	0	0
1980	Philadelphia	19	0	4	4	50	0	0	0
1981	Quebec	1	0	0	0	0	0	0	0
1982	Quebec	16	0	3	3	18	0	0	0
1983	Quebec	4	0	0	0	8	0	0	0
Playoff Totals		**140**	**14**	**18**	**32**	**352**	**3**	**0**	**2**
DUPONT, Jerome	Defense								
1984	Chicago	4	0	0	0	15	0	0	0
1985	Chicago	15	0	2	2	41	0	0	0
1986	Chicago	1	0	0	0	0	0	0	0
Playoff Totals		**20**	**0**	**2**	**2**	**56**	**0**	**0**	**0**
•DuPONT, Micki *No Playoffs*	Defense								
DUPONT, Norm	Left wing								
1980	Montreal	8	1	1	2	0	0	0	1
1982	Winnipeg	4	2	0	2	0	2	0	0
1983	Winnipeg	1	1	1	2	0	1	0	0
Playoff Totals		**13**	**4**	**2**	**6**	**0**	**3**	**0**	**1**
DUPRE, Yanick *No Playoffs*	Left wing								
•DUPUIS, Pascal *No Playoffs*	Left wing								
DURBANO, Steve	Defense								
1973	St. Louis	5	0	2	2	8	0	0	0
Playoff Totals		**5**	**0**	**2**	**2**	**8**	**0**	**0**	**0**
DURIS, Vitezslav	Defense								
1981	Toronto	3	0	1	1	2	0	0	0
Playoff Totals		**3**	**0**	**1**	**1**	**2**	**0**	**0**	**0**

Season	Team	GP	G	A	Pts	PIM	PP	SH	GW
DUSSAULT, Norm	Center								
1949	Montreal	2	0	0	0	0	....	....	....
1950	Montreal	5	3	1	4	0	....	....	....
Playoff Totals		**7**	**3**	**1**	**4**	**0**	....	....	....
DUTTON, Red	Defense								
1927	Mtl. Maroons	2	0	0	0	4	....	....	....
1928	Mtl. Maroons	9	1	0	1	27	....	....	....
1930	Mtl. Maroons	4	0	0	0	2	....	....	....
1936	NY Americans	3	0	0	0	0	....	....	....
Playoff Totals		**18**	**1**	**0**	**1**	**33**	....	....	....
DVORAK, Miroslav	Defense								
1983	Philadelphia	3	0	1	1	0	0	0	0
1984	Philadelphia	2	0	0	0	2	0	0	0
1985	Philadelphia	13	0	1	1	4	0	0	0
Playoff Totals		**18**	**0**	**2**	**2**	**6**	**0**	**0**	**0**
•DVORAK, Radek	Right wing								
1996	Florida	16	1	3	4	0	0	0	0
1997	Florida	3	0	0	0	0	0	0	0
Playoff Totals		**19**	**1**	**3**	**4**	**0**	**0**	**0**	**0**
•DWYER, Gordie *No Playoffs*	Left wing								
DWYER, Mike	Left wing								
1981	Calgary	1	1	0	1	0	0	0	0
Playoff Totals		**1**	**1**	**0**	**1**	**0**	**0**	**0**	**0**
DYCK, Henry *No Playoffs*	Center/Left wing								
DYE, Babe	Right wing								
1921	Toronto	2	0	0	0	7	....	....	....
1922♦	Toronto	2	2	0	2	2	....	....	....
1925	Toronto	2	0	0	0	0	....	....	....
1927	Chicago	2	0	0	0	2	....	....	....
1929	NY Americans	2	0	0	0	0	....	....	....
Playoff Totals		**10**	**2**	**0**	**2**	**11**	....	....	....
•DYKHUIS, Karl	Defense								
1995	Philadelphia	15	4	4	8	14	2	0	2
1996	Philadelphia	12	2	2	4	22	1	0	0
1997	Philadelphia	18	0	3	3	2	0	0	0
1999	Philadelphia	5	1	0	1	4	0	0	0
2002	Montreal	12	1	1	2	8	0	0	0
Playoff Totals		**62**	**8**	**10**	**18**	**50**	**3**	**0**	**2**
DYKSTRA, Steve	Defense								
1989	Pittsburgh	1	0	0	0	2	0	0	0
Playoff Totals		**1**	**0**	**0**	**0**	**2**	**0**	**0**	**0**
DYTE, Jack *No Playoffs*	Defense								
DZIEDZIC, Joe	Left wing								
1996	Pittsburgh	16	1	2	3	19	0	0	0
1997	Pittsburgh	5	0	1	1	4	0	0	0
Playoff Totals		**21**	**1**	**3**	**4**	**23**	**0**	**0**	**0**
EAGLES, Mike	Center/Left wing								
1986	Quebec	3	0	0	0	2	0	0	0
1987	Quebec	4	1	0	1	10	0	0	0
1992	Winnipeg	7	0	0	0	8	0	0	0
1993	Winnipeg	5	0	1	1	6	0	0	0
1995	Washington	7	0	2	2	4	0	0	0
1996	Washington	6	1	1	2	2	0	0	0
1998	Washington	12	0	2	2	2	0	0	0
Playoff Totals		**44**	**2**	**6**	**8**	**34**	**0**	**0**	**0**
EAKIN, Bruce *No Playoffs*	Center								
•EAKINS, Dallas	Defense								
1997	NY Rangers	4	0	0	0	4	0	0	0
1999	Toronto	1	0	0	0	0	0	0	0
Playoff Totals		**5**	**0**	**0**	**0**	**4**	**0**	**0**	**0**
•EASTWOOD, Mike	Center								
1993	Toronto	10	1	2	3	8	0	0	0
1994	Toronto	18	3	2	5	12	1	0	1
1996	Winnipeg	6	0	1	1	2	0	0	0
1997	NY Rangers	15	1	2	3	22	0	0	0
1998	St. Louis	3	1	0	1	0	0	0	1
1999	St. Louis	13	1	1	2	6	0	0	0
2000	St. Louis	7	1	1	2	6	0	0	0
2001	St. Louis	15	0	2	2	2	0	0	0
2002	St. Louis	10	0	0	0	6	0	0	0
Playoff Totals		**97**	**8**	**11**	**19**	**64**	**1**	**0**	**2**
•EATON, Mark	Defense								
2000	Philadelphia	7	0	0	0	0	0	0	0
Playoff Totals		**7**	**0**	**0**	**0**	**0**	**0**	**0**	**0**
EATOUGH, Jeff *No Playoffs*	Right wing								
EAVES, Mike	Center								
1980	Minnesota	15	2	5	7	4	0	0	0
1983	Minnesota	9	0	0	0	0	0	0	0
1984	Calgary	11	4	4	8	2	1	1	1
1986	Calgary	8	1	1	2	8	0	0	0
Playoff Totals		**43**	**7**	**10**	**17**	**14**	**1**	**1**	**1**
EAVES, Murray	Center								
1984	Winnipeg	2	0	0	0	2	0	0	0
1985	Winnipeg	2	0	1	1	0	0	0	0
Playoff Totals		**4**	**0**	**1**	**1**	**2**	**0**	**0**	**0**

Season	Team	GP	G	A	Pts	PIM	PP	SH	GW
ECCLESTONE, Tim									Left wing
1968	St. Louis	12	1	2	3	2	0	0	0
1969	St. Louis	12	2	2	4	20	0	0	0
1970	St. Louis	16	3	4	7	48	1	0	1
1974	Toronto	4	0	1	1	0	0	0	0
1977	Atlanta	3	0	2	2	6	0	0	0
1978	Atlanta	1	0	0	0	0	0	0	0
Playoff Totals		**48**	**6**	**11**	**17**	**76**	**1**	**0**	**1**
EDBERG, Rolf *No Playoffs*									Center
EDDOLLS, Frank									Defense
1945	Montreal	3	0	0	0	0	0	0	0
1946♦	Montreal	8	0	1	1	2	0	0	0
1947	Montreal	7	0	0	0	4	0	0	0
1948	NY Rangers	2	0	0	0	0	0	0	0
1950	NY Rangers	11	0	1	1	4	0	0	0
Playoff Totals		**31**	**0**	**2**	**2**	**10**	**0**	**0**	**0**
EDESTRAND, Darryl									Defense
1972	Pittsburgh	4	0	2	2	0	0	0	0
1974	Boston	16	1	2	3	15	0	0	0
1975	Boston	3	0	1	1	7	0	0	0
1976	Boston	12	1	3	4	23	0	0	0
1977	Boston	3	0	0	0	2	0	0	0
1978	Los Angeles	2	1	1	2	4	0	0	0
1979	Los Angeles	2	0	0	0	6	0	0	0
Playoff Totals		**42**	**3**	**9**	**12**	**57**	**0**	**0**	**0**
EDMUNDSON, Garry									Left wing
1952	Montreal	2	0	0	0	4	0	0	0
1960	Toronto	9	0	1	1	4	0	0	0
Playoff Totals		**11**	**0**	**1**	**1**	**8**	**0**	**0**	**0**
EDUR, Tom *No Playoffs*									Defense
EGAN, Pat									Defense
1940	NY Americans	2	0	0	0	4	....	....	....
1945	Boston	7	2	0	2	6	....	....	....
1946	Boston	10	3	0	3	8	....	....	....
1947	Boston	5	0	2	2	6	....	....	....
1948	Boston	5	1	1	2	2	....	....	....
1949	Boston	5	0	0	0	16	....	....	....
1950	NY Rangers	12	3	1	4	6	....	....	....
Playoff Totals		**46**	**9**	**4**	**13**	**48**	....	....	....
EGELAND, Allan *No Playoffs*									Center
EGERS, Jack									Right wing
1970	NY Rangers	5	3	1	4	10	1	0	0
1971	NY Rangers	3	0	0	0	2	0	0	0
1972	St. Louis	11	1	4	5	14	0	0	0
1973	St. Louis	5	0	1	1	2	0	0	0
1974	NY Rangers	8	1	0	1	4	0	0	0
Playoff Totals		**32**	**5**	**6**	**11**	**32**	**1**	**0**	**0**
EHMAN, Gerry									Right wing
1959	Toronto	12	6	7	13	8	2	0	2
1960	Toronto	9	0	0	0	0	0	0	0
1964♦	Toronto	9	1	0	1	4	0	0	0
1969	Oakland	7	2	2	4	0	0	0	0
1970	Oakland	4	1	1	2	0	1	0	0
Playoff Totals		**41**	**10**	**10**	**20**	**12**	**3**	**0**	**2**
EISENHUT, Neil *No Playoffs*									Center
EKLUND, Pelle									Center
1986	Philadelphia	5	0	2	2	0	0	0	0
1987	Philadelphia	26	7	20	27	2	2	0	0
1988	Philadelphia	7	0	3	3	0	0	0	0
1989	Philadelphia	19	3	8	11	2	3	0	1
1994	Dallas	9	0	3	3	4	0	0	0
Playoff Totals		**66**	**10**	**36**	**46**	**8**	**5**	**0**	**1**
•EKMAN, Nils *No Playoffs*									Left wing
ELDEBRINK, Anders									Defense
1982	Vancouver	13	0	0	0	10	0	0	0
1983	Quebec	1	0	0	0	0	0	0	0
Playoff Totals		**14**	**0**	**0**	**0**	**10**	**0**	**0**	**0**
•ELIAS, Patrik									Center
1997	New Jersey	8	2	3	5	4	1	0	0
1998	New Jersey	4	0	1	1	0	0	0	0
1999	New Jersey	7	0	5	5	6	0	0	0
2000♦	New Jersey	23	7	*13	20	9	2	1	1
2001	New Jersey	25	9	14	23	10	3	1	2
2002	New Jersey	6	2	4	6	6	2	0	0
Playoff Totals		**73**	**20**	**40**	**60**	**35**	**8**	**2**	**3**
•ELICH, Matt *No Playoffs*									Right wing
ELIK, Bo *No Playoffs*									Left wing
ELIK, Todd									Center
1990	Los Angeles	10	3	9	12	10	1	0	0
1991	Los Angeles	12	2	7	9	6	0	0	0
1992	Minnesota	5	1	1	2	2	0	0	1
1994	San Jose	14	5	5	10	12	1	0	0
1995	St. Louis	7	4	3	7	2	1	1	0
1996	Boston	4	0	2	2	16	0	0	0
Playoff Totals		**52**	**15**	**27**	**42**	**48**	**3**	**1**	**1**

Season	Team	GP	G	A	Pts	PIM	PP	SH	GW
ELLETT, Dave									Defense
1985	Winnipeg	8	1	5	6	4	1	0	0
1986	Winnipeg	3	0	1	1	0	0	0	0
1987	Winnipeg	10	0	8	8	2	0	0	0
1988	Winnipeg	5	1	2	3	10	1	0	0
1990	Winnipeg	7	2	0	2	6	2	0	1
1993	Toronto	21	4	8	12	8	2	0	0
1994	Toronto	18	3	15	18	31	3	0	0
1995	Toronto	7	0	2	2	0	0	0	0
1996	Toronto	6	0	0	0	4	0	0	0
1997	New Jersey	10	0	3	3	10	0	0	0
1998	Boston	6	0	1	1	6	0	0	0
1999	Boston	8	0	0	0	4	0	0	0
2000	St. Louis	7	0	1	1	2	0	0	0
Playoff Totals		**116**	**11**	**46**	**57**	**87**	**9**	**0**	**1**
ELLIOTT, Fred *No Playoffs*									Right wing
ELLIS, Ron									Right wing
1965	Toronto	6	3	0	3	2	0	0	0
1966	Toronto	4	0	0	0	2	0	0	0
1967♦	Toronto	12	2	1	3	4	0	0	0
1969	Toronto	4	2	1	3	2	1	0	0
1971	Toronto	6	1	1	2	2	1	0	0
1972	Toronto	5	1	1	2	4	1	0	0
1974	Toronto	4	2	1	3	0	0	0	0
1975	Toronto	7	3	0	3	2	1	0	0
1978	Toronto	13	3	2	5	0	0	0	2
1979	Toronto	6	1	1	2	2	0	0	0
1980	Toronto	3	0	0	0	0	0	0	0
Playoff Totals		**70**	**18**	**8**	**26**	**20**	**4**	**0**	**2**
•ELOMO, Miika *No Playoffs*									Left wing
ELORANTA, Kari									Defense
1982	St. Louis	5	0	0	0	0	0	0	0
1983	Calgary	9	1	3	4	17	0	0	0
1984	Calgary	6	0	2	2	2	0	0	0
1987	Calgary	6	0	2	2	0	0	0	0
Playoff Totals		**26**	**1**	**7**	**8**	**19**	**0**	**0**	**0**
•ELORANTA, Mikko									Left wing
2002	Los Angeles	7	1	1	2	2	0	0	0
Playoff Totals		**7**	**1**	**1**	**2**	**2**	**0**	**0**	**0**
ELYNUIK, Pat									Right wing
1990	Winnipeg	7	2	4	6	2	0	0	0
1992	Winnipeg	7	2	2	4	4	2	0	0
1993	Washington	6	2	3	5	19	0	0	0
Playoff Totals		**20**	**6**	**9**	**15**	**25**	**2**	**0**	**0**
EMBERG, Eddie									Center
1945	Montreal	2	1	0	1	0	....	....	....
Playoff Totals		**2**	**1**	**0**	**1**	**0**	....	....	....
•EMERSON, Nelson									Right wing
1992	St. Louis	6	3	3	6	21	2	0	0
1993	St. Louis	11	1	6	7	6	0	0	0
1999	Ottawa	4	1	3	4	0	0	0	0
2000	Los Angeles	1	0	0	0	0	0	0	0
2001	Los Angeles	13	2	2	4	4	0	0	0
2002	Los Angeles	5	0	1	1	2	0	0	0
Playoff Totals		**40**	**7**	**15**	**22**	**33**	**2**	**0**	**0**
•EMINGER, Steve *No Playoffs*									Defense
•EMMA, David *No Playoffs*									Center
EMMONS, Gary *No Playoffs*									Center
•EMMONS, John *No Playoffs*									Center
EMMS, Hap									Left wing/Defense
1932	Detroit	2	0	0	0	2	0	0	0
1933	Detroit	4	0	0	0	8	0	0	0
1934	Detroit	8	0	0	0	2	0	0	0
Playoff Totals		**14**	**0**	**0**	**0**	**12**	**0**	**0**	**0**
ENDEAN, Craig *No Playoffs*									Left wing
•ENDICOTT, Shane *No Playoffs*									Center
ENGBLOM, Brian									Defense
1977♦	Montreal	2	0	0	0	2	0	0	0
1978♦	Montreal	5	0	0	0	2	0	0	0
1979♦	Montreal	16	0	1	1	11	0	0	0
1980	Montreal	10	2	4	6	6	1	0	1
1981	Montreal	3	1	0	1	4	0	0	0
1982	Montreal	5	0	2	2	14	0	0	0
1983	Washington	4	0	2	2	2	0	0	0
1985	Los Angeles	3	0	0	0	2	0	0	0
Playoff Totals		**48**	**3**	**9**	**12**	**43**	**1**	**0**	**1**
ENGELE, Jerry									Defense
1977	Minnesota	2	0	1	1	0	0	0	0
Playoff Totals		**2**	**0**	**1**	**1**	**0**	**0**	**0**	**0**
ENGLISH, John									Defense
1988	Los Angeles	1	0	0	0	0	0	0	0
Playoff Totals		**1**	**0**	**0**	**0**	**0**	**0**	**0**	**0**
ENNIS, Jim *No Playoffs*									Defense
•ERAT, Martin *No Playoffs*									Left wing
ERICKSON, Aut									Defense
1964	Chicago	6	0	0	0	0	0	0	0
1967♦	Toronto	1	0	0	0	2	0	0	0
Playoff Totals		**7**	**0**	**0**	**0**	**2**	**0**	**0**	**0**

Season	Team	GP	G	A	Pts	PIM	PP	SH	GW
ERICKSON, Bryan									Right wing
1984	Washington	8	2	3	5	7	1	0	0
1987	Los Angeles	3	1	1	2	0	0	0	0
1993	Winnipeg	3	0	0	0	0	0	0	0
Playoff Totals		**14**	**3**	**4**	**7**	**7**	**1**	**0**	**0**
ERICKSON, Grant *No Playoffs*									Left wing
•ERIKSSON, Anders									Defense
1996	Detroit	3	0	0	0	0	0	0	0
1998♦	Detroit	18	0	5	5	16	0	0	0
2002	Toronto	10	0	0	0	0	0	0	0
Playoff Totals		**31**	**0**	**5**	**5**	**16**	**0**	**0**	**0**
ERIKSSON, Peter *No Playoffs*									Left wing
ERIKSSON, Roland									Center
1977	Minnesota	2	1	0	1	0	0	0	0
Playoff Totals		**2**	**1**	**0**	**1**	**0**	**0**	**0**	**0**
ERIKSSON, Thomas									Defense
1981	Philadelphia	7	0	2	2	6	0	0	0
1984	Philadelphia	3	0	1	1	0	0	0	0
1985	Philadelphia	9	0	0	0	6	0	0	0
Playoff Totals		**19**	**0**	**3**	**3**	**12**	**0**	**0**	**0**
ERIXON, Jan									Left wing
1984	NY Rangers	5	2	0	2	4	0	0	1
1985	NY Rangers	2	0	0	0	2	0	0	0
1986	NY Rangers	12	0	1	1	4	0	0	0
1987	NY Rangers	6	1	0	1	0	0	0	0
1989	NY Rangers	4	0	1	1	2	0	0	0
1990	NY Rangers	10	1	0	1	2	0	1	0
1991	NY Rangers	6	1	2	3	0	0	0	0
1992	NY Rangers	13	2	3	5	2	0	1	1
Playoff Totals		**58**	**7**	**7**	**14**	**16**	**0**	**2**	**2**
ERREY, Bob									Left wing
1989	Pittsburgh	11	1	2	3	12	0	0	0
1991♦	Pittsburgh	24	5	2	7	29	0	1	0
1992♦	Pittsburgh	14	3	0	3	10	0	1	0
1993	Buffalo	4	0	1	1	10	0	0	0
1994	San Jose	14	3	2	5	10	1	0	0
1995	Detroit	18	1	5	6	30	1	0	0
1996	Detroit	14	0	4	4	8	0	0	0
Playoff Totals		**99**	**13**	**16**	**29**	**109**	**2**	**2**	**0**
•ERSKINE, John *No Playoffs*									Defense
ESAU, Len *No Playoffs*									Defense
ESPOSITO, Phil									Center
1964	Chicago	4	0	0	0	0	0	0	0
1965	Chicago	13	3	3	6	15	0	0	0
1966	Chicago	6	1	1	2	2	1	0	0
1967	Chicago	6	0	0	0	7	0	0	0
1968	Boston	4	0	3	3	0	0	0	0
1969	Boston	10	*8	*10	*18	8	5	2	0
1970♦	Boston	14	*13	*14	*27	16	4	2	0
1971	Boston	7	3	7	10	6	2	0	0
1972♦	Boston	15	9	15	*24	24	2	0	3
1973	Boston	2	0	1	1	2	0	0	0
1974	Boston	16	9	5	14	25	4	0	2
1975	Boston	3	4	1	5	0	1	0	0
1978	NY Rangers	3	0	1	1	5	0	0	0
1979	NY Rangers	18	8	12	20	20	2	0	2
1980	NY Rangers	9	3	3	6	8	1	0	1
Playoff Totals		**130**	**61**	**76**	**137**	**138**	**22**	**4**	**8**
EVANS, Chris									Defense
1972	St. Louis	7	1	0	1	4	0	0	0
1973	St. Louis	5	0	1	1	4	0	0	0
Playoff Totals		**12**	**1**	**1**	**2**	**8**	**0**	**0**	**0**
EVANS, Daryl									Left wing
1982	Los Angeles	10	5	8	13	12	1	0	1
1987	Toronto	1	0	0	0	0	0	0	0
Playoff Totals		**11**	**5**	**8**	**13**	**12**	**1**	**0**	**1**
EVANS, Doug									Left wing
1987	St. Louis	5	0	0	0	10	0	0	0
1988	St. Louis	2	0	0	0	0	0	0	0
1989	St. Louis	7	1	2	3	16	0	0	0
1990	Winnipeg	7	2	2	4	10	0	0	0
1992	Winnipeg	1	0	0	0	2	0	0	0
Playoff Totals		**22**	**3**	**4**	**7**	**38**	**0**	**0**	**0**
EVANS, Jack									Defense
1956	NY Rangers	5	1	0	1	18	....	....	....
1957	NY Rangers	5	0	1	1	4	....	....	....
1958	NY Rangers	6	0	0	0	17	....	....	....
1959	Chicago	6	0	0	0	10	....	....	....
1960	Chicago	4	0	0	0	4	....	....	....
1961♦	Chicago	12	1	1	2	14	....	....	....
1962	Chicago	12	0	0	0	26	....	....	....
1963	Chicago	5	0	0	0	4	....	....	....
Playoff Totals		**56**	**2**	**2**	**4**	**97**	....	....	....
EVANS, John Paul									Center
1983	Philadelphia	1	0	0	0	0	0	0	0
Playoff Totals		**1**	**0**	**0**	**0**	**0**	**0**	**0**	**0**
EVANS, Kevin *No Playoffs*									Left wing

Season	Team	GP	G	A	Pts	PIM	PP	SH	GW
EVANS, Paul	Center/Left wing								
1977	Toronto	2	0	0	0	0	0	0	0
Playoff Totals		**2**	**0**	**0**	**0**	**0**	**0**	**0**	**0**
EVANS, Shawn *No Playoffs*	Defense								
EVANS, Stewart	Defense								
1933	Detroit	4	0	0	0	6	0	0	0
1934	Mtl. Maroons	4	0	0	0	4	0	0	0
1935♦	Mtl. Maroons	7	0	0	0	8	0	0	0
1936	Mtl. Maroons	3	0	0	0	0	0	0	0
1937	Mtl. Maroons	5	0	0	0	0	0	0	0
1939	Montreal	3	0	0	0	2	0	0	0
Playoff Totals		**26**	**0**	**0**	**0**	**20**	**0**	**0**	**0**
EVASON, Dean	Center								
1986	Hartford	10	1	4	5	10	0	0	0
1987	Hartford	5	3	2	5	35	0	0	0
1988	Hartford	6	1	1	2	2	0	0	0
1989	Hartford	4	1	2	3	10	0	1	0
1990	Hartford	7	2	2	4	22	0	0	0
1991	Hartford	6	0	4	4	29	0	0	0
1994	Dallas	9	0	2	2	12	0	0	0
1995	Dallas	5	1	2	3	12	0	1	0
1996	Calgary	3	0	1	1	0	0	0	0
Playoff Totals		**55**	**9**	**20**	**29**	**132**	**0**	**2**	**0**
EWEN, Todd	Right wing								
1987	St. Louis	4	0	0	0	23	0	0	0
1988	St. Louis	6	0	0	0	21	0	0	0
1989	St. Louis	2	0	0	0	21	0	0	0
1990	Montreal	10	0	0	0	4	0	0	0
1992	Montreal	3	0	0	0	18	0	0	0
1993♦	Montreal	1	0	0	0	0	0	0	0
Playoff Totals		**26**	**0**	**0**	**0**	**87**	**0**	**0**	**0**
EZINICKI, Bill	Right wing								
1947♦	Toronto	11	0	2	2	30	....	....	....
1948♦	Toronto	9	3	1	4	6	....	....	....
1949♦	Toronto	9	1	4	5	20	....	....	....
1950	Toronto	5	0	0	0	13	....	....	....
1951	Boston	6	1	1	2	18	....	....	....
Playoff Totals		**40**	**5**	**8**	**13**	**87**	....	....	....
•FAHEY, Jim *No Playoffs*	Defense								
FAHEY, Trevor *No Playoffs*	Left wing								
FAIRBAIRN, Bill	Right wing								
1970	NY Rangers	6	0	1	1	10	0	0	0
1971	NY Rangers	4	0	0	0	0	0	0	0
1972	NY Rangers	16	5	7	12	11	2	0	1
1973	NY Rangers	10	1	8	9	2	0	0	0
1974	NY Rangers	13	3	5	8	6	0	0	0
1975	NY Rangers	3	4	0	4	13	2	1	0
1977	Minnesota	2	0	1	1	0	0	0	0
Playoff Totals		**54**	**13**	**22**	**35**	**42**	**4**	**1**	**1**
•FAIRCHILD, Kelly *No Playoffs*	Center								
FALKENBERG, Bob *No Playoffs*	Defense								
FALLOON, Pat	Right wing								
1994	San Jose	14	1	2	3	6	0	0	0
1995	San Jose	11	3	1	4	0	0	0	0
1996	Philadelphia	12	3	2	5	2	2	0	0
1997	Philadelphia	14	3	1	4	2	1	0	0
1998	Ottawa	1	0	0	0	0	0	0	0
1999	Edmonton	4	0	1	1	4	0	0	0
2000	Pittsburgh	10	1	0	1	2	0	0	0
Playoff Totals		**66**	**11**	**7**	**18**	**16**	**3**	**0**	**0**
•FARKAS, Jeff	Right wing								
2000	Toronto	3	1	0	1	0	0	0	0
2002	Toronto	2	0	0	0	0	0	0	0
Playoff Totals		**5**	**1**	**0**	**1**	**0**	**0**	**0**	**0**
FARRANT, Walt *No Playoffs*	Right wing								
•FARRELL, Michael *No Playoffs*	Right wing								
FARRISH, Dave	Defense								
1978	NY Rangers	3	0	0	0	0	0	0	0
1979	NY Rangers	7	0	2	2	14	0	0	0
1980	Toronto	3	0	0	0	10	0	0	0
1981	Toronto	1	0	0	0	0	0	0	0
Playoff Totals		**14**	**0**	**2**	**2**	**24**	**0**	**0**	**0**
FASHOWAY, Gordie *No Playoffs*	Left wing								
•FATA, Rico *No Playoffs*	Center								
FAUBERT, Mario	Defense								
1977	Pittsburgh	3	1	0	1	2	1	0	0
1980	Pittsburgh	2	0	1	1	0	0	0	0
1981	Pittsburgh	5	1	1	2	4	1	0	0
Playoff Totals		**10**	**2**	**2**	**4**	**6**	**2**	**0**	**0**
FAULKNER, Alex	Center								
1963	Detroit	8	5	0	5	2	1	0	3
1964	Detroit	4	0	0	0	0	0	0	0
Playoff Totals		**12**	**5**	**0**	**5**	**2**	**1**	**0**	**3**
FAUSS, Ted *No Playoffs*	Defense								
FAUST, Andre *No Playoffs*	Center								

Season	Team	GP	G	A	Pts	PIM	PP	SH	GW
FEAMSTER, Dave	Defense								
1982	Chicago	15	2	4	6	53	0	0	1
1983	Chicago	13	1	0	1	4	0	0	0
1984	Chicago	5	0	1	1	4	0	0	0
Playoff Totals		**33**	**3**	**5**	**8**	**61**	**0**	**0**	**1**
FEATHERSTONE, Glen	Defense								
1989	St. Louis	6	0	0	0	25	0	0	0
1990	St. Louis	12	0	2	2	47	0	0	0
1991	St. Louis	9	0	0	0	31	0	0	0
1994	Boston	1	0	0	0	0	0	0	0
Playoff Totals		**28**	**0**	**2**	**2**	**103**	**0**	**0**	**0**
FEATHERSTONE, Tony	Right wing								
1970	Oakland	2	0	0	0	0	0	0	0
Playoff Totals		**2**	**0**	**0**	**0**	**0**	**0**	**0**	**0**
FEDERKO, Bernie	Center								
1977	St. Louis	4	1	1	2	2	0	0	0
1980	St. Louis	3	1	0	1	2	0	0	0
1981	St. Louis	11	8	10	18	2	4	0	1
1982	St. Louis	10	3	15	18	10	1	0	1
1983	St. Louis	4	2	3	5	0	1	0	0
1984	St. Louis	11	4	4	8	10	1	0	1
1985	St. Louis	3	0	2	2	4	0	0	0
1986	St. Louis	19	7	14	*21	17	1	0	1
1987	St. Louis	6	3	3	6	18	1	0	0
1988	St. Louis	10	2	6	8	18	2	0	0
1989	St. Louis	10	4	8	12	0	2	0	0
Playoff Totals		**91**	**35**	**66**	**101**	**83**	**13**	**0**	**4**
•FEDOROV, Fedor *No Playoffs*	Left wing								
•FEDOROV, Sergei	Center								
1991	Detroit	7	1	5	6	4	0	0	1
1992	Detroit	11	5	5	10	8	1	2	1
1993	Detroit	7	3	6	9	23	1	1	0
1994	Detroit	7	1	7	8	6	0	0	0
1995	Detroit	17	7	*17	*24	6	3	0	0
1996	Detroit	19	2	*18	20	10	0	0	2
1997♦	Detroit	20	8	12	20	12	3	0	4
1998♦	Detroit	22	*10	10	20	12	2	1	1
1999	Detroit	10	1	8	9	8	0	0	0
2000	Detroit	9	4	4	8	4	2	0	1
2001	Detroit	6	2	5	7	0	1	0	1
2002♦	Detroit	23	5	14	19	20	2	1	0
Playoff Totals		**158**	**49**	**111**	**160**	**113**	**15**	**5**	**11**
•FEDORUK, Todd	Left wing								
2001	Philadelphia	2	0	0	0	20	0	0	0
2002	Philadelphia	3	0	0	0	0	0	0	0
Playoff Totals		**5**	**0**	**0**	**0**	**20**	**0**	**0**	**0**
•FEDOTENKO, Ruslan	Left wing								
2001	Philadelphia	6	0	1	1	4	0	0	0
2002	Philadelphia	5	1	0	1	2	0	0	1
Playoff Totals		**11**	**1**	**1**	**2**	**6**	**0**	**0**	**1**
FEDOTOV, Anatoli *No Playoffs*	Defense								
FEDYK, Brent	Left wing								
1991	Detroit	6	1	0	1	2	0	0	1
1992	Detroit	1	0	0	0	2	0	0	0
1995	Philadelphia	9	2	2	4	8	0	0	0
Playoff Totals		**16**	**3**	**2**	**5**	**12**	**0**	**0**	**1**
FELIX, Chris	Defense								
1988	Washington	1	0	0	0	0	0	0	0
1989	Washington	1	0	1	1	0	0	0	0
Playoff Totals		**2**	**0**	**1**	**1**	**0**	**0**	**0**	**0**
FELSNER, Brian *No Playoffs*	Left wing								
FELSNER, Denny	Left wing								
1992	St. Louis	1	0	0	0	0	0	0	0
1993	St. Louis	9	2	3	5	2	1	0	0
Playoff Totals		**10**	**2**	**3**	**5**	**2**	**1**	**0**	**0**
FELTRIN, Tony *No Playoffs*	Defense								
FENTON, Paul	Left wing								
1988	Los Angeles	5	2	1	3	2	1	0	0
1990	Winnipeg	7	2	0	2	23	2	0	0
1991	Calgary	5	0	0	0	2	0	0	0
Playoff Totals		**17**	**4**	**1**	**5**	**27**	**3**	**0**	**0**
FENYVES, David	Defense								
1983	Buffalo	4	0	0	0	0	0	0	0
1984	Buffalo	2	0	0	0	7	0	0	0
1985	Buffalo	5	0	0	0	2	0	0	0
Playoff Totals		**11**	**0**	**0**	**0**	**9**	**0**	**0**	**0**
•FERENCE, Andrew	Defense								
2001	Pittsburgh	18	3	7	10	16	1	0	1
Playoff Totals		**18**	**3**	**7**	**10**	**16**	**1**	**0**	**1**
•FERENCE, Brad *No Playoffs*	Defense								

Season	Team	GP	G	A	Pts	PIM	PP	SH	GW
FERGUS, Tom	Center								
1982	Boston	6	3	0	3	0	2	0	0
1983	Boston	15	2	2	4	15	0	0	0
1984	Boston	3	2	0	2	9	1	0	0
1985	Boston	5	0	0	0	4	0	0	0
1986	Toronto	10	5	7	12	6	3	0	1
1987	Toronto	2	0	1	1	2	0	0	0
1988	Toronto	6	2	3	5	2	0	1	0
1990	Toronto	5	2	1	3	4	0	0	0
1992	Vancouver	13	5	3	8	6	0	0	1
Playoff Totals		**65**	**21**	**17**	**38**	**48**	**6**	**1**	**2**
FERGUSON, Craig *No Playoffs*	Center								
FERGUSON, George	Center								
1974	Toronto	3	0	1	1	2	0	0	0
1975	Toronto	7	1	0	1	7	0	0	0
1976	Toronto	10	2	4	6	2	0	0	1
1977	Toronto	9	0	3	3	7	0	0	0
1978	Toronto	13	5	1	6	7	0	0	0
1979	Pittsburgh	7	2	1	3	0	0	0	1
1980	Pittsburgh	5	0	3	3	4	0	0	0
1981	Pittsburgh	5	2	6	8	9	0	0	0
1982	Pittsburgh	5	0	1	1	0	0	0	0
1983	Minnesota	9	0	3	3	4	0	0	0
1984	Minnesota	13	2	0	2	2	0	0	1
Playoff Totals		**86**	**14**	**23**	**37**	**44**	**0**	**0**	**3**
FERGUSON, John	Left wing								
1964	Montreal	7	0	1	1	25	0	0	0
1965♦	Montreal	13	3	1	4	28	0	0	0
1966♦	Montreal	10	2	0	2	*44	0	0	0
1967	Montreal	10	4	2	6	22	1	0	2
1968♦	Montreal	13	3	5	8	25	0	0	1
1969♦	Montreal	14	4	3	7	*80	2	2	0
1971♦	Montreal	18	4	6	10	36	1	0	1
Playoff Totals		**85**	**20**	**18**	**38**	**260**	**4**	**2**	**4**
FERGUSON, Lorne	Left wing								
1951	Boston	6	1	0	1	2	....	....	....
1955	Boston	4	1	0	1	2	....	....	....
1956	Detroit	10	1	2	3	12	....	....	....
1957	Detroit	5	1	0	1	6	....	....	....
1959	Chicago	6	2	1	3	2	....	....	....
Playoff Totals		**31**	**6**	**3**	**9**	**24**	....	....	....
FERGUSON, Norm	Right wing								
1969	Oakland	7	1	4	5	7	0	0	0
1970	Oakland	3	0	0	0	0	0	0	0
Playoff Totals		**10**	**1**	**4**	**5**	**7**	**0**	**0**	**0**
•FERGUSON, Scott	Defense								
2001	Edmonton	6	0	0	0	0	0	0	0
Playoff Totals		**6**	**0**	**0**	**0**	**0**	**0**	**0**	**0**
FERNER, Mark *No Playoffs*	Defense								
•FERRARO, Chris *No Playoffs*	Center								
•FERRARO, Peter	Right wing								
1997	NY Rangers	2	0	0	0	0	0	0	0
Playoff Totals		**2**	**0**	**0**	**0**	**0**	**0**	**0**	**0**
•FERRARO, Ray	Center								
1986	Hartford	10	3	6	9	4	3	0	0
1987	Hartford	6	1	1	2	8	0	0	0
1988	Hartford	6	1	1	2	6	1	0	0
1989	Hartford	4	2	0	2	4	0	0	0
1990	Hartford	7	0	3	3	2	0	0	0
1993	NY Islanders	18	13	7	20	18	0	0	0
1994	NY Islanders	4	1	0	1	6	0	0	0
1998	Los Angeles	3	0	1	1	2	0	0	0
2002	St. Louis	10	0	3	3	4	0	0	0
Playoff Totals		**68**	**21**	**22**	**43**	**54**	**4**	**0**	**0**
FETISOV, Viacheslav	Defense								
1990	New Jersey	6	0	2	2	10	0	0	0
1991	New Jersey	7	0	0	0	17	0	0	0
1992	New Jersey	6	0	3	3	8	0	0	0
1993	New Jersey	5	0	2	2	4	0	0	0
1994	New Jersey	14	1	0	1	8	0	0	0
1995	Detroit	18	0	8	8	14	0	0	0
1996	Detroit	19	1	4	5	34	0	0	1
1997♦	Detroit	20	0	4	4	42	0	0	0
1998♦	Detroit	21	0	3	3	10	0	0	0
Playoff Totals		**116**	**2**	**26**	**28**	**147**	**0**	**0**	**1**
•FIDDLER, Vernon *No Playoffs*	Center								
FIDLER, Mike *No Playoffs*	Left wing								
FIELD, Wilf	Defense								
1939	NY Americans	2	0	0	0	2	0	0	0
Playoff Totals		**2**	**0**	**0**	**0**	**2**	**0**	**0**	**0**
FIELDER, Guyle	Center								
1953	Detroit	4	0	0	0	0	0	0	0
1954	Boston	2	0	0	0	2	0	0	0
Playoff Totals		**6**	**0**	**0**	**0**	**2**	**0**	**0**	**0**
FILIMONOV, Dmitri *No Playoffs*	Defense								

Season	Team	GP	G	A	Pts	PIM	PP	SH	GW
FILLION, Bob									Left wing
1944♦	Montreal	3	0	0	0	0	....	....	....
1945	Montreal	1	3	0	3	0	....	....	....
1946♦	Montreal	9	4	3	7	6	....	....	....
1947	Montreal	8	0	0	0	0	....	....	....
1949	Montreal	7	0	1	1	4	....	....	....
1950	Montreal	5	0	0	0	0	....	....	....
Playoff Totals		**33**	**7**	**4**	**11**	**10**	....	....	....
FILLION, Marcel *No Playoffs*									Left wing
FILMORE, Tommy *No Playoffs*									Right wing
FINKBEINER, Lloyd *No Playoffs*									Left wing/Defense
•FINLEY, Jeff									Defense
1988	NY Islanders	1	0	0	0	2	0	0	0
1990	NY Islanders	5	0	2	2	2	0	0	0
1996	Winnipeg	6	0	0	0	4	0	0	0
1997	Phoenix	1	0	0	0	2	0	0	0
1999	St. Louis	13	1	2	3	8	0	0	1
2000	St. Louis	7	0	2	2	4	0	0	0
2001	St. Louis	2	0	0	0	0	0	0	0
2002	St. Louis	10	0	0	0	8	0	0	0
Playoff Totals		**45**	**1**	**6**	**7**	**30**	**0**	**0**	**1**
FINN, Steven									Defense
1987	Quebec	13	0	2	2	29	0	0	0
1993	Quebec	6	0	1	1	8	0	0	0
1995	Quebec	4	0	1	1	2	0	0	0
Playoff Totals		**23**	**0**	**4**	**4**	**39**	**0**	**0**	**0**
FINNEY, Sid									Center
1953	Chicago	7	0	2	2	0	0	0	0
Playoff Totals		**7**	**0**	**2**	**2**	**0**	**0**	**0**	**0**
FINNIGAN, Ed *No Playoffs*									Left wing
FINNIGAN, Frank									Right wing
1924	Ottawa	2	0	0	0	2	....	....	....
1926	Ottawa	2	0	0	0	0	....	....	....
1927♦	Ottawa	6	3	0	3	0	....	....	....
1928	Ottawa	2	0	1	1	6	....	....	....
1930	Ottawa	1	0	0	0	4	....	....	....
1932♦	Toronto	7	2	3	5	8	....	....	....
1935	Toronto	7	1	2	3	2	....	....	....
1936	Toronto	9	0	3	3	0	....	....	....
1937	Toronto	2	0	0	0	0	....	....	....
Playoff Totals		**38**	**6**	**9**	**15**	**22**	....	....	....
FIORENTINO, Peter *No Playoffs*									Defense
•FISCHER, Jiri									Defense
2001	Detroit	5	0	0	0	9	0	0	0
2002♦	Detroit	22	3	3	6	30	0	0	1
Playoff Totals		**27**	**3**	**3**	**6**	**39**	**0**	**0**	**1**
FISCHER, Ron *No Playoffs*									Defense
FISHER, Alvin *No Playoffs*									Right wing
FISHER, Craig *No Playoffs*									Center
FISHER, Dunc									Right wing
1948	NY Rangers	1	0	1	1	0	....	....	....
1950	NY Rangers	12	3	3	6	14	....	....	....
1951	Boston	6	1	0	1	0	....	....	....
1952	Boston	2	0	0	0	0	....	....	....
Playoff Totals		**21**	**4**	**4**	**8**	**14**	....	....	....
FISHER, Joe									Right wing
1940	Detroit	5	1	1	2	0	....	....	....
1941	Detroit	5	1	0	1	6	....	....	....
1942	Detroit	1	0	0	0	0	....	....	....
1943♦	Detroit	1	0	0	0	0	....	....	....
Playoff Totals		**12**	**2**	**1**	**3**	**6**	....	....	....
•FISHER, Mike									Center
2001	Ottawa	4	0	1	1	4	0	0	0
2002	Ottawa	10	2	1	3	0	0	0	0
Playoff Totals		**14**	**2**	**2**	**4**	**4**	**0**	**0**	**0**
FITCHNER, Bob									Center
1981	Quebec	3	0	0	0	10	0	0	0
Playoff Totals		**3**	**0**	**0**	**0**	**10**	**0**	**0**	**0**
FITZGERALD, Rusty									Center
1995	Pittsburgh	5	0	0	0	4	0	0	0
Playoff Totals		**5**	**0**	**0**	**0**	**4**	**0**	**0**	**0**
•FITZGERALD, Tom									Right wing/Center
1990	NY Islanders	4	1	0	1	4	0	0	0
1993	NY Islanders	18	2	5	7	18	0	0	0
1996	Florida	22	4	4	8	34	0	0	2
1997	Florida	5	0	1	1	0	0	0	0
1998	Colorado	7	0	1	1	20	0	0	0
2002	Chicago	5	0	0	0	4	0	0	0
Playoff Totals		**61**	**7**	**11**	**18**	**80**	**0**	**0**	**2**
•FITZPATRICK, Rory									Defense
1996	Montreal	6	1	1	2	0	0	0	0
Playoff Totals		**6**	**1**	**1**	**2**	**0**	**0**	**0**	**0**
FITZPATRICK, Ross *No Playoffs*									Center
FITZPATRICK, Sandy									Center
1968	Minnesota	12	0	0	0	0	0	0	0
Playoff Totals		**12**	**0**	**0**	**0**	**0**	**0**	**0**	**0**

Season	Team	GP	G	A	Pts	PIM	PP	SH	GW
FLAMAN, Fern									Defense
1947	Boston	5	0	0	0	8	....	....	....
1948	Boston	5	0	0	0	12	....	....	....
1949	Boston	5	0	1	1	8	....	....	....
1951♦	Toronto	9	1	0	1	8	....	....	....
1952	Toronto	4	0	2	2	18	....	....	....
1954	Toronto	2	0	0	0	0	....	....	....
1955	Boston	4	1	0	1	2	....	....	....
1957	Boston	10	0	3	3	19	....	....	....
1958	Boston	12	2	2	4	10	....	....	....
1959	Boston	7	0	0	0	8	....	....	....
Playoff Totals		**63**	**4**	**8**	**12**	**93**	....	....	....
FLATLEY, Pat									Right wing
1984	NY Islanders	21	9	6	15	14	1	0	1
1985	NY Islanders	4	1	0	1	6	0	0	0
1986	NY Islanders	3	0	0	0	21	0	0	0
1987	NY Islanders	11	3	2	5	6	0	0	0
1990	NY Islanders	5	3	0	3	2	2	0	0
1993	NY Islanders	15	2	7	9	12	0	0	0
1997	NY Rangers	11	0	0	0	14	0	0	0
Playoff Totals		**70**	**18**	**15**	**33**	**75**	**3**	**0**	**1**
FLEMING, Gerry *No Playoffs*									Left wing
FLEMING, Reggie									Defense/Left wing
1961♦	Chicago	12	1	0	1	12	0	1	0
1962	Chicago	12	2	2	4	27	0	0	1
1963	Chicago	6	0	0	0	27	0	0	0
1964	Chicago	7	0	0	0	18	0	0	0
1967	NY Rangers	4	0	2	2	11	0	0	0
1968	NY Rangers	6	0	2	2	4	0	0	0
1969	NY Rangers	3	0	0	0	7	0	0	0
Playoff Totals		**50**	**3**	**6**	**9**	**106**	**0**	**1**	**1**
FLESCH, John *No Playoffs*									Left wing
FLETCHER, Steven									Left wing/Defense
1988	Montreal	1	0	0	0	5	0	0	0
Playoff Totals		**1**	**0**	**0**	**0**	**5**	**0**	**0**	**0**
FLETT, Bill									Right wing
1968	Los Angeles	7	1	2	3	8	0	0	0
1969	Los Angeles	10	3	4	7	11	1	1	0
1973	Philadelphia	11	3	4	7	0	0	1	1
1974♦	Philadelphia	17	0	6	6	21	0	0	0
1975	Toronto	5	0	0	0	2	0	0	0
1976	Atlanta	2	0	0	0	0	0	0	0
Playoff Totals		**52**	**7**	**16**	**23**	**42**	**1**	**2**	**1**
•FLEURY, Theoren									Right wing
1989♦	Calgary	22	5	6	11	24	3	0	3
1990	Calgary	6	2	3	5	10	0	0	0
1991	Calgary	7	2	5	7	14	0	0	1
1993	Calgary	6	5	7	12	27	3	1	0
1994	Calgary	7	6	4	10	5	1	0	2
1995	Calgary	7	7	7	14	2	2	1	0
1996	Calgary	4	2	1	3	14	0	0	0
1999	Colorado	18	5	12	17	20	2	0	0
Playoff Totals		**77**	**34**	**45**	**79**	**116**	**11**	**2**	**6**
FLICHEL, Todd *No Playoffs*									Defense
•FLINN, Ryan *No Playoffs*									Left wing
FLOCKHART, Rob									Left wing
1980	Minnesota	1	1	0	1	2	0	0	0
Playoff Totals		**1**	**1**	**0**	**1**	**2**	**0**	**0**	**0**
FLOCKHART, Ron									Center
1981	Philadelphia	3	1	0	1	2	0	0	0
1982	Philadelphia	4	0	1	1	2	0	0	0
1983	Philadelphia	2	1	1	2	2	1	0	0
1985	Montreal	2	1	1	2	2	0	0	1
1986	St. Louis	8	1	3	4	6	0	0	0
Playoff Totals		**19**	**4**	**6**	**10**	**14**	**1**	**0**	**1**
FLOYD, Larry *No Playoffs*									Center
•FOCHT, Dan									Defense
2002	Phoenix	1	0	1	1	0	0	0	0
Playoff Totals		**1**	**0**	**1**	**1**	**0**	**0**	**0**	**0**
FOGARTY, Bryan *No Playoffs*									Defense
FOGOLIN, Lee									Defense
1948	Detroit	2	0	1	1	6	0	0	0
1949	Detroit	9	0	0	0	4	0	0	0
1950♦	Detroit	10	0	0	0	16	0	0	0
1953	Chicago	7	0	1	1	4	0	0	0
Playoff Totals		**28**	**0**	**2**	**2**	**30**	**0**	**0**	**0**
FOGOLIN, Lee Jr.									Defense
1975	Buffalo	8	0	0	0	6	0	0	0
1976	Buffalo	9	0	4	4	23	0	0	0
1977	Buffalo	4	0	0	0	2	0	0	0
1978	Buffalo	6	0	2	2	23	0	0	0
1979	Buffalo	3	0	0	0	4	0	0	0
1980	Edmonton	3	0	0	0	4	0	0	0
1981	Edmonton	9	0	0	0	12	0	0	0
1982	Edmonton	5	1	1	2	14	0	1	0
1983	Edmonton	16	0	5	5	36	0	0	0
1984♦	Edmonton	19	1	4	5	23	0	0	0
1985♦	Edmonton	18	3	1	4	16	0	0	1
1986	Edmonton	8	0	2	2	10	0	0	0
Playoff Totals		**108**	**5**	**19**	**24**	**173**	**0**	**1**	**1**

Season	Team	GP	G	A	Pts	PIM	PP	SH	GW
FOLCO, Peter *No Playoffs*									Defense
FOLEY, Gerry									Right wing
1957	NY Rangers	3	0	0	0	0	0	0	0
1958	NY Rangers	6	0	1	1	2	0	0	0
Playoff Totals		**9**	**0**	**1**	**1**	**2**	**0**	**0**	**0**
FOLEY, Rick									Defense
1971	Chicago	4	0	1	1	4	0	0	0
Playoff Totals		**4**	**0**	**1**	**1**	**4**	**0**	**0**	**0**
FOLIGNO, Mike									Right wing
1982	Buffalo	4	2	0	2	9	2	0	0
1983	Buffalo	10	2	3	5	39	0	0	0
1984	Buffalo	3	2	1	3	19	0	0	0
1985	Buffalo	5	1	3	4	12	0	0	0
1988	Buffalo	6	3	2	5	31	0	0	0
1989	Buffalo	5	3	1	4	21	1	1	1
1990	Buffalo	6	0	1	1	12	0	0	0
1993	Toronto	18	2	6	8	42	1	0	2
Playoff Totals		**57**	**15**	**17**	**32**	**185**	**4**	**1**	**3**
FOLK, Bill *No Playoffs*									Defense
FONTAINE, Len *No Playoffs*									Right wing
FONTAS, Jon *No Playoffs*									Center
FONTEYNE, Val									Left wing
1960	Detroit	6	0	4	4	0	0	0	0
1961	Detroit	11	2	3	5	0	0	0	0
1963	Detroit	11	0	0	0	2	0	0	0
1965	Detroit	5	0	1	1	0	0	0	0
1966	Detroit	12	1	0	1	4	0	1	0
1970	Pittsburgh	10	0	2	2	0	0	0	0
1972	Pittsburgh	4	0	0	0	2	0	0	0
Playoff Totals		**59**	**3**	**10**	**13**	**8**	**0**	**1**	**0**
FONTINATO, Lou									Defense
1956	NY Rangers	4	0	0	0	6	0	0	0
1957	NY Rangers	5	0	0	0	7	0	0	0
1958	NY Rangers	6	0	1	1	6	0	0	0
1962	Montreal	6	0	1	1	23	0	0	0
Playoff Totals		**21**	**0**	**2**	**2**	**42**	**0**	**0**	**0**
•FOOTE, Adam									Defense
1993	Quebec	6	0	1	1	2	0	0	0
1995	Quebec	6	0	1	1	14	0	0	0
1996♦	Colorado	22	1	3	4	36	0	0	0
1997	Colorado	17	0	4	4	62	0	0	0
1998	Colorado	7	0	0	0	23	0	0	0
1999	Colorado	19	2	3	5	24	1	0	0
2000	Colorado	16	0	7	7	28	0	0	0
2001♦	Colorado	23	3	4	7	*47	1	0	1
2002	Colorado	21	1	6	7	28	0	0	0
Playoff Totals		**137**	**7**	**29**	**36**	**264**	**2**	**0**	**1**
•FORBES, Colin									Left wing
1997	Philadelphia	3	0	0	0	0	0	0	0
1998	Philadelphia	5	0	0	0	2	0	0	0
2000	Ottawa	5	1	0	1	14	0	0	0
Playoff Totals		**13**	**1**	**0**	**1**	**16**	**0**	**0**	**0**
FORBES, Dave									Left wing
1974	Boston	16	0	2	2	6	0	0	0
1975	Boston	3	0	0	0	0	0	0	0
1976	Boston	12	1	1	2	5	0	1	0
1977	Boston	14	0	1	1	2	0	0	0
Playoff Totals		**45**	**1**	**4**	**5**	**13**	**0**	**1**	**0**
FORBES, Mike *No Playoffs*									Defense
FOREY, Connie *No Playoffs*									Left wing
•FORSBERG, Peter									Center
1995	Quebec	6	2	4	6	4	1	0	0
1996♦	Colorado	22	10	11	21	18	3	0	1
1997	Colorado	14	5	12	17	10	3	0	0
1998	Colorado	7	6	5	11	12	2	0	0
1999	Colorado	19	8	16	*24	31	1	1	0
2000	Colorado	16	7	8	15	12	2	1	4
2001♦	Colorado	11	4	10	14	6	1	0	2
2002	Colorado	20	9	*18	*27	20	0	0	4
Playoff Totals		**115**	**51**	**84**	**135**	**113**	**13**	**2**	**11**
FORSEY, Jack									Right wing
1943	Toronto	3	0	1	1	0	0	0	0
Playoff Totals		**3**	**0**	**1**	**1**	**0**	**0**	**0**	**0**
FORSLUND, Gus *No Playoffs*									Right wing
FORSLUND, Tomas *No Playoffs*									Right wing
FORSYTH, Alex *No Playoffs*									Center
FORTIER, Dave									Defense
1975	NY Islanders	14	0	2	2	33	0	0	0
1976	NY Islanders	6	0	0	0	0	0	0	0
Playoff Totals		**20**	**0**	**2**	**2**	**33**	**0**	**0**	**0**
FORTIER, Marc *No Playoffs*									Center
•FORTIN, Jean-Francois *No Playoffs*									Defense
FORTIN, Ray									Defense
1968	St. Louis	3	0	0	0	2	0	0	0
1970	St. Louis	3	0	0	0	6	0	0	0
Playoff Totals		**6**	**0**	**0**	**0**	**8**	**0**	**0**	**0**

Season	Team	GP	G	A	Pts	PIM	PP	SH	GW
FOSTER, Corey									Defense
1996	Pittsburgh	3	0	0	0	4	0	0	0
Playoff Totals		**3**	**0**	**0**	**0**	**4**	**0**	**0**	**0**
FOSTER, Dwight									Right wing
1979	Boston	11	1	3	4	0	0	0	0
1980	Boston	9	3	5	8	2	0	1	1
1981	Boston	3	1	1	2	0	0	0	0
1984	Detroit	3	0	1	1	0	0	0	0
1985	Detroit	3	0	0	0	0	0	0	0
1986	Boston	3	0	2	2	2	0	0	0
1987	Boston	3	0	0	0	0	0	0	0
Playoff Totals		**35**	**5**	**12**	**17**	**4**	**0**	**1**	**1**
FOSTER, Herb *No Playoffs*									Left wing
FOSTER, Yip *No Playoffs*									Defense
FOTIU, Nick									Left wing
1978	NY Rangers	3	0	0	0	5	0	0	0
1979	NY Rangers	4	0	0	0	6	0	0	0
1980	Hartford	3	0	0	0	6	0	0	0
1981	NY Rangers	2	0	0	0	4	0	0	0
1982	NY Rangers	10	0	2	2	6	0	0	0
1983	NY Rangers	5	0	1	1	6	0	0	0
1986	Calgary	11	0	1	1	34	0	0	0
Playoff Totals		**38**	**0**	**4**	**4**	**67**	**0**	**0**	**0**
FOWLER, Jimmy									Defense
1937	Toronto	2	0	0	0	0	0	0	0
1938	Toronto	7	0	2	2	0	0	0	0
1939	Toronto	9	0	1	1	2	0	0	0
Playoff Totals		**18**	**0**	**3**	**3**	**2**	**0**	**0**	**0**
FOWLER, Tom *No Playoffs*									Center
FOX, Greg									Defense
1978	Atlanta	2	0	1	1	8	0	0	0
1979	Chicago	4	0	1	1	0	0	0	0
1980	Chicago	7	0	0	0	8	0	0	0
1981	Chicago	3	0	1	1	2	0	0	0
1982	Chicago	15	1	3	4	27	0	0	1
1983	Chicago	13	0	3	3	22	0	0	0
Playoff Totals		**44**	**1**	**9**	**10**	**67**	**0**	**0**	**1**
FOX, Jim									Right wing
1981	Los Angeles	4	0	1	1	0	0	0	0
1982	Los Angeles	9	1	4	5	0	0	0	0
1985	Los Angeles	3	0	1	1	0	0	0	0
1987	Los Angeles	5	3	2	5	0	1	0	0
1988	Los Angeles	1	0	0	0	0	0	0	0
Playoff Totals		**22**	**4**	**8**	**12**	**0**	**1**	**0**	**0**
FOYSTON, Frank *No Playoffs*									Center/Right wing
FRAMPTON, Bob									Left wing
1950	Montreal	3	0	0	0	0	0	0	0
Playoff Totals		**3**	**0**	**0**	**0**	**0**	**0**	**0**	**0**
FRANCESCHETTI, Lou									Right wing
1984	Washington	3	0	0	0	8	0	0	0
1985	Washington	5	1	1	2	15	0	0	0
1986	Washington	8	0	0	0	15	0	0	0
1987	Washington	7	0	0	0	23	0	0	0
1988	Washington	4	0	0	0	14	0	0	0
1989	Washington	6	1	0	1	8	0	0	1
1990	Toronto	5	0	1	1	26	0	0	0
1991	Buffalo	6	1	0	1	2	0	0	0
Playoff Totals		**44**	**3**	**2**	**5**	**111**	**0**	**0**	**1**
FRANCIS, Bobby *No Playoffs*									Center
•FRANCIS, Ron									Center
1986	Hartford	10	1	2	3	4	0	0	0
1987	Hartford	6	2	2	4	6	1	0	0
1988	Hartford	6	2	5	7	2	1	0	0
1989	Hartford	4	0	2	2	0	0	0	0
1990	Hartford	7	3	3	6	8	1	0	0
1991♦	Pittsburgh	24	7	10	17	24	0	0	4
1992♦	Pittsburgh	21	8	*19	27	6	2	0	2
1993	Pittsburgh	12	6	11	17	19	1	0	1
1994	Pittsburgh	6	0	2	2	6	0	0	0
1995	Pittsburgh	12	6	13	19	4	2	0	0
1996	Pittsburgh	11	3	6	9	4	2	0	1
1997	Pittsburgh	5	1	2	3	2	1	0	0
1998	Pittsburgh	6	1	5	6	2	0	0	0
1999	Carolina	3	0	1	1	0	0	0	0
2001	Carolina	3	0	0	0	0	0	0	0
2002	Carolina	23	6	10	16	6	4	0	3
Playoff Totals		**159**	**46**	**93**	**139**	**93**	**15**	**0**	**11**
FRASER, Archie *No Playoffs*									Center
FRASER, Charles *No Playoffs*									Defense
FRASER, Curt									Left wing
1979	Vancouver	3	0	2	2	6	0	0	0
1980	Vancouver	4	0	0	0	2	0	0	0
1981	Vancouver	3	1	0	1	2	0	0	0
1982	Vancouver	17	3	7	10	98	0	0	0
1983	Chicago	13	4	4	8	18	1	0	1
1984	Chicago	5	0	0	0	14	0	0	0
1985	Chicago	15	6	3	9	36	0	0	1
1986	Chicago	3	0	1	1	12	0	0	0
1987	Chicago	2	1	1	2	10	0	0	0
Playoff Totals		**65**	**15**	**18**	**33**	**198**	**1**	**0**	**2**

Season	Team	GP	G	A	Pts	PIM	PP	SH	GW
FRASER, Gord									Defense
1927	Chicago	2	1	0	1	6	....	....	....
Playoff Totals		**2**	**1**	**0**	**1**	**6**	....	....	....
FRASER, Harvey *No Playoffs*									Center
FRASER, Iain									Center
1996	Winnipeg	4	0	0	0	0	0	0	0
Playoff Totals		**4**	**0**	**0**	**0**	**0**	**0**	**0**	**0**
FRASER, Scott									Center
1998	Edmonton	11	1	1	2	0	0	0	0
Playoff Totals		**11**	**1**	**1**	**2**	**0**	**0**	**0**	**0**
FRAWLEY, Dan									Right wing
1985	Chicago	1	0	0	0	0	0	0	0
Playoff Totals		**1**	**0**	**0**	**0**	**0**	**0**	**0**	**0**
•FREADRICH, Kyle *No Playoffs*									Left wing
FREDRICKSON, Frank									Center
1927	Boston	8	2	2	4	20	....	....	....
1928	Boston	2	0	1	1	4	....	....	....
Playoff Totals		**10**	**2**	**3**	**5**	**24**	....	....	....
FREER, Mark *No Playoffs*									Center
FREW, Irv									Defense
1934	Mtl. Maroons	4	0	0	0	6	0	0	0
Playoff Totals		**4**	**0**	**0**	**0**	**6**	**0**	**0**	**0**
FRIDAY, Tim *No Playoffs*									Defense
FRIDGEN, Dan *No Playoffs*									Left wing
FRIEDMAN, Doug *No Playoffs*									Left wing
•FRIESEN, Jeff									Left wing
1995	San Jose	11	1	5	6	4	0	0	0
1998	San Jose	6	0	1	1	2	0	0	0
1999	San Jose	6	2	2	4	14	1	0	0
2000	San Jose	11	2	2	4	10	0	0	0
Playoff Totals		**34**	**5**	**10**	**15**	**30**	**1**	**0**	**0**
FRIEST, Ron									Left wing
1982	Minnesota	2	0	0	0	5	0	0	0
1983	Minnesota	4	1	0	1	2	0	0	0
Playoff Totals		**6**	**1**	**0**	**1**	**7**	**0**	**0**	**0**
FRIG, Len									Defense
1973	Chicago	4	1	1	2	0	1	0	0
1974	Chicago	7	1	0	1	0	1	0	0
1980	St. Louis	3	0	0	0	0	0	0	0
Playoff Totals		**14**	**2**	**1**	**3**	**0**	**2**	**0**	**0**
•FROLOV, Alexander *No Playoffs*									Left wing
FROST, Harry									Right wing
1939♦	Boston	1	0	0	0	0	0	0	0
Playoff Totals		**1**	**0**	**0**	**0**	**0**	**0**	**0**	**0**
FRYCER, Miroslav									Right wing
1983	Toronto	4	2	5	7	0	0	0	0
1986	Toronto	10	1	3	4	10	0	0	0
1988	Toronto	3	0	0	0	6	0	0	0
Playoff Totals		**17**	**3**	**8**	**11**	**16**	**0**	**0**	**0**
FRYDAY, Bob *No Playoffs*									Right wing
FTOREK, Robbie									Center/Left wing
1981	Quebec	5	1	2	3	17	1	0	0
1982	NY Rangers	10	7	4	11	11	4	0	1
1983	NY Rangers	4	1	0	1	0	0	0	0
Playoff Totals		**19**	**9**	**6**	**15**	**28**	**5**	**0**	**1**
FULLAN, Larry *No Playoffs*									Left wing
FUSCO, Mark *No Playoffs*									Defense
•GABORIK, Marian *No Playoffs*									Left wing
GADSBY, Bill									Defense
1953	Chicago	7	0	1	1	4	....	....	....
1956	NY Rangers	5	1	3	4	4	....	....	....
1957	NY Rangers	5	1	2	3	2	....	....	....
1958	NY Rangers	6	0	3	3	4	....	....	....
1963	Detroit	11	1	4	5	*36	....	....	....
1964	Detroit	14	0	4	4	22	....	....	....
1965	Detroit	7	0	3	3	8	....	....	....
1966	Detroit	12	1	3	4	12	....	....	....
Playoff Totals		**67**	**4**	**23**	**27**	**92**	....	....	....
GAETZ, Link *No Playoffs*									Defense
GAGE, Jody *No Playoffs*									Right wing
GAGNE, Art									Right wing
1927	Montreal	4	0	0	0	0	....	....	....
1928	Montreal	2	1	1	2	4	....	....	....
1929	Montreal	3	0	0	0	12	....	....	....
1930	Ottawa	2	1	0	1	4	....	....	....
Playoff Totals		**11**	**2**	**1**	**3**	**20**	....	....	....
GAGNE, Paul *No Playoffs*									Left wing
GAGNE, Pierre *No Playoffs*									Left wing
•GAGNE, Simon									Left wing
2000	Philadelphia	17	5	5	10	2	2	0	1
2001	Philadelphia	6	3	0	3	0	2	0	0
2002	Philadelphia	5	0	0	0	2	0	0	0
Playoff Totals		**28**	**8**	**5**	**13**	**4**	**4**	**0**	**1**

Season	Team	GP	G	A	Pts	PIM	PP	SH	GW
GAGNER, Dave									Center
1990	Minnesota	7	2	3	5	16	1	0	0
1991	Minnesota	23	12	15	27	28	6	1	1
1992	Minnesota	7	2	4	6	8	2	0	0
1994	Dallas	9	5	1	6	2	3	0	0
1995	Dallas	5	1	1	2	4	1	0	0
1996	Toronto	6	0	2	2	6	0	0	0
Playoff Totals		**57**	**22**	**26**	**48**	**64**	**13**	**1**	**1**
GAGNON, Germain									Left wing
1974	Chicago	11	2	2	4	2	1	0	1
1975	Chicago	8	0	1	1	0	0	0	0
Playoff Totals		**19**	**2**	**3**	**5**	**2**	**1**	**0**	**1**
GAGNON, Johnny									Right wing
1931♦	Montreal	10	*6	2	8	8	....	....	....
1932	Montreal	4	1	1	2	4	....	....	....
1933	Montreal	2	0	2	2	0	....	....	....
1934	Montreal	2	1	0	1	2	....	....	....
1935	Montreal	2	0	1	1	2	....	....	....
1937	Montreal	5	2	1	3	9	....	....	....
1938	Montreal	3	1	3	4	2	....	....	....
1939	Montreal	3	0	2	2	10	....	....	....
1940	NY Americans	1	1	0	1	0	....	....	....
Playoff Totals		**32**	**12**	**12**	**24**	**37**	....	....	....
•GAGNON, Sean *No Playoffs*									Defense
GAINEY, Bob									Left wing
1974	Montreal	6	0	0	0	6	0	0	0
1975	Montreal	11	2	4	6	4	0	0	1
1976♦	Montreal	13	1	3	4	20	0	0	0
1977♦	Montreal	14	4	1	5	25	0	1	1
1978♦	Montreal	15	2	7	9	14	0	1	0
1979♦	Montreal	16	6	10	16	10	0	0	1
1980	Montreal	10	1	1	2	4	0	0	1
1981	Montreal	3	0	0	0	2	0	0	0
1982	Montreal	5	0	1	1	8	0	0	0
1983	Montreal	3	0	0	0	4	0	0	0
1984	Montreal	15	1	5	6	9	0	0	0
1985	Montreal	12	1	3	4	13	0	0	0
1986♦	Montreal	20	5	5	10	12	0	1	3
1987	Montreal	17	1	3	4	6	0	0	0
1988	Montreal	6	0	1	1	6	0	0	0
1989	Montreal	16	1	4	5	8	0	0	0
Playoff Totals		**182**	**25**	**48**	**73**	**151**	**0**	**3**	**7**
•GAINEY, Steve *No Playoffs*									Left wing
GAINOR, Dutch									Center
1928	Boston	2	0	0	0	6	....	....	....
1929♦	Boston	5	2	0	2	4	....	....	....
1930	Boston	3	0	0	0	0	....	....	....
1931	Boston	5	0	1	1	2	....	....	....
1932	NY Rangers	7	0	0	0	2	....	....	....
1935♦	Mtl. Maroons	....	....	....	....	....	....	....	....
Playoff Totals		**22**	**2**	**1**	**3**	**14**	....	....	....
•GALANOV, Maxim									Defense
1999	Pittsburgh	1	0	0	0	0	0	0	0
Playoff Totals		**1**	**0**	**0**	**0**	**0**	**0**	**0**	**0**
GALARNEAU, Michel *No Playoffs*									Center
GALBRAITH, Percy									Left wing/Defense
1927	Boston	8	3	*3	*6	2	....	....	....
1928	Boston	2	0	1	1	6	....	....	....
1929♦	Boston	5	0	0	0	2	....	....	....
1930	Boston	6	1	3	4	8	....	....	....
1931	Boston	5	0	0	0	6	....	....	....
1933	Boston	5	0	0	0	0	....	....	....
Playoff Totals		**31**	**4**	**7**	**11**	**24**	....	....	....
GALLAGHER, John									Defense
1931	Mtl. Maroons	2	0	0	0	0	....	....	....
1933	Detroit	4	1	1	2	4	....	....	....
1937♦	Detroit	10	1	0	1	17	....	....	....
1938	NY Americans	6	0	2	2	6	....	....	....
1939	NY Americans	2	0	0	0	0	....	....	....
Playoff Totals		**24**	**2**	**3**	**5**	**27**	....	....	....
GALLANT, Gerard									Left wing
1985	Detroit	3	0	0	0	11	0	0	0
1987	Detroit	16	8	6	14	43	2	0	0
1988	Detroit	16	6	9	15	55	1	0	1
1989	Detroit	6	1	2	3	40	0	0	0
1992	Detroit	11	2	2	4	25	0	0	1
1993	Detroit	6	1	2	3	4	0	0	0
Playoff Totals		**58**	**18**	**21**	**39**	**178**	**3**	**0**	**2**
GALLEY, Garry									Defense
1985	Los Angeles	3	1	0	1	2	0	0	0
1987	Washington	2	0	0	0	0	0	0	0
1988	Washington	13	2	4	6	13	0	0	0
1989	Boston	9	0	1	1	33	0	0	0
1990	Boston	21	3	3	6	34	1	0	2
1991	Boston	16	1	5	6	17	0	0	0
1995	Buffalo	5	0	3	3	4	0	0	0
1997	Buffalo	12	0	6	6	14	0	0	0
1998	Los Angeles	4	0	1	1	2	0	0	0
2000	Los Angeles	4	0	0	0	0	0	0	0
Playoff Totals		**89**	**7**	**23**	**30**	**119**	**1**	**0**	**2**
GALLIMORE, Jamie *No Playoffs*									Right wing

Season	Team	GP	G	A	Pts	PIM	PP	SH	GW
GALLINGER, Don									Center
1943	Boston	9	3	1	4	10	....	....	....
1946	Boston	10	2	4	6	2	....	....	....
1947	Boston	4	0	0	0	7	....	....	....
Playoff Totals		**23**	**5**	**5**	**10**	**19**	....	....	....
GAMBLE, Dick									Left wing
1952	Montreal	7	0	2	2	0	....	....	....
1953♦	Montreal	5	1	0	1	2	....	....	....
1955	Montreal	2	0	0	0	2	....	....	....
Playoff Totals		**14**	**1**	**2**	**3**	**4**	....	....	....
GAMBUCCI, Gary *No Playoffs*									Center
GANCHAR, Perry									Right wing
1984	St. Louis	7	3	1	4	0	2	0	0
Playoff Totals		**7**	**3**	**1**	**4**	**0**	**2**	**0**	**0**
GANS, Dave *No Playoffs*									Center
•GARDINER, Bruce									Right wing
1997	Ottawa	7	0	1	1	2	0	0	0
1998	Ottawa	11	1	3	4	2	0	0	1
1999	Ottawa	3	0	0	0	4	0	0	0
Playoff Totals		**21**	**1**	**4**	**5**	**8**	**0**	**0**	**1**
GARDINER, Herb									Defense
1927	Montreal	4	0	0	0	10	0	0	0
1928	Montreal	2	0	1	1	4	0	0	0
1929	Montreal	3	0	0	0	2	0	0	0
Playoff Totals		**9**	**0**	**1**	**1**	**16**	**0**	**0**	**0**
GARDNER, Bill									Center
1982	Chicago	15	1	4	5	6	0	0	0
1983	Chicago	13	1	0	1	9	1	0	0
1984	Chicago	5	0	1	1	0	0	0	0
1985	Chicago	12	1	3	4	2	0	0	0
Playoff Totals		**45**	**3**	**8**	**11**	**17**	**1**	**0**	**0**
GARDNER, Cal									Center
1948	NY Rangers	5	0	0	0	0	....	....	....
1949♦	Toronto	9	2	5	7	0	....	....	....
1950	Toronto	7	1	0	1	4	....	....	....
1951♦	Toronto	11	1	1	2	4	....	....	....
1952	Toronto	3	0	0	0	2	....	....	....
1953	Chicago	7	0	2	2	4	....	....	....
1954	Boston	4	1	1	2	0	....	....	....
1955	Boston	5	0	0	0	4	....	....	....
1957	Boston	10	2	1	3	2	....	....	....
Playoff Totals		**61**	**7**	**10**	**17**	**20**	....	....	....
GARDNER, Dave *No Playoffs*									Center
GARDNER, Paul									Center
1979	Toronto	6	0	1	1	4	0	0	0
1981	Pittsburgh	5	1	0	1	8	1	0	0
1982	Pittsburgh	5	1	5	6	2	1	0	0
Playoff Totals		**16**	**2**	**6**	**8**	**14**	**2**	**0**	**0**
GARE, Danny									Right wing
1975	Buffalo	17	7	6	13	19	0	0	1
1976	Buffalo	9	5	2	7	21	0	0	2
1977	Buffalo	4	0	0	0	18	0	0	0
1978	Buffalo	8	4	6	10	37	2	0	0
1979	Buffalo	3	0	0	0	9	0	0	0
1980	Buffalo	14	4	7	11	35	4	0	1
1981	Buffalo	3	3	0	3	8	2	0	1
1984	Detroit	4	2	0	2	38	0	0	0
1985	Detroit	2	0	0	0	10	0	0	0
Playoff Totals		**64**	**25**	**21**	**46**	**195**	**8**	**0**	**5**
GARIEPY, Ray *No Playoffs*									Defense
GARLAND, Scott									Center
1976	Toronto	7	1	2	3	35	1	0	0
Playoff Totals		**7**	**1**	**2**	**3**	**35**	**1**	**0**	**0**
GARNER, Rob *No Playoffs*									Center
GARPENLOV, Johan									Left wing
1991	Detroit	6	0	1	1	4	0	0	0
1994	San Jose	14	4	6	10	6	0	0	2
1996	Florida	20	4	2	6	8	0	0	0
1997	Florida	4	2	0	2	4	2	0	1
Playoff Totals		**44**	**10**	**9**	**19**	**22**	**2**	**0**	**3**
GARRETT, Red *No Playoffs*									Defense
GARTNER, Mike									Right wing
1983	Washington	4	0	0	0	4	0	0	0
1984	Washington	8	3	7	10	16	2	0	0
1985	Washington	5	4	3	7	9	1	0	1
1986	Washington	9	2	10	12	4	0	0	0
1987	Washington	7	4	3	7	14	0	0	0
1988	Washington	14	3	4	7	14	1	0	0
1989	Minnesota	5	0	0	0	6	0	0	0
1990	NY Rangers	10	5	3	8	12	4	0	1
1991	NY Rangers	6	1	1	2	0	1	0	0
1992	NY Rangers	13	8	8	16	4	3	0	1
1994	Toronto	18	5	6	11	14	1	0	3
1995	Toronto	5	2	2	4	2	0	0	0
1996	Toronto	6	4	1	5	4	2	0	1
1997	Phoenix	7	1	2	3	4	0	0	0
1998	Phoenix	5	1	0	1	18	1	0	0
Playoff Totals		**122**	**43**	**50**	**93**	**125**	**16**	**0**	**7**

Season	Team	GP	G	A	Pts	PIM	PP	SH	GW
GASSOFF, Bob									Defense
1975	St. Louis	2	0	0	0	0	0	0	0
1976	St. Louis	3	0	0	0	6	0	0	0
1977	St. Louis	4	0	1	1	10	0	0	0
Playoff Totals		**9**	**0**	**1**	**1**	**16**	**0**	**0**	**0**
GASSOFF, Brad									Left wing
1979	Vancouver	3	0	0	0	0	0	0	0
Playoff Totals		**3**	**0**	**0**	**0**	**0**	**0**	**0**	**0**
GATZOS, Steve									Right wing
1982	Pittsburgh	1	0	0	0	0	0	0	0
Playoff Totals		**1**	**0**	**0**	**0**	**0**	**0**	**0**	**0**
GAUDREAU, Rob									Right wing
1994	San Jose	14	2	0	2	0	1	1	0
Playoff Totals		**14**	**2**	**0**	**2**	**0**	**1**	**1**	**0**
GAUDREAULT, Armand									Left wing
1945	Boston	7	0	2	2	8	0	0	0
Playoff Totals		**7**	**0**	**2**	**2**	**8**	**0**	**0**	**0**
GAUDREAULT, Leo *No Playoffs*									Left wing/Center
•GAUL, Mike *No Playoffs*									Defense
GAULIN, Jean-Marc									Right wing
1985	Quebec	1	0	0	0	0	0	0	0
Playoff Totals		**1**	**0**	**0**	**0**	**0**	**0**	**0**	**0**
GAUME, Dallas *No Playoffs*									Center
GAUTHIER, Art									Center
1927	Montreal	1	0	0	0	0	0	0	0
Playoff Totals		**1**	**0**	**0**	**0**	**0**	**0**	**0**	**0**
GAUTHIER, Daniel *No Playoffs*									Left wing
•GAUTHIER, Denis *No Playoffs*									Defense
GAUTHIER, Fern									Right wing
1945	Montreal	4	0	0	0	0	....	....	....
1946	Detroit	5	3	0	3	2	....	....	....
1947	Detroit	3	1	0	1	0	....	....	....
1948	Detroit	10	1	1	2	5	....	....	....
Playoff Totals		**22**	**5**	**1**	**6**	**7**	....	....	....
GAUTHIER, Jean									Defense
1963	Montreal	5	0	0	0	12	0	0	0
1965♦	Montreal	2	0	0	0	4	0	0	0
1968	Philadelphia	7	1	3	4	6	1	0	0
Playoff Totals		**14**	**1**	**3**	**4**	**22**	**1**	**0**	**0**
GAUTHIER, Luc *No Playoffs*									Defense
GAUVREAU, Jocelyn *No Playoffs*									Defense
•GAVEY, Aaron									Center
1996	Tampa Bay	6	0	0	0	4	0	0	0
2000	Dallas	13	1	2	3	10	0	0	1
Playoff Totals		**19**	**1**	**2**	**3**	**14**	**0**	**0**	**1**
GAVIN, Stew									Left wing
1983	Toronto	4	0	0	0	0	0	0	0
1986	Hartford	10	4	1	5	13	0	0	0
1987	Hartford	6	2	4	6	10	0	0	0
1988	Hartford	6	2	2	4	4	0	0	0
1989	Minnesota	5	3	1	4	10	0	0	0
1990	Minnesota	7	0	2	2	12	0	0	0
1991	Minnesota	21	3	10	13	20	0	1	1
1992	Minnesota	7	0	0	0	6	0	0	0
Playoff Totals		**66**	**14**	**20**	**34**	**75**	**0**	**1**	**1**
GEALE, Bob *No Playoffs*									Center
GEE, George									Center
1946	Chicago	4	1	1	2	4	....	....	....
1949	Detroit	10	1	3	4	22	....	....	....
1950♦	Detroit	14	3	*6	9	0	....	....	....
1951	Detroit	6	0	1	1	0	....	....	....
1953	Chicago	7	1	2	3	6	....	....	....
Playoff Totals		**41**	**6**	**13**	**19**	**32**	....	....	....
GELDART, Gary *No Playoffs*									Defense
•GELINAS, Martin									Left wing
1990♦	Edmonton	20	2	3	5	6	0	0	0
1991	Edmonton	18	3	6	9	25	0	0	1
1992	Edmonton	15	1	3	4	10	0	0	0
1994	Vancouver	24	5	4	9	14	2	0	1
1995	Vancouver	3	0	1	1	0	0	0	0
1996	Vancouver	6	1	1	2	12	1	0	0
1999	Carolina	6	0	3	3	2	0	0	0
2001	Carolina	6	0	1	1	6	0	0	0
2002	Carolina	23	3	4	7	10	0	0	1
Playoff Totals		**121**	**15**	**26**	**41**	**85**	**3**	**0**	**3**
GENDRON, Jean-Guy									Left wing
1956	NY Rangers	5	2	1	3	2	1	0	0
1957	NY Rangers	5	0	1	1	6	0	0	0
1958	NY Rangers	6	1	0	1	11	0	0	1
1959	Boston	7	1	0	1	18	0	0	1
1961	Montreal	5	0	0	0	2	0	0	0
1962	NY Rangers	6	3	1	4	2	0	0	0
1969	Philadelphia	4	0	0	0	6	0	0	0
1971	Philadelphia	4	0	1	1	0	0	0	0
Playoff Totals		**42**	**7**	**4**	**11**	**47**	**1**	**0**	**2**
GENDRON, Martin *No Playoffs*									Right wing

Season	Team	GP	G	A	Pts	PIM	PP	SH	GW
GEOFFRION, Bernie									Right wing
1951	Montreal	11	1	1	2	6	....	....	....
1952	Montreal	11	3	1	4	6	....	....	....
1953♦	Montreal	12	6	4	10	12	....	....	....
1954	Montreal	11	*6	5	11	18	....	....	....
1955	Montreal	12	8	5	13	8	....	....	....
1956♦	Montreal	10	5	9	14	6	....	....	....
1957♦	Montreal	10	*11	7	*18	2	....	....	....
1958♦	Montreal	10	6	5	11	2	....	....	....
1959♦	Montreal	11	5	8	13	10	....	....	....
1960♦	Montreal	8	2	*10	*12	4	....	....	....
1961	Montreal	4	2	1	3	0	....	....	....
1962	Montreal	5	0	1	1	6	....	....	....
1963	Montreal	5	0	1	1	4	....	....	....
1964	Montreal	7	1	1	2	4	....	....	....
1967	NY Rangers	4	2	0	2	0	....	....	....
1968	NY Rangers	1	0	1	1	0	0	0	0
Playoff Totals		**132**	**58**	**60**	**118**	**88**	**0**	**0**	**0**
GEOFFRION, Danny									Right wing
1980	Montreal	2	0	0	0	7	0	0	0
Playoff Totals		**2**	**0**	**0**	**0**	**7**	**0**	**0**	**0**
GERAN, Gerry *No Playoffs*									Center
GERARD, Eddie									Left wing/Defense
1919	Ottawa	5	3	0	3	3	....	....	....
1920♦	Ottawa	....	....	....	....	....	....	....	....
1921♦	Ottawa	7	1	0	1	*50	....	....	....
1922	Ottawa	2	0	0	0	8	....	....	....
1923♦	Ottawa	2	0	0	0	0	....	....	....
Playoff Totals		**16**	**4**	**0**	**4**	**61**	....	....	....
GERMAIN, Eric									Defense
1988	Los Angeles	1	0	0	0	4	0	0	0
Playoff Totals		**1**	**0**	**0**	**0**	**4**	**0**	**0**	**0**
•GERNANDER, Ken									Center
1996	NY Rangers	6	0	0	0	0	0	0	0
1997	NY Rangers	9	0	0	0	0	0	0	0
Playoff Totals		**15**	**0**	**0**	**0**	**0**	**0**	**0**	**0**
GETLIFFE, Ray									Center/Left wing
1936	Boston	2	0	0	0	0	....	....	....
1937	Boston	3	2	1	3	2	....	....	....
1938	Boston	3	0	1	1	2	....	....	....
1939♦	Boston	11	1	1	2	2	....	....	....
1941	Montreal	3	1	1	2	0	....	....	....
1942	Montreal	3	0	0	0	0	....	....	....
1943	Montreal	5	0	1	1	8	....	....	....
1944♦	Montreal	9	5	4	9	16	....	....	....
1945	Montreal	6	0	1	1	0	....	....	....
Playoff Totals		**45**	**9**	**10**	**19**	**30**	....	....	....
GIALLONARDO, Mario *No Playoffs*									Defense
GIBBS, Barry									Defense
1970	Minnesota	6	1	0	1	7	1	0	0
1971	Minnesota	12	0	1	1	47	0	0	0
1972	Minnesota	7	1	1	2	9	0	0	0
1973	Minnesota	5	1	0	1	0	1	0	0
1976	Atlanta	2	1	0	1	2	0	0	0
1977	Atlanta	3	0	0	0	2	0	0	0
1980	Los Angeles	1	0	0	0	0	0	0	0
Playoff Totals		**36**	**4**	**2**	**6**	**67**	**2**	**0**	**0**
GIBSON, Don *No Playoffs*									Defense
GIBSON, Doug									Center
1974	Boston	1	0	0	0	0	0	0	0
Playoff Totals		**1**	**0**	**0**	**0**	**0**	**0**	**0**	**0**
GIBSON, John *No Playoffs*									Defense
GIESEBRECHT, Gus									Center
1939	Detroit	6	0	2	2	0	....	....	....
1941	Detroit	9	2	1	3	0	....	....	....
1942	Detroit	2	0	0	0	0	....	....	....
Playoff Totals		**17**	**2**	**3**	**5**	**0**	....	....	....
GIFFIN, Lee *No Playoffs*									Right wing
GILBERT, Ed *No Playoffs*									Center
GILBERT, Greg									Left wing
1982♦	NY Islanders	4	1	1	2	2	0	0	0
1983♦	NY Islanders	10	1	0	1	14	0	0	0
1984	NY Islanders	21	5	7	12	39	2	0	1
1986	NY Islanders	2	0	0	0	9	0	0	0
1987	NY Islanders	10	2	2	4	6	0	0	1
1988	NY Islanders	4	0	0	0	6	0	0	0
1989	Chicago	15	1	5	6	20	0	0	0
1990	Chicago	19	5	8	13	34	0	0	0
1991	Chicago	5	0	1	1	2	0	0	0
1992	Chicago	10	1	3	4	16	0	0	1
1993	Chicago	3	0	0	0	0	0	0	0
1994♦	NY Rangers	23	1	3	4	8	0	0	0
1995	St. Louis	7	0	3	3	6	0	0	0
Playoff Totals		**133**	**17**	**33**	**50**	**162**	**2**	**0**	**3**
GILBERT, Jeannot *No Playoffs*									Center

Season	Team	GP	G	A	Pts	PIM	PP	SH	GW
GILBERT, Rod									Right wing
1962	NY Rangers	4	2	3	5	4	0	0	0
1967	NY Rangers	4	2	2	4	6	1	0	0
1968	NY Rangers	6	5	0	5	4	0	0	0
1969	NY Rangers	4	1	0	1	2	0	0	0
1970	NY Rangers	6	4	5	9	0	3	0	0
1971	NY Rangers	13	4	6	10	8	1	0	1
1972	NY Rangers	16	7	8	15	11	4	0	2
1973	NY Rangers	10	5	1	6	2	0	0	1
1974	NY Rangers	13	3	5	8	4	1	0	1
1975	NY Rangers	3	1	3	4	2	0	0	0
Playoff Totals		**79**	**34**	**33**	**67**	**43**	**10**	**0**	**5**
GILBERTSON, Stan									Left wing
1976	Pittsburgh	3	1	1	2	2	0	0	0
Playoff Totals		**3**	**1**	**1**	**2**	**2**	**0**	**0**	**0**
•GILCHRIST, Brent									Left wing
1989	Montreal	9	1	1	2	10	0	0	0
1990	Montreal	8	2	0	2	2	0	0	0
1991	Montreal	13	5	3	8	6	0	0	1
1992	Montreal	11	2	4	6	6	1	0	0
1994	Dallas	9	3	1	4	2	1	0	0
1995	Dallas	5	0	1	1	2	0	0	0
1997	Dallas	6	2	2	4	2	0	0	0
1998♦	Detroit	15	2	1	3	12	0	0	0
1999	Detroit	3	0	0	0	0	0	0	0
2000	Detroit	6	0	0	0	6	0	0	0
2001	Detroit	5	0	1	1	0	0	0	0
Playoff Totals		**90**	**17**	**14**	**31**	**48**	**2**	**0**	**1**
GILES, Curt									Defense
1980	Minnesota	12	2	4	6	10	2	0	0
1981	Minnesota	19	1	4	5	14	0	0	0
1982	Minnesota	4	0	0	0	2	0	0	0
1983	Minnesota	5	0	2	2	6	0	0	0
1984	Minnesota	16	1	3	4	25	1	0	0
1985	Minnesota	9	0	0	0	17	0	0	0
1986	Minnesota	5	0	1	1	10	0	0	0
1987	NY Rangers	5	0	0	0	6	0	0	0
1989	Minnesota	5	0	0	0	4	0	0	0
1990	Minnesota	7	0	1	1	6	0	0	0
1991	Minnesota	10	1	0	1	16	0	0	0
1992	St. Louis	3	1	1	2	0	1	0	0
1993	St. Louis	3	0	0	0	2	0	0	0
Playoff Totals		**103**	**6**	**16**	**22**	**118**	**4**	**0**	**0**
GILHEN, Randy									Center
1988	Winnipeg	4	1	0	1	10	0	1	1
1991♦	Pittsburgh	16	1	0	1	14	0	0	0
1992	NY Rangers	13	1	2	3	2	0	0	0
Playoff Totals		**33**	**3**	**2**	**5**	**26**	**0**	**1**	**1**
•GILL, Hal									Defense
1998	Boston	6	0	0	0	4	0	0	0
1999	Boston	12	0	0	0	14	0	0	0
2002	Boston	6	0	1	1	2	0	0	0
Playoff Totals		**24**	**0**	**1**	**1**	**20**	**0**	**0**	**0**
•GILL, Todd									Defense
1986	Toronto	1	0	0	0	0	0	0	0
1987	Toronto	13	2	2	4	42	0	0	0
1988	Toronto	6	1	3	4	20	1	0	0
1990	Toronto	5	0	3	3	16	0	0	0
1993	Toronto	21	1	10	11	26	0	0	0
1994	Toronto	18	1	5	6	37	0	0	1
1995	Toronto	7	0	3	3	6	0	0	0
1996	Toronto	6	0	0	0	24	0	0	0
1998	St. Louis	10	2	2	4	10	1	1	0
1999	Detroit	2	0	1	1	0	0	0	0
2000	Detroit	9	0	1	1	4	0	0	0
2001	Detroit	5	0	0	0	8	0	0	0
Playoff Totals		**103**	**7**	**30**	**37**	**193**	**2**	**1**	**1**
GILLEN, Don *No Playoffs*									Right wing
GILLIE, Farrand *No Playoffs*									Left wing/Defense
GILLIES, Clark									Left wing
1975	NY Islanders	17	4	2	6	36	0	0	2
1976	NY Islanders	13	2	4	6	16	0	0	1
1977	NY Islanders	12	4	4	8	15	0	0	4
1978	NY Islanders	7	2	0	2	15	1	0	0
1979	NY Islanders	10	1	2	3	11	0	0	0
1980♦	NY Islanders	21	6	10	16	63	1	0	2
1981♦	NY Islanders	18	6	9	15	28	3	0	0
1982♦	NY Islanders	19	8	6	14	34	4	0	3
1983♦	NY Islanders	8	0	2	2	10	0	0	0
1984	NY Islanders	21	12	7	19	19	3	0	0
1985	NY Islanders	10	1	0	1	9	0	0	0
1986	NY Islanders	3	1	0	1	6	0	0	0
1988	Buffalo	5	0	1	1	25	0	0	0
Playoff Totals		**164**	**47**	**47**	**94**	**287**	**12**	**0**	**12**
GILLIS, Jere									Left wing
1979	Vancouver	1	0	1	1	0	0	0	0
1981	NY Rangers	14	2	5	7	9	0	0	0
1984	Vancouver	4	2	1	3	0	0	0	0
Playoff Totals		**19**	**4**	**7**	**11**	**9**	**0**	**0**	**0**

Season	Team	GP	G	A	Pts	PIM	PP	SH	GW
GILLIS, Mike									Left wing
1981	Boston	1	0	0	0	0	0	0	0
1982	Boston	11	1	2	3	6	0	0	0
1983	Boston	12	1	3	4	2	0	0	0
1984	Boston	3	0	0	0	2	0	0	0
Playoff Totals		**27**	**2**	**5**	**7**	**10**	**0**	**0**	**0**
GILLIS, Paul									Center
1984	Quebec	1	0	0	0	2	0	0	0
1985	Quebec	18	1	7	8	73	0	0	0
1986	Quebec	3	0	2	2	14	0	0	0
1987	Quebec	13	2	4	6	65	0	0	0
1991	Chicago	2	0	0	0	2	0	0	0
1992	Hartford	5	0	1	1	0	0	0	0
Playoff Totals		**42**	**3**	**14**	**17**	**156**	**0**	**0**	**0**
•GILMOUR, Doug									Center/Left wing
1984	St. Louis	11	2	9	11	10	1	0	1
1985	St. Louis	3	1	1	2	2	0	0	0
1986	St. Louis	19	9	12	*21	25	1	2	2
1987	St. Louis	6	2	2	4	16	1	0	1
1988	St. Louis	10	3	14	17	18	1	0	0
1989♦	Calgary	22	11	11	22	20	3	0	3
1990	Calgary	6	3	1	4	8	0	0	1
1991	Calgary	7	1	1	2	0	0	0	1
1993	Toronto	21	10	*25	35	30	4	0	1
1994	Toronto	18	6	22	28	42	5	0	1
1995	Toronto	7	0	6	6	6	0	0	0
1996	Toronto	6	1	7	8	12	1	0	0
1997	New Jersey	10	0	4	4	14	0	0	0
1998	New Jersey	6	5	2	7	4	1	0	1
2000	Buffalo	5	0	1	1	0	0	0	0
2001	Buffalo	13	2	4	6	12	1	0	1
2002	Montreal	12	4	6	10	16	1	0	0
Playoff Totals		**182**	**60**	**128**	**188**	**235**	**20**	**2**	**13**
GINGRAS, Gaston									Defense
1980	Montreal	10	1	6	7	8	0	0	0
1981	Montreal	1	1	0	1	0	1	0	0
1982	Montreal	5	0	1	1	0	0	0	0
1983	Toronto	3	1	2	3	2	0	0	0
1986♦	Montreal	11	2	3	5	4	1	0	0
1987	Montreal	5	0	2	2	0	0	0	0
1988	St. Louis	10	1	3	4	4	0	0	0
1989	St. Louis	7	0	1	1	2	0	0	0
Playoff Totals		**52**	**6**	**18**	**24**	**20**	**2**	**0**	**0**
•GIONTA, Brian									Right wing
2002	New Jersey	6	2	2	4	0	0	1	2
Playoff Totals		**6**	**2**	**2**	**4**	**0**	**0**	**1**	**2**
GIRARD, Bob *No Playoffs*									Left wing
•GIRARD, Jonathan									Defense
2002	Boston	1	0	0	0	2	0	0	0
Playoff Totals		**1**	**0**	**0**	**0**	**2**	**0**	**0**	**0**
GIRARD, Kenny *No Playoffs*									Right wing
GIROUX, Art									Right wing
1933	Montreal	2	0	0	0	0	0	0	0
Playoff Totals		**2**	**0**	**0**	**0**	**0**	**0**	**0**	**0**
GIROUX, Larry									Defense
1978	Detroit	2	0	0	0	2	0	0	0
1980	Hartford	3	0	0	0	2	0	0	0
Playoff Totals		**5**	**0**	**0**	**0**	**4**	**0**	**0**	**0**
GIROUX, Pierre *No Playoffs*									Center
•GIROUX, Raymond *No Playoffs*									Defense
GLADNEY, Bob *No Playoffs*									Defense
GLADU, Jean-Paul									Left wing
1945	Boston	7	2	2	4	0	....	....	....
Playoff Totals		**7**	**2**	**2**	**4**	**0**	....	....	....
GLENNIE, Brian									Defense
1971	Toronto	3	0	0	0	0	0	0	0
1972	Toronto	5	0	0	0	25	0	0	0
1974	Toronto	3	0	0	0	10	0	0	0
1976	Toronto	6	0	1	1	15	0	0	0
1977	Toronto	2	0	0	0	0	0	0	0
1978	Toronto	13	0	0	0	16	0	0	0
Playoff Totals		**32**	**0**	**1**	**1**	**66**	**0**	**0**	**0**
GLENNON, Matt *No Playoffs*									Left wing
GLOECKNER, Lorry *No Playoffs*									Defense
GLOOR, Dan *No Playoffs*									Center
GLOVER, Fred									Center
1949	Detroit	2	0	0	0	0	0	0	0
1951	Detroit	6	0	0	0	0	0	0	0
1952♦	Detroit	....	....	....	....	....	....	....	....
Playoff Totals		**8**	**0**	**0**	**0**	**0**	**0**	**0**	**0**
GLOVER, Howie									Right wing
1961	Detroit	11	1	2	3	2	1	0	0
Playoff Totals		**11**	**1**	**2**	**3**	**2**	**1**	**0**	**0**

Season	Team	GP	G	A	Pts	PIM	PP	SH	GW
GLYNN, Brian									Defense
1988	Calgary	1	0	0	0	0	0	0	0
1991	Minnesota	23	2	6	8	18	2	0	0
1992	Edmonton	16	4	1	5	12	1	0	1
1994	Vancouver	17	0	3	3	10	0	0	0
Playoff Totals		**57**	**6**	**10**	**16**	**40**	**3**	**0**	**1**
•GOC, Sascha *No Playoffs*									Defense
•GODARD, Eric *No Playoffs*									Right wing
GODDEN, Ernie *No Playoffs*									Center
GODFREY, Warren									Defense
1953	Boston	11	0	1	1	2	0	0	0
1954	Boston	4	0	0	0	4	0	0	0
1955	Boston	3	0	0	0	0	0	0	0
1957	Detroit	5	0	0	0	6	0	0	0
1958	Detroit	4	0	0	0	0	0	0	0
1960	Detroit	6	1	0	1	10	0	0	0
1961	Detroit	11	0	2	2	18	0	0	0
1965	Detroit	4	0	1	1	2	0	0	0
1966	Detroit	4	0	0	0	0	0	0	0
Playoff Totals		**52**	**1**	**4**	**5**	**42**	**0**	**0**	**0**
GODIN, Eddy *No Playoffs*									Right wing
GODIN, Sam *No Playoffs*									Right wing
GODYNYUK, Alexander *No Playoffs*									Defense
GOEGAN, Pete									Defense
1958	Detroit	4	0	0	0	18	0	0	0
1960	Detroit	6	1	0	1	13	0	0	0
1961	Detroit	11	0	1	1	18	0	0	0
1963	Detroit	11	0	2	2	12	0	0	0
1966	Detroit	1	0	0	0	0	0	0	0
Playoff Totals		**33**	**1**	**3**	**4**	**61**	**0**	**0**	**0**
GOERTZ, Dave *No Playoffs*									Defense
GOLDHAM, Bob									Defense
1942♦	Toronto	13	2	2	4	31	....	....	....
1947♦	Toronto	....	....	....	....	....	....	....	....
1951	Detroit	6	0	1	1	2	....	....	....
1952♦	Detroit	8	0	1	1	8	....	....	....
1953	Detroit	6	1	1	2	2	....	....	....
1954♦	Detroit	12	0	2	2	2	....	....	....
1955♦	Detroit	11	0	4	4	4	....	....	....
1956	Detroit	10	0	3	3	4	....	....	....
Playoff Totals		**66**	**3**	**14**	**17**	**53**	....	....	....
•GOLDMANN, Erich *No Playoffs*									Defense
GOLDSWORTHY, Bill									Right wing
1968	Minnesota	14	*8	7	*15	12	1	0	1
1970	Minnesota	6	4	3	7	6	3	2	0
1971	Minnesota	7	2	4	6	6	0	0	0
1972	Minnesota	7	2	3	5	6	0	0	1
1973	Minnesota	6	2	2	4	0	1	0	0
Playoff Totals		**40**	**18**	**19**	**37**	**30**	**5**	**2**	**2**
GOLDSWORTHY, Leroy									Right wing
1929	NY Rangers	1	0	0	0	0	....	....	....
1930	NY Rangers	4	0	0	0	2	....	....	....
1933	Detroit	2	0	0	0	0	....	....	....
1934♦	Chicago	7	0	0	0	0	....	....	....
1935	Montreal	2	1	0	1	0	....	....	....
1937	Boston	3	0	0	0	0	....	....	....
1938	Boston	3	0	0	0	2	....	....	....
1939	NY Americans	2	0	0	0	0	....	....	....
Playoff Totals		**24**	**1**	**0**	**1**	**4**	....	....	....
GOLDUP, Glenn									Right wing
1977	Los Angeles	8	2	2	4	2	0	0	0
1978	Los Angeles	2	1	0	1	11	0	0	0
1979	Los Angeles	2	0	1	1	9	0	0	0
1980	Los Angeles	4	1	0	1	0	0	0	0
Playoff Totals		**16**	**4**	**3**	**7**	**22**	**0**	**0**	**0**
GOLDUP, Hank									Left wing
1940	Toronto	10	*5	1	6	4	....	....	....
1941	Toronto	7	0	0	0	0	....	....	....
1942♦	Toronto	9	0	0	0	2	....	....	....
Playoff Totals		**26**	**5**	**1**	**6**	**6**	....	....	....
•GOLUBOVSKY, Yan *No Playoffs*									Defense
•GOMEZ, Scott									Center
2000♦	New Jersey	23	4	6	10	4	1	0	2
2001	New Jersey	25	5	9	14	24	0	0	0
Playoff Totals		**48**	**9**	**15**	**24**	**28**	**1**	**0**	**2**
•GONCHAR, Sergei									Defense
1995	Washington	7	2	2	4	2	0	0	1
1996	Washington	6	2	4	6	4	1	0	0
1998	Washington	21	7	4	11	30	3	1	2
2000	Washington	5	1	0	1	6	0	0	0
2001	Washington	6	1	3	4	2	1	0	0
Playoff Totals		**45**	**13**	**13**	**26**	**44**	**5**	**1**	**3**
GONEAU, Daniel *No Playoffs*									Left wing
GOODEN, Bill *No Playoffs*									Left wing

Season	Team	GP	G	A	Pts	PIM	PP	SH	GW
GOODENOUGH, Larry									Defense
1975♦	Philadelphia	5	0	4	4	2	0	0	0
1976	Philadelphia	16	3	11	14	6	1	0	0
1979	Vancouver	1	0	0	0	2	0	0	0
Playoff Totals		**22**	**3**	**15**	**18**	**10**	**1**	**0**	**0**
GOODFELLOW, Ebbie									Center/Defense
1932	Detroit	2	0	0	0	0	....	....	....
1933	Detroit	4	1	0	1	11	....	....	....
1934	Detroit	9	4	3	7	12	....	....	....
1936♦	Detroit	7	1	0	1	4	....	....	....
1937♦	Detroit	9	2	2	4	12	....	....	....
1939	Detroit	6	0	0	0	8	....	....	....
1940	Detroit	5	0	2	2	9	....	....	....
1941	Detroit	3	0	1	1	9	....	....	....
1943♦	Detroit	....	....	....	....	....	....	....	....
Playoff Totals		**45**	**8**	**8**	**16**	**65**	....	....	....
GORDIOUK, Viktor *No Playoffs*									Left wing
GORDON, Fred									Right wing
1928	Boston	2	0	0	0	0	0	0	0
Playoff Totals		**2**	**0**	**0**	**0**	**0**	**0**	**0**	**0**
GORDON, Jack									Center
1950	NY Rangers	9	1	1	2	7	....	....	....
Playoff Totals		**9**	**1**	**1**	**2**	**7**	....	....	....
GORDON, Robb *No Playoffs*									Center
•GOREN, Lee *No Playoffs*									Right wing
GORENCE, Tom									Right wing
1979	Philadelphia	7	3	1	4	0	1	0	0
1980	Philadelphia	15	3	3	6	18	1	0	0
1981	Philadelphia	12	3	2	5	29	0	0	0
1982	Philadelphia	3	0	0	0	0	0	0	0
Playoff Totals		**37**	**9**	**6**	**15**	**47**	**2**	**0**	**0**
GORING, Butch									Center
1974	Los Angeles	5	0	1	1	0	0	0	0
1975	Los Angeles	3	0	0	0	0	0	0	0
1976	Los Angeles	9	2	3	5	4	1	0	2
1977	Los Angeles	9	7	5	12	0	3	0	2
1978	Los Angeles	2	0	0	0	2	0	0	0
1979	Los Angeles	2	0	0	0	0	0	0	0
1980♦	NY Islanders	21	7	12	19	2	1	0	0
1981♦	NY Islanders	18	10	10	20	6	4	2	2
1982♦	NY Islanders	19	6	5	11	12	1	0	2
1983♦	NY Islanders	20	4	8	12	4	0	0	1
1984	NY Islanders	21	1	5	6	2	1	0	0
1985	Boston	5	1	1	2	0	0	0	0
Playoff Totals		**134**	**38**	**50**	**88**	**32**	**11**	**2**	**9**
GORMAN, Dave *No Playoffs*									Right wing
GORMAN, Ed									Defense
1926	Ottawa	2	0	0	0	2	0	0	0
1927♦	Ottawa	6	0	0	0	0	0	0	0
Playoff Totals		**8**	**0**	**0**	**0**	**2**	**0**	**0**	**0**
GOSSELIN, Benoit *No Playoffs*									Left wing
•GOSSELIN, David *No Playoffs*									Right wing
GOSSELIN, Guy *No Playoffs*									Defense
GOTAAS, Steve									Center
1989	Minnesota	3	0	1	1	5	0	0	0
Playoff Totals		**3**	**0**	**1**	**1**	**5**	**0**	**0**	**0**
GOTTSELIG, Johnny									Left wing
1930	Chicago	2	0	0	0	4	....	....	....
1931	Chicago	9	3	3	6	2	....	....	....
1932	Chicago	2	0	0	0	2	....	....	....
1934♦	Chicago	8	4	3	7	4	....	....	....
1935	Chicago	2	0	0	0	0	....	....	....
1936	Chicago	2	0	2	2	0	....	....	....
1938♦	Chicago	10	5	3	*8	4	....	....	....
1940	Chicago	2	0	1	1	0	....	....	....
1944	Chicago	6	1	1	2	2	....	....	....
Playoff Totals		**43**	**13**	**13**	**26**	**18**	....	....	....
GOULD, Bobby									Right wing
1981	Calgary	11	3	1	4	4	0	0	0
1983	Washington	4	5	0	5	4	1	0	1
1984	Washington	5	0	2	2	4	0	0	0
1985	Washington	5	0	1	1	2	0	0	0
1986	Washington	9	4	3	7	11	0	0	0
1987	Washington	7	0	3	3	8	0	0	0
1988	Washington	14	3	1	4	21	0	2	0
1989	Washington	6	0	2	2	0	0	0	0
1990	Boston	17	0	0	0	4	0	0	0
Playoff Totals		**78**	**15**	**13**	**28**	**58**	**1**	**2**	**1**
GOULD, John									Right wing
1975	Vancouver	5	2	2	4	0	1	0	0
1976	Vancouver	2	1	0	1	0	0	1	0
1977	Atlanta	3	0	0	0	2	0	0	0
1978	Atlanta	2	0	0	0	2	0	0	0
1979	Atlanta	2	0	0	0	0	0	0	0
Playoff Totals		**14**	**3**	**2**	**5**	**4**	**1**	**1**	**0**
GOULD, Larry *No Playoffs*									Left wing

Season	Team	GP	G	A	Pts	PIM	PP	SH	GW
GOULET, Michel									Left wing
1981	Quebec	4	3	4	7	7	0	0	1
1982	Quebec	16	8	5	13	6	2	2	0
1983	Quebec	4	0	0	0	6	0	0	0
1984	Quebec	9	2	4	6	17	0	0	0
1985	Quebec	17	11	10	21	17	7	0	0
1986	Quebec	3	1	2	3	10	1	0	0
1987	Quebec	13	9	5	14	35	4	0	2
1990	Chicago	14	2	4	6	6	0	0	0
1992	Chicago	9	3	4	7	6	0	0	1
1993	Chicago	3	0	1	1	0	0	0	0
Playoff Totals		**92**	**39**	**39**	**78**	**110**	**14**	**2**	**4**
GOUPILLE, Red									Defense
1938	Montreal	3	2	0	2	4	....	....	....
1941	Montreal	2	0	0	0	0	....	....	....
1942	Montreal	3	0	0	0	2	....	....	....
Playoff Totals		**8**	**2**	**0**	**2**	**6**	....	....	....
GOVEDARIS, Chris									Left wing
1990	Hartford	2	0	0	0	2	0	0	0
1994	Toronto	2	0	0	0	0	0	0	0
Playoff Totals		**4**	**0**	**0**	**0**	**2**	**0**	**0**	**0**
GOYER, Gerry									Center
1968	Chicago	3	0	0	0	2	0	0	0
Playoff Totals		**3**	**0**	**0**	**0**	**2**	**0**	**0**	**0**
GOYETTE, Phil									Center
1957♦	Montreal	10	2	1	3	4	....	....	....
1958♦	Montreal	10	4	1	5	4	....	....	....
1959♦	Montreal	10	0	4	4	0	....	....	....
1960♦	Montreal	8	2	1	3	4	....	....	....
1961	Montreal	6	3	3	6	0	....	....	....
1962	Montreal	6	1	4	5	2	....	....	....
1963	Montreal	2	0	0	0	0	....	....	....
1967	NY Rangers	4	1	0	1	0	....	....	....
1968	NY Rangers	6	0	1	1	4	0	0	0
1969	NY Rangers	3	0	0	0	0	0	0	0
1970	St. Louis	16	3	11	14	6	1	2	0
1972	NY Rangers	13	1	3	4	2	1	0	0
Playoff Totals		**94**	**17**	**29**	**46**	**26**	**2**	**2**	**0**
GRABOSKI, Tony									Left wing/Defense
1941	Montreal	3	0	0	0	6	0	0	0
Playoff Totals		**3**	**0**	**0**	**0**	**6**	**0**	**0**	**0**
GRACIE, Bob									Center/Left wing
1931	Toronto	2	0	0	0	0	....	....	....
1932♦	Toronto	7	3	1	4	0	....	....	....
1933	Toronto	9	0	1	1	0	....	....	....
1935♦	Mtl. Maroons	7	0	2	2	2	....	....	....
1936	Mtl. Maroons	3	0	1	1	0	....	....	....
1937	Mtl. Maroons	5	1	2	3	2	....	....	....
Playoff Totals		**33**	**4**	**7**	**11**	**4**	....	....	....
GRADIN, Thomas									Center
1979	Vancouver	3	4	1	5	4	0	0	0
1980	Vancouver	4	0	2	2	0	0	0	0
1981	Vancouver	3	1	3	4	0	0	0	0
1982	Vancouver	17	9	10	19	10	4	0	0
1983	Vancouver	4	1	3	4	2	0	0	0
1984	Vancouver	4	0	1	1	2	0	0	0
1986	Vancouver	3	2	1	3	2	0	0	0
1987	Boston	4	0	4	4	0	0	0	0
Playoff Totals		**42**	**17**	**25**	**42**	**20**	**4**	**0**	**0**
GRAHAM, Dirk									Right/left wing
1984	Minnesota	1	0	0	0	2	0	0	0
1985	Minnesota	9	0	4	4	7	0	0	0
1986	Minnesota	5	3	1	4	2	0	1	2
1988	Chicago	4	1	2	3	4	0	0	0
1989	Chicago	16	2	4	6	38	1	0	0
1990	Chicago	5	1	5	6	2	0	1	0
1991	Chicago	6	1	2	3	17	0	0	0
1992	Chicago	18	7	5	12	8	0	0	1
1993	Chicago	4	0	0	0	0	0	0	0
1994	Chicago	6	0	1	1	4	0	0	0
1995	Chicago	16	2	3	5	8	0	0	1
Playoff Totals		**90**	**17**	**27**	**44**	**92**	**1**	**2**	**4**
GRAHAM, Leth									Left wing
1921♦	Ottawa	1	0	0	0	0	0	0	0
Playoff Totals		**1**	**0**	**0**	**0**	**0**	**0**	**0**	**0**
GRAHAM, Pat									Left wing
1982	Pittsburgh	4	0	0	0	2	0	0	0
Playoff Totals		**4**	**0**	**0**	**0**	**2**	**0**	**0**	**0**
GRAHAM, Rod *No Playoffs*									Left wing
GRAHAM, Ted									Defense
1930	Chicago	2	0	0	0	8	....	....	....
1931	Chicago	9	0	0	0	12	....	....	....
1932	Chicago	2	0	0	0	2	....	....	....
1934	Detroit	9	3	1	4	8	....	....	....
1936	Boston	2	0	0	0	0	....	....	....
Playoff Totals		**24**	**3**	**1**	**4**	**30**	....	....	....

Season	Team	GP	G	A	Pts	PIM	PP	SH	GW
GRANATO, Tony									Right wing
1989	NY Rangers	4	1	1	2	21	0	0	0
1990	Los Angeles	10	5	4	9	12	2	1	2
1991	Los Angeles	12	1	4	5	28	0	0	0
1992	Los Angeles	6	1	5	6	10	0	0	0
1993	Los Angeles	24	6	11	17	50	1	0	1
1998	San Jose	1	0	0	0	0	0	0	0
1999	San Jose	6	1	1	2	2	0	0	0
2000	San Jose	12	0	1	1	14	0	0	0
2001	San Jose	4	1	0	1	4	0	0	0
Playoff Totals		**79**	**16**	**27**	**43**	**141**	**3**	**1**	**3**
•GRAND-PIERRE, Jean-Luc									Defense
2000	Buffalo	4	0	0	0	4	0	0	0
Playoff Totals		**4**	**0**	**0**	**0**	**4**	**0**	**0**	**0**
GRANT, Danny									Right wing
1968♦	Montreal	10	0	3	3	5	0	0	0
1970	Minnesota	6	0	2	2	4	0	0	0
1971	Minnesota	12	5	5	10	8	3	0	1
1972	Minnesota	7	2	1	3	0	0	0	0
1973	Minnesota	6	3	1	4	0	0	0	0
1978	Los Angeles	2	0	2	2	2	0	0	0
Playoff Totals		**43**	**10**	**14**	**24**	**19**	**3**	**0**	**1**
•GRATTON, Benoit *No Playoffs*									Left wing
•GRATTON, Chris									Center
1996	Tampa Bay	6	0	2	2	27	0	0	0
1998	Philadelphia	5	2	0	2	10	0	0	0
2000	Buffalo	5	0	1	1	4	0	0	0
2001	Buffalo	13	6	4	10	14	2	0	1
Playoff Totals		**29**	**8**	**7**	**15**	**55**	**2**	**0**	**1**
GRATTON, Dan *No Playoffs*									Center
GRATTON, Norm									Left wing
1973	Buffalo	6	0	1	1	2	0	0	0
Playoff Totals		**6**	**0**	**1**	**1**	**2**	**0**	**0**	**0**
GRAVELLE, Leo									Right wing
1947	Montreal	6	2	0	2	2	....	....	....
1949	Montreal	7	2	1	3	0	....	....	....
1950	Montreal	4	0	0	0	0	....	....	....
Playoff Totals		**17**	**4**	**1**	**5**	**2**	....	....	....
•GRAVES, Adam									Center
1989	Detroit	5	0	0	0	4	0	0	0
1990♦	Edmonton	22	5	6	11	17	0	0	1
1991	Edmonton	18	2	4	6	22	0	0	0
1992	NY Rangers	10	5	3	8	22	1	0	1
1994♦	NY Rangers	23	10	7	17	24	3	0	0
1995	NY Rangers	10	4	4	8	8	2	0	0
1996	NY Rangers	10	7	1	8	4	6	0	2
1997	NY Rangers	15	2	1	3	12	1	0	2
2002	San Jose	12	3	1	4	6	0	0	2
Playoff Totals		**125**	**38**	**27**	**65**	**119**	**13**	**0**	**8**
GRAVES, Hilliard									Right wing
1976	Atlanta	2	0	0	0	0	0	0	0
Playoff Totals		**2**	**0**	**0**	**0**	**0**	**0**	**0**	**0**
GRAVES, Steve *No Playoffs*									Left wing
GRAY, Alex									Right wing
1928♦	NY Rangers	9	1	0	1	0	....	....	....
1929	Toronto	4	0	0	0	0	....	....	....
Playoff Totals		**13**	**1**	**0**	**1**	**0**	....	....	....
GRAY, Terry									Right wing
1968	Los Angeles	7	0	2	2	10	0	0	0
1969	St. Louis	11	3	2	5	8	1	0	0
1970	St. Louis	16	2	1	3	4	1	1	0
1971	St. Louis	1	0	0	0	0	0	0	0
Playoff Totals		**35**	**5**	**5**	**10**	**22**	**2**	**1**	**0**
•GREEN, Josh									Left wing
2001	Edmonton	3	0	0	0	0	0	0	0
Playoff Totals		**3**	**0**	**0**	**0**	**0**	**0**	**0**	**0**
GREEN, Red									Left wing
1929♦	Boston	1	0	0	0	0	0	0	0
Playoff Totals		**1**	**0**	**0**	**0**	**0**	**0**	**0**	**0**
GREEN, Rick									Defense
1983	Montreal	3	0	0	0	2	0	0	0
1984	Montreal	15	1	2	3	33	0	0	0
1985	Montreal	12	0	3	3	14	0	0	0
1986♦	Montreal	18	1	4	5	8	0	0	0
1987	Montreal	17	0	4	4	8	0	0	0
1988	Montreal	11	0	2	2	2	0	0	0
1989	Montreal	21	1	1	2	6	0	0	0
1991	Detroit	3	0	0	0	0	0	0	0
Playoff Totals		**100**	**3**	**16**	**19**	**73**	**0**	**0**	**0**
GREEN, Shorty *No Playoffs*									Right wing
GREEN, Ted									Defense
1968	Boston	4	1	1	2	11	1	0	0
1969	Boston	10	2	7	9	18	0	0	0
1971	Boston	7	1	0	1	25	0	0	0
1972♦	Boston	10	0	0	0	0	0	0	0
Playoff Totals		**31**	**4**	**8**	**12**	**54**	**1**	**0**	**0**

Season	Team	GP	G	A	Pts	PIM	PP	SH	GW
•GREEN, Travis	Center								
1993	NY Islanders	12	3	1	4	6	0	0	0
1994	NY Islanders	4	0	0	0	2	0	0	0
1999	Anaheim	4	0	1	1	4	0	0	0
2000	Phoenix	5	2	1	3	2	0	0	0
2002	Toronto	20	3	6	9	34	0	0	1
Playoff Totals		**45**	**8**	**9**	**17**	**48**	**0**	**0**	**1**
GREENLAW, Jeff	Left wing								
1988	Washington	1	0	0	0	19	0	0	0
1991	Washington	1	0	0	0	2	0	0	0
Playoff Totals		**2**	**0**	**0**	**0**	**21**	**0**	**0**	**0**
GREGG, Randy	Defense								
1982	Edmonton	4	0	0	0	0	0	0	0
1983	Edmonton	16	2	4	6	13	0	1	1
1984♦	Edmonton	19	3	7	10	21	0	0	1
1985♦	Edmonton	17	0	6	6	12	0	0	0
1986	Edmonton	10	1	0	1	12	0	0	0
1987♦	Edmonton	18	3	6	9	17	1	0	1
1988♦	Edmonton	19	1	8	9	24	0	0	1
1989	Edmonton	7	1	0	1	4	0	0	0
1990♦	Edmonton	20	2	6	8	16	1	0	0
1992	Vancouver	7	0	1	1	8	0	0	0
Playoff Totals		**137**	**13**	**38**	**51**	**127**	**2**	**1**	**4**
GREIG, Bruce *No Playoffs*	Left wing								
•GREIG, Mark	Right wing								
1999	Philadelphia	2	0	1	1	0	0	0	0
2000	Philadelphia	3	0	0	0	0	0	0	0
Playoff Totals		**5**	**0**	**1**	**1**	**0**	**0**	**0**	**0**
GRENIER, Lucien	Right wing								
1969♦	Montreal	2	0	0	0	0	0	0	0
Playoff Totals		**2**	**0**	**0**	**0**	**0**	**0**	**0**	**0**
•GRENIER, Martin *No Playoffs*	Defense								
GRENIER, Richard *No Playoffs*	Center								
GRESCHNER, Ron	Defense								
1975	NY Rangers	3	0	1	1	2	0	0	0
1978	NY Rangers	3	0	0	0	2	0	0	0
1979	NY Rangers	18	7	5	12	16	4	1	3
1980	NY Rangers	9	0	6	6	10	0	0	0
1981	NY Rangers	14	4	8	12	17	1	0	0
1983	NY Rangers	8	2	2	4	12	2	0	0
1984	NY Rangers	2	1	0	1	2	0	0	0
1985	NY Rangers	2	0	3	3	12	0	0	0
1986	NY Rangers	5	3	1	4	11	0	0	0
1987	NY Rangers	6	0	5	5	0	0	0	0
1989	NY Rangers	4	0	1	1	6	0	0	0
1990	NY Rangers	10	0	0	0	16	0	0	0
Playoff Totals		**84**	**17**	**32**	**49**	**106**	**7**	**1**	**3**
GRETZKY, Brent *No Playoffs*	Center								
GRETZKY, Wayne	Center								
1980	Edmonton	3	2	1	3	0	0	0	0
1981	Edmonton	9	7	14	21	4	2	1	1
1982	Edmonton	5	5	7	12	8	1	1	1
1983	Edmonton	16	12	*26	*38	4	2	3	3
1984♦	Edmonton	19	13	*22	*35	12	2	0	3
1985♦	Edmonton	18	17	*30	*47	4	4	2	3
1986	Edmonton	10	8	11	19	2	4	1	2
1987♦	Edmonton	21	5	*29	*34	6	2	0	0
1988♦	Edmonton	19	12	*31	*43	16	5	1	3
1989	Los Angeles	11	5	17	22	0	1	1	0
1990	Los Angeles	7	3	7	10	0	1	0	0
1991	Los Angeles	12	4	11	15	2	1	0	2
1992	Los Angeles	6	2	5	7	2	1	0	0
1993	Los Angeles	24	*15	*25	*40	4	4	1	3
1996	St. Louis	13	2	14	16	0	1	0	1
1997	NY Rangers	15	10	10	20	2	3	0	2
Playoff Totals		**208**	***122**	***260**	***382**	**66**	**34**	**11**	***24**
•GRIER, Mike	Right wing								
1997	Edmonton	12	3	1	4	4	1	0	1
1998	Edmonton	12	2	2	4	13	0	0	1
1999	Edmonton	4	1	1	2	6	0	0	0
2001	Edmonton	6	0	0	0	8	0	0	0
Playoff Totals		**34**	**6**	**4**	**10**	**31**	**1**	**0**	**2**
GRIEVE, Brent *No Playoffs*	Left wing								
GRIGOR, George	Center								
1944	Chicago	1	0	0	0	0	0	0	0
Playoff Totals		**1**	**0**	**0**	**0**	**0**	**0**	**0**	**0**
•GRIMSON, Stu	Left wing								
1991	Chicago	5	0	0	0	46	0	0	0
1992	Chicago	14	0	1	1	10	0	0	0
1993	Chicago	2	0	0	0	4	0	0	0
1995	Detroit	11	1	0	1	26	0	0	0
1996	Detroit	2	0	0	0	0	0	0	0
1999	Anaheim	3	0	0	0	30	0	0	0
2001	Los Angeles	5	0	0	0	4	0	0	0
Playoff Totals		**42**	**1**	**1**	**2**	**120**	**0**	**0**	**0**
GRISDALE, John	Defense								
1975	Vancouver	5	0	1	1	13	0	0	0
1976	Vancouver	2	0	0	0	0	0	0	0
1979	Vancouver	3	0	0	0	2	0	0	0
Playoff Totals		**10**	**0**	**1**	**1**	**15**	**0**	**0**	**0**

Season	Team	GP	G	A	Pts	PIM	PP	SH	GW
GROLEAU, Francois *No Playoffs*	Defense								
•GRON, Stanislav *No Playoffs*	Right wing								
GRONMAN, Tuomas	Defense								
1998	Pittsburgh	1	0	0	0	0	0	0	0
Playoff Totals		**1**	**0**	**0**	**0**	**0**	**0**	**0**	**0**
GRONSDAHL, Lloyd *No Playoffs*	Right wing								
GRONSTRAND, Jari	Defense								
1990	NY Islanders	3	0	0	0	4	0	0	0
Playoff Totals		**3**	**0**	**0**	**0**	**4**	**0**	**0**	**0**
•GROSEK, Michal	Left wing								
1997	Buffalo	12	3	3	6	8	0	0	0
1998	Buffalo	15	6	4	10	28	2	0	3
1999	Buffalo	13	0	4	4	28	0	0	0
Playoff Totals		**40**	**9**	**11**	**20**	**64**	**2**	**0**	**3**
GROSS, Lloyd	Left wing								
1934	Detroit	1	0	0	0	0	0	0	0
Playoff Totals		**1**	**0**	**0**	**0**	**0**	**0**	**0**	**0**
GROSSO, Don	Left wing/Center								
1939	Detroit	3	1	2	3	7	....	....	....
1940	Detroit	5	0	0	0	0	....	....	....
1941	Detroit	9	1	4	5	0	....	....	....
1942	Detroit	12	*8	6	*14	29	....	....	....
1943♦	Detroit	10	4	2	6	10	....	....	....
1944	Detroit	5	1	0	1	0	....	....	....
1946	Chicago	4	0	0	0	17	....	....	....
Playoff Totals		**48**	**15**	**14**	**29**	**63**	....	....	....
GROSVENOR, Len	Center/Right wing								
1928	Ottawa	2	0	0	0	2	0	0	0
1933	Montreal	2	0	0	0	0	0	0	0
Playoff Totals		**4**	**0**	**0**	**0**	**2**	**0**	**0**	**0**
GROULX, Wayne *No Playoffs*	Center								
•GRUDEN, John	Defense								
1996	Boston	3	0	1	1	0	0	0	0
Playoff Totals		**3**	**0**	**1**	**1**	**0**	**0**	**0**	**0**
GRUEN, Danny *No Playoffs*	Left wing								
GRUHL, Scott *No Playoffs*	Left wing								
GRYP, Bob *No Playoffs*	Left wing								
GUAY, Francois *No Playoffs*	Center								
GUAY, Paul	Right wing								
1984	Philadelphia	3	0	0	0	4	0	0	0
1987	Los Angeles	2	0	0	0	0	0	0	0
1988	Los Angeles	4	0	1	1	8	0	0	0
Playoff Totals		**9**	**0**	**1**	**1**	**12**	**0**	**0**	**0**
GUERARD, Daniel *No Playoffs*	Right wing								
GUERARD, Stephane *No Playoffs*	Defense								
•GUERIN, Bill	Right wing								
1992	New Jersey	6	3	0	3	4	0	0	0
1993	New Jersey	5	1	1	2	4	0	0	0
1994	New Jersey	17	2	1	3	35	0	0	1
1995♦	New Jersey	20	3	8	11	30	1	0	0
1997	New Jersey	8	2	1	3	18	1	0	1
1998	Edmonton	12	7	1	8	17	4	0	0
1999	Edmonton	3	0	2	2	2	0	0	0
2000	Edmonton	5	3	2	5	9	1	0	0
2002	Boston	6	4	2	6	6	3	0	0
Playoff Totals		**82**	**25**	**18**	**43**	**125**	**10**	**0**	**2**
GUEVREMONT, Jocelyn	Defense								
1975	Buffalo	17	0	6	6	14	0	0	0
1976	Buffalo	9	0	5	5	2	0	0	0
1977	Buffalo	6	3	4	7	0	1	0	0
1978	Buffalo	8	1	2	3	2	0	0	0
Playoff Totals		**40**	**4**	**17**	**21**	**18**	**1**	**0**	**0**
GUIDOLIN, Aldo *No Playoffs*	Right wing/Defense								
GUIDOLIN, Bep	Left wing								
1943	Boston	9	0	4	4	12	....	....	....
1946	Boston	10	5	2	7	13	....	....	....
1947	Boston	3	0	1	1	6	....	....	....
1948	Detroit	2	0	0	0	4	....	....	....
Playoff Totals		**24**	**5**	**7**	**12**	**35**			
GUINDON, Bobby *No Playoffs*	Left wing								
•GUOLLA, Stephen *No Playoffs*	Center								
•GUREN, Miloslav *No Playoffs*	Defense								
GUSAROV, Alexei	Defense								
1993	Quebec	5	0	1	1	0	0	0	0
1996♦	Colorado	21	0	9	9	12	0	0	0
1997	Colorado	17	0	3	3	14	0	0	0
1998	Colorado	7	0	1	1	6	0	0	0
1999	Colorado	5	0	0	0	2	0	0	0
2001	St. Louis	13	0	0	0	4	0	0	0
Playoff Totals		**68**	**0**	**14**	**14**	**38**	**0**	**0**	**0**
•GUSEV, Sergey *No Playoffs*	Defense								
•GUSMANOV, Ravil *No Playoffs*	Left wing								

Season	Team	GP	G	A	Pts	PIM	PP	SH	GW
GUSTAFSSON, Bengt-Ake	Right wing								
1983	Washington	4	0	1	1	4	0	0	0
1984	Washington	5	2	3	5	0	2	0	0
1985	Washington	5	1	3	4	0	1	0	0
1988	Washington	14	4	9	13	6	2	0	1
1989	Washington	4	2	3	5	6	1	0	0
Playoff Totals		**32**	**9**	**19**	**28**	**16**	**6**	**0**	**1**
GUSTAFSSON, Per	Defense								
1998	Ottawa	1	0	0	0	0	0	0	0
Playoff Totals		**1**	**0**	**0**	**0**	**0**	**0**	**0**	**0**
GUSTAVSSON, Peter *No Playoffs*	Left wing								
GUY, Kevan	Defense								
1987	Calgary	4	0	1	1	23	0	0	0
1989	Vancouver	1	0	0	0	0	0	0	0
Playoff Totals		**5**	**0**	**1**	**1**	**23**	**0**	**0**	**0**
•HAAKANA, Kari *No Playoffs*	Defense								
HAANPAA, Ari	Right wing								
1987	NY Islanders	6	0	0	0	10	0	0	0
Playoff Totals		**6**	**0**	**0**	**0**	**10**	**0**	**0**	**0**
HAAS, David *No Playoffs*	Left wing								
HABSCHEID, Marc	Right wing/Center								
1986	Minnesota	2	0	0	0	0	0	0	0
1989	Minnesota	5	1	3	4	13	0	0	0
1991	Detroit	5	0	0	0	0	0	0	0
Playoff Totals		**12**	**1**	**3**	**4**	**13**	**0**	**0**	**0**
HACHBORN, Len	Center								
1984	Philadelphia	3	0	0	0	7	0	0	0
1985	Philadelphia	4	0	3	3	0	0	0	0
Playoff Totals		**7**	**0**	**3**	**3**	**7**	**0**	**0**	**0**
HADDON, Lloyd	Defense								
1960	Detroit	1	0	0	0	0	0	0	0
Playoff Totals		**1**	**0**	**0**	**0**	**0**	**0**	**0**	**0**
HADFIELD, Vic	Left wing								
1962	NY Rangers	4	0	0	0	2	0	0	0
1967	NY Rangers	4	1	0	1	17	0	0	0
1968	NY Rangers	6	1	2	3	6	1	0	0
1969	NY Rangers	4	2	1	3	2	0	0	0
1971	NY Rangers	12	8	5	13	46	1	0	1
1972	NY Rangers	16	7	9	16	22	2	0	1
1973	NY Rangers	9	2	2	4	11	0	0	1
1974	NY Rangers	6	1	0	1	0	0	0	0
1975	Pittsburgh	9	4	2	6	0	0	1	0
1976	Pittsburgh	3	1	0	1	11	0	0	0
Playoff Totals		**73**	**27**	**21**	**48**	**117**	**4**	**1**	**3**
HAGGARTY, Jim	Left wing								
1942	Montreal	3	2	1	3	0	....	....	....
Playoff Totals		**3**	**2**	**1**	**3**	**0**	....	....	....
•HAGGERTY, Sean *No Playoffs*	Left wing								
HAGGLUND, Roger *No Playoffs*	Defense								
HAGMAN, Matti	Center								
1977	Boston	8	0	1	1	0	0	0	0
1981	Edmonton	9	4	1	5	6	0	0	2
1982	Edmonton	3	1	0	1	0	0	0	0
Playoff Totals		**20**	**5**	**2**	**7**	**6**	**0**	**0**	**2**
•HAGMAN, Niklas *No Playoffs*	Left wing								
•HAHL, Riku	Center								
2002	Colorado	21	1	2	3	0	0	0	0
Playoff Totals		**21**	**1**	**2**	**3**	**0**	**0**	**0**	**0**
HAIDY, Gord	Right wing								
1950♦	Detroit	1	0	0	0	0	0	0	0
Playoff Totals		**1**	**0**	**0**	**0**	**0**	**0**	**0**	**0**
•HAINSEY, Ron *No Playoffs*	Defense								
HAJDU, Richard *No Playoffs*	Left wing								
HAJT, Bill	Defense								
1975	Buffalo	17	1	4	5	18	0	0	0
1976	Buffalo	9	0	1	1	15	0	0	0
1977	Buffalo	6	0	1	1	4	0	0	0
1978	Buffalo	8	0	0	0	2	0	0	0
1980	Buffalo	14	0	5	5	4	0	0	0
1981	Buffalo	8	0	2	2	17	0	0	0
1982	Buffalo	2	0	0	0	0	0	0	0
1983	Buffalo	10	0	0	0	4	0	0	0
1984	Buffalo	3	0	0	0	0	0	0	0
1985	Buffalo	3	1	3	4	6	0	0	0
Playoff Totals		**80**	**2**	**16**	**18**	**70**	**0**	**0**	**0**
•HAJT, Chris *No Playoffs*	Defense								
HAKANSSON, Anders	Left wing								
1982	Minnesota	3	0	0	0	2	0	0	0
1985	Los Angeles	3	0	0	0	0	0	0	0
Playoff Totals		**6**	**0**	**0**	**0**	**2**	**0**	**0**	**0**
HALDERSON, Harold *No Playoffs*	Defense								
HALE, Larry	Defense								
1969	Philadelphia	4	0	0	0	10	0	0	0
1971	Philadelphia	4	0	0	0	2	0	0	0
Playoff Totals		**8**	**0**	**0**	**0**	**12**	**0**	**0**	**0**

Season	Team	GP	G	A	Pts	PIM	PP	SH	GW
HALEY, Len									Right wing
1960	Detroit	6	1	3	4	6	0	0	1
Playoff Totals		**6**	**1**	**3**	**4**	**6**	**0**	**0**	**1**
HALKIDIS, Bob									Defense
1985	Buffalo	4	0	0	0	19	0	0	0
1988	Buffalo	4	0	0	0	22	0	0	0
1990	Los Angeles	8	0	1	1	8	0	0	0
1991	Los Angeles	3	0	0	0	0	0	0	0
1994	Detroit	1	0	0	0	2	0	0	0
Playoff Totals		**20**	**0**	**1**	**1**	**51**	**0**	**0**	**0**
•HALKO, Steven									Defense
1999	Carolina	4	0	0	0	2	0	0	0
Playoff Totals		**4**	**0**	**0**	**0**	**2**	**0**	**0**	**0**
•HALL, Adam	*No Playoffs*								Right wing
HALL, Bob	*No Playoffs*								Forward
HALL, Del	*No Playoffs*								Center
HALL, Joe									Defense
1918	Montreal	2	0	1	1	12	0	0	0
1919	Montreal	5	0	0	0	*17	0	0	0
Playoff Totals		**7**	**0**	**1**	**1**	**29**	**0**	**0**	**0**
HALL, Murray									Right wing
1963	Chicago	4	0	0	0	0	0	0	0
1965	Detroit	1	0	0	0	0	0	0	0
1966	Detroit	1	0	0	0	0	0	0	0
Playoff Totals		**6**	**0**	**0**	**0**	**0**	**0**	**0**	**0**
HALL, Taylor	*No Playoffs*								Left wing
HALL, Wayne	*No Playoffs*								Left wing
•HALLER, Kevin									Defense
1991	Buffalo	6	1	4	5	10	0	0	0
1992	Montreal	9	0	0	0	6	0	0	0
1993♦	Montreal	17	1	6	7	16	1	0	0
1994	Montreal	7	1	1	2	19	0	0	0
1995	Philadelphia	15	4	4	8	10	0	1	1
1996	Philadelphia	6	0	1	1	8	0	0	0
1999	Anaheim	4	0	0	0	2	0	0	0
Playoff Totals		**64**	**7**	**16**	**23**	**71**	**1**	**1**	**1**
HALLIDAY, Milt									Left wing
1927♦	Ottawa	6	0	0	0	0	0	0	0
Playoff Totals		**6**	**0**	**0**	**0**	**0**	**0**	**0**	**0**
HALLIN, Mats									Left wing
1983♦	NY Islanders	7	1	0	1	6	0	0	1
1984	NY Islanders	6	0	0	0	7	0	0	0
1985	NY Islanders	1	0	0	0	0	0	0	0
1986	Minnesota	1	0	0	0	0	0	0	0
Playoff Totals		**15**	**1**	**0**	**1**	**13**	**0**	**0**	**1**
•HALPERN, Jeff									Center
2000	Washington	5	2	1	3	0	1	0	1
2001	Washington	6	2	3	5	17	1	0	1
Playoff Totals		**11**	**4**	**4**	**8**	**17**	**2**	**0**	**2**
HALVERSON, Trevor	*No Playoffs*								Left wing
HALWARD, Doug									Defense
1976	Boston	1	0	0	0	0	0	0	0
1977	Boston	6	0	0	0	4	0	0	0
1979	Los Angeles	1	0	0	0	12	0	0	0
1980	Los Angeles	1	0	0	0	2	0	0	0
1981	Vancouver	2	0	1	1	6	0	0	0
1982	Vancouver	15	2	4	6	44	0	0	1
1983	Vancouver	4	1	0	1	21	0	0	0
1984	Vancouver	4	3	1	4	2	2	0	0
1986	Vancouver	3	0	0	0	4	0	0	0
1988	Detroit	8	1	4	5	18	0	0	0
1989	Edmonton	2	0	0	0	0	0	0	0
Playoff Totals		**47**	**7**	**10**	**17**	**113**	**2**	**0**	**1**
•HAMEL, Denis	*No Playoffs*								Left wing
HAMEL, Gilles									Left wing
1981	Buffalo	5	0	1	1	4	0	0	0
1983	Buffalo	9	2	2	4	2	1	0	0
1984	Buffalo	3	0	2	2	2	0	0	0
1985	Buffalo	1	0	0	0	0	0	0	0
1987	Winnipeg	8	2	0	2	2	0	0	2
1988	Winnipeg	1	0	0	0	0	0	0	0
Playoff Totals		**27**	**4**	**5**	**9**	**10**	**1**	**0**	**2**
HAMEL, Herb	*No Playoffs*								Right wing
HAMEL, Jean									Defense
1973	St. Louis	2	0	0	0	0	0	0	0
1978	Detroit	7	0	0	0	10	0	0	0
1982	Quebec	5	0	0	0	16	0	0	0
1983	Quebec	4	0	0	0	2	0	0	0
1984	Montreal	15	0	2	2	16	0	0	0
Playoff Totals		**33**	**0**	**2**	**2**	**44**	**0**	**0**	**0**
HAMILL, Red									Left wing
1939♦	Boston	12	0	0	0	8	....	....	....
1940	Boston	5	0	1	1	5	....	....	....
1942	Chicago	3	0	1	1	0	....	....	....
1946	Chicago	4	1	0	1	7	....	....	....
Playoff Totals		**24**	**1**	**2**	**3**	**20**	....	....	....

Season	Team	GP	G	A	Pts	PIM	PP	SH	GW
HAMILTON, Al									Defense
1969	NY Rangers	1	0	0	0	0	0	0	0
1970	NY Rangers	5	0	0	0	2	0	0	0
1980	Edmonton	1	0	0	0	0	0	0	0
Playoff Totals		**7**	**0**	**0**	**0**	**2**	**0**	**0**	**0**
HAMILTON, Chuck	*No Playoffs*								Left wing
HAMILTON, Jack									Center
1943	Toronto	6	1	1	2	0	....	....	....
1944	Toronto	5	1	0	1	0	....	....	....
Playoff Totals		**11**	**2**	**1**	**3**	**0**	....	....	....
HAMILTON, Jim									Right wing
1979	Pittsburgh	5	3	0	3	0	1	0	0
1981	Pittsburgh	1	0	0	0	0	0	0	0
Playoff Totals		**6**	**3**	**0**	**3**	**0**	**1**	**0**	**0**
HAMILTON, Reg									Defense
1937	Toronto	2	0	1	1	2	....	....	....
1938	Toronto	7	0	1	1	2	....	....	....
1939	Toronto	10	0	2	2	4	....	....	....
1940	Toronto	10	0	0	0	0	....	....	....
1941	Toronto	7	1	2	3	13	....	....	....
1942♦	Toronto	....	....	....	....	....	....	....	....
1943	Toronto	6	1	1	2	9	....	....	....
1944	Toronto	5	1	0	1	8	....	....	....
1945♦	Toronto	13	0	0	0	6	....	....	....
1946	Chicago	4	0	1	1	2	....	....	....
Playoff Totals		**64**	**3**	**8**	**11**	**46**	....	....	....
HAMMARSTROM, Inge									Left wing
1974	Toronto	4	1	0	1	0	0	0	0
1975	Toronto	7	1	3	4	4	0	0	1
1977	Toronto	2	0	0	0	0	0	0	0
Playoff Totals		**13**	**2**	**3**	**5**	**4**	**0**	**0**	**1**
HAMMOND, Ken									Defense
1985	Los Angeles	3	0	0	0	4	0	0	0
1988	Los Angeles	2	0	0	0	4	0	0	0
1991	Boston	8	0	0	0	10	0	0	0
1992	Vancouver	2	0	0	0	6	0	0	0
Playoff Totals		**15**	**0**	**0**	**0**	**24**	**0**	**0**	**0**
HAMPSON, Gord	*No Playoffs*								Left wing
HAMPSON, Ted									Center
1962	NY Rangers	6	0	1	1	0	0	0	0
1969	Oakland	7	3	4	7	2	2	0	0
1970	Oakland	4	1	1	2	0	0	0	0
1971	Minnesota	11	3	3	6	0	1	0	0
1972	Minnesota	7	0	1	1	0	0	0	0
Playoff Totals		**35**	**7**	**10**	**17**	**2**	**3**	**0**	**0**
HAMPTON, Rick									Left wing/Defense
1979	Los Angeles	2	0	0	0	0	0	0	0
Playoff Totals		**2**	**0**	**0**	**0**	**0**	**0**	**0**	**0**
HAMR, Radek	*No Playoffs*								Defense
•HAMRLIK, Roman									Defense
1996	Tampa Bay	5	0	1	1	4	0	0	0
1998	Edmonton	12	0	6	6	12	0	0	0
1999	Edmonton	3	0	0	0	2	0	0	0
2000	Edmonton	5	0	1	1	4	0	0	0
2002	NY Islanders	7	1	6	7	6	0	0	0
Playoff Totals		**32**	**1**	**14**	**15**	**28**	**0**	**0**	**0**
HAMWAY, Mark									Right wing
1986	NY Islanders	1	0	0	0	0	0	0	0
Playoff Totals		**1**	**0**	**0**	**0**	**0**	**0**	**0**	**0**
HANDY, Ron	*No Playoffs*								Left wing
•HANDZUS, Michal									Center
1999	St. Louis	11	0	2	2	8	0	0	0
2000	St. Louis	7	0	3	3	6	0	0	0
2002	Phoenix	5	0	0	0	2	0	0	0
Playoff Totals		**23**	**0**	**5**	**5**	**16**	**0**	**0**	**0**
HANGSLEBEN, Al	*No Playoffs*								Defense
HANKINSON, Ben									Right wing
1994	New Jersey	2	1	0	1	4	0	0	0
Playoff Totals		**2**	**1**	**0**	**1**	**4**	**0**	**0**	**0**
•HANKINSON, Casey	*No Playoffs*								Left wing
HANNA, John	*No Playoffs*								Defense
HANNAN, Dave									Center
1988♦	Edmonton	12	1	1	2	8	0	0	1
1989	Pittsburgh	8	0	1	1	4	0	0	0
1990	Toronto	3	1	0	1	4	0	0	1
1992	Buffalo	7	2	0	2	2	2	0	0
1993	Buffalo	8	1	1	2	18	0	0	0
1994	Buffalo	7	1	0	1	6	0	0	1
1995	Buffalo	5	0	2	2	2	0	0	0
1996♦	Colorado	13	0	2	2	2	0	0	0
Playoff Totals		**63**	**6**	**7**	**13**	**46**	**2**	**0**	**3**
•HANNAN, Scott									Defense
2000	San Jose	1	0	1	1	0	0	0	0
2001	San Jose	6	0	1	1	6	0	0	0
2002	San Jose	12	0	2	2	12	0	0	0
Playoff Totals		**19**	**0**	**4**	**4**	**18**	**0**	**0**	**0**

Season	Team	GP	G	A	Pts	PIM	PP	SH	GW
HANNIGAN, Gord									Center
1954	Toronto	5	2	0	2	4	1	0	1
1956	Toronto	4	0	0	0	4	0	0	0
Playoff Totals		**9**	**2**	**0**	**2**	**8**	**1**	**0**	**1**
HANNIGAN, Pat									Left wing
1962	NY Rangers	4	0	0	0	2	0	0	0
1968	Philadelphia	7	1	2	3	9	0	0	0
Playoff Totals		**11**	**1**	**2**	**3**	**11**	**0**	**0**	**0**
HANNIGAN, Ray	*No Playoffs*								Right wing
HANSEN, Richie	*No Playoffs*								Center
•HANSEN, Tavis									Center
1999	Phoenix	2	0	0	0	0	0	0	0
Playoff Totals		**2**	**0**	**0**	**0**	**0**	**0**	**0**	**0**
HANSON, Dave	*No Playoffs*								Defense
HANSON, Emil	*No Playoffs*								Right wing/Defense
HANSON, Keith	*No Playoffs*								Defense
HANSON, Oscar	*No Playoffs*								Center
HARBARUK, Nick									Right wing
1970	Pittsburgh	10	3	0	3	20	0	1	0
1972	Pittsburgh	4	0	1	1	0	0	0	0
Playoff Totals		**14**	**3**	**1**	**4**	**20**	**0**	**1**	**0**
HARDING, Jeff	*No Playoffs*								Right wing
HARDY, Joe									Center
1970	Oakland	4	0	0	0	0	0	0	0
Playoff Totals		**4**	**0**	**0**	**0**	**0**	**0**	**0**	**0**
HARDY, Mark									Defense
1980	Los Angeles	4	1	1	2	9	0	0	0
1981	Los Angeles	4	1	2	3	4	1	0	0
1982	Los Angeles	10	1	2	3	9	0	0	0
1985	Los Angeles	3	0	1	1	2	0	0	0
1987	Los Angeles	5	1	2	3	10	0	0	0
1989	NY Rangers	4	0	1	1	31	0	0	0
1990	NY Rangers	3	0	1	1	2	0	0	0
1991	NY Rangers	6	0	1	1	30	0	0	0
1992	NY Rangers	13	0	3	3	31	0	0	0
1993	Los Angeles	15	1	2	3	30	0	0	0
Playoff Totals		**67**	**5**	**16**	**21**	**158**	**1**	**0**	**0**
HARGREAVES, Jim	*No Playoffs*								Defense
•HARKINS, Brett	*No Playoffs*								Left wing
HARKINS, Todd	*No Playoffs*								Center
•HARLOCK, David	*No Playoffs*								Defense
HARLOW, Scott	*No Playoffs*								Left wing
HARMON, Glen									Defense
1943	Montreal	5	0	1	1	2	....	....	....
1944♦	Montreal	9	1	2	3	4	....	....	....
1945	Montreal	6	1	0	1	2	....	....	....
1946♦	Montreal	9	1	4	5	0	....	....	....
1947	Montreal	11	1	1	2	4	....	....	....
1949	Montreal	7	1	1	2	4	....	....	....
1950	Montreal	5	0	1	1	21	....	....	....
1951	Montreal	1	0	0	0	0	....	....	....
Playoff Totals		**53**	**5**	**10**	**15**	**37**	....	....	....
HARMS, John									Right wing
1944	Chicago	4	3	0	3	2	....	....	....
Playoff Totals		**4**	**3**	**0**	**3**	**2**	....	....	....
HARNOTT, Walter	*No Playoffs*								Left wing
HARPER, Terry									Defense
1963	Montreal	5	1	0	1	8	0	0	0
1964	Montreal	7	0	0	0	6	0	0	0
1965♦	Montreal	13	0	0	0	19	0	0	0
1966♦	Montreal	10	2	3	5	18	0	0	1
1967	Montreal	10	0	1	1	15	0	0	0
1968♦	Montreal	13	0	1	1	8	0	0	0
1969♦	Montreal	11	0	0	0	8	0	0	0
1971♦	Montreal	20	0	6	6	28	0	0	0
1972	Montreal	5	1	1	2	6	0	0	0
1974	Los Angeles	5	0	0	0	16	0	0	0
1975	Los Angeles	3	0	0	0	2	0	0	0
1978	Detroit	7	0	1	1	4	0	0	0
1980	St. Louis	3	0	0	0	2	0	0	0
Playoff Totals		**112**	**4**	**13**	**17**	**140**	**0**	**0**	**1**
HARRER, Tim	*No Playoffs*								Right wing
HARRINGTON, Hago									Left wing
1928	Boston	2	0	0	0	0	....	....	....
1933	Montreal	2	1	0	1	2	....	....	....
Playoff Totals		**4**	**1**	**0**	**1**	**2**	....	....	....
HARRIS, Billy									Right wing
1975	NY Islanders	17	3	7	10	12	2	0	1
1976	NY Islanders	13	5	2	7	10	1	0	0
1977	NY Islanders	12	7	7	14	8	2	0	1
1978	NY Islanders	7	0	0	0	4	0	0	0
1979	NY Islanders	10	2	1	3	10	1	0	1
1980	Los Angeles	4	0	0	0	2	0	0	0
1981	Los Angeles	4	2	1	3	0	0	0	0
1983	Toronto	4	0	1	1	2	0	0	0
Playoff Totals		**71**	**19**	**19**	**38**	**48**	**6**	**0**	**3**

Season	Team	GP	G	A	Pts	PIM	PP	SH	GW
HARRIS, Billy									Center
1956	Toronto	5	1	0	1	4	....	....	....
1959	Toronto	12	3	4	7	16	....	....	....
1960	Toronto	9	0	3	3	4	....	....	....
1961	Toronto	5	1	0	1	0	....	....	....
1962♦	Toronto	12	2	1	3	2	....	....	....
1963♦	Toronto	10	0	1	1	0	....	....	....
1964♦	Toronto	9	1	1	2	4	....	....	....
Playoff Totals		**62**	**8**	**10**	**18**	**30**	....	....	....
HARRIS, Duke	*No Playoffs*								Right wing
HARRIS, Henry	*No Playoffs*								Right wing
HARRIS, Hugh									Center
1973	Buffalo	3	0	0	0	0	0	0	0
Playoff Totals		**3**	**0**	**0**	**0**	**0**	**0**	**0**	**0**
HARRIS, Ron									Defense
1970	Detroit	4	0	0	0	8	0	0	0
1973	NY Rangers	10	0	3	3	2	0	0	0
1974	NY Rangers	11	3	0	3	14	0	0	2
1975	NY Rangers	3	1	0	1	9	0	0	1
Playoff Totals		**28**	**4**	**3**	**7**	**33**	**0**	**0**	**3**
HARRIS, Smokey	*No Playoffs*								Left wing
HARRIS, Ted									Defense
1965♦	Montreal	13	0	5	5	45	0	0	0
1966♦	Montreal	10	0	0	0	38	0	0	0
1967	Montreal	10	0	1	1	19	0	0	0
1968♦	Montreal	13	0	4	4	22	0	0	0
1969♦	Montreal	14	1	2	3	34	0	0	0
1971	Minnesota	12	0	4	4	36	0	0	0
1972	Minnesota	7	0	1	1	17	0	0	0
1973	Minnesota	5	0	1	1	15	0	0	0
1975♦	Philadelphia	16	0	4	4	4	0	0	0
Playoff Totals		**100**	**1**	**22**	**23**	**230**	**0**	**0**	**0**
HARRISON, Ed									Center/Left wing
1948	Boston	5	1	0	1	2	....	....	....
1949	Boston	4	0	0	0	0	....	....	....
Playoff Totals		**9**	**1**	**0**	**1**	**2**	....	....	....
HARRISON, Jim									Center
1971	Toronto	6	0	1	1	33	0	0	0
1972	Toronto	5	1	0	1	10	0	0	1
1977	Chicago	2	0	0	0	0	0	0	0
Playoff Totals		**13**	**1**	**1**	**2**	**43**	**0**	**0**	**1**
HART, Gerry									Defense
1975	NY Islanders	17	2	2	4	42	0	0	1
1976	NY Islanders	13	1	3	4	24	0	0	0
1977	NY Islanders	12	0	2	2	23	0	0	0
1978	NY Islanders	7	0	0	0	16	0	0	0
1979	NY Islanders	9	0	2	2	10	0	0	0
1981	St. Louis	10	0	0	0	27	0	0	0
1982	St. Louis	10	0	3	3	33	0	0	0
Playoff Totals		**78**	**3**	**12**	**15**	**175**	**0**	**0**	**1**
HART, Gizzy									Left wing
1927	Montreal	4	0	0	0	0	0	0	0
1928	Montreal	2	0	0	0	0	0	0	0
1933	Montreal	2	0	1	1	0	0	0	0
Playoff Totals		**8**	**0**	**1**	**1**	**0**	**0**	**0**	**0**
•HARTIGAN, Mark	*No Playoffs*								Right wing
HARTMAN, Mike									Left wing
1988	Buffalo	6	0	0	0	35	0	0	0
1989	Buffalo	5	0	0	0	34	0	0	0
1990	Buffalo	6	0	0	0	18	0	0	0
1991	Buffalo	2	0	0	0	17	0	0	0
1992	Winnipeg	2	0	0	0	2	0	0	0
1994♦	NY Rangers	....	....	....	....	....	....	....	....
Playoff Totals		**21**	**0**	**0**	**0**	**106**	**0**	**0**	**0**
•HARTNELL, Scott	*No Playoffs*								Left wing
HARTSBURG, Craig									Defense
1980	Minnesota	15	3	1	4	17	2	0	0
1981	Minnesota	19	3	12	15	16	3	0	0
1982	Minnesota	4	1	2	3	14	0	0	0
1983	Minnesota	9	3	8	11	7	2	0	0
1985	Minnesota	9	5	3	8	14	3	0	0
1986	Minnesota	5	0	1	1	2	0	0	0
Playoff Totals		**61**	**15**	**27**	**42**	**70**	**10**	**0**	**0**
HARVEY, Buster									Right wing
1971	Minnesota	7	0	0	0	4	0	0	0
1972	Minnesota	1	0	0	0	0	0	0	0
1973	Minnesota	6	0	2	2	4	0	0	0
Playoff Totals		**14**	**0**	**2**	**2**	**8**	**0**	**0**	**0**

Season	Team	GP	G	A	Pts	PIM	PP	SH	GW
HARVEY, Doug									Defense
1949	Montreal	7	0	1	1	10	....	....	....
1950	Montreal	5	0	2	2	10	....	....	....
1951	Montreal	11	0	5	5	12	....	....	....
1952	Montreal	11	0	3	3	8	....	....	....
1953♦	Montreal	12	0	5	5	8	....	....	....
1954	Montreal	10	0	2	2	12	....	....	....
1955	Montreal	12	0	8	8	6	....	....	....
1956♦	Montreal	10	2	5	7	10	....	....	....
1957♦	Montreal	10	0	7	7	10	....	....	....
1958♦	Montreal	10	2	9	11	16	....	....	....
1959♦	Montreal	11	1	11	12	22	....	....	....
1960♦	Montreal	8	3	0	3	6	....	....	....
1961	Montreal	6	0	1	1	8	....	....	....
1962	NY Rangers	6	0	1	1	2	....	....	....
1968	St. Louis	8	0	4	4	12	....	....	....
Playoff Totals		**137**	**8**	**64**	**72**	**152**	....	....	....
HARVEY, Hugh	*No Playoffs*								Center/Left wing
•HARVEY, Todd									Center
1995	Dallas	5	0	0	0	8	0	0	0
1997	Dallas	7	0	1	1	10	0	0	0
2000	San Jose	12	1	0	1	8	1	0	0
2001	San Jose	6	0	0	0	8	0	0	0
2002	San Jose	12	0	2	2	12	0	0	0
Playoff Totals		**42**	**1**	**3**	**4**	**46**	**1**	**0**	**0**
HASSARD, Bob	*No Playoffs*								Center
•HATCHER, Derian									Defense
1992	Minnesota	5	0	2	2	8	0	0	0
1994	Dallas	9	0	2	2	14	0	0	0
1997	Dallas	7	0	2	2	20	0	0	0
1998	Dallas	17	3	3	6	39	2	0	0
1999♦	Dallas	18	1	6	7	24	0	0	0
2000	Dallas	23	1	3	4	29	0	0	0
2001	Dallas	10	0	1	1	16	0	0	0
Playoff Totals		**89**	**5**	**19**	**24**	**150**	**2**	**0**	**0**
HATCHER, Kevin									Defense
1985	Washington	1	0	0	0	0	0	0	0
1986	Washington	9	1	1	2	19	0	0	0
1987	Washington	7	1	0	1	20	0	0	0
1988	Washington	14	5	7	12	55	1	0	1
1989	Washington	6	1	4	5	20	1	0	0
1990	Washington	11	0	8	8	32	0	0	0
1991	Washington	11	3	3	6	8	2	0	0
1992	Washington	7	2	4	6	19	0	1	0
1993	Washington	6	0	1	1	14	0	0	0
1994	Washington	11	3	4	7	37	0	1	0
1995	Dallas	5	2	1	3	2	1	0	1
1997	Pittsburgh	5	1	1	2	4	1	0	0
1998	Pittsburgh	6	1	0	1	12	1	0	0
1999	Pittsburgh	13	2	3	5	4	1	0	0
2001	Carolina	6	0	0	0	6	0	0	0
Playoff Totals		**118**	**22**	**37**	**59**	**252**	**8**	**2**	**2**
HATOUM, Ed	*No Playoffs*								Right wing
•HAUER, Brett	*No Playoffs*								Defense
•HAVELID, Niclas	*No Playoffs*								Defense
•HAVLAT, Martin									Center
2001	Ottawa	4	0	0	0	2	0	0	0
2002	Ottawa	12	2	5	7	14	2	0	2
Playoff Totals		**16**	**2**	**5**	**7**	**16**	**2**	**0**	**2**
HAWERCHUK, Dale									Center
1982	Winnipeg	4	1	7	8	5	0	0	0
1983	Winnipeg	3	1	4	5	8	1	0	0
1984	Winnipeg	3	1	1	2	0	1	0	0
1985	Winnipeg	3	2	1	3	4	1	0	0
1986	Winnipeg	3	0	3	3	0	0	0	0
1987	Winnipeg	10	5	8	13	4	3	0	0
1988	Winnipeg	5	3	4	7	16	2	0	0
1990	Winnipeg	7	3	5	8	2	0	0	1
1991	Buffalo	6	2	4	6	10	1	0	0
1992	Buffalo	7	2	5	7	0	0	0	0
1993	Buffalo	8	5	9	14	2	3	0	0
1994	Buffalo	7	0	7	7	4	0	0	0
1995	Buffalo	2	0	0	0	0	0	0	0
1996	Philadelphia	12	3	6	9	12	1	0	0
1997	Philadelphia	17	2	5	7	0	1	0	1
Playoff Totals		**97**	**30**	**69**	**99**	**67**	**14**	**0**	**2**
•HAWGOOD, Greg									Defense
1988	Boston	3	1	0	1	0	0	0	0
1989	Boston	10	0	2	2	2	0	0	0
1990	Boston	15	1	3	4	12	1	0	0
1992	Edmonton	13	0	3	3	23	0	0	0
1994	Pittsburgh	1	0	0	0	0	0	0	0
Playoff Totals		**42**	**2**	**8**	**10**	**37**	**1**	**0**	**0**
HAWKINS, Todd	*No Playoffs*								Wing

Season	Team	GP	G	A	Pts	PIM	PP	SH	GW
HAWORTH, Alan									Center
1981	Buffalo	7	4	4	8	2	3	0	1
1982	Buffalo	3	0	1	1	2	0	0	0
1983	Washington	4	0	0	0	2	0	0	0
1984	Washington	8	3	2	5	4	1	0	0
1985	Washington	5	1	0	1	0	0	0	1
1986	Washington	9	4	6	10	11	1	0	0
1987	Washington	6	0	3	3	7	0	0	0
Playoff Totals		**42**	**12**	**16**	**28**	**28**	**5**	**0**	**2**
HAWORTH, Gord	*No Playoffs*								Center
HAWRYLIW, Neil	*No Playoffs*								Right wing
HAY, Bill									Center
1960	Chicago	4	1	2	3	2	....	....	....
1961♦	Chicago	12	2	5	7	20	....	....	....
1962	Chicago	12	3	7	10	18	....	....	....
1963	Chicago	6	3	2	5	6	....	....	....
1964	Chicago	7	3	1	4	4	....	....	....
1965	Chicago	14	3	1	4	4	....	....	....
1966	Chicago	6	0	2	2	4	....	....	....
1967	Chicago	6	0	1	1	4	....	....	....
Playoff Totals		**67**	**15**	**21**	**36**	**62**	....	....	....
•HAY, Dwayne	*No Playoffs*								Left wing
HAY, George									Left wing
1927	Chicago	2	1	2	3	2	....	....	....
1929	Detroit	2	1	0	1	0	....	....	....
1933	Detroit	4	0	1	1	0	....	....	....
Playoff Totals		**8**	**2**	**3**	**5**	**2**	....	....	....
HAY, Jim									Defense
1953	Detroit	4	0	0	0	2	0	0	0
1955♦	Detroit	5	1	0	1	0	0	0	0
Playoff Totals		**9**	**1**	**0**	**1**	**2**	**0**	**0**	**0**
•HAYDAR, Darren	*No Playoffs*								Right wing
HAYEK, Peter	*No Playoffs*								Defense
HAYES, Chris									Left wing
1972♦	Boston	1	0	0	0	0	0	0	0
Playoff Totals		**1**	**0**	**0**	**0**	**0**	**0**	**0**	**0**
HAYNES, Paul									Center
1932	Mtl. Maroons	4	0	0	0	0	....	....	....
1933	Mtl. Maroons	2	0	0	0	2	....	....	....
1934	Mtl. Maroons	4	0	1	1	2	....	....	....
1935	Boston	3	0	0	0	0	....	....	....
1937	Montreal	5	2	3	5	0	....	....	....
1938	Montreal	3	0	4	4	5	....	....	....
1939	Montreal	3	0	0	0	4	....	....	....
Playoff Totals		**24**	**2**	**8**	**10**	**13**	....	....	....
HAYWARD, Rick	*No Playoffs*								Defense
HAZLETT, Steve	*No Playoffs*								Left wing
HEAD, Galen	*No Playoffs*								Right wing
HEADLEY, Fern									Defense
1925	Montreal	1	0	0	0	0	0	0	0
Playoff Totals		**1**	**0**	**0**	**0**	**0**	**0**	**0**	**0**
•HEALEY, Paul									Right wing
2002	Toronto	18	0	1	1	2	0	0	0
Playoff Totals		**18**	**0**	**1**	**1**	**2**	**0**	**0**	**0**
HEALEY, Rich	*No Playoffs*								Defense
HEAPHY, Shawn	*No Playoffs*								Center
HEASLIP, Mark									Right wing
1978	NY Rangers	3	0	0	0	0	0	0	0
1979	Los Angeles	2	0	0	0	2	0	0	0
Playoff Totals		**5**	**0**	**0**	**0**	**2**	**0**	**0**	**0**
HEATH, Randy	*No Playoffs*								Left wing
•HEATLEY, Dany	*No Playoffs*								Right wing
HEBENTON, Andy									Right wing
1956	NY Rangers	5	1	0	1	2	....	....	....
1957	NY Rangers	5	2	0	2	2	....	....	....
1958	NY Rangers	6	2	3	5	4	....	....	....
1962	NY Rangers	6	1	2	3	0	....	....	....
Playoff Totals		**22**	**6**	**5**	**11**	**8**	....	....	....
•HECHT, Jochen									Center
1999	St. Louis	5	2	0	2	0	0	0	0
2000	St. Louis	7	4	6	10	2	1	0	1
2001	St. Louis	15	2	4	6	4	0	0	0
Playoff Totals		**27**	**8**	**10**	**18**	**6**	**1**	**0**	**1**
•HECL, Radoslav	*No Playoffs*								Defense
HEDBERG, Anders									Right wing
1979	NY Rangers	18	4	5	9	12	0	1	1
1980	NY Rangers	9	3	2	5	7	0	0	1
1981	NY Rangers	14	8	8	16	6	3	0	0
1983	NY Rangers	9	4	8	12	4	1	0	0
1984	NY Rangers	5	1	0	1	0	0	0	0
1985	NY Rangers	3	2	1	3	2	0	0	0
Playoff Totals		**58**	**22**	**24**	**46**	**31**	**4**	**1**	**2**

Season	Team	GP	G	A	Pts	PIM	PP	SH	GW
•HEDICAN, Bret									Defense
1992	St. Louis	5	0	0	0	0	0	0	0
1993	St. Louis	10	0	0	0	14	0	0	0
1994	Vancouver	24	1	6	7	16	0	0	0
1995	Vancouver	11	0	2	2	6	0	0	0
1996	Vancouver	6	0	1	1	10	0	0	0
2000	Florida	4	0	0	0	0	0	0	0
2002	Carolina	23	1	4	5	20	0	0	0
Playoff Totals		**83**	**2**	**13**	**15**	**66**	**0**	**0**	**0**
•HEDSTROM, Jonathan	*No Playoffs*								Right wing
•HEEREMA, Jeff	*No Playoffs*								Right wing
HEFFERNAN, Frank	*No Playoffs*								Defense
HEFFERNAN, Gerry									Right wing
1942	Montreal	2	2	1	3	0	....	....	....
1943	Montreal	2	0	0	0	0	....	....	....
1944♦	Montreal	7	1	2	3	8	....	....	....
Playoff Totals		**11**	**3**	**3**	**6**	**8**	....	....	....
HEIDT, Mike	*No Playoffs*								Defense
HEINDL, Bill	*No Playoffs*								Left wing
HEINRICH, Lionel	*No Playoffs*								Left wing
•HEINS, Shawn									Defense
2001	San Jose	2	0	0	0	0	0	0	0
Playoff Totals		**2**	**0**	**0**	**0**	**0**	**0**	**0**	**0**
•HEINZE, Steve									Right wing
1992	Boston	7	0	3	3	17	0	0	0
1993	Boston	4	1	1	2	2	0	0	0
1994	Boston	13	2	3	5	7	0	0	0
1995	Boston	5	0	0	0	0	0	0	0
1996	Boston	5	1	1	2	4	0	1	0
1998	Boston	6	0	0	0	6	0	0	0
1999	Boston	12	4	3	7	0	2	0	0
2001	Buffalo	13	3	4	7	10	3	0	0
2002	Los Angeles	4	0	0	0	2	0	0	0
Playoff Totals		**69**	**11**	**15**	**26**	**48**	**5**	**1**	**0**
HEISKALA, Earl	*No Playoffs*								Left wing
•HEISTEN, Barrett	*No Playoffs*								Left wing
•HEJDUK, Milan									Right wing
1999	Colorado	16	6	6	12	4	1	0	3
2000	Colorado	17	5	4	9	6	3	0	1
2001♦	Colorado	23	7	*16	23	6	4	0	1
2002	Colorado	16	3	3	6	4	1	0	0
Playoff Totals		**72**	**21**	**29**	**50**	**20**	**9**	**0**	**5**
HELANDER, Peter	*No Playoffs*								Defense
•HELENIUS, Sami									Defense
2001	Dallas	1	0	0	0	0	0	0	0
Playoff Totals		**1**	**0**	**0**	**0**	**0**	**0**	**0**	**0**
HELLER, Ott									Defense
1932	NY Rangers	7	3	1	4	8	....	....	....
1933♦	NY Rangers	8	3	0	3	10	....	....	....
1934	NY Rangers	2	0	0	0	0	....	....	....
1935	NY Rangers	4	0	1	1	4	....	....	....
1937	NY Rangers	9	0	0	0	11	....	....	....
1938	NY Rangers	3	0	1	1	2	....	....	....
1939	NY Rangers	7	0	1	1	10	....	....	....
1940♦	NY Rangers	12	0	3	3	12	....	....	....
1941	NY Rangers	3	0	1	1	4	....	....	....
1942	NY Rangers	6	0	0	0	0	....	....	....
Playoff Totals		**61**	**6**	**8**	**14**	**61**	....	....	....
HELMAN, Harry									Right wing
1923♦	Ottawa	2	0	0	0	0	0	0	0
Playoff Totals		**2**	**0**	**0**	**0**	**0**	**0**	**0**	**0**
•HELMER, Bryan									Defense
2002	Vancouver	6	0	0	0	0	0	0	0
Playoff Totals		**6**	**0**	**0**	**0**	**0**	**0**	**0**	**0**
HELMINEN, Raimo									Center
1986	NY Rangers	2	0	0	0	0	0	0	0
Playoff Totals		**2**	**0**	**0**	**0**	**0**	**0**	**0**	**0**
HEMMERLING, Tony	*No Playoffs*								Left wing
•HEMSKY, Ales	*No Playoffs*								Right wing
HENDERSON, Archie	*No Playoffs*								Right wing
•HENDERSON, Jay	*No Playoffs*								Left wing
•HENDERSON, Matt	*No Playoffs*								Right wing
HENDERSON, Murray									Defense
1945	Boston	7	0	1	1	2	....	....	....
1946	Boston	10	1	1	2	4	....	....	....
1947	Boston	4	0	0	0	4	....	....	....
1948	Boston	3	1	0	1	5	....	....	....
1949	Boston	5	0	1	1	2	....	....	....
1951	Boston	5	0	0	0	2	....	....	....
1952	Boston	7	0	0	0	4	....	....	....
Playoff Totals		**41**	**2**	**3**	**5**	**23**	....	....	....
HENDERSON, Paul									Right wing
1964	Detroit	14	2	3	5	6	0	0	0
1965	Detroit	7	0	2	2	0	0	0	0
1966	Detroit	12	3	3	6	10	1	0	2
1969	Toronto	4	0	1	1	0	0	0	0
1971	Toronto	6	5	1	6	4	1	0	2
1972	Toronto	5	1	2	3	6	0	0	0
1974	Toronto	4	0	2	2	2	0	0	0
1980	Atlanta	4	0	0	0	0	0	0	0
Playoff Totals		**56**	**11**	**14**	**25**	**28**	**2**	**0**	**4**
•HENDRICKSON, Darby									Center
1994	Toronto	2	0	0	0	0	0	0	0
Playoff Totals		**2**	**0**	**0**	**0**	**0**	**0**	**0**	**0**
HENDRICKSON, John	*No Playoffs*								Defense
HENNING, Lorne									Center
1975	NY Islanders	17	0	2	2	0	0	0	0
1976	NY Islanders	13	2	0	2	2	1	1	0
1977	NY Islanders	12	0	1	1	0	0	0	0
1978	NY Islanders	7	0	0	0	4	0	0	0
1979	NY Islanders	10	2	0	2	0	0	1	0
1980♦	NY Islanders	21	3	4	7	2	0	3	1
1981♦	NY Islanders	1	0	0	0	0	0	0	0
Playoff Totals		**81**	**7**	**7**	**14**	**8**	**1**	**5**	**1**
•HENRY, Alex	*No Playoffs*								Defense
•HENRY, Burke	*No Playoffs*								Defense
HENRY, Camille									Center
1957	NY Rangers	5	2	3	5	0	1	0	0
1958	NY Rangers	6	1	4	5	5	1	0	0
1962	NY Rangers	5	0	0	0	0	0	0	0
1965	Chicago	14	1	0	1	2	1	0	0
1968	NY Rangers	6	0	0	0	0	0	0	0
1969	St. Louis	11	2	5	7	0	1	0	0
Playoff Totals		**47**	**6**	**12**	**18**	**7**	**4**	**0**	**0**
HENRY, Dale									Left wing
1987	NY Islanders	8	0	0	0	2	0	0	0
1988	NY Islanders	6	1	0	1	17	0	1	0
Playoff Totals		**14**	**1**	**0**	**1**	**19**	**0**	**1**	**0**
•HENTUNEN, Jukka	*No Playoffs*								Right wing
HEPPLE, Alan	*No Playoffs*								Defense
HERBERS, Ian	*No Playoffs*								Defense
HERBERT, Jimmy									Center/Right wing
1927	Boston	8	3	0	3	8	....	....	....
1929	Detroit	1	0	0	0	2	....	....	....
Playoff Totals		**9**	**3**	**0**	**3**	**10**	....	....	....
HERCHENRATTER, Art	*No Playoffs*								Left wing
HERGERTS, Fred	*No Playoffs*								Center
HERGESHEIMER, Phil									Right wing
1940	Chicago	1	0	0	0	0	0	0	0
1941	Chicago	5	0	0	0	2	0	0	0
Playoff Totals		**6**	**0**	**0**	**0**	**2**	**0**	**0**	**0**
HERGESHEIMER, Wally									Right wing
1956	NY Rangers	5	1	0	1	0	0	0	0
Playoff Totals		**5**	**1**	**0**	**1**	**0**	**0**	**0**	**0**
HERON, Red									Center
1939	Toronto	2	0	0	0	4	....	....	....
1940	Toronto	9	2	0	2	2	....	....	....
1941	Toronto	7	0	2	2	0	....	....	....
1942	Montreal	3	0	0	0	0	....	....	....
Playoff Totals		**21**	**2**	**2**	**4**	**6**	....	....	....
HEROUX, Yves	*No Playoffs*								Right wing
•HERPERGER, Chris	*No Playoffs*								Left wing
•HERR, Matt	*No Playoffs*								Center
HERTER, Jason	*No Playoffs*								Defense
HERVEY, Matt									Defense
1992	Boston	5	0	0	0	6	0	0	0
Playoff Totals		**5**	**0**	**0**	**0**	**6**	**0**	**0**	**0**
HESS, Bob									Defense
1975	St. Louis	1	0	0	0	2	0	0	0
1976	St. Louis	1	0	1	1	0	0	0	0
1977	St. Louis	1	0	0	0	0	0	0	0
1981	Buffalo	1	1	0	1	0	0	0	0
Playoff Totals		**4**	**1**	**1**	**2**	**2**	**0**	**0**	**0**
•HEWARD, Jamie	*No Playoffs*								Defense
HEXIMER, Obs									Left wing/Center
1933	Boston	5	0	0	0	2	0	0	0
Playoff Totals		**5**	**0**	**0**	**0**	**2**	**0**	**0**	**0**
HEXTALL, Bryan									Right wing
1938	NY Rangers	3	2	0	2	0	....	....	....
1939	NY Rangers	7	0	1	1	4	....	....	....
1940♦	NY Rangers	12	4	3	7	11	....	....	....
1941	NY Rangers	3	0	1	1	0	....	....	....
1942	NY Rangers	6	1	1	2	4	....	....	....
1948	NY Rangers	6	1	3	4	0	....	....	....
Playoff Totals		**37**	**8**	**9**	**17**	**19**	....	....	....
HEXTALL, Bryan Jr.									Center
1970	Pittsburgh	10	0	1	1	34	0	0	0
1972	Pittsburgh	4	0	2	2	9	0	0	0
1974	Atlanta	4	0	1	1	16	0	0	0
Playoff Totals		**18**	**0**	**4**	**4**	**59**	**0**	**0**	**0**
HEXTALL, Dennis									Left wing
1968	NY Rangers	2	0	0	0	0	0	0	0
1972	Minnesota	7	0	2	2	19	0	0	0
1973	Minnesota	6	2	0	2	16	0	0	2
1978	Detroit	7	1	1	2	10	0	1	1
Playoff Totals		**22**	**3**	**3**	**6**	**45**	**0**	**1**	**3**
HEYLIGER, Vic	*No Playoffs*								Center
HICKE, Bill									Right wing
1959♦	Montreal	1	0	0	0	0	0	0	0
1960♦	Montreal	7	1	2	3	0	0	0	1
1961	Montreal	5	2	0	2	19	0	0	1
1962	Montreal	6	0	2	2	14	0	0	0
1963	Montreal	5	0	0	0	0	0	0	0
1964	Montreal	7	0	2	2	2	0	0	0
1969	Oakland	7	0	3	3	4	0	0	0
1970	Oakland	4	0	1	1	2	0	0	0
Playoff Totals		**42**	**3**	**10**	**13**	**41**	**0**	**0**	**2**
HICKE, Ernie									Left wing
1977	Minnesota	2	1	0	1	0	0	0	0
Playoff Totals		**2**	**1**	**0**	**1**	**0**	**0**	**0**	**0**
HICKEY, Greg	*No Playoffs*								Left wing
HICKEY, Pat									Left wing
1978	NY Rangers	3	2	0	2	0	1	0	0
1979	NY Rangers	18	1	7	8	6	0	0	0
1980	Toronto	3	0	0	0	2	0	0	0
1981	Toronto	2	0	0	0	0	0	0	0
1982	Quebec	15	1	3	4	21	1	0	0
1984	St. Louis	11	1	1	2	6	0	1	0
1985	St. Louis	3	0	0	0	2	0	0	0
Playoff Totals		**55**	**5**	**11**	**16**	**37**	**2**	**1**	**0**
HICKS, Alex									Left wing
1997	Pittsburgh	5	0	1	1	2	0	0	0
1998	Pittsburgh	6	0	0	0	2	0	0	0
2000	Florida	4	0	1	1	4	0	0	0
Playoff Totals		**15**	**0**	**2**	**2**	**8**	**0**	**0**	**0**
HICKS, Doug									Defense
1977	Minnesota	2	0	0	0	7	0	0	0
1978	Chicago	4	1	0	1	2	1	0	0
1980	Edmonton	3	0	0	0	2	0	0	0
1981	Edmonton	9	1	1	2	4	0	0	0
Playoff Totals		**18**	**2**	**1**	**3**	**15**	**1**	**0**	**0**
HICKS, Glenn	*No Playoffs*								Left wing
HICKS, Henry	*No Playoffs*								Defense
HICKS, Wayne									Right wing
1960	Chicago	1	0	1	1	0	0	0	0
1961♦	Chicago	1	0	0	0	2	0	0	0
Playoff Totals		**2**	**0**	**1**	**1**	**2**	**0**	**0**	**0**
HIDI, Andre									Left wing
1984	Washington	2	0	0	0	0	0	0	0
Playoff Totals		**2**	**0**	**0**	**0**	**0**	**0**	**0**	**0**
HIEMER, Uli	*No Playoffs*								Defense
•HIGGINS, Matt	*No Playoffs*								Center
HIGGINS, Paul									Right wing
1983	Toronto	1	0	0	0	0	0	0	0
Playoff Totals		**1**	**0**	**0**	**0**	**0**	**0**	**0**	**0**
HIGGINS, Tim									Right wing
1979	Chicago	4	0	0	0	0	0	0	0
1980	Chicago	7	0	3	3	10	0	0	0
1981	Chicago	3	0	0	0	0	0	0	0
1982	Chicago	12	3	1	4	15	0	0	0
1983	Chicago	13	1	3	4	10	0	0	0
1987	Detroit	12	0	1	1	16	0	0	0
1988	Detroit	13	1	0	1	26	0	0	1
1989	Detroit	1	0	0	0	0	0	0	0
Playoff Totals		**65**	**5**	**8**	**13**	**77**	**0**	**0**	**1**
•HILBERT, Andy	*No Playoffs*								Center
HILDEBRAND, Ike	*No Playoffs*								Right wing
HILL, Al									Center
1979	Philadelphia	7	1	0	1	2	0	0	0
1980	Philadelphia	19	3	5	8	19	1	0	0
1981	Philadelphia	12	2	4	6	18	0	0	1
1982	Philadelphia	3	0	0	0	0	0	0	0
1987	Philadelphia	9	2	1	3	0	0	0	0
1988	Philadelphia	1	0	1	1	4	0	0	0
Playoff Totals		**51**	**8**	**11**	**19**	**43**	**1**	**0**	**1**
HILL, Brian	*No Playoffs*								Right wing

Season	Team	GP	G	A	Pts	PIM	PP	SH	GW
HILL, Mel	Right wing								
1938	Boston	1	0	0	0	0	....	....	....
1939♦	Boston	12	6	3	9	12	....	....	....
1940	Boston	3	0	0	0	0	....	....	....
1941♦	Boston	8	1	1	2	0	....	....	....
1943	Toronto	6	3	0	3	0	....	....	....
1945♦	Toronto	13	2	3	5	6	....	....	....
Playoff Totals		**43**	**12**	**7**	**19**	**18**	....	....	....
•HILL, Sean	Defense								
1991	Montreal	1	0	0	0	0	0	0	0
1992	Montreal	4	1	0	1	2	0	0	0
1993♦	Montreal	3	0	0	0	4	0	0	0
2001	St. Louis	15	0	1	1	12	0	0	0
2002	Carolina	23	4	4	8	20	4	0	1
Playoff Totals		**46**	**5**	**5**	**10**	**38**	**4**	**0**	**1**
HILLER, Dutch	Left wing								
1938	NY Rangers	1	0	0	0	0	....	....	....
1939	NY Rangers	7	1	0	1	9	....	....	....
1940♦	NY Rangers	12	2	4	6	2	....	....	....
1941	NY Rangers	3	0	0	0	0	....	....	....
1942	Boston	5	0	1	1	0	....	....	....
1943	Montreal	5	1	0	1	4	....	....	....
1945	Montreal	6	1	1	2	4	....	....	....
1946♦	Montreal	9	4	2	6	2	....	....	....
Playoff Totals		**48**	**9**	**8**	**17**	**21**	....	....	....
HILLER, Jim	Right wing								
1993	Detroit	2	0	0	0	4	0	0	0
Playoff Totals		**2**	**0**	**0**	**0**	**4**	**0**	**0**	**0**
HILLIER, Randy	Defense								
1982	Boston	8	0	1	1	16	0	0	0
1983	Boston	3	0	0	0	4	0	0	0
1989	Pittsburgh	9	0	1	1	49	0	0	0
1991♦	Pittsburgh	8	0	0	0	24	0	0	0
Playoff Totals		**28**	**0**	**2**	**2**	**93**	**0**	**0**	**0**
HILLMAN, Floyd *No Playoffs*	Defense								
HILLMAN, Larry	Defense								
1955♦	Detroit	3	0	0	0	0	0	0	0
1956	Detroit	10	0	1	1	6	0	0	0
1958	Boston	11	0	2	2	6	0	0	0
1959	Boston	7	0	1	1	0	0	0	0
1961	Toronto	5	0	0	0	0	0	0	0
1962♦	Toronto	....	....	....	....	....	....	....	....
1963♦	Toronto	....	....	....	....	....	....	....	....
1964♦	Toronto	11	0	0	0	2	0	0	0
1966	Toronto	4	1	1	2	6	0	0	0
1967♦	Toronto	12	1	2	3	0	0	0	0
1969♦	Montreal	1	0	0	0	0	0	0	0
1971	Philadelphia	4	0	2	2	2	0	0	0
1973	Buffalo	6	0	0	0	8	0	0	0
Playoff Totals		**74**	**2**	**9**	**11**	**30**	**0**	**0**	**0**
HILLMAN, Wayne	Defense								
1961♦	Chicago	1	0	0	0	0	0	0	0
1963	Chicago	6	0	2	2	2	0	0	0
1964	Chicago	7	0	1	1	15	0	0	0
1967	NY Rangers	4	0	0	0	2	0	0	0
1968	NY Rangers	2	0	0	0	0	0	0	0
1973	Philadelphia	8	0	0	0	0	0	0	0
Playoff Totals		**28**	**0**	**3**	**3**	**19**	**0**	**0**	**0**
HILWORTH, John *No Playoffs*	Defense								
HIMES, Normie	Center								
1929	NY Americans	2	0	0	0	0	0	0	0
Playoff Totals		**2**	**0**	**0**	**0**	**0**	**0**	**0**	**0**
HINDMARCH, Dave	Right wing								
1981	Calgary	6	0	0	0	2	0	0	0
1983	Calgary	4	0	0	0	4	0	0	0
Playoff Totals		**10**	**0**	**0**	**0**	**6**	**0**	**0**	**0**
•HINOTE, Dan	Right wing								
2001♦	Colorado	23	2	4	6	21	0	0	0
2002	Colorado	19	1	2	3	9	0	0	0
Playoff Totals		**42**	**3**	**6**	**9**	**30**	**0**	**0**	**0**
HINSE, Andre *No Playoffs*	Left wing								
HINTON, Dan *No Playoffs*	Left wing								
HIRSCH, Tom	Defense								
1984	Minnesota	12	0	0	0	6	0	0	0
Playoff Totals		**12**	**0**	**0**	**0**	**6**	**0**	**0**	**0**
HIRSCHFELD, Bert	Left wing								
1950	Montreal	5	1	0	1	0	....	....	....
Playoff Totals		**5**	**1**	**0**	**1**	**0**	....	....	....
HISLOP, Jamie	Right wing								
1981	Calgary	16	3	0	3	5	1	0	1
1982	Calgary	3	0	0	0	0	0	0	0
1983	Calgary	9	0	2	2	6	0	0	0
Playoff Totals		**28**	**3**	**2**	**5**	**11**	**1**	**0**	**1**

Season	Team	GP	G	A	Pts	PIM	PP	SH	GW
HITCHMAN, Lionel	Defense								
1923♦	Ottawa	2	0	0	0	0	....	....	....
1924	Ottawa	2	0	0	0	4	....	....	....
1927	Boston	8	1	0	1	31	....	....	....
1928	Boston	2	0	0	0	2	....	....	....
1929♦	Boston	5	0	1	1	22	....	....	....
1930	Boston	6	1	0	1	14	....	....	....
1931	Boston	5	0	0	0	0	....	....	....
1933	Boston	5	1	0	1	0	....	....	....
Playoff Totals		**35**	**3**	**1**	**4**	**73**	....	....	....
•HLAVAC, Jan	Left wing								
2002	Vancouver	5	0	1	1	0	0	0	0
Playoff Totals		**5**	**0**	**1**	**1**	**0**	**0**	**0**	**0**
HLINKA, Ivan	Center								
1982	Vancouver	12	2	6	8	4	2	0	0
1983	Vancouver	4	1	4	5	4	0	0	0
Playoff Totals		**16**	**3**	**10**	**13**	**8**	**2**	**0**	**0**
HLUSHKO, Todd	Center								
1995	Calgary	1	0	0	0	2	0	0	0
1999	Pittsburgh	2	0	0	0	0	0	0	0
Playoff Totals		**3**	**0**	**0**	**0**	**2**	**0**	**0**	**0**
•HNIDY, Shane	Defense								
2001	Ottawa	1	0	0	0	0	0	0	0
2002	Ottawa	12	1	1	2	12	0	0	0
Playoff Totals		**13**	**1**	**1**	**2**	**12**	**0**	**0**	**0**
HOCKING, Justin *No Playoffs*	Defense								
HODGE, Ken	Right wing								
1966	Chicago	5	0	0	0	8	0	0	0
1967	Chicago	6	0	0	0	4	0	0	0
1968	Boston	4	3	0	3	2	0	0	0
1969	Boston	10	5	7	12	4	2	0	0
1970♦	Boston	14	3	10	13	7	0	1	0
1971	Boston	7	2	5	7	6	0	0	0
1972♦	Boston	15	9	8	17	*62	2	1	3
1973	Boston	5	1	0	1	7	1	0	0
1974	Boston	16	6	10	16	16	1	0	1
1975	Boston	3	1	1	2	0	1	0	0
1976	Boston	12	4	6	10	4	4	0	1
Playoff Totals		**97**	**34**	**47**	**81**	**120**	**11**	**2**	**5**
HODGE, Ken	Center/Right wing								
1991	Boston	15	4	6	10	6	1	0	1
Playoff Totals		**15**	**4**	**6**	**10**	**6**	**1**	**0**	**1**
HODGSON, Dan *No Playoffs*	Center								
HODGSON, Rick	Defense								
1980	Hartford	1	0	0	0	0	0	0	0
Playoff Totals		**1**	**0**	**0**	**0**	**0**	**0**	**0**	**0**
HODGSON, Ted *No Playoffs*	Right wing								
HOEKSTRA, Cec *No Playoffs*	Center								
HOEKSTRA, Ed	Center								
1968	Philadelphia	7	0	1	1	0	0	0	0
Playoff Totals		**7**	**0**	**1**	**1**	**0**	**0**	**0**	**0**
HOENE, Phil *No Playoffs*	Left wing								
HOFFINGER, Val *No Playoffs*	Defense								
HOFFMAN, Mike *No Playoffs*	Left wing								
HOFFMEYER, Bob	Defense								
1982	Philadelphia	2	0	1	1	25	0	0	0
1983	Philadelphia	1	0	0	0	0	0	0	0
Playoff Totals		**3**	**0**	**1**	**1**	**25**	**0**	**0**	**0**
HOFFORD, Jim *No Playoffs*	Defense								
HOGABOAM, Bill	Center								
1977	Minnesota	2	0	0	0	0	0	0	0
Playoff Totals		**2**	**0**	**0**	**0**	**0**	**0**	**0**	**0**
HOGANSON, Dale	Defense								
1981	Quebec	5	0	3	3	10	0	0	0
1982	Quebec	6	0	0	0	2	0	0	0
Playoff Totals		**11**	**0**	**3**	**3**	**12**	**0**	**0**	**0**
•HOGLUND, Jonas	Right wing								
1998	Montreal	10	2	0	2	0	0	0	0
2000	Toronto	12	2	4	6	2	0	0	0
2001	Toronto	10	0	0	0	4	0	0	0
2002	Toronto	20	4	6	10	2	3	0	1
Playoff Totals		**52**	**8**	**10**	**18**	**8**	**3**	**0**	**1**
•HOGUE, Benoit	Center								
1989	Buffalo	5	0	0	0	17	0	0	0
1990	Buffalo	3	0	0	0	10	0	0	0
1991	Buffalo	5	3	1	4	10	0	0	0
1993	NY Islanders	18	6	6	12	31	0	0	0
1994	NY Islanders	4	0	1	1	4	0	0	0
1995	Toronto	7	0	0	0	6	0	0	0
1997	Dallas	7	2	2	4	6	1	0	0
1998	Dallas	17	4	2	6	16	1	0	2
1999♦	Dallas	14	0	2	2	16	0	0	0
2000	Phoenix	5	1	2	3	2	0	0	0
2001	Dallas	7	1	0	1	6	0	0	1
Playoff Totals		**92**	**17**	**16**	**33**	**124**	**2**	**0**	**3**
HOLAN, Milos *No Playoffs*	Defense								

Season	Team	GP	G	A	Pts	PIM	PP	SH	GW
HOLBROOK, Terry	Right wing								
1973	Minnesota	6	0	0	0	0	0	0	0
Playoff Totals		**6**	**0**	**0**	**0**	**0**	**0**	**0**	**0**
•HOLDEN, Josh *No Playoffs*	Center								
•HOLIK, Bobby	Center								
1991	Hartford	6	0	0	0	7	0	0	0
1992	Hartford	7	0	1	1	6	0	0	0
1993	New Jersey	5	1	1	2	6	0	0	0
1994	New Jersey	20	0	3	3	6	0	0	0
1995♦	New Jersey	20	4	4	8	22	2	0	1
1997	New Jersey	10	2	3	5	4	1	0	0
1998	New Jersey	5	0	0	0	8	0	0	0
1999	New Jersey	7	0	7	7	6	0	0	0
2000♦	New Jersey	23	3	7	10	14	0	0	1
2001	New Jersey	25	6	10	16	37	1	0	3
2002	New Jersey	6	4	1	5	2	1	0	0
Playoff Totals		**134**	**20**	**37**	**57**	**118**	**5**	**0**	**5**
•HOLLAND, Jason	Defense								
2000	Buffalo	1	0	0	0	0	0	0	0
Playoff Totals		**1**	**0**	**0**	**0**	**0**	**0**	**0**	**0**
HOLLAND, Jerry *No Playoffs*	Left wing								
HOLLETT, Flash	Defense								
1935	Toronto	7	0	0	0	6	....	....	....
1937	Boston	3	0	0	0	2	....	....	....
1938	Boston	3	0	1	1	0	....	....	....
1939♦	Boston	12	1	3	4	2	....	....	....
1940	Boston	5	1	2	3	2	....	....	....
1941♦	Boston	11	3	4	7	8	....	....	....
1942	Boston	5	0	1	1	2	....	....	....
1943	Boston	9	0	9	9	4	....	....	....
1944	Detroit	5	0	0	0	6	....	....	....
1945	Detroit	14	3	4	7	6	....	....	....
1946	Detroit	5	0	2	2	0	....	....	....
Playoff Totals		**79**	**8**	**26**	**34**	**38**	....	....	....
HOLLINGER, Terry *No Playoffs*	Defense								
HOLLINGWORTH, Gord	Defense								
1956	Detroit	3	0	0	0	2	0	0	0
Playoff Totals		**3**	**0**	**0**	**0**	**2**	**0**	**0**	**0**
HOLLOWAY, Bruce *No Playoffs*	Defense								
HOLMES, Bill *No Playoffs*	Center								
HOLMES, Chuck *No Playoffs*	Right wing								
HOLMES, Lou	Center/Left wing								
1932	Chicago	2	0	0	0	2	0	0	0
Playoff Totals		**2**	**0**	**0**	**0**	**2**	**0**	**0**	**0**
HOLMES, Warren *No Playoffs*	Center								
HOLMGREN, Paul	Right wing								
1977	Philadelphia	10	1	1	2	25	0	0	0
1978	Philadelphia	12	1	4	5	26	0	0	0
1979	Philadelphia	8	1	5	6	22	0	0	0
1980	Philadelphia	18	10	10	20	47	3	0	1
1981	Philadelphia	12	5	9	14	49	2	0	1
1982	Philadelphia	4	1	2	3	6	0	0	0
1983	Philadelphia	3	0	0	0	6	0	0	0
1984	Minnesota	12	0	1	1	6	0	0	0
1985	Minnesota	3	0	0	0	8	0	0	0
Playoff Totals		**82**	**19**	**32**	**51**	**195**	**5**	**0**	**2**
•HOLMSTROM, Tomas	Left wing								
1997♦	Detroit	1	0	0	0	0	0	0	0
1998♦	Detroit	22	7	12	19	16	2	0	0
1999	Detroit	10	4	3	7	4	2	0	1
2000	Detroit	9	3	1	4	16	1	0	1
2001	Detroit	6	1	3	4	8	1	0	0
2002♦	Detroit	23	8	3	11	8	3	0	2
Playoff Totals		**71**	**23**	**22**	**45**	**52**	**9**	**0**	**4**
HOLOTA, John *No Playoffs*	Center								
HOLST, Greg *No Playoffs*	Center								
HOLT, Gary *No Playoffs*	Left wing								
HOLT, Randy	Defense								
1977	Chicago	2	0	0	0	7	0	0	0
1979	Los Angeles	2	0	0	0	4	0	0	0
1981	Calgary	13	2	2	4	52	0	0	1
1983	Washington	4	0	1	1	20	0	0	0
Playoff Totals		**21**	**2**	**3**	**5**	**83**	**0**	**0**	**1**
HOLWAY, Albert	Defense								
1925	Toronto	2	0	0	0	0	0	0	0
1926♦	Mtl. Maroons	4	0	0	0	0	0	0	0
Playoff Totals		**6**	**0**	**0**	**0**	**0**	**0**	**0**	**0**
•HOLZINGER, Brian	Center								
1995	Buffalo	4	2	1	3	2	1	0	0
1997	Buffalo	12	2	5	7	8	0	1	0
1998	Buffalo	15	4	7	11	18	1	1	0
1999	Buffalo	21	3	5	8	33	1	0	0
Playoff Totals		**52**	**11**	**18**	**29**	**61**	**3**	**2**	**0**
HOMENUKE, Ron *No Playoffs*	Right wing								
HOOVER, Ron	Center								
1991	Boston	8	0	0	0	18	0	0	0
Playoff Totals		**8**	**0**	**0**	**0**	**18**	**0**	**0**	**0**

Season	Team	GP	G	A	Pts	PIM	PP	SH	GW
HOPKINS, Dean	Right wing								
1980	Los Angeles	4	0	1	1	5	0	0	0
1981	Los Angeles	4	1	0	1	9	0	0	1
1982	Los Angeles	10	0	4	4	15	0	0	0
Playoff Totals		**18**	**1**	**5**	**6**	**29**	**0**	**0**	**1**
HOPKINS, Larry	Left wing								
1982	Winnipeg	4	0	0	0	2	0	0	0
1983	Winnipeg	2	0	0	0	0	0	0	0
Playoff Totals		**6**	**0**	**0**	**0**	**2**	**0**	**0**	**0**
HORACEK, Tony	Left wing								
1992	Chicago	2	1	0	1	2	0	0	0
Playoff Totals		**2**	**1**	**0**	**1**	**2**	**0**	**0**	**0**
HORAVA, Miloslav	Defense								
1990	NY Rangers	2	0	1	1	0	0	0	0
Playoff Totals		**2**	**0**	**1**	**1**	**0**	**0**	**0**	**0**
HORBUL, Doug *No Playoffs*	Left wing								
•**HORCOFF, Shawn**	Center								
2001	Edmonton	5	0	0	0	0	0	0	0
Playoff Totals		**5**	**0**	**0**	**0**	**0**	**0**	**0**	**0**
•**HORDICHUK, Darcy** *No Playoffs*	Left wing								
HORDY, Mike *No Playoffs*	Defense								
HORECK, Pete	Left wing								
1946	Chicago	4	0	0	0	2	....	....	....
1947	Detroit	5	2	0	2	6	....	....	....
1948	Detroit	10	3	*7	10	12	....	....	....
1949	Detroit	11	1	1	2	10	....	....	....
1951	Boston	4	0	0	0	13	....	....	....
Playoff Totals		**34**	**6**	**8**	**14**	**43**	....	....	....
HORNE, George	Right wing								
1926◆	Mtl. Maroons	....	....	....	....	....	....	....	....
1929	Toronto	4	0	0	0	4	0	0	0
Playoff Totals		**4**	**0**	**0**	**0**	**4**	**0**	**0**	**0**
HORNER, Red	Defense								
1929	Toronto	4	1	0	1	2	....	....	....
1931	Toronto	2	0	0	0	4	....	....	....
1932◆	Toronto	7	2	2	4	20	....	....	....
1933	Toronto	9	1	0	1	10	....	....	....
1934	Toronto	5	1	0	1	6	....	....	....
1935	Toronto	7	0	1	1	4	....	....	....
1936	Toronto	9	1	2	3	*22	....	....	....
1937	Toronto	2	0	0	0	7	....	....	....
1938	Toronto	7	0	1	1	14	....	....	....
1939	Toronto	10	1	2	3	*26	....	....	....
1940	Toronto	9	0	2	2	55	....	....	....
Playoff Totals		**71**	**7**	**10**	**17**	**170**	....	....	....
HORNUNG, Larry	Defense								
1972	St. Louis	11	0	2	2	2	0	0	0
Playoff Totals		**11**	**0**	**2**	**2**	**2**	**0**	**0**	**0**
HORTON, Tim	Defense								
1950	Toronto	1	0	0	0	2	....	....	....
1954	Toronto	5	1	1	2	4	....	....	....
1956	Toronto	2	0	0	0	4	....	....	....
1959	Toronto	12	0	3	3	16	....	....	....
1960	Toronto	10	0	1	1	6	....	....	....
1961	Toronto	5	0	0	0	0	....	....	....
1962◆	Toronto	12	3	13	16	16	....	....	....
1963◆	Toronto	10	1	3	4	10	....	....	....
1964◆	Toronto	14	0	4	4	20	....	....	....
1965	Toronto	6	0	2	2	13	....	....	....
1966	Toronto	4	1	0	1	12	....	....	....
1967◆	Toronto	12	3	5	8	25	....	....	....
1969	Toronto	4	0	0	0	7	0	0	0
1970	NY Rangers	6	1	1	2	28	0	0	0
1971	NY Rangers	13	1	4	5	14	0	0	0
1972	Pittsburgh	4	0	1	1	2	0	0	0
1973	Buffalo	6	0	1	1	4	0	0	0
Playoff Totals		**126**	**11**	**39**	**50**	**183**	**0**	**0**	**0**
HORVATH, Bronco	Center								
1956	NY Rangers	5	1	2	3	4	....	....	....
1958	Boston	12	5	3	8	8	....	....	....
1959	Boston	7	2	3	5	0	....	....	....
1962	Chicago	12	4	1	5	6	....	....	....
Playoff Totals		**36**	**12**	**9**	**21**	**18**	....	....	....
HOSPODAR, Ed	Defense								
1980	NY Rangers	7	1	0	1	42	0	0	1
1981	NY Rangers	12	2	0	2	*93	0	0	0
1985	Philadelphia	18	1	1	2	69	0	0	0
1986	Minnesota	2	0	0	0	2	0	0	0
1987	Philadelphia	5	0	0	0	2	0	0	0
Playoff Totals		**44**	**4**	**1**	**5**	**208**	**0**	**0**	**1**
•**HOSSA, Marcel** *No Playoffs*	Center								
•**HOSSA, Marian**	Left wing								
1999	Ottawa	4	0	2	2	4	0	0	0
2000	Ottawa	6	0	0	0	2	0	0	0
2001	Ottawa	4	1	1	2	4	0	0	0
2002	Ottawa	12	4	6	10	2	1	0	0
Playoff Totals		**26**	**5**	**9**	**14**	**12**	**1**	**0**	**0**
HOSTAK, Martin *No Playoffs*	Center								

Season	Team	GP	G	A	Pts	PIM	PP	SH	GW
HOTHAM, Greg	Defense								
1982	Pittsburgh	5	0	3	3	6	0	0	0
Playoff Totals		**5**	**0**	**3**	**3**	**6**	**0**	**0**	**0**
HOUCK, Paul *No Playoffs*	Right wing								
•**HOUDA, Doug**	Defense								
1989	Detroit	6	0	1	1	0	0	0	0
1991	Hartford	6	0	0	0	8	0	0	0
1992	Hartford	6	0	2	2	13	0	0	0
Playoff Totals		**18**	**0**	**3**	**3**	**21**	**0**	**0**	**0**
HOUDE, Claude *No Playoffs*	Defense								
HOUDE, Eric *No Playoffs*	Center								
HOUGH, Mike	Left wing								
1987	Quebec	9	0	3	3	26	0	0	0
1993	Quebec	6	0	1	1	2	0	0	0
1996	Florida	22	4	1	5	8	0	0	2
1997	Florida	5	1	0	1	2	0	0	0
Playoff Totals		**42**	**5**	**5**	**10**	**38**	**0**	**0**	**2**
•**HOULDER, Bill**	Defense								
1993	Buffalo	8	0	2	2	4	0	0	0
1995	St. Louis	4	1	1	2	0	0	0	0
1996	Tampa Bay	6	0	1	1	4	0	0	0
1998	San Jose	6	1	2	3	2	0	0	0
1999	San Jose	6	3	0	3	4	3	0	0
Playoff Totals		**30**	**5**	**6**	**11**	**14**	**3**	**0**	**0**
HOULE, Rejean	Wing								
1971◆	Montreal	20	2	5	7	20	0	0	1
1972	Montreal	6	0	0	0	2	0	0	0
1973◆	Montreal	17	3	6	9	0	0	0	0
1977◆	Montreal	6	0	1	1	4	0	0	0
1978◆	Montreal	15	3	8	11	14	0	0	0
1979◆	Montreal	7	1	5	6	2	0	0	0
1980	Montreal	10	4	5	9	12	1	0	0
1981	Montreal	3	1	0	1	6	0	0	0
1982	Montreal	5	0	4	4	6	0	0	0
1983	Montreal	1	0	0	0	0	0	0	0
Playoff Totals		**90**	**14**	**34**	**48**	**66**	**1**	**0**	**1**
•**HOUSLEY, Phil**	Defense								
1983	Buffalo	10	3	4	7	2	1	0	0
1984	Buffalo	3	0	0	0	6	0	0	0
1985	Buffalo	5	3	2	5	2	0	0	0
1988	Buffalo	6	2	4	6	6	1	0	0
1989	Buffalo	5	1	3	4	2	0	0	0
1990	Buffalo	6	1	4	5	4	1	0	0
1992	Winnipeg	7	1	4	5	0	1	0	1
1993	Winnipeg	6	0	7	7	2	0	0	0
1994	St. Louis	4	2	1	3	4	2	0	0
1995	Calgary	7	0	9	9	0	0	0	0
1998	Washington	18	0	4	4	4	0	0	0
2002	Chicago	5	0	1	1	4	0	0	0
Playoff Totals		**82**	**13**	**43**	**56**	**36**	**6**	**0**	**1**
HOUSTON, Ken	Right wing								
1976	Atlanta	2	0	0	0	0	0	0	0
1977	Atlanta	3	0	0	0	4	0	0	0
1978	Atlanta	2	0	0	0	0	0	0	0
1979	Atlanta	1	0	0	0	16	0	0	0
1980	Atlanta	4	1	1	2	10	0	0	0
1981	Calgary	16	7	8	15	28	5	0	1
1982	Calgary	3	1	0	1	4	0	0	0
1983	Washington	4	1	0	1	4	0	0	0
Playoff Totals		**35**	**10**	**9**	**19**	**66**	**5**	**0**	**1**
HOWARD, Jack *No Playoffs*	Defense								
HOWATT, Garry	Left wing								
1975	NY Islanders	17	3	3	6	59	0	0	1
1976	NY Islanders	13	5	5	10	23	0	0	1
1977	NY Islanders	12	1	1	2	28	0	0	0
1978	NY Islanders	7	0	1	1	62	0	0	0
1979	NY Islanders	9	0	1	1	18	0	0	0
1980◆	NY Islanders	21	3	1	4	84	0	0	1
1981◆	NY Islanders	8	0	2	2	15	0	0	0
Playoff Totals		**87**	**12**	**14**	**26**	**289**	**0**	**0**	**3**

Season	Team	GP	G	A	Pts	PIM	PP	SH	GW
HOWE, Gordie	Right wing								
1947	Detroit	5	0	0	0	18	....	....	....
1948	Detroit	10	1	1	2	11	....	....	....
1949	Detroit	11	*8	3	*11	19	....	....	....
1950◆	Detroit	1	0	0	0	7	....	....	....
1951	Detroit	6	4	3	7	4	....	....	....
1952◆	Detroit	8	2	*5	*7	2	....	....	....
1953	Detroit	6	2	5	7	2	....	....	....
1954◆	Detroit	12	4	5	9	*31	....	....	....
1955◆	Detroit	11	*9	*11	*20	24	....	....	....
1956	Detroit	10	3	9	12	8	....	....	....
1957	Detroit	5	2	5	7	6	....	....	....
1958	Detroit	4	1	1	2	0	....	....	....
1960	Detroit	6	1	5	6	4	....	....	....
1961	Detroit	11	4	11	*15	10	....	....	....
1963	Detroit	11	7	9	*16	22	....	....	....
1964	Detroit	14	*9	10	*19	16	....	....	....
1965	Detroit	7	4	2	6	20	....	....	....
1966	Detroit	12	4	6	10	12	....	....	....
1970	Detroit	4	2	0	2	2	1	0	0
1980	Hartford	3	1	1	2	2	0	0	0
Playoff Totals		**157**	**68**	**92**	**160**	**220**	**1**	**0**	**0**
HOWE, Mark	Defense								
1980	Hartford	3	1	2	3	2	0	0	0
1983	Philadelphia	3	0	2	2	4	0	0	0
1984	Philadelphia	3	0	0	0	2	0	0	0
1985	Philadelphia	19	3	8	11	6	1	0	1
1986	Philadelphia	5	0	4	4	0	0	0	0
1987	Philadelphia	26	2	10	12	4	0	0	0
1988	Philadelphia	7	3	6	9	4	0	0	0
1989	Philadelphia	19	0	15	15	10	0	0	0
1993	Detroit	7	1	3	4	2	0	0	0
1994	Detroit	6	0	1	1	0	0	0	0
1995	Detroit	3	0	0	0	0	0	0	0
Playoff Totals		**101**	**10**	**51**	**61**	**34**	**1**	**0**	**1**
HOWE, Marty	Defense								
1980	Hartford	3	1	1	2	0	0	0	0
1983	Boston	12	0	1	1	9	0	0	0
Playoff Totals		**15**	**1**	**2**	**3**	**9**	**0**	**0**	**0**
HOWE, Syd	Center/Left wing								
1930	Ottawa	2	0	0	0	0	....	....	....
1936◆	Detroit	7	3	3	6	2	....	....	....
1937◆	Detroit	10	2	5	7	0	....	....	....
1939	Detroit	6	3	1	4	4	....	....	....
1940	Detroit	5	2	2	4	2	....	....	....
1941	Detroit	9	1	*7	8	0	....	....	....
1942	Detroit	12	3	5	8	0	....	....	....
1943◆	Detroit	7	1	2	3	0	....	....	....
1944	Detroit	5	2	2	4	0	....	....	....
1945	Detroit	7	0	0	0	2	....	....	....
Playoff Totals		**70**	**17**	**27**	**44**	**10**	....	....	....
HOWE, Vic *No Playoffs*	Right wing								
HOWELL, Harry	Defense								
1956	NY Rangers	5	0	1	1	4	....	....	....
1957	NY Rangers	5	1	0	1	6	....	....	....
1958	NY Rangers	6	1	0	1	8	....	....	....
1962	NY Rangers	6	0	1	1	8	....	....	....
1967	NY Rangers	4	0	0	0	4	....	....	....
1968	NY Rangers	6	1	0	1	0	1	0	1
1969	NY Rangers	2	0	0	0	0	0	0	0
1970	Oakland	4	0	1	1	2	0	0	0
Playoff Totals		**38**	**3**	**3**	**6**	**32**	**1**	**0**	**1**
HOWELL, Ron *No Playoffs*	Defense/Left wing								
HOWSE, Don	Left wing								
1980	Los Angeles	2	0	0	0	0	0	0	0
Playoff Totals		**2**	**0**	**0**	**0**	**0**	**0**	**0**	**0**
HOWSON, Scott *No Playoffs*	Center								
HOYDA, Dave	Left wing								
1978	Philadelphia	9	0	0	0	17	0	0	0
1979	Philadelphia	3	0	0	0	0	0	0	0
Playoff Totals		**12**	**0**	**0**	**0**	**17**	**0**	**0**	**0**
•**HRDINA, Jan**	Center								
1999	Pittsburgh	13	4	1	5	12	1	0	1
2000	Pittsburgh	9	4	8	12	2	1	0	0
2001	Pittsburgh	18	2	5	7	8	0	0	0
Playoff Totals		**40**	**10**	**14**	**24**	**22**	**2**	**0**	**1**
HRDINA, Jiri	Center								
1988	Calgary	1	0	0	0	0	0	0	0
1989◆	Calgary	4	0	0	0	0	0	0	0
1990	Calgary	6	0	1	1	2	0	0	0
1991◆	Pittsburgh	14	2	2	4	6	0	0	1
1992◆	Pittsburgh	21	0	2	2	16	0	0	0
Playoff Totals		**46**	**2**	**5**	**7**	**24**	**0**	**0**	**1**
HRECHKOSY, Dave	Left wing								
1976	St. Louis	3	1	0	1	2	0	0	0
Playoff Totals		**3**	**1**	**0**	**1**	**2**	**0**	**0**	**0**

Season	Team	GP	G	A	Pts	PIM	PP	SH	GW
•HRKAC, Tony	Center								
1987	St. Louis	3	0	0	0	0	0	0	0
1988	St. Louis	10	6	1	7	4	3	1	1
1989	St. Louis	4	1	1	2	0	0	0	1
1992	Chicago	3	0	0	0	2	0	0	0
1994	St. Louis	4	0	0	0	0	0	0	0
1998	Edmonton	12	0	3	3	2	0	0	0
1999♦	Dallas	5	0	2	2	4	0	0	0
Playoff Totals		**41**	**7**	**7**	**14**	**12**	**3**	**1**	**2**
HRYCUIK, Jim *No Playoffs*	Center								
HRYMNAK, Steve	Defense								
1953	Detroit	2	0	0	0	0	0	0	0
Playoff Totals		**2**	**0**	**0**	**0**	**0**	**0**	**0**	**0**
HRYNEWICH, Tim *No Playoffs*	Left wing								
HUARD, Bill	Left wing								
1995	Quebec	1	0	0	0	0	0	0	0
1998	Edmonton	4	0	0	0	2	0	0	0
Playoff Totals		**5**	**0**	**0**	**0**	**2**	**0**	**0**	**0**
HUARD, Rolly *No Playoffs*	Center								
•HUBACEK, Petr *No Playoffs*	Center								
HUBER, Willie	Defense								
1984	NY Rangers	4	1	1	2	9	0	0	0
1985	NY Rangers	2	1	0	1	2	1	0	0
1986	NY Rangers	16	3	2	5	16	2	0	0
1987	NY Rangers	6	0	2	2	6	0	0	0
1988	Philadelphia	5	0	0	0	2	0	0	0
Playoff Totals		**33**	**5**	**5**	**10**	**35**	**3**	**0**	**0**
HUBICK, Greg *No Playoffs*	Defense								
HUCK, Fran	Center								
1971	St. Louis	6	1	2	3	2	0	0	0
1973	St. Louis	5	2	2	4	0	1	0	0
Playoff Totals		**11**	**3**	**4**	**7**	**2**	**1**	**0**	**0**
HUCUL, Fred	Defense								
1953	Chicago	6	1	0	1	10	....	....	....
Playoff Totals		**6**	**1**	**0**	**1**	**10**	....	....	....
HUDDY, Charlie	Defense								
1982	Edmonton	5	1	2	3	14	0	1	0
1983	Edmonton	15	1	6	7	10	0	0	0
1984♦	Edmonton	12	1	9	10	8	0	0	0
1985♦	Edmonton	18	3	17	20	17	1	0	0
1986	Edmonton	7	0	2	2	0	0	0	0
1987♦	Edmonton	21	1	7	8	21	0	0	0
1988♦	Edmonton	13	4	5	9	10	2	0	0
1989	Edmonton	7	2	0	2	4	1	0	0
1990♦	Edmonton	22	0	6	6	11	0	0	0
1991	Edmonton	18	3	7	10	10	1	0	0
1992	Los Angeles	6	1	1	2	10	0	0	1
1993	Los Angeles	23	1	4	5	12	0	0	0
1995	Buffalo	3	0	0	0	0	0	0	0
1996	St. Louis	13	1	0	1	8	0	0	0
Playoff Totals		**183**	**19**	**66**	**85**	**135**	**5**	**1**	**1**
HUDSON, Dave	Center								
1978	Colorado	2	1	1	2	0	0	0	0
Playoff Totals		**2**	**1**	**1**	**2**	**0**	**0**	**0**	**0**
HUDSON, Lex	Defense								
1979	Pittsburgh	2	0	0	0	0	0	0	0
Playoff Totals		**2**	**0**	**0**	**0**	**0**	**0**	**0**	**0**
HUDSON, Mike	Center/Left wing								
1989	Chicago	10	1	2	3	18	1	0	0
1990	Chicago	4	0	0	0	2	0	0	0
1991	Chicago	6	0	2	2	8	0	0	0
1992	Chicago	16	3	5	8	26	0	0	0
1994♦	NY Rangers	....	....	....	....	....	....	....	....
1995	Pittsburgh	11	0	0	0	6	0	0	0
1996	St. Louis	2	0	1	1	4	0	0	0
Playoff Totals		**49**	**4**	**10**	**14**	**64**	**1**	**0**	**0**
HUDSON, Ron *No Playoffs*	Center								
HUFFMAN, Kerry	Defense								
1988	Philadelphia	2	0	0	0	0	0	0	0
1993	Quebec	3	0	0	0	0	0	0	0
1996	Philadelphia	6	0	0	0	2	0	0	0
Playoff Totals		**11**	**0**	**0**	**0**	**2**	**0**	**0**	**0**
HUGGINS, Al *No Playoffs*	Left wing								
HUGHES, Albert *No Playoffs*	Center/Left wing								
HUGHES, Brent	Left wing								
1992	Boston	10	2	0	2	20	0	0	0
1993	Boston	1	0	0	0	2	0	0	0
1994	Boston	13	2	1	3	27	0	0	1
1995	Boston	5	0	0	0	4	0	0	0
Playoff Totals		**29**	**4**	**1**	**5**	**53**	**0**	**0**	**1**
HUGHES, Brent	Defense								
1968	Los Angeles	7	0	0	0	10	0	0	0
1969	Los Angeles	11	1	3	4	37	0	0	0
1971	Philadelphia	4	0	0	0	6	0	0	0
Playoff Totals		**22**	**1**	**3**	**4**	**53**	**0**	**0**	**0**
HUGHES, Frank *No Playoffs*	Left wing								

Season	Team	GP	G	A	Pts	PIM	PP	SH	GW
HUGHES, Howie	Right wing								
1968	Los Angeles	7	2	0	2	0	1	0	0
1969	Los Angeles	7	0	0	0	2	0	0	0
Playoff Totals		**14**	**2**	**0**	**2**	**2**	**1**	**0**	**0**
HUGHES, Jack *No Playoffs*	Defense								
HUGHES, James *No Playoffs*	Defense								
HUGHES, John	Defense								
1980	Vancouver	4	0	0	0	10	0	0	0
1981	NY Rangers	3	0	1	1	6	0	0	0
Playoff Totals		**7**	**0**	**1**	**1**	**16**	**0**	**0**	**0**
HUGHES, Pat	Right wing								
1979♦	Montreal	8	1	2	3	4	0	0	0
1980	Pittsburgh	5	0	0	0	21	0	0	0
1981	Edmonton	5	0	5	5	16	0	0	0
1982	Edmonton	5	2	1	3	6	0	0	0
1983	Edmonton	16	2	5	7	14	0	0	1
1984♦	Edmonton	19	2	11	13	12	0	0	0
1985♦	Edmonton	10	1	1	2	4	0	0	0
1987	Hartford	3	0	0	0	0	0	0	0
Playoff Totals		**71**	**8**	**25**	**33**	**77**	**0**	**0**	**1**
HUGHES, Ryan *No Playoffs*	Center								
•HULBIG, Joe	Left wing								
1997	Edmonton	6	0	1	1	2	0	0	0
Playoff Totals		**6**	**0**	**1**	**1**	**2**	**0**	**0**	**0**
HULL, Bobby	Left wing								
1959	Chicago	6	1	1	2	2	....	....	....
1960	Chicago	3	1	0	1	2	....	....	....
1961♦	Chicago	12	4	10	14	4	....	....	....
1962	Chicago	12	*8	6	14	12	....	....	....
1963	Chicago	5	*8	2	10	4	....	....	....
1964	Chicago	7	2	5	7	2	....	....	....
1965	Chicago	14	*10	7	*17	27	....	....	....
1966	Chicago	6	2	2	4	10	....	....	....
1967	Chicago	6	4	2	6	0	....	....	....
1968	Chicago	11	4	6	10	15	1	1	1
1970	Chicago	8	3	8	11	2	0	0	0
1971	Chicago	18	11	14	25	16	6	0	4
1972	Chicago	8	4	4	8	6	0	1	0
1980	Hartford	3	0	0	0	0	0	0	0
Playoff Totals		**119**	**62**	**67**	**129**	**102**	**7**	**2**	**5**
•HULL, Brett	Right wing								
1986	Calgary	2	0	0	0	0	0	0	0
1987	Calgary	4	2	1	3	0	0	0	0
1988	St. Louis	10	7	2	9	4	4	0	3
1989	St. Louis	10	5	5	10	6	1	0	2
1990	St. Louis	12	13	8	21	17	7	0	3
1991	St. Louis	13	11	8	19	4	3	0	2
1992	St. Louis	6	4	4	8	4	1	1	1
1993	St. Louis	11	8	5	13	2	5	0	2
1994	St. Louis	4	2	1	3	0	1	0	0
1995	St. Louis	7	6	2	8	0	2	0	0
1996	St. Louis	13	6	5	11	10	2	1	1
1997	St. Louis	6	2	7	9	2	0	0	0
1998	St. Louis	10	3	3	6	2	1	0	1
1999♦	Dallas	22	8	7	15	4	3	0	2
2000	Dallas	23	*11	*13	*24	4	3	0	4
2001	Dallas	10	2	5	7	6	1	0	0
2002♦	Detroit	23	*10	8	18	4	3	2	2
Playoff Totals		**186**	**100**	**84**	**184**	**69**	***37**	**4**	**23**
HULL, Dennis	Left wing								
1965	Chicago	6	0	0	0	0	0	0	0
1966	Chicago	3	0	0	0	0	0	0	0
1967	Chicago	6	0	1	1	12	0	0	0
1968	Chicago	11	1	3	4	6	0	0	1
1970	Chicago	8	5	2	7	0	0	1	0
1971	Chicago	18	7	6	13	2	2	0	1
1972	Chicago	8	4	2	6	4	1	0	0
1973	Chicago	16	9	*15	24	4	4	0	1
1974	Chicago	10	6	3	9	0	1	0	1
1975	Chicago	5	0	2	2	0	0	0	0
1976	Chicago	4	0	0	0	0	0	0	0
1977	Chicago	2	1	0	1	0	1	0	0
1978	Detroit	7	0	0	0	2	0	0	0
Playoff Totals		**104**	**33**	**34**	**67**	**30**	**9**	**1**	**4**
•HULL, Jody	Right wing								
1989	Hartford	1	0	0	0	2	0	0	0
1990	Hartford	5	0	1	1	2	0	0	0
1996	Florida	14	3	2	5	0	0	0	0
1997	Florida	5	0	0	0	0	0	0	0
1999	Philadelphia	6	0	0	0	4	0	0	0
2000	Philadelphia	18	0	1	1	0	0	0	0
2001	Philadelphia	6	0	0	0	4	0	0	0
2002	Ottawa	12	1	1	2	2	0	0	0
Playoff Totals		**67**	**4**	**5**	**9**	**14**	**0**	**0**	**0**
•HULSE, Cale	Defense								
1996	Calgary	1	0	0	0	0	0	0	0
Playoff Totals		**1**	**0**	**0**	**0**	**0**	**0**	**0**	**0**
•HUML, Ivan *No Playoffs*	Left wing								
HUNT, Fred *No Playoffs*	Right wing								

Season	Team	GP	G	A	Pts	PIM	PP	SH	GW
HUNTER, Dale	Center								
1981	Quebec	5	4	2	6	34	0	0	1
1982	Quebec	16	3	7	10	52	1	0	2
1983	Quebec	4	2	1	3	24	0	1	0
1984	Quebec	9	2	3	5	41	0	0	0
1985	Quebec	17	4	6	10	*97	0	1	2
1986	Quebec	3	0	0	0	15	0	0	0
1987	Quebec	13	1	7	8	56	1	0	0
1988	Washington	14	7	5	12	98	4	0	1
1989	Washington	6	0	4	4	29	0	0	0
1990	Washington	15	4	8	12	61	1	0	0
1991	Washington	11	1	9	10	41	0	0	0
1992	Washington	7	1	4	5	16	0	0	0
1993	Washington	6	7	1	8	35	4	0	1
1994	Washington	7	0	3	3	14	0	0	0
1995	Washington	7	4	4	8	24	2	0	0
1996	Washington	6	1	5	6	24	0	0	0
1998	Washington	21	0	4	4	30	0	0	0
1999	Colorado	19	1	3	4	38	0	0	0
Playoff Totals		**186**	**42**	**76**	**118**	**729**	**13**	**2**	**7**
HUNTER, Dave	Left wing								
1980	Edmonton	3	0	0	0	7	0	0	0
1981	Edmonton	9	0	0	0	28	0	0	0
1982	Edmonton	5	0	1	1	26	0	0	0
1983	Edmonton	16	4	7	11	60	0	0	0
1984♦	Edmonton	17	5	5	10	14	1	1	0
1985♦	Edmonton	18	2	5	7	33	0	0	0
1986	Edmonton	10	2	3	5	23	0	0	0
1987♦	Edmonton	21	3	3	6	20	0	0	0
1989	Edmonton	6	0	0	0	0	0	0	0
Playoff Totals		**105**	**16**	**24**	**40**	**211**	**1**	**1**	**0**
HUNTER, Mark	Right wing								
1982	Montreal	5	0	0	0	20	0	0	0
1984	Montreal	14	2	1	3	69	0	0	0
1985	Montreal	11	0	3	3	13	0	0	0
1986	St. Louis	19	7	7	14	48	2	0	1
1987	St. Louis	5	0	3	3	10	0	0	0
1988	St. Louis	5	2	3	5	24	1	0	0
1989♦	Calgary	10	2	2	4	23	0	0	0
1991	Hartford	6	5	1	6	17	3	0	0
1992	Hartford	4	0	0	0	6	0	0	0
Playoff Totals		**79**	**18**	**20**	**38**	**230**	**6**	**0**	**1**
HUNTER, Tim	Right wing								
1983	Calgary	9	1	0	1	*70	1	0	0
1984	Calgary	7	0	0	0	21	0	0	0
1985	Calgary	4	0	0	0	24	0	0	0
1986	Calgary	19	0	3	3	108	0	0	0
1987	Calgary	6	0	0	0	51	0	0	0
1988	Calgary	9	4	0	4	32	0	0	2
1989♦	Calgary	19	0	4	4	32	0	0	0
1990	Calgary	6	0	0	0	4	0	0	0
1991	Calgary	7	0	0	0	10	0	0	0
1993	Vancouver	11	0	0	0	26	0	0	0
1994	Vancouver	24	0	0	0	26	0	0	0
1995	Vancouver	11	0	0	0	22	0	0	0
Playoff Totals		**132**	**5**	**7**	**12**	**426**	**1**	**0**	**2**
•HUNTER, Trent	Right wing								
2002	NY Islanders	4	1	1	2	2	0	0	0
Playoff Totals		**4**	**1**	**1**	**2**	**2**	**0**	**0**	**0**
HURAS, Larry *No Playoffs*	Defense								
HURLBURT, Bob *No Playoffs*	Left wing								
•HURLBUT, Mike *No Playoffs*	Defense								
HURLEY, Paul *No Playoffs*	Defense								
HURST, Ron	Right wing								
1956	Toronto	3	0	2	2	4	0	0	0
Playoff Totals		**3**	**0**	**2**	**2**	**4**	**0**	**0**	**0**
HUSCROFT, Jamie	Defense								
1990	New Jersey	5	0	0	0	16	0	0	0
1991	New Jersey	3	0	0	0	6	0	0	0
1994	Boston	4	0	0	0	9	0	0	0
1995	Boston	5	0	0	0	11	0	0	0
1996	Calgary	4	0	1	1	4	0	0	0
Playoff Totals		**21**	**0**	**1**	**1**	**46**	**0**	**0**	**0**
•HUSELIUS, Kristian *No Playoffs*	Right wing								
HUSKA, Ryan *No Playoffs*	Left wing								
HUSTON, Ron *No Playoffs*	Center								
HUTCHINSON, Ron *No Playoffs*	Center								
HUTCHISON, Dave	Defense								
1975	Los Angeles	2	0	0	0	22	0	0	0
1976	Los Angeles	9	0	3	3	29	0	0	0
1977	Los Angeles	9	1	4	5	17	0	0	0
1979	Toronto	6	0	3	3	23	0	0	0
1980	Chicago	6	0	0	0	12	0	0	0
1981	Chicago	2	0	0	0	2	0	0	0
1982	Chicago	14	1	2	3	44	0	0	0
Playoff Totals		**48**	**2**	**12**	**14**	**149**	**0**	**0**	**0**
HUTTON, Bill	Defense/Right wing								
1930	Ottawa	2	0	0	0	0	0	0	0
Playoff Totals		**2**	**0**	**0**	**0**	**0**	**0**	**0**	**0**
HYLAND, Harry *No Playoffs*	Right wing								

HYNES, Dave *No Playoffs* Left wing

HYNES, Gord Defense

Season	Team	GP	G	A	Pts	PIM	PP	SH	GW
1992	Boston	12	1	2	3	6	0	0	0
Playoff Totals		**12**	**1**	**2**	**3**	**6**	**0**	**0**	**0**

•HYVONEN, Hannes *No Playoffs* Right wing

IAFRATE, Al Defense

Season	Team	GP	G	A	Pts	PIM	PP	SH	GW
1986	Toronto	10	0	3	3	4	0	0	0
1987	Toronto	13	1	3	4	11	1	0	0
1988	Toronto	6	3	4	7	6	2	0	0
1991	Washington	10	1	3	4	22	0	0	1
1992	Washington	7	4	2	6	14	1	0	0
1993	Washington	6	6	0	6	4	3	0	1
1994	Boston	13	3	1	4	6	1	0	1
1998	San Jose	6	1	0	1	10	1	0	0
Playoff Totals		**71**	**19**	**16**	**35**	**77**	**9**	**0**	**3**

•IGINLA, Jarome Right wing

Season	Team	GP	G	A	Pts	PIM	PP	SH	GW
1996	Calgary	2	1	1	2	0	0	0	0
Playoff Totals		**2**	**1**	**1**	**2**	**0**	**0**	**0**	**0**

•IGNATJEV, Victor Defense

Season	Team	GP	G	A	Pts	PIM	PP	SH	GW
1999	Pittsburgh	1	0	0	0	2	0	0	0
Playoff Totals		**1**	**0**	**0**	**0**	**2**	**0**	**0**	**0**

IHNACAK, Miroslav Left wing

Season	Team	GP	G	A	Pts	PIM	PP	SH	GW
1987	Toronto	1	0	0	0	0	0	0	0
Playoff Totals		**1**	**0**	**0**	**0**	**0**	**0**	**0**	**0**

IHNACAK, Peter Center

Season	Team	GP	G	A	Pts	PIM	PP	SH	GW
1986	Toronto	10	2	3	5	12	0	0	1
1987	Toronto	13	2	4	6	9	0	0	0
1988	Toronto	5	0	3	3	4	0	0	0
Playoff Totals		**28**	**4**	**10**	**14**	**25**	**0**	**0**	**1**

IMLACH, Brent *No Playoffs* Forward

INGARFIELD, Earl Center

Season	Team	GP	G	A	Pts	PIM	PP	SH	GW
1962	NY Rangers	6	3	2	5	2	1	0	0
1967	NY Rangers	4	1	0	1	2	0	0	0
1969	Oakland	7	4	6	10	2	0	1	1
1970	Oakland	4	1	0	1	4	1	0	0
Playoff Totals		**21**	**9**	**8**	**17**	**10**	**2**	**1**	**1**

INGARFIELD, Earl Jr. Center

Season	Team	GP	G	A	Pts	PIM	PP	SH	GW
1980	Atlanta	2	0	1	1	0	0	0	0
Playoff Totals		**2**	**0**	**1**	**1**	**0**	**0**	**0**	**0**

INGLIS, Billy Center

Season	Team	GP	G	A	Pts	PIM	PP	SH	GW
1969	Los Angeles	11	1	2	3	4	0	0	0
Playoff Totals		**11**	**1**	**2**	**3**	**4**	**0**	**0**	**0**

INGOLDSBY, Johnny *No Playoffs* Right wing/Defense

INGRAM, Frank Right wing

Season	Team	GP	G	A	Pts	PIM	PP	SH	GW
1930	Chicago	2	0	0	0	0	0	0	0
1931	Chicago	9	0	1	1	2	0	0	0
Playoff Totals		**11**	**0**	**1**	**1**	**2**	**0**	**0**	**0**

INGRAM, John J. *No Playoffs* Center

INGRAM, Ron Defense

Season	Team	GP	G	A	Pts	PIM	PP	SH	GW
1963	Chicago	2	0	0	0	0	0	0	0
Playoff Totals		**2**	**0**	**0**	**0**	**0**	**0**	**0**	**0**

INTRANUOVO, Ralph *No Playoffs* Center

IRVIN, Dick Center

Season	Team	GP	G	A	Pts	PIM	PP	SH	GW
1927	Chicago	2	2	0	2	4	....	....	....
Playoff Totals		**2**	**2**	**0**	**2**	**4**	....	....	....

IRVINE, Ted Left wing

Season	Team	GP	G	A	Pts	PIM	PP	SH	GW
1968	Los Angeles	6	1	3	4	2	0	0	0
1969	Los Angeles	11	5	1	6	7	1	1	0
1970	NY Rangers	6	1	2	3	8	0	1	0
1971	NY Rangers	12	1	2	3	28	0	0	0
1972	NY Rangers	16	4	5	9	19	0	0	0
1973	NY Rangers	10	1	3	4	20	1	0	0
1974	NY Rangers	13	3	5	8	16	0	0	0
1975	NY Rangers	3	0	1	1	11	0	0	0
1976	St. Louis	3	0	2	2	2	0	0	0
1977	St. Louis	3	0	0	0	2	0	0	0
Playoff Totals		**83**	**16**	**24**	**40**	**115**	**2**	**2**	**0**

IRWIN, Ivan Defense

Season	Team	GP	G	A	Pts	PIM	PP	SH	GW
1956	NY Rangers	5	0	0	0	8	0	0	0
Playoff Totals		**5**	**0**	**0**	**0**	**8**	**0**	**0**	**0**

ISAKSSON, Ulf *No Playoffs* Left wing

•ISBISTER, Brad Left wing

Season	Team	GP	G	A	Pts	PIM	PP	SH	GW
1998	Phoenix	5	0	0	0	2	0	0	0
2002	NY Islanders	3	1	1	2	17	1	0	1
Playoff Totals		**8**	**1**	**1**	**2**	**19**	**1**	**0**	**1**

ISSEL, Kim *No Playoffs* Right wing

•JACKMAN, Barret Defense

Season	Team	GP	G	A	Pts	PIM	PP	SH	GW
2002	St. Louis	1	0	0	0	2	0	0	0
Playoff Totals		**1**	**0**	**0**	**0**	**2**	**0**	**0**	**0**

•JACKMAN, Richard *No Playoffs* Defense

JACKSON, Art Center

Season	Team	GP	G	A	Pts	PIM	PP	SH	GW
1935	Toronto	1	0	0	0	2	....	....	....
1936	Toronto	8	0	3	3	2	....	....	....
1938	Boston	3	0	0	0	0	....	....	....
1939	NY Americans	2	0	0	0	2	....	....	....
1940	Boston	5	1	2	3	0	....	....	....
1941♦	Boston	11	1	3	4	16	....	....	....
1942	Boston	5	0	1	1	0	....	....	....
1943	Boston	9	6	3	9	7	....	....	....
1945♦	Toronto	8	0	0	0	0	....	....	....
Playoff Totals		**52**	**8**	**12**	**20**	**29**	....	....	....

JACKSON, Busher Left wing

Season	Team	GP	G	A	Pts	PIM	PP	SH	GW
1931	Toronto	2	0	0	0	0	....	....	....
1932♦	Toronto	7	5	2	7	13	....	....	....
1933	Toronto	9	3	1	4	2	....	....	....
1934	Toronto	5	1	0	1	8	....	....	....
1935	Toronto	7	3	2	*5	2	....	....	....
1936	Toronto	9	3	2	5	4	....	....	....
1937	Toronto	2	1	0	1	2	....	....	....
1938	Toronto	6	1	0	1	8	....	....	....
1939	Toronto	7	0	1	1	2	....	....	....
1940	NY Americans	3	0	1	1	2	....	....	....
1942	Boston	5	0	1	1	0	....	....	....
1943	Boston	9	1	2	3	10	....	....	....
Playoff Totals		**71**	**18**	**12**	**30**	**53**	....	....	....

•JACKSON, Dane Right wing

Season	Team	GP	G	A	Pts	PIM	PP	SH	GW
1995	Vancouver	6	0	0	0	10	0	0	0
Playoff Totals		**6**	**0**	**0**	**0**	**10**	**0**	**0**	**0**

JACKSON, Don Defense

Season	Team	GP	G	A	Pts	PIM	PP	SH	GW
1980	Minnesota	1	0	0	0	0	0	0	0
1983	Edmonton	16	3	3	6	30	0	0	0
1984♦	Edmonton	19	1	2	3	32	0	0	0
1985♦	Edmonton	9	0	0	0	64	0	0	0
1986	Edmonton	8	0	0	0	21	0	0	0
Playoff Totals		**53**	**4**	**5**	**9**	**147**	**0**	**0**	**0**

JACKSON, Harold Defense

Season	Team	GP	G	A	Pts	PIM	PP	SH	GW
1938♦	Chicago	1	0	0	0	2	....	....	....
1943♦	Detroit	6	0	1	1	4	....	....	....
1944	Detroit	5	0	0	0	11	....	....	....
1945	Detroit	14	1	1	2	10	....	....	....
1946	Detroit	5	0	0	0	6	....	....	....
Playoff Totals		**31**	**1**	**2**	**3**	**33**	....	....	....

JACKSON, Jack *No Playoffs* Defense

JACKSON, Jeff Left wing

Season	Team	GP	G	A	Pts	PIM	PP	SH	GW
1987	NY Rangers	6	1	1	2	16	0	0	0
Playoff Totals		**6**	**1**	**1**	**2**	**16**	**0**	**0**	**0**

JACKSON, Jim Left wing

Season	Team	GP	G	A	Pts	PIM	PP	SH	GW
1983	Calgary	8	2	1	3	2	0	0	0
1984	Calgary	6	1	1	2	4	0	1	0
Playoff Totals		**14**	**3**	**2**	**5**	**6**	**0**	**1**	**0**

JACKSON, Lloyd *No Playoffs* Center

JACKSON, Stan *No Playoffs* Left wing

JACKSON, Walter *No Playoffs* Left wing

JACOBS, Paul *No Playoffs* Defense

JACOBS, Tim *No Playoffs* Defense

•JAGR, Jaromir Right wing

Season	Team	GP	G	A	Pts	PIM	PP	SH	GW
1991♦	Pittsburgh	24	3	10	13	6	1	0	1
1992♦	Pittsburgh	21	11	13	24	6	2	0	4
1993	Pittsburgh	12	5	4	9	23	1	0	1
1994	Pittsburgh	6	2	4	6	16	0	0	1
1995	Pittsburgh	12	10	5	15	6	2	1	1
1996	Pittsburgh	18	11	12	23	18	5	1	1
1997	Pittsburgh	5	4	4	8	4	2	0	0
1998	Pittsburgh	6	4	5	9	2	1	0	0
1999	Pittsburgh	9	5	7	12	16	1	0	1
2000	Pittsburgh	11	8	8	16	6	2	0	4
2001	Pittsburgh	16	2	10	12	18	2	0	0
Playoff Totals		**140**	**65**	**82**	**147**	**121**	**19**	**2**	**14**

•JAKOPIN, John *No Playoffs* Defense

JALO, Risto *No Playoffs* Center

JALONEN, Kari Center

Season	Team	GP	G	A	Pts	PIM	PP	SH	GW
1983	Calgary	5	1	0	1	0	0	0	0
Playoff Totals		**5**	**1**	**0**	**1**	**0**	**0**	**0**	**0**

JAMES, Gerry Right wing

Season	Team	GP	G	A	Pts	PIM	PP	SH	GW
1956	Toronto	5	1	0	1	8	0	1	0
1960	Toronto	10	0	0	0	0	0	0	0
Playoff Totals		**15**	**1**	**0**	**1**	**8**	**0**	**1**	**0**

JAMES, Val *No Playoffs* Left wing

JAMIESON, Jim *No Playoffs* Defense

JANKOWSKI, Lou Center/Right wing

Season	Team	GP	G	A	Pts	PIM	PP	SH	GW
1953	Detroit	1	0	0	0	0	0	0	0
Playoff Totals		**1**	**0**	**0**	**0**	**0**	**0**	**0**	**0**

JANNEY, Craig Center

Season	Team	GP	G	A	Pts	PIM	PP	SH	GW
1988	Boston	23	6	10	16	11	4	0	1
1989	Boston	10	4	9	13	21	0	0	0
1990	Boston	18	3	19	22	2	1	0	2
1991	Boston	18	4	18	22	11	4	0	0
1992	St. Louis	6	0	6	6	0	0	0	0
1993	St. Louis	11	2	9	11	0	1	0	2
1994	St. Louis	4	1	3	4	0	0	0	0
1995	San Jose	11	3	4	7	4	0	0	1
1996	Winnipeg	6	1	2	3	0	0	0	0
1997	Phoenix	7	0	3	3	4	0	0	0
1998	Phoenix	6	0	3	3	0	0	0	0
Playoff Totals		**120**	**24**	**86**	**110**	**53**	**10**	**0**	**6**

JANSSENS, Mark Center

Season	Team	GP	G	A	Pts	PIM	PP	SH	GW
1990	NY Rangers	9	2	1	3	10	0	0	1
1991	NY Rangers	6	3	0	3	6	0	0	0
1997	Anaheim	11	0	0	0	15	0	0	0
1998	Phoenix	1	0	0	0	2	0	0	0
Playoff Totals		**27**	**5**	**1**	**6**	**33**	**0**	**0**	**1**

JANTUNEN, Marko *No Playoffs* Center

•JARDINE, Ryan *No Playoffs* Left wing

JARRETT, Doug Defense

Season	Team	GP	G	A	Pts	PIM	PP	SH	GW
1965	Chicago	11	1	0	1	10	0	0	0
1966	Chicago	5	0	1	1	9	0	0	0
1967	Chicago	6	0	3	3	8	0	0	0
1968	Chicago	11	4	0	4	9	0	0	0
1970	Chicago	8	1	0	1	4	0	0	0
1971	Chicago	18	1	6	7	14	0	0	0
1972	Chicago	8	0	2	2	16	0	0	0
1973	Chicago	15	0	3	3	2	0	0	0
1974	Chicago	10	0	1	1	6	0	0	0
1975	Chicago	7	0	0	0	4	0	0	0
Playoff Totals		**99**	**7**	**16**	**23**	**82**	**0**	**0**	**0**

JARRETT, Gary Left wing

Season	Team	GP	G	A	Pts	PIM	PP	SH	GW
1969	Oakland	7	2	1	3	4	0	1	0
1970	Oakland	4	1	0	1	5	1	0	0
Playoff Totals		**11**	**3**	**1**	**4**	**9**	**1**	**1**	**0**

JARRY, Pierre Left wing

Season	Team	GP	G	A	Pts	PIM	PP	SH	GW
1972	Toronto	5	0	1	1	0	0	0	0
Playoff Totals		**5**	**0**	**1**	**1**	**0**	**0**	**0**	**0**

JARVENPAA, Hannu *No Playoffs* Right wing

•JARVENTIE, Martti *No Playoffs* Defense

JARVI, Iiro *No Playoffs* Right wing

JARVIS, Doug Center

Season	Team	GP	G	A	Pts	PIM	PP	SH	GW
1976♦	Montreal	13	2	1	3	2	0	0	0
1977♦	Montreal	14	0	7	7	2	0	0	0
1978♦	Montreal	15	3	5	8	12	1	0	1
1979♦	Montreal	12	1	3	4	4	0	0	0
1980	Montreal	10	4	4	8	2	0	1	0
1981	Montreal	3	0	0	0	0	0	0	0
1982	Montreal	5	1	0	1	4	0	1	0
1983	Washington	4	0	1	1	0	0	0	0
1984	Washington	8	2	3	5	6	0	0	0
1985	Washington	5	1	0	1	2	0	0	0
1986	Hartford	10	0	3	3	4	0	0	0
1987	Hartford	6	0	0	0	4	0	0	0
Playoff Totals		**105**	**14**	**27**	**41**	**42**	**1**	**2**	**1**

JARVIS, James *No Playoffs* Left wing

JARVIS, Wes Center

Season	Team	GP	G	A	Pts	PIM	PP	SH	GW
1987	Toronto	2	0	0	0	2	0	0	0
Playoff Totals		**2**	**0**	**0**	**0**	**2**	**0**	**0**	**0**

•JASPERS, Jason *No Playoffs* Center/Left wing

JAVANAINEN, Arto *No Playoffs* Right wing

JAY, Bob *No Playoffs* Defense

JEFFREY, Larry Left wing

Season	Team	GP	G	A	Pts	PIM	PP	SH	GW
1963	Detroit	9	3	3	6	8	1	0	0
1964	Detroit	14	1	6	7	28	0	0	1
1965	Detroit	2	0	0	0	0	0	0	0
1967♦	Toronto	6	0	1	1	4	0	0	0
1968	NY Rangers	3	0	0	0	0	0	0	0
1969	NY Rangers	4	0	0	0	2	0	0	0
Playoff Totals		**38**	**4**	**10**	**14**	**42**	**1**	**0**	**1**

JELINEK, Tomas *No Playoffs* Right wing

JENKINS, Dean *No Playoffs* Right wing

JENKINS, Roger Right wing/Defense

Season	Team	GP	G	A	Pts	PIM	PP	SH	GW
1931	Chicago	3	0	0	0	0	....	....	....
1934♦	Chicago	8	0	0	0	0	....	....	....
1935	Montreal	2	1	0	1	2	....	....	....
1936	Boston	2	0	1	1	2	....	....	....
1938♦	Chicago	10	0	*6	6	8	....	....	....
Playoff Totals		**25**	**1**	**7**	**8**	**12**	....	....	....

JENNINGS, Bill Right wing

Season	Team	GP	G	A	Pts	PIM	PP	SH	GW
1941	Detroit	9	2	2	4	0	....	....	....
1944	Detroit	4	0	0	0	0	....	....	....
1945	Boston	7	2	2	4	6	....	....	....
Playoff Totals		**20**	**4**	**4**	**8**	**6**	....	....	....

Season	Team	GP	G	A	Pts	PIM	PP	SH	GW
JENNINGS, Grant	Defense								
1988	Washington	1	0	0	0	0	0	0	0
1989	Hartford	4	1	0	1	17	1	0	0
1990	Hartford	7	0	0	0	13	0	0	0
1991◆	Pittsburgh	13	1	1	2	16	0	0	0
1992◆	Pittsburgh	10	0	0	0	12	0	0	0
1993	Pittsburgh	12	0	0	0	8	0	0	0
1994	Pittsburgh	3	0	0	0	2	0	0	0
1995	Toronto	4	0	0	0	0	0	0	0
Playoff Totals		**54**	**2**	**1**	**3**	**68**	**1**	**0**	**0**
JENSEN, Chris *No Playoffs*	Right wing								
JENSEN, David *No Playoffs*	Defense								
JENSEN, David	Center								
1986	Washington	4	0	0	0	0	0	0	0
1987	Washington	7	0	0	0	2	0	0	0
Playoff Totals		**11**	**0**	**0**	**0**	**2**	**0**	**0**	**0**
JENSEN, Steve	Left wing								
1977	Minnesota	2	0	1	1	0	0	0	0
1979	Los Angeles	2	0	0	0	0	0	0	0
1980	Los Angeles	4	0	0	0	2	0	0	0
1981	Los Angeles	4	0	2	2	7	0	0	0
Playoff Totals		**12**	**0**	**3**	**3**	**9**	**0**	**0**	**0**
JEREMIAH, Ed *No Playoffs*	Right wing/Defense								
JERRARD, Paul *No Playoffs*	Defense								
JERWA, Frank *No Playoffs*	Left wing/Defense								
JERWA, Joe	Defense								
1931	NY Rangers	4	0	0	0	4	....	....	....
1936	NY Americans	5	2	3	5	2	....	....	....
1938	NY Americans	6	0	0	0	8	....	....	....
1939	NY Americans	2	0	0	0	2	....	....	....
Playoff Totals		**17**	**2**	**3**	**5**	**16**	....	....	....
•JILLSON, Jeff	Defense								
2002	San Jose	4	0	0	0	0	0	0	0
Playoff Totals		**4**	**0**	**0**	**0**	**0**	**0**	**0**	**0**
JIRIK, Jaroslav *No Playoffs*	left wing								
JOANETTE, Rosario *No Playoffs*	Center								
JODZIO, Rick *No Playoffs*	Left wing								
JOHANNESEN, Glenn *No Playoffs*	Left wing								
JOHANNSON, John *No Playoffs*	Center								
JOHANSEN, Bill *No Playoffs*	Center/Right wing								
JOHANSEN, Trevor	Defense								
1978	Toronto	13	0	3	3	21	0	0	0
Playoff Totals		**13**	**0**	**3**	**3**	**21**	**0**	**0**	**0**
•JOHANSSON, Andreas	Center								
1998	Pittsburgh	1	0	0	0	0	0	0	0
1999	Ottawa	2	0	0	0	0	0	0	0
Playoff Totals		**3**	**0**	**0**	**0**	**0**	**0**	**0**	**0**
JOHANSSON, Bjorn *No Playoffs*	Defense								
•JOHANSSON, Calle	Defense								
1988	Buffalo	6	0	1	1	0	0	0	0
1989	Washington	6	1	2	3	0	1	0	0
1990	Washington	15	1	6	7	4	0	0	0
1991	Washington	10	2	7	9	8	1	0	0
1992	Washington	7	0	5	5	4	0	0	0
1993	Washington	6	0	5	5	4	0	0	0
1994	Washington	6	1	3	4	4	0	0	1
1995	Washington	7	3	1	4	0	1	0	0
1998	Washington	21	2	8	10	16	0	0	0
2000	Washington	5	1	2	3	0	1	0	0
2001	Washington	6	1	2	3	2	0	0	0
Playoff Totals		**95**	**12**	**42**	**54**	**42**	**4**	**0**	**1**
•JOHANSSON, Mathias *No Playoffs*	Center								
JOHANSSON, Roger	Defense								
1993	Calgary	5	0	1	1	2	0	0	0
Playoff Totals		**5**	**0**	**1**	**1**	**2**	**0**	**0**	**0**
JOHNS, Don *No Playoffs*	Defense								
JOHNSON, Allan	Right wing/Center								
1961	Detroit	11	2	2	4	6	0	0	1
Playoff Totals		**11**	**2**	**2**	**4**	**6**	**0**	**0**	**1**
JOHNSON, Brian *No Playoffs*	Right wing								
JOHNSON, Ching	Defense								
1927	NY Rangers	2	0	0	0	8	....	....	....
1928◆	NY Rangers	9	1	1	2	*46	....	....	....
1929	NY Rangers	6	0	0	0	26	....	....	....
1930	NY Rangers	4	0	0	0	14	....	....	....
1931	NY Rangers	4	1	0	1	17	....	....	....
1932	NY Rangers	7	2	0	2	*24	....	....	....
1933◆	NY Rangers	8	1	0	1	14	....	....	....
1934	NY Rangers	2	0	0	0	4	....	....	....
1935	NY Rangers	4	0	0	0	2	....	....	....
1937	NY Rangers	9	0	1	1	4	....	....	....
1938	NY Americans	6	0	0	0	2	....	....	....
Playoff Totals		**61**	**5**	**2**	**7**	**161**	....	....	....

Season	Team	GP	G	A	Pts	PIM	PP	SH	GW
•JOHNSON, Craig	Left wing								
1995	St. Louis	1	0	0	0	2	0	0	0
1998	Los Angeles	4	1	0	1	4	0	0	0
2000	Los Angeles	4	1	0	1	2	0	0	0
2002	Los Angeles	7	1	2	3	2	0	0	1
Playoff Totals		**16**	**3**	**2**	**5**	**10**	**0**	**0**	**1**
JOHNSON, Danny *No Playoffs*	Center								
JOHNSON, Earl *No Playoffs*	Left wing								
•JOHNSON, Greg	Center								
1994	Detroit	7	2	2	4	2	1	0	0
1995	Detroit	1	0	0	0	0	0	0	0
1996	Detroit	13	3	1	4	8	0	0	0
1997	Pittsburgh	5	1	0	1	2	0	0	0
Playoff Totals		**26**	**6**	**3**	**9**	**12**	**1**	**0**	**0**
JOHNSON, Jim	Center								
1969	Philadelphia	3	0	0	0	2	0	0	0
1971	Philadelphia	4	0	2	2	0	0	0	0
Playoff Totals		**7**	**0**	**2**	**2**	**2**	**0**	**0**	**0**
JOHNSON, Jim	Defense								
1989	Pittsburgh	11	0	5	5	44	0	0	0
1991	Minnesota	14	0	1	1	52	0	0	0
1992	Minnesota	7	1	3	4	18	0	0	0
1995	Washington	7	0	2	2	8	0	0	0
1996	Washington	6	0	0	0	6	0	0	0
1997	Phoenix	6	0	0	0	4	0	0	0
Playoff Totals		**51**	**1**	**11**	**12**	**132**	**0**	**0**	**0**
JOHNSON, Mark	Center								
1980	Pittsburgh	5	2	2	4	0	1	0	1
1981	Pittsburgh	5	2	1	3	6	1	0	0
1982	Minnesota	4	2	0	2	0	1	0	0
1985	St. Louis	3	0	1	1	0	0	0	0
1988	New Jersey	18	10	8	18	4	5	0	1
1990	New Jersey	2	0	0	0	0	0	0	0
Playoff Totals		**37**	**16**	**12**	**28**	**10**	**8**	**0**	**2**
•JOHNSON, Matt	Left wing								
1998	Los Angeles	4	0	0	0	6	0	0	0
Playoff Totals		**4**	**0**	**0**	**0**	**6**	**0**	**0**	**0**
•JOHNSON, Mike	Right wing								
1999	Toronto	17	3	2	5	4	0	0	1
2002	Phoenix	5	1	1	2	6	0	0	0
Playoff Totals		**22**	**4**	**3**	**7**	**10**	**0**	**0**	**1**
JOHNSON, Norm	Center								
1958	Boston	12	4	0	4	6	....	....	....
1960	Chicago	2	0	0	0	0	....	....	....
Playoff Totals		**14**	**4**	**0**	**4**	**6**	....	....	....
•JOHNSON, Ryan *No Playoffs*	Center								
JOHNSON, Terry	Defense								
1981	Quebec	2	0	0	0	0	0	0	0
1984	St. Louis	11	0	1	1	25	0	0	0
1985	St. Louis	3	0	0	0	19	0	0	0
1986	Calgary	17	0	3	3	64	0	0	0
1987	Toronto	2	0	0	0	0	0	0	0
1988	Toronto	3	0	0	0	10	0	0	0
Playoff Totals		**38**	**0**	**4**	**4**	**118**	**0**	**0**	**0**
JOHNSON, Tom	Defense								
1950	Montreal	1	0	0	0	0	....	....	....
1951	Montreal	11	0	0	0	6	....	....	....
1952	Montreal	11	1	0	1	2	....	....	....
1953◆	Montreal	12	2	3	5	8	....	....	....
1954	Montreal	11	1	2	3	30	....	....	....
1955	Montreal	12	2	0	2	22	....	....	....
1956◆	Montreal	10	0	2	2	8	....	....	....
1957◆	Montreal	10	0	2	2	13	....	....	....
1958◆	Montreal	2	0	0	0	0	....	....	....
1959◆	Montreal	11	2	3	5	8	....	....	....
1960◆	Montreal	8	0	1	1	4	....	....	....
1961	Montreal	6	0	1	1	8	....	....	....
1962	Montreal	6	0	1	1	0	....	....	....
Playoff Totals		**111**	**8**	**15**	**23**	**109**	....	....	....
JOHNSON, Virgil	Defense								
1938◆	Chicago	10	0	0	0	0	0	0	0
1944	Chicago	9	0	3	3	4	0	0	0
Playoff Totals		**19**	**0**	**3**	**3**	**4**	**0**	**0**	**0**
•JOHNSSON, Kim	Defense								
2002	Philadelphia	5	0	0	0	2	0	0	0
Playoff Totals		**5**	**0**	**0**	**0**	**2**	**0**	**0**	**0**
JOHNSTON, Bernie	Center								
1980	Hartford	3	0	1	1	0	0	0	0
Playoff Totals		**3**	**0**	**1**	**1**	**0**	**0**	**0**	**0**
JOHNSTON, George *No Playoffs*	Right wing								
JOHNSTON, Greg	Right wing								
1987	Boston	4	0	0	0	0	0	0	0
1988	Boston	3	0	1	1	2	0	0	0
1989	Boston	10	1	0	1	6	0	1	0
1990	Boston	5	1	0	1	4	0	0	1
Playoff Totals		**22**	**2**	**1**	**3**	**12**	**0**	**1**	**1**
JOHNSTON, Jay *No Playoffs*	Defense								
JOHNSTON, Joey *No Playoffs*	Left wing								

Season	Team	GP	G	A	Pts	PIM	PP	SH	GW
JOHNSTON, Larry *No Playoffs*	Defense								
JOHNSTON, Marshall	Defense								
1970	Minnesota	6	0	0	0	2	0	0	0
Playoff Totals		**6**	**0**	**0**	**0**	**2**	**0**	**0**	**0**
JOHNSTON, Randy *No Playoffs*	Defense								
JOHNSTONE, Eddie	Right wing								
1979	NY Rangers	17	5	0	5	10	0	1	1
1980	NY Rangers	9	0	1	1	25	0	0	0
1981	NY Rangers	8	2	2	4	4	0	0	1
1982	NY Rangers	10	2	6	8	25	1	0	0
1983	NY Rangers	9	4	1	5	19	1	1	0
1984	Detroit	2	0	0	0	0	0	0	0
Playoff Totals		**55**	**13**	**10**	**23**	**83**	**2**	**2**	**2**
JOHNSTONE, Ross	Defense								
1944	Toronto	3	0	0	0	0	0	0	0
1945◆	Toronto	....	....	....	....	....	....	....	....
Playoff Totals		**3**	**0**	**0**	**0**	**0**	**0**	**0**	**0**
•JOKELA, Mikko *No Playoffs*	Defense								
•JOKINEN, Olli *No Playoffs*	Center								
JOLIAT, Aurel	Left wing								
1923	Montreal	2	1	0	1	11	....	....	....
1924◆	Montreal	2	1	1	2	0	....	....	....
1925	Montreal	1	0	0	0	5	....	....	....
1927	Montreal	4	1	0	1	10	....	....	....
1928	Montreal	2	0	0	0	4	....	....	....
1929	Montreal	3	1	1	2	10	....	....	....
1930◆	Montreal	6	0	2	2	6	....	....	....
1931◆	Montreal	10	0	*4	4	12	....	....	....
1932	Montreal	4	2	0	2	4	....	....	....
1933	Montreal	2	2	1	3	2	....	....	....
1934	Montreal	3	0	1	1	0	....	....	....
1935	Montreal	2	1	0	1	0	....	....	....
1937	Montreal	5	0	3	3	2	....	....	....
Playoff Totals		**46**	**9**	**13**	**22**	**66**	....	....	....
JOLIAT, Rene *No Playoffs*	Right wing/Defense								
JOLY, Greg	Defense								
1978	Detroit	5	0	0	0	8	0	0	0
Playoff Totals		**5**	**0**	**0**	**0**	**8**	**0**	**0**	**0**
JOLY, Yvan	Right wing								
1980	Montreal	1	0	0	0	0	0	0	0
Playoff Totals		**1**	**0**	**0**	**0**	**0**	**0**	**0**	**0**
JOMPHE, Jean-Francois *No Playoffs*	Center								
JONATHAN, Stan	Left wing								
1977	Boston	14	4	2	6	24	0	0	1
1978	Boston	15	0	1	1	36	0	0	0
1979	Boston	11	4	1	5	12	0	0	0
1980	Boston	9	0	0	0	29	0	0	0
1981	Boston	3	0	0	0	30	0	0	0
1982	Boston	11	0	0	0	6	0	0	0
Playoff Totals		**63**	**8**	**4**	**12**	**137**	**0**	**0**	**1**
JONES, Bob *No Playoffs*	Left wing								
JONES, Brad	Left wing								
1988	Winnipeg	1	0	0	0	0	0	0	0
1991	Los Angeles	8	1	1	2	2	0	0	1
Playoff Totals		**9**	**1**	**1**	**2**	**2**	**0**	**0**	**1**
JONES, Buck	Defense								
1939	Detroit	6	0	1	1	10	0	0	0
1943	Toronto	6	0	0	0	8	0	0	0
Playoff Totals		**12**	**0**	**1**	**1**	**18**	**0**	**0**	**0**
JONES, Jim *No Playoffs*	Defense								
JONES, Jimmy	Right wing								
1978	Toronto	13	1	5	6	7	0	0	0
1979	Toronto	6	0	0	0	4	0	0	0
Playoff Totals		**19**	**1**	**5**	**6**	**11**	**0**	**0**	**0**
JONES, Keith	Right wing								
1993	Washington	6	0	0	0	10	0	0	0
1994	Washington	11	0	1	1	36	0	0	0
1995	Washington	7	4	4	8	22	1	0	0
1996	Washington	2	0	0	0	7	0	0	0
1997	Colorado	6	3	3	6	4	1	0	0
1998	Colorado	7	0	0	0	13	0	0	0
1999	Philadelphia	6	2	1	3	14	0	0	0
2000	Philadelphia	18	3	3	6	14	1	0	0
Playoff Totals		**63**	**12**	**12**	**24**	**120**	**3**	**0**	**0**
JONES, Ron *No Playoffs*	Defense								
•JONES, Ty *No Playoffs*	Right wing								
•JONSSON, Hans	Defense								
2000	Pittsburgh	11	0	1	1	6	0	0	0
2001	Pittsburgh	16	0	0	0	8	0	0	0
Playoff Totals		**27**	**0**	**1**	**1**	**14**	**0**	**0**	**0**
•JONSSON, Jorgen *No Playoffs*	Left wing								
•JONSSON, Kenny	Defense								
1995	Toronto	4	0	0	0	0	0	0	0
2002	NY Islanders	5	1	2	3	4	1	0	0
Playoff Totals		**9**	**1**	**2**	**3**	**4**	**1**	**0**	**0**

Season	Team	GP	G	A	Pts	PIM	PP	SH	GW
JONSSON, Tomas									Defense
1982♦	NY Islanders	10	0	2	2	21	0	0	0
1983♦	NY Islanders	20	2	10	12	18	0	0	0
1984	NY Islanders	21	3	5	8	22	2	0	0
1985	NY Islanders	7	1	2	3	10	1	0	0
1986	NY Islanders	3	0	1	1	4	0	0	0
1987	NY Islanders	10	1	4	5	6	1	0	0
1988	NY Islanders	5	2	2	4	10	1	0	0
1989	Edmonton	4	2	0	2	6	2	0	0
Playoff Totals		**80**	**11**	**26**	**37**	**97**	**7**	**0**	**0**
•JOSEPH, Chris									Defense
1992	Edmonton	5	1	3	4	2	0	0	0
1995	Pittsburgh	10	1	1	2	12	0	0	0
1996	Pittsburgh	15	1	0	1	8	0	0	0
1998	Philadelphia	1	0	0	0	2	0	0	0
Playoff Totals		**31**	**3**	**4**	**7**	**24**	**0**	**0**	**0**
JOSEPH, Tony *No Playoffs*									Right wing
•JOVANOVSKI, Ed									Defense
1996	Florida	22	1	8	9	52	0	0	0
1997	Florida	5	0	0	0	4	0	0	0
2001	Vancouver	4	1	1	2	0	0	0	0
2002	Vancouver	6	1	4	5	8	1	0	0
Playoff Totals		**37**	**3**	**13**	**16**	**64**	**1**	**0**	**0**
JOYAL, Eddie									Center
1963	Detroit	11	1	0	1	2	1	0	0
1964	Detroit	14	2	3	5	10	0	0	1
1965	Detroit	7	1	1	2	4	1	0	0
1968	Los Angeles	7	4	1	5	2	3	0	1
1969	Los Angeles	11	3	3	6	0	1	0	0
Playoff Totals		**50**	**11**	**8**	**19**	**18**	**6**	**0**	**2**
JOYCE, Bob									Left wing
1988	Boston	23	8	6	14	18	3	0	1
1989	Boston	9	5	2	7	2	0	0	0
1990	Washington	14	2	1	3	9	0	0	0
Playoff Totals		**46**	**15**	**9**	**24**	**29**	**3**	**0**	**1**
JOYCE, Duane *No Playoffs*									Defense
JUCKES, Bing *No Playoffs*									Left wing
JUHLIN, Patrik									Left wing
1995	Philadelphia	13	1	0	1	2	0	0	0
Playoff Totals		**13**	**1**	**0**	**1**	**2**	**0**	**0**	**0**
JULIEN, Claude *No Playoffs*									Defense
•JUNEAU, Joe									Center
1992	Boston	15	4	8	12	21	2	0	0
1993	Boston	4	2	4	6	6	2	0	0
1994	Washington	11	4	5	9	6	2	0	1
1995	Washington	7	2	6	8	2	0	0	0
1996	Washington	5	0	7	7	6	0	0	0
1998	Washington	21	7	10	17	8	1	1	4
1999	Buffalo	20	3	8	11	10	0	1	0
2000	Ottawa	6	2	1	3	0	0	0	0
2002	Montreal	12	1	4	5	6	0	0	0
Playoff Totals		**101**	**25**	**53**	**78**	**65**	**7**	**2**	**5**
JUNKER, Steve									Left wing
1993	NY Islanders	3	0	1	1	0	0	0	0
Playoff Totals		**3**	**0**	**1**	**1**	**0**	**0**	**0**	**0**
JUTILA, Timo *No Playoffs*									Defense
JUZDA, Bill									Defense
1942	NY Rangers	6	0	1	1	4	0	0	0
1948	NY Rangers	6	0	0	0	9	0	0	0
1949♦	Toronto	9	0	2	2	8	0	0	0
1950	Toronto	7	0	0	0	16	0	0	0
1951♦	Toronto	11	0	0	0	7	0	0	0
1952	Toronto	3	0	0	0	2	0	0	0
Playoff Totals		**42**	**0**	**3**	**3**	**46**	**0**	**0**	**0**
KABEL, Bob *No Playoffs*									Center
•KABERLE, Frantisek *No Playoffs*									Defense
•KABERLE, Tomas									Defense
1999	Toronto	14	0	3	3	2	0	0	0
2000	Toronto	12	1	4	5	0	0	0	1
2001	Toronto	11	1	3	4	0	0	0	1
2002	Toronto	20	2	8	10	16	0	0	0
Playoff Totals		**57**	**4**	**18**	**22**	**18**	**0**	**0**	**2**
KACHOWSKI, Mark *No Playoffs*									Left wing
KACHUR, Ed *No Playoffs*									Right wing
KAESE, Trent *No Playoffs*									Right wing
KAISER, Vern									Left wing
1951	Montreal	2	0	0	0	0	0	0	0
Playoff Totals		**2**	**0**	**0**	**0**	**0**	**0**	**0**	**0**
KALBFLEISH, Walter									Defense
1936	NY Americans	5	0	0	0	2	0	0	0
Playoff Totals		**5**	**0**	**0**	**0**	**2**	**0**	**0**	**0**
KALETA, Alex									Left wing
1942	Chicago	3	1	2	3	0	....	....	....
1946	Chicago	4	0	1	1	2	....	....	....
1950	NY Rangers	10	0	3	3	0	....	....	....
Playoff Totals		**17**	**1**	**6**	**7**	**2**	....	....	....

Season	Team	GP	G	A	Pts	PIM	PP	SH	GW
•KALININ, Dmitri									Defense
2001	Buffalo	13	0	2	2	4	0	0	0
Playoff Totals		**13**	**0**	**2**	**2**	**4**	**0**	**0**	**0**
•KALLIO, Tomi *No Playoffs*									Left wing
KALLUR, Anders									Right wing
1980♦	NY Islanders	....	....	....	....	....	....	....	....
1981♦	NY Islanders	12	4	3	7	10	0	2	0
1982♦	NY Islanders	19	1	6	7	8	0	1	0
1983♦	NY Islanders	20	3	12	15	12	1	1	0
1984	NY Islanders	17	2	2	4	2	0	1	1
1985	NY Islanders	10	2	0	2	0	0	0	0
Playoff Totals		**78**	**12**	**23**	**35**	**32**	**1**	**5**	**1**
•KAMENSKY, Valeri									Left wing
1993	Quebec	6	0	1	1	6	0	0	0
1995	Quebec	2	1	0	1	0	0	0	0
1996♦	Colorado	22	10	12	22	28	3	0	2
1997	Colorado	17	8	14	22	16	5	0	2
1998	Colorado	7	2	3	5	18	1	0	0
1999	Colorado	10	4	5	9	4	1	0	1
2002	New Jersey	2	0	0	0	0	0	0	0
Playoff Totals		**66**	**25**	**35**	**60**	**72**	**10**	**0**	**5**
KAMINSKI, Kevin									Center
1995	Washington	5	0	0	0	36	0	0	0
1996	Washington	3	0	0	0	16	0	0	0
Playoff Totals		**8**	**0**	**0**	**0**	**52**	**0**	**0**	**0**
KAMINSKY, Max									Center
1935	Boston	4	0	0	0	0	0	0	0
Playoff Totals		**4**	**0**	**0**	**0**	**0**	**0**	**0**	**0**
KAMINSKY, Yan									Right wing
1994	NY Islanders	2	0	0	0	4	0	0	0
Playoff Totals		**2**	**0**	**0**	**0**	**4**	**0**	**0**	**0**
KAMPMAN, Bingo									Defense
1938	Toronto	7	0	1	1	6	....	....	....
1939	Toronto	10	1	1	2	20	....	....	....
1940	Toronto	10	0	0	0	0	....	....	....
1941	Toronto	7	0	0	0	0	....	....	....
1942♦	Toronto	13	0	2	2	12	....	....	....
Playoff Totals		**47**	**1**	**4**	**5**	**38**	....	....	....
KANE, Francis *No Playoffs*									Defense
KANNEGIESSER, Gord *No Playoffs*									Defense
KANNEGIESSER, Sheldon									Defense
1973	NY Rangers	1	0	0	0	2	0	0	0
1974	Los Angeles	5	0	1	1	0	0	0	0
1975	Los Angeles	3	0	1	1	4	0	0	0
1976	Los Angeles	9	0	0	0	4	0	0	0
Playoff Totals		**18**	**0**	**2**	**2**	**10**	**0**	**0**	**0**
•KAPANEN, Niko *No Playoffs*									Center
•KAPANEN, Sami									Left wing
1999	Carolina	5	1	1	2	0	0	0	0
2001	Carolina	6	2	3	5	0	1	0	0
2002	Carolina	23	1	8	9	6	0	0	0
Playoff Totals		**34**	**4**	**12**	**16**	**6**	**1**	**0**	**0**
KARABIN, Ladislav *No Playoffs*									Left wing
•KARALAHTI, Jere									Defense
2000	Los Angeles	4	0	1	1	2	0	0	0
2001	Los Angeles	13	0	0	0	18	0	0	0
Playoff Totals		**17**	**0**	**1**	**1**	**20**	**0**	**0**	**0**
KARAMNOV, Vitali									Left wing
1995	St. Louis	2	0	0	0	2	0	0	0
Playoff Totals		**2**	**0**	**0**	**0**	**2**	**0**	**0**	**0**
•KARIYA, Paul									Left wing
1997	Anaheim	11	7	6	13	4	4	0	1
1999	Anaheim	3	1	3	4	0	0	0	0
Playoff Totals		**14**	**8**	**9**	**17**	**4**	**4**	**0**	**1**
•KARIYA, Steve *No Playoffs*									Left wing
KARJALAINEN, Kyosti									Right wing
1992	Los Angeles	3	0	1	1	2	0	0	0
Playoff Totals		**3**	**0**	**1**	**1**	**2**	**0**	**0**	**0**
KARLANDER, Al									Center
1970	Detroit	4	0	1	1	0	0	0	0
Playoff Totals		**4**	**0**	**1**	**1**	**0**	**0**	**0**	**0**
•KARLSSON, Andreas *No Playoffs*									Center
•KARPA, Dave									Defense
1993	Quebec	3	0	0	0	0	0	0	0
1997	Anaheim	8	1	1	2	20	0	0	1
1999	Carolina	2	0	0	0	2	0	0	0
2001	Carolina	6	0	0	0	17	0	0	0
Playoff Totals		**19**	**1**	**1**	**2**	**39**	**0**	**0**	**1**
KARPOV, Valeri *No Playoffs*									Right wing

Season	Team	GP	G	A	Pts	PIM	PP	SH	GW
•KARPOVTSEV, Alexander									Defense
1994♦	NY Rangers	17	0	4	4	12	0	0	0
1995	NY Rangers	8	1	0	1	0	0	0	0
1996	NY Rangers	6	0	1	1	4	0	0	0
1997	NY Rangers	13	1	3	4	20	1	0	0
1999	Toronto	14	1	3	4	12	1	0	0
2000	Toronto	11	0	3	3	4	0	0	0
2002	Chicago	5	1	0	1	0	0	0	1
Playoff Totals		**74**	**4**	**14**	**18**	**52**	**2**	**0**	**1**
KASATONOV, Alexei									Defense
1990	New Jersey	6	0	3	3	14	0	0	0
1991	New Jersey	7	1	3	4	10	0	0	0
1992	New Jersey	7	1	1	2	12	0	0	0
1993	New Jersey	4	0	0	0	0	0	0	0
1994	St. Louis	4	2	0	2	2	0	0	0
1995	Boston	5	0	0	0	2	0	0	0
Playoff Totals		**33**	**4**	**7**	**11**	**40**	**0**	**0**	**0**
•KASPARAITIS, Darius									Defense
1993	NY Islanders	18	0	5	5	31	0	0	0
1994	NY Islanders	4	0	0	0	8	0	0	0
1997	Pittsburgh	5	0	0	0	6	0	0	0
1998	Pittsburgh	5	0	0	0	8	0	0	0
2000	Pittsburgh	11	1	1	2	10	0	0	0
2001	Pittsburgh	17	1	1	2	26	0	0	1
2002	Colorado	21	0	3	3	18	0	0	0
Playoff Totals		**81**	**2**	**10**	**12**	**107**	**0**	**0**	**1**
KASPER, Steve									Center
1981	Boston	3	0	1	1	0	0	0	0
1982	Boston	11	3	6	9	22	1	0	0
1983	Boston	12	2	1	3	10	0	1	0
1984	Boston	3	0	0	0	7	0	0	0
1985	Boston	5	1	0	1	9	0	0	0
1986	Boston	3	1	0	1	4	0	1	0
1987	Boston	3	0	2	2	0	0	0	0
1988	Boston	23	7	6	13	10	0	1	0
1989	Los Angeles	11	1	5	6	10	0	0	0
1990	Los Angeles	10	1	1	2	2	0	0	0
1991	Los Angeles	10	4	6	10	8	0	1	0
Playoff Totals		**94**	**20**	**28**	**48**	**82**	**1**	**4**	**0**
KASTELIC, Ed									Wing
1987	Washington	5	1	0	1	13	1	0	0
1988	Washington	1	0	0	0	19	0	0	0
1990	Hartford	2	0	0	0	0	0	0	0
Playoff Totals		**8**	**1**	**0**	**1**	**32**	**1**	**0**	**0**
KASZYCKI, Mike									Center
1978	NY Islanders	7	1	3	4	4	0	0	0
1979	NY Islanders	10	1	3	4	4	0	0	0
1980	Toronto	2	0	0	0	2	0	0	0
Playoff Totals		**19**	**2**	**6**	**8**	**10**	**0**	**0**	**0**
•KAVANAGH, Pat									Right wing
2001	Vancouver	3	0	0	0	2	0	0	0
Playoff Totals		**3**	**0**	**0**	**0**	**2**	**0**	**0**	**0**
KEA, Ed									Defense
1976	Atlanta	2	0	0	0	7	0	0	0
1977	Atlanta	3	0	1	1	2	0	0	0
1978	Atlanta	1	0	0	0	0	0	0	0
1979	Atlanta	2	0	0	0	0	0	0	0
1980	St. Louis	3	0	0	0	2	0	0	0
1981	St. Louis	11	1	2	3	12	0	0	0
1982	St. Louis	10	1	1	2	16	0	0	0
Playoff Totals		**32**	**2**	**4**	**6**	**39**	**0**	**0**	**0**
•KEANE, Mike									Right wing
1989	Montreal	21	4	3	7	17	2	0	0
1990	Montreal	11	0	1	1	8	0	0	0
1991	Montreal	12	3	2	5	6	0	0	0
1992	Montreal	8	1	1	2	16	0	0	0
1993♦	Montreal	19	2	13	15	6	0	0	0
1994	Montreal	6	3	1	4	4	0	0	0
1996♦	Colorado	22	3	2	5	16	0	0	1
1997	Colorado	17	3	1	4	24	0	0	1
1998	Dallas	17	4	4	8	0	0	1	1
1999♦	Dallas	23	5	2	7	6	0	1	1
2000	Dallas	23	2	4	6	14	0	0	0
2001	Dallas	10	3	2	5	4	0	0	0
2002	Colorado	18	1	4	5	8	0	0	0
Playoff Totals		**207**	**34**	**40**	**74**	**129**	**2**	**2**	**4**
KEARNS, Dennis									Defense
1975	Vancouver	4	0	0	0	4	0	0	0
1976	Vancouver	2	0	1	1	0	0	0	0
1979	Vancouver	3	1	1	2	2	1	0	0
1980	Vancouver	2	0	0	0	2	0	0	0
Playoff Totals		**11**	**1**	**2**	**3**	**8**	**1**	**0**	**0**
KEATING, Jack *No Playoffs*									Left wing
KEATING, John *No Playoffs*									Left wing
KEATING, Mike *No Playoffs*									Left wing
KEATS, Duke *No Playoffs*									Center

Season	Team	GP	G	A	Pts	PIM	PP	SH	GW
KECZMER, Dan	Defense								
1994	Calgary	3	0	0	0	4	0	0	0
1995	Calgary	7	0	1	1	2	0	0	0
1998	Dallas	2	0	0	0	2	0	0	0
Playoff Totals		**12**	**0**	**1**	**1**	**8**	**0**	**0**	**0**
•KEEFE, Sheldon *No Playoffs*	Right wing								
KEELING, Butch	Left wing								
1929	NY Rangers	6	*3	0	*3	2	....	....	....
1930	NY Rangers	4	0	3	3	8	....	....	....
1931	NY Rangers	4	1	1	2	0	....	....	....
1932	NY Rangers	7	2	1	3	12	....	....	....
1933♦	NY Rangers	8	0	2	2	8	....	....	....
1934	NY Rangers	2	0	0	0	0	....	....	....
1935	NY Rangers	4	2	1	3	0	....	....	....
1937	NY Rangers	9	3	2	5	2	....	....	....
1938	NY Rangers	3	0	1	1	2	....	....	....
Playoff Totals		**47**	**11**	**11**	**22**	**34**	....	....	....
KEENAN, Larry	Left wing								
1968	St. Louis	18	4	5	9	4	1	0	2
1969	St. Louis	12	4	5	9	8	1	2	0
1970	St. Louis	16	7	6	13	0	4	2	0
Playoff Totals		**46**	**15**	**16**	**31**	**12**	**6**	**4**	**2**
KEHOE, Rick	Right wing								
1972	Toronto	2	0	0	0	2	0	0	0
1975	Pittsburgh	9	0	2	2	0	0	0	0
1976	Pittsburgh	3	0	0	0	0	0	0	0
1977	Pittsburgh	3	0	2	2	0	0	0	0
1979	Pittsburgh	7	0	2	2	0	0	0	0
1980	Pittsburgh	5	2	5	7	0	2	0	0
1981	Pittsburgh	5	0	3	3	0	0	0	0
1982	Pittsburgh	5	2	3	5	2	0	0	2
Playoff Totals		**39**	**4**	**17**	**21**	**4**	**2**	**0**	**2**
KEKALAINEN, Jarmo *No Playoffs*	Left wing								
•KELLEHER, Chris *No Playoffs*	Defense								
KELLER, Ralph *No Playoffs*	Defense								
KELLGREN, Christer *No Playoffs*	Right wing								
KELLY, Bob	Left wing								
1975	Pittsburgh	9	5	3	8	17	1	0	0
1976	Pittsburgh	3	0	0	0	2	0	0	0
1977	Pittsburgh	3	1	0	1	4	0	0	0
1978	Chicago	4	0	0	0	8	0	0	0
1979	Chicago	4	0	0	0	9	0	0	0
Playoff Totals		**23**	**6**	**3**	**9**	**40**	**1**	**0**	**0**
KELLY, Bob	Left wing								
1971	Philadelphia	4	1	0	1	2	0	0	0
1973	Philadelphia	11	0	1	1	8	0	0	0
1974♦	Philadelphia	5	0	0	0	11	0	0	0
1975♦	Philadelphia	16	3	3	6	15	0	0	1
1976	Philadelphia	16	0	2	2	44	0	0	0
1977	Philadelphia	10	0	1	1	18	0	0	0
1978	Philadelphia	12	3	5	8	26	0	0	0
1979	Philadelphia	8	1	1	2	10	1	0	0
1980	Philadelphia	19	1	1	2	38	0	0	0
Playoff Totals		**101**	**9**	**14**	**23**	**172**	**1**	**0**	**1**
KELLY, Dave *No Playoffs*	Right wing								
KELLY, John Paul	Left wing								
1980	Los Angeles	3	0	0	0	2	0	0	0
1981	Los Angeles	4	0	1	1	25	0	0	0
1982	Los Angeles	10	1	0	1	14	1	0	0
1985	Los Angeles	1	0	0	0	0	0	0	0
Playoff Totals		**18**	**1**	**1**	**2**	**41**	**1**	**0**	**0**
KELLY, Pep	Right wing								
1935	Toronto	7	2	0	2	4	....	....	....
1936	Toronto	9	2	3	5	4	....	....	....
1938	Toronto	7	2	2	4	2	....	....	....
1939	Toronto	9	1	0	1	0	....	....	....
1940	Toronto	6	0	1	1	0	....	....	....
Playoff Totals		**38**	**7**	**6**	**13**	**10**	....	....	....
KELLY, Pete	Right wing								
1936♦	Detroit	7	1	1	2	2	....	....	....
1937♦	Detroit	8	2	0	2	0	....	....	....
1939	Detroit	4	0	0	0	0	....	....	....
Playoff Totals		**19**	**3**	**1**	**4**	**2**	....	....	....

Season	Team	GP	G	A	Pts	PIM	PP	SH	GW
KELLY, Red	Defense/Center								
1948	Detroit	10	3	2	5	2	....	....	....
1949	Detroit	11	1	1	2	10	....	....	....
1950♦	Detroit	14	1	3	4	2	....	....	....
1951	Detroit	6	0	1	1	0	....	....	....
1952♦	Detroit	5	1	0	1	0	....	....	....
1953	Detroit	6	0	4	4	0	....	....	....
1954♦	Detroit	12	5	1	6	0	....	....	....
1955♦	Detroit	11	2	4	6	17	....	....	....
1956	Detroit	10	2	4	6	2	....	....	....
1957	Detroit	5	1	0	1	0	....	....	....
1958	Detroit	4	0	1	1	2	....	....	....
1960	Toronto	10	3	8	11	2	....	....	....
1961	Toronto	2	1	0	1	0	....	....	....
1962♦	Toronto	12	4	6	10	0	....	....	....
1963♦	Toronto	10	2	6	8	6	....	....	....
1964♦	Toronto	14	4	9	13	4	....	....	....
1965	Toronto	6	3	2	5	2	....	....	....
1966	Toronto	4	0	2	2	0	....	....	....
1967♦	Toronto	12	0	5	5	2	....	....	....
Playoff Totals		**164**	**33**	**59**	**92**	**51**	....	....	....
•KELLY, Steve	Center								
1997	Edmonton	6	0	0	0	2	0	0	0
2000♦	New Jersey	10	0	0	0	4	0	0	0
2001	Los Angeles	8	0	0	0	2	0	0	0
2002	Los Angeles	1	0	0	0	0	0	0	0
Playoff Totals		**25**	**0**	**0**	**0**	**8**	**0**	**0**	**0**
KEMP, Kevin *No Playoffs*	Defense								
KEMP, Stan *No Playoffs*	Defense								
•KENADY, Chris *No Playoffs*	Right wing								
KENDALL, Bill	Right wing								
1934♦	Chicago	2	0	0	0	0	0	0	0
1935	Chicago	2	0	0	0	0	0	0	0
1936	Chicago	2	0	0	0	0	0	0	0
Playoff Totals		**6**	**0**	**0**	**0**	**0**	**0**	**0**	**0**
KENNEDY, Dean	Defense								
1987	Los Angeles	5	0	2	2	10	0	0	0
1988	Los Angeles	4	0	1	1	10	0	0	0
1989	Los Angeles	11	0	2	2	8	0	0	0
1990	Buffalo	6	1	1	2	12	0	0	0
1991	Buffalo	2	0	1	1	17	0	0	0
1992	Winnipeg	2	0	0	0	0	0	0	0
1993	Winnipeg	6	0	0	0	2	0	0	0
Playoff Totals		**36**	**1**	**7**	**8**	**59**	**0**	**0**	**0**
KENNEDY, Forbes	Center								
1958	Detroit	4	1	0	1	12	0	0	1
1968	Philadelphia	7	1	4	5	14	0	1	0
1969	Toronto	1	0	0	0	38	0	0	0
Playoff Totals		**12**	**2**	**4**	**6**	**64**	**0**	**1**	**1**
KENNEDY, Mike	Center								
1995	Dallas	5	0	0	0	9	0	0	0
Playoff Totals		**5**	**0**	**0**	**0**	**9**	**0**	**0**	**0**
KENNEDY, Sheldon	Right wing								
1993	Detroit	7	1	1	2	2	0	0	0
1994	Detroit	7	1	2	3	0	0	0	0
1995	Calgary	7	3	1	4	16	0	1	0
1996	Calgary	3	1	0	1	2	0	0	0
Playoff Totals		**24**	**6**	**4**	**10**	**20**	**0**	**1**	**0**
KENNEDY, Ted	Center								
1944	Toronto	5	1	1	2	4	....	....	....
1945♦	Toronto	13	*7	2	9	2	....	....	....
1947♦	Toronto	11	4	5	9	4	....	....	....
1948♦	Toronto	9	*8	6	*14	0	....	....	....
1949♦	Toronto	9	2	*6	8	2	....	....	....
1950	Toronto	7	1	2	3	8	....	....	....
1951♦	Toronto	11	4	5	9	6	....	....	....
1952	Toronto	4	0	0	0	4	....	....	....
1954	Toronto	5	1	1	2	2	....	....	....
1955	Toronto	4	1	3	4	0	....	....	....
Playoff Totals		**78**	**29**	**31**	**60**	**32**	....	....	....
KENNY, Ernest *No Playoffs*	Defense								
KEON, Dave	Center								
1961	Toronto	5	1	1	2	0	....	....	....
1962♦	Toronto	12	5	3	8	0	....	....	....
1963♦	Toronto	10	7	5	12	0	....	....	....
1964♦	Toronto	14	7	2	9	2	....	....	....
1965	Toronto	6	2	2	4	2	....	....	....
1966	Toronto	4	0	2	2	0	....	....	....
1967♦	Toronto	12	3	5	8	0	....	....	....
1969	Toronto	4	1	3	4	2	0	0	1
1971	Toronto	6	3	2	5	0	0	0	0
1972	Toronto	5	2	3	5	0	0	0	0
1974	Toronto	4	1	2	3	0	0	0	0
1975	Toronto	7	0	5	5	0	0	0	0
1980	Hartford	3	0	1	1	0	0	0	0
Playoff Totals		**92**	**32**	**36**	**68**	**6**	**0**	**0**	**1**
KERCH, Alexander *No Playoffs*	Left wing								

Season	Team	GP	G	A	Pts	PIM	PP	SH	GW
KERR, Alan	Right wing								
1985	NY Islanders	4	1	0	1	4	1	0	0
1986	NY Islanders	1	0	0	0	0	0	0	0
1987	NY Islanders	14	1	4	5	25	0	0	0
1988	NY Islanders	6	1	0	1	14	0	0	0
1990	NY Islanders	4	0	0	0	10	0	0	0
1992	Detroit	9	2	0	2	17	0	0	0
Playoff Totals		**38**	**5**	**4**	**9**	**70**	**1**	**0**	**0**
KERR, Reg	Left wing								
1979	Chicago	4	1	0	1	5	0	0	0
1981	Chicago	3	0	0	0	2	0	0	0
Playoff Totals		**7**	**1**	**0**	**1**	**7**	**0**	**0**	**0**
KERR, Tim	Center/Right wing								
1981	Philadelphia	10	1	3	4	2	1	0	0
1982	Philadelphia	4	0	2	2	2	0	0	0
1983	Philadelphia	2	2	0	2	0	0	0	0
1984	Philadelphia	3	0	0	0	0	0	0	0
1985	Philadelphia	12	10	4	14	13	4	0	1
1986	Philadelphia	5	3	3	6	8	1	0	0
1987	Philadelphia	12	8	5	13	2	5	0	3
1988	Philadelphia	6	1	3	4	4	1	0	0
1989	Philadelphia	19	14	11	25	27	8	0	2
1992	NY Rangers	8	1	0	1	0	1	0	0
Playoff Totals		**81**	**40**	**31**	**71**	**58**	**21**	**0**	**6**
KESA, Dan	Right wing								
1999	Pittsburgh	13	1	0	1	0	1	0	1
Playoff Totals		**13**	**1**	**0**	**1**	**0**	**1**	**0**	**1**
KESSELL, Rick *No Playoffs*	Center								
KETOLA, Veli-Pekka *No Playoffs*	Center								
KETTER, Kerry *No Playoffs*	Defense								
KHARIN, Sergei *No Playoffs*	Right wing								
•KHARITONOV, Alexander *No Playoffs*	Left wing								
•KHAVANOV, Alexander	Defense								
2001	St. Louis	15	3	2	5	14	1	0	0
2002	St. Louis	4	0	0	0	2	0	0	0
Playoff Totals		**19**	**3**	**2**	**5**	**16**	**1**	**0**	**0**
KHMYLEV, Yuri	Left wing								
1993	Buffalo	8	4	3	7	4	1	0	1
1994	Buffalo	7	3	1	4	8	0	0	0
1995	Buffalo	5	0	1	1	8	0	0	0
1996	St. Louis	6	1	1	2	4	0	0	1
Playoff Totals		**26**	**8**	**6**	**14**	**24**	**1**	**0**	**2**
•KHRISTICH, Dmitri	Left wing/Center								
1991	Washington	11	1	3	4	6	0	0	0
1992	Washington	7	3	2	5	15	3	0	1
1993	Washington	6	2	5	7	2	1	0	0
1994	Washington	11	2	3	5	10	0	0	0
1995	Washington	7	1	4	5	0	0	0	0
1998	Boston	6	2	2	4	2	2	0	0
1999	Boston	12	3	4	7	6	0	0	1
2000	Toronto	12	1	2	3	0	1	0	0
2001	Washington	3	0	0	0	0	0	0	0
Playoff Totals		**75**	**15**	**25**	**40**	**41**	**7**	**0**	**2**
KIDD, Ian *No Playoffs*	Defense								
KIESSLING, Udo *No Playoffs*	Defense								
•KILGER, Chad	Center								
1996	Winnipeg	4	1	0	1	0	0	0	1
1999	Edmonton	4	0	0	0	4	0	0	0
2000	Edmonton	3	0	0	0	0	0	0	0
2002	Montreal	12	0	1	1	9	0	0	0
Playoff Totals		**23**	**1**	**1**	**2**	**13**	**0**	**0**	**1**
KILREA, Brian *No Playoffs*	Center								
KILREA, Hec	Left wing								
1926	Ottawa	2	0	0	0	0	....	....	....
1927♦	Ottawa	6	1	1	2	4	....	....	....
1928	Ottawa	2	1	0	1	0	....	....	....
1930	Ottawa	2	0	0	0	4	....	....	....
1932	Detroit	2	0	0	0	0	....	....	....
1934	Toronto	5	2	0	2	2	....	....	....
1935	Toronto	6	0	0	0	4	....	....	....
1936♦	Detroit	7	0	3	3	2	....	....	....
1937♦	Detroit	10	3	1	4	2	....	....	....
1939	Detroit	6	1	2	3	0	....	....	....
Playoff Totals		**48**	**8**	**7**	**15**	**18**	....	....	....
KILREA, Ken	Left wing								
1939	Detroit	3	1	1	2	4	....	....	....
1940	Detroit	5	1	1	2	0	....	....	....
1941	Detroit	5	0	0	0	0	....	....	....
1944	Detroit	2	0	0	0	0	....	....	....
Playoff Totals		**15**	**2**	**2**	**4**	**4**	....	....	....
KILREA, Wally	Right wing/Center								
1930	Ottawa	2	0	0	0	0	....	....	....
1933	Mtl. Maroons	2	0	0	0	0	....	....	....
1934	Mtl. Maroons	4	0	0	0	0	....	....	....
1936♦	Detroit	7	2	2	4	2	....	....	....
1937♦	Detroit	10	0	2	2	4	....	....	....
Playoff Totals		**25**	**2**	**4**	**6**	**6**	....	....	....

Season	Team	GP	G	A	Pts	PIM	PP	SH	GW
KIMBLE, Darin	Right wing								
1991	St. Louis	13	0	0	0	38	0	0	0
1992	St. Louis	5	0	0	0	7	0	0	0
1993	Boston	4	0	0	0	2	0	0	0
1994	Chicago	1	0	0	0	5	0	0	0
Playoff Totals		**23**	**0**	**0**	**0**	**52**	**0**	**0**	**0**
KINDRACHUK, Orest	Center								
1974♦	Philadelphia	17	5	4	9	17	0	0	0
1975♦	Philadelphia	14	0	2	2	12	0	0	0
1976	Philadelphia	16	4	7	11	4	1	0	2
1977	Philadelphia	10	2	1	3	0	1	0	0
1978	Philadelphia	12	5	5	10	13	2	0	1
1979	Pittsburgh	7	4	1	5	7	0	0	1
Playoff Totals		**76**	**20**	**20**	**40**	**53**	**4**	**0**	**4**
•KING, Derek	Left wing								
1988	NY Islanders	5	0	2	2	2	0	0	0
1990	NY Islanders	4	0	0	0	4	0	0	0
1993	NY Islanders	18	3	11	14	14	0	0	0
1994	NY Islanders	4	0	1	1	0	0	0	0
1999	Toronto	16	1	3	4	4	0	0	0
Playoff Totals		**47**	**4**	**17**	**21**	**24**	**0**	**0**	**0**
KING, Frank *No Playoffs*	Center								
KING, Kris	Left wing								
1989	Detroit	2	0	0	0	2	0	0	0
1990	NY Rangers	10	0	1	1	38	0	0	0
1991	NY Rangers	6	2	0	2	36	0	0	1
1992	NY Rangers	13	4	1	5	14	0	0	3
1993	Winnipeg	6	1	1	2	4	0	0	0
1996	Winnipeg	5	0	1	1	4	0	0	0
1997	Phoenix	7	0	0	0	17	0	0	0
1999	Toronto	17	1	1	2	25	0	0	0
2000	Toronto	1	0	0	0	2	0	0	0
Playoff Totals		**67**	**8**	**5**	**13**	**142**	**0**	**0**	**4**
KING, Steven *No Playoffs*	Right wing								
KING, Wayne *No Playoffs*	Center								
KINNEAR, Geordie *No Playoffs*	Defense								
KINSELLA, Brian *No Playoffs*	Center								
KINSELLA, Ray *No Playoffs*	Left wing								
•KIPRUSOFF, Marko *No Playoffs*	Defense								
KIRK, Bobby *No Playoffs*	Right wing								
KIRKPATRICK, Bob *No Playoffs*	Center								
KIRTON, Mark	Center								
1983	Vancouver	4	1	2	3	7	0	0	0
Playoff Totals		**4**	**1**	**2**	**3**	**7**	**0**	**0**	**0**
KISIO, Kelly	Center								
1984	Detroit	4	1	0	1	4	0	0	0
1985	Detroit	3	0	2	2	2	0	0	0
1987	NY Rangers	4	0	1	1	2	0	0	0
1989	NY Rangers	4	0	0	0	9	0	0	0
1990	NY Rangers	10	2	8	10	8	0	1	0
1994	Calgary	7	0	2	2	8	0	0	0
1995	Calgary	7	3	2	5	19	1	0	0
Playoff Totals		**39**	**6**	**15**	**21**	**52**	**1**	**1**	**0**
KITCHEN, Bill	Defense								
1982	Montreal	3	0	1	1	0	0	0	0
Playoff Totals		**3**	**0**	**1**	**1**	**0**	**0**	**0**	**0**
KITCHEN, Hobie *No Playoffs*	Defense								
KITCHEN, Mike	Defense								
1978	Colorado	2	0	0	0	2	0	0	0
Playoff Totals		**2**	**0**	**0**	**0**	**2**	**0**	**0**	**0**
•KJELLBERG, Patric *No Playoffs*	Right wing								
KLASSEN, Ralph	Center								
1978	Colorado	2	0	0	0	0	0	0	0
1980	St. Louis	3	0	0	0	0	0	0	0
1981	St. Louis	11	2	0	2	2	0	0	0
1982	St. Louis	10	2	2	4	10	0	0	0
Playoff Totals		**26**	**4**	**2**	**6**	**12**	**0**	**0**	**0**
•KLATT, Trent	Right wing								
1992	Minnesota	6	0	0	0	2	0	0	0
1994	Dallas	9	2	1	3	4	1	0	0
1995	Dallas	5	1	0	1	0	1	0	0
1996	Philadelphia	12	4	1	5	0	0	0	0
1997	Philadelphia	19	4	3	7	12	0	0	2
1998	Philadelphia	5	0	0	0	0	0	0	0
2001	Vancouver	4	3	0	3	0	2	0	0
Playoff Totals		**60**	**14**	**5**	**19**	**18**	**4**	**0**	**2**
•KLEE, Ken	Defense								
1995	Washington	7	0	0	0	4	0	0	0
1996	Washington	1	0	0	0	0	0	0	0
1998	Washington	9	1	0	1	10	0	0	0
2000	Washington	5	0	1	1	10	0	0	0
2001	Washington	6	0	1	1	8	0	0	0
Playoff Totals		**28**	**1**	**2**	**3**	**32**	**0**	**0**	**0**
KLEIN, Lloyd	Left wing								
1929♦	Boston	....	....	....	....	....	....	....	....
1936	NY Americans	5	0	0	0	2	0	0	0
Playoff Totals		**5**	**0**	**0**	**0**	**2**	**0**	**0**	**0**

Season	Team	GP	G	A	Pts	PIM	PP	SH	GW
KLEINENDORST, Scot	Defense								
1983	NY Rangers	6	0	2	2	2	0	0	0
1986	Hartford	10	0	1	1	18	0	0	0
1987	Hartford	4	1	3	4	20	0	0	0
1988	Hartford	3	1	1	2	0	0	0	0
1990	Washington	3	0	0	0	0	0	0	0
Playoff Totals		**26**	**2**	**7**	**9**	**40**	**0**	**0**	**0**
•KLEMM, Jon	Defense								
1996♦	Colorado	15	2	1	3	0	1	0	0
1997	Colorado	17	1	1	2	6	0	0	0
1998	Colorado	4	0	0	0	0	0	0	0
1999	Colorado	19	0	1	1	10	0	0	0
2000	Colorado	17	2	1	3	9	0	0	0
2001♦	Colorado	22	1	2	3	16	0	0	1
2002	Chicago	5	0	1	1	4	0	0	0
Playoff Totals		**99**	**6**	**7**	**13**	**45**	**1**	**0**	**1**
•KLESLA, Rostislav *No Playoffs*	Defense								
KLIMA, Petr	Wing								
1987	Detroit	13	1	2	3	4	0	0	0
1988	Detroit	12	10	8	18	10	2	1	4
1989	Detroit	6	2	4	6	19	1	0	0
1990♦	Edmonton	21	5	0	5	8	1	0	1
1991	Edmonton	18	7	6	13	16	1	0	3
1992	Edmonton	15	1	4	5	8	0	0	0
1996	Tampa Bay	4	2	0	2	14	2	0	0
1997	Edmonton	6	0	0	0	4	0	0	0
Playoff Totals		**95**	**28**	**24**	**52**	**83**	**7**	**1**	**8**
KLIMOVICH, Sergei *No Playoffs*	Center								
KLINGBEIL, Ike *No Playoffs*	Defense								
•KLOUCEK, Tomas *No Playoffs*	Defense								
KLUKAY, Joe	Left wing								
1943	Toronto	1	0	0	0	0	....	....	....
1947♦	Toronto	11	1	0	1	0	....	....	....
1948♦	Toronto	9	1	1	2	2	....	....	....
1949♦	Toronto	9	2	3	5	4	....	....	....
1950	Toronto	7	3	0	3	4	....	....	....
1951♦	Toronto	11	4	3	7	0	....	....	....
1952	Toronto	4	1	1	2	0	....	....	....
1953	Boston	11	1	2	3	9	....	....	....
1954	Boston	4	0	0	0	0	....	....	....
1955	Toronto	4	0	0	0	4	....	....	....
Playoff Totals		**71**	**13**	**10**	**23**	**23**	....	....	....
KLUZAK, Gord	Defense								
1983	Boston	17	1	4	5	54	0	0	0
1984	Boston	3	0	0	0	0	0	0	0
1986	Boston	3	1	1	2	16	1	0	0
1988	Boston	23	4	8	12	59	0	1	1
Playoff Totals		**46**	**6**	**13**	**19**	**129**	**1**	**1**	**1**
KNIBBS, Bill *No Playoffs*	Center								
KNIPSCHEER, Fred	Center								
1994	Boston	12	2	1	3	6	0	0	1
1995	Boston	4	0	0	0	0	0	0	0
Playoff Totals		**16**	**2**	**1**	**3**	**6**	**0**	**0**	**1**
KNOTT, Nick *No Playoffs*	Defense								
KNOX, Paul *No Playoffs*	Right wing								
•KNUBLE, Mike	Right wing								
1998♦	Detroit	3	0	1	1	0	0	0	0
2002	Boston	2	0	0	0	0	0	0	0
Playoff Totals		**5**	**0**	**1**	**1**	**0**	**0**	**0**	**0**
•KNUTSEN, Espen *No Playoffs*	Center								
•KOBASEW, Chuck *No Playoffs*	Right wing								
KOCUR, Joe	Right wing								
1985	Detroit	3	1	0	1	5	0	0	0
1987	Detroit	16	2	3	5	71	1	0	2
1988	Detroit	10	0	1	1	13	0	0	0
1989	Detroit	3	0	1	1	6	0	0	0
1991	NY Rangers	6	0	2	2	21	0	0	0
1992	NY Rangers	12	1	1	2	38	0	0	0
1994♦	NY Rangers	20	1	1	2	17	0	0	0
1995	NY Rangers	10	0	0	0	8	0	0	0
1996	Vancouver	1	0	0	0	0	0	0	0
1997♦	Detroit	19	1	3	4	22	0	0	0
1998♦	Detroit	18	4	0	4	30	0	0	0
Playoff Totals		**118**	**10**	**12**	**22**	**231**	**1**	**0**	**2**
•KOEHLER, Greg *No Playoffs*	Center								
•KOHN, Ladislav	Right wing								
1999	Toronto	2	0	0	0	5	0	0	0
Playoff Totals		**2**	**0**	**0**	**0**	**5**	**0**	**0**	**0**
•KOIVISTO, Tom *No Playoffs*	Defense								
•KOIVU, Saku	Center								
1996	Montreal	6	3	1	4	8	0	0	0
1997	Montreal	5	1	3	4	10	0	0	0
1998	Montreal	6	2	3	5	2	1	0	0
2002	Montreal	12	4	6	10	4	1	0	1
Playoff Totals		**29**	**10**	**13**	**23**	**24**	**2**	**0**	**1**
•KOLANOS, Krys	Center								
2002	Phoenix	2	0	0	0	6	0	0	0
Playoff Totals		**2**	**0**	**0**	**0**	**6**	**0**	**0**	**0**

Season	Team	GP	G	A	Pts	PIM	PP	SH	GW
•KOLARIK, Pavel *No Playoffs*	Defense								
KOLESAR, Mark	Left wing								
1996	Toronto	3	1	0	1	2	0	1	0
Playoff Totals		**3**	**1**	**0**	**1**	**2**	**0**	**1**	**0**
•KOLNIK, Juraj *No Playoffs*	Right wing								
KOLSTAD, Dean *No Playoffs*	Defense								
•KOLTSOV, Konstantin *No Playoffs*	Right wing								
KOMADOSKI, Neil	Defense								
1974	Los Angeles	2	0	0	0	12	0	0	0
1975	Los Angeles	3	0	0	0	2	0	0	0
1976	Los Angeles	9	0	0	0	18	0	0	0
1977	Los Angeles	9	0	2	2	15	0	0	0
Playoff Totals		**23**	**0**	**2**	**2**	**47**	**0**	**0**	**0**
•KOMARNISKI, Zenith *No Playoffs*	Defense								
•KOMISAREK, Mike *No Playoffs*	Defense								
KONIK, George *No Playoffs*	Defense/Left wing								
•KONOWALCHUK, Steve	Center								
1993	Washington	2	0	1	1	0	0	0	0
1994	Washington	11	0	1	1	10	0	0	0
1995	Washington	7	2	5	7	12	0	1	0
1996	Washington	2	0	2	2	0	0	0	0
2000	Washington	5	1	0	1	2	0	1	0
2001	Washington	6	2	3	5	14	2	0	0
Playoff Totals		**33**	**5**	**12**	**17**	**38**	**2**	**2**	**0**
KONROYD, Steve	Defense								
1982	Calgary	3	0	0	0	12	0	0	0
1983	Calgary	9	2	1	3	18	0	0	0
1984	Calgary	8	1	2	3	8	0	0	0
1985	Calgary	4	1	4	5	2	0	1	0
1986	NY Islanders	3	0	0	0	6	0	0	0
1987	NY Islanders	14	1	4	5	10	0	0	0
1988	NY Islanders	6	1	0	1	4	0	1	0
1989	Chicago	16	2	0	2	10	0	1	0
1990	Chicago	20	1	3	4	19	0	0	0
1991	Chicago	6	1	0	1	8	0	0	0
1992	Hartford	7	0	1	1	2	0	0	0
1993	Detroit	1	0	0	0	0	0	0	0
Playoff Totals		**97**	**10**	**15**	**25**	**99**	**0**	**3**	**0**
KONSTANTINOV, Vladimir	Defense								
1992	Detroit	11	0	1	1	16	0	0	0
1993	Detroit	7	0	1	1	8	0	0	0
1994	Detroit	7	0	2	2	4	0	0	0
1995	Detroit	18	1	1	2	22	0	0	1
1996	Detroit	19	4	5	9	28	0	1	0
1997♦	Detroit	20	0	4	4	29	0	0	0
Playoff Totals		**82**	**5**	**14**	**19**	**107**	**0**	**1**	**1**
KONTOS, Chris	Left wing/Center								
1988	Los Angeles	4	1	0	1	4	0	0	0
1989	Los Angeles	11	9	0	9	8	6	0	1
1990	Los Angeles	5	1	0	1	0	0	1	0
Playoff Totals		**20**	**11**	**0**	**11**	**12**	**6**	**1**	**1**
KOPAK, Russ *No Playoffs*	Center								
KORAB, Jerry	Defense								
1971	Chicago	7	1	0	1	20	0	0	0
1972	Chicago	8	0	1	1	20	0	0	0
1973	Chicago	15	0	0	0	22	0	0	0
1975	Buffalo	16	3	2	5	32	1	0	0
1976	Buffalo	9	1	3	4	12	0	0	0
1977	Buffalo	6	2	4	6	8	1	0	1
1978	Buffalo	8	0	5	5	6	0	0	0
1979	Buffalo	3	1	0	1	4	0	0	0
1980	Los Angeles	3	0	1	1	11	0	0	0
1981	Los Angeles	4	0	0	0	33	0	0	0
1982	Los Angeles	10	0	2	2	26	0	0	0
1984	Buffalo	3	0	0	0	5	0	0	0
1985	Buffalo	1	0	0	0	2	0	0	0
Playoff Totals		**93**	**8**	**18**	**26**	**201**	**2**	**0**	**1**
KORDIC, Dan	Left wing								
1997	Philadelphia	12	1	0	1	22	0	0	0
Playoff Totals		**12**	**1**	**0**	**1**	**22**	**0**	**0**	**0**
KORDIC, John	Right wing								
1986♦	Montreal	18	0	0	0	53	0	0	0
1987	Montreal	11	2	0	2	19	0	0	1
1988	Montreal	7	2	2	4	26	0	0	0
1990	Toronto	5	0	1	1	33	0	0	0
Playoff Totals		**41**	**4**	**3**	**7**	**131**	**0**	**0**	**1**
KORN, Jim	Defense/Left wing								
1983	Toronto	3	0	0	0	26	0	0	0
1988	New Jersey	9	0	2	2	71	0	0	0
1990	Calgary	4	1	0	1	12	0	0	0
Playoff Totals		**16**	**1**	**2**	**3**	**109**	**0**	**0**	**0**
KORNEY, Mike *No Playoffs*	Right wing								
•KOROLEV, Evgeny	Defense								
2002	NY Islanders	2	0	0	0	0	0	0	0
Playoff Totals		**2**	**0**	**0**	**0**	**0**	**0**	**0**	**0**

Season	Team	GP	G	A	Pts	PIM	PP	SH	GW
•KOROLEV, Igor									Center/Left wing
1993	St. Louis	3	0	0	0	0	0	0	0
1994	St. Louis	2	0	0	0	0	0	0	0
1996	Winnipeg	6	0	3	3	0	0	0	0
1997	Phoenix	1	0	0	0	0	0	0	0
1999	Toronto	1	0	0	0	0	0	0	0
2000	Toronto	12	0	4	4	6	0	0	0
2001	Toronto	11	0	0	0	0	0	0	0
2002	Chicago	5	0	1	1	0	0	0	0
Playoff Totals		**41**	**0**	**8**	**8**	**6**	**0**	**0**	**0**
KOROLL, Cliff									Right wing
1970	Chicago	8	1	4	5	9	0	0	0
1971	Chicago	18	7	9	16	18	3	0	1
1972	Chicago	8	0	0	0	11	0	0	0
1973	Chicago	16	4	6	10	6	0	0	0
1974	Chicago	11	2	5	7	13	1	0	0
1975	Chicago	8	3	5	8	8	2	0	0
1976	Chicago	4	1	0	1	0	1	0	0
1977	Chicago	2	0	0	0	0	0	0	0
1978	Chicago	4	1	0	1	0	0	0	0
1979	Chicago	4	0	0	0	0	0	0	0
1980	Chicago	2	0	0	0	2	0	0	0
Playoff Totals		**85**	**19**	**29**	**48**	**67**	**7**	**0**	**1**
•KOROLYUK, Alexander									Right wing
1999	San Jose	6	1	3	4	2	0	0	1
2000	San Jose	9	0	3	3	6	0	0	0
2001	San Jose	2	0	0	0	0	0	0	0
Playoff Totals		**17**	**1**	**6**	**7**	**8**	**0**	**0**	**1**
KORTKO, Roger									Center
1985	NY Islanders	10	0	3	3	17	0	0	0
Playoff Totals		**10**	**0**	**3**	**3**	**17**	**0**	**0**	**0**
•KOSTOPOULOS, Tom *No Playoffs*									Right wing
KOSTYNSKI, Doug *No Playoffs*									Center
•KOTALIK, Ales *No Playoffs*									Right wing
KOTANEN, Dick *No Playoffs*									Defense
KOTSOPOULOS, Chris									Defense
1981	NY Rangers	14	0	3	3	63	0	0	0
1986	Toronto	10	1	0	1	14	0	0	0
1987	Toronto	7	0	0	0	14	0	0	0
Playoff Totals		**31**	**1**	**3**	**4**	**91**	**0**	**0**	**0**
•KOVALCHUK, Ilya *No Playoffs*									Left wing
•KOVALENKO, Andrei									Right wing
1993	Quebec	4	1	0	1	2	0	0	0
1995	Quebec	6	0	1	1	2	0	0	0
1996	Montreal	6	0	0	0	6	0	0	0
1997	Edmonton	12	4	3	7	6	3	0	0
1998	Edmonton	1	0	0	0	2	0	0	0
1999	Carolina	4	0	2	2	2	0	0	0
Playoff Totals		**33**	**5**	**6**	**11**	**20**	**3**	**0**	**0**
•KOVALEV, Alexei									Right wing
1994♦	NY Rangers	23	9	12	21	18	5	0	2
1995	NY Rangers	10	4	7	11	10	0	0	0
1996	NY Rangers	11	3	4	7	14	0	0	1
1999	Pittsburgh	10	5	7	12	14	0	0	1
2000	Pittsburgh	11	1	5	6	10	0	0	0
2001	Pittsburgh	18	5	5	10	16	1	0	0
Playoff Totals		**83**	**27**	**40**	**67**	**82**	**6**	**0**	**4**
KOWAL, Joe									Left wing
1978	Buffalo	2	0	0	0	0	0	0	0
Playoff Totals		**2**	**0**	**0**	**0**	**0**	**0**	**0**	**0**
KOZAK, Don									Right wing
1974	Los Angeles	5	0	0	0	33	0	0	0
1975	Los Angeles	3	1	1	2	7	0	0	0
1976	Los Angeles	9	1	0	1	12	0	0	1
1977	Los Angeles	9	4	1	5	17	1	0	0
1979	Vancouver	3	1	0	1	0	0	0	0
Playoff Totals		**29**	**7**	**2**	**9**	**69**	**1**	**0**	**1**
KOZAK, Les *No Playoffs*									Left wing
•KOZLOV, Viktor									Center
2000	Florida	4	0	1	1	0	0	0	0
Playoff Totals		**4**	**0**	**1**	**1**	**0**	**0**	**0**	**0**
•KOZLOV, Vyacheslav									Center
1993	Detroit	4	0	2	2	2	0	0	0
1994	Detroit	7	2	5	7	12	0	0	0
1995	Detroit	18	9	7	16	10	1	0	4
1996	Detroit	19	5	7	12	10	2	0	1
1997♦	Detroit	20	8	5	13	14	4	0	2
1998♦	Detroit	22	6	8	14	10	1	0	4
1999	Detroit	10	6	1	7	4	3	0	0
2000	Detroit	8	2	1	3	12	1	0	1
2001	Detroit	6	4	1	5	2	2	0	0
Playoff Totals		**114**	**42**	**37**	**79**	**76**	**14**	**0**	**12**
•KRAFT, Milan									Center
2001	Pittsburgh	8	0	0	0	2	0	0	0
Playoff Totals		**8**	**0**	**0**	**0**	**2**	**0**	**0**	**0**
•KRAFT, Ryan *No Playoffs*									Center
KRAFTCHECK, Stephen									Defense
1951	Boston	6	0	0	0	7	0	0	0
Playoff Totals		**6**	**0**	**0**	**0**	**7**	**0**	**0**	**0**

Season	Team	GP	G	A	Pts	PIM	PP	SH	GW
•KRAJICEK, Lukas *No Playoffs*									Defense
KRAKE, Skip									Center
1968	Boston	4	0	0	0	2	0	0	0
1969	Los Angeles	6	1	0	1	15	0	0	0
Playoff Totals		**10**	**1**	**0**	**1**	**17**	**0**	**0**	**0**
•KRAVCHUK, Igor									Defense
1992	Chicago	18	2	6	8	8	1	0	0
1996	St. Louis	10	1	5	6	4	0	0	1
1997	St. Louis	2	0	0	0	2	0	0	0
1998	Ottawa	11	2	3	5	4	0	0	0
1999	Ottawa	4	0	0	0	0	0	0	0
2000	Ottawa	6	1	1	2	0	0	0	0
Playoff Totals		**51**	**6**	**15**	**21**	**18**	**1**	**0**	**1**
KRAVETS, Mikhail *No Playoffs*									Right wing
KRENTZ, Dale									Left wing
1988	Detroit	2	0	0	0	0	0	0	0
Playoff Totals		**2**	**0**	**0**	**0**	**0**	**0**	**0**	**0**
•KRESTANOVICH, Jordan *No Playoffs*									Left wing
•KRISTEK, Jaroslav *No Playoffs*									Right wing
•KRIVOKRASOV, Sergei									Right wing
1995	Chicago	10	0	0	0	8	0	0	0
1996	Chicago	5	1	0	1	2	0	0	1
1997	Chicago	6	1	0	1	4	0	0	0
Playoff Totals		**21**	**2**	**0**	**2**	**14**	**0**	**0**	**1**
•KROG, Jason *No Playoffs*									Center
KROL, Joe *No Playoffs*									Left wing
KROMM, Richard									Left wing
1984	Calgary	11	1	1	2	9	0	0	0
1985	Calgary	3	0	1	1	4	0	0	0
1986	NY Islanders	3	0	1	1	0	0	0	0
1987	NY Islanders	14	1	3	4	4	0	0	0
1988	NY Islanders	5	0	0	0	5	0	0	0
Playoff Totals		**36**	**2**	**6**	**8**	**22**	**0**	**0**	**0**
•KRON, Robert									Left wing
1992	Vancouver	11	1	2	3	2	0	1	0
1999	Carolina	5	2	0	2	0	0	0	1
Playoff Totals		**16**	**3**	**2**	**5**	**2**	**0**	**1**	**1**
KROOK, Kevin *No Playoffs*									Defense
KROUPA, Vlastimil									Defense
1994	San Jose	14	1	2	3	21	0	0	1
1995	San Jose	6	0	0	0	4	0	0	0
Playoff Totals		**20**	**1**	**2**	**3**	**25**	**0**	**0**	**1**
KRULICKI, Jim *No Playoffs*									Left wing
•KRUPP, Uwe									Defense
1988	Buffalo	6	0	0	0	15	0	0	0
1989	Buffalo	5	0	1	1	4	0	0	0
1990	Buffalo	6	0	0	0	4	0	0	0
1991	Buffalo	6	1	1	2	6	1	0	0
1993	NY Islanders	18	1	5	6	12	0	0	0
1994	NY Islanders	4	0	1	1	4	0	0	0
1995	Quebec	5	0	2	2	2	0	0	0
1996♦	Colorado	22	4	12	16	33	1	0	2
1998	Colorado	7	0	1	1	4	0	0	0
2002	Detroit	2	0	0	0	2	0	0	0
Playoff Totals		**81**	**6**	**23**	**29**	**86**	**2**	**0**	**2**
KRUPPKE, Gord *No Playoffs*									Defense
KRUSE, Paul									Left wing
1994	Calgary	7	0	0	0	14	0	0	0
1995	Calgary	7	4	2	6	10	0	1	0
1996	Calgary	3	0	0	0	4	0	0	0
1998	Buffalo	1	1	0	1	4	0	0	0
1999	Buffalo	10	0	0	0	4	0	0	0
Playoff Totals		**28**	**5**	**2**	**7**	**36**	**0**	**1**	**0**
KRUSHELNYSKI, Mike									Left wing/Center
1982	Boston	1	0	0	0	2	0	0	0
1983	Boston	17	8	6	14	12	2	0	0
1984	Boston	2	0	0	0	0	0	0	0
1985♦	Edmonton	18	5	8	13	22	2	0	2
1986	Edmonton	10	4	5	9	16	1	0	2
1987♦	Edmonton	21	3	4	7	18	0	0	1
1988♦	Edmonton	19	4	6	10	12	0	0	0
1989	Los Angeles	11	1	4	5	4	1	0	0
1990	Los Angeles	10	1	3	4	12	0	0	1
1993	Toronto	16	3	7	10	8	1	0	0
1994	Toronto	6	0	0	0	0	0	0	0
1995	Detroit	8	0	0	0	0	0	0	0
Playoff Totals		**139**	**29**	**43**	**72**	**106**	**7**	**0**	**6**
KRUTOV, Vladimir *No Playoffs*									Left wing
KRYGIER, Todd									Left wing
1990	Hartford	7	2	1	3	4	0	0	0
1991	Hartford	6	0	2	2	0	0	0	0
1992	Washington	5	2	1	3	4	0	0	0
1993	Washington	6	1	1	2	4	0	1	0
1994	Washington	5	2	0	2	10	0	0	0
1996	Washington	6	2	0	2	12	0	0	1
1998	Washington	13	1	2	3	6	0	0	1
Playoff Totals		**48**	**10**	**7**	**17**	**40**	**0**	**1**	**2**

Season	Team	GP	G	A	Pts	PIM	PP	SH	GW
KRYSKOW, Dave									Left wing
1973	Chicago	3	2	0	2	0	0	0	0
1974	Chicago	7	0	0	0	2	0	0	0
1976	Atlanta	2	0	0	0	2	0	0	0
Playoff Totals		**12**	**2**	**0**	**2**	**4**	**0**	**0**	**0**
KRYZANOWSKI, Ed									Defense
1949	Boston	5	0	1	1	2	0	0	0
1951	Boston	6	0	0	0	2	0	0	0
1952	Boston	7	0	0	0	0	0	0	0
Playoff Totals		**18**	**0**	**1**	**1**	**4**	**0**	**0**	**0**
•KUBA, Filip *No Playoffs*									Defense
•KUBINA, Pavel *No Playoffs*									Defense
•KUCERA, Frantisek									Defense
1992	Chicago	6	0	0	0	0	0	0	0
1996	Vancouver	6	0	1	1	0	0	0	0
Playoff Totals		**12**	**0**	**1**	**1**	**0**	**0**	**0**	**0**
KUDASHOV, Alexei *No Playoffs*									Center
KUDELSKI, Bob									Right wing
1990	Los Angeles	8	1	2	3	2	0	0	0
1991	Los Angeles	8	3	2	5	2	0	0	0
1992	Los Angeles	6	0	0	0	0	0	0	0
Playoff Totals		**22**	**4**	**4**	**8**	**4**	**0**	**0**	**0**
•KUDROC, Kristian *No Playoffs*									Defense
KUHN, Gord *No Playoffs*									Right wing
KUKULOWICZ, Aggie *No Playoffs*									Center
KULAK, Stu									Right wing
1987	NY Rangers	3	0	0	0	2	0	0	0
Playoff Totals		**3**	**0**	**0**	**0**	**2**	**0**	**0**	**0**
KULLMAN, Arnie *No Playoffs*									Center
KULLMAN, Eddie									Right wing
1948	NY Rangers	6	1	0	1	2	....	....	....
Playoff Totals		**6**	**1**	**0**	**1**	**2**	....	....	....
•KULTANEN, Jarno *No Playoffs*									Defense
KUMPEL, Mark									Right wing
1985	Quebec	18	3	4	7	4	0	0	1
1986	Quebec	2	1	0	1	0	0	0	0
1987	Detroit	8	0	0	0	4	0	0	0
1988	Winnipeg	4	0	0	0	4	0	0	0
1990	Winnipeg	7	2	0	2	2	0	0	0
Playoff Totals		**39**	**6**	**4**	**10**	**14**	**0**	**0**	**1**
KUNTZ, Alan									Left wing
1942	NY Rangers	6	1	0	1	2	....	....	....
Playoff Totals		**6**	**1**	**0**	**1**	**2**	....	....	....
KUNTZ, Murray *No Playoffs*									Left wing
KURRI, Jari									Right wing
1981	Edmonton	9	5	7	12	4	0	0	0
1982	Edmonton	5	2	5	7	10	0	0	0
1983	Edmonton	16	8	15	23	8	2	2	0
1984♦	Edmonton	19	*14	14	28	13	4	0	0
1985♦	Edmonton	18	*19	12	31	6	1	2	2
1986	Edmonton	10	2	10	12	4	0	1	0
1987♦	Edmonton	21	*15	10	25	20	4	1	5
1988♦	Edmonton	19	*14	17	31	12	5	0	3
1989	Edmonton	7	3	5	8	6	0	1	0
1990♦	Edmonton	22	10	15	25	18	6	0	3
1992	Los Angeles	4	1	2	3	4	1	0	0
1993	Los Angeles	24	9	8	17	12	2	2	0
1996	NY Rangers	11	3	5	8	2	0	1	1
1997	Anaheim	11	1	2	3	4	0	0	0
1998	Colorado	4	0	0	0	0	0	0	0
Playoff Totals		**200**	**106**	**127**	**233**	**123**	**25**	**10**	**14**
KURTENBACH, Orland									Center
1966	Toronto	4	0	0	0	20	0	0	0
1967	NY Rangers	3	0	2	2	0	0	0	0
1968	NY Rangers	6	1	0	1	26	0	0	0
1970	NY Rangers	6	1	2	3	24	0	0	0
Playoff Totals		**19**	**2**	**4**	**6**	**70**	**0**	**0**	**0**
•KURTZ, Justin *No Playoffs*									Defense
KURVERS, Tom									Defense
1985	Montreal	12	0	6	6	6	0	0	0
1986♦	Montreal	....	....	....	....	....	....	....	....
1988	New Jersey	19	6	9	15	38	3	0	1
1990	Toronto	5	0	3	3	4	0	0	0
1991	Vancouver	6	2	2	4	12	1	0	0
1993	NY Islanders	12	0	2	2	6	0	0	0
1994	NY Islanders	3	0	0	0	2	0	0	0
Playoff Totals		**57**	**8**	**22**	**30**	**68**	**4**	**0**	**1**
KURYLUK, Merv									Left wing
1962	Chicago	2	0	0	0	0	0	0	0
Playoff Totals		**2**	**0**	**0**	**0**	**0**	**0**	**0**	**0**
KUSHNER, Dale *No Playoffs*									Right wing
•KUTLAK, Zdenek *No Playoffs*									Defense
•KUZNETSOV, Maxim *No Playoffs*									Defense
•KUZNIK, Greg *No Playoffs*									Defense
KUZYK, Ken *No Playoffs*									Right wing

Season	Team	GP	G	A	Pts	PIM	PP	SH	GW
KVARTALNOV, Dmitri									Left wing
1993	Boston	4	0	0	0	0	0	0	0
Playoff Totals		**4**	**0**	**0**	**0**	**0**	**0**	**0**	**0**
•KVASHA, Oleg									Center/Left wing
2000	Florida	4	0	0	0	0	0	0	0
2002	NY Islanders	7	0	1	1	6	0	0	0
Playoff Totals		**11**	**0**	**1**	**1**	**6**	**0**	**0**	**0**
•KWIATKOWSKI, Joel *No Playoffs*									Defense
KWONG, Larry *No Playoffs*									Right wing
KYLE, Bill *No Playoffs*									Center
KYLE, Gus									Defense
1950	NY Rangers	12	1	2	3	30	....	....	....
1952	Boston	2	0	0	0	4	....	....	....
Playoff Totals		**14**	**1**	**2**	**3**	**34**	....	....	....
KYLLONEN, Markku *No Playoffs*									Left wing
KYPREOS, Nick									Left wing
1990	Washington	7	1	0	1	15	0	0	0
1991	Washington	9	0	1	1	38	0	0	0
1994♦	NY Rangers	3	0	0	0	2	0	0	0
1995	NY Rangers	10	0	2	2	6	0	0	0
1996	Toronto	5	0	0	0	4	0	0	0
Playoff Totals		**34**	**1**	**3**	**4**	**65**	**0**	**0**	**0**
KYTE, Jim									Defense
1984	Winnipeg	3	0	0	0	11	0	0	0
1985	Winnipeg	8	0	0	0	14	0	0	0
1986	Winnipeg	3	0	0	0	12	0	0	0
1987	Winnipeg	10	0	4	4	36	0	0	0
1991	Calgary	7	0	0	0	7	0	0	0
1995	San Jose	11	0	2	2	14	0	0	0
Playoff Totals		**42**	**0**	**6**	**6**	**94**	**0**	**0**	**0**
•LAAKSONEN, Antti *No Playoffs*									Left wing
LABADIE, Mike *No Playoffs*									Right wing
LABATTE, Neil *No Playoffs*									Center/Defense
L'ABBE, Moe *No Playoffs*									Right wing
LABELLE, Marc *No Playoffs*									Left wing
LABINE, Leo									Right wing
1952	Boston	5	0	1	1	4	....	....	....
1953	Boston	7	2	1	3	*19	....	....	....
1954	Boston	4	0	1	1	8	....	....	....
1955	Boston	5	2	1	3	11	....	....	....
1957	Boston	10	3	2	5	*14	....	....	....
1958	Boston	11	0	2	2	10	....	....	....
1959	Boston	7	2	1	3	12	....	....	....
1961	Detroit	11	3	2	5	4	....	....	....
Playoff Totals		**60**	**12**	**11**	**23**	**82**	....	....	....
LABOSSIERE, Gord									Center
1968	Los Angeles	7	2	3	5	24	0	0	0
1971	Minnesota	3	0	0	0	4	0	0	0
Playoff Totals		**10**	**2**	**3**	**5**	**28**	**0**	**0**	**0**
LABOVITCH, Max *No Playoffs*									Right wing
LABRAATEN, Dan									Left wing
1981	Calgary	5	1	0	1	4	1	0	1
1982	Calgary	3	0	0	0	0	0	0	0
Playoff Totals		**8**	**1**	**0**	**1**	**4**	**1**	**0**	**1**
LABRE, Yvon *No Playoffs*									Defense
LABRIE, Guy *No Playoffs*									Defense
LACH, Elmer									Center
1941	Montreal	3	1	0	1	0	....	....	....
1943	Montreal	5	2	4	6	6	....	....	....
1944♦	Montreal	9	2	*11	13	4	....	....	....
1945	Montreal	6	4	4	8	2	....	....	....
1946♦	Montreal	9	5	*12	*17	4	....	....	....
1949	Montreal	1	0	0	0	4	....	....	....
1950	Montreal	5	1	2	3	4	....	....	....
1951	Montreal	11	2	2	4	2	....	....	....
1952	Montreal	11	1	2	3	4	....	....	....
1953♦	Montreal	12	1	6	7	6	....	....	....
1954	Montreal	4	0	2	2	0	....	....	....
Playoff Totals		**76**	**19**	**45**	**64**	**36**	....	....	....
LACHANCE, Michel *No Playoffs*									Defense
•LACHANCE, Scott									Defense
1994	NY Islanders	3	0	0	0	0	0	0	0
2001	Vancouver	2	0	1	1	2	0	0	0
2002	Vancouver	6	1	1	2	4	0	0	1
Playoff Totals		**11**	**1**	**2**	**3**	**6**	**0**	**0**	**1**
LACOMBE, Francois									Defense
1969	Oakland	3	1	0	1	0	0	0	0
Playoff Totals		**3**	**1**	**0**	**1**	**0**	**0**	**0**	**0**
LACOMBE, Normand									Right wing
1988♦	Edmonton	19	3	0	3	28	0	0	1
1989	Edmonton	7	2	1	3	21	0	0	0
Playoff Totals		**26**	**5**	**1**	**6**	**49**	**0**	**0**	**1**
•LaCOUTURE, Dan									Left wing
2000	Edmonton	1	0	0	0	0	0	0	0
2001	Pittsburgh	5	0	0	0	2	0	0	0
Playoff Totals		**6**	**0**	**0**	**0**	**2**	**0**	**0**	**0**

Season	Team	GP	G	A	Pts	PIM	PP	SH	GW
LACROIX, Andre									Center
1968	Philadelphia	7	2	3	5	0	1	0	0
1969	Philadelphia	4	0	0	0	0	0	0	0
1971	Philadelphia	4	0	2	2	0	0	0	0
1972	Chicago	1	0	0	0	0	0	0	0
Playoff Totals		**16**	**2**	**5**	**7**	**0**	**1**	**0**	**0**
LACROIX, Daniel									Left wing
1997	Philadelphia	12	0	1	1	22	0	0	0
1998	Philadelphia	4	0	0	0	4	0	0	0
Playoff Totals		**16**	**0**	**1**	**1**	**26**	**0**	**0**	**0**
LACROIX, Eric									Left wing
1994	Toronto	2	0	0	0	0	0	0	0
1997	Colorado	17	1	4	5	19	0	0	0
1998	Colorado	7	0	0	0	6	0	0	0
2001	Ottawa	4	0	1	1	0	0	0	0
Playoff Totals		**30**	**1**	**5**	**6**	**25**	**0**	**0**	**0**
LACROIX, Pierre									Defense
1981	Quebec	5	0	2	2	10	0	0	0
1982	Quebec	3	0	0	0	0	0	0	0
Playoff Totals		**8**	**0**	**2**	**2**	**10**	**0**	**0**	**0**
LADOUCEUR, Randy									Defense
1984	Detroit	4	1	0	1	6	0	1	0
1985	Detroit	3	1	0	1	0	0	0	0
1987	Hartford	6	0	2	2	12	0	0	0
1988	Hartford	6	1	1	2	4	0	0	0
1989	Hartford	1	0	0	0	10	0	0	0
1990	Hartford	7	1	0	1	10	0	0	1
1991	Hartford	6	1	4	5	6	0	0	0
1992	Hartford	7	0	1	1	11	0	0	0
Playoff Totals		**40**	**5**	**8**	**13**	**59**	**0**	**1**	**1**
LaFAYETTE, Nathan									Center
1994	Vancouver	20	2	7	9	4	0	0	0
1995	NY Rangers	8	0	0	0	2	0	0	0
1998	Los Angeles	4	0	0	0	2	0	0	0
Playoff Totals		**32**	**2**	**7**	**9**	**8**	**0**	**0**	**0**
•LAFLAMME, Christian									Defense
1999	Edmonton	4	0	1	1	2	0	0	0
Playoff Totals		**4**	**0**	**1**	**1**	**2**	**0**	**0**	**0**
LAFLEUR, Guy									Right wing
1972	Montreal	6	1	4	5	2	0	0	0
1973♦	Montreal	17	3	5	8	9	2	0	1
1974	Montreal	6	0	1	1	4	0	0	0
1975	Montreal	11	*12	7	19	15	4	0	4
1976♦	Montreal	13	7	10	17	2	0	0	3
1977♦	Montreal	14	9	*17	*26	6	1	0	2
1978♦	Montreal	15	*10	11	*21	16	3	0	2
1979♦	Montreal	16	10	*13	*23	0	2	0	2
1980	Montreal	3	3	1	4	0	0	0	0
1981	Montreal	3	0	1	1	2	0	0	0
1982	Montreal	5	2	1	3	4	2	0	0
1983	Montreal	3	0	2	2	2	0	0	0
1984	Montreal	12	0	3	3	5	0	0	0
1989	NY Rangers	4	1	0	1	0	1	0	0
Playoff Totals		**128**	**58**	**76**	**134**	**67**	**15**	**0**	**14**
LAFLEUR, Roland *No Playoffs*									Left wing
LaFONTAINE, Pat									Center
1984	NY Islanders	16	3	6	9	8	0	0	0
1985	NY Islanders	9	1	2	3	4	0	0	0
1986	NY Islanders	3	1	0	1	0	1	0	0
1987	NY Islanders	14	5	7	12	10	1	0	2
1988	NY Islanders	6	4	5	9	8	1	0	1
1990	NY Islanders	2	0	1	1	0	0	0	0
1992	Buffalo	7	8	3	11	4	5	1	1
1993	Buffalo	7	2	10	12	0	1	0	0
1995	Buffalo	5	2	2	4	2	1	0	0
Playoff Totals		**69**	**26**	**36**	**62**	**36**	**10**	**1**	**4**
LAFORCE, Ernie *No Playoffs*									Defense
LaFOREST, Bob *No Playoffs*									Right wing
LAFORGE, Claude									Left wing
1968	Philadelphia	5	1	2	3	15	0	0	0
Playoff Totals		**5**	**1**	**2**	**3**	**15**	**0**	**0**	**0**
LAFORGE, Marc *No Playoffs*									Left wing
LAFRAMBOISE, Pete									Left wing/Center
1975	Pittsburgh	9	1	0	1	0	0	0	0
Playoff Totals		**9**	**1**	**0**	**1**	**0**	**0**	**0**	**0**
LAFRANCE, Adie									Left wing
1934	Montreal	2	0	0	0	0	0	0	0
Playoff Totals		**2**	**0**	**0**	**0**	**0**	**0**	**0**	**0**
LAFRANCE, Leo *No Playoffs*									Left wing
LAFRENIERE, Jason									Center
1987	Quebec	12	1	5	6	2	1	0	0
1989	NY Rangers	3	0	0	0	17	0	0	0
Playoff Totals		**15**	**1**	**5**	**6**	**19**	**1**	**0**	**0**
LAFRENIERE, Roger *No Playoffs*									Left wing
LAGACE, Jean-Guy *No Playoffs*									Defense

Season	Team	GP	G	A	Pts	PIM	PP	SH	GW
LAIDLAW, Tom									Defense
1981	NY Rangers	14	1	4	5	18	0	0	1
1982	NY Rangers	10	0	3	3	14	0	0	0
1983	NY Rangers	9	1	1	2	10	0	0	0
1984	NY Rangers	5	0	0	0	8	0	0	0
1985	NY Rangers	3	0	2	2	4	0	0	0
1986	NY Rangers	7	0	2	2	12	0	0	0
1987	Los Angeles	5	0	0	0	2	0	0	0
1988	Los Angeles	5	0	2	2	4	0	0	0
1989	Los Angeles	11	2	3	5	6	0	0	0
Playoff Totals		**69**	**4**	**17**	**21**	**78**	**0**	**0**	**1**
LAIRD, Robbie *No Playoffs*									Left wing
LAJEUNESSE, Serge *No Playoffs*									Defense/Right wing
•LAKOVIC, Sasha *No Playoffs*									Right wing
LALANDE, Hec *No Playoffs*									Center
LALONDE, Bobby									Center
1975	Vancouver	5	0	0	0	0	0	0	0
1976	Vancouver	1	0	0	0	2	0	0	0
1978	Atlanta	1	1	0	1	0	0	0	0
1979	Atlanta	2	1	0	1	0	1	0	0
1980	Boston	4	0	1	1	2	0	0	0
1981	Boston	3	2	1	3	2	0	2	0
Playoff Totals		**16**	**4**	**2**	**6**	**6**	**1**	**2**	**0**
LALONDE, Newsy									Center
1918	Montreal	2	4	2	6	17	....	....	....
1919	Montreal	5	*11	2	*13	6	....	....	....
Playoff Totals		**7**	**15**	**4**	**19**	**23**	....	....	....
LALONDE, Ron *No Playoffs*									Center
LALOR, Mike									Defense
1986♦	Montreal	17	1	2	3	29	0	0	1
1987	Montreal	13	2	1	3	29	0	0	0
1988	Montreal	11	0	0	0	11	0	0	0
1989	St. Louis	10	1	1	2	14	1	0	0
1990	St. Louis	12	0	2	2	31	0	0	0
1991	Washington	10	1	2	3	22	0	0	0
1992	Winnipeg	7	0	0	0	19	0	0	0
1993	Winnipeg	4	0	2	2	4	0	0	0
1994	Dallas	5	0	0	0	6	0	0	0
1995	Dallas	3	0	0	0	2	0	0	0
Playoff Totals		**92**	**5**	**10**	**15**	**167**	**1**	**0**	**1**
LAMB, Joe									Right wing
1928	Mtl. Maroons	8	1	0	1	32	....	....	....
1930	Ottawa	2	0	0	0	11	....	....	....
1933	Boston	5	0	1	1	6	....	....	....
1936	Mtl. Maroons	3	0	0	0	2	....	....	....
Playoff Totals		**18**	**1**	**1**	**2**	**51**	....	....	....
LAMB, Mark									Center
1987	Detroit	11	0	0	0	11	0	0	0
1989	Edmonton	6	0	2	2	8	0	0	0
1990♦	Edmonton	22	6	11	17	2	1	0	2
1991	Edmonton	15	0	5	5	20	0	0	0
1992	Edmonton	16	1	1	2	10	0	0	0
Playoff Totals		**70**	**7**	**19**	**26**	**51**	**1**	**0**	**2**
LAMBERT, Dan *No Playoffs*									Defense
•LAMBERT, Denny									Left wing
1997	Ottawa	6	0	1	1	9	0	0	0
1998	Ottawa	11	0	0	0	19	0	0	0
Playoff Totals		**17**	**0**	**1**	**1**	**28**	**0**	**0**	**0**
LAMBERT, Lane									Right wing
1984	Detroit	4	0	0	0	10	0	0	0
1987	Quebec	13	2	4	6	30	0	0	0
Playoff Totals		**17**	**2**	**4**	**6**	**40**	**0**	**0**	**0**
LAMBERT, Yvon									Left wing
1974	Montreal	5	0	0	0	7	0	0	0
1975	Montreal	11	4	2	6	0	2	0	0
1976♦	Montreal	12	2	3	5	18	0	0	1
1977♦	Montreal	14	3	3	6	12	1	0	0
1978♦	Montreal	15	2	4	6	6	1	0	1
1979♦	Montreal	16	5	6	11	16	2	0	1
1980	Montreal	10	8	4	12	4	1	0	1
1981	Montreal	3	0	0	0	2	0	0	0
1982	Buffalo	4	3	0	3	2	1	0	0
Playoff Totals		**90**	**27**	**22**	**49**	**67**	**8**	**0**	**4**
LAMBY, Dick *No Playoffs*									Defense
LAMIRANDE, Jean-Paul									Left wing/Defense
1948	NY Rangers	6	0	0	0	4	0	0	0
1950	NY Rangers	2	0	0	0	0	0	0	0
Playoff Totals		**8**	**0**	**0**	**0**	**4**	**0**	**0**	**0**
LAMMENS, Hank *No Playoffs*									Defense
LAMOUREUX, Leo									Center/Defense
1944♦	Montreal	9	0	3	3	8	....	....	....
1945	Montreal	6	1	1	2	2	....	....	....
1946♦	Montreal	9	0	2	2	2	....	....	....
1947	Montreal	4	0	0	0	4	....	....	....
Playoff Totals		**28**	**1**	**6**	**7**	**16**	....	....	....
LAMOUREUX, Mitch *No Playoffs*									Center
LAMPMAN, Mike *No Playoffs*									Left wing

Season	Team	GP	G	A	Pts	PIM	PP	SH	GW
LANCIEN, Jack									Defense
1948	NY Rangers	2	0	0	0	2	0	0	0
1950	NY Rangers	4	0	1	1	0	0	0	0
Playoff Totals		**6**	**0**	**1**	**1**	**2**	**0**	**0**	**0**
LANDON, Larry	*No Playoffs*								Right wing
•LANDRY, Eric	*No Playoffs*								Center
LANE, Gord									Defense
1980♦	NY Islanders	21	1	3	4	*85	0	0	0
1981♦	NY Islanders	12	1	5	6	32	0	0	0
1982♦	NY Islanders	19	0	4	4	61	0	0	0
1983♦	NY Islanders	18	1	2	3	32	0	0	1
1984	NY Islanders	4	0	0	0	2	0	0	0
1985	NY Islanders	1	0	0	0	2	0	0	0
Playoff Totals		**75**	**3**	**14**	**17**	**214**	**0**	**0**	**1**
LANE, Myles									Defense
1929♦	Boston	5	0	0	0	0	0	0	0
1930	Boston	6	0	0	0	0	0	0	0
Playoff Totals		**11**	**0**	**0**	**0**	**0**	**0**	**0**	**0**
•LANG, Robert									Center
1998	Pittsburgh	6	0	3	3	2	0	0	0
1999	Pittsburgh	12	0	2	2	0	0	0	0
2000	Pittsburgh	11	3	3	6	0	2	0	0
2001	Pittsburgh	16	4	4	8	4	0	0	0
Playoff Totals		**45**	**7**	**12**	**19**	**6**	**2**	**0**	**0**
•LANGDON, Darren									Left wing
1996	NY Rangers	2	0	0	0	0	0	0	0
1997	NY Rangers	10	0	0	0	2	0	0	0
2001	Carolina	4	0	0	0	12	0	0	0
Playoff Totals		**16**	**0**	**0**	**0**	**14**	**0**	**0**	**0**
LANGDON, Steve									Left wing
1976	Boston	4	0	0	0	0	0	0	0
Playoff Totals		**4**	**0**	**0**	**0**	**0**	**0**	**0**	**0**
LANGELLE, Pete									Center
1939	Toronto	11	1	2	3	2	....	....	....
1940	Toronto	10	0	3	3	0	....	....	....
1941	Toronto	7	1	1	2	0	....	....	....
1942♦	Toronto	13	3	3	6	2	....	....	....
Playoff Totals		**41**	**5**	**9**	**14**	**4**	....	....	....
•LANGENBRUNNER, Jamie									Right wing
1997	Dallas	5	1	1	2	14	0	0	1
1998	Dallas	16	1	4	5	14	0	0	1
1999♦	Dallas	23	10	7	17	16	4	0	3
2000	Dallas	15	1	7	8	18	1	0	0
2001	Dallas	10	2	2	4	6	0	0	1
2002	New Jersey	5	0	1	1	8	0	0	0
Playoff Totals		**74**	**15**	**22**	**37**	**76**	**5**	**0**	**6**
LANGEVIN, Chris	*No Playoffs*								Left wing
LANGEVIN, Dave									Defense
1980♦	NY Islanders	21	0	3	3	32	0	0	0
1981♦	NY Islanders	18	0	3	3	25	0	0	0
1982♦	NY Islanders	19	2	4	6	16	0	0	1
1983♦	NY Islanders	8	0	2	2	2	0	0	0
1984	NY Islanders	12	0	4	4	18	0	0	0
1985	NY Islanders	4	0	0	0	4	0	0	0
1986	Minnesota	5	0	1	1	9	0	0	0
Playoff Totals		**87**	**2**	**17**	**19**	**106**	**0**	**0**	**1**
•LANGFELD, Josh	*No Playoffs*								Right wing
•LANGKOW, Daymond									Center
1999	Philadelphia	6	0	2	2	2	0	0	0
2000	Philadelphia	16	5	5	10	23	1	1	2
2001	Philadelphia	6	2	4	6	2	1	0	0
2002	Phoenix	5	1	0	1	0	0	0	0
Playoff Totals		**33**	**8**	**11**	**19**	**27**	**2**	**1**	**2**
LANGLAIS, Alain	*No Playoffs*								Left wing
LANGLOIS, Albert									Defense
1958♦	Montreal	7	0	1	1	4	0	0	0
1959♦	Montreal	7	0	0	0	4	0	0	0
1960♦	Montreal	8	0	3	3	18	0	0	0
1961	Montreal	5	0	0	0	6	0	0	0
1962	NY Rangers	6	0	1	1	2	0	0	0
1964	Detroit	14	0	0	0	12	0	0	0
1965	Detroit	6	1	0	1	4	0	0	0
Playoff Totals		**53**	**1**	**5**	**6**	**50**	**0**	**0**	**0**
LANGLOIS, Charlie									Right wing/Defense
1928	Montreal	2	0	0	0	0	0	0	0
Playoff Totals		**2**	**0**	**0**	**0**	**0**	**0**	**0**	**0**

Season	Team	GP	G	A	Pts	PIM	PP	SH	GW
LANGWAY, Rod									Defense
1979♦	Montreal	8	0	0	0	16	0	0	0
1980	Montreal	10	3	3	6	2	1	0	0
1981	Montreal	3	0	0	0	6	0	0	0
1982	Montreal	5	0	3	3	18	0	0	0
1983	Washington	4	0	0	0	0	0	0	0
1984	Washington	8	0	5	5	7	0	0	0
1985	Washington	5	0	1	1	6	0	0	0
1986	Washington	9	1	2	3	6	1	0	0
1987	Washington	7	0	1	1	2	0	0	0
1988	Washington	6	0	0	0	8	0	0	0
1989	Washington	6	0	0	0	6	0	0	0
1990	Washington	15	1	4	5	12	0	0	1
1991	Washington	11	0	2	2	6	0	0	0
1992	Washington	7	0	1	1	2	0	0	0
Playoff Totals		**104**	**5**	**22**	**27**	**97**	**2**	**0**	**1**
LANK, Jeff	*No Playoffs*								Defense
LANTHIER, Jean-Marc	*No Playoffs*								Right wing
LANYON, Ted	*No Playoffs*								Defense
LANZ, Rick									Defense
1981	Vancouver	3	0	0	0	4	0	0	0
1983	Vancouver	4	2	1	3	0	1	0	0
1984	Vancouver	4	0	4	4	2	0	0	0
1986	Vancouver	3	0	0	0	0	0	0	0
1987	Toronto	13	1	3	4	27	0	0	1
1988	Toronto	1	0	0	0	2	0	0	0
Playoff Totals		**28**	**3**	**8**	**11**	**35**	**1**	**0**	**1**
LAPERRIERE, Daniel	*No Playoffs*								Defense
•LAPERRIERE, Ian									Center
1995	St. Louis	7	0	4	4	21	0	0	0
1998	Los Angeles	4	1	0	1	6	0	0	0
2000	Los Angeles	4	0	0	0	2	0	0	0
2001	Los Angeles	13	1	2	3	12	0	0	0
2002	Los Angeles	7	0	1	1	9	0	0	0
Playoff Totals		**35**	**2**	**7**	**9**	**50**	**0**	**0**	**0**
LAPERRIERE, Jacques									Defense
1963	Montreal	5	0	1	1	4	0	0	0
1964	Montreal	7	1	1	2	8	0	1	0
1965♦	Montreal	6	1	1	2	16	1	0	0
1966♦	Montreal	....	....	....	....	....	....	....	....
1967	Montreal	9	0	1	1	9	0	0	0
1968♦	Montreal	13	1	3	4	20	0	0	0
1969♦	Montreal	14	1	3	4	28	1	0	0
1971♦	Montreal	20	4	9	13	12	1	0	1
1972	Montreal	4	0	0	0	2	0	0	0
1973♦	Montreal	10	1	3	4	2	0	0	0
Playoff Totals		**88**	**9**	**22**	**31**	**101**	**3**	**1**	**1**
•LAPLANTE, Darryl	*No Playoffs*								Center
•LAPOINTE, Claude									Center
1993	Quebec	6	2	4	6	8	0	0	0
1995	Quebec	5	0	0	0	8	0	0	0
1996	Calgary	2	0	0	0	0	0	0	0
2002	NY Islanders	7	0	0	0	14	0	0	0
Playoff Totals		**20**	**2**	**4**	**6**	**30**	**0**	**0**	**0**
LAPOINTE, Guy									Defense
1971♦	Montreal	20	4	5	9	34	1	0	2
1972	Montreal	6	0	1	1	0	0	0	0
1973♦	Montreal	17	6	7	13	20	2	0	1
1974	Montreal	6	0	2	2	4	0	0	0
1975	Montreal	11	6	4	10	4	3	1	0
1976♦	Montreal	13	3	3	6	12	1	0	1
1977♦	Montreal	12	3	9	12	4	1	0	0
1978♦	Montreal	14	1	6	7	16	1	0	0
1979♦	Montreal	10	2	6	8	10	1	0	0
1980	Montreal	2	0	0	0	0	0	0	0
1981	Montreal	1	0	0	0	17	0	0	0
1982	St. Louis	7	1	0	1	8	1	0	1
1983	St. Louis	4	0	1	1	9	0	0	0
Playoff Totals		**123**	**26**	**44**	**70**	**138**	**11**	**1**	**5**
•LAPOINTE, Martin									Right wing
1992	Detroit	3	0	1	1	4	0	0	0
1994	Detroit	4	0	0	0	6	0	0	0
1995	Detroit	2	0	1	1	8	0	0	0
1996	Detroit	11	1	2	3	12	0	0	0
1997♦	Detroit	20	4	8	12	60	1	0	1
1998♦	Detroit	21	9	6	15	20	2	1	1
1999	Detroit	10	0	2	2	20	0	0	0
2000	Detroit	9	3	1	4	20	2	0	1
2001	Detroit	6	0	1	1	8	0	0	0
2002	Boston	6	1	2	3	12	1	0	1
Playoff Totals		**92**	**18**	**24**	**42**	**170**	**6**	**1**	**4**
LAPOINTE, Rick									Defense
1977	Philadelphia	10	0	0	0	7	0	0	0
1978	Philadelphia	12	0	3	3	19	0	0	0
1979	Philadelphia	7	0	1	1	14	0	0	0
1980	St. Louis	3	0	1	1	6	0	0	0
1981	St. Louis	8	2	2	4	12	0	0	0
1982	St. Louis	3	0	0	0	6	0	0	0
1984	Quebec	3	0	0	0	0	0	0	0
Playoff Totals		**46**	**2**	**7**	**9**	**64**	**0**	**0**	**0**
LAPPIN, Peter	*No Playoffs*								Right wing

Season	Team	GP	G	A	Pts	PIM	PP	SH	GW
LAPRADE, Edgar									Center
1948	NY Rangers	6	1	4	5	0	....	....	....
1950	NY Rangers	12	3	5	8	4	....	....	....
Playoff Totals		**18**	**4**	**9**	**13**	**4**	....	....	....
LaPRAIRIE, Benjamin	*No Playoffs*								Defense
•LARAQUE, Georges									Right wing
1999	Edmonton	4	0	0	0	2	0	0	0
2000	Edmonton	5	0	1	1	6	0	0	0
2001	Edmonton	6	1	1	2	8	0	0	0
Playoff Totals		**15**	**1**	**2**	**3**	**16**	**0**	**0**	**0**
•LARIONOV, Igor									Center
1991	Vancouver	6	1	0	1	6	0	0	0
1992	Vancouver	13	3	7	10	4	1	0	0
1994	San Jose	14	5	13	18	10	0	0	0
1995	San Jose	11	1	8	9	2	0	0	0
1996	Detroit	19	6	7	13	6	3	0	2
1997♦	Detroit	20	4	8	12	8	3	0	1
1998♦	Detroit	22	3	10	13	12	0	0	0
1999	Detroit	7	0	2	2	0	0	0	0
2000	Detroit	9	1	2	3	6	1	0	0
2001	Detroit	6	1	3	4	2	1	0	0
2002♦	Detroit	18	5	6	11	4	0	0	1
Playoff Totals		**145**	**30**	**66**	**96**	**60**	**9**	**0**	**4**
LARIVIERE, Garry									Defense
1981	Edmonton	9	0	3	3	8	0	0	0
1982	Edmonton	4	0	1	1	0	0	0	0
1983	Edmonton	1	0	1	1	0	0	0	0
Playoff Totals		**14**	**0**	**5**	**5**	**8**	**0**	**0**	**0**
LARMER, Jeff									Left wing
1984	Chicago	5	1	0	1	2	1	0	0
Playoff Totals		**5**	**1**	**0**	**1**	**2**	**1**	**0**	**0**
LARMER, Steve									Right wing
1983	Chicago	11	5	7	12	8	2	0	1
1984	Chicago	5	2	2	4	7	1	0	0
1985	Chicago	15	9	13	22	14	5	0	1
1986	Chicago	3	0	3	3	4	0	0	0
1987	Chicago	4	0	0	0	2	0	0	0
1988	Chicago	5	1	6	7	0	1	0	0
1989	Chicago	16	8	9	17	22	3	0	2
1990	Chicago	20	7	15	22	2	2	2	2
1991	Chicago	6	5	1	6	4	1	0	0
1992	Chicago	18	8	7	15	6	3	0	0
1993	Chicago	4	0	3	3	0	0	0	0
1994♦	NY Rangers	23	9	7	16	14	3	0	0
1995	NY Rangers	10	2	2	4	6	0	1	1
Playoff Totals		**140**	**56**	**75**	**131**	**89**	**21**	**3**	**7**
LAROCHELLE, Wildor									Right wing
1927	Montreal	4	0	0	0	0	....	....	....
1928	Montreal	2	0	0	0	0	....	....	....
1930♦	Montreal	6	1	0	1	12	....	....	....
1931♦	Montreal	10	1	2	3	8	....	....	....
1932	Montreal	4	2	1	3	4	....	....	....
1933	Montreal	2	1	0	1	0	....	....	....
1934	Montreal	2	1	1	2	0	....	....	....
1935	Montreal	2	0	0	0	0	....	....	....
1936	Chicago	2	0	0	0	0	....	....	....
Playoff Totals		**34**	**6**	**4**	**10**	**24**	....	....	....
LAROCQUE, Denis	*No Playoffs*								Defense
•LAROCQUE, Mario	*No Playoffs*								Defense
LAROSE, Bonner	*No Playoffs*								Left wing
LAROSE, Claude									Left wing
1982	NY Rangers	2	0	0	0	0	0	0	0
Playoff Totals		**2**	**0**	**0**	**0**	**0**	**0**	**0**	**0**
LAROSE, Claude									Right wing
1964	Montreal	2	1	0	1	0	0	0	0
1965♦	Montreal	13	0	1	1	14	0	0	0
1966♦	Montreal	6	0	1	1	31	0	0	0
1967	Montreal	10	1	5	6	15	0	0	0
1968♦	Montreal	12	3	2	5	8	0	0	0
1970	Minnesota	6	1	1	2	25	0	0	0
1971♦	Montreal	11	1	0	1	10	0	0	0
1972	Montreal	6	2	1	3	23	0	0	0
1973♦	Montreal	17	3	4	7	6	0	0	0
1974	Montreal	5	0	2	2	11	0	0	0
1975	St. Louis	2	1	1	2	0	0	0	0
1976	St. Louis	3	0	0	0	0	0	0	0
1977	St. Louis	4	1	0	1	0	0	0	0
Playoff Totals		**97**	**14**	**18**	**32**	**143**	**0**	**0**	**0**
LAROSE, Guy									Center
1995	Boston	4	0	0	0	0	0	0	0
Playoff Totals		**4**	**0**	**0**	**0**	**0**	**0**	**0**	**0**

Season	Team	GP	G	A	Pts	PIM	PP	SH	GW
LAROUCHE, Pierre									Center
1975	Pittsburgh	9	2	5	7	2	0	0	1
1976	Pittsburgh	3	0	1	1	0	0	0	0
1977	Pittsburgh	3	0	3	3	0	0	0	0
1978♦	Montreal	5	2	1	3	4	1	0	1
1979♦	Montreal	6	1	3	4	0	0	0	1
1980	Montreal	9	1	7	8	2	0	0	0
1981	Montreal	2	0	2	2	0	0	0	0
1984	NY Rangers	5	3	1	4	2	2	0	0
1986	NY Rangers	16	8	9	17	2	4	0	1
1987	NY Rangers	6	3	2	5	4	0	0	1
Playoff Totals		**64**	**20**	**34**	**54**	**16**	**7**	**0**	**5**
LAROUCHE, Steve *No Playoffs*									Center
•**LARSEN, Brad**									Left wing
2002	Colorado	21	1	1	2	13	0	0	0
Playoff Totals		**21**	**1**	**1**	**2**	**13**	**0**	**0**	**0**
LARSON, Norm *No Playoffs*									Right wing
LARSON, Reed									Defense
1978	Detroit	7	0	2	2	4	0	0	0
1984	Detroit	4	2	0	2	21	2	0	0
1985	Detroit	3	1	2	3	20	0	0	0
1986	Boston	3	1	0	1	6	1	0	0
1987	Boston	4	0	2	2	2	0	0	0
1988	Boston	8	0	1	1	6	0	0	0
1989	Minnesota	3	0	0	0	4	0	0	0
Playoff Totals		**32**	**4**	**7**	**11**	**63**	**3**	**0**	**0**
LARTER, Tyler *No Playoffs*									Center
LATAL, Jiri *No Playoffs*									Defense
LATOS, James *No Playoffs*									Right wing
LATREILLE, Phil *No Playoffs*									Center/Right wing
LATTA, David *No Playoffs*									Left wing
LAUDER, Martin *No Playoffs*									Defense/Center
LAUEN, Mike *No Playoffs*									Right wing
LAUER, Brad									Left wing
1987	NY Islanders	6	2	0	2	4	0	0	0
1988	NY Islanders	5	3	1	4	4	0	0	0
1990	NY Islanders	4	0	2	2	10	0	0	0
1992	Chicago	7	1	1	2	2	0	0	0
1996	Pittsburgh	12	1	1	2	4	0	0	0
Playoff Totals		**34**	**7**	**5**	**12**	**24**	**0**	**0**	**0**
LAUGHLIN, Craig									Right wing
1982	Montreal	3	0	1	1	0	0	0	0
1983	Washington	4	1	0	1	0	0	0	0
1984	Washington	8	4	2	6	6	1	0	3
1985	Washington	5	0	0	0	2	0	0	0
1986	Washington	9	1	2	3	10	0	0	1
1987	Washington	1	0	0	0	0	0	0	0
1988	Los Angeles	3	0	1	1	2	0	0	0
Playoff Totals		**33**	**6**	**6**	**12**	**20**	**1**	**0**	**4**
LAUGHTON, Mike									Center
1969	Oakland	7	2	3	5	0	0	0	0
1970	Oakland	4	0	1	1	0	0	0	0
Playoff Totals		**11**	**2**	**4**	**6**	**0**	**0**	**0**	**0**
•**LAUKKANEN, Janne**									Defense
1995	Quebec	6	1	0	1	2	0	0	0
1997	Ottawa	7	0	1	1	6	0	0	0
1998	Ottawa	11	2	2	4	8	1	0	1
1999	Ottawa	4	0	0	0	4	0	0	0
2000	Pittsburgh	11	2	4	6	10	1	0	1
2001	Pittsburgh	18	2	2	4	14	1	0	0
Playoff Totals		**57**	**7**	**9**	**16**	**44**	**3**	**0**	**2**
LAURENCE, Don *No Playoffs*									Center
•**LAUS, Paul**									Defense
1996	Florida	21	2	6	8	*62	0	0	0
1997	Florida	5	0	1	1	4	0	0	0
2000	Florida	4	0	0	0	8	0	0	0
Playoff Totals		**30**	**2**	**7**	**9**	**74**	**0**	**0**	**0**
LaVALLEE, Kevin									Left wing
1981	Calgary	8	2	3	5	4	1	0	1
1982	Calgary	3	0	0	0	7	0	0	0
1983	Calgary	8	1	3	4	4	0	0	0
1986	St. Louis	13	2	2	4	6	0	0	0
Playoff Totals		**32**	**5**	**8**	**13**	**21**	**1**	**0**	**1**
LaVARRE, Mark									Right wing
1988	Chicago	1	0	0	0	2	0	0	0
Playoff Totals		**1**	**0**	**0**	**0**	**2**	**0**	**0**	**0**
LAVENDER, Brian									Left wing
1972	St. Louis	3	0	0	0	2	0	0	0
Playoff Totals		**3**	**0**	**0**	**0**	**2**	**0**	**0**	**0**
LAVIGNE, Eric *No Playoffs*									Defense
LAVIOLETTE, Jack									Defense/Right wing
1918	Montreal	2	0	0	0	0	0	0	0
Playoff Totals		**2**	**0**	**0**	**0**	**0**	**0**	**0**	**0**
LAVIOLETTE, Peter *No Playoffs*									Defense
LAVOIE, Dominic *No Playoffs*									Defense
•**LAW, Kirby** *No Playoffs*									Right wing

Season	Team	GP	G	A	Pts	PIM	PP	SH	GW
LAWLESS, Paul									Left wing
1986	Hartford	1	0	0	0	0	0	0	0
1987	Hartford	2	0	2	2	2	0	0	0
Playoff Totals		**3**	**0**	**2**	**2**	**2**	**0**	**0**	**0**
LAWRENCE, Mark *No Playoffs*									Right wing
LAWSON, Danny									Right wing
1970	Minnesota	6	0	1	1	2	0	0	0
1971	Minnesota	10	0	0	0	0	0	0	0
Playoff Totals		**16**	**0**	**1**	**1**	**2**	**0**	**0**	**0**
LAWTON, Brian									Left wing
1984	Minnesota	5	0	0	0	10	0	0	0
1986	Minnesota	3	0	1	1	2	0	0	0
1989	Hartford	3	1	0	1	0	0	0	0
Playoff Totals		**11**	**1**	**1**	**2**	**12**	**0**	**0**	**0**
LAXDAL, Derek									Right wing
1990	NY Islanders	1	0	2	2	2	0	0	0
Playoff Totals		**1**	**0**	**2**	**2**	**2**	**0**	**0**	**0**
LAYCOE, Hal									Defense
1949	Montreal	7	0	1	1	13	....	....	....
1950	Montreal	2	0	0	0	0	....	....	....
1951	Boston	6	0	1	1	5	....	....	....
1952	Boston	7	1	1	2	11	....	....	....
1953	Boston	11	0	2	2	10	....	....	....
1954	Boston	2	0	0	0	0	....	....	....
1955	Boston	5	1	0	1	0	....	....	....
Playoff Totals		**40**	**2**	**5**	**7**	**39**	....	....	....
LAZARO, Jeff									Left wing
1991	Boston	19	3	2	5	30	0	0	0
1992	Boston	9	0	1	1	2	0	0	0
Playoff Totals		**28**	**3**	**3**	**6**	**32**	**0**	**0**	**0**
LEACH, Jamie *No Playoffs*									Right wing
LEACH, Larry									Center
1959	Boston	7	1	1	2	8	0	1	0
Playoff Totals		**7**	**1**	**1**	**2**	**8**	**0**	**1**	**0**
LEACH, Reggie									Right wing
1971	Boston	3	0	0	0	0	0	0	0
1975♦	Philadelphia	17	8	2	10	6	2	0	2
1976	Philadelphia	16	*19	5	*24	8	2	0	2
1977	Philadelphia	10	4	5	9	0	0	0	2
1978	Philadelphia	12	2	2	4	0	1	0	0
1979	Philadelphia	8	5	1	6	0	3	0	2
1980	Philadelphia	19	9	7	16	6	2	1	0
1981	Philadelphia	9	0	0	0	2	0	0	0
Playoff Totals		**94**	**47**	**22**	**69**	**22**	**10**	**1**	**8**
LEACH, Stephen									Right wing
1986	Washington	6	0	1	1	0	0	0	0
1988	Washington	9	2	1	3	0	0	0	1
1989	Washington	6	1	0	1	12	1	0	0
1990	Washington	14	2	2	4	8	0	0	0
1991	Washington	9	1	2	3	8	0	0	0
1992	Boston	15	4	0	4	10	0	0	1
1993	Boston	4	1	1	2	2	0	0	0
1994	Boston	5	0	1	1	2	0	0	0
1996	St. Louis	11	3	2	5	10	1	0	1
1997	St. Louis	6	0	0	0	33	0	0	0
1999	Phoenix	7	1	1	2	2	0	0	0
Playoff Totals		**92**	**15**	**11**	**26**	**87**	**2**	**0**	**3**
LEAVINS, Jim *No Playoffs*									Defense
LEBEAU, Patrick *No Playoffs*									Left wing
LEBEAU, Stephan									Center
1990	Montreal	2	3	0	3	0	0	0	1
1991	Montreal	7	2	1	3	2	0	0	0
1992	Montreal	8	1	3	4	4	1	0	0
1993♦	Montreal	13	3	3	6	6	1	0	1
Playoff Totals		**30**	**9**	**7**	**16**	**12**	**2**	**0**	**2**
LeBLANC, Fern *No Playoffs*									Center
LeBLANC, J.P.									Center
1978	Detroit	2	0	0	0	0	0	0	0
Playoff Totals		**2**	**0**	**0**	**0**	**0**	**0**	**0**	**0**
LeBLANC, John									Right wing
1989	Edmonton	1	0	0	0	0	0	0	0
Playoff Totals		**1**	**0**	**0**	**0**	**0**	**0**	**0**	**0**
LeBOUTILLIER, Peter *No Playoffs*									Right wing
LeBRUN, Al *No Playoffs*									Defense
LECAINE, Bill *No Playoffs*									Left wing
•**LECAVALIER, Vincent** *No Playoffs*									Center
LECLAIR, Jack									Center
1955	Montreal	12	5	0	5	2	1	0	0
1956♦	Montreal	8	1	1	2	4	0	0	0
1957♦	Montreal	....	....	....	....	....	....	....	....
Playoff Totals		**20**	**6**	**1**	**7**	**6**	**1**	**0**	**0**

Season	Team	GP	G	A	Pts	PIM	PP	SH	GW
•**LeCLAIR, John**									Left wing
1991	Montreal	3	0	0	0	0	0	0	0
1992	Montreal	8	1	1	2	4	0	0	0
1993♦	Montreal	20	4	6	10	14	0	0	3
1994	Montreal	7	2	1	3	8	1	0	0
1995	Philadelphia	15	5	7	12	4	1	0	1
1996	Philadelphia	11	6	5	11	6	4	0	1
1997	Philadelphia	19	9	12	21	10	4	0	3
1998	Philadelphia	5	1	1	2	8	1	0	1
1999	Philadelphia	6	3	0	3	12	2	0	0
2000	Philadelphia	18	6	7	13	6	4	0	2
2001	Philadelphia	6	1	2	3	2	0	0	0
2002	Philadelphia	5	0	0	0	2	0	0	0
Playoff Totals		**123**	**38**	**42**	**80**	**76**	**17**	**0**	**11**
•**LECLERC, Mike**									Left wing
1997	Anaheim	1	0	0	0	0	0	0	0
1999	Anaheim	1	0	0	0	0	0	0	0
Playoff Totals		**2**	**0**	**0**	**0**	**0**	**0**	**0**	**0**
LECLERC, Rene *No Playoffs*									Right wing
LECUYER, Doug									Left wing
1980	Chicago	7	4	0	4	15	0	0	1
Playoff Totals		**7**	**4**	**0**	**4**	**15**	**0**	**0**	**1**
LEDINGHAM, Walt *No Playoffs*									Left wing
LEDUC, Albert									Defense
1927	Montreal	4	0	0	0	2	....	....	....
1928	Montreal	2	1	0	1	5	....	....	....
1929	Montreal	3	1	0	1	4	....	....	....
1930♦	Montreal	6	1	3	4	8	....	....	....
1931♦	Montreal	7	0	2	2	9	....	....	....
1932	Montreal	4	1	1	2	2	....	....	....
1933	Montreal	2	1	0	1	2	....	....	....
Playoff Totals		**28**	**5**	**6**	**11**	**32**	....	....	....
LEDUC, Rich									Center
1974	Boston	5	0	0	0	9	0	0	0
Playoff Totals		**5**	**0**	**0**	**0**	**9**	**0**	**0**	**0**
•**LEDYARD, Grant**									Defense
1985	NY Rangers	3	0	2	2	4	0	0	0
1987	Los Angeles	5	0	0	0	10	0	0	0
1988	Washington	14	1	0	1	30	0	0	0
1989	Buffalo	5	1	2	3	2	0	0	0
1991	Buffalo	6	3	3	6	10	0	0	0
1993	Buffalo	8	0	0	0	8	0	0	0
1994	Dallas	9	1	2	3	6	0	0	1
1995	Dallas	3	0	0	0	2	0	0	0
1997	Dallas	7	0	2	2	0	0	0	0
1998	Boston	6	0	0	0	2	0	0	0
1999	Boston	2	0	0	0	2	0	0	0
2000	Ottawa	6	0	0	0	16	0	0	0
2001	Dallas	9	0	1	1	4	0	0	0
Playoff Totals		**83**	**6**	**12**	**18**	**96**	**0**	**0**	**1**
LEE, Bobby *No Playoffs*									Center
LEE, Edward *No Playoffs*									Right wing
LEE, Peter									Right wing
1979	Pittsburgh	7	0	3	3	0	0	0	0
1980	Pittsburgh	4	0	1	1	0	0	0	0
1981	Pittsburgh	5	0	4	4	4	0	0	0
1982	Pittsburgh	3	0	0	0	0	0	0	0
Playoff Totals		**19**	**0**	**8**	**8**	**4**	**0**	**0**	**0**
•**LEEB, Brad** *No Playoffs*									Right wing
•**LEEB, Greg** *No Playoffs*									Center
LEEMAN, Gary									Right wing
1983	Toronto	2	0	0	0	0	0	0	0
1986	Toronto	10	2	10	12	2	0	0	0
1987	Toronto	5	0	1	1	14	0	0	0
1988	Toronto	2	2	0	2	2	2	0	0
1990	Toronto	5	3	3	6	16	2	0	0
1993♦	Montreal	11	1	2	3	2	0	0	0
1994	Montreal	1	0	0	0	0	0	0	0
Playoff Totals		**36**	**8**	**16**	**24**	**36**	**4**	**0**	**0**
•**LEETCH, Brian**									Defense
1989	NY Rangers	4	3	2	5	2	2	0	0
1991	NY Rangers	6	1	3	4	0	0	0	0
1992	NY Rangers	13	4	11	15	4	1	1	0
1994♦	NY Rangers	23	11	*23	*34	6	4	0	4
1995	NY Rangers	10	6	8	14	8	3	0	1
1996	NY Rangers	11	1	6	7	4	1	0	0
1997	NY Rangers	15	2	8	10	6	1	0	1
Playoff Totals		**82**	**28**	**61**	**89**	**30**	**12**	**1**	**6**
•**LEFEBVRE, Guillaume** *No Playoffs*									Left wing
LEFEBVRE, Patrice *No Playoffs*									Right wing

Season	Team	GP	G	A	Pts	PIM	PP	SH	GW
•LEFEBVRE, Sylvain	Defense								
1990	Montreal	6	0	0	0	2	0	0	0
1991	Montreal	11	1	0	1	6	0	0	0
1992	Montreal	2	0	0	0	2	0	0	0
1993	Toronto	21	3	3	6	20	0	0	0
1994	Toronto	18	0	3	3	16	0	0	0
1995	Quebec	6	0	2	2	2	0	0	0
1996♦	Colorado	22	0	5	5	12	0	0	0
1997	Colorado	17	0	0	0	25	0	0	0
1998	Colorado	7	0	0	0	4	0	0	0
1999	Colorado	19	0	1	1	12	0	0	0
Playoff Totals		**129**	**4**	**14**	**18**	**101**	**0**	**0**	**0**
LEFLEY, Bryan	Defense/Left wing								
1978	Colorado	2	0	0	0	0	0	0	0
Playoff Totals		**2**	**0**	**0**	**0**	**0**	**0**	**0**	**0**
LEFLEY, Chuck	Left wing								
1971♦	Montreal	1	0	0	0	0	0	0	0
1973♦	Montreal	17	3	5	8	6	0	0	0
1974	Montreal	6	0	1	1	0	0	0	0
1975	St. Louis	2	0	0	0	2	0	0	0
1976	St. Louis	2	2	1	3	0	0	1	0
1977	St. Louis	1	0	1	1	2	0	0	0
Playoff Totals		**29**	**5**	**8**	**13**	**10**	**0**	**1**	**0**
LEGER, Roger	Defense								
1947	Montreal	11	0	6	6	10	0	0	0
1949	Montreal	5	0	1	1	2	0	0	0
1950	Montreal	4	0	0	0	2	0	0	0
Playoff Totals		**20**	**0**	**7**	**7**	**14**	**0**	**0**	**0**
LEGGE, Barry *No Playoffs*	Defense								
LEGGE, Randy *No Playoffs*	Defense								
•LEGWAND, David *No Playoffs*	Center								
LEHMAN, Tommy *No Playoffs*	Center								
•LEHTINEN, Jere	Right wing								
1997	Dallas	7	2	2	4	0	0	0	0
1998	Dallas	12	3	5	8	2	1	0	0
1999♦	Dallas	23	10	3	13	2	1	1	0
2000	Dallas	13	1	5	6	2	0	0	0
2001	Dallas	10	1	0	1	2	0	0	0
Playoff Totals		**65**	**17**	**15**	**32**	**8**	**2**	**1**	**0**
LEHTO, Petteri *No Playoffs*	Defense								
LEHTONEN, Antero *No Playoffs*	Left wing								
LEHVONEN, Henri *No Playoffs*	Defense								
LEIER, Edward *No Playoffs*	Center								
LEINONEN, Mikko	Center								
1982	NY Rangers	7	1	6	7	20	0	0	0
1983	NY Rangers	7	1	3	4	4	1	0	0
1984	NY Rangers	5	0	2	2	4	0	0	0
1985	Washington	1	0	0	0	0	0	0	0
Playoff Totals		**20**	**2**	**11**	**13**	**28**	**1**	**0**	**0**
LEITER, Bobby	Center								
1972	Pittsburgh	4	3	0	3	0	1	0	0
1974	Atlanta	4	0	0	0	2	0	0	0
Playoff Totals		**8**	**3**	**0**	**3**	**2**	**1**	**0**	**0**
LEITER, Ken	Defense								
1987	NY Islanders	11	0	5	5	6	0	0	0
1988	NY Islanders	4	0	1	1	2	0	0	0
Playoff Totals		**15**	**0**	**6**	**6**	**8**	**0**	**0**	**0**
LEMAIRE, Jacques	Center								
1968♦	Montreal	13	7	6	13	6	2	0	2
1969♦	Montreal	14	4	2	6	6	1	0	0
1971♦	Montreal	20	9	10	19	17	4	0	1
1972	Montreal	6	2	1	3	2	0	0	0
1973♦	Montreal	17	7	13	20	2	3	0	1
1974	Montreal	6	0	4	4	2	0	0	0
1975	Montreal	11	5	7	12	4	1	0	0
1976♦	Montreal	13	3	3	6	2	1	1	1
1977♦	Montreal	14	7	12	19	6	1	0	3
1978♦	Montreal	15	6	8	14	10	0	0	1
1979♦	Montreal	16	*11	12	*23	6	6	0	2
Playoff Totals		**145**	**61**	**78**	**139**	**63**	**19**	**1**	**11**
LEMAY, Moe	Left wing								
1984	Vancouver	4	0	0	0	12	0	0	0
1987♦	Edmonton	9	2	1	3	11	0	0	1
1988	Boston	15	4	2	6	32	0	0	0
Playoff Totals		**28**	**6**	**3**	**9**	**55**	**0**	**0**	**1**
LEMELIN, Roger *No Playoffs*	Defense								
LEMIEUX, Alain	Center								
1983	St. Louis	4	0	1	1	0	0	0	0
1985	Quebec	14	3	3	6	0	2	0	0
1986	Quebec	1	1	2	3	0	1	0	0
Playoff Totals		**19**	**4**	**6**	**10**	**0**	**3**	**0**	**0**
LEMIEUX, Bob *No Playoffs*	Defense								

Season	Team	GP	G	A	Pts	PIM	PP	SH	GW
•LEMIEUX, Claude	Right wing								
1986♦	Montreal	20	10	6	16	68	4	0	4
1987	Montreal	17	4	9	13	41	2	0	0
1988	Montreal	11	3	2	5	20	0	0	2
1989	Montreal	18	4	3	7	58	0	0	1
1990	Montreal	11	1	3	4	38	0	0	1
1991♦	New Jersey	7	4	0	4	34	2	0	1
1992	New Jersey	7	4	3	7	26	1	0	0
1993	New Jersey	5	2	0	2	19	1	0	0
1994	New Jersey	20	7	11	18	44	0	0	2
1995♦	New Jersey	20	*13	3	16	20	0	0	3
1996♦	Colorado	19	5	7	12	55	3	0	0
1997	Colorado	17	*13	10	23	32	4	0	4
1998	Colorado	7	3	3	6	8	1	0	1
1999	Colorado	19	3	11	14	26	1	0	0
2000♦	New Jersey	23	4	6	10	28	1	0	0
2002	Phoenix	5	0	0	0	2	0	0	0
Playoff Totals		**226**	**80**	**77**	**157**	**519**	**20**	**0**	**19**
LEMIEUX, Jacques	Defense								
1969	Los Angeles	1	0	0	0	0	0	0	0
Playoff Totals		**1**	**0**	**0**	**0**	**0**	**0**	**0**	**0**
LEMIEUX, Jean	Defense								
1974	Atlanta	3	1	1	2	0	1	0	0
Playoff Totals		**3**	**1**	**1**	**2**	**0**	**1**	**0**	**0**
LEMIEUX, Jocelyn	Right wing								
1987	St. Louis	5	0	1	1	6	0	0	0
1988	St. Louis	5	0	0	0	15	0	0	0
1990	Chicago	18	1	8	9	28	0	0	0
1991	Chicago	4	0	0	0	0	0	0	0
1992	Chicago	18	3	1	4	33	0	0	2
1993	Chicago	4	1	0	1	2	0	0	0
1996	Calgary	4	0	0	0	0	0	0	0
1997	Phoenix	2	0	0	0	4	0	0	0
Playoff Totals		**60**	**5**	**10**	**15**	**88**	**0**	**0**	**2**
•LEMIEUX, Mario	Center								
1989	Pittsburgh	11	12	7	19	16	7	1	0
1991♦	Pittsburgh	23	16	*28	*44	16	6	2	0
1992♦	Pittsburgh	15	*16	18	*34	2	8	2	5
1993	Pittsburgh	11	8	10	18	10	3	1	1
1994	Pittsburgh	6	4	3	7	2	1	0	0
1996	Pittsburgh	18	11	16	27	33	3	1	2
1997	Pittsburgh	5	3	3	6	4	0	0	0
2001	Pittsburgh	18	6	11	17	4	1	0	3
Playoff Totals		**107**	**76**	**96**	**172**	**87**	**29**	**7**	**11**
LEMIEUX, Real	Left wing								
1968	Los Angeles	7	1	1	2	0	0	0	0
1969	Los Angeles	11	1	3	4	10	1	0	0
Playoff Totals		**18**	**2**	**4**	**6**	**10**	**1**	**0**	**0**
LEMIEUX, Rich	Center								
1976	Atlanta	2	0	0	0	0	0	0	0
Playoff Totals		**2**	**0**	**0**	**0**	**0**	**0**	**0**	**0**
LENARDON, Tim *No Playoffs*	Center								
•LEOPOLD, Jordan *No Playoffs*	Defense								
LEPINE, Hec *No Playoffs*	Center								
LEPINE, Pit	Center								
1927	Montreal	4	0	0	0	4	....	....	....
1928	Montreal	1	0	0	0	0	....	....	....
1929	Montreal	3	0	0	0	2	....	....	....
1930♦	Montreal	6	2	2	4	6	....	....	....
1931♦	Montreal	10	4	2	6	6	....	....	....
1932	Montreal	3	1	0	1	4	....	....	....
1933	Montreal	2	0	0	0	2	....	....	....
1934	Montreal	2	0	0	0	0	....	....	....
1935	Montreal	2	0	0	0	2	....	....	....
1937	Montreal	5	0	1	1	0	....	....	....
1938	Montreal	3	0	0	0	0	....	....	....
Playoff Totals		**41**	**7**	**5**	**12**	**26**	....	....	....
•LEROUX, Francois	Defense								
1995	Pittsburgh	12	0	2	2	14	0	0	0
1996	Pittsburgh	18	1	1	2	20	0	0	1
1997	Pittsburgh	3	0	0	0	0	0	0	0
Playoff Totals		**33**	**1**	**3**	**4**	**34**	**0**	**0**	**1**
LEROUX, Gaston *No Playoffs*	Defense								
•LEROUX, Jean-Yves *No Playoffs*	Left wing								
•LESCHYSHYN, Curtis	Defense								
1993	Quebec	6	1	1	2	6	1	0	0
1995	Quebec	3	0	1	1	4	0	0	0
1996♦	Colorado	17	1	2	3	8	0	0	0
1999	Carolina	6	0	0	0	6	0	0	0
2001	Ottawa	4	0	0	0	0	0	0	0
2002	Ottawa	12	0	1	1	0	0	0	0
Playoff Totals		**48**	**2**	**5**	**7**	**24**	**1**	**0**	**0**
LESIEUR, Art	Defense								
1931♦	Montreal	10	0	0	0	4	0	0	0
1932	Montreal	4	0	0	0	0	0	0	0
Playoff Totals		**14**	**0**	**0**	**0**	**4**	**0**	**0**	**0**
•LESSARD, Francis *No Playoffs*	Defense								
LESSARD, Rick *No Playoffs*	Defense								

Season	Team	GP	G	A	Pts	PIM	PP	SH	GW
LESUK, Bill	Left wing								
1969	Boston	1	0	0	0	0	0	0	0
1970♦	Boston	2	0	0	0	0	0	0	0
1971	Philadelphia	4	1	0	1	8	1	0	0
1974	Los Angeles	2	0	0	0	4	0	0	0
Playoff Totals		**9**	**1**	**0**	**1**	**12**	**1**	**0**	**0**
LESWICK, Jack *No Playoffs*	Center								
LESWICK, Pete *No Playoffs*	Wing								
LESWICK, Tony	Wing								
1948	NY Rangers	6	3	2	5	8	....	....	....
1950	NY Rangers	12	2	4	6	12	....	....	....
1952♦	Detroit	8	3	1	4	22	....	....	....
1953	Detroit	6	1	0	1	11	....	....	....
1954♦	Detroit	12	3	1	4	18	....	....	....
1955♦	Detroit	11	1	2	3	20	....	....	....
1958	Detroit	4	0	0	0	0	....	....	....
Playoff Totals		**59**	**13**	**10**	**23**	**91**	....	....	....
•LETANG, Alan *No Playoffs*	Defense								
•LETOWSKI, Trevor	Center								
2000	Phoenix	5	1	1	2	4	0	0	0
2002	Vancouver	6	0	1	1	8	0	0	0
Playoff Totals		**11**	**1**	**2**	**3**	**12**	**0**	**0**	**0**
LEVANDOSKI, Joe *No Playoffs*	Right wing								
LEVEILLE, Normand *No Playoffs*	Left wing								
LEVEQUE, Guy *No Playoffs*	Center								
LEVER, Don	Left wing								
1975	Vancouver	5	0	1	1	4	0	0	0
1976	Vancouver	2	0	0	0	0	0	0	0
1979	Vancouver	3	2	1	3	2	1	0	1
1980	Atlanta	4	1	1	2	0	1	0	0
1981	Calgary	16	4	7	11	20	0	0	0
Playoff Totals		**30**	**7**	**10**	**17**	**26**	**2**	**0**	**1**
LEVIE, Craig	Defense								
1984	Minnesota	15	2	3	5	32	0	0	0
1985	St. Louis	1	0	0	0	0	0	0	0
Playoff Totals		**16**	**2**	**3**	**5**	**32**	**0**	**0**	**0**
LEVINS, Scott *No Playoffs*	Center/Right wing								
LEVINSKY, Alex	Defense								
1931	Toronto	2	0	0	0	0	....	....	....
1932♦	Toronto	7	0	0	0	6	....	....	....
1933	Toronto	9	1	0	1	14	....	....	....
1934	Toronto	5	0	0	0	6	....	....	....
1935	Chicago	2	0	0	0	0	....	....	....
1936	Chicago	2	0	1	1	0	....	....	....
1938♦	Chicago	10	1	0	1	0	....	....	....
Playoff Totals		**37**	**2**	**1**	**3**	**26**	....	....	....
LEVO, Tapio *No Playoffs*	Defense								
LEWICKI, Danny	Left wing								
1951♦	Toronto	9	0	0	0	0	0	0	0
1956	NY Rangers	5	0	3	3	0	0	0	0
1957	NY Rangers	5	0	1	1	2	0	0	0
1958	NY Rangers	6	0	0	0	6	0	0	0
1959	Chicago	3	0	0	0	0	0	0	0
Playoff Totals		**28**	**0**	**4**	**4**	**8**	**0**	**0**	**0**
LEWIS, Dale *No Playoffs*	Left wing								
LEWIS, Dave	Defense								
1975	NY Islanders	17	0	1	1	28	0	0	0
1976	NY Islanders	13	0	1	1	44	0	0	0
1977	NY Islanders	12	1	6	7	4	0	0	0
1978	NY Islanders	7	0	1	1	11	0	0	0
1979	NY Islanders	10	0	0	0	4	0	0	0
1980	Los Angeles	4	0	1	1	2	0	0	0
1981	Los Angeles	4	0	2	2	4	0	0	0
1982	Los Angeles	10	0	4	4	36	0	0	0
1987	Detroit	14	0	4	4	10	0	0	0
Playoff Totals		**91**	**1**	**20**	**21**	**143**	**0**	**0**	**0**
LEWIS, Doug *No Playoffs*	Left wing								
LEWIS, Herbie	Left wing								
1932	Detroit	2	0	0	0	0	....	....	....
1933	Detroit	4	1	0	1	0	....	....	....
1934	Detroit	9	*5	2	7	2	....	....	....
1936♦	Detroit	7	2	3	5	0	....	....	....
1937♦	Detroit	10	*4	3	7	4	....	....	....
1939	Detroit	6	1	2	3	0	....	....	....
Playoff Totals		**38**	**13**	**10**	**23**	**6**	....	....	....
LEY, Rick	Defense								
1969	Toronto	3	0	0	0	9	0	0	0
1971	Toronto	6	0	2	2	4	0	0	0
1972	Toronto	5	0	0	0	7	0	0	0
Playoff Totals		**14**	**0**	**2**	**2**	**20**	**0**	**0**	**0**
LIBA, Igor	Left wing								
1989	Los Angeles	2	0	0	0	2	0	0	0
Playoff Totals		**2**	**0**	**0**	**0**	**2**	**0**	**0**	**0**
LIBBY, Jeff *No Playoffs*	Defense								

Season	Team	GP	G	A	Pts	PIM	PP	SH	GW
LIBETT, Nick	Left wing								
1970	Detroit	4	2	0	2	2	1	0	0
1978	Detroit	7	3	1	4	0	1	0	0
1980	Pittsburgh	5	1	1	2	0	1	0	0
Playoff Totals		**16**	**6**	**2**	**8**	**2**	**3**	**0**	**0**
LICARI, Tony *No Playoffs*	Right wing								
LIDDINGTON, Bob *No Playoffs*	Left wing								
LIDSTER, Doug	Defense								
1984	Vancouver	2	0	1	1	0	0	0	0
1986	Vancouver	3	0	1	1	2	0	0	0
1989	Vancouver	7	1	1	2	9	0	0	0
1991	Vancouver	6	0	2	2	6	0	0	0
1992	Vancouver	11	1	2	3	11	0	0	0
1993	Vancouver	12	0	3	3	8	0	0	0
1994◆	NY Rangers	9	2	0	2	10	0	0	0
1995	St. Louis	4	0	0	0	2	0	0	0
1996	NY Rangers	7	1	0	1	6	1	0	0
1997	NY Rangers	15	1	5	6	8	0	0	0
1999	Dallas	4	0	0	0	2	0	0	0
Playoff Totals		**80**	**6**	**15**	**21**	**64**	**1**	**0**	**0**
•LIDSTROM, Nicklas	Defense								
1992	Detroit	11	1	2	3	0	1	0	0
1993	Detroit	7	1	0	1	0	1	0	0
1994	Detroit	7	3	2	5	0	1	1	0
1995	Detroit	18	4	12	16	8	3	0	2
1996	Detroit	19	5	9	14	10	1	0	0
1997◆	Detroit	20	2	6	8	2	0	0	0
1998◆	Detroit	22	6	13	19	8	2	0	2
1999	Detroit	10	2	9	11	4	2	0	0
2000	Detroit	9	2	4	6	4	1	0	0
2001	Detroit	6	1	7	8	0	0	0	0
2002◆	Detroit	23	5	11	16	2	2	1	2
Playoff Totals		**152**	**32**	**75**	**107**	**38**	**14**	**2**	**6**
•LILJA, Andreas	Defense								
2001	Los Angeles	1	0	0	0	0	0	0	0
2002	Los Angeles	5	0	0	0	6	0	0	0
Playoff Totals		**6**	**0**	**0**	**0**	**6**	**0**	**0**	**0**
LILLEY, John *No Playoffs*	Right wing								
•LIND, Juha	Center								
1998	Dallas	15	2	2	4	8	0	0	1
Playoff Totals		**15**	**2**	**2**	**4**	**8**	**0**	**0**	**1**
LINDBERG, Chris	Left wing								
1993	Calgary	2	0	1	1	2	0	0	0
Playoff Totals		**2**	**0**	**1**	**1**	**2**	**0**	**0**	**0**
LINDBOM, Johan *No Playoffs*	Left wing								
LINDEN, Jamie *No Playoffs*	Right wing								
•LINDEN, Trevor	Center/Right wing								
1989	Vancouver	7	3	4	7	8	2	1	0
1991	Vancouver	6	0	7	7	2	0	0	0
1992	Vancouver	13	4	8	12	6	2	0	1
1993	Vancouver	12	5	8	13	16	2	0	1
1994	Vancouver	24	12	13	25	18	5	1	1
1995	Vancouver	11	2	6	8	12	1	0	0
1996	Vancouver	6	4	4	8	6	2	0	0
2001	Washington	6	0	4	4	14	0	0	0
2002	Vancouver	6	1	4	5	0	0	0	0
Playoff Totals		**91**	**31**	**58**	**89**	**82**	**14**	**2**	**3**
LINDGREN, Lars	Defense								
1979	Vancouver	3	0	0	0	6	0	0	0
1980	Vancouver	2	0	1	1	0	0	0	0
1982	Vancouver	16	2	4	6	6	0	0	0
1983	Vancouver	4	1	1	2	2	0	0	0
1984	Minnesota	15	2	0	2	6	0	0	0
Playoff Totals		**40**	**5**	**6**	**11**	**20**	**0**	**0**	**0**
•LINDGREN, Mats	Center/Left wing								
1997	Edmonton	12	0	4	4	0	0	0	0
1998	Edmonton	12	1	1	2	10	0	0	0
Playoff Totals		**24**	**1**	**5**	**6**	**10**	**0**	**0**	**0**
LINDHOLM, Mikael *No Playoffs*	Center								
LINDQUIST, Fredrik *No Playoffs*	Center								
LINDROS, Brett *No Playoffs*	Right wing								
•LINDROS, Eric	Center								
1995	Philadelphia	12	4	11	15	18	0	0	1
1996	Philadelphia	12	6	6	12	43	3	0	2
1997	Philadelphia	19	12	14	*26	40	4	0	1
1998	Philadelphia	5	1	2	3	17	0	0	0
2000	Philadelphia	2	1	0	1	0	0	0	0
Playoff Totals		**50**	**24**	**33**	**57**	**118**	**7**	**0**	**4**
•LINDSAY, Bill	Left wing								
1996	Florida	22	5	5	10	18	0	1	1
1997	Florida	3	0	1	1	8	0	0	0
2001	San Jose	6	0	0	0	16	0	0	0
2002	Montreal	11	2	2	4	2	0	0	0
Playoff Totals		**42**	**7**	**8**	**15**	**44**	**0**	**1**	**1**

Season	Team	GP	G	A	Pts	PIM	PP	SH	GW
LINDSAY, Ted	Left wing								
1945	Detroit	14	2	0	2	6	....	....	....
1946	Detroit	5	0	1	1	0	....	....	....
1947	Detroit	5	2	2	4	10	....	....	....
1948	Detroit	10	3	1	4	6	....	....	....
1949	Detroit	11	2	*6	8	31	....	....	....
1950◆	Detroit	13	4	4	8	16	....	....	....
1951	Detroit	6	0	1	1	8	....	....	....
1952◆	Detroit	8	*5	2	*7	8	....	....	....
1953	Detroit	6	4	4	8	6	....	....	....
1954◆	Detroit	12	4	4	8	14	....	....	....
1955◆	Detroit	11	7	12	19	12	....	....	....
1956	Detroit	10	6	3	9	22	....	....	....
1957	Detroit	5	2	4	6	8	....	....	....
1959	Chicago	6	2	4	6	13	....	....	....
1960	Chicago	4	1	1	2	0	....	....	....
1965	Detroit	7	3	0	3	34	....	....	....
Playoff Totals		**133**	**47**	**49**	**96**	**194**	....	....	....
LINDSTROM, Willy	Right wing								
1982	Winnipeg	4	2	1	3	2	0	0	0
1983	Edmonton	16	2	11	13	4	1	0	0
1984◆	Edmonton	19	5	5	10	10	3	0	0
1985◆	Edmonton	18	5	1	6	8	0	0	1
Playoff Totals		**57**	**14**	**18**	**32**	**24**	**4**	**0**	**1**
•LING, David *No Playoffs*	Right wing								
LINSEMAN, Ken	Center								
1979	Philadelphia	8	2	6	8	22	0	0	1
1980	Philadelphia	17	4	*18	22	40	0	0	1
1981	Philadelphia	12	4	16	20	67	0	0	3
1982	Philadelphia	4	1	2	3	6	1	0	0
1983	Edmonton	16	6	8	14	22	1	0	1
1984◆	Edmonton	19	10	4	14	65	3	1	4
1985	Boston	5	4	6	10	8	0	0	1
1986	Boston	3	0	1	1	17	0	0	0
1987	Boston	4	1	1	2	22	0	0	0
1988	Boston	23	11	14	25	56	4	1	0
1991	Edmonton	2	0	1	1	0	0	0	0
Playoff Totals		**113**	**43**	**77**	**120**	**325**	**9**	**2**	**11**
•LINTNER, Richard *No Playoffs*	Defense								
LIPUMA, Chris *No Playoffs*	Defense								
LISCOMBE, Carl	Left wing								
1939	Detroit	6	0	0	0	2	....	....	....
1941	Detroit	8	4	3	7	12	....	....	....
1942	Detroit	12	6	6	12	2	....	....	....
1943◆	Detroit	10	*6	8	*14	2	....	....	....
1944	Detroit	5	1	0	1	2	....	....	....
1945	Detroit	14	4	2	6	0	....	....	....
1946	Detroit	4	1	0	1	0	....	....	....
Playoff Totals		**59**	**22**	**19**	**41**	**20**	....	....	....
LITZENBERGER, Ed	Center/Right wing								
1959	Chicago	6	3	5	8	8	....	....	....
1960	Chicago	4	0	1	1	4	....	....	....
1961◆	Chicago	10	1	3	4	2	....	....	....
1962◆	Toronto	10	0	2	2	4	....	....	....
1963◆	Toronto	9	1	2	3	6	....	....	....
1964◆	Toronto	1	0	0	0	10	....	....	....
Playoff Totals		**40**	**5**	**13**	**18**	**34**	....	....	....
LOACH, Lonnie	Left wing								
1993	Los Angeles	1	0	0	0	0	0	0	0
Playoff Totals		**1**	**0**	**0**	**0**	**0**	**0**	**0**	**0**
LOCAS, Jacques *No Playoffs*	Right wing								
LOCHEAD, Bill	Left wing								
1978	Detroit	7	3	0	3	6	0	0	1
Playoff Totals		**7**	**3**	**0**	**3**	**6**	**0**	**0**	**1**
LOCKING, Norm *No Playoffs*	Left wing/Center								
LOEWEN, Darcy *No Playoffs*	Left wing								
LOFTHOUSE, Mark *No Playoffs*	Right wing/Center								
LOGAN, Dave	Defense								
1978	Chicago	4	0	0	0	8	0	0	0
1979	Chicago	4	0	0	0	2	0	0	0
1980	Vancouver	4	0	0	0	0	0	0	0
Playoff Totals		**12**	**0**	**0**	**0**	**10**	**0**	**0**	**0**
LOGAN, Robert *No Playoffs*	Right wing								
LOISELLE, Claude	Center								
1985	Detroit	3	0	2	2	0	0	0	0
1988	New Jersey	20	4	6	10	48	0	2	0
1993	NY Islanders	18	0	3	3	10	0	0	0
Playoff Totals		**41**	**4**	**11**	**15**	**58**	**0**	**2**	**0**
LOMAKIN, Andrei *No Playoffs*	Right wing								
LONEY, Brian *No Playoffs*	Right wing								
LONEY, Troy	Left wing								
1989	Pittsburgh	11	1	3	4	24	0	0	0
1991◆	Pittsburgh	24	2	2	4	41	0	0	0
1992◆	Pittsburgh	21	4	5	9	32	0	0	0
1993	Pittsburgh	10	1	4	5	0	0	0	0
1995	NY Rangers	1	0	0	0	0	0	0	0
Playoff Totals		**67**	**8**	**14**	**22**	**97**	**0**	**0**	**0**

Season	Team	GP	G	A	Pts	PIM	PP	SH	GW
LONG, Barry	Defense								
1974	Los Angeles	5	0	1	1	18	0	0	0
Playoff Totals		**5**	**0**	**1**	**1**	**18**	**0**	**0**	**0**
LONG, Stan	Defense								
1952	Montreal	3	0	0	0	0	0	0	0
Playoff Totals		**3**	**0**	**0**	**0**	**0**	**0**	**0**	**0**
LONSBERRY, Ross	Left wing								
1973	Philadelphia	11	4	3	7	9	0	0	1
1974◆	Philadelphia	17	4	9	13	18	1	1	1
1975◆	Philadelphia	17	4	3	7	10	1	0	1
1976	Philadelphia	16	4	3	7	2	1	0	1
1977	Philadelphia	10	1	2	3	29	0	0	0
1978	Philadelphia	12	2	2	4	6	1	0	1
1979	Pittsburgh	7	0	2	2	9	0	0	0
1980	Pittsburgh	5	2	1	3	2	0	0	1
1981	Pittsburgh	5	0	0	0	2	0	0	0
Playoff Totals		**100**	**21**	**25**	**46**	**87**	**4**	**1**	**6**
LOOB, Hakan	Right wing								
1984	Calgary	11	2	3	5	2	1	0	2
1985	Calgary	4	3	3	6	0	0	1	0
1986	Calgary	22	4	10	14	6	1	2	0
1987	Calgary	5	1	2	3	0	0	1	0
1988	Calgary	9	8	1	9	4	2	2	0
1989◆	Calgary	22	8	9	17	4	2	2	1
Playoff Totals		**73**	**26**	**28**	**54**	**16**	**6**	**8**	**3**
LOOB, Peter *No Playoffs*	Defense								
LORENTZ, Jim	Center/Right wing								
1970◆	Boston	11	1	0	1	4	0	0	0
1971	St. Louis	6	0	1	1	4	0	0	0
1973	Buffalo	6	0	3	3	2	0	0	0
1975	Buffalo	16	6	4	10	6	0	0	2
1976	Buffalo	9	1	2	3	6	0	0	0
1977	Buffalo	6	4	0	4	8	0	0	0
Playoff Totals		**54**	**12**	**10**	**22**	**30**	**0**	**0**	**2**
LORIMER, Bob	Defense								
1979	NY Islanders	10	1	3	4	15	0	0	0
1980◆	NY Islanders	21	1	3	4	41	0	0	1
1981◆	NY Islanders	18	1	4	5	27	0	0	0
Playoff Totals		**49**	**3**	**10**	**13**	**83**	**0**	**0**	**1**
LORRAIN, Rod	Right wing								
1937	Montreal	5	0	0	0	0	0	0	0
1938	Montreal	3	0	0	0	0	0	0	0
1939	Montreal	3	0	3	3	0	0	0	0
Playoff Totals		**11**	**0**	**3**	**3**	**0**	**0**	**0**	**0**
LOUGHLIN, Clem *No Playoffs*	Defense								
LOUGHLIN, Wilf *No Playoffs*	Defense/Left wing								
LOVSIN, Ken *No Playoffs*	Defense								
•LOW, Reed *No Playoffs*	Right wing								
LOWDERMILK, Dwayne *No Playoffs*	Defense								
LOWE, Darren *No Playoffs*	Right wing								
LOWE, Kevin	Defense								
1980	Edmonton	3	0	1	1	0	0	0	0
1981	Edmonton	9	0	2	2	11	0	0	0
1982	Edmonton	5	0	3	3	0	0	0	0
1983	Edmonton	16	1	8	9	10	0	0	0
1984◆	Edmonton	19	3	7	10	16	0	0	0
1985◆	Edmonton	16	0	5	5	8	0	0	0
1986	Edmonton	10	1	3	4	15	0	0	0
1987◆	Edmonton	21	2	4	6	22	0	2	1
1988◆	Edmonton	19	0	2	2	26	0	0	0
1989	Edmonton	7	1	2	3	4	0	0	0
1990◆	Edmonton	20	0	2	2	10	0	0	0
1991	Edmonton	14	1	1	2	14	0	0	0
1992	Edmonton	11	0	3	3	16	0	0	0
1994◆	NY Rangers	22	1	0	1	20	0	0	0
1995	NY Rangers	10	0	1	1	12	0	0	0
1996	NY Rangers	10	0	4	4	4	0	0	0
1997	Edmonton	1	0	0	0	0	0	0	0
1998	Edmonton	1	0	0	0	4	0	0	0
Playoff Totals		**214**	**10**	**48**	**58**	**192**	**0**	**2**	**1**
LOWE, Odie *No Playoffs*	Center								
LOWE, Ross	Defense/Left wing								
1951	Montreal	2	0	0	0	0	0	0	0
Playoff Totals		**2**	**0**	**0**	**0**	**0**	**0**	**0**	**0**
LOWREY, Ed *No Playoffs*	Center								
LOWREY, Fred	Right wing								
1926	Pittsburgh	2	0	0	0	....	0	0	0
Playoff Totals		**2**	**0**	**0**	**0**	....	**0**	**0**	**0**
LOWREY, Gerry	Left wing								
1932	Chicago	2	1	0	1	2	....	....	....
Playoff Totals		**2**	**1**	**0**	**1**	**2**	....	....	....

Season	Team	GP	G	A	Pts	PIM	PP	SH	GW
•LOWRY, Dave									Left wing
1986	Vancouver	3	0	0	0	0	0	0	0
1989	St. Louis	10	0	5	5	4	0	0	0
1990	St. Louis	12	2	1	3	39	0	0	0
1991	St. Louis	13	1	4	5	35	0	0	0
1992	St. Louis	6	0	1	1	20	0	0	0
1993	St. Louis	11	2	0	2	14	0	1	0
1996	Florida	22	10	7	17	39	4	0	2
1997	Florida	5	0	0	0	0	0	0	0
1998	San Jose	6	0	0	0	18	0	0	0
1999	San Jose	1	0	0	0	0	0	0	0
2000	San Jose	12	1	2	3	6	0	0	0
Playoff Totals		**101**	**16**	**20**	**36**	**175**	**4**	**1**	**2**
LOYNS, Lynn *No Playoffs*									Left wing
LUCAS, Danny *No Playoffs*									Right wing
LUCAS, Dave *No Playoffs*									Defense
LUCE, Don									Center
1970	NY Rangers	5	0	1	1	4	0	0	0
1973	Buffalo	6	1	1	2	2	0	0	0
1975	Buffalo	16	5	8	13	19	0	1	0
1976	Buffalo	9	4	3	7	6	0	0	1
1977	Buffalo	6	3	1	4	2	2	0	0
1978	Buffalo	8	0	2	2	6	0	0	0
1979	Buffalo	3	1	1	2	0	0	0	0
1980	Buffalo	14	3	3	6	11	0	1	1
1981	Los Angeles	4	0	2	2	2	0	0	0
Playoff Totals		**71**	**17**	**22**	**39**	**52**	**2**	**2**	**2**
LUDVIG, Jan *No Playoffs*									Right wing
LUDWIG, Craig									Defense
1983	Montreal	3	0	0	0	2	0	0	0
1984	Montreal	15	0	3	3	23	0	0	0
1985	Montreal	12	0	2	2	6	0	0	0
1986♦	Montreal	20	0	1	1	48	0	0	0
1987	Montreal	17	2	3	5	30	0	0	1
1988	Montreal	11	1	1	2	6	0	0	0
1989	Montreal	21	0	2	2	24	0	0	0
1990	Montreal	11	0	1	1	16	0	0	0
1992	Minnesota	7	0	1	1	19	0	0	0
1994	Dallas	9	0	3	3	8	0	0	0
1995	Dallas	4	0	1	1	2	0	0	0
1997	Dallas	7	0	2	2	18	0	0	0
1998	Dallas	17	0	1	1	22	0	0	0
1999♦	Dallas	23	1	4	5	20	0	0	0
Playoff Totals		**177**	**4**	**25**	**29**	**244**	**0**	**0**	**1**
LUDZIK, Steve									Center
1983	Chicago	13	3	5	8	20	0	0	0
1984	Chicago	4	0	1	1	9	0	0	0
1985	Chicago	15	1	1	2	16	0	0	0
1986	Chicago	3	0	0	0	12	0	0	0
1987	Chicago	4	0	0	0	0	0	0	0
1988	Chicago	5	0	1	1	13	0	0	0
Playoff Totals		**44**	**4**	**8**	**12**	**70**	**0**	**0**	**0**
LUHNING, Warren *No Playoffs*									Right wing
LUKOWICH, Bernie									Right wing
1975	St. Louis	2	0	0	0	0	0	0	0
Playoff Totals		**2**	**0**	**0**	**0**	**0**	**0**	**0**	**0**
•LUKOWICH, Brad									Defense
1999	Dallas	8	0	1	1	4	0	0	0
2001	Dallas	10	1	0	1	4	0	0	0
Playoff Totals		**18**	**1**	**1**	**2**	**8**	**0**	**0**	**0**
LUKOWICH, Morris									Left wing
1982	Winnipeg	4	0	2	2	16	0	0	0
1984	Winnipeg	3	0	0	0	0	0	0	0
1985	Boston	1	0	0	0	0	0	0	0
1987	Los Angeles	3	0	0	0	8	0	0	0
Playoff Totals		**11**	**0**	**2**	**2**	**24**	**0**	**0**	**0**
LUKSA, Charlie *No Playoffs*									Defense
LUMLEY, Dave									Right wing
1980	Edmonton	3	1	0	1	12	1	0	0
1981	Edmonton	7	1	0	1	4	0	0	0
1982	Edmonton	5	2	1	3	21	0	0	0
1983	Edmonton	16	0	0	0	19	0	0	0
1984♦	Edmonton	19	2	5	7	44	0	0	0
1985♦	Edmonton	8	0	0	0	29	0	0	0
1986	Edmonton	3	0	2	2	2	0	0	0
Playoff Totals		**61**	**6**	**8**	**14**	**131**	**1**	**0**	**0**
•LUMME, Jyrki									Defense
1991	Vancouver	6	2	3	5	0	1	1	0
1992	Vancouver	13	2	3	5	4	1	0	1
1993	Vancouver	12	0	5	5	6	0	0	0
1994	Vancouver	24	2	11	13	16	2	0	1
1995	Vancouver	11	2	6	8	8	1	0	0
1996	Vancouver	6	1	3	4	2	1	0	0
1999	Phoenix	7	0	1	1	6	0	0	0
2000	Phoenix	5	0	1	1	2	0	0	0
2002	Toronto	14	0	0	0	4	0	0	0
Playoff Totals		**98**	**9**	**33**	**42**	**48**	**6**	**1**	**2**

Season	Team	GP	G	A	Pts	PIM	PP	SH	GW
LUND, Pentti									Right wing
1947	Boston	1	0	0	0	0	....	....	....
1948	Boston	2	0	0	0	0	....	....	....
1950	NY Rangers	12	*6	5	*11	0	....	....	....
1952	Boston	2	1	0	1	0	....	....	....
1953	Boston	2	0	0	0	0	....	....	....
Playoff Totals		**19**	**7**	**5**	**12**	**0**	....	....	....
LUNDBERG, Brian *No Playoffs*									Defense
LUNDE, Len									Center
1960	Detroit	6	1	2	3	0	1	0	0
1961	Detroit	10	2	0	2	0	2	0	0
1963	Chicago	4	0	0	0	2	0	0	0
Playoff Totals		**20**	**3**	**2**	**5**	**2**	**3**	**0**	**0**
LUNDHOLM, Bengt									Left wing
1982	Winnipeg	4	1	1	2	2	0	0	0
1983	Winnipeg	3	0	1	1	2	0	0	0
1985	Winnipeg	5	2	2	4	8	0	2	0
1986	Winnipeg	2	0	0	0	2	0	0	0
Playoff Totals		**14**	**3**	**4**	**7**	**14**	**0**	**2**	**0**
•LUNDMARK, Jamie *No Playoffs*									Center
LUNDRIGAN, Joe *No Playoffs*									Defense
LUNDSTROM, Tord *No Playoffs*									Left wing
LUNDY, Pat									Center
1946	Detroit	2	1	0	1	0	....	....	....
1947	Detroit	5	0	1	1	2	....	....	....
1948	Detroit	5	1	1	2	0	....	....	....
1949	Detroit	4	0	0	0	0	....	....	....
Playoff Totals		**16**	**2**	**2**	**4**	**2**	....	....	....
LUONGO, Chris *No Playoffs*									Defense
•LUPASCHUK, Ross *No Playoffs*									Defense
LUPIEN, Gilles									Defense
1978♦	Montreal	8	0	0	0	17	0	0	0
1979♦	Montreal	13	0	0	0	2	0	0	0
1980	Montreal	4	0	0	0	2	0	0	0
Playoff Totals		**25**	**0**	**0**	**0**	**21**	**0**	**0**	**0**
LUPUL, Gary									Center/Left wing
1980	Vancouver	4	1	0	1	0	1	0	0
1982	Vancouver	10	2	3	5	4	0	0	1
1983	Vancouver	4	1	3	4	0	0	0	0
1984	Vancouver	4	0	1	1	7	0	0	0
1986	Vancouver	3	0	0	0	0	0	0	0
Playoff Totals		**25**	**4**	**7**	**11**	**11**	**1**	**0**	**1**
•LYASHENKO, Roman									Center
2000	Dallas	16	2	1	3	0	0	0	2
2001	Dallas	1	0	0	0	0	0	0	0
Playoff Totals		**17**	**2**	**1**	**3**	**0**	**0**	**0**	**2**
•LYDMAN, Toni *No Playoffs*									Defense
LYLE, George *No Playoffs*									Left wing
LYNCH, Jack *No Playoffs*									Defense
LYNN, Vic									Left wing/Defense
1947♦	Toronto	11	4	1	5	16	....	....	....
1948♦	Toronto	9	2	5	7	*20	....	....	....
1949♦	Toronto	8	0	1	1	2	....	....	....
1950	Toronto	7	0	2	2	2	....	....	....
1951	Boston	5	0	0	0	2	....	....	....
1953	Chicago	7	1	1	2	4	....	....	....
Playoff Totals		**47**	**7**	**10**	**17**	**46**	....	....	....
LYON, Steve *No Playoffs*									Defense/Right wing
LYONS, Ron									Left wing
1931	Boston	5	0	0	0	0	0	0	0
Playoff Totals		**5**	**0**	**0**	**0**	**0**	**0**	**0**	**0**
LYSIAK, Tom									Center
1974	Atlanta	4	0	2	2	0	0	0	0
1976	Atlanta	2	0	0	0	2	0	0	0
1977	Atlanta	3	1	3	4	8	1	0	0
1978	Atlanta	2	1	0	1	2	0	0	0
1979	Chicago	4	0	0	0	2	0	0	0
1980	Chicago	7	4	4	8	0	4	0	0
1981	Chicago	3	0	3	3	0	0	0	0
1982	Chicago	15	6	9	15	13	3	0	0
1983	Chicago	13	6	7	13	8	2	0	2
1984	Chicago	5	1	1	2	2	0	0	0
1985	Chicago	15	4	8	12	10	0	0	0
1986	Chicago	3	2	1	3	2	0	0	0
Playoff Totals		**76**	**25**	**38**	**63**	**49**	**10**	**0**	**2**
MacADAM, Al									Right wing
1974♦	Philadelphia	1	0	0	0	0	0	0	0
1980	Minnesota	15	7	9	16	4	1	0	2
1981	Minnesota	19	9	10	19	4	1	1	1
1982	Minnesota	4	1	0	1	4	0	0	0
1983	Minnesota	9	2	1	3	2	0	0	0
1984	Minnesota	16	1	4	5	7	0	0	0
Playoff Totals		**64**	**20**	**24**	**44**	**21**	**2**	**1**	**3**

Season	Team	GP	G	A	Pts	PIM	PP	SH	GW
MacDERMID, Paul									Right wing
1986	Hartford	10	2	1	3	20	0	0	1
1987	Hartford	6	2	1	3	34	0	0	1
1988	Hartford	6	0	5	5	14	0	0	0
1989	Hartford	4	1	1	2	16	0	0	0
1990	Winnipeg	7	0	2	2	8	0	0	0
1992	Washington	7	0	1	1	22	0	0	0
1995	Quebec	3	0	0	0	2	0	0	0
Playoff Totals		**43**	**5**	**11**	**16**	**116**	**0**	**0**	**2**
MacDONALD, Blair									Right wing
1980	Edmonton	3	0	3	3	0	0	0	0
1981	Vancouver	3	0	1	1	2	0	0	0
1982	Vancouver	3	0	0	0	0	0	0	0
1983	Vancouver	2	0	2	2	0	0	0	0
Playoff Totals		**11**	**0**	**6**	**6**	**2**	**0**	**0**	**0**
MacDONALD, Brett *No Playoffs*									Defense
•MacDONALD, Craig									Center
1999	Carolina	1	0	0	0	0	0	0	0
2002	Carolina	4	0	0	0	2	0	0	0
Playoff Totals		**5**	**0**	**0**	**0**	**2**	**0**	**0**	**0**
MacDONALD, Doug *No Playoffs*									Left wing
MacDONALD, Kevin *No Playoffs*									Defense
MacDONALD, Kilby									Left wing
1940♦	NY Rangers	12	0	2	2	4	....	....	....
1941	NY Rangers	3	1	0	1	0	....	....	....
Playoff Totals		**15**	**1**	**2**	**3**	**4**	....	....	....
MacDONALD, Lowell									Left wing
1963	Detroit	1	0	0	0	2	0	0	0
1968	Los Angeles	7	3	4	7	2	1	0	1
1969	Los Angeles	7	2	3	5	0	0	1	0
1975	Pittsburgh	9	4	2	6	4	1	0	1
1976	Pittsburgh	3	1	0	1	0	1	0	1
1977	Pittsburgh	3	1	2	3	4	0	0	0
Playoff Totals		**30**	**11**	**11**	**22**	**12**	**3**	**1**	**3**
MacDONALD, Parker									Center
1955	Toronto	4	0	0	0	4	....	....	....
1957	NY Rangers	1	1	1	2	0	....	....	....
1958	NY Rangers	6	1	2	3	2	....	....	....
1961	Detroit	9	1	0	1	0	....	....	....
1963	Detroit	11	3	2	5	2	....	....	....
1964	Detroit	14	3	3	6	2	....	....	....
1965	Detroit	7	1	1	2	6	....	....	....
1966	Detroit	9	0	0	0	2	....	....	....
1968	Minnesota	14	4	5	9	2	0	0	2
Playoff Totals		**75**	**14**	**14**	**28**	**20**	**0**	**0**	**2**
MacDOUGALL, Kim *No Playoffs*									Defense
MacEACHERN, Shane *No Playoffs*									Center
MACEY, Hub									Left wing
1942	NY Rangers	1	0	0	0	0	0	0	0
1947	Montreal	7	0	0	0	0	0	0	0
Playoff Totals		**8**	**0**	**0**	**0**	**0**	**0**	**0**	**0**
MacGREGOR, Bruce									Center
1961	Detroit	8	1	2	3	6	....	....	....
1963	Detroit	10	1	4	5	10	....	....	....
1964	Detroit	14	5	2	7	12	....	....	....
1965	Detroit	7	0	2	2	2	....	....	....
1966	Detroit	12	1	4	5	2	....	....	....
1970	Detroit	4	1	0	1	2	0	0	0
1971	NY Rangers	13	0	4	4	2	0	0	0
1972	NY Rangers	16	2	6	8	4	0	1	0
1973	NY Rangers	10	2	2	4	2	0	0	0
1974	NY Rangers	13	6	2	8	2	0	0	2
Playoff Totals		**107**	**19**	**28**	**47**	**44**	**0**	**1**	**2**
MacGREGOR, Randy *No Playoffs*									Right wing
MacGUIGAN, Garth *No Playoffs*									Center
•MacINNIS, Al									Defense
1984	Calgary	11	2	12	14	13	2	0	1
1985	Calgary	4	1	2	3	8	1	0	0
1986	Calgary	21	4	*15	19	30	2	0	0
1987	Calgary	4	1	0	1	0	1	0	0
1988	Calgary	7	3	6	9	18	2	0	0
1989♦	Calgary	22	7	*24	*31	46	5	0	4
1990	Calgary	6	2	3	5	8	1	0	0
1991	Calgary	7	2	3	5	8	2	0	0
1993	Calgary	6	1	6	7	10	1	0	0
1994	Calgary	7	2	6	8	12	1	0	0
1995	St. Louis	7	1	5	6	10	0	0	0
1996	St. Louis	13	3	4	7	20	1	0	0
1997	St. Louis	6	1	2	3	4	1	0	0
1998	St. Louis	8	2	6	8	12	1	0	0
1999	St. Louis	13	4	8	12	20	2	0	0
2000	St. Louis	7	1	3	4	14	1	0	0
2001	St. Louis	15	2	8	10	18	2	0	0
2002	St. Louis	10	0	7	7	4	0	0	0
Playoff Totals		**174**	**39**	**120**	**159**	**255**	**26**	**0**	**5**
MacINTOSH, Ian *No Playoffs*									Right wing
MacIVER, Don *No Playoffs*									Defense

Season	Team	GP	G	A	Pts	PIM	PP	SH	GW
MACIVER, Norm									Defense
1989	Hartford	1	0	0	0	2	0	0	0
1991	Edmonton	18	0	4	4	8	0	0	0
1992	Edmonton	13	1	2	3	10	0	0	0
1995	Pittsburgh	12	1	4	5	8	0	0	1
1996	Winnipeg	6	1	0	1	2	0	0	0
1998	Phoenix	6	0	1	1	2	0	0	0
Playoff Totals		**56**	**3**	**11**	**14**	**32**	**0**	**0**	**1**
MacKASEY, Blair *No Playoffs*									Defense
MacKAY, Calum									Left wing
1950	Montreal	5	0	1	1	2	....	....	....
1951	Montreal	11	1	0	1	0	....	....	....
1953♦	Montreal	7	1	3	4	10	....	....	....
1954	Montreal	3	0	1	1	0	....	....	....
1955	Montreal	12	3	8	11	8	....	....	....
Playoff Totals		**38**	**5**	**13**	**18**	**20**	....	....	....
MacKAY, Dave									Defense
1941	Chicago	5	0	1	1	2	0	0	0
Playoff Totals		**5**	**0**	**1**	**1**	**2**	**0**	**0**	**0**
MacKAY, Mickey									Center
1927	Chicago	2	0	0	0	0	0	0	0
1929♦	Boston	3	0	0	0	2	0	0	0
1930	Boston	6	0	0	0	4	0	0	0
Playoff Totals		**11**	**0**	**0**	**0**	**6**	**0**	**0**	**0**
MacKAY, Murdo									Right wing/Center
1947	Montreal	9	0	1	1	0	....	....	....
1949	Montreal	6	1	1	2	0	....	....	....
Playoff Totals		**15**	**1**	**2**	**3**	**0**	....	....	....
MacKELL, Fleming									Center
1949♦	Toronto	9	2	4	6	4	....	....	....
1950	Toronto	7	1	1	2	11	....	....	....
1951♦	Toronto	11	2	3	5	9	....	....	....
1952	Boston	5	2	1	3	12	....	....	....
1953	Boston	11	2	*7	9	7	....	....	....
1954	Boston	4	1	1	2	8	....	....	....
1955	Boston	4	0	1	1	0	....	....	....
1957	Boston	10	5	3	8	4	....	....	....
1958	Boston	12	5	14	*19	12	....	....	....
1959	Boston	7	2	6	8	8	....	....	....
Playoff Totals		**80**	**22**	**41**	**63**	**75**	....	....	....
MacKELL, Jack									Right wing/Defense
1920♦	Ottawa	....	....	....	....	....	....	....	....
1921♦	Ottawa	2	0	0	0	0	0	0	0
Playoff Totals		**2**	**0**	**0**	**0**	**0**	**0**	**0**	**0**
MacKENZIE, Barry *No Playoffs*									Defense
MacKENZIE, Bill									Defense
1934	Mtl. Maroons	4	0	0	0	0	....	....	....
1935	NY Rangers	3	0	0	0	0	....	....	....
1937	Montreal	5	1	0	1	0	....	....	....
1938♦	Chicago	9	0	1	1	11	....	....	....
Playoff Totals		**21**	**1**	**1**	**2**	**11**	....	....	....
•MacKENZIE, Derek *No Playoffs*									Center
MACKEY, David									Left wing
1992	St. Louis	1	0	0	0	0	0	0	0
1994	St. Louis	2	0	0	0	2	0	0	0
Playoff Totals		**3**	**0**	**0**	**0**	**2**	**0**	**0**	**0**
MACKEY, Reg									Defense
1927	NY Rangers	1	0	0	0	0	0	0	0
Playoff Totals		**1**	**0**	**0**	**0**	**0**	**0**	**0**	**0**
MACKIE, Howie									Right wing/Defense
1937♦	Detroit	8	0	0	0	0	0	0	0
Playoff Totals		**8**	**0**	**0**	**0**	**0**	**0**	**0**	**0**
MacKINNON, Paul *No Playoffs*									Defense
•MacLEAN, Don									Center
2002	Toronto	3	0	0	0	0	0	0	0
Playoff Totals		**3**	**0**	**0**	**0**	**0**	**0**	**0**	**0**
•MacLEAN, John									Right wing
1988	New Jersey	20	7	11	18	60	2	0	2
1990	New Jersey	6	4	1	5	12	2	1	0
1991	New Jersey	7	5	3	8	20	1	0	0
1993	New Jersey	5	0	1	1	10	0	0	0
1994	New Jersey	20	6	10	16	22	2	0	1
1995♦	New Jersey	20	5	13	18	14	2	0	0
1997	New Jersey	10	4	5	9	4	2	1	1
1998	San Jose	6	2	3	5	4	1	0	0
2001	Dallas	10	2	1	3	6	0	0	0
Playoff Totals		**104**	**35**	**48**	**83**	**152**	**12**	**2**	**4**

Season	Team	GP	G	A	Pts	PIM	PP	SH	GW
MacLEAN, Paul									Right wing
1981	St. Louis	1	0	0	0	0	0	0	0
1982	Winnipeg	4	3	2	5	26	2	0	1
1983	Winnipeg	3	1	2	3	6	1	0	0
1984	Winnipeg	3	1	0	1	0	0	0	0
1985	Winnipeg	8	3	4	7	4	2	0	0
1986	Winnipeg	2	1	0	1	7	0	0	0
1987	Winnipeg	10	5	2	7	16	2	0	0
1988	Winnipeg	5	2	0	2	23	2	0	0
1989	Detroit	5	1	1	2	8	0	0	0
1990	St. Louis	12	4	3	7	20	3	0	0
Playoff Totals		**53**	**21**	**14**	**35**	**110**	**12**	**0**	**1**
MacLEISH, Rick									Center
1971	Philadelphia	4	1	0	1	0	0	0	0
1973	Philadelphia	10	3	4	7	2	2	0	1
1974♦	Philadelphia	17	*13	9	*22	20	5	0	4
1975♦	Philadelphia	17	11	9	*20	8	4	0	1
1977	Philadelphia	10	4	9	13	2	2	0	1
1978	Philadelphia	12	7	9	16	4	3	0	3
1979	Philadelphia	7	0	1	1	0	0	0	0
1980	Philadelphia	19	9	6	15	2	1	0	1
1981	Philadelphia	12	5	5	10	0	4	0	0
1982	Pittsburgh	5	1	1	2	0	0	0	0
1984	Detroit	1	0	0	0	0	0	0	0
Playoff Totals		**114**	**54**	**53**	**107**	**38**	**21**	**0**	**11**
MacLELLAN, Brian									Left wing
1985	Los Angeles	3	0	1	1	0	0	0	0
1986	NY Rangers	16	2	4	6	15	0	0	1
1989♦	Calgary	21	3	2	5	19	0	0	1
1990	Calgary	6	0	2	2	8	0	0	0
1991	Calgary	1	0	0	0	0	0	0	0
Playoff Totals		**47**	**5**	**9**	**14**	**42**	**0**	**0**	**2**
MacLEOD, Pat *No Playoffs*									Defense
MacMILLAN, Billy									Right wing
1971	Toronto	6	0	3	3	2	0	0	0
1972	Toronto	5	0	0	0	0	0	0	0
1975	NY Islanders	17	0	1	1	23	0	0	0
1976	NY Islanders	13	4	2	6	8	0	0	2
1977	NY Islanders	12	2	0	2	7	0	0	2
Playoff Totals		**53**	**6**	**6**	**12**	**40**	**0**	**0**	**4**
MacMILLAN, Bob									Right wing
1976	St. Louis	3	0	1	1	0	0	0	0
1977	St. Louis	4	0	1	1	0	0	0	0
1978	Atlanta	2	0	2	2	0	0	0	0
1979	Atlanta	2	0	1	1	0	0	0	0
1980	Atlanta	4	0	0	0	9	0	0	0
1981	Calgary	16	8	6	14	7	2	0	1
Playoff Totals		**31**	**8**	**11**	**19**	**16**	**2**	**0**	**1**
MacMILLAN, John									Right wing
1961	Toronto	4	0	0	0	0	0	0	0
1962♦	Toronto	3	0	0	0	0	0	0	0
1963♦	Toronto	1	0	0	0	0	0	0	0
1964	Detroit	4	0	1	1	2	0	0	0
Playoff Totals		**12**	**0**	**1**	**1**	**2**	**0**	**0**	**0**
MacNEIL, Al									Defense
1962	Montreal	5	0	0	0	2	0	0	0
1963	Chicago	4	0	1	1	4	0	0	0
1964	Chicago	7	0	2	2	25	0	0	0
1965	Chicago	14	0	1	1	34	0	0	0
1966	Chicago	3	0	0	0	0	0	0	0
1967	NY Rangers	4	0	0	0	2	0	0	0
Playoff Totals		**37**	**0**	**4**	**4**	**67**	**0**	**0**	**0**
MacNEIL, Bernie *No Playoffs*									Left wing
•MacNEIL, Ian *No Playoffs*									Center
MACOUN, Jamie									Defense
1983	Calgary	9	0	2	2	8	0	0	0
1984	Calgary	11	1	0	1	0	1	0	0
1985	Calgary	4	1	0	1	4	0	0	0
1986	Calgary	22	1	6	7	23	0	0	0
1987	Calgary	3	0	1	1	8	0	0	0
1989♦	Calgary	22	3	6	9	30	0	0	1
1990	Calgary	6	0	3	3	10	0	0	0
1991	Calgary	7	0	1	1	4	0	0	0
1993	Toronto	21	0	6	6	36	0	0	0
1994	Toronto	18	1	1	2	12	0	0	0
1995	Toronto	7	1	2	3	8	0	0	0
1996	Toronto	6	0	2	2	8	0	0	0
1998♦	Detroit	22	2	2	4	18	0	0	2
1999	Detroit	1	0	0	0	0	0	0	0
Playoff Totals		**159**	**10**	**32**	**42**	**169**	**1**	**0**	**3**
MacPHERSON, Bud									Defense
1951	Montreal	11	0	2	2	8	0	0	0
1952	Montreal	11	0	0	0	0	0	0	0
1953♦	Montreal	4	0	1	1	9	0	0	0
1954	Montreal	3	0	0	0	4	0	0	0
Playoff Totals		**29**	**0**	**3**	**3**	**21**	**0**	**0**	**0**
MacSWEYN, Ralph									Defense
1969	Philadelphia	4	0	0	0	4	0	0	0
1971	Philadelphia	4	0	0	0	2	0	0	0
Playoff Totals		**8**	**0**	**0**	**0**	**6**	**0**	**0**	**0**

Season	Team	GP	G	A	Pts	PIM	PP	SH	GW
MacTAVISH, Craig									Center
1980	Boston	10	2	3	5	7	0	0	0
1983	Boston	17	3	1	4	18	0	0	0
1984	Boston	1	0	0	0	0	0	0	0
1986	Edmonton	10	4	4	8	11	1	0	0
1987♦	Edmonton	21	1	9	10	16	0	0	0
1988♦	Edmonton	19	0	1	1	31	0	0	0
1989	Edmonton	7	0	1	1	8	0	0	0
1990♦	Edmonton	22	2	6	8	29	0	0	0
1991	Edmonton	18	3	3	6	20	0	0	1
1992	Edmonton	16	3	0	3	28	0	1	1
1994♦	NY Rangers	23	1	4	5	22	0	0	0
1995	Philadelphia	15	1	4	5	20	0	0	0
1996	St. Louis	13	0	2	2	6	0	0	0
1997	St. Louis	1	0	0	0	2	0	0	0
Playoff Totals		**193**	**20**	**38**	**58**	**218**	**1**	**1**	**2**
MacWILLIAM, Mike *No Playoffs*									Left wing
•MADDEN, John									Left wing
2000♦	New Jersey	20	3	4	7	0	0	1	2
2001	New Jersey	25	4	3	7	6	0	0	0
2002	New Jersey	6	0	0	0	0	0	0	0
Playoff Totals		**51**	**7**	**7**	**14**	**6**	**0**	**1**	**2**
MADIGAN, Connie									Defense
1973	St. Louis	5	0	0	0	4	0	0	0
Playoff Totals		**5**	**0**	**0**	**0**	**4**	**0**	**0**	**0**
MADILL, Jeff									Right wing
1991	New Jersey	7	0	2	2	8	0	0	0
Playoff Totals		**7**	**0**	**2**	**2**	**8**	**0**	**0**	**0**
MAGEE, Dean *No Playoffs*									Left wing
MAGGS, Daryl									Defense
1972	Chicago	4	0	0	0	0	0	0	0
Playoff Totals		**4**	**0**	**0**	**0**	**0**	**0**	**0**	**0**
MAGNAN, Marc *No Playoffs*									Left wing
MAGNUSON, Keith									Defense
1970	Chicago	8	1	2	3	17	0	0	0
1971	Chicago	18	0	2	2	*63	0	0	0
1972	Chicago	8	0	1	1	29	0	0	0
1973	Chicago	7	0	2	2	4	0	0	0
1974	Chicago	11	1	0	1	17	0	0	0
1975	Chicago	8	1	2	3	15	0	0	0
1976	Chicago	4	0	0	0	12	0	0	0
1978	Chicago	4	0	0	0	7	0	0	0
Playoff Totals		**68**	**3**	**9**	**12**	**164**	**0**	**0**	**0**
MAGUIRE, Kevin									Right wing
1987	Toronto	1	0	0	0	0	0	0	0
1988	Buffalo	5	0	0	0	50	0	0	0
1989	Buffalo	5	0	0	0	36	0	0	0
Playoff Totals		**11**	**0**	**0**	**0**	**86**	**0**	**0**	**0**
MAHAFFY, John									Center
1945	Montreal	1	0	1	1	0	0	0	0
Playoff Totals		**1**	**0**	**1**	**1**	**0**	**0**	**0**	**0**
MAHOVLICH, Frank									Left wing
1959	Toronto	12	6	5	11	18	....	....	....
1960	Toronto	10	3	1	4	27	....	....	....
1961	Toronto	5	1	1	2	6	....	....	....
1962♦	Toronto	12	6	6	12	*29	....	....	....
1963♦	Toronto	9	0	2	2	8	....	....	....
1964♦	Toronto	14	4	*11	15	20	....	....	....
1965	Toronto	6	0	3	3	9	....	....	....
1966	Toronto	4	1	0	1	10	....	....	....
1967♦	Toronto	12	3	7	10	8	....	....	....
1970	Detroit	4	0	0	0	2	0	0	0
1971♦	Montreal	20	*14	13	*27	18	1	0	0
1972	Montreal	6	3	2	5	2	0	0	1
1973♦	Montreal	17	9	14	23	6	1	0	0
1974	Montreal	6	1	2	3	0	0	0	0
Playoff Totals		**137**	**51**	**67**	**118**	**163**	**2**	**0**	**1**
MAHOVLICH, Pete									Center
1971♦	Montreal	20	10	6	16	43	1	1	1
1972	Montreal	6	0	2	2	12	0	0	0
1973♦	Montreal	17	4	9	13	22	2	1	0
1974	Montreal	6	2	1	3	4	1	0	0
1975	Montreal	11	6	10	16	10	1	0	1
1976♦	Montreal	13	4	8	12	24	2	0	1
1977♦	Montreal	13	4	5	9	19	2	0	1
1979	Pittsburgh	2	0	1	1	0	0	0	0
Playoff Totals		**88**	**30**	**42**	**72**	**134**	**9**	**2**	**4**
MAILHOT, Jacques *No Playoffs*									Left wing
MAILLEY, Frank *No Playoffs*									Defense
•MAIR, Adam									Center
1999	Toronto	5	1	0	1	14	0	0	0
2000	Toronto	5	0	0	0	8	0	0	0
Playoff Totals		**10**	**1**	**0**	**1**	**22**	**0**	**0**	**0**
MAIR, Jim									Defense
1971	Philadelphia	3	1	2	3	4	1	0	0
Playoff Totals		**3**	**1**	**2**	**3**	**4**	**1**	**0**	**0**

Season	Team	GP	G	A	Pts	PIM	PP	SH	GW
MAJEAU, Fern	Center/Left wing								
1944♦	Montreal	1	0	0	0	0	0	0	0
Playoff Totals		**1**	**0**	**0**	**0**	**0**	**0**	**0**	**0**
•MAJESKY, Ivan *No Playoffs*	Defense								
MAJOR, Bruce *No Playoffs*	Center								
MAJOR, Mark *No Playoffs*	Left wing								
MAKAROV, Sergei	Right wing								
1990	Calgary	6	0	6	6	0	0	0	0
1991	Calgary	3	1	0	1	0	0	0	0
1994	San Jose	14	8	2	10	4	3	0	2
1995	San Jose	11	3	3	6	4	0	0	0
Playoff Totals		**34**	**12**	**11**	**23**	**8**	**3**	**0**	**2**
MAKELA, Mikko	Left wing								
1987	NY Islanders	11	2	4	6	8	1	0	1
1988	NY Islanders	6	1	4	5	6	1	0	0
1990	Los Angeles	1	0	0	0	0	0	0	0
Playoff Totals		**18**	**3**	**8**	**11**	**14**	**2**	**0**	**1**
MAKI, Chico	Right wing								
1961♦	Chicago	1	0	0	0	0	0	0	0
1963	Chicago	6	0	1	1	2	0	0	0
1964	Chicago	7	0	0	0	15	0	0	0
1965	Chicago	14	3	9	12	8	1	0	0
1966	Chicago	3	1	1	2	0	1	0	0
1967	Chicago	6	0	0	0	0	0	0	0
1968	Chicago	11	2	5	7	4	0	0	1
1970	Chicago	8	2	2	4	2	1	1	0
1971	Chicago	18	6	5	11	6	1	0	0
1972	Chicago	8	1	4	5	4	0	0	1
1973	Chicago	16	2	8	10	0	0	0	0
1974	Chicago	11	0	1	1	2	0	0	0
1976	Chicago	4	0	0	0	0	0	0	0
Playoff Totals		**113**	**17**	**36**	**53**	**43**	**4**	**1**	**2**
MAKI, Wayne	Left wing								
1968	Chicago	2	1	0	1	2	0	0	0
Playoff Totals		**2**	**1**	**0**	**1**	**2**	**0**	**0**	**0**
MAKKONEN, Kari *No Playoffs*	Right wing								
•MALAKHOV, Vladimir	Defense								
1993	NY Islanders	17	3	6	9	12	0	0	0
1994	NY Islanders	4	0	0	0	6	0	0	0
1997	Montreal	5	0	0	0	6	0	0	0
1998	Montreal	9	3	4	7	10	2	0	0
2000♦	New Jersey	23	1	4	5	18	1	0	0
Playoff Totals		**58**	**7**	**14**	**21**	**52**	**3**	**0**	**0**
•MALEC, Tomas *No Playoffs*	Defense								
MALEY, David	Left wing								
1986♦	Montreal	7	1	3	4	2	0	0	0
1988	New Jersey	20	3	1	4	80	0	0	0
1990	New Jersey	6	0	0	0	25	0	0	0
1992	Edmonton	10	1	1	2	4	0	0	0
1994	NY Islanders	3	0	0	0	0	0	0	0
Playoff Totals		**46**	**5**	**5**	**10**	**111**	**0**	**0**	**0**
•MALGUNAS, Stewart *No Playoffs*	Defense								
•MALHOTRA, Manny *No Playoffs*	Center								
•MALIK, Marek	Defense								
1999	Carolina	4	0	0	0	4	0	0	0
2001	Carolina	3	0	0	0	6	0	0	0
2002	Carolina	23	0	3	3	18	0	0	0
Playoff Totals		**30**	**0**	**3**	**3**	**28**	**0**	**0**	**0**
MALINOWSKI, Merlin *No Playoffs*	Center								
MALKOC, Dean *No Playoffs*	Defense								
MALLETTE, Troy	Left wing								
1990	NY Rangers	10	2	2	4	81	0	0	0
1991	NY Rangers	5	0	0	0	18	0	0	0
Playoff Totals		**15**	**2**	**2**	**4**	**99**	**0**	**0**	**0**
MALONE, Cliff *No Playoffs*	Right wing								
MALONE, Greg	Center								
1977	Pittsburgh	3	1	1	2	2	0	0	1
1979	Pittsburgh	7	0	1	1	10	0	0	0
1981	Pittsburgh	5	2	3	5	16	0	0	0
1982	Pittsburgh	3	0	0	0	4	0	0	0
1986	Quebec	1	0	0	0	0	0	0	0
1987	Quebec	1	0	0	0	0	0	0	0
Playoff Totals		**20**	**3**	**5**	**8**	**32**	**0**	**0**	**1**
MALONE, Joe	Center/Left wing								
1918	Montreal	2	1	0	1	3	....	....	....
1919	Montreal	5	5	0	5	0	....	....	....
1923	Montreal	2	0	0	0	0	....	....	....
1924♦	Montreal	....	....	....	....	....	....	....	....
Playoff Totals		**9**	**6**	**0**	**6**	**3**	....	....	....
MALONEY, Dan	Left wing								
1971	Chicago	10	0	1	1	8	0	0	0
1974	Los Angeles	5	0	0	0	2	0	0	0
1975	Los Angeles	3	0	0	0	2	0	0	0
1978	Toronto	13	1	3	4	17	1	0	0
1979	Toronto	6	3	3	6	2	1	0	1
1981	Toronto	3	0	0	0	4	0	0	0
Playoff Totals		**40**	**4**	**7**	**11**	**35**	**2**	**0**	**1**

Season	Team	GP	G	A	Pts	PIM	PP	SH	GW
MALONEY, Dave	Defense								
1978	NY Rangers	3	0	0	0	11	0	0	0
1979	NY Rangers	17	3	4	7	45	0	1	0
1980	NY Rangers	8	2	1	3	8	0	1	0
1981	NY Rangers	2	0	2	2	9	0	0	0
1982	NY Rangers	10	1	4	5	6	1	0	1
1983	NY Rangers	7	1	6	7	10	0	0	0
1984	NY Rangers	1	0	0	0	2	0	0	0
1985	Buffalo	1	0	0	0	0	0	0	0
Playoff Totals		**49**	**7**	**17**	**24**	**91**	**1**	**2**	**1**
MALONEY, Don	Left wing								
1979	NY Rangers	18	7	*13	20	19	0	0	1
1980	NY Rangers	9	0	4	4	10	0	0	0
1981	NY Rangers	13	1	6	7	13	1	0	0
1982	NY Rangers	10	5	5	10	10	2	0	0
1983	NY Rangers	5	0	1	1	0	0	0	0
1984	NY Rangers	5	1	4	5	0	0	0	0
1985	NY Rangers	3	4	0	4	2	2	0	0
1986	NY Rangers	16	2	1	3	31	0	0	0
1987	NY Rangers	6	2	1	3	6	0	0	0
1989	Hartford	4	0	0	0	8	0	0	0
1990	NY Islanders	5	0	0	0	2	0	0	0
Playoff Totals		**94**	**22**	**35**	**57**	**101**	**5**	**0**	**1**
MALONEY, Phil	Center								
1959	Chicago	6	0	0	0	0	0	0	0
Playoff Totals		**6**	**0**	**0**	**0**	**0**	**0**	**0**	**0**
•MALTAIS, Steve	Left wing								
1990	Washington	1	0	0	0	0	0	0	0
Playoff Totals		**1**	**0**	**0**	**0**	**0**	**0**	**0**	**0**
•MALTBY, Kirk	Right wing								
1996	Detroit	8	0	1	1	4	0	0	0
1997♦	Detroit	20	5	2	7	24	0	1	1
1998♦	Detroit	22	3	1	4	30	0	1	0
1999	Detroit	10	1	0	1	8	0	0	1
2000	Detroit	8	0	1	1	4	0	0	0
2001	Detroit	6	0	0	0	6	0	0	0
2002♦	Detroit	23	3	3	6	32	0	2	0
Playoff Totals		**97**	**12**	**8**	**20**	**108**	**0**	**4**	**2**
MALUTA, Ray	Defense								
1976	Boston	2	0	0	0	0	0	0	0
Playoff Totals		**2**	**0**	**0**	**0**	**0**	**0**	**0**	**0**
MANASTERSKY, Tom *No Playoffs*	Defense								
MANCUSO, Gus *No Playoffs*	Right wing								
•MANDERVILLE, Kent	Center								
1993	Toronto	18	1	0	1	8	0	0	0
1994	Toronto	12	1	0	1	4	0	1	0
1995	Toronto	7	0	0	0	6	0	0	0
1999	Carolina	6	0	0	0	2	0	0	0
2000	Philadelphia	18	0	1	1	22	0	0	0
2001	Philadelphia	6	1	2	3	2	0	0	0
Playoff Totals		**67**	**3**	**3**	**6**	**44**	**0**	**1**	**0**
MANDICH, Dan	Defense								
1983	Minnesota	7	0	0	0	2	0	0	0
Playoff Totals		**7**	**0**	**0**	**0**	**2**	**0**	**0**	**0**
MANELUK, Mike *No Playoffs*	Left wing								
MANERY, Kris *No Playoffs*	Center/Right wing								
MANERY, Randy	Defense								
1974	Atlanta	4	0	2	2	4	0	0	0
1976	Atlanta	2	0	0	0	0	0	0	0
1977	Atlanta	3	0	0	0	0	0	0	0
1978	Los Angeles	2	0	0	0	2	0	0	0
1979	Los Angeles	2	0	0	0	6	0	0	0
Playoff Totals		**13**	**0**	**2**	**2**	**12**	**0**	**0**	**0**
•MANLOW, Eric *No Playoffs*	Center								
•MANN, Cameron	Right wing								
1999	Boston	1	0	0	0	0	0	0	0
Playoff Totals		**1**	**0**	**0**	**0**	**0**	**0**	**0**	**0**
MANN, Jack *No Playoffs*	Center								
MANN, Jimmy	Right wing								
1982	Winnipeg	3	0	0	0	7	0	0	0
1983	Winnipeg	1	0	0	0	0	0	0	0
1984	Quebec	3	0	0	0	22	0	0	0
1985	Quebec	13	0	0	0	41	0	0	0
1986	Quebec	2	0	0	0	19	0	0	0
Playoff Totals		**22**	**0**	**0**	**0**	**89**	**0**	**0**	**0**
MANN, Ken *No Playoffs*	Right wing								
MANN, Norm	Right wing/Center								
1936	Toronto	1	0	0	0	0	0	0	0
1941	Toronto	1	0	0	0	0	0	0	0
Playoff Totals		**2**	**0**	**0**	**0**	**0**	**0**	**0**	**0**
MANNERS, Rennison *No Playoffs*	Center								
•MANNING, Paul *No Playoffs*	Defense								

Season	Team	GP	G	A	Pts	PIM	PP	SH	GW
MANNO, Bob	Defense								
1979	Vancouver	3	0	1	1	4	0	0	0
1980	Vancouver	4	1	0	1	6	0	0	0
1981	Vancouver	3	0	0	0	2	0	0	0
1984	Detroit	4	0	3	3	0	0	0	0
1985	Detroit	3	1	0	1	0	0	0	0
Playoff Totals		**17**	**2**	**4**	**6**	**12**	**0**	**0**	**0**
•MANSON, Dave	Defense								
1987	Chicago	3	0	0	0	10	0	0	0
1988	Chicago	5	0	0	0	27	0	0	0
1989	Chicago	16	0	8	8	84	0	0	0
1990	Chicago	20	2	4	6	46	1	0	0
1991	Chicago	6	0	1	1	36	0	0	0
1992	Edmonton	16	3	9	12	44	1	0	0
1996	Winnipeg	6	2	1	3	30	0	0	1
1997	Montreal	5	0	0	0	17	0	0	0
1998	Montreal	10	0	1	1	14	0	0	0
2000	Dallas	23	0	0	0	33	0	0	0
2001	Toronto	2	0	0	0	2	0	0	0
Playoff Totals		**112**	**7**	**24**	**31**	**343**	**2**	**0**	**1**
MANSON, Ray *No Playoffs*	Left wing								
MANTHA, Georges	Defense/Left wing								
1929	Montreal	3	0	0	0	0	....	....	....
1930♦	Montreal	6	0	0	0	8	....	....	....
1931♦	Montreal	10	5	1	6	4	....	....	....
1932	Montreal	4	0	1	1	8	....	....	....
1935	Montreal	2	0	0	0	4	....	....	....
1937	Montreal	5	0	0	0	0	....	....	....
1938	Montreal	3	1	0	1	0	....	....	....
1939	Montreal	3	0	0	0	0	....	....	....
Playoff Totals		**36**	**6**	**2**	**8**	**24**	....	....	....
MANTHA, Moe	Defense								
1982	Winnipeg	4	1	3	4	16	0	0	0
1983	Winnipeg	2	2	2	4	0	2	0	0
1984	Winnipeg	3	1	0	1	0	0	1	0
1989	Philadelphia	1	0	0	0	0	0	0	0
1990	Winnipeg	7	1	5	6	2	0	0	0
Playoff Totals		**17**	**5**	**10**	**15**	**18**	**2**	**1**	**0**
MANTHA, Sylvio	Defense								
1924♦	Montreal	2	0	0	0	0	....	....	....
1925	Montreal	2	0	1	1	0	....	....	....
1927	Montreal	4	1	0	1	0	....	....	....
1928	Montreal	2	0	0	0	6	....	....	....
1929	Montreal	3	0	0	0	0	....	....	....
1930♦	Montreal	6	2	1	3	18	....	....	....
1931♦	Montreal	10	2	1	3	*26	....	....	....
1932	Montreal	4	0	1	1	8	....	....	....
1933	Montreal	2	0	1	1	2	....	....	....
1934	Montreal	2	0	0	0	2	....	....	....
1935	Montreal	2	0	0	0	2	....	....	....
Playoff Totals		**39**	**5**	**5**	**10**	**64**	....	....	....
•MAPLETOFT, Justin *No Playoffs*	Center								
•MARA, Paul	Defense								
2002	Phoenix	5	0	0	0	4	0	0	0
Playoff Totals		**5**	**0**	**0**	**0**	**4**	**0**	**0**	**0**
MARACLE, Bud	Left wing								
1931	NY Rangers	4	0	0	0	0	0	0	0
Playoff Totals		**4**	**0**	**0**	**0**	**0**	**0**	**0**	**0**
MARCETTA, Milan	Center								
1967♦	Toronto	3	0	0	0	0	0	0	0
1968	Minnesota	14	7	7	14	4	1	0	1
Playoff Totals		**17**	**7**	**7**	**14**	**4**	**1**	**0**	**1**
MARCH, Mush	Right wing								
1931	Chicago	9	3	1	4	11	....	....	....
1932	Chicago	2	0	0	0	2	....	....	....
1934♦	Chicago	8	2	2	4	6	....	....	....
1935	Chicago	2	0	0	0	0	....	....	....
1936	Chicago	2	2	3	5	0	....	....	....
1938♦	Chicago	9	2	4	6	12	....	....	....
1940	Chicago	2	1	0	1	2	....	....	....
1941	Chicago	4	2	3	5	0	....	....	....
1942	Chicago	3	0	2	2	4	....	....	....
1944	Chicago	4	0	0	0	4	....	....	....
Playoff Totals		**45**	**12**	**15**	**27**	**41**	....	....	....
•MARCHANT, Todd	Center								
1997	Edmonton	12	4	2	6	12	0	3	1
1998	Edmonton	12	1	1	2	10	0	0	0
1999	Edmonton	4	1	1	2	12	0	0	0
2000	Edmonton	3	1	0	1	2	0	0	0
2001	Edmonton	6	0	0	0	4	0	0	0
Playoff Totals		**37**	**7**	**4**	**11**	**40**	**0**	**3**	**1**
MARCHINKO, Brian *No Playoffs*	Center								

•MARCHMENT, Bryan — Defense

Season	Team	GP	G	A	Pts	PIM	PP	SH	GW
1992	Chicago	16	1	0	1	36	0	0	0
1993	Chicago	4	0	0	0	12	0	0	0
1997	Edmonton	3	0	0	0	4	0	0	0
1998	San Jose	6	0	0	0	10	0	0	0
1999	San Jose	6	0	0	0	4	0	0	0
2000	San Jose	11	2	1	3	12	0	0	0
2001	San Jose	5	0	1	1	2	0	0	0
2002	San Jose	12	1	1	2	10	0	0	0
Playoff Totals		**63**	**4**	**3**	**7**	**90**	**0**	**0**	**0**

MARCINYSHYN, Dave *No Playoffs* — Defense

MARCON, Lou *No Playoffs* — Defense

MARCOTTE, Don — Left wing

Season	Team	GP	G	A	Pts	PIM	PP	SH	GW
1970♦	Boston	14	2	0	2	11	0	0	1
1971	Boston	4	0	0	0	0	0	0	0
1972♦	Boston	14	3	0	3	6	0	1	1
1973	Boston	5	1	1	2	0	0	0	0
1974	Boston	16	4	2	6	8	0	0	1
1975	Boston	3	1	0	1	0	0	0	0
1976	Boston	12	4	2	6	8	1	0	0
1977	Boston	14	5	6	11	10	0	1	0
1978	Boston	15	5	4	9	8	1	0	1
1979	Boston	11	5	3	8	10	0	0	0
1980	Boston	10	2	3	5	4	0	0	1
1981	Boston	3	2	2	4	6	0	0	0
1982	Boston	11	0	4	4	10	0	0	0
Playoff Totals		**132**	**34**	**27**	**61**	**81**	**2**	**2**	**5**

•MARHA, Josef *No Playoffs* — Center

MARINI, Hector — Right wing

Season	Team	GP	G	A	Pts	PIM	PP	SH	GW
1979	NY Islanders	1	0	0	0	0	0	0	0
1981♦	NY Islanders	9	3	6	9	14	0	0	0
1982♦	NY Islanders	....	....	....	....	....	....	....	....
Playoff Totals		**10**	**3**	**6**	**9**	**14**	**0**	**0**	**0**

MARINUCCI, Chris *No Playoffs* — Center

MARIO, Frank *No Playoffs* — Center

MARIUCCI, John — Defense

Season	Team	GP	G	A	Pts	PIM	PP	SH	GW
1941	Chicago	5	0	2	2	16	0	0	0
1942	Chicago	3	0	0	0	0	0	0	0
1946	Chicago	4	0	1	1	10	0	0	0
Playoff Totals		**12**	**0**	**3**	**3**	**26**	**0**	**0**	**0**

MARK, Gordon *No Playoffs* — Defense

MARKELL, John *No Playoffs* — Left wing

MARKER, Gus — Right wing

Season	Team	GP	G	A	Pts	PIM	PP	SH	GW
1934	Detroit	4	0	0	0	2	....	....	....
1935♦	Mtl. Maroons	7	1	1	2	4	....	....	....
1936	Mtl. Maroons	3	1	0	1	2	....	....	....
1937	Mtl. Maroons	5	0	1	1	0	....	....	....
1939	Toronto	10	2	2	4	0	....	....	....
1940	Toronto	10	1	3	4	23	....	....	....
1941	Toronto	7	0	0	0	5	....	....	....
Playoff Totals		**46**	**5**	**7**	**12**	**36**	....	....	....

MARKHAM, Ray — Center

Season	Team	GP	G	A	Pts	PIM	PP	SH	GW
1980	NY Rangers	7	1	0	1	24	0	0	0
Playoff Totals		**7**	**1**	**0**	**1**	**24**	**0**	**0**	**0**

MARKLE, Jack *No Playoffs* — Right wing

•MARKOV, Andrei — Defense

Season	Team	GP	G	A	Pts	PIM	PP	SH	GW
2002	Montreal	12	1	3	4	8	0	0	1
Playoff Totals		**12**	**1**	**3**	**4**	**8**	**0**	**0**	**1**

•MARKOV, Danny — Defense

Season	Team	GP	G	A	Pts	PIM	PP	SH	GW
1999	Toronto	17	0	6	6	18	0	0	0
2000	Toronto	12	0	3	3	10	0	0	0
2001	Toronto	11	1	1	2	12	0	0	0
Playoff Totals		**40**	**1**	**10**	**11**	**40**	**0**	**0**	**0**

MARKS, Jack *No Playoffs* — Left wing/Defense

MARKS, John — Left wing

Season	Team	GP	G	A	Pts	PIM	PP	SH	GW
1973	Chicago	16	1	2	3	2	1	0	1
1974	Chicago	11	2	0	2	8	0	0	1
1975	Chicago	8	2	6	8	34	0	0	1
1976	Chicago	4	0	0	0	10	0	0	0
1977	Chicago	2	0	0	0	4	0	0	0
1978	Chicago	4	0	1	1	0	0	0	0
1979	Chicago	4	0	0	0	2	0	0	0
1980	Chicago	4	0	0	0	0	0	0	0
1981	Chicago	3	0	0	0	0	0	0	0
1982	Chicago	1	0	0	0	0	0	0	0
Playoff Totals		**57**	**5**	**9**	**14**	**60**	**1**	**0**	**3**

MARKWART, Nevin — Left wing

Season	Team	GP	G	A	Pts	PIM	PP	SH	GW
1985	Boston	1	0	0	0	0	0	0	0
1987	Boston	4	0	0	0	9	0	0	0
1988	Boston	2	0	0	0	2	0	0	0
1991	Boston	12	1	0	1	22	0	0	0
Playoff Totals		**19**	**1**	**0**	**1**	**33**	**0**	**0**	**0**

•MARLEAU, Patrick — Center

Season	Team	GP	G	A	Pts	PIM	PP	SH	GW
1998	San Jose	5	0	1	1	0	0	0	0
1999	San Jose	6	2	1	3	4	2	0	0
2000	San Jose	5	1	1	2	2	1	0	0
2001	San Jose	6	2	0	2	4	0	0	0
2002	San Jose	12	6	5	11	6	1	0	3
Playoff Totals		**34**	**11**	**8**	**19**	**16**	**4**	**0**	**3**

MAROIS, Daniel — Right wing

Season	Team	GP	G	A	Pts	PIM	PP	SH	GW
1988	Toronto	3	1	0	1	0	0	0	0
1990	Toronto	5	2	2	4	12	2	0	0
1994	Boston	11	0	1	1	16	0	0	0
Playoff Totals		**19**	**3**	**3**	**6**	**28**	**2**	**0**	**0**

MAROIS, Mario — Defense

Season	Team	GP	G	A	Pts	PIM	PP	SH	GW
1978	NY Rangers	1	0	0	0	5	0	0	0
1979	NY Rangers	18	0	6	6	29	0	0	0
1980	NY Rangers	9	0	2	2	8	0	0	0
1981	Quebec	5	0	1	1	6	0	0	0
1982	Quebec	13	1	2	3	44	0	0	0
1984	Quebec	9	1	4	5	6	0	0	0
1985	Quebec	18	0	8	8	12	0	0	0
1986	Winnipeg	3	1	4	5	6	1	0	0
1987	Winnipeg	10	1	3	4	23	0	0	1
1988	Winnipeg	5	0	4	4	6	0	0	0
1991	St. Louis	9	0	0	0	37	0	0	0
Playoff Totals		**100**	**4**	**34**	**38**	**182**	**1**	**0**	**1**

MAROTTE, Gilles — Defense

Season	Team	GP	G	A	Pts	PIM	PP	SH	GW
1968	Chicago	11	3	1	4	14	0	0	1
1974	NY Rangers	12	0	1	1	6	0	0	0
1975	NY Rangers	3	0	1	1	4	0	0	0
1977	St. Louis	3	0	0	0	2	0	0	0
Playoff Totals		**29**	**3**	**3**	**6**	**26**	**0**	**0**	**1**

MARQUESS, Mark — Right wing

Season	Team	GP	G	A	Pts	PIM	PP	SH	GW
1947	Boston	4	0	0	0	0	0	0	0
Playoff Totals		**4**	**0**	**0**	**0**	**0**	**0**	**0**	**0**

MARSH, Brad — Defense

Season	Team	GP	G	A	Pts	PIM	PP	SH	GW
1979	Atlanta	2	0	0	0	17	0	0	0
1980	Atlanta	4	0	1	1	2	0	0	0
1981	Calgary	16	0	5	5	8	0	0	0
1982	Philadelphia	4	0	0	0	2	0	0	0
1983	Philadelphia	2	0	1	1	0	0	0	0
1984	Philadelphia	3	1	1	2	2	0	0	0
1985	Philadelphia	19	0	6	6	65	0	0	0
1986	Philadelphia	5	0	0	0	2	0	0	0
1987	Philadelphia	26	3	4	7	16	0	1	0
1988	Philadelphia	7	1	0	1	8	0	0	0
1990	Toronto	5	1	0	1	2	0	0	0
1991	Detroit	1	0	0	0	0	0	0	0
1992	Detroit	3	0	0	0	0	0	0	0
Playoff Totals		**97**	**6**	**18**	**24**	**124**	**0**	**1**	**0**

MARSH, Gary *No Playoffs* — Left wing

MARSH, Peter — Right wing

Season	Team	GP	G	A	Pts	PIM	PP	SH	GW
1981	Chicago	2	1	1	2	2	0	0	0
1982	Chicago	12	0	2	2	31	0	0	0
1983	Chicago	12	0	2	2	0	0	0	0
Playoff Totals		**26**	**1**	**5**	**6**	**33**	**0**	**0**	**0**

MARSHALL, Bert — Defense

Season	Team	GP	G	A	Pts	PIM	PP	SH	GW
1966	Detroit	12	1	3	4	16	0	0	0
1969	Oakland	7	0	7	7	20	0	0	0
1970	Oakland	4	0	1	1	12	0	0	0
1973	NY Rangers	6	0	1	1	8	0	0	0
1975	NY Islanders	17	2	5	7	16	0	0	0
1976	NY Islanders	13	1	3	4	12	0	0	1
1977	NY Islanders	6	0	0	0	6	0	0	0
1978	NY Islanders	7	0	2	2	9	0	0	0
Playoff Totals		**72**	**4**	**22**	**26**	**99**	**0**	**0**	**1**

MARSHALL, Don — Left wing

Season	Team	GP	G	A	Pts	PIM	PP	SH	GW
1955	Montreal	12	1	1	2	2	0	0	1
1956♦	Montreal	10	1	0	1	0	0	1	0
1957♦	Montreal	10	1	3	4	2	0	0	0
1958♦	Montreal	10	0	2	2	4	0	0	0
1959♦	Montreal	11	0	2	2	2	0	0	0
1960♦	Montreal	8	2	2	4	0	0	0	0
1961	Montreal	6	0	2	2	0	0	0	0
1962	Montreal	6	0	1	1	2	0	0	0
1963	Montreal	5	0	0	0	0	0	0	0
1967	NY Rangers	4	0	1	1	2	0	0	0
1968	NY Rangers	6	2	1	3	0	0	0	1
1969	NY Rangers	4	1	0	1	0	0	0	0
1970	NY Rangers	1	0	0	0	0	0	0	0
1972	Toronto	1	0	0	0	0	0	0	0
Playoff Totals		**94**	**8**	**15**	**23**	**14**	**0**	**1**	**2**

•MARSHALL, Grant — Right wing

Season	Team	GP	G	A	Pts	PIM	PP	SH	GW
1997	Dallas	5	0	2	2	8	0	0	0
1998	Dallas	17	0	2	2	*47	0	0	0
1999♦	Dallas	14	0	3	3	20	0	0	0
2000	Dallas	14	0	1	1	4	0	0	0
2001	Dallas	9	0	0	0	0	0	0	0
Playoff Totals		**59**	**0**	**8**	**8**	**79**	**0**	**0**	**0**

•MARSHALL, Jason — Defense

Season	Team	GP	G	A	Pts	PIM	PP	SH	GW
1997	Anaheim	7	0	1	1	4	0	0	0
1999	Anaheim	4	1	0	1	10	1	0	0
Playoff Totals		**11**	**1**	**1**	**2**	**14**	**1**	**0**	**0**

MARSHALL, Paul — Left wing

Season	Team	GP	G	A	Pts	PIM	PP	SH	GW
1980	Pittsburgh	1	0	0	0	0	0	0	0
Playoff Totals		**1**	**0**	**0**	**0**	**0**	**0**	**0**	**0**

MARSHALL, Willie *No Playoffs* — Center

MARSON, Mike *No Playoffs* — Left wing

MARTIN, Clare — Defense

Season	Team	GP	G	A	Pts	PIM	PP	SH	GW
1942	Boston	5	0	0	0	0	0	0	0
1947	Boston	5	0	1	1	0	0	0	0
1948	Boston	5	0	0	0	6	0	0	0
1950♦	Detroit	10	0	1	1	0	0	0	0
1951	Detroit	2	0	0	0	0	0	0	0
Playoff Totals		**27**	**0**	**2**	**2**	**6**	**0**	**0**	**0**

MARTIN, Craig *No Playoffs* — Right wing

MARTIN, Frank — Defense

Season	Team	GP	G	A	Pts	PIM	PP	SH	GW
1953	Boston	6	0	1	1	2	0	0	0
1954	Boston	4	0	1	1	0	0	0	0
Playoff Totals		**10**	**0**	**2**	**2**	**2**	**0**	**0**	**0**

MARTIN, Grant — Left wing

Season	Team	GP	G	A	Pts	PIM	PP	SH	GW
1987	Washington	1	1	0	1	2	0	0	0
Playoff Totals		**1**	**1**	**0**	**1**	**2**	**0**	**0**	**0**

MARTIN, Jack *No Playoffs* — Center

MARTIN, Matt *No Playoffs* — Defense

MARTIN, Pit — Center

Season	Team	GP	G	A	Pts	PIM	PP	SH	GW
1964	Detroit	14	1	4	5	14	1	0	0
1965	Detroit	3	0	1	1	2	0	0	0
1968	Chicago	11	3	6	9	2	0	0	0
1970	Chicago	8	3	3	6	4	2	1	0
1971	Chicago	17	2	7	9	12	0	0	1
1972	Chicago	8	4	2	6	4	0	0	1
1973	Chicago	15	10	6	16	6	4	0	1
1974	Chicago	7	2	0	2	4	1	0	0
1975	Chicago	8	1	1	2	2	0	0	0
1976	Chicago	4	1	0	1	4	0	0	0
1977	Chicago	2	0	0	0	0	0	0	0
1979	Vancouver	3	0	1	1	2	0	0	0
Playoff Totals		**100**	**27**	**31**	**58**	**56**	**8**	**1**	**3**

MARTIN, Rick — Left wing

Season	Team	GP	G	A	Pts	PIM	PP	SH	GW
1973	Buffalo	6	3	2	5	12	2	0	0
1975	Buffalo	17	7	8	15	20	5	0	1
1976	Buffalo	9	4	7	11	12	2	0	1
1977	Buffalo	6	2	1	3	9	1	0	1
1978	Buffalo	7	2	4	6	13	1	0	1
1979	Buffalo	3	0	3	3	0	0	0	0
1980	Buffalo	14	6	4	10	8	1	0	0
1981	Los Angeles	1	0	0	0	0	0	0	0
Playoff Totals		**63**	**24**	**29**	**53**	**74**	**12**	**0**	**4**

MARTIN, Ron *No Playoffs* — Right wing

MARTIN, Terry — Left wing

Season	Team	GP	G	A	Pts	PIM	PP	SH	GW
1977	Buffalo	3	0	2	2	5	0	0	0
1978	Buffalo	8	2	0	2	5	0	0	0
1980	Toronto	3	2	0	2	7	0	0	0
1981	Toronto	3	0	0	0	0	0	0	0
1983	Toronto	4	0	0	0	9	0	0	0
Playoff Totals		**21**	**4**	**2**	**6**	**26**	**0**	**0**	**0**

MARTIN, Tom *No Playoffs* — Right wing

MARTIN, Tom — Left wing

Season	Team	GP	G	A	Pts	PIM	PP	SH	GW
1985	Winnipeg	3	0	0	0	2	0	0	0
1989	Hartford	1	0	0	0	4	0	0	0
Playoff Totals		**4**	**0**	**0**	**0**	**6**	**0**	**0**	**0**

MARTINEAU, Don *No Playoffs* — Right wing

•MARTINEK, Radek *No Playoffs* — Defense

MARTINI, Darcy *No Playoffs* — Defense

•MARTINS, Steve — Center

Season	Team	GP	G	A	Pts	PIM	PP	SH	GW
2002	Ottawa	2	0	0	0	0	0	0	0
Playoff Totals		**2**	**0**	**0**	**0**	**0**	**0**	**0**	**0**

MARTINSON, Steve — Left wing

Season	Team	GP	G	A	Pts	PIM	PP	SH	GW
1989	Montreal	1	0	0	0	10	0	0	0
Playoff Totals		**1**	**0**	**0**	**0**	**10**	**0**	**0**	**0**

MARUK, Dennis — Center

Season	Team	GP	G	A	Pts	PIM	PP	SH	GW
1983	Washington	4	1	1	2	2	0	0	0
1984	Minnesota	16	5	5	10	8	1	1	0
1985	Minnesota	9	4	7	11	12	3	0	1
1986	Minnesota	5	4	9	13	4	1	0	0
Playoff Totals		**34**	**14**	**22**	**36**	**26**	**5**	**1**	**1**

MASNICK, Paul — Center

Season	Team	GP	G	A	Pts	PIM	PP	SH	GW
1951	Montreal	11	2	1	3	4	....	....	....
1952	Montreal	6	1	0	1	12	....	....	....
1953♦	Montreal	6	1	0	1	7	....	....	....
1954	Montreal	10	0	4	4	4	....	....	....
Playoff Totals		**33**	**4**	**5**	**9**	**27**	....	....	....

MASON, Charley — Right wing

Season	Team	GP	G	A	Pts	PIM	PP	SH	GW
1935	NY Rangers	4	0	1	1	0	0	0	0
Playoff Totals		**4**	**0**	**1**	**1**	**0**	**0**	**0**	**0**

MASSECAR, George *No Playoffs* — Left wing

MASTERS, Jamie — Defense

Season	Team	GP	G	A	Pts	PIM	PP	SH	GW
1976	St. Louis	1	0	0	0	0	0	0	0
1977	St. Louis	1	0	0	0	0	0	0	0
Playoff Totals		**2**	**0**	**0**	**0**	**0**	**0**	**0**	**0**

MASTERTON, Bill *No Playoffs* — Center

MATHERS, Frank *No Playoffs* — Defense

MATHIASEN, Dwight *No Playoffs* — Right wing

MATHIESON, Jim *No Playoffs* — Defense

Season	Team	GP	G	A	Pts	PIM	PP	SH	GW
MATHIEU, Marquis *No Playoffs*	Center								
•MATTE, Christian *No Playoffs*	Right wing								
MATTE, Joe *No Playoffs*	Defense								
MATTE, Joe *No Playoffs*	Defense								
•MATTEAU, Stephane	Left wing								
1991	Calgary	5	0	1	1	0	0	0	0
1992	Chicago	18	4	6	10	24	1	1	0
1993	Chicago	3	0	1	1	2	0	0	0
1994♦	NY Rangers	23	6	3	9	20	1	0	2
1995	NY Rangers	9	0	1	1	10	0	0	0
1996	St. Louis	11	0	2	2	8	0	0	0
1997	St. Louis	5	0	0	0	0	0	0	0
1998	San Jose	4	0	1	1	0	0	0	0
1999	San Jose	5	0	0	0	6	0	0	0
2000	San Jose	10	0	2	2	8	0	0	0
2001	San Jose	6	1	3	4	0	0	0	0
2002	San Jose	10	1	2	3	2	0	0	0
Playoff Totals		**109**	**12**	**22**	**34**	**80**	**2**	**1**	**2**
•MATTEUCCI, Mike *No Playoffs*	Defense								
MATTIUSSI, Dick	Left wing								
1969	Oakland	7	0	1	1	6	0	0	0
1970	Oakland	1	0	0	0	0	0	0	0
Playoff Totals		**8**	**0**	**1**	**1**	**6**	**0**	**0**	**0**
•MATVICHUK, Richard	Defense								
1994	Dallas	7	1	1	2	12	1	0	0
1995	Dallas	5	0	2	2	4	0	0	0
1997	Dallas	7	0	1	1	20	0	0	0
1998	Dallas	16	1	1	2	14	0	0	0
1999♦	Dallas	22	1	5	6	20	0	0	0
2000	Dallas	23	2	5	7	14	0	0	0
2001	Dallas	10	0	0	0	14	0	0	0
Playoff Totals		**90**	**5**	**15**	**20**	**98**	**1**	**0**	**0**
MATZ, Johnny	Center								
1925	Montreal	1	0	0	0	0	0	0	0
Playoff Totals		**1**	**0**	**0**	**0**	**0**	**0**	**0**	**0**
MAXNER, Wayne *No Playoffs*	Left wing								
MAXWELL, Brad	Defense								
1980	Minnesota	11	0	8	8	20	0	0	0
1981	Minnesota	18	3	11	14	35	1	0	0
1982	Minnesota	4	0	3	3	13	0	0	0
1983	Minnesota	9	5	6	11	23	2	0	0
1984	Minnesota	16	2	11	13	40	1	0	0
1985	Quebec	18	2	9	11	35	1	0	0
1986	Toronto	3	0	1	1	12	0	0	0
Playoff Totals		**79**	**12**	**49**	**61**	**178**	**5**	**0**	**0**
MAXWELL, Bryan	Defense								
1980	St. Louis	1	0	0	0	9	0	0	0
1981	St. Louis	11	0	1	1	54	0	0	0
1983	Winnipeg	3	1	0	1	23	1	0	0
Playoff Totals		**15**	**1**	**1**	**2**	**86**	**1**	**0**	**0**
MAXWELL, Kevin	Center								
1981	Minnesota	16	3	4	7	24	0	1	0
Playoff Totals		**16**	**3**	**4**	**7**	**24**	**0**	**1**	**0**
MAXWELL, Wally *No Playoffs*	Center								
MAY, Alan	Right wing								
1990	Washington	15	0	0	0	37	0	0	0
1991	Washington	11	1	1	2	37	0	0	1
1992	Washington	7	0	0	0	0	0	0	0
1993	Washington	6	0	1	1	6	0	0	0
1994	Dallas	1	0	0	0	0	0	0	0
Playoff Totals		**40**	**1**	**2**	**3**	**80**	**0**	**0**	**1**
•MAY, Brad	Left wing								
1992	Buffalo	7	1	4	5	2	0	0	1
1993	Buffalo	8	1	1	2	14	0	0	1
1994	Buffalo	7	0	2	2	9	0	0	0
1995	Buffalo	4	0	0	0	2	0	0	0
1997	Buffalo	10	1	1	2	32	0	0	0
2002	Phoenix	5	0	0	0	0	0	0	0
Playoff Totals		**41**	**3**	**8**	**11**	**59**	**0**	**0**	**2**
MAYER, Derek *No Playoffs*	Defense								
MAYER, Jim *No Playoffs*	Right wing								
MAYER, Pat *No Playoffs*	Defense								
MAYER, Shep *No Playoffs*	Right wing								
•MAYERS, Jamal	Center								
1999	St. Louis	11	0	1	1	8	0	0	0
2000	St. Louis	7	0	4	4	2	0	0	0
2001	St. Louis	15	2	3	5	8	0	0	0
2002	St. Louis	10	3	0	3	2	0	0	2
Playoff Totals		**43**	**5**	**8**	**13**	**20**	**0**	**0**	**2**
MAZUR, Eddie	Defense/Left wing								
1951	Montreal	2	0	0	0	0	....	....	....
1952	Montreal	5	2	0	2	4	....	....	....
1953♦	Montreal	7	2	2	4	11	....	....	....
1954	Montreal	11	0	3	3	7	....	....	....
Playoff Totals		**25**	**4**	**5**	**9**	**22**	....	....	....
MAZUR, Jay	Center/Right wing								
1991	Vancouver	6	0	1	1	8	0	0	0
Playoff Totals		**6**	**0**	**1**	**1**	**8**	**0**	**0**	**0**

Season	Team	GP	G	A	Pts	PIM	PP	SH	GW
McADAM, Gary	Left wing								
1976	Buffalo	1	0	0	0	0	0	0	0
1977	Buffalo	6	1	0	1	0	0	0	0
1978	Buffalo	8	2	2	4	7	0	0	0
1979	Pittsburgh	7	2	1	3	0	0	0	0
1980	Pittsburgh	5	1	2	3	9	0	0	0
1982	Calgary	3	0	0	0	0	0	0	0
Playoff Totals		**30**	**6**	**5**	**11**	**16**	**0**	**0**	**0**
McADAM, Sam *No Playoffs*	Center/Left wing								
•McALLISTER, Chris	Defense								
1999	Toronto	6	0	1	1	4	0	0	0
2001	Philadelphia	2	0	0	0	0	0	0	0
Playoff Totals		**8**	**0**	**1**	**1**	**4**	**0**	**0**	**0**
•McALPINE, Chris	Defense								
1995♦	New Jersey	....	....	....	....	....	....	....	....
1997	St. Louis	4	0	1	1	0	0	0	0
1998	St. Louis	10	0	0	0	16	0	0	0
1999	St. Louis	13	0	0	0	2	0	0	0
2002	Chicago	1	0	0	0	0	0	0	0
Playoff Totals		**28**	**0**	**1**	**1**	**18**	**0**	**0**	**0**
•McAMMOND, Dean	Center								
1992	Chicago	3	0	0	0	2	0	0	0
1998	Edmonton	12	1	4	5	12	0	0	0
2001	Philadelphia	4	0	0	0	2	0	0	0
Playoff Totals		**19**	**1**	**4**	**5**	**16**	**0**	**0**	**0**
McANDREW, Hazen *No Playoffs*	Defense								
McANEELEY, Ted *No Playoffs*	Defense								
McATEE, Jud	Left wing								
1945	Detroit	14	2	1	3	0	....	....	....
Playoff Totals		**14**	**2**	**1**	**3**	**0**	....	....	....
McATEE, Norm *No Playoffs*	Center								
McAVOY, George	Defense								
1955	Montreal	4	0	0	0	0	0	0	0
Playoff Totals		**4**	**0**	**0**	**0**	**0**	**0**	**0**	**0**
McBAIN, Andrew	Right wing								
1984	Winnipeg	3	2	0	2	0	0	0	0
1985	Winnipeg	7	1	0	1	0	0	0	0
1987	Winnipeg	9	0	2	2	10	0	0	0
1988	Winnipeg	5	2	5	7	29	0	1	0
Playoff Totals		**24**	**5**	**7**	**12**	**39**	**0**	**1**	**0**
McBAIN, Jason *No Playoffs*	Defense								
McBAIN, Mike *No Playoffs*	Defense								
McBEAN, Wayne	Defense								
1990	NY Islanders	2	1	1	2	0	0	0	0
Playoff Totals		**2**	**1**	**1**	**2**	**0**	**0**	**0**	**0**
McBRIDE, Cliff *No Playoffs*	Right wing/Defense								
McBURNEY, Jim *No Playoffs*	Left wing								
•McCABE, Bryan	Defense								
2001	Toronto	11	2	3	5	16	1	0	0
2002	Toronto	20	5	5	10	30	3	0	1
Playoff Totals		**31**	**7**	**8**	**15**	**46**	**4**	**0**	**1**
McCABE, Stan *No Playoffs*	Left wing								
McCAFFREY, Bert	Right wing/Defense								
1925	Toronto	2	1	0	1	4	....	....	....
1930♦	Montreal	6	1	1	2	6	....	....	....
Playoff Totals		**8**	**2**	**1**	**3**	**10**	....	....	....
McCAHILL, John *No Playoffs*	Defense								
McCAIG, Doug	Defense								
1942	Detroit	2	0	0	0	6	0	0	0
1947	Detroit	5	0	1	1	4	0	0	0
Playoff Totals		**7**	**0**	**1**	**1**	**10**	**0**	**0**	**0**
McCALLUM, Dunc	Defense								
1970	Pittsburgh	10	1	2	3	12	0	0	0
Playoff Totals		**10**	**1**	**2**	**3**	**12**	**0**	**0**	**0**
McCALMON, Eddie *No Playoffs*	Right wing								
McCANN, Rick *No Playoffs*	Center								
McCARTHY, Dan *No Playoffs*	Center								
McCARTHY, Kevin	Defense								
1978	Philadelphia	10	0	1	1	8	0	0	0
1980	Vancouver	4	1	0	1	0	0	0	0
1981	Vancouver	3	0	1	1	0	0	0	0
1983	Vancouver	4	1	1	2	12	0	0	0
Playoff Totals		**21**	**2**	**3**	**5**	**20**	**0**	**0**	**0**
•McCARTHY, Sandy	Right wing								
1994	Calgary	7	0	0	0	34	0	0	0
1995	Calgary	6	0	1	1	17	0	0	0
1996	Calgary	4	0	0	0	10	0	0	0
1999	Philadelphia	6	0	1	1	0	0	0	0
Playoff Totals		**23**	**0**	**2**	**2**	**61**	**0**	**0**	**0**
•McCARTHY, Steve *No Playoffs*	Defense								
McCARTHY, Thomas *No Playoffs*	Right wing								
McCARTHY, Tom *No Playoffs*	Left wing								

Season	Team	GP	G	A	Pts	PIM	PP	SH	GW
McCARTHY, Tom	Left wing								
1980	Minnesota	15	5	6	11	20	3	0	0
1981	Minnesota	8	0	3	3	6	0	0	0
1982	Minnesota	4	0	2	2	4	0	0	0
1983	Minnesota	9	2	4	6	9	0	0	0
1984	Minnesota	8	1	4	5	6	1	0	1
1985	Minnesota	7	0	2	2	0	0	0	0
1987	Boston	4	1	1	2	4	1	0	0
1988	Boston	13	3	4	7	18	0	0	0
Playoff Totals		**68**	**12**	**26**	**38**	**67**	**5**	**0**	**1**
McCARTNEY, Walt *No Playoffs*	Left wing								
•McCARTY, Darren	Right wing								
1994	Detroit	7	2	2	4	8	0	0	0
1995	Detroit	18	3	2	5	14	0	0	0
1996	Detroit	19	3	2	5	20	0	0	1
1997♦	Detroit	20	3	4	7	34	0	0	2
1998♦	Detroit	22	3	8	11	34	0	0	1
1999	Detroit	10	1	1	2	23	0	0	0
2000	Detroit	9	0	1	1	12	0	0	0
2001	Detroit	6	1	0	1	2	0	0	0
2002♦	Detroit	23	4	4	8	34	0	0	1
Playoff Totals		**134**	**20**	**24**	**44**	**181**	**0**	**0**	**5**
McCASKILL, Ted *No Playoffs*	Center								
•McCAULEY, Alyn	Center								
2000	Toronto	5	0	0	0	6	0	0	0
2001	Toronto	10	0	0	0	2	0	0	0
2002	Toronto	20	5	10	15	4	1	0	2
Playoff Totals		**35**	**5**	**10**	**15**	**12**	**1**	**0**	**2**
McCLANAHAN, Rob	Center								
1980	Buffalo	10	0	1	1	4	0	0	0
1981	Buffalo	5	0	1	1	13	0	0	0
1982	NY Rangers	10	2	5	7	2	0	0	0
1983	NY Rangers	9	2	5	7	12	0	0	1
Playoff Totals		**34**	**4**	**12**	**16**	**31**	**0**	**0**	**1**
McCLEARY, Trent *No Playoffs*	Right wing								
McCLELLAND, Kevin	Right wing								
1982	Pittsburgh	5	1	1	2	5	0	0	0
1984♦	Edmonton	18	4	6	10	42	0	0	1
1985♦	Edmonton	18	1	3	4	75	0	0	0
1986	Edmonton	10	1	0	1	32	0	0	0
1987♦	Edmonton	21	2	3	5	43	0	0	0
1988♦	Edmonton	19	2	3	5	68	0	0	0
1989	Edmonton	7	0	2	2	16	0	0	0
Playoff Totals		**98**	**11**	**18**	**29**	**281**	**0**	**0**	**1**
McCORD, Bob	Defense								
1968	Minnesota	14	2	5	7	10	0	0	0
Playoff Totals		**14**	**2**	**5**	**7**	**10**	**0**	**0**	**0**
McCORD, Dennis *No Playoffs*	Defense								
McCORMACK, John	Center								
1950	Toronto	6	1	0	1	0	....	....	....
1951♦	Toronto	....	....	....	....	....	....	....	....
1953♦	Montreal	9	0	0	0	0	....	....	....
1954	Montreal	7	0	1	1	0	....	....	....
Playoff Totals		**22**	**1**	**1**	**2**	**0**	....	....	....
McCOSH, Shawn *No Playoffs*	Center								
McCOURT, Dale	Center								
1978	Detroit	7	4	2	6	2	2	0	0
1982	Buffalo	4	2	3	5	0	1	0	0
1983	Buffalo	10	3	2	5	4	2	0	1
Playoff Totals		**21**	**9**	**7**	**16**	**6**	**5**	**0**	**1**
McCREARY, Bill *No Playoffs*	Right wing								
McCREARY, Bill	Left wing								
1968	St. Louis	15	3	2	5	0	0	2	2
1969	St. Louis	12	1	5	6	14	1	1	0
1970	St. Louis	15	1	7	8	0	0	0	0
1971	St. Louis	6	1	2	3	0	0	0	0
Playoff Totals		**48**	**6**	**16**	**22**	**14**	**1**	**3**	**2**
McCREARY, Keith	Right wing								
1962	Montreal	1	0	0	0	0	0	0	0
1970	Pittsburgh	10	0	4	4	4	0	0	0
1972	Pittsburgh	1	0	0	0	2	0	0	0
1974	Atlanta	4	0	0	0	0	0	0	0
Playoff Totals		**16**	**0**	**4**	**4**	**6**	**0**	**0**	**0**
McCREEDY, John	Right wing								
1942♦	Toronto	13	4	3	7	6	....	....	....
1945♦	Toronto	8	0	0	0	10	....	....	....
Playoff Totals		**21**	**4**	**3**	**7**	**16**	....	....	....

Season	Team	GP	G	A	Pts	PIM	PP	SH	GW
McCRIMMON, Brad — Defense									
1980	Boston	10	1	1	2	28	0	0	0
1981	Boston	3	0	1	1	2	0	0	0
1982	Boston	2	0	0	0	2	0	0	0
1983	Philadelphia	3	0	0	0	4	0	0	0
1984	Philadelphia	1	0	0	0	4	0	0	0
1985	Philadelphia	11	2	1	3	15	0	0	0
1986	Philadelphia	5	2	0	2	2	0	0	1
1987	Philadelphia	26	3	5	8	30	1	0	1
1988	Calgary	9	2	3	5	22	2	0	0
1989♦	Calgary	22	0	3	3	30	0	0	0
1990	Calgary	6	0	2	2	8	0	0	0
1991	Detroit	7	1	1	2	21	0	0	0
1992	Detroit	11	0	1	1	8	0	0	0
Playoff Totals		**116**	**11**	**18**	**29**	**176**	**3**	**0**	**2**
McCRIMMON, Jim *No Playoffs* — Defense									
McCULLEY, Bob *No Playoffs* — Right wing/Defense									
McCURRY, Duke — Left wing									
1926	Pittsburgh	2	0	2	2	4	0	0	0
1928	Pittsburgh	2	0	0	0	0	0	0	0
Playoff Totals		**4**	**0**	**2**	**2**	**4**	**0**	**0**	**0**
McCUTCHEON, Brian *No Playoffs* — Left wing									
McCUTCHEON, Darwin *No Playoffs* — Defense									
McDILL, Jeff *No Playoffs* — Right wing									
McDONAGH, Bill *No Playoffs* — Left wing									
McDONALD, Ab — Left wing									
1958♦	Montreal	2	0	0	0	2	....	....	....
1959♦	Montreal	11	1	1	2	6	....	....	....
1960♦	Montreal	....	....	....	....	....	....	....	....
1961♦	Chicago	8	2	2	4	0	....	....	....
1962	Chicago	12	6	6	12	0	....	....	....
1963	Chicago	6	2	3	5	9	....	....	....
1964	Chicago	7	2	2	4	0	....	....	....
1966	Detroit	10	1	4	5	2	....	....	....
1969	St. Louis	12	2	1	3	10	0	0	0
1970	St. Louis	16	5	10	15	13	3	0	0
Playoff Totals		**84**	**21**	**29**	**50**	**42**	**3**	**0**	**0**
•**McDONALD, Andy** *No Playoffs* — Center									
McDONALD, Brian — Center									
1968	Chicago	8	0	0	0	2	0	0	0
Playoff Totals		**8**	**0**	**0**	**0**	**2**	**0**	**0**	**0**
McDONALD, Bucko — Defense									
1936♦	Detroit	7	3	0	3	10	....	....	....
1937♦	Detroit	10	0	0	0	2	....	....	....
1939	Toronto	10	0	0	0	4	....	....	....
1940	Toronto	1	0	0	0	0	....	....	....
1941	Toronto	7	2	0	2	2	....	....	....
1942♦	Toronto	9	0	1	1	2	....	....	....
1943	Toronto	6	1	0	1	4	....	....	....
Playoff Totals		**50**	**6**	**1**	**7**	**24**	....	....	....
McDONALD, Butch — Left wing/Center									
1940	Detroit	5	0	2	2	10	0	0	0
Playoff Totals		**5**	**0**	**2**	**2**	**10**	**0**	**0**	**0**
McDONALD, Gerry *No Playoffs* — Defense									
McDONALD, Jack *No Playoffs* — Right wing									
McDONALD, Jack — Left wing									
1918	Montreal	2	1	0	1	0	....	....	....
1919	Montreal	5	0	1	1	3	....	....	....
Playoff Totals		**7**	**1**	**1**	**2**	**3**	....	....	....
McDONALD, Lanny — Right wing									
1975	Toronto	7	0	0	0	2	0	0	0
1976	Toronto	10	4	4	8	4	2	0	1
1977	Toronto	9	10	7	17	6	3	0	1
1978	Toronto	13	3	4	7	10	1	0	2
1979	Toronto	6	3	2	5	0	0	0	0
1982	Calgary	3	0	1	1	6	0	0	0
1983	Calgary	7	3	4	7	19	1	0	0
1984	Calgary	11	6	7	13	6	3	0	1
1985	Calgary	1	0	0	0	0	0	0	0
1986	Calgary	22	11	7	18	30	4	0	2
1987	Calgary	5	0	0	0	2	0	0	0
1988	Calgary	9	3	1	4	6	0	0	0
1989♦	Calgary	14	1	3	4	29	0	0	0
Playoff Totals		**117**	**44**	**40**	**84**	**120**	**14**	**0**	**7**
McDONALD, Robert *No Playoffs* — Right wing									
McDONALD, Terry *No Playoffs* — Defense									
McDONNELL, Joe *No Playoffs* — Defense									
McDONNELL, Moylan *No Playoffs* — Defense									
McDONOUGH, Al — Right wing									
1972	Pittsburgh	4	0	1	1	0	0	0	0
1974	Atlanta	4	0	0	0	2	0	0	0
Playoff Totals		**8**	**0**	**1**	**1**	**2**	**0**	**0**	**0**
McDONOUGH, Hubie — Center									
1990	NY Islanders	5	1	0	1	4	0	0	0
Playoff Totals		**5**	**1**	**0**	**1**	**4**	**0**	**0**	**0**
McDOUGAL, Mike *No Playoffs* — Right wing									

Season	Team	GP	G	A	Pts	PIM	PP	SH	GW
McDOUGALL, Bill — Center									
1991	Detroit	1	0	0	0	0	0	0	0
Playoff Totals		**1**	**0**	**0**	**0**	**0**	**0**	**0**	**0**
•**McEACHERN, Shawn** — Left wing									
1992♦	Pittsburgh	19	2	7	9	4	0	0	0
1993	Pittsburgh	12	3	2	5	10	0	0	1
1994	Pittsburgh	6	1	0	1	2	0	0	0
1995	Pittsburgh	11	0	2	2	8	0	0	0
1996	Boston	5	2	1	3	8	0	0	0
1997	Ottawa	7	2	0	2	8	1	0	0
1998	Ottawa	11	0	4	4	8	0	0	0
1999	Ottawa	4	2	0	2	6	1	0	0
2000	Ottawa	6	0	3	3	4	0	0	0
2001	Ottawa	4	0	2	2	2	0	0	0
2002	Ottawa	12	0	4	4	2	0	0	0
Playoff Totals		**97**	**12**	**25**	**37**	**62**	**2**	**0**	**1**
McELMURY, Jim *No Playoffs* — Defense									
McEWEN, Mike — Defense									
1979	NY Rangers	18	2	11	13	8	2	0	1
1981♦	NY Islanders	17	6	8	14	6	4	0	0
1982♦	NY Islanders	15	3	7	10	18	2	0	0
1983♦	NY Islanders	12	0	2	2	4	0	0	0
1985	Washington	5	0	1	1	4	0	0	0
1986	Hartford	8	0	4	4	6	0	0	0
1987	Hartford	1	1	1	2	0	1	0	0
1988	Hartford	2	0	2	2	2	0	0	0
Playoff Totals		**78**	**12**	**36**	**48**	**48**	**9**	**0**	**1**
McFADDEN, Jim — Center									
1947	Detroit	4	0	2	2	0	....	....	....
1948	Detroit	10	5	3	8	10	....	....	....
1949	Detroit	8	0	1	1	6	....	....	....
1950♦	Detroit	14	2	3	5	8	....	....	....
1951	Detroit	6	0	0	0	2	....	....	....
1953	Chicago	7	3	0	3	4	....	....	....
Playoff Totals		**49**	**10**	**9**	**19**	**30**	....	....	....
McFADYEN, Don — Center/Left wing									
1934♦	Chicago	8	2	2	4	5	....	....	....
1935	Chicago	2	0	0	0	0	....	....	....
1936	Chicago	1	0	0	0	0	....	....	....
Playoff Totals		**11**	**2**	**2**	**4**	**5**	....	....	....
McFALL, Dan *No Playoffs* — Defense									
McFARLANE, Gord *No Playoffs* — Right wing/Defense									
McGEOUGH, Jim *No Playoffs* — Center									
McGIBBON, Irv *No Playoffs* — Right wing									
McGILL, Bob — Defense									
1986	Toronto	9	0	0	0	35	0	0	0
1987	Toronto	3	0	0	0	0	0	0	0
1988	Chicago	3	0	0	0	2	0	0	0
1989	Chicago	16	0	0	0	33	0	0	0
1990	Chicago	5	0	0	0	2	0	0	0
1991	Chicago	5	0	0	0	2	0	0	0
1992	Detroit	8	0	0	0	14	0	0	0
Playoff Totals		**49**	**0**	**0**	**0**	**88**	**0**	**0**	**0**
McGILL, Jack — Center									
1942	Boston	5	4	1	5	6	....	....	....
1945	Boston	7	3	3	6	0	....	....	....
1946	Boston	10	0	0	0	0	....	....	....
1947	Boston	5	0	0	0	11	....	....	....
Playoff Totals		**27**	**7**	**4**	**11**	**17**	....	....	....
McGILL, Jack — Left wing									
1935	Montreal	2	2	0	2	0	....	....	....
1937	Montreal	1	0	0	0	0	....	....	....
Playoff Totals		**3**	**2**	**0**	**2**	**0**	....	....	....
McGILL, Ryan *No Playoffs* — Defense									
•**McGILLIS, Dan** — Defense									
1997	Edmonton	12	0	5	5	24	0	0	0
1998	Philadelphia	5	1	2	3	10	1	0	0
1999	Philadelphia	6	0	1	1	12	0	0	0
2000	Philadelphia	18	2	6	8	12	0	0	0
2001	Philadelphia	6	1	0	1	6	0	1	0
2002	Philadelphia	5	1	0	1	8	1	0	0
Playoff Totals		**52**	**5**	**14**	**19**	**72**	**2**	**1**	**0**
McGREGOR, Sandy *No Playoffs* — Right wing									
McGUIRE, Mickey *No Playoffs* — Left wing									
McHUGH, Mike *No Playoffs* — Left wing									
McILHARGEY, Jack — Defense									
1976	Philadelphia	15	0	3	3	41	0	0	0
1979	Vancouver	3	0	0	0	2	0	0	0
1980	Philadelphia	9	0	0	0	25	0	0	0
Playoff Totals		**27**	**0**	**3**	**3**	**68**	**0**	**0**	**0**
McINENLY, Bert — Left wing/Defense									
1935	Boston	4	0	0	0	2	0	0	0
Playoff Totals		**4**	**0**	**0**	**0**	**2**	**0**	**0**	**0**

Season	Team	GP	G	A	Pts	PIM	PP	SH	GW
•**McINNIS, Marty** — Left wing									
1993	NY Islanders	3	0	1	1	0	0	0	0
1994	NY Islanders	4	0	0	0	0	0	0	0
1999	Anaheim	4	2	0	2	2	2	0	0
2002	Boston	6	0	1	1	0	0	0	0
Playoff Totals		**17**	**2**	**2**	**4**	**2**	**2**	**0**	**0**
McINTOSH, Bruce *No Playoffs* — Defense									
McINTOSH, Paul — Defense									
1975	Buffalo	1	0	0	0	0	0	0	0
1976	Buffalo	1	0	0	0	7	0	0	0
Playoff Totals		**2**	**0**	**0**	**0**	**7**	**0**	**0**	**0**
McINTYRE, Jack — Defense									
1951	Boston	2	0	0	0	0	....	....	....
1952	Boston	7	1	2	3	2	....	....	....
1953	Boston	10	4	2	6	2	....	....	....
1958	Detroit	4	1	1	2	0	....	....	....
1960	Detroit	6	1	1	2	0	....	....	....
Playoff Totals		**29**	**7**	**6**	**13**	**4**	....	....	....
McINTYRE, John — Center									
1990	Toronto	2	0	0	0	2	0	0	0
1991	Los Angeles	12	0	1	1	24	0	0	0
1992	Los Angeles	6	0	4	4	12	0	0	0
1994	Vancouver	24	0	1	1	16	0	0	0
Playoff Totals		**44**	**0**	**6**	**6**	**54**	**0**	**0**	**0**
McINTYRE, Larry *No Playoffs* — Defense									
McKAY, Doug — Left wing									
1950♦	Detroit	1	0	0	0	0	0	0	0
Playoff Totals		**1**	**0**	**0**	**0**	**0**	**0**	**0**	**0**
•**McKAY, Randy** — Right wing									
1989	Detroit	2	0	0	0	2	0	0	0
1991	Detroit	5	0	1	1	41	0	0	0
1992	New Jersey	7	1	3	4	10	1	0	0
1993	New Jersey	5	0	0	0	16	0	0	0
1994	New Jersey	20	1	2	3	24	0	0	0
1995♦	New Jersey	19	8	4	12	11	2	0	2
1997	New Jersey	10	1	1	2	0	0	0	0
1998	New Jersey	6	0	1	1	0	0	0	0
1999	New Jersey	7	3	2	5	2	0	0	1
2000♦	New Jersey	23	0	6	6	9	0	0	0
2001	New Jersey	19	6	3	9	8	2	0	1
Playoff Totals		**123**	**20**	**23**	**43**	**123**	**5**	**0**	**4**
McKAY, Ray *No Playoffs* — Defense									
McKAY, Scott *No Playoffs* — Center									
McKECHNIE, Walt — Center									
1968	Minnesota	9	3	2	5	0	0	0	0
1979	Toronto	6	4	3	7	7	0	1	1
Playoff Totals		**15**	**7**	**5**	**12**	**7**	**0**	**1**	**1**
•**McKEE, Jay** — Defense									
1997	Buffalo	3	0	0	0	0	0	0	0
1998	Buffalo	1	0	0	0	0	0	0	0
1999	Buffalo	21	0	3	3	24	0	0	0
2000	Buffalo	1	0	0	0	0	0	0	0
2001	Buffalo	8	1	0	1	6	0	0	1
Playoff Totals		**34**	**1**	**3**	**4**	**30**	**0**	**0**	**1**
McKEE, Mike *No Playoffs* — Left wing									
McKEGNEY, Ian *No Playoffs* — Defense									
McKEGNEY, Tony — Left wing									
1979	Buffalo	2	0	1	1	0	0	0	0
1980	Buffalo	14	3	4	7	2	0	0	0
1981	Buffalo	8	5	3	8	2	1	0	0
1982	Buffalo	4	0	0	0	2	0	0	0
1983	Buffalo	10	3	1	4	4	1	0	2
1984	Quebec	7	0	0	0	0	0	0	0
1985	Minnesota	9	8	6	14	0	2	0	1
1986	Minnesota	5	2	1	3	22	0	0	0
1987	NY Rangers	6	0	0	0	12	0	0	0
1988	St. Louis	9	3	6	9	8	1	0	1
1989	St. Louis	3	0	1	1	0	0	0	0
1991	Chicago	2	0	0	0	4	0	0	0
Playoff Totals		**79**	**24**	**23**	**47**	**56**	**5**	**0**	**4**
McKENDRY, Alex — Wing									
1980♦	NY Islanders	6	2	2	4	0	0	0	0
Playoff Totals		**6**	**2**	**2**	**4**	**0**	**0**	**0**	**0**
McKENNA, Sean — Right wing									
1984	Buffalo	3	1	0	1	2	0	0	0
1985	Buffalo	5	0	1	1	0	0	0	0
1987	Los Angeles	5	0	1	1	0	0	0	0
1988	Toronto	2	0	0	0	0	0	0	0
Playoff Totals		**15**	**1**	**2**	**3**	**2**	**0**	**0**	**0**
•**McKENNA, Steve** — Left wing									
1998	Los Angeles	3	0	1	1	8	0	0	0
Playoff Totals		**3**	**0**	**1**	**1**	**8**	**0**	**0**	**0**

Season	Team	GP	G	A	Pts	PIM	PP	SH	GW
McKENNEY, Don	Center								
1955	Boston	5	1	2	3	4	....	....	....
1957	Boston	10	1	5	6	4	....	....	....
1958	Boston	12	9	8	17	0	....	....	....
1959	Boston	7	2	5	7	0	....	....	....
1964♦	Toronto	12	4	8	12	0	....	....	....
1965	Toronto	6	0	0	0	0	....	....	....
1968	St. Louis	6	1	1	2	2	0	0	0
Playoff Totals		**58**	**18**	**29**	**47**	**10**	**0**	**0**	**0**
McKENNY, Jim	Defense								
1971	Toronto	6	2	1	3	2	1	0	0
1972	Toronto	5	3	0	3	2	2	1	0
1974	Toronto	4	0	2	2	0	0	0	0
1975	Toronto	7	0	1	1	2	0	0	0
1976	Toronto	6	2	3	5	2	1	0	1
1977	Toronto	9	0	2	2	2	0	0	0
Playoff Totals		**37**	**7**	**9**	**16**	**10**	**4**	**1**	**1**
McKENZIE, Brian *No Playoffs*	Left wing								
•**McKENZIE, Jim**	Left wing								
1991	Hartford	6	0	0	0	8	0	0	0
1994	Pittsburgh	3	0	0	0	0	0	0	0
1995	Pittsburgh	5	0	0	0	4	0	0	0
1996	Winnipeg	1	0	0	0	2	0	0	0
1997	Phoenix	7	0	0	0	2	0	0	0
1998	Phoenix	1	0	0	0	0	0	0	0
1999	Anaheim	4	0	0	0	4	0	0	0
2000	Washington	1	0	0	0	0	0	0	0
2001	New Jersey	3	0	0	0	2	0	0	0
2002	New Jersey	6	0	0	0	2	0	0	0
Playoff Totals		**37**	**0**	**0**	**0**	**24**	**0**	**0**	**0**
McKENZIE, John	Right wing								
1959	Chicago	2	0	0	0	2	0	0	0
1960	Detroit	2	0	0	0	0	0	0	0
1964	Chicago	4	0	1	1	6	0	0	0
1965	Chicago	11	0	1	1	6	0	0	0
1968	Boston	4	1	1	2	8	0	0	0
1969	Boston	10	2	2	4	17	1	0	0
1970♦	Boston	14	5	12	17	35	0	3	0
1971	Boston	7	2	3	5	22	1	0	1
1972♦	Boston	15	5	12	17	37	3	0	0
Playoff Totals		**69**	**15**	**32**	**47**	**133**	**5**	**3**	**1**
McKIM, Andrew *No Playoffs*	Center								
McKINNON, Alex *No Playoffs*	Right wing								
McKINNON, John	Defense								
1928	Pittsburgh	2	0	0	0	4	0	0	0
Playoff Totals		**2**	**0**	**0**	**0**	**4**	**0**	**0**	**0**
•**McLAREN, Kyle**	Defense								
1996	Boston	5	0	0	0	14	0	0	0
1998	Boston	6	1	0	1	4	1	0	0
1999	Boston	12	0	3	3	10	0	0	0
2002	Boston	4	0	0	0	20	0	0	0
Playoff Totals		**27**	**1**	**3**	**4**	**48**	**1**	**0**	**0**
•**McLEAN, Brett** *No Playoffs*	Center								
McLEAN, Don *No Playoffs*	Defense								
McLEAN, Fred *No Playoffs*	Defense								
McLEAN, Jack	Center/Right wing								
1943	Toronto	6	2	2	4	2	....	....	....
1944	Toronto	3	0	0	0	6	....	....	....
1945♦	Toronto	4	0	0	0	0	....	....	....
Playoff Totals		**13**	**2**	**2**	**4**	**8**	....	....	....
McLEAN, Jeff *No Playoffs*	Center								
McLELLAN, John *No Playoffs*	Center								
McLELLAN, Scott *No Playoffs*	Right wing								
McLELLAN, Todd *No Playoffs*	Center								
McLENAHAN, Rollie	Defense								
1946	Detroit	2	0	0	0	0	0	0	0
Playoff Totals		**2**	**0**	**0**	**0**	**0**	**0**	**0**	**0**
McLEOD, Al *No Playoffs*	Defense								
McLEOD, Jackie	Right wing								
1950	NY Rangers	7	0	0	0	0	0	0	0
Playoff Totals		**7**	**0**	**0**	**0**	**0**	**0**	**0**	**0**
McLLWAIN, Dave	Center/Right wing								
1989	Pittsburgh	3	0	1	1	0	0	0	0
1990	Winnipeg	7	0	1	1	2	0	0	0
1993	Toronto	4	0	0	0	0	0	0	0
1996	Pittsburgh	6	0	0	0	0	0	0	0
Playoff Totals		**20**	**0**	**2**	**2**	**2**	**0**	**0**	**0**
McMAHON, Mike	Defense								
1968	Minnesota	14	3	7	10	4	0	2	0
Playoff Totals		**14**	**3**	**7**	**10**	**4**	**0**	**2**	**0**
McMAHON, Mike	Defense								
1943	Montreal	5	0	0	0	14	....	....	....
1944♦	Montreal	8	1	2	3	16	....	....	....
Playoff Totals		**13**	**1**	**2**	**3**	**30**	....	....	....
McMANAMA, Bob	Center								
1975	Pittsburgh	8	0	1	1	6	0	0	0
Playoff Totals		**8**	**0**	**1**	**1**	**6**	**0**	**0**	**0**

Season	Team	GP	G	A	Pts	PIM	PP	SH	GW
McMANUS, Sammy	Left wing								
1935♦	Mtl. Maroons	1	0	0	0	0	0	0	0
Playoff Totals		**1**	**0**	**0**	**0**	**0**	**0**	**0**	**0**
McMURCHY, Tom *No Playoffs*	Right wing								
McNAB, Max	Center								
1948	Detroit	3	0	0	0	2	....	....	....
1949	Detroit	10	1	0	1	2	....	....	....
1950♦	Detroit	10	0	0	0	0	....	....	....
1951	Detroit	2	0	0	0	0	....	....	....
Playoff Totals		**25**	**1**	**0**	**1**	**4**	....	....	....
McNAB, Peter	Center								
1975	Buffalo	17	2	6	8	4	0	0	0
1976	Buffalo	8	0	0	0	0	0	0	0
1977	Boston	14	5	3	8	2	2	0	0
1978	Boston	15	8	11	19	2	0	0	2
1979	Boston	11	5	3	8	0	0	0	0
1980	Boston	10	8	6	14	2	3	0	1
1981	Boston	3	3	0	3	0	1	0	0
1982	Boston	11	6	8	14	6	2	0	1
1983	Boston	15	3	5	8	4	0	0	0
1984	Vancouver	3	0	0	0	0	0	0	0
Playoff Totals		**107**	**40**	**42**	**82**	**20**	**8**	**0**	**4**
McNABNEY, Sid	Center								
1951	Montreal	5	0	1	1	2	0	0	0
Playoff Totals		**5**	**0**	**1**	**1**	**2**	**0**	**0**	**0**
McNAMARA, Howard *No Playoffs*	Defense								
McNAUGHTON, George *No Playoffs*	Right wing/Center								
McNEILL, Billy	Right wing								
1958	Detroit	4	1	1	2	4	0	0	0
Playoff Totals		**4**	**1**	**1**	**2**	**4**	**0**	**0**	**0**
McNEILL, Mike *No Playoffs*	Right wing								
McNEILL, Stu *No Playoffs*	Center								
McPHEE, George	Left wing								
1983	NY Rangers	9	3	3	6	2	1	0	0
1985	NY Rangers	3	1	0	1	7	0	0	0
1986	NY Rangers	11	0	0	0	32	0	0	0
1987	NY Rangers	6	1	0	1	28	1	0	0
Playoff Totals		**29**	**5**	**3**	**8**	**69**	**2**	**0**	**0**
McPHEE, Mike	Left wing								
1984	Montreal	15	1	0	1	31	0	0	0
1985	Montreal	12	4	1	5	32	0	0	0
1986♦	Montreal	20	3	4	7	45	0	1	1
1987	Montreal	17	7	2	9	13	1	0	2
1988	Montreal	11	4	3	7	8	0	1	0
1989	Montreal	20	4	7	11	30	0	0	1
1990	Montreal	9	1	1	2	16	0	0	0
1991	Montreal	13	1	7	8	12	1	0	0
1992	Montreal	8	1	1	2	4	0	0	0
1994	Dallas	9	2	1	3	2	0	0	0
Playoff Totals		**134**	**28**	**27**	**55**	**193**	**2**	**2**	**4**
McRAE, Basil	Left wing								
1982	Quebec	9	1	0	1	34	0	0	0
1987	Quebec	13	3	1	4	*99	0	0	1
1989	Minnesota	5	0	0	0	58	0	0	0
1990	Minnesota	7	1	0	1	24	0	0	0
1991	Minnesota	22	1	1	2	*94	0	0	0
1993	St. Louis	11	0	1	1	24	0	0	0
1994	St. Louis	2	0	0	0	12	0	0	0
1995	St. Louis	7	2	1	3	4	0	0	0
1996	St. Louis	2	0	0	0	0	0	0	0
Playoff Totals		**78**	**8**	**4**	**12**	**349**	**0**	**0**	**1**
McRAE, Chris *No Playoffs*	Left wing								
McRAE, Ken	Center								
1994	Toronto	6	0	0	0	4	0	0	0
Playoff Totals		**6**	**0**	**0**	**0**	**4**	**0**	**0**	**0**
McREAVY, Pat	Center								
1941♦	Boston	11	2	2	4	5	....	....	....
1942	Detroit	11	1	1	2	4	....	....	....
Playoff Totals		**22**	**3**	**3**	**6**	**9**	....	....	....
McREYNOLDS, Brian *No Playoffs*	Center								
McSHEFFREY, Bryan *No Playoffs*	Right wing								
McSORLEY, Marty	Defense								
1986	Edmonton	8	0	2	2	50	0	0	0
1987♦	Edmonton	21	4	3	7	65	0	0	1
1988♦	Edmonton	16	0	3	3	67	0	0	0
1989	Los Angeles	11	0	2	2	33	0	0	0
1990	Los Angeles	10	1	3	4	18	1	0	0
1991	Los Angeles	12	0	0	0	58	0	0	0
1992	Los Angeles	6	1	0	1	21	0	0	0
1993	Los Angeles	24	4	6	10	*60	2	0	1
1996	NY Rangers	4	0	0	0	0	0	0	0
1999	Edmonton	3	0	0	0	2	0	0	0
Playoff Totals		**115**	**10**	**19**	**29**	**374**	**3**	**0**	**2**
McSWEEN, Don *No Playoffs*	Defense								
McTAGGART, Jim *No Playoffs*	Defense								
McTAVISH, Dale *No Playoffs*	Center								
McTAVISH, Gord *No Playoffs*	Center								

Season	Team	GP	G	A	Pts	PIM	PP	SH	GW
McVEIGH, Charley	Center/Left wing								
1927	Chicago	2	0	0	0	0	0	0	0
1929	NY Americans	2	0	0	0	2	0	0	0
Playoff Totals		**4**	**0**	**0**	**0**	**2**	**0**	**0**	**0**
McVICAR, Jack	Defense								
1931	Mtl. Maroons	2	0	0	0	2	0	0	0
1932	Mtl. Maroons	4	0	0	0	0	0	0	0
Playoff Totals		**6**	**0**	**0**	**0**	**2**	**0**	**0**	**0**
MEAGHER, Rick	Center								
1986	St. Louis	19	4	4	8	12	0	1	0
1987	St. Louis	6	0	0	0	11	0	0	0
1988	St. Louis	10	0	0	0	8	0	0	0
1989	St. Louis	10	3	2	5	6	0	0	1
1990	St. Louis	8	1	0	1	2	0	0	0
1991	St. Louis	9	0	1	1	2	0	0	0
Playoff Totals		**62**	**8**	**7**	**15**	**41**	**0**	**1**	**1**
MEEHAN, Gerry	Center								
1969	Philadelphia	4	0	0	0	0	0	0	0
1973	Buffalo	6	0	1	1	0	0	0	0
Playoff Totals		**10**	**0**	**1**	**1**	**0**	**0**	**0**	**0**
MEEKE, Brent *No Playoffs*	Defense								
MEEKER, Howie	Right wing								
1947♦	Toronto	11	3	3	6	6	....	....	....
1948♦	Toronto	9	2	4	6	15	....	....	....
1949♦	Toronto	....	....	....	....	....	....	....	....
1950	Toronto	7	0	1	1	4	....	....	....
1951♦	Toronto	11	1	1	2	14	....	....	....
1952	Toronto	4	0	0	0	11	....	....	....
Playoff Totals		**42**	**6**	**9**	**15**	**50**	....	....	....
MEEKER, Mike *No Playoffs*	Right wing								
MEEKING, Harry	Left wing								
1918	Toronto	2	3	0	3	6	....	....	....
1927	Boston	7	0	0	0	0	....	....	....
Playoff Totals		**9**	**3**	**0**	**3**	**6**	....	....	....
MEGER, Paul	Left wing								
1950	Montreal	2	0	0	0	2	....	....	....
1951	Montreal	11	1	3	4	4	....	....	....
1952	Montreal	11	0	3	3	2	....	....	....
1953♦	Montreal	5	1	2	3	4	....	....	....
1954	Montreal	6	1	0	1	4	....	....	....
Playoff Totals		**35**	**3**	**8**	**11**	**16**	....	....	....
MEIGHAN, Ron *No Playoffs*	Defense								
MEISSNER, Barrie *No Playoffs*	Left wing								
MEISSNER, Dick *No Playoffs*	Right wing								
MELAMETSA, Anssi *No Playoffs*	Left wing								
•**MELANSON, Dean** *No Playoffs*	Defense								
•**MELICHAR, Josef** *No Playoffs*	Defense								
MELIN, Roger *No Playoffs*	Left wing								
•**MELLANBY, Scott**	Right wing								
1987	Philadelphia	24	5	5	10	46	0	0	1
1988	Philadelphia	7	0	1	1	16	0	0	0
1989	Philadelphia	19	4	5	9	28	0	0	0
1992	Edmonton	16	2	1	3	29	1	0	1
1996	Florida	22	3	6	9	44	2	0	0
1997	Florida	5	0	2	2	4	0	0	0
2000	Florida	4	0	1	1	2	0	0	0
2001	St. Louis	15	3	3	6	17	2	0	0
2002	St. Louis	10	7	3	10	18	4	0	1
Playoff Totals		**122**	**24**	**27**	**51**	**204**	**9**	**0**	**3**
MELLOR, Tom *No Playoffs*	Defense								
MELNYK, Gerry	Center								
1956	Detroit	6	0	0	0	0	0	0	0
1960	Detroit	6	3	0	3	0	0	0	1
1961	Detroit	11	1	0	1	2	0	0	1
1962	Chicago	7	0	0	0	2	0	0	0
1965	Chicago	6	0	0	0	0	0	0	0
1968	St. Louis	17	2	6	8	2	1	1	0
Playoff Totals		**53**	**6**	**6**	**12**	**6**	**1**	**1**	**2**
MELNYK, Larry	Defense								
1982	Boston	11	0	3	3	40	0	0	0
1983	Boston	11	0	0	0	9	0	0	0
1984♦	Edmonton	6	0	1	1	0	0	0	0
1985♦	Edmonton	12	1	3	4	26	0	0	0
1986	NY Rangers	16	1	2	3	46	0	0	0
1987	NY Rangers	6	0	0	0	4	0	0	0
1989	Vancouver	4	0	0	0	2	0	0	0
Playoff Totals		**66**	**2**	**9**	**11**	**127**	**0**	**0**	**0**
•**MELOCHE, Eric** *No Playoffs*	Right wing								
MELROSE, Barry	Defense								
1981	Toronto	3	0	1	1	15	0	0	0
1983	Toronto	4	0	1	1	23	0	0	0
Playoff Totals		**7**	**0**	**2**	**2**	**38**	**0**	**0**	**0**
MENARD, Hillary *No Playoffs*	Left wing								
MENARD, Howie	Center								
1968	Los Angeles	7	0	5	5	24	0	0	0
1969	Los Angeles	11	3	2	5	12	1	0	0
1970	Oakland	1	0	0	0	0	0	0	0
Playoff Totals		**19**	**3**	**7**	**10**	**36**	**1**	**0**	**0**

Season	Team	GP	G	A	Pts	PIM	PP	SH	GW
MERCREDI, Vic *No Playoffs*	Center								
MEREDITH, Greg	Right wing								
1983	Calgary	5	3	1	4	4	0	1	2
Playoff Totals		**5**	**3**	**1**	**4**	**4**	**0**	**1**	**2**
MERKOSKY, Glenn *No Playoffs*	Center								
MERONEK, Bill	Center								
1943	Montreal	1	0	0	0	0	0	0	0
Playoff Totals		**1**	**0**	**0**	**0**	**0**	**0**	**0**	**0**
MERRICK, Wayne	Center								
1973	St. Louis	5	0	1	1	2	0	0	0
1975	St. Louis	2	1	1	2	0	1	0	0
1978	NY Islanders	7	1	0	1	0	0	0	0
1979	NY Islanders	10	2	3	5	2	0	0	0
1980♦	NY Islanders	21	2	4	6	2	0	0	1
1981♦	NY Islanders	18	6	12	18	8	0	0	1
1982♦	NY Islanders	19	6	6	12	6	0	0	1
1983♦	NY Islanders	19	1	3	4	10	0	0	0
1984	NY Islanders	1	0	0	0	0	0	0	0
Playoff Totals		**102**	**19**	**30**	**49**	**30**	**1**	**0**	**3**
MERRILL, Horace *No Playoffs*	Defense								
MERTZIG, Jan *No Playoffs*	Defense								
•MESSIER, Eric	Left wing								
1997	Colorado	6	0	0	0	4	0	0	0
1999	Colorado	3	0	0	0	0	0	0	0
2000	Colorado	14	0	1	1	4	0	0	0
2001♦	Colorado	23	2	2	4	14	0	0	0
2002	Colorado	21	1	2	3	0	0	0	0
Playoff Totals		**67**	**3**	**5**	**8**	**22**	**0**	**0**	**0**
MESSIER, Joby *No Playoffs*	Defense								
•MESSIER, Mark	Center								
1980	Edmonton	3	1	2	3	2	0	1	0
1981	Edmonton	9	2	5	7	13	0	0	0
1982	Edmonton	5	1	2	3	8	0	0	0
1983	Edmonton	15	15	6	21	14	4	2	0
1984♦	Edmonton	19	8	18	26	19	1	1	2
1985♦	Edmonton	18	12	13	25	12	1	1	1
1986	Edmonton	10	4	6	10	18	0	2	0
1987♦	Edmonton	21	12	16	28	16	1	2	1
1988♦	Edmonton	19	11	23	34	29	7	1	0
1989	Edmonton	7	1	11	12	8	0	0	0
1990♦	Edmonton	22	9	*22	*31	20	1	1	1
1991	Edmonton	18	4	11	15	16	1	0	0
1992	NY Rangers	11	7	7	14	6	2	2	0
1994♦	NY Rangers	23	12	18	30	33	2	1	4
1995	NY Rangers	10	3	10	13	8	2	0	1
1996	NY Rangers	11	4	7	11	16	2	0	1
1997	NY Rangers	15	3	9	12	6	0	0	1
Playoff Totals		**236**	**109**	**186**	**295**	**244**	**24**	***14**	**12**
MESSIER, Mitch *No Playoffs*	Center								
MESSIER, Paul *No Playoffs*	Center								
METCALFE, Scott *No Playoffs*	Left wing								
•METROPOLIT, Glen	Right wing								
2000	Washington	2	0	0	0	2	0	0	0
2001	Washington	1	0	0	0	0	0	0	0
Playoff Totals		**3**	**0**	**0**	**0**	**2**	**0**	**0**	**0**
METZ, Don	Right wing								
1939	Toronto	2	0	0	0	0	....	....	....
1940	Toronto	2	0	0	0	0	....	....	....
1941	Toronto	7	1	1	2	2	....	....	....
1942♦	Toronto	4	4	3	7	0	....	....	....
1945♦	Toronto	11	0	1	1	4	....	....	....
1947♦	Toronto	11	2	3	5	4	....	....	....
1948♦	Toronto	2	0	0	0	2	....	....	....
1949♦	Toronto	3	0	0	0	0	....	....	....
Playoff Totals		**42**	**7**	**8**	**15**	**12**	....	....	....
METZ, Nick	Left wing								
1935	Toronto	6	1	1	2	0	....	....	....
1937	Toronto	2	0	0	0	0	....	....	....
1938	Toronto	7	0	2	2	0	....	....	....
1939	Toronto	10	3	3	6	6	....	....	....
1940	Toronto	9	1	3	4	9	....	....	....
1941	Toronto	7	3	4	7	0	....	....	....
1942♦	Toronto	13	4	4	8	12	....	....	....
1945♦	Toronto	7	1	1	2	2	....	....	....
1947♦	Toronto	6	4	2	6	0	....	....	....
1948♦	Toronto	9	2	0	2	2	....	....	....
Playoff Totals		**76**	**19**	**20**	**39**	**31**	....	....	....
•MEZEI, Branislav *No Playoffs*	Defense								
MICHALUK, Art *No Playoffs*	Defense								
MICHALUK, John *No Playoffs*	Left wing								
MICHAYLUK, Dave	Left wing								
1992♦	Pittsburgh	7	1	1	2	0	0	0	0
Playoff Totals		**7**	**1**	**1**	**2**	**0**	**0**	**0**	**0**
MICHELETTI, Joe	Defense								
1981	St. Louis	11	1	11	12	10	1	0	0
Playoff Totals		**11**	**1**	**11**	**12**	**10**	**1**	**0**	**0**
MICHELETTI, Pat *No Playoffs*	Center								

Season	Team	GP	G	A	Pts	PIM	PP	SH	GW
MICKEY, Larry	Right wing								
1969	Toronto	3	0	0	0	5	0	0	0
1973	Buffalo	6	1	0	1	5	0	0	0
Playoff Totals		**9**	**1**	**0**	**1**	**10**	**0**	**0**	**0**
MICKOSKI, Nick	Left wing								
1948	NY Rangers	2	0	1	1	0	....	....	....
1950	NY Rangers	12	1	5	6	2	....	....	....
1958	Detroit	4	0	0	0	4	....	....	....
Playoff Totals		**18**	**1**	**6**	**7**	**6**	....	....	....
MIDDENDORF, Max *No Playoffs*	Right wing								
MIDDLETON, Rick	Right wing								
1975	NY Rangers	3	0	0	0	2	0	0	0
1977	Boston	13	5	4	9	0	0	0	1
1978	Boston	15	5	2	7	0	0	0	2
1979	Boston	11	4	8	12	0	2	0	1
1980	Boston	10	4	2	6	5	0	0	0
1981	Boston	3	0	1	1	2	0	0	0
1982	Boston	11	6	9	15	0	2	0	0
1983	Boston	17	11	22	33	6	4	1	1
1984	Boston	3	0	0	0	0	0	0	0
1985	Boston	5	3	0	3	0	0	0	0
1987	Boston	4	2	2	4	0	1	1	0
1988	Boston	19	5	5	10	4	0	1	3
Playoff Totals		**114**	**45**	**55**	**100**	**19**	**9**	**3**	**8**
MIEHM, Kevin	Center								
1993	St. Louis	2	0	1	1	0	0	0	0
Playoff Totals		**2**	**0**	**1**	**1**	**0**	**0**	**0**	**0**
MIGAY, Rudy	Center								
1954	Toronto	5	1	0	1	4	....	....	....
1955	Toronto	3	0	0	0	10	....	....	....
1956	Toronto	5	0	0	0	6	....	....	....
1959	Toronto	2	0	0	0	0	....	....	....
Playoff Totals		**15**	**1**	**0**	**1**	**20**	....	....	....
•MIKA, Petr *No Playoffs*	Left wing								
MIKITA, Stan	Center/Right wing								
1960	Chicago	3	0	1	1	2	....	....	....
1961♦	Chicago	12	*6	5	11	21	....	....	....
1962	Chicago	12	6	*15	*21	19	....	....	....
1963	Chicago	6	3	2	5	2	....	....	....
1964	Chicago	7	3	6	9	8	....	....	....
1965	Chicago	14	3	7	10	*53	....	....	....
1966	Chicago	6	1	2	3	2	....	....	....
1967	Chicago	6	2	2	4	2	....	....	....
1968	Chicago	11	5	7	12	6	2	1	0
1970	Chicago	8	4	6	10	2	3	1	0
1971	Chicago	18	5	13	18	16	1	0	1
1972	Chicago	8	3	1	4	4	0	0	0
1973	Chicago	15	7	13	20	8	1	0	2
1974	Chicago	11	5	6	11	8	1	0	1
1975	Chicago	8	3	4	7	12	1	0	1
1976	Chicago	4	0	0	0	4	0	0	0
1977	Chicago	2	0	1	1	0	0	0	0
1978	Chicago	4	3	0	3	0	2	0	0
Playoff Totals		**155**	**59**	**91**	**150**	**169**	**11**	**2**	**5**
MIKKELSON, Bill *No Playoffs*	Defense								
MIKOL, Jim *No Playoffs*	Left wing/Defense								
MIKULCHIK, Oleg *No Playoffs*	Defense								
MILBURY, Mike	Defense								
1976	Boston	11	0	0	0	29	0	0	0
1977	Boston	13	2	2	4	*47	0	0	1
1978	Boston	15	1	8	9	27	0	0	0
1979	Boston	11	1	7	8	7	0	0	1
1980	Boston	10	0	2	2	50	0	0	0
1981	Boston	2	0	1	1	10	0	0	0
1982	Boston	11	0	4	4	6	0	0	0
1984	Boston	3	0	0	0	12	0	0	0
1985	Boston	5	0	0	0	10	0	0	0
1986	Boston	1	0	0	0	17	0	0	0
1987	Boston	4	0	0	0	4	0	0	0
Playoff Totals		**86**	**4**	**24**	**28**	**219**	**0**	**0**	**2**
MILKS, Hib	Left wing/Center								
1926	Pittsburgh	2	0	0	0	0	0	0	0
1928	Pittsburgh	2	0	0	0	2	0	0	0
1932	NY Rangers	7	0	0	0	0	0	0	0
Playoff Totals		**11**	**0**	**0**	**0**	**2**	**0**	**0**	**0**
•MILLAR, Craig *No Playoffs*	Defense								
MILLAR, Hugh	Defense								
1947	Detroit	1	0	0	0	0	0	0	0
Playoff Totals		**1**	**0**	**0**	**0**	**0**	**0**	**0**	**0**
MILLAR, Mike *No Playoffs*	Right wing								
MILLEN, Corey	Center								
1991	NY Rangers	6	1	2	3	0	1	0	0
1992	Los Angeles	6	0	1	1	6	0	0	0
1993	Los Angeles	23	2	4	6	12	0	0	0
1994	New Jersey	7	1	0	1	2	0	0	1
1995	Dallas	5	1	0	1	2	0	0	0
Playoff Totals		**47**	**5**	**7**	**12**	**22**	**1**	**0**	**1**

Season	Team	GP	G	A	Pts	PIM	PP	SH	GW
•MILLER, Aaron	Defense								
1997	Colorado	17	1	2	3	10	0	0	0
1998	Colorado	7	0	0	0	8	0	0	0
1999	Colorado	19	1	5	6	10	0	0	0
2000	Colorado	17	1	1	2	6	0	0	0
2001	Los Angeles	13	0	1	1	6	0	0	0
2002	Los Angeles	7	0	0	0	0	0	0	0
Playoff Totals		**80**	**3**	**9**	**12**	**40**	**0**	**0**	**0**
MILLER, Bill	Center/Defense								
1935♦	Mtl. Maroons	7	0	0	0	0	0	0	0
1937	Montreal	5	0	0	0	0	0	0	0
Playoff Totals		**12**	**0**	**0**	**0**	**0**	**0**	**0**	**0**
MILLER, Bob	Center								
1978	Boston	13	0	3	3	15	0	0	0
1979	Boston	11	1	1	2	8	0	0	0
1980	Boston	10	3	2	5	4	0	1	0
1985	Los Angeles	2	0	1	1	0	0	0	0
Playoff Totals		**36**	**4**	**7**	**11**	**27**	**0**	**1**	**0**
MILLER, Brad *No Playoffs*	Defense								
MILLER, Earl	Left wing								
1930	Chicago	2	1	0	1	6	....	....	....
1931	Chicago	1	0	0	0	0	....	....	....
1932♦	Toronto	7	0	0	0	0	....	....	....
Playoff Totals		**10**	**1**	**0**	**1**	**6**	....	....	....
MILLER, Jack *No Playoffs*	Center								
MILLER, Jason *No Playoffs*	Left wing								
MILLER, Jay	Left wing								
1986	Boston	2	0	0	0	17	0	0	0
1988	Boston	12	0	0	0	*124	0	0	0
1989	Los Angeles	11	0	1	1	63	0	0	0
1990	Los Angeles	10	1	1	2	10	0	0	0
1991	Los Angeles	8	0	0	0	17	0	0	0
1992	Los Angeles	5	1	1	2	12	0	0	0
Playoff Totals		**48**	**2**	**3**	**5**	**243**	**0**	**0**	**0**
MILLER, Kelly	Left wing								
1985	NY Rangers	3	0	0	0	2	0	0	0
1986	NY Rangers	16	3	4	7	4	0	1	0
1987	Washington	7	2	2	4	0	0	0	0
1988	Washington	14	4	4	8	10	0	1	1
1989	Washington	6	1	0	1	2	0	0	1
1990	Washington	15	3	5	8	23	0	1	0
1991	Washington	11	4	2	6	6	0	1	0
1992	Washington	7	1	2	3	4	0	0	0
1993	Washington	6	0	3	3	2	0	0	0
1994	Washington	11	2	7	9	0	1	1	0
1995	Washington	7	0	3	3	4	0	0	0
1996	Washington	6	0	1	1	4	0	0	0
1998	Washington	10	0	1	1	4	0	0	0
Playoff Totals		**119**	**20**	**34**	**54**	**65**	**1**	**5**	**2**
•MILLER, Kevin	Center								
1990	NY Rangers	1	0	0	0	0	0	0	0
1991	Detroit	7	3	2	5	20	0	1	0
1992	Detroit	9	0	2	2	4	0	0	0
1993	St. Louis	10	0	3	3	11	0	0	0
1994	St. Louis	3	1	0	1	4	0	1	0
1995	San Jose	6	0	0	0	2	0	0	0
1996	Pittsburgh	18	3	2	5	8	0	0	0
1997	Chicago	6	0	1	1	0	0	0	0
2000	Ottawa	1	0	0	0	0	0	0	0
Playoff Totals		**61**	**7**	**10**	**17**	**49**	**0**	**2**	**0**
•MILLER, Kip	Center								
1999	Pittsburgh	13	2	7	9	19	1	0	0
2002	NY Islanders	7	4	2	6	2	2	0	1
Playoff Totals		**20**	**6**	**9**	**15**	**21**	**3**	**0**	**1**
MILLER, Paul *No Playoffs*	Center								
MILLER, Perry *No Playoffs*	Defense								
MILLER, Tom *No Playoffs*	Center								
MILLER, Warren	Right wing								
1980	NY Rangers	6	1	0	1	0	0	0	0
Playoff Totals		**6**	**1**	**0**	**1**	**0**	**0**	**0**	**0**
•MILLEY, Norm *No Playoffs*	Right wing								
•MILLS, Craig	Right wing								
1996	Winnipeg	1	0	0	0	0	0	0	0
Playoff Totals		**1**	**0**	**0**	**0**	**0**	**0**	**0**	**0**
MINER, John *No Playoffs*	Defense								
MINOR, Gerry	Center								
1981	Vancouver	3	0	0	0	8	0	0	0
1982	Vancouver	9	1	3	4	17	0	0	0
Playoff Totals		**12**	**1**	**3**	**4**	**25**	**0**	**0**	**0**
•MIRONOV, Boris	Defense								
1997	Edmonton	12	2	8	10	16	2	0	0
1998	Edmonton	12	3	3	6	27	1	0	1
2002	Chicago	1	0	0	0	2	0	0	0
Playoff Totals		**25**	**5**	**11**	**16**	**45**	**3**	**0**	**1**

Season	Team	GP	G	A	Pts	PIM	PP	SH	GW
•MIRONOV, Dmitri	Defense								
1993	Toronto	14	1	2	3	2	1	0	0
1994	Toronto	18	6	9	15	6	6	0	0
1995	Toronto	6	2	1	3	2	1	0	0
1996	Pittsburgh	15	0	1	1	10	0	0	0
1997	Anaheim	11	1	10	11	10	1	0	0
1998♦	Detroit	7	0	3	3	14	0	0	0
2000	Washington	4	0	0	0	4	0	0	0
Playoff Totals		**75**	**10**	**26**	**36**	**48**	**9**	**0**	**0**
MISZUK, John	Defense								
1964	Detroit	3	0	0	0	2	0	0	0
1966	Chicago	3	0	0	0	4	0	0	0
1967	Chicago	2	0	0	0	2	0	0	0
1968	Philadelphia	7	0	3	3	11	0	0	0
1969	Philadelphia	4	0	0	0	0	0	0	0
Playoff Totals		**19**	**0**	**3**	**3**	**19**	**0**	**0**	**0**
MITCHELL, Bill *No Playoffs*	Defense								
MITCHELL, Herb *No Playoffs*	Left wing								
MITCHELL, Jeff *No Playoffs*	Center/Right wing								
MITCHELL, Red *No Playoffs*	Defense								
MITCHELL, Roy *No Playoffs*	Defense								
•MITCHELL, Willie *No Playoffs*	Defense								
•MODANO, Mike	Center								
1989	Minnesota	2	0	0	0	0	0	0	0
1990	Minnesota	7	1	1	2	12	0	0	0
1991	Minnesota	23	8	12	20	16	3	0	1
1992	Minnesota	7	3	2	5	4	1	0	0
1994	Dallas	9	7	3	10	16	2	0	2
1997	Dallas	7	4	1	5	0	1	1	2
1998	Dallas	17	4	10	14	12	1	0	1
1999♦	Dallas	23	5	*18	23	16	1	1	1
2000	Dallas	23	10	*13	23	10	4	0	2
2001	Dallas	9	3	4	7	0	2	0	0
Playoff Totals		**127**	**45**	**64**	**109**	**86**	**15**	**2**	**9**
•MODIN, Fredrik	Left wing								
1999	Toronto	8	0	0	0	6	0	0	0
Playoff Totals		**8**	**0**	**0**	**0**	**6**	**0**	**0**	**0**
•MODRY, Jaroslav	Defense								
2000	Los Angeles	2	0	0	0	2	0	0	0
2001	Los Angeles	10	1	0	1	4	1	0	1
2002	Los Angeles	7	0	2	2	0	0	0	0
Playoff Totals		**19**	**1**	**2**	**3**	**6**	**1**	**0**	**1**
MOE, Bill	Defense								
1948	NY Rangers	1	0	0	0	0	0	0	0
Playoff Totals		**1**	**0**	**0**	**0**	**0**	**0**	**0**	**0**
MOFFAT, Lyle *No Playoffs*	Left wing								
MOFFAT, Ron	Left wing								
1933	Detroit	4	0	0	0	0	0	0	0
1934	Detroit	3	0	0	0	0	0	0	0
Playoff Totals		**7**	**0**	**0**	**0**	**0**	**0**	**0**	**0**
MOGER, Sandy	Center								
1996	Boston	5	2	2	4	12	1	0	0
Playoff Totals		**5**	**2**	**2**	**4**	**12**	**1**	**0**	**0**
•MOGILNY, Alexander	Right wing								
1990	Buffalo	4	0	1	1	2	0	0	0
1991	Buffalo	6	0	6	6	2	0	0	0
1992	Buffalo	2	0	2	2	0	0	0	0
1993	Buffalo	7	7	3	10	6	2	0	0
1994	Buffalo	7	4	2	6	6	1	0	0
1995	Buffalo	5	3	2	5	2	0	0	0
1996	Vancouver	6	1	8	9	8	0	0	0
2000♦	New Jersey	23	4	3	7	4	2	0	1
2001	New Jersey	25	5	11	16	8	1	0	2
2002	Toronto	20	8	3	11	8	2	0	2
Playoff Totals		**105**	**32**	**41**	**73**	**46**	**8**	**0**	**5**
MOHER, Mike *No Playoffs*	Right wing								
MOHNS, Doug	Left wing/Defense								
1954	Boston	4	1	0	1	4	....	....	....
1955	Boston	5	0	0	0	4	....	....	....
1957	Boston	10	2	3	5	2	....	....	....
1958	Boston	12	3	10	13	18	....	....	....
1959	Boston	4	0	2	2	12	....	....	....
1965	Chicago	14	3	4	7	21	....	....	....
1966	Chicago	5	1	0	1	4	....	....	....
1967	Chicago	5	0	5	5	8	....	....	....
1968	Chicago	11	1	5	6	12	0	0	0
1970	Chicago	8	0	2	2	15	0	0	0
1971	Minnesota	6	2	2	4	10	1	0	0
1972	Minnesota	4	1	2	3	10	1	0	0
1973	Minnesota	6	0	1	1	2	0	0	0
Playoff Totals		**94**	**14**	**36**	**50**	**122**	**2**	**0**	**0**
MOHNS, Lloyd *No Playoffs*	Defense								
MOKOSAK, Carl	Left wing								
1989	Boston	1	0	0	0	0	0	0	0
Playoff Totals		**1**	**0**	**0**	**0**	**0**	**0**	**0**	**0**
MOKOSAK, John *No Playoffs*	Defense								

Season	Team	GP	G	A	Pts	PIM	PP	SH	GW
MOLIN, Lars	Left wing								
1982	Vancouver	17	2	9	11	7	0	0	2
1984	Vancouver	2	0	0	0	0	0	0	0
Playoff Totals		**19**	**2**	**9**	**11**	**7**	**0**	**0**	**2**
MOLLER, Mike	Right wing								
1981	Buffalo	3	0	1	1	0	0	0	0
Playoff Totals		**3**	**0**	**1**	**1**	**0**	**0**	**0**	**0**
MOLLER, Randy	Defense								
1982	Quebec	1	0	0	0	0	0	0	0
1983	Quebec	4	1	0	1	4	1	0	1
1984	Quebec	9	1	0	1	45	0	0	0
1985	Quebec	18	2	2	4	40	1	0	0
1986	Quebec	3	0	0	0	26	0	0	0
1987	Quebec	13	1	4	5	23	0	0	0
1990	NY Rangers	10	1	6	7	32	0	0	0
1991	NY Rangers	6	0	2	2	11	0	0	0
1992	Buffalo	7	0	0	0	8	0	0	0
1994	Buffalo	7	0	2	2	8	0	0	0
Playoff Totals		**78**	**6**	**16**	**22**	**197**	**2**	**0**	**1**
MOLLOY, Mitch *No Playoffs*	Left wing								
MOLYNEAUX, Larry	Defense								
1938	NY Rangers	3	0	0	0	8	0	0	0
1939	NY Rangers	7	0	0	0	0	0	0	0
Playoff Totals		**10**	**0**	**0**	**0**	**8**	**0**	**0**	**0**
MOMESSO, Sergio	Left wing								
1987	Montreal	11	1	3	4	31	0	0	0
1988	Montreal	6	0	2	2	16	0	0	0
1989	St. Louis	10	2	5	7	24	0	0	0
1990	St. Louis	12	3	2	5	63	0	0	1
1991	Vancouver	6	0	3	3	25	0	0	0
1992	Vancouver	13	0	5	5	30	0	0	0
1993	Vancouver	12	3	0	3	30	0	0	1
1994	Vancouver	24	3	4	7	56	0	0	1
1995	Vancouver	11	3	1	4	16	1	0	0
1996	NY Rangers	11	3	1	4	14	0	0	0
1997	St. Louis	3	0	0	0	6	0	0	0
Playoff Totals		**119**	**18**	**26**	**44**	**311**	**1**	**0**	**3**
MONAHAN, Garry	Left wing								
1971	Toronto	6	2	0	2	2	0	0	0
1972	Toronto	5	0	0	0	0	0	0	0
1974	Toronto	4	0	1	1	7	0	0	0
1975	Vancouver	5	1	0	1	2	0	0	1
1976	Vancouver	2	0	0	0	2	0	0	0
Playoff Totals		**22**	**3**	**1**	**4**	**13**	**0**	**0**	**1**
MONAHAN, Hartland	Right wing								
1978	Los Angeles	2	0	0	0	0	0	0	0
1980	St. Louis	3	0	0	0	0	0	0	0
1981	St. Louis	1	0	0	0	4	0	0	0
Playoff Totals		**6**	**0**	**0**	**0**	**4**	**0**	**0**	**0**
MONDOU, Armand	Left wing								
1929	Montreal	3	0	0	0	2	....	....	....
1930♦	Montreal	6	1	1	2	6	....	....	....
1931♦	Montreal	8	0	0	0	0	....	....	....
1932	Montreal	4	1	2	3	2	....	....	....
1934	Montreal	1	0	1	1	0	....	....	....
1935	Montreal	2	0	1	1	0	....	....	....
1937	Montreal	5	0	0	0	0	....	....	....
1939	Montreal	3	1	0	1	2	....	....	....
Playoff Totals		**32**	**3**	**5**	**8**	**12**	....	....	....
MONDOU, Pierre	Center								
1977♦	Montreal	4	0	0	0	0	0	0	0
1978♦	Montreal	15	3	7	10	4	2	0	1
1979♦	Montreal	16	3	6	9	4	1	0	0
1980	Montreal	4	1	4	5	4	0	0	0
1981	Montreal	3	0	1	1	0	0	0	0
1982	Montreal	5	2	5	7	8	1	1	0
1983	Montreal	3	0	1	1	2	0	0	0
1984	Montreal	14	6	3	9	2	1	0	1
1985	Montreal	5	2	1	3	2	0	0	0
Playoff Totals		**69**	**17**	**28**	**45**	**26**	**5**	**1**	**2**
MONGEAU, Michel	Center								
1990	St. Louis	2	0	1	1	0	0	0	0
Playoff Totals		**2**	**0**	**1**	**1**	**0**	**0**	**0**	**0**
MONGRAIN, Bob	Center								
1980	Buffalo	9	1	2	3	2	0	0	0
1982	Buffalo	1	0	0	0	0	0	0	0
1984	Buffalo	1	0	0	0	0	0	0	0
Playoff Totals		**11**	**1**	**2**	**3**	**2**	**0**	**0**	**0**
•MONTADOR, Steve *No Playoffs*	Defense								
MONTEITH, Hank	Left wing								
1970	Detroit	4	0	0	0	0	0	0	0
Playoff Totals		**4**	**0**	**0**	**0**	**0**	**0**	**0**	**0**
•MONTGOMERY, Jim	Center								
1995	Philadelphia	7	1	0	1	2	0	0	0
1996	Philadelphia	1	0	0	0	0	0	0	0
Playoff Totals		**8**	**1**	**0**	**1**	**2**	**0**	**0**	**0**
•MOORE, Barrie *No Playoffs*	Left wing								

Season	Team	GP	G	A	Pts	PIM	PP	SH	GW
MOORE, Dickie	Left wing								
1952	Montreal	11	1	1	2	12	....	....	....
1953♦	Montreal	12	3	2	5	13	....	....	....
1954	Montreal	11	5	*8	*13	8	....	....	....
1955	Montreal	12	1	5	6	22	....	....	....
1956♦	Montreal	10	3	6	9	12	....	....	....
1957♦	Montreal	10	3	7	10	4	....	....	....
1958♦	Montreal	10	4	7	11	4	....	....	....
1959♦	Montreal	11	5	*12	*17	8	....	....	....
1960♦	Montreal	8	*6	4	10	4	....	....	....
1961	Montreal	6	3	1	4	4	....	....	....
1962	Montreal	6	4	2	6	8	....	....	....
1963	Montreal	5	0	1	1	2	....	....	....
1965	Toronto	5	1	1	2	6	....	....	....
1968	St. Louis	18	7	7	14	15	2	0	1
Playoff Totals		**135**	**46**	**64**	**110**	**122**	**2**	**0**	**1**
•MOORE, Steve *No Playoffs*	Center								
MORAN, Amby *No Playoffs*	Defense								
•MORAN, Brad *No Playoffs*	Center								
•MORAN, Ian	Defense								
1995	Pittsburgh	8	0	0	0	0	0	0	0
1997	Pittsburgh	5	1	2	3	4	0	0	0
1998	Pittsburgh	6	0	0	0	2	0	0	0
1999	Pittsburgh	13	0	2	2	8	0	0	0
2000	Pittsburgh	11	0	1	1	2	0	0	0
2001	Pittsburgh	18	0	1	1	4	0	0	0
Playoff Totals		**61**	**1**	**6**	**7**	**20**	**0**	**0**	**0**
•MORAVEC, David *No Playoffs*	Right wing								
MORE, Jay	Defense								
1994	San Jose	13	0	2	2	32	0	0	0
1995	San Jose	11	0	4	4	6	0	0	0
1997	Phoenix	7	0	0	0	7	0	0	0
Playoff Totals		**31**	**0**	**6**	**6**	**45**	**0**	**0**	**0**
•MOREAU, Ethan	Left wing								
1997	Chicago	6	1	0	1	9	0	0	0
1999	Edmonton	4	0	3	3	6	0	0	0
2000	Edmonton	5	0	1	1	0	0	0	0
2001	Edmonton	4	0	0	0	2	0	0	0
Playoff Totals		**19**	**1**	**4**	**5**	**17**	**0**	**0**	**0**
MORENZ, Howie	Center								
1924♦	Montreal	2	3	1	4	6	....	....	....
1925	Montreal	2	3	0	3	4	....	....	....
1927	Montreal	4	1	0	1	4	....	....	....
1928	Montreal	2	0	0	0	12	....	....	....
1929	Montreal	3	0	0	0	6	....	....	....
1930♦	Montreal	6	3	0	3	10	....	....	....
1931♦	Montreal	10	1	*4	5	10	....	....	....
1932	Montreal	4	1	0	1	4	....	....	....
1933	Montreal	2	0	3	3	2	....	....	....
1934	Montreal	2	1	1	2	0	....	....	....
1935	Chicago	2	0	0	0	0	....	....	....
Playoff Totals		**39**	**13**	**9**	**22**	**58**	....	....	....
MORETTO, Angelo *No Playoffs*	Center								
•MORGAN, Jason *No Playoffs*	Center								
MORIN, Pete	Left wing								
1942	Montreal	1	0	0	0	0	0	0	0
Playoff Totals		**1**	**0**	**0**	**0**	**0**	**0**	**0**	**0**
MORIN, Stephane *No Playoffs*	Center								
•MORISSET, Dave *No Playoffs*	Right wing								
MORISSETTE, Dave *No Playoffs*	Left wing								
•MORO, Marc *No Playoffs*	Defense								
•MOROZOV, Aleksey	Right wing								
1998	Pittsburgh	6	0	1	1	2	0	0	0
1999	Pittsburgh	10	1	1	2	0	0	0	0
2000	Pittsburgh	5	0	0	0	0	0	0	0
2001	Pittsburgh	18	3	3	6	6	0	1	0
Playoff Totals		**39**	**4**	**5**	**9**	**8**	**0**	**1**	**0**
MORRIS, Bernie *No Playoffs*	Center/Right wing								
•MORRIS, Derek *No Playoffs*	Defense								
MORRIS, Jon	Center								
1990	New Jersey	6	1	3	4	23	1	0	0
1991	New Jersey	5	0	4	4	2	0	0	0
Playoff Totals		**11**	**1**	**7**	**8**	**25**	**1**	**0**	**0**
MORRIS, Moe	Defense								
1944	Toronto	5	1	2	3	2	....	....	....
1945♦	Toronto	13	3	0	3	*14	....	....	....
Playoff Totals		**18**	**4**	**2**	**6**	**16**	....	....	....
•MORRISON, Brendan	Center								
1998	New Jersey	3	0	1	1	0	0	0	0
1999	New Jersey	7	0	2	2	0	0	0	0
2001	Vancouver	4	1	2	3	0	1	0	0
2002	Vancouver	6	0	2	2	6	0	0	0
Playoff Totals		**20**	**1**	**7**	**8**	**6**	**1**	**0**	**0**
MORRISON, Dave *No Playoffs*	Right wing								
MORRISON, Don	Center								
1948	Detroit	3	0	1	1	0	0	0	0
Playoff Totals		**3**	**0**	**1**	**1**	**0**	**0**	**0**	**0**

Season	Team	GP	G	A	Pts	PIM	PP	SH	GW
MORRISON, Doug *No Playoffs*	Right wing								
MORRISON, Gary	Right wing								
1980	Philadelphia	5	0	1	1	2	0	0	0
Playoff Totals		**5**	**0**	**1**	**1**	**2**	**0**	**0**	**0**
MORRISON, George	Left wing								
1971	St. Louis	3	0	0	0	0	0	0	0
Playoff Totals		**3**	**0**	**0**	**0**	**0**	**0**	**0**	**0**
MORRISON, Jim	Defense								
1952	Toronto	2	0	0	0	0	0	0	0
1954	Toronto	5	0	0	0	4	0	0	0
1955	Toronto	4	0	1	1	4	0	0	0
1956	Toronto	5	0	0	0	4	0	0	0
1959	Boston	6	0	6	6	16	0	0	0
1960	Detroit	6	0	2	2	0	0	0	0
1970	Pittsburgh	8	0	3	3	10	0	0	0
Playoff Totals		**36**	**0**	**12**	**12**	**38**	**0**	**0**	**0**
MORRISON, John *No Playoffs*	Left wing								
MORRISON, Kevin *No Playoffs*	Defense								
MORRISON, Lew	Right wing								
1971	Philadelphia	4	0	0	0	2	0	0	0
1975	Pittsburgh	9	0	0	0	0	0	0	0
1976	Pittsburgh	3	0	0	0	0	0	0	0
1977	Pittsburgh	1	0	0	0	0	0	0	0
Playoff Totals		**17**	**0**	**0**	**0**	**2**	**0**	**0**	**0**
MORRISON, Mark *No Playoffs*	Center								
MORRISON, Rod	Right wing								
1948	Detroit	3	0	0	0	0	0	0	0
Playoff Totals		**3**	**0**	**0**	**0**	**0**	**0**	**0**	**0**
•**MORRISONN, Shaone** *No Playoffs*	Defense								
•**MORROW, Brenden**	Left wing								
2000	Dallas	21	2	4	6	22	1	0	0
2001	Dallas	10	0	3	3	12	0	0	0
Playoff Totals		**31**	**2**	**7**	**9**	**34**	**1**	**0**	**0**
MORROW, Ken	Defense								
1980♦	NY Islanders	20	1	2	3	12	0	0	1
1981♦	NY Islanders	18	3	4	7	8	0	0	1
1982♦	NY Islanders	19	0	4	4	8	0	0	0
1983♦	NY Islanders	19	5	7	12	18	0	0	0
1984	NY Islanders	20	1	2	3	20	0	0	1
1985	NY Islanders	10	0	0	0	17	0	0	0
1986	NY Islanders	2	0	0	0	4	0	0	0
1987	NY Islanders	13	1	3	4	2	0	0	0
1988	NY Islanders	6	0	0	0	8	0	0	0
Playoff Totals		**127**	**11**	**22**	**33**	**97**	**0**	**0**	**3**
MORROW, Scott *No Playoffs*	Left wing								
MORTON, Dean *No Playoffs*	Defense								
MORTSON, Gus	Defense								
1947♦	Toronto	11	1	3	4	22	....	....	....
1948♦	Toronto	5	1	2	3	2	....	....	....
1949♦	Toronto	9	2	1	3	8	....	....	....
1950	Toronto	7	0	0	0	18	....	....	....
1951♦	Toronto	11	0	1	1	4	....	....	....
1952	Toronto	4	0	0	0	8	....	....	....
1953	Chicago	7	1	1	2	6	....	....	....
Playoff Totals		**54**	**5**	**8**	**13**	**68**	....	....	....
MOSDELL, Ken	Center								
1946♦	Montreal	9	4	1	5	6	....	....	....
1947	Montreal	4	2	0	2	4	....	....	....
1949	Montreal	7	1	1	2	4	....	....	....
1950	Montreal	5	0	0	0	12	....	....	....
1951	Montreal	11	1	1	2	4	....	....	....
1952	Montreal	2	1	0	1	0	....	....	....
1953♦	Montreal	7	3	2	5	4	....	....	....
1954	Montreal	11	1	0	1	4	....	....	....
1955	Montreal	12	2	7	9	8	....	....	....
1956♦	Montreal	9	1	1	2	2	....	....	....
1959♦	Montreal	3	0	0	0	0	....	....	....
Playoff Totals		**80**	**16**	**13**	**29**	**48**	....	....	....
MOSIENKO, Bill	Right wing								
1942	Chicago	3	2	0	2	0	....	....	....
1944	Chicago	8	2	2	4	6	....	....	....
1946	Chicago	4	2	0	2	2	....	....	....
1953	Chicago	7	4	2	6	7	....	....	....
Playoff Totals		**22**	**10**	**4**	**14**	**15**	....	....	....
MOTT, Morris *No Playoffs*	Right wing								
•**MOTTAU, Mike** *No Playoffs*	Defense								
MOTTER, Alex	Center								
1935	Boston	4	0	0	0	0	....	....	....
1936	Boston	2	0	0	0	0	....	....	....
1939	Detroit	4	0	1	1	0	....	....	....
1940	Detroit	5	1	1	2	15	....	....	....
1941	Detroit	9	1	3	4	4	....	....	....
1942	Detroit	12	1	3	4	20	....	....	....
1943♦	Detroit	5	0	1	1	2	....	....	....
Playoff Totals		**41**	**3**	**9**	**12**	**41**	....	....	....
•**MOWERS, Mark** *No Playoffs*	Center								
MOXEY, Jim *No Playoffs*	Right wing								
•**MUCKALT, Bill** *No Playoffs*	Right wing								

Season	Team	GP	G	A	Pts	PIM	PP	SH	GW
•**MUIR, Bryan**	Defense								
1997	Edmonton	5	0	0	0	4	0	0	0
2001	Colorado	3	0	0	0	0	0	0	0
2002	Colorado	21	0	0	0	2	0	0	0
Playoff Totals		**29**	**0**	**0**	**0**	**6**	**0**	**0**	**0**
MULHERN, Richard	Defense								
1977	Atlanta	3	0	2	2	5	0	0	0
1978	Atlanta	2	0	1	1	0	0	0	0
1979	Los Angeles	1	0	0	0	0	0	0	0
1980	Toronto	1	0	0	0	0	0	0	0
Playoff Totals		**7**	**0**	**3**	**3**	**5**	**0**	**0**	**0**
MULHERN, Ryan *No Playoffs*	Center								
MULLEN, Brian	Right wing								
1983	Winnipeg	3	1	0	1	0	0	0	0
1984	Winnipeg	3	0	3	3	6	0	0	0
1985	Winnipeg	8	1	2	3	4	0	0	1
1986	Winnipeg	3	1	2	3	6	1	0	0
1987	Winnipeg	9	4	2	6	0	2	0	0
1989	NY Rangers	3	0	1	1	4	0	0	0
1990	NY Rangers	10	2	2	4	8	2	0	0
1991	NY Rangers	5	0	2	2	0	0	0	0
1993	NY Islanders	18	3	4	7	2	0	0	0
Playoff Totals		**62**	**12**	**18**	**30**	**30**	**5**	**0**	**1**
MULLEN, Joe	Right wing								
1980	St. Louis	1	0	0	0	0	0	0	0
1982	St. Louis	10	7	11	18	4	1	0	0
1984	St. Louis	6	2	0	2	0	0	0	0
1985	St. Louis	3	0	0	0	0	0	0	0
1986	Calgary	21	*12	7	19	4	4	0	2
1987	Calgary	6	2	1	3	0	1	0	1
1988	Calgary	7	2	4	6	10	0	0	0
1989♦	Calgary	21	*16	8	24	4	6	0	1
1990	Calgary	6	3	0	3	0	0	1	0
1991♦	Pittsburgh	22	8	9	17	4	1	0	1
1992♦	Pittsburgh	9	3	1	4	4	1	0	0
1993	Pittsburgh	12	4	2	6	6	0	1	1
1994	Pittsburgh	6	1	0	1	2	0	0	0
1995	Pittsburgh	12	0	3	3	4	0	0	0
1997	Pittsburgh	1	0	0	0	0	0	0	0
Playoff Totals		**143**	**60**	**46**	**106**	**42**	**14**	**2**	**6**
•**MULLER, Kirk**	Left wing								
1988	New Jersey	20	4	8	12	37	0	0	0
1990	New Jersey	6	1	3	4	11	0	0	0
1991	New Jersey	7	0	2	2	10	0	0	0
1992	Montreal	11	4	3	7	31	2	1	1
1993♦	Montreal	20	10	7	17	18	3	0	3
1994	Montreal	7	6	2	8	4	3	0	2
1996	Toronto	6	3	2	5	0	2	0	0
1997	Florida	5	1	2	3	4	1	0	0
2000	Dallas	23	2	3	5	18	0	0	1
2001	Dallas	10	1	3	4	12	0	0	1
Playoff Totals		**115**	**32**	**35**	**67**	**145**	**11**	**1**	**8**
MULOIN, Wayne	Defense								
1970	Oakland	4	0	0	0	0	0	0	0
1971	Minnesota	7	0	0	0	2	0	0	0
Playoff Totals		**11**	**0**	**0**	**0**	**2**	**0**	**0**	**0**
MULVENNA, Glenn *No Playoffs*	Center								
MULVEY, Grant	Right wing								
1975	Chicago	6	2	0	2	6	0	0	0
1976	Chicago	4	0	0	0	2	0	0	0
1977	Chicago	2	1	0	1	2	1	0	0
1978	Chicago	4	2	2	4	0	1	0	0
1979	Chicago	1	0	0	0	2	0	0	0
1980	Chicago	7	1	1	2	8	0	0	0
1981	Chicago	3	0	0	0	0	0	0	0
1982	Chicago	15	4	2	6	50	1	0	0
Playoff Totals		**42**	**10**	**5**	**15**	**70**	**3**	**0**	**0**
MULVEY, Paul *No Playoffs*	Left wing								
MUMMERY, Harry	Defense								
1918♦	Toronto	2	1	*1	2	17	....	....	....
Playoff Totals		**2**	**1**	**1**	**2**	**17**	....	....	....
MUNI, Craig	Defense								
1987♦	Edmonton	14	0	2	2	17	0	0	0
1988♦	Edmonton	19	0	4	4	31	0	0	0
1989	Edmonton	7	0	3	3	8	0	0	0
1990♦	Edmonton	22	0	3	3	16	0	0	0
1991	Edmonton	18	0	3	3	20	0	0	0
1992	Edmonton	3	0	0	0	2	0	0	0
1993	Chicago	4	0	0	0	2	0	0	0
1994	Buffalo	7	0	0	0	4	0	0	0
1995	Buffalo	5	0	1	1	2	0	0	0
1996	Winnipeg	6	0	1	1	2	0	0	0
1997	Pittsburgh	3	0	0	0	0	0	0	0
1998	Dallas	5	0	0	0	4	0	0	0
Playoff Totals		**113**	**0**	**17**	**17**	**108**	**0**	**0**	**0**

Season	Team	GP	G	A	Pts	PIM	PP	SH	GW
MUNRO, Dunc	Defense								
1926♦	Mtl. Maroons	2	0	0	0	0	....	....	....
1927	Mtl. Maroons	2	0	0	0	4	....	....	....
1928	Mtl. Maroons	9	0	2	2	8	....	....	....
1930	Mtl. Maroons	4	2	0	2	4	....	....	....
1932	Montreal	4	0	0	0	2	....	....	....
Playoff Totals		**21**	**2**	**2**	**4**	**18**	....	....	....
MUNRO, Gerry *No Playoffs*	Defense								
MURDOCH, Bob *No Playoffs*	Right wing								
MURDOCH, Bob	Defense								
1971♦	Montreal	2	0	0	0	0	0	0	0
1972	Montreal	1	0	0	0	0	0	0	0
1973♦	Montreal	13	0	3	3	10	0	0	0
1974	Los Angeles	5	0	0	0	2	0	0	0
1975	Los Angeles	3	0	1	1	4	0	0	0
1976	Los Angeles	9	0	5	5	15	0	0	0
1977	Los Angeles	9	2	3	5	14	1	0	1
1978	Los Angeles	2	0	1	1	5	0	0	0
1979	Atlanta	2	0	0	0	4	0	0	0
1980	Atlanta	4	1	1	2	2	0	0	0
1981	Calgary	16	1	4	5	36	0	0	0
1982	Calgary	3	0	0	0	0	0	0	0
Playoff Totals		**69**	**4**	**18**	**22**	**92**	**1**	**0**	**1**
MURDOCH, Don	Right wing								
1978	NY Rangers	3	1	3	4	4	0	0	1
1979	NY Rangers	18	7	5	12	12	3	0	1
1980	Edmonton	3	2	0	2	0	0	0	0
Playoff Totals		**24**	**10**	**8**	**18**	**16**	**3**	**0**	**2**
MURDOCH, Murray	Left wing								
1927	NY Rangers	2	0	0	0	0	....	....	....
1928♦	NY Rangers	9	2	1	3	12	....	....	....
1929	NY Rangers	6	0	0	0	2	....	....	....
1930	NY Rangers	4	3	0	3	6	....	....	....
1931	NY Rangers	4	0	2	2	0	....	....	....
1932	NY Rangers	7	0	2	2	2	....	....	....
1933♦	NY Rangers	8	3	*4	7	2	....	....	....
1934	NY Rangers	2	0	0	0	0	....	....	....
1935	NY Rangers	4	0	2	2	4	....	....	....
1937	NY Rangers	9	1	1	2	0	....	....	....
Playoff Totals		**55**	**9**	**12**	**21**	**28**	....	....	....
MURPHY, Brian *No Playoffs*	Center/Left wing								
•**MURPHY, Curtis** *No Playoffs*	Defense								
MURPHY, Gord	Defense								
1989	Philadelphia	19	2	7	9	13	1	0	1
1992	Boston	15	1	0	1	12	0	0	0
1996	Florida	14	0	4	4	6	0	0	0
1997	Florida	5	0	5	5	4	0	0	0
Playoff Totals		**53**	**3**	**16**	**19**	**35**	**1**	**0**	**1**
MURPHY, Joe	Right wing								
1988	Detroit	8	0	1	1	6	0	0	0
1990♦	Edmonton	22	6	8	14	16	0	0	2
1991	Edmonton	15	2	5	7	14	1	0	1
1992	Edmonton	16	8	16	24	12	4	0	2
1993	Chicago	4	0	0	0	8	0	0	0
1994	Chicago	6	1	3	4	25	0	0	0
1995	Chicago	16	9	3	12	29	3	0	3
1996	Chicago	10	6	2	8	33	0	0	2
1997	St. Louis	6	1	1	2	10	1	0	0
1998	San Jose	6	1	1	2	20	1	0	0
1999	San Jose	6	0	3	3	4	0	0	0
2000	Washington	5	0	0	0	8	0	0	0
Playoff Totals		**120**	**34**	**43**	**77**	**185**	**10**	**0**	**10**
MURPHY, Larry	Defense								
1981	Los Angeles	4	3	0	3	2	1	0	0
1982	Los Angeles	10	2	8	10	12	1	0	0
1984	Washington	8	0	3	3	6	0	0	0
1985	Washington	5	2	3	5	0	2	0	0
1986	Washington	9	1	5	6	6	1	0	0
1987	Washington	7	2	2	4	6	0	0	1
1988	Washington	13	4	4	8	33	2	0	1
1989	Minnesota	5	0	2	2	8	0	0	0
1990	Minnesota	7	1	2	3	31	0	0	1
1991♦	Pittsburgh	23	5	18	23	44	4	0	0
1992♦	Pittsburgh	21	6	10	16	19	3	0	1
1993	Pittsburgh	12	2	11	13	10	2	0	1
1994	Pittsburgh	6	0	5	5	0	0	0	0
1995	Pittsburgh	12	2	13	15	0	1	0	0
1996	Toronto	6	0	2	2	4	0	0	0
1997♦	Detroit	20	2	9	11	8	1	0	1
1998♦	Detroit	22	3	12	15	2	1	2	1
1999	Detroit	10	0	2	2	8	0	0	0
2000	Detroit	9	2	3	5	2	1	1	0
2001	Detroit	6	0	1	1	0	0	0	0
Playoff Totals		**215**	**37**	**115**	**152**	**201**	**20**	**3**	**7**

Season	Team	GP	G	A	Pts	PIM	PP	SH	GW
MURPHY, Mike	Right wing								
1972	St. Louis	11	2	3	5	6	1	0	0
1973	NY Rangers	10	0	0	0	0	0	0	0
1974	Los Angeles	5	0	4	4	0	0	0	0
1975	Los Angeles	3	3	0	3	4	2	0	1
1976	Los Angeles	9	1	4	5	6	1	0	0
1977	Los Angeles	9	4	9	13	4	1	0	0
1978	Los Angeles	2	0	0	0	0	0	0	0
1979	Los Angeles	2	0	1	1	0	0	0	0
1980	Los Angeles	4	1	0	1	2	0	1	0
1981	Los Angeles	1	0	1	1	0	0	0	0
1982	Los Angeles	10	2	1	3	32	0	0	0
Playoff Totals		**66**	**13**	**23**	**36**	**54**	**5**	**1**	**1**
MURPHY, Rob	Center								
1991	Vancouver	4	0	0	0	2	0	0	0
Playoff Totals		**4**	**0**	**0**	**0**	**2**	**0**	**0**	**0**
MURPHY, Ron	Left wing								
1956	NY Rangers	5	0	1	1	2	0	0	0
1957	NY Rangers	5	0	0	0	0	0	0	0
1960	Chicago	4	1	0	1	0	0	0	1
1961♦	Chicago	12	2	1	3	0	0	0	1
1963	Chicago	1	0	0	0	0	0	0	0
1964	Chicago	7	0	1	1	8	0	0	0
1965	Detroit	5	0	1	1	4	0	0	0
1968	Boston	4	0	0	0	0	0	0	0
1969	Boston	10	4	4	8	12	0	0	0
Playoff Totals		**53**	**7**	**8**	**15**	**26**	**0**	**0**	**2**
MURRAY, Allan	Defense								
1936	NY Americans	5	0	0	0	2	0	0	0
1938	NY Americans	6	0	0	0	6	0	0	0
1940	NY Americans	3	0	0	0	2	0	0	0
Playoff Totals		**14**	**0**	**0**	**0**	**10**	**0**	**0**	**0**
MURRAY, Bob	Defense								
1977	Chicago	2	0	1	1	2	0	0	0
1978	Chicago	4	1	4	5	2	0	0	0
1979	Chicago	4	1	0	1	6	0	0	0
1980	Chicago	7	2	4	6	6	0	0	0
1981	Chicago	3	0	0	0	2	0	0	0
1982	Chicago	15	1	6	7	16	0	0	0
1983	Chicago	13	2	3	5	10	1	0	0
1984	Chicago	5	3	1	4	6	1	0	0
1985	Chicago	15	3	6	9	20	1	0	0
1986	Chicago	3	0	2	2	0	0	0	0
1987	Chicago	4	1	0	1	4	0	0	0
1988	Chicago	5	1	3	4	2	1	0	0
1989	Chicago	16	2	3	5	22	1	0	0
1990	Chicago	16	2	4	6	8	0	0	0
Playoff Totals		**112**	**19**	**37**	**56**	**106**	**5**	**0**	**0**
MURRAY, Bob	Defense								
1974	Atlanta	4	1	0	1	2	0	0	0
1975	Vancouver	5	0	1	1	13	0	0	0
1976	Vancouver	1	0	0	0	0	0	0	0
Playoff Totals		**10**	**1**	**1**	**2**	**15**	**0**	**0**	**0**
MURRAY, Chris	Right wing								
1996	Montreal	4	0	0	0	4	0	0	0
1998	Ottawa	11	1	0	1	8	0	0	0
Playoff Totals		**15**	**1**	**0**	**1**	**12**	**0**	**0**	**0**
•MURRAY, Glen	Right wing								
1992	Boston	15	4	2	6	10	1	0	0
1994	Boston	13	4	5	9	14	0	0	0
1995	Boston	2	0	0	0	2	0	0	0
1996	Pittsburgh	18	2	6	8	10	0	0	1
1998	Los Angeles	4	2	0	2	6	0	0	0
2000	Los Angeles	4	0	0	0	2	0	0	0
2001	Los Angeles	13	4	3	7	4	1	0	1
2002	Boston	6	1	4	5	4	0	0	0
Playoff Totals		**75**	**17**	**20**	**37**	**52**	**2**	**0**	**2**
MURRAY, Jim *No Playoffs*	Defense								
MURRAY, Ken *No Playoffs*	Defense								
MURRAY, Leo *No Playoffs*	Center/Left wing								
•MURRAY, Marty	Center								
2002	Philadelphia	5	0	1	1	0	0	0	0
Playoff Totals		**5**	**0**	**1**	**1**	**0**	**0**	**0**	**0**
MURRAY, Mike *No Playoffs*	Center								
MURRAY, Pat *No Playoffs*	Left wing								
MURRAY, Randy *No Playoffs*	Defense								
•MURRAY, Rem	Center/Left wing								
1997	Edmonton	12	1	2	3	4	0	0	0
1998	Edmonton	11	1	4	5	2	0	0	0
1999	Edmonton	4	1	1	2	2	0	0	0
2000	Edmonton	5	0	1	1	2	0	0	0
2001	Edmonton	6	2	0	2	6	1	0	0
Playoff Totals		**38**	**5**	**8**	**13**	**16**	**1**	**0**	**0**
•MURRAY, Rob	Center								
1990	Washington	9	0	0	0	18	0	0	0
Playoff Totals		**9**	**0**	**0**	**0**	**18**	**0**	**0**	**0**
MURRAY, Terry	Defense								
1976	Philadelphia	6	0	1	1	0	0	0	0
1981	Philadelphia	12	2	1	3	10	0	0	0
Playoff Totals		**18**	**2**	**2**	**4**	**10**	**0**	**0**	**0**

Season	Team	GP	G	A	Pts	PIM	PP	SH	GW
MURRAY, Troy	Center								
1982	Chicago	7	1	0	1	5	0	0	0
1983	Chicago	2	0	0	0	0	0	0	0
1984	Chicago	5	1	0	1	7	0	0	1
1985	Chicago	15	5	14	19	24	1	0	0
1986	Chicago	2	0	0	0	2	0	0	0
1987	Chicago	4	0	0	0	5	0	0	0
1988	Chicago	5	1	0	1	8	1	0	0
1989	Chicago	16	3	6	9	25	1	0	0
1990	Chicago	20	4	4	8	22	1	0	0
1991	Chicago	6	0	1	1	12	0	0	0
1992	Winnipeg	7	0	0	0	2	0	0	0
1993	Chicago	4	0	0	0	2	0	0	0
1995	Pittsburgh	12	2	1	3	12	0	0	0
1996♦	Colorado	8	0	0	0	19	0	0	0
Playoff Totals		**113**	**17**	**26**	**43**	**145**	**4**	**0**	**1**
MURZYN, Dana	Defense								
1986	Hartford	4	0	0	0	10	0	0	0
1987	Hartford	6	2	1	3	29	1	0	1
1988	Calgary	5	2	0	2	13	0	0	0
1989♦	Calgary	21	0	3	3	20	0	0	0
1990	Calgary	6	2	2	4	2	0	0	0
1991	Vancouver	6	0	1	1	8	0	0	0
1992	Vancouver	1	0	0	0	15	0	0	0
1993	Vancouver	12	3	2	5	18	0	0	0
1994	Vancouver	7	0	0	0	4	0	0	0
1995	Vancouver	8	0	1	1	22	0	0	0
1996	Vancouver	6	0	0	0	25	0	0	0
Playoff Totals		**82**	**9**	**10**	**19**	**166**	**1**	**0**	**1**
•MUSIL, Frantisek	Defense								
1989	Minnesota	5	1	1	2	4	0	0	0
1990	Minnesota	4	0	0	0	14	0	0	0
1991	Calgary	7	0	0	0	10	0	0	0
1993	Calgary	6	1	1	2	7	0	0	0
1994	Calgary	7	0	1	1	4	0	0	0
1995	Calgary	5	0	1	1	0	0	0	0
1998	Edmonton	7	0	0	0	6	0	0	0
1999	Edmonton	1	0	0	0	2	0	0	0
Playoff Totals		**42**	**2**	**4**	**6**	**47**	**0**	**0**	**0**
MYERS, Hap *No Playoffs*	Defense								
MYHRES, Brantt *No Playoffs*	Right wing								
MYLES, Vic *No Playoffs*	Defense								
•MYRVOLD, Anders *No Playoffs*	Defense								
•NABOKOV, Dmitri *No Playoffs*	Center/Left wing								
NACHBAUR, Don	Center								
1983	Edmonton	2	0	0	0	7	0	0	0
1987	Philadelphia	7	1	1	2	15	0	0	1
1988	Philadelphia	2	0	0	0	2	0	0	0
Playoff Totals		**11**	**1**	**1**	**2**	**24**	**0**	**0**	**1**
•NAGY, Ladislav	Center								
2000	St. Louis	6	1	1	2	0	0	0	0
2002	Phoenix	5	0	0	0	21	0	0	0
Playoff Totals		**11**	**1**	**1**	**2**	**21**	**0**	**0**	**0**
NAHRGANG, Jim *No Playoffs*	Defense								
•NAMESTNIKOV, John	Defense								
1995	Vancouver	1	0	0	0	2	0	0	0
1996	Vancouver	1	0	0	0	0	0	0	0
Playoff Totals		**2**	**0**	**0**	**0**	**2**	**0**	**0**	**0**
NANNE, Lou	Defense/Right wing								
1970	Minnesota	5	0	2	2	2	0	0	0
1971	Minnesota	12	3	6	9	4	0	0	2
1972	Minnesota	7	0	0	0	0	0	0	0
1973	Minnesota	6	1	2	3	0	0	0	0
1977	Minnesota	2	0	0	0	2	0	0	0
Playoff Totals		**32**	**4**	**10**	**14**	**8**	**0**	**0**	**2**
NANTAIS, Rich *No Playoffs*	Left wing								
NAPIER, Mark	Right wing								
1979♦	Montreal	12	3	2	5	2	0	0	0
1980	Montreal	10	2	6	8	0	1	0	0
1981	Montreal	3	0	0	0	2	0	0	0
1982	Montreal	5	3	2	5	0	1	1	1
1983	Montreal	3	0	0	0	0	0	0	0
1984	Minnesota	12	3	2	5	0	3	0	0
1985♦	Edmonton	18	5	5	10	7	1	0	0
1986	Edmonton	10	1	4	5	0	0	0	0
1988	Buffalo	6	0	3	3	0	0	0	0
1989	Buffalo	3	1	0	1	0	0	0	0
Playoff Totals		**82**	**18**	**24**	**42**	**11**	**6**	**1**	**1**
•NASH, Rick *No Playoffs*	Left wing								
•NASH, Tyson	Left wing								
1999	St. Louis	1	0	0	0	2	0	0	0
2000	St. Louis	6	1	0	1	24	0	0	0
2002	St. Louis	9	0	1	1	20	0	0	0
Playoff Totals		**16**	**1**	**1**	**2**	**46**	**0**	**0**	**0**
•NASLUND, Markus	Right wing								
1996	Vancouver	6	1	2	3	8	1	0	0
2002	Vancouver	6	1	1	2	2	0	0	0
Playoff Totals		**12**	**2**	**3**	**5**	**10**	**1**	**0**	**0**

Season	Team	GP	G	A	Pts	PIM	PP	SH	GW
NASLUND, Mats	Left wing								
1983	Montreal	3	1	0	1	0	1	0	0
1984	Montreal	15	6	8	14	4	3	1	3
1985	Montreal	12	7	4	11	6	3	0	2
1986♦	Montreal	20	8	11	19	4	4	0	0
1987	Montreal	17	7	15	22	11	4	0	3
1988	Montreal	6	0	7	7	2	0	0	0
1989	Montreal	21	4	11	15	6	1	0	0
1990	Montreal	3	1	1	2	0	0	0	1
1995	Boston	5	1	0	1	0	0	0	0
Playoff Totals		**102**	**35**	**57**	**92**	**33**	**16**	**1**	**9**
•NASREDDINE, Alain *No Playoffs*	Defense								
NATTRASS, Ralph *No Playoffs*	Defense								
NATTRESS, Ric	Defense								
1983	Montreal	3	0	0	0	10	0	0	0
1985	Montreal	2	0	0	0	2	0	0	0
1986	St. Louis	18	1	4	5	24	0	0	0
1987	St. Louis	6	0	0	0	2	0	0	0
1988	Calgary	6	1	3	4	0	0	0	0
1989♦	Calgary	19	0	3	3	20	0	0	0
1990	Calgary	6	2	0	2	0	0	0	0
1991	Calgary	7	1	0	1	2	0	0	1
Playoff Totals		**67**	**5**	**10**	**15**	**60**	**0**	**0**	**1**
NATYSHAK, Mike *No Playoffs*	Right wing								
•NAZAROV, Andrei	Left wing								
1995	San Jose	6	0	0	0	9	0	0	0
2002	Phoenix	3	0	0	0	2	0	0	0
Playoff Totals		**9**	**0**	**0**	**0**	**11**	**0**	**0**	**0**
•NDUR, Rumun *No Playoffs*	Defense								
NEATON, Pat *No Playoffs*	Defense								
NECHAEV, Viktor *No Playoffs*	Center								
•NECKAR, Stan	Defense								
1998	Ottawa	9	0	0	0	2	0	0	0
1999	Phoenix	6	0	1	1	4	0	0	0
2000	Phoenix	5	0	0	0	0	0	0	0
Playoff Totals		**20**	**0**	**1**	**1**	**6**	**0**	**0**	**0**
NEDOMANSKY, Vaclav	Right wing								
1978	Detroit	7	3	5	8	0	1	0	0
Playoff Totals		**7**	**3**	**5**	**8**	**0**	**1**	**0**	**0**
•NEDOROST, Andrej *No Playoffs*	Center								
•NEDOROST, Vaclav *No Playoffs*	Center								
•NEDVED, Petr	Center								
1991	Vancouver	6	0	1	1	0	0	0	0
1992	Vancouver	10	1	4	5	16	0	0	0
1993	Vancouver	12	2	3	5	2	0	0	0
1994	St. Louis	4	0	1	1	4	0	0	0
1995	NY Rangers	10	3	2	5	6	2	0	0
1996	Pittsburgh	18	10	10	20	16	4	0	2
1997	Pittsburgh	5	1	2	3	12	0	1	0
Playoff Totals		**65**	**17**	**23**	**40**	**56**	**6**	**1**	**2**
NEDVED, Zdenek *No Playoffs*	Right wing								
NEEDHAM, Mike	Right wing								
1992♦	Pittsburgh	5	1	0	1	2	0	0	0
1993	Pittsburgh	9	1	0	1	2	0	0	0
Playoff Totals		**14**	**2**	**0**	**2**	**4**	**0**	**0**	**0**
NEELY, Bob	Left wing								
1974	Toronto	4	1	3	4	0	0	0	0
1975	Toronto	3	0	0	0	2	0	0	0
1976	Toronto	10	3	1	4	7	2	0	0
1977	Toronto	9	1	3	4	6	1	0	0
Playoff Totals		**26**	**5**	**7**	**12**	**15**	**3**	**0**	**0**
NEELY, Cam	Right wing								
1984	Vancouver	4	2	0	2	2	1	0	0
1986	Vancouver	3	0	0	0	6	0	0	0
1987	Boston	4	5	1	6	8	3	0	0
1988	Boston	23	9	8	17	51	2	0	2
1989	Boston	10	7	2	9	8	4	0	2
1990	Boston	21	12	16	28	51	4	1	2
1991	Boston	19	16	4	20	36	9	0	4
1993	Boston	4	4	1	5	4	1	0	0
1995	Boston	5	2	0	2	2	1	0	1
Playoff Totals		**93**	**57**	**32**	**89**	**168**	**25**	**1**	**11**
•NEIL, Christopher	Right wing								
2002	Ottawa	12	0	0	0	12	0	0	0
Playoff Totals		**12**	**0**	**0**	**0**	**12**	**0**	**0**	**0**
NEILSON, Jim	Defense								
1967	NY Rangers	4	1	0	1	0	1	0	0
1968	NY Rangers	6	0	2	2	4	0	0	0
1969	NY Rangers	4	0	3	3	5	0	0	0
1970	NY Rangers	6	0	1	1	8	0	0	0
1971	NY Rangers	13	0	3	3	30	0	0	0
1972	NY Rangers	10	0	3	3	8	0	0	0
1973	NY Rangers	10	0	4	4	2	0	0	0
1974	NY Rangers	12	0	1	1	4	0	0	0
Playoff Totals		**65**	**1**	**17**	**18**	**61**	**1**	**0**	**0**
NELSON, Gordie *No Playoffs*	Defense								

Season	Team	GP	G	A	Pts	PIM	PP	SH	GW
•NELSON, Jeff									Center
1996	Washington	3	0	0	0	4	0	0	0
Playoff Totals		**3**	**0**	**0**	**0**	**4**	**0**	**0**	**0**
NELSON, Todd									Defense
1994	Washington	4	0	0	0	0	0	0	0
Playoff Totals		**4**	**0**	**0**	**0**	**0**	**0**	**0**	**0**
•NEMCHINOV, Sergei									Left wing
1992	NY Rangers	13	1	4	5	8	0	0	0
1994♦	NY Rangers	23	2	5	7	6	0	0	0
1995	NY Rangers	10	4	5	9	2	0	0	1
1996	NY Rangers	6	0	1	1	2	0	0	0
1999	New Jersey	4	0	0	0	0	0	0	0
2000♦	New Jersey	21	3	2	5	2	1	0	0
2001	New Jersey	25	1	3	4	4	0	0	0
2002	New Jersey	3	0	0	0	0	0	0	0
Playoff Totals		**105**	**11**	**20**	**31**	**24**	**1**	**0**	**1**
•NEMECEK, Jan *No Playoffs*									Defense
NEMETH, Steve *No Playoffs*									Center
NEMIROVSKY, David									Right wing
1997	Florida	3	1	0	1	0	0	0	0
Playoff Totals		**3**	**1**	**0**	**1**	**0**	**0**	**0**	**0**
NESTERENKO, Eric									Right wing
1954	Toronto	5	0	1	1	9	....	....	....
1955	Toronto	4	0	1	1	6	....	....	....
1959	Chicago	6	2	2	4	8	....	....	....
1960	Chicago	4	0	0	0	2	....	....	....
1961♦	Chicago	11	2	3	5	6	....	....	....
1962	Chicago	12	0	5	5	22	....	....	....
1963	Chicago	6	2	3	5	8	....	....	....
1964	Chicago	7	2	1	3	8	....	....	....
1965	Chicago	14	2	2	4	16	....	....	....
1966	Chicago	6	1	0	1	4	....	....	....
1967	Chicago	6	1	2	3	2	....	....	....
1968	Chicago	10	0	1	1	2	0	0	0
1970	Chicago	7	1	2	3	4	0	0	0
1971	Chicago	18	0	1	1	19	0	0	0
1972	Chicago	8	0	0	0	11	0	0	0
Playoff Totals		**124**	**13**	**24**	**37**	**127**	**0**	**0**	**0**
NETHERY, Lance									Center
1981	NY Rangers	14	5	3	8	9	0	0	1
Playoff Totals		**14**	**5**	**3**	**8**	**9**	**0**	**0**	**1**
NEUFELD, Ray									Right wing
1980	Hartford	2	1	0	1	0	0	0	0
1986	Winnipeg	3	2	0	2	10	1	0	0
1987	Winnipeg	8	1	1	2	30	0	0	0
1988	Winnipeg	5	2	2	4	6	1	0	0
1989	Boston	10	2	3	5	9	0	0	1
Playoff Totals		**28**	**8**	**6**	**14**	**55**	**2**	**0**	**1**
NEVILLE, Mike									Center
1925	Toronto	2	0	0	0	0	0	0	0
Playoff Totals		**2**	**0**	**0**	**0**	**0**	**0**	**0**	**0**
NEVIN, Bob									Right wing
1961	Toronto	5	1	0	1	2	1	0	0
1962♦	Toronto	12	2	4	6	6	0	0	0
1963♦	Toronto	10	3	0	3	2	0	1	2
1967	NY Rangers	4	0	3	3	2	0	0	0
1968	NY Rangers	6	0	3	3	4	0	0	0
1969	NY Rangers	4	0	2	2	0	0	0	0
1970	NY Rangers	6	1	1	2	2	1	0	0
1971	NY Rangers	13	5	3	8	0	1	0	1
1972	Minnesota	7	1	1	2	0	0	0	0
1974	Los Angeles	5	1	0	1	2	0	0	0
1975	Los Angeles	3	0	0	0	0	0	0	0
1976	Los Angeles	9	2	1	3	4	0	0	1
Playoff Totals		**84**	**16**	**18**	**34**	**24**	**3**	**1**	**4**
NEWBERRY, John									Center
1983	Montreal	2	0	0	0	0	0	0	0
Playoff Totals		**2**	**0**	**0**	**0**	**0**	**0**	**0**	**0**
NEWELL, Rick *No Playoffs*									Defense
NEWMAN, Dan									Left wing
1978	NY Rangers	3	0	0	0	4	0	0	0
Playoff Totals		**3**	**0**	**0**	**0**	**4**	**0**	**0**	**0**
NEWMAN, John *No Playoffs*									Center/Left wing
•NICHOL, Scott *No Playoffs*									Center
NICHOLLS, Bernie									Center
1982	Los Angeles	10	4	0	4	23	0	0	1
1985	Los Angeles	3	1	1	2	9	0	0	0
1987	Los Angeles	5	2	5	7	6	1	0	0
1988	Los Angeles	5	2	6	8	11	1	0	0
1989	Los Angeles	11	7	9	16	12	3	0	1
1990	NY Rangers	10	7	5	12	16	3	0	0
1991	NY Rangers	5	4	3	7	8	0	0	1
1992	Edmonton	16	8	11	19	25	4	0	1
1993	New Jersey	5	0	0	0	6	0	0	0
1994	New Jersey	16	4	9	13	28	2	1	0
1995	Chicago	16	1	11	12	8	1	0	0
1996	Chicago	10	2	7	9	4	1	0	0
1998	San Jose	6	0	5	5	8	0	0	0
Playoff Totals		**118**	**42**	**72**	**114**	**164**	**16**	**1**	**4**

Season	Team	GP	G	A	Pts	PIM	PP	SH	GW
NICHOLSON, Al *No Playoffs*									Left wing
NICHOLSON, Ed *No Playoffs*									Defense
NICHOLSON, Hickey *No Playoffs*									Left wing
NICHOLSON, Neil									Defense
1970	Oakland	2	0	0	0	0	0	0	0
Playoff Totals		**2**	**0**	**0**	**0**	**0**	**0**	**0**	**0**
NICHOLSON, Paul *No Playoffs*									Left wing
•NICKULAS, Eric									Center
1999	Boston	1	0	0	0	2	0	0	0
Playoff Totals		**1**	**0**	**0**	**0**	**2**	**0**	**0**	**0**
NICOLSON, Graeme *No Playoffs*									Defense
NIECKAR, Barry *No Playoffs*									Left wing
•NIEDERMAYER, Rob									Center
1996	Florida	22	5	3	8	12	2	0	2
1997	Florida	5	2	1	3	6	1	0	0
2000	Florida	4	1	0	1	6	0	0	0
Playoff Totals		**31**	**8**	**4**	**12**	**24**	**3**	**0**	**2**
•NIEDERMAYER, Scott									Defense
1993	New Jersey	5	0	3	3	2	0	0	0
1994	New Jersey	20	2	2	4	8	1	0	0
1995♦	New Jersey	20	4	7	11	10	2	0	1
1997	New Jersey	10	2	4	6	6	2	0	1
1998	New Jersey	6	0	2	2	4	0	0	0
1999	New Jersey	7	1	3	4	18	1	0	0
2000♦	New Jersey	22	5	2	7	10	0	2	1
2001	New Jersey	21	0	6	6	14	0	0	0
2002	New Jersey	6	0	2	2	6	0	0	0
Playoff Totals		**117**	**14**	**31**	**45**	**78**	**6**	**2**	**3**
NIEKAMP, Jim *No Playoffs*									Defense
•NIELSEN, Chris *No Playoffs*									Center
NIELSEN, Jeff									Right wing
1999	Anaheim	4	0	0	0	2	0	0	0
Playoff Totals		**4**	**0**	**0**	**0**	**2**	**0**	**0**	**0**
NIELSEN, Kirk *No Playoffs*									Right wing
•NIEMI, Antti-Jussi *No Playoffs*									Defense
•NIEMINEN, Ville									Left wing
2001♦	Colorado	23	4	6	10	20	3	0	1
Playoff Totals		**23**	**4**	**6**	**10**	**20**	**3**	**0**	**1**
NIENHUIS, Kraig									Left wing
1986	Boston	2	0	0	0	14	0	0	0
Playoff Totals		**2**	**0**	**0**	**0**	**14**	**0**	**0**	**0**
•NIEUWENDYK, Joe									Center
1987	Calgary	6	2	2	4	0	0	0	0
1988	Calgary	8	3	4	7	2	1	0	0
1989♦	Calgary	22	10	4	14	10	6	0	1
1990	Calgary	6	4	6	10	4	1	0	0
1991	Calgary	7	4	1	5	10	2	0	0
1993	Calgary	6	3	6	9	10	1	0	0
1994	Calgary	6	2	2	4	0	1	0	0
1995	Calgary	5	4	3	7	0	2	0	1
1997	Dallas	7	2	2	4	6	0	0	0
1998	Dallas	1	1	0	1	0	0	0	0
1999♦	Dallas	23	*11	10	21	19	3	0	6
2000	Dallas	23	7	3	10	18	3	0	2
2001	Dallas	7	4	0	4	4	1	0	1
2002	New Jersey	5	0	1	1	0	0	0	0
Playoff Totals		**132**	**57**	**44**	**101**	**83**	**21**	**0**	**11**
NIGHBOR, Frank									Center
1919	Ottawa	2	0	2	2	3	....	....	....
1920♦	Ottawa	....	....	....	....	....	....	....	....
1921♦	Ottawa	2	1	3	4	2	....	....	....
1922	Ottawa	2	2	1	3	4	....	....	....
1923♦	Ottawa	2	0	1	1	0	....	....	....
1924	Ottawa	2	0	1	1	0	....	....	....
1926	Ottawa	2	0	0	0	2	....	....	....
1927♦	Ottawa	6	1	1	2	0	....	....	....
1928	Ottawa	2	0	0	0	2	....	....	....
Playoff Totals		**20**	**4**	**9**	**13**	**13**	....	....	....
NIGRO, Frank									Center
1983	Toronto	3	0	0	0	2	0	0	0
Playoff Totals		**3**	**0**	**0**	**0**	**2**	**0**	**0**	**0**
•NIINIMAA, Janne									Defense
1997	Philadelphia	19	1	12	13	16	1	0	1
1998	Edmonton	11	1	1	2	12	0	0	1
1999	Edmonton	4	0	0	0	2	0	0	0
2000	Edmonton	5	0	2	2	2	0	0	0
2001	Edmonton	6	0	2	2	6	0	0	0
Playoff Totals		**45**	**2**	**17**	**19**	**38**	**1**	**0**	**2**
•NIKOLISHIN, Andrei									Center
1998	Washington	21	1	13	14	12	1	0	0
2000	Washington	5	0	2	2	4	0	0	0
2001	Washington	6	0	0	0	2	0	0	0
Playoff Totals		**32**	**1**	**15**	**16**	**18**	**1**	**0**	**0**
NIKULIN, Igor									Right wing
1997	Anaheim	1	0	0	0	0	0	0	0
Playoff Totals		**1**	**0**	**0**	**0**	**0**	**0**	**0**	**0**

Season	Team	GP	G	A	Pts	PIM	PP	SH	GW
NILAN, Chris									Right wing
1980	Montreal	5	0	0	0	2	0	0	0
1981	Montreal	2	0	0	0	0	0	0	0
1982	Montreal	5	1	1	2	22	0	0	0
1983	Montreal	3	0	0	0	5	0	0	0
1984	Montreal	15	1	0	1	*81	0	0	0
1985	Montreal	12	2	1	3	81	1	0	1
1986♦	Montreal	18	1	2	3	*141	1	0	0
1987	Montreal	17	3	0	3	75	0	0	0
1989	NY Rangers	4	0	1	1	38	0	0	0
1990	NY Rangers	4	0	1	1	19	0	0	0
1991	Boston	19	0	2	2	62	0	0	0
1992	Montreal	7	0	1	1	15	0	0	0
Playoff Totals		**111**	**8**	**9**	**17**	**541**	**2**	**0**	**1**
NILL, Jim									Right wing
1982	Vancouver	16	4	3	7	67	1	0	1
1983	Vancouver	4	0	0	0	6	0	0	0
1984	Boston	3	0	0	0	4	0	0	0
1985	Winnipeg	8	0	1	1	28	0	0	0
1986	Winnipeg	3	0	0	0	4	0	0	0
1987	Winnipeg	3	0	0	0	7	0	0	0
1988	Detroit	16	6	1	7	62	0	1	0
1989	Detroit	6	0	0	0	25	0	0	0
Playoff Totals		**59**	**10**	**5**	**15**	**203**	**1**	**1**	**1**
•NILSON, Marcus *No Playoffs*									Right wing
NILSSON, Kent									Center
1980	Atlanta	4	0	0	0	2	0	0	0
1981	Calgary	14	3	9	12	2	0	0	0
1982	Calgary	3	0	3	3	2	0	0	0
1983	Calgary	9	1	11	12	2	1	0	0
1985	Calgary	3	0	1	1	0	0	0	0
1986	Minnesota	5	1	4	5	0	0	0	0
1987♦	Edmonton	21	6	13	19	6	2	0	0
Playoff Totals		**59**	**11**	**41**	**52**	**14**	**3**	**0**	**0**
NILSSON, Ulf									Center
1979	NY Rangers	2	0	0	0	2	0	0	0
1980	NY Rangers	9	0	6	6	2	0	0	0
1981	NY Rangers	14	8	8	16	23	3	0	1
Playoff Totals		**25**	**8**	**14**	**22**	**27**	**3**	**0**	**1**
NISTICO, Lou *No Playoffs*									Center
NOBLE, Reg									Center/Defense
1918♦	Toronto	2	1	1	2	9	....	....	....
1921	Toronto	2	0	0	0	0	....	....	....
1922♦	Toronto	2	0	0	0	12	....	....	....
1926♦	Mtl. Maroons	4	1	1	2	6	....	....	....
1927	Mtl. Maroons	2	0	0	0	2	....	....	....
1929	Detroit	2	0	0	0	2	....	....	....
1932	Detroit	2	0	0	0	0	....	....	....
1933	Mtl. Maroons	2	0	0	0	2	....	....	....
Playoff Totals		**18**	**2**	**2**	**4**	**33**	....	....	....
NOEL, Claude *No Playoffs*									Center
•NOLAN, Owen									Right wing
1993	Quebec	5	1	0	1	2	0	0	0
1995	Quebec	6	2	3	5	6	0	0	0
1998	San Jose	6	2	2	4	26	2	0	1
1999	San Jose	6	1	1	2	6	0	0	0
2000	San Jose	10	8	2	10	6	2	2	3
2001	San Jose	6	1	1	2	8	0	0	1
2002	San Jose	12	3	6	9	8	0	0	0
Playoff Totals		**51**	**18**	**15**	**33**	**62**	**4**	**2**	**5**
NOLAN, Paddy *No Playoffs*									Left wing/Defense
NOLAN, Ted *No Playoffs*									Center
NOLET, Simon									Right wing
1968	Philadelphia	1	0	0	0	0	0	0	0
1971	Philadelphia	4	2	1	3	0	1	0	0
1973	Philadelphia	11	3	1	4	4	0	0	0
1974♦	Philadelphia	15	1	1	2	4	0	0	0
1976	Pittsburgh	3	0	0	0	0	0	0	0
Playoff Totals		**34**	**6**	**3**	**9**	**8**	**1**	**0**	**0**
NOONAN, Brian									Right wing
1988	Chicago	3	0	0	0	4	0	0	0
1989	Chicago	1	0	0	0	0	0	0	0
1992	Chicago	18	6	9	15	30	3	0	1
1993	Chicago	4	3	0	3	4	1	0	0
1994♦	NY Rangers	22	4	7	11	17	2	0	1
1995	NY Rangers	5	0	0	0	8	0	0	0
1996	St. Louis	13	4	1	5	10	0	0	0
1999	Phoenix	5	0	2	2	4	0	0	0
Playoff Totals		**71**	**17**	**19**	**36**	**77**	**6**	**0**	**2**
NORDMARK, Robert									Defense
1989	Vancouver	7	3	2	5	8	2	0	0
Playoff Totals		**7**	**3**	**2**	**5**	**8**	**2**	**0**	**0**
•NORDSTROM, Peter *No Playoffs*									Center
NORIS, Joe *No Playoffs*									Center/Defense
NORRIS, Dwayne *No Playoffs*									Right wing
NORRISH, Rod *No Playoffs*									Left wing

•NORSTROM, Mattias Defense

Season	Team	GP	G	A	Pts	PIM	PP	SH	GW
1995	NY Rangers	3	0	0	0	0	0	0	0
1998	Los Angeles	4	0	0	0	2	0	0	0
2000	Los Angeles	4	0	0	0	6	0	0	0
2001	Los Angeles	13	0	2	2	18	0	0	0
2002	Los Angeles	7	0	0	0	4	0	0	0
Playoff Totals		**31**	**0**	**2**	**2**	**30**	**0**	**0**	**0**

NORTHCOTT, Baldy Defense/Left wing

Season	Team	GP	G	A	Pts	PIM	PP	SH	GW
1930	Mtl. Maroons	4	0	0	0	4	....	....	....
1931	Mtl. Maroons	2	0	1	1	0	....	....	....
1932	Mtl. Maroons	4	1	2	3	4	....	....	....
1933	Mtl. Maroons	2	0	0	0	4	....	....	....
1934	Mtl. Maroons	4	2	0	2	0	....	....	....
1935♦	Mtl. Maroons	7	*4	1	*5	0	....	....	....
1936	Mtl. Maroons	3	0	0	0	0	....	....	....
1937	Mtl. Maroons	5	1	1	2	2	....	....	....
Playoff Totals		**31**	**8**	**5**	**13**	**14**	....	....	....

•NORTON, Brad *No Playoffs* Defense

•NORTON, Jeff Defense

Season	Team	GP	G	A	Pts	PIM	PP	SH	GW
1988	NY Islanders	3	0	2	2	13	0	0	0
1990	NY Islanders	4	1	3	4	17	0	0	0
1993	NY Islanders	10	1	1	2	4	0	0	0
1994	San Jose	14	1	5	6	20	0	0	0
1995	St. Louis	7	1	1	2	11	0	0	0
1999	San Jose	6	0	7	7	10	0	0	0
2000	San Jose	12	0	1	1	7	0	0	0
2001	San Jose	6	0	1	1	2	0	0	0
2002	Boston	3	0	0	0	5	0	0	0
Playoff Totals		**65**	**4**	**21**	**25**	**89**	**0**	**0**	**0**

NORWICH, Craig *No Playoffs* Defense

NORWOOD, Lee Defense

Season	Team	GP	G	A	Pts	PIM	PP	SH	GW
1981	Quebec	3	0	0	0	2	0	0	0
1986	St. Louis	19	2	7	9	64	0	0	0
1987	Detroit	16	1	6	7	31	0	0	1
1988	Detroit	16	2	6	8	40	2	0	0
1989	Detroit	6	1	2	3	16	1	0	0
1991	New Jersey	4	0	0	0	18	0	0	0
1992	St. Louis	1	0	1	1	0	0	0	0
Playoff Totals		**65**	**6**	**22**	**28**	**171**	**3**	**0**	**1**

•NOVOSELTSEV, Ivan *No Playoffs* Left wing

NOVY, Milan Center

Season	Team	GP	G	A	Pts	PIM	PP	SH	GW
1983	Washington	2	0	0	0	0	0	0	0
Playoff Totals		**2**	**0**	**0**	**0**	**0**	**0**	**0**	**0**

NOWAK, Hank Left wing

Season	Team	GP	G	A	Pts	PIM	PP	SH	GW
1975	Boston	3	1	0	1	0	0	0	0
1976	Boston	10	0	0	0	8	0	0	0
Playoff Totals		**13**	**1**	**0**	**1**	**8**	**0**	**0**	**0**

•NUMMELIN, Petteri *No Playoffs* Defense

•NUMMINEN, Teppo Defense

Season	Team	GP	G	A	Pts	PIM	PP	SH	GW
1990	Winnipeg	7	1	2	3	10	0	0	0
1992	Winnipeg	7	0	0	0	0	0	0	0
1993	Winnipeg	6	1	1	2	2	1	0	0
1996	Winnipeg	6	0	0	0	2	0	0	0
1997	Phoenix	7	3	3	6	0	1	0	1
1998	Phoenix	1	0	0	0	0	0	0	0
1999	Phoenix	7	2	1	3	4	2	0	0
2000	Phoenix	5	1	1	2	0	0	0	0
2002	Phoenix	4	0	0	0	2	0	0	0
Playoff Totals		**50**	**8**	**8**	**16**	**20**	**4**	**0**	**1**

•NURMINEN, Kai *No Playoffs* Left wing

NYKOLUK, Mike *No Playoffs* Right wing

•NYLANDER, Michael Center

Season	Team	GP	G	A	Pts	PIM	PP	SH	GW
1994	Calgary	3	0	0	0	0	0	0	0
1995	Calgary	6	0	6	6	2	0	0	0
1996	Calgary	4	0	0	0	0	0	0	0
2002	Chicago	5	0	3	3	2	0	0	0
Playoff Totals		**18**	**0**	**9**	**9**	**4**	**0**	**0**	**0**

NYLUND, Gary Defense

Season	Team	GP	G	A	Pts	PIM	PP	SH	GW
1986	Toronto	10	0	2	2	25	0	0	0
1987	Chicago	4	0	2	2	11	0	0	0
1988	Chicago	5	0	0	0	10	0	0	0
1990	NY Islanders	5	0	2	2	17	0	0	0
Playoff Totals		**24**	**0**	**6**	**6**	**63**	**0**	**0**	**0**

NYROP, Bill Defense

Season	Team	GP	G	A	Pts	PIM	PP	SH	GW
1976♦	Montreal	13	0	3	3	12	0	0	0
1977♦	Montreal	8	1	0	1	4	0	0	0
1978♦	Montreal	12	0	4	4	6	0	0	0
1982	Minnesota	2	0	0	0	0	0	0	0
Playoff Totals		**35**	**1**	**7**	**8**	**22**	**0**	**0**	**0**

NYSTROM, Bob Right wing

Season	Team	GP	G	A	Pts	PIM	PP	SH	GW
1975	NY Islanders	17	1	3	4	27	0	0	0
1976	NY Islanders	13	3	6	9	30	1	0	0
1977	NY Islanders	12	0	2	2	7	0	0	0
1978	NY Islanders	7	3	1	4	14	1	0	2
1979	NY Islanders	10	3	2	5	4	0	0	1
1980♦	NY Islanders	20	9	9	18	50	0	0	3
1981♦	NY Islanders	18	6	6	12	20	0	0	1
1982♦	NY Islanders	15	5	5	10	32	0	0	0
1983♦	NY Islanders	20	7	6	13	15	0	0	0
1984	NY Islanders	15	0	2	2	8	0	0	0
1985	NY Islanders	10	2	2	4	29	0	0	0
Playoff Totals		**157**	**39**	**44**	**83**	**236**	**2**	**0**	**7**

•OATES, Adam Center

Season	Team	GP	G	A	Pts	PIM	PP	SH	GW
1987	Detroit	16	4	7	11	6	0	0	1
1988	Detroit	16	8	12	20	6	4	0	1
1989	Detroit	6	0	8	8	2	0	0	0
1990	St. Louis	12	2	12	14	4	1	0	0
1991	St. Louis	13	7	13	20	10	2	0	1
1992	Boston	15	5	14	19	4	3	0	2
1993	Boston	4	0	9	9	4	0	0	0
1994	Boston	13	3	9	12	8	2	0	0
1995	Boston	5	1	0	1	2	1	0	0
1996	Boston	5	2	5	7	2	0	1	0
1998	Washington	21	6	11	17	8	1	1	1
2000	Washington	5	0	3	3	4	0	0	0
2001	Washington	6	0	0	0	0	0	0	0
2002	Philadelphia	5	0	2	2	0	0	0	0
Playoff Totals		**142**	**38**	**105**	**143**	**60**	**14**	**2**	**6**

OATMAN, Russell Left wing

Season	Team	GP	G	A	Pts	PIM	PP	SH	GW
1927	Mtl. Maroons	2	0	0	0	0	....	....	....
1928	Mtl. Maroons	9	1	0	1	18	....	....	....
1929	NY Rangers	4	0	0	0	0	....	....	....
Playoff Totals		**15**	**1**	**0**	**1**	**18**	....	....	....

O'BRIEN, Dennis Defense

Season	Team	GP	G	A	Pts	PIM	PP	SH	GW
1971	Minnesota	9	0	0	0	20	0	0	0
1972	Minnesota	3	0	1	1	11	0	0	0
1973	Minnesota	6	1	0	1	38	0	0	0
1977	Minnesota	2	0	0	0	4	0	0	0
1978	Boston	14	0	1	1	28	0	0	0
Playoff Totals		**34**	**1**	**2**	**3**	**101**	**0**	**0**	**0**

O'BRIEN, Ellard *No Playoffs* Defense

•OBSUT, Jaroslav *No Playoffs* Defense

O'CALLAHAN, Jack Defense

Season	Team	GP	G	A	Pts	PIM	PP	SH	GW
1983	Chicago	5	0	2	2	2	0	0	0
1984	Chicago	2	0	0	0	2	0	0	0
1985	Chicago	15	3	5	8	25	0	0	0
1986	Chicago	3	0	1	1	4	0	0	0
1987	Chicago	2	0	0	0	2	0	0	0
1988	New Jersey	5	1	3	4	6	0	0	0
Playoff Totals		**32**	**4**	**11**	**15**	**41**	**0**	**0**	**0**

O'CONNELL, Mike Defense

Season	Team	GP	G	A	Pts	PIM	PP	SH	GW
1979	Chicago	4	0	0	0	4	0	0	0
1980	Chicago	7	0	1	1	0	0	0	0
1981	Boston	3	1	3	4	2	0	1	0
1982	Boston	11	2	2	4	20	0	0	0
1983	Boston	17	3	5	8	12	2	0	1
1984	Boston	3	0	0	0	0	0	0	0
1985	Boston	5	1	5	6	0	1	0	0
1987	Detroit	16	1	4	5	14	0	0	0
1988	Detroit	10	0	4	4	8	0	0	0
1989	Detroit	6	0	0	0	4	0	0	0
Playoff Totals		**82**	**8**	**24**	**32**	**64**	**3**	**1**	**1**

O'CONNOR, Buddy Center

Season	Team	GP	G	A	Pts	PIM	PP	SH	GW
1942	Montreal	3	0	1	1	0	....	....	....
1943	Montreal	5	4	5	9	0	....	....	....
1944♦	Montreal	8	1	2	3	2	....	....	....
1945	Montreal	2	0	0	0	0	....	....	....
1946♦	Montreal	9	2	3	5	0	....	....	....
1947	Montreal	8	3	4	7	0	....	....	....
1948	NY Rangers	6	1	4	5	0	....	....	....
1950	NY Rangers	12	4	2	6	4	....	....	....
Playoff Totals		**53**	**15**	**21**	**36**	**6**	....	....	....

O'CONNOR, Myles *No Playoffs* Defense

ODDLEIFSON, Chris Center

Season	Team	GP	G	A	Pts	PIM	PP	SH	GW
1975	Vancouver	5	0	3	3	2	0	0	0
1976	Vancouver	2	1	2	3	0	0	0	0
1979	Vancouver	3	0	1	1	2	0	0	0
1980	Vancouver	4	0	0	0	4	0	0	0
Playoff Totals		**14**	**1**	**6**	**7**	**8**	**0**	**0**	**0**

•ODELEIN, Lyle Defense

Season	Team	GP	G	A	Pts	PIM	PP	SH	GW
1991	Montreal	12	0	0	0	54	0	0	0
1992	Montreal	7	0	0	0	11	0	0	0
1993♦	Montreal	20	1	5	6	30	0	0	0
1994	Montreal	7	0	0	0	17	0	0	0
1996	Montreal	6	1	1	2	6	0	1	0
1997	New Jersey	10	2	2	4	19	1	0	0
1998	New Jersey	6	1	1	2	21	1	0	1
1999	New Jersey	7	0	3	3	10	0	0	0
2000	Phoenix	5	0	0	0	16	0	0	0
2002	Chicago	4	0	1	1	25	0	0	0
Playoff Totals		**84**	**5**	**13**	**18**	**209**	**2**	**1**	**1**

ODELEIN, Selmar *No Playoffs* Defense

•ODGERS, Jeff Right wing

Season	Team	GP	G	A	Pts	PIM	PP	SH	GW
1994	San Jose	11	0	0	0	11	0	0	0
1995	San Jose	11	1	1	2	23	0	0	0
1998	Colorado	6	0	0	0	25	0	0	0
1999	Colorado	15	1	0	1	14	0	0	1
2000	Colorado	4	0	0	0	0	0	0	0
Playoff Totals		**47**	**2**	**1**	**3**	**73**	**0**	**0**	**1**

•ODJICK, Gino Left wing

Season	Team	GP	G	A	Pts	PIM	PP	SH	GW
1991	Vancouver	6	0	0	0	18	0	0	0
1992	Vancouver	4	0	0	0	6	0	0	0
1993	Vancouver	1	0	0	0	0	0	0	0
1994	Vancouver	10	0	0	0	18	0	0	0
1995	Vancouver	5	0	0	0	47	0	0	0
1996	Vancouver	6	3	1	4	6	0	0	2
2002	Montreal	12	1	0	1	47	0	0	0
Playoff Totals		**44**	**4**	**1**	**5**	**142**	**0**	**0**	**2**

O'DONNELL, Fred Right wing

Season	Team	GP	G	A	Pts	PIM	PP	SH	GW
1973	Boston	5	0	1	1	5	0	0	0
Playoff Totals		**5**	**0**	**1**	**1**	**5**	**0**	**0**	**0**

•O'DONNELL, Sean Defense

Season	Team	GP	G	A	Pts	PIM	PP	SH	GW
1998	Los Angeles	4	1	0	1	36	0	0	0
2000	Los Angeles	4	1	0	1	4	0	0	0
2001	New Jersey	23	1	2	3	41	0	0	0
2002	Boston	6	0	2	2	4	0	0	0
Playoff Totals		**37**	**3**	**4**	**7**	**85**	**0**	**0**	**0**

O'DONOGHUE, Don Right wing

Season	Team	GP	G	A	Pts	PIM	PP	SH	GW
1970	Oakland	3	0	0	0	0	0	0	0
Playoff Totals		**3**	**0**	**0**	**0**	**0**	**0**	**0**	**0**

ODROWSKI, Gerry Defense

Season	Team	GP	G	A	Pts	PIM	PP	SH	GW
1961	Detroit	10	0	0	0	4	0	0	0
1963	Detroit	2	0	0	0	2	0	0	0
1969	Oakland	7	0	1	1	2	0	0	0
1972	St. Louis	11	0	0	0	8	0	0	0
Playoff Totals		**30**	**0**	**1**	**1**	**16**	**0**	**0**	**0**

O'DWYER, Bill Center

Season	Team	GP	G	A	Pts	PIM	PP	SH	GW
1988	Boston	9	0	0	0	0	0	0	0
1990	Boston	1	0	0	0	2	0	0	0
Playoff Totals		**10**	**0**	**0**	**0**	**2**	**0**	**0**	**0**

O'FLAHERTY, Gerry Left wing

Season	Team	GP	G	A	Pts	PIM	PP	SH	GW
1975	Vancouver	5	2	2	4	6	0	0	0
1976	Vancouver	2	0	0	0	0	0	0	0
Playoff Totals		**7**	**2**	**2**	**4**	**6**	**0**	**0**	**0**

O'FLAHERTY, Peanuts *No Playoffs* Right wing

OGILVIE, Brian *No Playoffs* Center

O'GRADY, George *No Playoffs* Defense

OGRODNICK, John Left wing

Season	Team	GP	G	A	Pts	PIM	PP	SH	GW
1984	Detroit	4	0	0	0	0	0	0	0
1985	Detroit	3	1	1	2	0	0	0	0
1987	Quebec	13	9	4	13	6	3	0	2
1989	NY Rangers	3	2	0	2	0	1	0	0
1990	NY Rangers	10	6	3	9	0	3	0	1
1991	NY Rangers	4	0	0	0	0	0	0	0
1992	NY Rangers	3	0	0	0	0	0	0	0
1993	Detroit	1	0	0	0	0	0	0	0
Playoff Totals		**41**	**18**	**8**	**26**	**6**	**7**	**0**	**3**

•OHLUND, Mattias Defense

Season	Team	GP	G	A	Pts	PIM	PP	SH	GW
2001	Vancouver	4	1	3	4	6	1	0	0
2002	Vancouver	6	1	1	2	6	0	0	0
Playoff Totals		**10**	**2**	**4**	**6**	**12**	**1**	**0**	**0**

OJANEN, Janne Center

Season	Team	GP	G	A	Pts	PIM	PP	SH	GW
1992	New Jersey	3	0	2	2	0	0	0	0
Playoff Totals		**3**	**0**	**2**	**2**	**0**	**0**	**0**	**0**

OKERLUND, Todd *No Playoffs* Right wing

OKSIUTA, Roman Right wing

Season	Team	GP	G	A	Pts	PIM	PP	SH	GW
1995	Vancouver	10	2	3	5	0	1	0	0
Playoff Totals		**10**	**2**	**3**	**5**	**0**	**1**	**0**	**0**

•OLAUSSON, Fredrik Defense

Season	Team	GP	G	A	Pts	PIM	PP	SH	GW
1987	Winnipeg	10	2	3	5	4	1	0	0
1988	Winnipeg	5	1	1	2	0	0	0	0
1990	Winnipeg	7	0	2	2	2	0	0	0
1992	Winnipeg	7	1	5	6	4	1	0	0
1993	Winnipeg	6	0	2	2	2	0	0	0
1997	Pittsburgh	4	0	1	1	0	0	0	0
1998	Pittsburgh	6	0	3	3	2	0	0	0
1999	Anaheim	4	0	2	2	4	0	0	0
2002♦	Detroit	21	2	4	6	10	1	0	1
Playoff Totals		**70**	**6**	**23**	**29**	**28**	**3**	**0**	**1**

Season	Team	GP	G	A	Pts	PIM	PP	SH	GW
OLCZYK, Ed — Center									
1985	Chicago	15	6	5	11	11	1	1	0
1986	Chicago	3	0	0	0	0	0	0	0
1987	Chicago	4	1	1	2	4	0	0	0
1988	Toronto	6	5	4	9	2	1	1	1
1990	Toronto	5	1	2	3	14	0	0	0
1992	Winnipeg	6	2	1	3	4	0	0	1
1994♦	NY Rangers	1	0	0	0	0	0	0	0
1996	Winnipeg	6	1	2	3	6	0	0	0
1997	Pittsburgh	5	1	0	1	12	0	1	1
1998	Pittsburgh	6	2	0	2	4	1	1	1
Playoff Totals		**57**	**19**	**15**	**34**	**57**	**3**	**4**	**4**
•OLIVER, David — Right wing									
1997	NY Rangers	3	0	0	0	0	0	0	0
Playoff Totals		**3**	**0**	**0**	**0**	**0**	**0**	**0**	**0**
OLIVER, Harry — Right wing									
1927	Boston	8	4	2	*6	4	....	....	....
1928	Boston	2	2	0	2	4	....	....	....
1929♦	Boston	5	1	1	2	8	....	....	....
1930	Boston	6	2	1	3	6	....	....	....
1931	Boston	4	0	0	0	2	....	....	....
1933	Boston	5	0	0	0	0	....	....	....
1936	NY Americans	5	1	2	3	0	....	....	....
Playoff Totals		**35**	**10**	**6**	**16**	**24**	....	....	....
OLIVER, Murray — Center									
1960	Detroit	6	1	0	1	4	0	0	0
1969	Toronto	4	1	2	3	0	0	0	0
1971	Minnesota	12	7	4	11	0	2	0	0
1972	Minnesota	7	0	6	6	4	0	0	0
1973	Minnesota	6	0	4	4	2	0	0	0
Playoff Totals		**35**	**9**	**16**	**25**	**10**	**2**	**0**	**0**
•OLIWA, Krzysztof — Left wing									
1998	New Jersey	6	0	0	0	23	0	0	0
1999	New Jersey	1	0	0	0	2	0	0	0
2000♦	New Jersey	....	....	....	....	....	....	....	....
2001	Pittsburgh	5	0	0	0	16	0	0	0
Playoff Totals		**12**	**0**	**0**	**0**	**41**	**0**	**0**	**0**
OLMSTEAD, Bert — Left wing									
1951	Montreal	11	2	4	6	9	....	....	....
1952	Montreal	11	0	1	1	4	....	....	....
1953♦	Montreal	12	2	2	4	4	....	....	....
1954	Montreal	11	0	1	1	19	....	....	....
1955	Montreal	12	0	4	4	21	....	....	....
1956♦	Montreal	10	4	*10	14	8	....	....	....
1957♦	Montreal	10	0	*9	9	13	....	....	....
1958♦	Montreal	9	0	3	3	0	....	....	....
1959	Toronto	12	4	2	6	13	....	....	....
1960	Toronto	10	3	4	7	0	....	....	....
1961	Toronto	3	1	2	3	10	....	....	....
1962♦	Toronto	4	0	1	1	0	....	....	....
Playoff Totals		**115**	**16**	**43**	**59**	**101**	....	....	....
OLSEN, Darryl *No Playoffs* — Defense									
OLSON, Dennis *No Playoffs* — Center									
OLSSON, Christer — Defense									
1996	St. Louis	3	0	0	0	0	0	0	0
Playoff Totals		**3**	**0**	**0**	**0**	**0**	**0**	**0**	**0**
•OLVESTAD, Jimmie *No Playoffs* — Left wing									
O'NEIL, Jim — Center/Right wing									
1935	Boston	4	0	0	0	9	....	....	....
1936	Boston	2	1	1	2	4	....	....	....
1941	Montreal	3	0	0	0	0	....	....	....
Playoff Totals		**9**	**1**	**1**	**2**	**13**	....	....	....
O'NEIL, Paul *No Playoffs* — Center/Right wing									
•O'NEILL, Jeff — Center									
1999	Carolina	6	0	1	1	0	0	0	0
2001	Carolina	6	1	2	3	10	0	0	1
2002	Carolina	22	8	5	13	27	3	0	1
Playoff Totals		**34**	**9**	**8**	**17**	**37**	**3**	**0**	**2**
O'NEILL, Tom — Right wing									
1944	Toronto	4	0	0	0	6	0	0	0
1945♦	Toronto	....	....	....	....	....	....	....	....
Playoff Totals		**4**	**0**	**0**	**0**	**6**	**0**	**0**	**0**
ORBAN, Bill — Center/Left wing									
1968	Chicago	3	0	0	0	0	0	0	0
Playoff Totals		**3**	**0**	**0**	**0**	**0**	**0**	**0**	**0**
O'REE, Willie *No Playoffs* — Wing									
O'REGAN, Tom *No Playoffs* — Center/Defense									

Season	Team	GP	G	A	Pts	PIM	PP	SH	GW
O'REILLY, Terry — Right wing									
1973	Boston	5	0	0	0	2	0	0	0
1974	Boston	16	2	5	7	38	0	0	0
1975	Boston	3	0	0	0	17	0	0	0
1976	Boston	12	3	1	4	25	0	0	0
1977	Boston	14	5	6	11	28	0	0	1
1978	Boston	15	5	10	15	40	1	0	1
1979	Boston	11	0	6	6	25	0	0	0
1980	Boston	10	3	6	9	69	2	0	1
1981	Boston	3	1	2	3	12	0	0	0
1982	Boston	11	5	4	9	56	0	0	1
1984	Boston	3	0	0	0	14	0	0	0
1985	Boston	5	1	2	3	9	0	0	0
Playoff Totals		**108**	**25**	**42**	**67**	**335**	**3**	**0**	**4**
ORLANDO, Gates — Center									
1985	Buffalo	5	0	4	4	14	0	0	0
Playoff Totals		**5**	**0**	**4**	**4**	**14**	**0**	**0**	**0**
ORLANDO, Jimmy — Defense									
1940	Detroit	5	0	0	0	15	0	0	0
1941	Detroit	9	0	2	2	31	0	0	0
1942	Detroit	12	0	4	4	45	0	0	0
1943♦	Detroit	10	0	3	3	14	0	0	0
Playoff Totals		**36**	**0**	**9**	**9**	**105**	**0**	**0**	**0**
ORLESKI, Dave *No Playoffs* — Left wing									
•ORPIK, Brooks *No Playoffs* — Defense									
ORR, Bobby — Defense									
1968	Boston	4	0	2	2	2	0	0	0
1969	Boston	10	1	7	8	10	0	0	0
1970♦	Boston	14	9	11	20	14	3	2	1
1971	Boston	7	5	7	12	25	1	1	1
1972♦	Boston	15	5	*19	*24	19	4	0	1
1973	Boston	5	1	1	2	7	0	0	0
1974	Boston	16	4	*14	18	28	1	0	2
1975	Boston	3	1	5	6	2	0	1	0
Playoff Totals		**74**	**26**	**66**	**92**	**107**	**9**	**4**	**5**
•ORSZAGH, Vladimir *No Playoffs* — Right wing									
OSBORNE, Keith *No Playoffs* — Right wing									
OSBORNE, Mark — Left wing									
1984	NY Rangers	5	0	1	1	7	0	0	0
1985	NY Rangers	3	0	0	0	4	0	0	0
1986	NY Rangers	15	2	3	5	26	0	1	1
1987	Toronto	9	1	3	4	6	0	0	0
1988	Toronto	6	1	3	4	16	0	0	1
1990	Toronto	5	2	3	5	12	0	1	0
1993	Toronto	19	1	1	2	16	0	0	0
1994	Toronto	18	4	2	6	52	0	2	1
1995	NY Rangers	7	1	0	1	2	0	0	0
Playoff Totals		**87**	**12**	**16**	**28**	**141**	**0**	**4**	**3**
OSBURN, Randy *No Playoffs* — Left wing									
O'SHEA, Danny — Center									
1970	Minnesota	6	1	0	1	8	0	0	0
1971	Chicago	18	2	5	7	15	0	0	0
1972	St. Louis	10	0	2	2	36	0	0	0
1973	St. Louis	5	0	0	0	2	0	0	0
Playoff Totals		**39**	**3**	**7**	**10**	**61**	**0**	**0**	**0**
O'SHEA, Kevin — Right wing									
1972	St. Louis	11	2	1	3	10	0	0	1
1973	St. Louis	1	0	0	0	0	0	0	0
Playoff Totals		**12**	**2**	**1**	**3**	**10**	**0**	**0**	**1**
OSIECKI, Mark *No Playoffs* — Defense									
•O'SULLIVAN, Chris *No Playoffs* — Defense									
OTEVREL, Jaroslav *No Playoffs* — Left wing									
•OTT, Steve *No Playoffs* — Center									
OTTO, Joel — Center									
1985	Calgary	3	2	1	3	10	1	0	1
1986	Calgary	22	5	10	15	80	3	0	1
1987	Calgary	2	0	2	2	6	0	0	0
1988	Calgary	9	3	2	5	26	1	0	1
1989♦	Calgary	22	6	13	19	46	2	1	1
1990	Calgary	6	2	2	4	2	0	0	0
1991	Calgary	7	1	2	3	8	0	0	0
1993	Calgary	6	4	2	6	4	0	1	1
1994	Calgary	3	0	1	1	4	0	0	0
1995	Calgary	7	0	3	3	2	0	0	0
1996	Philadelphia	12	3	4	7	11	1	0	1
1997	Philadelphia	18	1	5	6	8	0	0	0
1998	Philadelphia	5	0	0	0	0	0	0	0
Playoff Totals		**122**	**27**	**47**	**74**	**207**	**8**	**2**	**6**
OUELLETTE, Eddie — Center									
1936	Chicago	1	0	0	0	0	0	0	0
Playoff Totals		**1**	**0**	**0**	**0**	**0**	**0**	**0**	**0**
OUELLETTE, Gerry *No Playoffs* — Right wing									
OWCHAR, Dennis — Defense									
1975	Pittsburgh	6	0	1	1	4	0	0	0
1976	Pittsburgh	2	0	0	0	2	0	0	0
1978	Colorado	2	1	0	1	2	0	0	0
Playoff Totals		**10**	**1**	**1**	**2**	**8**	**0**	**0**	**0**

Season	Team	GP	G	A	Pts	PIM	PP	SH	GW
OWEN, George — Defense									
1929♦	Boston	5	0	0	0	0	....	....	....
1930	Boston	6	0	2	2	6	....	....	....
1931	Boston	5	2	3	5	13	....	....	....
1933	Boston	5	0	0	0	6	....	....	....
Playoff Totals		**21**	**2**	**5**	**7**	**25**	....	....	....
•OZOLINSH, Sandis — Defense									
1994	San Jose	14	0	10	10	8	0	0	0
1995	San Jose	11	3	2	5	6	1	0	0
1996♦	Colorado	22	5	14	19	16	2	0	1
1997	Colorado	17	4	13	17	24	2	0	1
1998	Colorado	7	0	7	7	14	0	0	0
1999	Colorado	19	4	8	12	22	3	0	1
2000	Colorado	17	5	5	10	20	3	0	1
2001	Carolina	6	0	2	2	5	0	0	0
Playoff Totals		**113**	**21**	**61**	**82**	**115**	**11**	**0**	**4**
PACHAL, Clayton *No Playoffs* — Center/Left wing									
PADDOCK, John — Right wing									
1980	Philadelphia	3	2	0	2	0	0	0	0
1981	Quebec	2	0	0	0	0	0	0	0
Playoff Totals		**5**	**2**	**0**	**2**	**0**	**0**	**0**	**0**
PAEK, Jim — Defense									
1991♦	Pittsburgh	8	1	0	1	2	0	0	0
1992♦	Pittsburgh	19	0	4	4	6	0	0	0
Playoff Totals		**27**	**1**	**4**	**5**	**8**	**0**	**0**	**0**
•PAHLSSON, Sami *No Playoffs* — Center									
PAIEMENT, Rosaire — Center									
1968	Philadelphia	3	3	0	3	0	2	0	1
Playoff Totals		**3**	**3**	**0**	**3**	**0**	**2**	**0**	**1**
PAIEMENT, Wilf — Right wing									
1978	Colorado	2	0	0	0	7	0	0	0
1980	Toronto	3	0	2	2	17	0	0	0
1981	Toronto	3	0	0	0	2	0	0	0
1982	Quebec	14	6	6	12	28	1	0	1
1983	Quebec	4	0	1	1	4	0	0	0
1984	Quebec	9	3	1	4	24	0	0	0
1985	Quebec	18	4	2	6	58	0	0	0
1986	NY Rangers	16	5	5	10	45	4	0	0
Playoff Totals		**69**	**18**	**17**	**35**	**185**	**5**	**0**	**1**
PALANGIO, Pete — Left wing									
1927	Montreal	4	0	0	0	0	0	0	0
1938♦	Chicago	3	0	0	0	0	0	0	0
Playoff Totals		**7**	**0**	**0**	**0**	**0**	**0**	**0**	**0**
PALAZZARI, Aldo *No Playoffs* — Right wing									
PALAZZARI, Doug — Center									
1975	St. Louis	2	0	0	0	0	0	0	0
Playoff Totals		**2**	**0**	**0**	**0**	**0**	**0**	**0**	**0**
•PALFFY, Ziggy — Right wing									
2000	Los Angeles	4	2	0	2	0	0	0	0
2001	Los Angeles	13	3	5	8	8	0	0	0
2002	Los Angeles	7	4	5	9	0	0	0	0
Playoff Totals		**24**	**9**	**10**	**19**	**8**	**0**	**0**	**0**
PALMER, Brad — Left wing									
1981	Minnesota	19	8	5	13	4	1	2	1
1982	Minnesota	3	0	0	0	12	0	0	0
1983	Boston	7	1	0	1	0	0	1	1
Playoff Totals		**29**	**9**	**5**	**14**	**16**	**1**	**3**	**2**
PALMER, Rob *No Playoffs* — Center									
PALMER, Robert — Defense									
1978	Los Angeles	2	0	0	0	0	0	0	0
1979	Los Angeles	2	0	0	0	2	0	0	0
1980	Los Angeles	4	1	2	3	4	0	0	0
Playoff Totals		**8**	**1**	**2**	**3**	**6**	**0**	**0**	**0**
PANAGABKO, Ed *No Playoffs* — Center									
•PANDOLFO, Jay — Left wing									
1997	New Jersey	6	0	1	1	0	0	0	0
1998	New Jersey	3	0	2	2	0	0	0	0
1999	New Jersey	7	1	0	1	0	0	0	0
2000♦	New Jersey	23	0	5	5	0	0	0	0
2001	New Jersey	25	1	4	5	4	0	0	0
2002	New Jersey	6	0	0	0	0	0	0	0
Playoff Totals		**70**	**2**	**12**	**14**	**4**	**0**	**0**	**0**
•PANKEWICZ, Greg *No Playoffs* — Right wing									
PANTELEEV, Grigori *No Playoffs* — Left wing									
PAPIKE, Joe — Right wing									
1941	Chicago	5	0	2	2	0	0	0	0
Playoff Totals		**5**	**0**	**2**	**2**	**0**	**0**	**0**	**0**
•PAPINEAU, Justin *No Playoffs* — Center									

Season	Team	GP	G	A	Pts	PIM	PP	SH	GW
PAPPIN, Jim	Right wing								
1964♦	Toronto	11	0	0	0	0	0	0	0
1967♦	Toronto	12	*7	8	*15	12	3	0	1
1970	Chicago	8	3	2	5	6	1	0	0
1971	Chicago	18	10	4	14	24	2	0	1
1972	Chicago	8	2	5	7	4	0	1	1
1973	Chicago	16	8	7	15	24	1	0	1
1974	Chicago	11	3	6	9	29	0	0	2
1975	Chicago	8	0	2	2	2	0	0	0
Playoff Totals		**92**	**33**	**34**	**67**	**101**	**7**	**1**	**6**
PARADISE, Bob	Defense								
1972	Minnesota	4	0	0	0	2	0	0	0
1975	Pittsburgh	6	0	1	1	17	0	0	0
1979	Pittsburgh	2	0	0	0	0	0	0	0
Playoff Totals		**12**	**0**	**1**	**1**	**19**	**0**	**0**	**0**
PARGETER, George	*No Playoffs* — Left wing								
PARISE, J.P.	Left wing								
1968	Minnesota	14	2	5	7	10	0	1	0
1970	Minnesota	6	3	2	5	2	2	0	0
1971	Minnesota	12	3	3	6	22	2	0	1
1972	Minnesota	7	3	3	6	6	2	0	0
1973	Minnesota	6	0	0	0	9	0	0	0
1975	NY Islanders	17	8	8	16	22	4	0	1
1976	NY Islanders	13	4	6	10	10	1	0	0
1977	NY Islanders	11	4	4	8	6	1	0	0
Playoff Totals		**86**	**27**	**31**	**58**	**87**	**12**	**1**	**2**
PARIZEAU, Michel	*No Playoffs* — Center								
PARK, Brad	Defense								
1969	NY Rangers	4	0	2	2	7	0	0	0
1970	NY Rangers	5	1	2	3	11	1	0	0
1971	NY Rangers	13	0	4	4	42	0	0	0
1972	NY Rangers	16	4	7	11	21	2	0	1
1973	NY Rangers	10	2	5	7	8	1	0	1
1974	NY Rangers	13	4	8	12	38	1	0	1
1975	NY Rangers	3	1	4	5	2	0	0	0
1976	Boston	11	3	8	11	14	1	1	0
1977	Boston	14	2	10	12	4	0	0	0
1978	Boston	15	9	11	20	14	4	0	0
1979	Boston	11	1	4	5	8	0	0	1
1980	Boston	10	3	6	9	4	0	0	0
1981	Boston	3	1	3	4	11	1	0	0
1982	Boston	11	1	4	5	4	0	0	1
1983	Boston	16	3	9	12	18	1	0	1
1984	Detroit	3	0	3	3	0	0	0	0
1985	Detroit	3	0	0	0	11	0	0	0
Playoff Totals		**161**	**35**	**90**	**125**	**217**	**12**	**1**	**6**
•PARK, Richard	Center								
1995	Pittsburgh	3	0	0	0	2	0	0	0
1996	Pittsburgh	1	0	0	0	0	0	0	0
1997	Anaheim	11	0	1	1	2	0	0	0
Playoff Totals		**15**	**0**	**1**	**1**	**4**	**0**	**0**	**0**
PARKER, Jeff	Right wing								
1989	Buffalo	5	0	0	0	26	0	0	0
Playoff Totals		**5**	**0**	**0**	**0**	**26**	**0**	**0**	**0**
•PARKER, Scott	Right wing								
2001♦	Colorado	4	0	0	0	2	0	0	0
Playoff Totals		**4**	**0**	**0**	**0**	**2**	**0**	**0**	**0**
PARKES, Ernie	*No Playoffs* — Right wing								
PARKS, Greg	Center								
1993	NY Islanders	2	0	0	0	0	0	0	0
Playoff Totals		**2**	**0**	**0**	**0**	**0**	**0**	**0**	**0**
•PARRISH, Mark	Right wing								
2000	Florida	4	0	1	1	0	0	0	0
2002	NY Islanders	7	2	1	3	6	2	0	0
Playoff Totals		**11**	**2**	**2**	**4**	**6**	**2**	**0**	**0**
PARSONS, George	Left wing								
1938	Toronto	7	3	2	5	11	....	....	....
Playoff Totals		**7**	**3**	**2**	**5**	**11**	....	....	....
•PARSSINEN, Timo	*No Playoffs* — Left wing								
PASEK, Dusan	Center								
1989	Minnesota	2	1	0	1	0	0	0	0
Playoff Totals		**2**	**1**	**0**	**1**	**0**	**0**	**0**	**0**
PASIN, Dave	Right wing								
1986	Boston	3	0	1	1	0	0	0	0
Playoff Totals		**3**	**0**	**1**	**1**	**0**	**0**	**0**	**0**
PASLAWSKI, Greg	Right wing								
1984	St. Louis	9	1	0	1	2	0	0	0
1985	St. Louis	3	0	0	0	2	0	0	0
1986	St. Louis	17	10	7	17	13	2	0	0
1987	St. Louis	6	1	1	2	4	0	0	0
1988	St. Louis	3	1	1	2	2	1	0	0
1989	St. Louis	9	2	1	3	2	1	0	0
1990	Winnipeg	7	1	3	4	0	0	0	0
1993	Calgary	6	3	0	3	0	0	0	1
Playoff Totals		**60**	**19**	**13**	**32**	**25**	**4**	**0**	**1**
•PATERA, Pavel	*No Playoffs* — Center								

Season	Team	GP	G	A	Pts	PIM	PP	SH	GW
PATERSON, Joe	Left wing								
1984	Detroit	3	0	0	0	7	0	0	0
1985	Philadelphia	17	3	4	7	70	1	0	0
1987	Los Angeles	2	0	0	0	0	0	0	0
Playoff Totals		**22**	**3**	**4**	**7**	**77**	**1**	**0**	**0**
PATERSON, Mark	*No Playoffs* — Defense								
PATERSON, Rick	Center								
1979	Chicago	1	0	1	1	0	0	0	0
1980	Chicago	7	0	0	0	5	0	0	0
1981	Chicago	2	1	0	1	0	0	1	0
1982	Chicago	15	3	2	5	21	0	0	0
1983	Chicago	13	1	1	2	4	0	1	1
1984	Chicago	5	1	1	2	6	0	1	0
1985	Chicago	15	1	5	6	15	0	0	0
1986	Chicago	3	0	0	0	0	0	0	0
Playoff Totals		**61**	**7**	**10**	**17**	**51**	**0**	**3**	**1**
PATEY, Doug	*No Playoffs* — Right wing								
PATEY, Larry	Center								
1976	St. Louis	3	1	1	2	2	1	0	1
1977	St. Louis	4	1	0	1	0	0	0	0
1980	St. Louis	3	1	0	1	2	0	0	0
1981	St. Louis	11	2	4	6	30	0	0	0
1982	St. Louis	10	2	4	6	13	0	1	0
1983	St. Louis	4	1	0	1	4	0	0	0
1984	NY Rangers	4	0	1	1	6	0	0	0
1985	NY Rangers	1	0	0	0	0	0	0	0
Playoff Totals		**40**	**8**	**10**	**18**	**57**	**1**	**1**	**1**
PATRICK, Craig	Right wing								
1975	St. Louis	2	0	1	1	0	0	0	0
Playoff Totals		**2**	**0**	**1**	**1**	**0**	**0**	**0**	**0**
PATRICK, Glenn	*No Playoffs* — Defense								
•PATRICK, James	Defense								
1984	NY Rangers	5	0	3	3	2	0	0	0
1985	NY Rangers	3	0	0	0	4	0	0	0
1986	NY Rangers	16	1	5	6	34	0	0	0
1987	NY Rangers	6	1	2	3	2	1	0	1
1989	NY Rangers	4	0	1	1	2	0	0	0
1990	NY Rangers	10	3	8	11	0	2	0	1
1991	NY Rangers	6	0	0	0	6	0	0	0
1992	NY Rangers	13	0	7	7	12	0	0	0
1994	Calgary	7	0	1	1	6	0	0	0
1995	Calgary	5	0	1	1	0	0	0	0
1996	Calgary	4	0	0	0	2	0	0	0
1999	Buffalo	20	0	1	1	12	0	0	0
2000	Buffalo	5	0	1	1	2	0	0	0
2001	Buffalo	13	1	2	3	2	0	0	0
Playoff Totals		**117**	**6**	**32**	**38**	**86**	**3**	**0**	**2**
PATRICK, Lester	*No Playoffs* — Defense								
PATRICK, Lynn	Center/Left wing								
1935	NY Rangers	4	2	2	4	0	....	....	....
1937	NY Rangers	9	3	0	3	2	....	....	....
1938	NY Rangers	3	0	1	1	2	....	....	....
1939	NY Rangers	7	1	1	2	0	....	....	....
1940♦	NY Rangers	12	2	2	4	4	....	....	....
1941	NY Rangers	3	1	0	1	14	....	....	....
1942	NY Rangers	6	1	0	1	0	....	....	....
Playoff Totals		**44**	**10**	**6**	**16**	**22**	....	....	....
PATRICK, Muzz	Defense								
1938	NY Rangers	3	0	0	0	2	....	....	....
1939	NY Rangers	7	1	0	1	17	....	....	....
1940♦	NY Rangers	12	3	0	3	13	....	....	....
1941	NY Rangers	3	0	0	0	2	....	....	....
Playoff Totals		**25**	**4**	**0**	**4**	**34**	....	....	....
PATRICK, Steve	Right wing								
1981	Buffalo	5	0	1	1	6	0	0	0
1983	Buffalo	2	0	0	0	0	0	0	0
1984	Buffalo	1	0	0	0	0	0	0	0
1985	NY Rangers	1	0	0	0	0	0	0	0
1986	Quebec	3	0	0	0	6	0	0	0
Playoff Totals		**12**	**0**	**1**	**1**	**12**	**0**	**0**	**0**
PATTERSON, Colin	Wing								
1984	Calgary	11	1	1	2	6	0	0	0
1985	Calgary	4	0	0	0	5	0	0	0
1986	Calgary	19	6	3	9	10	1	1	1
1987	Calgary	6	0	2	2	2	0	0	0
1988	Calgary	9	1	0	1	8	0	1	0
1989♦	Calgary	22	3	10	13	24	0	0	0
1991	Calgary	1	0	0	0	0	0	0	0
1992	Buffalo	5	1	0	1	0	0	0	0
1993	Buffalo	8	0	1	1	2	0	0	0
Playoff Totals		**85**	**12**	**17**	**29**	**57**	**1**	**2**	**1**
PATTERSON, Dennis	*No Playoffs* — Defense								
PATTERSON, Ed	*No Playoffs* — Right wing								
PATTERSON, George	Wing								
1929	Montreal	3	0	0	0	2	0	0	0
Playoff Totals		**3**	**0**	**0**	**0**	**2**	**0**	**0**	**0**
PAUL, Butch	*No Playoffs* — Center								
•PAUL, Jeff	*No Playoffs* — Defense								
PAULHUS, Rollie	*No Playoffs* — Defense								

Season	Team	GP	G	A	Pts	PIM	PP	SH	GW
PAVELICH, Mark	Center								
1982	NY Rangers	6	1	5	6	0	0	0	0
1983	NY Rangers	9	4	5	9	12	2	0	2
1984	NY Rangers	5	2	4	6	0	0	1	0
1985	NY Rangers	3	0	3	3	2	0	0	0
Playoff Totals		**23**	**7**	**17**	**24**	**14**	**2**	**1**	**2**
PAVELICH, Marty	Left wing								
1948	Detroit	10	2	2	4	6	....	....	....
1949	Detroit	9	0	1	1	8	....	....	....
1950♦	Detroit	14	4	2	6	13	....	....	....
1951	Detroit	6	0	1	1	2	....	....	....
1952♦	Detroit	8	2	2	4	2	....	....	....
1953	Detroit	6	2	1	3	7	....	....	....
1954♦	Detroit	12	2	2	4	4	....	....	....
1955♦	Detroit	11	1	3	4	12	....	....	....
1956	Detroit	10	0	1	1	14	....	....	....
1957	Detroit	5	0	0	0	6	....	....	....
Playoff Totals		**91**	**13**	**15**	**28**	**74**	....	....	....
PAVESE, Jim	Defense								
1982	St. Louis	3	0	3	3	2	0	0	0
1983	St. Louis	4	0	0	0	6	0	0	0
1985	St. Louis	1	0	0	0	5	0	0	0
1986	St. Louis	19	0	2	2	51	0	0	0
1987	St. Louis	2	0	0	0	2	0	0	0
1988	Detroit	4	0	1	1	15	0	0	0
1989	Hartford	1	0	0	0	0	0	0	0
Playoff Totals		**34**	**0**	**6**	**6**	**81**	**0**	**0**	**0**
PAYER, Evariste	*No Playoffs* — Center/Left wing								
•PAYER, Serge	*No Playoffs* — Center								
PAYNE, Davis	*No Playoffs* — Left wing								
PAYNE, Steve	Left wing								
1980	Minnesota	15	7	7	14	9	3	0	3
1981	Minnesota	19	17	12	29	6	6	0	4
1982	Minnesota	4	4	2	6	2	2	0	0
1983	Minnesota	9	3	6	9	19	1	0	0
1984	Minnesota	15	3	6	9	18	1	0	2
1985	Minnesota	9	1	2	3	6	0	0	0
Playoff Totals		**71**	**35**	**35**	**70**	**60**	**13**	**0**	**9**
PAYNTER, Kent	Defense								
1990	Washington	3	0	0	0	10	0	0	0
1991	Washington	1	0	0	0	0	0	0	0
Playoff Totals		**4**	**0**	**0**	**0**	**10**	**0**	**0**	**0**
PEAKE, Pat	Center								
1994	Washington	8	0	1	1	8	0	0	0
1996	Washington	5	2	1	3	12	2	0	0
Playoff Totals		**13**	**2**	**2**	**4**	**20**	**2**	**0**	**0**
PEARSON, Mel	*No Playoffs* — Left wing								
PEARSON, Rob	Right wing								
1993	Toronto	14	2	2	4	31	0	0	0
1994	Toronto	14	1	0	1	32	0	0	0
1995	Washington	3	1	0	1	17	0	0	1
1996	St. Louis	2	0	0	0	14	0	0	0
Playoff Totals		**33**	**4**	**2**	**6**	**94**	**0**	**0**	**1**
PEARSON, Scott	Left wing								
1990	Toronto	2	2	0	2	10	0	0	0
1993	Quebec	3	0	0	0	0	0	0	0
1995	Buffalo	5	0	0	0	4	0	0	0
Playoff Totals		**10**	**2**	**0**	**2**	**14**	**0**	**0**	**0**
•PEAT, Stephen	*No Playoffs* — Defense								
•PECA, Michael	Center								
1995	Vancouver	5	0	1	1	8	0	0	0
1997	Buffalo	10	0	2	2	8	0	0	0
1998	Buffalo	13	3	2	5	8	0	0	1
1999	Buffalo	21	5	8	13	18	2	1	0
2000	Buffalo	5	0	1	1	4	0	0	0
2002	NY Islanders	5	1	0	1	2	0	0	0
Playoff Totals		**59**	**9**	**14**	**23**	**48**	**2**	**1**	**1**
PEDERSEN, Allen	Defense								
1987	Boston	4	0	0	0	4	0	0	0
1988	Boston	21	0	0	0	34	0	0	0
1989	Boston	10	0	0	0	2	0	0	0
1990	Boston	21	0	0	0	41	0	0	0
1991	Boston	8	0	0	0	10	0	0	0
Playoff Totals		**64**	**0**	**0**	**0**	**91**	**0**	**0**	**0**
PEDERSON, Barry	Center								
1982	Boston	11	7	11	18	2	1	0	2
1983	Boston	17	14	18	32	21	1	1	2
1984	Boston	3	0	1	1	2	0	0	0
1986	Boston	3	1	0	1	0	0	0	0
1991♦	Pittsburgh	....	....	....	....	....	....	....	....
Playoff Totals		**34**	**22**	**30**	**52**	**25**	**2**	**1**	**4**
•PEDERSON, Denis	Center								
1997	New Jersey	9	0	0	0	2	0	0	0
1998	New Jersey	6	1	1	2	2	0	1	0
1999	New Jersey	3	0	1	1	0	0	0	0
2001	Vancouver	4	0	1	1	4	0	0	0
2002	Phoenix	5	0	2	2	0	0	0	0
Playoff Totals		**27**	**1**	**5**	**6**	**8**	**0**	**1**	**0**

Season	Team	GP	G	A	Pts	PIM	PP	SH	GW
PEDERSON, Mark	Left wing								
1990	Montreal	2	0	0	0	0	0	0	0
Playoff Totals		**2**	**0**	**0**	**0**	**0**	**0**	**0**	**0**
PEDERSON, Tom	Defense								
1994	San Jose	14	1	6	7	2	0	1	0
1995	San Jose	10	0	5	5	8	0	0	0
Playoff Totals		**24**	**1**	**11**	**12**	**10**	**0**	**1**	**0**
PEER, Bert *No Playoffs*	Right wing								
PEIRSON, Johnny	Right wing								
1948	Boston	5	3	2	5	0	....	....	....
1949	Boston	5	3	1	4	4	....	....	....
1951	Boston	2	1	1	2	2	....	....	....
1952	Boston	7	0	2	2	4	....	....	....
1953	Boston	11	3	6	9	2	....	....	....
1954	Boston	4	0	0	0	2	....	....	....
1957	Boston	10	0	3	3	12	....	....	....
1958	Boston	5	0	1	1	0	....	....	....
Playoff Totals		**49**	**10**	**16**	**26**	**26**	....	....	....
PELENSKY, Perry *No Playoffs*	Right wing								
•PELLERIN, Scott	Left wing								
1997	St. Louis	6	0	0	0	6	0	0	0
1998	St. Louis	10	0	2	2	10	0	0	0
1999	St. Louis	8	1	0	1	4	0	0	0
2000	St. Louis	7	0	0	0	2	0	0	0
2001	Carolina	6	0	0	0	4	0	0	0
Playoff Totals		**37**	**1**	**2**	**3**	**26**	**0**	**0**	**0**
PELLETIER, Roger *No Playoffs*	Defense								
PELOFFY, Andre *No Playoffs*	Center								
•PELTONEN, Ville *No Playoffs*	Left wing								
PELUSO, Mike	Left wing								
1991	Chicago	3	0	0	0	2	0	0	0
1992	Chicago	17	1	2	3	8	0	0	1
1994	New Jersey	17	1	0	1	*64	0	0	1
1995♦	New Jersey	20	1	2	3	8	0	0	0
1997	St. Louis	5	0	0	0	25	0	0	0
Playoff Totals		**62**	**3**	**4**	**7**	**107**	**0**	**0**	**2**
•PELUSO, Mike *No Playoffs*	Right wing								
PELYK, Mike	Defense								
1969	Toronto	4	0	0	0	8	0	0	0
1971	Toronto	6	0	0	0	10	0	0	0
1972	Toronto	5	0	0	0	8	0	0	0
1974	Toronto	4	0	0	0	4	0	0	0
1977	Toronto	9	0	2	2	4	0	0	0
1978	Toronto	12	0	1	1	7	0	0	0
Playoff Totals		**40**	**0**	**3**	**3**	**41**	**0**	**0**	**0**
PENNEY, Chad *No Playoffs*	Left wing								
PENNINGTON, Cliff *No Playoffs*	Center								
PEPLINSKI, Jim	Right wing								
1981	Calgary	16	2	3	5	41	0	0	0
1982	Calgary	3	1	0	1	13	1	0	0
1983	Calgary	8	1	1	2	45	0	0	0
1984	Calgary	11	3	4	7	21	0	0	0
1985	Calgary	4	1	3	4	11	0	0	0
1986	Calgary	22	5	9	14	107	0	0	0
1987	Calgary	6	1	0	1	24	0	0	0
1988	Calgary	9	0	5	5	45	0	0	0
1989♦	Calgary	20	1	6	7	75	0	0	0
Playoff Totals		**99**	**15**	**31**	**46**	**382**	**1**	**0**	**0**
PERLINI, Fred *No Playoffs*	Center								
PERREAULT, Fern *No Playoffs*	Left wing								
PERREAULT, Gilbert	Center								
1973	Buffalo	6	3	7	10	2	1	0	1
1975	Buffalo	17	6	9	15	10	4	0	1
1976	Buffalo	9	4	4	8	4	0	0	0
1977	Buffalo	6	1	8	9	4	0	0	0
1978	Buffalo	8	3	2	5	0	0	0	1
1979	Buffalo	3	1	0	1	2	1	0	0
1980	Buffalo	14	10	11	21	8	3	0	2
1981	Buffalo	8	2	10	12	2	0	0	0
1982	Buffalo	4	0	7	7	0	0	0	0
1983	Buffalo	10	0	7	7	8	0	0	0
1985	Buffalo	5	3	5	8	4	1	0	0
Playoff Totals		**90**	**33**	**70**	**103**	**44**	**10**	**0**	**5**
•PERREAULT, Yanic	Center								
1998	Los Angeles	4	1	2	3	6	1	0	0
1999	Toronto	17	3	6	9	6	0	0	2
2000	Toronto	1	0	1	1	0	0	0	0
2001	Toronto	11	2	3	5	4	1	0	1
2002	Montreal	11	3	5	8	0	2	0	1
Playoff Totals		**44**	**9**	**17**	**26**	**16**	**4**	**0**	**4**
•PERROTT, Nathan *No Playoffs*	Right wing								
PERRY, Brian	Center								
1969	Oakland	6	1	1	2	4	0	0	0
1970	Oakland	2	0	0	0	0	0	0	0
Playoff Totals		**8**	**1**	**1**	**2**	**4**	**0**	**0**	**0**

Season	Team	GP	G	A	Pts	PIM	PP	SH	GW
•PERSSON, Ricard	Defense								
1997	St. Louis	6	0	0	0	27	0	0	0
1999	St. Louis	13	0	3	3	17	0	0	0
2000	St. Louis	3	1	0	1	0	0	0	0
2001	Ottawa	2	0	0	0	0	0	0	0
2002	Ottawa	2	0	0	0	15	0	0	0
Playoff Totals		**26**	**1**	**3**	**4**	**59**	**0**	**0**	**0**
PERSSON, Stefan	Defense								
1978	NY Islanders	7	0	2	2	6	0	0	0
1979	NY Islanders	10	0	4	4	8	0	0	0
1980♦	NY Islanders	21	5	10	15	16	4	0	0
1981♦	NY Islanders	7	0	5	5	6	0	0	0
1982♦	NY Islanders	13	1	14	15	9	1	0	0
1983♦	NY Islanders	18	1	5	6	18	1	0	0
1984	NY Islanders	16	0	6	6	2	0	0	0
1985	NY Islanders	10	0	4	4	4	0	0	0
Playoff Totals		**102**	**7**	**50**	**57**	**69**	**6**	**0**	**0**
PESUT, George *No Playoffs*	Defense								
PETERS, Frank	Defense								
1931	NY Rangers	4	0	0	0	2	0	0	0
Playoff Totals		**4**	**0**	**0**	**0**	**2**	**0**	**0**	**0**
PETERS, Garry	Center								
1969	Philadelphia	4	1	1	2	16	0	0	1
1971	Philadelphia	4	1	1	2	15	0	0	0
1972♦	Boston	1	0	0	0	0	0	0	0
Playoff Totals		**9**	**2**	**2**	**4**	**31**	**0**	**0**	**1**
PETERS, Jimmy	Right wing								
1946♦	Montreal	9	3	1	4	6	....	....	....
1947	Montreal	11	1	2	3	10	....	....	....
1948	Boston	5	1	2	3	2	....	....	....
1949	Boston	4	0	1	1	0	....	....	....
1950♦	Detroit	8	0	2	2	0	....	....	....
1951	Detroit	6	0	0	0	0	....	....	....
1953	Chicago	7	0	1	1	4	....	....	....
1954♦	Detroit	10	0	0	0	0	....	....	....
Playoff Totals		**60**	**5**	**9**	**14**	**22**	....	....	....
PETERS, Jimmy Jr.	Center								
1969	Los Angeles	11	0	2	2	2	0	0	0
Playoff Totals		**11**	**0**	**2**	**2**	**2**	**0**	**0**	**0**
PETERS, Steve *No Playoffs*	Center								
•PETERSEN, Toby *No Playoffs*	Center								
PETERSON, Brent	Center								
1982	Buffalo	4	1	0	1	12	1	0	0
1983	Buffalo	10	1	2	3	28	0	0	1
1984	Buffalo	3	0	1	1	4	0	0	0
1985	Buffalo	5	0	0	0	6	0	0	0
1986	Vancouver	3	2	0	2	9	1	0	0
1988	Hartford	4	0	0	0	2	0	0	0
1989	Hartford	2	0	1	1	4	0	0	0
Playoff Totals		**31**	**4**	**4**	**8**	**65**	**2**	**0**	**1**
•PETERSON, Brent *No Playoffs*	Left wing								
PETIT, Michel	Defense								
1984	Vancouver	1	0	0	0	0	0	0	0
1989	NY Rangers	4	0	2	2	27	0	0	0
1996	Tampa Bay	6	0	0	0	20	0	0	0
1997	Philadelphia	3	0	0	0	6	0	0	0
1998	Phoenix	5	0	0	0	8	0	0	0
Playoff Totals		**19**	**0**	**2**	**2**	**61**	**0**	**0**	**0**
PETRENKO, Sergei *No Playoffs*	Left wing								
•PETROV, Oleg	Right wing								
1993	Montreal	1	0	0	0	0	0	0	0
1994	Montreal	2	0	0	0	0	0	0	0
1996	Montreal	5	0	1	1	0	0	0	0
2002	Montreal	12	1	5	6	2	0	0	1
Playoff Totals		**20**	**1**	**6**	**7**	**2**	**0**	**0**	**1**
•PETROVICKY, Robert	Center								
1997	St. Louis	2	0	0	0	0	0	0	0
Playoff Totals		**2**	**0**	**0**	**0**	**0**	**0**	**0**	**0**
•PETROVICKY, Ronald *No Playoffs*	Right wing								
PETTERSSON, Jorgen	Left wing								
1981	St. Louis	11	4	3	7	0	1	0	2
1982	St. Louis	7	1	2	3	0	1	0	0
1983	St. Louis	4	1	1	2	0	1	0	0
1984	St. Louis	11	7	3	10	2	2	0	1
1985	St. Louis	3	1	1	2	0	0	0	0
1986	Washington	8	1	2	3	2	1	0	0
Playoff Totals		**44**	**15**	**12**	**27**	**4**	**6**	**0**	**3**
•PETTINEN, Tomi *No Playoffs*	Defense								
PETTINGER, Eric	Left wing/Center								
1929	Toronto	4	1	0	1	8	....	....	....
Playoff Totals		**4**	**1**	**0**	**1**	**8**	....	....	....

Season	Team	GP	G	A	Pts	PIM	PP	SH	GW
PETTINGER, Gord	Center								
1933♦	NY Rangers	8	0	0	0	0	....	....	....
1934	Detroit	7	1	0	1	2	....	....	....
1936♦	Detroit	7	2	2	4	0	....	....	....
1937♦	Detroit	10	0	2	2	2	....	....	....
1938	Boston	3	0	0	0	0	....	....	....
1939♦	Boston	12	1	1	2	7	....	....	....
Playoff Totals		**47**	**4**	**5**	**9**	**11**	....	....	....
•PETTINGER, Matt *No Playoffs*	Left wing								
PHAIR, Lyle	Left wing								
1988	Los Angeles	1	0	0	0	0	0	0	0
Playoff Totals		**1**	**0**	**0**	**0**	**0**	**0**	**0**	**0**
PHILLIPOFF, Harold	Left wing								
1978	Atlanta	2	0	1	1	2	0	0	0
1979	Chicago	4	0	1	1	7	0	0	0
Playoff Totals		**6**	**0**	**2**	**2**	**9**	**0**	**0**	**0**
PHILLIPS, Bill	Center								
1930	Mtl. Maroons	4	0	0	0	2	0	0	0
Playoff Totals		**4**	**0**	**0**	**0**	**2**	**0**	**0**	**0**
PHILLIPS, Charlie *No Playoffs*	Defense								
•PHILLIPS, Chris	Defense								
1998	Ottawa	11	0	2	2	2	0	0	0
1999	Ottawa	3	0	0	0	0	0	0	0
2000	Ottawa	6	0	1	1	4	0	0	0
2001	Ottawa	1	1	0	1	0	0	0	0
2002	Ottawa	12	0	0	0	12	0	0	0
Playoff Totals		**33**	**1**	**3**	**4**	**18**	**0**	**0**	**0**
PHILLIPS, Merlyn	Center								
1926♦	Mtl. Maroons	4	3	0	3	4	....	....	....
1927	Mtl. Maroons	2	0	0	0	0	....	....	....
1928	Mtl. Maroons	9	2	1	3	9	....	....	....
1930	Mtl. Maroons	4	0	0	0	2	....	....	....
1931	Mtl. Maroons	1	0	0	0	2	....	....	....
1932	Mtl. Maroons	4	0	0	0	2	....	....	....
Playoff Totals		**24**	**5**	**1**	**6**	**19**	....	....	....
•PICARD, Michel	Left wing								
1999	St. Louis	5	0	0	0	2	0	0	0
Playoff Totals		**5**	**0**	**0**	**0**	**2**	**0**	**0**	**0**
PICARD, Noel	Defense								
1965♦	Montreal	3	0	1	1	0	0	0	0
1968	St. Louis	13	0	3	3	46	0	0	0
1969	St. Louis	12	1	4	5	30	0	0	0
1970	St. Louis	16	0	2	2	65	0	0	0
1971	St. Louis	6	1	1	2	26	1	0	0
Playoff Totals		**50**	**2**	**11**	**13**	**167**	**1**	**0**	**0**
PICARD, Robert	Defense								
1981	Montreal	1	0	0	0	0	0	0	0
1982	Montreal	5	1	1	2	7	0	0	0
1983	Montreal	3	0	0	0	0	0	0	0
1984	Winnipeg	3	0	0	0	12	0	0	0
1985	Winnipeg	8	2	2	4	8	1	0	0
1986	Quebec	3	0	2	2	2	0	0	0
1987	Quebec	13	2	10	12	10	1	0	0
Playoff Totals		**36**	**5**	**15**	**20**	**39**	**2**	**0**	**0**
PICARD, Roger *No Playoffs*	Right wing								
PICHETTE, Dave	Defense								
1981	Quebec	1	0	0	0	14	0	0	0
1982	Quebec	16	2	4	6	22	1	0	1
1983	Quebec	2	0	1	1	0	0	0	0
1984	St. Louis	9	1	2	3	18	0	0	0
Playoff Totals		**28**	**3**	**7**	**10**	**54**	**1**	**0**	**1**
PICKETTS, Hal *No Playoffs*	Right wing								
PIDHIRNY, Harry *No Playoffs*	Center								
PIERCE, Randy	Right wing								
1978	Colorado	2	0	0	0	0	0	0	0
Playoff Totals		**2**	**0**	**0**	**0**	**0**	**0**	**0**	**0**
PIKE, Alf	Left wing/Center								
1940♦	NY Rangers	12	3	1	4	6	....	....	....
1941	NY Rangers	3	0	1	1	2	....	....	....
1942	NY Rangers	6	1	0	1	4	....	....	....
Playoff Totals		**21**	**4**	**2**	**6**	**12**	....	....	....
•PILAR, Karel	Defense								
2002	Toronto	11	0	4	4	12	0	0	0
Playoff Totals		**11**	**0**	**4**	**4**	**12**	**0**	**0**	**0**
•PILON, Rich	Defense								
1993	NY Islanders	15	0	0	0	50	0	0	0
Playoff Totals		**15**	**0**	**0**	**0**	**50**	**0**	**0**	**0**

Season	Team	GP	G	A	Pts	PIM	PP	SH	GW
PILOTE, Pierre									Defense
1959	Chicago	6	0	2	2	10	0	0	0
1960	Chicago	4	0	1	1	8	0	0	0
1961♦	Chicago	12	3	*12	*15	8	1	0	0
1962	Chicago	12	0	7	7	8	0	0	0
1963	Chicago	6	0	8	8	8	0	0	0
1964	Chicago	7	2	6	8	6	0	0	1
1965	Chicago	12	0	7	7	22	0	0	0
1966	Chicago	6	0	2	2	10	0	0	0
1967	Chicago	6	2	4	6	6	0	0	0
1968	Chicago	11	1	3	4	12	1	0	0
1969	Toronto	4	0	1	1	4	0	0	0
Playoff Totals		**86**	**8**	**53**	**61**	**102**	**2**	**0**	**1**
PINDER, Gerry									Left wing
1970	Chicago	8	0	4	4	4	0	0	0
1971	Chicago	9	0	0	0	2	0	0	0
Playoff Totals		**17**	**0**	**4**	**4**	**6**	**0**	**0**	**0**
•PIRJETA, Lasse	*No Playoffs*								Center
•PIROS, Kamil	*No Playoffs*								Center
PIRUS, Alex									Right wing
1977	Minnesota	2	0	1	1	2	0	0	0
Playoff Totals		**2**	**0**	**1**	**1**	**2**	**0**	**0**	**0**
•PISA, Ales	*No Playoffs*								Defense
•PISANI, Fernando	*No Playoffs*								Center/Left wing
•PITLICK, Lance									Defense
1997	Ottawa	7	0	0	0	4	0	0	0
1998	Ottawa	11	0	1	1	17	0	0	0
1999	Ottawa	2	0	0	0	0	0	0	0
2000	Florida	4	0	1	1	0	0	0	0
Playoff Totals		**24**	**0**	**2**	**2**	**21**	**0**	**0**	**0**
PITRE, Didier									Right wing/Defense
1918	Montreal	2	0	1	1	13	....	....	....
1919	Montreal	5	2	*3	5	3	....	....	....
1923	Montreal	2	0	0	0	0	....	....	....
Playoff Totals		**9**	**2**	**4**	**6**	**16**	....	....	....
•PITTIS, Domenic									Center
2001	Edmonton	3	0	0	0	2	0	0	0
Playoff Totals		**3**	**0**	**0**	**0**	**2**	**0**	**0**	**0**
PIVONKA, Michal									Center
1987	Washington	7	1	1	2	2	0	0	0
1988	Washington	14	4	9	13	4	2	0	0
1989	Washington	6	3	1	4	10	0	1	0
1990	Washington	11	0	2	2	6	0	0	0
1991	Washington	11	2	3	5	8	0	0	0
1992	Washington	7	1	5	6	13	1	0	1
1993	Washington	6	0	2	2	0	0	0	0
1994	Washington	7	4	4	8	4	1	0	0
1995	Washington	7	1	4	5	21	0	0	0
1996	Washington	6	3	2	5	18	1	0	0
1998	Washington	13	0	3	3	0	0	0	0
Playoff Totals		**95**	**19**	**36**	**55**	**86**	**5**	**1**	**1**
PLAGER, Barclay									Defense
1968	St. Louis	18	2	5	7	*73	0	1	0
1969	St. Louis	12	0	4	4	31	0	0	0
1970	St. Louis	13	0	2	2	20	0	0	0
1971	St. Louis	6	0	3	3	10	0	0	0
1972	St. Louis	11	1	4	5	21	1	0	1
1973	St. Louis	5	0	1	1	0	0	0	0
1975	St. Louis	2	0	1	1	14	0	0	0
1976	St. Louis	1	0	0	0	13	0	0	0
Playoff Totals		**68**	**3**	**20**	**23**	**182**	**1**	**1**	**1**
PLAGER, Bill									Defense
1968	Minnesota	12	0	2	2	8	0	0	0
1969	St. Louis	4	0	0	0	4	0	0	0
1970	St. Louis	3	0	0	0	0	0	0	0
1971	St. Louis	1	0	0	0	2	0	0	0
1972	St. Louis	11	0	0	0	12	0	0	0
Playoff Totals		**31**	**0**	**2**	**2**	**26**	**0**	**0**	**0**
PLAGER, Bob									Defense
1968	St. Louis	18	1	2	3	69	0	0	0
1969	St. Louis	9	0	4	4	47	0	0	0
1970	St. Louis	16	0	3	3	46	0	0	0
1971	St. Louis	6	0	2	2	4	0	0	0
1972	St. Louis	11	1	4	5	5	0	0	0
1973	St. Louis	5	0	2	2	2	0	0	0
1975	St. Louis	2	0	0	0	20	0	0	0
1976	St. Louis	3	0	0	0	2	0	0	0
1977	St. Louis	4	0	0	0	0	0	0	0
Playoff Totals		**74**	**2**	**17**	**19**	**195**	**0**	**0**	**0**
PLAMONDON, Gerry									Left wing
1946♦	Montreal	1	0	0	0	0	....	....	....
1949	Montreal	7	5	1	6	0	....	....	....
1950	Montreal	3	0	1	1	2	....	....	....
Playoff Totals		**11**	**5**	**2**	**7**	**2**	....	....	....
PLANTE, Cam	*No Playoffs*								Defense
•PLANTE, Dan									Right wing
1994	NY Islanders	1	1	0	1	2	0	0	0
Playoff Totals		**1**	**1**	**0**	**1**	**2**	**0**	**0**	**0**

Season	Team	GP	G	A	Pts	PIM	PP	SH	GW
•PLANTE, Derek									Center
1994	Buffalo	7	1	0	1	0	0	0	0
1997	Buffalo	12	4	6	10	4	1	0	2
1998	Buffalo	11	0	3	3	10	0	0	0
1999♦	Dallas	6	1	0	1	4	0	0	0
2001	Philadelphia	5	0	1	1	0	0	0	0
Playoff Totals		**41**	**6**	**10**	**16**	**18**	**1**	**0**	**2**
PLANTE, Pierre									Right wing
1973	St. Louis	5	2	0	2	15	0	0	0
1975	St. Louis	2	0	0	0	8	0	0	0
1976	St. Louis	3	0	0	0	6	0	0	0
1977	St. Louis	4	0	0	0	2	0	0	0
1978	Chicago	1	0	0	0	0	0	0	0
1979	NY Rangers	18	0	6	6	20	0	0	0
Playoff Totals		**33**	**2**	**6**	**8**	**51**	**0**	**0**	**0**
PLANTERY, Mark	*No Playoffs*								Defense
PLAVSIC, Adrien									Defense
1992	Vancouver	13	1	7	8	4	0	0	0
Playoff Totals		**13**	**1**	**7**	**8**	**4**	**0**	**0**	**0**
PLAXTON, Hugh	*No Playoffs*								Left wing
PLAYFAIR, Jim	*No Playoffs*								Defense
PLAYFAIR, Larry									Defense
1980	Buffalo	14	0	2	2	29	0	0	0
1981	Buffalo	8	0	0	0	26	0	0	0
1982	Buffalo	4	0	0	0	22	0	0	0
1983	Buffalo	5	0	1	1	11	0	0	0
1984	Buffalo	3	0	0	0	0	0	0	0
1985	Buffalo	5	0	3	3	9	0	0	0
1988	Los Angeles	3	0	0	0	14	0	0	0
1989	Buffalo	1	0	0	0	0	0	0	0
Playoff Totals		**43**	**0**	**6**	**6**	**111**	**0**	**0**	**0**
PLEAU, Larry									Center
1972	Montreal	4	0	0	0	0	0	0	0
Playoff Totals		**4**	**0**	**0**	**0**	**0**	**0**	**0**	**0**
•PLETKA, Vaclav	*No Playoffs*								Right wing
PLETSCH, Charles	*No Playoffs*								Defense
PLETT, Willi									Right wing
1977	Atlanta	3	1	0	1	19	0	0	0
1979	Atlanta	2	1	0	1	29	0	0	0
1980	Atlanta	4	1	0	1	15	1	0	0
1981	Calgary	15	8	4	12	89	5	0	3
1982	Calgary	3	1	2	3	39	1	0	0
1983	Minnesota	9	1	3	4	38	0	0	0
1984	Minnesota	16	6	2	8	51	1	0	0
1985	Minnesota	9	3	6	9	67	1	0	0
1986	Minnesota	5	0	1	1	45	0	0	0
1988	Boston	17	2	4	6	74	0	0	1
Playoff Totals		**83**	**24**	**22**	**46**	**466**	**9**	**0**	**4**
PLUMB, Rob	*No Playoffs*								Left wing
PLUMB, Ron	*No Playoffs*								Defense
•POAPST, Steve									Defense
1996	Washington	6	0	0	0	0	0	0	0
2002	Chicago	5	0	0	0	0	0	0	0
Playoff Totals		**11**	**0**	**0**	**0**	**0**	**0**	**0**	**0**
POCZA, Harvie	*No Playoffs*								Left wing
PODDUBNY, Walt									Left wing
1983	Toronto	4	3	1	4	0	2	0	1
1986	Toronto	9	4	1	5	4	0	0	3
1987	NY Rangers	6	0	0	0	8	0	0	0
Playoff Totals		**19**	**7**	**2**	**9**	**12**	**2**	**0**	**4**
•PODEIN, Shjon									Left wing
1995	Philadelphia	15	1	3	4	10	0	0	0
1996	Philadelphia	12	1	2	3	50	0	0	1
1997	Philadelphia	19	4	3	7	16	0	0	1
1998	Philadelphia	5	0	0	0	10	0	0	0
1999	Colorado	19	1	1	2	12	0	0	0
2000	Colorado	17	5	0	5	8	0	0	1
2001♦	Colorado	23	2	3	5	14	0	0	1
2002	St. Louis	10	0	0	0	6	0	0	0
Playoff Totals		**120**	**14**	**12**	**26**	**126**	**0**	**0**	**4**
•PODKONICKY, Andrej	*No Playoffs*								Center
PODLOSKI, Ray	*No Playoffs*								Center
•PODOLLAN, Jason	*No Playoffs*								Right wing
PODOLSKY, Nels									Left wing
1949	Detroit	7	0	0	0	4	0	0	0
Playoff Totals		**7**	**0**	**0**	**0**	**4**	**0**	**0**	**0**
POESCHEK, Rudy									Right wing/Defense
1996	Tampa Bay	3	0	0	0	12	0	0	0
1998	St. Louis	2	0	0	0	6	0	0	0
Playoff Totals		**5**	**0**	**0**	**0**	**18**	**0**	**0**	**0**
POETA, Tony	*No Playoffs*								Right wing
POILE, Bud									Right wing
1943	Toronto	6	2	4	6	4	....	....	....
1947♦	Toronto	7	2	0	2	2	....	....	....
1949	Detroit	10	0	1	1	2	....	....	....
Playoff Totals		**23**	**4**	**5**	**9**	**8**	....	....	....

Season	Team	GP	G	A	Pts	PIM	PP	SH	GW
POILE, Don									Center
1958	Detroit	4	0	0	0	0	0	0	0
Playoff Totals		**4**	**0**	**0**	**0**	**0**	**0**	**0**	**0**
POIRER, Gordie	*No Playoffs*								Center
POLANIC, Tom									Defense
1970	Minnesota	5	1	1	2	4	0	0	0
Playoff Totals		**5**	**1**	**1**	**2**	**4**	**0**	**0**	**0**
POLICH, John	*No Playoffs*								Right wing
POLICH, Mike									Center/Left wing
1977♦	Montreal	5	0	0	0	0	0	0	0
1980	Minnesota	15	2	1	3	2	0	0	0
1981	Minnesota	3	0	0	0	0	0	0	0
Playoff Totals		**23**	**2**	**1**	**3**	**2**	**0**	**0**	**0**
POLIS, Greg									Left wing
1972	Pittsburgh	4	0	2	2	0	0	0	0
1975	NY Rangers	3	0	0	0	6	0	0	0
Playoff Totals		**7**	**0**	**2**	**2**	**6**	**0**	**0**	**0**
POLIZIANI, Dan									Right wing
1959	Boston	3	0	0	0	0	0	0	0
Playoff Totals		**3**	**0**	**0**	**0**	**0**	**0**	**0**	**0**
POLONICH, Dennis									Center/Right wing
1978	Detroit	7	1	0	1	19	0	0	0
Playoff Totals		**7**	**1**	**0**	**1**	**19**	**0**	**0**	**0**
•PONIKAROVSKY, Alexei									Right wing
2002	Toronto	10	0	0	0	4	0	0	0
Playoff Totals		**10**	**0**	**0**	**0**	**4**	**0**	**0**	**0**
POOLEY, Paul	*No Playoffs*								Center
POPEIN, Larry									Center
1956	NY Rangers	5	0	1	1	2	0	0	0
1957	NY Rangers	5	0	3	3	0	0	0	0
1958	NY Rangers	6	1	0	1	4	0	0	0
Playoff Totals		**16**	**1**	**4**	**5**	**6**	**0**	**0**	**0**
POPIEL, Poul									Defense
1968	Los Angeles	3	1	0	1	4	0	0	0
1970	Detroit	1	0	0	0	0	0	0	0
Playoff Totals		**4**	**1**	**0**	**1**	**4**	**0**	**0**	**0**
•POPOVIC, Peter									Defense
1994	Montreal	6	0	1	1	0	0	0	0
1996	Montreal	6	0	2	2	4	0	0	0
1997	Montreal	3	0	0	0	2	0	0	0
1998	Montreal	10	1	1	2	2	0	0	0
2000	Pittsburgh	10	0	0	0	10	0	0	0
Playoff Totals		**35**	**1**	**4**	**5**	**18**	**0**	**0**	**0**
PORTLAND, Jack									Defense
1934	Montreal	2	0	0	0	0	....	....	....
1937	Boston	3	0	0	0	4	....	....	....
1938	Boston	3	0	0	0	4	....	....	....
1939♦	Boston	12	0	0	0	11	....	....	....
1940	Chicago	2	0	0	0	2	....	....	....
1941	Montreal	3	0	1	1	2	....	....	....
1942	Montreal	3	0	0	0	0	....	....	....
1943	Montreal	5	1	2	3	2	....	....	....
Playoff Totals		**33**	**1**	**3**	**4**	**25**	....	....	....
PORVARI, Jukka	*No Playoffs*								Right wing
POSA, Victor	*No Playoffs*								Left wing/Defense
POSAVAD, Mike	*No Playoffs*								Defense
•POSMYK, Marek	*No Playoffs*								Defense
•POTHIER, Brian	*No Playoffs*								Defense
•POTI, Tom									Defense
1999	Edmonton	4	0	1	1	2	0	0	0
2000	Edmonton	5	0	1	1	0	0	0	0
2001	Edmonton	6	0	2	2	2	0	0	0
Playoff Totals		**15**	**0**	**4**	**4**	**4**	**0**	**0**	**0**
POTOMSKI, Barry	*No Playoffs*								Left wing
POTVIN, Denis									Defense
1975	NY Islanders	17	5	9	14	30	3	1	0
1976	NY Islanders	13	5	*14	19	32	2	0	1
1977	NY Islanders	12	6	4	10	20	2	0	0
1978	NY Islanders	7	2	2	4	6	0	0	0
1979	NY Islanders	10	4	7	11	8	0	0	1
1980♦	NY Islanders	21	6	13	19	24	4	0	1
1981♦	NY Islanders	18	8	17	25	16	6	1	2
1982♦	NY Islanders	19	5	16	21	30	3	0	0
1983♦	NY Islanders	20	8	12	20	22	4	0	1
1984	NY Islanders	20	1	5	6	28	1	0	0
1985	NY Islanders	10	3	2	5	10	1	0	1
1986	NY Islanders	3	0	1	1	0	0	0	0
1987	NY Islanders	10	2	2	4	21	1	0	0
1988	NY Islanders	5	1	4	5	6	1	0	0
Playoff Totals		**185**	**56**	**108**	**164**	**253**	**28**	**2**	**7**
POTVIN, Jean									Defense
1975	NY Islanders	15	2	4	6	9	0	0	0
1976	NY Islanders	13	0	1	1	2	0	0	0
1977	NY Islanders	11	0	4	4	6	0	0	0
1980♦	NY Islanders	....	....	....	....	....	....	....	....
Playoff Totals		**39**	**2**	**9**	**11**	**17**	**0**	**0**	**0**

Season	Team	GP	G	A	Pts	PIM	PP	SH	GW
POTVIN, Marc									Right wing
1991	Detroit	6	0	0	0	32	0	0	0
1992	Detroit	1	0	0	0	0	0	0	0
1993	Los Angeles	1	0	0	0	0	0	0	0
1996	Boston	5	0	1	1	18	0	0	0
Playoff Totals		**13**	**0**	**1**	**1**	**50**	**0**	**0**	**0**
POUDRIER, Daniel *No Playoffs*									Defense
POULIN, Daniel *No Playoffs*									Defense
POULIN, Dave									Center
1983	Philadelphia	3	1	3	4	9	0	0	0
1984	Philadelphia	3	0	0	0	2	0	0	0
1985	Philadelphia	11	3	5	8	6	0	2	0
1986	Philadelphia	5	2	0	2	2	1	0	0
1987	Philadelphia	15	3	3	6	14	1	1	0
1988	Philadelphia	7	2	6	8	4	1	0	1
1989	Philadelphia	19	6	5	11	16	0	2	2
1990	Boston	18	8	5	13	8	2	0	2
1991	Boston	16	0	9	9	20	0	0	0
1992	Boston	15	3	3	6	22	1	0	1
1993	Boston	4	1	1	2	10	0	1	0
1994	Washington	11	2	2	4	19	0	0	0
1995	Washington	2	0	0	0	0	0	0	0
Playoff Totals		**129**	**31**	**42**	**73**	**132**	**6**	**6**	**6**
•POULIN, Patrick									Center
1992	Hartford	7	2	1	3	0	1	0	0
1994	Chicago	4	0	0	0	0	0	0	0
1995	Chicago	16	4	1	5	8	1	0	0
1996	Tampa Bay	2	0	0	0	0	0	0	0
1998	Montreal	3	0	0	0	0	0	0	0
Playoff Totals		**32**	**6**	**2**	**8**	**8**	**2**	**0**	**0**
POUZAR, Jaroslav									Left wing
1983	Edmonton	1	2	0	2	0	1	0	1
1984♦	Edmonton	14	1	2	3	12	0	0	1
1985♦	Edmonton	9	2	1	3	2	0	0	0
1987♦	Edmonton	5	1	1	2	2	0	0	0
Playoff Totals		**29**	**6**	**4**	**10**	**16**	**1**	**0**	**2**
POWELL, Ray *No Playoffs*									Center
POWIS, Geoff *No Playoffs*									Center
POWIS, Lynn									Center
1974	Chicago	1	0	0	0	0	0	0	0
Playoff Totals		**1**	**0**	**0**	**0**	**0**	**0**	**0**	**0**
PRAJSLER, Petr									Defense
1989	Los Angeles	1	0	0	0	0	0	0	0
1990	Los Angeles	3	0	0	0	0	0	0	0
Playoff Totals		**4**	**0**	**0**	**0**	**0**	**0**	**0**	**0**
PRATT, Babe									Defense
1937	NY Rangers	9	3	1	4	11	....	....	....
1938	NY Rangers	2	0	0	0	2	....	....	....
1939	NY Rangers	7	1	2	3	9	....	....	....
1940♦	NY Rangers	12	3	1	4	18	....	....	....
1941	NY Rangers	3	1	1	2	6	....	....	....
1942	NY Rangers	6	1	3	4	24	....	....	....
1943	Toronto	6	1	2	3	8	....	....	....
1944	Toronto	5	0	3	3	4	....	....	....
1945♦	Toronto	13	2	4	6	8	....	....	....
Playoff Totals		**63**	**12**	**17**	**29**	**90**	....	....	....
PRATT, Jack									Center/Defense
1931	Boston	4	0	0	0	0	0	0	0
Playoff Totals		**4**	**0**	**0**	**0**	**0**	**0**	**0**	**0**
PRATT, Kelly *No Playoffs*									Right wing
•PRATT, Nolan									Defense
1999	Carolina	3	0	0	0	2	0	0	0
Playoff Totals		**3**	**0**	**0**	**0**	**2**	**0**	**0**	**0**
PRATT, Tracy									Defense
1970	Pittsburgh	10	0	1	1	51	0	0	0
1973	Buffalo	6	0	0	0	6	0	0	0
1975	Vancouver	3	0	0	0	5	0	0	0
1976	Vancouver	2	0	0	0	0	0	0	0
1977	Toronto	4	0	0	0	0	0	0	0
Playoff Totals		**25**	**0**	**1**	**1**	**62**	**0**	**0**	**0**
PRENTICE, Dean									Left wing
1956	NY Rangers	5	1	0	1	2	0	0	0
1957	NY Rangers	5	0	2	2	4	0	0	0
1958	NY Rangers	6	1	3	4	4	0	0	0
1962	NY Rangers	3	0	2	2	0	0	0	0
1966	Detroit	12	5	5	10	4	2	0	0
1970	Pittsburgh	10	2	5	7	8	1	0	0
1972	Minnesota	7	3	0	3	0	0	0	1
1973	Minnesota	6	1	0	1	16	1	0	0
Playoff Totals		**54**	**13**	**17**	**30**	**38**	**4**	**0**	**1**
PRENTICE, Eric *No Playoffs*									Left wing

Season	Team	GP	G	A	Pts	PIM	PP	SH	GW
PRESLEY, Wayne									Right wing
1986	Chicago	3	0	0	0	0	0	0	0
1987	Chicago	4	1	0	1	9	0	0	0
1988	Chicago	5	0	0	0	4	0	0	0
1989	Chicago	14	7	5	12	18	1	3	1
1990	Chicago	19	9	6	15	29	1	1	1
1991	Chicago	6	0	1	1	38	0	0	0
1992	Buffalo	7	3	3	6	14	0	0	0
1993	Buffalo	8	1	0	1	6	0	1	1
1994	Buffalo	7	2	1	3	14	1	0	1
1995	Buffalo	5	3	1	4	8	0	1	1
1996	Toronto	5	0	0	0	2	0	0	0
Playoff Totals		**83**	**26**	**17**	**43**	**142**	**3**	**6**	**5**
PRESTON, Rich									Right wing
1980	Chicago	7	0	3	3	2	0	0	0
1981	Chicago	3	0	1	1	0	0	0	0
1982	Chicago	15	2	4	6	21	0	0	0
1983	Chicago	13	2	7	9	25	0	0	1
1984	Chicago	5	0	1	1	4	0	0	0
1987	Chicago	4	0	2	2	4	0	0	0
Playoff Totals		**47**	**4**	**18**	**22**	**56**	**0**	**0**	**1**
PRESTON, Yves *No Playoffs*									Left wing
PRIAKIN, Sergei									Right wing
1989	Calgary	1	0	0	0	0	0	0	0
Playoff Totals		**1**	**0**	**0**	**0**	**0**	**0**	**0**	**0**
PRICE, Jack									Defense
1953	Chicago	4	0	0	0	0	0	0	0
Playoff Totals		**4**	**0**	**0**	**0**	**0**	**0**	**0**	**0**
PRICE, Noel									Defense
1959	Toronto	5	0	0	0	2	0	0	0
1966♦	Montreal	3	0	1	1	0	0	0	0
1974	Atlanta	4	0	0	0	6	0	0	0
Playoff Totals		**12**	**0**	**1**	**1**	**8**	**0**	**0**	**0**
PRICE, Pat									Defense
1977	NY Islanders	10	0	1	1	2	0	0	0
1978	NY Islanders	5	0	1	1	2	0	0	0
1979	NY Islanders	7	0	1	1	25	0	0	0
1980	Edmonton	3	0	0	0	11	0	0	0
1981	Pittsburgh	5	1	1	2	21	0	0	0
1982	Pittsburgh	5	0	0	0	28	0	0	0
1983	Quebec	4	0	0	0	14	0	0	0
1984	Quebec	9	1	0	1	10	0	0	0
1985	Quebec	17	0	4	4	51	0	0	0
1986	Quebec	3	0	1	1	4	0	0	0
1987	NY Rangers	6	0	1	1	27	0	0	0
Playoff Totals		**74**	**2**	**10**	**12**	**195**	**0**	**0**	**0**
PRICE, Tom *No Playoffs*									Defense
PRIESTLAY, Ken									Center
1988	Buffalo	6	0	0	0	11	0	0	0
1989	Buffalo	3	0	0	0	2	0	0	0
1990	Buffalo	5	0	0	0	8	0	0	0
1992♦	Pittsburgh	....	....	....	....	....	....	....	....
Playoff Totals		**14**	**0**	**0**	**0**	**21**	**0**	**0**	**0**
PRIMEAU, Joe									Center
1931	Toronto	2	0	0	0	0	....	....	....
1932♦	Toronto	7	0	*6	6	2	....	....	....
1933	Toronto	8	0	1	1	4	....	....	....
1934	Toronto	5	2	4	6	6	....	....	....
1935	Toronto	7	0	3	3	0	....	....	....
1936	Toronto	9	3	4	7	0	....	....	....
Playoff Totals		**38**	**5**	**18**	**23**	**12**	....	....	....
•PRIMEAU, Keith									Center
1991	Detroit	5	1	1	2	25	0	0	0
1992	Detroit	11	0	0	0	14	0	0	0
1993	Detroit	7	0	2	2	26	0	0	0
1994	Detroit	7	0	2	2	6	0	0	0
1995	Detroit	17	4	5	9	45	2	0	0
1996	Detroit	17	1	4	5	28	0	0	0
1999	Carolina	6	0	3	3	6	0	0	0
2000	Philadelphia	18	2	11	13	13	0	0	1
2001	Philadelphia	4	0	3	3	8	0	0	0
2002	Philadelphia	5	0	0	0	6	0	0	0
Playoff Totals		**97**	**8**	**31**	**39**	**177**	**2**	**0**	**1**
PRIMEAU, Kevin *No Playoffs*									Right wing
•PRIMEAU, Wayne									Center
1997	Buffalo	9	0	0	0	6	0	0	0
1998	Buffalo	14	1	3	4	6	0	0	0
1999	Buffalo	19	3	4	7	6	1	0	0
2001	Pittsburgh	18	1	3	4	2	0	0	0
Playoff Totals		**60**	**5**	**10**	**15**	**20**	**1**	**0**	**0**
PRINGLE, Ellie *No Playoffs*									Defense

Season	Team	GP	G	A	Pts	PIM	PP	SH	GW
•PROBERT, Bob									Left wing
1987	Detroit	16	3	4	7	63	1	0	1
1988	Detroit	16	8	13	21	51	5	0	1
1991	Detroit	6	1	2	3	50	0	0	0
1992	Detroit	11	1	6	7	28	0	0	0
1993	Detroit	7	0	3	3	10	0	0	0
1994	Detroit	7	1	1	2	8	0	0	0
1996	Chicago	10	0	2	2	23	0	0	0
1997	Chicago	6	2	1	3	41	0	0	0
2002	Chicago	2	0	0	0	0	0	0	0
Playoff Totals		**81**	**16**	**32**	**48**	**274**	**6**	**0**	**2**
•PROCHAZKA, Martin *No Playoffs*									Right wing
PRODGERS, Goldie *No Playoffs*									Forward/defense
PROKHOROV, Vitali									Left wing
1994	St. Louis	4	0	0	0	0	0	0	0
Playoff Totals		**4**	**0**	**0**	**0**	**0**	**0**	**0**	**0**
PROKOPEC, Mike *No Playoffs*									Right wing
•PRONGER, Chris									Defense
1996	St. Louis	13	1	5	6	16	0	0	0
1997	St. Louis	6	1	1	2	22	0	0	0
1998	St. Louis	10	1	9	10	26	0	0	0
1999	St. Louis	13	1	4	5	28	1	0	0
2000	St. Louis	7	3	4	7	32	2	0	2
2001	St. Louis	15	1	7	8	32	0	0	0
2002	St. Louis	9	1	7	8	24	0	0	0
Playoff Totals		**73**	**9**	**37**	**46**	**180**	**3**	**0**	**2**
•PRONGER, Sean									Center
1997	Anaheim	9	0	2	2	4	0	0	0
1998	Pittsburgh	5	0	0	0	4	0	0	0
Playoff Totals		**14**	**0**	**2**	**2**	**8**	**0**	**0**	**0**
PRONOVOST, Andre									Left wing
1957♦	Montreal	8	1	0	1	4	....	....	....
1958♦	Montreal	10	2	0	2	16	....	....	....
1959♦	Montreal	11	2	1	3	6	....	....	....
1960♦	Montreal	8	1	2	3	0	....	....	....
1963	Detroit	11	1	4	5	6	....	....	....
1964	Detroit	14	4	3	7	26	....	....	....
1968	Minnesota	8	0	1	1	0	0	0	0
Playoff Totals		**70**	**11**	**11**	**22**	**58**	**0**	**0**	**0**
PRONOVOST, Jean									Right wing
1970	Pittsburgh	10	3	4	7	2	1	1	0
1972	Pittsburgh	4	1	1	2	0	0	1	0
1975	Pittsburgh	9	3	3	6	6	0	0	0
1976	Pittsburgh	3	0	0	0	2	0	0	0
1977	Pittsburgh	3	2	1	3	2	1	0	0
1979	Atlanta	2	2	0	2	0	1	0	0
1980	Atlanta	4	0	0	0	2	0	0	0
Playoff Totals		**35**	**11**	**9**	**20**	**14**	**3**	**2**	**0**
PRONOVOST, Marcel									Defense
1950♦	Detroit	9	0	1	1	10	....	....	....
1951	Detroit	6	0	0	0	0	....	....	....
1952♦	Detroit	8	0	1	1	10	....	....	....
1953	Detroit	6	0	0	0	6	....	....	....
1954♦	Detroit	12	2	3	5	12	....	....	....
1955♦	Detroit	11	1	2	3	6	....	....	....
1956	Detroit	10	0	2	2	8	....	....	....
1957	Detroit	5	0	0	0	6	....	....	....
1958	Detroit	4	0	1	1	4	....	....	....
1960	Detroit	6	1	1	2	2	....	....	....
1961	Detroit	9	2	3	5	0	....	....	....
1963	Detroit	11	1	4	5	8	....	....	....
1964	Detroit	14	0	2	2	14	....	....	....
1965	Detroit	7	0	3	3	4	....	....	....
1966	Toronto	4	0	0	0	6	....	....	....
1967♦	Toronto	12	1	0	1	8	....	....	....
Playoff Totals		**134**	**8**	**23**	**31**	**104**	....	....	....
PROPP, Brian									Left wing
1980	Philadelphia	19	5	10	15	29	3	0	0
1981	Philadelphia	12	6	6	12	32	0	0	0
1982	Philadelphia	4	2	2	4	4	0	0	1
1983	Philadelphia	3	1	2	3	8	1	0	0
1984	Philadelphia	3	0	1	1	6	0	0	0
1985	Philadelphia	19	8	10	18	6	4	1	2
1986	Philadelphia	5	0	2	2	4	0	0	0
1987	Philadelphia	26	12	16	28	10	5	1	3
1988	Philadelphia	7	4	2	6	8	0	0	0
1989	Philadelphia	18	14	9	23	14	5	1	1
1990	Boston	20	4	9	13	2	1	0	2
1991	Minnesota	23	8	15	23	28	8	0	3
1992	Minnesota	1	0	0	0	0	0	0	0
Playoff Totals		**160**	**64**	**84**	**148**	**151**	**27**	**3**	**12**
•PROSPAL, Vaclav									Center
1997	Philadelphia	5	1	3	4	4	0	0	0
1998	Ottawa	6	0	0	0	0	0	0	0
1999	Ottawa	4	0	0	0	0	0	0	0
2000	Ottawa	6	0	4	4	4	0	0	0
Playoff Totals		**21**	**1**	**7**	**8**	**8**	**0**	**0**	**0**
PROULX, Christian *No Playoffs*									Defense

Season	Team	GP	G	A	Pts	PIM	PP	SH	GW
PROVOST, Claude									Right wing
1956♦	Montreal	10	3	3	6	12	....	....	....
1957♦	Montreal	10	0	1	1	8	....	....	....
1958♦	Montreal	10	1	3	4	8	....	....	....
1959♦	Montreal	11	6	2	8	2	....	....	....
1960♦	Montreal	8	1	1	2	0	....	....	....
1961	Montreal	6	1	3	4	4	....	....	....
1962	Montreal	6	2	2	4	2	....	....	....
1963	Montreal	5	0	1	1	2	....	....	....
1964	Montreal	7	2	2	4	22	....	....	....
1965♦	Montreal	13	2	6	8	12	....	....	....
1966♦	Montreal	10	2	3	5	2	....	....	....
1967	Montreal	7	1	1	2	0	....	....	....
1968♦	Montreal	13	2	8	10	10	1	0	1
1969♦	Montreal	10	2	2	4	2	0	0	0
Playoff Totals		**126**	**25**	**38**	**63**	**86**	**1**	**0**	**1**
•PRPIC, Joel *No Playoffs*									Center
PRYOR, Chris *No Playoffs*									Defense
PRYSTAI, Metro									Center
1951	Detroit	3	1	0	1	0	....	....	....
1952♦	Detroit	8	2	*5	*7	0	....	....	....
1953	Detroit	6	4	4	8	2	....	....	....
1954♦	Detroit	12	2	3	5	0	....	....	....
1956	Detroit	9	1	2	3	6	....	....	....
1957	Detroit	5	2	0	2	0	....	....	....
Playoff Totals		**43**	**12**	**14**	**26**	**8**	....	....	....
PUDAS, Al *No Playoffs*									Wing
PULFORD, Bob									Left wing
1959	Toronto	12	4	4	8	8	....	....	....
1960	Toronto	10	4	1	5	10	....	....	....
1961	Toronto	5	0	0	0	8	....	....	....
1962♦	Toronto	12	7	1	8	24	....	....	....
1963♦	Toronto	10	2	5	7	14	....	....	....
1964♦	Toronto	14	5	3	8	20	....	....	....
1965	Toronto	6	1	1	2	16	....	....	....
1966	Toronto	4	1	1	2	12	....	....	....
1967♦	Toronto	12	1	*10	11	12	....	....	....
1969	Toronto	4	0	0	0	2	0	0	0
Playoff Totals		**89**	**25**	**26**	**51**	**126**	**0**	**0**	**0**
PULKKINEN, Dave *No Playoffs*									Left wing/Defense
•PURINTON, Dale *No Playoffs*									Defense
PURPUR, Fido									Right wing
1944	Chicago	9	1	1	2	0	....	....	....
1945	Detroit	7	0	1	1	4	....	....	....
Playoff Totals		**16**	**1**	**2**	**3**	**4**	....	....	....
PURVES, John *No Playoffs*									Right wing
•PUSHOR, Jamie									Defense
1997♦	Detroit	5	0	1	1	5	0	0	0
1999	Anaheim	4	0	0	0	6	0	0	0
2000	Dallas	5	0	0	0	5	0	0	0
Playoff Totals		**14**	**0**	**1**	**1**	**16**	**0**	**0**	**0**
PUSIE, Jean									Defense
1931♦	Montreal	3	0	0	0	0	0	0	0
1935	Boston	4	0	0	0	0	0	0	0
Playoff Totals		**7**	**0**	**0**	**0**	**0**	**0**	**0**	**0**
PYATT, Nelson *No Playoffs*									Center
•PYATT, Taylor *No Playoffs*									Left wing
QUACKENBUSH, Bill									Defense
1944	Detroit	2	1	0	1	0	....	....	....
1945	Detroit	14	0	2	2	2	....	....	....
1946	Detroit	5	0	1	1	0	....	....	....
1947	Detroit	5	0	0	0	2	....	....	....
1948	Detroit	10	0	2	2	0	....	....	....
1949	Detroit	11	1	1	2	0	....	....	....
1951	Boston	6	0	1	1	0	....	....	....
1952	Boston	7	0	3	3	0	....	....	....
1953	Boston	11	0	4	4	4	....	....	....
1954	Boston	4	0	0	0	0	....	....	....
1955	Boston	5	0	5	5	0	....	....	....
Playoff Totals		**80**	**2**	**19**	**21**	**8**	....	....	....
QUACKENBUSH, Max									Defense
1951	Boston	6	0	0	0	4	0	0	0
Playoff Totals		**6**	**0**	**0**	**0**	**4**	**0**	**0**	**0**
QUENNEVILLE, Joel									Defense
1979	Toronto	6	0	1	1	4	0	0	0
1986	Hartford	10	0	2	2	12	0	0	0
1987	Hartford	6	0	0	0	0	0	0	0
1988	Hartford	6	0	2	2	2	0	0	0
1989	Hartford	4	0	3	3	4	0	0	0
Playoff Totals		**32**	**0**	**8**	**8**	**22**	**0**	**0**	**0**
QUENNEVILLE, Leo									Left wing/Center
1930	NY Rangers	3	0	0	0	0	0	0	0
Playoff Totals		**3**	**0**	**0**	**0**	**0**	**0**	**0**	**0**

Season	Team	GP	G	A	Pts	PIM	PP	SH	GW
QUILTY, John									Center
1941	Montreal	3	0	2	2	0	....	....	....
1942	Montreal	3	0	1	1	0	....	....	....
1947	Montreal	7	3	2	5	9	....	....	....
Playoff Totals		**13**	**3**	**5**	**8**	**9**	....	....	....
QUINN, Dan									Center
1984	Calgary	8	3	5	8	4	1	0	0
1985	Calgary	3	0	0	0	0	0	0	0
1986	Calgary	18	8	7	15	10	5	1	2
1989	Pittsburgh	11	6	3	9	10	4	0	1
1991	St. Louis	13	4	7	11	32	2	0	1
1996	Philadelphia	12	1	4	5	6	1	0	0
Playoff Totals		**65**	**22**	**26**	**48**	**62**	**13**	**1**	**4**
QUINN, Pat									Defense
1969	Toronto	4	0	0	0	13	0	0	0
1974	Atlanta	4	0	0	0	6	0	0	0
1976	Atlanta	2	0	1	1	2	0	0	0
1977	Atlanta	1	0	0	0	0	0	0	0
Playoff Totals		**11**	**0**	**1**	**1**	**21**	**0**	**0**	**0**
QUINNEY, Ken *No Playoffs*									Right wing
•QUINT, Deron									Defense
1997	Phoenix	7	0	2	2	0	0	0	0
Playoff Totals		**7**	**0**	**2**	**2**	**0**	**0**	**0**	**0**
•QUINTAL, Stephane									Defense
1991	Boston	3	0	1	1	7	0	0	0
1992	St. Louis	4	1	2	3	6	1	0	0
1993	St. Louis	9	0	0	0	8	0	0	0
1996	Montreal	6	0	1	1	6	0	0	0
1997	Montreal	5	0	1	1	6	0	0	0
1998	Montreal	9	0	2	2	4	0	0	0
2002	Montreal	12	1	3	4	12	0	0	0
Playoff Totals		**48**	**2**	**10**	**12**	**49**	**1**	**0**	**0**
QUINTIN, Jean-Francois *No Playoffs*									Left wing
•RACHUNEK, Karel									Defense
2001	Ottawa	3	0	0	0	0	0	0	0
Playoff Totals		**3**	**0**	**0**	**0**	**0**	**0**	**0**	**0**
RACINE, Yves									Defense
1991	Detroit	7	2	0	2	0	2	0	0
1992	Detroit	11	2	1	3	10	1	0	1
1993	Detroit	7	1	3	4	27	0	0	0
Playoff Totals		**25**	**5**	**4**	**9**	**37**	**3**	**0**	**1**
•RADIVOJEVIC, Branko									Right wing
2002	Phoenix	1	0	0	0	2	0	0	0
Playoff Totals		**1**	**0**	**0**	**0**	**2**	**0**	**0**	**0**
RADLEY, Yip *No Playoffs*									Defense
•RAFALSKI, Brian									Defense
2000♦	New Jersey	23	2	6	8	8	0	0	1
2001	New Jersey	25	7	11	18	7	1	0	3
2002	New Jersey	6	3	2	5	4	3	0	0
Playoff Totals		**54**	**12**	**19**	**31**	**19**	**4**	**0**	**4**
RAGLAN, Herb									Right wing
1986	St. Louis	10	1	1	2	24	0	0	0
1987	St. Louis	4	0	0	0	2	0	0	0
1988	St. Louis	10	1	3	4	11	0	0	0
1989	St. Louis	8	1	2	3	13	0	0	0
Playoff Totals		**32**	**3**	**6**	**9**	**50**	**0**	**0**	**0**
RAGLAN, Rags									Defense
1953	Chicago	3	0	0	0	0	0	0	0
Playoff Totals		**3**	**0**	**0**	**0**	**0**	**0**	**0**	**0**
•RAGNARSSON, Marcus									Defense
1998	San Jose	6	0	0	0	4	0	0	0
1999	San Jose	6	0	1	1	6	0	0	0
2000	San Jose	12	0	3	3	10	0	0	0
2001	San Jose	5	0	1	1	8	0	0	0
2002	San Jose	12	1	3	4	12	0	0	0
Playoff Totals		**41**	**1**	**8**	**9**	**40**	**0**	**0**	**0**
RALEIGH, Don									Center
1948	NY Rangers	6	2	0	2	2	....	....	....
1950	NY Rangers	12	4	5	9	4	....	....	....
Playoff Totals		**18**	**6**	**5**	**11**	**6**	....	....	....
•RALPH, Brad *No Playoffs*									Left wing
RAMAGE, Rob									Defense
1983	St. Louis	4	0	3	3	22	0	0	0
1984	St. Louis	11	1	8	9	32	1	0	1
1985	St. Louis	3	1	3	4	6	0	1	0
1986	St. Louis	19	1	10	11	66	0	0	0
1987	St. Louis	6	2	2	4	21	2	0	0
1988	Calgary	9	1	3	4	21	1	0	0
1989♦	Calgary	20	1	11	12	26	1	0	0
1990	Toronto	5	1	2	3	20	0	0	0
1993♦	Montreal	7	0	0	0	4	0	0	0
Playoff Totals		**84**	**8**	**42**	**50**	**218**	**5**	**1**	**1**
RAMSAY, Beattie *No Playoffs*									Defense

Season	Team	GP	G	A	Pts	PIM	PP	SH	GW
RAMSAY, Craig									Left wing
1973	Buffalo	6	1	1	2	0	0	0	0
1975	Buffalo	17	5	7	12	2	1	1	1
1976	Buffalo	9	1	2	3	2	0	1	0
1977	Buffalo	6	0	4	4	0	0	0	0
1978	Buffalo	8	3	1	4	9	1	0	1
1979	Buffalo	3	1	0	1	2	0	0	0
1980	Buffalo	10	0	6	6	4	0	0	0
1981	Buffalo	8	2	4	6	4	0	0	1
1982	Buffalo	4	1	1	2	0	0	0	1
1983	Buffalo	10	2	3	5	4	0	0	0
1984	Buffalo	3	0	1	1	0	0	0	0
1985	Buffalo	5	1	1	2	0	0	0	0
Playoff Totals		**89**	**17**	**31**	**48**	**27**	**2**	**2**	**4**
RAMSAY, Les *No Playoffs*									Left wing
RAMSEY, Mike									Defense
1980	Buffalo	13	1	2	3	12	1	0	1
1981	Buffalo	8	0	3	3	20	0	0	0
1982	Buffalo	4	1	1	2	14	0	0	0
1983	Buffalo	10	4	4	8	15	0	0	1
1984	Buffalo	3	0	1	1	6	0	0	0
1985	Buffalo	5	0	1	1	23	0	0	0
1988	Buffalo	6	0	3	3	29	0	0	0
1989	Buffalo	5	1	0	1	11	1	0	0
1990	Buffalo	6	0	1	1	8	0	0	0
1991	Buffalo	5	1	0	1	12	0	0	1
1992	Buffalo	7	0	2	2	8	0	0	0
1993	Pittsburgh	12	0	6	6	4	0	0	0
1994	Pittsburgh	1	0	0	0	0	0	0	0
1995	Detroit	15	0	1	1	4	0	0	0
1996	Detroit	15	0	4	4	10	0	0	0
Playoff Totals		**115**	**8**	**29**	**37**	**176**	**2**	**0**	**3**
RAMSEY, Wayne *No Playoffs*									Defense
RANDALL, Ken									Right wing/Defense
1918♦	Toronto	2	1	1	2	*12	....	....	....
1921	Toronto	2	0	0	0	11	....	....	....
1922♦	Toronto	2	1	0	1	4	....	....	....
Playoff Totals		**6**	**2**	**1**	**3**	**27**	....	....	....
•RANHEIM, Paul									Left wing
1990	Calgary	6	1	3	4	2	0	0	0
1991	Calgary	7	2	2	4	0	0	0	0
1993	Calgary	6	0	1	1	0	0	0	0
1999	Carolina	6	0	0	0	2	0	0	0
2001	Philadelphia	6	0	2	2	2	0	0	0
2002	Philadelphia	5	0	0	0	0	0	0	0
Playoff Totals		**36**	**3**	**8**	**11**	**6**	**0**	**0**	**0**
RANIERI, George *No Playoffs*									Left wing
•RASMUSSEN, Erik									Center/Left wing
1999	Buffalo	21	2	4	6	18	0	0	1
2000	Buffalo	3	0	0	0	4	0	0	0
2001	Buffalo	3	0	1	1	0	0	0	0
Playoff Totals		**27**	**2**	**5**	**7**	**22**	**0**	**0**	**1**
•RATCHUK, Peter *No Playoffs*									Defense
RATELLE, Jean									Center
1967	NY Rangers	4	0	0	0	2	0	0	0
1968	NY Rangers	6	0	4	4	2	0	0	0
1969	NY Rangers	4	1	0	1	0	1	0	0
1970	NY Rangers	6	1	3	4	0	0	0	0
1971	NY Rangers	13	2	9	11	8	0	0	0
1972	NY Rangers	6	0	1	1	0	0	0	0
1973	NY Rangers	10	2	7	9	0	1	0	0
1974	NY Rangers	13	2	4	6	0	0	0	1
1975	NY Rangers	3	1	5	6	2	1	0	0
1976	Boston	12	8	8	16	4	5	0	1
1977	Boston	14	5	12	17	4	1	0	1
1978	Boston	15	3	7	10	0	0	0	0
1979	Boston	11	7	6	13	2	2	0	2
1980	Boston	3	0	0	0	0	0	0	0
1981	Boston	3	0	0	0	0	0	0	0
Playoff Totals		**123**	**32**	**66**	**98**	**24**	**11**	**0**	**5**
•RATHJE, Mike									Defense
1994	San Jose	1	0	0	0	0	0	0	0
1995	San Jose	11	5	2	7	4	5	0	0
1998	San Jose	6	1	0	1	6	1	0	0
1999	San Jose	6	0	0	0	4	0	0	0
2000	San Jose	12	1	3	4	8	0	0	0
2001	San Jose	6	0	1	1	4	0	0	0
2002	San Jose	12	1	3	4	6	1	0	0
Playoff Totals		**54**	**8**	**9**	**17**	**32**	**7**	**0**	**0**
RATHWELL, Jake *No Playoffs*									Right wing
RATUSHNY, Dan *No Playoffs*									Defense
RAUSSE, Errol *No Playoffs*									Left wing
RAUTAKALLIO, Pekka									Defense
1980	Atlanta	4	0	1	1	2	0	0	0
1981	Calgary	16	2	4	6	6	1	0	0
1982	Calgary	3	0	0	0	0	0	0	0
Playoff Totals		**23**	**2**	**5**	**7**	**8**	**1**	**0**	**0**

Season	Team	GP	G	A	Pts	PIM	PP	SH	GW
RAVLICH, Matt									Defense
1965	Chicago	14	1	4	5	14	1	0	0
1966	Chicago	6	0	1	1	2	0	0	0
1968	Chicago	4	0	0	0	0	0	0	0
Playoff Totals		**24**	**1**	**5**	**6**	**16**	**1**	**0**	**0**
•RAY, Rob									Right wing
1991	Buffalo	6	1	1	2	56	0	0	1
1992	Buffalo	7	0	0	0	2	0	0	0
1994	Buffalo	7	1	0	1	43	0	0	0
1995	Buffalo	5	0	0	0	14	0	0	0
1997	Buffalo	12	0	1	1	28	0	0	0
1998	Buffalo	10	0	0	0	24	0	0	0
1999	Buffalo	5	1	0	1	0	0	0	1
2001	Buffalo	3	0	0	0	2	0	0	0
Playoff Totals		**55**	**3**	**2**	**5**	**169**	**0**	**0**	**2**
RAYMOND, Armand *No Playoffs*									Defense
RAYMOND, Paul									Right wing
1934	Montreal	2	0	0	0	0	0	0	0
1939	Montreal	3	0	0	0	2	0	0	0
Playoff Totals		**5**	**0**	**0**	**0**	**2**	**0**	**0**	**0**
READ, Mel *No Playoffs*									Center
REARDON, Ken									Defense
1941	Montreal	3	0	0	0	4	....	....	....
1942	Montreal	3	0	0	0	4	....	....	....
1946♦	Montreal	9	1	1	2	4	....	....	....
1947	Montreal	7	1	2	3	20	....	....	....
1949	Montreal	7	0	0	0	18	....	....	....
1950	Montreal	2	0	2	2	12	....	....	....
Playoff Totals		**31**	**2**	**5**	**7**	**62**	....	....	....
REARDON, Terry									Center/Right wing
1940	Boston	1	0	1	1	0	....	....	....
1941♦	Boston	11	2	4	6	6	....	....	....
1942	Montreal	3	2	2	4	2	....	....	....
1946	Boston	10	4	0	4	2	....	....	....
1947	Boston	5	0	3	3	2	....	....	....
Playoff Totals		**30**	**8**	**10**	**18**	**12**	....	....	....
•REASONER, Marty									Center
2000	St. Louis	7	2	1	3	4	1	0	0
2001	St. Louis	10	3	1	4	0	0	0	1
Playoff Totals		**17**	**5**	**2**	**7**	**4**	**1**	**0**	**1**
REAUME, Marc									Defense
1955	Toronto	4	0	0	0	2	0	0	0
1956	Toronto	5	0	2	2	6	0	0	0
1959	Toronto	10	0	0	0	0	0	0	0
1960	Detroit	2	0	0	0	0	0	0	0
Playoff Totals		**21**	**0**	**2**	**2**	**8**	**0**	**0**	**0**
REAY, Billy									Center
1946♦	Montreal	9	1	2	3	4	....	....	....
1947	Montreal	11	6	1	7	14	....	....	....
1949	Montreal	7	1	5	6	4	....	....	....
1950	Montreal	4	0	1	1	0	....	....	....
1951	Montreal	11	3	3	6	10	....	....	....
1952	Montreal	10	2	2	4	7	....	....	....
1953♦	Montreal	11	0	2	2	4	....	....	....
Playoff Totals		**63**	**13**	**16**	**29**	**43**	....	....	....
•RECCHI, Mark									Right wing
1991♦	Pittsburgh	24	10	24	34	33	5	0	2
1996	Montreal	6	3	3	6	0	3	0	0
1997	Montreal	5	4	2	6	2	0	0	0
1998	Montreal	10	4	8	12	6	0	0	2
1999	Philadelphia	6	0	1	1	2	0	0	0
2000	Philadelphia	18	6	12	18	6	2	0	1
2001	Philadelphia	6	2	2	4	2	1	0	1
2002	Philadelphia	4	0	0	0	2	0	0	0
Playoff Totals		**79**	**29**	**52**	**81**	**53**	**11**	**0**	**6**
REDAHL, Gord *No Playoffs*									Right wing
•REDDEN, Wade									Defense
1997	Ottawa	7	1	3	4	2	0	0	0
1998	Ottawa	9	0	2	2	2	0	0	0
1999	Ottawa	4	1	2	3	2	1	0	0
2001	Ottawa	4	0	0	0	0	0	0	0
2002	Ottawa	12	3	2	5	6	1	0	1
Playoff Totals		**36**	**5**	**9**	**14**	**12**	**2**	**0**	**1**
REDDING, George *No Playoffs*									Left wing/Defense
REDMOND, Craig									Defense
1985	Los Angeles	3	1	0	1	2	0	0	0
Playoff Totals		**3**	**1**	**0**	**1**	**2**	**0**	**0**	**0**
REDMOND, Dick									Defense
1973	Chicago	13	4	2	6	2	0	0	2
1974	Chicago	11	1	7	8	8	1	0	0
1975	Chicago	8	2	3	5	0	1	0	0
1976	Chicago	4	0	2	2	4	0	0	0
1977	Chicago	2	0	1	1	0	0	0	0
1978	Atlanta	2	1	0	1	0	0	0	0
1979	Boston	11	1	3	4	2	0	1	0
1980	Boston	10	0	3	3	9	0	0	0
1981	Boston	3	0	1	1	2	0	0	0
1982	Boston	2	0	0	0	0	0	0	0
Playoff Totals		**66**	**9**	**22**	**31**	**27**	**2**	**1**	**2**
REDMOND, Keith *No Playoffs*									Left wing

Season	Team	GP	G	A	Pts	PIM	PP	SH	GW
REDMOND, Mickey									Right wing
1968♦	Montreal	2	0	0	0	0	0	0	0
1969♦	Montreal	14	2	3	5	2	0	1	1
Playoff Totals		**16**	**2**	**3**	**5**	**2**	**0**	**1**	**1**
REEDS, Mark									Right wing
1982	St. Louis	10	0	1	1	2	0	0	0
1983	St. Louis	4	1	0	1	2	0	0	0
1984	St. Louis	11	3	3	6	15	0	1	1
1985	St. Louis	3	0	0	0	0	0	0	0
1986	St. Louis	19	4	4	8	2	0	0	1
1987	St. Louis	6	0	1	1	2	0	0	0
Playoff Totals		**53**	**8**	**9**	**17**	**23**	**0**	**1**	**2**
•REEKIE, Joe									Defense
1988	Buffalo	2	0	0	0	4	0	0	0
1994	Washington	11	2	1	3	29	0	1	1
1995	Washington	7	0	0	0	2	0	0	0
1998	Washington	21	1	2	3	20	0	0	0
2000	Washington	5	0	1	1	2	0	0	0
2001	Washington	4	0	0	0	4	0	0	0
2002	Chicago	1	0	0	0	2	0	0	0
Playoff Totals		**51**	**3**	**4**	**7**	**63**	**0**	**1**	**1**
REGAN, Bill									Defense
1930	NY Rangers	4	0	0	0	0	0	0	0
1931	NY Rangers	4	0	0	0	2	0	0	0
Playoff Totals		**8**	**0**	**0**	**0**	**2**	**0**	**0**	**0**
REGAN, Larry									Right wing
1957	Boston	8	0	2	2	10	....	....	....
1958	Boston	12	3	8	11	6	....	....	....
1959	Toronto	8	1	1	2	2	....	....	....
1960	Toronto	10	3	3	6	0	....	....	....
1961	Toronto	4	0	0	0	0	....	....	....
Playoff Totals		**42**	**7**	**14**	**21**	**18**	....	....	....
•REGEHR, Robyn *No Playoffs*									Defense
REGIER, Darcy *No Playoffs*									Defense
REIBEL, Dutch									Center
1954♦	Detroit	9	1	3	4	0	1	0	1
1955♦	Detroit	11	5	7	12	2	1	0	1
1956	Detroit	10	0	2	2	2	0	0	0
1957	Detroit	5	0	2	2	0	0	0	0
1959	Boston	4	0	0	0	0	0	0	0
Playoff Totals		**39**	**6**	**14**	**20**	**4**	**2**	**0**	**2**
•REICHEL, Robert									Center
1991	Calgary	6	1	1	2	0	1	0	0
1993	Calgary	6	2	4	6	2	2	0	0
1994	Calgary	7	0	5	5	0	0	0	0
1995	Calgary	7	2	4	6	4	0	0	1
1999	Phoenix	7	1	3	4	2	0	0	0
2002	Toronto	18	0	3	3	4	0	0	0
Playoff Totals		**51**	**6**	**20**	**26**	**12**	**3**	**0**	**1**
•REICHERT, Craig *No Playoffs*									Right wing
REID, Dave									Left wing
1985	Boston	5	1	0	1	0	0	0	0
1987	Boston	2	0	0	0	0	0	0	0
1990	Toronto	3	0	0	0	0	0	0	0
1992	Boston	15	2	5	7	4	0	0	1
1994	Boston	13	2	1	3	2	0	1	0
1995	Boston	5	0	0	0	0	0	0	0
1996	Boston	5	0	2	2	2	0	0	0
1997	Dallas	7	1	0	1	4	0	0	0
1998	Dallas	5	0	3	3	2	0	0	0
1999♦	Dallas	23	2	8	10	14	0	0	0
2000	Colorado	17	1	3	4	0	0	0	0
2001♦	Colorado	18	0	4	4	6	0	0	0
Playoff Totals		**118**	**9**	**26**	**35**	**34**	**0**	**1**	**1**
REID, Dave *No Playoffs*									Center
REID, Gerry									Center
1949	Detroit	2	0	0	0	2	0	0	0
Playoff Totals		**2**	**0**	**0**	**0**	**2**	**0**	**0**	**0**
REID, Gord *No Playoffs*									Defense
REID, Reg									Left wing
1925	Toronto	2	0	0	0	0	0	0	0
Playoff Totals		**2**	**0**	**0**	**0**	**0**	**0**	**0**	**0**
REID, Tom									Defense
1968	Chicago	9	0	0	0	2	0	0	0
1970	Minnesota	6	0	1	1	4	0	0	0
1971	Minnesota	12	0	6	6	20	0	0	0
1972	Minnesota	7	1	4	5	17	0	0	0
1973	Minnesota	6	0	2	2	4	0	0	0
1977	Minnesota	2	0	0	0	2	0	0	0
Playoff Totals		**42**	**1**	**13**	**14**	**49**	**0**	**0**	**0**
REIERSON, Dave *No Playoffs*									Defense
REIGLE, Ed *No Playoffs*									Defense

Season	Team	GP	G	A	Pts	PIM	PP	SH	GW
REINHART, Paul									Defense
1981	Calgary	16	1	14	15	16	1	0	0
1982	Calgary	3	0	1	1	2	0	0	0
1983	Calgary	9	6	3	9	2	4	1	0
1984	Calgary	11	6	11	17	2	0	1	0
1985	Calgary	4	1	1	2	0	0	0	0
1986	Calgary	21	5	13	18	4	4	0	0
1987	Calgary	4	0	1	1	6	0	0	0
1988	Calgary	8	2	7	9	6	1	0	0
1989	Vancouver	7	2	3	5	4	1	0	2
Playoff Totals		**83**	**23**	**54**	**77**	**42**	**11**	**2**	**2**
REINIKKA, Ollie *No Playoffs*									Center/Right wing
•REINPRECHT, Steve									Center
2001♦	Colorado	22	2	3	5	2	0	0	0
2002	Colorado	21	7	5	12	8	0	0	2
Playoff Totals		**43**	**9**	**8**	**17**	**10**	**0**	**0**	**2**
•REIRDEN, Todd									Defense
2000	St. Louis	4	0	1	1	0	0	0	0
2001	St. Louis	1	0	0	0	0	0	0	0
Playoff Totals		**5**	**0**	**1**	**1**	**0**	**0**	**0**	**0**
REISE, Leo									Defense
1929	NY Americans	2	0	0	0	0	0	0	0
1930	NY Rangers	4	0	0	0	16	0	0	0
Playoff Totals		**6**	**0**	**0**	**0**	**16**	**0**	**0**	**0**
REISE, Leo Jr.									Defense
1947	Detroit	5	0	1	1	4	....	....	....
1948	Detroit	10	2	1	3	12	....	....	....
1949	Detroit	11	1	0	1	4	....	....	....
1950♦	Detroit	14	2	0	2	19	....	....	....
1951	Detroit	6	2	3	5	2	....	....	....
1952♦	Detroit	6	1	0	1	*27	....	....	....
Playoff Totals		**52**	**8**	**5**	**13**	**68**	....	....	....
RENAUD, Mark *No Playoffs*									Defense
•RENBERG, Mikael									Right wing
1995	Philadelphia	15	6	7	13	6	2	0	0
1996	Philadelphia	11	3	6	9	14	1	0	0
1997	Philadelphia	18	5	6	11	4	2	0	0
1999	Philadelphia	6	0	1	1	0	0	0	0
2000	Phoenix	5	1	2	3	4	0	0	1
2002	Toronto	3	0	0	0	2	0	0	0
Playoff Totals		**58**	**15**	**22**	**37**	**30**	**5**	**0**	**1**
REYNOLDS, Bobby *No Playoffs*									Left wing
•RHEAUME, Pascal									Left wing
1998	St. Louis	10	1	3	4	8	1	0	0
1999	St. Louis	5	1	0	1	4	0	0	0
2001	St. Louis	3	0	1	1	0	0	0	0
Playoff Totals		**18**	**2**	**4**	**6**	**12**	**1**	**0**	**0**
RIBBLE, Pat									Defense
1977	Atlanta	2	0	0	0	6	0	0	0
1978	Atlanta	2	0	1	1	2	0	0	0
1979	Chicago	4	0	0	0	4	0	0	0
Playoff Totals		**8**	**0**	**1**	**1**	**12**	**0**	**0**	**0**
•RIBEIRO, Mike *No Playoffs*									Center
•RICCI, Mike									Center
1993	Quebec	6	0	6	6	8	0	0	0
1995	Quebec	6	1	3	4	8	0	0	0
1996♦	Colorado	22	6	11	17	18	3	0	1
1997	Colorado	17	2	4	6	17	0	0	1
1998	San Jose	6	1	3	4	6	0	0	0
1999	San Jose	6	2	3	5	10	1	0	0
2000	San Jose	12	5	1	6	2	3	0	1
2001	San Jose	6	0	3	3	0	0	0	0
2002	San Jose	12	4	6	10	4	0	0	1
Playoff Totals		**93**	**21**	**40**	**61**	**73**	**7**	**0**	**4**
RICE, Steven									Right wing
1991	NY Rangers	2	2	1	3	6	1	0	0
Playoff Totals		**2**	**2**	**1**	**3**	**6**	**1**	**0**	**0**
RICHARD, Henri									Center
1956♦	Montreal	10	4	4	8	21	....	....	....
1957♦	Montreal	10	2	6	8	10	....	....	....
1958♦	Montreal	10	1	7	8	11	....	....	....
1959♦	Montreal	11	3	8	11	13	....	....	....
1960♦	Montreal	8	3	9	*12	9	....	....	....
1961	Montreal	6	2	4	6	22	....	....	....
1963	Montreal	5	1	1	2	2	....	....	....
1964	Montreal	7	1	1	2	9	....	....	....
1965♦	Montreal	13	7	4	11	24	....	....	....
1966♦	Montreal	8	1	4	5	2	....	....	....
1967	Montreal	10	4	6	10	2	....	....	....
1968♦	Montreal	13	4	4	8	4	1	0	0
1969♦	Montreal	14	2	4	6	8	0	0	0
1971♦	Montreal	20	5	7	12	20	0	0	1
1972	Montreal	6	0	3	3	4	0	0	0
1973♦	Montreal	17	6	4	10	14	0	0	2
1974	Montreal	6	2	2	4	2	0	0	0
1975	Montreal	6	1	2	3	4	0	0	0
Playoff Totals		**180**	**49**	**80**	**129**	**181**	**1**	**0**	**3**

Season	Team	GP	G	A	Pts	PIM	PP	SH	GW
RICHARD, Jacques	Left wing								
1974	Atlanta	4	0	0	0	2	0	0	0
1976	Buffalo	9	1	1	2	7	0	0	0
1979	Buffalo	3	1	0	1	0	0	0	1
1981	Quebec	5	2	4	6	14	1	0	0
1982	Quebec	10	1	0	1	9	0	0	0
1983	Quebec	4	0	0	0	2	0	0	0
Playoff Totals		**35**	**5**	**5**	**10**	**34**	**1**	**0**	**1**
RICHARD, Jean-Marc *No Playoffs*	Defense								
RICHARD, Maurice	Right wing								
1944♦	Montreal	9	*12	5	17	10	....	....	....
1945	Montreal	6	6	2	8	10	....	....	....
1946♦	Montreal	9	*7	4	11	15	....	....	....
1947	Montreal	10	*6	5	*11	*44	....	....	....
1949	Montreal	7	2	1	3	14	....	....	....
1950	Montreal	5	1	1	2	6	....	....	....
1951	Montreal	11	*9	4	*13	13	....	....	....
1952	Montreal	11	4	2	6	6	....	....	....
1953♦	Montreal	12	7	1	8	2	....	....	....
1954	Montreal	11	3	0	3	22	....	....	....
1956♦	Montreal	10	5	9	14	*24	....	....	....
1957♦	Montreal	10	8	3	11	8	....	....	....
1958♦	Montreal	10	*11	4	15	10	....	....	....
1959♦	Montreal	4	0	0	0	2	....	....	....
1960♦	Montreal	8	1	3	4	2	....	....	....
Playoff Totals		**133**	**82**	**44**	**126**	**188**	....	....	....
RICHARD, Mike *No Playoffs*	Center								
•**RICHARDS, Brad** *No Playoffs*	Left wing								
RICHARDS, Todd	Defense								
1991	Hartford	6	0	0	0	2	0	0	0
1992	Hartford	5	0	3	3	4	0	0	0
Playoff Totals		**11**	**0**	**3**	**3**	**6**	**0**	**0**	**0**
•**RICHARDS, Travis** *No Playoffs*	Defense								
RICHARDSON, Dave *No Playoffs*	Left wing								
RICHARDSON, Glen *No Playoffs*	Left wing								
RICHARDSON, Ken *No Playoffs*	Center								
•**RICHARDSON, Luke**	Defense								
1988	Toronto	2	0	0	0	0	0	0	0
1990	Toronto	5	0	0	0	22	0	0	0
1992	Edmonton	16	0	5	5	45	0	0	0
1997	Edmonton	12	0	2	2	14	0	0	0
1998	Philadelphia	5	0	0	0	0	0	0	0
2000	Philadelphia	18	0	1	1	41	0	0	0
2001	Philadelphia	6	0	0	0	4	0	0	0
2002	Philadelphia	5	0	0	0	4	0	0	0
Playoff Totals		**69**	**0**	**8**	**8**	**130**	**0**	**0**	**0**
RICHER, Bob *No Playoffs*	Center								
RICHER, Stephane	Defense								
1993	Boston	3	0	0	0	0	0	0	0
Playoff Totals		**3**	**0**	**0**	**0**	**0**	**0**	**0**	**0**
RICHER, Stephane	Right wing								
1986♦	Montreal	16	4	1	5	23	3	0	1
1987	Montreal	5	3	2	5	0	0	0	1
1988	Montreal	8	7	5	12	6	1	0	2
1989	Montreal	21	6	5	11	14	2	0	3
1990	Montreal	9	7	3	10	2	1	0	1
1991	Montreal	13	9	5	14	6	1	0	1
1992	New Jersey	7	1	2	3	0	0	0	0
1993	New Jersey	5	2	2	4	2	1	0	0
1994	New Jersey	20	7	5	12	6	3	0	2
1995♦	New Jersey	19	6	15	21	2	3	1	2
1997	Montreal	5	0	0	0	0	0	0	0
2000	St. Louis	3	1	0	1	0	0	0	0
2002	New Jersey	3	0	0	0	0	0	0	0
Playoff Totals		**134**	**53**	**45**	**98**	**61**	**15**	**1**	**13**
RICHMOND, Steve	Defense								
1984	NY Rangers	4	0	0	0	12	0	0	0
Playoff Totals		**4**	**0**	**0**	**0**	**12**	**0**	**0**	**0**
•**RICHTER, Barry** *No Playoffs*	Defense								
RICHTER, Dave	Defense								
1984	Minnesota	8	0	0	0	20	0	0	0
1985	Minnesota	9	1	0	1	39	0	0	0
1986	Philadelphia	5	0	0	0	21	0	0	0
Playoff Totals		**22**	**1**	**0**	**1**	**80**	**0**	**0**	**0**
RIDLEY, Mike	Center								
1986	NY Rangers	16	6	8	14	26	2	0	1
1987	Washington	7	2	1	3	6	0	0	1
1988	Washington	14	6	5	11	10	1	0	0
1989	Washington	6	0	5	5	2	0	0	0
1990	Washington	14	3	4	7	8	0	1	0
1991	Washington	11	3	4	7	8	1	0	1
1992	Washington	7	0	11	11	0	0	0	0
1993	Washington	6	1	5	6	0	1	0	0
1994	Washington	11	4	6	10	6	0	0	0
1995	Toronto	7	3	1	4	2	1	0	1
1996	Vancouver	5	0	0	0	2	0	0	0
Playoff Totals		**104**	**28**	**50**	**78**	**70**	**6**	**1**	**4**
•**RIESEN, Michel** *No Playoffs*	Right wing								
RILEY, Bill *No Playoffs*	Right wing								

Season	Team	GP	G	A	Pts	PIM	PP	SH	GW
RILEY, Jack	Center								
1934	Montreal	2	0	1	1	0	0	0	0
1935	Montreal	2	0	2	2	0	0	0	0
Playoff Totals		**4**	**0**	**3**	**3**	**0**	**0**	**0**	**0**
RILEY, Jim *No Playoffs*	Left wing								
RIOPELLE, Rip	Left wing								
1949	Montreal	7	1	1	2	2	....	....	....
1950	Montreal	1	0	0	0	0	....	....	....
Playoff Totals		**8**	**1**	**1**	**2**	**2**	....	....	....
RIOUX, Gerry *No Playoffs*	Right wing								
RIOUX, Pierre *No Playoffs*	Right wing								
RIPLEY, Vic	Left wing								
1930	Chicago	2	0	0	0	2	....	....	....
1931	Chicago	9	2	1	3	4	....	....	....
1932	Chicago	2	0	0	0	0	....	....	....
1933	Boston	5	1	0	1	0	....	....	....
1934	NY Rangers	2	1	0	1	4	....	....	....
Playoff Totals		**20**	**4**	**1**	**5**	**10**	....	....	....
RISEBROUGH, Doug	Center								
1975	Montreal	11	3	5	8	37	0	0	0
1976♦	Montreal	13	0	3	3	30	0	0	0
1977♦	Montreal	12	2	3	5	16	0	0	0
1978♦	Montreal	15	2	2	4	17	0	1	1
1979♦	Montreal	15	1	6	7	32	0	0	1
1981	Montreal	3	1	0	1	0	1	0	0
1982	Montreal	5	2	1	3	11	0	0	0
1983	Calgary	9	1	3	4	18	0	0	0
1984	Calgary	11	2	1	3	25	0	0	0
1985	Calgary	4	0	3	3	12	0	0	0
1986	Calgary	22	7	9	16	38	0	1	1
1987	Calgary	4	0	1	1	2	0	0	0
Playoff Totals		**124**	**21**	**37**	**58**	**238**	**1**	**2**	**3**
RISSLING, Gary	Left wing								
1981	Pittsburgh	5	0	1	1	4	0	0	0
Playoff Totals		**5**	**0**	**1**	**1**	**4**	**0**	**0**	**0**
•**RITA, Jani** *No Playoffs*	Left wing								
RITCHIE, Bob *No Playoffs*	Left wing								
•**RITCHIE, Byron** *No Playoffs*	Center								
RITCHIE, Dave	Defense								
1925	Montreal	1	0	0	0	0	0	0	0
Playoff Totals		**1**	**0**	**0**	**0**	**0**	**0**	**0**	**0**
RITSON, Alex *No Playoffs*	Center								
RITTINGER, Alan *No Playoffs*	Wing								
RIVARD, Bob *No Playoffs*	Center/Left wing								
RIVERS, Gus	Right wing								
1930♦	Montreal	6	1	0	1	2	....	....	....
1931♦	Montreal	10	1	0	1	0	....	....	....
Playoff Totals		**16**	**2**	**0**	**2**	**2**	....	....	....
•**RIVERS, Jamie**	Defense								
1999	St. Louis	9	1	1	2	2	1	0	1
2001	Ottawa	1	0	0	0	4	0	0	0
2002	Boston	3	0	0	0	0	0	0	0
Playoff Totals		**13**	**1**	**1**	**2**	**6**	**1**	**0**	**1**
RIVERS, Shawn *No Playoffs*	Defense								
RIVERS, Wayne *No Playoffs*	Right wing								
•**RIVET, Craig**	Defense								
1997	Montreal	5	0	1	1	14	0	0	0
1998	Montreal	5	0	0	0	2	0	0	0
2002	Montreal	12	0	3	3	4	0	0	0
Playoff Totals		**22**	**0**	**4**	**4**	**20**	**0**	**0**	**0**
RIZZUTO, Garth *No Playoffs*	Center								
ROACH, Mickey *No Playoffs*	Center								
ROBERGE, Mario	Left wing								
1991	Montreal	12	0	0	0	24	0	0	0
1993♦	Montreal	3	0	0	0	0	0	0	0
Playoff Totals		**15**	**0**	**0**	**0**	**24**	**0**	**0**	**0**
ROBERGE, Serge *No Playoffs*	Right wing								
ROBERT, Claude *No Playoffs*	Left wing								
ROBERT, Rene	Right wing								
1973	Buffalo	6	5	3	8	2	1	0	1
1975	Buffalo	16	5	8	13	16	0	0	3
1976	Buffalo	9	3	2	5	6	0	0	0
1977	Buffalo	6	5	2	7	20	1	0	0
1978	Buffalo	7	2	0	2	23	0	0	0
1979	Buffalo	3	2	2	4	4	0	0	0
1981	Toronto	3	0	2	2	2	0	0	0
Playoff Totals		**50**	**22**	**19**	**41**	**73**	**2**	**0**	**4**
ROBERTO, Phil	Right wing								
1971♦	Montreal	15	0	1	1	36	0	0	0
1972	St. Louis	11	7	6	13	29	3	0	1
1973	St. Louis	5	2	1	3	4	0	0	0
Playoff Totals		**31**	**9**	**8**	**17**	**69**	**3**	**0**	**1**
ROBERTS, David	Left wing								
1994	St. Louis	3	0	0	0	12	0	0	0
1995	St. Louis	6	0	0	0	4	0	0	0
Playoff Totals		**9**	**0**	**0**	**0**	**16**	**0**	**0**	**0**

Season	Team	GP	G	A	Pts	PIM	PP	SH	GW
ROBERTS, Doug	Right wing								
1969	Oakland	7	0	1	1	34	0	0	0
1970	Oakland	4	0	2	2	6	0	0	0
1973	Boston	5	2	0	2	6	0	0	0
Playoff Totals		**16**	**2**	**3**	**5**	**46**	**0**	**0**	**0**
•**ROBERTS, Gary**	Left wing								
1987	Calgary	2	0	0	0	4	0	0	0
1988	Calgary	9	2	3	5	29	0	0	0
1989♦	Calgary	22	5	7	12	57	0	0	0
1990	Calgary	6	2	5	7	41	0	0	0
1991	Calgary	7	1	3	4	18	0	0	0
1993	Calgary	5	1	6	7	43	1	0	0
1994	Calgary	7	2	6	8	24	1	0	1
1999	Carolina	6	1	1	2	8	0	0	0
2001	Toronto	11	2	9	11	0	0	0	0
2002	Toronto	19	7	12	19	56	3	0	1
Playoff Totals		**94**	**23**	**52**	**75**	**280**	**5**	**0**	**2**
ROBERTS, Gordie	Defense								
1980	Hartford	3	1	1	2	2	0	0	0
1981	Minnesota	19	1	5	6	17	0	1	0
1982	Minnesota	4	0	3	3	27	0	0	0
1983	Minnesota	9	1	5	6	14	0	0	0
1984	Minnesota	15	3	7	10	23	1	1	0
1985	Minnesota	9	1	6	7	6	0	0	0
1986	Minnesota	5	0	4	4	8	0	0	0
1988	St. Louis	10	1	2	3	33	0	0	0
1989	St. Louis	10	1	7	8	8	0	0	0
1990	St. Louis	10	0	2	2	26	0	0	0
1991♦	Pittsburgh	24	1	2	3	63	0	0	0
1992♦	Pittsburgh	19	0	2	2	32	0	0	0
1993	Boston	4	0	0	0	6	0	0	0
1994	Boston	12	0	1	1	8	0	0	0
Playoff Totals		**153**	**10**	**47**	**57**	**273**	**1**	**2**	**0**
ROBERTS, Jim	Left wing								
1977	Minnesota	2	0	0	0	0	0	0	0
Playoff Totals		**2**	**0**	**0**	**0**	**0**	**0**	**0**	**0**
ROBERTS, Jimmy	Defense/Right wing								
1964	Montreal	7	0	1	1	14	0	0	0
1965♦	Montreal	13	0	0	0	30	0	0	0
1966♦	Montreal	10	1	1	2	10	0	1	0
1967	Montreal	4	1	0	1	0	0	0	0
1968	St. Louis	18	4	1	5	20	0	0	1
1969	St. Louis	12	1	4	5	10	0	0	0
1970	St. Louis	16	2	3	5	29	0	0	0
1971	St. Louis	6	2	1	3	11	0	0	0
1972	Montreal	6	1	0	1	0	0	0	1
1973♦	Montreal	17	0	2	2	22	0	0	0
1974	Montreal	6	0	0	0	4	0	0	0
1975	Montreal	11	2	2	4	2	0	0	0
1976♦	Montreal	13	3	1	4	2	0	1	0
1977♦	Montreal	14	3	0	3	6	0	1	1
Playoff Totals		**153**	**20**	**16**	**36**	**160**	**0**	**3**	**3**
ROBERTSON, Fred	Defense								
1932♦	Toronto	7	0	0	0	0	0	0	0
Playoff Totals		**7**	**0**	**0**	**0**	**0**	**0**	**0**	**0**
ROBERTSON, Geordie *No Playoffs*	Right wing								
ROBERTSON, George *No Playoffs*	Left wing/Center								
ROBERTSON, Torrie	Left wing								
1986	Hartford	10	1	0	1	67	0	0	0
1988	Hartford	6	0	1	1	6	0	0	0
1989	Detroit	6	1	0	1	17	0	0	0
Playoff Totals		**22**	**2**	**1**	**3**	**90**	**0**	**0**	**0**
•**ROBERTSSON, Bert**	Defense								
2000	Edmonton	5	0	0	0	0	0	0	0
Playoff Totals		**5**	**0**	**0**	**0**	**0**	**0**	**0**	**0**
•**ROBIDAS, Stephane**	Defense								
2002	Montreal	2	0	0	0	4	0	0	0
Playoff Totals		**2**	**0**	**0**	**0**	**4**	**0**	**0**	**0**
ROBIDOUX, Florent *No Playoffs*	Left wing								
ROBINSON, Doug	Left wing								
1964	Chicago	4	0	0	0	0	0	0	0
1968	Los Angeles	7	4	3	7	0	0	0	0
Playoff Totals		**11**	**4**	**3**	**7**	**0**	**0**	**0**	**0**
ROBINSON, Earl	Right wing/Center								
1930	Mtl. Maroons	4	0	0	0	0	....	....	....
1933	Mtl. Maroons	2	0	0	0	0	....	....	....
1934	Mtl. Maroons	4	2	0	2	0	....	....	....
1935♦	Mtl. Maroons	7	2	2	4	0	....	....	....
1936	Mtl. Maroons	3	0	0	0	0	....	....	....
1937	Mtl. Maroons	5	1	2	3	0	....	....	....
Playoff Totals		**25**	**5**	**4**	**9**	**0**	....	....	....

Season	Team	GP	G	A	Pts	PIM	PP	SH	GW
ROBINSON, Larry									Defense
1973♦	Montreal	11	1	4	5	9	0	0	1
1974	Montreal	6	0	1	1	26	0	0	0
1975	Montreal	11	0	4	4	27	0	0	0
1976♦	Montreal	13	3	3	6	10	0	0	1
1977♦	Montreal	14	2	10	12	12	1	0	0
1978♦	Montreal	15	4	*17	*21	6	2	0	0
1979♦	Montreal	16	6	9	15	8	1	0	1
1980	Montreal	10	0	4	4	2	0	0	0
1981	Montreal	3	0	1	1	2	0	0	0
1982	Montreal	5	0	1	1	8	0	0	0
1983	Montreal	3	0	0	0	2	0	0	0
1984	Montreal	15	0	5	5	22	0	0	0
1985	Montreal	12	3	8	11	8	1	0	0
1986♦	Montreal	20	0	13	13	22	0	0	0
1987	Montreal	17	3	17	20	6	2	0	0
1988	Montreal	11	1	4	5	4	0	0	0
1989	Montreal	21	2	8	10	12	0	0	0
1990	Los Angeles	10	2	3	5	10	0	0	0
1991	Los Angeles	12	1	4	5	15	0	0	0
1992	Los Angeles	2	0	0	0	0	0	0	0
Playoff Totals		**227**	**28**	**116**	**144**	**211**	**7**	**0**	**3**
ROBINSON, Moe *No Playoffs*									Defense
ROBINSON, Rob *No Playoffs*									Defense
ROBINSON, Scott *No Playoffs*									Right wing
•ROBITAILLE, Luc									Left wing
1987	Los Angeles	5	1	4	5	2	0	0	0
1988	Los Angeles	5	2	5	7	18	2	0	1
1989	Los Angeles	11	2	6	8	10	0	0	1
1990	Los Angeles	10	5	5	10	12	1	0	1
1991	Los Angeles	12	12	4	16	22	5	0	2
1992	Los Angeles	6	3	4	7	12	1	0	1
1993	Los Angeles	24	9	13	22	28	4	0	2
1995	Pittsburgh	12	7	4	11	26	0	0	2
1996	NY Rangers	11	1	5	6	8	0	0	0
1997	NY Rangers	15	4	7	11	4	0	0	0
1998	Los Angeles	4	1	2	3	6	0	0	0
2000	Los Angeles	4	2	2	4	6	0	0	0
2001	Los Angeles	13	4	3	7	10	1	0	1
2002♦	Detroit	23	4	5	9	10	1	0	1
Playoff Totals		**155**	**57**	**69**	**126**	**174**	**15**	**0**	**12**
ROBITAILLE, Mike									Defense
1973	Buffalo	6	0	0	0	0	0	0	0
1975	Vancouver	5	0	1	1	2	0	0	0
1976	Vancouver	2	0	0	0	2	0	0	0
Playoff Totals		**13**	**0**	**1**	**1**	**4**	**0**	**0**	**0**
•ROBITAILLE, Randy									Center
1999	Boston	1	0	0	0	0	0	0	0
Playoff Totals		**1**	**0**	**0**	**0**	**0**	**0**	**0**	**0**
•ROCHE, Dave									Left wing
1996	Pittsburgh	16	2	7	9	26	0	0	0
Playoff Totals		**16**	**2**	**7**	**9**	**26**	**0**	**0**	**0**
ROCHE, Des *No Playoffs*									Right wing
ROCHE, Earl									Left wing
1931	Mtl. Maroons	2	0	0	0	0	0	0	0
Playoff Totals		**2**	**0**	**0**	**0**	**0**	**0**	**0**	**0**
ROCHE, Ernie *No Playoffs*									Defense
•ROCHE, Travis *No Playoffs*									Defense
ROCHEFORT, Dave *No Playoffs*									Center
ROCHEFORT, Leon									Right wing
1966♦	Montreal	4	1	1	2	4	0	0	0
1967	Montreal	10	1	1	2	4	0	0	0
1968	Philadelphia	7	2	0	2	2	0	0	1
1969	Philadelphia	3	0	0	0	0	0	0	0
1971♦	Montreal	10	0	0	0	6	0	0	0
1975	Vancouver	5	0	2	2	0	0	0	0
Playoff Totals		**39**	**4**	**4**	**8**	**16**	**0**	**0**	**1**
ROCHEFORT, Normand									Defense
1981	Quebec	5	0	0	0	4	0	0	0
1982	Quebec	16	0	2	2	10	0	0	0
1983	Quebec	1	0	0	0	2	0	0	0
1984	Quebec	6	1	0	1	6	0	0	0
1985	Quebec	18	2	1	3	8	0	0	1
1987	Quebec	13	2	1	3	26	0	0	1
1990	NY Rangers	10	2	1	3	26	0	1	0
Playoff Totals		**69**	**7**	**5**	**12**	**82**	**0**	**1**	**2**
ROCKBURN, Harvey *No Playoffs*									Defense
RODDEN, Eddie									Center
1927	Chicago	2	0	1	1	0	0	0	0
Playoff Totals		**2**	**0**	**1**	**1**	**0**	**0**	**0**	**0**
RODGERS, Marc *No Playoffs*									Right wing
•ROENICK, Jeremy									Center
1989	Chicago	10	1	3	4	7	1	0	1
1990	Chicago	20	11	7	18	8	4	0	1
1991	Chicago	6	3	5	8	4	1	0	1
1992	Chicago	18	12	10	22	12	4	0	3
1993	Chicago	4	1	2	3	2	0	0	0
1994	Chicago	6	1	6	7	2	0	0	1
1995	Chicago	8	1	2	3	16	0	0	0
1996	Chicago	10	5	7	12	2	1	0	1
1997	Phoenix	6	2	4	6	4	0	0	0
1998	Phoenix	6	5	3	8	4	2	2	2
1999	Phoenix	1	0	0	0	0	0	0	0
2000	Phoenix	5	2	2	4	10	1	0	0
2002	Philadelphia	5	0	0	0	14	0	0	0
Playoff Totals		**105**	**44**	**51**	**95**	**85**	**14**	**2**	**10**
•ROEST, Stacy									Center
2000	Detroit	3	0	0	0	0	0	0	0
Playoff Totals		**3**	**0**	**0**	**0**	**0**	**0**	**0**	**0**
ROGERS, John *No Playoffs*									Right wing
ROGERS, Mike									Center
1980	Hartford	3	0	3	3	0	0	0	0
1982	NY Rangers	9	1	6	7	2	0	0	0
1983	NY Rangers	1	0	0	0	0	0	0	0
1984	NY Rangers	1	0	0	0	0	0	0	0
1985	NY Rangers	3	0	4	4	4	0	0	0
Playoff Totals		**17**	**1**	**13**	**14**	**6**	**0**	**0**	**0**
ROHLICEK, Jeff *No Playoffs*									Center
ROHLIN, Leif									Defense
1996	Vancouver	5	0	0	0	0	0	0	0
Playoff Totals		**5**	**0**	**0**	**0**	**0**	**0**	**0**	**0**
ROHLOFF, Jon									Defense
1995	Boston	5	0	0	0	6	0	0	0
1996	Boston	5	1	2	3	2	1	0	0
Playoff Totals		**10**	**1**	**2**	**3**	**8**	**1**	**0**	**0**
•ROHLOFF, Todd *No Playoffs*									Defense
ROLFE, Dale									Defense
1968	Los Angeles	7	0	1	1	14	0	0	0
1969	Los Angeles	10	0	4	4	8	0	0	0
1970	Detroit	4	0	2	2	8	0	0	0
1971	NY Rangers	13	0	1	1	14	0	0	0
1972	NY Rangers	16	4	3	7	16	0	0	1
1973	NY Rangers	8	0	5	5	6	0	0	0
1974	NY Rangers	13	1	8	9	23	0	0	0
Playoff Totals		**71**	**5**	**24**	**29**	**89**	**0**	**0**	**1**
•ROLSTON, Brian									Center
1995♦	New Jersey	6	2	1	3	4	1	0	0
1997	New Jersey	10	4	1	5	6	1	2	0
1998	New Jersey	6	1	0	1	2	0	1	0
1999	New Jersey	7	1	0	1	2	0	1	0
2002	Boston	6	4	1	5	0	1	1	0
Playoff Totals		**35**	**12**	**3**	**15**	**14**	**3**	**5**	**0**
ROMANCHYCH, Larry									Right wing
1974	Atlanta	4	2	2	4	4	0	0	0
1976	Atlanta	2	0	0	0	0	0	0	0
1977	Atlanta	1	0	0	0	0	0	0	0
Playoff Totals		**7**	**2**	**2**	**4**	**4**	**0**	**0**	**0**
ROMANIUK, Russell									Left wing
1993	Winnipeg	1	0	0	0	0	0	0	0
1996	Philadelphia	1	0	0	0	0	0	0	0
Playoff Totals		**2**	**0**	**0**	**0**	**0**	**0**	**0**	**0**
ROMBOUGH, Doug *No Playoffs*									Center
ROMINSKI, Dale *No Playoffs*									Right wing
ROMNES, Doc									Left wing/Center
1931	Chicago	9	1	1	2	2	....	....	....
1932	Chicago	2	0	0	0	0	....	....	....
1934♦	Chicago	8	2	*7	9	0	....	....	....
1935	Chicago	2	0	0	0	0	....	....	....
1936	Chicago	2	1	2	3	0	....	....	....
1938♦	Chicago	12	2	4	6	2	....	....	....
1939	Toronto	10	1	4	5	0	....	....	....
Playoff Totals		**45**	**7**	**18**	**25**	**4**	....	....	....
RONAN, Ed									Right wing
1993♦	Montreal	14	2	3	5	10	0	0	0
1994	Montreal	7	1	0	1	0	0	0	0
1997	Buffalo	6	1	0	1	6	0	0	1
Playoff Totals		**27**	**4**	**3**	**7**	**16**	**0**	**0**	**1**
RONAN, Skene *No Playoffs*									Defense/Center
•RONNING, Cliff									Center
1986	St. Louis	5	1	1	2	2	1	0	0
1987	St. Louis	4	0	1	1	0	0	0	0
1989	St. Louis	7	1	3	4	0	1	0	0
1991	Vancouver	6	6	3	9	12	2	0	2
1992	Vancouver	13	8	5	13	6	1	0	1
1993	Vancouver	12	2	9	11	6	0	0	0
1994	Vancouver	24	5	10	15	16	2	0	2
1995	Vancouver	11	3	5	8	2	1	0	2
1996	Vancouver	6	0	2	2	6	0	0	0
1997	Phoenix	7	0	7	7	12	0	0	0
1998	Phoenix	6	1	3	4	4	0	0	0
2002	Los Angeles	4	0	1	1	2	0	0	0
Playoff Totals		**105**	**27**	**50**	**77**	**68**	**8**	**0**	**7**
•RONNQVIST, Jonas *No Playoffs*									Right wing
RONSON, Len *No Playoffs*									Left wing
RONTY, Paul									Center
1948	Boston	5	0	4	4	0	....	....	....
1949	Boston	5	1	2	3	2	....	....	....
1951	Boston	6	0	1	1	2	....	....	....
1955	Montreal	5	0	0	0	2	....	....	....
Playoff Totals		**21**	**1**	**7**	**8**	**6**	....	....	....
ROONEY, Steve									Left wing
1985	Montreal	11	2	2	4	19	0	0	0
1986♦	Montreal	1	0	0	0	0	0	0	0
1987	Winnipeg	8	0	0	0	34	0	0	0
1988	Winnipeg	5	1	0	1	33	0	0	0
Playoff Totals		**25**	**3**	**2**	**5**	**86**	**0**	**0**	**0**
ROOT, Bill									Defense
1986	Toronto	7	0	2	2	13	0	0	0
1987	Toronto	13	1	0	1	12	0	0	0
1988	Philadelphia	2	0	0	0	0	0	0	0
Playoff Totals		**22**	**1**	**2**	**3**	**25**	**0**	**0**	**0**
•ROSA, Pavel *No Playoffs*									Right wing
ROSS, Art *No Playoffs*									Defense
ROSS, Jim *No Playoffs*									Defense
ROSSIGNOL, Roly									Right wing
1945	Montreal	1	0	0	0	2	0	0	0
Playoff Totals		**1**	**0**	**0**	**0**	**2**	**0**	**0**	**0**
•ROSSITER, Kyle *No Playoffs*									Defense
ROTA, Darcy									Left wing
1974	Chicago	11	3	0	3	11	0	0	0
1975	Chicago	7	0	1	1	24	0	0	0
1976	Chicago	4	1	0	1	2	1	0	0
1977	Chicago	2	0	0	0	0	0	0	0
1978	Chicago	4	0	0	0	2	0	0	0
1979	Atlanta	2	0	1	1	26	0	0	0
1980	Vancouver	4	2	0	2	8	0	0	0
1981	Vancouver	3	2	1	3	14	1	0	0
1982	Vancouver	17	6	3	9	54	2	0	1
1983	Vancouver	3	0	0	0	6	0	0	0
1984	Vancouver	3	0	1	1	0	0	0	0
Playoff Totals		**60**	**14**	**7**	**21**	**147**	**4**	**0**	**1**
ROTA, Randy									Center/Left wing
1974	Los Angeles	5	0	1	1	0	0	0	0
Playoff Totals		**5**	**0**	**1**	**1**	**0**	**0**	**0**	**0**
ROTHSCHILD, Sam									Left wing
1926♦	Mtl. Maroons	4	0	0	0	0	0	0	0
1927	Mtl. Maroons	2	0	0	0	0	0	0	0
Playoff Totals		**6**	**0**	**0**	**0**	**0**	**0**	**0**	**0**
ROULSTON, Rolly *No Playoffs*									Left wing/Defense
ROULSTON, Tom									Center/Right wing
1982	Edmonton	5	1	0	1	2	0	0	0
1983	Edmonton	16	1	2	3	0	0	0	0
Playoff Totals		**21**	**2**	**2**	**4**	**2**	**0**	**0**	**0**
ROUPE, Magnus *No Playoffs*									Left wing
ROUSE, Bob									Defense
1986	Minnesota	3	0	0	0	0	0	0	0
1989	Washington	6	2	0	2	4	0	0	0
1990	Washington	15	2	3	5	47	1	0	0
1993	Toronto	21	3	8	11	29	1	0	1
1994	Toronto	18	0	3	3	29	0	0	0
1995	Detroit	18	0	3	3	8	0	0	0
1996	Detroit	7	0	1	1	4	0	0	0
1997♦	Detroit	20	0	0	0	55	0	0	0
1998♦	Detroit	22	0	3	3	16	0	0	0
1999	San Jose	6	0	0	0	6	0	0	0
Playoff Totals		**136**	**7**	**21**	**28**	**198**	**2**	**0**	**1**

Season	Team	GP	G	A	Pts	PIM	PP	SH	GW
ROUSSEAU, Bobby	Right wing								
1962	Montreal	6	0	2	2	0	0	0	0
1963	Montreal	5	0	1	1	2	0	0	0
1964	Montreal	7	1	1	2	2	0	1	1
1965♦	Montreal	13	5	8	13	24	5	0	2
1966♦	Montreal	10	4	4	8	6	2	0	0
1967	Montreal	10	1	7	8	4	1	0	1
1968♦	Montreal	13	2	4	6	8	0	0	1
1969♦	Montreal	14	3	2	5	8	0	2	1
1971	Minnesota	12	2	6	8	0	1	0	1
1972	NY Rangers	16	6	11	17	7	0	0	1
1973	NY Rangers	10	2	3	5	4	0	0	0
1974	NY Rangers	12	1	8	9	4	1	0	0
Playoff Totals		**128**	**27**	**57**	**84**	**69**	**10**	**3**	**8**
ROUSSEAU, Guy *No Playoffs*	Left wing								
ROUSSEAU, Roland *No Playoffs*	Defense								
ROUTHIER, Jean-Marc *No Playoffs*	Right wing								
ROWE, Bobby *No Playoffs*	Right wing/Defense								
ROWE, Mike *No Playoffs*	Defense								
ROWE, Ron *No Playoffs*	Center/Left wing								
ROWE, Tom	Right wing								
1980	Hartford	3	2	0	2	0	0	0	0
Playoff Totals		**3**	**2**	**0**	**2**	**0**	**0**	**0**	**0**
•ROY, Andre	Left wing								
2000	Ottawa	5	0	0	0	2	0	0	0
2001	Ottawa	2	0	0	0	16	0	0	0
Playoff Totals		**7**	**0**	**0**	**0**	**18**	**0**	**0**	**0**
ROY, Jean-Yves *No Playoffs*	Right wing								
ROY, Stephane *No Playoffs*	Center								
•ROYER, Gaetan *No Playoffs*	Right wing								
ROYER, Remi *No Playoffs*	Defense								
•ROZSIVAL, Michal	Defense								
2000	Pittsburgh	2	0	0	0	4	0	0	0
Playoff Totals		**2**	**0**	**0**	**0**	**4**	**0**	**0**	**0**
ROZZINI, Gino	Center								
1945	Boston	6	1	2	3	6	....	....	....
Playoff Totals		**6**	**1**	**2**	**3**	**6**	....	....	....
•RUCCHIN, Steve	Center								
1997	Anaheim	8	1	2	3	10	0	0	0
1999	Anaheim	4	0	3	3	0	0	0	0
Playoff Totals		**12**	**1**	**5**	**6**	**10**	**0**	**0**	**0**
RUCINSKI, Mike	Center								
1988	Chicago	2	0	0	0	0	0	0	0
Playoff Totals		**2**	**0**	**0**	**0**	**0**	**0**	**0**	**0**
•RUCINSKI, Mike *No Playoffs*	Defense								
•RUCINSKY, Martin	Left wing								
1993	Quebec	6	1	1	2	4	1	0	0
1997	Montreal	5	0	0	0	4	0	0	0
1998	Montreal	10	3	0	3	4	1	0	0
Playoff Totals		**21**	**4**	**1**	**5**	**12**	**2**	**0**	**0**
RUELLE, Bernie *No Playoffs*	Left wing								
RUFF, Jason *No Playoffs*	Left wing								
RUFF, Lindy	Defense/Left wing								
1980	Buffalo	8	1	1	2	19	0	0	0
1981	Buffalo	6	3	1	4	23	1	0	1
1982	Buffalo	4	0	0	0	28	0	0	0
1983	Buffalo	10	4	2	6	47	0	0	0
1984	Buffalo	3	1	0	1	9	0	0	0
1985	Buffalo	5	2	4	6	15	1	0	0
1988	Buffalo	6	0	2	2	23	0	0	0
1989	NY Rangers	2	0	0	0	17	0	0	0
1990	NY Rangers	8	0	3	3	12	0	0	0
Playoff Totals		**52**	**11**	**13**	**24**	**193**	**2**	**0**	**1**
RUHNKE, Kent *No Playoffs*	Right wing								
•RUMBLE, Darren *No Playoffs*	Defense								
RUNDQVIST, Thomas *No Playoffs*	Center								
RUNGE, Paul	Center/Left wing								
1936	Boston	2	0	0	0	2	0	0	0
1937	Mtl. Maroons	5	0	0	0	4	0	0	0
Playoff Totals		**7**	**0**	**0**	**0**	**6**	**0**	**0**	**0**
RUOTSALAINEN, Reijo	Defense								
1982	NY Rangers	10	4	5	9	2	2	0	1
1983	NY Rangers	9	4	2	6	6	1	0	1
1984	NY Rangers	5	1	1	2	2	1	0	1
1985	NY Rangers	3	2	0	2	6	1	0	0
1986	NY Rangers	16	0	8	8	6	0	0	0
1987♦	Edmonton	21	2	5	7	10	1	0	1
1990♦	Edmonton	22	2	11	13	12	1	0	0
Playoff Totals		**86**	**15**	**32**	**47**	**44**	**7**	**0**	**4**
RUPP, Duane	Defense								
1970	Pittsburgh	6	2	2	4	2	0	0	0
1972	Pittsburgh	4	0	0	0	6	0	0	0
Playoff Totals		**10**	**2**	**2**	**4**	**8**	**0**	**0**	**0**
•RUPP, Mike *No Playoffs*	Right wing								

Season	Team	GP	G	A	Pts	PIM	PP	SH	GW
RUSKOWSKI, Terry	Center								
1980	Chicago	4	0	0	0	22	0	0	0
1981	Chicago	3	0	2	2	11	0	0	0
1982	Chicago	11	1	2	3	53	0	0	0
1985	Los Angeles	3	0	2	2	0	0	0	0
Playoff Totals		**21**	**1**	**6**	**7**	**86**	**0**	**0**	**0**
RUSSELL, Cam	Defense								
1990	Chicago	1	0	0	0	0	0	0	0
1991	Chicago	1	0	0	0	0	0	0	0
1992	Chicago	12	0	2	2	2	0	0	0
1993	Chicago	4	0	0	0	0	0	0	0
1995	Chicago	16	0	3	3	8	0	0	0
1996	Chicago	6	0	0	0	2	0	0	0
1997	Chicago	4	0	0	0	4	0	0	0
Playoff Totals		**44**	**0**	**5**	**5**	**16**	**0**	**0**	**0**
RUSSELL, Church *No Playoffs*	Left wing/Center								
RUSSELL, Phil	Defense								
1973	Chicago	16	0	3	3	49	0	0	0
1974	Chicago	9	0	1	1	41	0	0	0
1975	Chicago	8	1	3	4	23	0	0	0
1976	Chicago	4	0	1	1	17	0	0	0
1977	Chicago	2	0	1	1	2	0	0	0
1979	Atlanta	2	0	0	0	9	0	0	0
1980	Atlanta	4	0	1	1	6	0	0	0
1981	Calgary	16	2	7	9	29	0	0	0
1982	Calgary	3	0	1	1	2	0	0	0
1983	Calgary	9	1	4	5	24	0	0	0
Playoff Totals		**73**	**4**	**22**	**26**	**202**	**0**	**0**	**0**
RUUTTU, Christian	Center								
1988	Buffalo	6	2	5	7	4	1	0	0
1989	Buffalo	2	0	0	0	2	0	0	0
1990	Buffalo	6	0	0	0	4	0	0	0
1991	Buffalo	6	1	3	4	29	0	1	0
1992	Buffalo	3	0	0	0	6	0	0	0
1993	Chicago	4	0	0	0	2	0	0	0
1994	Chicago	6	0	0	0	2	0	0	0
1995	Vancouver	9	1	1	2	0	0	1	0
Playoff Totals		**42**	**4**	**9**	**13**	**49**	**1**	**2**	**0**
•RUUTU, Jarkko	Left wing								
2001	Vancouver	4	0	1	1	8	0	0	0
2002	Vancouver	1	0	0	0	0	0	0	0
Playoff Totals		**5**	**0**	**1**	**1**	**8**	**0**	**0**	**0**
RUZICKA, Vladimir	Center								
1991	Boston	17	2	11	13	0	1	0	2
1992	Boston	13	2	3	5	2	2	0	0
Playoff Totals		**30**	**4**	**14**	**18**	**2**	**3**	**0**	**2**
RYAN, Terry *No Playoffs*	Left wing								
RYCHEL, Warren	Left wing								
1991	Chicago	3	1	3	4	2	1	0	1
1993	Los Angeles	23	6	7	13	39	0	0	2
1995	Toronto	3	0	0	0	0	0	0	0
1996♦	Colorado	12	1	0	1	23	0	0	0
1997	Anaheim	11	0	2	2	19	0	0	0
1998	Colorado	6	0	0	0	24	0	0	0
1999	Colorado	12	0	1	1	14	0	0	0
Playoff Totals		**70**	**8**	**13**	**21**	**121**	**1**	**0**	**3**
•RYCROFT, Mark *No Playoffs*	Right wing								
RYMSHA, Andy *No Playoffs*	Defense								
SAARINEN, Simo *No Playoffs*	Defense								
SABOL, Shaun *No Playoffs*	Defense								
SABOURIN, Bob *No Playoffs*	Left wing								
SABOURIN, Gary	Right wing								
1968	St. Louis	18	4	2	6	30	1	0	1
1969	St. Louis	12	6	5	11	12	1	2	0
1970	St. Louis	16	5	0	5	10	0	1	1
1972	St. Louis	11	3	3	6	6	0	0	0
1973	St. Louis	5	1	1	2	0	0	0	1
Playoff Totals		**62**	**19**	**11**	**30**	**58**	**2**	**3**	**3**
SABOURIN, Ken	Defense								
1989	Calgary	1	0	0	0	0	0	0	0
1991	Washington	11	0	0	0	34	0	0	0
Playoff Totals		**12**	**0**	**0**	**0**	**34**	**0**	**0**	**0**
SACCO, David *No Playoffs*	Right wing								
•SACCO, Joe	Right wing								
1997	Anaheim	11	2	0	2	2	0	0	0
2000	Washington	5	0	0	0	4	0	0	0
2001	Washington	6	0	0	0	2	0	0	0
Playoff Totals		**22**	**2**	**0**	**2**	**8**	**0**	**0**	**0**
SACHARUK, Larry	Defense								
1975	St. Louis	2	1	1	2	2	0	0	0
Playoff Totals		**2**	**1**	**1**	**2**	**2**	**0**	**0**	**0**
•SAFRONOV, Kirill *No Playoffs*	Defense								
SAGANIUK, Rocky	Right wing/Center								
1979	Toronto	3	1	0	1	5	0	0	0
1980	Toronto	3	0	0	0	10	0	0	0
Playoff Totals		**6**	**1**	**0**	**1**	**15**	**0**	**0**	**0**
ST. AMOUR, Martin *No Playoffs*	Left wing								
•ST. JACQUES, Bruno *No Playoffs*	Defense								

Season	Team	GP	G	A	Pts	PIM	PP	SH	GW
ST. LAURENT, Andre	Center								
1975	NY Islanders	15	2	2	4	6	1	0	0
1976	NY Islanders	13	1	5	6	15	0	0	0
1977	NY Islanders	12	1	2	3	6	0	0	1
1978	Detroit	7	1	1	2	4	0	0	0
1980	Los Angeles	4	1	0	1	0	0	1	1
1981	Los Angeles	3	0	1	1	9	0	0	0
1982	Pittsburgh	5	2	1	3	8	0	0	0
Playoff Totals		**59**	**8**	**12**	**20**	**48**	**1**	**1**	**2**
ST. LAURENT, Dollard	Defense								
1952	Montreal	9	0	3	3	6	....	....	....
1953♦	Montreal	12	0	3	3	4	....	....	....
1954	Montreal	10	1	2	3	8	....	....	....
1955	Montreal	12	0	5	5	12	....	....	....
1956♦	Montreal	4	0	0	0	2	....	....	....
1957♦	Montreal	7	0	1	1	13	....	....	....
1958♦	Montreal	5	0	0	0	10	....	....	....
1959	Chicago	6	0	1	1	2	....	....	....
1960	Chicago	4	0	1	1	0	....	....	....
1961♦	Chicago	11	1	2	3	12	....	....	....
1962	Chicago	12	0	4	4	18	....	....	....
Playoff Totals		**92**	**2**	**22**	**24**	**87**	....	....	....
•ST. LOUIS, Martin *No Playoffs*	Right wing								
ST. MARSEILLE, Frank	Right wing								
1968	St. Louis	18	5	8	13	0	4	0	0
1969	St. Louis	12	3	3	6	2	0	0	0
1970	St. Louis	15	6	7	13	4	3	1	0
1971	St. Louis	6	2	1	3	4	2	0	1
1972	St. Louis	11	3	5	8	6	1	0	0
1974	Los Angeles	5	0	0	0	0	0	0	0
1975	Los Angeles	3	0	1	1	0	0	0	0
1976	Los Angeles	9	0	0	0	0	0	0	0
1977	Los Angeles	9	1	0	1	2	0	0	0
Playoff Totals		**88**	**20**	**25**	**45**	**18**	**10**	**1**	**1**
ST. SAUVEUR, Claude	Center								
1976	Atlanta	2	0	0	0	0	0	0	0
Playoff Totals		**2**	**0**	**0**	**0**	**0**	**0**	**0**	**0**
•SAKIC, Joe	Center								
1993	Quebec	6	3	3	6	2	1	0	0
1995	Quebec	6	4	1	5	0	1	1	1
1996♦	Colorado	22	*18	16	*34	14	6	0	6
1997	Colorado	17	8	*17	25	14	3	0	0
1998	Colorado	6	2	3	5	6	0	1	2
1999	Colorado	19	6	13	19	8	1	1	1
2000	Colorado	17	2	7	9	8	2	0	0
2001♦	Colorado	21	*13	13	*26	6	5	0	3
2002	Colorado	21	9	10	19	4	4	0	1
Playoff Totals		**135**	**65**	**83**	**148**	**62**	**23**	**3**	**14**
•SALEI, Ruslan	Defense								
1999	Anaheim	3	0	0	0	4	0	0	0
Playoff Totals		**3**	**0**	**0**	**0**	**4**	**0**	**0**	**0**
SALESKI, Don	Right wing								
1973	Philadelphia	11	1	2	3	4	0	0	0
1974♦	Philadelphia	17	2	7	9	24	0	0	0
1975♦	Philadelphia	17	2	3	5	25	0	0	1
1976	Philadelphia	16	6	5	11	47	0	1	1
1977	Philadelphia	10	0	0	0	12	0	0	0
1978	Philadelphia	11	2	0	2	19	0	0	1
Playoff Totals		**82**	**13**	**17**	**30**	**131**	**0**	**1**	**3**
SALMING, Borje	Defense								
1974	Toronto	4	0	1	1	4	0	0	0
1975	Toronto	7	0	4	4	6	0	0	0
1976	Toronto	10	3	4	7	9	1	0	0
1977	Toronto	9	3	6	9	6	2	0	0
1978	Toronto	6	2	2	4	6	0	0	1
1979	Toronto	6	0	1	1	8	0	0	0
1980	Toronto	3	1	1	2	2	1	0	0
1981	Toronto	3	0	2	2	4	0	0	0
1983	Toronto	4	1	4	5	10	1	0	0
1986	Toronto	10	1	6	7	14	0	0	0
1987	Toronto	13	0	3	3	14	0	0	0
1988	Toronto	6	1	3	4	8	0	0	0
Playoff Totals		**81**	**12**	**37**	**49**	**91**	**5**	**0**	**1**
•SALO, Sami	Defense								
1999	Ottawa	4	0	0	0	0	0	0	0
2000	Ottawa	6	1	1	2	0	1	0	0
2001	Ottawa	4	0	0	0	0	0	0	0
2002	Ottawa	12	2	1	3	4	0	0	0
Playoff Totals		**26**	**3**	**2**	**5**	**4**	**1**	**0**	**0**
•SALOMONSSON, Andreas	Right wing								
2002	New Jersey	4	0	1	1	0	0	0	0
Playoff Totals		**4**	**0**	**1**	**1**	**0**	**0**	**0**	**0**
SALOVAARA, Barry *No Playoffs*	Defense								
•SALVADOR, Bryce	Defense								
2001	St. Louis	14	2	0	2	18	0	0	1
2002	St. Louis	10	0	1	1	4	0	0	0
Playoff Totals		**24**	**2**	**1**	**3**	**22**	**0**	**0**	**1**
SALVIAN, Dave	Right wing								
1977	NY Islanders	1	0	1	1	2	0	0	0
Playoff Totals		**1**	**0**	**1**	**1**	**2**	**0**	**0**	**0**

Season	Team	GP	G	A	Pts	PIM	PP	SH	GW
SAMIS, Phil	Defense								
1948◆	Toronto	5	0	1	1	2	0	0	0
Playoff Totals		**5**	**0**	**1**	**1**	**2**	**0**	**0**	**0**
SAMPSON, Gary	Left wing								
1984	Washington	8	1	0	1	0	0	0	0
1985	Washington	4	0	0	0	0	0	0	0
Playoff Totals		**12**	**1**	**0**	**1**	**0**	**0**	**0**	**0**
•SAMSONOV, Sergei	Left wing								
1998	Boston	6	2	5	7	0	0	0	1
1999	Boston	11	3	1	4	0	0	0	0
2002	Boston	6	2	2	4	0	0	0	0
Playoff Totals		**23**	**7**	**8**	**15**	**0**	**0**	**0**	**1**
SAMUELSSON, Kjell	Defense								
1986	NY Rangers	9	0	1	1	8	0	0	0
1987	Philadelphia	26	0	4	4	25	0	0	0
1988	Philadelphia	7	2	5	7	23	0	0	1
1989	Philadelphia	19	1	3	4	24	0	0	0
1992◆	Pittsburgh	15	0	3	3	12	0	0	0
1993	Pittsburgh	12	0	3	3	2	0	0	0
1994	Pittsburgh	6	0	0	0	26	0	0	0
1995	Pittsburgh	11	0	1	1	32	0	0	0
1996	Philadelphia	12	1	0	1	24	0	0	0
1997	Philadelphia	5	0	0	0	2	0	0	0
1998	Philadelphia	1	0	0	0	0	0	0	0
Playoff Totals		**123**	**4**	**20**	**24**	**178**	**0**	**0**	**1**
•SAMUELSSON, Martin *No Playoffs*	Right wing								
•SAMUELSSON, Mikael *No Playoffs*	Right wing								
SAMUELSSON, Ulf	Defense								
1986	Hartford	10	1	2	3	38	0	0	1
1987	Hartford	5	0	1	1	41	0	0	0
1988	Hartford	5	0	0	0	8	0	0	0
1989	Hartford	4	0	2	2	4	0	0	0
1990	Hartford	7	1	0	1	2	0	0	0
1991◆	Pittsburgh	20	3	2	5	34	1	0	1
1992◆	Pittsburgh	21	0	2	2	39	0	0	0
1993	Pittsburgh	12	1	5	6	24	0	0	0
1994	Pittsburgh	6	0	1	1	18	0	0	0
1995	Pittsburgh	7	0	2	2	8	0	0	0
1996	NY Rangers	11	1	5	6	16	0	0	0
1997	NY Rangers	15	0	2	2	30	0	0	0
1999	Detroit	9	0	3	3	10	0	0	0
Playoff Totals		**132**	**7**	**27**	**34**	**272**	**1**	**0**	**2**
SANDELIN, Scott *No Playoffs*	Defense								
SANDERSON, Derek	Center								
1968	Boston	4	0	2	2	9	0	0	0
1969	Boston	9	*8	2	10	36	0	2	3
1970◆	Boston	14	5	4	9	*72	1	0	2
1971	Boston	7	2	1	3	13	0	0	0
1972◆	Boston	11	1	1	2	44	0	1	0
1973	Boston	5	1	2	3	13	0	0	0
1975	NY Rangers	3	0	0	0	0	0	0	0
1976	St. Louis	3	1	0	1	0	1	0	0
Playoff Totals		**56**	**18**	**12**	**30**	**187**	**2**	**3**	**5**
•SANDERSON, Geoff	Left wing								
1991	Hartford	3	0	0	0	0	0	0	0
1992	Hartford	7	1	0	1	2	0	0	0
1998	Buffalo	14	3	1	4	4	1	0	1
1999	Buffalo	19	4	6	10	14	0	0	1
2000	Buffalo	5	0	2	2	8	0	0	0
Playoff Totals		**48**	**8**	**9**	**17**	**28**	**1**	**0**	**2**
SANDFORD, Ed	Left wing								
1948	Boston	5	1	0	1	0	....	....	....
1949	Boston	5	1	3	4	2	....	....	....
1951	Boston	6	0	1	1	4	....	....	....
1952	Boston	7	2	2	4	0	....	....	....
1953	Boston	11	*8	3	*11	11	....	....	....
1954	Boston	3	0	1	1	4	....	....	....
1955	Boston	5	1	1	2	6	....	....	....
Playoff Totals		**42**	**13**	**11**	**24**	**27**	....	....	....
SANDLAK, Jim	Right wing								
1986	Vancouver	3	0	1	1	0	0	0	0
1989	Vancouver	6	1	1	2	2	0	0	0
1992	Vancouver	13	4	6	10	22	2	0	0
1993	Vancouver	6	2	2	4	4	0	0	0
1996	Vancouver	5	0	0	0	2	0	0	0
Playoff Totals		**33**	**7**	**10**	**17**	**30**	**2**	**0**	**0**
SANDS, Charlie	Center/Right wing								
1933	Toronto	9	2	2	4	2	....	....	....
1934	Toronto	5	1	0	1	0	....	....	....
1935	Boston	4	0	0	0	0	....	....	....
1936	Boston	2	0	0	0	0	....	....	....
1937	Boston	3	1	2	3	0	....	....	....
1938	Boston	3	1	1	2	0	....	....	....
1939◆	Boston	1	0	0	0	0	....	....	....
1941	Montreal	2	1	0	1	0	....	....	....
1942	Montreal	3	0	1	1	2	....	....	....
1943	Montreal	2	0	0	0	0	....	....	....
Playoff Totals		**34**	**6**	**6**	**12**	**4**	....	....	....
SANDSTROM, Tomas	Right wing								
1985	NY Rangers	3	0	2	2	0	0	0	0
1986	NY Rangers	16	4	6	10	20	0	0	1
1987	NY Rangers	6	1	2	3	20	0	0	0
1989	NY Rangers	4	3	2	5	12	2	0	0
1990	Los Angeles	10	5	4	9	19	0	0	0
1991	Los Angeles	10	4	4	8	14	3	0	0
1992	Los Angeles	6	0	3	3	8	0	0	0
1993	Los Angeles	24	8	17	25	12	2	0	2
1994	Pittsburgh	6	0	0	0	4	0	0	0
1995	Pittsburgh	12	3	3	6	16	2	0	0
1996	Pittsburgh	18	4	2	6	30	0	0	1
1997◆	Detroit	20	0	4	4	24	0	0	0
1999	Anaheim	4	0	0	0	4	0	0	0
Playoff Totals		**139**	**32**	**49**	**81**	**183**	**9**	**0**	**4**
SANDWITH, Terran *No Playoffs*	Defense								
SANIPASS, Everett	Left wing								
1988	Chicago	2	2	0	2	2	0	0	0
1989	Chicago	3	0	0	0	2	0	0	0
Playoff Totals		**5**	**2**	**0**	**2**	**4**	**0**	**0**	**0**
•SAPRYKIN, Oleg *No Playoffs*	Center								
•SARAULT, Yves	Left wing								
1997	Colorado	5	0	0	0	2	0	0	0
Playoff Totals		**5**	**0**	**0**	**0**	**2**	**0**	**0**	**0**
SARGENT, Gary	Defense								
1977	Los Angeles	9	3	4	7	6	2	0	0
1978	Los Angeles	2	0	0	0	0	0	0	0
1980	Minnesota	4	2	1	3	2	1	0	1
1983	Minnesota	5	0	2	2	0	0	0	0
Playoff Totals		**20**	**5**	**7**	**12**	**8**	**3**	**0**	**1**
•SARICH, Cory *No Playoffs*	Defense								
SARNER, Craig *No Playoffs*	Right wing								
SARRAZIN, Dick	Right wing								
1969	Philadelphia	4	0	0	0	0	0	0	0
Playoff Totals		**4**	**0**	**0**	**0**	**0**	**0**	**0**	**0**
SASAKAMOOSE, Fred *No Playoffs*	Center								
SASSER, Grant *No Playoffs*	Center								
•SATAN, Miroslav	Left wing								
1997	Buffalo	7	0	0	0	0	0	0	0
1998	Buffalo	14	5	4	9	4	4	0	1
1999	Buffalo	12	3	5	8	2	1	0	1
2000	Buffalo	5	3	2	5	0	0	0	0
2001	Buffalo	13	3	10	13	8	1	0	0
Playoff Totals		**51**	**14**	**21**	**35**	**14**	**6**	**0**	**2**
SATHER, Glen	Left wing								
1968	Boston	3	0	0	0	0	0	0	0
1969	Boston	10	0	0	0	18	0	0	0
1970	Pittsburgh	10	0	2	2	17	0	0	0
1971	NY Rangers	13	0	1	1	18	0	0	0
1972	NY Rangers	16	0	1	1	22	0	0	0
1973	NY Rangers	9	0	0	0	7	0	0	0
1975	Montreal	11	1	1	2	4	0	0	0
Playoff Totals		**72**	**1**	**5**	**6**	**86**	**0**	**0**	**0**
•SAUER, Kurt *No Playoffs*	Defense								
SAUNDERS, Bernie *No Playoffs*	Left wing								
SAUNDERS, David *No Playoffs*	Left wing								
SAUNDERS, Ted *No Playoffs*	Right wing								
SAUVE, Jean-Francois	Center								
1981	Buffalo	5	2	0	2	0	1	0	0
1982	Buffalo	2	0	2	2	0	0	0	0
1984	Quebec	9	2	5	7	2	2	0	1
1985	Quebec	18	5	5	10	8	2	0	0
1986	Quebec	2	0	0	0	0	0	0	0
Playoff Totals		**36**	**9**	**12**	**21**	**10**	**5**	**0**	**1**
•SAVAGE, Andre *No Playoffs*	Center								
•SAVAGE, Brian	Right wing								
1994	Montreal	3	0	2	2	0	0	0	0
1996	Montreal	6	0	2	2	2	0	0	0
1997	Montreal	5	1	1	2	0	0	0	0
1998	Montreal	9	0	2	2	6	0	0	0
2002	Phoenix	5	0	0	0	0	0	0	0
Playoff Totals		**28**	**1**	**7**	**8**	**8**	**0**	**0**	**0**
SAVAGE, Joel *No Playoffs*	Right wing								
•SAVAGE, Reggie *No Playoffs*	Center								
SAVAGE, Tony	Defense								
1935	Montreal	2	0	0	0	0	0	0	0
Playoff Totals		**2**	**0**	**0**	**0**	**0**	**0**	**0**	**0**
SAVARD, Andre	Center								
1974	Boston	16	3	2	5	24	0	0	0
1975	Boston	3	1	1	2	2	0	0	1
1976	Boston	12	1	4	5	9	0	0	0
1977	Buffalo	6	0	1	1	2	0	0	0
1978	Buffalo	6	0	0	0	4	0	0	0
1979	Buffalo	3	0	2	2	2	0	0	0
1980	Buffalo	8	1	1	2	2	0	0	0
1981	Buffalo	8	4	2	6	17	1	0	0
1982	Buffalo	4	0	1	1	5	0	0	0
1983	Buffalo	10	0	4	4	8	0	0	0
1984	Quebec	9	3	0	3	2	0	2	1
Playoff Totals		**85**	**13**	**18**	**31**	**77**	**1**	**2**	**2**
SAVARD, Denis	Center								
1981	Chicago	3	0	0	0	0	0	0	0
1982	Chicago	15	11	7	18	52	5	0	2
1983	Chicago	13	8	9	17	22	3	0	1
1984	Chicago	5	1	3	4	9	0	0	0
1985	Chicago	15	9	20	29	20	3	0	0
1986	Chicago	3	4	1	5	6	2	0	0
1987	Chicago	4	1	0	1	12	0	0	0
1988	Chicago	5	4	3	7	17	0	1	1
1989	Chicago	16	8	11	19	10	2	1	1
1990	Chicago	20	7	15	22	41	4	0	1
1991	Montreal	13	2	11	13	35	1	0	0
1992	Montreal	11	3	9	12	8	1	0	0
1993◆	Montreal	14	0	5	5	4	0	0	0
1995	Chicago	16	7	11	18	10	3	0	0
1996	Chicago	10	1	2	3	8	0	0	0
1997	Chicago	6	0	2	2	2	0	0	0
Playoff Totals		**169**	**66**	**109**	**175**	**256**	**24**	**2**	**6**
SAVARD, Jean *No Playoffs*	Center								
•SAVARD, Marc *No Playoffs*	Center								
SAVARD, Serge	Defense								
1968◆	Montreal	6	2	0	2	0	0	2	1
1969◆	Montreal	14	4	6	10	24	1	1	0
1971◆	Montreal	....	....	....	....	....	....	....	....
1972	Montreal	6	0	0	0	10	0	0	0
1973◆	Montreal	17	3	8	11	22	0	0	0
1974	Montreal	6	1	1	2	4	0	0	0
1975	Montreal	11	1	7	8	2	0	0	0
1976◆	Montreal	13	3	6	9	6	1	1	2
1977◆	Montreal	14	2	7	9	2	1	0	1
1978◆	Montreal	15	1	7	8	8	0	0	0
1979◆	Montreal	16	2	7	9	6	1	0	1
1980	Montreal	2	0	0	0	0	0	0	0
1981	Montreal	3	0	0	0	0	0	0	0
1982	Winnipeg	4	0	0	0	2	0	0	0
1983	Winnipeg	3	0	0	0	2	0	0	0
Playoff Totals		**130**	**19**	**49**	**68**	**88**	**4**	**4**	**5**
SAVOIA, Ryan *No Playoffs*	Center								
•SAWYER, Kevin *No Playoffs*	Left wing								
SCAMURRA, Peter *No Playoffs*	Defense								
•SCATCHARD, Dave	Center								
2002	NY Islanders	7	1	1	2	22	0	0	0
Playoff Totals		**7**	**1**	**1**	**2**	**22**	**0**	**0**	**0**
SCEVIOUR, Darin *No Playoffs*	Right wing								
•SCHAEFER, Peter	Left wing								
2001	Vancouver	3	0	0	0	0	0	0	0
Playoff Totals		**3**	**0**	**0**	**0**	**0**	**0**	**0**	**0**
SCHAEFFER, Butch *No Playoffs*	Defense								
SCHAMEHORN, Kevin *No Playoffs*	Right wing								
•SCHASTLIVY, Petr	Left wing								
2000	Ottawa	1	0	0	0	0	0	0	0
Playoff Totals		**1**	**0**	**0**	**0**	**0**	**0**	**0**	**0**
SCHELLA, John *No Playoffs*	Defense								
SCHERZA, Chuck *No Playoffs*	Left wing/Center								
SCHINKEL, Ken	Right wing								
1962	NY Rangers	2	1	0	1	0	0	0	0
1967	NY Rangers	4	0	1	1	0	0	0	0
1970	Pittsburgh	10	4	1	5	4	1	0	0
1972	Pittsburgh	3	2	0	2	0	0	0	0
Playoff Totals		**19**	**7**	**2**	**9**	**4**	**1**	**0**	**0**
SCHLEGEL, Brad	Defense								
1992	Washington	7	0	1	1	2	0	0	0
Playoff Totals		**7**	**0**	**1**	**1**	**2**	**0**	**0**	**0**
SCHLIEBENER, Andy	Defense								
1982	Vancouver	3	0	0	0	0	0	0	0
1984	Vancouver	3	0	0	0	0	0	0	0
Playoff Totals		**6**	**0**	**0**	**0**	**0**	**0**	**0**	**0**

Season	Team	GP	G	A	Pts	PIM	PP	SH	GW
SCHMAUTZ, Bobby	Right wing								
1968	Chicago	11	2	3	5	2	0	0	1
1974	Boston	16	3	6	9	44	0	0	0
1975	Boston	3	1	5	6	6	0	0	0
1976	Boston	11	2	8	10	13	0	0	1
1977	Boston	14	*11	1	12	10	4	0	1
1978	Boston	15	7	8	15	11	2	0	1
1979	Boston	11	2	2	4	6	1	0	0
1981	Vancouver	3	0	0	0	0	0	0	0
Playoff Totals		**84**	**28**	**33**	**61**	**92**	**7**	**0**	**4**
SCHMAUTZ, Cliff *No Playoffs*	Right wing								
•**SCHMIDT, Chris** *No Playoffs*	Center								
SCHMIDT, Clarence *No Playoffs*	Right wing								
SCHMIDT, Jackie	Left wing								
1943	Boston	5	0	0	0	0	0	0	0
Playoff Totals		**5**	**0**	**0**	**0**	**0**	**0**	**0**	**0**
SCHMIDT, Milt	Center/Defense								
1937	Boston	3	0	0	0	0	....	....	....
1938	Boston	3	0	0	0	0	....	....	....
1939♦	Boston	12	3	3	6	2	....	....	....
1940	Boston	6	0	0	0	0	....	....	....
1941♦	Boston	11	5	6	*11	9	....	....	....
1946	Boston	10	3	5	8	2	....	....	....
1947	Boston	5	3	1	4	4	....	....	....
1948	Boston	5	2	5	7	2	....	....	....
1949	Boston	4	0	2	2	8	....	....	....
1951	Boston	6	0	1	1	7	....	....	....
1952	Boston	7	2	1	3	0	....	....	....
1953	Boston	10	5	1	6	6	....	....	....
1954	Boston	4	1	0	1	20	....	....	....
Playoff Totals		**86**	**24**	**25**	**49**	**60**	....	....	....
SCHMIDT, Norm *No Playoffs*	Defense								
SCHMIDT, Otto *No Playoffs*	Defense								
•**SCHNABEL, Robert** *No Playoffs*	Defense								
SCHNARR, Werner *No Playoffs*	Center								
SCHNEIDER, Andy *No Playoffs*	Left wing								
•**SCHNEIDER, Mathieu**	Defense								
1990	Montreal	9	1	3	4	31	1	0	0
1991	Montreal	13	2	7	9	18	1	0	0
1992	Montreal	10	1	4	5	6	1	0	0
1993♦	Montreal	11	1	2	3	16	0	0	0
1994	Montreal	1	0	0	0	0	0	0	0
1996	Toronto	6	0	4	4	8	0	0	0
2001	Los Angeles	13	0	9	9	10	0	0	0
2002	Los Angeles	7	0	1	1	18	0	0	0
Playoff Totals		**70**	**5**	**30**	**35**	**107**	**3**	**0**	**0**
SCHOCK, Danny	Left wing								
1970♦	Boston	1	0	0	0	0	0	0	0
Playoff Totals		**1**	**0**	**0**	**0**	**0**	**0**	**0**	**0**
SCHOCK, Ron	Center								
1968	St. Louis	12	1	2	3	0	0	0	1
1969	St. Louis	12	1	2	3	6	0	0	0
1970	Pittsburgh	10	1	6	7	7	0	0	0
1972	Pittsburgh	4	1	0	1	6	0	0	0
1975	Pittsburgh	9	0	4	4	10	0	0	0
1976	Pittsburgh	3	0	1	1	0	0	0	0
1977	Pittsburgh	3	0	1	1	0	0	0	0
1978	Buffalo	2	0	0	0	0	0	0	0
Playoff Totals		**55**	**4**	**16**	**20**	**29**	**0**	**0**	**1**
SCHOENFELD, Jim	Defense								
1973	Buffalo	6	2	1	3	4	0	0	0
1975	Buffalo	17	1	4	5	38	1	0	0
1976	Buffalo	8	0	3	3	33	0	0	0
1977	Buffalo	6	0	0	0	12	0	0	0
1978	Buffalo	8	0	1	1	28	0	0	0
1979	Buffalo	3	0	1	1	0	0	0	0
1980	Buffalo	14	0	3	3	18	0	0	0
1981	Buffalo	8	0	0	0	14	0	0	0
1985	Buffalo	5	0	0	0	4	0	0	0
Playoff Totals		**75**	**3**	**13**	**16**	**151**	**1**	**0**	**0**
SCHOFIELD, Dwight	Defense								
1984	St. Louis	4	0	0	0	26	0	0	0
1985	St. Louis	2	0	0	0	15	0	0	0
1986	Washington	3	0	0	0	14	0	0	0
Playoff Totals		**9**	**0**	**0**	**0**	**55**	**0**	**0**	**0**
SCHREIBER, Wally *No Playoffs*	Right wing								
SCHRINER, Sweeney	Left wing								
1936	NY Americans	5	3	1	4	2	....	....	....
1938	NY Americans	6	1	0	1	0	....	....	....
1939	NY Americans	2	0	0	0	30	....	....	....
1940	Toronto	9	1	3	4	4	....	....	....
1941	Toronto	7	2	1	3	4	....	....	....
1942♦	Toronto	13	6	3	9	10	....	....	....
1943	Toronto	4	2	2	4	0	....	....	....
1945♦	Toronto	13	3	1	4	4	....	....	....
Playoff Totals		**59**	**18**	**11**	**29**	**54**	....	....	....
SCHULTE, Paxton *No Playoffs*	Left wing								

Season	Team	GP	G	A	Pts	PIM	PP	SH	GW
SCHULTZ, Dave	Left wing								
1973	Philadelphia	11	1	0	1	*51	0	0	0
1974♦	Philadelphia	17	2	4	6	*139	0	0	1
1975♦	Philadelphia	17	2	3	5	*83	0	0	0
1976	Philadelphia	16	2	2	4	*90	0	0	0
1977	Los Angeles	9	1	1	2	45	1	0	0
1979	Buffalo	3	0	2	2	4	0	0	0
Playoff Totals		**73**	**8**	**12**	**20**	**412**	**1**	**0**	**1**
•**SCHULTZ, Nick** *No Playoffs*	Defense								
•**SCHULTZ, Ray**	Defense								
2002	NY Islanders	2	0	0	0	2	0	0	0
Playoff Totals		**2**	**0**	**0**	**0**	**2**	**0**	**0**	**0**
SCHURMAN, Maynard *No Playoffs*	Left wing								
SCHUTT, Rod	Left wing								
1979	Pittsburgh	7	2	0	2	4	0	0	0
1980	Pittsburgh	5	2	1	3	6	0	0	0
1981	Pittsburgh	5	3	3	6	16	1	0	1
1982	Pittsburgh	5	1	2	3	0	0	0	0
Playoff Totals		**22**	**8**	**6**	**14**	**26**	**1**	**0**	**1**
SCISSONS, Scott	Center								
1993	NY Islanders	1	0	0	0	0	0	0	0
Playoff Totals		**1**	**0**	**0**	**0**	**0**	**0**	**0**	**0**
SCLISIZZI, Enio	Left wing								
1947	Detroit	1	0	0	0	0	0	0	0
1948	Detroit	6	0	0	0	4	0	0	0
1949	Detroit	6	0	0	0	2	0	0	0
Playoff Totals		**13**	**0**	**0**	**0**	**6**	**0**	**0**	**0**
SCOTT, Ganton *No Playoffs*	Right wing								
SCOTT, Laurie *No Playoffs*	Left wing/Center								
•**SCOTT, Richard** *No Playoffs*	Left wing								
•**SCOVILLE, Darrel** *No Playoffs*	Defense								
SCREMIN, Claudio *No Playoffs*	Defense								
SCRUTON, Howard *No Playoffs*	Defense								
SEABROOKE, Glen *No Playoffs*	Center								
SECORD, Al	Left wing								
1979	Boston	4	0	0	0	4	0	0	0
1980	Boston	10	0	3	3	65	0	0	0
1981	Chicago	3	4	0	4	14	0	0	0
1982	Chicago	15	2	5	7	61	2	0	1
1983	Chicago	12	4	7	11	66	1	0	0
1984	Chicago	5	3	4	7	28	0	0	1
1985	Chicago	15	7	9	16	42	1	0	1
1986	Chicago	2	0	2	2	26	0	0	0
1987	Chicago	4	0	0	0	21	0	0	0
1988	Toronto	6	1	0	1	16	0	0	0
1989	Philadelphia	14	0	4	4	31	0	0	0
1990	Chicago	12	0	0	0	8	0	0	0
Playoff Totals		**102**	**21**	**34**	**55**	**382**	**4**	**0**	**3**
•**SEDIN, Daniel**	Left wing								
2001	Vancouver	4	1	2	3	0	0	0	0
2002	Vancouver	6	0	1	1	0	0	0	0
Playoff Totals		**10**	**1**	**3**	**4**	**0**	**0**	**0**	**0**
•**SEDIN, Henrik**	Center								
2001	Vancouver	4	0	4	4	0	0	0	0
2002	Vancouver	6	3	0	3	0	0	0	1
Playoff Totals		**10**	**3**	**4**	**7**	**0**	**0**	**0**	**1**
SEDLBAUER, Ron	Left wing								
1975	Vancouver	5	0	0	0	10	0	0	0
1976	Vancouver	2	0	0	0	0	0	0	0
1979	Vancouver	3	0	1	1	9	0	0	0
1980	Chicago	7	1	1	2	6	1	0	1
1981	Toronto	2	0	1	1	2	0	0	0
Playoff Totals		**19**	**1**	**3**	**4**	**27**	**1**	**0**	**1**
SEFTEL, Steve *No Playoffs*	Left wing								
SEGUIN, Dan *No Playoffs*	Left wing								
SEGUIN, Steve *No Playoffs*	Wing								
SEIBERT, Earl	Defense								
1932	NY Rangers	7	1	2	3	14	....	....	....
1933♦	NY Rangers	8	1	0	1	14	....	....	....
1934	NY Rangers	2	0	0	0	4	....	....	....
1935	NY Rangers	4	0	0	0	6	....	....	....
1936	Chicago	2	2	0	2	0	....	....	....
1938♦	Chicago	10	5	2	7	12	....	....	....
1940	Chicago	2	0	1	1	8	....	....	....
1941	Chicago	5	0	0	0	12	....	....	....
1942	Chicago	3	0	0	0	0	....	....	....
1944	Chicago	9	0	2	2	2	....	....	....
1945	Detroit	14	2	1	3	4	....	....	....
Playoff Totals		**66**	**11**	**8**	**19**	**76**	....	....	....
•**SEIDENBERG, Dennis** *No Playoffs*	Defense								

Season	Team	GP	G	A	Pts	PIM	PP	SH	GW
SEILING, Ric	Right wing/Center								
1978	Buffalo	8	0	2	2	7	0	0	0
1979	Buffalo	3	0	1	1	2	0	0	0
1980	Buffalo	14	5	4	9	6	0	0	0
1981	Buffalo	8	2	2	4	2	0	0	0
1982	Buffalo	4	1	1	2	2	1	0	0
1983	Buffalo	10	2	3	5	6	0	0	0
1984	Buffalo	3	0	0	0	2	0	0	0
1985	Buffalo	5	4	1	5	4	0	0	0
1987	Detroit	7	0	0	0	5	0	0	0
Playoff Totals		**62**	**14**	**14**	**28**	**36**	**1**	**0**	**0**
SEILING, Rod	Defense								
1968	NY Rangers	6	1	1	2	4	0	0	0
1969	NY Rangers	4	1	0	1	2	0	0	0
1970	NY Rangers	2	0	0	0	0	0	0	0
1971	NY Rangers	13	1	0	1	12	0	0	0
1972	NY Rangers	16	1	4	5	10	1	0	0
1974	NY Rangers	13	0	2	2	19	0	0	0
1975	Toronto	7	0	0	0	0	0	0	0
1976	Toronto	10	0	1	1	6	0	0	0
1977	St. Louis	4	0	0	0	2	0	0	0
1979	Atlanta	2	0	0	0	0	0	0	0
Playoff Totals		**77**	**4**	**8**	**12**	**55**	**1**	**0**	**0**
SEJBA, Jiri *No Playoffs*	Left wing								
•**SEKERAS, Lubomir** *No Playoffs*	Defense								
•**SELANNE, Teemu**	Right wing								
1993	Winnipeg	6	4	2	6	2	2	0	2
1997	Anaheim	11	7	3	10	4	3	0	1
1999	Anaheim	4	2	2	4	2	1	0	0
2001	San Jose	6	0	2	2	2	0	0	0
2002	San Jose	12	5	3	8	2	2	0	1
Playoff Totals		**39**	**18**	**12**	**30**	**12**	**8**	**0**	**4**
SELBY, Brit	Left wing								
1966	Toronto	4	0	0	0	0	0	0	0
1968	Philadelphia	7	1	1	2	4	0	0	0
1969	Toronto	4	0	0	0	4	0	0	0
1971	St. Louis	1	0	0	0	0	0	0	0
Playoff Totals		**16**	**1**	**1**	**2**	**8**	**0**	**0**	**0**
SELF, Steve *No Playoffs*	Center								
•**SELIVANOV, Alex**	Right wing								
1996	Tampa Bay	6	2	2	4	6	0	0	1
1999	Edmonton	2	0	1	1	2	0	0	0
2000	Edmonton	5	0	0	0	8	0	0	0
Playoff Totals		**13**	**2**	**3**	**5**	**16**	**0**	**0**	**1**
•**SELLARS, Luke** *No Playoffs*	Defense								
•**SELMSER, Sean** *No Playoffs*	Left wing								
SELWOOD, Brad	Defense								
1972	Toronto	5	0	0	0	4	0	0	0
1980	Los Angeles	1	0	0	0	0	0	0	0
Playoff Totals		**6**	**0**	**0**	**0**	**4**	**0**	**0**	**0**
SEMAK, Alexander	Center								
1992	New Jersey	1	0	0	0	0	0	0	0
1993	New Jersey	5	1	1	2	0	0	0	0
1994	New Jersey	2	0	0	0	0	0	0	0
Playoff Totals		**8**	**1**	**1**	**2**	**0**	**0**	**0**	**0**
SEMCHUK, Brandy *No Playoffs*	Right wing								
SEMENKO, Dave	Left wing								
1980	Edmonton	3	0	0	0	2	0	0	0
1981	Edmonton	8	0	0	0	5	0	0	0
1982	Edmonton	4	0	0	0	2	0	0	0
1983	Edmonton	15	1	1	2	69	0	0	0
1984♦	Edmonton	19	5	5	10	44	0	0	1
1985♦	Edmonton	14	0	0	0	39	0	0	0
1986	Edmonton	6	0	0	0	32	0	0	0
1987	Hartford	4	0	0	0	15	0	0	0
Playoff Totals		**73**	**6**	**6**	**12**	**208**	**0**	**0**	**1**
•**SEMENOV, Alexei** *No Playoffs*	Defense								
SEMENOV, Anatoli	Center/Left wing								
1990	Edmonton	2	0	0	0	0	0	0	0
1991	Edmonton	12	5	5	10	6	0	0	0
1992	Edmonton	8	1	1	2	6	0	0	0
1993	Vancouver	12	1	3	4	0	0	0	0
1995	Philadelphia	15	2	4	6	0	0	0	0
Playoff Totals		**49**	**9**	**13**	**22**	**12**	**0**	**0**	**0**
SENICK, George *No Playoffs*	Left wing								
SEPPA, Jyrki *No Playoffs*	Defense								
SERAFINI, Ron *No Playoffs*	Defense								
SEROWIK, Jeff *No Playoffs*	Defense								
SERVINIS, George *No Playoffs*	Left wing								
SEVCIK, Jaroslav *No Playoffs*	Left wing								
SEVERYN, Brent	Left wing								
1997	Colorado	8	0	0	0	12	0	0	0
Playoff Totals		**8**	**0**	**0**	**0**	**12**	**0**	**0**	**0**
SEVIGNY, Pierre	Left wing								
1994	Montreal	3	0	1	1	0	0	0	0
Playoff Totals		**3**	**0**	**1**	**1**	**0**	**0**	**0**	**0**

Season	Team	GP	G	A	Pts	PIM	PP	SH	GW
SHACK, Eddie	Left wing								
1961	Toronto	4	0	0	0	2	0	0	0
1962♦	Toronto	9	0	0	0	18	0	0	0
1963♦	Toronto	10	2	1	3	11	0	0	2
1964♦	Toronto	13	0	1	1	25	0	0	0
1965	Toronto	5	1	0	1	8	0	0	0
1966	Toronto	4	2	1	3	33	1	0	0
1967♦	Toronto	8	0	0	0	8	0	0	0
1968	Boston	4	0	1	1	6	0	0	0
1969	Boston	9	0	2	2	23	0	0	0
1972	Pittsburgh	4	0	1	1	15	0	0	0
1974	Toronto	4	1	0	1	2	0	0	0
Playoff Totals		**74**	**6**	**7**	**13**	**151**	**1**	**0**	**2**
SHACK, Joe *No Playoffs*	Left wing								
SHAFRANOV, Konstantin *No Playoffs*	Right wing								
SHAKES, Paul *No Playoffs*	Defense								
SHALDYBIN, Yevgeny *No Playoffs*	Defense								
•SHANAHAN, Brendan	Left wing								
1988	New Jersey	12	2	1	3	44	1	0	0
1990	New Jersey	6	3	3	6	20	1	0	1
1991	New Jersey	7	3	5	8	12	2	0	0
1992	St. Louis	6	2	3	5	14	1	0	0
1993	St. Louis	11	4	3	7	18	2	0	0
1994	St. Louis	4	2	5	7	4	0	0	0
1995	St. Louis	5	4	5	9	14	1	0	1
1997♦	Detroit	20	9	8	17	43	2	0	2
1998♦	Detroit	20	5	4	9	22	3	0	2
1999	Detroit	10	3	7	10	6	1	0	1
2000	Detroit	9	3	2	5	10	0	0	0
2001	Detroit	2	2	2	4	0	0	0	1
2002♦	Detroit	23	8	11	19	20	1	0	2
Playoff Totals		**135**	**50**	**59**	**109**	**227**	**15**	**0**	**10**
SHANAHAN, Sean *No Playoffs*	Center/Right wing								
SHAND, Dave	Defense								
1977	Atlanta	3	0	0	0	33	0	0	0
1978	Atlanta	2	0	0	0	4	0	0	0
1979	Atlanta	2	0	0	0	20	0	0	0
1980	Atlanta	4	0	1	1	0	0	0	0
1981	Toronto	3	0	0	0	0	0	0	0
1983	Toronto	4	1	0	1	13	0	0	0
1984	Washington	8	0	1	1	13	0	0	0
Playoff Totals		**26**	**1**	**2**	**3**	**83**	**0**	**0**	**0**
SHANK, Daniel	Right wing								
1992	Hartford	5	0	0	0	22	0	0	0
Playoff Totals		**5**	**0**	**0**	**0**	**22**	**0**	**0**	**0**
SHANNON, Chuck *No Playoffs*	Defense								
SHANNON, Darrin	Left wing								
1989	Buffalo	2	0	0	0	0	0	0	0
1990	Buffalo	6	0	1	1	4	0	0	0
1991	Buffalo	6	1	2	3	4	0	0	0
1992	Winnipeg	7	0	1	1	10	0	0	0
1993	Winnipeg	6	2	4	6	6	1	0	0
1996	Winnipeg	6	1	0	1	6	0	0	0
1997	Phoenix	7	3	1	4	4	0	0	1
1998	Phoenix	5	0	1	1	4	0	0	0
Playoff Totals		**45**	**7**	**10**	**17**	**38**	**1**	**0**	**1**
•SHANNON, Darryl	Defense								
1997	Buffalo	12	2	3	5	8	1	0	0
1998	Buffalo	15	2	4	6	8	0	1	0
1999	Buffalo	2	0	0	0	0	0	0	0
Playoff Totals		**29**	**4**	**7**	**11**	**16**	**1**	**1**	**0**
SHANNON, Gerry	Left wing								
1935	Boston	4	0	0	0	2	0	0	0
1937	Mtl. Maroons	5	0	1	1	0	0	0	0
Playoff Totals		**9**	**0**	**1**	**1**	**2**	**0**	**0**	**0**
•SHANTZ, Jeff	Center								
1994	Chicago	6	0	0	0	6	0	0	0
1995	Chicago	16	3	1	4	2	0	0	0
1996	Chicago	10	2	3	5	6	0	0	0
1997	Chicago	6	0	4	4	6	0	0	0
Playoff Totals		**38**	**5**	**8**	**13**	**20**	**0**	**0**	**0**
•SHARIFIJANOV, Vadim	Right wing								
1999	New Jersey	4	0	0	0	0	0	0	0
Playoff Totals		**4**	**0**	**0**	**0**	**0**	**0**	**0**	**0**
•SHARP, Patrick *No Playoffs*	Center								
SHARPLES, Jeff	Defense								
1987	Detroit	2	0	0	0	2	0	0	0
1988	Detroit	4	0	3	3	4	0	0	0
1989	Detroit	1	0	0	0	0	0	0	0
Playoff Totals		**7**	**0**	**3**	**3**	**6**	**0**	**0**	**0**
SHARPLEY, Glen	Center								
1977	Minnesota	2	0	0	0	4	0	0	0
1980	Minnesota	9	1	6	7	4	0	0	0
1981	Chicago	1	0	2	2	0	0	0	0
1982	Chicago	15	6	3	9	16	0	0	0
Playoff Totals		**27**	**7**	**11**	**18**	**24**	**0**	**0**	**0**
SHAUNESSY, Scott *No Playoffs*	Defense/Left wing								

Season	Team	GP	G	A	Pts	PIM	PP	SH	GW
SHAW, Brad	Defense								
1989	Hartford	3	1	0	1	0	0	0	0
1990	Hartford	7	2	5	7	0	1	0	0
1991	Hartford	6	1	2	3	2	0	0	0
1992	Hartford	3	0	1	1	4	0	0	0
1999	St. Louis	4	0	0	0	0	0	0	0
Playoff Totals		**23**	**4**	**8**	**12**	**6**	**1**	**0**	**0**
SHAW, David	Defense								
1989	NY Rangers	4	0	2	2	30	0	0	0
1991	NY Rangers	6	0	0	0	11	0	0	0
1992	Minnesota	7	2	2	4	10	1	0	0
1993	Boston	4	0	1	1	6	0	0	0
1994	Boston	13	1	2	3	16	0	0	1
1995	Boston	5	0	1	1	4	0	0	0
1996	Tampa Bay	6	0	1	1	4	0	0	0
Playoff Totals		**45**	**3**	**9**	**12**	**81**	**1**	**0**	**1**
SHAY, Norm *No Playoffs*	Defense/Right wing								
SHEA, Pat *No Playoffs*	Defense								
•SHEARER, Rob *No Playoffs*	Center								
SHEDDEN, Doug *No Playoffs*	Center								
SHEEHAN, Bobby	Center								
1971♦	Montreal	6	0	0	0	0	0	0	0
1976	Chicago	4	0	0	0	0	0	0	0
1979	NY Rangers	15	4	3	7	8	1	0	0
Playoff Totals		**25**	**4**	**3**	**7**	**8**	**1**	**0**	**0**
SHEEHY, Neil	Defense								
1984	Calgary	4	0	0	0	4	0	0	0
1986	Calgary	22	0	2	2	79	0	0	0
1987	Calgary	6	0	0	0	21	0	0	0
1988	Hartford	1	0	0	0	7	0	0	0
1989	Washington	6	0	0	0	19	0	0	0
1990	Washington	13	0	1	1	92	0	0	0
1991	Washington	2	0	0	0	19	0	0	0
Playoff Totals		**54**	**0**	**3**	**3**	**241**	**0**	**0**	**0**
SHEEHY, Tim *No Playoffs*	Right wing								
•SHELLEY, Jody *No Playoffs*	Left wing								
SHELTON, Doug *No Playoffs*	Right wing								
SHEPPARD, Frank *No Playoffs*	Center/Left wing								
SHEPPARD, Gregg	Center								
1973	Boston	5	2	1	3	0	0	1	1
1974	Boston	16	11	8	19	4	0	2	2
1975	Boston	3	3	1	4	5	0	0	0
1976	Boston	12	5	6	11	6	1	0	1
1977	Boston	14	5	7	12	8	1	1	2
1978	Boston	15	2	10	12	6	0	0	0
1979	Pittsburgh	7	1	2	3	0	1	0	0
1980	Pittsburgh	5	1	1	2	0	0	0	0
1981	Pittsburgh	5	2	4	6	2	1	0	0
Playoff Totals		**82**	**32**	**40**	**72**	**31**	**4**	**4**	**6**
SHEPPARD, Johnny	Left wing								
1929	NY Americans	2	0	0	0	0	0	0	0
1934♦	Chicago	8	0	0	0	0	0	0	0
Playoff Totals		**10**	**0**	**0**	**0**	**0**	**0**	**0**	**0**
SHEPPARD, Ray	Right wing								
1988	Buffalo	6	1	1	2	2	1	0	0
1989	Buffalo	1	0	1	1	0	0	0	0
1992	Detroit	11	6	2	8	4	3	0	0
1993	Detroit	7	2	3	5	0	2	0	0
1994	Detroit	7	2	1	3	4	0	0	0
1995	Detroit	17	4	3	7	5	2	0	0
1996	Florida	21	8	8	16	4	3	0	0
1997	Florida	5	2	0	2	0	1	0	0
1999	Carolina	6	5	1	6	2	1	0	1
Playoff Totals		**81**	**30**	**20**	**50**	**21**	**13**	**0**	**1**
SHERF, John	Left wing								
1937♦	Detroit	5	0	1	1	2	0	0	0
1939	Detroit	3	0	0	0	0	0	0	0
Playoff Totals		**8**	**0**	**1**	**1**	**2**	**0**	**0**	**0**
SHERO, Fred	Defense								
1948	NY Rangers	6	0	1	1	6	0	0	0
1950	NY Rangers	7	0	1	1	2	0	0	0
Playoff Totals		**13**	**0**	**2**	**2**	**8**	**0**	**0**	**0**
SHERRITT, Gordon *No Playoffs*	Defense								
SHERVEN, Gord	Center								
1985	Minnesota	3	0	0	0	0	0	0	0
Playoff Totals		**3**	**0**	**0**	**0**	**0**	**0**	**0**	**0**
SHEVALIER, Jeff *No Playoffs*	Left wing								
SHEWCHUCK, Jack	Defense								
1940	Boston	6	0	0	0	0	0	0	0
1941♦	Boston	....	....	....	....	....	....	....	....
1942	Boston	5	0	1	1	7	0	0	0
1943	Boston	9	0	0	0	12	0	0	0
Playoff Totals		**20**	**0**	**1**	**1**	**19**	**0**	**0**	**0**

Season	Team	GP	G	A	Pts	PIM	PP	SH	GW
SHIBICKY, Alex	Right wing								
1937	NY Rangers	9	1	4	5	0	....	....	....
1938	NY Rangers	3	2	0	2	2	....	....	....
1939	NY Rangers	7	3	1	4	2	....	....	....
1940♦	NY Rangers	11	2	5	7	4	....	....	....
1941	NY Rangers	3	1	0	1	2	....	....	....
1942	NY Rangers	6	3	2	5	2	....	....	....
Playoff Totals		**39**	**12**	**12**	**24**	**12**	....	....	....
SHIELDS, Al	Defense								
1928	Ottawa	2	0	0	0	0	0	0	0
1930	Ottawa	2	0	0	0	0	0	0	0
1935♦	Mtl. Maroons	7	0	1	1	6	0	0	0
1936	Mtl. Maroons	3	0	0	0	6	0	0	0
1937	Boston	3	0	0	0	2	0	0	0
Playoff Totals		**17**	**0**	**1**	**1**	**14**	**0**	**0**	**0**
SHILL, Bill	Right wing								
1946	Boston	7	1	2	3	2	....	....	....
Playoff Totals		**7**	**1**	**2**	**3**	**2**	....	....	....
SHILL, Jack	Center								
1934	Toronto	2	0	0	0	0	....	....	....
1935	Boston	2	0	0	0	0	....	....	....
1936	Toronto	9	0	3	3	8	....	....	....
1937	Toronto	2	0	0	0	0	....	....	....
1938♦	Chicago	10	1	3	4	15	....	....	....
Playoff Totals		**25**	**1**	**6**	**7**	**23**	....	....	....
SHINSKE, Rick *No Playoffs*	Center								
SHIRES, Jim *No Playoffs*	Left wing								
SHMYR, Paul	Defense								
1970	Chicago	8	1	2	3	0	0	0	0
1971	Chicago	9	0	0	0	17	0	0	0
1980	Minnesota	14	2	1	3	23	1	0	1
1981	Minnesota	3	0	0	0	4	0	0	0
Playoff Totals		**34**	**3**	**3**	**6**	**44**	**1**	**0**	**1**
SHOEBOTTOM, Bruce	Defense								
1988	Boston	4	1	0	1	42	0	0	1
1989	Boston	10	0	2	2	35	0	0	0
Playoff Totals		**14**	**1**	**2**	**3**	**77**	**0**	**0**	**1**
SHORE, Eddie	Defense								
1927	Boston	8	1	1	2	*40	....	....	....
1928	Boston	2	0	0	0	8	....	....	....
1929♦	Boston	5	1	1	2	*28	....	....	....
1930	Boston	6	1	0	1	*26	....	....	....
1931	Boston	5	2	1	3	24	....	....	....
1933	Boston	5	0	1	1	14	....	....	....
1935	Boston	4	0	1	1	2	....	....	....
1936	Boston	2	1	1	2	12	....	....	....
1938	Boston	3	0	1	1	6	....	....	....
1939♦	Boston	12	0	4	4	19	....	....	....
1940	NY Americans	3	0	2	2	2	....	....	....
Playoff Totals		**55**	**6**	**13**	**19**	**181**	....	....	....
SHORE, Hamby *No Playoffs*	Defense/Left wing								
SHORT, Steve *No Playoffs*	Left wing								
SHUCHUK, Gary	Right wing								
1991	Detroit	3	0	0	0	0	0	0	0
1993	Los Angeles	17	2	2	4	12	0	0	1
Playoff Totals		**20**	**2**	**2**	**4**	**12**	**0**	**0**	**1**
SHUDRA, Ron *No Playoffs*	Defense								
SHUTT, Steve	Left wing								
1973♦	Montreal	1	0	0	0	0	0	0	0
1974	Montreal	6	5	3	8	9	1	0	0
1975	Montreal	9	1	6	7	4	0	0	0
1976♦	Montreal	13	7	8	15	2	3	0	0
1977♦	Montreal	14	8	10	18	2	2	0	3
1978♦	Montreal	15	9	8	17	20	3	0	0
1979♦	Montreal	11	4	7	11	6	1	0	0
1980	Montreal	10	6	3	9	6	2	0	2
1981	Montreal	3	2	1	3	4	0	0	0
1983	Montreal	3	1	0	1	0	0	0	0
1984	Montreal	11	7	2	9	8	2	0	0
1985	Los Angeles	3	0	0	0	4	0	0	0
Playoff Totals		**99**	**50**	**48**	**98**	**65**	**14**	**0**	**5**
•SHVIDKI, Denis *No Playoffs*	Right wing								
SIEBERT, Babe	Left wing/Defense								
1926♦	Mtl. Maroons	4	1	0	1	4	....	....	....
1927	Mtl. Maroons	2	1	0	1	2	....	....	....
1928	Mtl. Maroons	9	2	0	2	26	....	....	....
1930	Mtl. Maroons	3	0	0	0	0	....	....	....
1931	Mtl. Maroons	2	0	0	0	6	....	....	....
1932	Mtl. Maroons	4	0	1	1	4	....	....	....
1933♦	NY Rangers	8	1	0	1	12	....	....	....
1935	Boston	4	0	0	0	6	....	....	....
1936	Boston	2	0	1	1	0	....	....	....
1937	Montreal	5	1	2	3	2	....	....	....
1938	Montreal	3	1	1	2	0	....	....	....
1939	Montreal	3	0	0	0	0	....	....	....
Playoff Totals		**49**	**7**	**5**	**12**	**62**	....	....	....
•SIKLENKA, Mike *No Playoffs*	Right wing								

Season	Team	GP	G	A	Pts	PIM	PP	SH	GW
SILK, Dave	Right wing								
1982	NY Rangers	9	2	4	6	4	0	0	1
1984	Boston	3	0	0	0	7	0	0	0
1986	Winnipeg	1	0	0	0	2	0	0	0
Playoff Totals		**13**	**2**	**4**	**6**	**13**	**0**	**0**	**1**
•SILLINGER, Mike	Center								
1991	Detroit	3	0	1	1	0	0	0	0
1992	Detroit	8	2	2	4	2	0	0	0
1996	Vancouver	6	0	0	0	2	0	0	0
1998	Philadelphia	3	1	0	1	0	0	0	0
2000	Florida	4	2	1	3	2	0	0	0
2001	Ottawa	4	0	0	0	2	0	0	0
Playoff Totals		**28**	**5**	**4**	**9**	**8**	**0**	**0**	**0**
SILTALA, Mike *No Playoffs*	Right wing								
SILTANEN, Risto	Defense								
1980	Edmonton	2	0	0	0	2	0	0	0
1981	Edmonton	9	2	0	2	8	2	0	1
1982	Edmonton	5	3	2	5	10	1	0	0
1986	Quebec	3	0	1	1	2	0	0	0
1987	Quebec	13	1	9	10	8	1	0	0
Playoff Totals		**32**	**6**	**12**	**18**	**30**	**4**	**0**	**1**
•SIM, Jon	Center								
1999♦	Dallas	4	0	0	0	0	0	0	0
2000	Dallas	7	1	0	1	6	0	0	0
Playoff Totals		**11**	**1**	**0**	**1**	**6**	**0**	**0**	**0**
SIM, Trevor *No Playoffs*	Right wing								
SIMARD, Martin *No Playoffs*	Right wing								
•SIMICEK, Roman *No Playoffs*	Center								
SIMMER, Charlie	Left wing								
1979	Los Angeles	2	1	0	1	2	1	0	0
1980	Los Angeles	3	2	0	2	0	1	0	0
1982	Los Angeles	10	4	7	11	22	1	0	1
1985	Boston	5	2	2	4	2	0	0	0
1986	Boston	3	0	0	0	4	0	0	0
1987	Boston	1	0	0	0	2	0	0	0
Playoff Totals		**24**	**9**	**9**	**18**	**32**	**3**	**0**	**1**
SIMMONS, Al	Defense								
1974	Boston	1	0	0	0	0	0	0	0
Playoff Totals		**1**	**0**	**0**	**0**	**0**	**0**	**0**	**0**
•SIMON, Ben *No Playoffs*	Center								
•SIMON, Chris	Left wing								
1993	Quebec	5	0	0	0	26	0	0	0
1995	Quebec	6	1	1	2	19	0	0	1
1996♦	Colorado	12	1	2	3	11	0	0	0
1998	Washington	18	1	0	1	26	0	0	0
2000	Washington	4	2	0	2	24	0	0	0
2001	Washington	6	0	1	1	4	0	0	0
Playoff Totals		**51**	**5**	**4**	**9**	**110**	**0**	**0**	**1**
SIMON, Cully	Defense								
1943♦	Detroit	9	1	0	1	4	....	....	....
1944	Detroit	5	0	0	0	2	0	0	0
Playoff Totals		**14**	**1**	**0**	**1**	**6**	**0**	**0**	**0**
SIMON, Jason *No Playoffs*	Left wing								
SIMON, Thain *No Playoffs*	Defense								
SIMON, Todd	Center								
1994	Buffalo	5	1	0	1	0	1	0	1
Playoff Totals		**5**	**1**	**0**	**1**	**0**	**1**	**0**	**1**
SIMONETTI, Frank	Defense								
1985	Boston	5	0	1	1	2	0	0	0
1986	Boston	3	0	0	0	0	0	0	0
1987	Boston	4	0	0	0	6	0	0	0
Playoff Totals		**12**	**0**	**1**	**1**	**8**	**0**	**0**	**0**
SIMPSON, Bobby	Left wing								
1977	Atlanta	2	0	1	1	0	0	0	0
1978	Atlanta	2	0	0	0	2	0	0	0
1982	Pittsburgh	2	0	0	0	0	0	0	0
Playoff Totals		**6**	**0**	**1**	**1**	**2**	**0**	**0**	**0**
SIMPSON, Cliff	Center								
1947	Detroit	1	0	0	0	0	0	0	0
1948	Detroit	1	0	0	0	2	0	0	0
Playoff Totals		**2**	**0**	**0**	**0**	**2**	**0**	**0**	**0**
SIMPSON, Craig	Left wing								
1988♦	Edmonton	19	13	6	19	26	3	0	3
1989	Edmonton	7	2	0	2	10	1	0	1
1990♦	Edmonton	22	*16	15	*31	8	6	0	3
1991	Edmonton	18	5	11	16	12	1	0	0
1992	Edmonton	1	0	0	0	0	0	0	0
Playoff Totals		**67**	**36**	**32**	**68**	**56**	**11**	**0**	**7**
SIMPSON, Joe	Defense								
1929	NY Americans	2	0	0	0	0	0	0	0
Playoff Totals		**2**	**0**	**0**	**0**	**0**	**0**	**0**	**0**
•SIMPSON, Reid	Left wing								
1997	New Jersey	5	0	0	0	29	0	0	0
2001	St. Louis	5	0	0	0	2	0	0	0
Playoff Totals		**10**	**0**	**0**	**0**	**31**	**0**	**0**	**0**
•SIMPSON, Todd	Defense								
2000	Florida	4	0	0	0	4	0	0	0
2002	Phoenix	5	0	2	2	6	0	0	0
Playoff Totals		**9**	**0**	**2**	**2**	**10**	**0**	**0**	**0**
SIMS, Al	Defense								
1974	Boston	16	0	0	0	12	0	0	0
1976	Boston	1	0	0	0	0	0	0	0
1977	Boston	2	0	0	0	0	0	0	0
1978	Boston	8	0	0	0	0	0	0	0
1979	Boston	11	0	2	2	0	0	0	0
1980	Hartford	3	0	0	0	2	0	0	0
Playoff Totals		**41**	**0**	**2**	**2**	**14**	**0**	**0**	**0**
SINCLAIR, Reg	Right wing/Center								
1953	Detroit	3	1	0	1	0	....	....	....
Playoff Totals		**3**	**1**	**0**	**1**	**0**	....	....	....
SINGBUSH, Alex	Defense								
1941	Montreal	3	0	0	0	4	0	0	0
Playoff Totals		**3**	**0**	**0**	**0**	**4**	**0**	**0**	**0**
SINISALO, Ilkka	Right wing								
1982	Philadelphia	4	0	2	2	0	0	0	0
1983	Philadelphia	3	1	1	2	0	0	0	0
1984	Philadelphia	2	2	0	2	0	1	0	0
1985	Philadelphia	19	6	1	7	0	2	0	3
1986	Philadelphia	5	2	2	4	2	0	0	0
1987	Philadelphia	18	5	1	6	4	0	0	1
1988	Philadelphia	7	4	2	6	0	1	0	0
1989	Philadelphia	8	1	1	2	0	0	1	1
1991	Los Angeles	2	0	1	1	0	0	0	0
Playoff Totals		**68**	**21**	**11**	**32**	**6**	**4**	**1**	**5**
SIREN, Ville	Defense								
1989	Minnesota	4	0	0	0	4	0	0	0
1990	Minnesota	3	0	0	0	2	0	0	0
Playoff Totals		**7**	**0**	**0**	**0**	**6**	**0**	**0**	**0**
SIROIS, Bob *No Playoffs*	Right wing								
SITTLER, Darryl	Center								
1971	Toronto	6	2	1	3	31	1	0	0
1972	Toronto	3	0	0	0	2	0	0	0
1974	Toronto	4	2	1	3	6	1	0	0
1975	Toronto	7	2	1	3	15	1	0	0
1976	Toronto	10	5	7	12	19	2	0	1
1977	Toronto	9	5	16	21	4	3	0	0
1978	Toronto	13	3	8	11	12	2	0	0
1979	Toronto	6	5	4	9	17	2	0	0
1980	Toronto	3	1	2	3	10	1	0	0
1981	Toronto	3	0	0	0	4	0	0	0
1982	Philadelphia	4	3	1	4	6	1	0	0
1983	Philadelphia	3	1	0	1	4	0	0	0
1984	Philadelphia	3	0	2	2	7	0	0	0
1985	Detroit	2	0	2	2	0	0	0	0
Playoff Totals		**76**	**29**	**45**	**74**	**137**	**14**	**0**	**1**
•SIVEK, Michal *No Playoffs*	Center								
SJOBERG, Lars-Erik *No Playoffs*	Defense								
SJODIN, Tommy *No Playoffs*	Defense								
SKAARE, Bjorn *No Playoffs*	Center								
•SKALDE, Jarrod *No Playoffs*	Center								
SKARDA, Randy *No Playoffs*	Defense								
SKILTON, Raymie *No Playoffs*	Defense								
SKINNER, Alf	Right wing								
1918♦	Toronto	2	0	1	*1	9	....	....	....
Playoff Totals		**2**	**0**	**1**	**1**	**9**	....	....	....
SKINNER, Larry	Center								
1978	Colorado	2	0	0	0	0	0	0	0
Playoff Totals		**2**	**0**	**0**	**0**	**0**	**0**	**0**	**0**
•SKOPINTSEV, Andrei *No Playoffs*	Defense								
•SKOULA, Martin	Defense								
2000	Colorado	17	0	2	2	4	0	0	0
2001♦	Colorado	23	1	4	5	8	0	0	0
2002	Colorado	21	0	6	6	2	0	0	0
Playoff Totals		**61**	**1**	**12**	**13**	**14**	**0**	**0**	**0**
SKOV, Glen	Center/Left wing								
1951	Detroit	6	0	0	0	0	....	....	....
1952♦	Detroit	8	1	4	5	16	....	....	....
1953	Detroit	6	1	0	1	2	....	....	....
1954♦	Detroit	12	1	2	3	16	....	....	....
1955♦	Detroit	11	2	0	2	8	....	....	....
1959	Chicago	6	2	1	3	4	....	....	....
1960	Chicago	4	0	0	0	2	....	....	....
Playoff Totals		**53**	**7**	**7**	**14**	**48**	....	....	....
•SKRASTINS, Karlis *No Playoffs*	Defense								
•SKRBEK, Pavel *No Playoffs*	Defense								
SKRIKO, Petri	Left wing								
1986	Vancouver	3	0	0	0	0	0	0	0
1989	Vancouver	7	1	5	6	0	0	0	0
1991	Boston	18	4	4	8	4	3	0	0
Playoff Totals		**28**	**5**	**9**	**14**	**4**	**3**	**0**	**0**
SKRUDLAND, Brian	Center								
1986♦	Montreal	20	2	4	6	76	0	0	1
1987	Montreal	14	1	5	6	29	0	0	0
1988	Montreal	11	1	5	6	24	0	0	0
1989	Montreal	21	3	7	10	40	0	0	0
1990	Montreal	11	3	5	8	30	0	0	1
1991	Montreal	13	3	10	13	42	1	0	0
1992	Montreal	11	1	1	2	20	0	0	0
1993	Calgary	6	0	3	3	12	0	0	0
1996	Florida	21	1	3	4	18	0	0	0
1998	Dallas	17	0	1	1	16	0	0	0
1999♦	Dallas	19	0	2	2	16	0	0	0
Playoff Totals		**164**	**15**	**46**	**61**	**323**	**1**	**0**	**2**
•SLANEY, John	Defense								
1994	Washington	11	1	1	2	2	1	0	0
2000	Pittsburgh	2	1	0	1	2	1	0	0
2002	Philadelphia	1	0	0	0	0	0	0	0
Playoff Totals		**14**	**2**	**1**	**3**	**4**	**2**	**0**	**0**
SLEAVER, John *No Playoffs*	Center								
•SLEGR, Jiri	Defense								
1993	Vancouver	5	0	3	3	4	0	0	0
1998	Pittsburgh	6	0	4	4	2	0	0	0
1999	Pittsburgh	13	1	3	4	12	0	0	1
2000	Pittsburgh	10	2	3	5	19	0	0	1
2002♦	Detroit	1	0	0	0	2	0	0	0
Playoff Totals		**35**	**3**	**13**	**16**	**39**	**0**	**0**	**2**
SLEIGHER, Louis	Right wing								
1983	Quebec	4	0	0	0	4	0	0	0
1984	Quebec	7	1	1	2	42	0	0	0
1985	Boston	5	0	0	0	4	0	0	0
1986	Boston	1	0	0	0	14	0	0	0
Playoff Totals		**17**	**1**	**1**	**2**	**64**	**0**	**0**	**0**
•SLOAN, Blake	Right wing								
1999♦	Dallas	19	0	2	2	8	0	0	0
2000	Dallas	16	0	0	0	12	0	0	0
Playoff Totals		**35**	**0**	**2**	**2**	**20**	**0**	**0**	**0**
SLOAN, Tod	Center/Right wing								
1951♦	Toronto	11	4	5	9	18	....	....	....
1952	Toronto	4	0	0	0	10	....	....	....
1954	Toronto	5	1	1	2	4	....	....	....
1955	Toronto	4	0	0	0	2	....	....	....
1956	Toronto	2	0	0	0	5	....	....	....
1959	Chicago	6	3	5	8	0	....	....	....
1960	Chicago	3	0	0	0	0	....	....	....
1961♦	Chicago	12	1	1	2	8	....	....	....
Playoff Totals		**47**	**9**	**12**	**21**	**47**	....	....	....
SLOBODIAN, Peter *No Playoffs*	Defense								
SLOWINSKI, Ed	Right wing								
1948	NY Rangers	4	0	0	0	0	....	....	....
1950	NY Rangers	12	2	*6	8	6	....	....	....
Playoff Totals		**16**	**2**	**6**	**8**	**6**	....	....	....
SLY, Darryl *No Playoffs*	Defense								
SMAIL, Doug	Left wing								
1982	Winnipeg	4	0	0	0	0	0	0	0
1983	Winnipeg	3	0	0	0	6	0	0	0
1984	Winnipeg	3	0	1	1	7	0	0	0
1985	Winnipeg	8	2	1	3	4	0	1	0
1986	Winnipeg	3	1	0	1	0	0	0	0
1987	Winnipeg	10	4	0	4	10	0	1	0
1988	Winnipeg	5	1	0	1	22	0	0	0
1990	Winnipeg	5	1	0	1	0	0	0	0
1991	Minnesota	1	0	0	0	0	0	0	0
Playoff Totals		**42**	**9**	**2**	**11**	**49**	**0**	**2**	**0**
SMART, Alex *No Playoffs*	Left wing								
SMEDSMO, Dale *No Playoffs*	Left wing								
•SMEHLIK, Richard	Defense								
1993	Buffalo	8	0	4	4	2	0	0	0
1994	Buffalo	7	0	2	2	10	0	0	0
1995	Buffalo	5	0	0	0	2	0	0	0
1997	Buffalo	12	0	2	2	4	0	0	0
1998	Buffalo	15	0	2	2	6	0	0	0
1999	Buffalo	21	0	3	3	10	0	0	0
2000	Buffalo	5	1	0	1	0	0	0	0
2001	Buffalo	10	0	1	1	4	0	0	0
Playoff Totals		**83**	**1**	**14**	**15**	**38**	**0**	**0**	**0**
SMILLIE, Don *No Playoffs*	Left wing								
•SMIRNOV, Alexei *No Playoffs*	Left wing								
SMITH, Alex	Defense								
1926	Ottawa	2	0	0	0	2	0	0	0
1927♦	Ottawa	6	0	0	0	8	0	0	0
1928	Ottawa	2	0	0	0	4	0	0	0
1930	Ottawa	2	0	0	0	4	0	0	0
1932	Detroit	2	0	0	0	4	0	0	0
1933	Boston	5	0	2	2	6	0	0	0
Playoff Totals		**19**	**0**	**2**	**2**	**28**	**0**	**0**	**0**
SMITH, Art	Defense								
1929	Toronto	4	1	1	2	8	....	....	....
Playoff Totals		**4**	**1**	**1**	**2**	**8**	....	....	....
SMITH, Barry *No Playoffs*	Center								

Season	Team	GP	G	A	Pts	PIM	PP	SH	GW
SMITH, Bobby	Center								
1980	Minnesota	15	1	13	14	9	1	0	0
1981	Minnesota	19	8	17	25	13	2	0	0
1982	Minnesota	4	2	4	6	5	0	0	0
1983	Minnesota	9	6	4	10	17	3	0	2
1984	Montreal	15	2	7	9	8	1	0	1
1985	Montreal	12	5	6	11	30	3	0	1
1986♦	Montreal	20	7	8	15	22	3	0	3
1987	Montreal	17	9	9	18	19	2	0	0
1988	Montreal	11	3	4	7	8	1	0	0
1989	Montreal	21	11	8	19	46	5	0	1
1990	Montreal	11	1	4	5	6	0	0	0
1991	Minnesota	23	8	8	16	56	2	0	5
1992	Minnesota	7	1	4	5	6	1	0	0
Playoff Totals		**184**	**64**	**96**	**160**	**245**	**24**	**0**	**13**
SMITH, Brad	Right wing								
1985	Detroit	3	0	1	1	5	0	0	0
1986	Toronto	6	2	1	3	20	1	0	0
1987	Toronto	11	1	1	2	24	0	0	1
Playoff Totals		**20**	**3**	**3**	**6**	**49**	**1**	**0**	**1**
•SMITH, Brandon *No Playoffs*	Defense								
SMITH, Brian	Left wing								
1960	Detroit	5	0	0	0	0	0	0	0
Playoff Totals		**5**	**0**	**0**	**0**	**0**	**0**	**0**	**0**
SMITH, Brian	Left wing								
1968	Los Angeles	7	0	0	0	0	0	0	0
Playoff Totals		**7**	**0**	**0**	**0**	**0**	**0**	**0**	**0**
SMITH, Carl *No Playoffs*	Right wing								
SMITH, Clint	Center								
1938	NY Rangers	3	2	0	2	0	....	....	....
1939	NY Rangers	7	1	2	3	0	....	....	....
1940♦	NY Rangers	11	1	3	4	2	....	....	....
1941	NY Rangers	3	0	0	0	0	....	....	....
1942	NY Rangers	5	0	0	0	0	....	....	....
1944	Chicago	9	4	8	12	0	....	....	....
1946	Chicago	4	2	1	3	0	....	....	....
Playoff Totals		**42**	**10**	**14**	**24**	**2**	....	....	....
•SMITH, D.J. *No Playoffs*	Defense								
SMITH, Dallas	Defense								
1968	Boston	4	0	2	2	0	0	0	0
1969	Boston	10	0	3	3	16	0	0	0
1970♦	Boston	14	0	3	3	19	0	0	0
1971	Boston	7	0	3	3	26	0	0	0
1972♦	Boston	15	0	4	4	22	0	0	0
1973	Boston	5	0	2	2	2	0	0	0
1974	Boston	16	1	7	8	20	0	0	0
1975	Boston	3	0	2	2	4	0	0	0
1976	Boston	11	2	2	4	19	0	0	1
1978	NY Rangers	1	0	1	1	0	0	0	0
Playoff Totals		**86**	**3**	**29**	**32**	**128**	**0**	**0**	**1**
SMITH, Dan *No Playoffs*	Defense								
SMITH, Dennis *No Playoffs*	Defense								
SMITH, Derek	Center/Left wing								
1976	Buffalo	1	0	0	0	0	0	0	0
1978	Buffalo	8	3	3	6	7	0	0	0
1980	Buffalo	13	5	7	12	4	3	0	1
1981	Buffalo	8	1	4	5	2	1	0	0
Playoff Totals		**30**	**9**	**14**	**23**	**13**	**4**	**0**	**1**
SMITH, Derrick	Left wing								
1985	Philadelphia	19	2	5	7	16	0	0	0
1986	Philadelphia	4	0	0	0	10	0	0	0
1987	Philadelphia	26	6	4	10	26	0	0	1
1988	Philadelphia	7	0	0	0	6	0	0	0
1989	Philadelphia	19	5	2	7	12	0	2	1
1992	Minnesota	7	1	0	1	9	0	0	1
Playoff Totals		**82**	**14**	**11**	**25**	**79**	**0**	**2**	**3**
SMITH, Des	Defense								
1939	Montreal	3	0	0	0	4	....	....	....
1940	Boston	6	0	0	0	0	....	....	....
1941♦	Boston	11	0	2	2	12	....	....	....
1942	Boston	5	1	2	3	2	....	....	....
Playoff Totals		**25**	**1**	**4**	**5**	**18**	....	....	....
SMITH, Don	Left wing/Center								
1950	NY Rangers	1	0	0	0	0	0	0	0
Playoff Totals		**1**	**0**	**0**	**0**	**0**	**0**	**0**	**0**
SMITH, Don *No Playoffs*	Left wing/Center								
SMITH, Doug	Center								
1982	Los Angeles	10	3	2	5	11	1	0	0
1985	Los Angeles	3	1	0	1	4	0	0	0
1988	Buffalo	1	0	0	0	0	0	0	0
1989	Vancouver	4	0	0	0	6	0	0	0
Playoff Totals		**18**	**4**	**2**	**6**	**21**	**1**	**0**	**0**
SMITH, Floyd	Right wing								
1963	Detroit	11	2	3	5	4	0	0	0
1964	Detroit	14	4	3	7	4	2	0	0
1965	Detroit	7	1	3	4	4	0	0	0
1966	Detroit	12	5	2	7	4	2	0	1
1969	Toronto	4	0	0	0	0	0	0	0
Playoff Totals		**48**	**12**	**11**	**23**	**16**	**4**	**0**	**1**
SMITH, Geoff	Defense								
1990♦	Edmonton	3	0	0	0	0	0	0	0
1991	Edmonton	4	0	0	0	0	0	0	0
1992	Edmonton	5	0	1	1	6	0	0	0
1996	Florida	1	0	0	0	2	0	0	0
Playoff Totals		**13**	**0**	**1**	**1**	**8**	**0**	**0**	**0**
SMITH, Glen *No Playoffs*	Right wing								
SMITH, Glenn *No Playoffs*	Defense								
SMITH, Gord *No Playoffs*	Defense								
SMITH, Greg	Defense								
1980	Minnesota	12	0	1	1	9	0	0	0
1981	Minnesota	19	1	5	6	39	0	1	0
1984	Detroit	4	1	0	1	8	0	0	0
1985	Detroit	3	0	0	0	7	0	0	0
1986	Washington	9	2	1	3	9	0	1	0
1987	Washington	7	0	0	0	11	0	0	0
1988	Washington	9	0	0	0	23	0	0	0
Playoff Totals		**63**	**4**	**7**	**11**	**106**	**0**	**2**	**0**
SMITH, Hooley	Center/Right wing								
1926	Ottawa	2	0	0	0	14	....	....	....
1927♦	Ottawa	6	1	0	1	16	....	....	....
1928	Mtl. Maroons	9	2	1	3	23	....	....	....
1930	Mtl. Maroons	4	1	1	2	14	....	....	....
1932	Mtl. Maroons	4	2	1	3	2	....	....	....
1933	Mtl. Maroons	2	2	0	2	2	....	....	....
1934	Mtl. Maroons	4	0	1	1	6	....	....	....
1935♦	Mtl. Maroons	6	0	0	0	14	....	....	....
1936	Mtl. Maroons	3	0	0	0	2	....	....	....
1937	Boston	3	0	0	0	0	....	....	....
1938	NY Americans	6	0	3	3	0	....	....	....
1939	NY Americans	2	0	0	0	14	....	....	....
1940	NY Americans	3	3	1	4	2	....	....	....
Playoff Totals		**54**	**11**	**8**	**19**	**109**	....	....	....
•SMITH, Jason	Defense								
1994	New Jersey	6	0	0	0	7	0	0	0
1999	Edmonton	4	0	1	1	4	0	0	0
2000	Edmonton	5	0	1	1	4	0	0	0
2001	Edmonton	6	0	2	2	6	0	0	0
Playoff Totals		**21**	**0**	**4**	**4**	**21**	**0**	**0**	**0**
SMITH, Ken	Left wing								
1945	Boston	7	3	4	7	0	....	....	....
1946	Boston	8	0	4	4	0	....	....	....
1947	Boston	5	3	0	3	2	....	....	....
1948	Boston	5	2	3	5	0	....	....	....
1949	Boston	5	0	2	2	4	....	....	....
Playoff Totals		**30**	**8**	**13**	**21**	**6**	....	....	....
•SMITH, Mark *No Playoffs*	Center								
SMITH, Nakina *No Playoffs*	Center								
•SMITH, Nick *No Playoffs*	Center								
SMITH, Randy *No Playoffs*	Center								
SMITH, Rick	Defense								
1969	Boston	9	0	0	0	6	0	0	0
1970♦	Boston	14	1	3	4	17	0	0	0
1971	Boston	6	0	0	0	0	0	0	0
1976	St. Louis	3	0	1	1	4	0	0	0
1977	Boston	14	0	9	9	14	0	0	0
1978	Boston	15	1	5	6	18	0	0	0
1979	Boston	11	0	4	4	12	0	0	0
1980	Boston	6	1	1	2	2	0	0	0
Playoff Totals		**78**	**3**	**23**	**26**	**73**	**0**	**0**	**0**
SMITH, Rodger	Defense								
1926	Pittsburgh	2	1	0	1	0	....	....	....
1928	Pittsburgh	2	2	0	2	0	....	....	....
Playoff Totals		**4**	**3**	**0**	**3**	**0**	....	....	....
SMITH, Ron *No Playoffs*	Defense								
SMITH, Sid	Left wing								
1948♦	Toronto	2	0	0	0	0	....	....	....
1949♦	Toronto	6	5	2	7	0	....	....	....
1950	Toronto	7	0	3	3	2	....	....	....
1951♦	Toronto	11	7	3	10	0	....	....	....
1952	Toronto	4	0	0	0	0	....	....	....
1954	Toronto	5	1	1	2	0	....	....	....
1955	Toronto	4	3	1	4	0	....	....	....
1956	Toronto	5	1	0	1	0	....	....	....
Playoff Totals		**44**	**17**	**10**	**27**	**2**	....	....	....
SMITH, Stan	Center								
1940♦	NY Rangers	1	0	0	0	0	0	0	0
Playoff Totals		**1**	**0**	**0**	**0**	**0**	**0**	**0**	**0**
SMITH, Steve	Defense								
1986	Edmonton	6	0	1	1	14	0	0	0
1987♦	Edmonton	15	1	3	4	45	0	0	0
1988♦	Edmonton	19	1	11	12	55	1	0	0
1989	Edmonton	7	2	2	4	20	0	0	1
1990♦	Edmonton	22	5	10	15	37	0	1	1
1991	Edmonton	18	1	2	3	45	1	0	0
1992	Chicago	18	1	11	12	16	1	0	0
1993	Chicago	4	0	0	0	10	0	0	0
1995	Chicago	16	0	1	1	26	0	0	0
1996	Chicago	6	0	0	0	16	0	0	0
1997	Chicago	3	0	0	0	4	0	0	0
Playoff Totals		**134**	**11**	**41**	**52**	**288**	**3**	**1**	**2**
SMITH, Steve *No Playoffs*	Defense								
SMITH, Stu	Left wing								
1941	Montreal	1	0	0	0	0	0	0	0
Playoff Totals		**1**	**0**	**0**	**0**	**0**	**0**	**0**	**0**
SMITH, Stu *No Playoffs*	Defense								
SMITH, Tommy *No Playoffs*	Center								
SMITH, Vern *No Playoffs*	Defense								
SMITH, Wayne	Defense								
1967	Chicago	1	0	0	0	0	0	0	0
Playoff Totals		**1**	**0**	**0**	**0**	**0**	**0**	**0**	**0**
•SMITH, Wyatt *No Playoffs*	Center								
•SMITHSON, Jerred *No Playoffs*	Right wing								
•SMOLINSKI, Bryan	Center/Right wing								
1993	Boston	4	1	0	1	2	0	0	0
1994	Boston	13	5	4	9	4	2	0	0
1995	Boston	5	0	1	1	4	0	0	0
1996	Pittsburgh	18	5	4	9	10	0	0	1
2000	Los Angeles	4	0	0	0	2	0	0	0
2001	Los Angeles	13	1	5	6	14	0	0	0
2002	Los Angeles	7	2	0	2	2	1	0	0
Playoff Totals		**64**	**14**	**14**	**28**	**38**	**3**	**0**	**1**
•SMREK, Peter *No Playoffs*	Defense								
SMRKE, John *No Playoffs*	Left wing								
SMRKE, Stan *No Playoffs*	Left wing								
SMYL, Stan	Right wing								
1979	Vancouver	2	1	1	2	0	0	0	0
1980	Vancouver	4	0	2	2	14	0	0	0
1981	Vancouver	3	1	2	3	0	0	0	0
1982	Vancouver	17	9	9	18	25	1	0	1
1983	Vancouver	4	3	2	5	12	1	0	1
1984	Vancouver	4	2	1	3	4	0	0	0
1989	Vancouver	7	0	0	0	9	0	0	0
Playoff Totals		**41**	**16**	**17**	**33**	**64**	**2**	**0**	**2**
SMYLIE, Rod	Wing								
1921	Toronto	2	0	0	0	0	....	....	....
1922♦	Toronto	1	0	*0	0	2	....	....	....
1925	Toronto	1	0	0	0	0	....	....	....
Playoff Totals		**4**	**0**	**0**	**0**	**2**	....	....	....
•SMYTH, Brad *No Playoffs*	Right wing								
SMYTH, Greg	Defense								
1987	Philadelphia	1	0	0	0	2	0	0	0
1988	Philadelphia	5	0	0	0	38	0	0	0
1994	Chicago	6	0	0	0	0	0	0	0
Playoff Totals		**12**	**0**	**0**	**0**	**40**	**0**	**0**	**0**
SMYTH, Kevin *No Playoffs*	Left wing								
•SMYTH, Ryan	Left wing								
1997	Edmonton	12	5	5	10	12	1	0	2
1998	Edmonton	12	1	3	4	16	1	0	0
1999	Edmonton	3	3	0	3	0	2	0	0
2000	Edmonton	5	1	0	1	6	0	1	0
2001	Edmonton	6	3	4	7	4	0	0	0
Playoff Totals		**38**	**13**	**12**	**25**	**38**	**4**	**1**	**2**
SNELL, Chris *No Playoffs*	Defense								
SNELL, Ron *No Playoffs*	Right wing								
SNELL, Ted *No Playoffs*	Right wing								
SNEPSTS, Harold	Defense								
1976	Vancouver	2	0	0	0	4	0	0	0
1979	Vancouver	3	0	0	0	0	0	0	0
1980	Vancouver	4	0	2	2	8	0	0	0
1981	Vancouver	3	0	0	0	8	0	0	0
1982	Vancouver	17	0	4	4	50	0	0	0
1983	Vancouver	4	1	1	2	8	0	0	0
1984	Vancouver	4	0	1	1	15	0	0	0
1985	Minnesota	9	0	0	0	24	0	0	0
1987	Detroit	11	0	2	2	18	0	0	0
1988	Detroit	10	0	0	0	40	0	0	0
1989	Vancouver	7	0	1	1	6	0	0	0
1990	St. Louis	11	0	3	3	38	0	0	0
1991	St. Louis	8	0	0	0	12	0	0	0
Playoff Totals		**93**	**1**	**14**	**15**	**231**	**0**	**0**	**0**
SNOW, Sandy *No Playoffs*	Right wing								
SNUGGERUD, Dave	Right wing								
1990	Buffalo	6	0	0	0	2	0	0	0
1991	Buffalo	6	1	3	4	4	0	1	0
Playoff Totals		**12**	**1**	**3**	**4**	**6**	**0**	**1**	**0**

•SNYDER, Dan *No Playoffs* — Center

SOBCHUK, Dennis *No Playoffs* — Center

SOBCHUK, Gene *No Playoffs* — Left wing/Center

SOLHEIM, Ken — Left wing

Season	Team	GP	G	A	Pts	PIM	PP	SH	GW
1981	Minnesota	2	1	0	1	0	0	0	0
1982	Minnesota	1	0	1	1	2	0	0	0
Playoff Totals		**3**	**1**	**1**	**2**	**2**	**0**	**0**	**0**

SOLINGER, Bob *No Playoffs* — Wing

SOMERS, Art — Center

Season	Team	GP	G	A	Pts	PIM	PP	SH	GW
1930	Chicago	2	0	0	0	2	....	....	....
1931	Chicago	9	0	0	0	0	....	....	....
1932	NY Rangers	7	0	1	1	8	....	....	....
1933♦	NY Rangers	8	1	*4	5	8	....	....	....
1934	NY Rangers	2	0	0	0	0	....	....	....
1935	NY Rangers	2	0	0	0	2	....	....	....
Playoff Totals		**30**	**1**	**5**	**6**	**20**	....	....	....

•SOMIK, Radovan *No Playoffs* — Right wing

SOMMER, Roy *No Playoffs* — Left wing/Center

SONGIN, Tom *No Playoffs* — Right wing

SONMOR, Glen *No Playoffs* — Left wing

•SONNENBERG, Martin — Left wing

Season	Team	GP	G	A	Pts	PIM	PP	SH	GW
1999	Pittsburgh	7	0	0	0	0	0	0	0
Playoff Totals		**7**	**0**	**0**	**0**	**0**	**0**	**0**	**0**

•SOPEL, Brent — Defense

Season	Team	GP	G	A	Pts	PIM	PP	SH	GW
2001	Vancouver	4	0	0	0	2	0	0	0
2002	Vancouver	6	0	2	2	2	0	0	0
Playoff Totals		**10**	**0**	**2**	**2**	**4**	**0**	**0**	**0**

SOROCHAN, Lee *No Playoffs* — Defense

SORRELL, John — Left wing

Season	Team	GP	G	A	Pts	PIM	PP	SH	GW
1932	Detroit	2	1	0	1	0	....	....	....
1933	Detroit	4	2	2	4	4	....	....	....
1934	Detroit	8	0	2	2	0	....	....	....
1936♦	Detroit	7	3	4	7	0	....	....	....
1937♦	Detroit	10	2	4	6	2	....	....	....
1938	NY Americans	6	4	0	4	2	....	....	....
1939	NY Americans	2	0	0	0	0	....	....	....
1940	NY Americans	3	0	3	3	2	....	....	....
Playoff Totals		**42**	**12**	**15**	**27**	**10**	....	....	....

•SOURAY, Sheldon — Defense

Season	Team	GP	G	A	Pts	PIM	PP	SH	GW
1998	New Jersey	3	0	1	1	2	0	0	0
1999	New Jersey	2	0	1	1	0	0	0	0
2002	Montreal	12	0	1	1	16	0	0	0
Playoff Totals		**17**	**0**	**3**	**3**	**18**	**0**	**0**	**0**

•SPACEK, Jaroslav — Defense

Season	Team	GP	G	A	Pts	PIM	PP	SH	GW
2000	Florida	4	0	0	0	0	0	0	0
Playoff Totals		**4**	**0**	**0**	**0**	**0**	**0**	**0**	**0**

•SPANHEL, Martin *No Playoffs* — Right wing

SPARROW, Emory *No Playoffs* — Right wing/Center

SPECK, Fred *No Playoffs* — Center

SPEER, Bill — Defense

Season	Team	GP	G	A	Pts	PIM	PP	SH	GW
1970♦	Boston	8	1	0	1	4	0	0	0
Playoff Totals		**8**	**1**	**0**	**1**	**4**	**0**	**0**	**0**

SPEERS, Ted *No Playoffs* — Right wing

SPENCE, Gordon *No Playoffs* — Left wing

SPENCER, Brian — Left wing

Season	Team	GP	G	A	Pts	PIM	PP	SH	GW
1971	Toronto	6	0	1	1	17	0	0	0
1975	Buffalo	16	0	4	4	8	0	0	0
1976	Buffalo	9	1	0	1	4	0	0	0
1977	Buffalo	6	0	0	0	0	0	0	0
Playoff Totals		**37**	**1**	**5**	**6**	**29**	**0**	**0**	**0**

SPENCER, Irv — Defense

Season	Team	GP	G	A	Pts	PIM	PP	SH	GW
1962	NY Rangers	1	0	0	0	2	0	0	0
1964	Detroit	11	0	0	0	0	0	0	0
1965	Detroit	1	0	0	0	4	0	0	0
1966	Detroit	3	0	0	0	2	0	0	0
Playoff Totals		**16**	**0**	**0**	**0**	**8**	**0**	**0**	**0**

SPEYER, Chris *No Playoffs* — Defense

•SPEZZA, Jason *No Playoffs* — Center

SPRING, Corey *No Playoffs* — Right wing

SPRING, Don — Defense

Season	Team	GP	G	A	Pts	PIM	PP	SH	GW
1982	Winnipeg	4	0	0	0	4	0	0	0
1983	Winnipeg	2	0	0	0	6	0	0	0
Playoff Totals		**6**	**0**	**0**	**0**	**10**	**0**	**0**	**0**

SPRING, Frank *No Playoffs* — Right wing

SPRING, Jesse — Defense

Season	Team	GP	G	A	Pts	PIM	PP	SH	GW
1926	Pittsburgh	2	0	2	2	2	0	0	0
Playoff Totals		**2**	**0**	**2**	**2**	**2**	**0**	**0**	**0**

SPRUCE, Andy — Left wing

Season	Team	GP	G	A	Pts	PIM	PP	SH	GW
1978	Colorado	2	0	2	2	0	0	0	0
Playoff Totals		**2**	**0**	**2**	**2**	**0**	**0**	**0**	**0**

SRSEN, Tomas *No Playoffs* — Right wing

STACKHOUSE, Ron — Defense

Season	Team	GP	G	A	Pts	PIM	PP	SH	GW
1975	Pittsburgh	9	2	6	8	10	1	0	0
1976	Pittsburgh	3	0	0	0	0	0	0	0
1977	Pittsburgh	3	2	1	3	0	0	0	0
1979	Pittsburgh	7	0	0	0	4	0	0	0
1980	Pittsburgh	5	1	0	1	18	1	0	0
1981	Pittsburgh	4	0	1	1	6	0	0	0
1982	Pittsburgh	1	0	0	0	0	0	0	0
Playoff Totals		**32**	**5**	**8**	**13**	**38**	**2**	**0**	**0**

STACKHOUSE, Ted — Defense

Season	Team	GP	G	A	Pts	PIM	PP	SH	GW
1922♦	Toronto	1	0	0	0	0	0	0	0
Playoff Totals		**1**	**0**	**0**	**0**	**0**	**0**	**0**	**0**

STAHAN, Butch — Defense

Season	Team	GP	G	A	Pts	PIM	PP	SH	GW
1945	Montreal	3	0	1	1	2	0	0	0
Playoff Totals		**3**	**0**	**1**	**1**	**2**	**0**	**0**	**0**

•STAIOS, Steve — Defense

Season	Team	GP	G	A	Pts	PIM	PP	SH	GW
1996	Boston	3	0	0	0	0	0	0	0
Playoff Totals		**3**	**0**	**0**	**0**	**0**	**0**	**0**	**0**

STAJDUHAR, Nick *No Playoffs* — Defense

STALEY, Al *No Playoffs* — Center

STAMLER, Lorne *No Playoffs* — Left wing

STANDING, George *No Playoffs* — Right wing

STANFIELD, Fred — Left wing

Season	Team	GP	G	A	Pts	PIM	PP	SH	GW
1965	Chicago	14	2	1	3	2	0	0	0
1966	Chicago	5	0	0	0	2	0	0	0
1967	Chicago	1	0	0	0	0	0	0	0
1968	Boston	4	0	1	1	0	0	0	0
1969	Boston	10	2	2	4	0	1	0	0
1970♦	Boston	14	4	12	16	6	2	0	0
1971	Boston	7	3	4	7	0	1	0	0
1972♦	Boston	15	7	9	16	0	1	0	0
1973	Boston	5	1	1	2	0	0	0	0
1975	Buffalo	17	2	4	6	0	0	0	0
1976	Buffalo	9	0	1	1	0	0	0	0
1977	Buffalo	5	0	0	0	0	0	0	0
Playoff Totals		**106**	**21**	**35**	**56**	**10**	**5**	**0**	**0**

STANFIELD, Jack — Left wing

Season	Team	GP	G	A	Pts	PIM	PP	SH	GW
1966	Chicago	1	0	0	0	0	0	0	0
Playoff Totals		**1**	**0**	**0**	**0**	**0**	**0**	**0**	**0**

STANFIELD, Jim *No Playoffs* — Center/Right wing

STANKIEWICZ, Ed *No Playoffs* — Center

STANKIEWICZ, Myron — Left wing

Season	Team	GP	G	A	Pts	PIM	PP	SH	GW
1969	Philadelphia	1	0	0	0	0	0	0	0
Playoff Totals		**1**	**0**	**0**	**0**	**0**	**0**	**0**	**0**

STANLEY, Allan — Defense

Season	Team	GP	G	A	Pts	PIM	PP	SH	GW
1950	NY Rangers	12	2	5	7	10	....	....	....
1958	Boston	12	1	3	4	6	....	....	....
1959	Toronto	12	0	3	3	2	....	....	....
1960	Toronto	10	2	3	5	2	....	....	....
1961	Toronto	5	0	3	3	0	....	....	....
1962♦	Toronto	12	0	3	3	6	....	....	....
1963♦	Toronto	10	1	6	7	8	....	....	....
1964♦	Toronto	14	1	6	7	20	....	....	....
1965	Toronto	6	0	1	1	12	....	....	....
1966	Toronto	1	0	0	0	0	....	....	....
1967♦	Toronto	12	0	2	2	10	....	....	....
1969	Philadelphia	3	0	1	1	4	0	0	0
Playoff Totals		**109**	**7**	**36**	**43**	**80**	**0**	**0**	**0**

STANLEY, Barney *No Playoffs* — Right wing

STANLEY, Daryl — Defense/Left wing

Season	Team	GP	G	A	Pts	PIM	PP	SH	GW
1984	Philadelphia	3	0	0	0	19	0	0	0
1986	Philadelphia	1	0	0	0	2	0	0	0
1987	Philadelphia	13	0	0	0	9	0	0	0
Playoff Totals		**17**	**0**	**0**	**0**	**30**	**0**	**0**	**0**

STANOWSKI, Wally — Defense

Season	Team	GP	G	A	Pts	PIM	PP	SH	GW
1940	Toronto	10	1	0	1	2	....	....	....
1941	Toronto	7	0	3	3	2	....	....	....
1942♦	Toronto	13	2	8	10	2	....	....	....
1945♦	Toronto	13	0	1	1	5	....	....	....
1947♦	Toronto	8	0	0	0	0	....	....	....
1948♦	Toronto	9	0	2	2	2	....	....	....
Playoff Totals		**60**	**3**	**14**	**17**	**13**	....	....	....

STANTON, Paul — Defense

Season	Team	GP	G	A	Pts	PIM	PP	SH	GW
1991♦	Pittsburgh	22	1	2	3	24	0	0	0
1992♦	Pittsburgh	21	1	7	8	42	0	0	0
1993	Pittsburgh	1	0	1	1	0	0	0	0
Playoff Totals		**44**	**2**	**10**	**12**	**66**	**0**	**0**	**0**

STAPLETON, Brian *No Playoffs* — Right wing

•STAPLETON, Mike — Center

Season	Team	GP	G	A	Pts	PIM	PP	SH	GW
1987	Chicago	4	0	0	0	2	0	0	0
1993	Pittsburgh	4	0	0	0	0	0	0	0
1996	Winnipeg	6	0	0	0	21	0	0	0
1997	Phoenix	7	0	0	0	14	0	0	0
1998	Phoenix	6	0	0	0	2	0	0	0
1999	Phoenix	7	1	0	1	0	0	0	0
Playoff Totals		**34**	**1**	**0**	**1**	**39**	**0**	**0**	**0**

STAPLETON, Pat — Defense

Season	Team	GP	G	A	Pts	PIM	PP	SH	GW
1966	Chicago	6	2	3	5	4	1	0	0
1967	Chicago	6	1	1	2	12	0	0	0
1968	Chicago	11	0	4	4	4	0	0	0
1971	Chicago	18	3	14	17	4	1	1	0
1972	Chicago	8	2	2	4	4	2	0	0
1973	Chicago	16	2	*15	17	10	1	0	0
Playoff Totals		**65**	**10**	**39**	**49**	**38**	**5**	**1**	**0**

STARIKOV, Sergei *No Playoffs* — Defense

STARR, Harold — Defense

Season	Team	GP	G	A	Pts	PIM	PP	SH	GW
1930	Ottawa	2	1	0	1	0	....	....	....
1932	Mtl. Maroons	4	0	0	0	0	....	....	....
1933	Montreal	2	0	0	0	2	....	....	....
1934	Mtl. Maroons	3	0	0	0	0	....	....	....
1935	NY Rangers	4	0	0	0	2	....	....	....
Playoff Totals		**15**	**1**	**0**	**1**	**4**	....	....	....

STARR, Wilf — Center

Season	Team	GP	G	A	Pts	PIM	PP	SH	GW
1934	Detroit	7	0	2	2	2	0	0	0
Playoff Totals		**7**	**0**	**2**	**2**	**2**	**0**	**0**	**0**

STASIUK, Vic — Left wing

Season	Team	GP	G	A	Pts	PIM	PP	SH	GW
1952♦	Detroit	7	0	2	2	0	....	....	....
1954♦	Detroit	....	....	....	....	....	....	....	....
1955♦	Detroit	11	5	3	8	6	....	....	....
1957	Boston	10	2	1	3	2	....	....	....
1958	Boston	12	0	5	5	13	....	....	....
1959	Boston	7	4	2	6	11	....	....	....
1961	Detroit	11	2	5	7	4	....	....	....
1963	Detroit	11	3	0	3	4	....	....	....
Playoff Totals		**69**	**16**	**18**	**34**	**40**	....	....	....

STASTNY, Anton — Left wing

Season	Team	GP	G	A	Pts	PIM	PP	SH	GW
1981	Quebec	5	4	3	7	2	2	0	0
1982	Quebec	16	5	10	15	10	3	0	0
1983	Quebec	4	2	2	4	0	0	0	0
1984	Quebec	9	2	5	7	7	0	0	0
1985	Quebec	16	3	3	6	6	1	0	1
1986	Quebec	3	1	1	2	0	0	0	0
1987	Quebec	13	3	8	11	6	0	0	0
Playoff Totals		**66**	**20**	**32**	**52**	**31**	**6**	**0**	**1**

STASTNY, Marian — Right wing

Season	Team	GP	G	A	Pts	PIM	PP	SH	GW
1982	Quebec	16	3	14	17	5	1	0	0
1983	Quebec	2	0	0	0	0	0	0	0
1984	Quebec	9	2	3	5	2	0	0	1
1985	Quebec	2	0	0	0	0	0	0	0
1986	Toronto	3	0	0	0	0	0	0	0
Playoff Totals		**32**	**5**	**17**	**22**	**7**	**1**	**0**	**1**

STASTNY, Peter — Center

Season	Team	GP	G	A	Pts	PIM	PP	SH	GW
1981	Quebec	5	2	8	10	7	1	0	0
1982	Quebec	12	7	11	18	10	4	0	1
1983	Quebec	4	3	2	5	10	1	0	0
1984	Quebec	9	2	7	9	31	2	0	0
1985	Quebec	18	4	19	23	24	1	0	2
1986	Quebec	3	0	1	1	2	0	0	0
1987	Quebec	13	6	9	15	12	2	1	1
1990	New Jersey	6	3	2	5	2	1	0	1
1991	New Jersey	7	3	4	7	2	1	0	2
1992	New Jersey	7	3	7	10	19	0	0	0
1993	New Jersey	5	0	2	2	2	0	0	0
1994	St. Louis	4	0	0	0	2	0	0	0
Playoff Totals		**93**	**33**	**72**	**105**	**123**	**13**	**1**	**7**

STASZAK, Ray *No Playoffs* — Right wing

STEELE, Frank *No Playoffs* — Right wing/Defense

STEEN, Anders *No Playoffs* — Center

STEEN, Thomas — Center

Season	Team	GP	G	A	Pts	PIM	PP	SH	GW
1982	Winnipeg	4	0	4	4	2	0	0	0
1983	Winnipeg	3	0	2	2	0	0	0	0
1984	Winnipeg	3	0	1	1	9	0	0	0
1985	Winnipeg	8	2	3	5	17	2	0	0
1986	Winnipeg	3	1	1	2	4	0	1	0
1987	Winnipeg	10	3	4	7	8	0	1	1
1988	Winnipeg	5	1	5	6	2	1	0	0
1990	Winnipeg	7	2	5	7	16	1	0	0
1992	Winnipeg	7	2	4	6	2	2	0	0
1993	Winnipeg	6	1	3	4	2	1	0	0
Playoff Totals		**56**	**12**	**32**	**44**	**62**	**7**	**2**	**1**

•STEFAN, Patrik *No Playoffs* — Center

STEFANIW, Morris *No Playoffs* — Center

STEFANSKI, Bud *No Playoffs* — Center

STEMKOWSKI, Pete — Center

Season	Team	GP	G	A	Pts	PIM	PP	SH	GW
1965	Toronto	6	0	3	3	7	0	0	0
1966	Toronto	4	0	0	0	26	0	0	0
1967♦	Toronto	12	5	7	12	20	2	0	2
1970	Detroit	4	1	1	2	6	0	0	1
1971	NY Rangers	13	3	2	5	6	0	0	2
1972	NY Rangers	16	4	8	12	18	0	0	1
1973	NY Rangers	10	4	2	6	6	1	0	1
1974	NY Rangers	13	6	6	12	35	1	0	0
1975	NY Rangers	3	1	0	1	10	0	0	0
1978	Los Angeles	2	1	0	1	2	0	0	0
Playoff Totals		**83**	**25**	**29**	**54**	**136**	**4**	**0**	**7**

STENLUND, Vern *No Playoffs* — Center

Season	Team	GP	G	A	Pts	PIM	PP	SH	GW
•STEPHENS, Charlie	*No Playoffs* Center/Right wing								
STEPHENSON, Bob	*No Playoffs* Right wing								
STERN, Ron	Right wing								
1989	Vancouver	3	0	1	1	17	0	0	0
1991	Calgary	7	1	3	4	14	0	0	0
1993	Calgary	6	0	0	0	43	0	0	0
1994	Calgary	7	2	0	2	12	0	0	0
1995	Calgary	7	3	1	4	8	1	1	0
1996	Calgary	4	0	2	2	8	0	0	0
1999	San Jose	6	0	0	0	6	0	0	0
2000	San Jose	3	1	0	1	11	0	0	0
Playoff Totals		**43**	**7**	**7**	**14**	**119**	**1**	**1**	**0**
STERNER, Ulf	*No Playoffs* Left wing								
STEVENS, John	*No Playoffs* Defense								
STEVENS, Kevin	Left wing								
1989	Pittsburgh	11	3	7	10	16	0	0	0
1991♦	Pittsburgh	24	*17	16	33	53	7	0	4
1992♦	Pittsburgh	21	13	15	28	28	4	0	3
1993	Pittsburgh	12	5	11	16	22	4	0	0
1994	Pittsburgh	6	1	1	2	10	0	0	0
1995	Pittsburgh	12	4	7	11	21	3	0	1
2001	Pittsburgh	17	3	3	6	20	2	0	1
Playoff Totals		**103**	**46**	**60**	**106**	**170**	**20**	**0**	**9**
STEVENS, Mike	*No Playoffs* Left wing								
STEVENS, Phil	*No Playoffs* Center/Defense								
•STEVENS, Scott	Defense								
1983	Washington	4	1	0	1	26	0	0	0
1984	Washington	8	1	8	9	21	1	0	0
1985	Washington	5	0	1	1	20	0	0	0
1986	Washington	9	3	8	11	12	2	0	2
1987	Washington	7	0	5	5	19	0	0	0
1988	Washington	13	1	11	12	46	0	0	0
1989	Washington	6	1	4	5	11	0	0	0
1990	Washington	15	2	7	9	25	1	0	0
1991	St. Louis	13	0	3	3	36	0	0	0
1992	New Jersey	7	2	1	3	29	2	0	1
1993	New Jersey	5	2	2	4	10	1	0	0
1994	New Jersey	20	2	9	11	42	2	0	1
1995♦	New Jersey	20	1	7	8	24	0	0	1
1997	New Jersey	10	0	4	4	2	0	0	0
1998	New Jersey	6	1	0	1	8	0	0	0
1999	New Jersey	7	2	1	3	10	2	0	0
2000♦	New Jersey	23	3	8	11	6	0	0	2
2001	New Jersey	25	1	7	8	37	0	0	0
2002	New Jersey	6	0	0	0	4	0	0	0
Playoff Totals		**209**	**23**	**86**	**109**	**388**	**11**	**0**	**7**
•STEVENSON, Jeremy	*No Playoffs* Left wing								
STEVENSON, Shayne	*No Playoffs* Right wing								
•STEVENSON, Turner	Right wing								
1994	Montreal	3	0	2	2	0	0	0	0
1996	Montreal	6	0	1	1	2	0	0	0
1997	Montreal	5	1	1	2	2	0	0	0
1998	Montreal	10	3	4	7	12	0	0	0
2001	New Jersey	23	1	3	4	20	0	0	1
2002	New Jersey	1	0	0	0	4	0	0	0
Playoff Totals		**48**	**5**	**11**	**16**	**40**	**0**	**0**	**1**
STEWART, Allan	*No Playoffs* Left wing								
STEWART, Bill	Defense								
1978	Buffalo	8	0	2	2	0	0	0	0
1979	Buffalo	1	0	1	1	0	0	0	0
1981	St. Louis	4	1	0	1	11	0	0	0
Playoff Totals		**13**	**1**	**3**	**4**	**11**	**0**	**0**	**0**
STEWART, Blair	*No Playoffs* Center								
STEWART, Bob	Defense								
1980	Pittsburgh	5	1	1	2	2	0	0	0
Playoff Totals		**5**	**1**	**1**	**2**	**2**	**0**	**0**	**0**
STEWART, Cam	Left wing								
1994	Boston	8	0	3	3	7	0	0	0
1996	Boston	5	1	0	1	2	0	0	0
Playoff Totals		**13**	**1**	**3**	**4**	**9**	**0**	**0**	**0**
STEWART, Gaye	Left wing								
1942♦	Toronto	1	0	0	0	0	....	....	....
1943	Toronto	4	0	2	2	4	....	....	....
1947♦	Toronto	11	2	5	7	8	....	....	....
1951	Detroit	6	0	2	2	4	....	....	....
1954	Montreal	3	0	0	0	0	....	....	....
Playoff Totals		**25**	**2**	**9**	**11**	**16**	....	....	....
STEWART, Jack	Defense								
1940	Detroit	5	0	0	0	4	....	....	....
1941	Detroit	9	1	2	3	8	....	....	....
1942	Detroit	12	0	1	1	12	....	....	....
1943♦	Detroit	10	1	2	3	*35	....	....	....
1946	Detroit	5	0	0	0	14	....	....	....
1947	Detroit	5	0	1	1	12	....	....	....
1948	Detroit	9	1	3	4	6	....	....	....
1949	Detroit	11	1	1	2	*32	....	....	....
1950♦	Detroit	14	1	4	5	20	....	....	....
Playoff Totals		**80**	**5**	**14**	**19**	**143**	....	....	....
STEWART, John	*No Playoffs* Center								
STEWART, John	Left wing								
1974	Atlanta	4	0	0	0	10	0	0	0
Playoff Totals		**4**	**0**	**0**	**0**	**10**	**0**	**0**	**0**
STEWART, Ken	*No Playoffs* Defense								
STEWART, Nels	Center								
1926♦	Mtl. Maroons	4	0	2	2	10	....	....	....
1927	Mtl. Maroons	2	0	0	0	4	....	....	....
1928	Mtl. Maroons	9	2	2	4	13	....	....	....
1930	Mtl. Maroons	4	1	1	2	2	....	....	....
1931	Mtl. Maroons	2	1	0	1	6	....	....	....
1932	Mtl. Maroons	4	0	1	1	2	....	....	....
1933	Boston	5	2	0	2	4	....	....	....
1935	Boston	4	0	1	1	0	....	....	....
1936	NY Americans	5	1	2	3	4	....	....	....
1938	NY Americans	6	2	3	5	2	....	....	....
1939	NY Americans	2	0	0	0	0	....	....	....
1940	NY Americans	3	0	0	0	0	....	....	....
Playoff Totals		**50**	**9**	**12**	**21**	**47**	....	....	....
STEWART, Paul	*No Playoffs* Left wing/Defense								
STEWART, Ralph	Center								
1975	NY Islanders	13	3	3	6	2	1	0	0
1976	NY Islanders	6	1	1	2	0	1	0	0
Playoff Totals		**19**	**4**	**4**	**8**	**2**	**2**	**0**	**0**
STEWART, Ron	Right wing								
1954	Toronto	5	0	1	1	10	....	....	....
1955	Toronto	4	0	0	0	2	....	....	....
1956	Toronto	5	1	1	2	2	....	....	....
1959	Toronto	12	3	3	6	6	....	....	....
1960	Toronto	10	0	2	2	2	....	....	....
1961	Toronto	5	1	0	1	2	....	....	....
1962♦	Toronto	11	1	6	7	4	....	....	....
1963♦	Toronto	10	4	0	4	2	....	....	....
1964♦	Toronto	14	0	4	4	24	....	....	....
1965	Toronto	6	0	1	1	2	....	....	....
1968	NY Rangers	6	1	1	2	2	0	0	0
1969	NY Rangers	4	0	1	1	0	0	0	0
1970	NY Rangers	6	0	0	0	2	0	0	0
1971	NY Rangers	13	1	0	1	0	0	1	0
1972	NY Rangers	8	2	1	3	0	0	0	0
Playoff Totals		**119**	**14**	**21**	**35**	**60**	**0**	**1**	**0**
STEWART, Ryan	*No Playoffs* Center								
STIENBURG, Trevor	Right wing								
1986	Quebec	1	0	0	0	0	0	0	0
Playoff Totals		**1**	**0**	**0**	**0**	**0**	**0**	**0**	**0**
STILES, Tony	*No Playoffs* Defense								
•STILLMAN, Cory	Center								
1996	Calgary	2	1	1	2	0	0	0	0
2001	St. Louis	15	3	5	8	8	1	0	1
2002	St. Louis	9	0	2	2	2	0	0	0
Playoff Totals		**26**	**4**	**8**	**12**	**10**	**1**	**0**	**1**
•STOCK, P.J.	Left wing								
2001	Philadelphia	2	0	0	0	0	0	0	0
2002	Boston	6	1	0	1	19	0	0	0
Playoff Totals		**8**	**1**	**0**	**1**	**19**	**0**	**0**	**0**
STODDARD, Jack	*No Playoffs* Right wing								
STOJANOV, Alek	Right wing								
1995	Vancouver	5	0	0	0	2	0	0	0
1996	Pittsburgh	9	0	0	0	19	0	0	0
Playoff Totals		**14**	**0**	**0**	**0**	**21**	**0**	**0**	**0**
•STOLL, Jarret	*No Playoffs* Center								
STOLTZ, Roland	*No Playoffs* Right wing								
STONE, Steve	*No Playoffs* Right wing								
STORM, Jim	*No Playoffs* Left wing								
STOTHERS, Mike	Defense								
1986	Philadelphia	3	0	0	0	4	0	0	0
1987	Philadelphia	2	0	0	0	7	0	0	0
Playoff Totals		**5**	**0**	**0**	**0**	**11**	**0**	**0**	**0**
STOUGHTON, Blaine	Right wing								
1975	Toronto	7	4	2	6	2	1	0	1
1980	Hartford	1	0	0	0	0	0	0	0
Playoff Totals		**8**	**4**	**2**	**6**	**2**	**1**	**0**	**1**
STOYANOVICH, Steve	*No Playoffs* Center								
STRAIN, Neil	*No Playoffs* Left wing/Center								
•STRAKA, Martin	Center								
1993	Pittsburgh	11	2	1	3	2	0	0	0
1994	Pittsburgh	6	1	0	1	2	0	0	0
1996	Florida	13	2	2	4	2	0	0	0
1997	Florida	4	0	0	0	0	0	0	0
1998	Pittsburgh	6	2	0	2	2	0	1	0
1999	Pittsburgh	13	6	9	15	6	1	0	0
2000	Pittsburgh	11	3	9	12	10	1	0	0
2001	Pittsburgh	18	5	8	13	8	3	0	2
Playoff Totals		**82**	**21**	**29**	**50**	**32**	**5**	**1**	**2**
STRATE, Gord	*No Playoffs* Defense								
STRATTON, Art	Center/Left wing								
1968	Philadelphia	5	0	0	0	0	0	0	0
Playoff Totals		**5**	**0**	**0**	**0**	**0**	**0**	**0**	**0**
STROBEL, Art	*No Playoffs* Left wing								
STRONG, Ken	*No Playoffs* Left wing								
STRUCH, David	*No Playoffs* Center								
•STRUDWICK, Jason	Defense								
2001	Vancouver	2	0	0	0	0	0	0	0
Playoff Totals		**2**	**0**	**0**	**0**	**0**	**0**	**0**	**0**
STRUEBY, Todd	*No Playoffs* Left wing								
STUART, Billy	Defense								
1921	Toronto	2	0	0	0	0	....	....	....
1922♦	Toronto	2	1	1	2	0	....	....	....
1927	Boston	8	0	0	0	6	....	....	....
Playoff Totals		**12**	**1**	**1**	**2**	**6**	....	....	....
•STUART, Brad	Defense								
2000	San Jose	12	1	0	1	6	1	0	0
2001	San Jose	5	1	0	1	0	0	0	0
2002	San Jose	12	0	3	3	8	0	0	0
Playoff Totals		**29**	**2**	**3**	**5**	**14**	**1**	**0**	**0**
•STUMPEL, Jozef	Center								
1994	Boston	13	1	7	8	4	0	0	0
1995	Boston	5	0	0	0	0	0	0	0
1996	Boston	5	1	2	3	0	0	0	0
1998	Los Angeles	4	1	2	3	2	0	0	0
2000	Los Angeles	4	0	4	4	8	0	0	0
2001	Los Angeles	13	3	5	8	10	2	0	1
2002	Boston	6	0	2	2	0	0	0	0
Playoff Totals		**50**	**6**	**22**	**28**	**24**	**2**	**0**	**1**
STUMPF, Bob	*No Playoffs* Right wing/Defense								
STURGEON, Peter	*No Playoffs* Left wing								
•STURM, Marco	Center								
1998	San Jose	2	0	0	0	0	0	0	0
1999	San Jose	6	2	2	4	4	0	0	1
2000	San Jose	12	1	3	4	6	0	0	0
2001	San Jose	6	0	2	2	0	0	0	0
2002	San Jose	12	3	2	5	2	0	0	0
Playoff Totals		**38**	**6**	**9**	**15**	**12**	**0**	**0**	**1**
•SUCHY, Radoslav	Defense								
2000	Phoenix	5	0	1	1	0	0	0	0
2002	Phoenix	5	1	0	1	0	0	0	0
Playoff Totals		**10**	**1**	**1**	**2**	**0**	**0**	**0**	**0**
SUIKKANEN, Kai	*No Playoffs* Defense								
SULLIMAN, Doug	Right wing								
1981	NY Rangers	3	1	0	1	0	0	0	0
1988	New Jersey	9	0	3	3	2	0	0	0
1989	Philadelphia	4	0	0	0	0	0	0	0
Playoff Totals		**16**	**1**	**3**	**4**	**2**	**0**	**0**	**0**
SULLIVAN, Barry	*No Playoffs* Right wing								
SULLIVAN, Bob	*No Playoffs* Left wing								
SULLIVAN, Brian	*No Playoffs* Right wing								
SULLIVAN, Frank	*No Playoffs* Defense								
SULLIVAN, Mike	Center								
1994	Calgary	7	1	1	2	8	0	1	0
1995	Calgary	7	3	5	8	2	0	1	1
1996	Calgary	4	0	0	0	0	0	0	0
1998	Boston	6	0	1	1	2	0	0	0
1999	Phoenix	5	0	0	0	2	0	0	0
2000	Phoenix	5	0	1	1	0	0	0	0
Playoff Totals		**34**	**4**	**8**	**12**	**14**	**0**	**2**	**1**
SULLIVAN, Peter	*No Playoffs* Center								
SULLIVAN, Red	Center								
1951	Boston	2	0	0	0	2	0	0	0
1952	Boston	7	0	0	0	0	0	0	0
1953	Boston	3	0	0	0	0	0	0	0
1957	NY Rangers	5	1	2	3	4	0	0	0
1958	NY Rangers	1	0	0	0	0	0	0	0
Playoff Totals		**18**	**1**	**2**	**3**	**6**	**0**	**0**	**0**
•SULLIVAN, Steve	Right wing								
1999	Toronto	13	3	3	6	14	2	0	0
2002	Chicago	5	1	0	1	2	0	0	0
Playoff Totals		**18**	**4**	**3**	**7**	**16**	**2**	**0**	**0**
SUMMANEN, Raimo	Left wing								
1984	Edmonton	5	1	4	5	0	0	0	0
1986	Edmonton	5	1	1	2	0	0	0	0
Playoff Totals		**10**	**2**	**5**	**7**	**0**	**0**	**0**	**0**
SUMMERHILL, Bill	Right wing								
1938	Montreal	1	0	0	0	0	0	0	0
1939	Montreal	2	0	0	0	2	0	0	0
Playoff Totals		**3**	**0**	**0**	**0**	**2**	**0**	**0**	**0**
SUNDBLAD, Niklas	*No Playoffs* Right wing								
•SUNDIN, Mats	Center/Right wing								
1993	Quebec	6	3	1	4	6	1	0	0
1995	Toronto	7	5	4	9	4	2	0	1
1996	Toronto	6	3	1	4	4	2	0	1
1999	Toronto	17	8	8	16	16	3	0	2
2000	Toronto	12	3	5	8	10	2	0	1
2001	Toronto	11	6	7	13	14	2	1	1
2002	Toronto	8	2	5	7	4	0	0	0
Playoff Totals		**67**	**30**	**31**	**61**	**58**	**10**	**1**	**6**
SUNDIN, Ronnie	*No Playoffs* Defense								

Season	Team	GP	G	A	Pts	PIM	PP	SH	GW
•SUNDSTROM, Niklas									Left wing
1996	NY Rangers	11	4	3	7	4	1	0	0
1997	NY Rangers	9	0	5	5	2	0	0	0
2000	San Jose	12	0	2	2	2	0	0	0
2001	San Jose	6	0	3	3	2	0	0	0
2002	San Jose	12	1	6	7	6	0	0	0
Playoff Totals		**50**	**5**	**19**	**24**	**16**	**1**	**0**	**0**
SUNDSTROM, Patrik									Center
1983	Vancouver	4	0	0	0	2	0	0	0
1984	Vancouver	4	0	1	1	7	0	0	0
1986	Vancouver	3	1	0	1	0	1	0	0
1988	New Jersey	18	7	13	20	14	3	0	1
1990	New Jersey	6	1	3	4	2	0	0	0
1991	New Jersey	2	0	0	0	0	0	0	0
Playoff Totals		**37**	**9**	**17**	**26**	**25**	**4**	**0**	**1**
SUNDSTROM, Peter									Left wing
1984	NY Rangers	5	1	3	4	0	1	0	0
1985	NY Rangers	3	0	0	0	0	0	0	0
1986	NY Rangers	1	0	0	0	2	0	0	0
1988	Washington	14	2	0	2	6	0	1	1
Playoff Totals		**23**	**3**	**3**	**6**	**8**	**1**	**1**	**1**
SUOMI, Al *No Playoffs*									Left wing
•SUROVY, Tomas *No Playoffs*									Center
•SUSHINSKY, Maxim *No Playoffs*									Right wing
SUTER, Gary									Defense
1986	Calgary	10	2	8	10	8	0	0	1
1987	Calgary	6	0	3	3	10	0	0	0
1988	Calgary	9	1	9	10	6	0	1	0
1989♦	Calgary	5	0	3	3	10	0	0	0
1990	Calgary	6	0	1	1	14	0	0	0
1991	Calgary	7	1	6	7	12	1	0	0
1993	Calgary	6	2	3	5	8	0	1	0
1994	Chicago	6	3	2	5	6	2	0	0
1995	Chicago	12	2	5	7	10	1	0	0
1996	Chicago	10	3	3	6	8	2	0	1
1997	Chicago	6	1	4	5	8	0	0	0
2000	San Jose	12	2	5	7	12	1	0	1
2001	San Jose	1	0	0	0	0	0	0	0
2002	San Jose	12	0	4	4	8	0	0	0
Playoff Totals		**108**	**17**	**56**	**73**	**120**	**7**	**2**	**3**
•SUTHERBY, Brian *No Playoffs*									Center
SUTHERLAND, Bill									Center
1963	Montreal	2	0	0	0	0	0	0	0
1968	Philadelphia	7	1	3	4	0	1	0	0
1969	Philadelphia	4	1	1	2	0	1	0	0
1971	St. Louis	1	0	0	0	0	0	0	0
Playoff Totals		**14**	**2**	**4**	**6**	**0**	**2**	**0**	**0**
SUTHERLAND, Max *No Playoffs*									Left wing
SUTTER, Brent									Center
1982♦	NY Islanders	19	2	6	8	36	0	0	0
1983♦	NY Islanders	20	10	11	21	26	3	0	0
1984	NY Islanders	20	4	10	14	18	0	1	3
1985	NY Islanders	10	3	3	6	14	1	0	2
1986	NY Islanders	3	0	1	1	2	0	0	0
1987	NY Islanders	5	1	0	1	4	1	0	0
1988	NY Islanders	6	2	1	3	18	0	1	1
1990	NY Islanders	5	2	3	5	2	2	0	1
1992	Chicago	18	3	5	8	22	1	0	1
1993	Chicago	4	1	1	2	4	0	0	0
1994	Chicago	6	0	0	0	2	0	0	0
1995	Chicago	16	1	2	3	4	0	0	0
1996	Chicago	10	1	1	2	6	0	0	0
1997	Chicago	2	0	0	0	6	0	0	0
Playoff Totals		**144**	**30**	**44**	**74**	**164**	**8**	**2**	**8**
SUTTER, Brian									Left wing
1977	St. Louis	4	1	0	1	14	0	0	0
1980	St. Louis	3	0	0	0	4	0	0	0
1981	St. Louis	11	6	3	9	77	3	0	0
1982	St. Louis	10	8	6	14	49	0	0	1
1983	St. Louis	4	2	1	3	10	2	0	0
1984	St. Louis	11	1	5	6	22	1	0	0
1985	St. Louis	3	2	1	3	2	2	0	0
1986	St. Louis	9	1	2	3	22	0	0	0
1988	St. Louis	10	0	3	3	49	0	0	0
Playoff Totals		**65**	**21**	**21**	**42**	**249**	**8**	**0**	**1**
SUTTER, Darryl									Left wing
1980	Chicago	7	3	1	4	2	2	0	1
1981	Chicago	3	3	1	4	2	1	0	0
1982	Chicago	3	0	1	1	2	0	0	0
1983	Chicago	13	4	6	10	8	0	0	0
1984	Chicago	5	1	1	2	0	0	0	0
1985	Chicago	15	12	7	19	12	2	0	4
1986	Chicago	3	1	2	3	0	1	0	0
1987	Chicago	2	0	0	0	0	0	0	0
Playoff Totals		**51**	**24**	**19**	**43**	**26**	**6**	**0**	**5**
SUTTER, Duane									Right wing
1980♦	NY Islanders	21	3	7	10	74	0	0	0
1981♦	NY Islanders	12	3	1	4	10	0	0	0
1982♦	NY Islanders	19	5	5	10	57	0	0	2
1983♦	NY Islanders	20	9	12	21	43	2	0	1
1984	NY Islanders	21	1	3	4	48	0	0	0
1985	NY Islanders	10	0	2	2	47	0	0	0
1986	NY Islanders	3	0	0	0	16	0	0	0
1987	NY Islanders	14	1	0	1	26	0	0	0
1988	Chicago	5	0	0	0	21	0	0	0
1989	Chicago	16	3	1	4	15	0	0	2
1990	Chicago	20	1	1	2	48	0	0	0
Playoff Totals		**161**	**26**	**32**	**58**	**405**	**2**	**0**	**5**
SUTTER, Rich									Right wing
1984	Philadelphia	3	0	0	0	15	0	0	0
1985	Philadelphia	11	3	0	3	10	0	0	0
1986	Philadelphia	5	2	0	2	19	0	0	0
1989	Vancouver	7	2	1	3	12	0	0	0
1990	St. Louis	12	2	1	3	39	0	1	1
1991	St. Louis	13	4	2	6	16	0	0	1
1992	St. Louis	6	0	0	0	8	0	0	0
1993	St. Louis	11	0	1	1	10	0	0	0
1994	Chicago	6	0	0	0	2	0	0	0
1995	Toronto	4	0	0	0	2	0	0	0
Playoff Totals		**78**	**13**	**5**	**18**	**133**	**0**	**1**	**2**
SUTTER, Ron									Center
1984	Philadelphia	3	0	0	0	22	0	0	0
1985	Philadelphia	19	4	8	12	28	0	0	1
1986	Philadelphia	5	0	2	2	10	0	0	0
1987	Philadelphia	16	1	7	8	12	0	0	0
1988	Philadelphia	7	0	1	1	26	0	0	0
1989	Philadelphia	19	1	9	10	51	0	0	0
1992	St. Louis	6	1	3	4	8	1	0	0
1996	Boston	5	0	0	0	8	0	0	0
1998	San Jose	6	1	0	1	14	0	0	0
1999	San Jose	6	0	0	0	4	0	0	0
2000	San Jose	12	0	2	2	10	0	0	0
Playoff Totals		**104**	**8**	**32**	**40**	**193**	**1**	**0**	**1**
•SUTTON, Andy *No Playoffs*									Defense
SUZOR, Mark *No Playoffs*									Defense
•SVARTVADET, Per *No Playoffs*									Center
•SVEHLA, Robert									Defense
1996	Florida	22	0	6	6	32	0	0	0
1997	Florida	5	1	4	5	4	1	0	0
2000	Florida	4	0	1	1	4	0	0	0
Playoff Totals		**31**	**1**	**11**	**12**	**40**	**1**	**0**	**0**
SVEJKOVSKY, Jaroslav									Right wing
1998	Washington	1	0	0	0	2	0	0	0
Playoff Totals		**1**	**0**	**0**	**0**	**2**	**0**	**0**	**0**
SVENSSON, Leif *No Playoffs*									Defense
SVENSSON, Magnus *No Playoffs*									Defense
•SVITOV, Alexander *No Playoffs*									Center
•SVOBODA, Jaroslav									Left wing
2002	Carolina	23	1	4	5	28	1	0	1
Playoff Totals		**23**	**1**	**4**	**5**	**28**	**1**	**0**	**1**
SVOBODA, Petr									Defense
1985	Montreal	7	1	1	2	12	0	0	0
1986♦	Montreal	8	0	0	0	21	0	0	0
1987	Montreal	14	0	5	5	10	0	0	0
1988	Montreal	10	0	5	5	12	0	0	0
1989	Montreal	21	1	11	12	16	0	0	0
1990	Montreal	10	0	5	5	7	0	0	0
1991	Montreal	2	0	1	1	2	0	0	0
1992	Buffalo	7	1	4	5	6	0	1	0
1994	Buffalo	3	0	0	0	4	0	0	0
1995	Philadelphia	14	0	4	4	8	0	0	0
1996	Philadelphia	12	0	6	6	22	0	0	0
1997	Philadelphia	16	1	2	3	16	0	0	0
1998	Philadelphia	3	0	1	1	4	0	0	0
Playoff Totals		**127**	**4**	**45**	**49**	**140**	**0**	**1**	**0**
•SVOBODA, Petr *No Playoffs*									Defense
SWAIN, Garry *No Playoffs*									Center
•SWANSON, Brian *No Playoffs*									Center
SWARBRICK, George *No Playoffs*									Right wing
SWEENEY, Bill *No Playoffs*									Center
SWEENEY, Bob									Center/Right wing
1987	Boston	3	0	0	0	0	0	0	0
1988	Boston	23	6	8	14	66	1	1	1
1989	Boston	10	2	4	6	19	0	0	0
1990	Boston	20	0	2	2	30	0	0	0
1991	Boston	17	4	2	6	45	0	0	1
1992	Boston	14	1	0	1	25	0	1	0
1993	Buffalo	8	2	2	4	8	0	0	1
1994	Buffalo	1	0	0	0	0	0	0	0
1995	Buffalo	5	0	0	0	4	0	0	0
1996	Calgary	2	0	0	0	0	0	0	0
Playoff Totals		**103**	**15**	**18**	**33**	**197**	**1**	**2**	**3**
•SWEENEY, Don									Defense
1990	Boston	21	1	5	6	18	1	0	0
1991	Boston	19	3	0	3	25	0	0	0
1992	Boston	15	0	0	0	10	0	0	0
1993	Boston	4	0	0	0	4	0	0	0
1994	Boston	12	2	1	3	4	0	0	1
1995	Boston	5	0	0	0	4	0	0	0
1996	Boston	5	0	2	2	6	0	0	0
1999	Boston	11	3	0	3	6	1	0	0
2002	Boston	6	0	1	1	2	0	0	0
Playoff Totals		**98**	**9**	**9**	**18**	**79**	**2**	**0**	**1**
SWEENEY, Tim									Left wing
1993	Boston	3	0	0	0	0	0	0	0
1996	Boston	1	0	0	0	2	0	0	0
Playoff Totals		**4**	**0**	**0**	**0**	**2**	**0**	**0**	**0**
•SYDOR, Darryl									Defense
1993	Los Angeles	24	3	8	11	16	2	0	0
1997	Dallas	7	0	2	2	0	0	0	0
1998	Dallas	17	0	5	5	14	0	0	0
1999♦	Dallas	23	3	9	12	16	1	0	1
2000	Dallas	23	1	6	7	6	0	0	0
2001	Dallas	10	1	3	4	0	1	0	0
Playoff Totals		**104**	**8**	**33**	**41**	**52**	**4**	**0**	**1**
SYKES, Bob *No Playoffs*									Left wing
SYKES, Phil									Left wing
1985	Los Angeles	3	0	1	1	4	0	0	0
1987	Los Angeles	5	0	1	1	8	0	0	0
1988	Los Angeles	4	0	0	0	0	0	0	0
1989	Los Angeles	3	0	0	0	8	0	0	0
1990	Winnipeg	4	0	0	0	0	0	0	0
1992	Winnipeg	7	0	1	1	9	0	0	0
Playoff Totals		**26**	**0**	**3**	**3**	**29**	**0**	**0**	**0**
•SYKORA, Michal									Defense
1997	Chicago	1	0	0	0	0	0	0	0
2001	Philadelphia	6	0	1	1	0	0	0	0
Playoff Totals		**7**	**0**	**1**	**1**	**0**	**0**	**0**	**0**
•SYKORA, Petr									Right wing
1997	New Jersey	2	0	0	0	2	0	0	0
1998	New Jersey	2	0	0	0	0	0	0	0
1999	New Jersey	7	3	3	6	4	0	0	1
2000♦	New Jersey	23	9	8	17	10	1	0	3
2001	New Jersey	25	10	12	22	12	2	2	2
2002	New Jersey	4	0	1	1	0	0	0	0
Playoff Totals		**63**	**22**	**24**	**46**	**28**	**3**	**2**	**6**
•SYKORA, Petr *No Playoffs*									Center
SYLVESTER, Dean									Right wing
1999	Buffalo	4	0	0	0	0	0	0	0
Playoff Totals		**4**	**0**	**0**	**0**	**0**	**0**	**0**	**0**
SZURA, Joe									Center
1969	Oakland	7	2	3	5	2	1	0	0
Playoff Totals		**7**	**2**	**3**	**5**	**2**	**1**	**0**	**0**
•TAFFE, Jeff *No Playoffs*									Center
TAFT, John *No Playoffs*									Defense
TAGLIANETTI, Peter									Defense
1985	Winnipeg	1	0	0	0	0	0	0	0
1986	Winnipeg	3	0	0	0	2	0	0	0
1988	Winnipeg	5	1	1	2	12	0	0	0
1990	Winnipeg	5	0	0	0	6	0	0	0
1991♦	Pittsburgh	19	0	3	3	49	0	0	0
1992♦	Pittsburgh	....	....	....	....	....	....	....	....
1993	Pittsburgh	11	1	2	3	16	0	0	0
1994	Pittsburgh	5	0	2	2	16	0	0	0
1995	Pittsburgh	4	0	0	0	2	0	0	0
Playoff Totals		**53**	**2**	**8**	**10**	**103**	**0**	**0**	**0**
TALAFOUS, Dean									Right wing
1977	Minnesota	2	0	0	0	0	0	0	0
1980	NY Rangers	5	1	2	3	9	1	0	0
1981	NY Rangers	14	3	5	8	2	0	0	0
Playoff Totals		**21**	**4**	**7**	**11**	**11**	**1**	**0**	**0**
TALAKOSKI, Ron *No Playoffs*									Right wing
TALBOT, Jean-Guy									Defense
1956♦	Montreal	9	0	2	2	4	0	0	0
1957♦	Montreal	10	0	2	2	10	0	0	0
1958♦	Montreal	10	0	3	3	12	0	0	0
1959♦	Montreal	11	0	1	1	10	0	0	0
1960♦	Montreal	8	1	1	2	8	0	0	0
1961	Montreal	6	1	1	2	10	1	0	0
1962	Montreal	6	1	1	2	10	0	0	0
1963	Montreal	5	0	0	0	8	0	0	0
1964	Montreal	7	0	2	2	10	0	0	0
1965♦	Montreal	13	0	1	1	22	0	0	0
1966♦	Montreal	10	0	2	2	8	0	0	0
1967	Montreal	10	0	0	0	0	0	0	0
1968	St. Louis	17	0	2	2	8	0	0	0
1969	St. Louis	12	0	2	2	6	0	0	0
1970	St. Louis	16	1	6	7	16	0	0	0
Playoff Totals		**150**	**4**	**26**	**30**	**142**	**1**	**0**	**0**
•TALLINDER, Henrik *No Playoffs*									Defense

Season	Team	GP	G	A	Pts	PIM	PP	SH	GW
TALLON, Dale	Defense								
1974	Chicago	11	1	3	4	29	1	0	0
1975	Chicago	8	1	3	4	4	0	0	0
1976	Chicago	4	0	1	1	8	0	0	0
1977	Chicago	2	0	1	1	0	0	0	0
1978	Chicago	4	0	2	2	0	0	0	0
1980	Pittsburgh	4	0	0	0	4	0	0	0
Playoff Totals		**33**	**2**	**10**	**12**	**45**	**1**	**0**	**0**
TAMBELLINI, Steve	Center								
1980♦	NY Islanders	....	....	....	....	....	....	....	....
1984	Calgary	2	0	1	1	0	0	0	0
Playoff Totals		**2**	**0**	**1**	**1**	**0**	**0**	**0**	**0**
•TAMER, Chris	Defense								
1994	Pittsburgh	5	0	0	0	2	0	0	0
1995	Pittsburgh	4	0	0	0	18	0	0	0
1996	Pittsburgh	18	0	7	7	24	0	0	0
1997	Pittsburgh	4	0	0	0	4	0	0	0
1998	Pittsburgh	6	0	1	1	4	0	0	0
Playoff Totals		**37**	**0**	**8**	**8**	**52**	**0**	**0**	**0**
•TANABE, David	Defense								
2001	Carolina	6	2	0	2	12	2	0	0
2002	Carolina	1	0	1	1	0	0	0	0
Playoff Totals		**7**	**2**	**1**	**3**	**12**	**2**	**0**	**0**
TANCILL, Chris	Center								
1995	San Jose	11	1	1	2	8	0	0	0
Playoff Totals		**11**	**1**	**1**	**2**	**8**	**0**	**0**	**0**
•TANGUAY, Alex	Center								
2000	Colorado	17	2	1	3	2	1	0	1
2001♦	Colorado	23	6	15	21	8	1	0	2
2002	Colorado	19	5	8	13	0	3	0	0
Playoff Totals		**59**	**13**	**24**	**37**	**10**	**5**	**0**	**3**
TANGUAY, Christian *No Playoffs*	Right wing								
TANNAHILL, Don *No Playoffs*	Left wing								
TANTI, Tony	Right wing								
1983	Vancouver	4	0	1	1	0	0	0	0
1984	Vancouver	4	1	2	3	0	0	0	0
1986	Vancouver	3	0	1	1	11	0	0	0
1989	Vancouver	7	0	5	5	4	0	0	0
1991	Buffalo	5	2	0	2	8	1	0	0
1992	Buffalo	7	0	3	3	4	0	0	0
Playoff Totals		**30**	**3**	**12**	**15**	**27**	**1**	**0**	**0**
•TAPPER, Brad *No Playoffs*	Center								
TARDIF, Marc	Left wing								
1971♦	Montreal	20	3	1	4	40	0	0	0
1972	Montreal	6	2	3	5	9	0	0	1
1973♦	Montreal	14	6	6	12	6	2	0	2
1981	Quebec	5	1	3	4	2	0	0	0
1982	Quebec	13	1	2	3	16	0	0	0
1983	Quebec	4	0	0	0	2	0	0	0
Playoff Totals		**62**	**13**	**15**	**28**	**75**	**2**	**0**	**3**
TARDIF, Patrice *No Playoffs*	Center								
•TARNSTROM, Dick	Defense								
2002	NY Islanders	5	0	0	0	2	0	0	0
Playoff Totals		**5**	**0**	**0**	**0**	**2**	**0**	**0**	**0**
TATARINOV, Mikhail *No Playoffs*	Defense								
TATCHELL, Spence *No Playoffs*	Defense								
TAYLOR, Billy *No Playoffs*	Center								
TAYLOR, Billy	Center								
1940	Toronto	2	1	0	1	0	....	....	....
1941	Toronto	7	0	3	3	5	....	....	....
1942♦	Toronto	13	2	*8	10	4	....	....	....
1943	Toronto	6	2	2	4	0	....	....	....
1947	Detroit	5	1	5	6	4	....	....	....
Playoff Totals		**33**	**6**	**18**	**24**	**13**	....	....	....
TAYLOR, Bob *No Playoffs*	Right wing								
•TAYLOR, Chris	Center								
2000	Buffalo	2	0	0	0	2	0	0	0
Playoff Totals		**2**	**0**	**0**	**0**	**2**	**0**	**0**	**0**
TAYLOR, Dave	Right wing								
1978	Los Angeles	2	0	0	0	5	0	0	0
1979	Los Angeles	2	0	0	0	2	0	0	0
1980	Los Angeles	4	2	1	3	4	0	0	0
1981	Los Angeles	4	2	2	4	10	1	0	0
1982	Los Angeles	10	4	6	10	20	3	0	0
1985	Los Angeles	3	2	2	4	8	0	0	0
1987	Los Angeles	5	2	3	5	6	1	0	0
1988	Los Angeles	5	3	3	6	6	2	0	0
1989	Los Angeles	11	1	5	6	19	1	0	0
1990	Los Angeles	6	4	4	8	2	2	0	0
1991	Los Angeles	12	2	1	3	12	0	0	1
1992	Los Angeles	6	1	1	2	20	0	0	0
1993	Los Angeles	22	3	5	8	31	0	2	0
Playoff Totals		**92**	**26**	**33**	**59**	**145**	**10**	**2**	**1**
TAYLOR, Harry	Center								
1949♦	Toronto	1	0	0	0	0	0	0	0
Playoff Totals		**1**	**0**	**0**	**0**	**0**	**0**	**0**	**0**
TAYLOR, Mark	Center								
1983	Philadelphia	3	0	0	0	0	0	0	0
1986	Washington	3	0	0	0	0	0	0	0
Playoff Totals		**6**	**0**	**0**	**0**	**0**	**0**	**0**	**0**
TAYLOR, Ralph	Defense								
1930	NY Rangers	4	0	0	0	10	0	0	0
Playoff Totals		**4**	**0**	**0**	**0**	**10**	**0**	**0**	**0**
TAYLOR, Ted *No Playoffs*	Left wing								
•TAYLOR, Tim	Center								
1995	Detroit	6	0	1	1	12	0	0	0
1996	Detroit	18	0	4	4	4	0	0	0
1997♦	Detroit	2	0	0	0	0	0	0	0
1998	Boston	6	0	0	0	10	0	0	0
1999	Boston	12	0	3	3	8	0	0	0
Playoff Totals		**44**	**0**	**8**	**8**	**34**	**0**	**0**	**0**
TEAL, Jeff *No Playoffs*	Right wing								
TEAL, Skip *No Playoffs*	Center								
TEAL, Vic *No Playoffs*	Right wing								
TEBBUTT, Greg *No Playoffs*	Defense								
•TENKRAT, Petr *No Playoffs*	Right wing								
TEPPER, Stephen *No Playoffs*	Right wing								
TERBENCHE, Paul	Defense								
1968	Chicago	6	0	0	0	0	0	0	0
1973	Buffalo	6	0	0	0	0	0	0	0
Playoff Totals		**12**	**0**	**0**	**0**	**0**	**0**	**0**	**0**
TERRION, Greg	Left wing								
1981	Los Angeles	3	1	0	1	4	1	0	0
1983	Toronto	4	1	2	3	2	0	0	0
1986	Toronto	10	0	3	3	17	0	0	0
1987	Toronto	13	0	2	2	14	0	0	0
1988	Toronto	5	0	2	2	4	0	0	0
Playoff Totals		**35**	**2**	**9**	**11**	**41**	**1**	**0**	**0**
TERRY, Bill *No Playoffs*	Center								
TERTYSHNY, Dmitri	Defense								
1999	Philadelphia	1	0	0	0	0	0	0	0
Playoff Totals		**1**	**0**	**0**	**0**	**0**	**0**	**0**	**0**
TESSIER, Orval *No Playoffs*	Center								
•TETARENKO, Joey *No Playoffs*	Right wing								
•TEZIKOV, Alexei *No Playoffs*	Defense								
THEBERGE, Greg	Defense								
1983	Washington	4	0	1	1	0	0	0	0
Playoff Totals		**4**	**0**	**1**	**1**	**0**	**0**	**0**	**0**
THELIN, Mats	Defense								
1985	Boston	5	0	0	0	6	0	0	0
Playoff Totals		**5**	**0**	**0**	**0**	**6**	**0**	**0**	**0**
THELVEN, Michael	Defense								
1986	Boston	3	0	0	0	0	0	0	0
1988	Boston	21	3	3	6	26	1	0	0
1989	Boston	10	1	7	8	8	0	0	1
Playoff Totals		**34**	**4**	**10**	**14**	**34**	**1**	**0**	**1**
•THERIEN, Chris	Defense								
1995	Philadelphia	15	0	0	0	10	0	0	0
1996	Philadelphia	12	0	0	0	18	0	0	0
1997	Philadelphia	19	1	6	7	6	0	0	1
1998	Philadelphia	5	0	1	1	4	0	0	0
1999	Philadelphia	6	0	0	0	6	0	0	0
2000	Philadelphia	18	0	1	1	12	0	0	0
2001	Philadelphia	6	1	0	1	8	0	0	0
2002	Philadelphia	5	0	0	0	2	0	0	0
Playoff Totals		**86**	**2**	**8**	**10**	**66**	**0**	**0**	**1**
THERRIEN, Gaston	Defense								
1982	Quebec	9	0	1	1	4	0	0	0
Playoff Totals		**9**	**0**	**1**	**1**	**4**	**0**	**0**	**0**
THIBAUDEAU, Gilles	Center								
1988	Montreal	8	3	3	6	2	1	0	0
Playoff Totals		**8**	**3**	**3**	**6**	**2**	**1**	**0**	**0**
THIBEAULT, Lorrain *No Playoffs*	Left wing								
THIFFAULT, Leo	Left wing								
1968	Minnesota	5	0	0	0	0	0	0	0
Playoff Totals		**5**	**0**	**0**	**0**	**0**	**0**	**0**	**0**
THOMAS, Cy *No Playoffs*	Wing								
THOMAS, Reg *No Playoffs*	Left wing								
•THOMAS, Scott	Right wing								
2001	Los Angeles	12	1	0	1	4	1	0	0
Playoff Totals		**12**	**1**	**0**	**1**	**4**	**1**	**0**	**0**
•THOMAS, Steve	Right wing								
1986	Toronto	10	6	8	14	9	3	0	0
1987	Toronto	13	2	3	5	13	0	0	0
1988	Chicago	3	1	2	3	6	0	0	0
1989	Chicago	12	3	5	8	10	1	0	2
1990	Chicago	20	7	6	13	33	1	0	3
1991	Chicago	6	1	2	3	15	0	0	0
1993	NY Islanders	18	9	8	17	37	0	0	0
1994	NY Islanders	4	1	0	1	8	1	0	0
1997	New Jersey	10	1	1	2	18	0	0	0
1998	New Jersey	6	0	3	3	2	0	0	0
1999	Toronto	17	6	3	9	12	2	0	1
2000	Toronto	12	6	3	9	10	0	0	1
2001	Toronto	11	6	3	9	4	4	0	0
2002	Chicago	5	1	1	2	0	0	0	0
Playoff Totals		**147**	**50**	**48**	**98**	**177**	**12**	**0**	**7**
THOMLINSON, Dave	Left wing								
1991	St. Louis	9	3	1	4	4	1	0	1
Playoff Totals		**9**	**3**	**1**	**4**	**4**	**1**	**0**	**1**
•THOMPSON, Brent	Defense								
1992	Los Angeles	4	0	0	0	4	0	0	0
Playoff Totals		**4**	**0**	**0**	**0**	**4**	**0**	**0**	**0**
THOMPSON, Cliff *No Playoffs*	Defense								
THOMPSON, Errol	Left wing								
1974	Toronto	2	0	1	1	0	0	0	0
1975	Toronto	6	0	0	0	9	0	0	0
1976	Toronto	10	3	3	6	0	2	1	0
1977	Toronto	9	2	0	2	0	0	0	1
1978	Detroit	7	2	1	3	2	1	0	1
Playoff Totals		**34**	**7**	**5**	**12**	**11**	**3**	**1**	**2**
THOMPSON, Ken *No Playoffs*	Left wing/Center								
THOMPSON, Paul	Left wing								
1927	NY Rangers	2	0	0	0	0	....	....	....
1928♦	NY Rangers	8	0	0	0	30	....	....	....
1929	NY Rangers	6	0	*2	2	6	....	....	....
1930	NY Rangers	4	0	0	0	2	....	....	....
1931	NY Rangers	4	3	0	3	2	....	....	....
1932	Chicago	2	0	0	0	2	....	....	....
1934♦	Chicago	8	4	3	7	6	....	....	....
1935	Chicago	2	0	0	0	0	....	....	....
1936	Chicago	2	0	3	3	0	....	....	....
1938♦	Chicago	10	4	3	7	6	....	....	....
Playoff Totals		**48**	**11**	**11**	**22**	**54**	....	....	....
•THOMPSON, Rocky *No Playoffs*	Right wing								
THOMS, Bill	Center								
1933	Toronto	9	1	1	2	4	....	....	....
1934	Toronto	5	0	2	2	0	....	....	....
1935	Toronto	7	2	0	2	0	....	....	....
1936	Toronto	9	3	*5	8	0	....	....	....
1937	Toronto	2	0	0	0	0	....	....	....
1938	Toronto	7	0	1	1	0	....	....	....
1940	Chicago	1	0	0	0	0	....	....	....
1942	Chicago	3	0	1	1	0	....	....	....
1945	Boston	1	0	0	0	2	....	....	....
Playoff Totals		**44**	**6**	**10**	**16**	**6**	....	....	....
THOMSON, Bill	Center/Right wing								
1944	Detroit	2	0	0	0	0	0	0	0
Playoff Totals		**2**	**0**	**0**	**0**	**0**	**0**	**0**	**0**
THOMSON, Floyd	Left wing								
1973	St. Louis	5	0	1	1	2	0	0	0
1975	St. Louis	2	0	1	1	0	0	0	0
1977	St. Louis	3	0	0	0	4	0	0	0
Playoff Totals		**10**	**0**	**2**	**2**	**6**	**0**	**0**	**0**
THOMSON, Jim	Right wing								
1993	Los Angeles	1	0	0	0	0	0	0	0
Playoff Totals		**1**	**0**	**0**	**0**	**0**	**0**	**0**	**0**
THOMSON, Jimmy	Defense								
1947♦	Toronto	11	0	1	1	22	....	....	....
1948♦	Toronto	9	1	1	2	9	....	....	....
1949♦	Toronto	9	1	5	6	10	....	....	....
1950	Toronto	7	0	2	2	7	....	....	....
1951♦	Toronto	11	0	1	1	*34	....	....	....
1952	Toronto	4	0	0	0	25	....	....	....
1954	Toronto	3	0	0	0	2	....	....	....
1955	Toronto	4	0	0	0	16	....	....	....
1956	Toronto	5	0	3	3	10	....	....	....
Playoff Totals		**63**	**2**	**13**	**15**	**135**	....	....	....
THOMSON, Rhys *No Playoffs*	Defense								
THORNBURY, Tom *No Playoffs*	Defense								
•THORNTON, Joe	Center								
1998	Boston	6	0	0	0	9	0	0	0
1999	Boston	11	3	6	9	4	2	0	2
2002	Boston	6	2	4	6	10	0	0	0
Playoff Totals		**23**	**5**	**10**	**15**	**23**	**2**	**0**	**2**

Season	Team	GP	G	A	Pts	PIM	PP	SH	GW
•THORNTON, Scott	Center								
1992	Edmonton	1	0	0	0	0	0	0	0
1997	Montreal	5	1	0	1	2	0	0	0
1998	Montreal	9	0	2	2	10	0	0	0
2000	Dallas	23	2	7	9	28	0	0	1
2001	San Jose	6	3	0	3	8	0	0	1
2002	San Jose	12	3	3	6	6	0	0	0
Playoff Totals		**56**	**9**	**12**	**21**	**54**	**0**	**0**	**2**
•THORNTON, Shawn *No Playoffs*	Right wing								
THORSTEINSON, Joe *No Playoffs*	Right wing								
THURIER, Fred *No Playoffs*	Center								
THURLBY, Tom *No Playoffs*	Defense								
THYER, Mario	Center								
1990	Minnesota	1	0	0	0	2	0	0	0
Playoff Totals		**1**	**0**	**0**	**0**	**2**	**0**	**0**	**0**
•TIBBETTS, Billy *No Playoffs*	Right wing								
TICHY, Milan *No Playoffs*	Defense								
TIDEY, Alex	Right wing								
1977	Buffalo	2	0	0	0	0	0	0	0
Playoff Totals		**2**	**0**	**0**	**0**	**0**	**0**	**0**	**0**
TIKKANEN, Esa	Left wing								
1985♦	Edmonton	3	0	0	0	2	0	0	0
1986	Edmonton	8	3	2	5	7	0	0	0
1987♦	Edmonton	21	7	2	9	22	1	0	1
1988♦	Edmonton	19	10	17	27	72	5	0	1
1989	Edmonton	7	1	3	4	12	0	0	0
1990♦	Edmonton	22	13	11	24	26	2	2	0
1991	Edmonton	18	12	8	20	24	3	0	3
1992	Edmonton	16	5	3	8	8	1	0	1
1994♦	NY Rangers	23	4	4	8	34	0	0	1
1995	St. Louis	7	2	2	4	20	1	0	1
1996	Vancouver	6	3	2	5	2	2	0	0
1997	NY Rangers	15	9	3	12	26	3	1	3
1998	Washington	21	3	3	6	20	1	0	0
Playoff Totals		**186**	**72**	**60**	**132**	**275**	**19**	**3**	**11**
•TILEY, Brad	Defense								
1999	Phoenix	1	0	0	0	0	0	0	0
Playoff Totals		**1**	**0**	**0**	**0**	**0**	**0**	**0**	**0**
TILLEY, Tom	Defense								
1989	St. Louis	10	1	2	3	17	0	0	0
1994	St. Louis	4	0	1	1	2	0	0	0
Playoff Totals		**14**	**1**	**3**	**4**	**19**	**0**	**0**	**0**
•TIMANDER, Mattias	Defense								
1999	Boston	4	1	1	2	2	0	0	0
Playoff Totals		**4**	**1**	**1**	**2**	**2**	**0**	**0**	**0**
TIMGREN, Ray	Left wing								
1949♦	Toronto	9	3	3	6	2	....	....	....
1950	Toronto	6	0	4	4	2	....	....	....
1951♦	Toronto	11	0	1	1	2	....	....	....
1952	Toronto	4	0	1	1	0	....	....	....
Playoff Totals		**30**	**3**	**9**	**12**	**6**	....	....	....
•TIMONEN, Kimmo *No Playoffs*	Defense								
TINORDI, Mark	Defense								
1989	Minnesota	5	0	0	0	0	0	0	0
1990	Minnesota	7	0	1	1	16	0	0	0
1991	Minnesota	23	5	6	11	78	4	0	0
1992	Minnesota	7	1	2	3	11	0	0	0
1995	Washington	1	0	0	0	2	0	0	0
1996	Washington	6	0	0	0	16	0	0	0
1998	Washington	21	1	2	3	42	0	0	0
Playoff Totals		**70**	**7**	**11**	**18**	**165**	**4**	**0**	**0**
TIPPETT, Dave	Left wing								
1986	Hartford	10	2	2	4	4	0	1	0
1987	Hartford	6	0	2	2	4	0	0	0
1988	Hartford	6	0	0	0	2	0	0	0
1989	Hartford	4	0	1	1	0	0	0	0
1990	Hartford	7	1	3	4	2	0	0	0
1991	Washington	10	2	3	5	8	0	0	0
1992	Washington	7	0	1	1	0	0	0	0
1993	Pittsburgh	12	1	4	5	14	0	0	0
Playoff Totals		**62**	**6**	**16**	**22**	**34**	**0**	**1**	**0**
TITANIC, Morris *No Playoffs*	Left wing								
•TITOV, German	Center								
1994	Calgary	7	2	1	3	4	1	0	0
1995	Calgary	7	5	3	8	10	0	1	0
1996	Calgary	4	0	2	2	0	0	0	0
1999	Pittsburgh	11	3	5	8	4	0	0	0
2000	Edmonton	5	1	1	2	0	0	0	0
Playoff Totals		**34**	**11**	**12**	**23**	**18**	**1**	**1**	**0**
•TJARNQVIST, Daniel *No Playoffs*	Defense								
•TKACHUK, Keith	Left wing								
1992	Winnipeg	7	3	0	3	30	0	0	0
1993	Winnipeg	6	4	0	4	14	1	0	0
1996	Winnipeg	6	1	2	3	22	0	0	0
1997	Phoenix	7	6	0	6	7	2	0	0
1998	Phoenix	6	3	3	6	10	0	0	0
1999	Phoenix	7	1	3	4	13	1	0	0
2000	Phoenix	5	1	1	2	4	1	0	0
2001	St. Louis	15	2	7	9	20	2	0	1
2002	St. Louis	10	5	5	10	18	1	0	0
Playoff Totals		**69**	**26**	**21**	**47**	**138**	**8**	**0**	**1**
•TKACZUK, Daniel *No Playoffs*	Center								
TKACZUK, Walt	Center								
1969	NY Rangers	4	0	1	1	6	0	0	0
1970	NY Rangers	6	2	1	3	17	1	0	0
1971	NY Rangers	13	1	5	6	14	0	0	1
1972	NY Rangers	16	4	6	10	35	0	0	2
1973	NY Rangers	10	7	2	9	8	1	0	1
1974	NY Rangers	13	0	5	5	22	0	0	0
1975	NY Rangers	3	1	2	3	5	0	0	0
1978	NY Rangers	3	0	2	2	0	0	0	0
1979	NY Rangers	18	4	7	11	10	0	1	0
1980	NY Rangers	7	0	1	1	2	0	0	0
Playoff Totals		**93**	**19**	**32**	**51**	**119**	**2**	**1**	**4**
TOAL, Mike *No Playoffs*	Center								
•TOBLER, Ryan *No Playoffs*	Left wing								
TOCCHET, Rick	Right wing								
1985	Philadelphia	19	3	4	7	72	0	0	2
1986	Philadelphia	5	1	2	3	26	0	0	0
1987	Philadelphia	26	11	10	21	72	0	1	2
1988	Philadelphia	5	1	4	5	55	0	1	0
1989	Philadelphia	16	6	6	12	69	2	0	1
1992♦	Pittsburgh	14	6	13	19	24	3	0	1
1993	Pittsburgh	12	7	6	13	24	1	0	0
1994	Pittsburgh	6	2	3	5	20	1	0	1
1996	Boston	5	4	0	4	21	3	0	1
1998	Phoenix	6	6	2	8	25	3	0	0
1999	Phoenix	7	0	3	3	8	0	0	0
2000	Philadelphia	18	5	6	11	*49	2	0	1
2001	Philadelphia	6	0	1	1	6	0	0	0
Playoff Totals		**145**	**52**	**60**	**112**	**471**	**15**	**2**	**9**
TODD, Kevin	Center								
1991	New Jersey	1	0	0	0	6	0	0	0
1992	New Jersey	7	3	2	5	8	1	0	0
1997	Anaheim	4	0	0	0	2	0	0	0
Playoff Totals		**12**	**3**	**2**	**5**	**16**	**1**	**0**	**0**
TOMALTY, Glenn *No Playoffs*	Left wing								
TOMLAK, Mike	Center/Left wing								
1990	Hartford	7	0	1	1	2	0	0	0
1991	Hartford	3	0	0	0	2	0	0	0
Playoff Totals		**10**	**0**	**1**	**1**	**4**	**0**	**0**	**0**
TOMLINSON, Dave *No Playoffs*	Center								
TOMLINSON, Kirk *No Playoffs*	Center								
•TOMS, Jeff	Left wing								
1998	Washington	1	0	0	0	0	0	0	0
Playoff Totals		**1**	**0**	**0**	**0**	**0**	**0**	**0**	**0**
TOMSON, Jack	Defense								
1939	NY Americans	2	0	0	0	0	0	0	0
Playoff Totals		**2**	**0**	**0**	**0**	**0**	**0**	**0**	**0**
TONELLI, John	Left wing								
1979	NY Islanders	10	1	6	7	0	0	0	0
1980♦	NY Islanders	21	7	9	16	18	0	0	0
1981♦	NY Islanders	16	5	8	13	16	0	0	2
1982♦	NY Islanders	19	6	10	16	18	1	0	1
1983♦	NY Islanders	20	7	11	18	20	0	0	2
1984	NY Islanders	17	1	3	4	31	0	0	0
1985	NY Islanders	10	1	8	9	10	0	0	0
1986	Calgary	22	7	9	16	49	1	0	1
1987	Calgary	3	0	0	0	4	0	0	0
1988	Calgary	6	2	5	7	8	2	0	1
1989	Los Angeles	6	0	0	0	8	0	0	0
1990	Los Angeles	10	1	2	3	6	0	0	0
1991	Los Angeles	12	2	4	6	12	1	0	0
Playoff Totals		**172**	**40**	**75**	**115**	**200**	**5**	**0**	**7**
TOOKEY, Tim	Center								
1987	Philadelphia	10	1	3	4	2	0	0	0
Playoff Totals		**10**	**1**	**3**	**4**	**2**	**0**	**0**	**0**
TOOMEY, Sean *No Playoffs*	Left wing								
TOPOROWSKI, Shayne *No Playoffs*	Right wing								
TOPPAZZINI, Jerry	Right wing								
1953	Boston	11	0	3	3	9	....	....	....
1957	Boston	10	0	1	1	2	....	....	....
1958	Boston	12	9	3	12	2	....	....	....
1959	Boston	7	4	2	6	0	....	....	....
Playoff Totals		**40**	**13**	**9**	**22**	**13**	....	....	....
TOPPAZZINI, Zellio	Right wing								
1949	Boston	2	0	0	0	0	0	0	0
Playoff Totals		**2**	**0**	**0**	**0**	**0**	**0**	**0**	**0**
TORGAEV, Pavel	Left wing								
1996	Calgary	1	0	0	0	0	0	0	0
Playoff Totals		**1**	**0**	**0**	**0**	**0**	**0**	**0**	**0**
TORKKI, Jari *No Playoffs*	Left wing								
TORMANEN, Antti *No Playoffs*	Right wing								
•TORRES, Raffi *No Playoffs*	Left wing								
TOUHEY, Bill	Left wing								
1930	Ottawa	2	1	0	1	0	....	....	....
Playoff Totals		**2**	**1**	**0**	**1**	**0**	....	....	....
TOUPIN, Jacques	Right wing								
1944	Chicago	4	0	0	0	0	0	0	0
Playoff Totals		**4**	**0**	**0**	**0**	**0**	**0**	**0**	**0**
TOWNSEND, Art *No Playoffs*	Defense								
TOWNSHEND, Graeme *No Playoffs*	Right wing								
TRADER, Larry	Defense								
1985	Detroit	3	0	0	0	0	0	0	0
Playoff Totals		**3**	**0**	**0**	**0**	**0**	**0**	**0**	**0**
TRAINOR, Wes *No Playoffs*	Center/Left wing								
TRAPP, Bob	Defense								
1927	Chicago	2	0	0	0	4	0	0	0
Playoff Totals		**2**	**0**	**0**	**0**	**4**	**0**	**0**	**0**
TRAPP, Doug *No Playoffs*	Left wing								
TRAUB, Percy	Defense								
1927	Chicago	2	0	0	0	6	0	0	0
1929	Detroit	2	0	0	0	0	0	0	0
Playoff Totals		**4**	**0**	**0**	**0**	**6**	**0**	**0**	**0**
•TRAVERSE, Patrick	Defense								
2000	Ottawa	6	0	0	0	2	0	0	0
Playoff Totals		**6**	**0**	**0**	**0**	**2**	**0**	**0**	**0**
•TREBIL, Dan	Defense								
1997	Anaheim	9	0	1	1	6	0	0	0
1999	Anaheim	1	0	0	0	2	0	0	0
Playoff Totals		**10**	**0**	**1**	**1**	**8**	**0**	**0**	**0**
TREDWAY, Brock	Right wing								
1982	Los Angeles	1	0	0	0	0	0	0	0
Playoff Totals		**1**	**0**	**0**	**0**	**0**	**0**	**0**	**0**
TREMBLAY, Brent *No Playoffs*	Defense								
TREMBLAY, Gilles	Left wing								
1961	Montreal	6	1	3	4	0	0	0	0
1962	Montreal	6	1	0	1	2	0	0	0
1963	Montreal	5	2	0	2	0	2	0	1
1964	Montreal	2	0	0	0	0	0	0	0
1966♦	Montreal	10	4	5	9	0	3	0	1
1967	Montreal	10	0	1	1	0	0	0	0
1968♦	Montreal	9	1	5	6	2	0	0	0
1969♦	Montreal	....	....	....	....	....	....	....	....
Playoff Totals		**48**	**9**	**14**	**23**	**4**	**5**	**0**	**2**
TREMBLAY, J.C.	Defense								
1961	Montreal	5	0	0	0	2	0	0	0
1962	Montreal	6	0	2	2	2	0	0	0
1963	Montreal	5	0	0	0	0	0	0	0
1964	Montreal	7	2	1	3	9	0	1	0
1965♦	Montreal	13	1	*9	10	18	0	1	0
1966♦	Montreal	10	2	9	11	2	2	0	0
1967	Montreal	10	2	4	6	2	0	0	0
1968♦	Montreal	13	3	6	9	2	0	1	1
1969♦	Montreal	13	1	4	5	6	0	1	0
1971♦	Montreal	20	3	14	17	15	1	0	3
1972	Montreal	6	0	2	2	0	0	0	0
Playoff Totals		**108**	**14**	**51**	**65**	**58**	**3**	**4**	**4**
TREMBLAY, Marcel *No Playoffs*	Right wing								
TREMBLAY, Mario	Right wing								
1975	Montreal	11	0	1	1	7	0	0	0
1976♦	Montreal	10	0	1	1	27	0	0	0
1977♦	Montreal	14	3	0	3	9	0	0	0
1978♦	Montreal	5	2	1	3	16	0	0	1
1979♦	Montreal	13	3	4	7	13	0	0	1
1980	Montreal	10	0	11	11	14	0	0	0
1981	Montreal	3	0	0	0	9	0	0	0
1982	Montreal	5	4	1	5	24	0	0	1
1983	Montreal	3	0	1	1	7	0	0	0
1984	Montreal	15	6	3	9	31	0	0	1
1985	Montreal	12	2	6	8	30	1	0	0
1986♦	Montreal	....	....	....	....	....	....	....	....
Playoff Totals		**101**	**20**	**29**	**49**	**187**	**1**	**0**	**4**
TREMBLAY, Nils	Center								
1945	Montreal	2	0	0	0	0	0	0	0
Playoff Totals		**2**	**0**	**0**	**0**	**0**	**0**	**0**	**0**
•TREMBLAY, Yannick *No Playoffs*	Defense								
•TREPANIER, Pascal	Defense								
2002	Colorado	2	0	0	0	0	0	0	0
Playoff Totals		**2**	**0**	**0**	**0**	**0**	**0**	**0**	**0**
TRIMPER, Tim	Left wing								
1980	Chicago	1	0	0	0	2	0	0	0
1982	Winnipeg	1	0	0	0	0	0	0	0
Playoff Totals		**2**	**0**	**0**	**0**	**2**	**0**	**0**	**0**

TRIPP, John *No Playoffs* — Right wing

•TRNKA, Pavel — Defense

Season	Team	GP	G	A	Pts	PIM	PP	SH	GW
1999	Anaheim	4	0	1	1	2	0	0	0
Playoff Totals		**4**	**0**	**1**	**1**	**2**	**0**	**0**	**0**

TROTTIER, Bryan — Center

Season	Team	GP	G	A	Pts	PIM	PP	SH	GW
1976	NY Islanders	13	1	7	8	8	0	0	0
1977	NY Islanders	12	2	8	10	2	0	0	0
1978	NY Islanders	7	0	3	3	4	0	0	0
1979	NY Islanders	10	2	4	6	13	0	0	1
1980♦	NY Islanders	21	*12	17	*29	16	4	2	2
1981♦	NY Islanders	*18	11	*18	29	34	4	2	1
1982♦	NY Islanders	19	6	*23	*29	40	2	0	2
1983♦	NY Islanders	17	8	12	20	18	3	0	1
1984	NY Islanders	21	8	6	14	49	1	0	0
1985	NY Islanders	10	4	2	6	8	1	0	1
1986	NY Islanders	3	1	1	2	2	0	0	0
1987	NY Islanders	14	8	5	13	12	3	0	2
1988	NY Islanders	6	0	0	0	10	0	0	0
1990	NY Islanders	4	1	0	1	4	0	0	0
1991♦	Pittsburgh	23	3	4	7	49	0	0	2
1992♦	Pittsburgh	21	4	3	7	8	0	0	0
1994	Pittsburgh	2	0	0	0	0	0	0	0
Playoff Totals		**221**	**71**	**113**	**184**	**277**	**18**	**4**	**12**

TROTTIER, Dave — Left wing

Season	Team	GP	G	A	Pts	PIM	PP	SH	GW
1930	Mtl. Maroons	4	0	2	2	8	....	....	....
1931	Mtl. Maroons	2	0	0	0	6	....	....	....
1932	Mtl. Maroons	4	1	0	1	0	....	....	....
1933	Mtl. Maroons	2	0	0	0	6	....	....	....
1934	Mtl. Maroons	4	0	0	0	6	....	....	....
1935♦	Mtl. Maroons	7	2	1	3	4	....	....	....
1936	Mtl. Maroons	3	0	0	0	4	....	....	....
1937	Mtl. Maroons	5	1	0	1	5	....	....	....
Playoff Totals		**31**	**4**	**3**	**7**	**39**	....	....	....

TROTTIER, Guy — Right wing

Season	Team	GP	G	A	Pts	PIM	PP	SH	GW
1971	Toronto	5	0	0	0	0	0	0	0
1972	Toronto	4	1	0	1	16	0	0	0
Playoff Totals		**9**	**1**	**0**	**1**	**16**	**0**	**0**	**0**

TROTTIER, Rocky *No Playoffs* — Right wing

•TRUDEL, Jean-Guy *No Playoffs* — Left wing

TRUDEL, Lou — Left wing

Season	Team	GP	G	A	Pts	PIM	PP	SH	GW
1934♦	Chicago	7	0	0	0	0	....	....	....
1935	Chicago	2	0	0	0	0	....	....	....
1936	Chicago	2	0	0	0	2	....	....	....
1938♦	Chicago	10	0	3	3	2	....	....	....
1939	Montreal	3	1	0	1	0	....	....	....
Playoff Totals		**24**	**1**	**3**	**4**	**4**	....	....	....

TRUDELL, Rene — Right wing

Season	Team	GP	G	A	Pts	PIM	PP	SH	GW
1948	NY Rangers	5	0	0	0	2	0	0	0
Playoff Totals		**5**	**0**	**0**	**0**	**2**	**0**	**0**	**0**

•TSELIOS, Nikos *No Playoffs* — Defense

TSULYGIN, Nikolai *No Playoffs* — Defense

TSYGUROV, Denis *No Playoffs* — Defense

•TSYPLAKOV, Vladimir — Left wing

Season	Team	GP	G	A	Pts	PIM	PP	SH	GW
1998	Los Angeles	4	0	1	1	8	0	0	0
2000	Buffalo	5	0	1	1	4	0	0	0
2001	Buffalo	9	1	0	1	4	0	0	0
Playoff Totals		**18**	**1**	**2**	**3**	**16**	**0**	**0**	**0**

•TUCKER, Darcy — Center

Season	Team	GP	G	A	Pts	PIM	PP	SH	GW
1997	Montreal	4	0	0	0	0	0	0	0
2000	Toronto	12	4	2	6	15	1	0	2
2001	Toronto	11	0	2	2	6	0	0	0
2002	Toronto	17	4	4	8	38	1	0	1
Playoff Totals		**44**	**8**	**8**	**16**	**59**	**2**	**0**	**3**

TUCKER, John — Center

Season	Team	GP	G	A	Pts	PIM	PP	SH	GW
1984	Buffalo	3	1	0	1	0	0	0	0
1985	Buffalo	5	1	5	6	0	0	0	0
1988	Buffalo	6	7	3	10	18	4	0	2
1989	Buffalo	3	0	3	3	0	0	0	0
1990	Washington	12	1	7	8	4	0	0	0
1996	Tampa Bay	2	0	0	0	2	0	0	0
Playoff Totals		**31**	**10**	**18**	**28**	**24**	**4**	**0**	**2**

TUDIN, Connie *No Playoffs* — Center

TUDOR, Rob — Right wing/Center

Season	Team	GP	G	A	Pts	PIM	PP	SH	GW
1979	Vancouver	2	0	0	0	0	0	0	0
1980	Vancouver	1	0	0	0	0	0	0	0
Playoff Totals		**3**	**0**	**0**	**0**	**0**	**0**	**0**	**0**

TUER, Allan *No Playoffs* — Defense

•TUOMAINEN, Marko — Right wing

Season	Team	GP	G	A	Pts	PIM	PP	SH	GW
2000	Los Angeles	1	0	0	0	0	0	0	0
Playoff Totals		**1**	**0**	**0**	**0**	**0**	**0**	**0**	**0**

TURCOTTE, Alfie — Center

Season	Team	GP	G	A	Pts	PIM	PP	SH	GW
1985	Montreal	5	0	0	0	0	0	0	0
Playoff Totals		**5**	**0**	**0**	**0**	**0**	**0**	**0**	**0**

TURCOTTE, Darren — Center

Season	Team	GP	G	A	Pts	PIM	PP	SH	GW
1989	NY Rangers	1	0	0	0	0	0	0	0
1990	NY Rangers	10	1	6	7	4	0	0	1
1991	NY Rangers	6	1	2	3	0	1	0	0
1992	NY Rangers	8	4	0	4	6	2	1	0
1998	St. Louis	10	0	0	0	2	0	0	0
Playoff Totals		**35**	**6**	**8**	**14**	**12**	**3**	**1**	**1**

•TURGEON, Pierre — Center

Season	Team	GP	G	A	Pts	PIM	PP	SH	GW
1988	Buffalo	6	4	3	7	4	3	0	0
1989	Buffalo	5	3	5	8	2	1	0	0
1990	Buffalo	6	2	4	6	2	0	0	1
1991	Buffalo	6	3	1	4	6	1	0	0
1993	NY Islanders	11	6	7	13	0	0	0	0
1994	NY Islanders	4	0	1	1	0	0	0	0
1996	Montreal	6	2	4	6	2	0	0	0
1997	St. Louis	5	1	1	2	2	1	0	0
1998	St. Louis	10	4	4	8	2	2	0	0
1999	St. Louis	13	4	9	13	6	0	0	2
2000	St. Louis	7	0	7	7	0	0	0	0
2001	St. Louis	15	5	10	15	2	1	0	0
Playoff Totals		**94**	**34**	**56**	**90**	**28**	**9**	**0**	**3**

TURGEON, Sylvain — Left wing

Season	Team	GP	G	A	Pts	PIM	PP	SH	GW
1986	Hartford	9	2	3	5	4	0	0	0
1987	Hartford	6	1	2	3	4	0	0	0
1988	Hartford	6	0	0	0	4	0	0	0
1989	Hartford	4	0	2	2	4	0	0	0
1990	New Jersey	1	0	0	0	0	0	0	0
1991	Montreal	5	0	0	0	2	0	0	0
1992	Montreal	5	1	0	1	4	0	0	0
Playoff Totals		**36**	**4**	**7**	**11**	**22**	**0**	**0**	**0**

TURLICK, Gord *No Playoffs* — Left wing/Center

TURNBULL, Ian — Defense

Season	Team	GP	G	A	Pts	PIM	PP	SH	GW
1974	Toronto	4	0	0	0	8	0	0	0
1975	Toronto	7	0	2	2	4	0	0	0
1976	Toronto	10	2	9	11	29	1	0	0
1977	Toronto	9	4	4	8	10	4	0	0
1978	Toronto	13	6	10	16	10	1	0	0
1979	Toronto	6	0	4	4	27	0	0	0
1980	Toronto	3	0	3	3	2	0	0	0
1981	Toronto	3	1	0	1	4	0	0	0
Playoff Totals		**55**	**13**	**32**	**45**	**94**	**6**	**0**	**0**

TURNBULL, Perry — Center

Season	Team	GP	G	A	Pts	PIM	PP	SH	GW
1980	St. Louis	3	1	1	2	2	1	0	0
1982	St. Louis	5	3	2	5	11	1	0	0
1983	St. Louis	4	1	0	1	14	0	0	0
1984	Montreal	9	1	2	3	10	0	0	0
1985	Winnipeg	8	0	1	1	26	0	0	0
1986	Winnipeg	3	0	1	1	11	0	0	0
1987	Winnipeg	1	0	0	0	10	0	0	0
1988	St. Louis	1	0	0	0	2	0	0	0
Playoff Totals		**34**	**6**	**7**	**13**	**86**	**2**	**0**	**0**

TURNBULL, Randy *No Playoffs* — Defense

TURNER, Bob — Defense

Season	Team	GP	G	A	Pts	PIM	PP	SH	GW
1956♦	Montreal	10	0	1	1	10	0	0	0
1957♦	Montreal	6	0	1	1	0	0	0	0
1958♦	Montreal	10	0	0	0	2	0	0	0
1959♦	Montreal	11	0	2	2	20	0	0	0
1960♦	Montreal	8	0	0	0	0	0	0	0
1961	Montreal	5	0	0	0	0	0	0	0
1962	Chicago	12	1	0	1	6	0	1	0
1963	Chicago	6	0	0	0	6	0	0	0
Playoff Totals		**68**	**1**	**4**	**5**	**44**	**0**	**1**	**0**

TURNER, Brad *No Playoffs* — Defense

TURNER, Dean *No Playoffs* — Defense

TUSTIN, Norm *No Playoffs* — Left wing

TUTEN, Aud *No Playoffs* — Defense

TUTT, Brian *No Playoffs* — Defense

TUTTLE, Steve — Right wing

Season	Team	GP	G	A	Pts	PIM	PP	SH	GW
1989	St. Louis	6	1	2	3	0	0	0	0
1990	St. Louis	5	0	1	1	2	0	0	0
1991	St. Louis	6	0	3	3	0	0	0	0
Playoff Totals		**17**	**1**	**6**	**7**	**2**	**0**	**0**	**0**

•TUZZOLINO, Tony *No Playoffs* — Right wing

•TVERDOVSKY, Oleg — Defense

Season	Team	GP	G	A	Pts	PIM	PP	SH	GW
1996	Winnipeg	6	0	1	1	0	0	0	0
1997	Phoenix	7	0	1	1	0	0	0	0
1998	Phoenix	6	0	7	7	0	0	0	0
1999	Phoenix	6	0	2	2	6	0	0	0
Playoff Totals		**25**	**0**	**11**	**11**	**6**	**0**	**0**	**0**

TWIST, Tony — Left wing

Season	Team	GP	G	A	Pts	PIM	PP	SH	GW
1995	St. Louis	1	0	0	0	6	0	0	0
1996	St. Louis	10	1	1	2	16	0	0	0
1997	St. Louis	6	0	0	0	0	0	0	0
1999	St. Louis	1	0	0	0	0	0	0	0
Playoff Totals		**18**	**1**	**1**	**2**	**22**	**0**	**0**	**0**

UBRIACO, Gene — Left wing/Center

Season	Team	GP	G	A	Pts	PIM	PP	SH	GW
1969	Oakland	7	2	0	2	2	0	0	0
1970	Chicago	4	0	0	0	2	0	0	0
Playoff Totals		**11**	**2**	**0**	**2**	**4**	**0**	**0**	**0**

•ULANOV, Igor — Defense

Season	Team	GP	G	A	Pts	PIM	PP	SH	GW
1992	Winnipeg	7	0	0	0	39	0	0	0
1993	Winnipeg	4	0	0	0	4	0	0	0
1995	Washington	2	0	0	0	4	0	0	0
1996	Tampa Bay	5	0	0	0	15	0	0	0
1998	Montreal	10	1	4	5	12	0	0	0
2000	Edmonton	5	0	0	0	6	0	0	0
2001	Edmonton	6	0	0	0	4	0	0	0
Playoff Totals		**39**	**1**	**4**	**5**	**84**	**0**	**0**	**0**

ULLMAN, Norm — Center

Season	Team	GP	G	A	Pts	PIM	PP	SH	GW
1956	Detroit	10	1	3	4	13	....	....	....
1957	Detroit	5	1	1	2	6	....	....	....
1958	Detroit	4	0	2	2	4	....	....	....
1960	Detroit	6	2	2	4	0	....	....	....
1961	Detroit	11	0	4	4	4	....	....	....
1963	Detroit	11	4	*12	*16	14	....	....	....
1964	Detroit	14	7	10	17	6	....	....	....
1965	Detroit	7	6	4	10	2	....	....	....
1966	Detroit	12	*6	9	*15	12	....	....	....
1969	Toronto	4	1	0	1	0	0	0	0
1971	Toronto	6	0	2	2	2	0	0	0
1972	Toronto	5	1	3	4	2	0	0	0
1974	Toronto	4	1	1	2	0	0	0	0
1975	Toronto	7	0	0	0	2	0	0	0
Playoff Totals		**106**	**30**	**53**	**83**	**67**	**0**	**0**	**0**

•ULMER, Jeff *No Playoffs* — Right wing

UNGER, Garry — Center

Season	Team	GP	G	A	Pts	PIM	PP	SH	GW
1970	Detroit	4	0	1	1	6	0	0	0
1971	St. Louis	6	3	2	5	20	0	1	0
1972	St. Louis	11	4	5	9	35	2	0	1
1973	St. Louis	5	1	2	3	2	0	0	0
1975	St. Louis	2	1	3	4	6	0	0	0
1976	St. Louis	3	2	1	3	7	0	0	0
1977	St. Louis	4	0	1	1	2	0	0	0
1980	Atlanta	4	0	3	3	2	0	0	0
1981	Edmonton	8	0	0	0	2	0	0	0
1982	Edmonton	4	1	0	1	23	0	0	0
1983	Edmonton	1	0	0	0	0	0	0	0
Playoff Totals		**52**	**12**	**18**	**30**	**105**	**2**	**1**	**1**

•UPSHALL, Scottie *No Playoffs* — Right wing

USTORF, Stefan — Center

Season	Team	GP	G	A	Pts	PIM	PP	SH	GW
1996	Washington	5	0	0	0	0	0	0	0
Playoff Totals		**5**	**0**	**0**	**0**	**0**	**0**	**0**	**0**

•VAANANEN, Ossi — Defense

Season	Team	GP	G	A	Pts	PIM	PP	SH	GW
2002	Phoenix	5	0	0	0	6	0	0	0
Playoff Totals		**5**	**0**	**0**	**0**	**6**	**0**	**0**	**0**

VACHON, Nick *No Playoffs* — Center

VADNAIS, Carol — Defense

Season	Team	GP	G	A	Pts	PIM	PP	SH	GW
1967	Montreal	1	0	0	0	2	0	0	0
1968♦	Montreal	1	0	0	0	0	0	0	0
1969	Oakland	7	1	4	5	10	1	0	0
1970	Oakland	4	2	1	3	15	2	0	0
1972♦	Boston	15	0	2	2	43	0	0	0
1973	Boston	5	0	0	0	8	0	0	0
1974	Boston	16	1	12	13	42	1	0	0
1975	Boston	3	1	5	6	0	0	0	0
1978	NY Rangers	3	0	2	2	16	0	0	0
1979	NY Rangers	18	2	9	11	13	0	0	0
1980	NY Rangers	9	1	2	3	6	0	0	0
1981	NY Rangers	14	1	3	4	26	0	0	0
1982	NY Rangers	10	1	0	1	4	0	0	0
Playoff Totals		**106**	**10**	**40**	**50**	**185**	**4**	**0**	**0**

VAIC, Lubomir *No Playoffs* — Center

VAIL, Eric — Left wing

Season	Team	GP	G	A	Pts	PIM	PP	SH	GW
1974	Atlanta	1	0	0	0	2	0	0	0
1976	Atlanta	2	0	0	0	0	0	0	0
1977	Atlanta	3	1	3	4	0	0	0	1
1978	Atlanta	2	1	1	2	0	0	0	0
1979	Atlanta	2	0	1	1	2	0	0	0
1980	Atlanta	4	3	1	4	2	1	0	1
1981	Calgary	6	0	0	0	0	0	0	0
Playoff Totals		**20**	**5**	**6**	**11**	**6**	**1**	**0**	**2**

VAIL, Sparky — Defense/Left wing

Season	Team	GP	G	A	Pts	PIM	PP	SH	GW
1929	NY Rangers	6	0	0	0	2	0	0	0
1930	NY Rangers	4	0	0	0	0	0	0	0
Playoff Totals		**10**	**0**	**0**	**0**	**2**	**0**	**0**	**0**

VAIVE, Rick — Right wing

Season	Team	GP	G	A	Pts	PIM	PP	SH	GW
1980	Toronto	3	1	0	1	11	0	0	0
1981	Toronto	3	1	0	1	4	0	0	0
1983	Toronto	4	2	5	7	6	0	0	0
1986	Toronto	9	6	2	8	9	3	0	0
1987	Toronto	13	4	2	6	23	1	0	0
1988	Chicago	5	6	2	8	38	5	0	0
1989	Buffalo	5	2	1	3	8	2	0	0
1990	Buffalo	6	4	2	6	6	4	0	1
1991	Buffalo	6	1	2	3	6	1	0	0
Playoff Totals		**54**	**27**	**16**	**43**	**111**	**16**	**0**	**1**

VALENTINE, Chris — Center

Season	Team	GP	G	A	Pts	PIM	PP	SH	GW
1983	Washington	2	0	0	0	4	0	0	0
Playoff Totals		**2**	**0**	**0**	**0**	**4**	**0**	**0**	**0**

•VALICEVIC, Rob *No Playoffs* — Right wing

Season	Team	GP	G	A	Pts	PIM	PP	SH	GW
VALIQUETTE, Jack	Center								
1976	Toronto	10	2	3	5	2	0	0	0
1978	Toronto	13	1	3	4	2	1	0	0
Playoff Totals		**23**	**3**	**6**	**9**	**4**	**1**	**0**	**0**
•VALK, Garry	Right wing								
1991	Vancouver	5	0	0	0	20	0	0	0
1992	Vancouver	4	0	0	0	5	0	0	0
1993	Vancouver	7	0	1	1	12	0	0	0
1999	Toronto	17	3	4	7	22	0	0	1
2000	Toronto	12	1	2	3	14	0	0	0
2001	Toronto	5	1	0	1	2	0	0	0
2002	Toronto	11	1	0	1	4	0	0	0
Playoff Totals		**61**	**6**	**7**	**13**	**79**	**0**	**0**	**1**
VALLIS, Lindsay	*No Playoffs* Defense								
•VAN ALLEN, Shaun	Center								
1997	Ottawa	7	0	1	1	4	0	0	0
1998	Ottawa	11	0	1	1	10	0	0	0
1999	Ottawa	4	0	0	0	0	0	0	0
2000	Ottawa	6	0	1	1	9	0	0	0
2001	Dallas	8	0	2	2	8	0	0	0
2002	Montreal	7	0	1	1	2	0	0	0
Playoff Totals		**43**	**0**	**6**	**6**	**33**	**0**	**0**	**0**
VAN BOXMEER, John	Defense								
1974	Montreal	1	0	0	0	0	0	0	0
1976♦	Montreal	....	....	....	....	....	....	....	....
1978	Colorado	2	0	1	1	2	0	0	0
1980	Buffalo	14	3	5	8	12	2	0	2
1981	Buffalo	8	1	8	9	7	0	0	0
1982	Buffalo	4	0	1	1	6	0	0	0
1983	Buffalo	9	1	0	1	10	1	0	0
Playoff Totals		**38**	**5**	**15**	**20**	**37**	**3**	**0**	**2**
•VANDENBUSSCHE, Ryan	Right wing								
2002	Chicago	1	0	0	0	0	0	0	0
Playoff Totals		**1**	**0**	**0**	**0**	**0**	**0**	**0**	**0**
•VANDERMEER, Jim	*No Playoffs* Defense								
VAN DORP, Wayne	Left wing								
1987	Edmonton	3	0	0	0	2	0	0	0
1989	Chicago	16	0	1	1	17	0	0	0
1990	Chicago	8	0	0	0	23	0	0	0
Playoff Totals		**27**	**0**	**1**	**1**	**42**	**0**	**0**	**0**
VAN DRUNEN, David	*No Playoffs* Defense								
•VAN IMPE, Darren	Defense								
1997	Anaheim	9	0	2	2	16	0	0	0
1998	Boston	6	2	1	3	0	1	0	1
1999	Boston	11	1	2	3	4	1	0	0
2002	NY Islanders	7	0	4	4	8	0	0	0
Playoff Totals		**33**	**3**	**9**	**12**	**28**	**2**	**0**	**1**
VAN IMPE, Ed	Defense								
1967	Chicago	6	0	0	0	8	0	0	0
1968	Philadelphia	7	0	4	4	11	0	0	0
1969	Philadelphia	1	0	0	0	17	0	0	0
1971	Philadelphia	4	0	1	1	8	0	0	0
1973	Philadelphia	11	0	0	0	16	0	0	0
1974♦	Philadelphia	17	1	2	3	41	0	0	0
1975♦	Philadelphia	17	0	4	4	28	0	0	0
1976	Pittsburgh	3	0	1	1	2	0	0	0
Playoff Totals		**66**	**1**	**12**	**13**	**131**	**0**	**0**	**0**
•VAN RYN, Mike	Defense								
2002	St. Louis	9	0	0	0	0	0	0	0
Playoff Totals		**9**	**0**	**0**	**0**	**0**	**0**	**0**	**0**
•VARADA, Vaclav	Right wing								
1998	Buffalo	15	3	4	7	18	0	0	0
1999	Buffalo	21	5	4	9	14	1	0	0
2000	Buffalo	5	0	0	0	8	0	0	0
2001	Buffalo	13	0	4	4	8	0	0	0
Playoff Totals		**54**	**8**	**12**	**20**	**48**	**1**	**0**	**0**
VARIS, Petri	*No Playoffs* Left wing								
•VARLAMOV, Sergei	Left wing								
2002	St. Louis	1	0	0	0	2	0	0	0
Playoff Totals		**1**	**0**	**0**	**0**	**2**	**0**	**0**	**0**
VARVIO, Jarkko	*No Playoffs* Right wing								
•VASICEK, Josef	Center								
2001	Carolina	6	2	0	2	0	0	0	0
2002	Carolina	23	3	2	5	12	0	0	1
Playoff Totals		**29**	**5**	**2**	**7**	**12**	**0**	**0**	**1**
VASILEVSKI, Alexander	*No Playoffs* Right wing								
•VASILIEV, Alexei	*No Playoffs* Defense								
•VASILJEVS, Herbert	*No Playoffs* Center								
VASILYEV, Andrei	*No Playoffs* Left wing								
VASKE, Dennis	Defense								
1993	NY Islanders	18	0	6	6	14	0	0	0
1994	NY Islanders	4	0	1	1	2	0	0	0
Playoff Totals		**22**	**0**	**7**	**7**	**16**	**0**	**0**	**0**

Season	Team	GP	G	A	Pts	PIM	PP	SH	GW
VASKO, Moose	Defense								
1959	Chicago	6	0	1	1	4	0	0	0
1960	Chicago	4	0	0	0	0	0	0	0
1961♦	Chicago	12	1	1	2	23	1	0	1
1962	Chicago	12	0	0	0	4	0	0	0
1963	Chicago	6	0	1	1	8	0	0	0
1964	Chicago	7	0	0	0	4	0	0	0
1965	Chicago	14	1	2	3	20	0	0	0
1966	Chicago	3	0	0	0	4	0	0	0
1968	Minnesota	14	0	2	2	6	0	0	0
Playoff Totals		**78**	**2**	**7**	**9**	**73**	**1**	**0**	**1**
VASKO, Rick	*No Playoffs* Defense								
VAUTOUR, Yvon	*No Playoffs* Right wing								
VAYDIK, Greg	*No Playoffs* Center								
•VEILLEUX, Stephane	*No Playoffs* Right wing								
VEITCH, Darren	Defense								
1984	Washington	5	0	1	1	15	0	0	0
1985	Washington	5	0	1	1	4	0	0	0
1987	Detroit	12	3	4	7	8	2	0	1
1988	Detroit	11	1	5	6	6	1	0	0
Playoff Totals		**33**	**4**	**11**	**15**	**33**	**3**	**0**	**1**
VELISCHEK, Randy	Defense								
1983	Minnesota	9	0	0	0	0	0	0	0
1984	Minnesota	1	0	0	0	0	0	0	0
1985	Minnesota	9	2	3	5	8	0	0	0
1988	New Jersey	19	0	2	2	20	0	0	0
1990	New Jersey	6	0	0	0	4	0	0	0
Playoff Totals		**44**	**2**	**5**	**7**	**32**	**0**	**0**	**0**
VELLUCCI, Mike	*No Playoffs* Defense								
VENASKY, Vic	Center								
1976	Los Angeles	9	0	1	1	6	0	0	0
1977	Los Angeles	9	1	4	5	6	1	0	0
1978	Los Angeles	1	0	0	0	0	0	0	0
1979	Los Angeles	2	0	0	0	0	0	0	0
Playoff Totals		**21**	**1**	**5**	**6**	**12**	**1**	**0**	**0**
VENERUZZO, Gary	Wing								
1968	St. Louis	9	0	2	2	2	0	0	0
Playoff Totals		**9**	**0**	**2**	**2**	**2**	**0**	**0**	**0**
•VERBEEK, Pat	Right wing								
1988	New Jersey	20	4	8	12	51	2	0	1
1990	Hartford	7	2	2	4	26	1	0	1
1991	Hartford	6	3	2	5	40	2	0	0
1992	Hartford	7	0	2	2	12	0	0	0
1995	NY Rangers	10	4	6	10	20	3	0	0
1996	NY Rangers	11	3	6	9	12	1	0	0
1997	Dallas	7	1	3	4	16	1	0	0
1998	Dallas	17	3	2	5	26	2	0	1
1999♦	Dallas	18	3	4	7	14	0	0	1
2000	Detroit	9	1	1	2	2	1	0	1
2001	Detroit	5	2	0	2	6	2	0	0
Playoff Totals		**117**	**26**	**36**	**62**	**225**	**15**	**0**	**5**
VERMETTE, Mark	*No Playoffs* Right wing								
•VERNARSKY, Kris	*No Playoffs* Center								
VERRET, Claude	*No Playoffs* Center								
VERSTRAETE, Leigh	*No Playoffs* Right wing								
VERVERGAERT, Dennis	Right wing								
1975	Vancouver	1	0	0	0	0	0	0	0
1976	Vancouver	2	1	0	1	4	1	0	0
1979	Philadelphia	3	0	2	2	2	0	0	0
1980	Philadelphia	2	0	0	0	0	0	0	0
Playoff Totals		**8**	**1**	**2**	**3**	**6**	**1**	**0**	**0**
VESEY, Jim	*No Playoffs* Center/Right wing								
VEYSEY, Sid	*No Playoffs* Center								
VIAL, Dennis	*No Playoffs* Defense/Left wing								
VICKERS, Steve	Left wing								
1973	NY Rangers	10	5	4	9	4	0	0	0
1974	NY Rangers	13	4	4	8	17	2	0	0
1975	NY Rangers	3	2	4	6	6	0	0	0
1978	NY Rangers	3	2	1	3	0	0	0	0
1979	NY Rangers	18	5	3	8	13	1	0	1
1980	NY Rangers	9	2	2	4	4	0	0	1
1981	NY Rangers	12	4	7	11	14	1	0	0
Playoff Totals		**68**	**24**	**25**	**49**	**58**	**4**	**0**	**2**
•VIGIER, Jean-Pierre	*No Playoffs* Right wing								
VIGNEAULT, Alain	Defense								
1983	St. Louis	4	0	1	1	26	0	0	0
Playoff Totals		**4**	**0**	**1**	**1**	**26**	**0**	**0**	**0**
VIITAKOSKI, Vesa	*No Playoffs* Left wing								
VILGRAIN, Claude	Right wing								
1990	New Jersey	4	0	0	0	0	0	0	0
1992	New Jersey	7	1	1	2	17	0	0	0
Playoff Totals		**11**	**1**	**1**	**2**	**17**	**0**	**0**	**0**
VINCELETTE, Dan	Left wing								
1987	Chicago	3	0	0	0	0	0	0	0
1988	Chicago	4	0	0	0	0	0	0	0
1989	Chicago	5	0	0	0	4	0	0	0
Playoff Totals		**12**	**0**	**0**	**0**	**4**	**0**	**0**	**0**
VIPOND, Pete	*No Playoffs* Left wing								

Season	Team	GP	G	A	Pts	PIM	PP	SH	GW
VIRTA, Hannu	Defense								
1982	Buffalo	4	0	1	1	0	0	0	0
1983	Buffalo	10	1	2	3	4	0	0	0
1984	Buffalo	3	0	0	0	2	0	0	0
Playoff Totals		**17**	**1**	**3**	**4**	**6**	**0**	**0**	**0**
•VIRTA, Tony	*No Playoffs* Right wing								
•VIRTUE, Terry	*No Playoffs* Defense								
VISHEAU, Mark	*No Playoffs* Defense								
•VISHNEVSKI, Vitaly	*No Playoffs* Defense								
•VISNOVSKY, Lubomir	Defense								
2001	Los Angeles	8	0	0	0	0	0	0	0
2002	Los Angeles	4	0	1	1	0	0	0	0
Playoff Totals		**12**	**0**	**1**	**1**	**0**	**0**	**0**	**0**
VITOLINSH, Harijs	*No Playoffs* Center								
VIVEIROS, Emanuel	*No Playoffs* Defense								
•VLASAK, Tomas	*No Playoffs* Center								
VOKES, Ed	*No Playoffs* Left wing								
VOLCAN, Mickey	*No Playoffs* Defense								
•VOLCHENKOV, Anton	*No Playoffs* Defense								
VOLCHKOV, Alexandre	*No Playoffs* Center								
VOLEK, David	Wing								
1990	NY Islanders	5	1	4	5	0	0	0	0
1993	NY Islanders	10	4	1	5	2	0	0	1
Playoff Totals		**15**	**5**	**5**	**10**	**2**	**0**	**0**	**1**
VOLMAR, Doug	Right wing								
1970	Detroit	2	1	0	1	0	0	0	0
Playoff Totals		**2**	**1**	**0**	**1**	**0**	**0**	**0**	**0**
•VON ARX, Reto	*No Playoffs* Center								
VON STEFENELLI, Phil	*No Playoffs* Defense								
VOPAT, Jan	Defense								
1998	Los Angeles	2	0	1	1	2	0	0	0
Playoff Totals		**2**	**0**	**1**	**1**	**2**	**0**	**0**	**0**
VOPAT, Roman	*No Playoffs* Center								
VOROBIEV, Vladimir	Left wing								
1999	Edmonton	1	0	0	0	0	0	0	0
Playoff Totals		**1**	**0**	**0**	**0**	**0**	**0**	**0**	**0**
VOSS, Carl	Center								
1933	Detroit	4	1	1	2	0	....	....	....
1936	NY Americans	5	0	0	0	0	....	....	....
1937	Mtl. Maroons	5	1	0	1	0	....	....	....
1938♦	Chicago	10	3	2	5	0	....	....	....
Playoff Totals		**24**	**5**	**3**	**8**	**0**	....	....	....
•VRBATA, Radim	Right wing								
2002	Colorado	9	0	0	0	0	0	0	0
Playoff Totals		**9**	**0**	**0**	**0**	**0**	**0**	**0**	**0**
•VUJTEK, Vladimir	*No Playoffs* Left wing								
VUKOTA, Mick	Right wing								
1988	NY Islanders	2	0	0	0	23	0	0	0
1990	NY Islanders	1	0	0	0	17	0	0	0
1993	NY Islanders	15	0	0	0	16	0	0	0
1994	NY Islanders	4	0	0	0	17	0	0	0
1998	Montreal	1	0	0	0	0	0	0	0
Playoff Totals		**23**	**0**	**0**	**0**	**73**	**0**	**0**	**0**
VYAZMIKIN, Igor	*No Playoffs* Wing								
•VYBORNY, David	*No Playoffs* Right wing								
•VYSHEDKEVICH, Sergei	*No Playoffs* Defense								
WADDELL, Don	*No Playoffs* Defense								
WAITE, Frank	*No Playoffs* Center								
WALKER, Gord	*No Playoffs* Right wing								
WALKER, Howard	*No Playoffs* Defense								
WALKER, Jack	*No Playoffs* Forward								
WALKER, Kurt	Defense								
1976	Toronto	6	0	0	0	24	0	0	0
1978	Toronto	10	0	0	0	10	0	0	0
Playoff Totals		**16**	**0**	**0**	**0**	**34**	**0**	**0**	**0**
•WALKER, Matt	*No Playoffs* Defense								
WALKER, Russ	*No Playoffs* Right wing								
•WALKER, Scott	*No Playoffs* Center								
WALL, Bob	Defense								
1965	Detroit	1	0	0	0	0	0	0	0
1966	Detroit	6	0	0	0	2	0	0	0
1968	Los Angeles	7	0	1	1	0	0	0	0
1969	Los Angeles	8	0	2	2	0	0	0	0
Playoff Totals		**22**	**0**	**3**	**3**	**2**	**0**	**0**	**0**
•WALLIN, Jesse	*No Playoffs* Defense								
•WALLIN, Niclas	Defense								
2001	Carolina	3	0	0	0	2	0	0	0
2002	Carolina	23	2	1	3	12	0	0	2
Playoff Totals		**26**	**2**	**1**	**3**	**14**	**0**	**0**	**2**
WALLIN, Peter	Right wing								
1981	NY Rangers	14	2	6	8	6	0	0	0
Playoff Totals		**14**	**2**	**6**	**8**	**6**	**0**	**0**	**0**
•WALLIN, Rickard	*No Playoffs* Center								

Season	Team	GP	G	A	Pts	PIM	PP	SH	GW
•WALSER, Derrick	*No Playoffs*								Defense
WALSH, Jim	*No Playoffs*								Defense
WALSH, Mike	*No Playoffs*								Wing
WALTER, Ryan									Center/Left wing
1983	Montreal	3	0	0	0	11	0	0	0
1984	Montreal	15	2	1	3	4	1	0	1
1985	Montreal	12	2	7	9	13	0	0	0
1986♦	Montreal	5	0	1	1	2	0	0	0
1987	Montreal	17	7	12	19	10	2	1	1
1988	Montreal	11	2	4	6	6	2	0	1
1989	Montreal	21	3	5	8	6	0	1	2
1990	Montreal	11	0	2	2	0	0	0	0
1991	Montreal	5	0	0	0	2	0	0	0
1992	Vancouver	13	0	3	3	8	0	0	0
Playoff Totals		**113**	**16**	**35**	**51**	**62**	**5**	**2**	**5**
WALTON, Bobby	*No Playoffs*								Center/Right wing
WALTON, Mike									Center
1967♦	Toronto	12	4	3	7	2	3	0	1
1969	Toronto	4	0	0	0	4	0	0	0
1971	Boston	5	2	0	2	19	1	0	0
1972♦	Boston	15	6	6	12	13	1	0	2
1973	Boston	5	1	1	2	2	0	0	0
1976	Vancouver	2	0	0	0	5	0	0	0
1979	Chicago	4	1	0	1	0	0	0	0
Playoff Totals		**47**	**14**	**10**	**24**	**45**	**5**	**0**	**3**
•WALZ, Wes									Center
1991	Boston	2	0	0	0	0	0	0	0
1994	Calgary	6	3	0	3	2	0	0	0
1995	Calgary	1	0	0	0	0	0	0	0
Playoff Totals		**9**	**3**	**0**	**3**	**2**	**0**	**0**	**0**
•WANVIG, Kyle	*No Playoffs*								Right wing
WAPPEL, Gord									Defense
1980	Atlanta	2	0	0	0	4	0	0	0
Playoff Totals		**2**	**0**	**0**	**0**	**4**	**0**	**0**	**0**
•WARD, Aaron									Defense
1997♦	Detroit	19	0	0	0	17	0	0	0
1998♦	Detroit	....	....	....	....	....	....	....	....
1999	Detroit	8	0	1	1	8	0	0	0
2000	Detroit	3	0	0	0	0	0	0	0
2002	Carolina	23	1	1	2	22	0	0	0
Playoff Totals		**53**	**1**	**2**	**3**	**47**	**0**	**0**	**0**
•WARD, Dixon									Right wing
1993	Vancouver	9	2	3	5	0	2	0	0
1997	Buffalo	12	2	3	5	6	0	0	1
1998	Buffalo	15	3	8	11	6	0	0	0
1999	Buffalo	21	7	5	12	32	0	2	3
2000	Buffalo	5	0	1	1	2	0	0	0
Playoff Totals		**62**	**14**	**20**	**34**	**46**	**2**	**2**	**4**
WARD, Don	*No Playoffs*								Defense
•WARD, Ed	*No Playoffs*								Right wing
•WARD, Jason	*No Playoffs*								Right wing
WARD, Jimmy									Right wing
1928	Mtl. Maroons	9	1	1	2	6	....	....	....
1930	Mtl. Maroons	4	0	1	1	12	....	....	....
1931	Mtl. Maroons	2	0	0	0	2	....	....	....
1932	Mtl. Maroons	4	2	1	3	0	....	....	....
1933	Mtl. Maroons	2	0	0	0	0	....	....	....
1934	Mtl. Maroons	4	0	0	0	0	....	....	....
1935♦	Mtl. Maroons	7	1	1	2	0	....	....	....
1936	Mtl. Maroons	3	0	0	0	6	....	....	....
1939	Montreal	1	0	0	0	0	....	....	....
Playoff Totals		**36**	**4**	**4**	**8**	**26**	....	....	....
WARD, Joe	*No Playoffs*								Center
•WARD, Lance	*No Playoffs*								Defense
WARD, Ron	*No Playoffs*								Center
WARE, Jeff	*No Playoffs*								Defense
WARE, Michael	*No Playoffs*								Right wing
WARES, Eddie									Defense/Right wing
1939	Detroit	6	1	0	1	8	....	....	....
1940	Detroit	5	0	0	0	0	....	....	....
1941	Detroit	9	0	0	0	0	....	....	....
1942	Detroit	12	1	3	4	22	....	....	....
1943♦	Detroit	10	3	3	6	4	....	....	....
1946	Chicago	3	0	1	1	0	....	....	....
Playoff Totals		**45**	**5**	**7**	**12**	**34**	....	....	....
WARNER, Bob									Defense
1976	Toronto	2	0	0	0	0	0	0	0
1977	Toronto	2	0	0	0	0	0	0	0
Playoff Totals		**4**	**0**	**0**	**0**	**0**	**0**	**0**	**0**
WARNER, Jim	*No Playoffs*								Right wing
•WARRENER, Rhett									Defense
1996	Florida	21	0	1	1	0	0	0	0
1997	Florida	5	0	0	0	0	0	0	0
1999	Buffalo	20	1	3	4	32	0	0	0
2000	Buffalo	5	0	0	0	2	0	0	0
2001	Buffalo	13	0	2	2	4	0	0	0
Playoff Totals		**64**	**1**	**6**	**7**	**38**	**0**	**0**	**0**

Season	Team	GP	G	A	Pts	PIM	PP	SH	GW
•WARRINER, Todd									Left wing
1996	Toronto	6	1	1	2	2	0	0	0
1999	Toronto	9	0	0	0	2	0	0	0
2002	Vancouver	6	1	0	1	2	0	0	0
Playoff Totals		**21**	**2**	**1**	**3**	**6**	**0**	**0**	**0**
WARWICK, Bill	*No Playoffs*								Left wing
WARWICK, Grant									Right wing
1942	NY Rangers	6	0	1	1	2	....	....	....
1948	Boston	5	0	3	3	4	....	....	....
1949	Boston	5	2	0	2	0	....	....	....
Playoff Totals		**16**	**2**	**4**	**6**	**6**	....	....	....
•WASHBURN, Steve									Center
1996	Florida	1	0	1	1	0	0	0	0
Playoff Totals		**1**	**0**	**1**	**1**	**0**	**0**	**0**	**0**
WASNIE, Nick									Right wing
1930♦	Montreal	6	2	2	4	12	....	....	....
1931♦	Montreal	10	4	1	5	8	....	....	....
1932	Montreal	4	0	0	0	0	....	....	....
Playoff Totals		**20**	**6**	**3**	**9**	**20**	....	....	....
WATSON, Bill									Right wing
1986	Chicago	2	0	1	1	0	0	0	0
1987	Chicago	4	0	1	1	0	0	0	0
Playoff Totals		**6**	**0**	**2**	**2**	**0**	**0**	**0**	**0**
WATSON, Bryan									Defense
1964	Montreal	6	0	0	0	2	0	0	0
1966	Detroit	12	2	0	2	30	0	0	0
1970	Pittsburgh	10	0	0	0	17	0	0	0
1972	Pittsburgh	4	0	0	0	21	0	0	0
Playoff Totals		**32**	**2**	**0**	**2**	**70**	**0**	**0**	**0**
WATSON, Dave	*No Playoffs*								Left wing
WATSON, Harry									Left wing
1943♦	Detroit	7	0	0	0	0	....	....	....
1946	Detroit	5	2	0	2	0	....	....	....
1947♦	Toronto	11	3	2	5	6	....	....	....
1948♦	Toronto	9	5	2	7	9	....	....	....
1949♦	Toronto	9	4	2	6	2	....	....	....
1950	Toronto	7	0	0	0	2	....	....	....
1951♦	Toronto	5	1	2	3	4	....	....	....
1952	Toronto	4	1	0	1	2	....	....	....
1954	Toronto	5	0	1	1	2	....	....	....
Playoff Totals		**62**	**16**	**9**	**25**	**27**	....	....	....
WATSON, Jim	*No Playoffs*								Defense
WATSON, Jimmy									Defense
1973	Philadelphia	2	0	0	0	0	0	0	0
1974♦	Philadelphia	17	1	2	3	41	1	0	0
1975♦	Philadelphia	17	1	8	9	10	0	0	0
1976	Philadelphia	16	1	8	9	6	0	0	0
1977	Philadelphia	10	1	2	3	2	0	0	1
1978	Philadelphia	12	1	7	8	6	0	0	0
1979	Philadelphia	8	0	2	2	2	0	0	0
1980	Philadelphia	15	0	4	4	20	0	0	0
1982	Philadelphia	4	0	1	1	2	0	0	0
Playoff Totals		**101**	**5**	**34**	**39**	**89**	**1**	**0**	**1**
WATSON, Joe									Defense
1968	Philadelphia	7	1	1	2	28	0	0	0
1969	Philadelphia	4	0	0	0	0	0	0	0
1971	Philadelphia	1	0	0	0	0	0	0	0
1973	Philadelphia	11	0	2	2	12	0	0	0
1974♦	Philadelphia	17	1	4	5	24	0	0	0
1975♦	Philadelphia	17	0	4	4	6	0	0	0
1976	Philadelphia	16	1	1	2	10	0	0	0
1977	Philadelphia	10	0	0	0	2	0	0	0
1978	Philadelphia	1	0	0	0	0	0	0	0
Playoff Totals		**84**	**3**	**12**	**15**	**82**	**0**	**0**	**0**
WATSON, Phil									Right wing/Center
1937	NY Rangers	9	0	2	2	9	....	....	....
1938	NY Rangers	3	0	2	2	0	....	....	....
1939	NY Rangers	7	1	1	2	7	....	....	....
1940♦	NY Rangers	12	3	6	*9	16	....	....	....
1941	NY Rangers	3	0	2	2	9	....	....	....
1942	NY Rangers	6	1	4	5	8	....	....	....
1944♦	Montreal	9	3	5	8	16	....	....	....
1948	NY Rangers	5	2	3	5	2	....	....	....
Playoff Totals		**54**	**10**	**25**	**35**	**67**	....	....	....
•WATT, Mike	*No Playoffs*								Left wing
WATTERS, Tim									Defense
1982	Winnipeg	4	0	1	1	8	0	0	0
1983	Winnipeg	3	0	0	0	2	0	0	0
1984	Winnipeg	3	1	0	1	2	0	0	0
1985	Winnipeg	8	0	1	1	16	0	0	0
1987	Winnipeg	10	0	0	0	21	0	0	0
1988	Winnipeg	4	0	0	0	4	0	0	0
1989	Los Angeles	11	0	1	1	6	0	0	0
1990	Los Angeles	4	0	0	0	6	0	0	0
1991	Los Angeles	7	0	0	0	12	0	0	0
1992	Los Angeles	6	0	0	0	8	0	0	0
1993	Los Angeles	22	0	2	2	30	0	0	0
Playoff Totals		**82**	**1**	**5**	**6**	**115**	**0**	**0**	**0**
WATTS, Brian	*No Playoffs*								Left wing

Season	Team	GP	G	A	Pts	PIM	PP	SH	GW
•WEAVER, Mike	*No Playoffs*								Defense
•WEBB, Steve									Right wing
2002	NY Islanders	7	0	0	0	12	0	0	0
Playoff Totals		**7**	**0**	**0**	**0**	**12**	**0**	**0**	**0**
WEBSTER, Aubrey	*No Playoffs*								Right wing
WEBSTER, Don									Left wing
1944	Toronto	5	0	0	0	12	0	0	0
Playoff Totals		**5**	**0**	**0**	**0**	**12**	**0**	**0**	**0**
WEBSTER, John	*No Playoffs*								Center
WEBSTER, Tom									Right wing
1969	Boston	1	0	0	0	0	0	0	0
Playoff Totals		**1**	**0**	**0**	**0**	**0**	**0**	**0**	**0**
•WEIGHT, Doug									Center
1991	NY Rangers	1	0	0	0	0	0	0	0
1992	NY Rangers	7	2	2	4	0	1	0	0
1997	Edmonton	12	3	8	11	8	0	0	0
1998	Edmonton	12	2	7	9	14	2	0	1
1999	Edmonton	4	1	1	2	15	0	0	0
2000	Edmonton	5	3	2	5	4	2	0	1
2001	Edmonton	6	1	5	6	17	0	0	0
2002	St. Louis	10	1	1	2	4	1	0	1
Playoff Totals		**57**	**13**	**26**	**39**	**62**	**6**	**0**	**3**
WEILAND, Cooney									Center
1929♦	Boston	5	2	0	2	2	....	....	....
1930	Boston	6	1	*5	*6	2	....	....	....
1931	Boston	5	*6	3	*9	2	....	....	....
1934	Detroit	9	2	2	4	4	....	....	....
1936	Boston	2	1	0	1	2	....	....	....
1937	Boston	3	0	0	0	0	....	....	....
1938	Boston	3	0	0	0	0	....	....	....
1939♦	Boston	12	0	0	0	0	....	....	....
Playoff Totals		**45**	**12**	**10**	**22**	**12**	....	....	....
•WEINHANDL, Mattias	*No Playoffs*								Right wing
•WEINRICH, Eric									Defense
1990	New Jersey	6	1	3	4	17	0	0	0
1991	New Jersey	7	1	2	3	6	1	0	0
1992	New Jersey	7	0	2	2	4	0	0	0
1994	Chicago	6	0	2	2	6	0	0	0
1995	Chicago	16	1	5	6	4	0	0	0
1996	Chicago	10	1	4	5	10	1	0	0
1997	Chicago	6	0	1	1	4	0	0	0
2002	Philadelphia	5	0	0	0	4	0	0	0
Playoff Totals		**63**	**4**	**19**	**23**	**55**	**2**	**0**	**0**
WEIR, Stan									Center
1976	Toronto	9	1	3	4	0	1	0	1
1977	Toronto	7	2	1	3	0	1	0	1
1978	Toronto	13	3	1	4	0	1	0	1
1980	Edmonton	3	0	0	0	2	0	0	0
1981	Edmonton	5	0	0	0	2	0	0	0
Playoff Totals		**37**	**6**	**5**	**11**	**4**	**3**	**0**	**3**
WEIR, Wally									Defense
1981	Quebec	3	0	0	0	15	0	0	0
1982	Quebec	15	0	0	0	45	0	0	0
1983	Quebec	4	0	1	1	19	0	0	0
1984	Quebec	1	0	0	0	17	0	0	0
Playoff Totals		**23**	**0**	**1**	**1**	**96**	**0**	**0**	**0**
•WEISS, Stephen	*No Playoffs*								Center
WELLINGTON, Alex	*No Playoffs*								Right wing
WELLS, Chris									Center
1997	Florida	3	0	0	0	0	0	0	0
Playoff Totals		**3**	**0**	**0**	**0**	**0**	**0**	**0**	**0**
WELLS, Jay									Defense
1980	Los Angeles	4	0	0	0	11	0	0	0
1981	Los Angeles	4	0	0	0	27	0	0	0
1982	Los Angeles	10	1	3	4	41	0	0	0
1985	Los Angeles	3	0	1	1	0	0	0	0
1987	Los Angeles	5	1	2	3	10	1	0	0
1988	Los Angeles	5	1	2	3	21	0	0	0
1989	Philadelphia	18	0	2	2	51	0	0	0
1990	Buffalo	6	0	0	0	12	0	0	0
1991	Buffalo	1	0	1	1	0	0	0	0
1992	NY Rangers	13	0	2	2	10	0	0	0
1994♦	NY Rangers	23	0	0	0	20	0	0	0
1995	NY Rangers	10	0	0	0	8	0	0	0
1996	St. Louis	12	0	1	1	2	0	0	0
Playoff Totals		**114**	**3**	**14**	**17**	**213**	**1**	**0**	**0**
WENSINK, John									Left wing
1977	Boston	13	0	3	3	8	0	0	0
1978	Boston	15	2	2	4	54	0	0	0
1979	Boston	8	0	1	1	19	0	0	0
1980	Boston	4	0	0	0	5	0	0	0
1981	Quebec	3	0	0	0	0	0	0	0
Playoff Totals		**43**	**2**	**6**	**8**	**86**	**0**	**0**	**0**

WENTWORTH, Cy Defense

Season	Team	GP	G	A	Pts	PIM	PP	SH	GW
1931	Chicago	9	1	1	2	14	....	....	....
1932	Chicago	2	0	0	0	0	....	....	....
1933	Mtl. Maroons	2	0	1	1	0	....	....	....
1934	Mtl. Maroons	4	0	2	2	2	....	....	....
1935♦	Mtl. Maroons	7	3	2	*5	0	....	....	....
1936	Mtl. Maroons	3	0	0	0	0	....	....	....
1937	Mtl. Maroons	5	1	0	1	0	....	....	....
1939	Montreal	3	0	0	0	4	....	....	....
Playoff Totals		**35**	**5**	**6**	**11**	**20**	....	....	....

WERENKA, Brad Defense

Season	Team	GP	G	A	Pts	PIM	PP	SH	GW
1998	Pittsburgh	6	1	0	1	8	0	1	0
1999	Pittsburgh	13	1	1	2	6	0	0	0
Playoff Totals		**19**	**2**	**1**	**3**	**14**	**0**	**1**	**0**

WESENBERG, Brian *No Playoffs* Right wing

WESLEY, Blake Defense

Season	Team	GP	G	A	Pts	PIM	PP	SH	GW
1983	Quebec	4	0	0	0	2	0	0	0
1984	Quebec	9	1	2	3	20	0	0	1
1985	Quebec	6	1	0	1	8	0	0	0
Playoff Totals		**19**	**2**	**2**	**4**	**30**	**0**	**0**	**1**

•WESLEY, Glen Defense

Season	Team	GP	G	A	Pts	PIM	PP	SH	GW
1988	Boston	23	6	8	14	22	4	1	0
1989	Boston	10	0	2	2	4	0	0	0
1990	Boston	21	2	6	8	36	0	0	1
1991	Boston	19	2	9	11	19	2	0	0
1992	Boston	15	2	4	6	16	0	0	0
1993	Boston	4	0	0	0	0	0	0	0
1994	Boston	13	3	3	6	12	1	0	0
1999	Carolina	6	0	0	0	2	0	0	0
2001	Carolina	6	0	0	0	0	0	0	0
2002	Carolina	22	0	2	2	12	0	0	0
Playoff Totals		**139**	**15**	**34**	**49**	**123**	**7**	**1**	**1**

•WESTCOTT, Duvie *No Playoffs* Defense

WESTFALL, Ed Defense/Right wing

Season	Team	GP	G	A	Pts	PIM	PP	SH	GW
1968	Boston	4	2	0	2	2	0	0	0
1969	Boston	10	3	7	10	11	0	2	2
1970♦	Boston	14	3	5	8	4	0	1	1
1971	Boston	7	1	2	3	2	0	1	0
1972♦	Boston	15	4	3	7	10	0	2	1
1975	NY Islanders	17	5	10	15	12	2	1	2
1976	NY Islanders	8	2	3	5	0	1	0	0
1977	NY Islanders	12	1	5	6	0	0	1	0
1978	NY Islanders	2	0	0	0	0	0	0	0
1979	NY Islanders	6	1	2	3	0	0	0	0
Playoff Totals		**95**	**22**	**37**	**59**	**41**	**3**	**8**	**6**

•WESTLUND, Tommy Right wing

Season	Team	GP	G	A	Pts	PIM	PP	SH	GW
2001	Carolina	6	0	0	0	17	0	0	0
2002	Carolina	19	1	0	1	0	0	0	0
Playoff Totals		**25**	**1**	**0**	**1**	**17**	**0**	**0**	**0**

WHARRAM, Kenny Right wing/Center

Season	Team	GP	G	A	Pts	PIM	PP	SH	GW
1959	Chicago	6	0	2	2	2	....	....	....
1960	Chicago	4	1	1	2	0	....	....	....
1961♦	Chicago	12	3	5	8	12	....	....	....
1962	Chicago	12	3	4	7	8	....	....	....
1963	Chicago	6	1	5	6	0	....	....	....
1964	Chicago	7	2	2	4	6	....	....	....
1965	Chicago	12	2	3	5	4	....	....	....
1966	Chicago	6	1	0	1	4	....	....	....
1967	Chicago	6	2	2	4	2	....	....	....
1968	Chicago	9	1	3	4	0	0	0	0
Playoff Totals		**80**	**16**	**27**	**43**	**38**	**0**	**0**	**0**

WHARTON, Len *No Playoffs* Defense

WHEELDON, Simon *No Playoffs* Center

WHELDON, Don *No Playoffs* Defense

WHELTON, Bill *No Playoffs* Defense

WHISTLE, Rob Defense

Season	Team	GP	G	A	Pts	PIM	PP	SH	GW
1986	NY Rangers	3	0	0	0	2	0	0	0
1988	St. Louis	1	0	0	0	0	0	0	0
Playoff Totals		**4**	**0**	**0**	**0**	**2**	**0**	**0**	**0**

WHITE, Bill Defense

Season	Team	GP	G	A	Pts	PIM	PP	SH	GW
1968	Los Angeles	7	2	2	4	4	0	0	1
1969	Los Angeles	11	1	4	5	8	0	0	0
1970	Chicago	8	1	2	3	8	0	0	0
1971	Chicago	18	1	4	5	20	0	0	1
1972	Chicago	8	0	3	3	6	0	0	0
1973	Chicago	16	1	6	7	10	0	1	0
1974	Chicago	11	1	7	8	14	1	0	0
1975	Chicago	8	0	3	3	4	0	0	0
1976	Chicago	4	0	1	1	2	0	0	0
Playoff Totals		**91**	**7**	**32**	**39**	**76**	**1**	**1**	**2**

•WHITE, Brian *No Playoffs* Defense

•WHITE, Colin Defense

Season	Team	GP	G	A	Pts	PIM	PP	SH	GW
2000♦	New Jersey	23	1	5	6	18	0	0	1
2001	New Jersey	25	0	3	3	42	0	0	0
2002	New Jersey	6	0	0	0	2	0	0	0
Playoff Totals		**54**	**1**	**8**	**9**	**62**	**0**	**0**	**1**

WHITE, Moe *No Playoffs* Left wing/Center

•WHITE, Peter Center

Season	Team	GP	G	A	Pts	PIM	PP	SH	GW
2000	Philadelphia	16	0	2	2	0	0	0	0
2001	Philadelphia	3	0	0	0	0	0	0	0
Playoff Totals		**19**	**0**	**2**	**2**	**0**	**0**	**0**	**0**

WHITE, Sherman *No Playoffs* Center

WHITE, Tex Right wing

Season	Team	GP	G	A	Pts	PIM	PP	SH	GW
1928	Pittsburgh	2	0	0	0	2	0	0	0
1929	NY Americans	2	0	0	0	2	0	0	0
Playoff Totals		**4**	**0**	**0**	**0**	**4**	**0**	**0**	**0**

•WHITE, Todd Center

Season	Team	GP	G	A	Pts	PIM	PP	SH	GW
2001	Ottawa	2	0	0	0	0	0	0	0
2002	Ottawa	12	2	2	4	6	0	0	0
Playoff Totals		**14**	**2**	**2**	**4**	**6**	**0**	**0**	**0**

WHITE, Tony *No Playoffs* Left wing

WHITELAW, Bob Defense

Season	Team	GP	G	A	Pts	PIM	PP	SH	GW
1941	Detroit	8	0	0	0	0	0	0	0
Playoff Totals		**8**	**0**	**0**	**0**	**0**	**0**	**0**	**0**

•WHITFIELD, Trent Center

Season	Team	GP	G	A	Pts	PIM	PP	SH	GW
2000	Washington	3	0	0	0	0	0	0	0
2001	Washington	5	0	0	0	2	0	0	0
Playoff Totals		**8**	**0**	**0**	**0**	**2**	**0**	**0**	**0**

WHITLOCK, Bob *No Playoffs* Center

•WHITNEY, Ray Left wing

Season	Team	GP	G	A	Pts	PIM	PP	SH	GW
1994	San Jose	14	0	4	4	8	0	0	0
1995	San Jose	11	4	4	8	2	0	0	1
2000	Florida	4	1	0	1	4	0	0	0
Playoff Totals		**29**	**5**	**8**	**13**	**14**	**0**	**0**	**1**

WHYTE, Sean *No Playoffs* Right wing

WICKENHEISER, Doug Center

Season	Team	GP	G	A	Pts	PIM	PP	SH	GW
1984	St. Louis	11	2	2	4	2	0	1	1
1986	St. Louis	19	2	5	7	12	1	0	1
1987	St. Louis	6	0	0	0	2	0	0	0
1989	Washington	5	0	0	0	2	0	0	0
Playoff Totals		**41**	**4**	**7**	**11**	**18**	**1**	**1**	**2**

WIDING, Juha Center

Season	Team	GP	G	A	Pts	PIM	PP	SH	GW
1974	Los Angeles	5	1	0	1	2	0	0	1
1975	Los Angeles	3	0	2	2	0	0	0	0
Playoff Totals		**8**	**1**	**2**	**3**	**2**	**0**	**0**	**1**

WIDMER, Jason *No Playoffs* Defense

WIEBE, Art Defense

Season	Team	GP	G	A	Pts	PIM	PP	SH	GW
1935	Chicago	2	0	0	0	2	....	....	....
1936	Chicago	2	0	0	0	0	....	....	....
1938♦	Chicago	10	0	1	1	2	....	....	....
1940	Chicago	2	1	0	1	2	....	....	....
1941	Chicago	4	0	0	0	0	....	....	....
1942	Chicago	3	0	0	0	0	....	....	....
1944	Chicago	8	0	2	2	4	....	....	....
Playoff Totals		**31**	**1**	**3**	**4**	**10**	....	....	....

•WIEMER, Jason Center

Season	Team	GP	G	A	Pts	PIM	PP	SH	GW
1996	Tampa Bay	6	1	0	1	28	1	0	0
Playoff Totals		**6**	**1**	**0**	**1**	**28**	**1**	**0**	**0**

WIEMER, Jim Defense

Season	Team	GP	G	A	Pts	PIM	PP	SH	GW
1983	Buffalo	1	0	0	0	0	0	0	0
1985	NY Rangers	1	0	0	0	0	0	0	0
1986	NY Rangers	8	1	0	1	6	1	0	1
1988	Edmonton	2	0	0	0	2	0	0	0
1989	Los Angeles	10	2	1	3	19	0	0	1
1990	Boston	8	0	1	1	4	0	0	0
1991	Boston	16	1	3	4	14	1	0	0
1992	Boston	15	1	3	4	14	0	0	1
1993	Boston	1	0	0	0	4	0	0	0
Playoff Totals		**62**	**5**	**8**	**13**	**63**	**2**	**0**	**3**

WILCOX, Archie Right wing/Defense

Season	Team	GP	G	A	Pts	PIM	PP	SH	GW
1930	Mtl. Maroons	4	1	0	1	2	....	....	....
1931	Mtl. Maroons	2	0	0	0	2	....	....	....
1932	Mtl. Maroons	4	0	0	0	4	....	....	....
1933	Mtl. Maroons	2	0	0	0	0	....	....	....
Playoff Totals		**12**	**1**	**0**	**1**	**8**	....	....	....

WILCOX, Barry *No Playoffs* Right wing

WILDER, Arch *No Playoffs* Left wing

WILEY, Jim *No Playoffs* Center

WILKIE, Bob *No Playoffs* Defense

•WILKIE, David Defense

Season	Team	GP	G	A	Pts	PIM	PP	SH	GW
1996	Montreal	6	1	2	3	12	0	0	0
1997	Montreal	2	0	0	0	2	0	0	0
Playoff Totals		**8**	**1**	**2**	**3**	**14**	**0**	**0**	**0**

WILKINS, Barry Defense

Season	Team	GP	G	A	Pts	PIM	PP	SH	GW
1975	Pittsburgh	3	0	0	0	0	0	0	0
1976	Pittsburgh	3	0	1	1	4	0	0	0
Playoff Totals		**6**	**0**	**1**	**1**	**4**	**0**	**0**	**0**

WILKINSON, John *No Playoffs* Defense

WILKINSON, Neil Defense

Season	Team	GP	G	A	Pts	PIM	PP	SH	GW
1990	Minnesota	7	0	2	2	11	0	0	0
1991	Minnesota	22	3	3	6	12	1	0	0
1994	Chicago	4	0	0	0	0	0	0	0
1996	Pittsburgh	15	0	1	1	14	0	0	0
1997	Pittsburgh	5	0	0	0	4	0	0	0
Playoff Totals		**53**	**3**	**6**	**9**	**41**	**1**	**0**	**0**

WILKS, Brian *No Playoffs* Center

WILLARD, Rod *No Playoffs* Left wing

WILLIAMS, Burr Defense

Season	Team	GP	G	A	Pts	PIM	PP	SH	GW
1934	Detroit	7	0	0	0	8	0	0	0
Playoff Totals		**7**	**0**	**0**	**0**	**8**	**0**	**0**	**0**

WILLIAMS, Butch *No Playoffs* Right wing

WILLIAMS, Darryl *No Playoffs* Left wing

WILLIAMS, David *No Playoffs* Defense

WILLIAMS, Fred *No Playoffs* Center

WILLIAMS, Gord *No Playoffs* Right wing

•WILLIAMS, Jason Center

Season	Team	GP	G	A	Pts	PIM	PP	SH	GW
2001	Detroit	2	0	0	0	0	0	0	0
2002♦	Detroit	9	0	0	0	2	0	0	0
Playoff Totals		**11**	**0**	**0**	**0**	**2**	**0**	**0**	**0**

•WILLIAMS, Justin Right wing

Season	Team	GP	G	A	Pts	PIM	PP	SH	GW
2002	Philadelphia	5	0	0	0	4	0	0	0
Playoff Totals		**5**	**0**	**0**	**0**	**4**	**0**	**0**	**0**

WILLIAMS, Sean *No Playoffs* Center

WILLIAMS, Tiger Left wing

Season	Team	GP	G	A	Pts	PIM	PP	SH	GW
1975	Toronto	7	1	3	4	25	1	0	0
1976	Toronto	10	0	0	0	75	0	0	0
1977	Toronto	9	3	6	9	29	0	0	1
1978	Toronto	12	1	2	3	*63	0	0	0
1979	Toronto	6	0	0	0	*48	0	0	0
1980	Vancouver	3	0	0	0	20	0	0	0
1981	Vancouver	3	0	0	0	20	0	0	0
1982	Vancouver	17	3	7	10	*116	0	0	2
1983	Vancouver	4	0	3	3	12	0	0	0
1984	Vancouver	4	1	0	1	13	0	0	0
1985	Los Angeles	3	0	0	0	4	0	0	0
1987	Los Angeles	5	3	2	5	30	0	0	1
Playoff Totals		**83**	**12**	**23**	**35**	**455**	**1**	**0**	**4**

Season	Team	GP	G	A	Pts	PIM	PP	SH	GW
WILLIAMS, Tom									Left wing
1974	Los Angeles	5	3	1	4	0	1	0	0
1975	Los Angeles	3	0	0	0	0	0	0	0
1976	Los Angeles	9	2	2	4	2	0	0	0
1977	Los Angeles	9	3	4	7	2	1	0	0
1978	Los Angeles	2	0	0	0	0	0	0	0
1979	Los Angeles	1	0	0	0	0	0	0	0
Playoff Totals		**29**	**8**	**7**	**15**	**4**	**2**	**0**	**0**
WILLIAMS, Tommy									Right wing
1968	Boston	4	1	0	1	2	0	0	0
1970	Minnesota	6	1	5	6	0	0	0	0
Playoff Totals		**10**	**2**	**5**	**7**	**2**	**0**	**0**	**0**
•WILLIS, Shane									Right wing
2001	Carolina	2	0	0	0	0	0	0	0
Playoff Totals		**2**	**0**	**0**	**0**	**0**	**0**	**0**	**0**
•WILLSIE, Brian									Right wing
2002	Colorado	4	0	1	1	2	0	0	0
Playoff Totals		**4**	**0**	**1**	**1**	**2**	**0**	**0**	**0**
WILLSON, Don									Center
1938	Montreal	3	0	0	0	0	0	0	0
Playoff Totals		**3**	**0**	**0**	**0**	**0**	**0**	**0**	**0**
•WILM, Clarke *No Playoffs*									Center
WILSON, Behn									Defense
1979	Philadelphia	5	1	0	1	8	0	0	0
1980	Philadelphia	19	4	9	13	66	0	0	2
1981	Philadelphia	12	2	10	12	36	1	0	0
1982	Philadelphia	4	1	4	5	10	1	0	0
1983	Philadelphia	3	0	1	1	2	0	0	0
1984	Chicago	4	0	0	0	0	0	0	0
1985	Chicago	15	4	5	9	60	1	0	1
1986	Chicago	2	0	0	0	2	0	0	0
1988	Chicago	3	0	0	0	6	0	0	0
Playoff Totals		**67**	**12**	**29**	**41**	**190**	**3**	**0**	**3**
WILSON, Bert									Left wing
1976	Los Angeles	8	0	0	0	24	0	0	0
1977	Los Angeles	8	0	2	2	12	0	0	0
1978	Los Angeles	2	0	0	0	2	0	0	0
1980	Los Angeles	2	0	0	0	4	0	0	0
1981	Calgary	1	0	0	0	0	0	0	0
Playoff Totals		**21**	**0**	**2**	**2**	**42**	**0**	**0**	**0**
WILSON, Bob *No Playoffs*									Defense
WILSON, Carey									Center
1984	Calgary	6	3	1	4	2	0	0	1
1985	Calgary	4	0	0	0	0	0	0	0
1986	Calgary	9	0	2	2	2	0	0	0
1987	Calgary	6	1	1	2	6	0	0	0
1988	Hartford	6	2	4	6	2	1	0	1
1989	NY Rangers	4	1	2	3	2	0	0	0
1990	NY Rangers	10	2	1	3	0	1	0	0
1991	Calgary	7	2	2	4	0	1	0	0
Playoff Totals		**52**	**11**	**13**	**24**	**14**	**3**	**0**	**2**
WILSON, Cully									Right wing
1927	Chicago	2	1	0	1	6	....	....	....
Playoff Totals		**2**	**1**	**0**	**1**	**6**	....	....	....
WILSON, Doug									Defense
1978	Chicago	4	0	0	0	0	0	0	0
1980	Chicago	7	2	8	10	6	0	0	0
1981	Chicago	3	0	3	3	2	0	0	0
1982	Chicago	15	3	10	13	32	0	1	1
1983	Chicago	13	4	11	15	12	0	1	0
1984	Chicago	5	0	3	3	2	0	0	0
1985	Chicago	12	3	10	13	12	2	0	0
1986	Chicago	3	1	1	2	2	0	0	0
1987	Chicago	4	0	0	0	0	0	0	0
1989	Chicago	4	1	2	3	0	1	0	0
1990	Chicago	20	3	12	15	18	1	0	1
1991	Chicago	5	2	1	3	2	2	0	0
Playoff Totals		**95**	**19**	**61**	**80**	**88**	**6**	**2**	**2**
WILSON, Gord									Left wing
1955	Boston	2	0	0	0	0	0	0	0
Playoff Totals		**2**	**0**	**0**	**0**	**0**	**0**	**0**	**0**
WILSON, Hub *No Playoffs*									Left wing
WILSON, Jerry *No Playoffs*									Center
WILSON, Johnny									Left wing
1950♦	Detroit	8	0	1	1	0	....	....	....
1951	Detroit	1	0	0	0	0	....	....	....
1952♦	Detroit	8	4	1	5	5	....	....	....
1953	Detroit	6	2	5	7	0	....	....	....
1954♦	Detroit	12	3	0	3	0	....	....	....
1955♦	Detroit	11	0	1	1	0	....	....	....
1958	Detroit	4	2	1	3	0	....	....	....
1960	Toronto	10	1	2	3	2	....	....	....
1962	NY Rangers	6	2	2	4	4	....	....	....
Playoff Totals		**66**	**14**	**13**	**27**	**11**	....	....	....
•WILSON, Landon									Right wing
1998	Boston	1	0	0	0	0	0	0	0
1999	Boston	8	1	1	2	8	1	0	1
2002	Phoenix	4	0	0	0	12	0	0	0
Playoff Totals		**13**	**1**	**1**	**2**	**20**	**1**	**0**	**1**

Season	Team	GP	G	A	Pts	PIM	PP	SH	GW
WILSON, Larry									Center
1950♦	Detroit	4	0	0	0	0	0	0	0
Playoff Totals		**4**	**0**	**0**	**0**	**0**	**0**	**0**	**0**
•WILSON, Mike									Defense
1997	Buffalo	10	0	1	1	2	0	0	0
1998	Buffalo	15	0	1	1	13	0	0	0
2000	Florida	4	0	0	0	0	0	0	0
Playoff Totals		**29**	**0**	**2**	**2**	**15**	**0**	**0**	**0**
WILSON, Mitch *No Playoffs*									Center
WILSON, Murray									Left wing
1973♦	Montreal	16	2	4	6	6	0	0	1
1974	Montreal	5	1	0	1	2	0	0	0
1975	Montreal	5	0	3	3	4	0	0	0
1976♦	Montreal	12	1	1	2	6	0	0	0
1977♦	Montreal	14	1	6	7	14	0	0	0
1978♦	Montreal	....	....	....	....	....	....	....	....
1979	Los Angeles	1	0	0	0	0	0	0	0
Playoff Totals		**53**	**5**	**14**	**19**	**32**	**0**	**0**	**1**
WILSON, Rick									Defense
1975	St. Louis	2	0	0	0	0	0	0	0
1976	St. Louis	1	0	0	0	0	0	0	0
Playoff Totals		**3**	**0**	**0**	**0**	**0**	**0**	**0**	**0**
WILSON, Rik									Defense
1982	St. Louis	9	0	3	3	14	0	0	0
1984	St. Louis	11	0	0	0	9	0	0	0
1985	St. Louis	2	0	1	1	0	0	0	0
Playoff Totals		**22**	**0**	**4**	**4**	**23**	**0**	**0**	**0**
WILSON, Roger *No Playoffs*									Defense
WILSON, Ron									Defense
1979	Toronto	3	0	1	1	0	0	0	0
1980	Toronto	3	1	2	3	2	1	0	0
1985	Minnesota	9	1	6	7	2	1	0	0
1986	Minnesota	5	2	4	6	4	1	0	0
Playoff Totals		**20**	**4**	**13**	**17**	**8**	**3**	**0**	**0**
WILSON, Ron									Center
1983	Winnipeg	3	2	2	4	2	0	0	0
1985	Winnipeg	8	4	2	6	2	0	0	1
1986	Winnipeg	1	0	0	0	0	0	0	0
1987	Winnipeg	10	1	2	3	0	0	0	0
1988	Winnipeg	1	0	0	0	2	0	0	0
1990	St. Louis	12	3	5	8	18	2	0	0
1991	St. Louis	7	0	0	0	28	0	0	0
1992	St. Louis	6	0	1	1	0	0	0	0
1993	St. Louis	11	0	0	0	12	0	0	0
1994	Montreal	4	0	0	0	0	0	0	0
Playoff Totals		**63**	**10**	**12**	**22**	**64**	**2**	**0**	**1**
WILSON, Wally									Center
1948	Boston	1	0	0	0	0	0	0	0
Playoff Totals		**1**	**0**	**0**	**0**	**0**	**0**	**0**	**0**
WING, Murray *No Playoffs*									Defense
WINNES, Chris									Right wing
1991	Boston	1	0	0	0	0	0	0	0
Playoff Totals		**1**	**0**	**0**	**0**	**0**	**0**	**0**	**0**
WISEMAN, Brian *No Playoffs*									Center
WISEMAN, Eddie									Right wing
1933	Detroit	2	0	0	0	0	....	....	....
1934	Detroit	7	0	1	1	4	....	....	....
1936	NY Americans	4	2	1	3	0	....	....	....
1938	NY Americans	6	0	4	4	10	....	....	....
1939	NY Americans	2	0	0	0	0	....	....	....
1940	Boston	6	2	1	3	2	....	....	....
1941♦	Boston	11	*6	2	8	0	....	....	....
1942	Boston	5	0	1	1	0	....	....	....
Playoff Totals		**43**	**10**	**10**	**20**	**16**	....	....	....
WISTE, Jim *No Playoffs*									Center
•WITEHALL, Johan *No Playoffs*									Left wing
WITHERSPOON, Jim *No Playoffs*									Defense
WITIUK, Steve *No Playoffs*									Right wing
•WITT, Brendan									Defense
1998	Washington	16	1	0	1	14	0	0	0
2000	Washington	3	0	0	0	0	0	0	0
2001	Washington	6	2	0	2	12	1	0	0
Playoff Totals		**25**	**3**	**0**	**3**	**26**	**1**	**0**	**0**
WOIT, Benny									Right wing/Defense
1951	Detroit	4	0	0	0	2	....	....	....
1952♦	Detroit	8	1	1	2	2	....	....	....
1953	Detroit	6	1	3	4	0	....	....	....
1954♦	Detroit	12	0	1	1	8	....	....	....
1955♦	Detroit	11	0	1	1	6	....	....	....
Playoff Totals		**41**	**2**	**6**	**8**	**18**	....	....	....
WOJCIECHOWSKI, Steve									Right wing
1945	Detroit	6	0	1	1	0	0	0	0
Playoff Totals		**6**	**0**	**1**	**1**	**0**	**0**	**0**	**0**

Season	Team	GP	G	A	Pts	PIM	PP	SH	GW
WOLANIN, Craig									Defense
1988	New Jersey	18	2	5	7	51	1	0	0
1993	Quebec	4	0	0	0	4	0	0	0
1995	Quebec	6	1	1	2	4	0	0	0
1996♦	Colorado	7	1	0	1	8	0	0	1
Playoff Totals		**35**	**4**	**6**	**10**	**67**	**1**	**0**	**1**
WOLF, Bennett *No Playoffs*									Defense
WONG, Mike *No Playoffs*									Center
WOOD, Dody *No Playoffs*									Center
WOOD, Randy									Left wing/Center
1987	NY Islanders	13	1	3	4	14	0	0	1
1988	NY Islanders	5	1	0	1	6	0	0	0
1990	NY Islanders	5	1	1	2	4	0	0	0
1992	Buffalo	7	2	1	3	6	0	0	0
1993	Buffalo	8	1	4	5	4	1	0	0
1994	Buffalo	6	0	0	0	0	0	0	0
1995	Toronto	7	2	0	2	6	1	0	1
Playoff Totals		**51**	**8**	**9**	**17**	**40**	**2**	**0**	**2**
WOOD, Robert *No Playoffs*									Defense
WOODLEY, Dan *No Playoffs*									Right wing
WOODS, Paul									Left wing
1978	Detroit	7	0	5	5	4	0	0	0
Playoff Totals		**7**	**0**	**5**	**5**	**4**	**0**	**0**	**0**
•WOOLLEY, Jason									Defense
1994	Washington	4	1	0	1	4	0	0	1
1996	Florida	13	2	6	8	14	1	0	1
1997	Pittsburgh	5	0	3	3	0	0	0	0
1998	Buffalo	15	2	9	11	12	1	0	1
1999	Buffalo	21	4	11	15	10	2	0	1
2000	Buffalo	5	0	2	2	2	0	0	0
2001	Buffalo	8	1	5	6	2	0	0	1
Playoff Totals		**71**	**10**	**36**	**46**	**44**	**4**	**0**	**5**
•WORRELL, Peter									Left wing
2000	Florida	4	1	0	1	8	0	0	0
Playoff Totals		**4**	**1**	**0**	**1**	**8**	**0**	**0**	**0**
WORTMAN, Kevin *No Playoffs*									Defense
•WOTTON, Mark									Defense
1995	Vancouver	5	0	0	0	4	0	0	0
Playoff Totals		**5**	**0**	**0**	**0**	**4**	**0**	**0**	**0**
WOYTOWICH, Bob									Defense
1968	Minnesota	14	0	1	1	18	0	0	0
1970	Pittsburgh	10	1	2	3	2	0	0	0
Playoff Totals		**24**	**1**	**3**	**4**	**20**	**0**	**0**	**0**
•WREN, Bob									Center
2002	Toronto	1	0	0	0	0	0	0	0
Playoff Totals		**1**	**0**	**0**	**0**	**0**	**0**	**0**	**0**
•WRIGHT, Jamie									Left wing
1998	Dallas	5	0	0	0	0	0	0	0
Playoff Totals		**5**	**0**	**0**	**0**	**0**	**0**	**0**	**0**
WRIGHT, John *No Playoffs*									Center
WRIGHT, Keith *No Playoffs*									Left wing
WRIGHT, Larry *No Playoffs*									Center
•WRIGHT, Tyler									Center
1998	Pittsburgh	6	0	1	1	4	0	0	0
1999	Pittsburgh	13	0	0	0	19	0	0	0
2000	Pittsburgh	11	3	1	4	17	0	0	0
Playoff Totals		**30**	**3**	**2**	**5**	**40**	**0**	**0**	**0**
WYCHERLEY, Ralph *No Playoffs*									Left wing
WYLIE, Bill *No Playoffs*									Center
WYLIE, Duane *No Playoffs*									Center
WYROZUB, Randy *No Playoffs*									Center
•YACHMENEV, Vitali *No Playoffs*									Left wing
YACKEL, Ken									Right wing
1959	Boston	2	0	0	0	2	0	0	0
Playoff Totals		**2**	**0**	**0**	**0**	**2**	**0**	**0**	**0**
•YAKE, Terry									Center
1991	Hartford	6	1	1	2	16	0	1	0
1998	St. Louis	10	2	1	3	6	2	0	1
1999	St. Louis	13	1	2	3	14	1	0	0
2000	Washington	3	0	0	0	0	0	0	0
Playoff Totals		**32**	**4**	**4**	**8**	**36**	**3**	**1**	**1**
•YAKUSHIN, Dmitri *No Playoffs*									Defense
YAREMCHUK, Gary *No Playoffs*									Center
YAREMCHUK, Ken									Center
1984	Chicago	1	0	0	0	0	0	0	0
1985	Chicago	15	5	5	10	37	0	0	1
1986	Chicago	3	1	1	2	2	0	0	0
1987	Toronto	6	0	0	0	0	0	0	0
1988	Toronto	6	0	2	2	10	0	0	0
Playoff Totals		**31**	**6**	**8**	**14**	**49**	**0**	**0**	**1**

•YASHIN, Alexei — Center

Season	Team	GP	G	A	Pts	PIM	PP	SH	GW
1997	Ottawa	7	1	5	6	2	1	0	0
1998	Ottawa	11	5	3	8	8	3	0	2
1999	Ottawa	4	0	0	0	10	0	0	0
2001	Ottawa	4	0	1	1	0	0	0	0
2002	NY Islanders	7	3	4	7	2	1	0	0
Playoff Totals		**33**	**9**	**13**	**22**	**22**	**5**	**0**	**2**

YATES, Ross *No Playoffs* — Center

YAWNEY, Trent — Defense

Season	Team	GP	G	A	Pts	PIM	PP	SH	GW
1988	Chicago	5	0	4	4	8	0	0	0
1989	Chicago	15	3	6	9	20	0	1	0
1990	Chicago	20	3	5	8	27	3	0	1
1991	Chicago	1	0	0	0	0	0	0	0
1993	Calgary	6	3	2	5	6	1	0	0
1994	Calgary	7	0	0	0	16	0	0	0
1995	Calgary	2	0	0	0	2	0	0	0
1996	Calgary	4	0	0	0	2	0	0	0
Playoff Totals		**60**	**9**	**17**	**26**	**81**	**4**	**1**	**1**

YEGOROV, Alexei *No Playoffs* — Right wing

•YELLE, Stephane — Center

Season	Team	GP	G	A	Pts	PIM	PP	SH	GW
1996♦	Colorado	22	1	4	5	8	0	1	0
1997	Colorado	12	1	6	7	2	0	0	0
1998	Colorado	7	1	0	1	12	0	0	0
1999	Colorado	10	0	1	1	6	0	0	0
2000	Colorado	17	1	2	3	4	0	0	0
2001♦	Colorado	23	1	2	3	8	0	0	1
2002	Colorado	20	0	2	2	14	0	0	0
Playoff Totals		**111**	**5**	**17**	**22**	**54**	**0**	**1**	**1**

•YLONEN, Juha — Center

Season	Team	GP	G	A	Pts	PIM	PP	SH	GW
1999	Phoenix	2	0	2	2	2	0	0	0
2000	Phoenix	1	0	0	0	0	0	0	0
2002	Ottawa	12	0	5	5	2	0	0	0
Playoff Totals		**15**	**0**	**7**	**7**	**4**	**0**	**0**	**0**

•YONKMAN, Nolan *No Playoffs* — Defense

YORK, Harry — Center

Season	Team	GP	G	A	Pts	PIM	PP	SH	GW
1997	St. Louis	5	0	0	0	2	0	0	0
Playoff Totals		**5**	**0**	**0**	**0**	**2**	**0**	**0**	**0**

•YORK, Jason — Defense

Season	Team	GP	G	A	Pts	PIM	PP	SH	GW
1997	Ottawa	7	0	0	0	4	0	0	0
1998	Ottawa	7	1	1	2	7	1	0	0
1999	Ottawa	4	1	1	2	4	0	0	0
2000	Ottawa	6	0	2	2	2	0	0	0
2001	Ottawa	4	0	0	0	4	0	0	0
Playoff Totals		**28**	**2**	**4**	**6**	**21**	**1**	**0**	**0**

•YORK, Mike *No Playoffs* — Center

YOUNG, B.J. *No Playoffs* — Right wing

YOUNG, Brian *No Playoffs* — Defense

YOUNG, C.J. *No Playoffs* — Right wing

YOUNG, Doug — Defense

Season	Team	GP	G	A	Pts	PIM	PP	SH	GW
1932	Detroit	2	0	0	0	2	....	....	....
1933	Detroit	4	1	1	2	0	....	....	....
1934	Detroit	9	0	0	0	10	....	....	....
1936♦	Detroit	7	0	2	2	0	....	....	....
1937♦	Detroit	....	....	....	....	....	....	....	....
1939	Detroit	6	0	2	2	4	....	....	....
Playoff Totals		**28**	**1**	**5**	**6**	**16**	....	....	....

YOUNG, Howie — Defense/Right wing

Season	Team	GP	G	A	Pts	PIM	PP	SH	GW
1961	Detroit	11	2	2	4	*30	0	0	0
1963	Detroit	8	0	2	2	16	0	0	0
Playoff Totals		**19**	**2**	**4**	**6**	**46**	**0**	**0**	**0**

•YOUNG, Scott — Right wing

Season	Team	GP	G	A	Pts	PIM	PP	SH	GW
1988	Hartford	4	1	0	1	0	0	0	0
1989	Hartford	4	2	0	2	4	0	0	0
1990	Hartford	7	2	0	2	2	0	0	0
1991♦	Pittsburgh	17	1	6	7	2	1	0	0
1993	Quebec	6	4	1	5	0	0	0	2
1995	Quebec	6	3	3	6	2	0	1	0
1996♦	Colorado	22	3	12	15	10	0	0	0
1997	Colorado	17	4	2	6	14	2	0	0
1999	St. Louis	13	4	7	11	10	1	0	1
2000	St. Louis	6	6	2	8	8	3	0	0
2001	St. Louis	15	6	7	13	2	0	2	3
2002	St. Louis	10	3	0	3	2	1	1	0
Playoff Totals		**127**	**39**	**40**	**79**	**56**	**8**	**4**	**6**

YOUNG, Tim — Center

Season	Team	GP	G	A	Pts	PIM	PP	SH	GW
1977	Minnesota	2	1	1	2	2	0	0	0
1980	Minnesota	15	2	5	7	4	1	1	0
1981	Minnesota	12	3	14	17	9	0	0	1
1982	Minnesota	4	1	1	2	10	0	0	0
1983	Minnesota	2	0	2	2	2	0	0	0
1984	Winnipeg	1	0	1	1	0	0	0	0
Playoff Totals		**36**	**7**	**24**	**31**	**27**	**1**	**1**	**1**

YOUNG, Warren *No Playoffs* — Center

YOUNGHANS, Tom — Right wing

Season	Team	GP	G	A	Pts	PIM	PP	SH	GW
1977	Minnesota	2	0	0	0	0	0	0	0
1980	Minnesota	15	2	1	3	17	0	2	0
1981	Minnesota	5	0	0	0	4	0	0	0
1982	NY Rangers	2	0	0	0	0	0	0	0
Playoff Totals		**24**	**2**	**1**	**3**	**21**	**0**	**2**	**0**

YSEBAERT, Paul — Center

Season	Team	GP	G	A	Pts	PIM	PP	SH	GW
1991	Detroit	2	0	2	2	0	0	0	0
1992	Detroit	10	1	0	1	10	0	0	0
1993	Detroit	7	3	1	4	2	0	1	1
1994	Chicago	6	0	0	0	8	0	0	0
1996	Tampa Bay	5	0	0	0	0	0	0	0
Playoff Totals		**30**	**4**	**3**	**7**	**20**	**0**	**1**	**1**

•YUSHKEVICH, Dmitry — Defense

Season	Team	GP	G	A	Pts	PIM	PP	SH	GW
1995	Philadelphia	15	1	5	6	12	0	0	0
1996	Toronto	4	0	0	0	0	0	0	0
1999	Toronto	17	1	5	6	22	1	0	0
2000	Toronto	12	1	1	2	4	0	0	0
2001	Toronto	11	0	4	4	12	0	0	0
Playoff Totals		**59**	**3**	**15**	**18**	**50**	**1**	**0**	**0**

•YZERMAN, Steve — Center

Season	Team	GP	G	A	Pts	PIM	PP	SH	GW
1984	Detroit	4	3	3	6	0	1	0	1
1985	Detroit	3	2	1	3	2	0	0	0
1987	Detroit	16	5	13	18	8	1	0	0
1988	Detroit	3	1	3	4	6	0	0	0
1989	Detroit	6	5	5	10	2	2	0	0
1991	Detroit	7	3	3	6	4	1	0	0
1992	Detroit	11	3	5	8	12	0	1	1
1993	Detroit	7	4	3	7	4	1	1	1
1994	Detroit	3	1	3	4	0	0	0	0
1995	Detroit	15	4	8	12	0	2	0	1
1996	Detroit	18	8	12	20	4	4	0	1
1997♦	Detroit	20	7	6	13	4	3	0	2
1998♦	Detroit	22	6	*18	*24	22	3	1	0
1999	Detroit	10	9	4	13	0	4	0	2
2000	Detroit	8	0	4	4	0	0	0	0
2001	Detroit	1	0	0	0	0	0	0	0
2002♦	Detroit	23	6	17	23	10	4	0	2
Playoff Totals		**177**	**67**	**108**	**175**	**78**	**26**	**3**	**11**

ZABRANSKY, Libor *No Playoffs* — Defense

ZAHARKO, Miles — Defense

Season	Team	GP	G	A	Pts	PIM	PP	SH	GW
1978	Atlanta	1	0	0	0	0	0	0	0
1981	Chicago	2	0	0	0	0	0	0	0
Playoff Totals		**3**	**0**	**0**	**0**	**0**	**0**	**0**	**0**

ZAINE, Rod *No Playoffs* — Center

ZALAPSKI, Zarley — Defense

Season	Team	GP	G	A	Pts	PIM	PP	SH	GW
1989	Pittsburgh	11	1	8	9	13	1	0	0
1991	Hartford	6	1	3	4	8	0	0	1
1992	Hartford	7	2	3	5	6	0	0	0
1994	Calgary	7	0	3	3	2	0	0	0
1995	Calgary	7	0	4	4	4	0	0	0
1996	Calgary	4	0	1	1	10	0	0	0
1998	Montreal	6	0	1	1	4	0	0	0
Playoff Totals		**48**	**4**	**23**	**27**	**47**	**1**	**0**	**1**

•ZAMUNER, Rob — Left wing

Season	Team	GP	G	A	Pts	PIM	PP	SH	GW
1996	Tampa Bay	6	2	3	5	10	0	1	0
2000	Ottawa	6	2	0	2	2	0	0	1
2001	Ottawa	4	0	0	0	6	0	0	0
2002	Boston	6	0	2	2	4	0	0	0
Playoff Totals		**22**	**4**	**5**	**9**	**22**	**0**	**1**	**1**

ZANUSSI, Joe — Defense

Season	Team	GP	G	A	Pts	PIM	PP	SH	GW
1976	Boston	4	0	1	1	2	0	0	0
Playoff Totals		**4**	**0**	**1**	**1**	**2**	**0**	**0**	**0**

ZANUSSI, Ron — Right wing

Season	Team	GP	G	A	Pts	PIM	PP	SH	GW
1980	Minnesota	14	0	4	4	17	0	0	0
1981	Toronto	3	0	0	0	0	0	0	0
Playoff Totals		**17**	**0**	**4**	**4**	**17**	**0**	**0**	**0**

ZAVISHA, Brad *No Playoffs* — Left wing

•ZEDNIK, Richard — Left wing

Season	Team	GP	G	A	Pts	PIM	PP	SH	GW
1998	Washington	17	7	3	10	16	2	0	0
2000	Washington	5	0	0	0	5	0	0	0
2002	Montreal	4	4	4	8	6	2	0	0
Playoff Totals		**26**	**11**	**7**	**18**	**27**	**4**	**0**	**0**

ZEHR, Jeff *No Playoffs* — Left wing

ZEIDEL, Larry — Defense

Season	Team	GP	G	A	Pts	PIM	PP	SH	GW
1952♦	Detroit	5	0	0	0	0	0	0	0
1968	Philadelphia	7	0	1	1	12	0	0	0
Playoff Totals		**12**	**0**	**1**	**1**	**12**	**0**	**0**	**0**

•ZELEPUKIN, Valeri — Left wing

Season	Team	GP	G	A	Pts	PIM	PP	SH	GW
1992	New Jersey	4	1	1	2	2	0	0	0
1993	New Jersey	5	0	2	2	0	0	0	0
1994	New Jersey	20	5	2	7	14	1	0	0
1995♦	New Jersey	18	1	2	3	12	0	0	1
1997	New Jersey	8	3	2	5	2	1	0	1
1998	Edmonton	8	1	2	3	2	0	0	0
1999	Philadelphia	4	1	0	1	4	0	0	1
2000	Philadelphia	18	1	2	3	12	1	0	0
Playoff Totals		**85**	**13**	**13**	**26**	**48**	**3**	**0**	**3**

ZEMLAK, Richard — Right wing

Season	Team	GP	G	A	Pts	PIM	PP	SH	GW
1989	Pittsburgh	1	0	0	0	10	0	0	0
Playoff Totals		**1**	**0**	**0**	**0**	**10**	**0**	**0**	**0**

ZENIUK, Ed *No Playoffs* — Defense

ZENT, Jason *No Playoffs* — Left wing

•ZETTERBERG, Henrik *No Playoffs* — Left wing

ZETTERSTROM, Lars *No Playoffs* — Defense

ZETTLER, Rob — Defense

Season	Team	GP	G	A	Pts	PIM	PP	SH	GW
1995	Philadelphia	1	0	0	0	2	0	0	0
1996	Toronto	2	0	0	0	0	0	0	0
2000	Washington	5	0	0	0	2	0	0	0
2001	Washington	6	0	0	0	0	0	0	0
Playoff Totals		**14**	**0**	**0**	**0**	**4**	**0**	**0**	**0**

ZEZEL, Peter — Center

Season	Team	GP	G	A	Pts	PIM	PP	SH	GW
1985	Philadelphia	19	1	8	9	28	1	0	0
1986	Philadelphia	5	3	1	4	4	1	0	1
1987	Philadelphia	25	3	10	13	10	1	1	1
1988	Philadelphia	7	3	2	5	7	0	0	0
1989	St. Louis	10	6	6	12	4	1	1	1
1990	St. Louis	12	1	7	8	4	1	0	0
1993	Toronto	20	2	1	3	6	0	0	0
1994	Toronto	18	2	4	6	8	0	0	1
1995	Dallas	3	1	0	1	0	0	0	0
1996	St. Louis	10	3	0	3	2	0	1	0
1997	New Jersey	2	0	0	0	10	0	0	0
Playoff Totals		**131**	**25**	**39**	**64**	**83**	**5**	**3**	**4**

•ZHAMNOV, Alexei — Center

Season	Team	GP	G	A	Pts	PIM	PP	SH	GW
1993	Winnipeg	6	0	2	2	2	0	0	0
1996	Winnipeg	6	2	1	3	8	0	0	0
2002	Chicago	5	0	0	0	0	0	0	0
Playoff Totals		**17**	**2**	**3**	**5**	**10**	**0**	**0**	**0**

•ZHITNIK, Alexei — Defense

Season	Team	GP	G	A	Pts	PIM	PP	SH	GW
1993	Los Angeles	24	3	9	12	26	2	0	1
1995	Buffalo	5	0	1	1	14	0	0	0
1997	Buffalo	12	1	0	1	16	0	0	0
1998	Buffalo	15	0	3	3	36	0	0	0
1999	Buffalo	21	4	11	15	*52	4	0	2
2000	Buffalo	4	0	0	0	8	0	0	0
2001	Buffalo	13	1	6	7	12	0	0	0
Playoff Totals		**94**	**9**	**30**	**39**	**164**	**6**	**0**	**3**

•ZHOLTOK, Sergei — Center

Season	Team	GP	G	A	Pts	PIM	PP	SH	GW
1997	Ottawa	7	1	1	2	0	1	0	0
1998	Ottawa	11	0	2	2	0	0	0	0
2001	Edmonton	3	0	0	0	0	0	0	0
Playoff Totals		**21**	**1**	**3**	**4**	**0**	**1**	**0**	**0**

ZIEGLER, Thomas *No Playoffs* — Right wing

•ZIZKA, Tomas *No Playoffs* — Defense

ZMOLEK, Doug — Defense

Season	Team	GP	G	A	Pts	PIM	PP	SH	GW
1994	Dallas	7	0	1	1	4	0	0	0
1995	Dallas	5	0	0	0	10	0	0	0
1998	Los Angeles	2	0	0	0	2	0	0	0
Playoff Totals		**14**	**0**	**1**	**1**	**16**	**0**	**0**	**0**

ZOBOROSKY, Marty *No Playoffs* — Defense

ZOMBO, Rick — Defense

Season	Team	GP	G	A	Pts	PIM	PP	SH	GW
1987	Detroit	7	0	1	1	9	0	0	0
1988	Detroit	16	0	6	6	55	0	0	0
1989	Detroit	6	0	1	1	16	0	0	0
1991	Detroit	7	1	0	1	10	0	0	0
1992	St. Louis	6	0	2	2	12	0	0	0
1993	St. Louis	11	0	1	1	12	0	0	0
1994	St. Louis	4	0	0	0	11	0	0	0
1995	St. Louis	3	0	0	0	2	0	0	0
Playoff Totals		**60**	**1**	**11**	**12**	**127**	**0**	**0**	**0**

•ZUBOV, Sergei — Defense

Season	Team	GP	G	A	Pts	PIM	PP	SH	GW
1994♦	NY Rangers	22	5	14	19	0	2	0	0
1995	NY Rangers	10	3	8	11	2	1	0	0
1996	Pittsburgh	18	1	14	15	26	1	0	0
1997	Dallas	7	0	3	3	2	0	0	0
1998	Dallas	17	4	5	9	2	3	0	1
1999♦	Dallas	23	1	12	13	4	0	0	0
2000	Dallas	18	2	7	9	6	1	1	0
2001	Dallas	10	1	5	6	4	0	0	0
Playoff Totals		**125**	**17**	**68**	**85**	**46**	**8**	**1**	**1**

•ZUBRUS, Dainius — Right wing

Season	Team	GP	G	A	Pts	PIM	PP	SH	GW
1997	Philadelphia	19	5	4	9	12	1	0	1
1998	Philadelphia	5	0	1	1	2	0	0	0
2001	Washington	6	0	0	0	2	0	0	0
Playoff Totals		**30**	**5**	**5**	**10**	**16**	**1**	**0**	**1**

ZUKE, Mike — Center

Season	Team	GP	G	A	Pts	PIM	PP	SH	GW
1980	St. Louis	3	0	0	0	2	0	0	0
1981	St. Louis	11	4	5	9	4	3	0	0
1982	St. Louis	8	1	1	2	2	0	0	0
1983	St. Louis	4	1	0	1	4	0	0	1
Playoff Totals		**26**	**6**	**6**	**12**	**12**	**3**	**0**	**1**

ZUNICH, Rudy *No Playoffs* — Defense

•ZYUZIN, Andrei — Defense

Season	Team	GP	G	A	Pts	PIM	PP	SH	GW
1998	San Jose	6	1	0	1	14	0	0	1
Playoff Totals		**6**	**1**	**0**	**1**	**14**	**0**	**0**	**1**

CHAPTER 23

Goaltender Register

Career NHL Playoff Records, 1918-2002

Abbreviations: Avg – goals against average; **GA** – goals against; **GP** – games played; **L** – losses; **Mins** – minutes played; **S%** – save percentage; **SA** – shots against; **SAPG** – shots against per 60 minutes; **SO** – shutouts; **T** – ties; **W** – wins; • – active goaltender; * – league-leading total; ♦ – member of Stanley Cup winning team. Statistics for 1918 to 1926 are NHL only and do not include series vs. PCHA/WCHL/WHL opponents. Player Register begins on page 145.

AUBRY, Serge No Playoffs
ABBOTT, George No Playoffs
ADAMS, John No Playoffs
•**AEBISCHER, David**

Season Team	GP	W	L	T	Mins	GA	SO	Avg	SA	S%	SAPG
2001♦ Colorado	1	0	0	....	1	0	0	0.00	0	.000	0.0
2002 Colorado	1	0	0	....	34	1	0	1.76	14	.929	24.7
Playoff Totals	**2**	**0**	**0**	....	**35**	**1**	**0**	**1.71**	**14**	**.929**	**24.0**

•**AHONEN, Ari** No Playoffs
AIKEN, Don No Playoffs
AITKENHEAD, Andy

Season Team	GP	W	L	T	Mins	GA	SO	Avg	SA	S%	SAPG
1933♦ NY Rangers	8	*6	1	1	488	13	*2	1.60			
1934 NY Rangers	2	0	1	1	120	2	1	1.00			
Playoff Totals	**10**	**6**	**2**	**2**	**608**	**15**	**3**	**1.48**			

ALMAS, Red

Season Team	GP	W	L	T	Mins	GA	SO	Avg	SA	S%	SAPG
1947 Detroit	5	1	3	....	263	13	0	2.97			
Playoff Totals	**5**	**1**	**3**	....	**263**	**13**	**0**	**2.97**			

ANDERSON, Craig No Playoffs
ANDERSON, Lorne No Playoffs
•**ASKEY, Tom**

Season Team	GP	W	L	T	Mins	GA	SO	Avg	SA	S%	SAPG
1999 Anaheim	1	0	1	....	30	2	0	4.00	11	.818	22.0
Playoff Totals	**1**	**0**	**1**	....	**30**	**2**	**0**	**4.00**	**11**	**.818**	**22.0**

ASTROM, Hardy No Playoffs
•**AUBIN, Jean-Sebastien**

Season Team	GP	W	L	T	Mins	GA	SO	Avg	SA	S%	SAPG
2001 Pittsburgh	1	0	0	....	1	0	0	0.00	0	.000	0.0
Playoff Totals	**1**	**0**	**0**	....	**1**	**0**	**0**	**0.00**	**0**	**.000**	**0.0**

•**AULD, Alexander** No Playoffs
BACH, Ryan No Playoffs
BAILEY, Scott No Playoffs
BAKER, Steve

Season Team	GP	W	L	T	Mins	GA	SO	Avg	SA	S%	SAPG
1981 NY Rangers	14	7	7	....	826	55	0	4.00			
Playoff Totals	**14**	**7**	**7**	....	**826**	**55**	**0**	**4.00**			

BALES, Mike No Playoffs
BANNERMAN, Murray

Season Team	GP	W	L	T	Mins	GA	SO	Avg	SA	S%	SAPG
1982 Chicago	10	5	4	....	555	35	0	3.78			
1983 Chicago	8	4	4	....	480	32	0	4.00			
1984 Chicago	5	2	3	....	300	17	0	3.40	171	.901	34.2
1985 Chicago	15	9	6	....	906	72	0	4.77	547	.868	36.2
1986 Chicago	2	0	1	....	81	9	0	6.67	40	.775	29.6
Playoff Totals	**40**	**20**	**18**	....	**2322**	**165**	**0**	**4.26**			

BARON, Marco

Season Team	GP	W	L	T	Mins	GA	SO	Avg	SA	S%	SAPG
1981 Boston	1	0	1	....	20	3	0	9.00			
Playoff Totals	**1**	**0**	**1**	....	**20**	**3**	**0**	**9.00**			

•**BARRASSO, Tom**

Season Team	GP	W	L	T	Mins	GA	SO	Avg	SA	S%	SAPG
1984 Buffalo	3	0	2	....	139	8	0	3.45	59	.864	25.5
1985 Buffalo	5	2	3	....	300	22	0	4.40	151	.854	30.2
1988 Buffalo	4	1	3	....	224	16	0	4.29	120	.867	32.1
1989 Pittsburgh	11	7	4	....	631	40	0	3.80	389	.897	37.0
1991♦ Pittsburgh	20	12	7	....	1175	51	*1	*2.60	629	.919	32.1
1992♦ Pittsburgh	*21	*16	5	....	*1233	58	1	2.82	622	.907	30.3
1993 Pittsburgh	12	7	5	....	722	35	*2	2.91	370	.905	30.7
1994 Pittsburgh	6	2	4	....	356	17	0	2.87	162	.895	27.3
1995 Pittsburgh	2	0	1	....	80	8	0	6.00	41	.805	30.8
1996 Pittsburgh	10	4	5	....	558	26	1	2.80	337	.923	36.2
1998 Pittsburgh	6	2	4	....	376	17	0	2.71	171	.901	27.3
1999 Pittsburgh	13	6	7	....	787	35	1	2.67	350	.900	26.7
2000 Ottawa	6	2	4	....	372	16	0	2.58	168	.905	27.1
Playoff Totals	**119**	**61**	**54**	....	**6953**	**349**	**6**	**3.01**	**3569**	**.902**	**30.8**

BASSEN, Hank

Season Team	GP	W	L	T	Mins	GA	SO	Avg	SA	S%	SAPG
1961 Detroit	4	1	2	....	220	9	0	2.45			
1966 Detroit	1	0	1	....	54	2	0	2.22			
Playoff Totals	**5**	**1**	**3**	....	**274**	**11**	**0**	**2.41**			

BASTIEN, Baz No Playoffs
BAUMAN, Gary No Playoffs

BEAUPRE, Don

Season Team	GP	W	L	T	Mins	GA	SO	Avg	SA	S%	SAPG
1981 Minnesota	6	4	2	....	360	26	0	4.33			
1982 Minnesota	2	0	1	....	60	4	0	4.00			
1983 Minnesota	4	2	2	....	245	20	0	4.90			
1984 Minnesota	13	6	7	....	782	40	1	3.07	380	.895	29.2
1985 Minnesota	4	1	1	....	184	12	0	3.91	80	.850	26.1
1986 Minnesota	5	2	3	....	300	17	0	3.40	158	.892	31.6
1990 Washington	8	4	3	....	401	18	0	2.69	187	.904	28.0
1991 Washington	11	5	5	....	624	29	*1	2.79	294	.901	28.3
1992 Washington	7	3	4	....	419	22	0	3.15	212	.896	30.4
1993 Washington	2	1	1	....	119	9	0	4.54	65	.862	32.8
1994 Washington	8	5	2	....	429	21	1	2.94	191	.890	26.7
1996 Toronto	2	0	0	....	20	2	0	6.00	13	.846	39.0
Playoff Totals	**72**	**33**	**31**	....	**3943**	**220**	**3**	**3.35**			

BEAUREGARD, Stephane

Season Team	GP	W	L	T	Mins	GA	SO	Avg	SA	S%	SAPG
1990 Winnipeg	4	1	3	....	238	12	0	3.03	105	.886	26.5
Playoff Totals	**4**	**1**	**3**	....	**238**	**12**	**0**	**3.03**	**105**	**.886**	**26.5**

BEDARD, Jim No Playoffs
BEHREND, Marc

Season Team	GP	W	L	T	Mins	GA	SO	Avg	SA	S%	SAPG
1984 Winnipeg	2	0	2	0	121	9	0	4.46	91	.901	45.1
1985 Winnipeg	4	1	1	0	179	10	0	3.35	98	.898	32.8
1986 Winnipeg	1	0	0	0	12	0	0	0.00	7	1.000	35.0
Playoff Totals	**7**	**1**	**3**	**0**	**312**	**19**	**0**	**3.65**	**196**	**.903**	**37.7**

BELANGER, Yves No Playoffs
•**BELFOUR, Ed**

Season Team	GP	W	L	T	Mins	GA	SO	Avg	SA	S%	SAPG
1990 Chicago	9	4	2	....	409	17	0	2.49	200	.915	29.3
1991 Chicago	6	2	4	....	295	20	0	4.07	183	.891	37.2
1992 Chicago	18	12	4	....	949	39	1	*2.47	398	.902	25.2
1993 Chicago	4	0	4	....	249	13	0	3.13	97	.866	23.4
1994 Chicago	6	2	4	....	360	15	0	2.50	191	.921	31.8
1995 Chicago	16	9	7	....	1014	37	1	2.19	479	.923	28.3
1996 Chicago	9	6	3	....	666	23	1	2.07	323	.929	29.1
1998 Dallas	17	10	7	....	1039	31	1	*1.79	399	.922	23.0
1999♦ Dallas	*23	*16	7	....	*1544	43	*3	1.67	617	.930	24.0
2000 Dallas	*23	14	9	....	1443	45	*4	1.87	651	.931	27.1
2001 Dallas	10	4	6	....	671	25	0	2.24	277	.910	24.8
Playoff Totals	**141**	**79**	**57**	....	**8639**	**308**	**11**	**2.14**	**3815**	**.919**	**26.5**

BELHUMEUR, Michel

Season Team	GP	W	L	T	Mins	GA	SO	Avg	SA	S%	SAPG
1973 Philadelphia	1	0	0	....	10	1	0	6.00			
Playoff Totals	**1**	**0**	**0**	....	**10**	**1**	**0**	**6.00**			

BELL, Gordie

Season Team	GP	W	L	T	Mins	GA	SO	Avg	SA	S%	SAPG
1956 NY Rangers	2	1	1	....	120	9	0	4.50			
Playoff Totals	**2**	**1**	**1**	....	**120**	**9**	**0**	**4.50**			

BENEDICT, Clint

Season Team	GP	W	L	T	Mins	GA	SO	Avg	SA	S%	SAPG
1919 Ottawa	5	1	4	0	300	26	0	5.20			
1920♦ Ottawa	....										
1921♦ Ottawa	2	2	0	0	120	0	2	0.00			
1922 Ottawa	2	0	1	1	120	5	1	2.50			
1923♦ Ottawa	2	2	0	0	120	2	1	1.00			
1924 Ottawa	2	0	2	0	120	5	0	2.50			
1926♦ Mtl. Maroons	4	2	0	0	240	5	1	1.25			
1927 Mtl. Maroons	2	0	1	1	132	2	0	0.91			
1928 Mtl. Maroons	*9	*5	3	1	*555	8	*4	*0.86			
Playoff Totals	**28**	**12**	**11**	**3**	**1707**	**53**	**9**	**1.86**			

BENNETT, Harvey No Playoffs
BERGERON, Jean-Claude No Playoffs
BERNHARDT, Tim No Playoffs
BERTHIAUME, Daniel

Season Team	GP	W	L	T	Mins	GA	SO	Avg	SA	S%	SAPG
1986 Winnipeg	1	0	1	....	68	4	0	3.53	43	.907	37.9
1987 Winnipeg	8	4	4	....	439	21	0	2.87	210	.900	28.7
1988 Winnipeg	5	1	4	....	300	25	0	5.00	154	.838	30.8
Playoff Totals	**14**	**5**	**9**	....	**807**	**50**	**0**	**3.72**	**407**	**.877**	**30.3**

BESTER, Allan

Season Team	GP	W	L	T	Mins	GA	SO	Avg	SA	S%	SAPG
1987 Toronto	1	0	0	....	39	1	0	1.54	17	.941	26.2
1988 Toronto	5	2	3	....	253	21	0	4.98	135	.844	32.0
1990 Toronto	4	0	3	....	196	14	0	4.29	120	.883	36.7
1991 Detroit	1	0	0	....	20	1	0	3.00	12	.917	36.0
Playoff Totals	**11**	**2**	**6**	....	**508**	**37**	**0**	**4.37**	**284**	**.870**	**33.5**

BEVERIDGE, Bill

Season Team	GP	W	L	T	Mins	GA	SO	Avg	SA	S%	SAPG
1937 Mtl. Maroons	5	2	3	....	300	11	0	2.20			
Playoff Totals	**5**	**2**	**3**	....	**300**	**11**	**0**	**2.20**			

Season	Team	GP	W	L	T	Mins	GA	SO	Avg	SA	S%	SAPG
BIBEAULT, Paul												
1942	Montreal	3	1	2	....	180	8	*1	2.67	....	....	....
1943	Montreal	5	1	4	....	320	18	1	3.38	....	....	....
1944	Toronto	5	1	4	....	300	23	0	4.60	....	....	....
1945	Boston	7	3	4	....	437	22	0	3.02	....	....	....
Playoff Totals		20	6	14	....	1237	71	2	3.44	....	....	....
•**BIERK, Zac** *No Playoffs*												
•**BILLINGTON, Craig**												
1993	New Jersey	2	0	1	....	78	5	0	3.85	39	.872	30.0
1995	Boston	1	0	0	....	25	1	0	2.40	10	.900	24.0
1996	Boston	1	0	1	....	60	6	0	6.00	28	.786	28.0
1997	Colorado	1	0	0	....	20	1	0	3.00	13	.923	39.0
1998	Colorado	1	0	0	....	1	0	0	0.00	0	.000	0.0
1999	Colorado	1	0	0	....	9	1	0	6.67	6	.833	40.0
2000	Washington	1	0	0	....	20	1	0	3.00	6	.833	18.0
Playoff Totals		8	0	2	....	213	15	0	4.23	102	.853	28.7
BINETTE, Andre *No Playoffs*												
BINKLEY, Les												
1970	Pittsburgh	7	5	2	....	428	15	0	2.10	....	....	....
Playoff Totals		7	5	2	....	428	15	0	2.10	....	....	....
•**BIRON, Martin** *No Playoffs*												
BITTNER, Richard *No Playoffs*												
•**BLACKBURN, Dan** *No Playoffs*												
BLAKE, Mike *No Playoffs*												
BLUE, John												
1993	Boston	2	0	1	....	96	5	0	3.13	49	.898	30.6
Playoff Totals		2	0	1	....	96	5	0	3.13	49	.898	30.6
BOISVERT, Gilles *No Playoffs*												
BOUCHARD, Dan												
1974	Atlanta	1	0	1	....	60	4	0	4.00	....	....	....
1976	Atlanta	2	0	2	....	120	3	0	1.50	....	....	....
1977	Atlanta	1	0	1	....	60	5	0	5.00	....	....	....
1978	Atlanta	2	0	2	....	120	7	0	3.50	....	....	....
1979	Atlanta	2	0	2	....	100	9	0	5.40	....	....	....
1980	Atlanta	4	1	3	....	241	14	0	3.49	....	....	....
1981	Quebec	5	2	3	....	286	19	*1	3.99	....	....	....
1982	Quebec	11	4	7	....	677	38	0	3.37	....	....	....
1983	Quebec	4	1	3	....	242	11	0	2.73	....	....	....
1984	Quebec	9	5	4	....	543	25	0	2.76	224	.888	24.8
1985	Quebec	1	0	1	....	60	7	0	7.00	24	.708	24.0
1986	Winnipeg	1	0	1	....	40	5	0	7.50	22	.773	33.0
Playoff Totals		43	13	30	....	2549	147	1	3.46	....	....	....
•**BOUCHER, Brian**												
2000	Philadelphia	18	11	7	....	1183	40	1	2.03	484	.917	24.5
2001	Philadelphia	1	0	0	....	37	3	0	4.86	17	.824	27.6
2002	Philadelphia	2	0	1	....	88	2	0	1.36	33	.939	22.5
Playoff Totals		21	11	8	....	1308	45	1	2.06	534	.916	24.5
BOURQUE, Claude												
1939	Montreal	3	1	2	....	188	8	1	2.55	....	....	....
Playoff Totals		3	1	2	....	188	8	1	2.55	....	....	....
BOUTIN, Rollie *No Playoffs*												
BOUVRETTE, Lionel *No Playoffs*												
BOWER, Johnny												
1959	Toronto	*12	5	7	....	*746	38	0	3.06	....	....	....
1960	Toronto	*10	4	6	....	*645	31	0	2.88	....	....	....
1961	Toronto	3	0	3	....	180	8	0	2.67	....	....	....
1962♦	Toronto	10	*6	3	....	579	20	0	*2.07	....	....	....
1963♦	Toronto	10	*8	2	....	600	16	*2	*1.60	....	....	....
1964♦	Toronto	*14	*8	6	....	*850	30	*2	*2.12	....	....	....
1965	Toronto	5	2	3	....	321	13	0	2.43	....	....	....
1966	Toronto	2	0	2	....	120	8	0	4.00	....	....	....
1967♦	Toronto	4	2	0	....	183	5	*1	1.64	....	....	....
1969	Toronto	4	0	2	....	154	11	0	4.29	....	....	....
Playoff Totals		74	35	34	....	4378	180	5	2.47	....	....	....
•**BRATHWAITE, Fred**												
2002	St. Louis	1	0	0	....	1	0	0	0.00	0	.000	0.0
Playoff Totals		1	0	0	....	1	0	0	0.00	0	.000	0.0
BRIMSEK, Frank												
1939♦	Boston	*12	*8	4	....	*863	18	1	*1.25	....	....	....
1940	Boston	6	2	4	....	360	15	0	2.50	....	....	....
1941♦	Boston	*11	*8	3	....	*678	23	*1	*2.04	....	....	....
1942	Boston	5	2	3	....	307	16	0	3.13	....	....	....
1943	Boston	9	4	5	....	560	33	0	3.54	....	....	....
1946	Boston	*10	5	5	....	*651	29	0	2.67	....	....	....
1947	Boston	5	1	4	....	343	16	0	2.80	....	....	....
1948	Boston	5	1	4	....	317	20	0	3.79	....	....	....
1949	Boston	5	1	4	....	316	16	0	3.04	....	....	....
Playoff Totals		68	32	36	....	4395	186	2	2.54	....	....	....
•**BROCHU, Martin** *No Playoffs*												

Season	Team	GP	W	L	T	Mins	GA	SO	Avg	SA	S%	SAPG
BRODA, Turk												
1937	Toronto	2	0	2	....	133	5	0	2.26	....	....	....
1938	Toronto	7	4	3	....	452	13	1	1.73	....	....	....
1939	Toronto	10	5	5	....	617	20	*2	1.94	....	....	....
1940	Toronto	10	6	4	....	657	19	1	1.74	....	....	....
1941	Toronto	7	3	4	....	438	15	0	2.05	....	....	....
1942♦	Toronto	*13	*8	5	....	*780	31	*1	2.38	....	....	....
1943	Toronto	6	2	4	....	439	20	0	2.73	....	....	....
1947♦	Toronto	*11	*8	3	....	680	27	*1	2.38	....	....	....
1948♦	Toronto	9	*8	1	....	557	20	*1	*2.15	....	....	....
1949♦	Toronto	9	*8	1	....	574	15	*1	*1.57	....	....	....
1950	Toronto	7	3	4	....	450	10	*3	*1.33	....	....	....
1951♦	Toronto	8	*5	1	....	492	9	*2	1.10	....	....	....
1952	Toronto	2	0	2	....	120	7	0	3.50	....	....	....
Playoff Totals		101	60	39	....	6389	211	13	1.98	....	....	....
BRODERICK, Ken *No Playoffs*												
BRODERICK, Len *No Playoffs*												
•**BRODEUR, Martin**												
1992	New Jersey	1	0	1	....	32	3	0	5.63	15	.800	28.1
1994	New Jersey	17	8	9	....	1171	38	1	1.95	531	.928	27.2
1995♦	New Jersey	*20	*16	4	....	*1222	34	*3	*1.67	463	.927	22.7
1997	New Jersey	10	5	5	....	659	19	2	*1.73	268	.929	24.4
1998	New Jersey	6	2	4	....	366	12	0	1.97	164	.927	26.9
1999	New Jersey	7	3	4	....	425	20	0	2.82	139	.856	19.6
2000♦	New Jersey	*23	*16	7	....	*1450	39	2	*1.61	537	.927	22.2
2001	New Jersey	*25	15	10	....	*1505	52	*4	2.07	507	.897	20.2
2002	New Jersey	6	2	4	....	381	9	1	1.42	145	.938	22.8
Playoff Totals		115	67	48	....	7211	226	13	1.88	2769	.918	23.0
BRODEUR, Richard												
1981	Vancouver	3	0	3	....	185	13	0	4.22	....	....	....
1982	Vancouver	17	11	6	....	1089	49	0	2.70	....	....	....
1983	Vancouver	3	0	3	....	193	13	0	4.04	....	....	....
1984	Vancouver	4	1	3	....	222	12	1	3.24	115	.896	31.1
1986	Vancouver	2	0	2	....	120	12	0	6.00	79	.848	39.5
1988	Hartford	4	1	3	....	200	12	0	3.60	87	.862	26.1
Playoff Totals		33	13	20	....	2009	111	1	3.32	....	....	....
BROMLEY, Gary												
1979	Vancouver	3	1	2	....	180	14	0	4.67	....	....	....
1980	Vancouver	4	1	3	....	100	11	0	3.67	....	....	....
Playoff Totals		7	2	5	....	360	25	0	4.17	....	....	....
BROOKS, Art *No Playoffs*												
BROOKS, Ross												
1973	Boston	1	0	0	....	20	3	0	9.00	....	....	....
Playoff Totals		1	0	0	....	20	3	0	9.00	....	....	....
BROPHY, Frank *No Playoffs*												
BROWN, Andy *No Playoffs*												
BROWN, Ken *No Playoffs*												
BRUNETTA, Mario *No Playoffs*												
•**BRYZGALOV, Ilja** *No Playoffs*												
BULLOCK, Bruce *No Playoffs*												
•**BURKE, Sean**												
1988	New Jersey	17	9	8	....	1001	57	*1	3.42	515	.889	30.9
1990	New Jersey	2	0	2	....	125	8	0	3.84	57	.860	27.4
1998	Philadelphia	5	1	4	....	283	17	0	3.60	121	.860	25.7
2000	Phoenix	5	1	4	....	296	16	0	3.24	167	.904	33.9
2002	Phoenix	5	1	4	....	297	13	0	2.63	133	.902	26.9
Playoff Totals		34	12	22	....	2002	111	1	3.33	993	.888	29.8
BUZINSKI, Steve *No Playoffs*												
CALEY, Don *No Playoffs*												
CAPRICE, Frank *No Playoffs*												
CAREY, Jim												
1995	Washington	7	2	4	....	358	25	0	4.19	151	.834	25.3
1996	Washington	3	0	1	....	97	10	0	6.19	39	.744	24.1
Playoff Totals		10	2	5	....	455	35	0	4.62	190	.816	25.1
CARON, Jacques												
1972	St. Louis	9	4	5	....	499	26	0	3.13	....	....	....
1973	St. Louis	3	0	2	....	140	8	0	3.43	....	....	....
Playoff Totals		12	4	7	....	639	34	0	3.19	....	....	....
CARTER, Lyle *No Playoffs*												
CASEY, Jon												
1989	Minnesota	4	1	3	....	211	16	0	4.55	121	.868	34.4
1990	Minnesota	7	3	4	....	415	21	1	3.04	219	.904	31.7
1991	Minnesota	*23	*14	7	....	*1205	61	*1	3.04	571	.893	28.4
1992	Minnesota	7	3	4	....	437	22	0	3.02	225	.902	30.9
1994	Boston	11	5	6	....	698	34	0	2.92	308	.890	26.5
1995	St. Louis	2	0	1	....	30	2	0	4.00	10	.800	20.0
1996	St. Louis	12	6	6	....	747	36	1	2.89	378	.905	30.4
Playoff Totals		66	32	31	....	3743	192	3	3.08	1832	.895	29.4
•**CASSIVI, Frederic** *No Playoffs*												
•**CECHMANEK, Roman**												
2001	Philadelphia	6	2	4	....	347	18	0	3.11	165	.891	28.5
2002	Philadelphia	4	1	3	....	227	7	1	1.85	109	.936	28.8
Playoff Totals		10	3	7	....	574	25	1	2.61	274	.909	28.6
•**CENTOMO, Sebastien** *No Playoffs*												
CHABOT, Frederic *No Playoffs*												

Season	Team	GP	W	L	T	Mins	GA	SO	Avg	SA	S%	SAPG
CHABOT, Lorne												
1927	NY Rangers	2	0	1	1	120	3	1	1.50	....	....	....
1928♦	NY Rangers	6	2	2	1	321	8	1	1.50	....	....	....
1929	Toronto	4	2	2	0	242	5	0	1.24	....	....	....
1931	Toronto	2	0	1	1	139	4	0	1.73	....	....	....
1932♦	Toronto	*7	*5	1	1	438	15	0	2.05	....	....	....
1933	Toronto	*9	4	5	0	*686	18	*2	1.57	....	....	....
1934	Montreal	2	0	1	1	131	4	0	1.83	....	....	....
1935	Chicago	2	0	1	1	124	1	1	0.48	....	....	....
1936	Mtl. Maroons	3	0	3	0	297	6	0	*1.21	....	....	....
Playoff Totals		**37**	**13**	**17**	**6**	**2498**	**64**	**5**	**1.54**	....	....	....
CHADWICK, Ed *No Playoffs*												
CHAMPOUX, Bob												
1964	Detroit	1	1	0	....	55	4	0	4.36	....	....	....
Playoff Totals		**1**	**1**	**0**	....	**55**	**4**	**0**	**4.36**	....	....	....
•CHARPENTIER, Sebastien *No Playoffs*												
CHEEVERS, Gerry												
1968	Boston	4	0	4	....	240	15	0	3.75	....	....	....
1969	Boston	9	6	3	....	572	16	*3	1.68	....	....	....
1970♦	Boston	*13	*12	1	....	*781	29	0	2.23	....	....	....
1971	Boston	6	3	3	....	360	21	0	3.50	....	....	....
1972♦	Boston	8	*6	2	....	483	21	*2	2.61	....	....	....
1976	Boston	6	2	4	....	392	14	1	2.14	....	....	....
1977	Boston	*14	8	5	....	*858	44	1	3.08	....	....	....
1978	Boston	12	8	4	....	731	35	1	2.87	....	....	....
1979	Boston	6	4	2	....	360	15	0	2.50	....	....	....
1980	Boston	10	4	6	....	619	32	0	3.10	....	....	....
Playoff Totals		**88**	**53**	**34**	....	**5396**	**242**	**8**	**2.69**	....	....	....
CHEVELDAE, Tim												
1991	Detroit	7	3	4	....	398	22	0	3.32	208	.894	31.4
1992	Detroit	11	3	7	....	597	25	*2	2.51	277	.910	27.8
1993	Detroit	7	3	4	....	423	24	0	3.40	200	.880	28.4
Playoff Totals		**25**	**9**	**15**	....	**1418**	**71**	**2**	**3.00**	**685**	**.896**	**29.0**
CHEVRIER, Alain												
1989	Chicago	16	9	7	....	1013	44	0	2.61	484	.909	28.7
Playoff Totals		**16**	**9**	**7**	....	**1013**	**44**	**0**	**2.61**	**484**	**.909**	**28.7**
•CLEMMENSEN, Scott *No Playoffs*												
CLIFFORD, Chris *No Playoffs*												
•CLOUTIER, Dan												
2001	Vancouver	2	0	2	....	117	9	0	4.62	57	.842	29.2
2002	Vancouver	6	2	3	....	273	16	0	3.52	123	.870	27.0
Playoff Totals		**8**	**2**	**5**	....	**390**	**25**	**0**	**3.85**	**180**	**.861**	**27.7**
•CLOUTIER, Frederic *No Playoffs*												
CLOUTIER, Jacques												
1989	Buffalo	4	1	3	....	238	10	1	2.52	108	.907	27.2
1990	Chicago	4	0	2	....	175	8	0	2.74	75	.893	25.7
Playoff Totals		**8**	**1**	**5**	....	**413**	**18**	**1**	**2.62**	**183**	**.902**	**26.6**
COLVIN, Les *No Playoffs*												
•CONKLIN, Ty *No Playoffs*												
CONNELL, Alex												
1926	Ottawa	2	0	1	1	120	2	0	*1.00	....	....	....
1927♦	Ottawa	6	*3	0	3	400	4	*2	*0.60	....	....	....
1928	Ottawa	2	0	2	0	120	3	0	1.50	....	....	....
1930	Ottawa	2	0	1	1	120	6	0	3.00	....	....	....
1932	Detroit	2	0	1	1	120	3	0	1.50	....	....	....
1935♦	Mtl. Maroons	*7	*5	0	2	429	8	*2	*1.12	....	....	....
Playoff Totals		**21**	**8**	**5**	**8**	**1309**	**26**	**4**	**1.19**	....	....	....
CORSI, Jim *No Playoffs*												
COURTEAU, Maurice *No Playoffs*												
COUSINEAU, Marcel *No Playoffs*												
COWLEY, Wayne *No Playoffs*												
COX, Abbie *No Playoffs*												
CRAIG, Jim *No Playoffs*												
CRHA, Jiri												
1980	Toronto	2	0	2	....	121	10	0	4.96	....	....	....
1981	Toronto	3	0	2	....	65	11	0	10.15	....	....	....
Playoff Totals		**5**	**0**	**4**	....	**186**	**21**	**0**	**6.77**	....	....	....
CROZIER, Roger												
1964	Detroit	3	0	2	....	126	5	0	2.38	....	....	....
1965	Detroit	7	3	4	....	420	23	0	3.29	....	....	....
1966	Detroit	*12	6	5	....	*668	26	*1	2.34	....	....	....
1970	Detroit	1	0	1	....	34	3	0	5.29	....	....	....
1973	Buffalo	4	2	2	....	249	11	0	2.65	....	....	....
1975	Buffalo	5	3	2	....	292	14	0	2.88	....	....	....
Playoff Totals		**32**	**14**	**16**	....	**1789**	**82**	**1**	**2.75**	....	....	....
CUDE, Wilf												
1934	Detroit	*9	4	5	0	*593	21	1	2.12	....	....	....
1935	Montreal	2	0	1	1	120	6	0	3.00	....	....	....
1937	Montreal	5	2	3	....	352	13	0	2.22	....	....	....
1938	Montreal	3	1	2	....	192	11	0	3.44	....	....	....
Playoff Totals		**19**	**7**	**11**	**1**	**1257**	**51**	**1**	**2.43**	....	....	....
CUTTS, Don *No Playoffs*												
CYR, Claude *No Playoffs*												
DADSWELL, Doug *No Playoffs*												

Season	Team	GP	W	L	T	Mins	GA	SO	Avg	SA	S%	SAPG
•DAFOE, Byron												
1994	Washington	2	0	2	....	118	5	0	2.54	39	.872	19.8
1995	Washington	1	0	0	....	20	1	0	3.00	3	.667	9.0
1998	Boston	6	2	4	....	422	14	1	1.99	159	.912	22.6
1999	Boston	12	6	6	....	768	26	2	2.03	330	.921	25.8
2002	Boston	6	2	4	....	358	19	0	3.18	141	.865	23.6
Playoff Totals		**27**	**10**	**16**	....	**1686**	**65**	**3**	**2.31**	**672**	**.903**	**23.9**
D'ALESSIO, Corrie *No Playoffs*												
DALEY, Joe *No Playoffs*												
DAMORE, Nick *No Playoffs*												
D'AMOUR, Marc *No Playoffs*												
•DAMPHOUSSE, Jean-Francois *No Playoffs*												
DARRAGH, Jack *No Playoffs*												
DASKALAKIS, Cleon *No Playoffs*												
DAVIDSON, John												
1975	St. Louis	1	0	1	....	60	4	0	4.00	....	....	....
1978	NY Rangers	2	1	1	....	122	7	0	3.44	....	....	....
1979	NY Rangers	*18	11	7	....	*1106	42	*1	2.28	....	....	....
1980	NY Rangers	9	4	5	....	541	21	0	2.33	....	....	....
1982	NY Rangers	1	0	0	....	33	3	0	5.45	....	....	....
Playoff Totals		**31**	**16**	**14**	....	**1862**	**77**	**1**	**2.48**	....	....	....
DECOURCY, Bob *No Playoffs*												
DEFELICE, Norm *No Playoffs*												
DeJORDY, Denis												
1961♦	Chicago	....	....	....	....	....	....	....	....	....	....	....
1964	Chicago	1	0	0	....	20	2	0	6.00	....	....	....
1965	Chicago	2	0	1	....	80	9	0	6.75	....	....	....
1967	Chicago	4	1	2	....	184	10	0	3.26	....	....	....
1968	Chicago	11	5	6	....	662	34	0	3.08	....	....	....
Playoff Totals		**18**	**6**	**9**	....	**946**	**55**	**0**	**3.49**	....	....	....
DELGUIDICE, Matt *No Playoffs*												
•DENIS, Marc *No Playoffs*												
DeROUVILLE, Philippe *No Playoffs*												
DESJARDINS, Gerry												
1969	Los Angeles	9	3	4	....	431	28	0	3.90	....	....	....
1972	Chicago	1	1	0	....	60	5	0	5.00	....	....	....
1975	Buffalo	*15	7	5	....	760	43	0	3.39	....	....	....
1976	Buffalo	9	4	5	....	563	28	0	2.98	....	....	....
1977	Buffalo	1	0	1	....	60	4	0	4.00	....	....	....
Playoff Totals		**35**	**15**	**15**	....	**1874**	**108**	**0**	**3.46**	....	....	....
•DesROCHERS, Patrick *No Playoffs*												
DICKIE, Bill *No Playoffs*												
DION, Connie												
1944	Detroit	5	1	4	....	300	17	0	3.40	....	....	....
Playoff Totals		**5**	**1**	**4**	....	**300**	**17**	**0**	**3.40**	....	....	....
DION, Michel												
1982	Pittsburgh	5	2	3	....	304	22	0	4.34	....	....	....
Playoff Totals		**5**	**2**	**3**	....	**304**	**22**	**0**	**4.34**	....	....	....
•DiPIETRO, Rick *No Playoffs*												
•DIVIS, Reinhard *No Playoffs*												
DOLSON, Dolly												
1929	Detroit	2	0	2	0	120	7	0	3.50	....	....	....
Playoff Totals		**2**	**0**	**2**	**0**	**120**	**7**	**0**	**3.50**	....	....	....
DOPSON, Rob *No Playoffs*												
DOWIE, Bruce *No Playoffs*												
DRAPER, Tom												
1992	Buffalo	7	3	4	....	433	19	1	2.63	201	.905	27.9
Playoff Totals		**7**	**3**	**4**	....	**433**	**19**	**1**	**2.63**	**201**	**.905**	**27.9**
DRYDEN, Dave												
1966	Chicago	1	0	0	....	13	0	0	0.00	....	....	....
1973	Buffalo	2	0	2	....	120	9	0	4.50	....	....	....
Playoff Totals		**3**	**0**	**2**	....	**133**	**9**	**0**	**4.06**	....	....	....
DRYDEN, Ken												
1971♦	Montreal	*20	*12	8	....	*1221	61	0	3.00	....	....	....
1972	Montreal	6	2	4	....	360	17	0	2.83	....	....	....
1973♦	Montreal	*17	*12	5	....	*1039	50	1	2.89	....	....	....
1975	Montreal	11	6	5	....	688	29	2	2.53	....	....	....
1976♦	Montreal	*13	*12	1	....	*780	25	1	*1.92	....	....	....
1977♦	Montreal	*14	*12	2	....	849	22	*4	*1.55	....	....	....
1978♦	Montreal	*15	*12	3	....	*919	29	*2	*1.89	....	....	....
1979♦	Montreal	16	*12	4	....	990	41	0	2.48	....	....	....
Playoff Totals		**112**	**80**	**32**	....	**6846**	**274**	**10**	**2.40**	....	....	....
DUFFUS, Parris *No Playoffs*												
DUMAS, Michel												
1975	Chicago	1	0	0	....	19	1	0	3.16	....	....	....
Playoff Totals		**1**	**0**	**0**	....	**19**	**1**	**0**	**3.16**	....	....	....
•DUNHAM, Mike *No Playoffs*												
DUPUIS, Bob *No Playoffs*												

Season Team	GP	W	L	T	Mins	GA	SO	Avg	SA	S%	SAPG
DURNAN, Bill											
1944♦ Montreal	*9	*8	1	....	*549	14	*1	*1.53	....	....	....
1945 Montreal	6	2	4	....	373	15	0	2.41	....	....	....
1946♦ Montreal	9	*8	1	....	581	20	0	*2.07	....	....	....
1947 Montreal	*11	6	5	....	*720	23	*1	*1.92	....	....	....
1949 Montreal	7	3	4	....	468	17	0	2.18	....	....	....
1950 Montreal	3	0	3	....	180	10	0	3.33	....	....	....
Playoff Totals	45	27	18	....	2871	99	2	2.07	....	....	....
DYCK, Ed *No Playoffs*											
EDWARDS, Don											
1977 Buffalo	5	2	3	....	300	15	0	3.00			
1978 Buffalo	8	3	5	....	482	22	0	2.74			
1980 Buffalo	6	3	3	....	360	17	1	2.83			
1981 Buffalo	8	4	4	....	503	28	0	3.34			
1982 Buffalo	4	1	3	....	214	16	0	4.49			
1983 Calgary	5	1	2	....	226	22	0	5.84			
1984 Calgary	6	2	1	....	217	12	0	3.32	133	.910	36.8
Playoff Totals	42	16	21	....	2302	132	1	3.44			
EDWARDS, Gary											
1974 Los Angeles	1	1	0	....	60	1	0	1.00			
1976 Los Angeles	2	1	1	....	120	9	0	4.50			
1980 Minnesota	7	3	3	....	337	22	0	3.92			
1981 Edmonton	1	0	0	....	20	2	0	6.00			
Playoff Totals	11	5	4	....	537	34	0	3.80			
EDWARDS, Marv *No Playoffs*											
EDWARDS, Roy											
1970 Detroit	4	0	3	....	206	11	0	3.20			
Playoff Totals	4	0	3	....	206	11	0	3.20			
ELIOT, Darren											
1987 Los Angeles	1	0	0	....	40	7	0	10.50	29	.759	43.5
Playoff Totals	1	0	0	....	40	7	0	10.50	29	.759	43.5
ELLACOTT, Ken *No Playoffs*											
•**EMERY, Ray** *No Playoffs*											
ERICKSON, Chad *No Playoffs*											
•**ESCHE, Robert** *No Playoffs*											
ESPOSITO, Tony											
1969♦ Montreal	....	....	....	....	....	....	....				
1970 Chicago	8	4	4	....	480	27	0	3.38			
1971 Chicago	18	11	7	....	1151	42	*2	*2.19			
1972 Chicago	5	2	3	....	300	16	0	3.20			
1973 Chicago	15	10	5	....	895	46	1	3.08			
1974 Chicago	10	6	4	....	584	28	*2	2.88			
1975 Chicago	8	3	5	....	472	34	0	4.32			
1976 Chicago	4	0	4	....	240	13	0	3.25			
1977 Chicago	2	0	2	....	120	6	0	3.00			
1978 Chicago	4	0	4	....	252	19	0	4.52			
1979 Chicago	4	0	4	....	243	14	0	3.46			
1980 Chicago	6	3	3	....	373	14	0	2.25			
1981 Chicago	3	0	3	....	215	15	0	4.19			
1982 Chicago	7	3	3	....	381	16	*1	2.52			
1983 Chicago	5	3	2	....	311	18	0	3.47			
Playoff Totals	99	45	53	....	6017	308	6	3.07			
ESSENSA, Bob											
1990 Winnipeg	4	2	1	....	206	12	0	3.50	100	.880	29.1
1992 Winnipeg	1	0	0	....	33	3	0	5.45	17	.824	30.9
1993 Winnipeg	6	2	4	....	367	20	0	3.27	183	.891	29.9
1994 Detroit	2	0	2	....	109	9	0	4.95	43	.791	23.7
1998 Edmonton	1	0	0	....	27	1	0	2.22	11	.909	24.4
2001 Vancouver	2	0	2	....	122	6	0	2.95	58	.897	28.5
Playoff Totals	16	4	9	....	864	51	0	3.54	412	.876	28.6
EVANS, Claude *No Playoffs*											
EXELBY, Randy *No Playoffs*											
•**FANKHOUSER, Scott** *No Playoffs*											
FARR, Rocky *No Playoffs*											
FAVELL, Doug											
1968 Philadelphia	2	1	1	....	120	8	0	4.00			
1969 Philadelphia	1	0	1	....	60	5	0	5.00			
1971 Philadelphia	2	0	2	....	120	8	0	4.00			
1973 Philadelphia	11	5	6	....	669	29	1	2.60			
1974 Toronto	3	0	3	....	181	10	0	3.31			
1978 Colorado	2	0	2	....	120	6	0	3.00			
Playoff Totals	21	6	15	....	1270	66	1	3.12			
•**FERNANDEZ, Manny**											
1998 Dallas	1	0	0	....	2	0	0	0.00	0	.000	0.0
2000 Dallas	1	0	0	....	17	1	0	3.53	8	.875	28.2
Playoff Totals	2	0	0	....	19	1	0	3.16	8	.875	25.3
•**FICHAUD, Eric** *No Playoffs*											
•**FISET, Stephane**											
1993 Quebec	1	0	0	....	21	1	0	2.86	12	.917	34.3
1995 Quebec	4	1	2	....	209	16	0	4.59	115	.861	33.0
1996♦ Colorado	1	0	0	....	1	0	0	0.00	0	.000	0.0
1998 Los Angeles	2	0	2	....	93	7	0	4.52	61	.885	39.4
2000 Los Angeles	4	0	3	....	200	10	0	3.00	98	.898	29.4
2001 Los Angeles	1	0	0	....	1	0	0	0.00	0	.000	0.0
2002 Montreal	1	0	0	....	38	3	0	4.74	19	.842	30.0
Playoff Totals	14	1	7	....	563	37	0	3.94	305	.879	32.5
FITZPATRICK, Mark											
1990 NY Islanders	4	0	2	....	152	13	0	5.13	71	.817	28.0
1993 NY Islanders	3	0	1	....	77	4	0	3.12	23	.826	17.9
1996 Florida	2	0	0	....	60	6	0	6.00	30	.800	30.0
Playoff Totals	9	0	3	....	289	23	0	4.78	124	.815	25.7
•**FLAHERTY, Wade**											
1995 San Jose	7	2	3	....	377	31	0	4.93	221	.860	35.2
Playoff Totals	7	2	3	....	377	31	0	4.93	221	.860	35.2
FORBES, Jake											
1921 Toronto	2	0	2	0	120	7	0	3.50			
Playoff Totals	2	0	2	0	120	7	0	3.50			
FORD, Brian *No Playoffs*											
FOSTER, Norm *No Playoffs*											
•**FOUNTAIN, Mike** *No Playoffs*											
FOWLER, Hec *No Playoffs*											
FRANCIS, Emile *No Playoffs*											
FRANKS, Jimmy											
1937♦ Detroit	1	0	1	....	30	2	0	4.00			
Playoff Totals	1	0	1	....	30	2	0	4.00			
FREDERICK, Ray *No Playoffs*											
FRIESEN, Karl *No Playoffs*											
FROESE, Bob											
1984 Philadelphia	3	0	2	....	154	11	0	4.29	77	.857	30.0
1985 Philadelphia	4	0	1	....	146	11	0	4.52	71	.845	29.2
1986 Philadelphia	5	2	3	....	293	15	0	3.07	125	.880	25.6
1987 NY Rangers	4	1	1	....	165	10	0	3.64	96	.896	34.9
1989 NY Rangers	2	0	2	....	72	8	0	6.67	51	.843	42.5
Playoff Totals	18	3	9	....	830	55	0	3.98	420	.869	30.4
FUHR, Grant											
1982 Edmonton	5	2	3	....	309	26	0	5.05			
1983 Edmonton	1	0	0	....	11	0	0	0.00			
1984♦ Edmonton	16	11	4	....	883	44	1	2.99	491	.910	33.4
1985♦ Edmonton	*18	*15	3	....	1064	55	0	3.10	522	.895	29.4
1986 Edmonton	9	5	4	....	541	28	0	3.11	273	.897	30.3
1987♦ Edmonton	19	14	5	....	1148	47	0	2.46	511	.908	26.7
1988♦ Edmonton	*19	*16	2	....	*1136	55	0	2.90	471	.883	24.9
1989 Edmonton	7	3	4	....	417	24	1	3.45	227	.894	32.7
1990♦ Edmonton	....	....	....	....	....	....	....				
1991 Edmonton	17	8	7	....	1019	51	0	3.00	488	.895	28.7
1993 Buffalo	8	3	4	....	474	27	1	3.42	216	.875	27.3
1996 St. Louis	2	1	0	....	69	1	0	0.87	45	.978	39.1
1997 St. Louis	6	2	4	....	357	13	2	2.18	183	.920	30.8
1998 St. Louis	10	6	4	....	616	28	0	2.73	297	.906	28.9
1999 St. Louis	13	6	6	....	790	31	1	2.35	305	.898	23.2
Playoff Totals	150	92	50	....	8834	430	6	2.92			
GAGE, Joaquin *No Playoffs*											
GAGNON, David *No Playoffs*											
GAMBLE, Bruce											
1967♦ Toronto	....	....	....	....	....	....	....				
1969 Toronto	3	0	2	....	86	13	0	9.07			
1971 Philadelphia	2	0	2	....	120	12	0	6.00			
Playoff Totals	5	0	4	....	206	25	0	7.28			
GAMBLE, Troy											
1991 Vancouver	4	1	3	....	249	16	0	3.86	133	.880	32.0
Playoff Totals	4	1	3	....	249	16	0	3.86	133	.880	32.0
GARDINER, Bert											
1939 NY Rangers	6	3	3	....	433	12	0	1.66			
1941 Montreal	3	1	2	....	214	8	0	2.24			
Playoff Totals	9	4	5	....	647	20	0	1.85			
GARDINER, Charlie											
1930 Chicago	2	0	1	1	172	3	0	1.05			
1931 Chicago	9	5	3	1	638	14	*2	1.32			
1932 Chicago	2	1	1	0	120	6	*1	3.00			
1934♦ Chicago	8	*6	1	1	542	12	*2	*1.33			
Playoff Totals	21	12	6	3	1472	35	5	1.43			
GARDNER, George *No Playoffs*											
•**GARNER, Tyrone** *No Playoffs*											
•**GARON, Mathieu** *No Playoffs*											
GARRETT, John											
1980 Hartford	1	0	1	....	60	8	0	8.00			
1982 Quebec	5	3	2	....	323	21	0	3.90			
1983 Vancouver	1	1	0	....	60	4	0	4.00			
1984 Vancouver	2	0	0	....	18	0	0	0.00	5	1.000	16.7
Playoff Totals	9	4	3	....	461	33	0	4.30			
GATHERUM, Dave											
1954♦ Detroit	....	....	....	....	....	....	....				
GAUTHIER, Paul *No Playoffs*											
GAUTHIER, Sean *No Playoffs*											
GELINEAU, Jack											
1951 Boston	4	1	2	....	260	7	1	1.62			
Playoff Totals	4	1	2	....	260	7	1	1.62			
•**GERBER, Martin** *No Playoffs*											

Season	Team	GP	W	L	T	Mins	GA	SO	Avg	SA	S%	SAPG
GIACOMIN, Ed												
1967	NY Rangers	4	0	4	....	246	14	0	3.41	....	....	....
1968	NY Rangers	6	2	4	....	360	18	0	3.00	....	....	....
1969	NY Rangers	3	0	3	....	180	10	0	3.33	....	....	....
1970	NY Rangers	5	2	3	....	280	19	0	4.07	....	....	....
1971	NY Rangers	12	7	5	....	759	28	0	2.21	....	....	....
1972	NY Rangers	*10	*6	4	....	*600	27	0	2.70	....	....	....
1973	NY Rangers	10	5	4	....	539	23	1	2.56	....	....	....
1974	NY Rangers	13	7	6	....	788	37	0	2.82	....	....	....
1975	NY Rangers	2	0	2	....	86	4	0	2.79	....	....	....
Playoff Totals		**65**	**29**	**35**	....	**3838**	**180**	**1**	**2.81**	....	....	....
•GIGUERE, Jean-Sebastien *No Playoffs*												
GILBERT, Gilles												
1973	Minnesota	1	0	1	....	60	4	0	4.00	....	....	....
1974	Boston	16	10	6	....	977	43	1	2.64	....	....	....
1975	Boston	3	1	2	....	188	12	0	3.83	....	....	....
1976	Boston	6	3	3	....	360	19	*2	3.17	....	....	....
1977	Boston	1	0	1	....	20	3	0	9.00	....	....	....
1979	Boston	5	3	2	....	314	16	0	3.06	....	....	....
Playoff Totals		**32**	**17**	**15**	....	**1919**	**97**	**3**	**3.03**	....	....	....
GILL, Andre *No Playoffs*												
GOODMAN, Paul												
1938♦	Chicago	1	0	1	....	60	5	0	5.00	....	....	....
1940	Chicago	2	0	2	....	127	5	0	2.36	....	....	....
Playoff Totals		**3**	**0**	**3**	....	**187**	**10**	**0**	**3.21**	....	....	....
GORDON, Scott *No Playoffs*												
GOSSELIN, Mario												
1985	Quebec	17	9	8	....	1059	54	0	3.06	473	.886	26.8
1986	Quebec	1	0	1	....	40	5	0	7.50	22	.773	33.0
1987	Quebec	11	7	4	....	654	37	0	3.39	326	.887	29.9
1990	Los Angeles	3	0	2	....	63	3	0	2.90	23	.870	21.9
Playoff Totals		**32**	**16**	**15**	....	**1816**	**99**	**0**	**3.27**	**844**	**.883**	**27.9**
GOVERDE, David *No Playoffs*												
•GRAHAME, John *No Playoffs*												
GRAHAME, Ron												
1978	Boston	4	2	1	....	202	7	0	2.08	....	....	....
Playoff Totals		**4**	**2**	**1**	....	**202**	**7**	**0**	**2.08**	....	....	....
GRANT, Benny *No Playoffs*												
GRANT, Doug *No Playoffs*												
GRATTON, Gilles *No Playoffs*												
GRAY, Gerry *No Playoffs*												
GRAY, Harrison *No Playoffs*												
GREENLAY, Mike *No Playoffs*												
GUENETTE, Steve *No Playoffs*												
•GUSTAFSON, Derek *No Playoffs*												
•HACKETT, Jeff												
1995	Chicago	2	0	0	....	26	1	0	2.31	11	.909	25.4
1996	Chicago	1	0	1	....	60	5	0	5.00	32	.844	32.0
1997	Chicago	6	2	4	....	345	25	0	4.35	190	.868	33.0
Playoff Totals		**9**	**2**	**5**	....	**431**	**31**	**0**	**4.32**	**233**	**.867**	**32.4**
HAINSWORTH, George												
1927	Montreal	4	1	1	2	252	6	1	1.43	....	....	....
1928	Montreal	2	0	1	1	128	3	0	1.41	....	....	....
1929	Montreal	3	0	3	0	180	5	0	1.67	....	....	....
1930♦	Montreal	*6	*5	0	1	*481	6	*3	*0.75	....	....	....
1931♦	Montreal	*10	*6	4	0	*722	21	*2	1.75	....	....	....
1932	Montreal	4	1	3	0	300	13	0	2.60	....	....	....
1933	Montreal	2	0	1	1	120	8	0	4.00	....	....	....
1934	Toronto	5	2	3	0	302	11	0	2.19	....	....	....
1935	Toronto	*7	3	4	0	*460	12	*2	1.57	....	....	....
1936	Toronto	*9	4	5	0	*541	27	0	2.99	....	....	....
Playoff Totals		**52**	**22**	**25**	**5**	**3486**	**112**	**8**	**1.93**	....	....	....
HALL, Glenn												
1952♦	Detroit	....	....	....	....	....	....	....	....	....	....	....
1956	Detroit	*10	5	5	....	*604	28	0	2.78	....	....	....
1957	Detroit	5	1	4	....	300	15	0	3.00	....	....	....
1959	Chicago	6	2	4	....	360	21	0	3.50	....	....	....
1960	Chicago	4	0	4	....	249	14	0	3.37	....	....	....
1961♦	Chicago	*12	*8	4	....	*772	26	*2	*2.02	....	....	....
1962	Chicago	*12	*6	6	....	*720	31	*2	2.58	....	....	....
1963	Chicago	6	2	4	....	360	25	0	4.17	....	....	....
1964	Chicago	7	3	4	....	408	22	0	3.24	....	....	....
1965	Chicago	*13	*7	6	....	*760	28	1	2.21	....	....	....
1966	Chicago	6	2	4	....	347	22	0	3.80	....	....	....
1967	Chicago	3	1	2	....	176	8	0	2.73	....	....	....
1968	St. Louis	*18	8	10	....	*1111	45	*1	2.43	....	....	....
1969	St. Louis	3	0	2	....	131	5	0	2.29	....	....	....
1970	St. Louis	7	4	3	....	421	21	0	2.99	....	....	....
1971	St. Louis	3	0	3	....	180	9	0	3.00	....	....	....
Playoff Totals		**115**	**49**	**65**	....	**6899**	**320**	**6**	**2.78**	....	....	....
HAMEL, Pierre *No Playoffs*												
HANLON, Glen												
1980	Vancouver	2	0	0	....	60	3	0	3.00	....	....	....
1982	St. Louis	3	0	2	....	109	9	0	4.95	....	....	....
1983	NY Rangers	1	0	1	....	60	5	0	5.00	....	....	....
1984	NY Rangers	5	2	3	....	308	13	1	2.53	166	.922	32.3
1985	NY Rangers	3	0	3	....	168	14	0	5.00	99	.859	35.4
1986	NY Rangers	3	0	0	....	75	6	0	4.80	32	.813	25.6
1987	Detroit	8	5	2	....	467	13	*2	*1.67	227	.943	29.2
1988	Detroit	8	4	3	....	431	22	*1	3.06	171	.871	23.8
1989	Detroit	2	0	1	....	78	7	0	5.38	47	.851	36.2
Playoff Totals		**35**	**11**	**15**	....	**1756**	**92**	**4**	**3.14**	....	....	....
•HARDING, Josh *No Playoffs*												
HARRISON, Paul												
1979	Toronto	2	0	1	....	91	7	0	4.62	....	....	....
1981	Toronto	1	0	0	....	40	1	0	1.50	....	....	....
1982	Buffalo	1	0	0	....	26	1	0	2.31	....	....	....
Playoff Totals		**4**	**0**	**1**	....	**157**	**9**	**0**	**3.44**	....	....	....
HASEK, Dominik												
1991	Chicago	3	0	0	....	69	3	0	2.61	39	.923	33.9
1992	Chicago	3	0	2	....	158	8	0	3.04	70	.886	26.6
1993	Buffalo	1	1	0	....	45	1	0	1.33	24	.958	32.0
1994	Buffalo	7	3	4	....	484	13	2	*1.61	261	.950	32.4
1995	Buffalo	5	1	4	....	309	18	0	3.50	131	.863	25.4
1997	Buffalo	3	1	1	....	153	5	0	1.96	68	.926	26.7
1998	Buffalo	15	10	5	....	948	32	1	2.03	514	.938	32.5
1999	Buffalo	19	13	6	....	1217	36	2	1.77	587	.939	28.9
2000	Buffalo	5	1	4	....	301	12	0	2.39	147	.918	29.3
2001	Buffalo	13	7	6	....	833	29	1	2.09	347	.916	25.0
2002♦	Detroit	*23	*16	7	....	*1455	45	*6	1.86	562	.920	23.2
Playoff Totals		**97**	**53**	**39**	....	**5972**	**202**	**12**	**2.03**	**2750**	**.927**	**27.6**
HAYWARD, Brian												
1983	Winnipeg	3	0	3	....	160	14	0	5.25	....	....	....
1985	Winnipeg	6	2	4	....	309	23	0	4.47	156	.853	30.3
1986	Winnipeg	2	0	1	....	68	6	0	5.29	31	.806	27.4
1987	Montreal	13	6	5	....	708	32	0	2.71	308	.896	26.1
1988	Montreal	4	2	2	....	230	9	0	2.35	85	.894	22.2
1989	Montreal	2	1	1	....	124	7	0	3.39	54	.870	26.1
1990	Montreal	1	0	0	....	33	2	0	3.64	18	.889	32.7
1991	Minnesota	6	0	2	....	171	11	0	3.86	75	.853	26.3
Playoff Totals		**37**	**11**	**18**	....	**1803**	**104**	**0**	**3.46**	....	....	....
HEAD, Don *No Playoffs*												
HEALY, Glenn												
1988	Los Angeles	4	1	3	....	240	20	0	5.00	128	.844	32.0
1989	Los Angeles	3	0	1	....	97	6	0	3.71	59	.898	36.5
1990	NY Islanders	4	1	2	....	166	9	0	3.25	79	.886	28.6
1993	NY Islanders	18	9	8	....	1109	59	0	3.19	524	.887	28.3
1994♦	NY Rangers	2	0	0	....	68	1	0	0.88	17	.941	15.0
1995	NY Rangers	5	2	1	....	230	13	0	3.39	93	.860	24.3
1999	Toronto	1	0	0	....	20	0	0	0.00	5	1.000	15.0
Playoff Totals		**37**	**13**	**15**	....	**1930**	**108**	**0**	**3.36**	**905**	**.881**	**28.1**
HEBERT, Guy												
1993	St. Louis	1	0	0	....	2	0	0	0.00	1	1.000	30.0
1997	Anaheim	9	4	4	....	534	18	1	2.02	255	.929	28.7
1999	Anaheim	4	0	3	....	208	15	0	4.33	124	.879	35.8
Playoff Totals		**14**	**4**	**7**	....	**744**	**33**	**1**	**2.66**	**380**	**.913**	**30.6**
HEBERT, Sammy *Backup goalie on Cup-winning team*												
1918♦	Toronto	....	....	....	....	....	....	....	....	....	....	....
•HEDBERG, Johan												
2001	Pittsburgh	18	9	9	....	1123	43	2	2.30	482	.911	25.8
Playoff Totals		**18**	**9**	**9**	....	**1123**	**43**	**2**	**2.30**	**482**	**.911**	**25.8**
HEINZ, Rick												
1984	St. Louis	1	0	0	....	8	1	0	7.50	....	....	....
Playoff Totals		**1**	**0**	**0**	....	**8**	**1**	**0**	**7.50**	....	....	....
HENDERSON, John												
1955	Boston	2	0	2	....	120	8	0	4.00	....	....	....
Playoff Totals		**2**	**0**	**2**	....	**120**	**8**	**0**	**4.00**	....	....	....
HENRY, Gord												
1951	Boston	2	0	2	....	120	10	0	5.00	....	....	....
1953	Boston	3	0	2	....	163	11	0	4.05	....	....	....
Playoff Totals		**5**	**0**	**4**	....	**283**	**21**	**0**	**4.45**	....	....	....
HENRY, Jim												
1942	NY Rangers	6	2	4	....	360	13	*1	*2.17	....	....	....
1952	Boston	7	3	4	....	448	18	1	2.41	....	....	....
1953	Boston	*9	5	4	....	*510	26	0	3.06	....	....	....
1954	Boston	4	0	4	....	240	16	0	4.00	....	....	....
1955	Boston	3	1	2	....	183	8	0	2.62	....	....	....
Playoff Totals		**29**	**11**	**18**	....	**1741**	**81**	**2**	**2.79**	....	....	....
HERRON, Denis												
1977	Pittsburgh	3	1	2	....	180	11	0	3.67	....	....	....
1979	Pittsburgh	7	2	5	....	421	24	0	3.42	....	....	....
1980	Montreal	5	2	3	....	300	15	0	3.00	....	....	....
Playoff Totals		**15**	**5**	**10**	....	**901**	**50**	**0**	**3.33**	....	....	....

Season	Team	GP	W	L	T	Mins	GA	SO	Avg	SA	S%	SAPG
HEXTALL, Ron												
1987	Philadelphia	*26	15	11	....	*1540	71	*2	2.77	769	.908	30.0
1988	Philadelphia	7	2	4	....	379	30	0	4.75	196	.847	31.0
1989	Philadelphia	15	8	7	....	886	49	0	3.32	445	.890	30.1
1993	Quebec	6	2	4	....	372	18	0	2.90	211	.915	34.0
1994	NY Islanders	3	0	3	....	158	16	0	6.08	80	.800	30.4
1995	Philadelphia	15	10	5	....	897	42	0	2.81	437	.904	29.2
1996	Philadelphia	12	6	6	....	760	27	0	2.13	319	.915	25.2
1997	Philadelphia	8	4	3	....	444	22	0	2.97	203	.892	27.4
1998	Philadelphia	1	0	0	....	20	1	0	3.00	8	.875	24.0
Playoff Totals		**93**	**47**	**43**	....	**5456**	**276**	**2**	**3.04**	**2668**	**.897**	**29.3**
HIGHTON, Hec *No Playoffs*												
•HIRSCH, Corey												
1996	Vancouver	6	2	3	....	338	21	0	3.73	166	.873	29.5
Playoff Totals		**6**	**2**	**3**	....	**338**	**21**	**0**	**3.73**	**166**	**.873**	**29.5**
•HNILICKA, Milan *No Playoffs*												
HODGE, Charlie												
1955	Montreal	4	1	2	....	84	6	0	4.29	....	....	....
1956♦	Montreal	....	....	....	....	....	....	....	....	....	....	....
1959♦	Montreal	....	....	....	....	....	....	....	....	....	....	....
1960♦	Montreal	....	....	....	....	....	....	....	....	....	....	....
1964	Montreal	7	3	4	....	420	16	1	2.29	....	....	....
1965♦	Montreal	5	3	2	....	300	10	1	2.00	....	....	....
1966♦	Montreal	....	....	....	....	....	....	....	....	....	....	....
Playoff Totals		**16**	**7**	**8**	....	**804**	**32**	**2**	**2.39**	....	....	....
•HODSON, Jamie *No Playoffs*												
•HODSON, Kevin												
1997♦	Detroit	....	....	....	....	....	....	....	....	....	....	....
1998♦	Detroit	1	0	0	....	1	0	0	0.00	0	.000	0.0
Playoff Totals		**1**	**0**	**0**	....	**1**	**0**	**0**	**0.00**	**0**	**.000**	**0.0**
HOFFORT, Bruce *No Playoffs*												
HOGANSON, Paul *No Playoffs*												
HOGOSTA, Goran *No Playoffs*												
HOLDEN, Mark *No Playoffs*												
HOLLAND, Ken *No Playoffs*												
HOLLAND, Robbie *No Playoffs*												
HOLMES, Hap												
1918♦	Toronto	*2	*1	1	0	*120	7	0	*3.50	....	....	....
Playoff Totals		**2**	**1**	**1**	**0**	**120**	**7**	**0**	**3.50**	....	....	....
•HOLMQVIST, Johan *No Playoffs*												
HRIVNAK, Jim *No Playoffs*												
HRUDEY, Kelly												
1985	NY Islanders	5	1	3	....	281	8	0	1.71	149	.946	31.8
1986	NY Islanders	2	0	2	....	120	6	0	3.00	59	.898	29.5
1987	NY Islanders	14	7	7	....	842	38	0	2.71	464	.918	33.1
1988	NY Islanders	6	2	4	....	381	23	0	3.62	154	.851	24.3
1989	Los Angeles	10	4	6	....	566	35	0	3.71	293	.881	31.1
1990	Los Angeles	9	4	4	....	539	39	0	4.34	265	.853	29.5
1991	Los Angeles	12	6	6	....	798	37	0	2.78	382	.903	28.7
1992	Los Angeles	6	2	4	....	355	22	0	3.72	179	.877	30.3
1993	Los Angeles	20	10	10	....	1261	74	0	3.52	656	.887	31.2
1998	San Jose	1	0	0	....	20	1	0	3.00	6	.833	18.0
Playoff Totals		**85**	**36**	**46**	....	**5163**	**283**	**0**	**3.29**	**2607**	**.891**	**30.3**
•HUET, Cristobal *No Playoffs*												
•HURME, Jani *No Playoffs*												
ING, Peter *No Playoffs*												
INNESS, Gary												
1975	Pittsburgh	9	5	4	....	540	24	0	2.67	....	....	....
Playoff Totals		**9**	**5**	**4**	....	**540**	**24**	**0**	**2.67**	....	....	....
•IRBE, Arturs												
1994	San Jose	14	7	7	....	806	50	0	3.72	399	.875	29.7
1995	San Jose	6	2	4	....	316	27	0	5.13	184	.853	34.9
1997	Dallas	1	0	0	....	13	0	0	0.00	4	1.000	18.5
1999	Carolina	6	2	4	....	408	15	0	2.21	181	.917	26.6
2001	Carolina	6	2	4	....	360	20	0	3.33	201	.900	33.5
2002	Carolina	18	10	8	....	1078	30	1	1.67	480	.938	26.7
Playoff Totals		**51**	**23**	**27**	....	**2981**	**142**	**1**	**2.86**	**1449**	**.902**	**29.2**
IRELAND, Randy *No Playoffs*												
IRONS, Robbie *No Playoffs*												
IRONSTONE, Joe *No Playoffs*												
JABLONSKI, Pat												
1991	St. Louis	3	0	0	....	90	5	0	3.33	35	.857	23.3
1996	Montreal	1	0	0	....	49	1	0	1.22	17	.941	20.8
Playoff Totals		**4**	**0**	**0**	....	**139**	**6**	**0**	**2.59**	**52**	**.885**	**22.4**
JACKSON, Doug *No Playoffs*												
JACKSON, Percy *No Playoffs*												
JAKS, Pauli *No Playoffs*												
JANASZAK, Steve *No Playoffs*												
JANECYK, Bob												
1985	Los Angeles	3	0	3	....	184	10	0	3.26	100	.900	32.6
Playoff Totals		**3**	**0**	**3**	....	**184**	**10**	**0**	**3.26**	**100**	**.900**	**32.6**
JENSEN, Al												
1983	Washington	3	1	2	....	139	10	0	4.32	....	....	....
1984	Washington	6	3	1	....	258	14	0	3.26	120	.883	27.9
1985	Washington	3	1	2	....	201	8	0	2.39	86	.907	25.7
Playoff Totals		**12**	**5**	**5**	....	**598**	**32**	**0**	**3.21**	....	....	....
JENSEN, Darren *No Playoffs*												
JOHNSON, Bob *No Playoffs*												
•JOHNSON, Brent												
2001	St. Louis	2	0	1	....	62	2	0	1.94	36	.944	34.8
2002	St. Louis	10	5	5	....	590	18	3	1.83	252	.929	25.6
Playoff Totals		**12**	**5**	**6**	....	**652**	**20**	**3**	**1.84**	**288**	**.931**	**26.5**
JOHNSTON, Eddie												
1969	Boston	1	0	1	....	65	4	0	3.69	....	....	....
1970♦	Boston	1	0	1	....	60	4	0	4.00	....	....	....
1971	Boston	1	0	1	....	60	7	0	7.00	....	....	....
1972♦	Boston	7	*6	1	....	420	13	1	*1.86	....	....	....
1973	Boston	3	1	2	....	160	9	0	3.38	....	....	....
1974	Toronto	1	0	1	....	60	6	0	6.00	....	....	....
1975	St. Louis	1	0	1	....	60	5	0	5.00	....	....	....
1977	St. Louis	3	0	2	....	138	9	0	3.91	....	....	....
Playoff Totals		**18**	**7**	**10**	....	**1023**	**57**	**1**	**3.34**	....	....	....
•JOSEPH, Curtis												
1990	St. Louis	6	4	1	....	327	18	0	3.30	167	.892	30.6
1992	St. Louis	6	2	4	....	379	23	0	3.64	217	.894	34.4
1993	St. Louis	11	7	4	....	715	27	*2	2.27	438	.938	36.8
1994	St. Louis	4	0	4	....	246	15	0	3.66	158	.905	38.5
1995	St. Louis	7	3	3	....	392	24	0	3.67	178	.865	27.2
1997	Edmonton	12	5	7	....	767	36	2	2.82	405	.911	31.7
1998	Edmonton	12	5	7	....	716	23	3	1.93	319	.928	26.7
1999	Toronto	17	9	8	....	1011	41	1	2.43	440	.907	26.1
2000	Toronto	12	6	6	....	729	25	1	2.06	369	.932	30.4
2001	Toronto	11	7	4	....	685	24	3	2.10	329	.927	28.8
2002	Toronto	20	10	10	....	1253	48	3	2.30	557	.914	26.7
Playoff Totals		**118**	**58**	**58**	....	**7220**	**304**	**15**	**2.53**	**3577**	**.915**	**29.7**
JUNKIN, Joe *No Playoffs*												
KAARELA, Jari *No Playoffs*												
KAMPPURI, Hannu *No Playoffs*												
KARAKAS, Mike												
1936	Chicago	2	1	1	0	120	7	0	3.50	....	....	....
1938♦	Chicago	*8	*6	2	....	*525	15	*2	1.71	....	....	....
1944	Chicago	*9	4	5	....	*549	24	*1	2.62	....	....	....
1946	Chicago	4	0	4	....	240	26	0	6.50	....	....	....
Playoff Totals		**23**	**11**	**12**	**0**	**1434**	**72**	**3**	**3.01**	....	....	....
KEANS, Doug												
1980	Los Angeles	1	0	1	....	40	7	0	10.50	....	....	....
1982	Los Angeles	2	0	1	....	32	1	0	1.88	....	....	....
1985	Boston	4	2	2	....	240	15	0	3.75	110	.864	27.5
1987	Boston	2	0	2	....	120	11	0	5.50	58	.810	29.0
Playoff Totals		**9**	**2**	**6**	....	**432**	**34**	**0**	**4.72**	....	....	....
KEENAN, Don *No Playoffs*												
KERR, Dave												
1931	Mtl. Maroons	2	0	2	0	120	8	0	4.00	....	....	....
1933	Mtl. Maroons	2	0	2	0	120	5	0	2.50	....	....	....
1934	Mtl. Maroons	4	1	2	1	240	7	1	1.75	....	....	....
1935	NY Rangers	4	1	1	2	240	10	0	2.50	....	....	....
1937	NY Rangers	*9	*6	3	....	*553	10	*4	*1.08	....	....	....
1938	NY Rangers	3	1	2	....	262	8	0	1.83	....	....	....
1939	NY Rangers	1	0	1	....	119	2	0	1.01	....	....	....
1940♦	NY Rangers	*12	*8	4	....	*770	20	*3	*1.56	....	....	....
1941	NY Rangers	3	1	2	....	192	6	0	1.88	....	....	....
Playoff Totals		**40**	**18**	**19**	**3**	**2616**	**76**	**8**	**1.74**	....	....	....
•KHABIBULIN, Nikolai												
1996	Winnipeg	6	2	4	....	359	19	0	3.18	214	.911	35.8
1997	Phoenix	7	3	4	....	426	15	1	2.11	222	.932	31.3
1998	Phoenix	4	2	1	....	185	13	0	4.22	106	.877	34.4
1999	Phoenix	7	3	4	....	449	18	0	2.41	236	.924	31.5
Playoff Totals		**24**	**10**	**13**	....	**1419**	**65**	**1**	**2.75**	**778**	**.916**	**32.9**
•KIDD, Trevor												
1995	Calgary	7	3	4	....	434	26	1	3.59	181	.856	25.0
1996	Calgary	2	0	1	....	83	9	0	6.51	40	.775	28.9
Playoff Totals		**9**	**3**	**5**	....	**517**	**35**	**1**	**4.06**	**221**	**.842**	**25.6**
KING, Scott *No Playoffs*												
•KIPRUSOFF, Miikka												
2001	San Jose	3	1	1	....	149	5	0	2.01	79	.937	31.8
2002	San Jose	1	0	0	....	8	0	0	0.00	2	1.000	15.0
Playoff Totals		**4**	**1**	**1**	....	**157**	**5**	**0**	**1.91**	**81**	**.938**	**31.0**
KLEISINGER, Terry *No Playoffs*												
KLYMKIW, Julian *No Playoffs*												
KNICKLE, Rick *No Playoffs*												
•KOCHAN, Dieter *No Playoffs*												
•KOLZIG, Olaf												
1995	Washington	2	1	0	....	44	1	0	1.36	21	.952	28.6
1996	Washington	5	2	3	....	341	11	0	*1.94	167	.934	29.4
1998	Washington	21	12	9	....	1351	44	*4	1.95	740	.941	32.9
2000	Washington	5	1	4	....	284	16	0	3.38	103	.845	21.8
2001	Washington	6	2	4	....	375	14	1	2.24	153	.908	24.5
Playoff Totals		**39**	**18**	**20**	....	**2395**	**86**	**5**	**2.15**	**1184**	**.927**	**29.7**
•KONSTANTINOV, Evgeny *No Playoffs*												

Season	Team	GP	W	L	T	Mins	GA	SO	Avg	SA	S%	SAPG
KUNTAR, Les *No Playoffs*												
KURT, Gary *No Playoffs*												
•LABARBERA, Jason *No Playoffs*												
•LABBE, Jean-Francois *No Playoffs*												
LABRECQUE, Patrick *No Playoffs*												
LACHER, Blaine												
1995	Boston	5	1	4	....	283	12	0	2.54	125	.904	26.5
Playoff Totals		**5**	**1**	**4**	....	**283**	**12**	**0**	**2.54**	**125**	**.904**	**26.5**
LACROIX, Frenchy *No Playoffs*												
LaFERRIERE, Rick *No Playoffs*												
LaFOREST, Mark												
1988	Philadelphia	2	1	0	....	48	1	0	1.25	12	.917	15.0
Playoff Totals		**2**	**1**	**0**	....	**48**	**1**	**0**	**1.25**	**12**	**.917**	**15.0**
•LAJEUNESSE, Simon *No Playoffs*												
•LALIME, Patrick												
2001	Ottawa	4	0	4	....	251	10	0	2.39	99	.899	23.7
2002	Ottawa	12	7	5	....	778	18	4	*1.39	332	.946	25.6
Playoff Totals		**16**	**7**	**9**	....	**1029**	**28**	**4**	**1.63**	**431**	**.935**	**25.1**
•LAMOTHE, Marc *No Playoffs*												
•LANGKOW, Scott *No Playoffs*												
LAROCQUE, Michel												
1974	Montreal	6	2	4	....	364	18	0	2.97	....	....	....
1976♦	Montreal	....	....	....	....	....	....	....	....	....	....	....
1977♦	Montreal	....	....	....	....	....	....	....	....	....	....	....
1978♦	Montreal	....	....	....	....	....	....	....	....	....	....	....
1979♦	Montreal	1	0	0	....	20	0	0	0.00	....	....	....
1980	Montreal	5	4	1	....	300	11	1	2.20	....	....	....
1981	Toronto	2	0	1	....	75	8	0	6.40	....	....	....
Playoff Totals		**14**	**6**	**6**	....	**759**	**37**	**1**	**2.92**	....	....	....
LAROCQUE, Michel *No Playoffs*												
•LASAK, Jan *No Playoffs*												
LASKOWSKI, Gary *No Playoffs*												
LAXTON, Gord *No Playoffs*												
LeBLANC, Ray *No Playoffs*												
•LECLAIRE, Pascal *No Playoffs*												
•LEGACE, Manny												
2002♦	Detroit	1	0	0	....	11	1	0	5.45	2	.500	10.9
Playoff Totals		**1**	**0**	**0**	....	**11**	**1**	**0**	**5.45**	**2**	**.500**	**10.9**
LEGRIS, Claude *No Playoffs*												
LEHMAN, Hugh												
1927	Chicago	2	0	1	1	120	10	0	5.00	....	....	....
Playoff Totals		**2**	**0**	**1**	**1**	**120**	**10**	**0**	**5.00**	....	....	....
LEMELIN, Reggie												
1979	Atlanta	1	0	0	....	20	0	0	0.00	....	....	....
1981	Calgary	6	3	3	....	366	22	0	3.61	....	....	....
1983	Calgary	7	3	3	....	327	27	0	4.95	....	....	....
1984	Calgary	8	4	4	....	448	32	0	4.29	290	.890	38.8
1985	Calgary	4	1	3	....	248	15	1	3.63	128	.883	31.0
1986	Calgary	3	0	1	....	109	7	0	3.85	48	.854	26.4
1987	Calgary	2	0	1	....	101	6	0	3.56	47	.872	27.9
1988	Boston	17	11	6	....	1027	45	*1	*2.63	430	.895	25.1
1989	Boston	4	1	3	....	252	16	0	3.81	112	.857	26.7
1990	Boston	3	0	1	....	135	13	0	5.78	57	.772	25.3
1991	Boston	2	0	0	....	32	0	0	0.00	18	1.000	33.8
1992	Boston	2	0	0	....	54	3	0	3.33	23	.870	25.6
Playoff Totals		**59**	**23**	**25**	....	**3119**	**186**	**2**	**3.58**	....	....	....
LENARDUZZI, Mike *No Playoffs*												
LESSARD, Mario												
1979	Los Angeles	2	0	2	....	126	8	0	3.81	....	....	....
1980	Los Angeles	4	1	2	....	207	14	0	4.06	....	....	....
1981	Los Angeles	4	1	3	....	220	20	0	5.45	....	....	....
1982	Los Angeles	10	4	5	....	583	41	0	4.22	....	....	....
Playoff Totals		**20**	**6**	**12**	....	**1136**	**83**	**0**	**4.38**	....	....	....
LEVASSEUR, Jean-Louis *No Playoffs*												
LINDBERGH, Pelle												
1983	Philadelphia	3	0	3	....	180	18	0	6.00	....	....	....
1984	Philadelphia	2	0	1	....	26	3	0	6.92	13	.769	30.0
1985	Philadelphia	*18	12	6	....	1008	42	*3	2.50	490	.914	29.2
Playoff Totals		**23**	**12**	**10**	....	**1214**	**63**	**3**	**3.11**	....	....	....
LINDSAY, Bert *No Playoffs*												
•LITTLE, Neil *No Playoffs*												
LITTMAN, David *No Playoffs*												
LIUT, Mike												
1980	St. Louis	3	0	3	....	193	12	0	3.73	....	....	....
1981	St. Louis	11	5	6	....	685	50	0	4.38	....	....	....
1982	St. Louis	10	5	3	....	494	27	0	3.28	....	....	....
1983	St. Louis	4	1	3	....	240	15	0	3.75	....	....	....
1984	St. Louis	11	6	5	....	714	29	1	2.44	362	.920	30.4
1986	Hartford	8	5	2	....	441	14	*1	*1.90	226	.938	30.7
1987	Hartford	6	2	4	....	332	25	0	4.52	159	.843	28.7
1988	Hartford	3	1	1	....	160	11	0	4.13	82	.866	30.8
1990	Washington	9	4	4	....	507	28	0	3.31	223	.874	26.4
1991	Washington	2	0	1	....	48	4	0	5.00	30	.867	37.5
Playoff Totals		**67**	**29**	**32**	....	**3814**	**215**	**2**	**3.38**	....	....	....
LOCKETT, Ken												
1975	Vancouver	1	0	1	....	60	6	0	6.00	....	....	....
Playoff Totals		**1**	**0**	**1**	....	**60**	**6**	**0**	**6.00**	....	....	....
LOCKHART, Howard *No Playoffs*												
LoPRESTI, Pete												
1977	Minnesota	2	0	2	....	77	6	0	4.68	....	....	....
Playoff Totals		**2**	**0**	**2**	....	**77**	**6**	**0**	**4.68**	....	....	....
LoPRESTI, Sam												
1941	Chicago	5	2	3	....	343	12	0	2.10	....	....	....
1942	Chicago	3	1	2	....	187	5	*1	1.60	....	....	....
Playoff Totals		**8**	**3**	**5**	....	**530**	**17**	**1**	**1.92**	....	....	....
LORENZ, Danny *No Playoffs*												
LOUSTEL, Ron *No Playoffs*												
LOW, Ron												
1978	Detroit	4	1	3	....	240	17	0	4.25	....	....	....
1980	Edmonton	3	0	3	....	212	12	0	3.40	....	....	....
Playoff Totals		**7**	**1**	**6**	....	**452**	**29**	**0**	**3.85**	....	....	....
LOZINSKI, Larry *No Playoffs*												
LUMLEY, Harry												
1945	Detroit	*14	7	7	....	*871	31	2	*2.14	....	....	....
1946	Detroit	5	1	4	....	310	16	*1	3.10	....	....	....
1948	Detroit	*10	4	6	....	*600	30	0	3.00	....	....	....
1949	Detroit	*11	4	7	....	*726	26	0	2.15	....	....	....
1950♦	Detroit	*14	*8	6	....	910	28	*3	1.85	....	....	....
1954	Toronto	5	1	4	....	321	15	0	2.80	....	....	....
1955	Toronto	4	0	4	....	240	14	0	3.50	....	....	....
1956	Toronto	5	1	4	....	304	13	1	2.57	....	....	....
1958	Boston	1	0	1	....	60	5	0	5.00	....	....	....
1959	Boston	7	3	4	....	436	20	0	2.75	....	....	....
Playoff Totals		**76**	**29**	**47**	....	**4778**	**198**	**7**	**2.49**	....	....	....
•LUONGO, Roberto *No Playoffs*												
MacKENZIE, Shawn *No Playoffs*												
MADELEY, Darrin *No Playoffs*												
MALARCHUK, Clint												
1986	Quebec	3	0	2	....	143	11	0	4.62	81	.864	34.0
1987	Quebec	3	0	2	....	140	8	0	3.43	56	.857	24.0
1988	Washington	4	0	2	....	193	15	0	4.66	95	.842	29.5
1989	Buffalo	1	0	1	0	59	5	0	5.08	32	.844	32.5
1991	Buffalo	4	2	2	....	246	17	0	4.15	116	.853	28.3
Playoff Totals		**15**	**2**	**9**	**0**	**781**	**56**	**0**	**4.30**	**380**	**.853**	**29.2**
MANELUK, George *No Playoffs*												
MANIAGO, Cesare												
1961	Toronto	2	1	1	....	145	6	0	2.48	....	....	....
1968	Minnesota	14	7	7	....	893	39	0	2.62	....	....	....
1970	Minnesota	3	1	2	....	180	6	*1	2.00	....	....	....
1971	Minnesota	8	3	5	....	480	28	0	3.50	....	....	....
1972	Minnesota	4	1	3	....	238	12	0	3.03	....	....	....
1973	Minnesota	5	2	3	....	309	9	*2	*1.75	....	....	....
Playoff Totals		**36**	**15**	**21**	....	**2245**	**100**	**3**	**2.67**	....	....	....
•MARACLE, Norm												
1999	Detroit	2	0	0	....	58	3	0	3.10	22	.864	22.8
Playoff Totals		**2**	**0**	**0**	....	**58**	**3**	**0**	**3.10**	**22**	**.864**	**22.8**
•MARKKANEN, Jussi *No Playoffs*												
MAROIS, Jean *No Playoffs*												
MARTIN, Seth												
1968	St. Louis	2	0	0	....	73	5	0	4.11	....	....	....
Playoff Totals		**2**	**0**	**0**	....	**73**	**5**	**0**	**4.11**	....	....	....
MASON, Bob												
1987	Washington	4	2	2	....	309	9	1	1.75	143	.937	27.8
1988	Chicago	1	0	1	....	60	3	0	3.00	31	.903	31.0
Playoff Totals		**5**	**2**	**3**	....	**369**	**12**	**1**	**1.95**	**174**	**.931**	**28.3**
•MASON, Chris *No Playoffs*												
MATTSSON, Markus *No Playoffs*												
MAY, Darrell *No Playoffs*												
MAYER, Gilles *No Playoffs*												
McAULEY, Ken *No Playoffs*												
McCARTAN, Jack *No Playoffs*												
McCOOL, Frank												
1945♦	Toronto	13	*8	5	....	807	30	*4	2.23	....	....	....
Playoff Totals		**13**	**8**	**5**	....	**807**	**30**	**4**	**2.23**	....	....	....
McDUFFE, Peter												
1972	St. Louis	1	0	1	....	60	7	0	7.00	....	....	....
Playoff Totals		**1**	**0**	**1**	....	**60**	**7**	**0**	**7.00**	....	....	....
McGRATTAN, Tom *No Playoffs*												
McKAY, Ross *No Playoffs*												
McKENZIE, Bill *No Playoffs*												
McKICHAN, Steve *No Playoffs*												
McLACHLAN, Murray *No Playoffs*												

Season	Team	GP	W	L	T	Mins	GA	SO	Avg	SA	S%	SAPG
McLEAN, Kirk												
1989	Vancouver	5	2	3	....	302	18	0	3.58	167	.892	33.2
1991	Vancouver	2	1	1	....	123	7	0	3.41	66	.894	32.2
1992	Vancouver	13	6	7	....	785	33	*2	2.52	364	.909	27.8
1993	Vancouver	12	6	6	....	754	42	0	3.34	369	.886	29.4
1994	Vancouver	*24	15	9	....	*1544	59	*4	2.29	820	.928	31.9
1995	Vancouver	11	4	7	....	660	36	0	3.27	336	.893	30.5
1996	Vancouver	1	0	1	....	21	3	0	8.57	12	.750	34.3
Playoff Totals		**68**	**34**	**34**	....	**4189**	**198**	**6**	**2.84**	**2134**	**.907**	**30.6**
McLELLAND, Dave *No Playoffs*												
•McLENNAN, Jamie												
1994	NY Islanders	2	0	1	....	82	6	0	4.39	47	.872	34.4
1998	St. Louis	1	0	0	....	14	1	0	4.29	4	.750	17.1
1999	St. Louis	1	0	1	....	37	0	0	0.00	7	1.000	11.4
Playoff Totals		**4**	**0**	**2**	....	**133**	**7**	**0**	**3.16**	**58**	**.879**	**26.2**
McLEOD, Don *No Playoffs*												
McLEOD, Jim *No Playoffs*												
McNAMARA, Gerry *No Playoffs*												
McNEIL, Gerry												
1950	Montreal	2	1	1	....	135	5	0	2.22	....	....	....
1951	Montreal	*11	*5	6	....	*785	25	1	1.91	....	....	....
1952	Montreal	*11	4	7	....	*688	23	1	2.01	....	....	....
1953♦	Montreal	8	*5	3	....	486	16	*2	1.98	....	....	....
1954	Montreal	3	2	1	....	190	3	1	0.95	....	....	....
1957♦	Montreal	....	....	....	....	....	....	....	....	....	....	....
1958♦	Montreal	....	....	....	....	....	....	....	....	....	....	....
Playoff Totals		**35**	**17**	**18**	....	**2284**	**72**	**5**	**1.89**	....	....	....
McRAE, Gord												
1975	Toronto	7	2	5	....	441	21	0	2.86	....	....	....
1976	Toronto	1	0	0	....	13	1	0	4.62	....	....	....
Playoff Totals		**8**	**2**	**5**	....	**454**	**22**	**0**	**2.91**	....	....	....
MELANSON, Roland												
1981♦	NY Islanders	3	1	0	....	92	6	0	3.91	....	....	....
1982♦	NY Islanders	3	0	1	....	64	5	0	4.69	....	....	....
1983♦	NY Islanders	5	2	2	....	238	10	0	2.52	....	....	....
1984	NY Islanders	6	0	1	....	87	5	0	3.45	32	.844	22.1
1987	Los Angeles	5	1	4	....	260	24	0	5.54	154	.844	35.5
1988	Los Angeles	1	0	1	....	60	9	0	9.00	50	.820	50.0
Playoff Totals		**23**	**4**	**9**	....	**801**	**59**	**0**	**4.42**	....	....	....
MELOCHE, Gilles												
1980	Minnesota	11	5	4	....	564	34	1	3.62	....	....	....
1981	Minnesota	13	8	5	....	802	47	0	3.52	....	....	....
1982	Minnesota	4	1	2	....	184	8	0	2.61	....	....	....
1983	Minnesota	5	2	3	....	319	18	0	3.39	....	....	....
1984	Minnesota	4	1	2	....	200	11	0	3.30	88	.875	26.4
1985	Minnesota	8	4	3	....	395	25	1	3.80	256	.902	38.9
Playoff Totals		**45**	**21**	**19**	....	**2464**	**143**	**2**	**3.48**	....	....	....
MICALEF, Corrado												
1984	Detroit	1	0	0	....	7	2	0	17.14	5	.600	42.9
1985	Detroit	2	0	0	....	42	6	0	8.57	18	.667	25.7
Playoff Totals		**3**	**0**	**0**	....	**49**	**8**	**0**	**9.80**	**23**	**.652**	**28.2**
•MICHAUD, Alfie *No Playoffs*												
•MICHAUD, Olivier *No Playoffs*												
MIDDLEBROOK, Lindsay *No Playoffs*												
MILLAR, Al *No Playoffs*												
MILLEN, Greg												
1980	Pittsburgh	5	2	3	....	300	21	0	4.20	....	....	....
1981	Pittsburgh	5	2	3	....	325	19	0	3.51	....	....	....
1985	St. Louis	1	0	1	....	60	2	0	2.00	35	.943	35.0
1986	St. Louis	10	6	3	....	586	29	0	2.97	330	.912	33.8
1987	St. Louis	4	1	3	....	250	10	0	2.40	122	.918	29.3
1988	St. Louis	10	5	5	....	600	38	0	3.80	252	.849	25.2
1989	St. Louis	10	5	5	....	649	34	0	3.14	308	.890	28.5
1990	Chicago	14	6	6	....	613	40	0	3.92	300	.867	29.4
Playoff Totals		**59**	**27**	**29**	....	**3383**	**193**	**0**	**3.42**	....	....	....
MILLER, Joe												
1928♦	NY Rangers	3	2	1	0	180	3	1	1.00	....	....	....
Playoff Totals		**3**	**2**	**1**	**0**	**180**	**3**	**1**	**1.00**	....	....	....
•MILLER, Ryan *No Playoffs*												
•MINARD, Mike *No Playoffs*												
MIO, Eddie												
1982	NY Rangers	8	4	3	....	443	28	0	3.79	....	....	....
1983	NY Rangers	8	5	3	....	480	32	0	4.00	....	....	....
1984	Detroit	1	0	1	....	63	3	0	2.86	24	.875	22.9
Playoff Totals		**17**	**9**	**7**	....	**986**	**63**	**0**	**3.83**	....	....	....
MITCHELL, Ivan *No Playoffs*												
1922♦	Toronto	....	....	....	....	....	....	....	....	....	....	....
MOFFAT, Mike												
1982	Boston	11	6	5	....	663	38	0	3.44	....	....	....
Playoff Totals		**11**	**6**	**5**	....	**663**	**38**	**0**	**3.44**	....	....	....

Season	Team	GP	W	L	T	Mins	GA	SO	Avg	SA	S%	SAPG
MOOG, Andy												
1981	Edmonton	9	5	4	....	526	32	0	3.65	....	....	....
1983	Edmonton	16	11	5	....	949	48	0	3.03	....	....	....
1984♦	Edmonton	7	4	0	....	263	12	0	2.74	110	.891	25.1
1985♦	Edmonton	2	0	0	....	20	0	0	0.00	3	1.000	9.0
1986	Edmonton	1	1	0	....	60	1	0	1.00	27	.963	27.0
1987♦	Edmonton	2	2	0	....	120	8	0	4.00	37	.784	18.5
1988	Boston	7	1	4	....	354	25	0	4.24	166	.849	28.1
1989	Boston	6	4	2	....	359	14	0	2.34	136	.897	22.7
1990	Boston	20	13	7	....	1195	44	*2	*2.21	486	.909	24.4
1991	Boston	19	10	9	....	1133	60	0	3.18	569	.895	30.1
1992	Boston	15	8	7	....	866	46	1	3.19	385	.881	26.7
1993	Boston	3	0	3	....	161	14	0	5.22	67	.791	25.0
1994	Dallas	4	1	3	....	246	12	0	2.93	121	.901	29.5
1995	Dallas	5	1	4	....	277	16	0	3.47	169	.905	36.6
1997	Dallas	7	3	4	....	449	21	0	2.81	214	.902	28.6
1998	Montreal	9	4	5	....	474	24	1	3.04	204	.882	25.8
Playoff Totals		**132**	**68**	**57**	....	**7452**	**377**	**4**	**3.04**	....	....	....
MOORE, Alfie												
1938♦	Chicago	1	1	0	....	60	1	0	1.00	....	....	....
1939	NY Americans	2	0	2	....	120	6	0	3.00	....	....	....
Playoff Totals		**3**	**1**	**2**	....	**180**	**7**	**0**	**2.33**	....	....	....
MOORE, Robbie												
1979	Philadelphia	5	3	2	....	268	18	0	4.03	....	....	....
Playoff Totals		**5**	**3**	**2**	....	**268**	**18**	**0**	**4.03**	....	....	....
MORISSETTE, Jean-Guy *No Playoffs*												
•MOSS, Tyler *No Playoffs*												
MOWERS, Johnny												
1941	Detroit	9	4	5	....	561	20	0	2.14	....	....	....
1942	Detroit	12	7	5	....	720	38	0	3.17	....	....	....
1943♦	Detroit	*10	*8	2	....	*679	22	*2	*1.94	....	....	....
1947	Detroit	1	0	1	....	40	5	0	7.50	....	....	....
Playoff Totals		**32**	**19**	**13**	....	**2000**	**85**	**2**	**2.55**	....	....	....
MRAZEK, Jerome *No Playoffs*												
MURPHY, Hal *No Playoffs*												
MURRAY, Mickey *No Playoffs*												
MUZZATTI, Jason *No Playoffs*												
MYLLYS, Jarmo *No Playoffs*												
MYLNIKOV, Sergei *No Playoffs*												
MYRE, Phil												
1971♦	Montreal	....	....	....	....	....	....	....	....	....	....	....
1974	Atlanta	3	0	3	....	186	13	0	4.19	....	....	....
1977	Atlanta	2	1	1	....	120	5	0	2.50	....	....	....
1980	Philadelphia	6	5	1	....	384	16	1	2.50	....	....	....
1983	Buffalo	1	0	0	....	57	7	0	7.37	....	....	....
Playoff Totals		**12**	**6**	**5**	....	**747**	**41**	**1**	**3.29**	....	....	....
•NABOKOV, Evgeni												
2000	San Jose	1	0	0	....	20	0	0	0.00	10	1.000	30.0
2001	San Jose	4	1	3	....	218	10	1	2.75	103	.903	28.3
2002	San Jose	12	7	5	....	712	31	0	2.61	322	.904	27.1
Playoff Totals		**17**	**8**	**8**	....	**950**	**41**	**1**	**2.59**	**435**	**.906**	**27.5**
•NAUMENKO, Gregg *No Playoffs*												
NEWTON, Cam *No Playoffs*												
•NORONEN, Mika *No Playoffs*												
NORRIS, Jack *No Playoffs*												
•NURMINEN, Pasi *No Playoffs*												
OLESCHUK, Bill *No Playoffs*												
OLESEVICH, Dan *No Playoffs*												
O'NEILL, Mike *No Playoffs*												
•OSGOOD, Chris												
1994	Detroit	6	3	2	....	307	12	1	2.35	110	.891	21.5
1995	Detroit	2	0	0	....	68	2	0	1.76	25	.920	22.1
1996	Detroit	15	8	7	....	936	33	2	2.12	322	.898	20.6
1997♦	Detroit	2	0	0	....	47	2	0	2.55	21	.905	26.8
1998♦	Detroit	*22	*16	6	....	*1361	48	2	2.12	588	.918	25.9
1999	Detroit	6	4	2	....	358	14	1	2.35	172	.919	28.8
2000	Detroit	9	5	4	....	547	18	2	1.97	237	.924	26.0
2001	Detroit	6	2	4	....	365	15	1	2.47	158	.905	26.0
2002	NY Islanders	7	3	4	....	392	17	0	2.60	193	.912	29.5
Playoff Totals		**75**	**41**	**29**	....	**4381**	**161**	**9**	**2.20**	**1826**	**.912**	**25.0**
•OUELLET, Maxime *No Playoffs*												
OUIMET, Ted *No Playoffs*												
PAGEAU, Paul *No Playoffs*												
PAILLE, Marcel *No Playoffs*												
PALMATEER, Mike												
1977	Toronto	6	3	3	....	360	16	0	2.67	....	....	....
1978	Toronto	13	6	7	....	795	32	*2	2.42	....	....	....
1979	Toronto	5	2	3	....	298	17	0	3.42	....	....	....
1980	Toronto	1	0	1	....	60	7	0	7.00	....	....	....
1983	Toronto	4	1	3	....	252	17	0	4.05	....	....	....
Playoff Totals		**29**	**12**	**17**	....	**1765**	**89**	**2**	**3.03**	....	....	....
PANG, Darren												
1988	Chicago	4	1	3	....	240	18	0	4.50	130	.862	32.5
1989	Chicago	2	0	0	....	10	0	0	0.00	4	1.000	24.0
Playoff Totals		**6**	**1**	**3**	....	**250**	**18**	**0**	**4.32**	**134**	**.866**	**32.2**

Season	Team	GP	W	L	T	Mins	GA	SO	Avg	SA	S%	SAPG
PARENT, Bernie												
1968	Philadelphia	5	2	3	....	355	8	0	*1.35	....	....	....
1969	Philadelphia	3	0	3	....	180	12	0	4.00	....	....	....
1971	Toronto	4	2	2	....	235	9	0	2.30	....	....	....
1972	Toronto	4	1	3	....	243	13	0	3.21	....	....	....
1974◆	Philadelphia	*17	*12	5	....	*1042	35	*2	2.02	....	....	....
1975◆	Philadelphia	*15	*10	5	....	*922	29	*4	*1.89	....	....	....
1976	Philadelphia	8	4	4	....	480	27	0	3.38	....	....	....
1977	Philadelphia	3	0	3	....	123	8	0	3.90	....	....	....
1978	Philadelphia	12	7	5	....	722	33	0	2.74	....	....	....
Playoff Totals		**71**	**38**	**33**	....	**4302**	**174**	**6**	**2.43**	....	....	....
PARENT, Bob *No Playoffs*												
PARENT, Rich *No Playoffs*												
PARRO, Dave *No Playoffs*												
•PASSMORE, Steve												
2002	Chicago	3	0	2	....	138	6	0	2.61	62	.903	27.0
Playoff Totals		**3**	**0**	**2**	....	**138**	**6**	**0**	**2.61**	**62**	**.903**	**27.0**
PEETERS, Pete												
1980	Philadelphia	13	8	5	....	799	37	1	2.78	....	....	....
1981	Philadelphia	3	2	1	....	180	12	0	4.00	....	....	....
1982	Philadelphia	4	1	2	....	220	17	0	4.64	....	....	....
1983	Boston	*17	9	8	....	*1024	61	1	3.57	....	....	....
1984	Boston	3	0	3	....	180	10	0	3.33	68	.853	22.7
1985	Boston	1	0	1	....	60	4	0	4.00	26	.846	26.0
1986	Washington	9	5	4	....	544	24	0	2.65	253	.905	27.9
1987	Washington	3	1	2	....	180	9	0	3.00	76	.882	25.3
1988	Washington	12	7	5	....	654	34	0	3.12	326	.896	29.9
1989	Washington	6	2	4	....	359	24	0	4.01	164	.854	27.4
Playoff Totals		**71**	**35**	**35**	....	**4200**	**232**	**2**	**3.31**	....	....	....
•PELLETIER, Jean-Marc *No Playoffs*												
PELLETIER, Marcel *No Playoffs*												
PENNEY, Steve												
1984	Montreal	15	9	6	....	871	32	*3	*2.20	354	.910	24.4
1985	Montreal	12	6	6	....	733	40	1	3.27	300	.867	24.6
Playoff Totals		**27**	**15**	**12**	....	**1604**	**72**	**4**	**2.69**	**654**	**.890**	**24.5**
PERREAULT, Bob *No Playoffs*												
PETTIE, Jim *No Playoffs*												
PIETRANGELO, Frank												
1991◆	Pittsburgh	5	4	1	....	288	15	*1	3.13	148	.899	30.8
1992	Hartford	7	3	4	....	425	19	0	2.68	244	.922	34.4
Playoff Totals		**12**	**7**	**5**	....	**713**	**34**	**1**	**2.86**	**392**	**.913**	**33.0**
PLANTE, Jacques												
1953◆	Montreal	4	3	1	....	240	7	1	*1.75	....	....	....
1954	Montreal	8	5	3	....	480	15	*2	1.88	....	....	....
1955	Montreal	*12	6	3	....	639	30	0	2.82	....	....	....
1956◆	Montreal	*10	*8	2	....	600	18	*2	*1.80	....	....	....
1957◆	Montreal	*10	*8	2	....	*616	17	1	*1.66	....	....	....
1958◆	Montreal	10	*8	2	....	618	20	*1	*1.94	....	....	....
1959◆	Montreal	11	*8	3	....	670	26	0	*2.33	....	....	....
1960◆	Montreal	8	*8	0	....	489	11	*3	*1.35	....	....	....
1961	Montreal	6	2	4	....	412	16	0	2.33	....	....	....
1962	Montreal	6	2	4	....	360	19	0	3.17	....	....	....
1963	Montreal	5	1	4	....	300	14	0	2.80	....	....	....
1969	St. Louis	*10	*8	2	....	*589	14	*3	1.43	....	....	....
1970	St. Louis	6	4	1	....	324	8	*1	*1.48	....	....	....
1971	Toronto	3	0	2	....	134	7	0	3.13	....	....	....
1972	Toronto	1	0	1	....	60	5	0	5.00	....	....	....
1973	Boston	2	0	2	....	120	10	0	5.00	....	....	....
Playoff Totals		**112**	**71**	**36**	....	**6651**	**237**	**14**	**2.14**	....	....	....
PLASSE, Michel												
1973◆	Montreal	....	....	....	....	....	....	....	....	....	....	....
1976	Pittsburgh	3	1	2	....	180	8	1	2.67	....	....	....
1981	Quebec	1	0	0	....	15	1	0	4.00	....	....	....
Playoff Totals		**4**	**1**	**2**	....	**195**	**9**	**1**	**2.77**	....	....	....
•POTVIN, Felix												
1993	Toronto	*21	11	10	....	*1308	62	1	2.84	636	.903	29.2
1994	Toronto	18	9	9	....	1124	46	3	2.46	520	.912	27.8
1995	Toronto	7	3	4	....	424	20	1	2.83	253	.921	35.8
1996	Toronto	6	2	4	....	350	19	0	3.26	198	.904	33.9
2001	Los Angeles	13	7	6	....	812	33	2	2.44	361	.909	26.7
2002	Los Angeles	7	3	4	....	417	15	1	2.16	201	.925	28.9
Playoff Totals		**72**	**35**	**37**	....	**4435**	**195**	**8**	**2.64**	**2169**	**.910**	**29.3**
PRONOVOST, Claude *No Playoffs*												
•PRUSEK, Martin *No Playoffs*												
PUPPA, Daren												
1988	Buffalo	3	1	1	....	142	11	0	4.65	67	.836	28.3
1990	Buffalo	6	2	4	....	370	15	0	2.43	192	.922	31.1
1991	Buffalo	2	0	1	....	81	10	0	7.41	46	.783	34.1
1993	Toronto	1	0	0	....	20	1	0	3.00	7	.857	21.0
1996	Tampa Bay	4	1	3	....	173	14	0	4.86	86	.837	29.8
Playoff Totals		**16**	**4**	**9**	....	**786**	**51**	**0**	**3.89**	**398**	**.872**	**30.4**
PUSEY, Chris *No Playoffs*												
RACICOT, Andre												
1991	Montreal	2	0	1	....	12	2	0	10.00	14	.857	70.0
1992	Montreal	1	0	0	....	1	0	0	0.00	1	1.000	60.0
1993◆	Montreal	1	0	0	....	18	2	0	6.67	9	.778	30.0
Playoff Totals		**4**	**0**	**1**	....	**31**	**4**	**0**	**7.74**	**24**	**.833**	**46.5**

Season	Team	GP	W	L	T	Mins	GA	SO	Avg	SA	S%	SAPG
RACINE, Bruce												
1996	St. Louis	1	0	0	....	1	0	0	0.00	0	.000	0.0
Playoff Totals		**1**	**0**	**0**	....	**1**	**0**	**0**	**0.00**	**0**	**.000**	**0.0**
RAM, Jamie *No Playoffs*												
RANFORD, Bill												
1986	Boston	2	0	2	....	120	7	0	3.50	44	.841	22.0
1987	Boston	2	0	2	....	123	8	0	3.90	55	.855	26.8
1988◆	Edmonton	....	....	....	....	....	....	....	....	....	....	....
1990◆	Edmonton	*22	*16	6	....	*1401	59	1	2.53	672	.912	28.8
1991	Edmonton	3	1	2	....	135	8	0	3.56	78	.897	34.7
1992	Edmonton	16	8	8	....	909	51	*2	3.37	484	.895	31.9
1996	Boston	4	1	3	....	239	16	0	4.02	112	.857	28.1
1999	Detroit	4	2	2	....	183	10	1	3.28	105	.905	34.4
Playoff Totals		**53**	**28**	**25**	....	**3110**	**159**	**4**	**3.07**	**1550**	**.897**	**29.9**
•RAYCROFT, Andrew *No Playoffs*												
RAYMOND, Alain *No Playoffs*												
RAYNER, Chuck												
1948	NY Rangers	6	2	4	....	360	17	0	2.83	....	....	....
1950	NY Rangers	12	7	5	....	775	29	1	2.25	....	....	....
Playoff Totals		**18**	**9**	**9**	....	**1135**	**46**	**1**	**2.43**	....	....	....
REAUGH, Daryl *No Playoffs*												
REDDICK, Pokey												
1987	Winnipeg	3	0	2	....	166	10	0	3.61	74	.865	26.7
1990◆	Edmonton	1	0	0	....	2	0	0	0.00	1	1.000	30.0
Playoff Totals		**4**	**0**	**2**	....	**168**	**10**	**0**	**3.57**	**75**	**.867**	**26.8**
REDDING, George *No Playoffs*												
REDQUEST, Greg *No Playoffs*												
REECE, Dave *No Playoffs*												
REESE, Jeff												
1990	Toronto	2	1	1	....	108	6	0	3.33	50	.880	27.8
1993	Calgary	4	1	3	....	209	17	0	4.88	91	.813	26.1
1996	Tampa Bay	5	1	1	....	198	12	0	3.64	100	.880	30.3
Playoff Totals		**11**	**3**	**5**	....	**515**	**35**	**0**	**4.08**	**241**	**.855**	**28.1**
RESCH, Glenn												
1975	NY Islanders	12	8	4	....	692	25	1	2.17	....	....	....
1976	NY Islanders	7	3	3	....	357	18	0	3.03	....	....	....
1977	NY Islanders	3	1	1	....	144	5	0	2.08	....	....	....
1978	NY Islanders	7	3	4	....	388	15	0	2.32	....	....	....
1979	NY Islanders	5	2	3	....	300	11	*1	2.20	....	....	....
1980◆	NY Islanders	4	0	2	....	120	9	0	4.50	....	....	....
1986	Philadelphia	1	0	0	....	7	1	0	8.57	1	.000	8.6
1987	Philadelphia	2	0	0	....	36	1	0	1.67	12	.917	20.0
Playoff Totals		**41**	**17**	**17**	....	**2044**	**85**	**2**	**2.50**	....	....	....
RHEAUME, Herb *No Playoffs*												
•RHODES, Damian												
1994	Toronto	1	0	0	....	1	0	0	0.00	0	.000	0.0
1998	Ottawa	10	5	5	....	590	21	0	2.14	236	.911	24.0
1999	Ottawa	2	0	2	....	150	6	0	2.40	65	.908	26.0
Playoff Totals		**13**	**5**	**7**	....	**741**	**27**	**0**	**2.19**	**301**	**.910**	**24.4**
RICCI, Nick *No Playoffs*												
RICHARDSON, Terry *No Playoffs*												
•RICHTER, Mike												
1989	NY Rangers	1	0	1	....	58	4	0	4.14	30	.867	31.0
1990	NY Rangers	6	3	2	....	330	19	0	3.45	182	.896	33.1
1991	NY Rangers	6	2	4	....	313	14	*1	2.68	182	.923	34.9
1992	NY Rangers	7	4	2	....	412	24	1	3.50	226	.894	32.9
1994◆	NY Rangers	23	*16	7	....	1417	49	*4	2.07	623	.921	26.4
1995	NY Rangers	7	2	5	....	384	23	0	3.59	189	.878	29.5
1996	NY Rangers	11	5	6	....	661	36	0	3.27	308	.883	28.0
1997	NY Rangers	15	9	6	....	939	33	*3	2.11	488	.932	31.2
Playoff Totals		**76**	**41**	**33**	....	**4514**	**202**	**9**	**2.68**	**2228**	**.909**	**29.6**
RIDLEY, Curt												
1976	Vancouver	2	0	2	....	120	8	0	4.00	....	....	....
Playoff Totals		**2**	**0**	**2**	....	**120**	**8**	**0**	**4.00**	....	....	....
RIENDEAU, Vincent												
1990	St. Louis	8	3	4	....	397	24	0	3.63	223	.892	33.7
1991	St. Louis	13	6	7	....	687	35	*1	3.06	294	.881	25.7
1992	Detroit	2	1	0	....	73	4	0	3.29	30	.867	24.7
1994	Boston	2	1	1	....	120	8	0	4.00	42	.810	21.0
Playoff Totals		**25**	**11**	**12**	....	**1277**	**71**	**1**	**3.34**	**589**	**.879**	**27.7**
RIGGIN, Dennis *No Playoffs*												
RIGGIN, Pat												
1981	Calgary	11	6	4	....	629	37	0	3.53	....	....	....
1982	Calgary	3	0	3	....	194	10	0	3.09	....	....	....
1983	Washington	3	0	1	....	101	8	0	4.75	....	....	....
1984	Washington	5	1	3	....	230	9	0	2.35	81	.889	21.1
1985	Washington	2	1	1	....	122	5	0	2.46	39	.872	19.2
1986	Boston	1	0	1	....	60	3	0	3.00	23	.870	23.0
Playoff Totals		**25**	**8**	**13**	....	**1336**	**72**	**0**	**3.23**	....	....	....
RING, Bob *No Playoffs*												
RIVARD, Fern *No Playoffs*												

Season	Team	GP	W	L	T	Mins	GA	SO	Avg	SA	S%	SAPG
ROACH, John Ross												
1922◆	Toronto	2	1	0	1	120	4	1	2.00	....	....	....
1925	Toronto	2	0	2	0	120	5	0	*2.50	....	....	....
1929	NY Rangers	*6	3	2	1	*392	5	*3	0.77	....	....	....
1930	NY Rangers	4	1	2	1	309	7	0	1.36	....	....	....
1931	NY Rangers	4	2	2	0	240	4	1	*1.00	....	....	....
1932	NY Rangers	*7	3	4	0	*480	27	*1	3.38	....	....	....
1933	Detroit	4	2	2	0	240	8	1	2.00	....	....	....
Playoff Totals		**29**	**12**	**14**	**3**	**1901**	**60**	**7**	**1.89**	....	....	....
ROBERTS, Moe *No Playoffs*												
ROBERTSON, Earl												
1937◆	Detroit	6	3	2	....	340	8	2	1.41	....	....	....
1938	NY Americans	6	3	3	....	475	12	0	*1.52	....	....	....
1940	NY Americans	3	1	2	....	180	9	0	3.00	....	....	....
Playoff Totals		**15**	**7**	**7**	....	**995**	**29**	**2**	**1.75**	....	....	....
ROLLINS, Al												
1951◆	Toronto	4	3	1	....	210	6	0	1.71	....	....	....
1952	Toronto	2	0	2	....	120	6	0	3.00	....	....	....
1953	Chicago	7	3	4	....	425	18	0	2.54	....	....	....
Playoff Totals		**13**	**6**	**7**	....	**755**	**30**	**0**	**2.38**	....	....	....
•ROLOSON, Dwayne												
1999	Buffalo	4	1	1	....	139	10	0	4.32	67	.851	28.9
Playoff Totals		**4**	**1**	**1**	....	**139**	**10**	**0**	**4.32**	**67**	**.851**	**28.9**
ROMANO, Roberto *No Playoffs*												
ROSATI, Mike *No Playoffs*												
ROUSSEL, Dominic												
1995	Philadelphia	1	0	0	....	23	0	0	0.00	8	1.000	20.9
Playoff Totals		**1**	**0**	**0**	....	**23**	**0**	**0**	**0.00**	**8**	**1.000**	**20.9**
•ROY, Patrick												
1986◆	Montreal	20	*15	5	....	1218	39	*1	1.92	506	.923	24.9
1987	Montreal	6	4	2	....	330	22	0	4.00	173	.873	31.5
1988	Montreal	8	3	4	....	430	24	0	3.35	218	.890	30.4
1989	Montreal	19	13	6	....	1206	42	2	*2.09	528	.920	26.3
1990	Montreal	11	5	6	....	641	26	1	2.43	292	.911	27.3
1991	Montreal	13	7	5	....	785	40	0	3.06	394	.898	30.1
1992	Montreal	11	4	7	....	686	30	1	2.62	312	.904	27.3
1993◆	Montreal	20	*16	4	....	1293	46	0	*2.13	647	.929	30.0
1994	Montreal	6	3	3	....	375	16	0	2.56	228	.930	36.5
1996◆	Colorado	*22	*16	6	....	*1454	51	*3	2.10	649	.921	26.8
1997	Colorado	17	10	7	....	1034	38	*3	2.21	559	.932	32.4
1998	Colorado	7	3	4	....	430	18	0	2.51	191	.906	26.7
1999	Colorado	19	11	8	....	1173	52	1	2.66	650	.920	33.2
2000	Colorado	17	11	6	....	1039	31	3	1.79	431	.928	24.9
2001◆	Colorado	23	*16	7	....	1451	41	*4	*1.70	622	.934	25.7
2002	Colorado	21	11	10	....	1241	52	3	2.51	572	.909	27.7
Playoff Totals		**240**	**148**	**90**	....	***14786**	**568**	***22**	**2.30**	***6972**	**.919**	**28.3**
•RUDKOWSKY, Cody *No Playoffs*												
RUPP, Pat *No Playoffs*												
RUTHERFORD, Jim												
1972	Pittsburgh	4	0	4	....	240	14	0	3.50	....	....	....
1978	Detroit	3	2	1	....	180	12	0	4.00	....	....	....
1981	Los Angeles	1	0	0	....	20	2	0	6.00	....	....	....
Playoff Totals		**8**	**2**	**5**	....	**440**	**28**	**0**	**3.82**	....	....	....
RUTLEDGE, Wayne												
1968	Los Angeles	3	1	1	....	149	8	0	3.22	....	....	....
1969	Los Angeles	5	1	3	....	229	12	0	3.14	....	....	....
Playoff Totals		**8**	**2**	**4**	....	**378**	**20**	**0**	**3.17**	....	....	....
•SABOURIN, Dany *No Playoffs*												
ST. CROIX, Rick												
1981	Philadelphia	9	4	5	....	541	27	*1	2.99	....	....	....
1982	Philadelphia	1	0	1	....	20	1	0	3.00	....	....	....
1983	Toronto	1	0	0	....	1	1	0	60.00	....	....	....
Playoff Totals		**11**	**4**	**6**	....	**562**	**29**	**1**	**3.10**	....	....	....
ST. LAURENT, Sam												
1988	Detroit	1	0	0	....	10	1	0	6.00	7	.857	42.0
Playoff Totals		**1**	**0**	**0**	....	**10**	**1**	**0**	**6.00**	**7**	**.857**	**42.0**
•SALO, Tommy												
1999	Edmonton	4	0	4	....	296	11	0	2.23	149	.926	30.2
2000	Edmonton	5	1	4	....	297	14	0	2.83	133	.895	26.9
2001	Edmonton	6	2	4	....	406	15	0	2.22	187	.920	27.6
Playoff Totals		**15**	**3**	**12**	....	**999**	**40**	**0**	**2.40**	**469**	**.915**	**28.2**
SANDS, Mike *No Playoffs*												
SANFORD, Curtis *No Playoffs*												
SARJEANT, Geoff *No Playoffs*												
SAUVE, Bob												
1979	Buffalo	3	1	2	....	181	9	0	2.98	....	....	....
1980	Buffalo	8	6	2	....	501	17	*2	*2.04	....	....	....
1983	Buffalo	10	6	4	....	545	28	*2	3.08	....	....	....
1984	Buffalo	2	0	1	....	41	5	0	7.32	14	.643	20.5
1986	Chicago	2	0	2	....	99	8	0	4.85	61	.869	37.0
1987	Chicago	4	0	4	....	245	15	0	3.67	136	.890	33.3
1988	New Jersey	5	2	1	....	238	13	0	3.28	118	.890	29.7
Playoff Totals		**34**	**15**	**16**	....	**1850**	**95**	**4**	**3.08**	....	....	....

Season	Team	GP	W	L	T	Mins	GA	SO	Avg	SA	S%	SAPG
SAWCHUK, Terry												
1951	Detroit	6	2	4	....	463	13	1	1.68	....	....	....
1952◆	Detroit	*8	*8	0	....	480	5	*4	*0.63	....	....	....
1953	Detroit	6	2	4	....	372	21	1	3.39	....	....	....
1954◆	Detroit	*12	*8	4	....	*751	20	*2	*1.60	....	....	....
1955◆	Detroit	11	*8	3	....	*660	26	*1	*2.36	....	....	....
1958	Detroit	4	0	4	....	252	19	0	4.52	....	....	....
1960	Detroit	6	2	4	....	405	20	0	2.96	....	....	....
1961	Detroit	8	5	3	....	465	18	1	2.32	....	....	....
1963	Detroit	*11	5	6	....	*660	35	0	3.18	....	....	....
1964	Detroit	13	6	5	....	677	31	1	2.75	....	....	....
1965	Toronto	1	0	1	....	60	3	0	3.00	....	....	....
1966	Toronto	2	0	2	....	120	6	0	3.00	....	....	....
1967◆	Toronto	*10	*6	4	....	*565	25	0	2.65	....	....	....
1968	Los Angeles	5	2	3	....	280	18	*1	3.86	....	....	....
1970	NY Rangers	3	0	1	....	80	6	0	4.50	....	....	....
Playoff Totals		**106**	**54**	**48**	....	**6290**	**266**	**12**	**2.54**	....	....	....
SCHAEFER, Joe *No Playoffs*												
SCHAFER, Paxton *No Playoffs*												
•SCHWAB, Corey												
2002	Toronto	1	0	0	....	12	0	0	0.00	5	1.000	25.0
Playoff Totals		**1**	**0**	**0**	....	**12**	**0**	**0**	**0.00**	**5**	**1.000**	**25.0**
SCOTT, Ron												
1990	Los Angeles	1	0	0	....	32	4	0	7.50	10	.600	18.8
Playoff Totals		**1**	**0**	**0**	....	**32**	**4**	**0**	**7.50**	**10**	**.600**	**18.8**
•SCOTT, Travis *No Playoffs*												
SEVIGNY, Richard												
1979◆	Montreal	....	....	....	....	....	....	....	....	....	....	....
1981	Montreal	3	0	3	....	180	13	0	4.33	....	....	....
1983	Montreal	1	0	0	....	28	0	0	0.00	....	....	....
Playoff Totals		**4**	**0**	**3**	....	**208**	**13**	**0**	**3.75**	....	....	....
SHARPLES, Scott *No Playoffs*												
•SHIELDS, Steve												
1997	Buffalo	10	4	6	....	570	26	1	2.74	334	.922	35.2
1999	San Jose	1	0	1	....	60	6	0	6.00	36	.833	36.0
2000	San Jose	12	5	7	....	696	36	0	3.10	323	.889	27.8
Playoff Totals		**23**	**9**	**14**	....	**1326**	**68**	**1**	**3.08**	**693**	**.902**	**31.4**
SHTALENKOV, Mikhail												
1997	Anaheim	4	0	3	....	211	10	0	2.84	162	.938	46.1
Playoff Totals		**4**	**0**	**3**	....	**211**	**10**	**0**	**2.84**	**162**	**.938**	**46.1**
SHULMISTRA, Richard *No Playoffs*												
SIDORKIEWICZ, Peter												
1989	Hartford	2	0	2	....	124	8	0	3.87	45	.822	21.8
1990	Hartford	7	3	4	....	429	23	0	3.22	193	.881	27.0
1991	Hartford	6	2	4	....	359	24	0	4.01	174	.862	29.1
Playoff Totals		**15**	**5**	**10**	....	**912**	**55**	**0**	**3.62**	**412**	**.867**	**27.1**
SIMMONS, Don												
1957	Boston	*10	5	5	....	600	29	*2	2.90	....	....	....
1958	Boston	*11	6	5	....	*671	25	*1	2.24	....	....	....
1962◆	Toronto	3	2	1	....	165	8	0	2.91	....	....	....
1963◆	Toronto	....	....	....	....	....	....	....	....	....	....	....
1964◆	Toronto	....	....	....	....	....	....	....	....	....	....	....
Playoff Totals		**24**	**13**	**11**	....	**1436**	**62**	**3**	**2.59**	....	....	....
SIMMONS, Gary												
1977	Los Angeles	1	0	0	....	20	1	0	3.00	....	....	....
Playoff Totals		**1**	**0**	**0**	....	**20**	**1**	**0**	**3.00**	....	....	....
SKIDMORE, Paul *No Playoffs*												
SKORODENSKI, Warren												
1985	Chicago	2	0	0	....	33	6	0	10.91	28	.786	50.9
Playoff Totals		**2**	**0**	**0**	....	**33**	**6**	**0**	**10.91**	**28**	**.786**	**50.9**
•SKUDRA, Peter												
2000	Pittsburgh	1	0	0	....	20	1	0	3.00	11	.909	33.0
2002	Vancouver	2	0	1	....	96	5	0	3.13	46	.891	28.8
Playoff Totals		**3**	**0**	**1**	....	**116**	**6**	**0**	**3.10**	**57**	**.895**	**29.5**
SMITH, Al												
1970	Pittsburgh	3	1	2	....	180	10	0	3.33	....	....	....
1976	Buffalo	1	0	0	....	17	1	0	3.53	....	....	....
1980	Hartford	2	0	2	....	120	10	0	5.00	....	....	....
Playoff Totals		**6**	**1**	**4**	....	**317**	**21**	**0**	**3.97**	....	....	....
SMITH, Billy												
1975	NY Islanders	6	1	4	....	333	23	0	4.14	....	....	....
1976	NY Islanders	8	4	3	....	437	21	0	2.88	....	....	....
1977	NY Islanders	10	7	3	....	580	27	0	2.79	....	....	....
1978	NY Islanders	1	0	0	....	47	1	0	1.28	....	....	....
1979	NY Islanders	5	4	1	....	315	10	*1	*1.90	....	....	....
1980◆	NY Islanders	*20	*15	4	....	*1198	56	1	2.80	....	....	....
1981◆	NY Islanders	*17	*14	3	....	*994	42	0	*2.54	....	....	....
1982◆	NY Islanders	*18	*15	3	....	*1120	47	*1	2.52	....	....	....
1983◆	NY Islanders	*17	*13	3	....	962	43	*2	*2.68	....	....	....
1984	NY Islanders	*21	*12	8	....	*1190	54	0	2.72	567	.905	28.6
1985	NY Islanders	6	3	3	....	342	19	0	3.33	182	.896	31.9
1986	NY Islanders	1	0	1	....	60	4	0	4.00	34	.882	34.0
1987	NY Islanders	2	0	0	....	67	1	0	0.90	22	.955	19.7
Playoff Totals		**132**	**88**	**36**	....	**7645**	**348**	**5**	**2.73**	....	....	....

Season	Team	GP	W	L	T	Mins	GA	SO	Avg	SA	S%	SAPG
SMITH, Gary												
1969	Oakland	7	3	4	....	420	23	0	3.29	....	....	....
1970	Oakland	4	0	4	....	248	13	0	3.15	....	....	....
1972	Chicago	2	1	1	....	120	3	1	1.50	....	....	....
1973	Chicago	2	0	1	....	65	5	0	4.62	....	....	....
1975	Vancouver	4	1	3	....	257	14	0	3.27	....	....	....
1977	Minnesota	1	0	0	....	43	4	0	5.58	....	....	....
Playoff Totals		**20**	**5**	**13**	....	**1153**	**62**	**1**	**3.23**	....	....	....
SMITH, Normie												
1936♦	Detroit	7	*6	1	0	538	12	*2	1.34	....	....	....
1937♦	Detroit	5	3	1	....	282	6	1	1.28	....	....	....
Playoff Totals		**12**	**9**	**2**	**0**	**820**	**18**	**3**	**1.32**	....	....	....
SNEDDON, Bob *No Playoffs*												
•SNOW, Garth												
1995	Quebec	1	0	0	....	9	1	0	6.67	3	.667	20.0
1996	Philadelphia	1	0	0	....	1	0	0	0.00	0	.000	0.0
1997	Philadelphia	12	8	4	....	699	33	0	2.83	305	.892	26.2
2002	NY Islanders	1	0	0	....	26	2	0	4.62	19	.895	43.8
Playoff Totals		**15**	**8**	**4**	....	**735**	**36**	**0**	**2.94**	**327**	**.890**	**26.7**
SODERSTROM, Tommy *No Playoffs*												
SOETAERT, Doug												
1982	Winnipeg	2	1	1	....	120	8	0	4.00	....	....	....
1983	Winnipeg	1	0	0	....	20	0	0	0.00	....	....	....
1984	Winnipeg	1	0	1	....	20	5	0	15.00	19	.737	57.0
1985	Montreal	1	0	0	....	20	1	0	3.00	9	.889	27.0
1986♦	Montreal	....	....	....	....	....	....	....	....	....	....	....
Playoff Totals		**5**	**1**	**2**	....	**180**	**14**	**0**	**4.67**	....	....	....
SOUCY, Christian *No Playoffs*												
SPOONER, Red *No Playoffs*												
STANIOWSKI, Ed												
1976	St. Louis	3	1	2	....	206	7	0	2.04	....	....	....
1977	St. Louis	3	0	2	....	102	9	0	5.29	....	....	....
1982	Winnipeg	2	0	2	....	120	12	0	6.00	....	....	....
Playoff Totals		**8**	**1**	**6**	....	**428**	**28**	**0**	**3.93**	....	....	....
STAUBER, Robb												
1993	Los Angeles	4	3	1	....	240	16	0	4.00	157	.898	39.3
Playoff Totals		**4**	**3**	**1**	....	**240**	**16**	**0**	**4.00**	**157**	**.898**	**39.3**
STEFAN, Greg												
1984	Detroit	3	1	2	....	210	8	0	2.29	86	.907	24.6
1985	Detroit	3	0	3	....	138	17	0	7.39	69	.754	30.0
1987	Detroit	9	4	5	....	508	24	0	2.83	252	.905	29.8
1988	Detroit	10	5	4	....	531	32	*1	3.62	236	.864	26.7
1989	Detroit	5	2	3	....	294	18	0	3.67	151	.881	30.8
Playoff Totals		**30**	**12**	**17**	....	**1681**	**99**	**1**	**3.53**	**794**	**.875**	**28.3**
STEIN, Phil *No Playoffs*												
STEPHENSON, Wayne												
1973	St. Louis	3	1	2	....	160	14	0	5.25	....	....	....
1975♦	Philadelphia	2	2	0	....	123	4	1	1.95	....	....	....
1976	Philadelphia	8	4	4	....	494	22	0	2.67	....	....	....
1977	Philadelphia	9	4	3	....	532	23	1	2.59	....	....	....
1979	Philadelphia	4	0	3	....	213	16	0	4.51	....	....	....
Playoff Totals		**26**	**11**	**12**	....	**1522**	**79**	**2**	**3.11**	....	....	....
STEVENSON, Doug *No Playoffs*												
STEWART, Charles *No Playoffs*												
STEWART, Jim *No Playoffs*												
•STORR, Jamie												
1998	Los Angeles	3	0	2	....	145	9	0	3.72	77	.883	31.9
2000	Los Angeles	1	0	1	....	36	2	0	3.33	25	.920	41.7
2002	Los Angeles	1	0	0	....	0	0	0	0.00	0	.000	0.0
Playoff Totals		**5**	**0**	**3**	....	**181**	**11**	**0**	**3.65**	**102**	**.892**	**33.8**
STUART, Herb *No Playoffs*												
SYLVESTRI, Don *No Playoffs*												
•SZUPER, Levente *No Playoffs*												
TABARACCI, Rick												
1992	Winnipeg	7	3	4	....	387	26	0	4.03	212	.877	32.9
1993	Washington	4	1	3	....	304	14	0	2.76	160	.913	31.6
1994	Washington	2	0	2	....	111	6	0	3.24	50	.880	27.0
1995	Calgary	1	0	0	....	19	0	0	0.00	9	1.000	28.4
1996	Calgary	3	0	3	....	204	7	0	2.06	84	.917	24.7
Playoff Totals		**17**	**4**	**12**	....	**1025**	**53**	**0**	**3.10**	**515**	**.897**	**30.1**
TAKKO, Kari												
1989	Minnesota	3	0	1	....	105	7	0	4.00	55	.873	31.4
1990	Minnesota	1	0	0	....	4	0	0	0.00	0	.000	0.0
Playoff Totals		**4**	**0**	**1**	....	**109**	**7**	**0**	**3.85**	**55**	**.873**	**30.3**
•TALLAS, Robbie *No Playoffs*												
TANNER, John *No Playoffs*												
TATARYN, Dave *No Playoffs*												
TAYLOR, Bobby *Backup goalie on Cup-winning team*												
1974♦	Philadelphia	....	....	....	....	....	....	....	....	....	....	....
TENO, Harvey *No Playoffs*												
TERRERI, Chris												
1990	New Jersey	4	2	2	....	238	13	0	3.28	103	.874	26.0
1991	New Jersey	7	3	4	....	428	21	0	2.94	216	.903	30.3
1992	New Jersey	7	3	3	....	386	23	0	3.58	203	.887	31.6
1993	New Jersey	4	1	3	....	219	17	0	4.66	118	.856	32.3
1994	New Jersey	4	3	0	....	200	9	0	2.70	111	.919	33.3
1995♦	New Jersey	1	0	0	....	8	0	0	0.00	2	1.000	15.0
1997	Chicago	2	0	0	....	44	3	0	4.09	28	.893	38.2
2000♦	New Jersey	....	....	....	....	....	....	....	....	....	....	....
Playoff Totals		**29**	**12**	**12**	....	**1523**	**86**	**0**	**3.39**	**781**	**.890**	**30.8**
•THEODORE, Jose												
1997	Montreal	2	1	1	....	168	7	0	2.50	108	.935	38.6
1998	Montreal	3	0	1	....	120	1	0	0.50	35	.971	17.5
2002	Montreal	12	6	6	....	686	35	0	3.06	413	.915	36.1
Playoff Totals		**17**	**7**	**8**	....	**974**	**43**	**0**	**2.65**	**556**	**.923**	**34.3**
•THIBAULT, Jocelyn												
1995	Quebec	3	1	2	....	148	8	0	3.24	76	.895	30.8
1996	Montreal	6	2	4	....	311	18	0	3.47	188	.904	36.3
1997	Montreal	3	0	3	....	179	13	0	4.36	101	.871	33.9
1998	Montreal	2	0	0	....	43	4	0	5.58	16	.750	22.3
2002	Chicago	3	1	2	....	159	7	0	2.64	77	.909	29.1
Playoff Totals		**17**	**4**	**11**	....	**840**	**50**	**0**	**3.57**	**458**	**.891**	**32.7**
•THOMAS, Tim *No Playoffs*												
THOMAS, Wayne												
1976	Toronto	10	5	5	....	587	34	1	3.48	....	....	....
1977	Toronto	4	1	2	....	202	12	0	3.56	....	....	....
1978	NY Rangers	1	0	1	....	60	4	0	4.00	....	....	....
Playoff Totals		**15**	**6**	**8**	....	**849**	**50**	**1**	**3.53**	....	....	....
THOMPSON, Tiny												
1929♦	Boston	5	*5	0	0	300	3	*3	*0.60	....	....	....
1930	Boston	*6	3	3	0	432	12	0	1.67	....	....	....
1931	Boston	5	2	3	0	343	13	0	2.27	....	....	....
1933	Boston	5	2	3	0	438	9	0	*1.23	....	....	....
1935	Boston	4	1	3	0	275	7	1	1.53	....	....	....
1936	Boston	2	1	1	0	120	8	1	4.00	....	....	....
1937	Boston	3	1	2	....	180	8	1	2.67	....	....	....
1938	Boston	3	0	3	....	212	6	0	1.70	....	....	....
1939	Detroit	6	3	3	....	374	15	1	2.41	....	....	....
1940	Detroit	5	2	3	....	300	12	0	2.40	....	....	....
Playoff Totals		**44**	**20**	**24**	**0**	**2974**	**93**	**7**	**1.88**	....	....	....
TORCHIA, Mike *No Playoffs*												
•TOSKALA, Vesa *No Playoffs*												
TREFILOV, Andrei												
1997	Buffalo	1	0	0	....	5	0	0	0.00	4	1.000	48.0
Playoff Totals		**1**	**0**	**0**	....	**5**	**0**	**0**	**0.00**	**4**	**1.000**	**48.0**
TREMBLAY, Vincent *No Playoffs*												
TUCKER, Ted *No Playoffs*												
•TUGNUTT, Ron												
1992	Edmonton	2	0	0	....	60	3	0	3.00	34	.912	34.0
1994	Montreal	1	0	1	....	59	5	0	5.08	25	.800	25.4
1997	Ottawa	7	3	4	....	425	14	1	1.98	169	.917	23.9
1998	Ottawa	2	0	1	....	74	6	0	4.86	25	.760	20.3
1999	Ottawa	2	0	2	....	118	6	0	3.05	41	.854	20.8
2000	Pittsburgh	11	6	5	....	746	22	2	1.77	398	.945	32.0
Playoff Totals		**25**	**9**	**13**	....	**1482**	**56**	**3**	**2.27**	**692**	**.919**	**28.0**
•TURCO, Marty *No Playoffs*												
•TUREK, Roman												
1999♦	Dallas	....	....	....	....	....	....	....	....	....	....	....
2000	St. Louis	7	3	4	....	415	19	0	2.75	161	.882	23.3
2001	St. Louis	14	9	5	....	908	31	0	2.05	382	.919	25.2
Playoff Totals		**21**	**12**	**9**	....	**1323**	**50**	**0**	**2.27**	**543**	**.908**	**24.6**
TURNER, Joe *No Playoffs*												
VACHON, Rogie												
1967	Montreal	9	*6	3	....	555	22	0	*2.38	....	....	....
1968♦	Montreal	2	1	1	....	113	4	0	2.12	....	....	....
1969♦	Montreal	8	7	1	....	507	12	1	1.42	....	....	....
1971♦	Montreal	....	....	....	....	....	....	....	....	....	....	....
1974	Los Angeles	4	0	4	....	240	7	0	1.75	....	....	....
1975	Los Angeles	3	1	2	....	199	7	0	2.11	....	....	....
1976	Los Angeles	7	4	3	....	438	17	1	2.33	....	....	....
1977	Los Angeles	9	4	5	....	520	36	0	4.15	....	....	....
1978	Los Angeles	2	0	2	....	120	11	0	5.50	....	....	....
1981	Boston	3	0	2	....	164	16	0	5.85	....	....	....
1982	Boston	1	0	0	....	20	1	0	3.00	....	....	....
Playoff Totals		**48**	**23**	**23**	....	**2876**	**133**	**2**	**2.77**	....	....	....
•VALIQUETTE, Stephen *No Playoffs*												
VANBIESBROUCK, John												
1984	NY Rangers	1	0	0	....	1	0	0	0.00	0	.000	0.0
1985	NY Rangers	1	0	0	....	20	0	0	0.00	12	1.000	36.0
1986	NY Rangers	16	8	8	....	899	49	*1	3.27	477	.897	31.8
1987	NY Rangers	4	1	3	....	195	11	1	3.38	110	.900	33.8
1989	NY Rangers	2	0	1	....	107	6	0	3.36	55	.891	30.8
1990	NY Rangers	6	2	3	....	298	15	0	3.02	153	.902	30.8
1991	NY Rangers	1	0	0	....	52	1	0	1.15	22	.955	25.4
1992	NY Rangers	7	2	5	....	368	23	0	3.75	179	.872	29.2
1996	Florida	*22	12	10	....	1332	50	1	2.25	735	.932	33.1
1997	Florida	5	1	4	....	328	13	1	2.38	184	.929	33.7
1999	Philadelphia	6	2	4	....	369	9	1	1.46	146	.938	23.7
Playoff Totals		**71**	**28**	**38**	....	**3969**	**177**	**5**	**2.68**	**2073**	**.915**	**31.3**

Season Team	GP	W	L	T	Mins	GA	SO	Avg	SA	S%	SAPG
VEISOR, Mike											
1974 Chicago	2	0	1	....	80	5	0	3.75	....	....	....
1980 Chicago	1	0	1	....	60	6	0	6.00	....	....	....
1984 Winnipeg	1	0	0	....	40	4	0	6.00	29	.862	43.5
Playoff Totals	4	0	2	....	180	15	0	5.00	....	....	....
VERNON, Mike											
1986 Calgary	*21	12	*9	....	*1229	60	0	2.93	583	.897	28.5
1987 Calgary	5	2	3	....	263	16	0	3.65	136	.882	31.0
1988 Calgary	9	4	4	....	515	34	0	3.96	210	.838	24.5
1989♦ Calgary	*22	*16	5	....	*1381	52	*3	2.26	550	.905	23.9
1990 Calgary	6	2	3	....	342	19	0	3.33	150	.873	26.3
1991 Calgary	7	3	4	....	427	21	0	2.95	204	.897	28.7
1993 Calgary	4	1	1	....	150	15	0	6.00	81	.815	32.4
1994 Calgary	7	3	4	....	466	23	0	2.96	220	.895	28.3
1995 Detroit	18	12	6	....	1063	41	1	2.31	370	.889	20.9
1996 Detroit	4	2	2	....	243	11	0	2.72	81	.864	20.0
1997♦ Detroit	*20	*16	4	....	*1229	36	0	1.76	494	.927	24.1
1998 San Jose	6	2	4	....	348	14	1	2.41	138	.899	23.8
1999 San Jose	5	2	3	....	321	13	0	2.43	172	.924	32.1
2000 Florida	4	0	4	....	237	12	0	3.04	136	.912	34.4
Playoff Totals	138	77	56	....	8214	367	6	2.68	3525	.896	25.7
VEZINA, Georges											
1918 Montreal	2	1	1	0	120	10	0	5.00	....	....	....
1919 Montreal	*5	*4	1	1	*300	18	*0	*3.60	....	....	....
1923 Montreal	2	0	2	0	120	4	0	2.00	....	....	....
1924♦ Montreal	2	2	0	0	120	2	1	1.00	....	....	....
1925 Montreal	2	2	0	0	120	2	1	1.00	....	....	....
Playoff Totals	13	9	4	1	780	36	2	2.77	....	....	....
VILLEMURE, Gilles											
1969 NY Rangers	1	0	1	....	60	4	0	4.00	....	....	....
1971 NY Rangers	2	0	1	....	80	6	0	4.50	....	....	....
1972 NY Rangers	6	4	2	....	360	14	0	2.33	....	....	....
1973 NY Rangers	2	0	1	....	61	2	0	1.97	....	....	....
1974 NY Rangers	1	0	0	....	1	0	0	0.00	....	....	....
1975 NY Rangers	2	1	0	....	94	6	0	3.83	....	....	....
Playoff Totals	14	5	5	....	656	32	0	2.93	....	....	....
•**VOKOUN, Tomas** No Playoffs											
WAITE, Jimmy											
1994 San Jose	2	0	0	....	40	3	0	4.50	17	.824	25.5
1998 Phoenix	4	0	3	....	171	11	0	3.86	97	.887	34.0
Playoff Totals	6	0	3	....	211	14	0	3.98	114	.877	32.4
WAKALUK, Darcy											
1991 Buffalo	2	0	1	....	37	2	0	3.24	22	.909	35.7
1994 Dallas	5	4	1	....	307	15	0	2.93	168	.911	32.8
1995 Dallas	1	0	0	....	20	1	0	3.00	9	.889	27.0
Playoff Totals	8	4	2	....	364	18	0	2.97	199	.910	32.8
WAKELY, Ernie											
1970 St. Louis	4	0	4	....	216	17	0	4.72	....	....	....
1971 St. Louis	3	2	1	....	180	7	1	2.33	....	....	....
1972 St. Louis	3	0	1	....	113	13	0	6.90	....	....	....
Playoff Totals	10	2	6	....	509	37	1	4.36	....	....	....
WALSH, Flat											
1930 Mtl. Maroons	4	1	3	0	312	11	1	2.12	....	....	....
1932 Mtl. Maroons	4	1	1	2	258	5	*1	*1.16	....	....	....
Playoff Totals	8	2	4	2	570	16	2	1.68	....	....	....
WAMSLEY, Rick											
1982 Montreal	5	2	3	....	300	11	0	*2.20	....	....	....
1983 Montreal	3	0	3	....	152	7	0	2.76	....	....	....
1984 Montreal	1	0	0	....	32	0	0	0.00	12	1.000	22.5
1985 St. Louis	3	0	2	....	120	7	0	3.50	56	.875	28.0
1986 St. Louis	10	4	6	....	569	37	0	3.90	307	.879	32.4
1987 St. Louis	2	1	1	....	120	5	0	2.50	54	.907	27.0
1988 Calgary	1	0	1	....	33	2	0	3.64	8	.750	14.5
1989♦ Calgary	1	0	1	....	20	2	0	6.00	10	.800	30.0
1990 Calgary	1	0	1	....	49	9	0	11.02	23	.609	28.2
1991 Calgary	1	0	0	....	2	1	0	30.00	2	.500	60.0
Playoff Totals	27	7	18	....	1397	81	0	3.48	....	....	....
WATT, Jim No Playoffs											

Season Team	GP	W	L	T	Mins	GA	SO	Avg	SA	S%	SAPG
•**WEEKES, Kevin**											
2002 Carolina	8	3	2	....	408	11	2	1.62	180	.939	26.5
Playoff Totals	8	3	2	....	408	11	2	1.62	180	.939	26.5
WEEKS, Steve											
1981 NY Rangers	1	0	0	....	14	1	0	4.29	....	....	....
1982 NY Rangers	4	1	2	....	127	9	0	4.25	....	....	....
1986 Hartford	3	1	2	....	169	8	0	2.84	64	.875	22.7
1987 Hartford	1	0	0	....	36	1	0	1.67	22	.955	36.7
1989 Vancouver	3	1	1	....	140	8	0	3.43	79	.899	33.9
Playoff Totals	12	3	5	....	486	27	0	3.33	....	....	....
WETZEL, Carl No Playoffs											
WHITMORE, Kay											
1989 Hartford	2	0	2	....	135	10	0	4.44	73	.863	32.4
1992 Hartford	1	0	0	....	19	1	0	3.16	5	.800	15.8
1995 Vancouver	1	0	0	....	20	2	0	6.00	18	.889	54.0
Playoff Totals	4	0	2	....	174	13	0	4.48	96	.865	33.1
WILKINSON, Derek No Playoffs											
WILLIS, Jordan No Playoffs											
WILSON, Dunc No Playoffs											
WILSON, Lefty No Playoffs											
WINKLER, Hal											
1927 Boston	*8	2	2	4	*520	13	*2	1.50	....	....	....
1928 Boston	2	0	1	1	120	5	0	2.50	....	....	....
Playoff Totals	10	2	3	5	640	18	2	1.69	....	....	....
WOLFE, Bernie No Playoffs											
WOOD, Alex No Playoffs											
WORSLEY, Gump											
1956 NY Rangers	3	0	3	....	180	14	0	4.67	....	....	....
1957 NY Rangers	5	1	4	....	316	21	0	3.99	....	....	....
1958 NY Rangers	6	2	4	....	365	28	0	4.60	....	....	....
1962 NY Rangers	6	2	4	....	384	21	0	3.28	....	....	....
1965♦ Montreal	8	5	3	....	501	14	*2	*1.68	....	....	....
1966♦ Montreal	10	*8	2	....	602	20	*1	*1.99	....	....	....
1967 Montreal	2	0	1	....	80	2	0	1.50	....	....	....
1968♦ Montreal	12	*11	0	....	672	21	*1	1.88	....	....	....
1969♦ Montreal	7	5	1	....	370	14	0	2.27	....	....	....
1970 Minnesota	3	1	2	....	180	14	0	4.67	....	....	....
1971 Minnesota	4	3	1	....	240	13	0	3.25	....	....	....
1972 Minnesota	4	2	1	....	194	7	1	2.16	....	....	....
Playoff Totals	70	40	26	....	4084	189	5	2.78	....	....	....
WORTERS, Roy											
1926 Pittsburgh	2	0	1	1	120	6	0	3.00	....	....	....
1928 Pittsburgh	2	1	1	0	120	6	0	3.00	....	....	....
1929 NY Americans	2	0	1	1	150	1	1	0.40	....	....	....
1936 NY Americans	5	2	3	0	300	11	*2	2.20	....	....	....
Playoff Totals	11	3	6	2	690	24	3	2.09	....	....	....
WORTHY, Chris No Playoffs											
WREGGET, Ken											
1986 Toronto	10	6	4	....	607	32	*1	3.16	323	.901	31.9
1987 Toronto	13	7	6	....	761	29	1	2.29	368	.921	29.0
1988 Toronto	2	0	1	....	108	11	0	6.11	62	.823	34.4
1989 Philadelphia	5	2	2	....	268	10	0	2.24	139	.928	31.1
1992 Pittsburgh	1	0	0	....	40	4	0	6.00	16	.750	24.0
1995 Pittsburgh	11	5	6	....	661	33	1	3.00	349	.905	31.7
1996 Pittsburgh	9	7	2	....	599	23	0	2.30	328	.930	32.9
1997 Pittsburgh	5	1	4	....	297	18	0	3.64	211	.915	42.6
Playoff Totals	56	28	25	....	3341	160	3	2.87	1796	.911	32.3
•**YEREMEYEV, Vitali** No Playoffs											
YOUNG, Wendell											
1986 Vancouver	1	0	1	....	60	5	0	5.00	32	.844	32.0
1989 Pittsburgh	1	0	0	....	39	1	0	1.54	11	.909	16.9
1991♦ Pittsburgh	....	....	....	....	....	....	....	....	....	....	....
1992♦ Pittsburgh	....	....	....	....	....	....	....	....	....	....	....
Playoff Totals	2	0	1	....	99	6	0	3.64	43	.860	26.1
ZANIER, Mike No Playoffs											

Stanley Cup Notebook

Name Game

After the New York Rangers captured the Cup in 1994, the team made a special request to Commissioner Bettman to have Ed Olczyk's name engraved on the Cup. Although he didn't meet the standard requirements – at least 41 games with the club or one game played in the Stanley Cup Finals – he had won the Rangers' "Good Guy" award and was only out of the lineup due to injury. Commissioner Bettman agreed with the team. Since then it has been possible for teams to petition the Commissioner for permission to have players' names put on the Cup if extenuating circumstances prevented them from being available to play.